MW00718214

Current Perspectives:
Working With Sexually Aggressive Youth And Youth With Sexual Behavior Problems

Editors:
Robert E. Longo
David S. Prescott

Current Perspectives: Working with Sexually Aggressive Youth and Youth with Sexual Behavior Problems

Copyright©2006
NEARI Press
2nd Printing 2011

Robert E. Longo and David S. Prescott (Editors)

Published by:

NEARI Press
70 North Summer Street
Holyoke, Massachusetts
01040 USA
413.540.0712

Order from:

NEARI Distribution
10 Water Street
PO Box 1220
Lebanon, New Hampshire
03766 USA
888.632.7412
603.448.0317

ISBN# 978-1-929657-26-1

DEDICATION AND ACKNOWLEDGEMENTS

This book is dedicated to all the professionals who work with young persons who have spent their time, personal resources, and effort to work with this challenging population.

In particular, we would like to dedicate this book to the late David O'Callaghan who was previously Co-director of GMAP in Manchester, England. Dave was accidentally killed during a hiking accident on March 5, 2004. Dave will be well remembered for his dedication and commitment to the field, his contributions to the literature, and his kind and gentle manner in working with people. This book is also dedicated to another colleague and friend John Michaud, who died of natural causes in December 2004. John was a dedicated professional who worked with Alaskan natives and had a kind and kindred spirit.

~~~

My work on this book has been inspired by the lives and memories of my father, Peter S. Prescott, my grandfather, Orville Prescott, and my grandmother, Eleanor Lake. Authors, critics, and editors themselves, they taught me the value and joy of words. I also thank my mother, Anne Lake Prescott, my wife, Louise, and my sister, Tonia, for their patience and support through all the years.
~ David S. Prescott

I would like to thank all of the authors who so generously gave of their time to write chapters for this book. I would also like to thank NEARI Press, and in particular Steve Bengis, Penny Cuninggim and Diane Langelier for their support, patience and courage to take this project to completion. Finally, I would like to dedicate this book to my late mother Shirley who was always my greatest fan and supporter, my father Earl who gave me my sense of humor, and my wife Debbie who has supported my writing projects and this project without hesitation. This book is also dedicated to my children Josh and Sandy. I hope they will live in a safer world.
~ Robert E. Longo

CURRENT PERSPECTIVES: WORKING WITH SEXUALLY AGGRESSIVE YOUTH AND YOUTH WITH SEXUAL BEHAVIOR PROBLEMS

PART I – Current Perspectives

PART II – <u>Special Populations</u>

PART III – <u>Special Issues</u>

PART IV – <u>Interventions</u>

CONTRIBUTING AUTHORS

Judith V. Becker, Ph.D.
Department of Psychology
University of Arizona
Tucson, AZ 85721 USA
Ph: 520.621.7455
E-mail: jvbecker@email.arizona.edu

Judith Becker is a professor of psychology and psychiatry at the University of Arizona. She is the past President of the Association for the Treatment of Sexual Abusers. She has published over 100 articles and book chapters on the topic of sexual violence.

Steven M. Bengis, Ed.D., LCSW
Executive Director
New England Adolescent Research Institute
70 North Summer Street
Holyoke, MA 01040 USA
Ph: 413.540.0712 Ext.12
E-mail: sbengis@aol.com

Steven Bengis is a nationally recognized consultant and trainer. He has offered workshops and keynoted conferences in over twenty-five states, in Israel, throughout Canada, and in New Zealand. He is a former member of the National Task Force on Juvenile Sexual Offending, Coordinator of the National Task Force on Residential Standards, and President of the Massachusetts Adolescent Sexual Offender Coalition, Inc. Together with his wife, Penny Cuninggim, Ed.D., he founded and currently serves as Executive Director of the New England Adolescent Research Institute, Inc. (NEARI) in Holyoke, Massachusetts. NEARI administers: 1) a day school that provides special education services to severely emotionally disturbed and behaviorally disordered youth, 2) an early intervention after-school program, "Jumpstart", for highly at-risk primarily Lationo youth, 3) the NEARI Press, a publishing company specializing in sex abuse-specific, educational and intervention resources for work with "at-risk youth"; and, 4) a training and consulting center.

Dr. Bengis, holds a doctorate in counseling psychology from the University of Massachusetts and has worked as a therapist both privately and in outpatient, residential and school settings.

John Bergman, MA, RDT, MT-BCT
Stonewall Arts Project Inc./Geese Theatre Co.
Melbourne, Australia
Ph: 04.222.55984
Mobile: 603.264.5245
E-mail: macflap@aol.com

John Bergman currently works in New Zealand, Romania, Australia, England, Bulgaria, and the USA. He is a registered Master Teacher in Dramatherapy (criminal justice), who has worked for 24 years in criminal justice. Mr Bergman has received awards for his work from the American Correctional Association and has contributed chapters to a number of books including *The Sex Offender*, Schwartz and Cellini Vols. 1 and 2 , *Drama Therapy for Juvenile & Adult Sex Offenders*, a Safer Society Press training video, T*he Sexual Predator*, Vols. 2 and 4 edited by Schlank, and a new treatment book with Saul Hewish, *Challenging Experience.*

Mr. Bergman splits his work between staff development, drama therapy-based ethics training for commissioners and administrators, training officers to work therapeutically with violent offenders, creating original theatre works with offenders and community members, and working as a drama therapist with violent and sexual offenders.

Mr. Bergman has just finished doing a mass set of trainings in ethics for the development of a statewide rehabilitation framework for the Office of the Correctional Services Commissioner, Department of Justice, Australia.

Steven M. Brown, Psy.D.
Traumatic Stress Institute/
Center for Adult & Adolescent Psychotherapy
(TSI/CAAP)
22 Morgan Farms Drive
South Windsor, CT 06074 USA
Ph: 860.644.2541
Fax: 860.644.6891
E-mail: stmbrown@worldnet.att.net

Steven Brown is a clinical psychologist at the Traumatic Stress Institute/Center for Adult & Adolescent Psychotherapy (TSI/CAAP) in S. Windsor, CT and Northampton, MA. At TSI/CAAP, he does psychotherapy with trauma survivors, evaluations of survivors and perpetrators of abuse, and professional training on a variety of issues including trauma treatment, vicarous traumatization, adolescent sexual health, and sexuality education. He is a sexuality educator/ trainer and co-author of *Streetwise to Sex-Wise: Sexuality Education for High Risk Youth*, 2nd Edition, a curricula used nationally by agencies and schools serving high risk youth. He is a member of the Board of Directors of Stop It Now!, a national sexual abuse prevention organization.

David L. Burton, MSW, Ph.D.
Smith College
New England Center for Change-Lilly Hall
Smith College School For Social Work
Northampton, MA 01053 USA
Ph: 413.585.7985
E-mail: dlburton@email.smith.edu

David has worked in the field of sexual aggression for over 15 years, primarily as a clinician with adolescents and children. He is a resident faculty member at Smith College School for Social Work in Massachusetts. He researches the trauma and etiology of child, adolescent and adult sexual abusers. Current research interests include attachment, cognitive behavioral theory and treatment, effectiveness of treatment for adolescent sexual abusers; racial discrimination of sexual abusers; and personality as an etiological factor for sexually abusive behavior. He has been published in several journals including, *Child Abuse and Neglect, Victims and Violence, Sexual Aggression, Evidenced Based Social Work, and Sexual Abuse: A Journal of Research and Practice.* Since 2001, Dr. Burton has been the Chair of the Association for the Treatment of Sexual Abusers' (ATSA) Education and Training Committee and a member of ATSA's executive board. He currently chairs the ATSA committee developing the adolescent guidelines for treatment.

Martin C. Calder, MA
Salford Child Protection Unit
Avon House
Avon Close, Little Hulton
Greater Manchester, M28 0LA UK
Ph: 0161 790 6332
Fax: 0161 790 4892
E-mail: martin.calder@salford.gov.uk or martinccalder@aol.com

Martin C. Calder manages a Child Protection Unit for Salford City Council in the UK. He has written, trained, and consulted extensively on a range of child protection matters, specializing in the field of child sexual abuse. Martin is driven to produce accessible, evidence-based assessment frameworks for frontline workers; to provide structures and procedures for local agencies to respond to the deficiencies within central government guidance; and has written in detail about the concerns associated with the demise of risk as a concept in the UK.

Deborah Cavanaugh, MA
Justice Resource Institute
63 Main Street
Bridgewater, MA 02324 USA
Ph: 508.697.2744
Fax: 508.697.2738
E-mail: DCAV7681@aol.com

Deborah Cavanaugh received her B.A. and M.A. degrees in Clinical Psychology from Bridgewater State College in Massachusetts. Her first research project, conducted at the Massachusetts Treatment Center for Sexually Dangerous Persons under the guidance of Dr. Robert Prentky and Dr. Martin Kafka, involved an examination of the relationship between childhood conduct disorder, ADHD, and handedness in adult sex offenders. This study was awarded the first "Theo Seghorn Memorial Scholarship" for "Most Promising Graduate Student" in the field of sexual abusers, from the Massachusetts Chapter of the Association for Treatment of Sexual Abusers (MATSA) in 2002. Theo Seghorn was one of the pioneers in the field of research and treatment of sexual offenders.

She currently works for Justice Resource Institute's Research Department on a project funded by the National Institute of Justice and the Massachusetts Department of Social Services (DSS) examining antecedents of sexually coercive behaviors in a sample of children and adolescents involved with the Massachusetts DSS. Ms. Cavanaugh presented the results of the initial stages of this project at the ATSA conference in October 2004. A follow-up phase to this study is currently under-way. Her current clinical interests include trauma and impact on the developing brain, as well as psychiatric disorders in juveniles with sexually coercive behaviors.

Mark Chaffin, Ph.D.
University of Oklahoma Health Sciences Center
PO Box 26901
Oklahoma City, OK 73190 USA
Ph: 405.271.8858
E-mail: mark-chaffin@ouhsc.edu

Mark Chaffin is a Psychologist, a Professor of Pediatrics, and Clinical Professor of Psychiatry and Behavioral Sciences at the University of Oklahoma Health Sciences Center in Oklahoma City, Oklahoma. He currently serves as Director of Research for Developmental and Behavioral Pediatrics. He conducts research in areas related to child abuse and neglect, including development and dissemination of evidence-based intervention models.

Kevin Creeden, MA, LMHC
Whitney Academy
85 Dr. Braley Road; P.O. Box 619
East Freetown, MA 02717 USA
Ph: 508.763.2202 Ext. 222
E-mail: kcreeden@whitneyacademy.org

Kevin Creeden is the Director of Assessment and Research at the Whitney Academy in East Freetown, Massachusetts. He has over 20 years of clinical experience working with children, adolescents, and adults engaging in sexually and physically aggressive behavior. Mr. Creeden co-led the first outpatient treatment group for juvenile sexual abusers in Massachusetts. He is past president of the Massachusetts chapter of the American Professional Society on the Abuse of Children (APSAC). Mr. Creeden trains and consults nationally to school, youth, community, and mental health service agencies.

Penny Cuninggim, Ed.D., MAT, MSW, LCSW
Director of Educational Services
New England Adolescent Research Institute
70 North Summer Street
Holyoke, MA 01040
Ph: 413.540.0712 ext. 24
E-mail: penepsc@aol.com
Penny Cuninggim has been working with emotionally disturbed children, youth, and

the staffs who serve them for 26 years. Working in a small agency has meant she has had the opportunity to study many fields in depth, and become proficient in a variety of capacities, including administrator, teacher, trainer, therapist and interventionist. She has a deep commitment to understanding the whole child, and using line staff experiences as the basis for effective education and treatment.

Currently, Penny is building an educational assessment and resource center which incorporates the latest research in science, psychology and special education as to how the brain learns best. Even the short term results she has seen with NEARI students using these new brain-based methods are astounding. For the complex youth with whom she works, many of these assessments and treatment tools are giving staff a new window into origins of learning problems, as well as new ways to not only remediate more effectively, but actually grow the brain for improved performance over the long term. She and her colleagues continue to learn about and pilot the best of both traditional and new brain based learning and brain self regulation tools available. She welcomes your ideas and experiences in this work.

Ronda L. Doonan, Ph.D.
Glendale, CA USA
E-mail: doonanr@aol.com

Ronda Doonan is a recent graduate of The California School of Professional Psychology, Los Angeles. She is currently serving a post-doctoral internship with the Julia Ann Singer Center and works as the clinical intake corrdinator for their parent agency, Vista Del Mar Child and Family Services.

Elissa McElrath Dyer, MA
University of Oklahoma
2709 Lawrence Avenue
Norman, OK 73019 USA
E-mail: elissa@ou.edu

Elissa Dyer completed a Master of Education in Community Counseling at the University of Oklahoma in 2000. She is a doctoral candidate at OU in Counseling Psychology and is currently completing her internship year with the Oklahoma Health Consortium. Her research interests include child abuse and neglect, adolescent sex offenders, and ethical issues.

Amanda M. Fanniff, MA
University of Arizona
Psychology Department
PO Box 210068
Tucson, AZ 85721-0068 USA
E-mail: fanniff@email.arizona.edu

Amanda Fanniff is a doctoral student at the University of Arizona. Her research interests include recidivism in juvenile sex offenders and competency to stand trial in juvenile offenders.

William N. Friedrich, Ph.D.
Mayo Clinic
200 1st St. SW
Ge 1B
Rochester, MN 55905 USA
Ph: 507.284.2088
Fax: 507.255.7383
E-mail: friedrich.william@mayo.edu

Dr. Friedrich is a Professor/Consultant at the Mayo Clinic and the Mayo Medical School. He is also a Diplomate with the American Board of Professional Psychology in both Clinical and Family Psychology. He is the author of seven books, 125 articles and 25 chapters, the majority of them dealing with the assessment and treatment of child maltreatment, particulary sexual abuse and sexual behavior problems in children. He is also the developer of the *Child Sexual Behavior Inventory*. He has been a Fulbright Scholar to Latvia and for six years was on the faculty of the Eastern European Children's Mental Health Alliance.

Lisa L. Frey, Ph.D.
University of Oklahoma
Assistant Professor
Counseling Psychology Program
Department of Educational Psychology
820 Van Vleet Oval, Room 321
Norman, OK 73019-2041 USA
Ph: 405.325.1503
Fax: 405.325.6655
E-mail: Melissa.Frey-1@ou.edu

Lisa Frey is an Assistant Professor in the Counseling Psychology Program of the Department of Educational Psychology at the University of Oklahoma. Prior to her move to academia, Dr. Frey had a private clinical and consulting practice for over twenty years focusing on sexually aggressive youth, youth with sexual behavior problems, and youth who experienced trauma. She has specific clinical and consulting experience in working with adolescent females who have engaged in sexually aggressive behavior. Dr. Frey's research interests include at-risk youth, particularly sexually aggressive behavior and female adolescent delinquent behavior; gender similarities and differences in relationship development; applications of relational-cultural therapy; and acculturation and worldview of international students and immigrants.

Jane F. Gilgun, Ph.D., LICSW
School of Social Work
University of Minnesota, Twin Cities
1404 Gortner Avenue
St. Paul, MN 55410 USA
Ph: 612.624.3643
Fax: 612.624.3744
E-mail: jgilgun@umn.edu

Jane F. Gilgun is professor, at the School of Social Work, University of Minnesota, Twin Cities. She has done research on resilience for more than twenty years, focusing on risks for violent behaviors, the meanings of violence to perpetrators, and why persons don't become violent when they have risks to do so. Her present research projects include the development of violent behaviors, adoptions of children with special needs, and the development of strategies to encourage help-seeking among perpetrators of child sexual abuse or those who are at risk. Other projects have been on strengths-based assessments for children and adolescents and outcome evaluations in family incest treatment. She has published widely, most recently on a new approach to assessment that includes resilience, cognitive schemas, gender issues, and neuropsychology as well as on the four cornerstones of evidence-based practice. She has presented locally, nationally, and internationally on resilience, violence, and treatment approaches that build on client strengths. She is the author of workbooks for children and their families where the children have a variety of adjustment issues associated with histories of adversity. These and other materials are available free of charge at ssw.che.umn.edu/Faculty_Profiles/Gilgun_Jane.html

David Harvey, Ph.D.
Counseling and Consulting
2430 E. 6th St
Tucson, AZ 85719 USA
E-mail: dharvey@counselingconsulting.org

David Harvey has provided specialized offender treatment services in community-based settings for the past twenty years. His consultation and training programs have served sex offender and domestic-violence treatment providers, criminal justice organizations, and policy makers in many communities. Dr. Harvey is the Executive Director of Counseling & Consulting Services, Inc. in Tucson, Arizona.

Saul Hewish
United Kingdom
E-mail: Saul@actingout.co.uk

Saul Hewish has worked extensively in both UK and USA criminal justice systems using drama and theatre as a medium for change. He was a founding member, and former director, of Geese Theatre (UK) (est 1987), a deputy director of Geese Theatre (USA), and since 1996 has worked in a freelance capacity developing drama-based responses to crime within youth offending teams, social services departments, and special educational settings across the UK. He is currently executive co-director of

Rideout (Creative Arts for Rehabilitation), a small arts-based company specialising in drama, theatre, and multi-arts based programmes in the UK prison system. He is a recipient of the Butler Trust Certificate Award, a national award which recognises exceptional work by staff in HM Prison Service. Saul also teaches a degree level course on Theatre in the Community at the University of Warwick, and is a member of the National Training Consortium on Arts in Criminal Justice.

John A. Hunter, Ph.D.
Louisiana State University Health Sciences Center
1600 Canal Street, Suite 1207
New Orleans, LA USA
Ph: 504.568.2526

John Hunter is Professor of Public Health, and state-wide Director of Mental Health for the School of Public Health's Juvenile Justice Program, at Louisiana State University in New Orleans, Louisiana. Dr. Hunter is well-known for his clinical and research expertise on juvenile sexual offending.

Dr. Hunter has published over 40 articles and book chapters on the subject of sexual offenders and sexual trauma, and has been the recipient of seven federal research grants in this area of study. Most recently, he received a "Career Development Award" from the National Institute of Mental Health to further study subtypes of sexually aggressive youth and their hypothesized differential developmental trajectories. Dr. Hunter has directed both community-based and residential treatment programs for juvenile and adult sexual offenders. He currently serves on the Kempe Center's National Task Force on Juvenile Sexual Offending, the National Advisory Committee of the University of Oklahoma's National Center on Sexual Behavior of Youth, and the Center for Sex Offender Management's National Resource Group.

Alan Jenkins
Nada Counselling, Consulting & Training
PO Box 773
Stirling, South Australia 5152
Ph: 618.8340.2240
Fax: 618.8370.8696
E-mail: alanjenkins@ozemail.com.au

Alan Jenkins has worked in a range of multi-undisciplinary teams addressing violence and abusive behaviour for 25 years. Rather than tire from this work, he has become increasingly intrigued with possibilities for the discovery of ethical and respectful ways of relating. The valuing of ethics, fairness, and the importance of protest against injustice has led him to stray considerably from the path prescribed in his early training as a psychologist towards a political analysis of abuse.

He is currently a director of Nada, an independent service, which provides intervention in family abuse, violence, and workplace harassment. He manages the Mary Street Program for young people who have sexually assaulted, their caregivers, and communities.

Bradley R. Johnson, MD
6812 N. Oracle Rd., #114
Tucson, AZ 85704 USA
Ph: 520.297.9878
Fax: 520.297.2242

Bradley Johnson is a psychiatrist in private practice who works with adults, adolescents, and children. In addition to his work in general psychiatry, he specializes in working in the subspecialty area of forensics, with particular emphasis on assessing and treating sexual offenders. He has worked for the Arizona Department of Corrections, taking care of inmates in the highest security units, including Condemned Row. He is currently the Chief of Psychiatry at the Arizona Community Protection and Treatment Center for sex offender civil commitment in Phoenix, Arizona.

Throughout his practice, Dr. Johnson has maintained a position as an Assistant Clinical Professor at the University of Arizona, Department of Psychiatry.

Toni Cavanagh Johnson, Ph.D.
Independent Practice
1101 Fremont Avenue
South Pasadena, CA 91030 USA
Ph: 626.799.4522
Fax: 818.790.0139
E-mail: toni@tcavjohn.com

Toni Cavanagh Johnson is a licensed clinical psychologist in private practice in South Pasadena, California. She has been working in the field of child abuse for 24 years as a researcher, trainer and clinician. For the past twenty years Dr. Johnson has provided highly specialized treatment for children below the age of twelve with sexual behavior problems. She has written five books, two booklets, published numerous articles in journals, as well as book chapters on the topic of children with sexual behavior problems.

Dr. Johnson has lectured on child abuse around the world. She provides consultation to protective service workers, mental health professionals, attorneys, the police, probation, and the courts in the area of sexual victimization and perpetration.

Robert Kinscherff, Ph.D., Esq.
Juvenile Court Department, MA Trial Court
MA School of Professional Psychology
Harvard Medical School
Boston University School of Law
AOTC-Juvenile Court
3 Center Plaza, Suite 520
Boston, MA 02108 USA
Ph: 617.788.6550
E-mail: kinscherff_r@jud.state.ma.us

Robert Kinscherff is a forensic psychologist and attorney who currently serves as Director of Juvenile Court Clinic Services for the Juvenile Court Department of the Massachusetts Trial Court. He is also Director of the Forensic Specialization Track at the Massachusetts Trial Court and holds teaching appointments through Harvard Medical School and Boston University School of Law. He previously has served as Director of Training (Adult Forensics) and Senior Psychologist of the Boston Juvenile Court Clinic while affiliated with the Law and Psychiatry Service of the Massachusetts General Hospital. He has served as Chair of the Ethics Committee and of the Committee on Legal Issues of the American Psychological Association. His areas of professional practice and research include adult and juvenile sexual offenders, violence risk assessment and management, child maltreatment, and legal and ethical issues in professional mental health practice.

Ian Lambie, Ph.D.
Senior Lecturer and Director of Clinical Psychology
Consultant to the SAFE Programme
Psychology Department; University of Auckland; Private Bag 92019
Auckland New Zealand
Ph: 64.9.3737.599 ext. 85012
Fax: 64.9.3737.450
E-mail: i.lambie@auckland.ac.nz

Ian Lambie is a Senior Lecturer and Director of Training in Clinical Psychology at the University of Auckland, New Zealand. He has been providing treatment for adolescent sexual offenders for over fifteen years. He is Clinical Consultant to the SAFE Programme, which provides community treatment to adolescent sexual offenders in Auckland. There he has an ongoing international research programme and undertakes clinical work. His clinical and research interests are youth forensic psychology, and, in particular, severe conduct disorder, adolescent sexual offending, and arson. Ian is a consultant to the New Zealand Government on youth offending and a member of the Ministry of Justice Independent Advisory Group on Youth Offending. Dr. Lambie is a consulting psychologist for the New Zealand Fire Service National Fire Awareness and Youth Intervention Programme. In 1999 he was awarded the graduate student award from The Association for the Treatment of Sexual Abusers for his research on resiliency in the victim-offender cycle in male sexual abuse. In 2001, he was the youngest recipient ever to receive the New Zealand Psychological Society Public Interest Award for his long-standing community work in developing adolescent sexual offender treatment in New Zealand.

Craig Latham, Ph.D.
Latham Consulting Group, LLC
Ten Union Street
Natick, MA 01760-4579 USA
Ph: 508.650.4800
Fax: 508.650.4004
E-mail: clatham@forensicdoc.com

Craig Latham received his Ph.D. in Personality and Developmental Psychology from Harvard University and completed his clinical training at the Judge Baker Children's Center. He has worked with violent and emotionally disturbed adolescents in a variety of capacities at the Massachusetts Departments of Mental Health, Social Services, and Youth Services since 1980.   Before leaving state service in 1990, Dr. Latham was the Senior Forensic Child Psychologist for the Massachusetts Department of Mental Health. In that position, he was responsible for forensic mental health services provided to children in Massachusetts, and he also served as a consultant to the United States Secret Service. Currently, Dr. Latham is in private practice, where he continues to serve as a consultant for various law enforcement and social service agencies in this country and abroad on the treatment of violent and sexually aggressive children and adolescents.

Elizabeth J. Letourneau, Ph.D.
Medical University of South Carolina
Department of Psychiatry and Behavioral Sciences
67 President St., Suite CPP
Box 250861
Charleston, SC 29425 USA
Ph: 843.876.1868
Fax: 843.876.1808
E-mail: letourej@musc.edu

Elizabeth Letourneau has conducted research with adult and juvenile sex offenders for the past fifteen years. She has numerous publications in this field and is active in the Association for the Treatment of Sexual Abusers (ATSA). For the past four years, Dr. Letourneau has conducted research at the Family Services Research Center in the Medical University of South Carolina. This center conducts research primarily on juvenile delinquency treatment effectiveness and Dr. Letourneau's research has focused on treatment effectiveness with juvenile sex offenders.

Robert E. Longo, MRC, LPC
Sexual Abuse Prevention &
Education Resources International
Charleston, SC USA
Ph: 843.345.5445
E-mail: RobertELongo@aol.com
Web: www.saperi.us

Robert E. Longo is an independent contractor, consultant, educator, trainer, and author dedicated to sexual abuse prevention and treatment. He was previously Corporate Director of Special Programming and Clinical Training for New Hope

Treatment Centers, Charleston, South Carolina. His focus is on sexual abuse prevention and treatment with youth. He has consulted and presented internationally in the field of sexual abuser assessment, treatment, and program development. He is an advisory board member of the National Adolescent Perpetrator Network, a national committee member of the Center for Sex Offender Management, a national advisory committee member to the National Center On Sexual Behavior of Youth, and an advisory team member to Darkness to Light.

Mr. Longo has published four books, five workbooks, and over forty chapters and articles in the field of sexual abuse treatment. He pioneered the adult sexual offender workbook series published by NEARI Press. He is the author of the books *New Hope Exercises for Youth: Experiential Exercises for Children and Adolescents*, and *Paths To Wellness*, and is co-author of *Men & Anger: Understanding and Managing Your Anger*, and *Sexual Abuse In America: Epidemic of the 21st Century*. He has specialized in the sexual abuse field and has worked with victims, and with juvenile and adult sex abusers in residential, hospital, prison, and community-based settings since 1978.

Tony Morrison
Independent Child Welfare Trainer and Consultant
3 Aintree Drive
Rochdale, Lancs 0L115SH UK
Ph: 4170.635.3399
E-mail: tonymorrison@btinternet.com

Tony Morrison is an independent social care trainer, practitioner and consultant from Rochdale UK. Tony works with staff in social services, health and other agencies on staff supervision, inter-agency collaboration, child welfare strategic planning, and emotional literacy development. His clinical interest is in holistic approaches to the management and treatment of young people who sexually abuse. He has a special interest in attachment and has been co-running a therapeutic service for the parents of young people who commit sexual offences with GMAP in Manchester. He is a practice consultant for two other programmes and has co-written assessment and therapeutic guides for work with the parents of young people who sexually abuse (in press AIM Project, Greater Manchester). His publications include *'Sexual Offending Against Children'* co-editor (Routledge 1994) , *'Supervision in Social Care'* (2nd edition, Pavilion, 2001), and a number of publications in the field of young people who sexually abuse. He is a Visiting Research Fellow at the University of Huddersfield and an external examiner for the Advanced Social Work Course at Queens University and University of Ulster, Northern Ireland.

Dave O'Callaghan
c/o G-MAP Services
1 Roebuck Lane
Sale, Chesire, M33 7SY UK
E-mail: office@g-map.org

Dave O'Callaghan sadly died in March 2004. He was a founder and Director of G-MAP, an independent specialist therapeutic service for young people who sexually harm, based in Manchester, UK.

Dave was a pioneer in developing services for young people with learning difficulties. His publications, presentations and training in this field of work have been highly influential amongst professionals for many years and his enthusiasm, creativity, and understanding will continue to inspire many more for a long time to come.

Ann M. Pimental, MSCJ/MHC
Justice Resource Institute, Research Department
63 Main Street
Bridgewater, MA 02324 USA
Ph: 508.697.2744 ext. 206
Fax: 508.697.2738
E-mail: apimental@jri.org

Ann Pimental received her B.S. from Bridgewater State College and two Master degrees from Suffolk University in the areas of Criminal Justice and Mental Health Counseling. She has worked with offenders and victims in various capacities. She began working in the field of sex offenders in 1997 at the Massachusetts Treatment Center for the non-profit organization, Justice Resource Institute (JRI). In 2001, she worked as a counselor and an advocate for surviors of domestic violence and sexual assault. During that same year, she began a new position for JRI as project coordinator for their newly developed research department. The first research project was a colloborate effort with the Massachusetts Department of Social Services. The research examined the Assessment for Safe and Appropriate Placement (ASAP) program, which was designed to flag children who demonstrate sexually aggressive behaviors. The research department received additional funding from the National Institute of Justice to conduct a follow-up study of these children. She also works with the Counseling and Psychotherapy Center conducting assessments on incarcerated juvenile sex offenders and training staff on the Juvenile Sex Offender Assessment Protocol-II.

Robert Prentky Ph.D.
Justice Resource Institute
Research Department
63 Main Street – Suite #6
Bridgewater, MA 02343 USA
Ph: 508.697.2744 x205
Fax: 508.697.2738
E-mail: rprentky@jri.org

Robert Prentky is currently in private practice with F & P Associates as a forensic psychologist. In addition, he teaches in the Graduate School of Criminal Justice at Northeastern University and is director of research for Justice Resource Institute. In his latter capacity, he has been conducting state (Massachusetts) and federally funded (NIJ) research since 2001 on risk factors and risk mitigative management strategies for highly abuse-reactive male and female adolescents and pre-adolescents. Dr. Prentky has been working in the field of sexual violence for the past 24 years.

David S. Prescott, LICSW
Sand Ridge Secure Treatment Center
P.O. Box 700
Mauston, WI 53948 USA
Ph: 608.847.4438
Fax: 608.847.1749
E-mail: VTPrescott@Earthlink.net

David Prescott has worked in and around inpatient settings since 1984, becoming involved in the assessment and treatment of sexual abuse shortly thereafter. Throughout this time, he has been fascinated by the processes involved in understanding and helping others, as well as how information is communicated amongst professionals and clients. A strong advocate of collaborative approaches towards reducing the harm of sexual abuse, Mr. Prescott is closely involved with the Association for the Treatment of Sexual Abusers, at both the state and national levels, and edits that organization's newsletter, *The Forum*.

Susan L. Robinson, LCSW
Progressive Therapy Systems
758 Sherman Street
Denver, Co 80203 USA
Ph: 303.831.9344 Ext. 17
Fax: 303.831.9347
E-mail: surobin@hotmail.com

Susan Robinson works in a private mental health agency specializing in forensic social work. She has been working in the field of sexual abuse for over ten years. She specializes in working with sexually abusive females and wrote the first workbook specifically designed for sexually abusive female adolescents entitled *Growing Beyond: A Workbook for Teenage Girls*. She speaks nationally on the subject of female sexual abuse and serves as a field instructor for the University of Denver's Master of Social Work Program.

Marlyn Robson
Practice 92
92 Owen's Road
Mt. Eden, Auckland, New Zealand
Ph: 649.238.6490
E-mail: marlynr@xtra.co.nz

Marlyn Robson is originally from Scotland but emigrated to New Zealand with her husband and two children 25 years ago.

She is a psychotherapist and psychodramatist working in private practice. She has been working with survivors of child sexual abuse for twenty years. However, ten years ago she started with SAFE Network, a community agency, working with people who sexually offend, adolescents and adults, males and females.

Lisa Saldana, Ph.D.
Family Services Research Center
Medical University of South Carolina
Charleston, SC USA
E-mail: saldanal@musc.edu

Lisa Saldana received her Ph.D. in clinical psychology from the University of Missouri-Columbia, in 2003. Currently, she is an assistant professor at the Family Services Research Center in the Department of Psychiatry and Behavioral Sciences at the Medical University of South Carolina. Dr. Saldana completed her clinical internship at La Rabida Children's Hospital in Chicago, with an emphasis in assessment and treatment of child maltreatment and trauma. Her research interests include development and validation of empirically supported interventions for intentional (i.e., maltreatment) and unintentional (i.e., accidental) child injuries, methods of providing services for disadvantaged children and their families, children's reactions to negative life events, and family preservation. Dr. Saldana is currently working on National Institute of Mental Health funded research grants evaluating the effectiveness of multisystemic therapy in the treatment of sexually aggressive youth and child maltreatment.

Matt Sanders
Counseling and Consulting

Joann Schladale, MA
Resources For Resolving Violence
28 Marshview Drive
Freeport, ME 04032 USA
Ph: 207.865.3111
E-mail: schladale@aol.com
Web: www.resourcesforresolvingviolence.com

Joann Schladale has been working in the field of family violence since 1981. In 1991, as faculty at the University of Louisville, she developed and coordinated the internationally acclaimed Juvenile Sexual Offender Counselor Certification Program. She continues to teach a series of courses that focus on a collaborative approach for treatment with adolescents and children who are violent and sexually abusive. She provides extensive consultation, program development and evaluation, clinical supervision, staff development, and training throughout North America. She is a clinical member, and approved supervisor, of the American Association for Marriage and Family Therapy, and a clinical member of the Association for the Treatment of Sexual Abusers, and the International Association for the Treatment of Sexual Offenders. She has received professional awards and made over a hundred presentations throughout North America and Europe focusing on violence and sexual abuse. Her publication, *"The T.O.P. Workbook for Taming Violence and Sexual Aggression,"* was published in June 2002.

Barbara K. Schwartz, Ph.D.
Justice Resource Institute
Research Department; 63 Main Street – Suite #6
Bridgewater, MA 02343 USA
Ph: 508.697.2452 x207
Fax: 508.697.2738
E-mail: drbsch@aol.com

Barbara Schwartz has been working with adult and juvenile sex offenders since 1971. She has directed programs for this population in New Mexico, Washington, Massachusetts, New Jersey, Missouri, and Connecticut. Her career has included consultation with over 40 states as well as Canada and Israel. Widely published, she has authored or edited eight books in the field including, *The Sex Offender, Volumes 1-5* and *Facing the Shadow*. Currently she is involved with her co-authors in this volume in a large research project studying sexually inappropriate behavior in children. In connection with her work for Justice Resource Institute, she treats juvenile sex offenders for the Massachusetts Department of Youth Services. She maintains a private practice dealing with the outpatient evaluation and treatment of adult and juvenile sex offenders through New England Forensic Associates. Dr. Schwartz received her Ph.D. in psychology/criminology from the University of New Mexico.

Carl Schwartz, Ph.D.
Prehab of Arizona
Tempe, AZ USA

Carl Schwartz has been working in the addictions and sexual abuse field for over 20 years. He has clinically directed an inpatient program for adolescents. He has presented and organized clinical methods for increasing empathic structures for clients using high impact imagery and highly focused narrative methods. His overall approach is to combine the principles of restorative justice, emotional retribution, and the clarification of long-standing family themes and conflicts that have directly and indirectly contributed to a client's sexually abusive scripts.

Leslie A. Sim, Ph.D.
Mayo Clinic
Department of Psychiatry and Psychology
200 1st Street
SW Rochester, MN 55902 USA
Ph: 507.284.2088
E-mail: Sim.Leslie@mayo.edu

Leslie Sim is an Associate Consultant at the Mayo Clinic and an instructor at the Mayo Medical School. Her research interests focus on emotion regulation and child psychopathology.

Melissa Sisco
University of Arizona
Psychology Department, Rm #312
1503 E. University Blvd.
Tucson, AZ 85721-0068 USA
Ph: 520.621.7447
E-mail: sisco@u.arizona.edu

Melissa Sisco is a doctoral student at the University of Arizona. Her research interests include restorative justice, domestic violence, and sexual aggression.

Cynthia Cupit Swenson, Ph.D.
Medical University of South Carolina
67 President Street-Suite CPP
PO Box 250861
Charleston, SC 29425 USA
Ph: 843.876.1800
Fax: 843.876.1808
E-mail: swensocc@musc.edu

Cynthia Cupit Swenson received her Ph.D. in clinical psychology with a sub-specialty in school psychology from Florida State University. Currently she is associate professor and associate director at the Family Services Research Center in the Department of Psychiatry and Behavioral Sciences of the Medical University of South Carolina. She is principle investigator on the National Institue of Mental Health-funded randomized clinical trial comparing parent training and multisystemic therapy with physically abused adolescents and their families.

Dr. Swenson has worked extensively with children and families over the last 25 years. Her research is community-based and focuses on community violence, child maltreatment, youth aggression and substance abuse. She has published over 30 journal articles and book chapters, and a recent book on treating community violence and troubled neighborhoods. Dr. Swenson is currently on the Board of the American Professional Society on the Abuse of Children.

Jerry D. Thomas, MA
J. Thomas Consulting and Training Services
1799 Linden Avenue
Memphis, TN 38104 USA
E-mail: thom5741@bellsouth.net

Jerry Thomas is an independent consultant who specializes in work with sexually abusive youth. She has always been a strong advocate of family involvement in treatment and her chapter "Family Treatment," in the book *Juvenile Sexual Offending: Causes and Consequences*, edited by, Ryan and Lane (1998) was the first written on this subject. A member of the National Task Force on Juvenile Sexual Offending, she participated in the development of The Task Force Report, which was published by the National Counsel of Juvenile and Family Court Judges. She also participated in the

National Task Force on Offense Specific Residential Programs, and collaborated in the development of residential standards of practice.

Patrick Tidmarsh, MA (Criminology)
Melbourne Adolescent Program for Positive Sexuality
900 Park St
Melbourne, Victoria, Australia 3052
Ph: 613.9389.4273
E-mail: MAPPS@rch.org.au

Patrick Tidmarsh is a former founding member of Geese Theatre Co., UK. He worked at Gracewell Clinic as the foremost proponent of drama therapy, and then moved to Melbourne, Australia where he was the developer and director of MAPPS (Melbourne Adolescent Program for Positive Sexuality). Currently he is the program director for Adolescent Forensic Health Services, on the board of directors of Child Wise and a consultant to Melbourne police and child care workers on issues to do with child sexual assault, and rape.

C. Wilson Viar, III
Viar Services

C. Wilson Viar is an independent research and writing consultant focusing primarily on problematic social issues and creative efforts to solve them. Since 1996 he has co-authored a wide variety of articles, chapters, handbooks, seminars and training materials with Ms. Jerry Thomas on topics spanning the field.

EDITORS' NOTE:
MISSION, PURPOSE, AND STYLE

This book compiles new perspectives in understanding and treating youthful sexual abusers. It began as a casual conversation in which the editors discovered we were trying to build similar projects. We believe that the fundamental strength of the chapters is in the knowledge and passion of each contributor. This however, presents several dilemmas.

The first dilemma is whether the ultimate message of the book might get lost within the diversity of the chapters. To be clear: the unifying theme of this book is the necessity for a holistic approach towards youth that integrates aspects of their entire functioning, context, and development. Our field has a history of understanding and treating youthful sexual aggression separately from other aspects of their lives. It does not serve youth to understand or rehabilitate them outside of a solid understanding of their co-existing psychiatric conditions (see Bradley Johnson's chapter), their family (see Schladale's and Thomas' chapters), or a full accounting of their own histories of abuse (see chapters by Schwartz, Cavanaugh, & Prentky, and Creeden). Our hope is to inspire others to provide rehabilitation based on the long-term development of youth rather than solely on short-term solutions.

Another dilemma is to what extent editors should shape the voices of individual chapters in order to create a smooth flow throughout a volume. On one hand, a book that presents a similar voice across all chapters has obvious appeal to readers and editors alike. On the other hand, we have deliberately sought out contributors from around the world who come from often very different backgrounds (hence the plural title "Current Perspectives"). We have placed our editorial priority on highlighting the individual voice of each contributor over ensuring a unified voice. We have done this with the belief that readers can gain from each turn of a phrase and each difference in chapter structure. This is a result of our having learned from the contributors as individuals as much as we have learned from them as authors.

Another dilemma involves the research that provides the foundation for these chapters. Anyone reading scholarly journals frequently sees the disclaimer that "more research is needed", and yet many chapters state that "the research clearly shows…" Worse, it seems that our entire field is willing to admit that much of what we thought we knew twenty years ago has turned out not to be true. Some chapters contain up-to-the-moment research, while others build their case on innovative thought around older research. What to do?

These chapters are a snapshot of a field experiencing both unprecedented growth (in treatment technique, research, and assessment instrumentation) and unprecedented pressures (such as those that come with life-long registration, civil commitment, increased media exposure, and initiatives for stiffer sentencing). Much of the information contained here is very much a work in progress. At a time when practitioners are desperate for resources, is it better to wait to publish assessment and treatment techniques, or do we have an obligation to keep current with both practice and research as they unfold? Must we wait for ideas to be proven to practice them, or should we develop ideas that we can later test?

The understanding and treatment of youthful sexual abusers still cries out for further refinement. However, the current states of knowledge and practice demand that new ideas challenge traditional practice. Those active in organizations such as the Association for the Treatment of Sexual Abusers and the National Adolescent Perpetration Network are familiar with the rapid growth of our field. Far from the final word, this book is intended to explore that growth and to inspire more.

FOREWORD

DAVID L. BURTON

While to some of us the field of treatment aimed at youth who have sexually abused or acted inappropriately in a sexual way feels old, it is really quite a new area of service provision, moving from a crawl to a teetering walk – even as we personally age. Many of us in the field started working with this group of abusers in the mid 1980's. As with any new field, ours struggles with challenges, revisions, zealots and resistance to change – this is especially true in the absence of much hard science or of proof of what is the best method of treatment for these youth.

The chapters in this volume take on diverse areas of practice and wide ranging paradigms ranging from an analysis of resistance to experiential therapy to techniques of engagement, legal issues facing adolescents who are sexually abusive, treatment of females that sexually abuse, neurology, family practice, and the relevance of victimization of youth who are abusive. This text covers many other areas as well, each important and useful and as a whole reading like a brochure for a very good conference on the treatment of children and adolescents. Contributors are an exciting combination of experienced researchers and authors from around the world, and a few new and talented voices. Nonetheless, themes emerge across the chapters which illuminate the barriers, boundaries, and areas for development of practice techniques, assessment, and future research in the field. Three of these themes are development, heterogeneity of the populations, and advanced techniques for treatment.

Development

Development implies *change over time* and is addressed by the authors in several ways. First, the development of the field is evident in some of the chapters as previously asked questions have been answered by new research and recent conceptualizations of difficult behaviors. The second, and perhaps most salient, area of development addressed by several of the authors is the need to consider biopsychosocial development of the youth. This is underlined as critical for appropriate design of interventions, as opposed to just taking programs and assumptions from extant adult programming, and for development of appropriate assessment methods for the youth. A third area of some discussion is understanding that our clients are sexual beings and that we need to not condemn them (be they prepubescent children or adolescents) for normal sexual behavior, and we should encourage their healthy sexual development. Developmental concerns are also addressed in treatment discussions regarding sexually abusive youth who are developmentally delayed and in understanding the development of healthy and healing relationships – with potential of development gone awry in each case and suggestions for remediation. Another important area of development that has been stressed by one of the editors previously is that of societal development that needs to address sexual abuse as a public health issue (Freeman-Longo & Blanchard, 1998) rather than as personal failing of the victim or as a sad but rare event.

Heterogeneity

A second emergent theme in this text is that of the heterogeneity of the youth. They have distinctly different pathways of development (Knight & Sims-Knight, 2004), different family experiences, different background in terms of victimization, different narratives, and understandings of their world and behavior – all of which leads to the absolute need for individualized assessment and treatment. While mental health practitioners laud research and desire evidence-based practice methods, this is difficult to do in our field when witnessing how different symptoms, situations, capacities, and resilience patterns present themselves in clients. Especially when research supports an amazing amount of heterogeneity among youth, we must never assume a "one size fits all" (or even most) model in program design or treatment delivery. This theme is highlighted by John Hunter's chapter and echoed throughout the text.

Advanced Techniques

The third and final theme I will discuss here is that of advanced techniques. While guidelines for treatment of adolescent abusers exist (National Adolescent Perpetration Network, 1993) and are being developed by ATSA, these are currently tentative and based on very little science. We desperately need research on the effectiveness of elements or components of treatment (e.g., cycle, trauma, and relapse prevention work), iatrogenic effects of group therapy[1], group processes (i.e., should we increase cohesion in a group of sexual abusers given potential iatrogenic effects), length of stay, and many other areas. Other than the early work with MST – some of which is presented in the text – and recidivism studies, we know little about treatment. Yet there are many ways of knowing and learning information and, as has been the case in a number of mental health fields, practice frequently guides research on adolescent sexual abusers.

While unabashedly discussing limits of recent research, the authors contend with the real-world dilemma of the need to deliver treatment and base observations, detailed descriptions of techniques and methods of treatment from a post modern perspective of multiple truths – the authors describe what they see as working while genuinely inviting the reader's feedback and participation in a journey towards the development of best practices for the amelioration of adolescent sexual aggression. How wonderful and refreshing!

Conclusion

As a researcher and clinician who has had the good luck to work in and with many programs and to read and follow the work and arduous efforts of the two editors of this text, I conclude this forward with three final points that arise from the chapters. First, I challenge the reader to accept and even embrace the ambiguity of our field. In doing this I recommend always remembering that we must be committed to helping youth in every way that we can, that we do not yet know what is best, but that through communication, learning, collaboration, and training we can work towards the shared goal of stopping this serious problem. Second, I seriously challenge the reader to contribute to the science in the field. Join the National Adolescent Perpetration Network[2] (NAPN) and the Association for the Treatment of Sexual

Abusers[3] (ATSA) and find research efforts to which you can contribute[4]. All of us with professional credentials have an ethical requirement to assist in the development of knowledge, to evaluate our practice, to be open to learning the newest and best methods of treatment[5]. Join us in research efforts to increase sample sizes, to advocate for randomized control trials and contribute to the development of knowledge in our field. Third, even though many of us are caught between roles of incarceration and/or reporter of probation violations and treatment provider, we must also develop sincere therapeutic relationships with these youth to effect change. In support of some of the authors in this text, therapeutic alliance is of particular value in work with adolescents in general (Digiusuppe, Linscott, & Jilton, 1996; Horvath & Greenberg, 1994; Horvath & Symonds, 1991; Shirk & Russell, 1996). More specifically, this method is empirically supported for work with delinquent youth. For example, a positive therapeutic alliance is associated with psychological improvement and decreased recidivism for delinquent youth (Florsheim, Shotorbani, Guest-Warnick, Barrat & Hwang, 2000). Moreover, delinquent youth are more responsive and compliant when they share a stronger therapeutic alliance with their therapist (Langer & Nieli, 1999).

Enjoy the book and the learning. I'll see you at the conferences!

David L. Burton
Northampton, Massachusetts
Smith College School for Social Work
Northeast Center for Youth and Families

End Notes

[1] Poulin, F., Dishion, T. J & Burraston (2001) found that less severe delinquents became more severe evidently due to exposure to more severe youth in a cognitive behavioral group program.
[2] http://www.kempe.org/napn/
[3] http://atsa.com/
[4] For example, the Collaboration for Adolescent Research: Mentoring & Advancement (CARMA) meets at ATSA every year. Please contact David Burton for information at dlburton@email.smith.edu.
[5] Psychology:http://www.apa.org/ethics/homepage.html.SocialWork: http://www.socialworkers.org/pubs/code/code.asp.
[6] http://www.ncsby.org/pages/publications/What%20Research%20Shows%20About%20Adolescent%20Sex%20Offenders%2020060404.pdf - retrieved January 5, 2005.
[7] http://www.fbi.gov/ucr/cius_03/pdf/03sec4.pdf

References

Digiuseppe, R., Linscott, J., & Jilton, R. (1996). Developing the therapeutic alliance in child-adolescent psychotherapy. *Applied & Preventive Psychology*, 5:85-100.

Florsheim, P., Shotorbani, S., Guest-Warnick, G. , Barratt, T., & Hwang, W. (2000). Role of the working alliance in the treatment of delinquent boys in community-based programs. *Journal of Clinical Child Psychology*, 29 (1), 94-107.

Freeman-Longo, R. & Blanchard, G. (1998) *Sexual abuse in America: Epidemic in the 21st century*. Brandon, VT, Safer Society Press.

Horvath, A. O., & Greenburg, L. S. (1994). The working alliance: *Theory, research, and practice*. New York, NY: John Wiley and Sons.

Horvath, A. O., & Symonds, B. D. (1991). Relation between working alliance and outcome in psychotherapy: A meta-analysis. *Journal of Counseling Psychology*, 38(2), 139-149.

Knight, R. A., & Sims-Knight, J. E. (2004). Testing an etiological model for juvenile sexual offending against women. In R. Geffner, K. C. Franey, T. G. Arnold, & R. Falconer (Eds.), *Identifying and treating youths who sexually offend: Current approaches, techniques, and research*. New York: Haworth Press.

Langer, N. (1999). Culturally competent professionals in therapeutic alliances enhance patient compliance. *Journal of Health Care for the Poor & Underserved*, 10(1), 19-26.

National Adolescent Perpetration Network (1993). The Revised Report from the National Task Force on Juvenile Sexual Offending. *Juvenile and Family Court Journal*, 44, 1-120.

Poulin, F., Dishion, T. J & Burraston, B. (2001). 3-Year iatrogenic effects associated with aggregating high-risk adolescents in cognitive-behavioral preventive interventions. *Applied Developmental Science*, 5(4), pp. 214-224.

Shirk, S. R., & Russell, R. L. (1996). *Change processes in child psychotherapy: Revitalizing treatment and research*. New York, NY: The Guildford Press.

INTRODUCTION

ROBERT E. LONGO
AND
DAVID S. PRESCOTT

A Brief History of Treating Youth with Sexual Behavior Problems

A deep understanding of evaluating and treating sexually abusive youth requires that that we first know our history and ourselves. Many who began this work in the 1980s have since concluded that much of what we thought we knew turned out to be wrong. This introduction outlines many of the accomplishments in understanding young people who have sexually abused since the mid-20th century.

Although unfamiliar to many, Kurt Freund was a pioneer in the field of human sexuality. Living in Czechoslovakia, Freund helped to develop and research the volumetric penile plethysmograph, a device that measures penile engorgement in response to auditory and/or visual stimuli. The military used his early research to help detect homosexuals joining the ranks. While the plethysmograph often raised more questions than it answered regarding the nature of sexual arousal and interest, it was the first objective measure of its kind. It provided a common and unified area of study. Freund eventually left Czechoslovakia and settled at Clarke University in Toronto, where his research continued in many areas, ranging from the use of plethysmography with sexual abusers to the construct of "courtship disorder."

The plethysmograph began to find use outside the research laboratory in subsequent decades, particularly following public awareness of sexual abuse as a topic of societal concern. The advent of the women's movement (e.g. Brownmiller, 1975) certainly helped bring the issue of sexual abuse to the forefront of discussion.

One of the first documents published about the sex offender treatment movement was written by Edward Brecher (1978) and supported by a grant from the National Institute of Law Enforcement and Criminal Justice, the law enforcement assistance administration of the U.S. Department of Justice. The grant funds were awarded to the American Correctional Association under the Omnibus Crime Control and Safe Streets Act of 1968. In the abstract, Brecher notes,

> *"What should be done about sex offenders after they have been sentenced and turned over to the correctional system? … Nothing in particular is being done about the vast majority of them and little or no attention is being paid to the partic-*

ular factors which made these men sex offenders—and which may (or may not) lead them to commit future sex offenses. There are however, some notable exceptions. This survey report presents information on 20 treatment programs in 12 states which are directly concerned with the existing sexual problems and future of correctional inmates, probationers and parolees. Three additional programs which are no longer in operation, but have considerable historical interest are also described..." (p. v).

The programs in Brecher's monograph were identified, in part, through the help of several people, including Fay Honey Knopp, founder of the Prison Research Education Action Project of Westport, Connecticut. This evolved into the Safer Society Program of Orwell, Vermont. Robert E. Longo (published as Robert E. Freeman-Longo, between 1982 and 2001) became the director of the Safer Society Program in 1993 and transformed it in 1994 into the current Safer Society Foundation in Brandon, Vermont. Brecher goes on to say:

> *"The first four American programs for sex offenders were established by California in 1948, by Wisconsin in 1951, and by Massachusetts and Washington State in 1958."* (p. 5)

Since Brecher's publication, the Safer Society has continued to track the existence and development of sex offender treatment programs with monographs dated from 1982 through 2002.

Many of the earliest programs cited in Brecher's monograph, as well as those that developed through the 1970s and 1980s, were created as the result of specific horrific crimes publicized at state and national levels. Several of these crimes included the abduction, rape, and murder of a child or adult woman.

Brecher's monograph identified twenty programs in twelve states. Only one program (in Seattle) treated juveniles. This clinic operated out of the School of Medicine at the University of Washington. Programs in Florida treated both adult and juvenile sexual offenders. It was at the North Florida Evaluation and Treatment Center in Gainesville, Florida that Longo and his colleagues decided to separate younger clients from the adults and develop specialized housing and programming for them (Longo & McFadin, 1981).

In 1982, Fay Honey Knopp continued to identify and explore treatment for sexually abusive youth, publishing *Remedial Intervention in Adolescent Sex Offenses: Nine Program Descriptions* (Knopp, 1982). This was the first report on adolescent sex offenders and their treatment. The nine programs consisted of five community–based and four residential treatment programs located in Washington, Minnesota, Colorado, and Washington, D.C.

Knopp's initial publication was followed by *A Preliminary Survey of Adolescent Sex Offenses in New York: Remedies and Recommendations* (Jackson, 1984), also published by the Safer Society. By 1986, the Safer Society Press had begun a journey, which continues today, of reporting on programs that treat sexual offenders (Knopp, Rosenberg, &

Stevenson, 1986). In the 1986 survey, the Safer Society Program had identified a total of 297 programs treating adult sex offenders and 346 treating juvenile sexual offenders.

The majority of programs at that time used family therapy, peer-group treatment groups, cognitive restructuring, and behavioral treatment methods. Some used penile plethysmography and aversive conditioning. Psycho-educational models were most common, and concepts such as aftercare did not exist for those youth who came out of residential treatment programs. The use of phallometry with adult sex offenders was a heated debate, and sparingly used (in 12% of the reported programs) with juveniles.

1982 saw the beginnings of the Association for the Treatment of Sexual Abusers (ATSA), now an international organization. At the Oregon State Hospital in Salem, Robert Longo began weekly brown-bag luncheon meetings to discuss issues related to the evaluation and treatment of sex offenders. This included concerns around the use and misuse of the penile plethysmograph, which was being used in some cases to determine guilt or innocence in legal settings. In one case, a local evaluator was conducting evaluations of eight hours' duration. By 1983 other professionals in community-based treatment programs outside Oregon State Hospital joined this small group of individuals.

As this group's knowledge expanded and concerns deepened, the individuals involved decided to form an organization. On December 18, 1984, they officially established the Association for the Behavioral Treatment of Sexual Aggressors (ABTSA) in Salem, Oregon. Robert Longo served as ABTSA's first President. On April 30, 1986, ABTSA filed its new name, The Association for the Behavioral Treatment of Sexual Abusers, and it was several years later that the name was changed to its current name, The Association for the Treatment of Sexual Abusers (ATSA).

ATSA began as a state organization focused on the assessment and treatment of adult sexual offenders. It wasn't until the late 1980s that ATSA began to spread its scope to include juvenile sexual abusers. Today it also addresses issues related to sexually reactive children. In February 1986, the 5th Annual Conference on Sexual Aggression, sponsored by the National Institute of Mental Health and Florida Mental Health Institute, was held in Tampa, Florida. This would be the last in the series of national meetings funded under grants from the National Institute of Mental Health (NIMH) held by Dr. Gene Abel (in cooperation with Dr. Judith Becker), and later, Dr. D. Richard Laws.

After this meeting, Robert Longo contacted Dr. James Brieling with NIMH to see whether the annual Research and Treatment conference could be continued if funding were found. It was from this collaboration that ATSA's successful annual conferences emerged, first organized by Robert Longo and several ABTSA Board members, including Jim Haaven, and Jan Hindman. In May 1987, the 6th Annual Conference on Sexual Aggression: Assessment & Treatment, Association for the Behavioral Treatment of Sexual Abusers took place in Newport, Oregon.

The Safer Society released its next survey in 1988 (Knopp & Stevenson, 1988). By this time, the field was growing and with it a rising concern about juvenile sexual abusers.

Knopp and Stevenson reported a total of 573 identified programs treating juvenile sexual offenders, and 429 programs treating adult sex offenders.

Gail Ryan began the National Adolescent Perpetrator Network (NAPN) at the C. Henry Kempe Center of the University of Colorado in 1983 and up to the present has been its principle architect. Noting the lack of research treating juvenile sexual offenders, Ryan formed a task force with four honorary appointments: Gail Ryan served as Facilitator, Fay Honey Knopp served as Honorary Chairperson, Brandt Steele served as Honorary Advisor, and Alison Stickrod served as Reporter. The National Task Force on Juvenile Sexual Offending consisted of twenty participant members and twenty advisory members selected from NAPN's membership.

The task force reviewed virtually every document published on youthful sexual abusers and created the initial working draft of the *Preliminary Report from The National Task Force on Juvenile Sexual Offending*, first published in the Juvenile and Family Court Journal in 1988.

In 1990, the Safer Society Foundation released its next survey on sex offender treatment programs (Knopp & Stevenson, 1990). This report identified a total of 626 programs treating juvenile sex offenders and 541 programs treating adult sex offenders. The foundation's next survey on sex offender treatment programs (Knopp, Freeman-Longo, & Stevenson, 1992) identified a total of 755 programs treating juvenile sex offenders and 745 programs treating adult sex offenders. It tracked more detail in both the treatment models and modalities used in these programs. Ten different models identified by treatment providers were now being tracked. Programs serving both juveniles and adults reported using over 50 treatment modalities and five treatment modes. In 1993, after several meetings of original and added task force and advisory members, the National Adolescent Perpetration Network published its *Revised Report from The National Task Force on Juvenile Sexual Offending in the Juvenile And Family Court Journal*.

The Safer Society Foundation documented continued growth in the field (Freeman-Longo, Bird, Stevenson, & Fiske, 1995). *The 1994 Nationwide Survey of Treatment Programs & Models Serving Abuse-reactive Children and Adolescent & Adult Sex Offenders*, noted for the first time the number of programs treating children under the age of twelve. It cited a total of 390 programs treating children and 684 programs treating adolescents. The leading treatment model for both populations was behavioral-cognitive (40% of reporting programs) followed by programs using relapse prevention (37%).

The next Safer Society report was the 1996 Nationwide Survey (Burton, & Smith-Darden, with Levins, Fiske, & Freeman-Longo, 2000). A variety of complications delayed publication of this report until 2000. The format of the 1996 survey was lengthier and more detailed. The smaller return rate of the questionnaire was presumed to result from three factors: closure of programs due to the economy, the merger of residential programs for adolescents, and the survey took more time and effort to complete than previous surveys. This report provided a summary of the previous ten years of the national survey summarized below:

Comparison of Treatment Provider Response Since 1986

Year	Adult	Juvenile	Child	Total
1986	297	346	N/A	643
1988	429	573	N/A	1,002
1990	541	626	N/A	1,167
1992	745	755	N/A	1,500
1994	710	684	390	1,784
1996	527	539	314	1,380

In 2001, the Safer Society Foundation published the next report (Burton, & Smith-Darden, 2001). This report saw a further decrease in the number of programs reporting:

Comparison of the Number of Programs by Age Group, 1986-2000

Year	Adult	Juvenile	Child	Total
1986	297	346	N/A	643
1988	429	573	N/A	1,002
1990	541	626	N/A	1,167
1992	745	755	N/A	1,500
1994	710	684	390	1,784
1996	527	539	314	1,380
2000	461	291	66	818

Again, it was noted in the 2000 report that funding issues for sex offender treatment programs continues to be a concern.

The Safer Society Foundation published its most recent report in 2003 (McGrath, Cumming, & Burchard, 2003). This report was a collaborative effort; the Safer Society used membership lists from both ATSA and NAPN, resulting in 2,289 responses.

Number of Programs in Each Survey 1986-2002

Year	Adult	Juvenile	Child	Total
1986	297	346	N/A	643
1988	429	573	N/A	1,002
1990	541	626	N/A	1,167
1992	745	755	N/A	1,500
1994	710	684	390	1,784
1996	527	539	314	1,380
2000	461	291	66	818
2002	951	937	410	2,289

This was the most comprehensive report conducted by the Safer Society Foundation. It included information about treatment models and modalities, assessment, and the use of various technologies. For example, it noted that of 937 juvenile programs, 19 used penile plethysmography, 74 used polygraph, and 42 used viewing time measures (e.g. Abel Screen). Core treatment targets for children and adolescents included offense responsibility, cognitive restructuring, intimacy/relationship skills, social skills training, victim awareness and empathy, relapse prevention, arousal control, and family support networks.

This survey also asked questions regarding sexual arousal reconditioning techniques such as aversive behavioral rehearsal, covert sensitization, masturbatory satiation, odor aversion, and a technique called "minimal arousal conditioning", where the youth interrupts a fantasy as soon as it becomes arousing. The results are as follows:

Male adolescent residential: 56.4% of programs use one or more.
Male adolescent outpatient: 49.4% of programs use one or more.
Female adolescent residential: 48.5% of programs use one or more.
Female adolescent outpatient: 37.2% of programs use one or more.

The most remarkable aspect of these findings is that there is no research to support the idea that youthful sexual abusers experience sexual disorders in the same ways that adults do. As mentioned elsewhere in this volume, there is evidence that sexual arousal is fluid and dynamic across adolescence (Hunter & Becker, 1994). Although sexually abusive youth can engage in sexually deviant behavior, it appears that true sexual deviance has yet to be established as a treatment target for the majority of them, while the willingness to act on sexually deviant thoughts or impulses may be more important and more amenable.

In the midst of these developments, a number of programs began to reconsider their approach towards sexually abusive youth. In Vermont, David Prescott coordinated a program that directed treatment toward developing relationships within a collaborative context. Point-and-level systems were replaced by more direct communication regarding treatment progress. Activities and family contact became fundamental components of treatment, rather than privileges. Treatment targeting sexual deviance was adjusted in accordance with the youths' development. A prevailing belief that treatment should include full and meaningful participation by all students guided the program's development and implementation. Many aspects of that program have been described elsewhere (Prescott, 2002).

Looking Toward the Future

The field of treating children and adolescents has grown remarkably during the past two decades. Not only has the number of programs grown, but our knowledge, treatment methods, and technology have evolved, resulting in significant changes in what we know and do today.

Understanding and working with youth is a complex and comprehensive endeavor. When young people experience mental health problems and/or become involved with the juvenile justice system, the complexity intensifies. Youth must be understood from medical, psychological, developmental, contextual, and behavioral perspectives. The recent research on brain development, family violence, trauma impact, and emerging treatment methods and models addressed in this book requires us to consistently improve our assessment and treatment methods. This is especially true for sexually abusive youth, a population that generates sobering statistics.

The National Center on Sexual Behavior of Youth (NCSBY[1]), defines *"adolescent sex offenders"* as "adolescents from 13 to 17 who commit illegal sexual behavior as defined by the sex crime statutes of their jurisdictions." While statistics vary, the Federal Bureau of Investigation crime data indicate that in 2000, juveniles accounted for 16% of arrests for forcible rape and 19% of arrests for all other sex crimes. The FBI's Uniform Crime Reports[2] for 2003 indicate that juveniles committed 16.1% of forcible rapes, 20.0% of sex offenses (except forcible rape and prostitution), and 16.3% of crimes in all categories. Hunter, Hazelwood, and Slesinger (2000) note that current estimates are that youthful offenders account for as many as one third of rapes and half of all child molestation in the United States. Freeman-Longo and Blanchard (1998) report that 30-60% of all child sexual abuse is perpetrated by juveniles. The NCSBY reports that adolescent sexual offenders commit a substantial number of sex crimes, including 17% of all arrests for sex crimes and approximately one third of all sex offenses against children. Females under the age of 18, account for 8% of arrests for sex offenses. Younger children, ages twelve and under also have sexual behavior problems. NCSBY reports that of school-age children with sexual behavior problems, about one-third are female, while a recent study on preschool children found that a majority are girls.

Children are the majority of victims sexually abused by youth. Righthand and Welch (2002) state that "girls are targeted most frequently, however, boys represent up to 25% of some victim samples. Victims usually are substantially younger than the youth who offend. Victims are usually relatives or acquaintances; rarely are they strangers." Thus, it is no surprise that the effective assessment and treatment of youth is a strong step in the prevention of further sexual victimization of children.

The "trickle-down phenomenon" of using adult-based treatment methods and models for sex offenders has occurred since the first programs for youth emerged decades ago (Chaffin and Bonner, 1998; Developmental Services Group 2000, Longo, 2003). The trickle-down phenomenon is the use of adult-based models and modalities to treat children and adolescents with sexual behavior problems and sexually aggressive behaviors. These models do not generally account for developmental factors, learning styles, and the impact of trauma in treating sexual abusers. In most cases they are sex-offender specific and seldom focus on areas outside of the sexual offending behavior. They are often forensic models developed to work with normal-functioning adults in prison-like settings. During the last few years, however, the use of adult-based treatment modals and modalities has been challenged and has come under increased scrutiny as inadequate and/or inappropriate for working with children and adolescents (Ryan & Lane, 1997; Longo, 2003; Rich, 2003).

Our new century finds growing support for the holistic/integrated model of treatment promoted in this book. It is no longer prudent to ignore the emerging research and information on child maltreatment, family violence, trauma, post-traumatic stress disorder, brain development, attachment disorders, and their respective impact on youth. The current state of our knowledge obligates us to be familiar with the latest research into assessment and treatment.

Precise language is vital to understanding and treating those who have sexually abused. Unfortunately, the terms "sex offender", "juvenile sex offender", and even "predator" and "mini-perp" have become such popular vernacular that our field has used them regardless of age, developmental stage, cognitive ability, or diagnosis. Such labels often cause harm by establishing a sense of identity more than they accurately identify behavior. By telling kids who they are rather than accurately describing what they've done, we do further disservice to tomorrow's adults. Additionally, not all children or adolescents with sexual behavior problems are "JSO's" because not all have criminal convictions. Many youth charged with crimes such as statutory rape are not (other than by legal definition) sexual offenders with the intent and motivation to willfully commit a sexual offense. Not all youth with criminal charges for committing a sexual offense have a true sexual disorder, and by definition very few of them can be diagnosed as such. For example, six-year-old children who act out sexually simply do not have the motivations of older adolescents or adults. In the final analysis, we should remember that youth are more vulnerable than adults, especially with respect to the labels that we use. It is possible to confront the problem of sexual abuse while reducing the harm of the labels we use.

When working with young people, we should keep in mind that behavior is part of a person, not the whole person (Longo, 2003). Professionals must separate the person from their behavior and use precise language that promotes both accountability and optimism. As Chaffin and Bonner (1998) note:

> *"Fifteen years ago, our battle was getting the system to take cases seriously. We may have been too successful. Where we previously encountered public reluctance to identify the problem, we now sometimes encounter not only the willingness but also zeal. We see the labels of offender and perp placed on preschoolers. In many instances, this has extended to affixing the label of sex offender, even in advance of any actual inappropriate behavior."*

Programs will do best to operate based with developmental, contextual framework. Righthand and Welch (2002) state that, *"A review of the literature conducted by the authors suggest that programs for these youths frequently have been based on knowledge and interventions designed for adult offenders without adequate consideration of the developmental issues and needs unique to juveniles. There are important distinctions that differentiate juveniles from adult sex offenders."* Many programs do not use individualized treatment plans. Few of these programs undergo periodic program evaluation, and many are based upon older models or outdated literature, and may use treatment models and modalities not suitable for young clients. Some programs are not even based upon scientific literature. The most glaring example is found in the Safer Society's national survey of treatment programs and models. The 2000 survey conducted and published by the Safer Society Foundation, Inc., (Burton & Smith-Darden, 2001) shows that over 80% of all programs, 87.3% treating adolescents and 79.3% treating children use relapse prevention as the guiding treatment model for clients. Despite this occurrence, there are no scientific studies to support the use of relapse prevention as being more effective than any other model to treat sex offenders, and specifically children and adolescents with sexual behavior problems.

In fact, there is growing evidence (e.g., Laws, Hudson, and Ward, 2000) that the original relapse prevention model (Gray & Pithers, 1993) is not as effective as once believed. Some (e.g., Ward, Laws, & Hudson, 2003) have observed that not all abusers intend to stop abusing. In papers on pedophilia and its treatment, Nathaniel

McConaghy (1998, 1999) states that "relapse prevention treatment has been shown to be ineffective for incarcerated child molesters." Dr. James Breiling (2002) of the National Institute of Mental Health has noted:

> *"From McConaghy's paper in the ATSA journal Sexual Abuse, I am confident that his argument that relapse prevention has been shown to be ineffective for incarcerated child molesters reflects the outcome data from the exemplarily well designed treatments and experimental research design of SOTEP, the evaluation of relapse prevention for sex offenders that Janice Marques directed.*
>
> *I weigh findings differentially, giving the most weight to well-designed, implemented and evaluated studies, and SOTEP is at the top of the list on all those criteria, so the lack of conclusive evidence for a treatment effect should force a serious reconsideration of the use of this model (just as strong positive findings, had they been obtained (I wish they had been) would have been a powerful launch pad for vigorous advocacy for the use of the relapse prevention model).*

Youth who have sexually abused are a heterogeneous group of clients. They differ in important ways, including victim and offense characteristics, types of offending behaviors, histories of maltreatment, social and interpersonal skills levels and abilities, sexual knowledge and experience, academic, cognitive functions and mental health issues (Righthand & Welch, 2002; Longo, 2003). Their risk factors for reoffense vary, and their characteristics often do not differ significantly from youth who commit other types of crimes (Hunter et al., 2000). While relapse prevention can contribute to treatment, it can no longer be viewed as the only model. Many of the treatment models associated with relapse prevention (i.e., arousal reconditioning) may be counterproductive or harmful (Chaffin & Bonner, 1998; Chaffin, this volume). There is sparse literature suggesting that relapse prevention is useful or effective with children or adolescents, yet there are several programs that continue to use this model.

Another element found to be ineffective is the use of hostile or confrontational treatment styles. Although fewer programs openly endorse a harsh treatment style, current research stresses that a warm, empathic, rewarding, and directive approach can produce better outcomes in treating sexual abusers (Marshall, Fernandez, Serran, Mulloy, Thornton, Mann, & Anderson, 2003). Confrontational styles may also result in symptoms associated with trauma. Clinicians should re-think their goals and interactional style (Jenkins, 1990). It is worthwhile to remember that Righthand and Welch (2002) found that, "Juveniles who have offended typically are less violent than adult sex offenders."

Other aspects of what constitutes good treatment have also changed within our field. For example, the 1992, 1994, and 1996, nationwide surveys conducted by the Safer Society Foundation saw empathy enhancement emerge to be the leading treatment modality in both juvenile and adult programs (Knopp, Freeman-Longo, & Stevenson, 1992; Freeman-Longo, Bird, Stevenson, & Fiske, 1995; Burton, Smith-Darden, Levins, Fiske, & Freeman-Longo, 2000). However, in the 2000 survey (Burton & Smith-Darden, 2001), empathy training had dropped off to where it was being used by less than 7% of programs treating adolescents and adults.

From a holistic or integrated perspective, sexual behavior problems are part of a bigger picture (Longo, 2001; Longo, 2002, Longo & Longo, 2003). One can hardly expect to treat a young person who has stolen underwear without addressing his ecology and willingness to break rules. All too few treatment programs are based in a developmental framework.

Questions remain around intensity and dosage of treatment. At this time, managed care and tight budgets have led some programs to reduce the length of treatment. This has been an ongoing dialog among some programs for nearly a decade. According to the Safer Society nationwide survey 2000 (Burton & Smith-Darden, 2001), the average length of treatment for community-based programs ranges predominantly between 12-24 months for adolescents and 6-12 months for children. Some programs are less than twelve months and in some cases are six months, while others keep clients for over 24 months. Residential programs for adolescents range between 12-24 months, and from under six months to over 24 months for children. The average is eighteen months for both residential and community-based treatment for adolescents and seven months for community-based treatment, and thirteen months for residential treatment with children.

Significant differences among research findings became highly apparent during our research for this book. Such differences might reflect the diversity of the populations studied. One would expect to see differences between youth in a community-based versus secure residential treatment program. However, we do not see uniformity between programs in the use of psychometric measures, risk assessment strategies, and program design. Some programs do not work with youth with mental illness, while others do. The use of different treatment models, treatment modalities, length of treatment, acceptance criteria, discharge criteria, what constitutes program completion, etc., likely all factor into the differences we see in the literature. So, at the very least, one must be cautious about what we read.

The chapters in this book address these and other issues. Despite the politics and economics that often govern our work, we believe that professionals must always be cognizant of emerging issues and changes in the field. We hope the chapters in this book will lend insight as well as challenge the ways that we do our work.

Summary

The rapid advances in the study of sexually abusive youth, although well meaning and praiseworthy, has often narrowed our focus to elusive sexual aspects at the expense of a full accounting of the youth's development and ecology. While there is much in youthful development to distract us from a clear understanding of potential re-offense processes, we can no longer allow adult programming to be the sole source of assessing and treating young people. It is for this reason we have collected the chapters in this book.

End Notes

[1]http://www.ncsby.org/pages/publications/What%20Research%20Shows%20Abou t%20Adolescent%20Sex%20Offenders%20060404.pdf - retrieved January 5, 2005.
[2]http://www.fbi.gov/ucr/cius_03/pdf/03sec4.pdf

References

Brecher, E.M. (1978). *Treatment programs for sex offenders.* Washington, DC: U.S. Department of Justice; Law Enforcement Assistance Administration.

Breiling, James. E-mail dated 4/3/2002, posted to the ATSA List Serve.

Brownmiller, S. (1975). *Against our will: Men, women and rape.* New York: Simon and Schuster.

Burton, D.L., and Smith-Darden, J.P., with Levins, J., Fiske, J.A. and Freeman-Longo, R.E. (2000). 1996 *Nationwide survey: A survey of treatment programs & models serving children with sexual behavior problems, adolescent sex offenders, and adult sex-offenders.* Brandon, VT: Safer Society Press.

Burton, D.L., and Smith-Darden, J.P. (2001). *North American survey of sexual abuser treatment and models summary data 2000.* Brandon, VT: Safer Society Press.

Chaffin, M. and Bonner, B. (1998). "Editor's Introduction: 'Don't shoot, we're your children': Have we gone too far in our response to adolescent sexual abusers and children with sexual behavior problems?" *Child Maltreatment,* 3 (4): 314-316.

Development Services Group (2000). *Understanding treatment and accountability in juvenile sex offending: results and recommendations from an OJJDP Focus Group* (Prepared for Office of Juvenile Justice and Delinquency Prevention Training and Technical Assistance Division). Bethesda, MD: Author.

Freeman-Longo, R., Bird, S., Stevenson, W.F., and Fiske, J.A. (1995). *1994 Nationwide survey of treatment programs & models serving abuse-reactive children and adolescent & adult sex-offenders.* Brandon, VT: Safer Society Press.

Freeman-Longo, R.E. & Blanchard, G.T. (1998). *Sexual Abuse in America: Epidemic of the 21st Century.* Brandon, VT: Safer Society Press.

Gray, A.S. & Pithers, W.D. (1993). Relapse prevention with sexually aggressive adolescents and children: Expanding treatment and supervision. In H.E. Barbaree, W.L. Marshall, & S.M. Hudson (Eds.). *The Juvenile Sex Offender* (pp. 289-320). New York: Guilford Press.

Hunter, J.A., Hazelwood, R.R., and Slesinger, D. (2000). Juvenile-perpetrated sex crimes: patterns of offending and predictors of violence. *Journal of Family Violence.* Vol.15, No 1. pp 81-93.

Hunter, J.A. & Becker, J.V. (1994). The role of deviant sexual arousal in juvenile sexual offending: Etiology, evaluation, and treatment, *Criminal Justice and Behavior* 21, 132-149.

Hunter, J. and Longo, R.E. (2004). Relapse prevention with juvenile sexual abusers: A holistic/integrated approach. In G. O'Reilly, W. Marshall, A. Carr, & R. Beckett (Eds.) *Handbook of clinical intervention with young people who sexually abuse.* Sussex, UK: Brunner-Routledge.

Jackson, I.F., (1984). *A preliminary survey of adolescent sex offenses in New York: Remedies and recommendations.* Syracuse, NY: Safer Society Press.

Jenkins, Alan (1990). *Invitations to Responsibility.* Adelaide, Australia: Dulwich Centre Publications.

Knopp, F.H., (1982). *Remedial intervention in adolescent sex offenses: Nine program descriptions.* Orwell, VT: Safer Society Press.

Knopp, F.H., Rosenberg, J., and Stevenson, W., (1986). *Report on nationwide survey of juvenile and adult sex-offender treatment programs and providers,* 1986. Orwell, VT: Safer Society Press.

Knopp, F.H. and Stevenson, W.F., (1988). *Nationwide survey of juvenile & adult sex-offender treatment programs,* 1988. Orwell, VT: Safer Society Press.

Knopp, F.H., Freeman-Longo, R.E., and Stevenson, W.F., (1992). *Nationwide survey of juvenile & adult sex-offender treatment programs & models,* 1992. Orwell, VT: Safer Society Press.

Knopp, F.H. and Stevenson, W.F., (1990). *Nationwide survey of juvenile & adult sex-offender treatment programs, 1990.* Orwell, VT: Safer Society Press.

Laws, D.R., Hudson, S.M., and Ward, T. (2000). *Remaking Relapse prevention with sex offenders: A sourcebook.* Thousand Oaks, CA: Sage Publications.

Longo, R.E. (2001). *Paths to Wellness: A Holistic Approach and Guide for Personal Recovery.* Holyoke, MA: NEARI Press.

Longo, R.E. (2002). A Holistic Approach to Treating Juvenile Sexual Abusers, in In M. C. Calder (Ed.) *Young people who sexually abuse: building the evidence base for your practice.* Dorset, England: Russell House Publishing.

Longo, R.E. (2003). Emerging Issues, Policy Changes, and the Future of Treating Children with Sexual Behavior Problems. In R.A. Prentky, E.S. Janus, & M.C. Seto (eds.), *Sexually coercive behavior: understanding and management.* Annals of the New York Academy of Sciences. Vol. 989.

Longo, R.E. & McFadin, J.B. (1981). Florida: the adolescent sex offender. New York: TSA News, 4 (2).

Longo, R.E. & Longo, D.P. (2003). *New Hope Exercises for Youth: Experiential Exercises for Children and Adolescents*. Holyoke, MA: NEARI Press.

Marshall, W.L., Fernandez, Y.M., Serran, G., Mulloy, R., Thornton, D., Mann, R.E. , & Anderson, D. (2003). Process variables in the treatment of sexual offenders: A review of the relevent literature. *Aggression and Violent Behavior*, 8, 205-234.

McConaghy, Nathaniel (1998). Paedophilia: A review of the evidence. *Australian &New Zealand Journal of Psychiatry*, 32(2), 252-265.

McConaghy, Nathaniel (1999). Methodological issues concerning evaluation of treatment for sexual offenders: randomization, treatment dropouts, untreated controls, and within-treatment studies. *Sexual Abuse: A Journal of Research and Treatment*, 11(3), 183-194.

McGrath, R.J., Cumming, G.F. and Burchard, B.L. (2003). *Current practices and trends in sexual abuser management: The Safer Society 2002 nationwide survey*. Brandon, VT: Safer Society Press.

National Adolescent Perpetrator Network (1988). Preliminary report from the national task force on juvenile sexual offending, 1988. *Juvenile and Family Court Journal*. 39 (2).

National Adolescent Perpetrator Network (1993). The revised report from the national task force on juvenile sexual offending, 1993 of the National Adolescent Perpetrator Network. *Juvenile And Family Court Journal*, 44 (4), pages, 1-121.

Rich, P. (2003) *Understanding, Assessing and Rehabilitating Juvenile Sex Offenders*. Hoboken, New Jersey: John Wiley and Sons.

Righthand, S. and Welch, C. (2002) Juveniles who have sexually offended: an introduction. *The Prevention Researcher*, 9 (4), pp. 1-3.

Ryan, G. & Lane, S. (1997). Juvenile Sexual Offending: Causes, Consequences, and Correction. San Francisco: Jossey-Bass.

Laws, D.R., Hudson, S.M. & Ward, T. (2000). *Remaking relapse prevention with sex offenders: A sourcebook*. CA: Sage.

CHAPTER ONE

CURRENT PERSPECTIVES: WORKING WITH YOUNG PEOPLE WHO SEXUALLY ABUSE

DAVID S. PRESCOTT
AND
ROBERT E. LONGO

"Good people do bad things."

Introduction

The treatment of youth with sexual behavior problems has advanced in directions few could have imagined two decades ago. Of primary importance has been the development of a public health perspective in understanding sexual abusers (Freeman-Longo & Blanchard, 1998). Researchers and practitioners alike have come to recognize that the widespread problem of sexual abuse requires global prevention (Longo, 2003; Longo & Blanchard, 2002, Freeman-Longo, 1998; Freeman-Longo & Blanchard, 1998; Klein & Tabachnick, 2002). Specialized organizations such as Darkness to Light and Stop it Now! have worked to increase public awareness, the latter specifically partnering with treatment provider organizations such as the Association for the Treatment of Sexual Abusers (ATSA).

Within the past five years, organizations such as the National Adolescent Perpetrator Network (NAPN) and ATSA have also acknowledged the need to address sexual abuse as a public health problem. However, it was former Surgeon General C. Everett Koop who had the vision to look at all violence, including sexual violence as a public health problem. In 1985, Dr. Koop wrote:

> *Identifying violence as a public health issue is a relatively new idea. Traditionally, when confronted by the circumstances of violence, the health professionals have deferred to the criminal justice system. Over the years we've tacitly and, I believe, mistakenly agreed that violence was the exclusive province of the police, the courts, and the penal system. To be sure, those agents of public safety and justice have served us well. But when we ask them to concentrate more on the prevention of violence and to provide additional services for victims, we may begin to burden the criminal justice system beyond reason. At that point, the professionals of medicine, nursing, and the health-related social services must come forward and recognize violence as their issue, also, one which profoundly affects the public health ... Henry David Thoreau in his book, "Walden," wrote: "It is characteristic of wisdom not to*

do desperate things." I think we have worked with patience and wisdom. And hope-fully the time of desperation is over.

In order to grasp the full spectrum of sexual abuse, we must understand that it exists in our own neighborhoods and communities, perhaps even in our own families. We cannot afford to take an "us-against-them" approach toward sexual abusers, espe-cially youthful sexual abusers. It is natural to be horrified by sexual aggression. However, believing ourselves to be superior to abusers can only make our attempts to foster change more problematic. Accepting sexual abuse as a public health issue enables us to distinguish youth from their actions, and provides the support and encouragement necessary for them to confront their harmful behavior. At a societal level, this perspective allows society to go about the work of healing and prevention.

The trickle-down phenomenon

The trickle-down phenomenon is the importation of adult treatment strategies to the juvenile field. At present, this has continued for well over two decades (Developmental Services Group, 2000), and has pervaded our field (Chaffin & Bonner, 1998). The influence of adult models can keep youth in treatment longer than neces-sary because youthful sexual abusers are often perceived in a one-size-fits-all per-spective inherited from "the adult world". Youth are too often considered as a high risk to the community, untreatable, and as "predators". Chaffin and Bonner (1998) note that many adult treatments are controversial and may include involuntary treat-ments (i.e., phallometry, polygraphy, and arousal reconditioning) for purposes of public safety, rather than for rehabilitative reasons. Further, there is no shortage of evidence that, in North American samples, the base rate of sexual recidivism by youth is considerably lower than among adults (Alexander, 1999; Prescott, in press; Worling & Curwen, 2000).

Unlike their adult counterparts, sexually abusive youth are still developing at the rapid pace that defines adolescence. Yet in a growing number of jurisdictions, many youthful sexual abusers are being waived into adult courts, based in part on the pub-lic's growing concerns for personal and family safety (Hunter, Hazelwood, & Slesinger, 2000; Levesque, 1996). Whatever the crime, these young people are still growing physically, cognitively, morally, and emotionally. In our experience, they can often be far more idealistic than their behaviors would suggest.

Younger children's beliefs and values can be altered or distorted through exposure to family violence and abuse. One often hears the phrase "children without a con-science", with respect to sexually abusive and violent youth. However, children leav-ing this impression often have understandable reasons for behaving as they do (see Schwartz et al., Chapter 18). Although they must become responsible for their behav-iors, it is vital to remember adolescents aged 13-18 are still in development, can change rapidly, and can be better served without pejorative labels.

Histories of abuse, neglect, and trauma do not make growing up any easier. Even healthy youth are clarifying their understanding of what it means to be responsible. Society does not give them the full complement of adult responsibilities, and practi-tioners should not think that we can arbitrarily single out particular behaviors (crim-inal or otherwise) to selectively treat them as adults. Chaffin and Bonner (1998) write:

"To the extent we can identify those truly at risk and work productively with them, our communities will be safer. But in the process, we should not forget that these are our children. And as professionals committed to children's rights and welfare, we should think carefully about their rights and welfare before responding to their behavior."

Sadly, over the course of the past two decades, our field has been subject to the pendulum effect, swinging back and forth between the rehabilitation and punishment of youth (Leversee & Pearson, 2001). While treatment strategies have become more effective (Hanson, Gordon, Harris, Marques, Murphy, Quinsey, & Seto, 2002), we have also witnessed greater emphasis on punishment in many jurisdictions. Rehabilitation of youthful sexual abusers must take into account their developmental abilities as well as potential developmental lags. Many adolescents with sexual behavior problems also have learning disabilities (see Creeden, Chapter 16). These youth, as well as their families and communities, would all benefit if the legal and mental health systems took such factors into account.

Typologies and risk assessment

Typologies of sexual abusers provide useful information for assessment and treatment planning. Initial typology research suggests two broad categories of youthful sexual abusers, those who rape peers and adults, and those who sexually abuse children (Hunter et al., 2000; Hunter & Longo, 2004; Hunter, this volume). The current state of these typologies is discussed further in Chapter Two.

Further typological research will help to guide the development of risk assessment tools. There are several scales currently in use, including the Juvenile Sex Offender Assessment Protocol (J-SOAP-II; Prentky & Righthand, 2003) the Estimate of Risk of Adolescent Sexual Offense Recidivism (ERASOR; Worling & Curwen, 2000, 2001, 2002), the Juvenile (Clinical) Risk Assessment Tool (J-RAT; Rich, 2003), and the Juvenile Sex Offender Reoffense Risk Assessment Tool (J-SORRAT; Epperson, Ralston, DeWitt, & Fowers, 2005). The Protective Factors Scale (Bremer, 2001) examines the various assets a young person possesses in order to assist in placement decisions. While the current tools all show promise, additional research is necessary for further development and validation (Prescott, in press). There remains no empirically validated means for accurately assessing the risk of a young person to recidivate sexually.

At this time there is no empirically validated typology or risk assessment tool for children (ages twelve and under) who sexually abuse, With the growing number of programs treating children in this age group, this is essential for advancing the field.

As our field grows, ongoing research will continue to help refine typologies, and clarify risk factors for youth. Ryan (in press) states:

"Emerging research has demonstrated that: (1) childhood neglect, physical abuse, and witnessing family violence may precede sexual offending even more often than sexual abuse; (2) many child victims recover without long-term damage or dysfunction, even without treatment; (3) sexually abusive youth are less at risk for sexual offense recidivism than for non-sexual reoffense; and juveniles reoffend less often

than adult sex offenders, especially after treatment; and (4) only a small portion of juveniles who sexually abuse have deviant sexual arousal patterns. Combining offense-specific theories with developmental, contextual, and ecological theories, a new set of hypotheses developed and were described by Ryan and Associates."

Risk assessment and the need for evidenced-based strategies are further addressed by Chaffin (Chapter 28).

Static and dynamic risk factors

Current investigation into risk factors for sexually abusive youth suggests there are two types of risk factors associated with them (Andrews & Bonta, 2003; Rich, 2003; Prescott, in press). Static risk factors are established in an individual's history and are permanent in nature (i.e., previous sex offense convictions, age of onset, numbers of victims, histories of abuse and neglect). Dynamic risk factors are those factors that can be changed over time (e.g., low self-esteem, poor anger management skills, self-reported and/or documented sexual arousal to paraphilias, treatment experience).

Ryan (in press) recommends that practitioners consider three types of risk factors:

> 1) Static (e.g., permanent disabilities, family of origin, early life experience);
> 2) Stable (life spanning, but potentially changeable) risk factors (e.g., temperament, intellectual potential, physical attributes, heritable neurological characteristics); and
> 3) Dynamic risk factors (e.g., situational, cognitive, emotional, and behavioral factors that may change throughout the individual's life).

Some common etiological factors associated with sexually abusive youth include prior sexual aggression, entrenched patterns of deviant sexual arousal, stranger victims, having child victims, a history of child abuse, general delinquency, deficits in self-esteem, deficits in assertiveness, inadequate interpersonal skills, poor life management skills, and lack of family support (Worling, & Curwen, 2000; Worling, & Curwen, 2002; Prentky, Harris, Frizzell, & Righthand, 2002; Caldwell, 2002). However, the factors that contribute to first offense are not necessarily those that signal a propensity for re-offense (Prescott, in press). Ryan (in press) considers other factors when addressing static risk factors:

> *Defining static factors as those which are retrospective/historical variables, we know that these factors cannot be changed because we cannot change history. Such factors might include: (1) the condition at birth; (2) permanent disabilities; (3) family of origin; and (4) early life experience.*

Ryan proposes that an additional type of risk factor, "stable" risk factors, should be considered in assessing youth. She describes stable risk factors as, "risk factors, which may be relevant to the risk of dysfunctional behaviors, may include such things as difficult temperament, low intellect or learning disabilities, negative internal working model, heritable psychiatric disorders, and chronic PTSD reactivity" (Ryan, in press).

The need to clarify our understanding of dynamic risk factors for children and adolescents who sexually abuse is apparent. Some of the risk-assessment scales mentioned above include dynamic risk factors, but are not comprehensive. Many are simply "laundry lists" of risk factors, and do not address the interactive effects of static and dynamic risk factors.

Some of the dynamic risk factors for adolescents with sexual behavior problems that are now being recognized include attitudes toward offending, negative peer influence, emotional self-regulation, general self-regulation, intimacy deficits, resistance to treatment, anger management, deficits in self-esteem, deficits in self-confidence, deficits in independence, deficits in assertiveness, deficits in self-satisfaction, deficits in competency skills, inadequate interpersonal skills, inadequate social skills/social competence, and poor life management skills.

Ryan (in press) notes:

> *Risk assessment and treatment models based solely on unchangeable risk factors in the past are likely to over-estimate risk, as well as miss important opportunities in treatment to change what is changeable. By balancing offense specific interventions with preventive interventions to increase healthy functioning, outcomes may improve, and iatrogenic risks may be reduced.*

Many of these risk factors have their origins in child maltreatment and neglect. These have a demonstrated role in the etiology of aggressive conduct problems (Ryan & Associates, 1999). Further, the impact on the brain of abuse and neglect is established (Creeden, Chapter 16). Childhood maltreatment is a crucial treatment need. It can contribute to biologically based vulnerabilities (such as impulsivity and hypervigilance) as well as the thoughts, beliefs, and attitudes that contribute to re-offense.

Unfortunately, some of the impact on the brain is not reversible. However, children are resilient (Gilgun, Chapter 15), and we can promote health and recovery by addressing dynamic risk factors.

Finally, there are risk factors previously thought to be associated with sexual recidivism among youth whose roles are questionable or not supported by research. These include denial, empathy deficits, and victim penetration (Worling & Curwen, 2002). Although each of these is worthy of a volume itself, they serve as a reminder that what may appear important is not always supported empirically. There are several possible reasons why these elements have not been found to contribute to sexual recidivism. The first is that denial and empathy deficits are so common among sexually abusive youth as to provide no discrimination between high and low risk. It is also possible that by looking at denial and empathy deficits, practitioners are distracted from understanding their contribution to risk. Although they might stand as proxies for genuine risk factors under some circumstances, they are not necessarily markers in themselves. For example, denial might in one situation mean only that the practitioner has not provided a supportive environment where the youth can disclose. In other circumstances, denial might signal the very attitudes that contribute to re-offense. On its own, victim penetration has been found to be more indicative of future violence (Langstrom & Grann, 2000).

Other research cautions us that the sexual arousal patterns of youth are "fluid" and dynamic, and may be less of a concern in youth than in their adult counterparts (Hunter & Becker, 1994). Many of us practicing in this field twenty years ago discovered that much of what we believed turned out not to be true.

Female sexually abusive youth

Our field has only just begun to focus on special populations. The development of strategies for treating young females (Robinson, Chapter 11; Frey, Chapter 10) is particularly important. While strategies inherited from adult programs may inform work with young people and vice versa, they are not necessarily appropriate for female children and adolescents with sexual behavior problems (Robinson, 2002; Guambana, 2001). The treatment needs of males differ from those of girls in several areas. Boys and girls develop and experience life differently, and cognitive and emotional differences exist between them (Robinson, 2002). The growth of programs for young women has been sporadic, and Guambana (2001) notes a lack of gender-specific programs for adolescent females.

Statistically, the majority of adolescent sex offenders are male. However, research during the past ten years has shown that female adolescents also engage in harmful sexual behaviors. Studies of hospital, child welfare agency, and treatment programs have found that females comprise between 3% - 10% of the sex offender population (Bear, 1993). Importantly, however, Risin & Koss (1987) note that general population and victimization surveys report significantly higher numbers and extend the range up to 50% and some report higher figures depending on the victim sample population studied (Johnson & Shrier, 1987).

Sexual abuse by female adolescents is often hard to detect because few people question the close interactions of females with children. Frequently, sexual abuse by female adolescents occurs when they are babysitting. Their victims are predominantly acquaintances and young children. Adolescent females, like males, also offend against partners in same sex relationships (Bear, 1993; Davin, Hislop, & Dunbar, 1999).

Developmentally delayed sexual abusers

Developmentally delayed clients (also referred to as lower functioning, MR/DD, intellectually disabled) are another population requiring specialized attention and the development of resources (O'Callaghan, Chapter 12). Often, this type of patient is most difficult to serve. Community-based programs are often reluctant to take these clients, and not all foster homes or group care situations have adequate training for their needs.

Professionals face many challenges with youth. Age, developmental and contextual issues, learning abilities and styles, etiology, cultural issues, spirituality, and gender differences must all be taken into account. Our field still needs programs that work within these areas while improving sensitivity to cultural issues (Lewis, 1999).

Families

The lack of investigation into helping the families of sexually abusive youth reflects poorly on our field. Despite the vast literature on family therapy, there is precious little research into successful family interventions. One might attend any number of conferences and not find a workshop on this topic. While this often reflects the egregious circumstances in which youthful abusers are raised, the fact remains that our field is better at the short-term solution of separating family members rather than the longer-term solution of reconciliation and growth. While the former is often necessary as an initial measure, the latter is too often left out of both research and practice.

Continuum of care

Sexually abusive youth are best rehabilitated with a continuum of care (Bengis 1986, 2002a). The NCSBY proposes a continuum developed by Chaffin and Longo (2003):

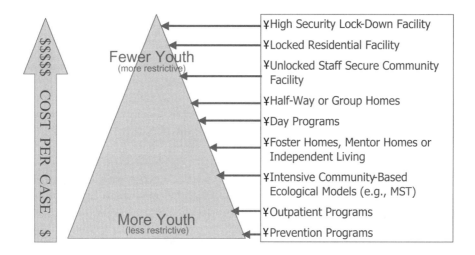

Examples of Continuum Levels of Care[1] (beginning with least restrictive)

At the base of the continuum is the Prevention Level.[2] Prevention consists of two types:

> 1) Primary Prevention Programs are public and private school systems that provide age-appropriate or educational program on human sexuality and human sexual behavior, including materials on sexual assault and child sexual abuse.

> 2) Secondary Prevention Programs are community-based mental health, behavior problem, victim treatment, or delinquency programs that provide a short-term age-appropriate collateral psycho-educational module on human sexuality and human sexual behavior, including detailed material on sexual assault and child sexual abuse definitions, consequences, and strategies for identifying, avoiding and coping with risky sexual behavior situations.

Next, the Outpatient Program Level generally provides individual, group or family therapy providing traditional ad hoc mental health services (with variations in focus, model, and duration). These programs usually practice in an abuse-specific fashion, employing cognitive-behavioral models. They often include modules based on relapse prevention, increasing self-monitoring of behavior, and understanding patterns, consequences and strategies for managing inappropriate sexual behavior, etc.

The next level is Intensive Community-Based Intervention Level, such as Multi-systemic Therapy (MST) or Functional Family Therapy (FFT). These are short-term (four months in some models), highly intensive (sometimes including daily in-home contacts, low caseloads, 24-hour availability) interventions designed for seriously delinquent adolescents and their families. Both emphasize the role of families and obtaining immediate and maximal behavior change on assessment-driven goals.

The fourth level is Foster Home and Independent Living Home Level. Foster parents are usually lay individuals who have been screened and provided with brief basic training. Youth in foster care attend school in the community, and live a more normal family life. Foster homes are not physically secured and cannot realistically provide constant supervision.

The fifth level is Day Program Level. In most cases these programs are attached to a residential or inpatient milieu program, where youth participate in the treatment milieu and programming, but live in the community and return home in the evenings and on weekends. Day programs usually incorporate specialized classroom schooling/vocational training and therapeutic components similar to those found in residential programs.

The sixth level is Group Home Level. A group home is typically a small, structured, home-like facility, often in a residential neighborhood, housing a group of adolescents under 24-hour staff supervision. Group homes may be locked at night, and the activities of residents generally supervised, but they are not physically secure facilities designed to contain inmates, provide constant supervision, or prevent escape. Group home residents may attend school in the community, or may hold jobs in the community, but typically there are rules that do not allow them to move freely in and out of the facility. Group homes may provide on-site counselors or offer on-site services such as group therapy, or they may arrange for those services off site.

The seventh level is the Unlocked Staff-Secure Residential Program Level. These programs are typically year-round structured program with staff-supervised dormitories or cottages designed to provide therapeutic, educational, recreational, and behavior management services to children and adolescents who have long standing emotional and/or behavioral difficulties, but are not acutely psychiatrically ill. Residents commonly receive weekly individual/group/family therapy and periodic medical or psychiatric services. Residents are usually restricted to the campus, but may have "grounds privileges" based upon behavior and treatment plan progress. Lengths of stays in these facilities are often quite long term. Some of these facilities have specialized sex-offender cottages or campuses segregated from other youth and/or specialized sex-offender programming.

The eighth level is Locked Residential Treatment Centers. These centers are generally a locked controlled-access unit, either freestanding or a more controlled unit within an overall residential campus, where resident activities and movements are controlled or monitored by staff on a 24-hour basis, and there is a strong emphasis on structure, intensive behavior management, and containment. These facilities provide on-site schooling as well as frequent and intensive psychological or psychiatric services delivered by on-site professional staff. These facilities often have seclusion and restraint capacity and rely upon behavioral systems or level systems to gain compliance from residents.

The ninth and final level is High-Security Lock Down. Most common are juvenile correctional facilities with guards, high security, and multiple barriers preventing escape (e.g., razor wire fences, remote-controlled hardened doors or gates, etc.). These facilities may provide some professional psychological or psychiatric treatment services and may use a level system. Participation in school or GED services usually is required for residents. Behavior change is often pursued via control and application of sanctions. Staff are typically security officers rather than treatment or nursing staff.

Bengis (2002 a, b) notes that use of a continuum requires special attention to the following criteria as a guideline for placement of clients:

1) The placement should correspond to the level of risk posed by the patient.
2) The level of client risk should be determined by examining both:
    a) the client's level of self-control (the bottom-line acting-out which the
    b) placement has been designed to contain), and
    the staff-client ratios present on-line to contain these behaviors.
3) Whenever legally possible, movement along the continuum should be based on the competency level achieved by the patient.
4) Required competency levels should correspond to the level of internal-control required for safe placement at each level of the continuum.
5) Initially, clients can be referred to any level of the continuum that corresponds to their diagnosed level of risk. However, decisions regarding movement to less restrictive placements should be competency-based.
6) The entire continuum of care should use the same sex abuser-specific assessment and treatment criteria. While specific placements may emphasize different aspects of sex abuser-specific treatment (e.g., one program may emphasize learning the assault cycle and another may emphasize arousal reduction) all placements should adhere to the guidelines established by the National Task Force On Juvenile Sexual Offending (1993). Sex abuser-specific treatment that takes place in other than outpatient settings, i.e., residential or day programs, should incorporate sexual abuser-specific milieu treatment. As such all staff in those placements should be trained:
    a) to provide abuser-specific interventions as part of their work on-line with youth;
    b) to integrate the basics of abuser specific treatment into interventions that do not involve sexually abusive behaviors; and
    c) to integrate abuser-specific issues into vocational and educational curricula.

Programs offering specialized assessments and specialized groups, but do not provide specialized milieu treatment, should not be considered sex abuser-specific programs.

7) Whenever possible, caregivers should remain consistent as a youth moves from one level of the continuum to another (i.e., probation officer, case worker, therapists).

8) Placements along the continuum should be evaluated:

    a) by professionals trained in both evaluation methodology and abuser specific assessment and treatment; and

    b) according to sex abuser specific criteria agreed to in advance by evaluators and those being evaluated.

9) The continuum should include long-term self-help and require community relapse prevention components.

10) Day programs and educational placements should be thoroughly integrated into the continuum of care and be required to provide sex abuser specific treatment.

11) All youth placed in programs anywhere along the continuum should receive pre and post abuser specific evaluations. These evaluations should be the basis for initial placement and for discharge to less restrictive settings. These evaluations should also screen the patient according to more traditional clinical criteria (i.e., thought disorders, clinical depression, ADHD, and other neurological criteria).

12) In unlocked settings, failure to meaningfully participate in treatment over reasonably appropriate periods of time should be criteria for discharge from a program. Ideally, such a discharge would also constitute violation of probation and/or court orders and subject the youth to placement in a more restrictive and/or locked setting. For youth who are not court involved, such discharge should also result in placement in a more restrictive setting.

In locked correctional settings, treatment should be considered a privilege. Youth refusing to meaningfully participate in treatment over reasonably appropriate periods of time should be discharged from treatment groups and not be provided with additional benefits or perquisites. They should also be required to serve the maximum sentence imposed by a judge. However, the option of participating in treatment should be available to these youth at any time during their incarceration.

Best practice

The definition of best practice in treating sexually abusive youth is still in question (Chaffin & Bonner, 1998; Developmental Services Group, 2000, Hunter & Longo, 2004). While the field is not new, conceptualization of what constitutes effective treatment for this population is still evolving (Chaffin, Chapter 28; Hunter and Longo, 2004).

All too often, clinical approaches have overlooked developmental and contextual issues. Many programs have focused treatment on areas that may not be relevant for the juvenile sex offender population, such as deviant sexual arousal (Freeman-Longo, 2002; Hunter, 1999; Hunter & Becker, 1994). Techniques and modalities used in treating adult sexual offenders have been directly applied to youth, or modified only slightly to make materials more easily understood, without taking into consideration learning styles and intelligence variations of these clients (Gardner, 1983). High levels of confrontation are still used in many programs. When used with traumatized youth, these techniques may serve to re-traumatize them instead of promoting healing, forgiveness, and respect for self and others. Even the recent research with adult sex offenders demonstrates that warm, empathic, rewarding, and directive therapeutic styles can produce better treatment outcomes than harsh and confrontational methods (Marshall, Fernandez, Serran, Mulloy, Thornton, Mann, & Anderson, 2003).

As of 2002, the majority of juvenile sexual offender treatment programs still adhere to a traditional adult sex-offender model (Burton & Smith-Darden, 2001). According to national surveys, the most popular treatments for both adult and juvenile sex offenders include relapse prevention, the sexual abuse cycle, empathy training, anger management, social and interpersonal skills training, cognitive restructuring, assertiveness training, journaling, and sex education (Freeman-Longo, Bird, Stevenson, & Fiske, 1995; Becker & Hunter, 1997; Hunter, 1999; Burton, Smith-Darden, Levins, Fiske, & Freeman-Longo, 2000; Burton & Smith-Darden, 2001). Questions about the appropriateness and effectiveness of these approaches requires the development and testing of juvenile-specific intervention programs (Hunter & Longo, 2004; Prescott, 2002).

Throughout this book, we endorse the use of a holistic/integrated approach to treating youthful sexual abusers (Longo, 2001; Hunter & Longo, 2004). This approach blends traditional aspects of sexual abuser treatment into a holistic, humanistic and developmentally consistent model for working with youth (Morrison, Chapter 13). While cognitive-behavioral treatment methods appear promising, treatment must go beyond the sexual problems, and address "growth and development, social ecology, increasing health, social skills, resiliency, and incorporate treatment for the offender's own victimization and co-occurring disorders" (Developmental Services Group, 2000). If successful risk reduction involves changing thoughts and behaviors, then a holistic, integrated model prepares the youth to make these changes while respecting his long-term development.

Standards of care

The first standards of care for sex offender treatment appeared in the late 1980s, when ATSA published its first set of standards and guidelines for its members. Since then these standards have been revised several times to its current version (ATSA, 2004). Although comprehensive, its focus is more oriented to adult sex offenders than children or adolescents. ATSA is currently establishing guidelines specific to youthful sexual abusers. Coleman and Dwyer (1990) proposed a set of standards for care for the treatment of adult sex offenders. These standards were later revised and updated in 1996 and again in 2001 (Coleman, Dwyer, Abel, Berner, Breiling, Eher, Hindman, Langevin, Langfeldt, Miner, Pfafflin, & Weiss, 2001). These standards have also focused specifically on adult sex offenders.

In 1996 the National Offense-Specific Residential Standards Task Force was developed and over the course of three years this small independent group researched, developed, and published standards of care for the residential treatment of juvenile sexual abusers (Bengis, Brown, Freeman-Longo, Matsuda, Ross, Singer, and Thomas, 1999; Longo, 2002b). This was the first successful attempt to produce and publish standards for juvenile sexual abusers.

While there have been several independent efforts to establish standards of care, there is no national standard that is endorsed by a national agency or organization. Even the independently published standards do not provide consistently applied standards across the country.

Summary

One may well argue that the field of treating children and adolescents is itself barely out of adolescence. The past two decades have seen the recognition of sexual abuse by youth, but it is only recently that research and treatment have come to appreciate the heterogeneity of this population. We have imported many of our strategies for understanding, assessing, treating, and managing youth from adult populations. However, youth are, by definition, different. They exist in a different context and at different developmental stages. They often have unresolved histories of trauma, both physical and psychological.

Although treatment strategies aimed at thoughts and behaviors are promising, we cannot expect youth to respond to them without also attending to their needs at a more holistic level or incorporating the assets they bring into treatment (Longo, 2002a; Longo, 2004). We believe that the best practitioners are warm and empathic, addressing all aspects of the youth's functioning, while maintaining a focus on those areas demonstrated to be associated with risk. We also believe that interventions that do not take the youth's family circumstances into consideration may well do harm in the long run.

Finally, the field has struggled to develop standards and a continuum of care based on treatment needs and community safety. While many decisions around sexually abusive youth have been, and remain, driven by public fear and furor – not to mention economics – we remain confident and optimistic that efforts in these areas will continue to bear fruit in the long run. To that end, we hope the chapters that follow are helpful.

End Notes

[1] We recognize that this continuum is not exhaustive and that the points along it may not accurately characterize a particular individual facility. This continuum does not include all existing, necessary, or desirable levels of care. Also, an individual facility may or may not fit the description we have offered for that type of facility. For example, there may be group homes that provide a much higher level of security, or a juvenile correctional facility that provides far more services.

[2] In this continuum, the prevention level describes services that would be appropriate across a range of populations, including some identified case populations as well as general populations of children (primary prevention levels) and at-risk populations (secondary prevention levels).

References

Alexander, M. (1999). Sexual Offender Treatment Efficacy Revisited, *Sexual Abuse: A Journal of Research and Treatment*, 11, 101-116.

Andrews, D.A. & Bonta, J.L. (2003). T*he Psychology of Criminal Conduct, Third Edition*. Cincinnati: Anderson Publishing.

Association for the Treatment of Sexual Abusers (2004). *Practice standards and guidelines for members of the association for the Treatment of sexual abusers*. Beaverton, OR: Author.

Bauman, S. (2002). Types of juvenile sex offenders. T*he Prevention Researcher*, 9(4), 11-13.

Bear, E. (1993). *Inpatient treatment of adult survivors of sexual abuse: a summary of data from 22 programs*. Brandon, VT: Safer Society Press.

Becker, J. V., & Hunter, J. A. (1997). Understanding and treating child and adolescent sexual offenders. *Advances in Clinical Child Psychology*, 19, 177-197.

Bengis, S.M. (1986). A comprehensive service-delivery system with a continuum of care for adolescent sexual offenders. Shoreham, VT. Safer Society Program.

Bengis, S.M. (2002a). A state-of-the-art continuum of care for youth who engage in sexually abusive behavior. Unpublished manuscript.

Bengis, S.M. (2002b), unpublished manuscript). Principles guiding the development of a competency-based continuum of care for sexually abusive youth.

Bengis, S., Brown, A., Freeman-Longo, R.E., Matsuda, B., Ross, J., Singer, K., & Thomas, J. (1999). *Standards of Care for Youth in Sex Offense-Specific Residential Programs*. National Offense-Specific Residential Standards Task Force; Holyoke, MA: NEARI Press.

Bremer, J.F. (2001) "The Protective Factors Scale: assessing youth with sexual concerns". Plenary address at the 16th annual conference of the National Adolescent Perpetration Network, Kansas City, Mo. May 7, 2001.

Burton, D.L., & Smith-Darden, J. (2001). *North American survey of sexual abuser treatment and models: summary data 2000*. Brandon, VT: Safer Society Press.

Burton, D.L., Smith-Darden, J.P., Levins, J., Fiske, J.A. & Freeman-Longo, R.E., (2000). *1996 Nationwide survey: a survey of treatment programs & models serving children with sexual behavior problems, adolescent sex offenders, and adult sex offenders*. Brandon, VT: Safer Society Press.

Caldwell, M.F. (2002). What we do not know about juvenile sex offender reoffense risk. *Child Maltreatment*, 7(4), pp. 291-302.

Chaffin, M. & Bonner, B. (1998). "Editor's Introduction: 'Don't shoot, we're your children': Have we gone to far in our response to adolescent sexual abusers and children with sexual behavior problems?" *Child Maltreatment* 3(4): 314-316.

Chaffin, M. & Longo, R. (2003). Guidelines for Placement Within a Continuum of Care for Adolescent Sex Offenders (ASOs) and Children with Sexual Behavior Problems (CSBPs). National Center on the Sexual Behavior of Youth. http://www.ncsby.org/index.cfm

Coleman, E. & Dwyer, S.M. (1990). Proposed standards of care for the treatment of adult sex offenders. *Journal of Offender Rehabilitation*, 16(?), 93-106.

Coleman, E., Dwyer, S.M., Abel, G., Berner, W., Breiling, J., Hindman, J., Knopp, F. H., Langevin, R., & Phafflin, F. (1996). Standards of care for the treatment of adult sex offenders. *Journal of Offender Rehabilitation*, 22 (3/4).

Coleman, E., Dwyer, S.M., Abel, G., Berner, W., Breiling, J., Eher, R., Hindman, J. Langevin, R., Langfeldt, T., Miner, M., Pfafflin, F., & Weiss, P. (2001). Standards of care for the treatment of adult sex offenders. In Miner, M. & Coleman, E. (Eds). *Sex Offender Treatment: Accomplishments, Challenges and Future Directions.* Binghamton, NY: Haworth Press.

Davin, P.A., Hislop, J.C.R., & Dunbar, P. (1999). *Female sexual abusers: three views.* Brandon, VT: Safer Society Press.

Development Services Group (2000). *Understanding Treatment and Accountability in Juvenile Sex Offending: Results and Recommendations From an OJJDP Focus Group* (Prepared for Office of Juvenile Justice and Delinquency Prevention Training and Technical Assistance Division). Bethesda, MD. Author.

Epperson, D. L., Ralston, C. A., Fowers, D., & Dewitt, J. (2005, February). *Optimal predictors of Juvenile sexual recidivism in a large scale study of Utah adolescents who have offended sexually.* Paper presented at the 20th Annual Conference of the National Adolescent Perpetration Network, Denver, CO.

Freeman-Longo, R.E. (1998). A Public Health Model for Sexual Abuse. In Whitman, C., Zimmerman, J., & Miller, T. (eds.) Frontiers of Justice: Volume 2: Coddling or Common Cause. Biddle Publishing Co. Brunswick, ME 04011.

Freeman-Longo, R. E. (2002). Myths and Facts About Sex Offenders. Center For Sex Offender Management. Silver Spring, MD.

Freeman-Longo, R.E. & Blanchard, G.T. (1998). *Sexual Abuse in America: Epidemic of the 21st Century.* Brandon, VT: Safer Society Press.

Freeman-Longo, R.E., Bird, S. Stevenson, W.F. & Fiske, J.A. (1995). 1994 Nationwide survey of treatment programs & models: Serving abuse reactive children and adolescent & adult sexual offenders. Brandon, VT: Safer Society Press.

Gardner, H. (1983). Frames of Mind: The Theory of Multiple Intelligences, New York, Basic Books.

Guambana, A. (2001). *Staff Training: Gender-Specific Differences*. Juvenile Accountability: New & Views. OJJDP. 3(1) p. 3.

Hanson, R.K., Gordon, A., Harris, A.J.R., Marques, J.K., Murphy, W., Quinsey, V.L., & Seto, M.C. (2002). First report of the collaborative outcome data project on the effectiveness of psychological treatment for sex offenders. *Sexual Abuse: A Journal of Research and Treatment*, 14, 169-194.

Hunter, J.A. (1999). Adolescent Sex Offenders (pp. 117-130). In V.B. Van Hasselt & M. Hersen, *Handbook of Psychological Approaches with Violent Offenders*. Plenum: New York.

Hunter, J.A. & Becker, J.V. (1994). The role of deviant sexual arousal in juvenile sexual offending: Etiology, evaluation, and treatment, *Criminal Justice and Behavior* 21, 132-149.

Hunter, J. A., Hazelwood, R. R., & Slesinger, D. (2000). Juvenile-perpetrated sex crimes: patterns of offending and predictors of violence. *Journal of Family Violence*. Vol.15, No 1. pp 81-93.

Hunter, J. & Longo, R.E. (2004). Relapse Prevention with Juvenile Sexual Abusers: A Holistic/Integrated Approach. In G. O'Reilly & W. Marshall, A. Carr, & R. Beckett (Eds.), *Handbook of clinical intervention with young people who sexually abuse*. Sussex, UK: Brunner-Routledge.

Johnson, R.L., & Shrier, D. (1987). "Past sexual victimization by females of male patients in an adolescent medicine clinic population." *American Journal of Psychiatry*, 144(5).

Klein, A. & Tabachnick, J (2002). Finding ways to effectively prevent sexual abuse by youth. *The Prevention Researcher*. Vol. # (No 4. pp. 8-10.

Langstrom, N., & Grann, M. (2000). Risk for criminal recidivism among young sex offenders, *Journal of Interpersonal Violence*, 15, 855-871.

Leversee, T. & Pearson, C. (2001). Eliminating the pendulum effect: a balanced approach to the assessment, treatment, and management of sexually abusive youth. *Journal of the Center for Families, Children, & The Courts*. Pp. 45-57.

Levesque, R. J. R. (1996). Is there still a place for violent youth in juvenile justice? *Aggression and Violent Behavior*, I, 69-79.

Lewis, A. D. (1999). *Cultural Diversity in Sexual Abuser Treatment: Issues and Approaches*. Brandon, VT: Safer Society Press.

Longo, R.E. (2001). *Paths to Wellness: A Holistic Approach and Guide for Personal Recovery.* Holyoke, MA: NEARI Press.

Longo, R.E. (2002a). A Holistic Approach to Treating Juvenile Sexual Abusers, In Martin C. Calder (Ed.) *Young People Who Sexually Abuse: Building the Evidence Base for Your Practice.* Dorset, England: Russell House Publishing

Longo, R.E. (2002b). Residential Standards of Care for Adolescent Sexual Abusers, in Young People Who Sexually Abuse: Building the Evidence Base for Your Practice. Martin C. Calder (Ed.) Dorset, England: Russell House Publishing.

Longo, R.E. (2003). Emerging Issues, Policy Changes, and the Future of Treating Children with Sexual Behavior Problems. In R.A. Prentky, E.S. Janus, & M.C. Seto (eds.) Sexually coercive behavior: understanding and management. Annals of the New York Academy of Sciences. Vol. 989.

Longo, R.E. (2004). A Integrated Experiential Approach to Treating Young People Who Sexually Abuse. In Geffner, R. (Ed.) *Sex Offenders: Assessment and Treatment.* Family Violence and Sexual Assault Institute.

Longo, R.E. & Blanchard, G.T. (2002). Prevention of sexual offending by among adolescents. *The Prevention Researcher.* Vol. 9, No 4. pp. 5-8.

Marshall, W.L., Fernandez, Y.M., Serran, G., Mulloy, R., Thornton, D., Mann, R.E. , & Anderson, D. (2003). Process variables in the treatment of sexual offenders: A review of the relevent literature. *Aggression and Violent Behavior*, 8, 205-234.

Prentky, R., Harris, B., Frizzell, K. & Righthand, S. (2002). An actuarial procedure for assessing risk with juvenile sex offenders. *Sexual Abuse: A Journal of Research and Treatment.* Vol.12 No 2. pp-71-94.

Prentky, R. & Righthand, S. (2003). Juvenile Sex Offender Assessment Protocol – II (JSOAP – II). Available from Center for Sex Offender Management at www.csom.org.

Prescott, D.S. (2002). Collaborative treatment for sexual behavior problems in an adolescent residential center. In Miner, M.H., & Coleman, E., Ed.s (2002). *Sex Offender Treatment: Accomplishments, Challenges, and Future Directions.* Binghamton, NY: Haworth Press.

Prescott, D.S. (in press). The Current State of Adolescent Risk Assessment. In Schwartz, B. *The Sex Offender.* New York: Civic Research Institute.

Rich, P. (2001). Personal communication.

Rich, P. (2003). Understanding, assessing, and rehabilitating juvenile sexual offenders. New Jersey: Wiley.

Risin, L. & Koss, M. (1987). The sexual abuse of boys: Prevalence and descriptive characteristics of childhood victimization. *Journal of Interpersonal Violence,* 2(3).

Robinson, S. L. (2002). Growing Beyond: A Workbook for Sexually Abusive Teenage Girls - Treatment Manual. Holyoke, MA: NEARI Press.

Ryan, G. & Associates (1999). Web of Meaning: A Developmental-Contextual Approach in Sexual Abuse Treatment. Brandon, VT. Safer Society Press.

Ryan, G. (in press). Static, Stable and Dynamic Risks and Assets Relevant to the Prevention and Treatment of Abusive Behavior. (Poster Presentation at the First National Sexual Violence Prevention Conference, May. Dallas, Texas).

Worling, J.R., & Curwen, T., (2000). Adolescent sexual offender recidivism: success of specialized treatment and implications for risk prediction. Child Abuse and Neglect, 24, 965-982.

Worling, J. R., & Curwen, T. (2001). Estimate of Risk of Adolescent Sexual Offense Recidivism (Version 2.0: The "ERASOR"). In M. C. Calder, *Juveniles and children who sexually abuse: Frameworks for assessment (pp. 372-397).* Lyme Regis, Dorset, UK: Russell House Publishing.

Worling, J. R. & Curwen, T. (2002). The "ERASOR" estimate of risk of adolescent sexual offense recidivism. Version 1.2. SAFE-T Program, Thistletown Regional Centre. Canada.

CHAPTER TWO

UNDERSTANDING DIVERSITY IN JUVENILE SEXUAL OFFENDERS: IMPLICATIONS FOR ASSESSMENT, TREATMENT, AND LEGAL MANAGEMENT

JOHN A. HUNTER

Introduction

Adolescent males who present to the criminal justice system for the perpetration of sexual crimes have been seen as manifesting a wide range of offense related characteristics. Differences amongst these youth can be observed in the persistence of their sexual offending behavior, their selection of victims, and the type of sexual behavior displayed. While some youth appear to have begun offending sexually in childhood or early adolescence and continued to offend over the course of years, others appear to have engaged in only transient offending behavior. Similarly, some youth apparently exclusively offend against prepubescent children of one gender, while others primarily offend against peer-age or adult females or show variability in victim age and gender across time. Likewise, considerable variation is seen amongst youth in how they access victims, and the means by which they gain victim compliance. For example, while some youth primarily rely on physical force or violence and inflict serious injury on their victims, others employ more psychological methods, such as manipulation and trickery.

Clinical observation and record review, suggest that adolescent male sexual offenders also vary on several other potentially important dimensions, including: the extent of their involvement in non-sexual crime, their personality characteristics, and whether they manifest associated psychiatric co-morbidity. In this regard, some youth appear primarily antisocial in their personality make-up and have long histories of engagement in a variety criminal behavior. Others appear depressed and anxious, and have little or no previous involvement with the criminal justice system. Still others show evidence of long-standing deviant sexual interests and behaviors, or have lengthy histories of mental health treatment and hospitalization.

It is the author's contention that effective intervention with adolescent male sexual offenders requires an understanding of their described diversity, including their uniqueness from, and similarity to, other populations of youth who present to the criminal justice and mental health systems for aggressive and delinquent behaviors.

Successful intervention is thought to be largely contingent on gaining a clear understanding of the underlying determinants of their problematic behaviors. It is proposed in this chapter that there are multiple determinants of the sexual and non-sexual delinquency of sexually abusive youth, ranging from endogenous personality factors to family, peer, and community systems influences. Furthermore, it is suggested that it may be possible to classify youth on the basis of differential determinants, manifestation, and developmental course of the sexual behavior problem. The remainder of this chapter is devoted to reviewing research that supports the viability of classifying adolescent male sexual offenders into clinically meaningful subtypes, and the potential implications that such efforts have for clinical and legal management practices.

Research Exploring Diversity in Juvenile Sexual Offenders

Clinical interest in observed differences amongst juveniles that have perpetrated sexual abuse is long-standing (O'Brien, 1991); however, empirical research in this area is a relatively recent endeavor. Much of the conducted research has focused on comparison of subgroups of youth based on developmental history and offense characteristics.

Comparisons based on developmental characteristics

In one of the earliest studies of differential characteristics, Worling (1995) examined the sexual abuse histories of adolescent male sex offenders and found that victimization rates were higher in those adolescents who had sexually offended against male children. Kaufman, Hiliker, and Daleiden (1996) similarly found that a history of sexual abuse in the adolescent perpetrator was linked to the selection of male, and younger, victims. Veneziano, Veneziano, & LeGrand (2000), in their review of 74 cases of adolescent male sexual offending, commented on the parallels between the childhood victimization experiences of these youth and their patterns of emergent sexual offending.

In a subsequent study, Hunter, Figueredo, Malamuth, & Becker (2003) found support for the association between a history of sexual victimization by male perpetrators and the selection of male child victims in adolescent male sex offenders. It is noted that the latter study suggested that this association was limited to sexual victimization experiences perpetrated by non-relatives and those where a high level of force or violence was not employed. Together, the reviewed studies suggest that there may be some modeling or conditioning effect associated with sexual abuse experiences that helps shape the sexual offending behavior of some youthful perpetrators.

Comparisons based on victim characteristics

The referenced research by Kaufman and associates (Kaufman et al., 1996) also suggested that there may be differences in the modus operandi of adolescent males who perpetrate against siblings, and those who target non-family members. Specifically, the former group of youth appeared to rely more on manipulation and other psychological methods than physical force or coercion. Worling (1995) found sibling incest to be linked to family system dysfunction, including marital discord, parental rejection, physical discipline and childhood sexual abuse, and a negative family environment.

Richardson, Kelly, and Graham (1997), and Hunter, Hazelwood, and Slesinger (2000), both found that adolescent males who targeted peers and adults were more likely to commit the sexual offense along with a co-offender. These youth were also more likely to commit a non-sexual offense in conjunction with the sexual crime, and have a previous arrest record than those who targeted prepubescent children. The former group of youth, have also been found to almost exclusively offend against females (Stermac and Mathews, 1987; Worling, 1995), and to be more violent in the commission of their sexual offenses (Hunter et al., 2000).

The preceding research served as a conceptual basis for Hunter et al.'s (2003) comparison of adolescent males who targeted peer or adult females to those that targeted younger male or female children. These investigators found that offenders of peers and adults were more likely to target strangers or acquaintances, employ force or violence, and use a weapon in the commission of the sexual offense than offenders of children. The former group of youth were also more likely to be under the influence of drugs or alcohol at the time of commission of the sexual offense, commit the offense outside of the home of the victim or perpetrator, and have a prior arrest record for a non-sexual offense. Overall, these results are consistent with the interpretation that peer-adult offenders tend to be more antisocial or criminal in their personality make-up.

Comparisons based on personality characteristics

Study of diversity within adolescent male sex offenders has also focused on the personality characteristics of these youth. Worling (1995) did not find that youth that targeted female peers and adults differed from those assaulting children on the basis of interpersonal functioning, self-perception, or sexual attitudes. However, Hunter et al. (2003) found that the latter group of youth did manifest more deficits in psychosocial functioning, including lower social esteem and higher levels of anxiety and depression. Johnson and Knight (2000) found support for the association between hyper-masculinity and misogynistic fantasy, and sexually coercive behavior in adolescent male sex offenders. Endorsement of rape myths has also been found to be associated with a higher self-reported rate of sexual assault in a non-clinical sample of adolescent males (Maxwell, Robinson, & Post, 2003).

Personality characteristics were the basis for grouping adolescent male sex offenders in studies conducted by Worling (2001) and Hunter, Figueredo, Malamuth, Becker, and Conaway (2004). They are also the basis for a current longitudinal study by the author. In the Worling (2001) study, 112 male sexual offenders between the ages of 12 and 19 were categorized on the basis of their scores on the California Psychological Inventory. This resulted in four identifiable clusters of youth: Antisocial/Impulsive, Unusual/Isolated, Over Controlled/Reserved, and Confident/Aggressive. Subgroup membership was not found to be associated with victim gender or age, or offender history of sexual victimization. However, recidivism data did suggest that the Antisocial/Impulsive and Unusual/Isolated groups were at higher risk for committing a subsequent violent (sexual or non-sexual) or nonviolent offense.

Hunter, Figueredo, Malamuth, & Becker (2004) sequentially clustered 256 adolescent male sex offenders on the basis of scores on the following personality constructs: a) pedophilic interests; b) hostile masculinity, egotistical-antagonistic masculinity, and lifestyle delinquency; and c) psychosocial deficits. Pedophilic interests were measured using the Revised Attraction Scale (Malamuth, 1989), and consisted of multidimensional and multi-contextual ratings of sexual interest in children. The studied hostile masculinity construct reflected negative, stereotypic views of females as controlling and rejecting. Hostile masculinity previously has been found to be associated with sexual aggression in young adult males (Malamuth & Malamuth, 1999; Hall, Sue, Narang & Lilly, 2000).

The egotistical-antagonistic construct reflected dominance traits and a propensity to employ aggression as a means of resolving intra-sexual conflict in males (Hunter, Figueredo, Malamuth, & Becker, 2004). Lifestyle delinquency described psychopathic and impulsive personality traits, whereas the psychosocial construct measured low social self-esteem and related feelings of anxiety and depression.

The described research represented a preliminary effort to identify three prototypic subtypes of adolescent male sexual offenders: "Life-Style Persistent"; "Adolescent Onset, Non-Paraphilic", and "Early Adolescent Onset, Paraphilic".This preliminary typology of adolescent male sexual offenders builds on the work of Moffitt (1993), who has developed a typology of delinquent and aggressive youth.

"Life Style Persistent" youth, consistent with Moffitt's theoretical predictions, are thought to represent youth who begin to engage in oppositional and aggressive behaviors early in life and continue to manifest conduct-related problems into adolescence and beyond. The developmental trajectory of these youth is believed to be negative and downward spiraling, reflecting underlying trait-like psychopathy and impulsivity. The author has hypothesized that the coupling of the described character pathology with the aforementioned hostile masculinity construct propels these youth toward the sexual assault of pubescent and post-pubescent females. This group of youth is also thought to engage in more general antisocial behavior than the other two subtypes.

The "Adolescent Onset, Non-Paraphilic" subtype describes youth who engage in transient sexual offending. The sexual offending is thought to represent either adolescent experimentation or compensatory psychosexual behavior. The latter would represent those youth who lack the social skills and self-confidence to form and maintain age-appropriate relations with peers. It is hypothesized that the majority of youth in this subtype sexually offend against prepubescent females. The prognosis of these youth is thought to be positive if they do not become ensnared in drug and alcohol abuse, or negative peer affiliations that alter their developmental trajectory.

The "Early Adolescent Onset, Paraphilic" subtype is believed to represent cases of developing pedophilia. Thus, these youth are thought to sexually offend against prepubescent children because of emerging deviant sexual interests and arousal. Based on previous research (Hunter, Goodwin, & Becker, 1994; Hunter & Becker, 1994), it is predicted that these youth will have more prepubescent male victims than the other two subtypes. These youth are thought to be at high risk for continued sexual offending into adulthood.

The referenced cluster analysis identified five groups of youth: 1) those that scored high on the pedophilia construct; 2) those that scored high on hostile masculinity, egotistical-antagonistic masculinity, and lifestyle delinquency, and low on psychosocial deficits; 3) those that scored high on the above three constructs and high on psychosocial deficits; 4) those that scored low on all of the measured constructs; and 5) those that scored high on psychosocial deficits and low on the other constructs. The first group was thought to represent the "Early Adolescent Onset, Paraphilic" subtype, the second and third groups the "Life Course Persistent" subtype, and the latter groups the "Adolescent Onset, Non-Paraphilic" subtype.

Consistent with this hypothesis, the group scoring high on the pedophilic construct had the highest composite index of sexual offending against male children based on record review. As predicted, the groups believed to represent the "Life Course Persistent" youth had the highest self-reported level of engagement in non-sexual violence in the twelve months preceding the study, the highest archival record documented percent of arrests for non-sexual crimes, and the highest percent of sexual assaults against pubescent or post-pubescent females.

The author's study of the described prototypic subtypes of sexually aggressive youth is continuing with the support of a grant from the National Institute of Mental Health. The study design involves the longitudinal tracking of 330 adolescent males from their enrollment in specialized institutional and community-based treatment programs for juvenile sex offenders, through their post-treatment release and adjustment in the community. Youth are tracked altogether for four to five years. Measured outcomes include: response to treatment, long-term psychosocial and psychosexual adjustment, and sexual and non-sexual recidivism.

It is predicted that the "Life-Style Delinquent" youth will manifest the poorest response to treatment and have the highest post-treatment percent of arrests for non-sexual crimes. It is also hypothesized that they will have the highest post-treatment percent of arrests for sexual offenses against pubescent and post-pubescent females. Furthermore, it is predicted that this group of youth will demonstrate the poorest long-term psychosocial adjustment.

"Early Adolescent Onset, Paraphilic" youth are predicted to have the highest post-treatment percent of arrests for sexual offenses against children, and poorest long-term psychosexual adjustment. The "Adolescent Onset, Non-Paraphilic" group is predicted to show the best response to treatment, have the lowest post-treatment percent of arrests for sexual or non-sexual crimes, and show the most favorable psychosocial and psychosexual adjustment. Table 1 summarizes the prototypic subtypes and their hypothesized features.

TABLE 1: Prototypic Subtypes of Adolescent Male Sexual Offenders

Subtype	Hypothesized Features
"Adolescent Onset, Non-paraphilic" experimentation or positive response to if does not and/or drug and alcohol	Transient sexual offending reflective of compensatory behavior. Predicted to have treatment and favorable long-term adjustment, become ensnared in negative peer group abuse.
"Early Adolescent Onset, Paraphilic" pedophilia. Chief sexual interest in sexual offending.	Thought to represent cases of juvenile onset clinical feature is pronounced and sustained children. Believed to be at long-term risk for
"Life Course Persistent" problems. Sexual behavior. Sexual thought to reflect masculinity. thought to be poor.	Early developmental onset for conduct-related offending embedded in overall antisocial aggression toward adolescent and adult females underlying character pathology and hostile Treatment response and long-term prognosis

Study of Psychiatric Co-morbidity

Considerable diversity is also seen in the psychiatric co-morbidity of adolescent male sexual offenders. Nearly half of juvenile sex offenders in community-based programming have been found to meet diagnostic criteria for Conduct Disorder (Kavoussi, Kaplan, & Becker, 1988). This rate is likely to be even higher in residential samples. The detected high prevalence of general conduct disorder in these youth is supported by the observation that non-sexual recidivism rates in these youth is typically two to four times higher than sexual recidivism rates (Becker, 1998).

ADHD is likewise believed to be present in a significant percentage of juvenile male sexual offenders (Kavoussi et al., 1988), and may directly contribute to the observed problems that many of these youth have with sexual impulse control and inhibition.

In a recent study of 72 youth between the ages of six and seventeen who had engaged in "hands-on" sexual offending, Fago (2003) found evidence that 82% met diagnostic criteria for ADHD or showed evidence of other neurodevelopmental disorders associated with deficits in executive function. Furthermore, 44% of this community-based sample of youth had documented histories of a specific learning disability or showed evidence of school failure.

Mood disorders and substance abuse have also been found to be prevalent in samples of juvenile male sex offenders (Becker, Kaplan, Tenke, & Taraglini, 1991; Matthews, Hunter, & Vuz, 1997; Hunter et al., 2003). The previously discussed study by Hunter et al. (2003) suggests that experienced anxiety and depression in these youth may be associated with low social self-esteem and perceived emotional isolation.

Family and Peer Influences

While not as well-studied in samples of juvenile sex offenders, there is an emergent literature that suggests that delinquent behavior in youth is heavily influenced by both the family and peer-affiliation systems. For example, Eddy and Chamberlain (2000) found that family management skills and deviant peer association mediated the treatment effect of adolescent males with histories of chronic delinquency. In general, families of violent adolescents have been found to be less effective disciplinarians, less cohesive, and less involved than controls (Gorman-Smith, Tolan, Zelli, Huesmann, & Rowell, 1996). Youth who are low in perceived self-regulatory efficacy may have more difficulty warding off negative peer influences and communicating with parents about problems experienced outside of the home (Carpara, Scabini, Barbaranelli, Pastorelli, Regalia, & Bandura (1998). In one of the few studies involving juvenile sex offenders, Blaske, Borduin, Henggeler, and Mann (1989) found that sexually offending youth and their mothers evidenced less positive communication than non-delinquent controls, and that the mothers of sexually offending youth viewed their sons as having more difficulty emotionally bonding with peers.

Implications for Assessment

The above findings suggest that adolescent male sex offenders present with an array of developmental, offense, personality, familial, and peer relationship characteristics that directly or indirectly influence their response to treatment and risk of sexual and non-sexual recidivism. Furthermore, they display a wide range of associated mental health and behavioral problems. The author suggests that the described characteristics and behaviors cluster in a manner that is potentially diagnostically meaningful, and that clinical assessments should be conducted in a manner that helps illuminate differential developmental processes and disorder type. While a comprehensive discussion of the issues and methods of clinical assessment of juvenile sex offenders is beyond the scope of this chapter, four potentially critical diagnostic and treatment planning issues are discussed below.

Determining differential personality, sexual interest, and developmental characteristics

The reviewed typology research suggests that there may be differential personality and developmental characteristics in adolescent male sexual offenders that have relevance for understanding their amenability to treatment, intervention needs, and risk of re-offending. It is recommended that clinicians do two things germane to making such differential diagnoses:

> 1) examine the developmental context of the sexual offending behavior; and
> 2) employ measures that are specific to relevant personality constructs and sexual attitudes and interests.

As it relates to the former, it is thought important to achieve through extensive mental health, school, and legal record review, along with self-report and collateral interviews of family members, a perspective on the youth's overall development. Pertinent issues here include: early childhood behavior and temperament, level and type of parental attachment, achievement of developmental milestones, social relatedness and ability to make and keep friends, and academic progress. Also relevant, are assessments of quality of parenting, stability of the home environment, exposure to violence, and maltreatment experiences. It is believed that examination of the developmental context in which the sexual offending behavior occurs greatly assists the diagnostic process. While too voluminous to review for the purposes of this chapter, there are a number of studies that suggest that there is continuity in the antisocial and aggressive behavior of male youth, and that early onset delinquency portends a more negative developmental trajectory (Broidy, Nagin, Tremblay, et al., 2003). Furthermore, such early onset delinquency may reflect a stronger genetic influence than delinquency that emerges during adolescence (Taylor, Iacono, & McGue, 2000).

With regard to psychological assessment, it is recommended that measures specific to the following constructs be included in the test battery: psychopathy, dominance, delinquent and antisocial attitudes, impulsivity, social self-esteem, depression and anxiety, and empathy. To the extent possible, and so as to help attenuate biases in self-reporting, assessments should rely on multi-informant data. In that regard, the observations of parents, teachers, and others in a care-taking or service delivery role, are often quite helpful.

Clinicians should also, through both interview and psychometric assessment, try and determine whether there is evidence of paraphilic interests and arousal. Where appropriate (see Hunter & Lexier, 1998 for guidelines), these assessments may involve psychophysiological measures. Clinical observation, and preliminary typology research, suggests that established patterns of paraphilic arousal and interests may be limited to a relatively small subset of adolescent male sexual offenders. However, where present, such patterns have considerable diagnostic and treatment planning significance.

Expanding assessment to the larger social-ecological context

Traditionally, clinical assessment has almost exclusively focused on endogenous or intrapsychic characteristics of these youth. As reviewed, there is an emerging research literature that documents the importance of familial, peer, and cultural influences on a youth's delinquent behavior. These influences may have direct or indirect bearing on the youth's sexual behavior problem and/or willingness to engage in and benefit from treatment.

It is therefore important that assessments focus on each of these potentially significant systems. Clinicians are encouraged to use both observational and self-report measures that are specific to the following: overall family functioning, family cohesiveness and adaptability, parental disciplinary style and method, level and type of parental supervision and monitoring, sibling influences, peer affiliation, and cultural attitudes and beliefs.

Identifying psychiatric co-morbidity

As discussed by Hunter, Gilbertson, Vedros, and Morton (2004), effective treatment planning requires the identification and proper addressing of all of the emotional and behavioral problems exhibited by the youth. The interview and assessment process should therefore have a focus beyond that of the demonstrated sexual behavior problem. If such a comprehensive, holistic assessment is beyond the skills or means of the evaluator, then it is recommended that collateral evaluations be sought. This is particularly important where there is evidence or suggestion of the following: more pervasive developmental delays or neurological problems (including intellectual deficits and ADHD), a history of significant substance abuse, mood instability and/or suicidal ideation, and disorders of thinking or reality testing.

Delineating risk and specific treatment issues and needs

Clinicians are encouraged to use assessment data to form a diagnostic conceptualization of the type and nature of a youth's sexual behavior problem. It is recommended that this conceptualization encompass a judged risk for sexual and non-sexual re-offending, and the recommendations regarding required level and intensity of care. Within this diagnostic conceptualization, there should be the identification of specific treatment issues and needs within the intrapsychic, interpersonal, familial, academic, peer, and cultural community spheres. Treatment recommendations should not be generic, but specific to the youth and his individual intervention and management needs. Case conceptualization should extend to support to legal professionals in formulating an effective, and complementary, legal management and supervision plan.

Implications for Treatment and Legal Management

The discussed diversity of the juvenile sexual offender population also has potential implications for effective clinical and legal management. The following issues are discussed in support of integrating an understanding of diversity into service development and intervention planning.

Need for a continuum of care

Because of the range in psychopathology and risk seen in adolescent male sexual offenders, there must be a variety of treatment and placement options available to meet their individual needs. These options should range from comprehensive community-based programming, to secure residential and correctional placement.

As discussed by Hunter et al. (2004), few states have developed a continuum of care for adolescent sexual offenders, with most states relying on secure residential care for all but the most mildly maladjusted youth. The reviewed typology research suggests that many adolescent male sexual offenders can be safely and effectively managed in the community if proper services are in place. In fact, it can be argued that it is clinically counterproductive and fiscally irresponsible to place less characterologically disturbed and sexually deviant youth in residential programs.

As it relates to the former, research suggests that exposure of younger and less antisocial youth to older and more antisocial peers, may result in harmful long-term effects (Dishion, McCord, & Poulin, 1999). In essence, younger and less disturbed youth may incorporate the negative, antisocial values of older and more delinquent youth and experience social reinforcement of their delinquent attitudes and behavior (i.e. deviancy training). Fiscally, the cost of 24-hour residential care is typically two to three times higher than community-based services, even after factoring in the cost of group and/or foster homes (Hunter et al., 2004). Such costs can make it difficult for communities to provide treatment funding for more than a handful of juvenile sex offenders.

Critical to the viability of community-based programming for adolescent male sexual offenders is; a) the development of comprehensive and well-integrated clinical and legal management programming to meet the varied needs of these youth and their families/caretakers, and b) the proper screening of individual youth to determine their appropriateness for this level of care. The latter should take into consideration differential offending patterns and dynamics, and include formal risk and needs assessment. In general, it is recommended that community-based treatment be limited to the less sexually predatory and characterologically impaired youth, and those without pronounced paraphilic interests. However, with the availability of alternative living placements (e.g. group home) and the provision of comprehensive wraparound services, community-based programs can serve large numbers of adolescent male sexual offenders and reduce residential utilization (Hunter et al., 2004b).

Caution in mixing youth in treatment settings

As discussed above, the diversity seen in adolescent male sexual offenders provides reason for caution in combining youth for placement purposes. However, this caution should extend to any setting where youth are congregated for treatment purposes—including group therapy. Group therapy has traditionally been a staple of juvenile and adult sex offender treatment programming, and it has been argued that it is the preferred modality of treatment for sex offenders (Sawyer, 2002; Jennings & Sawyer, 2003; McGraph, Cummings, & Burchard, 2003). Unfortunately, there is a paucity of empirical support for this conventional clinical wisdom. Furthermore, the aforementioned research on iatrogenic treatment effects raises the possibility that uninformed combining of sexually offending youth in therapy groups may do more harm than good.

Clinicians who desire to utilize group therapy with this population, whether in community-based or institutional settings, should carefully assess youth and not mix younger and less characterologically and psychosexually impaired youth, with older and more disturbed ones. Careful screening, with attention to the previously discussed personality, social-ecological, and developmental factors, is essential to sound clinical practice in this area.

Need for greater treatment specificity

Continued typology research will ultimately enable the field to define clinically discrete subtypes of adolescent male sexual offenders with differential developmental trajectories. The achievement of this goal could lead to subtype-specific interventions. The latter would represent highly focused and specialized approaches based on an understanding of the unique developmental, clinical, and legal characteristics of each subtype. Such advancement would hold promise for improved clinical outcomes and enhanced legal management planning.[1]

Until research advances to the above-referenced point, clinicians must rely on their own judgment in formulating treatment plans for individual youth. Clinicians are encouraged to utilize assessment data to identify the salient personality, peer and family systems, and developmental characteristics of the youth and to fashion a treatment plan that addresses each of these issues. Consistent with a social-ecological approach (see Henggeler, Schoenwald, Borduin, Rowland, and Cunningham, 1998 for a comprehensive discussion of such approaches), clinicians should be particularly sensitive to the dynamic nature of these systems and the manner in which systems interact and exert reciprocal influences on one another.

Integrated and risk-adjusted clinical and legal case management

Observation of the apparent diversity in adolescent male sexual offenders should foster a keen appreciation for the importance of integrated, risk-adjusted clinical and legal case management services. Given that these youth appear to differ in offending dynamics and risk, it is imperative that mental health and legal professionals work in a closely coordinated manner to effect a comprehensive and individualized case management plan. This integrated plan of services should be aimed at both maximizing community safety, and ensuring that the youth and his family/caretakers are afforded the intervention services they need.

In support of achievement of the above, the author assisted the Virginia Department of Juvenile Justice in developing a model risk-adjusted case management protocol for juvenile sexual offenders. These protocols were informed by existent typology research and clinical observation of differences amongst these youth in offending dynamics and characteristics. They also reflect, in large part, a "best practices" model for community-based management of juvenile sexual offenders piloted by the Norfolk Court Services Unit under the support of a U.S. Office of Justice Department grant. However, it should be noted that the protocols have not been validated through research and should be viewed as the professional opinion of the author.

[1]*The author would like to emphasize that the discussed prototypic subtypes are restricted to adolescent males who have engaged in "hands-on" sexual offending. Subtype descriptions do not necessarily apply to prepubescent youth or to adolescent females who have engaged in sexually abusive behavior. Readers are directed to Pithers, Gray, Busconi, and Houchens (1998) for a discussion of the differential characteristics of children who engage in aggressive and inappropriate sexual behavior, and to Hunter, Becker, and Lexier (in press) for description of clinically observed subtypes of sexually abusive adolescent females.*

The protocols apply to those youth placed on community supervision following adjudication and sentencing, and youth returning to the community following court-ordered correctional or residential placement. The guidelines were specifically developed to provide decision support to probation and parole officers in making three determinations: 1) the appropriateness of community care for an individual offender given the nature and severity of his sexual and other psychological and behavioral problems, 2) the type and level of intensity of supervisory and intervention services an offender requires to maintain public safety and ensure his successful rehabilitation, and 3) the offender's readiness for "step-down" or termination of clinical and legal services. The guidelines and accompanying probation and parole supervision matrices can be found on the Center for Sex Offender Management website (CSOM.org), under "Other Resources"/"Juveniles Who Commit Sexual Offenses".

Summary

Adolescent male sexual offenders appear to constitute a heterogeneous clinical population representing various offending dynamics and levels of risk. Although typology research is still in its infancy, preliminary findings suggest that it may be possible to identify distinct subtypes of youth with differential developmental, personality, and offending characteristics. It is suggested that clinical practice can be enhanced by an understanding and appreciation for the diversity observed in the population. The author has summarized research in this area, and discussed its potential implications for new and improved approaches to clinical assessment and clinical/legal management.

References

Becker, J.V. (1998). What we know about the characteristics and treatment of adolescents who have committed sexual offenses. *Child Maltreatment: Journal of the American Professional Society on the Abuse of Children*, 3(4), 317-329.

Becker, J.V., Kaplan, M.S., Tenke, C.E., & Tartaglini, A. (1991). The incidence of depressive symptomatology in juvenile sex offenders with a history of abuse. *Child Abuse & Neglect*, 15(4), 531-536.

Blaske, D.M., Borduin, C.M., Henggeler, S.W., & Mann, B.J. (1989). Individual, family, and peer characteristics of adolescent sex offenders and assaultive offenders. *Developmental Psychology*, 25(5), 846-855.

Broidy, L.M., Nagin, D.S., Tremblay, R.E., Bates, J.E., Brame, B., Dodge, K.A., Fergusson, D., Horwood, J.L., Loeber, R., Laird, R., Lynam, D.R., Moffitt, T.E., Pettit, G.S., & Vitaro, F. (2003). Developmental trajectories of childhood disruptive behaviors and adolescent delinquency: A six-site, cross-national study. *Developmental Psychology*, 39(2), 222-245.

Caprara, G.V., Scabini, E., Barbaranelli, C., Pastorelli, C., Regalia, C., & Bandura, A. (1998). *European Psychologist*, 3(2), 125-132.
Center for Sex Offender Management (www.csom.org)

Dishion, T. J., McCord, J. & Poulin, F. (1999). When interventions harm: Peer groups and problem behavior. *American Psychologist*, 54(9), 755-764.

Eddy, J.M. & Chamberlain, P. (2000). Family management and deviant peer association as mediators of the impact of treatment condition on youth antisocial behavior. *Journal of Consulting & Clinical Psychology*, 68(5), 857-863.

Fago, D.P. (2003). Evaluation and treatment of neurodevelopmental deficits in sexually aggressive children and adolescents. *Professional Psychology: Research and Practice*, 34(3), 248-257.

Gorman-Smith, D., Tolan, P.H., Zelli, A., Huesmann, L.R. & Rowell (1996). The relation of family functioning to violence among inner-city minority youths. *Journal of Family Psychology*, 10(2), Jun 1996, 115-129

Hall, G.C.N., Sue, S., Narang, D.S., & Lilly, R.S. (2000). Culture-specific models of men's sexual aggression: Intra- and interpersonal determinants. *Cultural Diversity & Ethnic Minority Psychology*, 6(3), 252-268.

Henggeler, S.W., Schoenwald, S.K., Borduin, C.M., Rowland, M.D., & Cunningham, P.B. (1998). *Multisystemic treatment of antisocial behavior in children and adolescents. Treatment manuals for practitioners*, New York, NY, US: Guilford Press, 287pp.

Hunter, J.A. & Becker, J.V. (1994). The role of deviant sexual arousal in juvenile sexual offending: Etiology, evaluation, and treatment. *Criminal Justice & Behavior*, 21(1), 132-14.

Hunter, J.A., Becker, J.V. & Lexier, L. (in press). The Female Juvenile Sex Offender. In H.E. Barbaree and W.L. Marshall (Editors), *The Juvenile Sex Offender*, Second Edition. Guilford Publications.

Hunter, J.A., Goodwin, D.W., & Becker, J.V. (1994). The relationship between phallometrically measured deviant sexual arousal and clinical characteristics in juvenile sexual offenders. *Behaviour Research & Therapy*, 32(5), 533-538.

Hunter, J.A. & Lexier, L.J. (1998) (invited article). Ethical and legal issues in the assessment and treatment of juvenile sex offenders. *Child Maltreatment*, 3(4), 339-348.

Hunter, J.A., Hazelwood, R.R., & Slesinger, D., (2000). Juvenile-perpetrated sex crimes: Patterns of offending and predictors of violence. *Journal of Family Violence*, 15(1), 81-93.

Hunter, J.A., Figueredo, A.J., Malamuth, N., & Becker, J.V. (2003). Juvenile sex offenders: Toward the development of a typology. *Sexual Abuse: A Journal of Research and Treatment*.

Hunter, J.A., Gilbertson, S., Vedros, D., & Morton, M. (2004a). Strengthening community-based programming for juvenile sexual offenders: Key concepts and paradigm shifts. *Child Maltreatment*, 9(2), 177-189.

Hunter, J.A., Figueredo, A.J., Malamuth, N., & Becker, J.V. (2004b). Developmental pathways in youth sexual aggression and delinquency. *Journal of Family Violence,* 19(4), 233-242.

Hunter, J.A., Figueredo, A.J., Malamuth, N., Becker, J.V., & Conaway, M. (2004-manuscript in preparation). The development of a juvenile sex offender typology: A report of on-going research.

Jennings, J.L., & Sawyer S. (2003). Principles and techniques for maximizing the effectiveness of group therapy with sex offenders. *Sexual Abuse: A Journal of research and Treatment,* 15, 251-267.

Johnson, G. M., & Knight, R. A. (2000). Developmental antecedents of sexual coercion in juvenile sexual offenders. *Sexual Abuse: A Journal of Research and Treatment,* 12(3), 165-178.

Kaufman, K. L., Hilliker, D. R., & Daleiden, E. L. (1996). Subgroup differences in the modus operandi of adolescent sexual offenders. *Child Maltreatment: Journal of the American Professional Society on the Abuse of Children,* 1(1), 17-24.

Kavoussi, R. J., Kaplan, M. & Becker, J. V. (1988). Psychiatric diagnoses in adolescent sex offenders. *Journal of the American Academy of Child and Adolescent Psychiatry,* 27(2), 241-243.

Malamuth, N. M. (1989). The attraction to sexual aggression scale: I. *Journal of Sex Research,* 26(1), 26-49.

Malamuth, N.M. & Malamuth, E.Z. (1999). Integrating multiple levels of scientific analysis and the confluence model of sexual coercers. *Jurimetrics,* 39, 157-179.

Mathews, R., Hunter, J.A. & Vuz, J. (1997). Juvenile female sexual offenders: Clinical characteristics and treatment issues. *Sexual Abuse: A Journal of Research and Treatment,* 9(3), 187-199.

Maxwell, C.D., Robinson, A.L. & Post, L.A. (2003). The Nature and Predictors of Sexual Victimization and Offending Among Adolescents. *Journal of Youth & Adolescence,* 32(6), 465-477.

McGraph, R.J., Cumming, G. F. & Burchard, B.L. (2003). *Current practices and trends in sexual abuser management: The Safer Society 2002 nationwide survey.* Brandon, VT: Safer Society.

Moffit, T.E. (1993). Adolescence-limited and life-course-persistent antisocial behavior: A developmental taxonomy. *Psychological Review,* 100(4), 674-701.

O'Brien, Michael J. (1991). Taking sibling incest seriously. In Michael Quinn Patton (Ed), *Family sexual abuse: Frontline research and evaluation* (pp. 75-92). Sage Publications: Thousand Oaks, CA.

Pithers, W.D., Gray, A, Busconi, A., & Houchens, P., (1998). Children with sexual behavior problems: Identification of five distinct child types and related treatment considerations. *Child Maltreatment: Journal of the American Professional Society on the Abuse of Children*, 3(4), 384-406.

Richardson, G., Kelly, T. P. & Graham, F. (1997). Group differences in abuser and abuse characteristics in a British sample of sexually abusive adolescents. *Sexual Abuse: Journal of Research & Treatment*, 9(3), 239-257.

Sawyer, S. (2002). Group therapy with adult sex offenders. In B.K. Schwartz (Ed.), *The sex offender: Current treatment modalities and systems issues* (pp. 14.1-14.15). Kingston, NJ: Civic Research Institute.

Stermac, L. & Mathews, F. (1987). *Adolescent sex offenders: Towards a profile.* Toronto: Central Toronto Youth Services.

Taylor, J., Iacono, W.G. & McGue, M. (2000). Evidence for a genetic etiology of early-onset delinquency. *Journal of Abnormal Psychology*, 109(4), 634-643.

Veneziano, C., Veneziano, L. & LeGrand, S. (2000). The relationship between adolescent sex offender behaviors and victim characteristics with prior victimization. *Journal of Interpersonal Violence*, 15(4), 363-374.

Worling, J.R. (1995). Sexual abuse histories of adolescent male sex offenders: Differences on the basis of the age and gender of the victims. *Journal of Abnormal Psychology*, 104, 610-613.

Worling, J. A. (2001). Personality-based typology of adolescent male sexual offenders: Differences in recidivism rates, victim-selection characteristics, and personal victimization histories. *Sexual Abuse: Journal of Research and Treatment*, 13(3), 149-166.

CHAPTER THREE

CHILDREN TWELVE AND YOUNGER
WITH SEXUAL BEHAVIOR PROBLEMS:
What We Know in 2005 That We Didn't Know in 1985

TONI CAVANAGH JOHNSON
AND
RONDA DOONAN

Introduction

While this chapter talks about the "sexual behaviors" of children, this term could be misleading. The behaviors that most of these children engage in are behaviors that are related to sex and sexuality but are not "sexual" behaviors in the same way we conceive of adult sexual behaviors. The behaviors of young children often mimic the behaviors of adults, as they touch their own and others' genitals and explore adult gender roles and the pairing/coupling behaviors of adults ("dating," "marrying," "playing house," "playing doctor," "dirty dancing," and/or "humping"). Unlike adults, children are generally not seeking emotional connections and intimate relationships in their "sexual" behaviors. Most of the "sexual" behaviors engaged in by young children are not driven by the desire for sexual arousal, physical gratification, and orgasm. Yet, children's bodies are equipped from birth for arousal and pleasure, and infants can experience orgasms even in utero. Generally, children experience pleasurable sensations from genital touching. Some children experience sexual arousal while others experience orgasm. Sexual arousal and orgasm are more frequently found in older children entering puberty. Therefore, the term "sexual behavior" is used for the sake of brevity; otherwise the phrase that is more apt is "behaviors related to sex and sexuality" (Johnson, 2000).

Nomenclature

At this time in the United States the term "children with sexual behavior problems" is used frequently, but different people use it differently. Some use the term when referring to children who are sexually offending, some use it to refer to children who are engaging in problematic sexual behavior of far less seriousness, and some use it to refer to the whole range of sexual behavior problems in children. This lack of precision can lead to confusion. For instance, someone may refer to the "victim" of a child with a sexual behavior problem. If the language (victim) were being used precisely, this would mean that a child has been "sexually abused" by another child. Yet, upon questioning, it may be that the person uses the language of victimization but is talking about a sexual behavior that was mutually agreed upon but developmentally advanced for children of their age.

Due to the lack of definitions, some people equate all children with sexual behavior problems as offenders or on a trajectory to sexual offending. When definitions and language are not precise and clearly delineated, children labeled as having problems with sexual behaviors can receive serious legal consequences that can affect their entire lives. Unfortunately, with the advent of sex offender registries and Megan's Law, the stakes have become very high. There are states that register children as sex offenders, even as young as seven years of age. The lack of agreement in the use of terminology and definitions is a problem that needs further work.

Beginning in 1987, Johnson (1993) developed a continuum of sexual behaviors to better delineate the children being referred to Children's Institute International. There are four groups along the continuum. The first group, which is by far the largest, includes children with "natural and healthy sexual behaviors"; the next three groups pertain to children with problematic sexual behavior. These three groups are as follows: "sexually-reactive," "children engaged in extensive mutual sexual behaviors," and "children who molest." Johnson uses the term "children with sexual behavior problems" to refer to all three groups of children who are not engaging in natural and healthy sexual behaviors. The three groups of children with sexual behavior problems engage in increasingly disturbed sexual behaviors. Only one group, children who molest engage in sexually abusive behavior. (See section; Identifying the Seriousness of the Child's Problematic Sexual Behavior below for further information.) These groups were conceptualized based on the first author's clinical experience and have never been subjected to empirical verification. Interestingly, typologies developed by Hall using complex statistical methods derived very similar groups (Hall, Mathews et al. 1998; Hall, Mathews et al. 2002).

The confusion in language and group designation can be seen in Schwartz's 1995 book. She uses "abuse-reactive" synonymously with "perpetrator" and "children who sexually assault." "Another population of perpetrators, which has only recently been identified, are children who sexually assault other children. These perpetrators, who have themselves been victims of sexual abuse, are now being referred to as 'abuse reactive' children" (Schwartz et al., 1995, p. 3-4). The implication is that all abuse-reactive children are perpetrators and all have themselves been victims of sexual abuse. In the first author's designation the "abuse-reactive" child may or may not be a victim of abuse and has no intention of harming another child when engaging in sexual behaviors with him or her. Sometimes the term "inappropriate" is used to designate children who are offending (Adams, McClellan et al. 1995). The term "sexually intrusive" is used by some to indicate interpersonal but unplanned, impulsive and non-aggressive behavior (Bonner, Walker et al. 1999; Bonner, Walker et al. 1999). Others use "sexually intrusive" as more synonymous to perpetration behaviors by adult and adolescent sex offenders (Friedrich, Davies et al. 2003). The term "sexually intrusive" is used in Canada with no consensus as to its definition.

It is the belief of the authors that it is important for the field to develop a consensus of some subsets of "children with sexual behavior problems" or develop terminology that defines levels of seriousness. This will aid mental health professionals, child protective services (CPS), law enforcement, and the judiciary to communicate with one another in a meaningful way regarding the level of severity of the sexual behavior(s) in question, thus allowing for effective case management, treatment, placement and safety planning for each child.

Are All Children with Sexual Behavior Problems Victims of Abuse?

In the mid-1980s there was a belief that the major etiological factor for children with sexual behavior problems was that they had been sexually abused. This belief was based on the incorrect notion that virtually all adult sex offenders had been sexually abused, and that the abuse was the cause for their sexual offending.

Several articles were published in the late 1980s about children who molest other children. This category represents the most seriously disturbed of all children with sexual behavior problems. A study of 14 boys and 4 girls (Friedrich and Luecke, 1988) found that 75% of the "sexually-aggressive" boys and 100% of the "sexually-aggressive" girls had been sexually abused. A study of 47 boys, (Johnson, 1988) found that overall, 50% of the "children who molested" had been sexually abused, with a higher percentage of the younger children being sexually abused and 30% of the children between 11-12 years old being sexually abused. Virtually all of the boys had sustained pervasive harsh physical punishment. In an article on 13 girls who molest, Johnson (1989) found that all of the girls had been sexually abused and they had sustained pervasive harsh physical punishment. Early studies did not confirm a history of sexual abuse in all male and female children who molested.

Even after the above studies, the belief persisted that the reason for children sexually offending other children was a recapitulation of their own sexual abuse. As more children who were molesting other children were brought into treatment, it was found that many did not disclose sexual abuse. As most of the children who did not disclose sexual abuse were boys, a belief developed that the reason more sexual abuse was not being found in their history was due to it being difficult for boys to disclose sexual abuse.

While the samples of children who molest were small, the lower than expected incidence of sexual abuse in boys was corroborated by information gathered on adult sex offenders. Murphy and Peters (1992) state:

> There is a good deal of clinical lore that a history of being sexually victimized is predominant in the backgrounds of sex offenders. However, there are a number of problems when extrapolating the clinical lore to the legal arena. First, one must realize that estimates currently suggest that somewhere between 1 in 9 children to 1 in 10 young males will be sexually abused before the age of 18 (Finkelhor, Hotaling et al. 1990). The vast majority of these children do not grow up to be sex offenders and therefore one could not classify someone as a sex offender based on the fact that they have been sexually abused. In addition, reviewed data on 1,717 offenders included in 18 different studies found that the average rate of sexual abuse across studies was 28%. (Hanson and Slater, 1988)

Although the empirical literature indicates that not all children who molest other children are themselves victims of sexual abuse, this belief has persisted in the minds of the general public, and in some police, CPS workers and mental health professionals (Friedrich and Chaffin, 2000). As with children who sexually offend, it is also true of the entire range of children with sexual behavior problems that sexual abuse is not pervasive in their history. Drach, Wientzen et al., (2001) found no significant relationship between being a victim of sexual abuse and the presence or absence of sexual behavior problems in a sample of children referred for sexual abuse evaluation. Silovsky and Nice, (2002) likewise found that in a sample of children with sexual behavior problems, 65% had no history of sexual abuse. In this study the percentage of children who had been physically abused was 47%, and 58% had witnessed domestic violence.

It is important to counteract this belief in professionals, as some may influence children with sexual behavior problems to make a disclosure of sexual abuse when there has been none. Children may believe that there is only one acceptable explanation for their worrisome sexual behavior and move to satisfy the belief of the therapist by fabricating a history of sexual abuse. It is also important that children who have been molested and are now engaging in problematic sexual behavior not think that being molested is the sole reason for their problematic sexual behavior. This could act as a reason, a justification, or provide a lessening of resolve to curtail problematic sexual behaviors. It could make them feel less competent to cease from engaging in this behavior. This belief can also dishearten parents who may feel that their children who have been sexually abused are destined to engage in problematic sexual behavior.

The belief that sexually abused children will molest others has the effect on many in the general public of seeing child sexual abuse victims as potential threats to other children. Children who have been sexually abused are unjustifiably seen as at substantial risk to molest (Friedrich and Chaffin, 2000; Johnson, 2004). In schools, foster homes and even in the child's biological home, sexual behavior by a sexually abused child is often seen as far more disturbed than the same sexual behavior by a child who has not been sexually abused. (See section below, How Many Victims Of Childhood Sexual Abuse Will Sexually Offend In Adulthood)

What Are the Factors that Come Together to Bring Forward Sexual Behavior Problems in Children?

Understanding the etiological factors for the wide range of children who engage in problematic sexual behavior is still developing. Early studies (Gomes-Schwartz, Horowitz et al., 1985; Friedrich, Beilke et al. 1988; Gale, Thompson et al. 1988; Gomes-Schwartz, Horowitz et al., 1990; Kendall-Tackett, Williams, et al., 1993) found the area that differentiated nonsexually abused children from sexually abused children who were all receiving mental health services was their reported sexual behaviors. Friedrich, Grambsch et al., (1992) found that parents of children with a history of sexual abuse report on the Child Sexual Behavior Inventory (CSBI) that their children engage in more frequent and intrusive sexual behaviors when compared to children without a history of sexual abuse. In 1995, after reviewing many studies of sexually abused children in an effort to identify indicators that could be used to help determine when a child had been sexually abused, Slusser (1995) states, "These studies empirically support the growing impression among clinicians that overt sexual behavior, inappropriate for their age, is an indication of sexual abuse."

Due to the confluence of research that found a strong relationship between sexual abuse and sexual behavior, Dr. William Friedrich analyzed his data from the Child Sexual Behavior Inventory (CSBI) to determine if certain sexual behaviors in which children engaged could distinguish between children who had been sexually abused and children who had not been sexually abused. Dr. Friedrich indicated certain sexual behaviors were highly correlated with a history of sexual abuse and developed a system of scoring the reported sexual behaviors, together with data from other sources that could be helpful in pointing to a diagnosis of sexual abuse. Yet, he stressed in the manual (Friedrich, 1997) that the sexual behaviors of a child are not sufficient to make a diagnosis of sexual abuse.

As research on the sexual behaviors of sexually abused and non-abused children continued, alternate findings emerged. While sexual abuse is in the history of some children with sexual behavior problems, there are other demographic and environmental factors that are more pervasive and which may be more instrumental in providing fodder for the development of sexual behavior problems in children.

Recent research points out, that sexually abused children cannot be distinguished from children in outpatient psychiatric clinics based on their sexual behaviors. Dr. Friedrich (2002) used data gathered on the Child Sexual Behavior Inventory (CSBI) to attempt to distinguish between a population of children with no known history of sexual abuse, a non-abused psychiatric population and a clinical sample of sexually abused children. The non-abused psychiatric sample and the sexually abused sample could not be differentiated based on their sexual behaviors. Friedrich found that the populations were quite similar based on their sexual behaviors. Additionally, Dr. Friedrich found that many of the factors in the backgrounds of the non-abused psychiatric population of children, such as poverty, poorly educated single parents and stressful life events, were also factors in the lives of the sexually abused children. He concluded, "Sexual abuse may be only one of several significant stressors in the life of the typically sexually abused child." (Friedrich, 2002).

Freidrich's finding lead to further exploration of the backgrounds of sexually abused children. "Recent data suggest that sexually abused children who are symptomatic are significantly more likely than nonsymptomatic sexually abused children to have experienced more overall life stress, come from more troubled and disrupted families, and have experienced more maternal rejection." (Friedrich and Fehrer, 2004)

Understanding that sexually abused children who engage in problematic sexual behaviors have similar backgrounds to symptomatic nonsexually abused children led to further study. In a 2003 article, Friedrich took three sexual behaviors ("Touches another child's sex parts," "Tries to have sexual intercourse with another child or adult," and "Puts mouth on another child/adults' sex parts") from the CSBI and called them "Sexually Intrusive Behavior" (SIB). Using two large samples, one sexually abused and one non-abused, he determined statistically that the highest correlation to SIB are the Child Behavior Checklist (CBCL). Externalizing and Internalizing subscales, followed by (in order of statistical significance) low family income, low education, single parent, domestic violence, physical abuse, and sexual abuse. Sexual abuse was defined as involving penetration, being incestuous, occurring when the child was very young or including multiple perpetrators, consisting of a long duration, and including physical abuse.

Friedrich also found that SIB is inversely correlated with age and has no significant correlation to gender. He notes that the young age of the children likely indicates that the behavior may be related to immaturity and reactivity to the environment. He notes that this population of children with intrusive sexual behavior is "not similar to adults or adolescents with intrusive sexuality as those are mainly male."

Summarizing his findings regarding the etiology of "sexually intrusive behaviors" in children, Friedrich, Davies et al., (2003) state, "It does appear that a four-component model has heuristic validity. As demonstrated with the current data, the elements are family adversity, modeling of coercion, modeling of sexuality, and a vulnerable/predisposed child substrate."

Although children who sexually offend do not necessarily engage in the types of sexual behaviors Friedrich describes as SIB, his model is consistent with the clinical findings of the first author who, over the last 20 years, has studied the etiology of children who molest. Regarding the modeling of coercion and sexuality in Friedrich's model, not only have the majority of the children who molest been physically abused, but they have almost universally witnessed domestic violence between their caretakers. It is hypothesized (Johnson, 1999) that some children who live in homes with domestic violence believe that sex and aggression are complementary. Children who live in homes with partner violence often hear intense arguments in which one partner accuses the other of sexual misconduct, attempts to control all of the behaviors of that partner and emotionally and/or physically hurts the other partner as a payback for alleged or real infidelity. These children often hear angry sexual language, and witness violent interactions between parental figures in which one parent violates the other's sexual rights. These children do not learn that sex is an expression of love between two people. Constant fighting and jealousy by parents relating to sex, teaches children that people use sex to hurt other people and that violence in relation to sex is natural. Often, sexual contact appears to be a caring act only after violence has occurred. This pairing of sex and aggression can cause confusion for the child's developing template for sexual relationships. In the homes of children who molest, the children are very aware of the trauma and violence in the parents'/caretakers' lives and often become part of the drama as one or the other parent pulls them in as an ally or a scapegoat. It is not infrequent that when one parent does not have a partner, or when the partner explodes and leaves, the child is used for emotional sustenance for the remaining parent. The child feels overwhelmed by the parent's needs but feels he or she needs to take care of the parent. When the other parent returns, the child is generally thrust aside to feel abandoned, jealous, angry and confused.

Ralph, age 10, is a good example of a boy whose aggressive sexual behaviors led his therapists, teachers and CPS to search for who sexually abused him. They thought that if they found out, this would help him stop the behaviors. When he denied being sexually abused they were stymied. After several years of therapy working with both

Ralph and his mother it became clear that Ralph's aggressive sexual behaviors emanated not from being directly (hands-on) sexually abused, but from his anxiety over witnessing his mother having sex many times with men he did not know, seeing her beaten up by these men, being physically and emotionally abused himself by her and many of her boyfriends, and living in a continual atmosphere of boundariless sexuality.

It should be stressed that many children live in homes with this level of dysfunction and do not start molesting others. Yet, children who sexually offend have almost always lived in these chaotic homes with multiple forms of abuse, neglect and violence.

How Many Victims of Childhood Sexual Abuse Will Sexually Offend in Adulthood?

The belief that sexual abuse was the major etiological factor for sexually abusive behavior in children spawned the alternate belief that children who were sexually abused were likely to sexually abuse other children. This belief persists, in spite of literature to the contrary. As Kaufman and Zigler (1987) have observed:

> *The findings of the different investigations are not easily integrated because of their methodological variations. Nonetheless, the best estimate of intergenerational transmission appears to be 30% plus or minus 5%. This suggests that approximately one-third of all individuals who were physically abused, sexually abused, or extremely neglected will subject their offspring to one of these forms of maltreatment, while the remaining two-thirds will provide adequate care for their children…The rate of abuse among individuals with a history of abuse (30% plus or minus 5%) is approximately six times higher than the base rate for abuse in the general population (5%). Being maltreated as a child puts one at risk for becoming abusive but the path between these two points is far from direct or inevitable. In the past, unqualified acceptance of the intergenerational hypothesis has had many negative consequences. Adults who were maltreated have been told so many times that they will abuse their child that for some it has become a self-fulfilling prophecy. Many who have broken the cycle are left feeling like walking time bombs. In addition, persistent acceptance of this belief has impeded progress in understanding the etiology of abuse and led to misguided judicial and social policy interventions. The time has come for the intergenerational myth to be put aside and for researchers to cease asking, "Do abused children become abusive parents?" and ask, instead, "Under what conditions is the transmission of abuse most likely to occur."*

In Widom's 1994 article, entitled "Criminal Consequences of Childhood Sexual Victimization," she states that compared to other types of child abuse and neglect, childhood sexual abuse does not uniquely increase an individual's risk for later delinquent and adult criminal behavior. As adults, child sexual abuse victims are at increased risk of arrest for sex crimes, although they are no more likely than victims of nonsexual abuse to have such an arrest. That is, all three of the abuse groups (physical abuse, sexual abuse and neglect) are significantly more likely to commit a sexual offense than the controls. (Those who had been abused or neglected as children are more likely to be arrested as juveniles [27 percent versus 17 percent], adults [42 percent versus 33 percent], and for a violent crime [18 percent versus 14 percent]). Thus, the criminogenic effect associated with sexual offending may not result from sexual abuse uniquely, but rather may be associated with the trauma and stress of these early childhood experiences or society's response to the event. Additionally, childhood sexual abuse victims in this longitudinal study are not at increased risk of arrest for a violent sex crime (rape and/or sodomy). Rather, the findings suggest an association between childhood physical abuse and later arrests for violent sex crimes (rape and/or sodomy) in males. In Widom and Maxfield's (2001) update on this longitudinal study of the effects of abuse and neglect she found that victims of neglect, as well as victims of physical abuse, are likely to develop later violent criminal behavior.

Johnson (2004) estimated that less than .5% of sexually abused children would go on to sexually abuse other children during childhood. In fact, specialized residential treatment programs for children who molest are generally unable to find sufficient numbers of children with the severest level of sexual behavior problems to fill their beds (Johnson, 2004). Unable to fill all of their beds with children who sexually offend, these facilities accept children with a lesser degree of sexual problems. This can present a danger to children who are sexualized but who are not offending.

"Not Normal" Sexual Behavior is Not Necessarily Abusive

Delineating what is "normal" sexual behavior for children has been the subject of much concern and research (Friedrich, Grambsch et al., 1991; Johnson, 1991; Friedrich, Grambsch et al., 1992; Friedrich, Fisher et al., 1998; Johnson, 2004; Johnson, 1999). Friedrich asked mothers to fill out the Child Sexual Behavior Inventory and subsequently defined certain behaviors as "normative" based on at least 20% of mothers observing this behavior in their children (Friedrich, 1997; Friedrich, Fisher et al., 1998). Defining this has helped us to know what are the most expected behaviors in children as per parent report.

Johnson (2004) stated that:

> *Natural and healthy sexual exploration during childhood is an information gathering process wherein children explore each other's bodies, by looking and touching (e.g. playing doctor), as well as explore gender roles and behaviors (e.g. playing house). Children involved in natural and healthy sexual play are of similar age, size and developmental status and participate on a voluntary basis. While siblings engage in mutual sexual exploration, most sexual play is between children who have an ongoing mutually enjoyable play and/or school friendship. The sexual behaviors are limited in type and frequency and occur in several periods of the child's life. The child's interest in sex and sexuality is balanced by curiosity about other aspects of his or her life. Natural and healthy sexual exploration may result in embarrassment but does not usually leave children with deep feelings of anger, shame, fear or anxiety. If the children are discovered in sexual exploration and instructed to stop, the behavior generally diminishes, at least in the view of adults. The feelings of the children regarding the sexual behavior is generally light-hearted and spontaneous. Generally, children experience pleasurable sensations from genital touching, some children experience sexual arousal, while some children experience orgasm. Sexual arousal and orgasm are more frequently found in older children entering puberty.*

A behavior that is not expected or considered "normative" in children cannot necessarily be defined as abusive. There has been a tendency to label developmentally advanced behaviors as abusive. For instance, Burton, D. et al., (1997) "defined 'simulated intercourse' between any children 12 and younger as 'sexually abnormal behavior' and then equated this with 'sexually-aggressive' behavior." Whereas this behavior by young children may not be acceptable, engaging in it does not necessarily mean that one child is forcing the other. It means that it is more advanced than the adults discovering it would like to find.

This transformation of developmentally advanced sexual behaviors into abusive behaviors happens with some regularity in everyday practice. Oral-genital contact is certainly not a behavior that is considered "normal" for children. Yet because it occurs between two children does not mean one of the children is abusing the other. A startled preschool teacher who finds two boys in the corner of the classroom with their pants down and one child approaching the genitals of the other with his mouth may describe the approaching child as a "perpetrator." If the teacher discovers that both children have put their mouths on the penis of the other, the teacher may describe the more outspoken or bold, older, or larger child as a "perpetrator." This immediate reaction has lead to serious consequences for children and families. While suspected child abuse is a mandatory reporting issue, a thoughtful approach will allow for some assessment of the circumstances surrounding the discovered events.

Johnson (1998b, 2003b) encourages examining the characteristics of the sexual behavior being engaged in between children, not the behavior alone, when trying to determine if sexual abuse has occurred (See Part IV of the Child Sexual Behavior Checklist in section below on Assessment). Young children look at and touch each other's body parts, genital or nongenital, by way of exploration. They also tend to reenact what they have seen and are not as good, nor diligent, as older children in hiding their behavior. It has been found that oral-genital contact between children is found more frequently in younger children and that boys and girls both engage in the behavior (Friedrich, Davies et al. 2003).

Any sexual behavior can be abusive, not only developmentally advanced behaviors. Some children find it fun to tell dirty jokes, touch each other's bottoms, and use scatological language, while other children may not like it at all. If one child persists in these types of behaviors while the other child feels very uncomfortable and consistently requests the child stop, this can feel like abusive behavior. If the child doing the behaviors to another child is aware of the child's discomfort, and after repeated requests to stop by the child and adults, does not care what the other child wants or feels and gets pleasure (not necessarily sexual) out of being mean to the other child, this is sexually abusive behavior.

Another issue of great concern is the situation in which a teacher sees an advanced, developmentally inappropriate sexual behavior between children. If the teacher is aware that one of the children is a victim of child sexual abuse, this may lead directly to the sexual abuse victim being called a perpetrator. In the late 1990s, the highly pejorative term "predator" began being used referring to young children, usually sexually abused children, who had engaged in problematic sexual behavior.

This delineation of a developmentally advanced or inappropriate behavior being seen as abusive also happens in the criminal justice system. In late 2003 the first author was seeing an 11-year old girl in therapy who was charged with lewd and lascivious behavior with a minor. This is a felony offense. This young girl asked a five-year old boy she knew from her daycare to go with her into a toilet stall in the girl's bathroom. She wanted to see his penis. She had seen some male genitals on the Internet (including multiple advertisements for increasing the size of the male penis) and wanted to see a real penis. When the young boy said he didn't want to take down his pants, she asked him again and he did. There was no force, anger or yelling. She touched his penis one time with her hand for approximately two seconds. Nothing else happened. There were no previous incidents. Her charges were as follows: On 03/03/03 within the County of Los Angeles, the crime of LEWD ACT UPON A CHILD, in violation of PENAL CODE 288(A), a Felony, was committed by said minor, who did willfully, unlawfully, and lewdly commit a lewd and lascivious act upon and with the body and certain parts and members thereof of (name withheld), a child under the age of fourteen years, with the intent of arousing, appealing to, and gratifying the lust, passions, and sexual desires of the said minor or the said child. Because she was not incarcerated in the California Youth Authority, she is not subject to taking her DNA or sex offender registration.

Legal Implications for Children Labeled as Sexual Offenders

On July 29, 1994 in New Jersey, a 7-year-old named Megan Kanka was brutally raped and murdered by a previously convicted sex offender living in her neighborhood. At the time of Megan's death, New Jersey law did not allow the release of information on registered sex offenders to the public. In response to overwhelming public outcry, on October 31, 1994, New Jersey enacted Megan's Law. This law requires sex offenders who are convicted, adjudicated delinquent, or found not guilty by reason of insanity to register with local law enforcement agencies for the remainder of their lives. Under Megan's law, notification for moderate- and high-risk offenders consists of a recent photograph, a physical description of the offender, a description of the offense, the name of the offender, the name of the offender's work or school, and a description and the license plate of the offender's vehicle. Sex offenders must verify their address periodically.

A federal statue known as the Jacob Wetterling Crimes Against Children and Sexually Violent Offender Registration Program (1994) was passed requiring all states to create registration programs for convicted sex offenders. On May 17, 1996 the federal Megan's Law amendment was signed by President Clinton requiring the release of information on sex offenders for the purpose of community notification and safety. This law, which amended the Wetterling Act, requires that registrant information be available to the public, but allows states to set their own criteria for disclosure.

All 50 United States, and the District of Columbia, have sex offender registration and some form of community notification. Each state can set its own standards regarding who registers and for how long and what type of notification will be made to the public. In at least 22 states (as of 2003), juveniles (which can include children under 12) are subject to registration as sex offenders. Some states offer public access to their registries over the internet while others require individuals to go into a law enforcement agency to view the information via intranet or CD-ROM.

The registration and notification statutes in some states fail to differentiate the severity of the offense. For example, a juvenile who has been convicted of multiple rapes would appear no differently than a juvenile who had touched the breast of a female schoolmate (Trivits and Repucci, 2002). In Texas, 1,389 of the 26,769 sex offenders posted on the state's Internet registry in the fall of 2000 were between 11 and 16 years old (Williams, 2000), including offenders with relatively minor crimes. For instance, one of the postings is a 12-year-old boy who mooned a group of 5- and 6-year-old children (Trivits and Repucci, 2002).

In California, if a child 12 years old or younger is adjudicated on a serious sex charge, he can be sent to the California Youth Authority, which houses adolescents. After the child's term is up, his DNA is taken for forensic purposes; he has to check in regularly with his probation officer. The child can be registered for life as a sex offender.

In some states in the United States, if a child is registered for life, there is no mechanism for him or her to get off the list. Until July 2001 this was true in New Jersey. In a bold action the State Supreme Court of New Jersey ruled unanimously that offenders found guilty before their 14th birthday should have a chance to escape those sanctions at 18 by presenting evidence that they do not pose a risk of committing another sex crime. Justice Stein wrote that the court was troubled by the lack of evidence to support the charge that J.G., as a 10-year-old, had committed an act of sexual penetration on his cousin. Although J.G. admitted to the crime in 1996, when he was 11, the justice noted that a detective who investigated the case was not convinced that penetration had occurred. In addition, a therapist for J.G. testified in a lower-court hearing that the boy had a learning disability and had difficulty reading and spelling simple words, and that she did not believe that he understood the terms "sex," "rape" or "penetration" when he admitted the crime.

The New Jersey case is very instructive of the errors in assessment of children's sexual behaviors. Not only is there a lack of understanding of children's cognitive, emotional, and sexual development, but there are no good criteria to define what is sexual offending by children.

Since there is no empirical evidence, either longitudinal or retrospective, to indicate that when children molest (or engage in developmentally advanced sexual behavior) at a young age they will continue to sexually offend, and there are no guidelines for assessment of children with sexual behavior problems, it is cruel and unusual punishment to condemn them to a lifetime stigma as a sex offender.

Children Should Not be Judged by Adult Standards Regarding Their Sexual Behaviors

Defining Sexual Abuse Between Children

Some of the confusion experienced by professionals working with young children with sexual behavior problems has occurred due to a reliance on standards for adult sexual offending. It is a great deal more clear-cut when defining what is sexually abusive when one of the persons involved in the sexual activity is an adult and the other is a child, rather than two children twelve and younger engaging in sexual behavior together. An adult being sexual with a child is clearly sexual abuse. This is largely not the case when children twelve and younger behave in a sexual manner with other children. While the greater the age difference between the children, the more concern there is about the sexual behavior, it is very infrequently sexually abusive when a child engages in sexual behavior with children younger than themselves. Unfortunately, if adult laws are applied to children's sexual contact, misinterpretations can be made and nonabusive sexual contact between children can be criminalized. When children are experimenting and trying to gather knowledge about sex and sexuality, they are not thinking about the adult laws regarding sexual contact and they are not trying to conform their exploration to this unknown set of restrictions.

Consider the eight year old brother who wants to see what a vagina looks like and asks his only sister to show him hers. She is three and willingly shows him while she is taking a bath. He looks and then touches between the labia with his finger to see what it feels like. For the 3 seconds it takes place they both giggle and that is the end of it. Is it legitimate to call this a sexual offense, as it would be construed if an adult engaged in the same behavior? No, but it could be construed this way in the current climate in some jurisdictions in the United States. The data on a police charge sheet might look like this, "8 year old male digitally penetrates vagina of 3 year-old sister."

When the police or a Child Protective Services worker believes, based on the sexual behavior, that a child has sexually abused another child, the child often has little or no ability to explain what he or she was thinking or what his or her motivation was for engaging in the sexual behavior. If the boy in the example above tried to explain, if he were allowed, it might be perceived as a rationalization, or trying to lie to get out of trouble, or that the child is denying or minimizing (terms used with adolescent and adult sexual offenders) the behavior. Because police, CPS and mental health professionals tend to believe they only know the "tip of the iceberg," the child may be continually questioned about additional sexual behaviors. If the child acknowledges further behaviors, this can further cement the CPS or police officer's perception that the child is a sexual offender. In some cases, the term "sexual predator" may be used if multiple children or multiple acts are discovered. The child's reality is often not taken into account. The adult demands that the child see the behavior from the adult's perspective while the adult refuses to see the behavior from the child's perspective. Many practitioners, following the belief that "all sex offenders lie" do not listen to the children and develop their own picture of the events surrounding the discovered sexual behaviors.

Sexual Arousal and Sexual Offending

Some penal codes that deal with sexual offending require that the individual have the "intent of arousing, appealing to, and gratifying the lust, passions, and sexual desires of that person or the child." (California Penal Code 288(a)[1]. This code section is frequently used when dealing with children's interpersonal sexual behaviors. While it is possible that a child is seeking pleasant sexual feelings, or even sexual arousal, most of the sexual behaviors engaged in by young children are not for the purpose of sexual arousal. Sexual stimulation (as an adult might feel), was reported by 5.3% of adults recalling their sexual experiences at 6-10 years of age and 17.4% recalling their sexual experiences at 11-12 years of age (Johnson, Huang et al., under review).

If it can be proved, and this is difficult in young children, that the child who engaged in a sexual behavior has experienced sexual arousal while engaging in the behavior, is that adequate to label the behavior an offense? Consider the five-year old child, Jeannie, who likes the genital sensations she feels when she is masturbating. As she is trying to sleep, Jeannie frequently overhears her alcoholic father and his drug addicted girl friend having intercourse in the living room while they talk about the sexual pleasure they feel and describe the pleasuring they want from the other. Jeannie, listening to this night after night, gets in bed with her older or younger brother and simulates intercourse with him trying to recreate what she thinks is going on in the other bedroom. She feels sexual arousal while she is engaging in the behavior. Is this sexual offending?

There have been several appellate decisions dealing with young children that relied upon PC 288(a). In Jerry M. (1997) 59 Ca.App. 4th 289, the California Court of Appeal ruled an 11 year old touching three different girls' breasts on four separate occasions cannot be convicted of PC 288 (a), where there was no evidence that minor had reached puberty or that any of the touching was intended to accomplish sexual arousal. The appellate court relied on: there was no evidence of sexual arousal, or of whether the minor had reached puberty; the victims each knew the minor; the conduct was in public, during the daytime, and occurred in the presence of others, without any attempt or opportunity to avoid detection; there was no clandestine activity preceding the touching; "There was no attempt to prolong the touching beyond the initial momentary contact; there was no caressing. The record shows Jerry was a brazen 11-year-old whose conduct was more consistent with an intent to annoy and obtain attention than with sexual arousal. Under these circumstances Jerry was perhaps guilty of battery (§ 242), but the record does not support a true finding beyond a reasonable doubt of conduct intended sexually to exploit a child—the "gist" of section 288, subdivision (a)."

Billie Y. (1990) 220 Cal. App. 3d 127 states that there must be lewd and lascivious intent proven, as well as knowledge of its wrongfulness.

Motivation and Sexual Offending in Children

Whereas the motivation for a sexual behavior is not a valid way of discriminating when sexual behaviors between an adult and a child are sexually abusive, it is very important when two children are involved. If a child is engaging in the sexual behavior due to curiosity, desire for knowledge, experimentation, anxiety, confusion, or if the child is replaying something he or she has seen or heard about or something that was done to him or her, and there is no element of anger, revenge, payback or desire for harm, then the behavior generally should not be categorized as an offense. Instead of trying to figure things out by reading about them or directly asking for help, children often play out their concerns, worries and confusion. Children are concrete thinkers and learn most effectively when it is experiential. This is also the case for learning about their sexual selves.

Consider the sexually abused child who touches the penis of another child in a re-creation of what was done to him. He does not force the child or hold the child down. He finds a child who will allow the behavior and does it in an attempt to make sense of what was done to him. If he tries the behavior on a child who says "no," he will not force that child. He will go and try it with another child. Is this sexual abuse?

Children's Knowledge of Legal Standards

Whereas it is assumed that an adult knows that acting in a sexual way with a child is wrong and illegal, this cannot be assumed with young children. Trying out sexual behaviors with other children has been going on throughout history. Eighty-four percent of adults reporting about their sexual behaviors when they were twelve or younger said they engaged in solitary sexual behaviors, and eighty-one percent said they engaged in sexual behaviors with other children (Johnson, Huang et al., under review).

In a culture with extensive sexually explicit public media and advertising which encourages children to explore sex and sexuality, adults' messages to children are generally punitive if they see children mimic the sexual behaviors they see. Even young children who engage in sexual behaviors with other children learn that grownups get uncomfortable when they mimic adult sexual behaviors. For this reason, children usually hide when they engage in sexual conversations or sexual behavior with one another. Hence when being questioned by the police or Child Protective Services, children will acknowledge that they know it is wrong to engage in sexual behaviors with another child. Yet, the wrong to which they refer is not morally wrong or legally wrong.

Children do not think in terms of age differences and legal standards. They are almost never aware that their behavior could lead to criminal prosecution. Most children engage in sexual behaviors with their friends who are of a similar age, size and developmental status (Johnson, 1991; Johnson, 2004; Johnson, 2000). Yet, some children who have no same age children available, or are developmentally delayed, or socially inadequate, or have neurological disorders may play with substantially younger children and hence might choose to sexually experiment with them. There are frequently cases of children with ADD or ADHD who get caught up in the criminal justice system or CPS because they touch younger children. It is frequently not taken in to account that younger children are the play-mates of children with ADD and ADHD because children their own age will not play with them due to their immaturity and impulsiveness. Children do not know about laws that declare a three, four or five year age difference illegal sexual behaviors. Children who engage in natural and healthy sexual behaviors do so with available children who are friendly with them and seemingly interested, regardless of their age. It is implausible to think that a child would ask the age of a play-mate to see if he or she fits within the legally accepted ages for consensual sexual behavior with them. Adults and adolescents, unless intellectually impaired, know that sex with children is illegal. This is not the case with children 12 and younger. Knowledge that their behavior is illegal should not be taken for granted.

Children and Consent

Whereas agreement between people engaged in sexual behaviors is an essential ingredient when defining consensual sexual behavior between adults, it is a developmentally advanced concept for young children. Children understand that physical force is not acceptable in any behaviors. They know that if they purposely hit someone and hurt her or him, this is never acceptable. But one child may not pay close attention to whether the other child really wants to do something with them (consents) that he or she wants to do. Children tend to be more self-focused than other-focused. This is particularly true of children with ADD or ADHD or children who are developmentally delayed or poorly socialized. For instance, two children have water guns and are shooting at each other. After some time one wants to stop and the other does not. The one child may continue, semi-oblivious to the protestations of the other. The child would generally not be thinking he or she is harming the other child, just that he or she is having fun and wants to continue. This can also be true with sexual behaviors between children. Children do not necessarily differentiate between one kind of play behavior and another.

When an adult sexual offender provides children with toys or special privileges, these bribes create an atmosphere that leads the child to want to please the grownup. These bribes are an indirect form of manipulation and subtle coercion. Children also use bribery and coercive techniques to get their way. For example, if one child wants to play catch and the other wants to play soccer, one child may say he will not play with the other child ever again, if the other child does not play soccer. Or, one child may bribe the other child by saying he will give him extra time on a video game, if he plays soccer. We must be careful not to over interpret these persuasive methods as sexually coercive or grooming behavior when it comes to sexual behavior between children. This would be using concepts derived from adult sex offender behavior to interpret children's behavior. This potentially leads to false conclusions.

Miranda Rights

Before children are queried by the police regarding their sexual behavior they are often read their Miranda Rights, just as an adult offender would be read his or her Miranda Rights. This warning, originally written for use with adults, is frequently not understood by children, and they can become entrapped by it. Children believe they have to do what grownups say and, if they do not, they will get in trouble. This is particularly true of children and police officers in uniform.

Timothy, age 10, had been caught 6 months previously humping his six-year old cousin. He had been in therapy for five months regarding this behavior.

Timothy was in class when a person from the attendance office came and took him to the main office. There he met a woman who said she needed to speak to him. She took him into a separate area. At that time she read him his Miranda Rights. Six months after this event Timothy described his feelings at that time. "I wasn't sure what was happening. I didn't have time to think. I didn't know that this woman was from the police. I thought she was a therapist. I was in therapy, and I thought it was just another therapist. I didn't think anything bad would happen if I did what she wanted. I've always been told it's better to tell the truth then be caught in a lie. I wasn't sure, so I agreed to everything"

Timothy did not realize that he was talking to a police officer until well into the interview. During the interview, after Timothy had told the detective what he had done, the detective asked Timothy what he thought his adult cousins would do if they found out. Timothy responded that maybe the cousins would go to the police and press charges. At that point, the detective said, "I am the police." Timothy said he kept talking because he thought she might take him to jail if he didn't, and that would make it worse for him. He said, "I felt like I wanted to tell her to stop, but I thought maybe I would get arrested. Like if I said something about her, like she was rude, she might tell that in court." At no point did he think he could stop talking, even after he realized that it was the police.

In reviewing the actual phrases used in Miranda six months later, Timothy was still unclear what they meant. When asked to paraphrase the first two Miranda questions (1. You have the right to remain silent. Do you understand? 2. Anything you say may be used against you in a court of law. Do you understand?) Timothy said, "If I said something she didn't like, she could use it against me in court or if you say anything wrong, it can be used against you in court." Timothy did not comprehend at all that he had a choice at any time to simply say, "No, I don't want to answer your questions." Regarding having an attorney present Timothy said, "But I didn't have an attorney, and I didn't have time to think about what it all meant."

A recent decision by the U.S, Supreme Court says, "The police need not always warn a teenage crime suspect of his rights before formally questioning him, the Supreme Court said Tuesday. The 5-4 ruling gives police a bit more leeway to question suspects without warning them of their Miranda Rights, and it says that a suspect's youth is not reason enough to treat him with more caution." (Savage, 2004).

Once a Sex Offender Always a Sex Offender

An additional problem with assuming that information about adult sex offenders fits for children who sexually abuse is that most people believe that adults who sexually offend will always sexually offend. This static approach to a developing child's sexuality is unwarranted. There is no empirical evidence to support that once a child has engaged in sexually abusive behavior, the child will continue to engage in sexually abusive behavior throughout his or her lifetime. Likewise, it is untrue that adults and adolescents who sexually abuse will all continue to sexually abuse others. (See section in this chapter, Misinformation On The Recidivism Rates Of Adult And Adolescent Sex Offenders Taints Perception Of Children Who Sexually Abuse.)

Less Guilty by Reason of Preadolescence

Juvenile offenders are held to answer for their crimes in Juvenile Court and are not generally tried as adults. Steinberg and Scott (2003) argue in *Less Guilty by Reason of Adolescence*, that emerging knowledge about cognitive, psychosocial, and neurobiological development in adolescence supports the conclusion that juveniles should not be held to the same standards of criminal responsibility as adults. "Under standard, well-accepted principles of criminal law, the developmental immaturity of juveniles mitigates their criminal culpability and, accordingly, should moderate the severity of their punishment." Steinberg and Scott (2003) distinguish between an "excuse for bad behavior" and "mitigation. " "In legal parlance, *excuse* refers to the complete exculpation of a criminal defendant; he or she bears no responsibility for the crime and should receive no punishment." (p.1010) "Unlike excuse, which calls for a binary judgment – guilty or not guilty – *mitigation* places the culpability of the guilty actor somewhere on a continuum of criminal culpability and, by extension, a continuum of punishment." (p. 1010). Steinberg and Scott (2003) continue "…we argue that the developmental immaturity of adolescence mitigates culpability and justifies more lenient punishment, but that it is not, generally, a basis for excuse – except in the case of very young, preadolescent offenders." (p. 1010). Preadolescent offenders, in the case of this article, are children who sexually offend.

When discussing mitigation, Steinberg and Scott (2003) report:

> *In general, factors that reduce criminal culpability can be grouped roughly into three categories. The first category includes endogenous impairments or deficiencies in the actor's decision-making capacity, which affect his or her choice to engage in criminal activity. Under the second category, culpability is reduced when the external circumstances faced by the actor are so compelling that an ordinary (or "reasonable") person might have succumbed to the pressure in the same way as did the defendant (Morse, 1994). The third category of mitigation includes evidence that the criminal act was out of character for the actor and that, unlike the typical criminal act, his or her crime was not the product of bad character.*

The major impetus of the Steinberg and Scott (2003) article is to persuade against the use of the death penalty for juveniles. Yet, these categories that reduce culpability for adolescents are salient to an argument for not using adult criteria and laws to adjudicate preadolescents regarding their sexual behaviors and are certainly strong reasons for mitigating their culpability regarding punishment.

Regarding Steinberg and Scott's (2003) first mitigating factor, the ability to engage in reasoning and sound decision-making regarding sexual behaviors is only rarely developed in preadolescents in general, and virtually never in children who sexually offend. Children who sexually offend model their behavior off of the adult role models with whom they live, as well as television, music videos, song lyrics, their friends, the Internet and printed material, often of a questionable nature, found around their homes. It has been found that the vast majority of children who engage in sexual offending live in families with poor emotional, physical and sexual boundaries and have generally observed domestic violence. These children have frequently been exposed to explicit adult sex *in vivo* and given little, if any healthy education regarding sexual mores and values. Their role models are their parents' whose lives are generally fraught with marital breakups, a history of abuse, incarcerations, drug and alcohol addiction, and overall poor social and emotional adjustment. The problem-solving ability of the parents is often as deficient as that of the children.

Regarding heightened vulnerability to coercive circumstances, Steinberg and Scott's (2003) second mitigating factor, the psychosocial immaturity of preadolescents makes them extremely vulnerable to being led into bad behavior. Being surrounded by sexual confusion and sexual tension provides a premature sexualization of the child and an impetus to problematic sexual expression. While preadolescents who sexually offend are not generally coerced into engaging in abusive behavior, most are sur-rounded in their families by people who violate the law and others' rights on a con-sistent basis. These children's caretakers provide coercive and aggressive role models. Generally there have been a series of males who have been sexually, physically and emotionally abusive to the child's mother, which the child has witnessed on an ongo-ing basis. Steinberg and Scott (2003) state, "Adolescents' claim to mitigation on this ground is particularly compelling in that, as legal minors, they lack the freedom that adults have to extricate themselves from a criminogenic setting" (Fagan, 2000). This is even truer of children 12 and under.

The third category of mitigation includes evidence that the criminal act was out of character for the individual and that it was not the product of bad character. The crim-inal law implicitly assumes that harmful conduct reflects the person's bad character, but if there is evidence that this assumption is not accurate this can mitigate culpa-bility (Duff, 1993; Vuoso, 1986). Steinberg and Scott (2003) believe that most adoles-cents' identity is not formed into a developed self until late adolescence or early adulthood, therefore their crimes are less culpable than those of typical adult crimi-nals. Preadolescents' character is by nature of their age, unformed. There is no data to support that all or most preadolescents who engage in sexual offending behavior will continue to engage in the behavior into adolescence. In fact, studies of criminal or delinquent behavior in adolescents' indicate that the majority desist from criminal activity as they mature into adulthood (Farrington, 1986).

Misinformation on the Recidivism Rates of Adult and Adolescent Sex Offenders Taints Perception of Children who Sexually Abuse

There has been an ongoing misperception by the public, as well as many profession-als who work in the field of sexual offending, about the recidivism rates of adult and adolescent sex offenders. While accurate recidivism rates are extremely difficult to calculate due to the element of secrecy in both victims and offenders (Schwartz et al, 1995), even if the true rates are 200% higher than the published rates, they are still lower than most people believe.

The general perception has been, "Once a Sex Offender, Always a Sex Offender." This has severely affected children with sexual behavior problems. Because so many peo-ple do not differentiate between the levels of seriousness of sexual behaviors in chil-dren, many school teachers, day care providers, and foster parents will not care for a child who has engaged in problematic sexual behavior. If the behavior by the child has been labeled "sexual offending," many children are totally separated from other children for years based on the presumption that they will soon "strike" again.

The reported recidivism rates for adult sex offenders vary depending on whether the offender has or has not received treatment. A recent meta-analytic study by Hanson, Gordon et al., (2002) that examined the effectiveness of treatment for sex offenders revealed sexual recidivism rates of 17.3 percent for untreated offenders, compared with 9.9 percent for treated offenders. There was also a large difference in general recidivism from 51% for untreated sex offenders and 32% for treated sex offenders. A Wisconsin study (Alexander, 1999) suggests a dramatic decrease in sexual recidivism rates when child molesters are treated. Overall, in an analysis of 11,350 sex offenders from 79 treatment outcome studies, recidivism for child molesters in most categories was less than 11%.

A meta-analytic study of eight studies (Alexander, 1999) totaling over 1000 juveniles who participated in offense-specific treatment in a variety of settings found the combined recidivism rate for all of these youths was 7.1% in 3-5 year follow-up.

A comparison study of juveniles treated in an offense-specific, multi-systemic treatment versus nonspecific traditional counseling found that the multi-systemic approach resulted in an 83% reduction in the rate of sexual offense recidivism (as well as a 50% reduction in non-sexual recidivism), compared to that of youth who received traditional nonspecific therapy. Sexual recidivism was 12.5% in the specialized treatment (Borduin, Henggler, Blaske, & Stein, 1990).

James Worling (Worling and Curwen, 2000) reports that his program in Canada obtained records from all Canadian jurisdictions of any new (juvenile or adult) charges filed against two groups of sexually abusive youth, an average of 6 years after they were identified and assessed. One group had successfully completed offense-specific group treatment along with treatment aimed at enhancing family and peer relationships, and the second group had been assessed for treatment due to similar sexual offenses, but had either not entered treatment or had dropped out of treatment prematurely. They found that the treated group had a 72% reduction in sexual recidivism, along with a 41% reduction in non-sexual violence charges and a 59% reduction of non-violent/non-sexual charges. In comparing the treated and untreated samples, 18% of the untreated boys had new charges, compared to 5% of those who had successfully completed treatment.

It is assumed that sexual recidivism rates among juveniles are very high. Yet, the studies that have been conducted on reoffense behavior indicate that official recidivism rates for sexual offenses are actually lower than anticipated. The official sexual recidivism rates for juveniles (even when followed into early adulthood) appear to range from 2% to 14%. Most juvenile sex offenders do not go on to become adult sex offenders. However, there may be a subset of chronic sex offenders who need to be identified. The key concern should be how to identify these high risk offenders, as opposed to assuming that all sex offenders are at high risk to reoffend (Milloy, 1998).

Are We Damaging Children's Sexual Development?

Many children who are not molesting children but who have problematic sexual behaviors are given the label of "perpetrator," "abuser," 'sex offender," or "molester." This can seriously affect the life of the child and family. There are children who have been mislabeled throughout the world. When a child is continually told he or she is a "sex offender," and it is not accurate, the child will likely have extreme difficulty in understanding not only what constitutes offending behavior but also what constitutes healthy sexual behavior. Healthy sexual development for children includes natural curiosity about their bodies, others' bodies, finding out the differences between the genders, trying to discover how babies are made, experiencing genital feelings, etc. We must guard against making children feel it is wrong to exercise their interest in this natural experience of childhood.

In a study that asked mental health and child protective services professionals to report on their sexual experiences when they were twelve and younger, 33.9% said when they were engaging in sexual behavior they felt "good" about it, 39.5% said they felt "silly, giggly", and 22.7% said they felt excited (not sexually) (Johnson, Huang et al., under review). It is possibly very damaging to children's natural exploration of their sexual selves to have this behavior made "bad." The same study by Johnson et al. indicates that 11.8% of the respondents felt "bad" when they were engaging in sexual behaviors, 19.1% felt "scared," 37.8% felt "guilty," and 31.6% felt "confused." It would be extremely unfortunate for the children of today to grow up and report significantly higher percentages of negative feelings about their childhood sexual behaviors.

It has become increasingly clear that children in therapy for sexual issues are beginning to believe that all contact with the genitals is bad and that they are bad if they do it. The responses to vignettes, which were given as part of a pilot study of an instrument to understand children's thinking about interpersonal sexual behavior, are indicative of this problem. The first author created six vignettes that describe different scenarios related to genital touching or other sexual behaviors between children, between children and adults, and between adolescents and children. The answers of 49 children in four different residential facilities were tabulated. Each child who was in therapy for sexual behavior problems was asked by her or his therapist to respond to the series of vignettes. The therapist read the vignette and made sure the child understood it. The age of the child in the vignette was changed to correspond to the child's age that was being asked the questions. Each question was asked following the vignette, and a response was received before the next question was asked. The answers to the first vignette are illustrative of the children's thinking about mutual versus victimizing sexual behaviors.

Vignette: Johnny (use the age of the child you are asking) has always wanted to see a girl's private parts. Suzie has always wanted to see a boy's private parts. They are good friends and agree to go in Suzie's bedroom and look at each other's private parts. A friend of theirs sees them.

> 1) What do you think the friend does? Will the friend who sees them tell anyone? Why? Why not?
> 2) Is what Johnny and Suzie did okay? Why? Why not?
> 3) If two good friends agree to look at each others' private parts would that ever be considered sexual abuse? If so, who is the abuser and who is the victim?

Virtually all children said the friend would tell because what the children were doing was "not right," "bad," "wrong."

The vast majority of children said that Johnny and Suzie were both abusers. A few said they were both "victims and abusers." Only one child said they had not hurt one another.

The first author evaluated a child (10 years old) in November 2003 who was just entering into individual therapy. He was living at home with his grandmother. He had been removed from his mother for neglect. As part of the evaluation he respond-ed to a series of vignettes. He had been in group therapy for sexual behavior prob-lems.

Vignette: Two children (10 years old) agreed to kiss. The teacher caught them on the far side of the playground.

      1) What will the teacher do?
      2) Will the teacher tell anyone else?

The child said that the teacher would call the police and the boy would be taken to jail for sexual harassment. When he was reminded they had agreed to kiss, and was asked if this made a difference in his answer, he said "no." "He sexually abused her." This young boy had little or no concept of consensual sexual behaviors between two children. The boy's saying the boy is the abuser is consistent with a gender bias ascribing abusive behavior to males more often than to females.

It is of great concern that children's experiences of sex and sexuality are being pathol-ogized (Krivacska, 1991; Okami, 1992). The concepts of "good touch" and "bad touch" have become equated in many children's minds as "good touch" is "healthy touch" and "bad touch" is "sexual touch." Many children see everything that has to do with sex as being "bad," "dangerous," and/or "harmful." Some programs for chil-dren with sexual behavior problems have "sexual behavior rules" that the children learn. Children who are in the groups have broken a rule and need to talk about this and listen to other children talk about the rule(s) they broke. These rules often leave the children feeling that anything that has to do with sex and sexuality is "wrong" or "rule breaking." Healthy sexual behaviors are generally not discussed.

An additional concern about the treatment process for children with sexual behavior problems is that many programs have "no touch" policies. This is sometimes true in group treatment, day treatment and residential care. In these programs there is to be no physical contact at any time between the children. In a very few programs this pol-icy relaxes as the child learns how to have healthy and nonintrusive physical contact. Other programs, perhaps the majority, never allow touch. Some programs tell chil-dren they are in a bubble and their bubble is not to touch the bubble of any other child. Some use a hula-hoop analogy in much the same way. One program said that the children could not come within an arm's length of any other child. What are we teaching the children about themselves? Touching is dangerous? They are dangerous? All touching is sexual touching, which is dangerous? They cannot control themselves and so they cannot touch anyone? They will never control themselves, so they can never touch anyone? Once you engage in a "bad touch" you will remain dangerous? The negative self-percepts are endless.

There are also elementary schools with "no touch" policies in the United States where children are literally not to touch one another. Many schools have sexual harassment prevention programs that are taught to all of the students. Students can be suspend-ed or expelled for sexually harassing another child. In a book entitled *STOP IT NOW-A Guide For the Prevention of Sexual Harassment* the following behaviors are given as examples of sexual harassment: (Davis, 1998)

For K-2nd Grade

"I am in second grade. I like school but I don't like it that two of the girls in my class keep trying to hug me and tell me that I am 'cute.' One of them kissed me in the hall. I want them to stop it!"

For grades 3-6

Jamal picks up the phone and hears a girl giggling. The girl says, 'I want to kiss you.' This is the sixth call Jamal has gotten from the girl today, even though he has asked her to leave him alone.

Behaviors such as in the above examples have been happening in schools forever. While they may need to stop, examples such as these trivialize and over generalize the term sexual harassment. Just as with using the term "perpetrator" for a young child with sexual behavior problems, using the term "sexual harassment" for normal childhood behaviors is problematic. Children's behaviors related to sex and sexuality are not the same as adults' sexual behaviors. The intent, motivation and pleasure seeking are not the same as adults'. It is essential to understand children's thinking about sex and sexuality and not confuse it with adult sexuality. When a young girl calls a boy and says she wants to kiss him, or tells a boy he is cute and hugs him, she is not intending any harm, nor would she think that any harm could come to him. She is not thinking about sex in a negative or hurtful way. She (and likely her friends) is having fun. They are giggling as they engage in the childhood games between the genders. We must not pathologize behaviors that have occurred over the centuries and for which there is no evidence of harm. The behavior should not be encouraged but the child should not be made to feel stigmatized as a bad person.

Assessment

This section will not instruct the reader "how to" do an assessment, but rather discusses issues that have arisen over the last 20 years that modifies the focus of previous assessments.

Data Gathering

All children with behavior problems require a thorough assessment of their early life history, prenatal care, prenatal drug exposure, developmental milestones, day-care, school history including performance both academically and interpersonally, any behavioral or psychological problems and when they arose, child and family's strengths and weaknesses, primary caretakers, attachment figures, problems with siblings, deaths, divorces and incarcerations of parents or parental figures, out-of-home placements, etc. Checklists such as the Child Behavior Checklist (CBCL) and the Trauma Symptom Checklist for Children (TSCC) are very good normed instruments for gathering additional behavioral information. These can be used to establish a baseline and used again later in treatment.

The Child Behavior Checklist (CBCL) is used to describe the everyday problems of children. The CBCL has been normed on a clinical and nonclinical population. Output from the computerized scoring indicates when a child is performing in the clinical range and when the child's behavior is more like children in the community who do not require mental health services. There are eight scales: Withdrawn, Somatic Complaints, Anxious/Depressed, Social Problems, Thought Problems, Attention Problems, Delinquent Behavior, and Aggressive Behavior. Adults who know the child well complete it.

The Trauma Symptom Checklist for Children (TSCC) is a self-report measure of post-traumatic distress and related psychological symptomatology in male and female children aged 8 – 16 years. It is useful in the evaluation of children who have experienced traumatic events, including physical and sexual assault, victimization by peers, major losses, the witnessing of violence done to others and natural disasters. The Validity scales are Under-Response and Hyper-Response. The Clinical scales are Anxiety, Depression, Anger, Post Traumatic Stress Disorder, Dissociation, and Sexual Concerns. It identifies eight critical items.

Previously it was believed that being a victim of sexual abuse was the main determinant for developing sexual behavior problems. Consistent with recent research (Friedrich, 2002; Friedrich, Davies et al., 2003; Silovsky and Nice, 2002) on children with sexual behavior problems, Kordich-Hall, Mathews et al., 1998) found a significant relationship between children with interpersonal sexual behavior problems and multiple forms of abuse (sexual, physical and emotional), single parent (mother), high stress, and poor boundaries regarding privacy and sexuality.

Based on our current understanding, assessment of a child with sexual behavior problems should investigate all forms of abuse and neglect. Domestic violence should be investigated as this is almost universal in the histories of children who sexually abuse (Johnson, 1999). The assessor should no longer feel that the answer has been found to the child's troubles, just because the child has disclosed sexual abuse. This is particularly true if the sexual abuse happened many years previously. If a child, 12 and under, is going to show problematic sexual behaviors, it is more likely to happen in close proximity to the sexual abuse rather than years later.

For instance, if a foster mother complains that her eight-year old foster child who was sexually abused at three has just started masturbating excessively, there are more plausible explanations to pursue than the sexual abuse five years earlier. While all avenues should be explored, including any lingering issues related to sexual abuse, environmental, emotional and physical issues in the child's current circumstances should not be excluded. For instance, what is "excessive" masturbation to the foster mother? Is the boy masturbating in public? Is he trying to be discrete? When did this start? Are there older children in the foster home? What is the sexual environment in the foster home? Has he been evaluated for any medical conditions? Does he have other behaviors that are impulsive and unplanned? Is the masturbation planned to annoy someone? How long has he been in this foster home? Did he do this in previous foster homes?

There are endless circumstances in the present that may be coming into play with newly discovered masturbatory behavior that might have something to do with the early sexual abuse or nothing to do with it. Since the problem is in the present, it is best to look for the solution in the present. If the behavior is linked emotionally with the past, the child can learn that later. Telling a child (or adult) she is doing something today because of something that happened when she was three provides no relief. If the events are connected, we learn the present precipitants help the child get them under control and then deal with latent emotional issues.

Recent research (Friedrich, 2003) points us to the parents' and the child's environment as important in the etiology of the child's problems. This is particularly salient if the child is living with biological parents who may have a history of abuse, neglect or domestic violence that is making them less able to deal with their child's problems. Some parents had a history of sexual behavior problems themselves that may impinge on their ability to help their children. Since the parents will need to provide a stable environment for the children to heal, assessment and remediation of issues for the parents will be important (Johnson, 2004b).

Research findings also point us to a thorough evaluation of the child's environment. There are several instruments that have been developed for this purpose. The Family Practices Questionnaires (Johnson, 2003a, 2003b) ask parents/caregivers of the child up to what age they believe children and parents should sleep, shower, bathe, and change clothes together; kiss on the mouth give full body hugs, etc. The Family Roles, Relationships, Behaviors and Practices Questionnaire (Johnson, 1998b, 2003b) is four pages of items regarding emotional, physical and sexual boundary violations from the fairly benign to more egregious. For both questionnaires, each parent is separately asked to indicate which of these occurred in the home in which they grew up. In subsequent clinical interviews, the parents are told that most parents parent the way they were brought up. It is very usual for parents to bring into their own home, the same practices that were engaged in their family of origin. Each parent is then asked which of the boundary violations occur in their present home.

The first two pages of the Family Roles, Relationships, Behaviors and Practices Questionnaire (Johnson 1998b, 2003b) are used with children eight and older. These pages can be used to check on the parent's veracity. Most children are more truthful than their parents. The items on the questionnaire were developed through work with the families of children with sexual behavior problems and can be used throughout treatment. These boundary violations are often the substrata for the anxiety and confusion that the children are acting out in their worrisome sexual behaviors.

There are two instruments that have been developed specifically to assess children's sexual behaviors: the Child Sexual Behavior Inventory (CSBI) (Friedrich 1997) and the Child Sexual Behavior Checklist (CSBCL) (Johnson 1998b 2003b). The CSBI was initially developed to try to distinguish between sexually abused and nonsexually abused children. It has approximately 34 items. There is normative data that indicates from the sample of mothers of nonsexually abused children the frequency with which they saw each of the sexual behaviors listed. There is also data that indicates which behaviors are developmentally unexpected.

The CSBCL offers a descriptive history or summary record of a child's sexual behaviors from the perspective of the parent/caregiver(s). Part I of the CSBCL contains over

150 behaviors of children related to sex and sexuality ranging from natural and healthy childhood sexual exploration to behaviors of children experiencing severe difficulties in the area of sexuality. Part II asks about aspects of the child's life which might increase the frequency of sexual behaviors, e.g. access to pornography, the Internet, nudity, abuse history, sleeping and bathing arrangements and whether the child has seen violence between people he or she knows. Part III provides a more detailed description of sexual behaviors engaged in with other children. Part IV should be completed by the therapist/evaluator with the parent/caregiver if it appears the child may have a sexual behavior problem. This section is comprised of 26 characteristics of children's sexual behaviors that raise concern. The seriousness of the child's sexual behavior problems increases in direct proportion to the number and type of the characteristics that fit the child's sexual behaviors. The 26 characteristics fall into nine factors that indicate where the child's problems are, if the child has problem sexual behavior. The factors are as follows:

1) Child's sexual development is different than same age peers.
2) Child shows anxiety, guilt, and/or shame about sex.
3) Child has a greater than expected emphasis on sex and sexuality.
4) Child does not respond to limit setting.
5) Child is confused regarding sexual boundaries.
6) Child shows adult-like sexual behaviors.
7) Child disregards or objectifies others.
8) Child has angry feelings about sex.
9) Child uses coercion or hurts others with sex.

Part IV of the CSBCL was developed to assist the evaluator to use more than the advanced nature of the sexual behavior to determine if the behavior is abusive. The nine factors on the CSBCL can be used to help distinguish the type, frequency, range and level of severity of the child's sexual problems.

There are projective tests such as the Roberts Apperception Test, (Roberts, 1982) and the *Projective Storytelling Cards* (Caruso, 1987) that can be useful in understanding how the child sees relationships between adults and children, parents, boyfriends and girlfriends, siblings, and playmates. The child's world-view often arises out of the stories given in response to the projective cards. Issues of violence, sexuality, love, hatred, vengeance, and jealousy often arise. While these stories cannot be taken at face value, repeated themes can form the basis of hypotheses to explore with the child.

It is also important to gather information on the siblings or children living in the home with the child with sexual behavior problems. It may be that the identified child was caught engaging in problematic sexual behaviors with a neighbor but is also engaging in problematic sexual behaviors with siblings or relatives. It is possible that there is a sibling with sexual behavior problems who initiated the present behavior with this child. Older siblings may be exposing younger siblings to sexual material or experiences that are too advanced for the child. Interviewing all of the siblings of a child always provides a good balance of information about the child, parents and home-life.

Every effort should be made to get accurate information about the other children involved in the sexual behaviors, their social and sexual history with the identified child, any sexual or behavioral problems they have, their account of what happened leading up to the known behaviors, and their detailed account of the actual behaviors that brought the identified child for evaluation. It will be important to know where the behaviors occurred, why they occurred there, who decided on the behaviors, who else was present, had the children done these before at any one else's suggestion, etc. (Johnson, 1992).

Although the guidelines of the Association for the Treatment of Sexual Abusers (ATSA) and the American Polygraph Association are silent on the issue of age when using the polygraph, there are no studies of its use with children with sexual behavior problems. The guidelines of the California Coalition on Sexual Offending (CCOSO) state, "Particular caution is warranted with clients who are between the age of thirteen and eighteen."

Phallometric testing using penile plethysmography involves the measurement of changes in penile circumference or volume in response to sexual and nonsexual stimuli. This is not suitable for children as little is known about sexual arousal in prepubertal or newly pubertal children. The procedure itself may feel victimizing, highly embarrassing, frightening or arousing to the child absent the stimuli. The stimuli used to measure arousal may be shocking to the child due to the child's age and developmental level. There is no base-line data on children to determine what is normal and not normal responding.

Interviewing clinicians about what they have learned in working with children with sexual behavior problems always brings forth the exclamation, "don't rely on the referral information!" This caveat is exceptionally important when working with young children and sexual issues. Initial investigators have very little time when sent out on a call about a child engaging in sexual behaviors. They determine what they need for their agency and send the matter on. Some children look very frightening and highly pathological on paper. This may occur because as adults we fill in the gaps in information the way we would if the child were an adult doing the sexual things noted. It is also possible that the facts that were available were misconstrued and the investigator saw everything from the point of view of an adult offender and did not take into account child sexuality. There are many, many cases where the facts are wrong, the previous history of the children is not known, the child's motivation for the behavior is not understood, and a child is named a perpetrator or predator based on the type of behavior attempted or engaged in. Each person doing an assessment of a child with sexual behavior problems should try to get as many source documents as possible and talk to as many people who know the child well over as long a period as possible, and get people who are in every day contact with the child for extended periods to fill out (with proper authorization) the CSBI or the CSBCL.

Each data gathering instrument should be completed by as many people who know the child as possible (with proper authorization). It is helpful if people outside the family, including the schoolteacher, fills out the CSBI or CSBCL and the CBCL. Different people report different things depending on when and under what circumstances they see the child, and their input provides perspective. The greater the number of informants, the broader the perspective. It is possible that some behaviors, including sexual behavior, only occur under certain circumstances. This will be important for understanding the child's sexual behavior and treatment planning.

Identifying the Seriousness of the Child's Problematic Sexual Behavior

After detailed assessment, it is helpful to have some framework in which to conceptualize the child and family so that a treatment plan can be developed. While empirically derived typologies have not been successful to date (Chaffin, Letourneau et al., 2002), a clinically derived continuum of sexual behaviors has provided a rudimentary template for understanding the myriad of different sexual behaviors of young children. This continuum attempts to categorize the sexual behaviors of children, 12 and younger, into four large groups. The first group is "natural and healthy sexual behaviors" (see definition under section above entitled, "Not Normal" Sexual Behavior is not Necessarily Abusive) that is by far the largest group; the next three pertain to children with problematic sexual behavior. These three groups are: "sexually-reactive," "children engaged in extensive mutual sexual behaviors," and "children who sexually abuse." Children, if they move from Group 1 where each child starts, first move to being "sexually-reactive." No child goes from group one to being sexually abusive, group four. If there is movement out of group one, it is to group two. If children's behavior becomes more serious, generally due to a feeling of abandonment and lack of attachment to caring adults, children can move to group three or group four.

Most children who engage in problematic sexual behaviors fall into the category of "sexually-reactive." "Sexually-reactive" children engage in self-stimulating behaviors and also engage in sexual behaviors with other children and, sometimes, with adults. Generally, this type of sexual behavior is in response to environmental cues that are overly stimulating or reminiscent of previous abuse or feelings that reawaken traumatic or painful memories. The child may respond directly by masturbating or engaging in other sexual behaviors alone or with others. Hiding the sexual behaviors or finding friends to engage in the behaviors in private may not always be possible as the sexual behavior is a way of coping with overwhelming feelings of which they cannot make sense. The behaviors are often impulsive but are sometimes planned. Sexually reactive behavior is often not within the full conscious control of the child. In some situations children are trying to make sense of something sexual done to them by doing it to someone else. These children do not coerce others into sexual behaviors but act out their confusion on them. Many of these children do not understand their own or others' rights to privacy. While there is no intent to hurt or be mean to others, receiving sexual behaviors can be confusing for the other child and may feel like a violation or abuse (Johnson, 1999).

Because "sexually-reactive" children may impulsively act out on other children, they are often confused with children who sexually abuse. Yet, the "sexually-reactive" child has no ill feelings toward the other child, and does not think he can or will hurt the other child. The "sexually-reactive" child is trying to work out his own premature sexualization or confusion about sexual matters. (It can occur that a child with whom a "sexually-reactive" child acts out can feel victimized based on his or her own history whereas the "sexually-reactive" child had no intention to harm the child.)

Consider the boys, ages 9 and 7, whose mother is an alcoholic and drug addict, and leaves the boys alone frequently. One night she leaves them with a 4 year old girl cousin while she is "partying." The children find a pornographic video and watch it. Later that night the boys hump the little girl and each tries to put his penis inside her. A neighbor who can see the children from his window, reports to the police that all the children were laughing and giggling while this went on. It lasted about 2-3 minutes. After interviews and testing, no history of other sexual problems was found for any of the children. They were doing relatively well at school and had no problems with peers at home or at school. There was a history of ADHD for the 9-year old. The little girl said she thought it was fun and had no aftereffects that could be noted. The major problem was the mother's neglect and lack of supervision with pornographic videos readily available. The initial evaluator agreed with the facts, as just stated, but encouraged adjudication based on the advanced nature of the sexual behaviors.

The second group of children with sexual behavior problems that is seen in clinical populations is "children who engage in extensive, mutual sexual behaviors." Often distrustful, chronically hurt and abandoned by adults, they relate best to other children. In the absence of close, supportive relationships to adults, the sexual behaviors become a way of making a connection to other children. They use sex as a way to cope with their feelings of abandonment, hurt, sadness, anxiety, and often despair. These children do not coerce other children into sexual behaviors but find other similarly lonely children who will engage with them. Almost all of these children have been emotionally abused and neglected. All have lived in sexualized environments with no real parental supervision and love. They look to other children to help meet their emotional needs and their need for physical contact (Johnson, 1999). All of these children have previously been "sexually reactive" children who are now using sexual behavior as a coping mechanism to cope with their overwhelming fears of abandonment and potential annihilation.

John, a ten-year-old, and Jim, an eleven-year-old, are both boys at a residential treatment facility. Jim and John became friends at the residential unit. Both were emotionally needy and confused. Late one night a staff member caught Jim and John in the bathroom with Jim applying Vaseline to his penis while standing behind John. Jim was a year older than John, much bigger, more aggressive, and was standing in a position to insert his penis in John's rectum. It was for these reasons that it was decided that Jim was an offender and John was the intended victim.

Before entering the facility, John lived with his mother and stepfather. John's mother had been physically, emotionally, and sexually abused as a child and had given birth to John when she was seventeen and unmarried. She worked hard to keep John and his sister at home and safe but eventually married a man who was physically and emotionally abusive.

Child protective services removed John and his sister from their mother and stepfather because the children were engaging in sexual behavior with one another. The social workers were unaware of any emotional, sexual, or physical abuse the children might have endured when they removed them from their home. The children were placed in separate institutions for fear that they would continue to engage in sexual behaviors if they remained together. John was very depressed, anxious, and fearful when he entered the residential center. John missed his sister and asked to see her frequently. His requests were denied. John didn't ask about his mother or stepfather. He wasn't actively aggressive toward staff or other children and although superficially compliant, at most times he was distrustful and emotionally disconnected from staff. Jim was brought to the residential center after being hospitalized for severe depression and suicidal ideation. He alternated between being physically aggressive with his peers, and being totally withdrawn. He'd been abandoned as a young child by his mother and father and lived off and on in foster care for many years. On several occasions Jim was returned to his mother only to be removed due to her drug and alcohol problems. Jim was emotionally and physically neglected by his mother and often left alone for long periods when his mother went on binges. In the last four foster homes Jim had engaged in sexually reactive behaviors with other foster children. When they were caught, they were punished. In one of his foster homes, Jim's hands had been tied to the sides of his bed to stop him from masturbating when he was falling asleep at night.

When interviewed about the incident in the bathroom with the Vaseline, both John and Jim said it was the other one's idea, both said they wanted to do it, both denied being forced, and both said it made them feel better. Jim, the 11 year old, was not believed and it was felt that John, the 10-year old, was intimidated into silence. Jim was removed to a sexual offender treatment program.

Both John and Jim are examples of children engaged in extensive but mutual sexual behaviors. Jim started out as a sexually reactive child, but moved into group three as he became more alienated from his family and more despairing about adults. Sex had become an important part of his life. The only close and comforting relationship he had had was with an adult neighbor who sexually abused him at one of his foster homes; he did not share this fact with anyone. Confusing sex with caring and love, he sought out John as a source of emotional and physical comfort. John and his sister had been physically and sexually abused on a regular basis by their stepfather. Their stepfather frequently accused John of having sexual thoughts about his mother. John had already engaged in a sexual relationship with his sister before he left home. He and his sister clung to each other in a sexual way to overcome the abandonment feelings in the highly charged sexual environment of their home.

Both John and Jim had engaged in many problematic sexual behaviors alone and with other children before seeking each other out. Their sexual contact was being used as a coping mechanism for the depression, disconnectedness, and despair they both felt. Both boys denied any homosexual feelings. Yet when living in a dorm full of boys, they felt temporary relief while engaging in the sexual behaviors. John and his sister and then John and Jim are examples of children engaged in extensive, mutual sexual behaviors who use sex to cope with their intense alienation and feelings of abandonment and aloneness in a scary world.

The third group of children who have sexual behavior problems are children who molest (Johnson, 1999).There has been difficulty with children engaging in adult-like sexual behaviors being labeled as children who sexual abuse. The over-identification of children as "sexual offenders" generally stems from an exaggeration and misinterpretation of the sexual behavior in which the child engaged.

There are only a small number of children who engage in sexually abusive acts. A child may engage in a sexually abusive act but may not necessarily be defined clinically, or for purposes of treatment, as a "child who molests." While the legal system can prosecute a child for one offense and the child can be defined legally as a "sexual offender" this may not describe the thoughts, feelings and behavior of the child as they relate to his or her sexuality and may therefore incorrectly label a child for life for a behavior which was an aberration or the result of transient modeling.

Children, 11 and under who molest other children have all of the following characteristics:

1) A child, eleven years or younger, who intentionally touches the sexual organs or other intimate parts of another person, or orchestrates other children into sexual behaviors.
2) The child's problematic sexual behaviors have occurred across time and in different situations.
3) The child has demonstrated a continuing unwillingness to accept "no" when pressing another person to engage in sexual activity.
4) The child's motivation for engaging in the sexual behavior is to act out negative emotions toward the person with whom he or she engages in the sexual behavior, to upset a third person (such as parent of a sibling), or to act out generalized negative emotions using sex as the vehicle. There are a few children who are cut off from their own and other's emotions and orchestrate children into sexual behaviors to control them.
5) The child uses force, fear, physical or emotional intimidation, manipulation, bribery, and/or trickery to coerce another person into sexual behavior.
6) The child's problematic sexual behavior is unresponsive to consistent adult intervention and supervision. (See number four below.)

The following are important points related to children who molest:

1) When children are asked if they know if it is right or wrong to engage in sexual behaviors, they say it is wrong. By this statement, they do not mean that sexual behavior is wrong because it is abusive or against the law. They mean that children are not supposed to engage in sexual behavior. Children almost universally receive negative reactions from adults when they use bad words, tell dirty jokes, try to watch others engaged in sexual behaviors, look at R-rated movies or magazines with naked pictures, or touch their own or others' genitals. Even children who are not castigated consistently for these types of behaviors know they are "wrong" for children to do.

The response by adults to children's sexual expression is complicated by adults' apparent acceptance of sexual messages via the media that bombard children and enter virtually every home. In the homes of children who sexually abuse, there are almost always sexual, physical and emotional boundary violations that impinge directly on them propagated by the adults with whom they live.

2) Sections in laws about sexual offenses written for adolescents and adults refer to touching that is done with the specific intent to arouse, appeal to, or gratify the lust, passions, or sexual desires of either person. Sexual arousal and/or sexual pleasure may or may not be involved when children engage in behaviors related to sex and sexuality. Most frequently, it is not involved. A child can sexually abuse another child without any intention for sexual arousal.

3) Any sexual behaviors from kissing to penetrative acts can constitute abusive behavior. Sexual abuse is not defined by the sexual behavior alone. For instance, oral-genital contact or humping by young children does not necessarily constitute sexual abuse, whereas it would be sexual abuse if done by an adult with a child. Oral-genital contact or humping by young children is sexual abuse, if all of the criteria of the above definition is met.

4) Many children who engage in abusive sexual behavior will stop the behavior when their home environment is stabilized, or after they are placed in a stable environment, and learn healthy emotional, physical and sexual boundaries. Therefore, it is important to reassess the child prior to each court report to determine if the child remains at risk for aggressive sexual behavior, and whether the intervention plan, including placement, is the least restrictive and the most health producing.

5) Children sexually abuse children as well as people older than themselves. The age and size differential are not definers of whether or not a child has molested.

Treatment of Children With Sexual Behavior Problems

There has been a tendency in all realms of working with children with sexual behavior problems to equate them with adult and adolescent sexual offenders. Because the sexual behaviors are similar, there is a temptation to use treatment techniques with children akin to those used with older clients. Even as late as 1995, professionals were suggesting "a modified version of adult offender treatment" for children and adolescents (Cashwell and Bloss, 1995). As late as 2000, assessment and treatment of adolescents and children were considered to be so similar that separate sections were not written to describe them (Shaw, 2000).

It has become crystal clear that children with sexual behavior problems are not just miniature versions of adult and adolescent sexual offenders. In the first place, the variation in the severity of the problems is much greater. Most importantly, only one subset of children with sexual behavior problems, children who molest, engages in abusive sexual behaviors. The majority of children with sexual behavior problems are not coercing other children into sexual behaviors. Hence, therapy that is based on reducing sexual offending completely misses the mark for most children with sexual behavior problems. Even when working with children who sexually abuse, the strong confrontation used with adult offenders is not justifiable. There is no evidence that it will work with children (Marshall, Serran et al., 2002; Marshall, Fernandez et al., 2003; Marshall, Serran et al., 2003).

The first published group treatment approach (Johnson and Berry, 1989) proposed parallel treatment of the children who molested and their parents. Based on a cognitive-behavioral model, the children were grouped by age and gender with structured experiential exercises aimed at increasing their self-management skills (problem-solving, anxiety reduction, self-soothing, etc.) and gaining a cognitive understanding of their problematic sexual behavior and interpersonal problems. The parallel parents' group focused on boundary issues, parenting skills, parent-child relationships and healthy sexuality. Issues of all forms of abuse were addressed in both the parents' and the children's groups. A great deal of attention was paid to integrating the group work with the child and family's home, school life and day-care.

There have been two randomized clinical studies of children (ages 6 to 12) with sexual behavior problems funded by the National Center on Child Abuse and Neglect (NCCAN). One was in Oklahoma (Bonner, Walker et al. 1999) and the other in Vermont (Gray, Busconi et al. 1997; Pithers 1998). Each program tested two different treatment methods on randomly assigned children and parents. In the Bonner study (http://ccan.ouhsc.edu/publications.asp) 12 sessions of either a structured cognitive-behavioral approach or an unstructured psychodynamic play therapy approach was used for both the children and in parallel groups for the parents/caretakers. In the cognitive-behavioral approach sexual behaviors were mentioned frequently; in the unstructured approach, sexual behaviors were only discussed if brought up by the clients. Both had approximately the same success in decreasing problematic sexual behaviors.

In the Pithers' study (Pithers, Gray et al., 1998; Pithers, 1998), 32-week group treatment programs were compared: a structured relapse prevention program and a sexual behavior focused expressive therapy program. Parallel caregiver groups were provided. There were no appreciable differences in the results based on reduction of sexual behaviors. Pithers did conclude that relapse prevention treatment is not useful for children with generic sexual behavior problems. He thought it might be useful, with many modifications, for some severely traumatized and/or sexually aggressive children.

Four different treatment methodologies were used between the two programs with no significant differences in rate of reoccurrence of the problematic sexual behaviors. Therefore, there are no research-based guidelines that can be offered as far as the best theoretical framework on which to base treatment. The one thing that was consistent between the programs was the presence of at least one parent in parallel treatment groups. As has been found in the work of Johnson (Johnson and Berry, 1989; Johnson, 2004b), the work with the parents was very important (Chaffin, Letourneau et al., 2002).

Unfortunately, this coordination of the treatment of children with their parents is not always done. Some practitioners attempt to treat children with sexual behavior problems in isolation from their parents or caregivers. This may be due to their conceptualization of the problem. If the clinician believes that the problem resides within the child or because of an event that has happened to him/her, and believes that the child has the strength to overcome the problem with help of the therapist alone, the work may proceed without the child's parents or caretakers. The problems of young children with sexual behavior problems generally emanate not from within, but from circumstances in their lives. Because the home environment, including the parents and others they bring into the home, are often a significant factor in precipitating and sustaining the sexual behavior, working with the parents/caretakers is essential.

Young children with sexual behavior problems are generally trying to solve feelings of confusion, anxiety, shame, or anger about sex and sexuality through their acting out. It takes the form of sexual behavior due to sexualized circumstances that have occurred in their young lives. These children need adults who understand them and to whom they can talk who will help solve their problems. Fundamental to the problem is generally a lack of close attachment of the children to the parents/caregivers. The parents are not attuned to the children's needs and worries. As the children become more overwhelmed by the circumstances in their lives and do not feel that their parents will take care of them, they attempt to solve their problems on their own. Unable to do this, they escalate and eventually come to the attention of the authorities.

If the children live with their biological parents and have grown up with them, the parents and the environment they provide will likely be a significant part of the problem and therefore, a major part of the solution. Young children's sexual behavior problems evolve from what has happened to them, as well as from what they have learned and seen when growing up. The children need a healthy sexual environment with good boundaries and parents who support their growth to overcome sexual behavior problems. Working with the parents to determine the elements in the child's relationship to them, and boundary issues in the environment that may be fundamental to the child's problems, is essential. The parents will be needed to help the child decrease the problematic sexual behaviors. A modified behavior management approach with the target behaviors, reinforcers, and substitute behaviors decided on by the parents and the child together has been found to be highly effective in decreasing problematic sexual behaviors. If the children's sexual problems have arisen out of confusion due to extrafamilial sexual abuse or other inappropriate sexual exposure outside the home, the child's parents will need to be active agents in the child's learning to change.

If the child lives in a foster home, it is important to involve the foster parents. Children need to learn skills and be supported by their caregivers in modifying problematic sexual behaviors. A plan will need to be developed with the child and foster parents to assist the child in achieving their treatment goals. If there are problems in the foster home that are causing or exacerbating the child's sexual behavior problems, these problems need to be assessed and changes put in place. Even if there are no problems in the foster home, a plan will need to be developed with the child and foster parents to decrease the sexual behaviors.

If the child lives in a residential facility with rotating staff, it is important to have the same caregiver transport the child to therapy and take a strong interest in the child's development. Fostering an attachment between the caregiver and the child will assist the child in understanding relationships and help her or him feel less isolated and alone. In some cases the sexual behavior with another child is an attempt to feel attached to someone (Johnson, 1999). This attachment should be to adults, not children.

Placement in residential care that is specifically focused on the sexual behavior problems will only be appropriate for a very few children. The problems in young children who exhibit problematic sexual behaviors are very broad. In only a few cases will the sexual behaviors be a central issue. Focusing too much attention on the sexual aspect may put too much emphasis where it is not needed and fixate the child on that aspect of his or her development.

A problem that frequently arises with the placement of children in programs specifically focused on sexual behaviors is that children are placed with adolescents who sexually offend. Due to developmental differences and differences in types and severity of sexual problems, the younger children are exposed to pathology that is far beyond their own and developmentally too advanced. Children who are not sexually offending but have less serious problems should never be placed with adolescents who sexually offend. Even children who are sexually abusing should never be put with older adolescents. Some residential facilities house 9-14 year olds together. The developmental differences from a social/emotional perspective and differences in sexual feelings, attitudes and behaviors between 9-10 year olds and 13-14 year olds are too great. The younger children will be negatively affected.

Whereas many people feel that once a child has sexual behavior problems he or she will continue, this is not the case. The sexual behavior problems of most children are very amenable to treatment. As demonstrated in the programs funded by NCCAN, only about 15% of the children engaged in the problematic sexual behaviors after the 12-week treatment. Some children's problems require greater assistance and always in combination with their parents/caregivers.

The level of seriousness of the child's sexual behaviors and the strengths and weaknesses of the child's family are essential in determining the treatment. Treatment will need to be fashioned for the child and family. When children are grouped together for treatment it is advised that children who sexually abuse not be in the same groups as children who do not abuse. The thinking, emotional problems, level of severity of other behavior problems and complexity of the family's problems are generally far greater than those of children with lesser sexual behavior problems.

Whether the child and parents need individual, group or family therapy and in what combination will depend on the assessment of the child and family's problems. All children with sexual behavior problems will need family work during the treatment process. When there are other children in the family, or sibling incest occurs, the safety of all of the siblings using the support of the parents will be a significant part of the family work. Whereas some providers recommend not telling the other children in the family, whether it be a biological or foster family about the events that have occurred, this is ill-advised. Openness, with sensitivity, compassion and objectivity is far better than secrecy. It helps the child with the sexual behavior problem know that others are there to help him or her stop engaging in problematic sexual behavior.

When children with serious sexual problems may cause a risk to other children, the treatment will need to be coordinated with the school, day care and other locations. It is generally most helpful to develop a plan about how to manage the behaviors that can be operationalized in these other settings. It is not advisable to call a school principal or school counselor and say a child is acting in sexual ways with other children without suggesting a safety plan based on the one developed in the overall treatment plan for the child. Some school officials will ask for the child to be removed from the school unless the treatment provider details a plan, and sometimes even if there is a detailed plan. This is likely due to schools being held liable in the United States based on the US Supreme Court decision (1999) Davis v. Monroe County if they allow a hostile learning environment to occur. One of the definitions of a hostile learning environment is not providing students with reasonable protection from sexual harassment from other students.

Safety planning should be based in a developmental context. The plan should meet the child's needs at the time and change as the child develops better self control, understands the parameters around sexual contact, and is capable of more freedom. Some plans leave children completely isolated from other children with no chance to develop the social skills they need as they grow and develop. The children then feel as if they are dangerous and pariahs.

When selecting treatment providers for children with sexual behavior problems, the major criteria should be that they understand and relate to "the child" in these children. For far too long, treatment providers have come from a background of working with adult or adolescent offenders and look for the "offender" not "the child." It is far better to come to the work with an openness to learn and understand the children's problems from their perspective with no basic assumptions based on sexual offending in adults and adolescents.

Conclusion

Children with sexual behavior problems are not miniature adult or adolescent sexual offenders. Only a very small number of these children are sexually offending; most are engaging in sexual behaviors which are developmentally too advanced and need to be curtailed. Not only is children's sexuality different than adults and adolescents, their emotional, social, and cognitive awareness and relationship to the world is different. It is dangerous to children that we do not recognize the differences and treat the child, not our projections onto the child.

End Notes

[1]288. a) Any person who willfully and lewdly commits any lewd or lascivious act, including any of the acts constituting other crimes provided for in Part 1, upon or with the body, or any part or member thereof, of a child who is under the age of 14 years, with the intent of arousing, appealing to, or gratifying the lust, passions, or sexual desires of that person or the child, is guilty of a felony and shall be punished by imprisonment in the state prison for three, six, or eight years.

References

Achenbach, T. M. (1991). *Manual for the Child Behavior Checklist and Revised Child Behavior Checklist/ 4-18 & 1991 Profile.* Burlington: University of Vermont Department of Psychiatry.

Adams, J., McClellan, D., McCurry, C., & Storck, M. (1995). Sexually inappropriate behaviors in seriously mentally ill children and adolescents. *Child Abuse & Neglect, 19*(5), 555-568.

Alexander, M. (1999). Sexual offender treatment efficacy revisited. *Sexual Abuse: A Journal of Research and Treatment, 11*(2), 101-116.

Bonner, B., Walker, C. E., & Berliner, L. (1999a). *Treatment manual for cognitive-behavioral group treatment for parents/caregivers of children with sexual behavior problems,* from http://nccanch.acf.hhs.gov/

Bonner, B., Walker, C. E., & Berliner, L. (1999b). *Treatment manual for dynamic group play therapy for children with sexual behavior problems and their parent/caregivers,* from http://nccanch.acf.hhs.gov/

Borduin, C. M., Henggler, S. W., Blaske, D. M., & Stein, R. (1990). Multisystemic treatment of adolescent sexual offenders. *International Journal of Offender Therapy and Comparative Criminology, 34,* 105-114.

Briere, J. (1996). *Trauma symptom checklist for children.* Odessa, FL: Psychological Asessment Resources.

Burton, D., L., N., A., A., & Badten, L. (1997). Clinician's views on sexually aggressive children and their families: A theoretical exploration. *Child Abuse & Neglect, 21*(2), 157-170.

Caruso, K. (1987). *Projective storytelling cards.* Redding, California: Northwest Psychological Publishers, Inc.

Cashwell, C., & Bloss, K. (1995). From victim to client: Preventing the cycle of sexual reactivity. *School Counselor, 42*(3), 233-240.

Chaffin, M., Letourneau, E., & Silovsky, J. (2002). Adults, adolescents, and children who sexually abuse children. In J. Myers, L. Berliner, J. Briere, C. Hendrix, C. Jenny & R. T. (Eds.), *The APSAC Handbook on Child Maltreatment* (Second Edition ed.). Thousand Oaks: Sage.

Davis, D. (1998). *STOP IT, NOW - A guide for the prevention of sexual harassment for elementary school children.* Seattle, Washington: Help Yourself Books.

Drach, K., Wientzen, & Ricci, L. (2001). The diagnostic utility of sexual behavior problems in diagnosing sexual abuse in a forensic child abuse evaluation clinic. *Child Abuse & Neglect, 25,* 489-503.

Duff, R. (1993). Choice, character, and criminal liability. *Law and Philosophy, 12,* 345-383.

Fagan, I., & Zimring, F. (2000). *The changing borders of juvenile justice: Transfer of adolescents to the criminal court.* Chicago: University of Chicago Press.

Farrington, D. (1986). Age and crime. In M. Tonry & N. Morris (Eds.), *Crime and Justice: An annual review of research* (pp. 189-217). Chicago: University of Chicago.

Finkelhor, D., Hotaling, G., Lewis, I., & Smith, C. (1990). Sexual abuse in a national survey of men and women: Prevalence, characteristics, and risk factors. *Child Abuse and Neglect, 14,* 19-28.

Friedrich, W. (1997). *Child sexual behavior inventory Professional manual.* Odessa, Florida: Psychological Assessment Resources, Inc.

Friedrich, W. (2002). Child sexual behavior inventory: Normative, psychiatric and sexual abuse comparisons. *Child Maltreatment, 6*(1), 37-49.

Friedrich, W., Beilke, R., & Urquiza, A. (1988). Behavior problems in young sexually abused boys. *Journal of Interpersonal Violence, 3*(1), 21-27.

Friedrich, W., & Chaffin, M. (2000, November 4, 2000). *Developmental-systemic perspectives on children with sexual behavior problems.* Paper presented at the Association for the Treatment of Sexual Abusers, San Diego.

Friedrich, W., & Fehrer, E. (2004). Correlates of behavior problems in a clinical sample of sexually abused children. *Under review.*

Friedrich, W., Fisher, J., Broughton, D., Houston, M., & Shafran, C. (1998). Normative sexual behavior in children: A contemporary sample. *Pediatrics, 101*(4).

Friedrich, W., Grambsch, P., Broughton, D., Kuiper, J., & Beilke, R. (1991). Normative sexual behavior in children. *Pediatrics, 88*(3), 456-464.

Friedrich, W., Grambsch, P., Damon, L., Hewitt, S., Koverola, C., Lang, R., et al. (1992). The child sexual behavior inventory: Normative and clinical comparisons. *Psychological Assessment, 4(3),* 303-311.

Friedrich, W., & Luecke, W. (1988). Young school-age sexually aggressive children. *Professional Psychology Research and Practice, 19*(2), 155-164.

Friedrich, W. N., Davies, W., Fehrer, E., & Wright, J. (2003). Sexual behavior problems in preteen children: Developmental, ecological, and behavioral correlates. *Annals of the New York Academy of Sciences, 989,* 95-104.

Gale, J., Thompson, R.J., Moran, T., & Sack, W.H. (1988). Sexual abuse in young children: Its clinical presentation and characteristic patterns. *Child Abuse & Neglect, 12,* 163-170.

Gomes-Schwartz, B., & Horowitz, J. M. (1985). Sexual abuse in young children. Its clinical presentation and charateristic patterns. *Child Abuse & Neglect, 163-170.*

Gomes-Schwartz, B., Horowitz, J. M., & Cardarelli, A. (1990). *Child abuse: The initial effects.* Newbury Park, CA: Sage.

Gray, A., Busconi, A., Houchens, P., & Pithers, W. (1997). Children with sexual behavior problems and their caregivers: Demographics, functioning, and clinical patterns. *Sexual Abuse: A Journal of Research and Treatment, 9*(4), 267-290.

Hall, D. K., Mathews, F., & Pearce, J. (1998). *Problematic sexual behavior in sexually abused children: A preliminary typology.* Paper presented at the National Adolescent Perpetrator Network International Conference, Winnipeg.

Hall, D. K., Mathews, F., & Pearce, J. (2002). Sexual behavior problems in sexually abused children: A preliminary typology. *Child Abuse and Neglect, 26,* 289-312.

Hanson, K., Gordon, A., Harris, A., Marques, J., Murphy, W., Quinsey, V., et al. (2002). First report of the collaborative outcome data project on the effectiveness of psychological treatment for sex offenders. *Sexual Abuse: A Journal of Research and Treatment, 14*(2), 169-194.

Hanson, R. K., & Slater, S. (1988). Sexual victimization in the history of sexual abusers: A review. *Annals of Sex Research, 1,* 485-499.

Johnson, T. C. (1988). Child perpetrators - children who molest other children: preliminary findings. *Child Abuse & Neglect, 12,* 219-229.

Johnson, T. C. (1989). Female child perpetrators: children who molest other children. *Child Abuse & Neglect, 13*(4), 571-585.

Johnson, T. C. (1991). Understanding the sexual behaviors of young children. *SIECUS Report, August/September.*

Johnson, T. C. (1992). Investigating allegation of sexual behaviors between children. 1101 Fremont Ave. South Pasadena, CA 91030: Author. www.tcavjohn.com

Johnson, T. C. (1993). Sexual behaviors: A continuum. In E. Gil & T. C. Johnson (Eds.), *Sexualized children :Assessment and treatment of sexualized children and children who molest* (pp. 41-52). Rockville, MD.: Launch Press.

Johnson, T. C. (1999). *Understanding your child's sexual behavior.* Oakland, California: New Harbinger Publications.

Johnson, T. C. (2000). Children with sexual behavior problems. *SEICUS, 29*(1), 35-39.

Johnson, T. C. (2002). *Treatment exercises for abused children and children with sexual behavior problems.* South Pasadena, CA: Author. www.tcavjohn.com

Johnson, T. C. (2003b). Assessment packet for children with sexual behavior problems. South Pasadena, California 91030. www.tcavjohn.com

Johnson, T. C. (2003c). Child sexual behavior checklist-Revised. In *Assessment packet for children with sexual behavior problems.* South Pasadena. CA: Author. www.tcavjohn.com

Johnson, T. C. (2004a). *Understanding children's sexual behaviors - What's natural and healthy* - Updated. South Pasadena, CA: Author. www.tcavjohn.com

Johnson, T. C. (2004b). *Helping children with sexual behavior problems - A guidebook for parents and substitute caregivers 2nd Edition.* South Pasadena, Ca: Author. www.tcavjohn.com

Johnson, T. C., & Berry, C. (1989). Children who molest other children: a treatment program. *Journal of Interpersonal Violence, 4*(2), 185-203.

Johnson, T. C., & Hooper, R. (2003a). Boundaries and family practices: Implications for assessing child abuse. *Journal of Child Sexual Abuse, 12*(3/4), 103-126.

Johnson, T. C., Huang, E., Simpson, P., & Doonan, R. (2004c). A retrospective study of children's (twelve and younger) sexual behaviors. *Under review.*

Kaufman, J., & Zigler, E. (1987). Do abused children become abusive parents? *American Journal of Orthopsychiatry, 57*(2), 186-192.

Kendall-Tackett, K., Williams, L., & Finkelhor, D. (1993). Impact of sexual abuse on children: A review and synthesis of recent empirical studies. *Psychological Bulletin, 113*(1), 164-180.

Krivacska, J. J. (1991). Child sexual abuse prevention programs; The need for childhood sexuality education. *SIECUS Report, 19*(6), 1-7.

Marshall, W., Fernandez, Y., Serran, G., Mulloy, R., Thornton, D., Mann, R., et al. (2003). Process variables in the treatment of sexual offenders: A review of the relevant literature. *Aggression and Violent Behavior: A Review Journal, 8*(2), 205-234.

Marshall, W., Serran, G., Fernandez, Y., Mulloy, R., Mann, R., & Thornton, D. (2003). Therapist characteristics in the treatment of sexual offenders: Tentative data on their relationship with indices of behaviour changes. *Journal of Sexual Aggression, 9,* 25-30.

Marshall, W., Serran, G., Moulden, H., Mulloy, R., Fernandez, Y., Mann, R., et al. (2002). Therapist features in sexual offender treatment: Their reliable identification and influence on behavior change. *Clinical Psychology and Psychotherapy, 9,* 395-405.

Milloy, C. (1998). Specialized treatment for juvenile sex offenders: A closer look. *Journal of Interpersonal Violence, 13*(5), 653-656.

Morse, S. (1994). Culpability and control. Pennsylvania Law Review(142), 1587-1660.

Murphy, W. D., & Peters, J. M. (1992). Profiling child sexual abusers: Psychological considerations. *Criminal Justice and Behavior, 19,* 24-37.

Okami, P. (1992). "Child perpetrators of sexual abuse": The emergence of a problematic deviant category. *The Journal of Sex Research, 29*(1), 109-130.

Pithers, W., Gray, A., Busconi, A., & Houchens, P. (1998a). Caregivers of children with sexual behavior problems: Psychological and family functioning. *Child Abuse & Neglect, 22*(2), 129-141.

Pithers, W. D., Gray, A., Busconi, A., Houchens, P. (1998b). Children with sexual behavior problems: Identification of five distinct child types and related treatment considerations. *Child Maltreatment, 3*(4), 384-406.

Roberts, G. (1982). Roberts apperception test. Los Angeles: Western Psychological Services.

Savage, D. (2004, June 2). Teens' miranda rights redefined. *New York Times.*

Schwartz, B. K., & Colleen, H. R. (Eds.). (1995). *The sex offender: Corrections, treatment and legal practice.* Kingston, New Jersey: Civic Research Institute, Inc.

Shaw, J. (2000). Summary of the practice parameters for the assessment and treatment of children and adolescents who are sexually abusive of others. *Journal of the American Academy of Child and Adolescent Psychiatrists, 39*(1), 127-130.

Silovsky, J., & Niec, L. (2002). Characteristics of young children with sexual behavior problems: A pilot study. *Child Maltreatment, 7*(3), 187-197.

Slusser, M. (1995). Manifestations of sexual abuse in preschool-aged children. *Issues in Mental Health Nursing, 16*, 481-491.

Steinberg, L., & Scott, E. (2003). Less guilty by reason of adolescence -- Developmental immaturity, diminished responsibility, and the juvenile death penalty. *American Psychologist, 58*(12), 1009-1018.

Trivits, L., & Repucci, N. (2002). Application of megans' law to juveniles. *American Psychologist, 57*(9), 690-704.

Vuoso, G. (1986). Background, responsibility, and excuse. *Yale Law Review, 96*, 1661-1686.

Widom, C., & Ames, M. (1994). Criminal consequences of childhood sexual victimization. *Child Abuse & Neglect, 18*(4), 303-318.

Widom, C., & Maxfield, M. (2001). *An update on the "cycle of violence."* NCJRS.

Worling, J., & Curwen, T. (2000). Adolescent sexual offender recidivism: Success of specialized treatment and implications for risk predication. *Child Abuse & Neglect, 24*(7), 965-982.

CHAPTER FOUR

DEVELOPMENTAL CONSIDERATIONS IN WORKING WITH JUVENILE SEX OFFENDERS

AMANDA M. FANNIFF
AND
JUDITH V. BECKER

Introduction

A considerable number of juveniles are responsible for cases of sexual abuse and assault in our society. The FBI Uniform Crime Report indicates that in 2002, juveniles represented 16.7% of arrests for forcible rapes and 20.6% of arrests for other sex offenses (US Department of Justice, 2003). Since not all youth who commit sex offenses are arrested, it is important to note that this figure is likely to underestimate the number of sexual assaults committed by youth. While the professional literature on characteristics, assessment and treatment of juveniles who have committed sexual offenses has increased over the past two decades (e.g., Davis & Leitenberg, 1987; Becker, 1998; Brown & Kolko, 1998; Worling & Curwen, 2000; Hunter, Figueredo, Malamuth, Becker, & Mack, 2003), the majority of these articles do not address developmental issues. People who work with juveniles with sexual behavior problems need to be knowledgeable about child and adolescent development, theories of juvenile delinquency, and developmental pathways to sexual aggression. It is not enough to be knowledgeable about adult sex offenders and apply that knowledge to juveniles. All children and adolescents are different from adults in important ways, and this is also true for juvenile sex offenders. There is a variety of evidence to suggest that juvenile sex offenders are in fact quite different from adult offenders. The purpose of this chapter is to provide to individuals who will be involved in the assessment and treatment of juvenile sex offenders a broad overview of development, pathways to delinquent behavior, pathways to sexually aggressive behavior, and recent research on both assessment and treatment.

Areas of Development

Developmental factors are important to consider in understanding, assessing, and treating juvenile sex offenders because juveniles are still maturing in many different areas. Both biological factors, such as neuropsychological deficits, and environmental factors, such as parental responsiveness, play a part in developmental outcome. A youth's current developmental level can affect the meaning of experiences to the youth, as well as affect specific behaviors. Important areas of development to consider are the nature of the youth's brain development, attachment to caregivers, cognitive development, social development, moral development and sexual development.

Biological development

Kendall-Tackett (2003) provides a summary of brain development, including the regions of the brain, its constituent parts, age of developmental activity, functional maturity and the key functions of specific brain regions. Emotional and behavioral regulation are important functions to master in becoming a prosocial person. The limbic system, whose key function is memory, emotional regulation and primary sensory integration, experiences its greatest developmental activity during early childhood. However, functional maturity is not reached until puberty. If trauma or damage to the constituent parts of the limbic system occurs during a youth's development, the ability to regulate emotions may be compromised. The frontal lobes do not achieve maturity until adulthood, an important consideration given that the frontal lobes are essential to the inhibition of emotion and behavior, problem solving, and reasoning.

Kendall-Tackett (2003) notes that traumatic events manifested either psychologically or by brain trauma can influence brain development. Traumatic stress can cause alterations in the frontal-limbic connections. Youth who are being raised in homes where they are exposed to either physical or emotional abuse can experience chronic stress that may alter the hypothalamic-pituitary-adrenal axis leading to the symptom of hyperarousal. Abused children have shown elevations in morning cortisol levels, supporting this hypothesis (Kendall-Tackett, 2003). Ishikawa and Raine (2003) suggest that some individuals suffer early health and family environment risk factors that interrupt both maturation of the frontal lobes and socialization processes. These risk factors include prenatal exposure to substances, birth complications, and maternal rejection in infancy. Children with frontal lobe deficits fail to learn to inhibit aggressive responses and are largely unresponsive to discipline. Consequently, these children may act out in school, be rejected by peers, associate with deviant peers, and show disregard for authority. All these are factors known to be associated with antisocial behavior. While a number of studies consider early abuse experiences as a potential developmental precursor to juvenile offending, the majority of research of juvenile sexual and nonsexual offenders has not examined neuropsychological functioning. The relationship between damage to the brain in early development, emotion and behavior regulation, and the development of antisocial behaviors should be examined in future research.

Social development

Early social development occurs within the family, as infants interact mostly with caregivers. Secure attachment to a caregiver, which can be described as "confidence that supportive care is available" which "supports confident exploration of the environment and ease of settling when distressed" (p. 85), has been related to numerous positive outcomes, including self-esteem, prosocial behavior, and overall adjustment (reviewed in Sroufe, Duggal, Weinfield, & Carlson, 2000). Insecure attachment, on the other hand, is associated with a number of negative outcomes including psychopathology. Sroufe and colleagues (2000) emphasize the importance of the caregiver relationship in learning to regulate emotion. Caregivers soothe infants and respond to their needs based on their emotional displays, and through this process children learn to organize their emotions and behavior. This forms the basis for the child's goal-directed behavior starting around 6 months of age and encourages the child to believe in his or her own ability to maintain regulation. Youth with inconsistent or toxic caregiving experiences may form an insecure attachment and may be at risk for experiencing difficulty in developing prosocial peer relationships that include empathic responding. Research has demonstrated that children with histories of secure attachment are rated to be better self-regulators, more self-reliant, to have higher self-esteem, and to be better able to form close relationships with friends and to function successfully in mixed-gender peer groups in adolescence (Sroufe et al., 2000). Particularly important is the finding that children with histories of secure attachment "positively engage and respond to other children, are able to sustain interactions even in the face of conflict and challenge, and are notably empathic" (Sroufe et al., 2000, p. 85). In comparison, children with histories of anxious/resistant attachment have been shown to be easily frustrated, to have difficulty coping with stress, and "are unable to sustain interactions with peers" (Sroufe et al., 2000, p. 86). Additionally, negative attachment histories have been found to be related to aggression, conduct disturbances, and other disorders.

These findings support the hypothesis that insecure attachment during early stages of development may affect the developing sex offender's ability to attain intimacy in relationships and ability to develop empathy (e.g., Marshall, 1989). Research has begun to explore the attachment patterns found in adult sex offenders (e.g., Smallbone & Dadds, 2000), yet there is a lack of research connecting attachment experiences to juvenile sex offending. Research on adult sex offenders suggests they use sexual coping strategies to deal with loneliness and intimacy deficits more frequently than other offenders (Cortoni & Marshall, 2001) and that sex offenders who were sexually abused as children demonstrate an earlier onset of masturbatory behavior (Smallbone & McCabe, 2003). Results that do not fit well into an attachment theory of sex offending have also been published. Smallbone & McCabe (2003) report differences between subgroups of sex offenders on paternal but not maternal attachment. Another study reports few differences between sex offenders and other types of offenders on measurements of attachment (Ward, Hudson, & Marshall, 1996). This can be interpreted as indicative of the generally problematic childhoods of incarcerated offenders. Given the variety of findings, it appears that attachment should be considered one of many factors that can influence the development of a range of antisocial behaviors, including sex offending. Sexual coping strategies may be forms of self-soothing. Self-soothing behaviors may also include fantasies or play enactment where juveniles envision themselves in powerful situations or fantasize about harming people. Self-harm (cutting) and alcohol or illegal substance abuse may also be utilized to reduce their emotional pain.

Cognitive development

The level of the youth's cognitive development is important to assess in considering the youth's responsibility for his/her behavior and in devising a treatment plan.

Piaget (2000) has outlined stages of cognitive development. They include the senso-rimotor stage (birth to 2 years of age), during which children learn to coordinate sensory perceptions and simple motor behaviors. The pre-operational stage is usually attained between ages 2-6. Children are able to represent reality to themselves via symbols. During the concrete operational stage (6-12 years of age), youth are able to understand perspectives of others and during the formal operational stage (12 and up), youth begin to be able to think abstractly (Piaget, 2000). This suggests that children still in an early stage of development are not necessarily capable of complex planning, such as the planning that is often observed in adult sex offenders. Also, the younger the youth, the more difficulty he or she may have in understanding the perspectives of others. This would make it difficult for a child to exhibit or even to learn empathy. Younger children have more limited repertoires of coping strategies. Research regarding the cognitive development of juvenile sex offenders and the relationship of cognitive development to the development of offending behaviors or to treatment has not been explored.

Moral development

Kohlberg (1963) has outlined six stages of moral development. The first stages are labeled the preconventional level, usually attained from pre-school to middle childhood, where children learn to follow rules, avoid punishment, and learn to be obedient. The highest levels of moral development are in the post-conventional level, where there is an obligation to law, a desire to do the greatest good for the greatest number of people, or adherence to self-chosen ethical principles. Research has demonstrated differences in the moral behavior of maltreated children in comparison to nonmaltreated children (Koenig, Cicchetti, & Rogosch, 2004). The scientific literature is devoid of studies exploring the relationship between moral development and juvenile sexual offending.

Sexual development

There is an expected course of sexual development in the life course of an individual. DeLamater and Friedrich (2002) describe this normal sexual development. They note that the capacity for a sexual response is present from birth. Male infants experience erections and female infants experience vaginal lubrication. These phenomena, however, are not cognitively processed as sexual by infants. Young children occasionally fondle their own genitals. A number of children engage in a variety of sexual play experiences when they are young. The behavior becomes more covert as they learn that such behaviors are not approved of by adults (DeLamater & Friedrich, 2002). During early childhood, usually by age 3, children form a gender identity. Some children, however, do not identify with their genetic sex and develop a gender identity disorder (DeLamater & Friedrich, 2002). During ages 8-12, children are usually more comfortable socially with members of their own gender. During puberty, biological changes occur with the maturation of the gonads, other genitalia, and secondary sex characteristics leading to an increase in sexual interest. Whether youth act on this sexual interest depends on a number of factors including cultural, moral, religious, and parental attitudes and opportunity (DeLamater & Friedrich, 2002). Not all children follow a pattern of "normative" or expected development. Some children develop sexual behavior problems, others develop sexual disorders and still others commit sexual offenses. Research comparing the sexual development of juvenile sex offenders to controls over the early years of life may provide useful information regarding the development of deviant sexual behaviors.

Summary

There is an extensive body of research regarding expected bio-psycho-social development in childhood, and a paucity of research connecting such development to the experiences of juvenile sex offenders. In several areas, information regarding the effect of child abuse on development has been noted. The effect of child abuse is a topic more amenable to research than differences in the development of juvenile sex offenders. This is due to the fact that the effects of child abuse occur after the child has come to the attention of public officials. Understanding developmental processes in juvenile sex offenders requires retrospective analysis of what happened before the child came to the attention of public officials. Future research on juvenile sex offenders and children with sexual behavior problems could provide valuable information by explicitly addressing what differentiates the experiences of juvenile sex offenders from typical developmental experiences. Such results can aid in the development of maximally effective interventions.

Developmental Pathways to Delinquency

While there is limited research comparing the development of juvenile sex offenders to the development of juvenile nonoffenders across different domains, an extensive body of literature exists that examines specific developmental pathways to sexual and nonsexual criminal offending. These approaches look to the individual and environmental characteristics and experiences of offenders to determine the precursors to antisocial behavior, and there is some overlap in the experiences considered important (e.g., abuse experiences). While not a developmental model, Gottfredson and Hirschi's (1990) general theory of crime offers an explanation of offending behavior that may be important in understanding juvenile sex offenders. Gottfredson and Hirschi (1990) suggest that all offenders are generalists who commit whatever crimes they have the opportunity to commit because of a lack of self-control and an inability to delay gratification or consider long-term consequences. Therefore, juvenile sex offenders would be expected to be characterized by conduct disorder, antisocial behavior, and non-sexual offending. The sex offending behavior can be considered "opportunistic" because according to the general theory of crime (Gottfredson & Hirschi, 1990) it is the lack of impulse control plus an opportunity that presented itself that caused the juvenile to engage in the offense.

Coercion theory

Patterson (2002) describes one model of the development of antisocial behaviors based on coercion theory. According to this model, the child's temperament interacts with the caregiving environment to produce antisocial behavior. This occurs through what Patterson (2002) refers to as a coercive process, in which children are reinforced for aversive behaviors starting as early as 10 to 18 months of age. Snyder and Stoolmiller (2002) describe this negative reinforcement process, illustrated by the following examples: "Hitting a sibling in response to the sibling's teasing will be performed if it terminates the teasing. A child's noncompliance to parental commands will promote similar behavior in the future if it deflects the command" (p. 75).

Children may also be positively reinforced for aversive behaviors in receiving attention or other rewards they desire. Aggressive children have been found to be "more likely to engage in unprovoked aggression, to reciprocate the aversive behavior of another family member, and to persist in aversive behavior once they have initiated it" (Snyder & Stoolmiller, 2002, p.70) than nonaggressive children, and their family members have been found to be more likely to engage in all of these behaviors than the family members of nonaggressive children (Snyder & Stoolmiller, 2002). Children with conduct problems meet with greater success in achieving the reinforcement desired when they engage in coercive rather than constructive tactics, while the reverse is true for normative children (Snyder & Stoolmiller, 2002). Coercion theory has been shown to be a good predictor of antisocial behavior.

Adolescence-limited vs. life-course persistent antisocial behavior

Another model of the development of juvenile offending is offered by Moffitt (1993) to explain the differences between individuals with a persistent pattern of antisocial behavior and individuals who engage in antisocial behavior in a temporary fashion. Individuals who engage in antisocial behavior consistently across developmental periods are termed life-course-persistent offenders, and Moffitt (1993) states that these offenders are not only consistent across time but also across situations, engaging in a variety of antisocial behaviors in a variety of contexts as new opportunities appear. These individuals may be born with neuropsychological deficits that affect their activity level, temperament, behavioral development and cognitive development. Additionally, these youth are disproportionately raised in disadvantaged environments by parents who may share their child's vulnerabilities. These factors then interact, as the child's characteristics evoke certain parental responses that are toxic to the child. For example, a difficult child may create stress in the family, compromising the parents' already limited skills. The parent's responses to the child then become more negative, thereby exacerbating the child's problems. Individuals who engage in antisocial behavior only during adolescence and young adulthood represent the majority of adolescent offenders and are termed adolescence-limited offenders. Moffitt (1993) points to the prevalence of antisocial behavior in adolescence and suggests that it is normative behavior. These adolescents generally are not consistent in their antisocial behavior across situations (e.g., break rules at the mall with friends but follow rules at school) and can choose antisocial or prosocial behaviors based on which strategy will be more profitable to them in a given situation. Moffitt (1993) argues that these youth engage in these behaviors to achieve perceived maturity, power, and privilege that they are lacking in the extended delay before achieving adult status in modern society. Thus as the privileges of adulthood become available to them legitimately, these individuals no longer engage in antisocial behaviors. In a review of the past decade of research, Moffitt (2003) described considerable evidence for the hypothesis that life-course-persistent antisocial behavior develops from early biological and family-environment deficits and has a greater genetic loading than adolescence-limited antisocial behavior. There is less evidence for the theory regarding the development of the adolescence-limited behavior and there is some evidence that a third type exists consisting of low-level chronic offenders (Moffitt, 2003).

Biopsychosocial models

This approach focuses on the interactions between various influences on the development of antisocial behavior. This model suggests that biological predisposition (genetic influences, prenatal and perinatal complications, executive functioning deficits, etc. as described above) and sociocultural context (exposure to violence, handgun availability, and cultural values such as a culture of honor) influence the parenting practices of the family (e.g., coercive processes, lack of warmth) and peer relationships (particularly peer rejection; Dodge & Pettit, 2003). All four of these factors then have a direct effect on mental processes, which then have a direct effect on the development of symptoms of conduct disorder. Dodge (2003) emphasizes the proximal role of social information processing on the development of antisocial behavior and the commission of antisocial acts. Early childhood experiences lead to the formation of "multidimensional, stable, and unique patterns of processing social stimuli" during middle childhood (Dodge, 2003, p. 253). Dodge (2003) emphasizes that while other causes influence antisocial behavior, the relationship is mediated by the individual's cognitions. An individual's behavior in any given situation is determined by her or his cognitive processes. Perception of threat, hostile attributions, poor ability to evaluate consequences of multiple choices, and other social information processes will make an aggressive or antisocial response more likely.

Summary

These models are quite complementary, each providing important information to understand juvenile offending. Moffitt (1993) attempts to explain the difference between two major types of offenders; coercion theory and the biopsychosocial model do not attempt to address this problem. Coercion theory provides a more detailed explanation of the transactions in the environment that lead to the development of antisocial behavior and has been used to successfully intervene with delinquent adolescents, but the theory does not sufficiently acknowledge the role of genetic transmission of antisocial and aggressive traits. The biopsychosocial model offers an explanation of the proximal cause of antisocial behavior, cognition, which is influenced by factors such as those outlined in the other two theories.

Developmental Pathways to Sexual Coercion

Developmental pathways to juvenile offending suggest that at least some juvenile sex offenders are very similar to juvenile nonsex offenders. Becker and Kaplan (1988) offers a developmental theory of sex offense patterns, suggesting that some juveniles engage in inappropriate sexual behavior in the context of an established pattern of conduct disordered behavior, others commit such acts in the context of a developing paraphilia, and others commit such acts in the context of otherwise normal development. Thus, Becker and Kaplan (1988) predict that some will desist in their offending behavior after a single incident, some will continue breaking the law in a generalized conduct disordered pattern, and others will continue to specialize in sex offending.

The work of Malamuth, Sockloskie, Koss, and Tanaka (1991) and Johnson and Knight (2000) offer another perspective on the development of sexually coercive behaviors. Malamuth and colleagues (1991) tested a model of the development of aggression against women using a sample of male college students. The results suggested distal factors such as parental violence and child abuse are related to the development of delinquency, which in turn influences the development of sexual promiscuity. Sexual promiscuity paired with hostile masculinity predicted sexual aggression in this sample. Hostile masculinity is conceptualized as "dominance motives associated with negative perceptions of women and interpersonal rejection experiences" (Hunter, Figueredo, Malamuth, & Becker, 2003, p. 34).

This model has also been applied to understanding sexual coercion in juvenile sex offenders (Johnson and Knight, 2000). This study found that sexual abuse, misogynistic fantasies, and teenage alcohol abuse each have a direct effect upon sexual coercion. Misogynistic fantasies were directly impacted by sexual compulsivity and hypermasculinity, a construct defined as "attitudes supporting male dominance, both sexually and intellectually, and behaviors such as driving recklessly and relying on violence as a means of dealing with conflict" (Johnson & Knight, 2000, p. 170). Sexual compulsivity was predicted by peer aggression (which was influenced by physical abuse) and sexual abuse. Hypermasculinity was influenced by peer aggression and teenage alcohol abuse, both of which were predicted by physical abuse. This model demonstrates a complicated pattern of distal and proximal effects of experiences and attitudes on sexually coercive behavior across the adolescent's life span. Another study utilizing structural equations modeling to test hypotheses regarding adolescent deviant sexual aggression found that sexual abuse by males and physical abuse by one's father were predictive of sexual aggression whereas attachment to one's mother had a negative relationship with deviant sexual aggression (Kobayashi, Sales, Becker, Figueredo, & Kaplan, 1995). This study provides support for a social learning explanation or an ethological explanation of sexually aggressive behavior, as well as support for the impact of attachment or social control as seen in the relationship with the mother.

Each of these studies provides important information, yet the results are not easily condensed into a single set of findings. In a more recent study, cluster analysis of juvenile sex offenders was conducted based on personality characteristics and sexual attitude/interest variables that tie typology research to developmental research (Hunter, Figueredo, Malamuth, Becker, and Mack, 2003). One cluster appeared to be those youth who were developing paraphilias, based on a high score on the "pedophilic interest" factor; further analysis demonstrated that these youth were more likely than the other clusters to have offended against a male child (Hunter, Figueredo, Malamuth, Becker, and Mack, 2003). Two clusters appeared to fit with Moffit's (1993) description of youth with life-course-persistent antisocial behavior. The youth in these two clusters do not appear to have pedophilic interests but did score highly on "egotistical antagonistic masculinity," "hostile masculinity," and "lifestyle delinquency." Consistent with hypotheses based on Moffit's (1993) typology of juvenile offenders, these juveniles reported: more nonsexual violent behavior in the prior 12 months; higher levels of exposure to male-modeled violent behavior; more substance abuse and exposure to pornography prior to age 12; and were more likely to have a nonsexual arrest record than other clusters. Additionally, the highest percentage of pubescent or post-pubescent female victims was found in these clusters (Hunter, Figueredo, Malamuth, Becker, and Mack, 2003). The final two clusters appear consistent with an "Adolescent Onset, Nonparaphilic" subtype of juvenile sex offenders. Youth in these two clusters had low scores for the three factors on which the life-course persistent group scored highly. These youth can be considered "experimental" in their inappropriate sexual behaviors and are not likely paraphilic or engaged in an antisocial lifestyle (Hunter, Figueredo, Malamuth, Becker, and Mack, 2003). Future research demonstrating that these categories are distinguishable in an independent sample and relating the categories to future behavior would provide important evidence for the validity of this model.

The typology approach has also been applied to prepubescent children who engage in sexually inappropriate behaviors. Pithers, Gray, Busconi, and Houchens (1998) outline an empirically derived categorization system for children with sexual behavior problems. In this study a cluster analysis of the characteristics of 127 6-12 year olds with such behavior problems was conducted. The resulting five categories are sexually aggressive, nonsymptomatic, highly traumatized, rule breaker, and abuse reactive. These groups differ from each other on a number of characteristics such as the predominant gender of group members, internalizing and externalizing problems, age of onset of sexual behavior problem, number of victims, and a variety of other measures (Pithers et al., 1998).

One of the first steps in this developing research area should be replication, demonstrating that different models of the development of inappropriate sexual behavior are consistently supported in different samples. Given that these youth are still developing in a variety of areas (cognitive, moral, social, etc.), classifying juveniles into different types that show consistency over time may prove difficult. Looking at deviant arousal and fantasies may be an important way to distinguish types of offenders. Future work in the area of developmental trajectories and empirically based typologies needs to examine whether the factors that contribute to the development of sexually inappropriate behavior are the same factors that contribute to the maintenance of the behavior. Additional research could explore the implications of these pathways to antisocial behavior and sexually coercive behavior for creating or selecting appropriate interventions.

Assessment

The intervention chosen for any specific individual offender should be based on the needs of that particular juvenile, using an ecological approach focusing on relevant family, peer, and community factors as well as the topography of the criminal acts. Assessment of juveniles must be comprehensive and assess for co-morbid problems, both within the individual and within the family. Interventions should be chosen based on the needs of the child and family as determined by this comprehensive assessment rather than applied in a one size fits all manner. Interventions should also be tailored to the developmental level of the child or adolescent. Assessment of different developmental areas may be conducted in a variety of ways. Moral and social developmental level may be inferred from the behavior and communications of the youth, perhaps, instead of a formal assessment. Other areas may be assessed with specialized instruments.

When selecting any assessment tool, psychologists must consider whether the instrument has demonstrated sound psychometric properties and whether the type of individual you plan to assess was represented in the standardization sample. The ethical guidelines of the American Psychological Association explicitly require that instruments with known validity and reliability for members of the population being tested be used, or psychologists must describe strengths and limitations of testing results (APA Ethics Committee, 2002). Therefore, instruments with proven validity and reliability for the populations being tested should be used. Reliability and validity of tests used should be included in written reports. If those values are not known for a test used, or if a test is selected which was not normed on an appropriate standardization sample, this must be noted in any written report. Clinicians and researchers looking for such information to aid in selecting instruments may find it useful to consult sources such as the Mental Measurements Yearbook. While specific instruments are described below, these are simply examples of appropriate tests and not meant to be comprehensive recommendations.

Biological assessment

If a treatment provider suspects a youth has neuropsychological deficits, that youth should be referred to a professional qualified to assess such problems in children and adolescents specifically. There are numerous neuropsychological assessments designed for use with younger populations, such as the Behavior Rating Inventory of Executive Function (BRIEF, Gioia, Isquith, Guy, & Kenworthy, 2000) and the Wide Range Assessment of Memory and Learning, 2nd edition (WRAML2; Sheslow & Adams, 1990). These instruments are both appropriate for use with children and adolescents ages 5-18, both demonstrate good reliability, and were normed on diverse national samples. These and other tests could be selected by a child neuropsychologist to assess specific suspected deficits.

Cognitive assessment

Cognitive functioning can be assessed using a short instrument designed to estimate IQ, such as the Kaufman Brief Intelligence Test (K-BIT; Kaufman & Kaufman, 1990) or a full test battery such as the Wechsler Intelligence Scale for Children-IV (WISC-IV, Wechsler, 2003). Again, tests must be selected to be appropriate for the age of the juvenile being evaluated, therefore some 16 or 17 year olds may be better assessed using instruments designed for adults, such as the Wechsler Adult Intelligence Scale-III (WAIS-III; Wechsler, 1997).

Sexual assessment

A psychosexual history is a standard and important aspect of the assessment of juvenile sex offenders. This involves interviews of the youth and the parents to gather important information about the juvenile's sexual development. Sexual development may also be assessed with standardized instruments. The Multiphasic Sex Inventory for male adolescents can serve as a structured assessment of a range of sexual behaviors and attitudes (Nichols & Molinder, 2001). For children ages 2 to 12 with sexual behavior problems, the Child Sexual Behavior Inventory (Friedrich, 1997) will provide information regarding whether the child's behavior is truly unusual compared to a normative sample. A scale for use with adolescents, the Adolescent Clinical Sexual Behavior Inventory (ASCBI) is currently in development (Friedrich, Lysne,

Sim, & Shamos, 2004). This instrument is designed for use with adolescents in clinical settings, not juvenile sex offenders. The benefit of such an instrument, however, may lie in its potential to differentiate between juvenile sex offenders with serious sexual problems and those who are more similar to other youth sexually. This would provide important information for treatment planning, as youth who need sexually focused treatment could receive it, while other youth can receive more general interventions for antisocial behavior.

Other areas of interest

Assessment of other relevant information should also be conducted in light of the juvenile's stage of development. For example, specialized instruments for the assessment of depression and anxiety in children are available, such as the Children's Depression Inventory (CDI; Kovacs, 1992) and the State-Trait Anxiety Inventory for Children (Spielberger, 1973). Broader assessment instruments of general psychopathology that may be useful include the Minnesota Multiphasic Personality Inventory for Adolescents (MMPI-A; Butcher et al., 1992), and the Diagnostic Interview Schedule for Children (DISC; Shaffer et al., 1996). Assessment of behavioral and psychological problems can be conducted with such age appropriate instruments like the Child Behavior Checklist and its related teacher-report and child-report forms (Achenbach & Rescorla, 2001). Such instruments should be favored over instruments developed for and normed on adults. Clinicians concerned about the impact of trauma on a child's mental health, a common and legitimate concern in work with juvenile sex offenders, should use an instrument developed specifically for children such as the Trauma Symptom Checklist for Children (TSCC; Briere, 1996).

Treatment

Ideally, treatment or interventions for youth and family members would follow from the particular needs of the youth. Appropriate interventions, based on the current literature, are quite varied and include educating a youth regarding the inappropriateness of his or her behavior and providing individual, group, or family interventions that may be sex offender specific or more general interventions for criminal deviance. As the research on developmental pathways to offending expands, the nature of those needs may become more clear. If, for example, research demonstrates that the main cause of the behavior in some youth is pedophilic interest while in others it is hostile masculinity and lifestyle delinquency, appropriate interventions can be chosen for each. For youth with pedophilic interest, sex offender specific cognitive behavioral treatments may be most effective. For adolescents demonstrating a pattern of problematic forms of masculinity and lifestyle delinquency, treatments shown to be efficacious in the treatment of general juvenile offenders may be most effective.

Currently, the research is not at a point where clinicians can categorize juvenile sex offenders and pick an empirically supported treatment for that type of juvenile. However, given the importance of the family context in the development of antisocial behavior in youth (e.g., Patterson, 2002; Moffitt, 1993), as well as in the development of sexually coercive behavior (Malamuth et al., 1991; Kobayashi et al., 1995), it seems logical to intervene within the family. Other etiological factors, such as neurological impairments, may not be amenable to treatment and therefore are an unlikely target of intervention. Consequently, malleable aspects of the causes of offending behaviors should be targeted. It makes intuitive sense that if we can effect a change in the etiological factors related to non-normative behaviors, we will create a lasting change in the behavior. Additionally, as children and adolescents are still developing on multiple fronts, treating them in their natural environment and treating the environment itself may be more likely to produce sustainable results than an intervention that treats the youth in isolation. By creating change in the youth's natural environment, the environment may be more likely to sustain changes that occur in the juvenile than if the changes occur in the juvenile while the environment is left untreated.

Evidence-based treatments

Two major approaches to the treatment of juvenile offending have been developed that are geared toward changing the juvenile's family system. These approaches try to provide families with the tools necessary to effectively monitor and discipline their children and therefore decrease non-normative behaviors. They give the power to shape the juvenile's behavior back to the family, the most powerful institution in the youth's life. One of these approaches, multidimensional treatment foster care (Chamberlain & Reid, 1998), was developed in connection with the research on the coercion model of the development of delinquency described above (Patterson, 2002). The second, which has been tested with juvenile sex offenders specifically in addition to other juvenile offenders, is multisystemic treatment (Henggeler, Schoenwald, Borduin, Rowland, & Cunningham, 1998). These two treatments were selected from a number of promising approaches for working with family environments. The first, MTFC, was chosen because of its unique approach to treating the family while the juvenile is removed from the home. This unique aspect of the treatment seems to make it a logical choice for juvenile sex offenders as they often must be removed from the home they share with their victim. The second, MST, was selected due to the vast body of research supporting its efficacy and the quality of research demonstrating its efficacy with juvenile sex offenders.

Both approaches teach families about parental monitoring, consistent and effective discipline, and aim to decrease a child's affiliation with delinquent peers. Both approaches make assistance to the family housing the child available 24 hours a day. Both offer individual treatment to the juveniles as well. In MTFC, it is assumed additionally that antisocial behavior wears down the family to the point at which "the family is no longer capable of supervising, mentoring, setting limits, or negotiating with the youngster" (Chamberlain & Reid, 1998, p. 625). Therefore children are removed from the home and placed in a new nuclear family-type setting. Both the foster family and natural family receive treatment. In MST, interventions address the many interacting systems that affect the juvenile's behavior, such as school, family, and peers. Treatment is typically provided in the home, although it is sometimes provided in other community settings. Interventions are drawn from empirically supported treatments to address the specific needs of the family (Henggeler, et al., 1998). While the majority of research on these two approaches has been conducted with non-sex offending samples, they hold great promise for the effective treatment of juvenile sex offenders, given the similarity between the majority of juvenile sex offenders and juvenile non-sex offenders.

Both of these approaches have documented empirical support. Results comparing MTFC to community-based group care (GC) demonstrate that the boys in MTFC were less likely to run away, more likely to complete their programs, spent less time detained, spent more time living with their natural families, and showed larger drops in official criminal referral rates (Chamberlain & Reid, 1998). Compared to an at-risk sample of youth involved in a longitudinal study, both MTFC and GC boys had greater rates of referral before than after treatment. While 41% of MTFC boys had no referrals in the year after treatment, 7% of boys in the GC treatment had no referrals during this period. A follow-up study demonstrated the continued effects of treatment, which influenced outcome through changes in deviant peer association, supervision, discipline, and positive adult-youth relationships (Eddy & Chamberlain, 2000). Treatment effects continued to explain more of the variance in antisocial behavior than pretreatment behavior upon follow-up, an encouraging finding given the predictive power of past behavior.

Research has consistently shown MST to be superior to alternative treatments or to control groups in the treatment of juvenile offenders (e.g., Henggeler, Rodick, Borduin, et al., 1986; Henggeler, Melton, & Smith, 1992; Hengeller, Melton, Smith, et al., 1993; Borduin et al., 1995; Henggeler, Cunningham, Pickrel, Schoenwald, & Brondino, 1996). The effectiveness of treatment appears to be related to improved family functioning (cohesion, parental monitoring) which decreases delinquent peer affiliation and delinquent behavior (Huey, Henggeler, Brondino, & Pickrel, 2000). MST has also been demonstrated to be effective specifically in the treatment of juvenile sex offenders. The research on MST is the most methodologically sound research available in the literature on the treatment of juvenile sex offenders. In a study comparing outcomes of male juvenile sex offenders who were randomly assigned to receive MST or individual treatment (IT), recidivism rates for the MST group and the IT group were 12.5% and 75%, respectively, for sexual recidivism and 25% and 50% for nonsexual recidivism (Borduin, Henggeler, Blaske, & Stein, 1990). The differences between the two groups are significant. The individual therapy group was also found to have a greater frequency of rearrest for sexual offenses, although not for nonsexual offenses. This study had a very small sample, making it difficult to draw definitive conclusions. A follow-up study referenced by Borduin and Schaeffer (2001) that is currently being updated has found that at 8-year follow-up, 12.5% of youth who received MST recidivated sexually compared to 41.7% of those who received treatment as usual. Juveniles receiving MST were also less likely to recidivate nonsexually (29.2%) than those who received treatment as usual (62.5%) (Borduin & Schaeffer, 2001). Juveniles who received MST also demonstrated improvements in school functioning and relating to peers (Borduin & Schaeffer, 2001). MST is one of the most promising treatments available for juvenile sex offenders. This approach demonstrates how effective noninstitutional approaches can be, not just with general juvenile offenders, but with juvenile sex offenders.

The results from studies of MTFC and MST suggest that treatments that focus on family interaction (parental monitoring, consistent discipline, positive relationship with caretakers, and family involvement in decreasing delinquent peer affiliation) hold great promise for successful treatment of juvenile offenders regardless of age, age of onset of antisocial behavior, or severity of antisocial behavior. Other family-focused approaches have also demonstrated efficacy in the treatment of juvenile offenders (e.g., Kazdin & Whitley, 2003; Szapocznik & Williams, 2000). One potential explanation for the superiority of family therapy may be that traditional treatments often rely on the use of peer groups despite the fact that research continuously demonstrates the iatrogenic effects of delinquent peer influence, in treatment or otherwise (e.g., Dishion, McCord, & Poulin, 1999). The success of MST with juvenile sex offenders provides reason to believe that these ecologically based approaches can be effective with this population.

Another successful program for working with juvenile sex offenders, the Sexual Abuse, Family Education and Treatment (SAFE-T) Program, also has a family focus, as seen in the following statement describing the approach: "we believe that the family is an important system in the adolescent's life and that the most significant change will result from family participation, whenever possible" (Worling & Curwen, 2000, p. 968). This treatment utilizes a cognitive-behavioral and relapse prevention framework to intervene at the peer group, individual, and family levels, addressing sexual and nonsexual problems. Participants in the evaluation of this approach were living in a variety of settings, including home, secure-custody facilities, and group homes. The comparison group consisted of youth who received only assessment, received treatment elsewhere, refused treatment, or dropped out of treatment. Significant differences at post treatment assessment were found between the treatment and comparison groups on sexual assault recidivism (5% and 18% respectively), violent nonsexual offenses (19% to 32% respectively), and nonviolent offenses (21% and 50% respectively) (Worling & Curwen, 2000). This is another well-conducted study of juvenile sex offender treatment. Although lacking random assignment, it provides important support for addressing the systemic context of a juvenile sex offender's behavior. While cognitive behavioral and relapse prevention approaches to treating sex offending are based in a different understanding of the etiology of sex offending behavior than the other approaches, the SAFE-T program shares the emphasis on family and other systems in the youth's life. While some participants in the program were living in institutions, this is not necessary for the intervention to be successful nor is it a cost-effective strategy.

Institutions, such as juvenile detention centers and therapeutic group homes, are disconnected from the factors shown to be related to the development of antisocial behavior. Interventions that do not address these factors and treat the juvenile in isolation from his or her usual environment may have less promise for effective long-term change in the behavior. Given the evidence that antisocial and sexually inappropriate behaviors develop in the context of the family and environment, creating change in that environment may be a more effective intervention. In the literature on the treatment of juvenile sex offenders, a number of studies focus on treatment provided in institutional settings. Most of these studies do not include a comparison group (Hagan & Gust-Brey, 2000; Miner, Sieker, & Ackland, 1997; Brannon & Troyer, 1995; Hagan, King, & Patros, 1994; Hunter & Goodwin, 1992; Schram, Milloy, & Rowe, 1991). Only one study of an institutional program included a comparison group and investigated recidivism. Unfortunately, the comparison group consisted of juvenile delinquents who committed nonsex offenses who received the same treatment as the sex offending juveniles, therefore no conclusions about the effectiveness of treatment can be drawn (Brannon & Troyer, 1991). This problem is not limited to investigations of institutional programs; it is a common problem in outcome research for juvenile sex offenders, likely because of special concerns in dealing with this population. Many studies of noninstitutional interventions utilize a pre-test/post-test design to measure outcomes other than recidivism (Kaplan, Morales, & Becker, 1993; Becker, Kaplan, & Kavoussi, 1988; Kaplan, Becker, & Tenke, 1991; Hunter & Santos, 1990) or report recidivism of a treatment group without using a comparison group (Mazur & Michael, 1992). Other studies have shown the superiority of a treatment group to a control group when assessing outcomes other than recidivism (Graves, Openshaw, & Adams, 1992; Weinrott, Riggan, & Frothingham, 1997).

Future research should provide information that will be helpful in making treatment decisions. Randomized, controlled trials of treatments for juvenile sex offenders would provide clinicians with important information regarding what treatments can be considered empirically supported, information not available based on current research. Developments in risk assessment, either through actuarial or typology approaches, may provide information that can be useful in choosing an intervention for a particular youth. If instruments are developed that identify youth at risk for sexual recidivism or nonsexual recidivism, more appropriate treatment decisions could be made. For example, if the typology constructed by Hunter and colleagues (2003) gathers more empirical support, and results in the development of an assessment tool, clinicians may make treatment decisions based on the similarity of a juvenile to a given offender type. These are hypotheses that need to be tested in randomized, controlled studies of treatments that investigate the differential impact of various treatment approaches on each type of juvenile sex offender.

Recommendations

Treatment recommendations can grow from each of the research areas reviewed above. The literature on normal development could be utilized to design interventions to address deficits in the development of juvenile sex offenders. For example, if research demonstrates that juvenile sex offenders are behind in their cognitive and moral development, an intervention could be designed with the goal of helping juveniles move from one stage of development to the next. The connections between cognitive and moral development suggest these two areas could be treated simultaneously. Alternatively, if research shows that predominantly poor social development as a result of poor attachment experiences predicts sex offending, juveniles' families could receive treatment to improve family relationships and juveniles could receive social skills training.

Specific approaches may be more effective given their sensitivity to levels of development. Unfortunately, there are no interventions that repair any neuropsychological deficits. If assessment confirms that a particular child has a neuropsychological impairment, therapists should reevaluate how appropriate their treatment plan is in light of the individual's abilities. When trying to teach empathy to juvenile sex offenders, therapists should consider their cognitive developmental level. If youth appear to be in the concrete operational stage, they may have a hard time with perspective-taking abilities. Special attention should be given to learning the skill of perspective taking before it is applied to learning empathy for victims. In working with pre-pubescent children who have sexual behavior problems, one should consider utilizing a rules-based approach such as that employed by Bonner, Walker, and Berliner (n.d.), where children learn sexual behavior rules. This strategy is appropriate to the moral reasoning ability of youth in the preconventional level of reasoning. In treating youth with sexual behavior problems, it is important to remember that some sexual behavior is normative, and not all expressions of sexuality should be considered deviant and addressed in treatment. Knowledge of normative sexual development will help practitioners to distinguish between normative and inappropriate sexual behavior, and the use of specialized instruments such as the CSBI (Friedrich, 1997) and ACSBI (Friedrich et al., 2004) may help distinguish normative from non-normative behaviors.

Research on developmental pathways to offending can also provide clues into what treatments may be effective. Given the importance of parenting abilities in several theories (Patterson, 2002; Moffitt, 1993), approaches like MTFC and MST seem particularly promising because they attempt to teach families how to manage a child's behavior more effectively. By changing the patterns of reinforcement a child is exposed to, the child's behavior can be reshaped into a more socially desirable pattern. Additionally, programs that do not have access to families to conduct such an intervention should still be aware of the reinforcement contingencies operating on youth under their care. Treatment programs should ensure that youth are not able to achieve their goals through aversive behaviors. Moffitt (1993) suggests that a major difference between life-course persistent offenders and adolescence limited offenders lies in the ability of adolescence limited offenders to choose appropriate behaviors in different situations. This suggests that problem-solving training may be beneficial to youth. This would likely need to include training in producing a variety of options when facing a problem and ways to evaluate the outcome of each option.

Research on developmental pathways to juvenile sex offending may also inform treatment decisions. The importance of hostile masculinity, egotistical antagonistic masculinity, sexual promiscuity, sexual compulsivity, misogynistic fantasies, teenage alcohol abuse, and lifestyle delinquency in the development of sexual coercion suggest that treatments should consider focusing on altering these factors. Treatments proven effective for use with juvenile delinquents may be likely candidates for the treatment of these factors, as other juvenile offenders likely share many of these characteristics. Substance abuse problems should be addressed in treatment programs that service juvenile offenders.

The importance of environmental influences on the development of antisocial behavior, particularly the influence of the family, provides justification for favoring treatment in the community. There is no evidence that institutional treatment is more effective than those noninstitutional programs described. Additionally, given that these juveniles generally do not pose a specific risk to the community in terms of sexual crime (e.g., Caldwell, 2002), incarceration should not be used solely as a strategy to contain sexual risk to the community. Family factors are implicated in each of the developmental pathways discussed, indicating the family's prominent role as one of the most influential factors in the development of sexual and nonsexual offending. Even more important is the fact that family interactions are amenable to treatment. The best designed studies of treatment of juvenile sex offenders to demonstrate reductions in recidivism rates involved family interventions (Borduin et. al., 1995; Borduin & Schaeffer, 2001; Worling & Curwen, 2000). Based on this information, unless substantial new evidence suggests institutional treatment is superior to noninstitutional treatments, the noninstitutional treatments should be favored. Noninstitutional treatments have a stronger theoretical basis, particularly regarding treating etiological factors, and have more empirical support demonstrating effectiveness. Furthermore these programs are typically found to be more cost effective than institutional programs (e.g., Henggeler, 1999).

Conclusion

Over the past two decades, advances have been made in assessing characteristics of youthful sexual offenders and evaluating intervention programs. Future directions should include replication of typology studies, investigation of factors related to sexual recidivism, exploration of the differences in development between juvenile sex offenders and well-adjusted youth, and controlled treatment outcome studies. Juveniles are not the same as adults; therefore adjustments should be made accordingly in assessment and treatment strategies. Treatment and intervention strategies should be devised that are specific to the etiological factors identified in developmental pathway research and to the developmental abilities of the juvenile. Future research should also focus on secondary and primary prevention efforts based on this developmental literature.

References

Achenbach, T.M. & Rescorla, L.A. (2001). *Manual for the ASEBA School-Age Forms & Profiles*. Burlington, VT: University of Vermont, Research Center for Children, Youth, & Families.

American Psychological Association Ethic Committee (2002). Ethical principles of psychologists and code of conduct. *American Psychologist*, 57, 1060-1073.

Becker, J.V. (1998). What we know about the characteristics and treatment of adolescents who have committed sexual offenses. *Child Maltreatment*, 3, 317-329.

Becker, J.V., & Kaplan, M.S. (1988). The assessment of adolescent sexual offenders. In R. Prinz (Ed.), *Advances in Behavioral Assessment of Children and Families*, Vol. 4, 97-118. Greenwich, CT: JAI Press

Becker, J.V., Kaplan, M.S., & Kavoussi, R. (1988). Measuring the effectiveness of treatment for the aggressive adolescent sexual offender. *Annals of the New York Academy of Sciences*, 528, 215-222.

Bonner, B.L., Walker, C.E., Berliner, L. (n.d.). *Treatment manual for cognitive behavioral group therapy for children with sexual behavior problems*. National Center on Child Abuse and Neglect, Grant No. 90-CA-1469. Washington, D.C.: U.S. Department of Health and Human Services.

Borduin, C.M., Henggeler, S.W., Blaske, D.M., & Stein, R.J. (1990). Multisystemic treatment of juvenile sex offenders. *International Journal of Offender Therapy and Comparative Criminology*, 34, 105-113.

Borduin, C.M., Mann, B.J., Cone L.T., Henggeler, S.W., Fucci, B.R., Blaske, D.M., & Williams, R.A. (1995). Multisystemic treatment of serious juvenile offenders: Long term prevention of criminality and violence. *Journal of Consulting and Clinical Psychology*, 63, 569-578.

Borduin, C.M. & Schaeffer, C.M. (2001). Multisystemic treatment of juvenile sexual offenders : A progress report. *Journal of Psychology and Human Sexuality*, 13(3/4), 25-42.

Brannon, J.M. & Troyer, R. (1991). Peer group counseling: A normalized residential alternative to the specialized treatment of adolescent sex offenders. *International Journal of Offender Therapy and Comparative Criminology*, 35, 225-234.

Brannon, J.M. & Troyer, R. (1995). Adolescent sex offenders: Investigating adult commitment-rates four years later. *International Journal of Offender Therapy and Comparative Criminology*, 39, 317-326.

Briere, J. (1996). *Trauma Symptom Checklist for Children, Professional Manual*. Odessa, FL: Psychological Assessment Resources, Inc.

Brown, E.J., & Kolko, D.G. (1998). Treatment efficacy and program evaluation with juvenile sexual abusers: A critique with directions for service delivery and research. *Child Maltreatment*, 3, 362-373.

Butcher, J.N., Williams, C.L., Graham, J.R., Archer, R.P., Tellegen, A., Ben-Porath, Y.S., & Kaemmer, B. (1992). *Minnesota Multiphasic Personality Inventory-Adolescent (MMPI-A), Manual for Administration, Scoring, and Interpretation*. Minneapolis, MN: University of Minnesota Press.

Caldwell, M.F. (2002). What we do not know about juvenile sexual reoffense risk. *Child Maltreatment*, 7(4), 291-302.

Chamberlain, P. & Reid, J.B. (1998). Comparison of two community alternative to incarceration for chronic juvenile offenders. *Journal of Consulting and Clinical Psychology*, 66(4), 624-633.

Cortoni, F. & Marshall, W.L. (2001). Sex as a coping strategy and its relationship to juvenile sexual history and intimacy in sexual offenders. *Sexual Abuse: A Journal of Research and Treatment*, 13(1), 27-43.

Davis, G.E., & Leitenberg, H. (1987). Juvenile sexual offenders. *Psychological Bulletin*, 101, 417-427.

DeLamater, J. & Friedrich, W.N. (2002). Human sexual development. *Journal of Sex Research*, 39, 10-15.

Dishion, T.J., McCord, J., & Poulin, F. (1999). When interventions harm: Peer groups and problem behavior. *American Psychologist*, 54(9), 755-764.

Dodge, K.A. (2003). Do social information-processing patterns mediate aggressive behavior? In: B.B. Lahey, T.E. Moffitt, & A. Caspi (Eds), *Causes of Conduct Disorder and Juvenile Delinquency*. New York: Guilford Press.

Dodge, K.A. & Pettit, G.S. (2003). A biopsychosocial model of the development of chronic conduct problems in adolescence. *Developmental Psychology*, 39(2), 349-371.

Eddy, J.M. & Chamberlain, P. (2000). Family management and deviant peer association as mediators of the impact of treatment condition on youth antisocial behavior. *Journal of Consulting and Clinical Psychology*, 68(5), 857-863.

Friedrich, W.N. (1997). *Child Sexual Behavior Inventory professional manual*. Odessa, FL: Psychological Assessment Resources.

Friedrich, W.N., Lysne, M., Sim, L., & Shamos, S. (2004). Assessing sexual behavior in high-risk adolescents with the Adolescent Clinical Sexual Behavior Inventory (ACSBI). *Child Maltreatment*, 9, 239-250.

Gioia, G.A., Isquith, P.K., Guy, S.C., & Kenworthy, L. (2000). *Behavior Rating Inventory of Executive Function- Manual*. Odessa, FL: Psychological Assessment Resources, Inc.

Gottfredson, M.R. & Hirschi, T. (1990). *A general theory of crime*. Stanford CA: Stanford University Press.

Graves, R., Openshaw, D.K., & Adams, G.R. (1992). Adolescent sex offenders and social skills training. *International Journal of Offender Therapy and Comparative Criminology*, 36, 139-153.

Hagan, M.P. & Gust-Brey, K.L. (2000). A ten-year longitudinal study of adolescent perpetrators of sexual assault against children. *Journal of Offender Rehabilitation*, 31, 117-126.

Hagan, M.P., King, R.P., & Patros, R.L. (1994). The efficacy of a serious sex offenders treatment program for adolescent rapists. *International Journal of Offender Therapy and Comparative Criminology*, 38, 141-150.

Henggeler, S.W. (1999). Multisystemic therapy: An overview of clinical procedures, outcomes, and policy implications. *Child Psychology and Psychiatry Review*, 4(1), 2-10.

Henggeler, S.W., Cunningham, P.B., Pickrel, S.G., Schoenwald, S.K., & Brondino, M.J. (1996). Multisystemic therapy: An effective violence prevention approach for serious juvenile offenders. *Journal of Adolescence*, 19, 47-61.

Henggeler, S.W., Melton, G.B., & Smith, L.A. (1992). Family preservation using multisystemic therapy: An effective alternative to incarcerating serious juvenile offenders. *Journal of Consulting and Clinical Psychology*, 60, 953-961.

Henggeler, S.W., Melton, G.B., Smith, L.A., Schoenwald, S.K., Hanley, J.H. (1993). Family preservation using multisystemic treatment: Long-term follow-up to a clinical trial with serious juvenile offenders. *Journal Child and Family Studies*, 2, 283-293.

Henggeler, S.W., Rodick, J., Borduin, D., Hanson, C., Watson, S., & Urey, J. (1986). Multisystemic treatment of juveniles offenders: Effects on adolescent behavior and family interaction. *Developmental Psychology*, 22, 132-141.

Henggeler, S.W., Schoenwald, S.K., Borduin, C.M., Rowland, M.D., & Cunningham, P.B. (1998). *Multisystemic Treatment of Antisocial Behavior in Children and Adolescents*. New York: Guildford Press.

Huey, S.J., Henggeler, S.W., Brondino, M.J., & Pickrel, S.G. (2000). Mechanisms of change in multisystemic therapy: Reducing delinquent behavior through therapist adherence and improved family and peer functioning. *Journal of Consulting and Clinical Psychology*, 68, 451-467.

Hunter, J.A., Figueredo, A.J., Malamuth, N., & Becker, J.V. (2003). Juvenile sex offenders: Toward the development of a typology. *Sexual Abuse: A Journal of Research and Treatment*, 15, 27-48.

Hunter, J.A., Figueredo, A.J., Malamuth, N., Becker, J.V., & Mack, J. (2003). Juvenile Sex Offender Typology: Final Report. *Submitted to the Office of Juvenile Justice and Delinquency Prevention*, July 7, 2003.

Hunter, J.A. & Goodwin, D.W. (1992). The clinical utility of satiation therapy with juvenile sexual offenders: Variations and efficacy. *Annals of Sex Research*, 5, 71-80.

Hunter, J.A., & Santos, D.R. (1990). The use of specialized cognitive behavior therapies in the treatment of juvenile sex offenders. *International Journal of Offender Therapy and Comparative Criminology*, 34, 239-247.

Ishikawa, S.S. & Raine, A. (2003). Prefrontal deficits and antisocial behavior: A causal model. In: B.B. Lahey, T.E. Moffitt, & A. Caspi (Eds), *Causes of Conduct Disorder and Juvenile Delinquency*. New York: Guilford Press.

Johnson, G.M., & Knight, R.A. (2000). Developmental antecedents of sexual coercion in juvenile sex offenders. *Sexual Abuse: A Journal of Research and Treatment*, 12(3), 165-178.

Kaplan, M.S., Becker, J.V., & Tenke, C.E. (1991). Assessment of sexual knowledge and attitudes in an adolescent sex offender population. *Journal of Sex Education & Therapy*, 17, 217-225.

Kaplan, M.S., Morales, M., & Becker, J.V. (1993). The impact of verbal satiation on adolescent sex offenders: A preliminary report. *Journal of Child Sexual Abuse*, 2, 81-88.

Kaufman, A.S. & Kaufman, N.L. (1990). *Kaufman Brief Intelligence Test- Manual*. Circle Pines, MN: American Guidance Service.

Kazdin, A.E. & Whitley, M.K. (2003). Treatment of parental stress to enhance therapeutic change among children referred for aggressive and antisocial behavior. *Journal of Consulting and Clinical Psychology*, 71(3), 504-515.

Kendall-Tackett, K. (2003). *Treating the Lifetime Heath Effects of Childhood Victimization.* Kingston, NJ: Civic Research Institute.

Kobayashi, J., Sales, B.D., & Becker, J.V., Figueredo, A.J., & Kaplan, M.S. (1995). Perceived parental deviance, parent-child bonding, child abuse, and child sexual aggression. *Sexual Abuse: A Journal of Research & Treatment*, 7, 25-44.

Koenig, A.L., Cicchetti, D., & Rogosch, F.A. (2004). Moral development: The association between maltreatment and young children's prosocial behaviors and moral transgressions. *Social Development*, 13, 97-106.

Kohlberg, L. (1963). The development of children's orientation towards a moral order: I. Sequence in the development of moral thought. *Vita Humana*, 6, 11-33.

Kovacs, M. (1992). *Children's Depression Inventory.* North Tonawanda, New York: Multi-Health Systems.

Malamuth, N.M., Sockloskie, R.J., Koss, M.P., & Tanaka, J.S. (1991). Characteristics of aggressors against women: Testing a model using a national sample of college students. *Journal of Consulting and Clinical Psychology*, 59(5), 670-681.

Marshall, W.L. (1989). Intimacy, loneliness, and sexual offenders. *Behaviour Research and Therapy*, 27, 491-503.

Mazur, T., & Michael, P.M. (1992). Outpatient treatment for juveniles with sexually inappropriate behavior: Program description and 6-month follow-up. *Journal of Offender Rehabilitation*, 18, 191-203.

Miner, M.H., Siekert, G.P., & Ackland, M. (1997). Evaluation: Juvenile sex offender treatment program, Minnesota Correctional Facility-Sauk Centre. Final Report-Biennium 1995-1997, Contract Number 085388011. *Submitted to the State of Minnesota*, July 1997.

Moffitt, T.M. (1993). Adolescence-limited and life-course-persistent antisocial behavior: A developmental taxonomy. *Psychological Review*, 100(4), 674-701.

Moffitt, T.M. (2003). Life-course-persistent and adolescence-limited antisocial behavior: A 10-year research review and a research agenda. In B.B. Lahey, T.E. Moffitt, & A. Caspi (Eds.), *Causes of Conduct Disorder and Juvenile Delinquency*. New York: The Guilford Press.

Nichols & Molinder (2001). *Multiphasic Sex Inventory-II, Adolescent Male Form*. Fircrest, WA: Nichols & Molinder Assessments.

Patterson, G.R. (2002). The early development of coercive family process. In: J.B. Reid, G.R. Patterson, & J. Synder (Eds.), *Antisocial Behavior in Children and Adolescents: A Developmental Analysis and Model for Intervention.* Washington DC: American Psychological Association.

Piaget, J. (2000). Piaget's theory. In: K. Lee (Ed.), *Childhood cognitive development: The essential readings.* Malden, MA: Blackwell Publishers, pp. 33-47.

Pithers, W.D., Gray, A., Busconi, A., & Houchens, P. (1998). Children with sexual behavior problems: Identification of five distinct child types and related treatment considerations. *Child Maltreatment*, 3(4), 384-406.

Shaffer, D., Fisher, P., Dulcan,M.K., Davies, M., Piacentini, J., Schwab-Stone, M.E., Lahey, B.B., Bourdon, K., Jensen, P.S., Bird, H.R., Canino, G., & Regier, D.A. (1996). The NIMH Diagnostic Interview Schedule for Children Version 2.3 (DISC-2.3): description, acceptability, prevalence rates, and performance in the MECA Study. *Journal of the American Academy of Child and Adolescent Psychiatry*, 35, 865-877.

Sheslow, D. & Adams, W. (1990). *Wide Range Assessment of Memory and Learning, 2nd edition- Manual.* Wilmington, DE: Jastak Associates, Inc.

Schram, D.D., Milloy, C.D., & Rowe, W.E. (1991). Juvenile sex offenders: A follow-up study of reoffense behavior. *Report submitted to the Washington State Institute for Public Policy*, September 1991.

Smallbone, S.W. & Dadds, M.R. (2000). Attachment and coercive sexual behavior. *Sexual Abuse: A Journal of Research and Treament*, 13(1), 3-15.

Smallbone, S.W. & McCabe, B. (2003). Childhood attachment, childhood sexual abuse, and onset of masturbation among adult sexual offenders. *Sexual Abuse: A Journal of Research and Treament*, 15(1), 1-9.

Snyder, J. & Stoolmiller, M. (2002). Reinforcement and coercion mechanisms in the development of antisocial behavior: The family. In: J.B. Reid, G.R. Patterson, & J. Synder (Eds.), *Antisocial Behavior in Children and Adolescents: A Developmental Analysis and Model for Intervention.* Washington DC: American Psychological Association.

Spielberger, C.S. (1973). *State-Trait Anxiety Inventory for Child- Manual.* Palo Alto, CA: Mind Garden.

Sroufe, L.A., Duggal, S., Weinfield, N., & Carlson, E. (2000). Relationships, development, and psychopathology. In: A.J. Sameroff, M. Lewis, & S.M. Miller (Eds.), *Handbook of Developmental Psychopathology, 2nd edition*, pp. 75-91. New York: Kluwer Academic/Plenum Publishers.

Szapocznik, J., & Williams, R.A. (2000). Brief strategic family therapy: Twenty-five years of interplay among theory, research, and practice in adolescent behavior problems and drug abuse. *Clinical Child and Family Psychology Review*, 3(2), 117-134.

United States Department of Justice (2003). Uniform crime reports, 2002. Federal Bureau of Investigation. Washington, DC: U.S. Government Printing Office..

Ward, T., Hudson, S.M., Marshall, W.L. (1996). Attachment style in sex offenders: A preliminary study. *The Journal of Sex Research*, 33, 17-26.

Wechsler, D. (1997). *Wechsler Adult Intelligence Scale,3rd* edition. San Antonio, TX: Harcourt Assessment, Inc.

Wechsler, D. (2003). *Wechsler Intelligence Scale for Children, 4th edition*. San Antonio, TX: Harcourt Assessment, Inc.

Weinrott, M.R., Riggan, M., & Frothingham, S. (1997). Reducing deviant arousal in juvenile sex offenders using vicarious sensitization. *Journal of Interpersonal Violence*, 12, 704-728.

Worling, J.R., & Curwen, T. (2000). Adolescent sexual recidivism: Success of specialized treatment and implications for risk prediction. *Child Abuse and Neglect*, 24(7), 965-982.

CHAPTER FIVE

THE POLITICS OF INTERVENTION: FAIRNESS AND ETHICS

ALAN JENKINS

Introduction

An invitational model of engagement and intervention is designed to assist adolescents to find motivation to discover their own preferences and capacities for respectful ways of being and relating. Processes of inquiry are developed to invite young people to make choices in relation to undertaking and investing in an ethical journey towards responsibility and respect of self and others. Such a journey promotes the cessation of abusive practices. This model has been previously described and documented (Jenkins, 1990; 1999).

An invitational model is concerned with enabling readiness for the young man to:

- declare his ethics
- establish his own goals in relation to these stated ethics
- develop his own motivation to achieve them
- examine his ethics and actions as expressions of a preferred
  sense of identity

The young person is invited to make his own decisions, based on his own ethics and preferences, whether or not to undertake a journey towards responsibility and respect. We invite a fundamental shift in focus from the initial investments of young people in accommodation to the wishes of workers or parents and adversarial battles centred around resistance to their influence, to the possibility of choosing to embark upon a personal journey. It must be the young person's journey - one which he has chosen for himself.

The invitational model promotes the discovery and co-construction of a sense of identity, which is informed by qualities and practices of responsibility and respect, as opposed to an identity of "sex offender". The young person is afforded opportunities to develop a sense of self-respect and respect of others as he discovers his own sense of justice, courage, honour, and integrity.

Principles of Intervention

This five principles of intervention; safety, responsibility, accountability, respect, and fairness, have been documented (Jenkins, 1999). It is the principle of fairness which will be explored in this chapter.

The principle of fairness in an unfair world

I have become increasingly preoccupied with the principle of fairness, particularly when working with young people who have been subjected to disadvantage, oppression, or abuse and who have sexually abused others.

In the face of oppressive secrecy, under-reporting, unmitigated suffering, and ineffectual community responses for victims of sexual abuse, it is easy to overlook or underestimate the importance of fairness in working with young people who have abused. Well-intended efforts to prevent abuse and hold young people accountable for their actions have resulted in fairness being the one principle most often overlooked or disregarded in policy and practice, especially with those who have experienced disadvantage.

It can be extremely challenging to find balance in intervention practice which privileges safety, responsibility, and accountability on one hand, along with respect and fairness on the other. However, this is a vital balance. Young people are only likely to find their own motivation and make their own investment in a journey towards ceasing abusive practices, if the context of intervention feels fair.

This chapter concerns dilemmas in intervention, which are at the heart of the principle of fairness:

- How can we intervene with young people who have abused, without reproducing dominant abusive practices?
- How can we respectfully address young people's experiences of disadvantage and victimisation, without sacrificing the priority on responsibility and accountability for their abusive actions?

Political contexts for intervention

When we attempt to assist young people to cease abuse and develop respectful practices, we are conducting our intervention within several contexts that mitigate against a sense of fairness and justice.

Young disadvantaged persons are generally subjected to an ongoing sense of inequity, exploitation, and marginalisation in a hierarchical and competitive dominant culture. They are also more likely to face police and judicial consequences for their abusive acts than those who are privileged and who have access to a wide range of economic, legal and cultural mechanisms and structures to avoid being held accountable for their actions.

Furthermore, young people's needs are frequently sacrificed in western cultures in order to maintain economic structures that support the needs of privileged adults. This is particularly evident when there are policies that lead to high youth unemployment but derogatory and critical attitudes towards young people when they are unable to get work. When children commit serious crimes, they can even lose the protections of their childhood status and be dealt with as adults. When children offend the powers that be, they may do so at the expense of their childhood.

Young people, especially those who are disadvantaged, frequently experience a sense of 'being done to' where their own ethics and beliefs are ignored or overlooked, and any attempts to protest injustice are not taken seriously or suppressed.

For some young people, their only experience of being heard or noticed is when their protest is loud and aggressive, or when it involves violence or "anti-social behaviour". In these circumstances, the violence is often responded to, usually with attempts to suppress or punish the young person. However, the protest is frequently overlooked.

> *Joe, aged sixteen, is a young indigenous man who was court mandated to attend an intervention program to address several sexual assaults upon younger children, in a variety of foster placements. Joe had himself been subjected to severe physical and sexual assaults and neglect in his first nine years of life, after which he endured a series of foster placements where he suffered further sexual assaults on two occasions.*
>
> *Joe is an intelligent and creative young man. However, his experience at school was characterised by enormous difficulties in fitting with conventional educational and teaching structures and strategies. He also experienced racial harassment on a daily basis throughout his school attendance. At school, Joe was subjected to the usual sifting and sorting processes, which serve to separate 'winners' from 'losers' and favour the privileged (Connell, 1993). The myth of equality, which proposes that anyone can succeed if they are bright enough and work hard enough, was inadvertently rubbed in Joe's face.*
>
> *Joe was initially assessed as "learning disordered" but "failed to respond" to remedial intervention strategies. When attempts to help Joe were not helpful, he was described in assessment reports as "possible ADHD" with a suspected "bad attitude." The alternative diagnosis suggested that Joe might be "lazy." As Joe was relegated to the "loser" bin and increasingly harassed at school, he lost interest in the curriculum and protested. His protests were at first ignored and later regarded as, "attention seeking", "provocative", and finally "deliberately disruptive and abusive", when they were associated with violence towards property and other people. Joe's protests were disqualified but his violence and aggression was noticed resulting in a diagnosis of "conduct disorder".*
>
> *Just prior to my first meeting with Joe, he and two "whitefellas" had been charged with the offence of stealing a car. The "whitefellas" were released on bail but Joe was remanded in custody.*

Disadvantaged young men such as Joe are constantly confronted with their lack of privilege. Attempts at protest are regarded as evidence of a lack of respectful ethics.

Joe was regarded as irresponsible and disrespectful; in effect, as a "loser" who "doesn't care about anyone but himself", "has no remorse", etc. These disabling descriptions were supported by documented, professional opinions that detailed and labelled conditions and syndromes, such as "conduct disorder", "empathy deficit", and disorders of "impulse control".

It is hardly surprising that young men like Joe experience a life of "being done to" and eventually come to believe others' judgements that they may in fact be worthless and insufficient. Life becomes a struggle to "become somebody", through the only culturally prescribed means available; violence and aggression (Wexler, 1992). These young men engage in desperate attempts to avoid the "evidence" that highlights a humiliating sense of identity as "loser".

The politics of intervention

In traditional statutory and therapeutic intervention programmes, there has been a tendency to ignore the politics of disadvantage and the politics of adult-child relations, both in theory and practice. Little attention has been paid to examining the abusive behaviour of adolescents within the developmental context of childhood. The political context of power relations concerning a child living in adult-focussed world is often overlooked in psycho-educational curricula, which may have been developed in adult programmes and then imposed upon young people.

Statutory and therapeutic authorities have tended to develop models of intervention in white, middle class contexts and then proceed to impose psychological assessment and intervention procedures upon young people who may live in extremely disadvantaged and vastly different circumstances.

This raises a major dilemma

What does it mean if we expect young people to be respectful and understanding of their victim's experiences and feelings (and refrain from imposing unwanted ideas and practices upon others), but we fail to understand or take account of their own experiences of disadvantage and deprivation (and attempt to impose our own ideas and practices upon them)?

We can actively serve to promote fairness and provide opportunities for atonement, restitution and restoration. Alternatively we can collude with a kind of "justice" that masks a form of colonisation that promotes confrontation, correction, and retribution. Colonisation practices may be well-intended but always lead to the inevitable consequences of protest and insurrection or passive accommodation.

If a young person experiences our intervention as a form of colonisation, with accompanying practices of psychological invasion and benevolent bullying, we only serve to provide yet another experience of "being done to" which is very familiar to most disadvantaged young people. The effect on identity is to confirm the young person's marginalised state and a sense of judgement that he really is a worthless "loser".

Most disadvantaged young people have learned to accommodate and have survived invasions and violations that will have involved much more sinister tactics than those utilised in our interventions. However, each experience of "being done to" adds to the sense of marginalisation and to a sense of identity, which may serve to foster greater risk of harm to self and others.

What is Fairness?

The invitational model draws upon Foucault's descriptions of power and Derrida's concepts of justice (Ransom, 1997; Larner, 1999).

Fairness is an ongoing ethical responsibility which aspires to the establishment of "a non-violative relationship to the other" which respects and sustains the other's difference and singularity. Such a relationship fosters critique and subversion of dominant power relations.

Through fairness, we aspire to enact "a power that is non-hegemonic"; one that does not align itself with dominant power relations; one "that allows the other to 'say everything'… to think their own thoughts, to have their own feelings… to write their own narrative." This might be regarded as a political "position taking" towards discourses of power which aligns itself with the voices of the marginalised and the many (Larner, 1999).

The ethics that inform the concept of fairness in an invitational model, are based on a requirement for consideration of others needs and feelings, rather than appeals to universal concepts of 'human rights' or 'equal opportunity'. Derrida's concept of 'hospitality' requires those with privilege to recognise and attend to the needs and feelings of those who may be experiencing disadvantage (Derrida & Dufourmantelle, 2000). Fairness requires an ongoing critique of power relations in which the personal and political are intimately connected.

Establishing a context for fairness – responsibility overload

What does it mean to talk about fairness when working with a disadvantaged young person who already has a history of marginalisation in a dominant culture that fosters inequality and injustice? We cannot reverse injustices or make the world entirely fair for young people. However, if we begin to promote fairness in our work and attend to the various political contexts, within which our interventions are situated, we can challenge and subvert the effects of dominant power relations. We can establish safe and enabling environments for our work, which will foster responsibility and respect.

Two major themes of inquiry are of vital significance in establishing a context for fairness:

- attending to ethics in the face of adversity
- honouring young people's protest

I work with many disadvantaged young men who have experienced considerable abuse, oppression, and neglect and who feel a strong sense of injustice in their own lives. Most of these young men have never felt that anyone has ever been genuinely interested in understanding their experiences of injustice, abuse, and victimisation-let alone appreciating their capacities for survival and ethical action. Young Aboriginal Australians and other economically disadvantaged youth in intervention pro- grammes have experiences of disadvantage and marginalisation that are seldom understood or acknowledged. These young men often experience a profound sense of injustice and may have been subjected to a range of extreme abuses, yet there is an expectation that they will address their own abusive behaviour. This expectation often constitutes a set of unreasonable and unrealistic expectations and, in an invita- tional model, is referred to as responsibility overload. The following dilemmas relate to responsibility overload:

- • What does it mean for a context of fairness if we expect young people to take responsibility for and understand the effects of their abusive behaviours, if others are not prepared to take responsibility for or understand the effects of abuses done to the young person?
- • To what extent might we expect young people to take steps that others have never been prepared to take on their behalf?

The issue of responsibility overload is pivotal in establishing a context for fairness. Responsibility overload exists whenever we hold unrealistic or unfair expectations of the young man. We may unrealistically expect him to provide something that has never been provided for him, such as:

- • acknowledge responsibility for his actions
- • demonstrate consideration or understanding of other's
- • demonstrate remorse or shame
- • take for granted any ethical actions undertaken by the young person in the face of extreme adversity
- • overlook current or past injustices experienced by the young person, whilst encouraging him to face responsibility for his own unjust actions
- • overlook or disrespect significant cultural values, relevant to the young person, whilst at the same time expecting him to adopt our cultural values

Establishing a context for fairness - ethics in the face of adversity

I am continually astonished and amazed at the tenacity and determination of my young clients to hold on to respectful ethics and preferences in the face of what seems to be overwhelming injustice and oppression.

Before I had even met Joe, I was informed that he had sexually assaulted five young children in several foster care families. I was furnished with a history of his violent and abusive actions. This history was accompanied by attributions which included: "He is bad"; "He has an evil mind"; "He doesn't care about anyone but himself".

Over time I learned about an appalling variety of abuses and injustices to which Joe had been subjected throughout his sixteen years of life. He had been physically and sexually abused by two of his uncles and some older children in his fist nine years of life. Joe was frequently neglected as a little child and learned to look after his siblings and his mother, while he "grew himself up". He had been subjected to racist harassment and taunts throughout his life, in school, and a variety of other settings. Joe was removed from his home and community at the age of ten and placed in a series of non-aboriginal foster placements, in two of which he was further sexually abused. For six years, he was deprived of contact with his own family, community, and culture.

However, after only a few conversations with Joe, I discovered that he felt intense shame about his sexual assault of several little children. When I inquired about this, he showed some recognition of the fact that these children had looked up to him and that he had betrayed their vulnerability and trust.

How could such realisations be made, given the descriptions of "empathy deficit" and "conduct disorder" which had been documented in his psychological assessments. It occurred to me that perhaps he had never been observed in a context where empathy or compassion might be expressed or noticed.

I began to wonder:

> *How is it that Joe is able to begin to consider his own abusive actions and their consequences, the hurts he had caused others, when he has felt and continues to feel so much hurt himself?*

> *How was Joe able to care for and protect his mother and siblings, as a little child, when he experienced so little protection and care and so much neglect himself?*

> *What does this say about Joe in the face of the adversity he has experienced?*

I noticed that few others seemed interested in these dilemmas. Most tended either to distrust Joe's expressions of remorse or to take them for granted: "Well he damn well should feel ashamed for what he has done, he is a sex offender", "Anyway, we don't want him in our school; he has a bad attitude".

Few opportunities are afforded to enable young men like Joe to find a fair and respectful space to consider, let alone express ethics that might support a capacity for empathy, compassion, or caring and concern. These young men lose sight of their ethical beliefs and values and have few means to be able to incorporate them into a sense of respectful identity. When disabling stories and labels concerning empathy deficits, conduct disorder, and cycles of abusive behaviour, are privileged in considerations about young men like Joe, they become the influences that inform his sense of identity.

Addressing responsibility overload – individual level

Young people most often present to an intervention programme as the result of external coercion, often following police intervention and with a justice system mandate. Disadvantaged young people, with a history of "being done to", come to intervention programmes accompanied by a selection of disabling descriptions, labels, diagnoses and stories. The young person may anticipate his time in the intervention programme as, yet another chapter in the history of his experience of injustice and marginalisation. In this context, he can appear extremely irresponsible and unmotivated.

However, despite all appearances and suggestions to the contrary, many of these young people are struggling with a pervasive sense of shame in relation to their abusive actions, and are engaging in desperate attempts to avoid this experience. Attributions of worthlessness, insufficiency, and the risk of further entrenchment of a sense of identity as a "loser," are at the centre of these struggles.

It is both logical and sensible that the young person is preoccupied with survival and self defence at this time. We should not be surprised when our initial inquiries, regardless of how much they might be informed by motives of caring and concern, elicit hostile or avoidance reactions.

> *Jake (aged fifteen) is attending his fist appointment following a court-mandate, after having raped his six year-old half sister repeatedly over an eighteen month period of time, beaten her up following her disclosures and later beaten up his mother. On introduction, he rolls his eyes upwards and exclaims, "Whatever!"*

> *Mike (aged fourteen) exclaims, "This is all bullshit!" despite having partially acknowledged repeated rape of his five year old cousin.*

> *Steve (aged fourteen) looks sullen and resentful whilst frequently glancing at his watch. He begins to challenge, "When is this gonna be finished? I've gotta meet my mates in half an hour."*

These responses, when taken at face value, provide a powerful and challenging invitation for a therapist to confirm disabling descriptions and stories about the young person - to regard him as deficient in ethics of empathy, care and concern. In these circumstances, it can be difficult to decline the invitation to adopt coercive practices of confrontation and challenge.

> *Jake had partially acknowledged the abuse of his half sister but greatly minimised its nature and impact. "I dunno what the fuss is about. It didn't hurt her. Why do I have to come here? This sucks!"*

> *Jake's mother is beside herself with worry. She laments, "He doesn't care. He just goes on like nothing has happened. He's turning out just like his (abusive) step-father."*

We can easily "prove" the disabling premise that young men like Jake have no remorse, are conduct disordered, and are indeed turning out just like their abusive parent, by replicating the violence they witnessed or to which they were subjected. We may even inadvertently encourage these young men to believe such disabling ideas themselves.

In order to address and prevent responsibility overload, it is vital that we maintain openness and curiosity regarding the possibility that the young person may have and may be open to embrace respectful ethical preferences. This requires that we ensure that we do not expect anything of the young person which we are not prepared to provide for him. To practice fairness, we must at all times be engaged with the following dilemmas:

> *How can we ensure that any of the young person's experiences of injustice are acknowledged and appreciated, before we establish expectations about his own unjust behaviour?*

> *How can we appreciate and acknowledge the young person's experiences of injustice and marginalisation, without sacrificing the focus on responsibility whereby these experiences are regarded as excuses or justifications for abusive behaviour?*

Confrontation and coercion may have their place in police and some statutory contexts, where arrest, stopping a crime and ensuring the safety of individuals in immediate danger, are primary considerations. However, unsolicited coercion has no helpful place in therapeutic intervention and should be regarded as a power play, which serves to reproduce and promote abusive and disrespectful practices.

It is often helpful to respond to hostile or avoiding reactions with inquiries about fairness:

> *"I know you have been told by the court that you have to come here, but has anyone taken the trouble to find out what you think or how you see the whole situation?"*

> *"You have got people trying to tell you what to do or what to think, but is anyone bothering to listen to you or find out what you think?"*

This type of inquiry may be broadened to a wider context:

> *"I have a hunch that for a lot of your life you have probably had heaps of unfair things pushed on to you, with people trying to tell you what to do and think, but nobody taking the trouble to listen to what you think or care about what you feel?"*

> *"I imagine that coming here probably feels like just another unfair thing that has been pushed on to you?"*

This can culminate in a formal proposal:

> *"You have to come here. You have no choice in that. But you don't have to put up with being pushed around or made to do things that are unfair."*

> *"I have no right to try to make you talk about things you don't want to talk about."*

> *"In fact, there is no way I'd even think about talking to you about what happened with your sister, if I didn't understand what is important to you and where you stand."*

> *"You have the right to speak out or refuse to do or talk about anything that feels unfair. I will respect this and butt out if you do speak out. You should not have to put up with anything that is unfair in here."*

These inquiries and proposals must be complemented with statements of the purpose of intervention in order to establish fair and respectful reasons for conducting the interviews in the first place. The broad aims of intervention can be stated in an open and up front manner. I generally make repeated statements of purpose in a general and non-confrontational manner in the early interviews:

> *"You are here because of what happened with your sister. My job is to try to help find ways to put things right which are fair for you, fair for your sister and fair for your mum."*

These statements of purpose can be made increasingly specific with gradual shifts in naming practices from, "what happened with your sister," towards, "hurting your sister" and eventually "abusing your sister", as engagement with the young person allows for readiness to assume greater levels of responsibility.

As the purpose of intervention becomes established, the priority of fairness is gradually developed and extended by raising a series of basic fairness dilemmas that expose and highlight potential responsibility overloads:

> *"Other people are worried about what you have done to your sister. They are expecting you to stop and think about unfair things you have done to her, but how much have you had to put up with things that have been heaps unfair to you in your life?"*

> *"How much has anyone bothered to stop and think about what you have been through and what it has been like for you?"*

> *"How fair would it be to expect you to face up to what you did and think about your sister's feelings, if nobody takes the trouble to stop and think about what you have been through and what it has been like for you?"*

These forms of inquiry state basic fairness dilemmas and serve to name responsibility overloads which may be active in the context of therapeutic intervention, family, and community.

When a responsibility overload is named, potential injustices are anticipated and means can be found to avoid perpetrating further unfairness. The young person can be invited to speak out or protest, if processes are felt to be unfair, thus promoting a form of legitimising and honouring of protest. Workers can unite with the young person to remain vigilant in identifying and taking stands against unfairness.

In this way, the young person's hostile or avoiding behaviour may be regarded as a form of legitimate protest that is respected rather than disqualified or pathologised.

When protest is encouraged in a context of fairness, young people seldom use or take advantage of these inquiries to justify or excuse their own abusive behaviour. Protest becomes directed towards genuine injustices rather than being wasted through impotent avoidance practices. The young person may eventually be invited to protest in ways that are increasingly more direct and less aggressive or harmful to others.

Discovering and Naming Ethics

At the heart of the context for fairness and respect, is a requirement for us to be open to believe in the young person's capacity to discover his own respectful ethics, evaluate his own behaviour, and plan respectful actions that accord with his ethics. If we underestimate this capacity, intervention is likely to become highly colonising and disqualifying of the young person's sense of integrity and agency. Such underestimation serves only to provide yet another example of "being done to" and an implicit judgement of the young person's insufficiency and worthlessness.

If we remain carefully attuned and vigilant in the anticipation of responsibility overloads, whilst promoting a context for fairness, the young person's ethics readily become evident and accessible.

When disadvantaged young people experience a pervasive sense of injustice, the ethic concerning protest against injustice is often accessible for discovery and naming. When the young person has little experience of others being interested in his feelings and needs, a simple inquiry may assist in the respectful naming of and invitation to practice protest:

> *"Do you believe in speaking out/standing up for yourself, when something is unfair?"*

> *"Will you stand up for yourself if I say or do anything that's unfair?"*

The young person is invited to engage in a legitimate activity to challenge injustice, rather than submit to suppression or pathologising of his protest. These inquiries may be broadened to a wider context:

> *"Have you had to look out for yourself/stand up for yourself a fair bit in your life?"*

> *"Have you had to put up with unfair things a lot?"*

> *"Has anyone stood by you/stood up for you, or have you had to handle this on your own?"*

Many disadvantaged young people gradually reveal a painful but courageous story of survival in which they learned to "look out for themselves" or "grow themselves up," with little support and in the face of considerable adversity.

The ethic of protest against injustice can be explored in conversation about challenges the young person has faced or is facing. Initial contexts for this inquiry, which may feel safe enough to speak about, can include living out of the family, living in residential care, police intervention, and at school. Contexts that relate to being subjected to abuse and exploitation, or family betrayal and neglect, may require a level of trust in engagement, before they are accessible by inquiry. Opportunities for inquiry often arise quite serendipitously:

Jake was describing an incident at school in which he had observed a teacher hitting a student in a classroom with a steel-edged ruler. Jake walked up to the teacher and took the ruler from his hand. The teacher was outraged and sent Jake to the principal's office. The principal chastised Jake for disrespectful behaviour towards the teacher (and for possessing cigarettes found whilst checking Jake's pockets). It was evident that no one noticed or enquired about Jake's motivation for challenging the teacher.

I was unable to resist, "Why did you do that, Jake?"

He looked surprised, perhaps regarding this as a stupid question. I persisted until Jake eventually explained, "A teacher can't do that to a kid."

I enquired further as to why not? Jake again looked surprised but eventually explained his actions as being informed by his understanding that the teacher had breached a duty of care and had violated a smaller person who was less powerful and in a vulnerable situation. It was evident that Jake, like many young people, had engaged in few conversations about his ethics, especially with adults.

I obtained Jake's permission to make further inquiries:

"How much do you believe in sticking up for other people who are being treated unfairly?"

"How important is it to you to stick up for the little guy, if he is being picked on by a bigger person?"

These inquiries can later be broadened in a wide range of contexts which can include family circumstances involving abuse and neglect. Many disadvantaged young people have, as younger children, witnessed and experienced severe domestic violence:

"How much did your father/stepfather stand by you and how much did you have to look out for yourself?"

"What sort of things did your family have to put up with?"

"What sort of things did your mum have to put up with?"

"How much did (your stepfather) hurt your mum and your family?"

"Did you worry about your mum?"

"How much did you worry about your mum?"

These initial inquiries are best focussed upon other family members and not the young person himself, who may not feel ready to acknowledge high levels of hurt and fear that he experienced through abuse directed towards him personally. However, when these inquiries do focus upon others within the family, it often emerges that the young person was "worried sick" about his mother or other family members. He may even have tried to stand up for or protect others in the family. Such experience and action may begin to highlight qualities such as caring, concern, loyalty, and protectiveness as valued ethics.

However, the meaning of his experiences must be canvassed and clarified in order to avoid the possibility of colonising his ethics with our labels, descriptions, and good intentions. This is not an exercise in "reinforcing the good" in others according to our standards. The young person must be invited to make meaning of his own experience, name the ethics it reflects, and decide what value he places upon them:

> *"When did you first try to stick up for your mum?"*

> *"How did you manage that when you were only a little guy of seven years old?"*

> *"Why do you think you did that?"*

> *"How did you manage to think about other people's feelings when you were heaps scared and hurt yourself?"*

> *"When you look back at yourself then, what kind of person do you see?"*

> *"What does this say about you?"*

> *"How does it fit with what you believe in?"*

Inquiries that employ concepts of connection through difference, can help to subvert the oppressive "inter-generational cycle of violence" ideology which proposes that the young person is acting like (and is perhaps similar to) the older abusive person. These inquiries highlight differences in thinking and action that have previously been developed by the young person but may have been lost or suppressed along the way:

> *"When you saw your stepfather hurting people smaller than him, what did you think?"*

> *"Do you think your stepfather ever took the trouble to stop and think about what he was doing to you guys/how much he was hurting your family?"*

> *"How did you manage to see what he wasn't seeing when you were only a little kid?"*

> *"Who understands that you were trying to stand up against unfairness in your family?"*

The young person can be gradually invited to clarify and name his ethics:

> *"What is it that you were standing up for in your family?'"*

> *"What is it that you believe in, that you were fighting for back then?"*

These initial conversations about protest against injustice can appear somewhat alarming, when a young person begins to describe ways that he has stood up for himself or stood up for other people, using violence or unjust behaviour to achieve this goal. Young people will frequently describe terrible acts of vengeance and threaten to enact them upon an abusive adult who has caused considerable hurt and pain towards themselves and their families.

It is helpful to decline the invitation to become alarmed and corrective in response to these violent descriptions, and to focus instead upon the young person's motivation and intent. Then we can appreciate the ethics that he has been struggling to enact. There will be plenty of opportunity for the young person to discover preferred, respectful means of protest at a later time, if the concepts of fairness and protest are legitimised and honoured in the present.

Exploring Injustices Without Sacrificing Responsibility

If intervention is conducted in the spirit of fairness, it can enable a responsible exploration of the nature and impact of injustices and challenges experienced by the young person, as well as the abuse he has perpetrated. If inquiry about injustice and responsibility overload is conducted alongside inquiry about ethics, it is unlikely that the young person will begin or continue to regard injustices as an excuse for his own abusive acts. In fact, minimisation and justification are more likely to have proffered when we act coercively or try to impose our ethics upon the young person.

When the young person begins to publicly name injustices that he has experienced, perhaps for the first time, further opportunities to name responsibility overload will arise. For example, a young person who has witnessed or experienced abuse from a parent or trusted adult may experience a strong sense of injustice, particularly when the adult has not been held accountable for his actions. It is vital that we name and highlight such overloads:

> *"Was your step father ever expected to face up to what he did to your family?"*

> *"How fair is it that you are expected to do something that he never had to do?"*

We may never be able to redress such a fundamental injustice, but what does it mean if we fail to acknowledge its existence and potential impact?

Responsibility overloads can be identified and named and respectful ethics discovered and highlighted. It is amazing and wondrous that these ethics can exist and inform behaviour despite the effects of extreme injustice and adversity. They have a history which demands exploration. Throughout our inquiries, we can honour ethics in the young person's thinking and behaviour and thus ensure that we do not take their existence for granted. In this way, ethical ideas and practices are co-constructed, developed, and strengthened throughout the intervention processes. This form of inquiry is called ethics or honour in the face of adversity.

"Does anyone understand what you were trying to do when you were sticking up for and trying to protect your mum/your brother?"

"People are worried about the hurt that you did to your sister but do they also realise the ways you tried to care for and protect people in your family?"

"How have you managed to think about other people's feelings when you have had so much unfairness and hurt done to you?"

"What does this say about you and what you believe in?"

"How does this fit with who you are as a person – your true colours?"

Establishing a context for fairness - naming abuse

As ethics are highlighted and honoured in the face of adversity, and injustices and responsibility overloads are named, the young person will usually begin to experience a great deal of dissonance. On one hand there is a gradual appreciation of ethics but, on the other, increasing discomfort in relation to awareness of having engaged in abusive behaviours that do not accord with these ethics. The young person will inevitably experience an increased sense of shame from within, rather than a sense of being shamed. Awareness of shame can serve to create an enabling context for him to begin to address his abusive behaviour.

If the young person has already made a limited or partial acknowledgement of abusive actions, enquiries may be initiated in the spirit of "inquiry of ethics" in the face of adversity:

'"How did you manage to start to face up to what you did to your sister?"

"What were you up against?"

"What stopped you from running away from it and calling your sister a total liar?"

"What did it take for you to start to face the truth?"

"How does this direction fit with the person you really are?"

When the young person begins to consider that his actions may have hurt others, these inquiries may help to further ethical realisations and create a respectful context for the acknowledgement of abusive actions:

"How are you managing to even begin to think abut the hurt you did to your sister when you are hurting so much about all the things that have been done to you?"

"How are you able to care about your sister's feelings when you have been through so much hurt yourself?"

"What does this say about you?"

"How does it fit with the kind of person you really are?"

Such a focus on what the young person is ready and able to acknowledge, whilst clearly labelling it as a beginning, establishes a radically different form of inquiry, compared with traditional attempts to challenge and confront the young person to be completely truthful and make full acknowledgments, right from the beginning. These enquiries highlight our refusal to participate in responsibility overload, by inviting the appreciation of ethical actions carried out in the face of adversity and never taking them for granted.

In fact, we find it more helpful to encourage the young person not to acknowledge full details until he knows that it is safe to do so:

> *"If there is more truth to come out (and there usually is) you would be nuts to face it:*
>
> *unless you knew for sure that it would*
> *- help the kid you did it to*
> *- and help you.*
>
> *unless you knew for sure that*
> *- it wouldn't be used against you*
> *- it wouldn't be used to put you down or make you feel small."*

"How would you know whether it was safe to speak out?"

A broader context for fairness - caregivers

Caregivers, including parents, extended family members, foster carers, residential care workers, and mentors, have a major influence on the young person's sense of fairness and justice in his everyday life. The nature of participation helps determine how effectively responsibility overloads are addressed and the successful establishment of a context for fairness.

When the parents are accessible, it is vital that we attempt to engage their ongoing participation in the young person's intervention program.

Parental attributions concerning the young person's abusive behaviour are often highly restraining for his journey towards respect:

> *"He doesn't care about what he has done."*
>
> *"He is turning out just like his father."*
>
> *"He's made his bed, now he can lie in it."*

Such attributions inadvertently contribute to responsibility overloads and underestimate the young person's capacity for ethical actions. They reiterate disabling ideas and promote selective perceptions and the biased collection of evidence to support them.

Caregivers can be invited to help in the acknowledgment and naming of injustices and challenges faced by the young person, along with maintaining expectations that he address his abusive behaviour. When they notice and honour the young person's early glimmers of ethical ideas and practices, caregivers can provide an appreciative audience to help him make his own meaning of the steps that he takes in his journey towards respect.

A great deal of careful attention must be paid to engagement with caregivers. Many parents will feel a degree of culpability in relation to the young person's abusive behaviour. Consequently they may hold fearful expectations that professional people will blame them or hold them responsible for the young person's actions.

Peter, aged fourteen, made a partial acknowledgement that he had sexually abused his seven-year-old cousin. However, he was described by police as "sneaky" and "evasive" and appeared highly distracted and avoiding of responsibility in our initial interviews. It emerged that Peter's father, Tom, had been and still was acting in a highly abusive manner towards Peter, particularly in his attempts to discipline his son. The implications for responsibility overload were obvious:

> *"What would it mean if we encouraged Peter to address his abusive behaviour but overlooked his father's abusive behaviour?"*

> *"What would it mean of we expected more of Peter than of his father?"*

This raised an enormous challenge. Peter's father appeared unwilling to participate, having indicated that he was "disgusted" with his son, whom he regarded as having 'made his bed and now must lie in it'. "He's on his own now."

Careful attempts to engage Tom's participation ran parallel with the process of engagement with Peter. Tom also felt an intense sense of injustice in his own life. Furthermore, he had experienced welfare attempts at intervention in the past as intrusive and disrespectful. However, it became apparent that, whilst Tom practiced a highly controlling and punitive style of parenting, he had held hopes of having a relationship with his son that would be vastly more satisfying than his own relationship with his father. Whist establishing a context for fairness, Tom was invited to reconsider a frustrated desire to "be mates" with Peter and to acknowledge the possibility of taking on a "real" leadership role for his son, by demonstrating responsibility in addressing behaviours that had been hurtful to Peter.

> *"What would it mean for Peter to know that his father feels ashamed about hurting his son?"*

> *"What would it mean for Peter if his father took steps to make amends for the hurtful behaviour?"*

> *"What example would Tom be setting for Peter in his journey to face his own abuse?"*

> *"Where might this lead their relationship in terms of 'being mates,' earning his son's admiration, and respect as opposed to his fear, etc."*

Once Tom had begun to participate actively and responsibly by acknowledging and addressing his abusive behaviour towards both his son and his partner, Peter quickly became more focused and took leaps forward in addressing his own abusive behaviour.

A context for fairness, without the highly restraining and burdening influences of responsibility overloads, greatly frees up the young person to discover his capacity to move forward in his journey.

Once Jake had begun to identify and name ethics relating to caring, loyalty, and protectiveness in his relationships with his mother and siblings - ethics which contrasted greatly with his sexual and physical violence towards these family members - I began to enquire about his readiness to participate in a meeting with his mother which might further address responsibility overload:

> *"Does your mum know, how much your worried about her and your family? What it was like for you when your stepfather was in your family? How you tried to stand up for yourself and your family?"*

> *"Do you think she would be interested in learning about what it's been like for you?"*

> *"How fair would it be to expect you to talk about what you did to your mum and your step sister, but not talk about what it's been like for you?"*

These inquiries were complemented with inquiries about Jake's readiness to let his Mum know about some of his initial realisations regarding his abuses within the family:

> *"Does your mum know that you feel bad about what you did to your sister? You realise you hurt your sister heaps? Would she still think that you think that it wasn't such a big deal?"*

> *"What difference would it make to let her know the truth?"*

> *"Are you ready to let her know?"*

> *"What tells you that you are ready?"*

> *"How does this fit with the kind of person you are?"*

Inquiries which establish readiness are vital:

> *"Do you think your mum made the right decision in refusing to put up with any more of your step father's violence?"*

160

"Do you think she should put up with any more violence from anyone?" "Even from her son?"

"Does your mum know that you feel bad about what you did to her or, does she only know that you think she was unfair?"

"What difference would it make to let her know the truth?"

"Are you ready to let her know?"

Meetings were also being conducted with Jake's mother, Jill, to engage her participation and determine her readiness to address responsibility overloads that might restrain Jake's progress in his journey. To be ready to assist her son, Jill needed first to reclaim her ethics about parenting, discover the strength and caring she used in surviving and protesting against abuse within her family, and recognise her own competence. Jill began to challenge a restraining view of herself as "weak" and defeated.

She then felt ready to talk with Jake about their survival of years of tyranny within the family and the qualities and strength that each had employed to make it through such ordeals. Jill was then invited to appreciate the potential responsibility overload, from a position of strength rather than insufficiency and guilt:

"Does Jake know how much you realise about what he has been through?"

"What would happen if Jake thought we were expecting him to face his abusive behaviour and the effects on his sister, but felt that no one had understood or acknowledged the challenges that he has been through himself?"

In three emotionally moving meetings, Jill and Jake were able to describe and name terrible injustices perpetrated by Jake's stepfather, along with a variety of loyal and protective actions that were aimed at providing mutual support and survival throughout this time. They were able to provide for each other, some of their realisations about the impact of these injustices and abuses upon each other and they started to acknowledge ways they felt that they had let each other down.

At one point, Jill achieved a clear and spontaneous realisation that she had indeed let Jake down. She told him that she could see how he had been desperately worried and trying to protect her, whilst only a little boy, when it was really her job to protect him. She declared the level of injustice that she perceived in this realisation. In the midst of tears and hugs, Jake was able to express in a meaningful way to his mother, his remorse about having hurt his sister and his mother, for the first time.

Acknowledgements such as this, whilst enabling the young person and his parents to reclaim a sense of connection and closeness, also have a significant effect on relieving the huge burden associated with the responsibility overload, in which he is expected to address injustices he has perpetrated without the benefit of having others address injustices he has suffered. The implications of this freeing up can be substantial.

One week after the third meeting between Jake and his mother, Jake telephoned me to make an urgent time to meet. When we met, he disclosed that he had also sexually assaulted one of his sister's friends who had been in the house for a sleepover several years back. This was the first time that this abuse had been disclosed. Jake's disclosure could be honoured because it furthered his integrity and enabled appropriate notification and responses to be made for the younger child.

When responsibility overload is effectively addressed, it often results in a sense of liberation or freedom from the burden of unfairness which the young person may have carried for a considerable period of time and which has consistently provided an obstacle in his journey towards respect. His capacity for respectful action will be opened up and become more accessible.

When parents, caregivers, residential care workers etc. are invited to: a) acknowledge injustices and challenges faced by the young person; b) acknowledge ethical stances and achievements they have observed; c) hear further evidence of ethical stances and achievements that others have observed with the young person, and make meaning of these stances and achievements, in the face of injustice and in context of the young person's sense of identity, they play a vital role in reducing the impact of responsibility overloads and in co-constructing and broadening ethical stances which inform a respectful sense of identity.

In this context, caregivers generally feel that they are part of the solution rather than part of the problem. The initial unhelpful attributions give way to respectful efforts to assist the young person to define his own ethical qualities. Caregivers provide an audience for honouring respectful ethics and behaviour.

Developing a broader context for fairness – peer group and culture

The young person's relationships with other young people provide a context in which the nature and influence of power hierarchies, and dominant ideologies concerning power, can be made open to critique in the light of fairness and ethics. Dominant recipes for gaining status and the uses and effects of violence in differentiating and determining young men's positions in social hierarchies, can emerge from limited awareness into sharper focus.

For example, a young person who has begun to establish and develop ethics which relate to "standing up against unfairness", "protection of other's rights", "standing by a friend in need", etc., can be invited to examine dominant ideas and practices which promote disrespectful recipes for gaining status. These include:

- put down (members of marginalised groups) to feel tough or strong
- the use of intimidation to get what you want at the expense of others
- strategies of revenge and retribution to "get even", avenge disrespect by others or reclaim a sense of lost honour
- the use of sex to obtain status

He may be encouraged to observe his peer group and critique these ideas and practices - to take a position in the light of his own ethics:

"Is the other person turning more towards using his head or using his fists to sort out his problems?"

"When you talk about respect, what kind of respect are you wanting?
- respect that comes from others being scared of you?
- respect that comes from others admiring you?"

"Does this fit with being tough or being yourself?"

"What do you respect most?"

"What do you think is fair?"

Young people can be invited to examine and critique specific, dominant ideas as "dangerous ideas" that inform violence and abusive practices through the process of externalisation which enables the idea to be made visible in its historical and cultural contexts and accessible for challenge (White, 1995). Cultural and peer support systems which encourage complicity with "dangerous ideas" along with patterns of resistance against their influence, can be understood and highlighted by the young person, in the context of his own life experience.

Developing a broader context for fairness - community and culture

The context for fairness can include school, church, and other community contexts that impact upon the family.

When Joe and members of his extended family began to demonstrate readiness to meet for the purposes of mutual acknowledgement and restitution, a dilemma arose that required consideration. Much of Joe's experience of injustice and victimisation had taken place in a range of inappropriate foster placements that had been sanctioned by the statutory child protection authority.

What would it mean if an expectation was maintained that Joe and members of his extended family acknowledge and take responsibility for abusive or neglectful actions that have harmed one another, their families, and their community – but the abusive and neglectful actions which took place under the auspice of the child protection authority, were overlooked or ignored?

This kind of responsibility overload is frequently experienced by members of disadvantaged and marginalised communities.

In this case, representatives of the statutory authority were prepared to meet with Joe and members of his extended family. They were prepared to listen to and review case records that documented well-intended, but ignorant and appalling decisions about Joe's placement and connection with his community. They were prepared to acknowledge the impact that this had upon Joe and his community. These acknowledgements contributed to an extremely moving discussion that surprised members of Joe's family who had never before experienced welfare authorities taking responsibility for inappropriate or harmful actions. As a consequence Joe was able to reconnect with his family and community, and the family was able, for the first time, to begin to forge a co-operative relationship with welfare authorities.

Developing a broader context for fairness - statutory justice

The idea of fairness has considerable implications for statutory justice systems and processes that traditionally have tended, inadvertently, to encourage young people to avoid responsibility for their actions and sanction punitive consequences for those who fully acknowledge responsibility. In the Youth Court of South Australia, these concerns have led to a shift away from concepts of mitigation of responsibility and the pathologising of young people's behaviour, towards responsibility-based assessment and decision-making criteria that promote acknowledgement of responsibility for abusive behaviour.

The development of youth conferencing processes in South Australia has enabled a majority of young people who commit sexual offences, to engage in a justice process which:

- provides an incentive for acknowledging responsibility in the form of a guilty plea.
- provides a forum in which people affected by the offences can express their experiences of the nature and affects of the abuse to the young person and others.
- provides a forum in which the young person and those effected by the abuse can participate in determining consequence of the offences in the form of undertakings or formal requirements.
- promotes a commitment by the young person to address his abusive behaviour in the context of accountability to the experiences of those who have been hurt by the abuse.

The nature and theory of conferencing processes, and their contributions to fairness and social justice, have been documented by Braithwaite (2000). Research regarding the effectiveness of these processes, in the context of adolescent sexual offending in South Australia, is described by Daly and Curtis-Fawley (2003).

We have found that statutory justice processes that privilege fairness and a sense of social justice, greatly facilitate young people successfully addressing and challenging their abusive behaviours and the ideologies that inform these behaviours. When justice processes are fair, they promote genuine desires and efforts by young people to make restitution to the specific individuals they have hurt and to their communities (Jenkins, Hall, & Joy, 2002).

In this context, we have discovered that 45% of young people attending our intervention programme will eventually make further disclosures of abuse of other children who have not yet disclosed themselves. These acknowledgements are made freely from the young person's sense of ethics, when he understands that such responsibility and honesty will be respected and will enable the possibility of helpful resolutions and outcomes which enhance a sense of respectful identity.

In this way, statutory justice systems can actually serve to promote fairness and respect, whilst holding a young person accountable for his actions and maintaining a priority on community safety.

References

Braithwaite, J. (2000). Shame and criminal justice. *Canadian Journal of Criminology.* July:281-298

Connell, R.W. (1993). *Schools and social justice.* Philadelphia, PA: Temple University Press.

Daly, K. (2001). *Sexual assault and restorative justice.* Paper presented at Restorative Justice and Family Violence Conference, Australian National University, Canberra, July 2000.

Daly, K. & Curtis-Fawley (2003). *Sexual offence cases finalised in court, by conference, and by formal caution in South Australia.* Presentation to National Practitioner's Forum. Adelaide. May, 2003.

Derrida, J & Dufourmantelle, A. (2000). Of hospitality: *Anne Dufourmantelle invites Jacques Derrida to respond.* Stanford, CA: Stanford University Press.

Jenkins, A., Hall, R. & Joy, M. (2002). Forgiveness in child sexual abuse: A matrix of meanings. In, *'The Question of Forgiveness.'* International Journal of Narrative Therapy and community Work. Issue 1.

Jenkins, A. (1999). Invitations to responsibility: Engaging adolescents and young men who have sexually abused. In William Marshal (Ed). *Sourcebook of treatment programs for sexual offenders.* NY: Plenum, pp163-189.

Jenkins, A. (1990). *Invitations to responsibility: The therapeutic engagement of men who are violent and abusive.* Adelaide, Australia: Dulwich Centre Publications.

Larner, G. (1999). Derrida and the deconstruction of power as context and topic in therapy. In Ian Parker (Ed). *Deconstructing psychotherapy.* London: Sage, pp 39-53.

Ransom. (1997). *Foucault's disciplines.* Durham, NC: Duke University Press.

Wexler, P. (1992). *Becoming somebody: Toward a social psychology of school.* London: Farmer Press.

White, M. (1995). *Re-authoring lives.* Adelaide, Australia: Dulwich Centre Publications.

<hr>

CHAPTER SIX

CO-MORBID DIAGNOSIS OF SEXUALLY ABUSIVE YOUTH

BRADLEY R. JOHNSON

Introduction

State of the art assessment and treatment of sexual offenders has become a more individualized process than it was in the past. This idea holds true for sexually aggressive youth, as well as youth with sexual behavior problems. Part of the unique process in working with these youngsters is the appropriate assessment and treatment of their co-morbid psychiatric disorders. Although there are a number of psychiatric problems that are more frequently seen in the sexually abusive population, it is likely that clinicians will come across just about any psychiatric disorder in their adolescent patients who have committed sexual crimes or struggle with sexual behavioral problems. This chapter will discuss the more commonly seen co-morbid psychiatric diagnoses in this population based on both research and this author's experience.

In taking a holistic and individualized approach in working with sexually aggressive youth, it is important that the clinician become familiar with the more commonly seen general psychiatric problems seen in this population. Perhaps patient consultation with a psychiatrist who has experience in working with youth who have struggled with behavioral problems can be considered on cases that have already been pre-screened for psychiatric disorders. There may even be cases in which the use of psychiatric medication may be necessary as part of the individualized treatment plan. Although some medications have been considered to treat paraphilic fantasies and behaviors, the medical treatment of co-morbid psychiatric diagnoses may also directly or indirectly decrease the chances of sexual offense recidivism in some patients, increase the overall functioning of the patient, and decrease unnecessary suffering. It has also been theorized that understanding the relationship between sexual violence and mental illness might lead to the development of more effective legal, correctional, and public health policies regarding sexual offenders (McElroy, Soutullo, Taylor, et al, 1999).

This chapter will first briefly discuss the research published on the topic of psychiatric co-morbidity with adult sexual offenders as a foundation to compare and contrast to adolescents. Next, we will review what is known about psychiatric co-morbidity and juveniles who commit non-sexual offenses. Finally, we will focus on what is known about the psychiatric co-morbid conditions that are commonly seen in juvenile sexual offender populations. The chapter will then conclude with a discussion about some of the more commonly seen psychiatric disorders in this last-mentioned population.

Psychiatric co-morbidity with adult sex offenders

Regarding the adult population, there have been many studies looking at the relationship between mental illness and violent crime (Marzuk, 1996; Monahan & Steadman, 1994; Swanson, 1993; Volavka, 1995). These studies concluded that the most common forms of mental illness seen in the violent adult population include psychotic disorders, depression, bipolar disorder, substance abuse disorders, and antisocial personality disorder. However, these studies did not break down the correlation by types of violence committed, including sexual offenses.

Until recently, research looking at the correlation between psychiatric disorders and sexual offense was flawed due to small sample sizes, lack of a structured means to diagnose, and poor methodology. Some studies came to contradictory conclusions. However, at the end of the last decade, McElroy, Soutullo, Taylor, et al (1999) assessed 36 adult male sexual offenders in a residential treatment facility based on structured clinical interviews for DSM-IV Axis I and II disorders. They concluded that 83% of the adult sexual offenders had a substance abuse disorder, 61% had a mood disorder (the most prevalent being bipolar disorder), 58% had a paraphilia, 39% had an impulse control disorder, 36% had an anxiety disorder, and 17% had an eating disorder. The most common Axis II disorder reported was antisocial personality disorder, seen in 72% of the population.

Similar results were seen in a study conducted by Raymond, Coleman, Ohlerking, et al (1999), evaluating 45 adult male subjects with pedophilia who were either in a residential or outpatient sex offender treatment program. They were interviewed using the Structured Clinical Interview for DSM-IV, in order to assess for Axis I and II comorbidity rates. In general, they concluded that 93% of their subjects suffered from an Axis I disorder. Sixty-seven percent of this group had a lifetime prevalence of a mood disorder, with 64% having an anxiety disorder, 60% a substance abuse disorder, and 24% a sexual dysfunction diagnosis. They also concluded that 53% of their population suffered from two or more paraphilias. Finally, they concluded that 60% of their population met criteria for an Axis II diagnosis, the most common type being a Cluster C personality disorder, although many also suffered from Cluster B symptomatology.

The largest group assessed to date of adult males with paraphilias or paraphilia-related disorders was by Kafka and Hennen (2002). They concluded that of 88 male subjects with paraphilias (60 having had committed sexual offenses), there was a higher self-report of a history of physical abuse, fewer years of completed education, a higher prevalence of learning and behavioral problems, more psychiatric and substance abuse hospitalizations, and a higher level of employment-related disability. In the combined data looking at those who suffered either from a paraphilia or a paraphilia-related disorder (n = 120), the most prevalent Axis I disorder was a mood disorder (71.6%). This broke down to 55% of this subgroup having a dysthymic disorder, and 39% suffering from a major depression. Approximately 38% of subjects had an anxiety disorder, the most common type being social phobia. Finally, 40.8% suffered from a substance abuse disorder, the most prevalent form being alcohol abuse.

This study also retrospectively looked at the diagnosis of attention deficit/hyperactivity disorder (ADHD), concluding that 35.8% of their population met criteria for the diagnosis. They also concluded that both ADHD and conduct disorder were associated with a higher propensity for suffering from multiple paraphilias, and a higher likelihood of incarceration. Finally, they concluded that those subjects who had committed sexual offenses were most likely to be diagnosed with a history of a conduct disorder, alcohol abuse, cocaine abuse, or a generalized anxiety disorder.

Campo, Nijman, Merckelbach, and Evers (2003) looked at a specific subgroup of adult paraphiliacs, those with gender identity disorder. They surveyed 584 subjects concluding that 61% had a co-morbid psychiatric disorder. The most common disorders seen in this study were mood disorders, dissociative disorders, psychotic disorders, and personality disorders.

A recent study examining 113 convicted adult sexual offenders determined that mood disorders, major depressive disorder, bipolar affective disorder Type I, and impulse control disorders were significantly more common among paraphilic sexual offenders (Dunsieth, 2002). More specifically, it was concluded that 23.9% of the study group suffered from a history of a major depression, and 24.8% suffered from bipolar disorder Type I. Eighty-five percent suffered from a form of substance abuse, 23% suffered from an anxiety disorder, and 38.1% with an impulse control disorder. When one looks at the subgroup of those offender subjects who were not diagnosed with suffering from a paraphilia (n = 26), it was noticed that they were significantly more likely than those sex offenders who could be diagnosed with a paraphilia to suffer from a substance abuse disorder.

Like many areas in both psychiatry as well as sexual offender literature, one cannot assume that what is known about adults applies to adolescents and children. Rather, the next sections will review the literature that is specific to youthful offenders. Additionally, although most of these studies have used some formal method of arriving at diagnostic conclusions, there are some diagnostic conclusions in this batch of literature that is based on less structured means. Inter-rater reliability is generally not discussed in these studies, and conclusions based on more subjective measures or survey questionnaires make one question results. Since similar results are reached in many of these studies, it is likely that despite these flaws, the conclusions are reasonable. However, it is important to understand that the literature is imperfect, and clinicians should be careful to realize such when applying these results to actual clinical practices.

Psychiatric co-morbidity in non-sexual juvenile offenders

Before looking at psychiatric co-morbidity issues with adolescent sexual offenders, it is appropriate to review a little of what is known about psychiatric co-morbidity with non-sexual violent juvenile offenders.

Haapasalo and Hamalainen (1996) studied the difference in young property and violent offenders, including the prevalence of disruptive behavior disorder, depression, and substance abuse. They did not find any statistically significant difference in regard to childhood physical or psychological abuse between the two groups.

Likewise, they did not find any difference between the two groups when looking at prevalence rates of family problems. However, 71% of the violent group had abused illicit drugs compared to 51% of the property offender group. The two groups also did not differ in regard to disruptive behavior disorders, alcohol abuse/dependence, or depression. Unfortunately, this study did not compare the two groups to adolescent non-offenders.

In a Canadian study by Ulzen and Hamilton (1998), the prevalence of psychiatric disorders and degree of psychiatric co-morbidity was measured, comparing age and sex-matched samples of 49 incarcerated adolescents with 49 non-delinquent adolescents. The diagnoses were determined via the Diagnostic Interview for Children and Adolescents – Revised (DICA-R). They determined that approximately 63.3% of incarcerated adolescents suffered from two or more co-morbid psychiatric disorders, the degree of psychiatric morbidity being directly related to such things as family adversity, physical abuse, other psychosocial variables, or substance abuse. They also noted that psychiatric co-morbidity was more frequent in females than it was in males, and that incarcerated adolescents were more likely to admit to thought-disordered symptoms.

A few years later, Kataoka, Zima, Dupre, et al (2001) published findings regarding the lifetime use of specialty mental health services and special education programs among incarcerated female juvenile offenders. They concluded that 80% of these female offenders suffered from an emotional disorder or a substance abuse problem. They also determined that almost two-thirds of this group had a history of recidivism, thus likely being more consistent with a conduct disordered diagnosis. Of those who suffered from an emotional disorder or substance abuse, 51% had sought specialty mental health services, and 58% had been in a special education program. When looking only at the youth who had a history of recidivism, 82% struggled with substance abuse, and 47% had sought specialty mental health services at some time during their life.

In the same year, another study was done retrospectively to determine the prevalence of child neuropsychiatric disorders, specifically assessing for pervasive developmental disorders, attention deficit/hyperactivity disorder, and Tourette's Syndrome in juvenile offenders (Siponmma, Kristiansson, Jonson, et al, 2001). This study looked at 126 general offenders between the ages of 15 and 22 who presented for initial forensic psychiatric evaluations. It was reported that most of the offenders in this study had committed serious offenses. Of the subjects studied, 15% had a firm diagnosis of ADHD, and another 15% suffered from a pervasive developmental disorder. Of this last group, 3% could be diagnosed with Asperger's Syndrome. None of the subjects could be diagnosed with actual autism, the remainder of this group being diagnosed with a pervasive developmental disorder not otherwise specified. Finally, only 2% of the cases were diagnosed with Tourette's Syndrome.

Finally, 1,829 African-American, Caucasian, and Hispanic youth were studied who had been arrested and detained in the area of Chicago, Illinois and its surrounding suburbs. In the first study of this population (Teplin, Abram, McClelland, et al, 2002), subjects were assessed via the Diagnostic Interview Schedule for Children Version 2.3, looking at six-month prevalence estimates for affective disorders (major depression episode, dysthymia, manic episode), anxiety (panic, separation anxiety, over-anxious, generalized anxiety, and obsessive compulsive disorders), psychosis, attention-deficit/hyperactivity disorder, disruptive behavior disorders (oppositional defiant disorder or conduct disorder), and substance use disorders (alcohol and other drugs). It was concluded that nearly two-thirds of the males, and almost three-quarters of females, met diagnostic criteria for one or more co-morbid psychiatric disorder. Half of the males and nearly half of the females studied suffered from a substance abuse disorder. More than 40% of the subjects met criteria for disruptive behavior disorder. Affective disorders were more prevalent in the females, nearly 20% of females meeting the criteria for major depression. Psychiatric disorders appeared to be more prevalent in the females, Caucasians, and older adolescents when they were looked at by age.

The same group of juvenile detainees from Chicago was assessed further in an attempt to determine specifics of psychiatric co-morbidity (Abram, Teplin, McClelland, & Dulcan, 2003). It was seen that 56.5% of females (vs. 45.9% of males) met the criteria for two or more generalized psychiatric disorders including: major depression, dysthymia, mania, psychosis, panic disorder, separation anxiety disorder, over-anxiousness, generalized anxiety disorder, obsessive compulsive disorder, attention deficit/hyperactivity disorder, conduct disorder, oppositional defiant disorder, an alcohol disorder, a marijuana disorder, or another type of substance abuse disorder. In comparison, only 17.3% of females and 20.4% of males in this study suffered from a single psychiatric disorder. Almost 14% of the females and 11% of the males studied suffered from both a major mental disorder (psychosis, manic episode, or major depressive episode) and a substance abuse disorder. They also concluded that those with a major mental disorder had significantly increased odds of also struggling with a substance abuse disorder.

Psychiatric co-morbidity with adolescent sexual offenders

After having just briefly reviewed the literature in regard to co-morbidity with non-sexual adolescent offenders, we will now review this same issue in populations where the adolescent crime committed has been a sexual offense.

Becker, Kaplan, Cunningham-Rather, and Kavoussi (1986) looked at 19 adolescent sex offenders who were officially diagnosed by a psychiatrist to determine the presence of co-morbid psychiatric disorders. Of the small group interviewed, only 26.3% could *not* be diagnosed with a DSM-III disorder. Thirteen of the 19 subjects were diagnosed with a conduct disorder, two with attention deficit disorder, two with adjustment disorders, two with social phobias, one with dysthymia, and one with post traumatic stress disorder. Finally, four of their 19 subjects were diagnosed with alcohol or marijuana abuse. They also noted that 22.7% of their subjects had a significant history of medical disease or physical trauma. A few years later, Kavoussi, Kaplan, and Becker (1988) set out to determine the psychiatric characteristics of 58 outpatient inner-city male adolescent sexual offenders, ages 13 to 18. All of their subjects had admitted to or been found guilty of a sexual crime, and each was interviewed via the Structured Clinical Interview for DSM-III and the Childrens' Schedule for Affective Disorders and Schizophrenia – Epidemiologic Version. The first of these semi-structured interviews was used to diagnose affective disorders, psychotic disorders, anxiety disorders, and substance abuse. The second was used to probe for conduct disorder and attention deficit disorder. The final diagnoses were made by a psychiatrist according to the DSM-III criteria based on the information from the interviews, as well as information obtained from the subject's families and referral sources. Eleven percent were Caucasian, 61% African American, and 28% Hispanic.

In this study, by far the most common psychiatric disorder seen in the adolescent sexual offender population was conduct disorder (48.3%). The next most common generalized co-morbid psychiatric disorder was an adjustment disorder or depressed mood (8.6%), followed by attention deficit disorder (6.9%). Additionally, 8.6% of subjects could be diagnosed with alcohol abuse, and 10.3% with marijuana abuse. What is quite interesting is when one looks at the number of adolescents who met any of the DSM-III criteria for a psychiatric disorder, even if not meeting the full criteria for a disorder. Approximately two-thirds of the youngsters interviewed had some symptoms of a conduct disorder, whereas just over one-third suffered from some symptoms of attention deficit disorder. Finally, just over 20% of their subjects suffered from an adjustment disorder/depressed mood, followed by smaller percentages of all other types of psychiatric disorders. They suggested that the high incidence of conduct disorder in their sample showed that many adolescent sexual offenses are likely committed as part of a larger impulse control and antisocial pattern.

During the same time period, other researchers also concluded that a history of non-sexual delinquency is seen in adolescent sexual offender groups. Fehrenbach, Smith, Monastersky, and Deisher (1986) looked at 293 male adolescent sexual offenders, concluding that 44% had committed non-sexual offenses prior to their first sexual offense. This would support the notion that this population is at high risk for suffering from a conduct disorder. A number of other researchers have concluded that low academic performance is another characteristic frequently seen in juvenile sex offender populations (Awad & Saunders, 1989; 1991; Fagen & Wexler, 1986; Schram, Milloy, & Rowe, 1991). In the Awad and Saunders study (1989), 83% of their juvenile sex offender population had serious learning problems, and 48% could be diagnosed with a learning disability.

Another characteristic frequently seen in the adolescent sex offender population is lack of impulse control. Smith, Monastersky, & Deisher (1987) studied 262 male adolescents who had committed less violent and less aggressive sexual offenses. They concluded that approximately 50% of the common variant was explained by their propensity to act out in an impulsive manner. They also demonstrated that many adolescent sexual offenders had below average skills in regard to anger control, a problem that may be secondary to impulsivity, or may be secondary to a conduct disorder.

A few years later, Becker, Kaplan, Tenke, & Tartaglini (1991) studied a much larger sample than these investigators had previously done, looking at 246 male adolescent sex offenders. Forty-two percent of their subjects were diagnosed with a major depression on the Beck Depression Inventory (BDI). The mean score that these adolescent offenders demonstrated on the BDI was 14.3, being double that usually seen in adolescents in general (Kaplan, Hong, & Weinhold, 1984).

Becker, Harris, & Sales (1993) admit that many of the studies done with adolescent sex offenders may have focused on conduct disordered characteristics. However, it is possible that although conduct disorder is an obvious psychiatric co-morbidity, other psychiatric disorders may be quite prevalent in this population.

Mathews, Hunter, & Vuz (1997) looked at juvenile female sexual offenders, studying 67 such youngsters who were in either a community-based or residential treatment program. They compared this group to 70 juvenile male sexual offenders regarding psychiatric characteristics. Approximately 50% of both the females and males studied had a previous history of mental health treatment, and approximately one-fourth of both groups had either attempted suicide or had suffered from suicidal ideations. Seventeen percent of the females versus 10% of the males could be diagnosed with alcohol or drug abuse. However, 31% of the males could be diagnosed with a learning disability, compared to only 15% of the females.

The high incidence of psychiatric co-morbidity demonstrated in the prior reviewed studies causes one to conclude that juvenile sexual offenders need to be carefully assessed with strong consideration of a psychiatric evaluation and possibly, at times, generalized psychological testing. If the clinician is uncomfortable in making such diagnoses, they should consult with those trained to do so.

In the remainder of this chapter, some of the frequently seen co-morbid psychiatric diagnoses discussed in this last section will be reviewed in further detail. Additionally, there will be occasional interspersed mention about other child psychiatric disorders that one may wish to watch for in the juvenile sex offender population. It is felt that the research done thus far has been limited, and further study is merited to look at the juvenile sex offender population and psychiatric co-morbidity. The studies listed thus far are imperfect and often with small groups. Therefore, it may be seen in future studies that additional psychiatric disorders that have been less well assessed in prior studies will prove to also exist in this population.

Co-Morbid Psychiatric Disorders

Conduct disorder

Problems with disruptive behaviors, oppositionality, and aggression present as the most common reason that children are referred for mental health intervention (Hill, 2002; Keenan & Wakschlag, 2000). The Diagnostic and Statistical Manual, 4th Edition, Text Revision (American Psychiatric Association, 2000) reviews that the essential feature of a conduct disorder is repetitive and persistent behavioral patterns in which the basic rights of others or major age-appropriate societal norms or rules are violated. It lists that these behaviors fall into four main sub-groupings: aggressive conduct that causes or threatens physical harm to other people or animals, non-aggressive conduct that causes property loss or damage, deceitfulness or theft, and serious violations of rules. In order to obtain the diagnosis, the patient has to demonstrate three or more of these characteristic behaviors during a period of the previous 12 months, with at least one behavior present in the last six months. Of course, the disturbance and behavior must cause clinically significant impairment in social, academic, or occupational functioning. It is also interesting to note that a conduct disorder may be diagnosed in individuals who are over the age of 18, but only if they do not meet the criteria for an anti-social personality disorder.

Assessing an adolescent for a conduct disorder is sometimes difficult, and improved predictive accuracy increases with age of the patient (Bennett & Offord, 2001). It is suggested that the adolescent may need to be seen on multiple occasions over a period of time in order to conclude with an accurate diagnosis. That is, without a sufficient history, a diagnosis of a conduct disorder is difficult to give when the adolescent is seen or interviewed only once. It appears that boys more frequently suffer from a conduct disorder than do girls, possibly as high as three to four times (Lahey, Miller, Gordon, & Riley, 1999). This fact combined with the overall commonality of this disorder seems to correlate with the fact that this is so commonly seen in adolescent sexual offenders, a group who are also predominantly male.

Jacobs, Kennedy, & Meyer (1997) studied incarcerated juvenile sexual offenders (n = 156), measuring delinquent history, intelligence, academic achievement, and psychopathology. They concluded that juvenile sexual offending might be one expression of antisocial and violent behavior by these youngsters. Therefore, they recommended that such juveniles should receive treatment that targets other aspects of their antisocial and violent behavior. In other words, it may be that sexual offenses committed by adolescents may be one expression or symptom of an overall conduct disordered presentation, thus concluding that conduct disorder may be an actual risk factor for adolescent sexual offenses.

Victim characteristics of 100 British sexually abusive male adolescents between the ages of 11 and 18 were evaluated (Richardson, Kelly, Bahte, & Graham, 1997). The findings from this study were consistent with that found in the North American literature, concluding that the primary psychiatric diagnosis seen in their subjects was conduct disorder. They concluded that none of the adolescents in their study groups suffered from a psychotic disorder or a major depressive disorder, however. They subdivided their subjects into those who had committed incestuous sexual offenses, general child sexual offenses, mixed sexual offenses, and offenses against peers and adults. The latter group, those who offended against peers and adults, had the highest incidence of conduct disorder (88%) compared to the others.

Hastings, Anderson, & Hemphill (1997) also published data on adolescent sexual offenders (n = 28), comparing them to a general conduct disordered group of youngsters (n = 33) and to a group of control adolescents (n = 34). They measured their levels of stress, coping, problem behavior, and cognitive distortions. The group that had a conduct disordered diagnosis scored higher than the adolescents who had only committed sexual offenses (but without conduct disorder) in regard to socialized aggression, aggressive coping, as well as coping by engaging in sexual behavior. However, the adolescent sexual offenders were similar to the conduct disordered group, and higher than the control group, when it came to negative automatic thoughts as well as problem behaviors including hyperactivity, anxiety, and an overall conduct disorder. Again, they showed that there is a similarity between these two groups, although there may still be some differences as well.

In 2000, Prentky, Harris, Frizzell, & Righthand, (2000) published the first actuarially derived procedure to assess the risk of reoffense by juvenile sexual offenders. They noted that one group of symptoms that consistently related to the risk of sexual reoffense was delinquency, antisocial behavior, and lack of impulse control. They included a number of items in their juvenile sex offender protocol (J-SOAP) that are related to symptoms of conduct disorder. Specifically, the scale includes the following: whether the offender had ever been arrested before the age of 16, if they had had school behavioral problems (school failure, repeated truancy, fighting with peers and/or teachers or other evidence of serious behavioral problems at school), school suspensions or expulsions, a history of conduct disorder, a history of multiple types of offenses, impulsivity, a history of alcohol abuse, evidence of empathy or guilt, poorly managed anger, stability in school, and quality of their peer relationships. Although there are other areas and symptoms that they included on their assessment protocol, it appears that many of the items that they listed on their scale are either directly or indirectly related to the diagnosis of a conduct disorder.

Finally, Butler and Seto (2002) attempted to distinguish between adolescent sexual offenders to non-sexual offenders according to their non-sexual offense history. They concluded that the adolescent sexual offenders were similar to their non-sexual offenders in their early childhood conduct problems, current behavioral adjustment, and pro-criminal attitudes and beliefs. Interestingly, they demonstrated that the sexual offender group had a lower than expected risk for future delinquency.

Before finishing this section, let's conclude with a few other interesting ideas about the origin of conduct disorder, its relationship to other childhood disorders, and symptoms or behaviors that are warning signs of a conduct disorder. In the first part of a comprehensive two-part review on oppositional defiant disorder and conduct disorder, Loeber, Berke, Lahey, et al (2000) summarized the most common co-morbid disorders seen with either of these behavioral disorders including childhood ADHD, anxiety, mood disorders, somatoform disorder, and substance use. In the second part of their review (Burke, Loeber, & Birmaher, 2002), they discussed that there may be a proportion of youth with oppositional defiant disorder that progress to conduct disorder. This review also discussed the fact that there may be a number of functional factors that affect children with conduct disorder including their temperament, attachment, neuropsychological functioning, intelligence and academic performance, reading problems, social cognition, sociomoral reasoning, and adolescent development. It was also discussed that parenting, child abuse, peer effects, and other life stressors may be psychosocial factors associated with the disorder. Another recent study concluded that a history of aggression, negative parent/child relationships in childhood, and a lower IQ, was more predictive of aggression and serious emotional disturbance (Vance, Bowen, Fernandez, & Thompson, 2002), thus making these likely predictive factors for the aggressive conduct disordered youngster.

Although there has been an increase in research into conduct disordered problems, more studies are yet needed. However, it is currently believed that conduct disorder is multi factorial in cause. It is estimated that 30% of conduct disordered adolescents have committed at least one violent act in the previous year, although only a small percentage of these youth will likely go on to become chronic adult offenders

(Srinivasaraghavan, 2004). They concluded that the majority of conduct disordered youth discontinue their antisocial or violent behavior by the end of their adolescence. Similar results were shown in a study by Ruchkin, Koposov, Vermeiren, & Schwab-Stone (2003) in which 358 incarcerated male juvenile delinquents were interviewed. Approximately 73% of their subjects met the criteria for a conduct disorder. This likely means that youngsters with a conduct disorder are at high risk of criminal behavior that leads to incarceration.

In the past, it has often been discussed that there is a triad of symptoms frequently associated with conduct disorder (or violence) including enuresis, fire setting, and cruelty to animals. Although these behaviors may be considered as being red flags to look for a conduct disorder or a future risk of violence, it has been proposed that they may not be the best predictive symptoms correlated with later violence (Justice, Justice, & Kraft, 1974). However, a history of animal cruelty during childhood has still been associated with antisocial personality disorder, antisocial personality traits, and substance abuse (Gleyzer, Felthouse, & Holzer, 2002). Likewise, fire setters still have been associated with conduct disordered problems as well as shyness and aggressiveness (Chen, Arria, & Anthony, 2003; Slavkin, 2002).

Attention deficit/hyperactivity disorder

As previously discussed, attention deficit/hyperactivity disorder is less commonly seen in adolescent sexual offenders than is conduct disorder, but is still a common psychiatric diagnosis associated with this population. ADHD occurs in approximately 3% to 7% of school-age children (American Psychiatric Association, 2000), and is the most common psychiatric disorder in children (Kratochvil, Heiligenstein, Dittmann, et al, 2002). Although there are numerous rating scales that may aid in the diagnosis of ADHD (Colett, Ohan, & Myers, 2003), the determination of ADHD is based on the criteria as currently outlined in the DSM-IV-TR (American Psychiatric Association, 2000).

In the past, individuals have frequently referred to this disorder as either "Attention Deficit Disorder" (ADD) or "Attention Deficit/Hyperactivity Disorder" (ADHD), depending on whether or not the attentional problem included a hyperactive component. However, the current way of looking at these disorders is to refer to them as Attention Deficit/Hyperactivity Disorder with either the Combined Type (both inattentive and hyperactive/impulsive symptoms), predominantly the Inattentive Type, or predominantly the Hyperactive/Impulsive Type (American Psychiatric Association, 2000). Inattentive symptoms may include such things as failing to give close attention to details and making careless mistakes in schoolwork or similar activities, having difficulty sustaining attention in tasks or play activities, having difficulty with organizing tasks or activities, or being easily distracted by extraneous stimuli. Hyperactive symptoms may include such things as fidgeting or squirming in seat, running about or climbing excessively in situations where it would be inappropriate, or talking excessively. Finally, impulsive symptoms may include such things as blurting out answers before questions have been completed, or having difficulty awaiting turn. Of course there are other symptoms that may be consistent with this diagnosis, but at least some of the symptoms need to have caused impairment in the individual before the age of seven, and symptoms must show some impairment in two or more settings such as in school, work, or home.

In regard to ADHD and sexuality, it has been demonstrated that adolescents with this disorder often begin to engage in sexual intercourse at an early age (Barkley, 1998). Additionally, adolescents with ADHD have a tendency to be more promiscuous, changing sexual partners more frequently than the average sexually active adolescent. They tend to be less cognizant of safe sexual practices, thus leading to higher rates of teenage pregnancy and sexually transmitted disease (Barkley, 2002).

As previously discussed, adolescent sexual offenders have a higher rate of ADHD co-morbidity than does the average adolescent non-offender. Kelly, Richardson, Hunter, & Knapp (2002) demonstrated this concept nicely when they assessed 36 adolescent male sexual offenders and 20 age-matched male adolescents, assessing them for attention and executive function. Attentional differences between the two groups were found to be highly significant. Thus, they encouraged the importance of neuropsychological investigation of adolescent sexual offenders, including seeking for attentional problems. One can only conclude that it is important to appropriately diagnose ADHD in that subgroup of adolescent sexual offenders, offering appropriate treatment to help decrease their impulsivity and improve their focus, attention, hyperactivity, and aggressive behavior.

One area that is of vital importance to adolescent sexual offenders is the relationship of ADHD to socialization and social skills. A survey of 255 parents of children with ADHD and 252 children without the condition concluded that children with ADHD were reported to have substantially increased problems of getting along with their peers, as well as suffering from other socialization problems (IMPACT Survey, 2001). This survey concluded that 43% of children with ADHD had been "picked" on by their peers, compared to only 18% of the comparison group. Likewise, 72% of the ADHD population had trouble getting along with their siblings and other family members, compared to only 53% of the comparison group. It is possible that the lack of some children with the ADHD to read social cues, as well as to have more difficulty in associating with pro-social youth, may lead to increased risk of impulsive behaviors, including impulsive sexual behavior. Perhaps this is one reason that adolescent sexual offenders more commonly suffer from ADHD.

Another interesting area is the association of ADHD with conduct disorder as previously touched upon in the section on conduct disorder. In fact, the general child psychiatry literature has long discussed the association between these two disorders, and it is well known that some youngsters with ADHD may develop into oppositional defiant disorder, and then on to a conduct disorder (Anderson, Williams, McGee, & Silva, 1987; Biederman, Newcorn, & Sprich, 1991). However, it is important to realize that this is the case with only a subpopulation of youngsters with ADHD.

MacDonald and Achenbach (1996) investigated the course of attention and conduct problems in a sample of adolescents over a six year period. They concluded that both boys and girls who show a combination of attention and conduct problems are at particular risk for persistence of conduct problems. At the same time, Taylor, Chadwick,

Heptinstall, & Danckaerts (1996) also conducted a follow up study of children who were identified as showing pervasive hyperactivity or conduct problems, or the co-morbid mixture of both problems. They compared the study group to a control group. These groups were initially identified at the ages of six and seven years old, and then followed through the ages of 16 to 18 years old. They concluded that hyperactivity was a risk factor for the later development or co-existence of conduct problems. They also concluded that hyperactivity was related with a higher likelihood of other psychiatric diagnoses, persistent hyperactivity, violence, other antisocial problems, and social and peer problems.

Satterfield and Schell (1997) conducted a prospective study following 89 adolescents with ADHD into adulthood, comparing them to 87 normal subjects. They concluded that the hyperactive subjects had significantly higher juvenile and adult arrest rates (46 vs. 11% and 21 vs. 1% respectively). However, they also demonstrated the childhood conduct problems predicted later criminality as did serious antisocial behavior in adolescents. Like prior studies, it appeared to be the combination of both the hyperactivity and the conduct problems that led to the increased chance of later criminality, and hyperactive children who do not have conduct problems did not appear to be at increased risk. Similar conclusions have been reached by other researchers in more recent studies, suggesting that ADHD may actually be a risk factor for future antisocial and substance related disorders, as well as aggression (Biederman, 2004; Mannuzza, Klein, Bessler, et al, 1998; Weller, Rowan, Weller, & Elia, 1999). In fact, the impulsivity component of ADHD is likely to be the best predictor of both psychopathy and conduct problems in adolescent males (Vitacco & Rogers, 2001).

It is the author's clinical experience that ADHD is often overlooked in the assessment of adolescent sexual offenders. The same has been hypothesized to be true in adult sexual offenders (Kafka & Hennen, 2002). Many times this population will express that they have engaged in a sexually inappropriate act without prior planning, in a rather impulsive manner. It is especially important in this subpopulation that one should look closely for ADHD symptoms. Such recognition and appropriate treatment for the disorder may greatly reduce the adolescent's chances of impulsivity, thus possibly reducing their risk of reoffense in the future. Although one should not merely ignore the sexually inappropriate behavior and assume it is only secondary to ADHD, doing just the opposite and only focusing on the sexual offense without treatment of the co-morbid disorder leads to a great disservice for the adolescent.

Oppositional defiant disorder

Although Oppositional Defiant Disorder is not as commonly seen with adolescent sexual offenders as is Conduct Disorder or Attention Deficit/Hyperactivity Disorder, it is important to understand the concept of this disorder given its close relationship to these other behavioral diagnoses that are seen in this population. We will review just a few thoughts about this disorder to round out the discussion on behavioral disorders.

The essential feature of Oppositional Defiant Disorder is a current pattern of negativistic, defiant, disobedient, and hostile behavior toward authority figures persisting for over six months and characterized by frequent occurrence of four or more problematic behaviors such as losing temper, arguing with adults, actively defying or refusing to comply with requests or rules of adults, deliberately doing things that will annoy other people, blaming others for their own mistakes or behaviors, being touchy or easily annoyed by others, being angry and resentful, or being spiteful or vindictive (American Psychiatric Association, 2000).

There is one further interesting study that looks at the relationship of ADHD, oppositional defiant disorder and conduct disorder in a slightly different way from the previously mentioned studies. Biederman, Faraone, Milberger, et al (1996), assessed 140 children with ADHD, and 120 normal controls at baseline and again four years later. Of those with the ADHD diagnosis at baseline, 65% had a co-morbid oppositional defiant disorder, and 22% had a co-morbid conduct disorder. When they looked further, of those with an oppositional defiant disorder, 32% had a co-morbid conduct disorder. Those children with both oppositional defiant disorder and conduct disorder had more severe symptoms of oppositional defiant disorder, as well as other co-morbid psychiatric disorders. They concluded that there are two sub types of Oppositional Defiant Disorder that are associated with Attention Deficit/Hyperactivity Disorder. First, they believe that one form is prodromal to conduct disorder, and the other is subsyndromal to conduct disorder, but not likely to actually progress to conduct disorder in later years. Further research would help us better delineate whether this proves to be true. However, understanding this relationship is quite important in regard to adolescent sexual offenders due to the high rate of conduct disorder in this population as previously discussed.

Depression

As previously stated, next to conduct disorder, the most common generalized co-morbid psychiatric disorder in the adolescent sexual offender population is an adjustment disorder or a depressed mood. This is a serious issue given the fact that suicide remains the third leading cause of death among U.S. adolescents, as well as the fact that the overall trend in suicide attempts rose from 7.3% in 1991 to 8.8% in 2001. However, at least in the adolescent population, the rates of suicide completion have actually fallen steadily since 1993 (Joe & Marcus, 2003).

Perhaps one of the reasons that there is an increased level of depression seen in sexually abusive youth is the fact that individuals who have been sexually abused as children are also shown to be at a higher risk for depression (Barbe, Bridge, Birmaher, et al, 2004; Putnam, 2003). This makes sense since many juvenile sexual offenders have been sexually abused in their own past. Likewise, childhood physical abuse by a father or stepfather and exposure to violence against females were found to be associated with higher levels of co-morbid depression in the juvenile sex offender population (Hunter, Figueredo, Malamuth, & Becker, 2003).

Another interesting offshoot of the adolescent sex offender population is the subgroup of these youth who are incarcerated or detained. First, however, we will review two studies that look at incarcerated adolescents in general. Domalanta, Risser, Roberts, & Risser (2003) evaluated 1024 incarcerated adolescents who completed self-administered questionnaires that included the Beck Depression Inventory. Two hundred sixty-one (25%) of their subjects suffered from moderate depression, and 223

(33%) suffered from severe depression. Sixty-one percent of their population suffered from more than one psychiatric disorder, particularly demonstrating a relationship between both depression and anxiety, and drug and alcohol abuse.

Sanisolow, Grilo, Fehon, et al, (2003) compared 81 adolescents in a short-term juvenile detention center with a matched group of 81 adolescent psychiatric inpatients using a clinical assessment battery of established instruments to assess for the risk of suicidal behavior. Although both groups reported similar levels of distress on measures of suicide risk, depression, impulsivity, and drug abuse, once the two groups were controlled for depression, impulsivity and drug abuse remained significantly associated with suicide risk scores in the juvenile detention group, but not in the psychiatric inpatient group. Therefore, one may conclude that of juvenile detainees, a presence of impulsivity and history of drug abuse may actually be correlated to suicide risk, especially of concern in those youth who are struggling with depression.

An interesting conclusion was seen in a small study by Lindsay and Lees (2003) in which the Beck Anxiety and Depression Inventories were used with a group of 16 sex offenders with mild intellectual disability and borderline intelligence, and 16 control participants with similar levels of intellectual disability. They concluded that there was a significant difference between the two groups, although the sex offenders reported significantly lower levels of anxiety and depression than did the control group. They explained their unusual findings by the thought that some psychopathic individuals have reported lower levels of anxiety, or that some sex offenders could simply be better adjusted in regard to anxiety and depression than others. However, one has to keep in mind that this was a small study and the ages of the participants were not delineated in the report.

Finally, there has been a great deal of recent research regarding the issue of lower self-esteem in both adolescent as well as adult sexual offenders, which has been proposed to be associated with loneliness or problems with intimacy that may be associated with the offensive behavior (Marshall, Champagne, Sturgeon, & Bryce, 1997; Monto, Zgourides & Harris, 1998). Lower self-esteem is another way of looking at feelings of worthlessness or excessive or inappropriate guilt, one of the criteria for a major depressed episode (American Psychiatric Association, 2000). When one sees low self-esteem in a youngster, it may be important to look for other criteria of a depressed episode including the subjective feelings of depression, anhedonia, changes in weight or changes in appetite, sleep disturbance, psychomotor agitation or retardation, fatigue or loss of energy, problems with concentration, or recurrent thoughts of death/suicide.

Bipolar disorder

It seems that recently, many children and adolescents who engage in criminalistic behaviors or interpersonal violent behaviors are diagnosed with Bipolar Disorder. The criteria for diagnosis of a manic episode are not considered to be different in children than they are with adults based on the current Diagnostic and Statistical Manual (American Psychiatric Association, 2000). Such symptoms include mood disturbance in addition to an inflated self-esteem/grandiosity, decreased need for sleep, pressured speech, flight of ideas, distractibility, increased goal directed activity, and excessive involvement in pleasurable activities that have a high potential for painful consequences. Some clinicians and researchers have proposed different criteria for child and adolescent Bipolar Disorder, but the debate still exists as to whether such an actual disorder in youngsters is valid, demonstrating irritability as the major presenting symptom as opposed to euphoria (Biederman, Mick, Faraone, et al, 2003; Leibenluft, Charney, Towbin, et al, 2003).

Although Bipolar Disorder has not been demonstrated to be a common co-morbid psychiatric disorder in studies thus far that look at adolescent sexual offenders, it has been demonstrated in the adult sex offender population (McElroy, Soutullo, Taylor, et al, 1999). One explanation is the fact that it is difficult to diagnose Bipolar Disorder in youngsters as well as the current controversy as to whether Bipolar Disorder actually exists very commonly in the adolescent population.

A recent study also suggested that manic symptoms in the adult population place bipolar patients at significant risk for criminal offending and arrest (Quanbeck, Stone, Scott, et al, 2004), although demonstrating such a correlation with risk of sexual offense has still yet to be determined. It is possible that once further research is done looking at the existence of Bipolar Disorder in adult sexual offenders, a similar correlation may be seen. Showing such a correlation in youth sexual offenders will be difficult until clinical criteria for Bipolar Disorder in adolescents is determined and agreed upon.

Anxiety disorders

Interestingly, anxiety disorders have not been seen frequently in the adolescent sexual offender population despite the assumption that they would. It is this author's experience that many youngsters who are undergoing legal ramifications or evaluations for sexual offense are acutely anxious early in the process for obvious reasons. Despite this, one would question as to whether anxiety disorders are being appropriately assessed in this population including generalized anxiety problems, obsessive/compulsive disorder, and especially post traumatic stress disorder. In the DSM-IV (American Psychiatric Association, 1994), anxiety disorders were defined quite differently than they had been previously. It has been proposed that sources for anxiety in the general adolescent population may include such issues as identity, sexuality, social acceptance, and independence conflicts (Bernstein, Borchardt, & Perwien, 1996). Therefore, it makes sense that at least a small relationship may exist between anxiety and individuals who suffer from a sexual disorder.

Cortoni and Marshall (2001) reported that sexual offenders consistently have reported using sexual activities, both consenting and non-consenting, as a coping strategy to deal with stressful and problematic situations. They also demonstrated that such offenders have shown evidence of sexual preoccupation during their adolescence, later being related to the use of sex as a coping strategy in adulthood. Perhaps there is a subpopulation of sexual offenders who use sex to deal with anxiety provoking situations that would be seen as stressful and problematic.

Many clinicians have talked about both adolescent as well as adult sexual offenders suffering from obsessive compulsive disorder, a specialized form of an anxiety disorder, as the reason behind their sexually offensive behavior. That is, one explanation that seems plausible to some is that a subgroup of sexual offenders have obsessive and compulsive problems with sexuality, thus leading to inappropriate sexual behavior. Interestingly, very little is noted in the literature regarding this correlation. In a recent meta-analysis by Hanson and Morton-Bourgon (2004), 95 different studies were quantitatively examined concerning recidivism risk factors for sexual offenders. The results identified new predictor variables when compared to prior such analytic studies, including both paraphilic and non-paraphilic sexual preoccupations were significantly related to sexual recidivism. One might assume that this conclusion is consistent with obsessive-compulsive thinking patterns. However, it is obvious that further study needs to be done in order to show if a similar correlation exists with actual obsessive compulsive disorder, especially with youthful offenders.

Likewise, very little has been shown to demonstrate a correlation between sexual offensive behaviors and posttraumatic stress disorder in adolescents, a specialized form of an anxiety disorder. However, there is likely an indirect correlation in that it is well known that many sexually abusive youth have been sexually and/or physically abused, a subpopulation that makes sense to be at higher risk for posttraumatic stress disorder due to their abuse.

Let's take this issue step by step. First, it has long been discussed that victims of sexual abuse may become the victimizer of sexual abuse (Ryan, 1989; Schwartz, 1995). Second, there is an association between childhood sexual and physical abuse and adverse psychological/psychosocial outcomes seeing that such individuals are at higher risk for major depression, suicide, conduct disorder, alcohol dependence, nicotine dependence, social anxiety, rape after the age of 18, divorce, adjustment problems, cognitive/academic impairment, aggression, as well as post traumatic stress disorder (Graham, 1996); Kaplan, Pelcovitz, & Labruna, 1999; Nelson, Heath, Madden, et al, 2002; Valle, Silovsky, 2002). Third, it has been shown that sexual abuse has been significantly associated with hypersexual, exposing, and victimizing sexual behaviors, the age of such abuse having the highest correlation (McClellan, McCurry, Ronnei, et al, 1996).

As one looks at the mechanism as to why abused youth may go on to be victimizers, a possible explanation would be that some of these youth have developed posttraumatic stress disorder, with their sexual acting out behaviors being part of the symptomatology. Additionally, there is a fair amount of evidence to suggest that adverse early-life experiences such as sexual abuse have a profound effect on the developing brain (Nemeroff, 2004). It is possible that those who are exposed to traumatic early-life experiences could have abnormal neural developments that are related to future abnormal behavior, including abnormal sexual acts.

Posttraumatic stress disorder is a fairly common psychiatric disorder that has an approximate 9% lifetime prevalence in the United States (Yehuda, 2004). It can be a condition that greatly affects functionality, including ones ability to engage in treatment, due to issues such as intrusive recollections of traumatic events, hyperarousal, avoidance of clues associated with traumas, and psychological numbing. Such disabling symptoms may be due to structural and functional brain changes that occur due to trauma (Nutt and Malizia, 2004), and needs to be taken into account when working with youngsters who have a background of physical, emotional, or sexual abuse. It is likely that these youth are at much higher risk for the development of depressive and other anxiety disorders later in life (Nemeroff, 2004), again making it more difficult for these youth to gain from treatment efforts. They are at higher risk to avoid therapy that focuses on their own history of abuse or that cause uncomfortable arousal, dissociation, anger, or somatic symptoms. They may be struggling with issues regarding trust, hope and despair.

In treating adolescent sex offenders with co-morbid posttraumatic stress disorder, the concepts of individualized treatment and flexibility may need to be emphasized. One may need to engage the youngster in both supportive and exploratory techniques, as well as focus on both here-and-now and historically traumatic material. The patient who is pushed too fast may become overwhelmed, and shut down the therapy process entirely. Clinicians should have a reasonable understanding of such concepts as repression, dissociation, isolation of affect, amnesia for parts of events, disguised traumatic dreams, holding of traumatic memories, conflicts and impacted affects in the unconscious over time, symbolic expression of anxiety, and identification with the aggressor (Blank, 1994). Experts in the field agree that more research is needed to improve diagnosis, treatment, and prevention of posttraumatic stress disorder including assessing the role of trauma type and severity, the individual response to trauma, and the concept of multiple trauma exposures after an initial event (Ballenger, Davidson, Lecrubier, et al, 2004).

Substance abuse

Substance abuse of all forms has been seen both in adults as well as adolescent sexual offender populations. Likewise, it has been seen as a risk factor for general violence in the adolescent population.

Peugh and Belenko (2001) used data from the Bureau of Justice & Statistics' national prison inmate survey to analyze alcohol and drug use and abuse patterns of men who are incarcerated in a state prison for sexual crimes. They concluded that two-thirds of their sex offense population was under the influence of alcohol or drugs at the time of their crime, had committed a crime to get money for drugs, had histories of regular illegal drug use, had received treatment for alcoholism, or had had a combination of a number of these characteristics.

Marx, Gross, and Adams (1999) studied the impact psychologically and pharmacologically of alcohol on the ability of sexually coercive and non-coercive men to discriminate when their female partner wants to bring a halt to sexual advances. They concluded that individuals who consumed, or expected to consume alcohol, took significantly longer to determine that they should refrain from attempting further sexual contact. Another interesting correlation was made by Williams (1999) who explained that one possible relationship between alcohol and sexual aggression or paraphilic behaviors is exposure to alcohol in utero (fetal alcohol syndrome). Finally, in a recent study (Abracen, Looman, & Anderson, 2000) it was seen that adult sexual offenders were more likely to abuse alcohol than were non-sexual violent offenders. Additionally, it was concluded that non-sexual offenders were significantly more likely to have had a history of other forms of substance abuse.

When one looks at general violent behavior in adolescents, two specific risk factors have stood out. First, violence directed at the adolescent seems to correlate with future violent behavior. Second, the adolescent's own drug use has demonstrated to be a significant risk factor (Brook, Brook, Rosen, et al, 2003). Myers, Stewart, & Brown (1998) concluded in a prospective longitudinal study that there was a high rate of progression to antisocial personality disorder among substance abusing adolescents who were diagnosed with a conduct disorder.

Conclusion

As one can see, the majority of information regarding general psychiatric disorders and sexual offense is from the adult sexual offender literature. However, there is still a small amount of literature regarding co-morbidity and adolescent youth who have engaged in inappropriate sexual behaviors. This chapter outlined what is known in regard to both of these populations, in addition to some discussions regarding adolescent non-sexual offenders. On top of the specific co-morbid diagnoses outlined and discussed, it has been suggestion that there are other possible psychiatric struggles with some sex offenders such as dissociation, attachment problems, and cognitive disabilities (Friedrich, Gerber, Kaplin, et al, 2001; Hawk, Rosenfeld, & Warren, 1993; Kenny, Keohy, & Seidler, 2001; Marshall, Serran, & Cortoni, 2000; Smallbone & Dadds, 2000). These were not outlined in further detail due to the fact that there is very little published on them in regard to their relationship to adolescent sexual offenders, or sexual offenders in general.

Further research is warranted in regard to co-morbidity with adolescent sexual offenders. However, given the increased interest in interrupting inappropriate sexual behavior when the offender is young, further research is likely to come forth in the future, better clarifying the limited amount that is known at this time. Despite this, it is encouraged that evaluators and those treating sexually abusive youth appropriately assess, or refer for assessment, their patients for psychiatric co-morbid problems. Youngsters should be treated for these difficulties as part of their overall treatment plan. Treating sexual issues without treating the entire person, including their psychiatric and medical problems, is not adequately addressing the needs of the adolescent.

References

Abracen, J., Looman, J., & Anderson, D. (2000). Alcohol and drug abuse in sexual and non-sexual violent offenders. *Sexual Abuse: A Journal of Research and Treatment*, 12:263-274.

Abram, K.M., Teplin, L.A., McClelland, G.M., & Dulcan, M.K. (2003). Co-morbid psychiatric disorders in youth in juvenile detention. *Archives of General Psychiatry*, 60:1097-1108.

American Psychiatric Association (1994), *Diagnostic and Statistical Manual of Mental Disorders*, 4th Edition (DSM-IV). Washington, D.C.: American Psychiatric Association.

American Psychiatric Association (2000), Diagnostic and Statistical Manual of Mental Disorders, 4th Edition – Text Revision (DSM-IV-TR). Washington, D.C.: American Psychiatric Association.

Anderson, J.C., Williams, S., McGee, R., & Silva, P.A. (1987). DSM-III Disorders in Pre-adolescent children: Prevalence in a large sample from the general population. *Archives of General Psychiatry*, 44:69-76.

Awad, G.A., & Saunders, E.B. (1989). Adolescent child molesters: Clinical observations. Child Psychiatry and Human Development, 19:195-206.

Awad, G.A., & Saunders, E.B. (1991). Male adolescent sexual assaulters: Clinical observations. *Journal of Interpersonal Violence*, 6:446-460.

Ballenger, J.C., Davidson, J.R.T., Lecrubier, Y., Nutt, D.J., Marshall, R.D., Nemeroff, C.B., Shalev, A.Y., & Yehuda, R. (2004). Consensus statement update on posttraumatic stress disorder from the Internal Consensus Group on Depression and Anxiety. *Journal of Clinical Psychiatry*, 65(supple 1):55-62.

Barbe, R.P., Bridge, J.A., Birmaher, B., Kolko, D.J., & Brent, D.A. (2004). Lifetime history of sexual abuse, clinical presentation, and outcome in a clinical trial for adolescent depression. *Journal of Clinical Psychiatry*, 65:77-83.

Barkley, R.A. (1998). *Attention-Deficit/Hyperactivity Disorder: A handbook for diagnosis and treatment, 2nd Edition*. New York, New York:Guilford Press.

Barkley, R.A. (2002). Major life activity and health outcomes associated with attention-deficit/hyperactivity disorder. *Journal of Clinical Psychiatry* (Suppl 12):10-15.

Becker, J.V., Kaplan, M.S., Cunningham-Rathner, J., & Kavoussi, R. (1986). Characteristics of adolescent incest sexual perpetrators: Preliminary findings. *Journal of Family Violence*, 1:85-97.

Becker, J.V., Kaplan, M.S., Tenke, C.E., & Tartaglini, A. (1991). The incidence of depressive symptomatology in juvenile sex offenders with a history of abuse. *Child Abuse and Neglect*, 15:531-536.

Becker, J.V., Harris, C.D., & Sales, B.D. (1993). Juveniles who commit sexual offenses: A critical review of research. In: *Sexual Aggression*, R.G. Hall, R. Hinschman, J. Graham, & M. Zaragoza (eds). Taylor-Francis Press. (pp. 215-228).

Bennett, K.J. & Offord, D.R. (2001). Screening for conduct problems: Does the predictive accuracy of conduct disorder symptoms improve with age? *Journal of the American Academy of Child and Adolescent Psychiatry*, 40:1418-1425.

Bernstein, G.A., Borchardt, C.M.,& Perwien, A.R. (1996). Anxiety disorders in children and adolescents: A review of the past ten years. *Journal of American Academy of Child and Adolescent Psychiatry*, 35:1110-1119.

Biederman, J. (2004). Impact of co-morbidity in adults with attention deficit/hyper-activity disorder. *Journal of Clinical Psychology*, 65(suppl 3):3-7.

Biederman, K.J., Faraone, S.V., Milberger, S., Getton, J.G., Chen, L., Mick, E., Greene, R.W., & Russell, R.L. (1996). Is childhood oppositional defiant disorder a precursor to adolescent conduct disorder? Findings from a four year follow up study of children with ADHD. *Journal of American Academy of Child and Adolescent Psychiatry*, 35:1193-1204.

Biederman, J., Mick, E., Faraone, S.V., Wilens, S.T., & Wozniak, J. (2003). Current concepts in the validity, diagnosis and treatment of paediatric bipolar disorder. *International Journal of europsychopharmacology*, 6:293-300.

Biedermanm, J., Newcorn, J. & Sprich, S. (1991). Co-morbidity of attention deficit/hyperactivity disorder with conduct, depressive, anxiety, and other disorders. *American J Psychiatry*, 148:564-577.

Blank, A.S. (1994). Clinical detection, diagnosis, and differential diagnosis of post-traumatic stress disorder. *American Journal of Psychiatry*, 143:908-910.

Brook, D.W., Brook, J.S., Rosen, Z., De la Rosa, M., Montoya, I.D., & Whiteman, M. (2003). Early risk factors for violence in Columbian adolescents. *American Journal of Psychiatry*, 160:1470-1478.

Burke, J.D., Loeber, R., & Birmaher, B. (2002). Oppositional defiant disorder and conduct disorder: A review of the past ten years, Part II. *Journal of the American Academy of Child and Adolescent Psychiatry*, 41:1275-1293.

Butler, S. & Seto, M.C. (2002). Distinguishing two types of adolescent sex offenders. *Journal of the American Academy of Child and Adolescent Psychiatry*, 41:83-90.

Campo, J., Nijman, H., Merckelbach, H., & Evers, C. (2003). Psychiatric co-morbidity of gender identity disorders: A survey among Dutch psychiatrists. *American Journal of Psychiatry*, 160:1332-1336.

Chen, Y., Arria, A.N., & Anthony, J.C. (2003). Fire setting in adolescence and being aggressive, shy, and rejected by peers: New epidemiologic evidence from a national sample survey. *The Journal of The American Academy of Psychiatry and the Law*, 31:44-52.

Colett, B.R., Ohan, J.L., & Myers, K.M. (2003). Ten-year review of rating scales. IV: scales assessing attention-deficit/hyperactivity disorder. *Journal of the American Academy of Child and Adolescent Psychiatry*, 42:1015-1037.

Cortoni, F. & Marshall, W.L. (2001). Sex as a coping strategy and its relationship to juvenile sexual history and intimacy in sexual offenders. *Sexual Abuse: A Journal of Research and Treatment*, 13:27-43.

Domalanta, D.D., Risser, W.L., Roberts, R.E., & Risser, J.M.H. (2003). Prevalence of depression and other psychiatric disorders among incarcerated youths. *Journal of the American Academy of Child and Adolescent Psychiatry*, 42:477-484.

Dunsieth, N.W. (2002). Flaws in the sexual addiction model. *Current Psychiatry*, 1:37-50.

Fagen, J. & Wexler, S. (1986). Explanations of sexual assault among violent delinquents. *Journal of Adolescent Research*, 3:363-385.

Fehrenbach, P.A., Smith, W., Monastersky, C., & Deisher, R.W. (1986). Adolescent sexual offenders: Offender and offense characteristics. *American Journal of Orthopsychiatry*, 56:225-233.

Friedrich, W.N., Gerber, P.N., Koplin, B., Davis, M., Giese, J., Mykelbust, C., & Franckowiak, D. (2001). Multimodal assessment of dissociation in adolescents: Inpatients and juvenile sex offenders. *Sexual Abuse: A Journal of Research and Treatment*, 13:167-177.

Gleyzer, R., Felthouse, A.R., & Holzer, C.E. (2002). Animal cruelty and psychiatric disorders. *Journal of the American Academy of Psychiatry and the Law*, 30:257-265.

Graham, K.R. (1996). The childhood victimization of sex offenders: An underestimated issue. *International Journal of Offender Therapy and Comparative Criminology*, 40:192-203.

Haapasalo, J. & Hamalainen, T. (1996). Childhood family problems and current psychiatric problems among young violent and property offenders. *Journal of The American Academy of Child and Adolescent Psychiatry*, 34:1394-1401.

Hanson, R.K. & Morton-Bourgon, K. (2004). *Predictors of sexual recidivism: An updated meta-analysis* 2004-03. Ottawa, ON.: Public Safety and Emergency Preparedness Canada (HQ72C2H257-2004).

Hastings, T., Anderson, S.J., & Hemphill, P. (1997). Comparisons of daily stress, coping, problem behavior, and cognitive distortions in adolescent sexual offenders and conduct-disordered youth. *Sexual Abuse: A Journal of Research and Treatment*, 9:29-43.

Hawk, G.L., Rosenfeld, B.D., & Warren, J.I. (1993). Prevalence of sexual offenses among mentally retarded criminal defendants. *Hospital and Community Psychiatry*, 44:784-786.

Hill, J. (2002). Biological, psychological, and social processes in conduct disorder. *Journal of Clinical Psychology and Psychiatry*, 43:133-164.

Hunter, J.A., Figueredo, A.J., Malamuth, N.M., & Becker, J.V. (2003). Juvenile sex offenders: Toward the development of a typology. *Sexual Abuse: A Journal of Research and Treatment*, 15:27-48.

I.M.P.A.C.T. (*Investigating the mindset of parents about AD/HD and children today*) Survey (2001). New York University Child Study Center. Available at http://www.about Our Kids.org.

Jacobs, W.L., Kennedy, W.A., & Meyer, J.B. (1997). Juvenile delinquents: A between-group comparison study of sexual and non-sexual offenders. *Sexual Abuse: A Journal of Research and Treatment*, 9:201-217.

Joe, S. & Marcus, S.C. (2003). Trends by race and gender in suicide attempts among U.S. adolescents, 1991-2001. Psychiatric Services, 54:454.

Justice, B., Justice, R., & Kraft, I.A. (1974). Early-warning signs of violence: Is a triad enough? *American Journal of Psychiatry*, 131:457-459.

Kafka, M.P. & Hennen, J. (2002). A DSM-IV Axis I co-morbidity study of males (n = 120) with paraphilias and paraphilia-related disorders. *Sexual Abuse: A Journal of Research and Treatment*, 14:349-66.

Kaplan, S.J., Pelcovitz, D., & Labruna, V. (1999). Child and adolescent abuse and neglect research: A review of the past 10 years. Part I: Physical and emotional abuse and neglect. *Journal of the American Academy of Child and Adolescent Psychiatry*, 38:1214-1221.

Kaplan, S., Hong, G., & Weinhold, C. (1984). Epidemiology of depressive sympto-matology in adolescents. *Journal of the Academy of Child Psychiatry*, 23:91-98.

Kataoka, S.H., Zima, B.T., Dupre, D.A., Moreno, K.A., Yang, X., & McCracken, J.T. (2001). Mental health problems and service use among female juvenile offenders: Their relationship to criminal history. *Journal of the American Academy of Child and Adolescent Psychiatry*, 40:549-555.

Kavoussi, R.J., Kaplan, M., & Becker, J.V. (1988). Psychiatric diagnoses in adolescent sex offenders. *Journal of the American Academy of Child and Adolescent Psychiatry*, 27:241-243.

Keenan, K.& Wakschlag, L.S. (2000). More than terrible twos: The nature and sever-ity of disruptive behavior problems in clinic-referred preschool children. *Journal of Abnormal Child Psychology*, 28:33-46.

Kelly, T., Richardson, G., Hunter, R., & Knapp, M. (2002). Attention and executive function deficits in adolescent sex offenders. *Neuropsychological Dev Cogn Sect C Child Neuropsycholy*, 8:138-143.

Kenny, D.T., Keogh, T., & Seidler, K. (2001). Predictors of recidivism in Australian juvenile sex offenders: Implications for treatment. *Sexual Abuse: A Journal of Research and Treatment*, 13:131-148.

Kratochvil, C.J., Heiligenstein, J.H., Spencer, T.J., Biederman, J., Wernicke, J., Newcorn, I.H., Casat, C., Milton, D., Michelson, D., & Dittmann, R., (2002). Tomoxetine and methylphenidate treatment in children with ADHD: A perspective, randomized, open-label trial. *Journal of the American Academy of Child and Adolescent Psychiatry*, 41:776-784.

Laehey, B.B., Miller, T.L., Gordon, R.A., & Riley, A.W. (1999). Developmental epidemiology of the disruptive behavior disorders. In: *Handbook of the Disruptive Behavior Disorders*, Quay, H.C., Hogan, A., (eds.). New York: Plenum, pp. 23-48).

Leibenluft, E., Charney, D.S., Towbin, K.E., Bhangoo, R.K., & Pine, D.S.(2003). Defining clinical phenotypes of juvenile mania. *American Journal of Psychiatry*, 160:430-437.

Lindsay, W.R., Lees, M.S. (2003). A comparison of anxiety and depression in sex offenders with intellectual disability and a control group with intellectual disability. *Sexual Abuse: A Journal of Research and Treatment*, 15:339-345.

Loeber, R., Burke, J.D., Lahey, B.B., Winters, A., & Zera, M. (2000). Oppositional defiant and conduct disorder: A review of the past ten years, Part I. *Journal of the American Academy of Child and Adolescent Psychiatry*, 39:1468-1484.

MacDonald, V.A. & Achenbach, T.M. (1996). Attention problems versus conduct problems as six-year predictors of problem scores in a national sample. *Journal of the American Academy of Child & Adolescent Psychiatry*, 35:1237-1246.

Mannuzza, S., Klein, R.G., Bessler, A., Malloy, P., & LaPadula, M. (1998). Adult psychiatric status of hyperactive boys grown up. *American Journal of Psychiatry*, 155:493-498.

Marshall, W.L., Champagne, F., Sturgeon, C., & Bryce, P. (1997). Increasing the self-esteem of child molesters. *Sexual Abuse: A Journal of Research and Treatment*, 9:321-333.

Marshall, W.L., Serran, G.A., & Cortoni, F.A. (2000). Childhood attachments, sexual abuse, and their relationship to adult coping and child molesters. *Sexual Abuse: A Journal of Research and Treatment*, 12:17-26.

Marx, B.P., Gross, A.M., & Adams, H.E. (1999). The effect of alcohol on the responses of sexually coercive and non-coercive men to an experimental rape analog. *Sexual Abuse: A Journal of Research and Treatment*, 11:131-145.

Marzuk, P.M. (1996). Violence, crime, and mental illness: How strong a link? *Archives of General Psychiatry*, 53:481-486.

Mathews, R., Hunter, J.A., & Vuz, J. (1997). Juvenile female sexual offenders: Clinical characteristics and treatment issues. *Sexual Abuse: A Journal of Research and Treatment*, 9:187-199.

McClellan, J., McCurry, C., Ronnei, M., Adams, J., Eisner, A., & Storck, N. (1996). Age of onset of sexual abuse: Relationship to sexually inappropriate behaviors. *Journal of the American Academy of Child and Adolescent Psychiatry*, 34:1375-1383.

McElroy, S.., Soutullo, C.A., Taylor, P., Nelson E.B., Beckman, D.A., Brusman, L.A., Ombaba, G.M., Strakowski, S.M., & Keck, P.E. (1999). Psychiatric features of 36 men convicted of sexual offenses. *Journal of Clinical Psychiatry*, 60:414-420.

Monahan, J., Steadman, H.J., eds. (1994). *Violence and mental disorder: Developments in risk assessment*. Chicago, ILL: University of Chicago Press.

Monto, M., Zgourides, G., & Harris, R. (1998). Empathy, self-esteem, and the adolescent sexual offender. *Sexual Abuse: A Journal of Research and Treatment*, 10:127-140.

Myers, M.G., Stewart, D.G., & Brown, S.A. (1998). Progression from conduct disorder to antisocial personality disorder following treatment for adolescent substance abuse. *American Journal of Psychiatry*, 155:479-485.

Nelson, E.C., Heath, A.C., Madden, P.A., Cooper, M.L., Dinwiddie, S.H., Bucholz, K.K., Glowinski, A., McLaughlin, T., Dunne, M.P., Statham, D.J., & Martin, N.G. (2002). Associations between self-reported childhood sexual abuse and adverse psychosocial outcomes. *Archives of General Psychiatry*, 59:139-145.

Nemeroff, C.B. (2004). Neurobiological consequences of childhood trauma. *Journal of Clinical Psychiatry*, 65(supple 1):18-27.

Nutt, D.J. & Malizia, A.L. (2004) Structural and Functional Brain Changes in Posttraumatic Stress Disorder. *J Clin Psychiatry*, 65 (suppl 1):11-17.

Peugh, J. & Belenko, S. (2001). Examining the substance use patterns and treatment needs of incarcerated sex offenders. *Sexual Abuse: A Journal of Research and Treatment*, 13:179-195.

Prentky, R., Harris, B., Frizzell, K. & Righthand, S. (2000). An actuarial procedure for assessing risk with juvenile sex offenders. *Sexual Abuse: A Journal of Research and Treatment*, 12:71-93.

Putnam, F.W. (2003). Ten-year research update review: Child sexual abuse. *Journal of the American Academy of Child and Adolescent Psychiatry*, 42:269-278.

Quanbeck, C.D., Stone, D.C., Scott, C.L., McDermott, B.E., Altshuler, L.L., and Frye, M.A. (2004). Clinical and legal correlates of inmates with Bipolar Disorder at the time of criminal arrest. *Journal of Clinical Psychiatry*, 65:198-203.

Raymond, N.C., Coleman, E., Ohlerking, F., Christenson, G.A., & Miner, M. (1999). Psychiatric co-morbidity in pedophilic sex offenders. *American Journal of Psychiatry*, 156:786-788.

Richardson, G., Kelly, T.P., Bahte, S.R. & Graham, F. (1997). Group differences in abuser and abuse characteristics in a British sample of sexually abusive adolescents. *Sexual Abuse: A Journal of Research and Treatment*, 9:239-257.

Ruchkin, V., Koposov, R., Vermeiren, R., & Schwab-Stone, M. (2003). Psychopathology and age at onset of conduct problems in juvenile delinquents. *Journal of Clinical Psychiatry*, 64:913-920.

Ryan, G. (1989). Victim to victimizer: Rethinking victim treatment. *Journal of Interpersonal Violence*, 4:325-341.

Sanisolow, C.A., Grilo, C.M., Fehon, D.C., Axelrod, S.R., & McGlashan, T.H. (2003). Correlates of suicide risk in juvenile detainees and adolescent inpatients. *Journal of the American Academy of Child and Adolescent Psychiatry*, 42:234-240.

Satterfield, J.H. & Schell, A. (1997). A prospective study of hyperactive boys with conduct problems and normal boys: Adolescent and adult criminality. *Journal of the American Academy of Child and Adolescent Psychiatry*, 36:1726-1735.

Schram, D.D., Milloy, C.D., & Rowe, W.E. (1991). Juvenile sex offenders: A follow up study of reoffense behavior. Unpublished manuscript.

Schwartz, M.F. (1995). In my opinion: Victim to victimizer. Sexual Addiction and Compulsivity, 2:81-88.

Siponmma, L., Kristiansson, M., Jonson, C., Nyden, A., & Gillberg, C. (2001). Juvenile and young adult mentally disordered offenders: The role of child neuropsychiatric disorders. *Journal of the American Academy of Psychiatry and the Law*, 29:420-426.

Slavkin, M.L. (2002). What every clinician needs to know about juvenile fire setters. *Psychiatric Services*, 53:1237-1238.

Smallbone, S.W. & Dadds, M.R. (2000). Attachment and coercive sexual behavior. *Sexual Abuse: A Journal of Research and Treatment*, 12:3-15.

Smith, W.R., Monastersky, C., & Deisher, R.M. (1987). MMPI-based personality types among juvenile sexual offenders. *Journal of Clinical Psychology*, 43:422-430.

Srinivasaraghavan, J. (2004). Violent adolescents. *American Academy of Psychiatry and the Law Newsletter*, 29:1-3.

Swanson, J.W. (1993). Alcohol abuse, mental disorder, and violent behavior: An epidemiologic inquiry. *Alcohol Health Res World*, 17:123-32.

Taylor, E., Chadwick, O., Heptinstall, E. & Danckaerts, M. (1996). Hyperactivity and conduct problems as risk factors for adolescent development. *Journal of the American Academy of Child and Adolescent Psychiatry*, 35:1213-1226.

Teplin, L.A., Abram, K.M., McClelland, G.M., Dulcan, M.K., & Merricle, A.A. (2002). Psychiatric disorders in youth in juvenile detention. *Archives of General Psychiatry*, 59:1133-1143.

Ulzen, T.P. & Hamilton, H. (1998). The nature and characteristics of psychiatric co-morbidity in incarcerated adolescents. *Canadian Journal of Psychiatry*, 43:57-63.

Valle, L.A. & Silovsky, J.F. (2002). Attributions and adjustment following child sexual and physical abuse. *Child Maltreatment*, 7:9-25.

Vance, J.E., Bowen, N.K., Fernandez, G., & Thompson, S. (2002). Risk and protective factors as predictors of outcome in adolescents with psychiatric disorder and aggression. *Journal of the American Academy of Child and Adolescent Psychiatry*, 41:36-43.

Vitacco, M.J. & Rogers, R. (2001). Predictors of adolescent psychopathy: The role of impulsivity, hyperactivity, and sensation seeking. *Journal of the American Academy of Psychiatry and the Law*, 29:374-382.

Volavka, J. (1995). *Neurobiology of violence*. Washington, D.C.: American Psychiatric Press.

Weller, E., Rowan, A., Weller, R., & Elia, J. (1999). Aggressive behavior associated with attention-deficit/hyperactivity disorder, conduct disorder, and developmental disabilities. *Journal of Clinical Psychiatry Monograph*, 17:2-7.

Williams, S. (1999). Alcohol's possible covert role: Brain dysfunction, paraphilias, and sexually aggressive behaviors. *Sexual Abuse: A Journal of Research and Treatment*, 11:147-158.

Yehuda, R. (2004). Risk and resilience in post traumatic stress disorder. *Journal of Clinical Psychiatry*, 65(suppl 1):29-36.

CHAPTER SEVEN

PROMOTING HEALTHY SEXUALITY IN SEXUALLY ABUSIVE YOUTH

STEVEN M. BROWN
AND
CARL SCHWARTZ

Introduction

"Promoting health," even "promoting sexual health" – who would disagree with that? Any well-meaning service provider working with sexually abusive young people would hope that their hard work is contributing to making a young person more sexually healthy. The problem seems to arise around the question of what we mean by sexual health for these troubled young people, a question that parallels a societal quandary about how to define adolescent sexual health generally. In addition, assuming we can agree on what we mean by sexual health, the question still remains how do we craft our treatment models to reach that goal with minimal unintended negative consequences.

As a culture, we are immensely conflicted about sexuality generally, especially child and adolescent sexuality. On our televisions, movie screens, video games and in our email boxes, sexual messages, images, innuendos are ever present. A 1997 study of prime time television revealed that the average adolescent in the U.S. views 1400 sexual references, jokes, and innuendos each year (Stasburger, 1997). However, only one in 85 of these references will mention abstinence, contraception, or marriage (Daves, 1995). Studies show that few parents talk with their children in a meaningful way about sexual health issues (Warren & Neer, 1992; Goldstein & Connelly, 1998; Durex Corporation, 1997) despite children's desire to hear their parents' views on the topic. The media screams "go for it," "everybody's doing it," "gotta be sexy." At the same time, our government will only pay for sex education that talks exclusively about sexual abstinence until marriage despite statistics revealing that, compared to previous generations, today's adolescents reach puberty earlier, have sexual intercourse earlier, and get married significantly later (Facing Facts, 1995).

Mirroring the general culture, there is also striking contradictions and ambivalences in the juvenile sex offender field about addressing healthy sexuality. There are hundreds of articles about how to help juvenile sex abusers recognize and avoid their sexually abusive behavior. In contrast, a recent search on the topic of healthy sexuality/sexuality education and sex offenders yielded fewer than ten articles on the subject. Treatment providers acknowledge that the majority of these young people will be returning to the community and need the knowledge and skills to negotiate future romantic and sexual relationships (Brown, 2000). Yet, because of the harm they have caused, it is difficult to imagine them having future sexual lives. While many providers encourage open communication about deviant sexuality, they fear that talking about *healthy* sexuality will over-stimulate youth and possibly give them permission to act out sexually. Because these young people have used sex abusively, there is a fear about how they will internalize and act upon messages about healthy sexuality. In the end, programs often settle for a "better safe than sorry" approach that focuses on interventions aimed at containing young peoples' sexuality. In short, we, in the juvenile offender field, have tended to avoid the reality that juvenile abusers are or will be sexual, rather than grapple with the complexity of how to help them become healthy sexual people.

Good intentions gone awry

Consider the following exchange with a 17-year-old boy who was approaching discharge after 2 years of intensive and quite successful treatment at a long term residential treatment program.

> Q: "What do you think it will be like 'out there' in the real world when you start to meet girls your age?"

> A: "I'm looking forward to it."

> Q: "What if you meet someone you really like, you're attracted to her, and you guys really hit it off?"

> A: He immediately interrupted saying, "Well, nothing will happen, I'll just use my urge control I've learned here."

> Q: Pressing him further, "But, let's say you really like her. You might like to ask her out on a date. You guys go out on a date and, at some point, you both might want to kiss, make out, or even go further?"

> A: Anxious and searching for the "right" answer, he said, "Well, I'll make sure I don't do anything or I'll keep my relapse prevention plan in mind."

> Q: "Well, what does your relapse prevention plan say?"

> A: "It says to avoid situations where I might be with someone who fits my 'victim profile.'"

> Q: "What's your victim profile?"

> A: "Little girls that are the same age as my victim."

Q: "So how's that gonna help you with a girl your own age who you're attracted to?"

A: Seeming frustrated, he blurted, "I don't know, I guess I'll just use my urge control. Nothing will happen. Don't worry, I'm not going to do anything. I've come too far to make that mistake again."

In recent years, some in the juvenile sex offender field have raised concern that sexually abusive youth often emerge from treatment programs with a sophisticated knowledge of what **not** to do with their sexual feelings, but little, if any, knowledge about healthy sexual expression (Brown, 2000; Perry and Ohm, 1998). They argue that many young people feel unprepared to enter the world of dating and romantic/sexual relationships. Some come to equate any sexual expression with deviant sexual expression. Others vow to put their sexuality away altogether, having the perception that, if they have eliminated their sexual feelings, they have succeeded in treatment.

Treatment Cultures and Practices that Discourage Healthy Sexual Development

If it is true that some clients internalize highly negative messages about their sexuality, how is it that they get such unbalanced sex-negative messages? The answer to this question, we believe, lies in the aspects of the treatment culture and treatment practices that historically have been, and currently still are, being used with sexually abusive youth. Here are some examples.

Historically, central to treatment has been the "sex offender introduction" requiring clients to talk about their offenses by first saying, "my name is _____ and I am a sex offender", then proceed to disclose the details of their offenses. Chaffin and Bonner (1998) discuss young teenagers, ages 13 to 15, who are forced on a daily basis to recite phrases such as "I am a pedophile and am not fit to live in human society...I can never be trusted...Everything I say is a lie...I can never be cured." While this example may be extreme, it is not difficult to imagine how young people, over time, adopt this identity as their own and can come to view all their sexual feelings, fantasies and actions as scary, dangerous, and needing to be repressed or contained.

Mirroring the juvenile offender literature, treatment programs and cultures are often organized around the goal of helping young people avoid sexually abusive patterns centering on concepts such as sex abuse cycles, thinking errors, and relapse prevention (Lane, 1997). In contrast, there is a relative absence of interventions aimed at promoting healthy sexuality. It is not surprising that youth, as a result, would glean from this approach that they can succeed in treatment by talking about abusive sexual behavior and should not discuss other aspects of sexuality.

Because these young people have been universally seen as being highly sexualized, compulsive, and manipulative, treatment programs often train their staff to be vigilant, and often hypervigilant, about any possible sign of "grooming" behavior. Staff can interpret things as simple as a look, stare, or playful joking as sexual and feel the need to limit this behavior. Over time, teens in treatment can learn that, in order to avoid charges of grooming and succeed in the program, they need to put away any behavior that is, or could possibly be construed as, sexual.

Finally, in a commonly used model of relapse prevention, the word "abstinence" is used to describe the baseline state prior to a client proceeding down the relapse chain (Steen, 1993). While the word abstinence presumably is intended to mean "abstinence from sexual offending," this is also the word commonly used to describe refraining from sexual behavior of any kind. It is not surprising that young people can get the message that the ultimate goal, and what treatment providers really want, is to for them to refrain from any sexual behavior, abusive or otherwise (Brown & Linder, 2001). This example, maybe more than any, illustrates how, in ways that we are often unaware, our treatment practices reflect our fear of what will happen when these young people enter sexual relationships and our unrealistic wish that they just be asexual.

Why this treatment culture and these treatment practices?

A number of explanations have been offered to account for the treatment culture and practices historically used with sexually abusive youth. In recent years, researchers and practitioners have pointed to the fact that current treatment models used with sexually abusive youth have trickled down from treatment work with adult sex offenders and pedophiles, usually in prison settings (Creeden, 1999; Longo, 2002; Chaffin & Bonner, 1998). As a result, they are rooted in dubious assumptions that are developmentally inappropriate when applied to adolescents and children. These include beliefs, for example, that sex offending is a compulsive behavior resulting in an extremely high recidivism rate; that sex offending is a life-long disorder that cannot be cured, only managed; that denial must be broken and manipulation challenged via a highly confrontational stance; that offenders engage in carefully planned and highly ritualized grooming behaviors to set up their victims; and that an ingrained pattern of deviant arousal and deviant fantasies are essential features. If we view sexually abusive youth as "little pedophiles" who can not be cured, only contained, then it makes sense to put in place highly restrictive treatment practices aimed at ensuring the goal of safety of peers and the community at all costs.

Treatment programs also exist within the wider culture and cannot help but be influenced by the views in the U.S. about sex offenders. In our society, sex offenders are the ultimate pariah. They are often viewed with irrational fear and are the target of rage and sometimes hysteria. It should not be surprising that these views are reflected in the attitudes of treatment providers, treatment practices, and treatment cultures. As well, treatment providers and programs feel an immense pressure from outside forces, whether they be probation officers, policy makers, child protective service workers, or parents, to do whatever they can to "**stop** these young people from doing what they are doing." This, combined with a fear of lawsuits resulting from clients engaging in sexual behavior while in care, propels providers and programs toward a containment and control approach under the guise of "better safe that sorry." As one workshop participant stated in reference to residential programs, "Programs can't be held liable for kids being woefully unprepared for life after treatment. The same can't be said for them sexually acting out in the program." Hence, it is easy for (and understandable why) residential programs would adopt a highly contained and restrictive approach that opts for short term order at the expense of longer term gains (Prescott, 2004).

Finally, still others explain these highly restrictive and confrontive treatment practices via the concept of "re-enactment." The concept of re-enactment refers to how clients, and especially clients with histories of trauma, unwittingly repeat aspects of their traumatic past in current relationships (Saakvitne, Gamble, Pearlman & Lev, 2000). Treatment providers inevitably are drawn into the re-enactment dance and also wittingly or unwittingly can replay abusive patterns in their relationships with clients. Traumatized young people, whether they be perpetrators or victims, are extremely adept at getting treatment providers and treatment systems to replicate the abusive environments in which they were raised. While most noticeable on a micro level between and individual client and treatment provider, whole systems also easily can develop in such a way that they re-enact the abusive dynamics of the populations they serve.

Potential consequences

First, it is important to remember that our first responsibility is to do no harm to our clients. As noted by Chaffin and Bonner (1998) this is particularly important in treatment situations that are mandated or coerced. They state,

> *"It is time for potentially harmful practices that are used in well-intentioned efforts to intervene with these children and adolescents to engage our professional attention...Punitive and aversive treatment approaches must be considered within the context of the current political climate that exaggerates our fear of juvenile crime...This combined with the emotionality and zeal surrounding sexual abuse and sex offenders...should alert us to the potential for harming youthful patients by swatting flies with sledge hammers."* (p. 315)

More specifically, by ignoring interventions to promote healthy sexuality, our concern is that we are "setting kids up for failure" by leaving them unprepared for the world of teen dating and relationships. The sole focus on stopping deviance violates a fundamental principal of therapeutic intervention – if you take away a maladaptive coping mechanism, you need to replace it with something more adaptive (Brown, 2000; Perry & Ohm, 1999). For example, these young people never learned through adult guidance and modeling the difference between a healthy and unhealthy romantic/sexual relationship; how to get to know someone who you have a crush on; what cues tell you someone might "like you back;" or what one actually does when things get sexual. We do sexually abusive youth a disservice and we do a disservice to the safety of the community if we do not grapple with how to teach them these kinds of skills.

Highly sex-negative treatment practices also parallel the family cultures of many of these young people. For these youth, sexuality is already emotionally linked with danger and fraught with anxiety, shame and guilt. In their experience, sex has been used in destructive ways and they have learned to use sex as a weapon or a way to gain power, control, acceptance, self-esteem or revenge. Gil and Johnson (1993) state, "children who molest are socialized to sex and aggression occurring in tandem...Touching is not for the child's comfort, but for someone else's pleasures. Anxiety, tension, anger, rage and cruelty become intimately associated with sex...Relationships are based on sex and need, not love and caring...The way to stop emotional emptiness and pain is through sex, which is often accompanied by hitting and violence and quick exits and loss..." Don Grief (1998) states, "excessive control (in treatment) runs the risk of reinforcing the idea that sex is simply dangerous or disgusting, something to be feared, not something to be valued. Consequences of too tight or rigid control is to discourage or squash any sexual thoughts, feelings, fantasies – in short, any developmentally normal curiosity or behavior." Reinforcing these negative messages seems likely at minimum to promote lives of troubled relationships and sexual dysfunction, and, quite possibly, further sexual offending.

Finally, if young people are taking from our treatment programs that they should repress, deny or avoid all their sexual feelings, their sexuality will find expression in other ways, ways that are often more dangerous and destructive. As is true with anger, putting the lid on tighter and tighter only works for so long and ultimately leads to disaster. Increased risk for re-offending is often linked to stress. There is hardly anything more stressful than trying to negotiate the world of dating, teen relationships, and physical intimacy with no skills and a feeling that your sexuality is bad and dangerous.

A Shift in Paradigm

The field of evaluation and treatment of sexually abusive youth has been evolving over the course of the past 25 years since its beginnings in the 1980's (Knopp, Freeman-Longo & Stevenson, 1992). As noted, the juvenile field has been most powerfully influenced by the adult sex offender field whose assumptions and practices have either trickled down to or been wholly imported into the treatment model for sexually abusive youth. However, in recent years, researchers and practitioners have asserted that there is little empirical evidence to support the notion that sexually abusive youth mirror adult sexual offenders. As one therapist and trainer who has been practicing in the field for nearly 15 years put it, "we have developed theory and notions about who juvenile offenders are based on the worst, most dangerous 15% of the adult offender population" (Creeden, 1999).

As professionals in the field have begun to question old assumptions, a paradigm shift has begun to take place. The notion of a paradigm shift, associated with the writing of Thomas Kuhn (1970), refers to a fundamental change in the assumptions underlying a particular discipline or field of study. Different authors have characterized this paradigm shift in different ways. Rich (2003) describes movement from simplistic approaches stressing either a forensic/correctional approach or a mental health approach to what he calls a "third direction" that integrates the forensic and the mental health perspectives. Longo (2002) contrasts traditional sex offender treatment models for treating juveniles that have trickled down from adult sex offender models with what he calls a more holistic approach.

In Table 1, we contrast the assumptions of a "traditional sex offender model" with a "holistic or integrated model." The purpose of contrasting these two models is not to portray the traditional model as a "straw man" and then tear it down with the notion of a holistic model. Rather, it is to contrast two very different ways of thinking or approaching work with sexually abusive youth as well as highlight the dialectical nature of how fields of study tend to evolve. A dialectical perspective (Linehan &

Kehrer, 1993) holds that, within any one thing or system including a field of study, there is polarity. The polar forces (the thesis and antithesis) exist in tension with each other and it is this tension that produces change and movement to a synthesis of the poles. Inherent in this synthesis are polar forces which result in a new synthesis thus making change and evolution continuous.

The holistic model views juvenile sexual offenders as developmentally distinct from adult offenders, especially pedophiles, the population for which many of the traditional treatment models were designed. Whereas pedophiles' primary motivation for offending stemmed from deviant arousal patterns and/or needs for power and control, the holistic model assumes that the motivation for offending is extremely varied, complex and individual. Traditional models assume high rates of recidivism typical of pedophiles and that offending behavior cannot be cured, only controlled. Research on juvenile offenders generally find relatively low rates of sexual recidivism even without treatment (Worling & Curwen, 2000) and there is no evidence to support that, similar to pedophiles, "once an abuser, always an abuser." As a result of the extremely high-risk population for which the model was designed, the traditional sex offender model places a very strong emphasis on control and containment of clients' sexual interests and behaviors. More holistic models attempt to balance the still important goals of control and containment with client collaboration. The traditional model has been drawn from the cognitive behavioral and substance abuse traditions and has tended to focus on eliminating clients' deficits. In contrast, the holistic model draws from numerous theoretical perspectives, tends to be more strength-based, and more focused on issues such as the therapeutic process and relationship. Finally, regarding clients' histories of victimization, the traditional model views this as of secondary importance or even dangerous because victimization can be used as an excuse for offending. The holistic model, in contrast, views clients' histories of trauma and victimization as important to understanding their anti-social, including offending, behavior.

Table 1
A Paradigm Shift: Traditional Sex Offender Model Versus Holistic/Integrated Model

Traditional Sex Offender Model	Holistic/Integrated Model
• Views juvenile offenders as similar to adult offenders	• Views juvenile offenders as distinct from adults (developmental perspective)
• Views power/control and deviant arousal as central motivators for offending	• Views motivators for offending as extremely varied and complex
• Sexual offending is typically a compulsive behavior with high recidivism rates	• There is great variation in juvenile sexual abusers. The recidivism rate is generally fairly low
• Emphasis on safety, control and containment.	• Balance safety/control/containment with collaboration
• Assumes you cannot cure sexual offending, only control it	• Assumes that elimination of sexual offending behavior (cure) is possible
• Cognitive-behavioral relapse prevention approach	• Integrative theoretical approach (cognitive-behavioral, humanistic, family systems, attachment/trauma, neurobiological, psychodynamic, addiction)
• Deficit- or problem-based	• Strength- or asset-based.
• Content focused	• Balance focus on content with process and the therapeutic relationship
• Stress on risk management	• Balance risk management goals with promotion of client development
• Sees addressing trauma/victimization as eroding accountability	• Sees trauma/victimization as important to understanding offending behavior

Table 2 contrasts the beliefs about sexuality that explicitly or implicitly grow out of the contrasting models and the assumptions delineated in Table 1. As one looks down Table 1 at the list of beliefs under the traditional model, it is apparent that many of these beliefs reflect beliefs about adolescent sexuality in our culture, a culture which refuses to view children as sexual beings and fears that information about sexuality equals permission. As noted earlier, if our assumption about sexually abusive youth is that they are "little pedophiles" with all that the label connotes – ingrained deviant arousal, predatory, high number of victims – then it makes sense to view expressions of their sexuality as dangerous, needing to be feared and carefully contained. However, when one begins to view sexually abusive youth as developmentally distinct from adult pedophiles, it becomes more reasonable to embrace a more open, positive, and balanced view of our clients developing sexuality.

Table 2
A Paradigm Shift: Implicit Beliefs About Sexuality in a Traditional Sex Offender Model Versus Holistic/Integrated Model

Traditional Sex Offender Model	Holistic/Integrated Model
• Sexuality is something to be feared.	• Sexuality is a critical life force in all people that can be used positively or negatively
• Focus solely on control of problem sexual behavior	• Balance focus on problem sexual behavior with focus on social and sexual competencies
• Problem sexual behavior is primarily about power and control, not sexuality	• Sexuality (in its broadest sense) is integral to problem sexual behavior
• Sexuality is a topic that needs to be treated with seriousness and gravity	• Sexuality is serious and is also associated with things fun, light, and humorous
• Education about sexuality should focus on its consequences/dangers	• Education about sexuality should balance a focus on benefits/pleasures with consequences/dangers
• Information about sexuality equals permission to engage in sexual behavior	• Information about sexuality satisfies curiosity and tends to make it less likely that young people will engage in sexual behavior
• All behaviors can be potentially sexual and a sign of grooming	• Clients social and sexual behavior must be assessed as to whether it is part of the grooming process
• Touch is dangerous. It can become easily sexualized and lead to sexual acting out	• Touch is important to healing. Clients can learn to experience touch in a non-sexual manner
• Sexuality viewed as separate from clients' ability to develop secure attachment	• Development of secure attachment is viewed as integral to healthy sexuality

What is normative when it comes to adolescent sexual health?

The paucity of literature on healthy sexuality in the juvenile offender field parallels the lack of social science literature about adolescent sexuality more generally. Because of the charged climate around sexuality in our culture, there are considerable barriers to researchers asking question of a sexual nature to young people. As a result, we have limited knowledge about adolescent sexuality, generally including issues such as what sexual behaviors teens are engaging in, what is normative and non-normative, what is healthy and problematic. The data that does exist about adolescent sexual health tends to focus on problems stemming from adolescent sexual behavior and rarely addresses the positive aspects of adolescent sexuality and what it means to be a sexually healthy adolescent (Erhardt, 1996).

However, in the last decade, an important, though limited, literature has evolved which attempts to define adolescent health in a more comprehensive and positive manner. In 1995, The National Commission on Adolescent Sexual Health published a consensus statement on adolescent sexual health which was endorsed by 50 national organizations and over 35 professional organizations (Facing Facts, 1995). In contrast to most approaches to sexual health, which are narrowly focused on avoiding unwanted pregnancy and disease, the Commission's statement was much more comprehensive in its approach and construed sexual health as a normative part of adolescent development. According to the statement, sexual health includes the abilities (a) to develop and maintain meaningful interpersonal relationships; (b) to appreciate one's own body; (c) to interact with both genders in respectful and appropriate ways; and (d) to express affection, love, and intimacy in ways consistent with one's own values. The Commission identified the characteristics and behaviors of a sexually healthy adolescent which are outlined in abbreviated form in Table 3. It is noteworthy that most of the qualities and behaviors identified also apply to sexually healthy adults, and, as applied to young people, can be seen as an ideal to aim toward.

Table 3
Characteristics of a Sexually Healthy Adolescent
(Facing Facts, 1995)

SELF
- Appreciates own body
- Takes responsibility for own behaviors
- Is knowledgeable about sexuality issues

RELATIONSHIPS WITH PARENTS AND FAMILY MEMBERS
- Communicates effectively with family about issues, including sexuality
- Understands and seeks information about parents' and family's values, and considers them in developing one's own values

PEERS
- Interacts with both genders in appropriate and respectful ways
- Acts on one's own values and beliefs when they conflict with peers

ROMANTIC PARTNERS
- Expresses love and intimacy in developmentally appropriate ways
- Has the skills to evaluate readiness for mature sexual relationships

---

In 2001, former U.S. Surgeon General David Satcher, in his Call to Action to Promote Sexual Health and Responsible Sexual Behavior (Satcher, 2001), acknowledged the broader aspects of sexual health. It offers this definition of sexual health:

> *"Sexual health is not limited to the absence of disease or dysfunction, nor is its importance confined to just the reproductive years. It includes the ability to understand and weigh the risks, responsibilities, outcomes and impacts of sexual actions and to practice abstinence when appropriate. It includes freedom from sexual abuse and discrimination and the ability of individuals to integrate their sexuality into their lives, derive pleasure from it, and to reproduce if they so choose."* (page 1)

Perry and Ohm (1999), in one of the few articles on promotion of healthy sexuality in sexually abusive youth, offer the following definition of healthy sexuality:

> *"The ability to appreciate one's own sexual feelings and act on them through a variety of channels (e.g. Abstention, masturbation, fantasies, consenting sexual relationships) without impinging on their own or others right to privacy, mastery and enjoyment/satisfaction. Sexuality, while it may be part of a relationship with another person, is neither the sole reason for the relationship nor does it take the place of meeting other relationship needs."* (p. 158)

Tolman, Striepe & Harmon (2003) propose a model of adolescent sexual health that highlights the importance of gender. This model, rooted in social constructivist theory, argues that the social contexts (peers, family, wider culture) within which an individual develops greatly impact his or her sexual health. Through examination of girls and boys narratives about sexuality, they have examined how, for example, girls' conceptions of romance disable them from feeling like agents and authentic when it comes to their bodies and sexual relationships. Boys, though they may have a genuine personal desire for emotional connection, feel the powerful socio-cultural expectation to be driven by sexual desire and seek sexual conquest with no interest in emotions or relationships.

Application to Sexually Abusive Youth

When applied to sexually abusive youth, the goals for sexual health discussed above can seem distant at best if not wholly unrealistic or impossible. How can we conceive of a young person being able to, "express love and intimacy toward a romantic partner in developmentally appropriate ways" (Facing Facts, 1995) when he, for example, struggles to respect basic physical boundaries in a controlled residential setting. While it is true that these goals might seem remote for sexually abusive youth, they also represent a distant ideal for many so-called mainstream adolescents as well as many adults for that matter. These models of adolescent sexual health are important in that they provide developmental goals or end points toward which we can work. Moreover, they can help keep treatment programs and providers on track amidst the pressures of the wider sex-negative culture and other external forces that can easily derail providers from these goals.

Gil and Johnson (1993) describe the challenge for treatment as being "how to support natural and expectable sexual development without overlooking problematic sexual behaviors that can result in an unsafe environment of sexual exploitation or abuse…Sexual development cannot be put on the back burner during the treatment of adolescent male sex offenders…" Perry and Ohm (1999) assert that "adolescents not only have to learn how not to offend…but they must find ways of meeting needs in healthy ways. Our program focuses on assisting the youth to develop a healthy lifestyle, with healthy sexuality being one component."

This is not an easy balancing act to accomplish, especially for multi-problem youth with complex psychopathology. With these young people, it is that much more difficult to keep an eye trained on healthy sexual development when their ability to engage in the most basic of relationships is so impaired.

Interventions to Promote Healthy Sexuality

The most commonly-used intervention to promote healthy sexuality is sex education groups. While sex education is important, we believe that alone it is not sufficient.

Below, we outline a list of interventions that can be implemented in programs to facilitate the development of healthy sexuality. Some of these measures apply to residential settings only, but most could be integrated into outpatient or community programs as well. The interventions span multiple levels of agency systems from executive administration to front-line workers. More specific intervention ideas will be discussed below when we describe what one program has instituted to promote healthy sexuality.

1) **Articulate an agency mission, policy and values related to promotion of healthy sexuality.** This ensures that agency administrators also have grappled with the difficult issues involved in doing this work and are committed to backing staff that are carrying out interventions to address healthy sexuality.

2) **Provide staff training related to promotion of healthy sexuality.** The goals of such training would be to clarify agency values and policies, provide guidance for staff on how to respond to young people in ways that promote healthy sexuality, have staff to examine their own learning and values about sexuality, and increase staff comfort addressing issues of sexuality.

3) **Establish a sexually healthy milieu culture** which balances the goals of challenging abusive use of sexuality with the promotion of healthy beliefs and feelings about sexuality. This would include, for example, working with staff on how to monitor behavior, including potentially sexualized behavior, to ensure safety without imposing an overly restrictive and rigid culture.

4) **Ensure that psychosexual assessments focus on all aspects of sexuality, not just the nature of client's abusive behavior.** It is important that psychosexual assessments include questions about client's history of more normative sexual behaviors. This is critical information because it helps providers assess the capacity for healthy romantic and sexual relationships which can be expanded and built upon during sex-offender specific treatment.

5) **Implement sensible policies around touch and use interventions to recondition touch.** The capacity to give and receive healthy touch is an important developmental task. Touch is a central mechanism of attachment and also a powerful trigger for young who have been traumatized. In sexually abusive youth, any touch is often mistaken for sexual touch. Policies and interventions related to touch must balance the need to protect against abusive touch and promote the learning of healthy non-sexual touch (Guidelines for Use of Touch, in Longo, R.E. & Longo, D.P., 2003).

6) **Implement sensible policies about normative sexual behaviors such as masturbation.** Such policies should seek again to balance safety concerns with goals of acknowledging normative sexual behaviors with as little shame and guilt attached to them as possible.

7) **Implement formal sexuality education groups.** In these groups, young people learn the information, attitudes and skills necessary to make healthy choices about their sexuality.

8) **Provide support for gay, lesbian, bisexual, transgender and questioning clients.** Because concerns related to sexual orientation and identity are common with sexually abusive youth, it is critical that they have a safe space to learn about and explore these issues.

9) **Provide psycho-educational groups for families to promote healthy sexuality.** The goal of such groups would be to educate families about healthy sexual development and facilitate communication between parents/guardians and teens about sexual issues and concerns.

10) **Integrate healthy sexuality as part of the general psycho-educational curricula.** Balance use of workbooks commonly used in offender programs (Kahn, 1996; Steen, 1993) which focus primarily on abusive sexuality, with material about healthy sexuality.

Sexuality education groups

Sexuality education groups are the most common intervention used to promote healthy sexuality in sexually abusive youth. For this reason we will discuss in more detail, the content and process of these groups. When taught well, sex education groups can be immensely powerful and therapeutic. If a safe and open atmosphere can be established in the group, young people (and observing staff), after initially being wary, often report that sex education is their favorite group. Staff often reflect upon how there is a palpable energy, fascination and engagement in the room that they see at few other times in the treatment setting. Treatment staff, for whom burnout and vicarious traumatization (Pearlman & Saakvine,1995) are common, often remark at how refreshing and energizing it is it to participate it the human sexuality groups.

What young people learn in sexuality education

One goal of sexuality education groups is to teach about important topics in human sexuality ranging from sexual and reproductive anatomy to dating and courtships skills. However, we believe that how the information is conveyed is equally, if not more important, than the information itself. The aim is to set a tone and atmosphere that communicates: that it is okay to talk openly, ask questions and learn about sexuality; that sexuality, while serious, is also sometimes funny, light and awkward; that there are adults who are willing to talk frankly about sex; and that young people can talk about sex (and perhaps even get aroused) and not act on it. For most of these teens, it is the first time in their lives that an adult has talked to them about sexuality in a manor that is both open yet with appropriate boundaries (Brown, 2000). Some have suggested it may reduce dependency on pornography because young people have the information they crave.

Content and process of sexuality education groups

In their Guidelines for Sexuality Education, the Sexuality Information and Education Council of the United States (SIECUS) lays out six key concept areas to be covered in a comprehensive sexuality education program (National Guidelines Task Force, 1996). They are: human development, relationships, personal skills, sexual behavior, sexual health, and society and culture. As shown in Table 4, each key concept has specific topic areas to be covered. Though not shown here, each topic area has developmental messages appropriate to four stages of development: middle childhood (ages 5-8); preadolescence (ages 9-12); early adolescence (ages 13-15); and adolescence (ages 16-18). (See the SIECUS Guidelines for further details). While it is rare and often impossible for sexuality education groups to cover all of these topics, this can be seen as a comprehensive list from which to choose topic areas.

Table 4
Key Concepts and Topics in a Comprehensive Sexuality Education Program

Key Concept 1: Human Development • Reproductive Anatomy and Physiology • Reproduction • Puberty • Body Image • Sexual Identity and Orientation	**Key Concept 4: Sexual Behavior** • Sexuality Throughout Life • Masturbation • Shared Sexual Behavior • Abstinence • Human Sexual Response • Fantasy • Sexual Dysfunction
Key Concept 2: Relationships • Families • Friendship • Love Dating • Marriage and Lifetime Commitments • Parenting	**Key Concept 5: Sexual Health** • Contraception • Abortion • Sexually Transmitted Diseases and HIV Infection • Sexual Abuse • Reproductive Health
Key Concept 3: Personal Skills • Values • Decision-making • Communication • Assertiveness • Negotiation • Finding Help	**Key Concept 6: Society and Culture** • Sexuality and Society • Gender Roles • Sexuality and the Law • Sexuality and Religion • Diversity • Sexuality and the Arts • Sexuality and the Media

Professionals teaching sexuality education to sexually abusive youth draw teaching materials and lesson plans from a variety of sources. For curricula, books, resources, websites used to teach sexuality education groups, see annotated bibliographies on the SIECUS website, www.siecus.org.

The curricula used for sexuality education groups should balance a focus on three learning domains: 1) information/knowledge; 2) attitudes/beliefs; and 3) skills. Commonly, too much emphasis is placed on information which, while important, is less critical than concrete skills needed to effect behavior change. For example, it would be more important to have group members role play asking someone out on a date rather than have a group discussion about what makes it hard to ask someone out on a date.

The curricula should also generally use a teaching methodology that: invites participation; balances a focus on the healthy and unhealthy aspects of sexuality; is age-appropriate; is appropriate to non-traditional learners; and is appropriate to their level of social maturity (Brown & Tavener, 2002).

Creating an atmosphere conducive to learning about sexuality

Sexuality is an uncomfortable and highly charged topic for most people, young and old alike. This is even more the case with sexually abusive youth. Young people expect adults not to talk with them about sexual issues. And, if adults do talk with them about sex, they anticipate the exchange to be awkward with adults lecturing them about what they should and should not do. Therefore, even before a group has started, group leaders are suspect in young people's eyes. Therefore, group leaders must demonstrate to young people that they are comfortable talking about sexuality, open to hearing young peoples ideas, generally non-judgmental, and knowledgeable about the subject. Hedgepeth and Helmich (1996) note:

> *"Educator credibility in the sexuality education classroom is easily perishable. Learners are quick to spot a hypocritical teacher in any topic area, but their 'radar' seems especially well tuned for those teaching sexuality education...sexuality educators face extraordinary expectations to fulfill their promises, practice their stated philosophy, and maintain a psychologically safe environment."* (p. 42)

Brown and Tavener (2002) set out a number of factors that promote an atmosphere conducive to learning about sexuality. These include such things as: establishing group ground rules; setting a balanced tone in the program that is "open yet not inappropriately personal, humorous but not silly, fun yet serious;" the presence of a group leader who is comfortable talking about sexuality; having a group leader who is willing to accept teens where they are; and using inclusive language meaning language that does not assume all group members are heterosexual.

Group leadership

Too often sexuality education groups are taught by staff that has little or no interest in teaching the topic or have no training that would prepare them for teaching it. It is not uncommon for administrators in programs to assign the task of leading a sexuality education group to a nurse, clinician, or even line-staff as an additional job responsibility without providing them with the time to plan and execute the group. When this occurs, not only are the groups ineffective, but there is increased likelihood that there will be disruptive behavior in the group, and that the negative behavior will spill over into other aspects of the program.

Though seemingly obvious, it is most important that sexuality education groups be taught by leaders who are teen-friendly and comfortable talking openly and frankly about sexuality. While it would be ideal that a staff member have prior experience or training teaching sexuality education, it is rare that staff have such experience. Fortunately, if someone is comfortable talking about sexuality, they can learn, both via formal or informal training, the skills for teaching sex education and the factual information about human sexuality. It is strongly suggested that group leaders eventually obtain some formal training in the methodology and knowledge base related to teaching sexuality education.

When possible, groups should be led by a male-female team. This enables group members to: benefit from both a male and female perspective on sexuality; observe both males and females talking openly and honestly about sex; observe the co-leaders talking with each other about sexual matters. Furthermore, it has the advantage of ensuring that at least one leader is the same gender as the group members (assuming the group is single sex). Having a single group leader talking explicitly about sexuality who is the opposite gender of group members can make it more difficult for group members (and the group leader) to feel safe and comfortable in the group.

Clinicians and/or nurses are generally (though by no means always) best prepared professionally to lead sexuality education groups. In residential settings, it can be ideal to have line-staff participate in these groups as co-leaders or assistants, but they rarely have the training to lead groups on their own. The clear advantage of having line-staff involved in these groups is that discussions about healthy sexuality can continue outside the group. Sexual learning can spill over into the milieu, and youth see staff with whom they spend most of their time as "askable" adults around sexuality.

Moving toward change

Anecdotal evidence seems to indicate that treatment providers and programs working with sexually abusive youth fall along a broad continuum when it comes to implementation of practices aimed at promoting healthy sexuality. Programs that adhere to a traditional sex offender model focusing on containment tend to place less emphasis on healthy sexuality. These programs typically have a time-limited sexuality education groups as their primary intervention to promote healthy sexuality. It is these programs that we believe run the greatest risk of doing harm to young people's developing sexuality.

Then there are programs, broadly speaking, that are in the midst of the paradigm shift discussed earlier, moving from a traditional treatment model to a more integrated or holistic model of treatment. These programs appear to be shifting their treatment cultures, policies, and interventions to ones that balance the goal of elimination of sexually abusive behavior with facilitating sexually healthy behavior. As this change process occurs, there tends to be more openness and importance placed on interventions to promote healthy sexuality. However, when programs are trying to change in these ways, they understandably encounter significant barriers that are inherent in moving from an old to a new paradigm.

Finally, there appear to be a handful of providers and programs that are unique in that they infuse all aspects of their treatment interventions with a mindset of promoting healthy sexuality. The goal of promoting healthy sexuality is explicit, intentional, proactive, and integral to their approach. Below is a more detailed description of one of these programs, the PREHAB of Arizona program in Mesa, Arizona (Schwartz & Brown, 2003).

PREHAB of Arizona

In contrast to many treatment programs that are only now working to integrate interventions to promote healthy sexuality, PREHAB of Arizona was designed with an emphasis on normative sexuality and has been operating under this guise for over 15 years. Also different from most others in the sex offender field, the program was designed by a sexologist (the co-author of this chapter, Dr. Carl Schwartz) who, from the outset, defined the problem of sexual offending as one of resolving adolescent sexual conflict rather than controlling or eliminating sexual offending.

PREHAB has two residential programs with a total of 45 beds serving adjudicated males, ages 11-17. The overall goals of the program integrate three clinical areas: 1) teaching clients the skills to regulate and manage their sexual urges; 2) uncovering and reconciling long existing individual and family conflicts; and 3) enhancing client competence by providing community-based opportunities to learn about and practice pro-social skills, including and especially skills related to normative social/sexual development. Client success and community safety are equally important.

Milieu culture

The milieu culture at PREHAB, based on the goals of safety and discovery, attempts to foster an atmosphere with respect to all aspects of clients' lives, including their sexual and erotic lives. They encourage explicit and frank discussion of all aspects of clients' sexuality, as free as possible from shame, guilt, fear, and secrecy. Staff attempt to model talking about sexual issues in a candid, comfortable way with safe boundaries. Such discussions are lighthearted and fun at times, serious at other times.

The teaching of appropriate touch is a constant part of the milieu. Students, unless 'officially' felt to be dangerous and deceitful, are not asked or required to keep distance. Staff and students, when appropriate, freely touch and hug one another and this is an accepted part of the milieu culture. Staff for the most part, do not need to keenly monitor clients' touch because the milieu culture places such a strong emphasis on clients policing themselves and each other.

Program perspective on sexual arousal

Sexual arousal is treated as universal, human, and important. The program teaches clients that sexual challenges are a normal part of everyone's life experience. A fundamental principle of the treatment philosophy is that clients' arousal takes many forms, both deviant and normative, and that these arousal interests are generally fluid – they coexist simultaneously, shift, and change. The program language reflects this principle. PREHAB clients and staff routinely and comfortably dialogue about clients' "male arousal," "female arousal," "child arousal," "same age arousal," "older female arousal" etc. The milieu is such that clients feel free to talk about, explore, and learn about all aspects of their arousal interests and patterns.

Psychosexual assessment and arousal redirection

There are numerous components to the comprehensive psychosexual assessment process, each of which is used to guide treatment interventions to redirect and shape arousal. First, each student within a week of entering the program undergoes a thorough interview exploring all aspects of their sexual history, both normative and abusive. Second, clients complete an "erotic timeline." All sexual experiences throughout their life are plotted and explained as one way to view the formation of desires, fixations, masturbatory practices, and other forms of sexual interest. Third, clients make a detailed drawing of their molest behavior. The drawing's specificity is intended to arouse both self disgust and/or erotic memories. This drawing is used as part of a personalized, computerized multi-media presentation that a student views multiple times during treatment to develop feelings of empathy, remorse, and hopefulness. Finally, each student engages in a careful interview to uncover and discover all traits that produce their arousal interests, what is called their "anatomy of arousal." These discussions assist clinicians in reshaping and evolving mature/erotic potential. Clinicians, for example, help clients to carefully sculpt their fantasies which are eventually crafted into an "Erotic Short Story" reflecting the client's relational values and erotic interests.

Teaching appropriate touch

The program directly teaches appropriate touch. It has a certified massage therapist on staff to work with clients on these issues. This form of intervention helps to break the automatic connection many clients have between touch and sexual/erotic feelings – the belief that all touch is sexual touch. Over time, they learn to experience the pleasure of non-sexual touch gained from feelings of closeness, intimacy, and affection. Through this contained and structured intervention, they also learn how to assign language to physical sensations in their body. By talking in explicit detail about their physical, emotional and sexual responses to the touch, they learn to put language and thought between feelings and action, instead of moving quickly and impulsively from feelings to action.

Massage sessions, during which clients remain fully clothed, include discussion about any conflicted feelings about arousal or mistrust. At various points in treatment, clients may do massage work with the massage therapist, with staff, and/or peers. The massage therapist is part of the multidisciplinary team, reporting on client progress and conflicts.

Socialization

The program also creates opportunities for learning social, courtship, and dating skills. It arranges for clients to socialize in the community after sufficient therapeutic work has been completed. Clients attend establishments where they can participate in activities like dancing, singing, and poetry reading. On trips to the mall, clients practice going up to and talking with peers. They work to overcome social anxieties as well as practice conversation skills and mature behavior management. The program prepares clients for these experiences with frequent role plays about social and dating situations. These supervised experiences can create confidence in an often highly under-socialized population. When ready, clients may date and form social bonds where they can strengthen skills for negotiating the conflicts that intimacy brings.

Sexuality education

Whereas in many programs formal sexuality education, if taught at all, takes place in a time-limited group. At PREHAB clients participate in weekly sex education groups throughout their entire stay. The importance placed on these groups is reflected not only in their frequency, but also in the fact that they are led by staff with experience and training in the field of sexual health and sexuality education. The groups cover a wide range of topics and a particular emphasis is placed on skill building, largely through role playing.

Risk management

A concern about treatment practices that directly promote normative sexuality is that they will increase the risk of clients acting out sexually in programs or in the community. PREHAB has found the opposite to be true; the more clients engage in normalized experiences, the less they engage in secret and inappropriate sexualized behavior. On the rare occasion when sexual acting out has occurred, rather than shifting to a treatment approach of containment as is the temptation, administration has consistently supported continuation of the model. Evaluating client risk to sexually act-out, is, of course, a constant concern. The program stresses education of families and clients, using the "offense cycle," about how common it is for clients to use negative behaviors, including sex offending, to compensate for negative feelings and insecurities. Risk is seen as dynamic and not static and clients are encouraged, with staff's help, to track attitudes and behaviors daily.

Case example

PREHAB sponsored a case where three brothers, ages 12, 14 and 16, were received into our treatment program simultaneously. These brothers had extensively sexualized each other and had been severely abused sexually by their biological father and his second wife. The non-offending biological mother and her extended family were all invited to participate in their treatment. Though the brothers clearly had difficulties with boundaries, we decided not to prohibit touch between the brothers, but rather to cultivate healthy touch in the spirit of wellness. The metaphor became "to become touch masters." In this case, we worked closely with our certified massage therapist, to institute a carefully worded behavioral contract that set boundaries and criteria for touch. Their touch, over time, became desensitized to erotic associations, and became sensitized to non-erotic aspects of touch. There was no sexual acting out from any boy (as verified by polygraph) during their stay.

Their extended family (about 25) was all invited to large family group meetings. This oversized format was used to create a forum where many long standing grievances with one another could be aired and reconciled, with all of the family as witnesses. These approaches were highly successful in rebuilding a strong family environment with the brothers as primary clients.

Dating activity and social contact were introduced for all the brothers to provide them with the emotional familiarity that comes from taking social risks and fostering trust. The brothers reported that this activity allowed them to feel the difference between the abusive touch they called "daddy's love" and their consensual interests in the girls they were meeting. Normalizing experiences reinforced the "believability" for these young men that they could change long held beliefs that "daddy's touch was love." Client willingness and family support allowed us to consider the risks of these interventions worthwhile in light of the therapeutic payoffs.

Conclusion

In this chapter, we have attempted to discuss the promotion of healthy sexuality within the context of the larger field of juvenile sex abuse treatment. We argue that historically not only has sex offender treatment ignored the important goal of facilitating sexual health, it may even do damage to young people's developing sexuality by communicating highly sex negative messages, and put the community at risk by implicitly encouraging youth to rid themselves of sexual feelings, thoughts and behaviors. In some ways, this treatment approach makes perfect sense when viewed within a traditional adult sex offender model from which the juvenile offender model evolved. However, in recent years, there has been a shift in paradigm to a more holistic and integrated treatment model. The assumptions of this new paradigm allow for a more open, positive, and balanced view of young peoples emerging sexuality. For example, rather than solely focusing on control of problem sexual behavior, a holistic model allows for a balance of focus on problem sexual behavior and social and sexual competencies. Rather than viewing sexuality as something to be feared, it is viewed as a critical life force in all people that can be used positively or negatively.

In addition, we discuss more concretely how to intervene with sexually abusive youth to promote sexual health. While for most programs facilitation of sexual health means sex education, we believe that, while critically important, sex education alone is not sufficient. We outline a wide range of interventions that integrate the goal of promoting healthy sexuality systemically throughout an agency doing this work.

Finally, we offer a detailed description of one residential treatment program, PRE-HAB of Arizona, which has succeeded in implementing the goal of promoting normative sexuality into every aspect of their program. Although using an approach that many providers might view as radical, or at least politically difficult to implement, they have been effectively working with youth in this manner for over 15 years. Hopefully, this chapter and the PREHAB program model will challenge us to re-consider assumptions we hold dearly and propel us to implement treatment practices that advance healthy sexual development.

References

Brown, S. (2000, October/November). Healthy sexuality and the treatment of sexually abusive youth. *SIECUS Report*, 29 (1), 40-46.

Brown, S. & Tavener, W. (2002). *Streetwise to sex-wise: Sexuality education for high risk youth, 2nd Edition.* Morristown, NJ: Planned Parenthood of Greater Northern New Jersey.

Brown, S. & Linder, P. (2001, November) *A missing link: healthy sexuality and the treatment of sexually abusive youth.* Workshop presented at the Annual Conference of the Association for the Treatment of Sexual Abusers (ATSA).

Chaffin, M. & Bonner, B. (1998). Don't shoot, we're your children: Have we gone too far in our response to adolescent sexual abusers and children with sexual behavior problems? *Child Maltreatment* 3 (4), pp 314-316.

Creeden, K. (1999, January). *Attachment and trauma with children and adolescents with sexual behavior problems.* Workshop presented at the Stetson School, Barre, MA.

Daves, J. A. (1995). Addressing television sexuality with adolescents. *Pediatric Annals*, 24, pp. 79-82.

Durex Corporation. (1997, October 1). *Truth for Youth, '97.* Press release and survey. Atlanta, GA.

Erhardt, A.A (1996). Our view of adolescent sexuality: A focus on risk behavior without the developmental context. *American Journal of Public Health*, 86, pp. 1523-1525.

Facing facts: Sexual health for America's adolescents. Report of the National Commission on Adolescent Sexual Health. (1995). Haffner, (Ed.) New York: Sexuality Information and Education Council of the United States (SIECUS).

Gil, E. & Johnson, T.C. (1993) *Sexualized children: Assessment and treatment of sexualized children and children who molest.* Rockville, MD: Launch Press.

Grief, D. (1998, Spring). *How to help the adolescent sex abuser develop a healthy sexual identity.* Workshop presented at the Massachusetts Association for the Treatment of Sexual Abusers (MATSA), Marlboro, MA.

Goldstein, L. & Connelly, M. (1998, April 30). Teen-age poll finds a turn to the traditional. *New York Times.*

Hedgepeth, E. & Helmich, J. (1996). *Teaching about sexuality and HIV: Principles and methods for effective education.* New York: New York University Press.

Kahn, T. (1996). *Pathways: A guided workbook for youth beginning treatment.* Orwell, VT: Safer Society Press.

Knopp, F.H., Freeman-Longo, R.E, & Stevenson, W.F. (1993). *Nationwide survey of juvenile and adult sex offender treatment programs and models.* Orwell, VT: Safer Society Press.

Kuhn, T.S. (1970). *The structure of scientific revolutions* (2nd ed.). Chicago: University of Chicago Press.

Lane, S (1997). The sexual abuse cycle. In G. Ryan & S. Lane (Eds.), *Juvenile sexual offending: Causes, consequences and corrections* (pp. 77-121). San Francisco: Jossey-Bass.

Linehan, M. M., & Kehrer, C.A. (1993). Borderline personality disorder. In D.H. Barlow (Ed.), *Clinical handbook of psychological disorders* (pp. 396-441). New York: Guilford.

Longo, R.E. (2002) A holistic approach to treating juvenile sexual abusers. In Martin C. Calder (Ed.) *Young people who sexually abuse: Building the evidence base for your practice*. Dorset, England: Russell House Publishing.

Longo, R. E. with Longo, D.P (2003) New Hope Exercises for Youth: Experiential Exercises for Children and Adolescents. Holyoke, MA: NEARI Press.

National Guidelines Task Force (1996). *Guidelines for comprehensive sexuality education: Kindergarten – 12th Grade, 2nd Edition*. New York: Sexuality Information and Education Coalition of the United States (SIECUS)

Pearlman, L.A. & Saakvitne, K.W. (1995). *Trauma and the therapist: Countertransference and vicarious traumatization in psychotherapy with incest survivors*. New York: Norton.

Perry, G., & Ohm, P. (1998). The role healthy sexuality plays in modifying abusive behaviours of adolescent sex offenders: Practical considerations for professionals. *Canadian Journal of Counseling*, 33 (2), pp. 157-169.

Prescott, D. (2004, January 8). Harsh confrontational approach. *Message posted on listserve of The Association for the Treatment of Sexual Abusers*.

Rich, P. (2003). *Understanding, assessing and rehabilitating juvenile sexual offenders*. Hoboken, N.J.: John Wiley & Sons.

Satcher, D. (2001) The Surgeon General's call to action to promote sexual health and responsible sexual behavior. Washington DC: US Department of Health and Human Services.

Saakvitne, K.W., Gamble, S., Pearlman, L.A., & Lev, B.T. (2000). *Risking connection: A training curriculum for working with survivors of childhood abuse*. Lutherville, MD: The Sidran Press.

Schwartz, C. & Brown, S. (2003, Summer). Promoting normative sexuality in the treatment of sexually abusive youth: The PREHAB of Arizona program model. *The ATSA Forum*, 15,pp. 7-9.

Stasburger, V.C. (1997). Sex, drugs, rock n' roll and the media: Are the media responsible for adolescent behavior. *Adolescent Medicine*, 8, pp.403-414.

Steen, C. (1993). *Relapse prevention: Workbook for youth in treatment*. Orwell, VT: Safer Society Press.

Tolman, D.L., Striepe, M.I., & Harmon, T. (February 2003). Gender matters: Constructing a model of adolescent sexual health. *Journal of Sex Research*, 40 (1), 4-12.

Warren, C. & Neer, B. (1992). Perspectives on international sex practices and American family sex communication relevant to teenage sexual behavior in the U.S. *Health Communication*, 4, 121-136.

Worling, J.R., & Curwen, T., (2000). Adolescent sexual offender recidivism: success of specialized treatment and implications for risk prediction. *Child Abuse and Neglect*, 24, 965-982.

CHAPTER EIGHT

LEGAL AND ETHICAL CONSIDERATIONS IN EVALUATIONS OF CHILDREN WITH SEXUAL BEHAVIOR PROBLEMS

CRAIG LATHAM
AND
ROBERT T. KINSCHERFF

A public defender representing an indigent juvenile charged with a violent sex offense has filed a motion to obtain funds from the Court to retain you as an expert witness for the defense, and the motion was allowed. The attorney asks you to conduct an evaluation of the juvenile in preparation for a possible plea negotiation, and the juvenile's parents, who have legal custody, give permission for such an evaluation. You conclude, based on your detailed assessment, that the offer being considered by the prosecution is far more favorable than you would recommend. Defense counsel thanks you and tells you there is no need to write a report because your opinion would adversely affect the plea negotiation. The judge knew that you were evaluating the defendant and orders you to prepare a report and turn it over to the Court, but the defense attorney refuses to waive attorney/client privilege. You are inclined to cooperate, most importantly because the Court has ordered you to file a report, but also because you feel some responsibility to insure that the juvenile gets adequate treatment and containment to protect public safety. What should you do?

Introduction

Clinicians are routinely called upon by attorneys, judges, policy makers, and other clinicians to provide information about the treatment needs and risk to others of children with sexual behavior problems. The decisions often involve fundamental rights and interests of parents and children, and they can have a profound affect on the lives of identified clients as well as potential victims. The framework of law, professional ethics, and professional practice standards exist to protect these fundamental rights or interests, to protect persons from harm or exploitation, and to enhance the effectiveness and reputation of professional practices. Legal and professional decision-making, which often reflects an effort to balance these rights and interests, can be quite complex, as illustrated by this brief case example.

For example, some professional relationships are offered privacy in the form of confidentiality and privilege. However, the privacy of professional mental health relationships is limited by mandated reporting requirements (an interest in protecting children and other vulnerable persons), duties to warn or protect against potential patient/client violence (an interest in protecting potential victims), and access by a court to otherwise protected information (to serve the interests of justice or the "best interests" of a child). The protections of attorney-client privilege reflect a judgment that the Constitutional presumption of a criminal defendant's innocence and guarantee of effective assistance of counsel require particularly stringent protections of the communications between the defendant and defense counsel. Similarly, there are many procedural safeguards for children accused of sexual misconduct that balance the Constitutional protection against self-incrimination with interests in determining the facts of a case.

There is also an expectation that mental health professionals who offer expert testimony rely upon methods or procedures that meet or exceed the ordinary standard of professional practice in providing particular kinds of evaluations or interventions. This is an attempt to balance the court's need for reliable information to make important decisions against such interests as the need to avoid injustice, the misuse of professional influence, and the preservation of the primary fact-finding role for the judge or jury.

The science on which forensic evaluations are based is constantly evolving, as are ethical standards and laws, so it will never be possible to provide a definitive manual that covers all aspects of work with children who have sexual behavior problems. We will, however, pose six questions that will help professionals involved in such cases identify key interests at stake and the duties and obligations that arise, however the law and science evolve. We will also suggest a way to analyze the competing interests, which we will illustrate with a number of clinical vignettes.

While we rely on general legal and ethical principles, law varies by jurisdiction, and the details of professional ethics vary by profession and professional association. Clinicians have a duty to be familiar with the laws and ethics codes relevant to their profession and areas of clinical expertise.

Who has legal custody of the child?

Persons who are under the age of eighteen are "legal incompetents" who ordinarily cannot make their own legally binding decisions about mental health evaluation or treatment. Except under "dire emergency" circumstances, a mental health professional providing evaluation or treatment services without proper authorization by the child's legal custodian may be acting illegally and unethically unless acting under another exception expressly provided under law.

With the exception of situations such as those described below, the parents of a child are the legal custodians, and proper informed consent must be obtained from the parent(s) before initiating any evaluation or treatment services. Where parents are divorced or were never married, professionals should determine whether both parents have legal custody, particularly where there is reason to believe that a parent may object to the provision of professional services. Where two parents each have legal custody, but disagree whether the professional should provide services to the child, the professional has the duty to seek resolution by court order or other means before providing services. A child may sometimes have a relative or other person who has been deemed the child's "legal guardian" by a court. The professional should determine that the authorization of mental health or other professional services is within the scope of the guardianship granted by the court.

Children who are in the legal custody of the state ordinarily will require authorization for professional services by a representative of the state agency holding legal custody of the child. This most often means obtaining a proper informed consent from the child's case worker. However, professionals must be cautious to determine who actually has the authority to authorize professional evaluation or treatment services. For example, a child may be in the legal custody of the state child protection agency but may have a case manager from the state mental health agency. In some jurisdictions, commitment of a delinquent child to the state juvenile justice authority means that the juvenile justice authority has legal custody during the period of commitment. In other jurisdictions, commitment to a juvenile justice authority means only that the authority controls physical custody and placement of the child but any form of treatment needs to be separately authorized by the child's legal custodian.

State and federal law vary about the circumstances under which a person under 18 may authorize their own medical or mental health care. Professionals should be familiar with practice areas that often have exceptions to the general rules that permit a minor to authorize their own care, such as substance abuse treatment or treatment related to reproductive health. Evaluations or treatment of children with sexual behavior problems would not usually be deemed to fall within these exceptions, but clinicians should know the law that applies in the jurisdiction where they practice.

Some states have provisions to legally "emancipate" minors by court order that permit these emancipated minors to authorize their own medical and mental health care. Other states do not formally emancipate minors by court order, but have provisions that allow a minor to authorize care where certain indicators of adult characteristics are present. These can include situations where the minor is serving in the armed forces, is pregnant or believes she is pregnant, has ever been married or divorced, has a child of his/her own, or has been supporting himself independently from a parent or other legal guardian for a significant period of time.

Who is the "client" for the professional services to be rendered?

A practitioner's professional duties and responsibilities arise from the special relationship that the law has established between the practitioner and the practitioner's identified "client." The legal client is the only party who can authorize, direct, modify, or terminate assessment or treatment provided by the practitioner. With the exception of mandated reporting requirements and other exceptions where the permission of the client is not required to release information, only the legal client can authorize releases of information or otherwise grant permission for information to go beyond the boundaries of confidentiality of the professional relationship.

The term "client" can often be confusing because it may not be used with precision. For example, practitioners may refer to the child they are assessing as the client because the child is the direct focus of the practitioner's assessment or treatment. However, a child who has a legal custodian cannot be the legal client if the child cannot authorize, direct, modify or terminate professional services or sign a legitimate release of information.

It is more precise to distinguish the "legal clients" who have such authority from the "ethical clients" to whom the practitioner owes ethical duties. For example, if a parent with legal custody has authorized an evaluation of sexualized behavior, the parent is the "legal client" and the child is the "ethical client" to whom the practitioner owes ethical duties such as professional competence and obtaining the child's assent (rather than consent for professional services, which can only come from the legal client).

If a court orders the professional services, the court is ordinarily the legal client and the professional activities and any reports or other "work products" generated by the activities belong to the court. When a court has ordered an evaluation of a juvenile sexual offender, the juvenile, the juvenile's attorney, and the juvenile's legal custodian(s) need to be informed of this fact. The nature and limits of confidentiality and privilege need to be understood by the juvenile, the juvenile's attorney, and whoever holds legal custody. Since the court is the legal client, any assessment reports or other reports of the practitioner's activities in the case should be provided directly and only to the court unless the court has specifically directed otherwise in advance. Since the court is the legal client, the juvenile's legal custodian or others who might otherwise have clear access to reports or authority to sign releases of information will not have this access and authority unless specifically permitted by the court.

The retaining attorney is the legal client if the practitioner is retained by the attorney to provide professional services in the case in anticipation of using them in the legal arena. If conducted for an attorney, the professional activities are covered by attorney-client privilege; the practitioner should clarify with the juvenile and the juvenile's legal custodian that the usual psychotherapist-patient privilege does not apply but that attorney-client privilege does apply.

Sometimes parents or others will bring a juvenile for professional services "because the attorney told us to get an evaluation or some treatment." In such circumstances, it is crucial that the practitioner communicate directly with the attorney before providing services to clarify whether the actual client is the attorney (with attorney-client privilege) or the parents of the juvenile referred (with psychotherapist-patient privilege).

One crucial implication of who is the actual legal client under these circumstances is the question of who gets to authorize release of the practitioner's work in the case. If the client is the attorney, only the attorney can authorize the release of the report or other work generated in the case. Having a parent or other legal custodian sign a release of information would not be adequate to permit the practitioner to provide information to a school system, therapist, or other party. However, if the parent is the legal client, the attorney has no basis to assert attorney-client privilege for the information nor to block its dissemination to third parties upon a valid release by the child's legal custodian.

If the attorney in any way contemplates relying upon a practitioner's work in a case before the court, practitioners are very strongly urged to clarify that it is the attorney who is the legal client, and to proceed as if the services being provided are forensic mental health services rather than clinical services. This has important implications for defining professional roles, since best professional practice is to avoid mixing forensic mental health and clinical roles if at all possible. Additionally, the competence of professional services and quality of documentation of the services are subject to higher expectations when acting in a forensic role.

Practitioners retained by defense attorneys in juvenile sexual offense matters must clarify before providing services how they will proceed if they learn about events that would ordinarily trigger a mandated reporting duty. For example, while assessing a juvenile charged with a sexual offense, a practitioner may learn of other sexual offenses against victims while the juvenile or the juvenile's parents were in a care taking role or other role that would trigger a mandated child abuse report.

Anecdotally, when we ask mental health practitioners whether their duty as mandated reporters trumps the protections of attorney-client privilege, the vast majority of licensed practitioners are certain that the mandated reporting duty would require them to file a child abuse report. When we ask defense attorneys the same question, the attorneys are equally certain that the information would be protected by attorney-client privilege, and that the practitioner would be barred from disclosing any information. In fact, we are unaware of any lawsuit or professional licensure case where this issue has been directly decided in any jurisdiction. Best practice is to notify the defense attorney of what you would do under such circumstances before accepting a retainer or providing services in the case to clarify mutual expectations.

Since prosecutors have a different role in a delinquency or criminal prosecution, practitioners retained by prosecutors will ordinarily have explained their mandated reporting obligations to the prosecutor, the juvenile, defense counsel, and the juvenile's legal custodian while obtaining informed consent. Practitioners providing court-ordered services or those serving as court clinicians who evaluate juveniles are not covered by the attorney-client privilege of defense counsel, and their obligation to file any mandated reports should be made clear as part of clarifying their role with the juvenile, the juvenile's defense attorney, and the juvenile's legal custodian.

Unless professional services are court-ordered or provided upon retainer by an attorney, assessment and treatment of children with histories of sexual misconduct are generally subject to authorization by the child's legal custodian(s). Practitioners who provide specialized sexual offender services to juveniles as a condition of probation or placement in a facility should establish before providing those services who has the legal standing to authorize them, who controls the sharing of information (such as reports back to probation or informing law enforcement of previously unknown sexual misconduct), and who has the authority to terminate the services (such as for failure to attend or effectively participate).

What is the practitioner's professional role in the case?

Proper informed consent to provide professional services requires clarity about the role that the practitioner will play in providing services. At the very least, this requires clarity about the practitioner's legal client in the case and the nature of the services to be provided. Discussion of the nature of the services to be provided includes discussion of whether the services are assessment and/or intervention services, and discussion at a relevant level of detail about the procedures to be relied upon. Additionally, the practitioner must be very clear about whether the professional services are forensic or clinical services.

Forensic mental health services are intended to generate legally defensible evidence in formal legal proceedings. Forensic mental health services may result in clinical benefits to those subject to the professional activities, such as juveniles being assessed as sexual offenders, but those clinical benefits are incidental to achieving the primary goal of forensic mental health activity. The legal client for forensic services is typically a court ordering the services, an attorney retaining them, or an organization seeking information that may be relied upon in a legal proceeding. These organizations may include treatment facilities gathering information regarding whether a juvenile may be subject to involuntary civil commitment, a sexual offender registration board seeking information for classification of a juvenile, or a state juvenile justice authority seeking information upon which to base an effort to extend a period of commitment for a juvenile in custody and deemed still at high risk to re-offend.

Clinical mental health services include assessments and interventions that are intended primarily to benefit the person receiving those services. For example, in providing juvenile sexual offender treatment groups, the goal is to benefit the participating juveniles by equipping them with information and skills that reduce their risk of re-offense. Of course, there is substantial benefit to potential future victims if that clinical intervention is successful, but potential future victims are neither the ethical nor the legal client from the perspective of the practitioner, nor is society at large. A goal of preventing future victims may well describe a practitioner's motives for working with offenders, but except for statutes mandating disclosures to protect potential victims in specifically defined circumstances, this goal cannot be the legal or ethical basis for decisions in a case. The legal custodian of the juvenile cannot authorize treatment on behalf of potential future victims, only on behalf of the juvenile being enrolled in the treatment group.

Many reasons are offered for distinguishing between forensic and clinical roles and for avoiding mixing or confusing them whenever possible. First, as discussed above, the primary goals of these roles differ and may readily be in conflict with each other. For example, a court may determine that punishment or public safety concerns warrant a period of extension in a juvenile justice facility while strictly clinical concerns may support a more prompt return to the community. Law may require registration of a juvenile on a sexual offender registry according to criteria set by the legislature or a board, although clinical assessment may suggest that the loss of privacy inherent in the registration process would interfere with the juvenile's treatment.

Second, forensic activity ordinarily relies upon multiple sources of information and independent corroboration of facts at issue to render opinions relevant to legal issues. Clinical activity ordinarily relies more upon individual relationship-building with a juvenile to gather information about their subjective experiences to guide clinical decision-making that may be irrelevant to legal decisions.

Third, clinicians who are pulled into forensic roles that lead them to disclose information provided in treatment or who must render unfavorable opinions subsequently relied upon by courts often find the treatment relationship is then significantly complicated or fatally compromised.

Fourth, the rules governing confidentiality and privilege differ significantly between forensic and clinical roles, making it difficult to obtain the proper informed consent when moving between clinical and forensic roles. Indeed, since in forensic work the legal client is typically not the legal custodian of the juvenile, who may offer informed consent for forensic or clinical activities can change across roles. Finally, professionals providing clinical services to children over extended periods are likely to develop opinions about the child's progress or lack thereof that are at least subtly influenced by the nature of their personal relationship with the child. For this reason, it is best practice to have an independent evaluator who has no prior professional relationship with the child provide any forensic services that may be required.

Circumstances may require or permit a mixing of forensic or clinical roles over time, particularly in rural areas, on institutional units with a limited number of qualified staff, or in communities where there are no other specialized practitioners reasonably available. In these circumstances, the burden will be upon the practitioner to show that there was no reasonable alternative available, and that proper steps were made to effectively clarify the practitioner's role, clients, and goals at each point.

For example, a court-appointed forensic evaluator who has assessed a youth found delinquent of a juvenile sexual offense should ordinarily refer the youth to another clinician for treatment if specialized intervention is recommended. However, if the evaluator also is the only reasonably available provider of the recommended juvenile sexual offender group, the evaluator will need to clearly establish the shift between evaluator and treating clinician, revisit the nature and limits of confidentiality, distinguish the goals of forensic assessment and clinical intervention, and secure an appropriate informed consent. Care should be taken to clarify whether the forensic evaluator, now having moved into the role of clinical provider, could ever again move back into the role of forensic evaluator.

What methods and procedures will be relied upon in the case?

Another standard element of informed consent is a discussion of the methods and procedures to be relied upon in the case. This discussion ordinarily comes in the context of disclosing the goals of the professional activity, any risks or benefits associated with relying upon the methods proposed, any reasonable alternative methods that could be used, and whether the proposed methods have some reasonable foundation in scientific literature or clinical practice.

A practitioner providing clinical services will be held to the prevailing "standard of care" for using clinical methods and procedures. The standard of care consists of what similar professionals in similar clinical circumstances would do when providing assessment and treatment services. The standard of care may shift over time in light of advances in research and practice, and clinical practitioners can be accountable for failing to keep up with such advances.

For example, recent developments in the area of juvenile sexual misconduct and offending include the descriptions of various clinical subtypes of youth presenting with sexually aggressive behavior. Clinicians practicing in this area increasingly appreciate the need to distinguish among these subtypes and to identify and understand the contributions to sexual misconduct that may arise from factors as diverse as substance abuse, delinquent socialization, trauma history, attachment disorders, psychiatric symptoms, learning disability, and developmental disorders.

Clinical assessments or interventions that rely upon "cookbook" identification of case characteristics but fail to integrate other relevant information into treatment planning and implementation are increasingly viewed as clinically inadequate. Routine enrollment of juveniles with histories of sexual misconduct into the same kinds of clinical interventions without taking into account individual features that may warrant another approach and/or additional interventions is also increasingly viewed as clinically inadequate. Clinical practitioners who accept a clinically heterogeneous population of juveniles into specialized sexual offender treatment interventions must be able to adapt the available interventions to take into account clinically relevant features such as cognitive level, degree of psychiatric impairment, degree of functional impairment arising from developmental disorder or learning disability, degree of emotional impairment due to trauma, and other potential obstacles to effective treatment.

Similarly, as research evolves that suggests a relatively high percentage of juveniles self-desist sexual misconduct upon detection, and that there are different rates of recidivism among different subtypes of juveniles, clinicians must increasingly be prepared to articulate why a particular juvenile should be labeled a "sexual offender" and referred for specialized sex offender treatment rather than held accountable like any other delinquent juvenile but without enrollment in a specialized sexual offender intervention.

Practitioners serving in a forensic role have an elevated duty to be familiar with research and practice in the area of juvenile sexual offenders. In states that rely on the older Frye case as the standard to determine admissibility of expert testimony, their forensic work will be assessed by courts to determine whether the methods and procedures relied upon in conducting their assessments are "generally accepted" among practitioners who do forensic work in juvenile sexual offender cases. In states that rely on Daubert and in federal courts, the methods and procedures relied upon by the forensic practitioner will be scrutinized in light of a flexible test of their "scientific reliability." These factors include, but are not limited to: (a) whether the method relied upon has been standardized; (b) whether there has been peer review of the method relied upon; and, (c) the known or potential rate of error of the method relied upon.

Particularly in Daubert jurisdictions, forensic practitioners now have a heightened obligation to be aware of the scientific basis for the methods they rely upon in conducting evaluations of juveniles before the courts. For example, if relying upon a particular juvenile sexual offender checklist or inventory, practitioners must be prepared to articulate the psychometric characteristics of the measure and its known or potential rate of error. They need to be familiar with the literature suggesting that unstructured clinical interview for diagnosis or for risk assessment is a flawed method that, at least when assessing mentally ill adults, is strongly skewed in the direction of "false positive" identification of persons as being a danger when they actually are not. The high rates of juveniles who stop engaging in delinquent or sexual misconduct simply as a result of being caught require that forensic practitioners be familiar with different developmental trajectories of antisocial conduct in youth.

Whether in a clinical or forensic role, persons providing information or testimony before a court or other decision-makers for a juvenile have duties to only offer opinions for which they have an adequate basis to support those opinions, to disclose any relevant limitations of the methods relied upon or the available information, and to reveal any plausible alternative ways of understanding the clinical or forensic information.

If court-involved or likely to be, what is the posture of the case?

Sexual misconduct may give rise to delinquency charges or, in some jurisdictions, may give rise to prosecution as an adult. Practitioners who are involved with youth who engage in sexual misconduct must be sensitive to the likelihood of charges being brought or, if already brought, the legal posture of the case as it moves from arraignment through disposition.

Sometimes youth engage in sexual misconduct in their homes, schools or treatment settings. The need to investigate such situations and to protect potential victims from further sexual misconduct warrants efforts by responsible adults to determine what happened and what steps need to be taken for safety. However, adults need to be aware of the potential legal consequences of their actions when sexual misconduct is alleged but has not yet been charged or prosecuted.

In some cases, a juvenile accused of sexual misconduct may be subject to some form of assessment before a decision is made about subsequent placement. For example, in Massachusetts, a child in state custody due to abuse or neglect who is accused of sexual misconduct or fire setting must undergo a formal risk assessment before the child can be placed in any home care setting. The goal of such assessments is simply to determine what level of supervision and risk management would be necessary simply to keep the child safe *if the allegations were true*. Possible outcomes include placing the child in a group home or in a foster home with only male children, only female children, only older children, or no children at all, depending on the nature of the alleged victims. Since the goal is risk management only, no offense-specific treatment is provided unless there is an admission by the child and/or unless the child's legal custodian feels the evidence is compelling enough to proceed with treatment. If the child is represented by an attorney for child welfare, status offense, or other delinquency matters, the attorney should be notified before the assessment occurs. The attorney may be concerned that the statements made to the risk screener will result in charges being pressed or, more generally, that any report systematically documenting alleged problematic sexual behavior is not helpful to the child's long-term liberty interest. In those cases, the attorney may instruct the child to not participate in the screening. However, an option that achieves both the goal of safe placement and limiting self-incrimination by this child is for the attorney to go to court to seek a protective order that prevents the child's statements from being introduced as self-incriminating statements, or otherwise make this arrangement with the prosecutor who would be responsible for pursuing the case in court.

If a child not facing delinquency charges is referred for assessment or treatment, clinical care providers should take prudent steps to assess the evidence of sexual misconduct. If the child acknowledges the sexual misconduct, clinical care providers are entitled to rely upon the acknowledgment of misconduct and the corroborating evidence supporting the allegations. However, clinical providers should take reasonable steps to obtain corroborating reports if there continue to be concerns about the accuracy of the allegations, even if the child acknowledges misconduct. We have both come across cases where a child has improperly been enrolled in specialized juvenile sexual offender treatment despite reason to doubt seriously either the original accounts of misconduct or the basis upon which the child was deemed at elevated risk for sexual re-offense and referred for specialized treatment.

If a child referred for assessment or treatment of sexual misconduct denies the allegations, clinical care providers should not only take prudent steps to assess the evidence for sexual misconduct, they should consider whether enrollment in a specialized intervention for sexual misconduct is warranted. A probationary period might be considered during which the child may participate without making acknowledgements of sexual misconduct. However, clinicians should be cautious about accepting a youth for extended or open-ended sexual offender interventions where he consistently denies the alleged misconduct and there has been no legal finding of fact. If clinicians decide to continue sexual offender treatment of a youth who denies sexual misconduct, they should carefully document the rationale for doing so with the understanding that the more ambiguous the basis for establishing the misconduct, the more they bear the burden of showing that the youth should be involved in this kind of specialized intervention and is likely to benefit from it.

Practitioners must be aware of the special obligations that arise when they are asked to provide services when charges have been pressed. Juveniles charged with sexual offenses are entitled to a presumption of innocence, and the state bears the prosecutorial burden of demonstrating that the juvenile defendant has committed the delinquent act.

Unless retained by the defense, practitioners asked to conduct sexual offender evaluations before admissions on the record or an adjudication of delinquency must be extremely circumspect regarding these evaluations. Where a juvenile is prepared to make admissions to the sexual offense charges for a plea bargain or other purposes, the evaluator should work with the attorneys and the court to make certain that the plea bargain is conditioned upon the juvenile defendant's willingness to maintain the admissions during evaluation or subsequent treatment. Evaluators should be particularly cautious when the plea bargain involves a "continued without a finding" or a so-called Alford plea where the juvenile defendant may not have to offer or maintain any acknowledgement of misconduct. We are both aware of many cases where a juvenile accepted a plea agreement that dropped the sexual element of the charge only to deny or recant any sexual misconduct during a subsequent evaluation or treatment.

In situations where the juvenile is referred for a court-ordered evaluation before adjudication, and the juvenile denies the allegations, it is improper for the sexual offender evaluation to proceed. There is no evidence that sexual offender evaluations conducted before adjudication on an alleged offender who denies sexual misconduct yields reliable determinations of what, if any, sexual misconduct occurred or a reliable estimate of risk. There is no evidence that under these circumstances an evaluator can reliably distinguish among: (a) an innocent defendant who is accurately denying misconduct; (b) a defendant who has engaged in the alleged misconduct and would like to admit it and seek help but is fearful of the potential consequences of making admissions; (c) a defendant who has engaged in the alleged misconduct and intends to offend again but is lying to avoid consequences for the misconduct; (d) a defendant who engaged in some, but not all, of the alleged misconduct and fears that making a partial admission may result in negative consequences; or, (e) a defendant who is so anxious and shamed by the sexual misconduct that they deny it even to themselves, and so are in a state of psychological denial where they cannot admit the reality of what they have done.

Evaluators who characterize a juvenile defendant who denies allegations of sexual misconduct prior to adjudication as "in denial" are: (a) making an assumption that the disputed allegations of sexual offense are true; (b) improperly usurping the fact-finding role of the court; (c) determining without adequate factual basis about the alleged misconduct or adequate clinical basis about the juvenile's experience that the juvenile is manifesting the defense mechanism of "denial" rather than simply lying; and (d) running the risk that their professional services will be improperly relied upon by a court making determinations of fact. Similarly, evaluators who conclude prior to an adjudication of the disputed facts that it is either "likely" or "unlikely" that the juvenile committed the specific alleged offenses are stepping well beyond the established bounds of the scientific reliability of assessment procedures and improperly usurping the fact-finding role of the court.

Because there is no established "profile" of a juvenile sexual offender, and because there is no forensic or clinical mental health method that can reliably determine whether a juvenile committed a particular sexual offense in a particular manner with a specific victim in a specific jurisdiction, sexual offender evaluations of a juvenile who is denying the allegations prior to an adjudication of the facts are dangerously unreliable and professionally irresponsible. Practitioners requested by the court or prosecution to conduct such evaluations should refrain from doing so and attempt to educate the court about why it would be improper clinically, legally, and ethically to conduct such an evaluation. Similarly, practitioners tempted to rely upon assessment tools that estimate risk of re-offense, where the statistical techniques on which the predictions depend assume a known first offense, should avoid using those tools when the juvenile has not yet admitted or been adjudicated a sexual offender. We have both encountered attorneys and practitioners who misinterpret this restriction as a procedural formality that could be cast aside when, in fact, it is a statistical premise on which the use of the tools is based.

Practitioners retained by the defense are in a somewhat different position due to the protections afforded by attorney-client privilege, but should still refrain from offering opinions about whether the defendant engaged in conduct the defendant denies. A practitioner retained by the defense may attempt to educate the defense attorney about the risk and protective factors for re-offense that are present in the case, any relevant clinical features and the needs of the defendant for clinical assessment or treatment, and the characteristics of the alleged incident or the defendant likely to be relevant at trial.

Where a juvenile charged with sexual offenses denies the allegations prior to adjudication, best practice is to defer assessment of sexual re-offense risk until the court adjudicates the case. Following adjudication, the court may order a juvenile sexual offender assessment as an aid in disposition, often in determining whether or not a juvenile should be maintained in the community or committed for services through the state juvenile justice authority. Following a finding of delinquency on a sexual offense, an evaluator is entitled to rely upon the findings of the court even if the juvenile continues to deny the offenses.

If the original charges have been reduced in a plea agreement, or the court has found the juvenile delinquent on lesser sexual offense charges, the evaluator should seek guidance from the court about the actual behavior to be evaluated. For example, if the case has been pled down from a rape to an indecent assault and battery, the evaluator should establish with the court whether the penetration that constitutes an element in the charge of rape is part of the evaluation, or if the inquiry is limited only to the elements of indecent assault and battery. Should a juvenile involved in a plea agreement tell the evaluator that "I really only admitted what I did because my lawyer told me to do it, but I did not really do anything," the evaluator should suspend the assessment pending clarification by the court whether or how to proceed in light of this disavowal.

The best posture for a case to be in when referred for a juvenile sexual offender evaluation is either when the juvenile has made specific admissions to particular sexual offense behavior under oath on the record as part of a plea agreement, or when the court has made findings of fact in adjudicating the case. However, courts that make a threshold determination that a juvenile will not be committed to juvenile justice authorities prior to making a referral for sexual offender evaluation must appreciate that they have already made a *de facto* risk determination. It is unfortunate to get a case referred for a sexual offender evaluation after the court has already decided to place the defendant on probation, only to determine during the evaluation that the defendant cannot be adequately served in the community and requires the containment or the specialized services available only through commitment to the state juvenile justice authority.

What are the nature and limits of confidentiality and privilege in the case?

The nature and limits of confidentiality and privilege that protect information obtained in the course of professional activities largely arise from the specifics of who is the identified legal client, the role (forensic or clinical) of the practitioner, the purpose to which information obtained will be used, and any rules governing application or exceptions to confidentiality and privilege.

Confidentiality is the general duty to keep private information that is received while providing professional services. There are, however, a number of clearly defined exceptions to this rule. Information must be shared when mandated reporting requirements or duty to protect requirements are triggered, when the need for emergency hospitalization arises, and in response to a legitimate release of information signed by the child's legal custodian. Some information may be shared when clinicians are seeking supervision or consultation about professional services, when defending themselves against allegations of professional misconduct, and when billing for professional services. Practitioners should be aware of federal law such as the Health Insurance Privacy and Portability Act (HIPPA) and specific state laws that together govern confidentiality when providing health care services, including psychotherapeutic interventions. Because of the specific interplay between federal and state confidentiality law, practitioners should be familiar with how the law effects their practice in their own state. Any information released should be as little as is required to achieve the goal or to be responsive to a legitimate request for information. For example, identifying information should not be used in securing case consultations unless proper permission is obtained or that information is critical to the substance of the case consultation. Patient information provided to secure third party insurance reimbursement should be limited to only that information that is required for release under the terms of the insurance contract.

Privilege is an exception to the general duty of citizens to testify about matters of which they have personal knowledge when called upon to do so in court. For example, a citizen who is a witness to a crime has a duty to testify about what she has witnessed and may be compelled to testify if necessary. Formally termed "testamentary privilege" in many jurisdictions, privilege is a firewall created by legislatures to protect the privacy of communications that occur within specific relationships. It is an effort to balance the interest of courts in accessing information that may become evidence in a legal proceeding against the interest in encouraging the privacy and safety of some kinds of relationships. Just as with confidentiality, it is largely a creature of state law and practice, and clinicians should know in detail how privilege operates where they offer services.

For example, the firewall that forbids compelling an unwilling spouse to testify against the other spouse is "spousal privilege," and it is intended to protect the privacy of communications between married persons. Attorney-client privilege is intended to protect communications between an attorney and her client, just as doctor-patient privilege is intended to encourage frank discussions about health concerns between a physician and her patient. The United States Supreme Court has ruled that communications between many mental health professionals and their clients are privileged in federal cases, and state legislatures have, to varying degrees for different licensed mental health professions in different states, created a similar privilege for professional communications between these licensed professionals and those to whom professional services are provided.

Generally, privilege protects the "professional communications" between the licensed professional and the person directly offering the protected communications. Unlicensed practitioners or those whose license has not been endowed with privilege by the legislature do not have the protection offered by privilege. For example, a client of an unlicensed psychotherapist cannot prevent the therapist from being compelled to testify in court about what the client has told the therapist. Sometimes the communications can be protected by privilege if the unlicensed therapist or student is operating under the supervision of a licensed mental health professional, but state law varies on that point, and practitioners are urged to establish whether local law extends the privilege in that way.

If clinicians do not keep the distinction between confidentiality and privilege clear, it will be difficult to decide how to protect professional communications. Testamentary privilege applies *only* when the content of those communications may be offered into evidence in a legal proceeding. It is confidentiality and not privilege that is involved when a legal custodian signs a release of information, or waiver of confidentiality, for a practitioner to provide records of treatment to another practitioner or to a utilization reviewer for an insurance company. Here, the boundaries of confidentiality are managed by the legal custodian of the juvenile. It is also confidentiality and not privilege that is involved when a practitioner makes a mandated child abuse report. Here, the boundaries of confidentiality are shaped by exceptions made to confidentiality by the state legislature when creating a mandated reporting duty.

When a juvenile communicates with a licensed mental health professional, the juvenile is entitled to the expectation of privilege unless otherwise informed prior to initiating services. This is why clinicians conducting court-ordered evaluations must inform a juvenile that any statements made during assessment can be reported to the court and potentially included in any testimony by the evaluator. Without such a warning, the juvenile could assert privilege and bar the evaluator from referring to statements made by the juvenile.

State law and practice regarding the status of privilege held by juveniles varies and is often unclear. In some jurisdictions, parents or other legal custodians are permitted to waive privilege on behalf of a juvenile. In other jurisdictions, the privilege is held by the juvenile who, as a legal incompetent, can neither assert nor waive the privilege on his own. In such jurisdictions, a Guardian *ad litem* may be appointed to make recommendations to the court as to whether the best interests of the juvenile are served by waiving privilege and permitting the practitioner to testify or by asserting privilege to protect the privacy of the practitioner's professional relationship with the juvenile. Note that in these jurisdictions, a parent or other legal guardian has no standing to either assert or waive the privilege on behalf of the juvenile. In still other jurisdictions, there is no clear direction in local law, and practice may vary widely.

Whatever the status of the law of privilege in a jurisdiction, practitioners have the duty to know their obligations regarding privilege in the event that they ever receive a court order, subpoena, or release of information from a legal custodian indicating that they should release records for use in legal proceedings or testify in court. Where the juvenile cannot be found (such as after the completion of treatment) or where the status of the juvenile's privilege is unclear, the practitioner has an obligation to assert the juvenile's protective privilege and decline to provide records or testimony until the privilege issue has been resolved.

The issue of privilege for juveniles is further complicated when group treatments are used. Each member of a juvenile sexual offender treatment group has individual privilege that can be asserted on an individual basis. Waiver of privilege to disclose information by one group member in testimony is not a waiver for testimony about the protected communications of any other group member. When families are involved in treatment of their child, it is important to clarify whether all of the family are the "treatment clients" of the practitioner (in which case they all have protective privilege) or whether family members are simply helpful participants in the treatment of the child (in which case they are covered by the confidentiality of the treatment but may not have a protective privilege since they are not the identified subject of treatment services).

Case Examples

We will now turn to four case examples, beginning with the case described at the beginning of this chapter, to illustrate how the answers to these six questions can help illuminate conflicts in practice.

Case One

> *A public defender representing an indigent juvenile charged with a violent sex offense has filed a motion to obtain funds from the Court to retain you as an expert witness for the defense, and the motion was allowed. The attorney asks you to conduct an evaluation of the juvenile in preparation for a possible plea negotiation, and the juvenile's parents, who have legal custody, give permission for such an evaluation. You conclude, based on your detailed assessment, that the offer being considered by the prosecution is far more favorable than you would recommend. Defense counsel thanks you and tells you there is no need to write a report because your opinion would adversely affect the plea negotiation. The judge knew that you were evaluating the defendant and orders you to prepare a report and turn it over to the Court, but the defense attorney refuses to waive attorney/client privilege. You are inclined to cooperate, most importantly because the Court has ordered you to file a report, but also because you feel some responsibility to insure that the juvenile gets adequate treatment and containment to protect public safety. What should you do?*

The juvenile is in the legal custody of his parents, who have given permission for an evaluation to assist the defense attorney. The ethical client is the juvenile, and the legal client is the defense attorney, who retained you as an expert for the defense. The fact that you are to be paid from funds approved by the court is irrelevant, because the funds were provided to allow defense counsel to retain an expert for the defense. Your role is to provide forensic services to the defense attorney, not the court. You have relied upon accepted methods and procedures to evaluate the juvenile, which are not in dispute in this case. Charges have been filed against the juvenile, and the case will go to trial if the plea negotiations are unsuccessful. Your communications with the juvenile are confidential except for your discussions with defense counsel, and they are protected by attorney/client privilege. In the face of a court order that appears to require you to violate state law and the ethical standards of your profession, you should inform the Court that the juvenile has not waived attorney/client privilege, and you are asserting it on his behalf for the Court to consider. You may also ask the Court to appoint a guardian *ad litem* to evaluate whether it is in the juvenile's best interest to waive attorney/client privilege.

Case Two

> *A sixteen year-old juvenile in the legal custody of his parents is charged with a sex offense. He retains counsel and enters a plea of not guilty at arraignment. The Court orders a pre-trial "sex offender evaluation" of the juvenile, and you are appointed to do the evaluation for the Court. You are unable to reach the juvenile's attorney by telephone. Should you proceed with the interview without the attorney's permission? Should you proceed with the interview if you reach the attorney and he gives you permission? If so, what kinds of observations could you make in your report?*

As in the first case, this juvenile is in the legal custody of his parents. However, neither his parents, who have legal custody, nor his attorney have given permission for him to participate in an evaluation that requires an informed consent to waive client/therapist privilege. Therefore, you should postpone your evaluation until you are able to get permission from the juvenile's attorney to proceed. If the juvenile's attorney refuses to give permission, you should advise the Court and ask for guidance. If the juvenile's attorney gives permission for you to conduct the evaluation, you are then faced with the issue of appropriate methods and procedures. As we outlined above, there is no way to determine whether a juvenile's assertion of innocence is truthful unless the evaluator improperly assumes the role of fact finder, weighing the evidence and making decisions about the relevance of facts that are still in dispute before the court. Similarly, there is no "profile" of a juvenile offender, and it is impermissible to offer such testimony in the guilt phase of a trial according to Federal law, most state's laws, and the ethical principles of virtually every mental health discipline whose members engage in forensic practice. Therefore, it is advisable to inform the Court that the results of any pre-trail evaluation of a juvenile who asserts his innocence would be limited to a general assessment of the juvenile's functioning and needs aside from those arising from any alleged sexual misconduct until the allegations are adjudicated. Best practice would be to ask the Court to delay the evaluation until the case is adjudicated if the court wants an assessment of re-offense risk or of offender-specific treatment needs.

Case Three

> *A fourteen year-old boy in the legal custody of state protective services has just been found guilty in adult court on four counts of indecent assault and battery. The judge refers the case to you, an employee of the Court Clinic, for sentencing recommendations. The case received extensive media coverage because the juvenile, who is diagnosed with Asperger syndrome, did not display any evidence of remorse in the courtroom, and even seemed to be mocking the court officers at one point. The judge indicates on the referral form that he expects the report to include the results of some actuarial instrument, preferably the J-SOAP, which he knows was created to use with juveniles, and the Static-99, because the child was tried as an adult. You obtain informed consent from the protective services worker to conduct the evaluation, and the child's attorney also gives permission for you to proceed. Should you*

incorporate results from either the J-SOAP or the Static-99?

This case example illustrates issues related to methods and procedures. In all situations where licensed mental health professionals practice, they retain responsibility for the methods and procedures they employ. This means that they have a duty to avoid methods and procedures that provide inaccurate or misleading results, even when there is a specific request by the referral source or the Court. In this case, the judge has asked that the report include the results of two instruments, the Static-99 and the J-SOAP. Although the Static-99 is an actuarial test that has been used extensively in risk assessments with adults, there are no data to establish its validity in predicting anything with juveniles or children. In the absence of validity studies with data from an appropriate comparison group, an actuarial test is just a list that may or may not be applicable and may be misleading. The fact that the juvenile has been tried as an adult is irrelevant; the Static-99 should not be used in this case because it has no demonstrated validity with juveniles.

While the J-SOAP was, in fact, designed to become an actuarial test for use with children and adolescents, there are insufficient data establishing that it predicts anything at this point. In addition, the research samples studied to date did not include a group of youth with pervasive developmental disorders, so the data that do exist may or may not be applicable to juveniles with Asperger syndrome. Since the J-SOAP may yield misleading results due to the lack of sufficient validity data with adolescents in general and with adolescents who have Asperger syndrome in particular, it should not be used in this case either. This is especially so because the Court may not be aware of the limitations of the J-SOAP and may place greater weight on the results of an instrument designed to be used with children.

Since both tests requested by the Court lack empirical evidence of their validity with juveniles, it would be a violation of professional ethics and, therefore, law in some jurisdictions to use them in this case. It would be advisable to inform the Court that there are insufficient data to support the use of either the J-SOAP or the Static-99 as actuarial assessments of risk in legal decision making with juveniles, and that to do so may subject the clinician to sanctions for unethical conduct.

Many jurisdictions have administrative bodies created by law, most notably state sex offender registry boards, that are required to employ a specified number of licensed psychologists. Some have argued that these psychologists are acting in a "ministerial" rather than "clinical" capacity, and are, therefore, not bound by the ethical duty to use appropriate methods and procedures. We maintain that ethical standards for psychologists, including the prohibition against the inappropriate use of test data, apply to anyone for whom licensure as a psychologist was a condition of employment. It would, therefore, be unethical for a licensed psychologist providing expert testimony to or serving as a member of such a board to use any test before the reliability and validity are established with the specific population in question.

Case Four

> *A colleague of yours, Dr. Thompson, is asked by the Court to perform a pre-adjudication evaluation of a juvenile accused of sexually assaulting a young*

neighbor. Specifically, the referral is for a "juvenile sex offender evaluation" with a request for assessment of risk of re-offense and recommendations for treatment. The juvenile denies having committed the offense, and the case is scheduled for a trial. Dr. Thompson contacts the juvenile's attorney and parents, who give permission for the evaluation to proceed. He then interviews the juvenile and his parents for several hours and administers the MMPI-A, the J-SOAP, and several self-report measures designed to assess cognitive distortions, deviant beliefs, and sexual interests. During the trial, Dr. Thompson testifies that "sixty-five out of one hundred juveniles with similar test results were subsequently convicted of sex offenses," and that "this defendant would be at moderate to high risk for re-offense." Has Dr. Thompson behaved unethically?

Unfortunately, Dr. Thompson has behaved problematically in three ways. First, although he had been asked by the Court to conduct a pre-adjudication evaluation of the juvenile, and the juvenile's attorney and parents had consented to the evaluation, Dr. Thompson undertook an evaluation for which there are no accepted standards and procedures and which risks usurping the fact-finding role of the Court. The only issue before the Court during a trial on the facts is whether or not the juvenile committed the sexual offense as alleged. When the juvenile denies the offense prior to trial, there are no scientifically-based methods by which the mental health professional can determine whether the juvenile committed the acts as alleged, nor any scientifically based methods by which the clinical significance of the juvenile's denial of the alleged offense can be assessed. Conducting a "juvenile sexual offender" evaluation under these circumstances improperly presumes exactly what is at issue: whether or not the juvenile has committed a sexual offense.

Second, Dr. Thompson offered testimony about how the juvenile compared to other juveniles who gave similar test responses who were subsequently determined by the Court to have committed a sexual offense. This testimony might lead a judge or jury to conclude that it is more likely than not that the juvenile defendant committed the alleged sexual offense. This type of testimony about the characteristics of a person in a delinquency or criminal trial, which is generally termed "profile testimony" or "syndrome testimony," is forbidden by case law in every jurisdiction with which we are familiar because it may mislead the judge or jury about the likelihood of innocence or guilt of the defendant before them. Even if the judge were to allow such testimony, the forensic evaluator has a duty to be familiar with the law relating to expert witness testimony and conduct him or herself accordingly. While profile testimony is inappropriate during the adjudication phase of any delinquency hearing or criminal trial because whether or not a sexual offense was committed by the defendant is precisely what is at issue, the same testimony would be appropriate at sentencing, in a civil commitment hearing, or any other proceeding where the fact of the sexual offense has already been established.

Third, there is no scientific basis upon which to base an assessment of risk of sexual offense recidivism if it has not been established that the defendant has committed a sexual offense in the first place. Therefore, by testifying as to the juvenile's risk of *re-offense*, Dr. Thompson is again both presuming precisely what is at issue—whether or not the juvenile committed a sexual offense—and potentially misleading the judge or jury by comparing the defendant (whose guilt has not been established) with sexual offense recidivists (whose history of sexual offense had been established).

Conclusion

Evaluations of children with sexual behavior problems are of great importance due to the obvious implications for both public safety and for the well-being of the children undergoing evaluation. In the best of all worlds, the legal, ethical, and moral issues that arise in these evaluations would all point toward a single, clear course of action for the forensic evaluator. Unfortunately, this is rarely the case, and mental health professionals are forced to analyze competing and conflicting demands. We have outlined some of the more common conflicts that arise, and we have posed six questions, the answers to which may help resolve some of the conflicts. Mental health professionals who evaluate children with sexual behavior problems should also be aware of laws and regulations that apply to their jurisdictions, and they may also seek advice from the ethics committees of national and state professional associations.

CHAPTER NINE

MALE ADOLESCENT SEXUALLY COERCIVE BEHAVIOR TARGETING PEERS AND ADULTS: A RELATIONAL PERSPECTIVE

**LISA L. FREY
AND
ELISSA MCELRATH DYER**

Introduction

This chapter explores three bodies of literature related to male adolescent sexually coercive behavior targeting peers and adults: the literature relating to sexual harassment, date and acquaintance sexual violence, and identified juvenile sexual offender populations. It is suggested that the lack of integration across these bodies of literature limits our understanding of peer and adult-directed sexually coercive behavior in adolescents. The relational-cultural model (e.g., Jordan, Kaplan, Miller, et al., 1991; Miller & Stiver, 1997) is presented as a framework from which to conceptualize the sexually coercive behavior evidenced by these youth. Specific treatment implications emerging from the philosophical orientation of this model are discussed.

The literature emphasizes the heterogeneity that exists within the population of adolescents who engage in sexually coercive behavior (Knight & Prentky, 1993; Murphy & Page, 2000; Richardson, Kelly, Bhate, & Graham, 1997). One example of this heterogeneity is found in recent research pointing to significant differences between youth who target child victims and those who target peer and/or adult victims (e.g., Hunter, Figueredo, Malamuth, & Becker, 2004; Hunter, Hazelwood, & Slesinger, 2000; Richardson et al.). This line of research is vital in order to develop effective, targeted, outcome-based interventions. For instance, there is some evidence that youth who target peer and/or adult victims have more delinquent profiles than those who target children (e.g., Hunter et al., 2004; Richardson et al.), a finding that has important implications for treatment providers and programs.

Absent in much of the literature, however, is an overarching conceptualization of sexually coercive behavior toward peers and/or adults as encompassing a range or continuum of sexual behaviors. For example, there is a body of research regarding sexual harassment in youth but there is rarely any cross-over between that body of literature and the literature on date or acquaintance rape among adolescents. Thus, two of the purposes of this chapter are to present a broad review of the available literature related to sexually coercive behaviors that adolescents direct toward peers and/or adults and to point to the limitations in the current literature.

Ryan and Lane (1997) suggest that the "coercive and exploitative patterns of interaction" (p. 277) evidenced by youth engaging in sexually coercive behavior reflect the chronic disconnections and lack of mutuality (Miller, 1991; Miller & Stiver, 1997) they have experienced within their own intimate relationships. The sociocultural context of their lives further complicates this issue through its influence on the shaping of gender role identity (e.g., Feltey, Ainslie, & Geib, 1991; Hird, 2000; Marciniak, 1998; Rosenthal, 1997). Consequently, a vital aspect of the change process in counseling these youths is the development of a connected, growth-enhancing relationship between the youth and the counselor (e.g., Ryan & Lane). This relationship must foster the exploration of difficult issues, such as the impact of sociocultural messages and experiences of chronic relational disconnections (see section on relational-cultural model), while simultaneously holding youth accountable for their behavior.

Unfortunately, the issue of relationship building is sometimes neglected in the treatment literature on juvenile sexual aggression, particularly in regard to the provision of a comprehensive framework for understanding relational development. This oversight is especially distressing in view of the challenges inherent in building relationships with a group of youth who are often hostile, detached, and untrusting. The relational-cultural model (e.g., Miller, 1991; Miller & Stiver, 1997) is a relevant framework from which relational development and sociocultural influences on gender role development in adolescents can be conceptualized. Thus, the third purpose of this chapter is to discuss how this model informs the understanding of adolescent sexually coercive behavior and relational development.

Defining the Population

This review will primarily focus on the incidence of peer and adult-directed sexually coercive behavior in adolescents between the ages of 13 and 18. However, because the reviewed studies sampled high school students, some included older students (over age 18) who were still in high school. These studies were considered as long as the mean of the participant group fell within the 13-18 year old range and all participants were high school students. Empirical studies investigating college student and adult populations were excluded, primarily because the developmental characteristics and contextual circumstances (e.g., status as minors vs. adults, living with parents vs. independently) of high school adolescents and those of college students/adults often differ significantly. For instance, dating and peer relationships in adolescence are typically more unstable than relationships in later adult life (Arriaga & Foshee, 2004) and, during adolescence, gendered attitudes toward sex are just beginning to coalesce (Feltey et al., 1991).

Relationship intimacy becomes a primary focus of many adolescents at the same time they are experiencing physiological changes that bring sexual issues to the forefront (Hird & Jackson, 2001). Adolescence is also a time when youth begin to experience greater gender role pressure (Brown & Gilligan, 1992; Hird & Jackson). Further, under some circumstances, such as in consensual peer relationships, adolescents are considered capable of giving voluntary consent for sexual activity. These factors combine to make adolescence a sensitive time during which youth may be at increased risk for engaging in or experiencing sexually coercive behavior (Feiring, Deblinger, Hoch-Espada, & Haworth, 2002; Feltey et al., 1991; Herman, 1990; Hird & Jackson). In order to develop an understanding of this behavior, though, sexual coercion as it applies to adolescents must be clearly defined. Thus, for purposes of this review, sexual coercion is defined as "any sexual or erotic behavior involving either verbal coercion such as continual arguments or verbal pressure, use of drugs and alcohol, or abuse of authority or the threat or use of physical force in order to obtain an unwanted contact with any part of the body" (Poitras & Lavoie, 1995, p. 299). In addition, it is assumed that the intent to obtain unwanted contact can be implicit or explicit (Hird, 2000; Poitras & Lavoie). This definition incorporates a continuum of sexually coercive behaviors ranging from non-physical coercion, including verbal pressure, manipulation, and harassment, to physical coercion, including the threat or use of physical force.

Subsequent to the previously defined parameters, the reviewed literature will be limited to studies that distinctly address the factors involved in sexual coercion. Empirical studies examining sexual coercion within the wider context of dating violence were not included if sexual aggression and physical violence were considered in aggregate form. For example, some dating violence studies combined sexual coercion with other types of aggression in conducting analyses, resulting in an inability to distinguish predictors and factors related only to sexual violence (e.g., Arriaga & Foshee, 2004; Feiring et al., 2002; Foshee, Linder, MacDougall, & Bangdiwala, 2001; O'Keefe & Treister, 1998). Also, studies investigating combined populations of adolescents who targeted peers and those who targeted children were not considered unless the two populations were considered separately. Differences in typology between these groups of offenders have been noted by researchers (Boyd, Hagan, & Cho, 2000; Carpenter, Peed, & Eastman, 1995; Hunter, et al., 2004; Hunter et al., 2000; Knight & Prentky, 1993; Worling, 1995) and, as such, important distinctions exist that may be overlooked if the populations are treated in aggregate.

Of necessity, this review focuses on male offenders due to the scarcity of studies examining female adolescents who engage in sexually coercive behavior toward peers and adults. However, it should be noted that prevalence rates for female offenders may be artificially lowered by a lack of identification and/or failure to acknowledge that this population exists (Frey, 2005), and by the reluctance of male victims to endorse items related to sexual victimization due to socialization regarding gender roles (Hird & Jackson, 2001).

A Review of the Literature

The extant literature regarding adolescent sexually coercive behavior directed toward peers and adults tends to be grouped into three areas: literature relating to sexual harassment, date and acquaintance sexual violence, and identified juvenile sexual offender populations. Literature in each of these areas will be reviewed, although it should be emphasized that this categorization may be misleading. The limitation imposed by such categorization is that it becomes difficult to determine whether youth who engage in each type of behavior (i.e., sexual harassment, dating or acquaintance sexual violence, juvenile corrections-identified sexual offending) are three distinct populations of youth or one population engaging in a continuum of behaviors. Considerable overlap likely exists among these categories. For example, a survey investigating sexual harassment initiation in a high school population almost certainly includes responders who have also engaged in acquaintance rape or have been previously charged with a sexual offense. Certainly there is also overlap in terms of the harmful and potentially long-lasting effects of all types of sexual coercion on victims.

Sexual Harassment as Sexually Coercive Behavior

Fineran and Bennett (1998) pointed out that sexual dating violence and sexual harassment in adolescence are treated separately in the literature despite research indicating that a sizeable number of youth, particularly girls, experience physical forms of sexual harassment, including sexual assault (e.g., American Association of University Women Educational Foundation [AAUW], 1993; AAUW, 2001; Fineran & Bennett, 1999). The consequences of this dichotomization may be societal minimization of the impact of sexual harassment on victims and the negation of the criminal nature of sexually harassing behavior (Fineran & Bennett, 1999). Lee, Croninger, Linn, and Chen (1996) emphasize this point when they state, "By definition, sexual harassment is victimization" (p. 407). Thus, the lack of empirical and theoretical studies integrating these two bodies of research is an issue that should be addressed.

Definition and incidence

The United States Supreme Court has defined two categories of sexual harassment: (a) quid pro quo, which occurs when a person in a power position, such as a supervisor or teacher, makes decisions about an individual's job or school grade based on compliance with the authority's demands for sexual contact; and (b) hostile environment, which occurs when harassing behavior in the workplace or school results in a hostile, intimidating, or offensive environment and interferes in an individual's ability to do her/his work (United States Equal Opportunity Commission, 1990). The literature on adolescents focuses on hostile environment as the most applicable to peer sexual harassment (Fineran & Bennett, 1998). An AAUW (2001) study of high schools in the United States defined sexual harassment as "…unwanted and unwelcome sexual behavior that interferes with your life. Sexual harassment is not behaviors that you like or want (for example wanted kissing, touching, or flirting)" (p. 2). Expanding on this definition, Timmerman (2003) indicated that sexual harassment is most often conceptualized as a continuum of behavior, ranging from mild to severe forms of unwanted sexual behavior.

The factor that differentiates sexual harassment from the verbal coercion that may be part of sexual violence in dating or acquaintance relationships is the context. In other words, sexual harassment refers to behavior that occurs in the context of the work or school environment, generally in public areas and/or in the presence of others (AAUW, 2001; Timmerman, 2003), whereas dating or acquaintance sexual violence may occur in a range of environments and most often in the context of a one-on-one relationship. As might be expected, however, the overlap between sexually harassing behaviors and sexually violent behaviors in dating relationships (see following section) has resulted in some confusion regarding the operational definition of sexual harassment. In an effort to more precisely define sexual harassment, Timmerman (2003) and Fitzgerald and Hesson-McInnis (1989) have differentiated between harassment involving sexual violence, referring to severe forms of sexual behavior such as rape, and that involving unwanted sexual behavior, referring to milder forms of sexual harassment such as unwanted remarks with sexual connotations.

The existing research suggests that a large number of adolescents report engaging in sexually harassing behaviors. For example, Lee et al. (1996) found 72% and the AAUW study (2001) found 54% of their adolescent participants reported engaging in such behaviors. Further, Lee et al. reported that 53% of male and female participants stated they had both experienced and perpetrated sexual harassment. While male adolescents report experiencing a significant amount of sexual harassment (e.g., 56% of the adolescent males in the AAUW study reported this experience), their reports also indicate they remain more likely to perpetrate sexual harassment than adolescent females (AAUW; Fineran & Bennett, 1999; Hand & Sanchez, 2000; Lee et al.; Timmerman, 2003). Hand and Sanchez found that the commission rate for each measured sexually harassing behavior, as well as for the additive index of behaviors, was nearly twice as high in male adolescents as compared to female adolescents. In addition, female adolescents were more likely than males to experience sexual harassment with greater frequency (AAUW; Fineran & Bennett; Hand & Sanchez; Lee et al.); that was more severe, physically intrusive, and/or intimidating (AAUW; Fineran & Bennett; Hand & Sanchez; Lee et al.; Timmerman); and that involved combined forms of harassment (AAUW). Caution must be taken, though, in comparing the results of these studies, which are limited by differences in the operationalization of sexually coercive behavior. For example, Fineran and Bennett asked participants to report behaviors experienced over a one year period of time, whereas the AAUW study asked participants to report experiences that occurred sometime during their school years.

Adolescent perpetrators of sexual harassment

Although the research indicates that adolescent males are more likely to perpetrate sexual harassment than adolescent females (see previous section), there is little in the literature clarifying the characteristics of these young men or the dynamics underlying their behavior. One exception is the AAUW (2001) study, which included limited information regarding the perpetrators of sexual harassment. In regard to male perpetrators, the study indicated that the most frequently reported reason for sexual harassing was that it was simply part of school life and many students engaged in the behavior, so it was not considered a "big deal" (AAUW, p. 41). Some ethnic differences in regard to victim selection were suggested, with African American males more likely than white or Hispanic males to report a female victim and white males more likely than African American or Hispanic males to report a male victim (AAUW).

Sexually Coercive Behavior in Dating or Acquaintance Relationships

As previously discussed, the importance placed on peer relationships and the sexual exploration that occurs during the developmental stage of adolescence can provide a forum in which sexually coercive behaviors in acquaintance and peer relationships are first expressed (Feiring et al., 2002; Hird & Jackson, 2001; Feltey et al., 1991). For instance, Maxwell, Robinson, and Post (2003) found that 80% of the incidents reported by female adolescent victims of coercion involved either an acquaintance or romantic partner. Similarly, studies have indicated that unwanted or coercive sexual activities among youth occur more often in long-term romantic relationships (Jackson, Cram, & Seymour, 2000) and are rated as more acceptable as adolescent relationships increase in seriousness and commitment (Feltey et al.).

Definition and incidence

Estimates of the number of male adolescents within high school populations who initiate sexually coercive behavior toward peers or acquaintances vary, with percentages ranging from 1% to 19% (e.g., Foshee, 1996; Hilton, Harris, & Rice, 2003; Maxwell et al., 2003; O'Keefe, 1997; Poitras & Lavoie, 1995; Schwartz, O'Leary, & Kendziora, 1997). However, the variability in definition and measurement of sexual coercion, ranging from unwanted kissing to forced intercourse and from measurement with one item to several items, complicates the generalizability of these estimates. Nonetheless, there is agreement in the majority of the research literature that male adolescents report engaging in sexual coercion toward peers and acquaintances significantly more often than female adolescents (e.g., Foshee; Feltey et al, 1991; Lodico, Gruber, & DiClemente, 1996; O'Keefe; Poitras & Lavoie).

The research conveys mixed results regarding the effects of race and ethnicity on sexually coercive acts in dating or acquaintance relationships. Davis, Peck, and Storment (1993) found that black male adolescents were significantly more likely to report that forcing sexual contact on a female was acceptable in some situations. Marciniak (1998) also reported that black male adolescents were significantly more likely to endorse acceptability of rape myths and gender-role stereotypes. Maxwell et al. (2003) & Lodico et al. (1996), in contrast, found no significant effects for race/ethnicity. Results of the effects of race/ethnicity are questionable for several reasons, including the significant sample attrition of black males in some studies, small overall numbers of minority research participants, and the confounding effects of not differentiating between experiencing or perpetrating forced sex. Overall, findings concerning the effects of race and ethnicity may be better accounted for by socioeconomic and sociocultural factors (Marciniak).

A complicating factor in defining and determining the incidence of sexual coercion in adolescent dating and acquaintance relationships is that much of the reported sexual coercion occurring in this context is not physically violent (Hird & Jackson, 2001). Verbal coercion is reportedly the most frequently indicated type of coercion used by both male and female adolescents (Poitras & Lavoie, 1995; Maxwell et al., 2003). Maxwell et al. found that 34% of male perpetrators endorsed the item "said things (to a female) he did not mean" (p. 472) in order to engage in sexual activity, and 42% of females indicated that males had pressured them into sexual activities in this way. Hird and Jackson reported that many of the male adolescents in their qualitative study indicated using verbal pressuring and unwanted sexual touching as coercive tactics. The understanding of persistent verbal coercion as a sexually coercive tactic is underscored by reports of adolescent females that such pressure "wearied them into submission" (Hird & Jackson, p. 37). Gender differences in communication regarding sexual coercion have also been suggested as influencing perceptions of such verbally coercive behavior (e.g., Hird & Jackson; Rosenthal, 1997). For instance, adolescents have been reported to perceive agreement to participate in sex as clearer communication than refusing sex (Rosenthal).

Risk factors

Sexual abuse history and the use of drugs or alcohol are potential risk factors that have been examined in the literature on perpetration of sexual violence directed toward peers or acquaintances. Lodico et al. (1996) found that adolescents with a history of childhood sexual abuse were two times more likely than nonabused adolescents to force an acquaintance or date into sexual contact. Although this finding held true for both genders who had experienced abuse, differential gender effects were also found with 13.4% of abused males (as compared to 1.9% of abused females) and 3% of nonabused males (as compared to 0.8% of nonabused females) reporting engaging in sexually aggressive behavior. The generalizability of this study is limited, however, because "forced sexual contact" was not specifically defined for participants. As a result, the range of sexual behaviors endorsed was unclear.

Poitras and Lavoie (1995) reported that 2.3% of male adolescents reported using alcohol and/or drugs as a sexually coercive strategy. In contrast, none of the female participants indicated they had used such a method to initiate sexual experiences. Maxwell et al. (2003) reported that 32% of male adolescents endorsed that they had engaged in sex with someone who was "very drunk, stoned, or unconscious" (p. 472). Overall, the research on sexual assault among adolescents largely supports alcohol and/or drug use as a risk factor for inflicting or experiencing sexual coercion (Maxwell et al.).

Gender role attitudes and sexual coercion toward peers and acquaintances

Hird and Jackson (2001) proposed that gender role socialization places males as initiators and females as passive and/or "gate-keepers" (p. 31) in sexual activities. Other sociocultural influences on adolescent gender role development have also been theoretically linked to sexually coercive behavior, including the beliefs that: (a) males have an increased sex drive and heterosexual sex proves masculinity (Hird & Jackson); (b) sexual aggression toward women is justified in some situations (Feltey et al., 1991); and (c) males should not be concerned about violence (Jackson et al., 2000; Marciniak, 1998).

Poitras and Lavoie (1995) pointed out that differences between males and females in defining verbal coercion or pressure are confusing to many adolescents, which may increase the risk of sexually coercive behavior. For instance, female adolescents who go against social norms and express sexual desire might be perceived as pressuring their partner verbally for sex (Poitras & Lavoie). In contrast, male adolescents responding to social norms encouraging initiation of sexual contact may be direct about their sexual desire, resulting in the experience of verbal pressure by their partners (Poitras & Lavoie). Nonetheless, despite these communication differences, implying that verbal coercion is a part of sexual exploration is inaccurate and potentially undermines the seriousness of the effects of sexual coercion on victims (Poitras & Lavoie).

As suggested by these observations, male and female adolescents may view sexual coercion from different perspectives. Research exploring attitudes toward sexual coercion in dating or acquaintance relationships has attempted to clarify these theorized gender differences. For example, Feltey et al. (1991) found that male adolescents were more likely than female adolescents to support sexually coercive behaviors, justifying aggression across 17 situations (e.g., male spending money on female, male being extremely sexually aroused, female dressing "sexy"). Maxwell et al. (2003) and Marciniak (1998) reported a relationship between the acceptance of rape myths and sexually coercive behavior toward peers or acquaintances. Reported sexually coercive behavior in male adolescents has been linked with increased age, less positive attitudes toward women, and less accurate legal knowledge about rape (Maxwell et al.).

Despite the growing body of research concerning sexually coercive behaviors in dating and acquaintance relationships, limitations related to study design and operational definition pose difficulties in obtaining a clear picture of how sexual coercion operates within such relationships. As previously discussed, variability in definitions of sexual coercion complicate interpretation of this research. Also, many study designs fail to discriminate between victims and perpetrators of sexually coercive behavior or consider sexual coercion only from the standpoint of being directed by males toward females, leaving questions about female aggressors unanswered. The widespread use of cross-sectional designs introduces ambiguity regarding whether the measured constructs, including attitudes about rape myths, sexually coercive behaviors, and male views of women, are antecedents of sexual coercion or consequences of aggressors trying to justify their sexually coercive behaviors.

Sexually Coercive Behavior in Identified Juvenile Sexual Offender Populations

Definition and incidence

Adolescents whose sexually coercive acts are identified as criminal or illegal behavior are often labeled as juvenile sexual offenders in the literature. One point of confusion, however, is that use of the term "offender" in the literature does not always mean that the juvenile justice system has been involved in labeling the behavior (Frey, 2005). Rather, the term juvenile sexual offender is also understood to refer to those youths who may not be involved in the juvenile justice system but are in specialized treatment placements consequent to engaging in sexually aggressive behavior.

Juvenile sexual offenders are often divided into two categories, those who offend against children (identified as "child group" in this review) and those who offend against peers and adults (identified as "peer/adult group" in this review). The majority of research investigating this typology focuses on personal characteristics, background variables, and potential recidivism. Most of these studies examine male adolescents who have targeted female victims, generally identified as the most frequently targeted peer/adult victim group (Hunter et al., 2000; Worling, 1995).

In regard to incidence, a few studies have extrapolated from retrospective information gathered from adults convicted of sexual crimes. For example, Knight and Prentky (1993) reported in a review of the literature that up to 50% of adult offenders indicated they first sexually assaulted someone during adolescence. According to the United

States Department of Justice (1997), 19% of rapes and sexual assaults involving one perpetrator and 7% involving multiple perpetrators were attributed to adolescents younger than age 18. Although the peer/adult and child groups are not specifically separated in the survey, it was noted that 20% of all rape and sexual assault victims were between the ages of 12 and 17 (United States Department of Justice). Despite several studies reporting relatively low recidivism rates for juvenile sexual offenders overall (e.g., Alexander, 1999; Association for the Treatment of Sexual Abusers, 2000; Becker, 1990; Chaffin & Bonner, 1998), it has been suggested that the peer/adult group may be more likely to recidivate than the child group (Nisbet, Wilson, & Smallbone, 2004; Smith & Monastersky, 1986).

Peer/adult-directed vs. child-directed adolescent sexual offenders

In order to better understand sexual coercion in juvenile sexual offender populations, it is important to be aware of differences between peer/adult and child group adolescent offenders. Several differences in offense characteristics have been suggested, including peer/adult offenders being older at the time of their first offense (Hsu & Starzynski, 1990), more likely to use force or a weapon (Hunter et al., 2004; Hunter et al., 2000; Nisbet et al, 2004), and more likely to be influenced by alcohol or drugs during the sex offense (Hunter et al., 2004).

Specific personality characteristics and background variables have also been associated with adolescents who offend against peers/adults. As a whole, peer/adult group offenders have been reported to be more impulsive, aggressive, and violent than those who aggress against younger children (Richardson et al., 1997). Peer/adult group adolescent offenders have also been identified as less schizoid and/or avoidant and to have decreased dependency-related issues as compared to child group adolescent offenders (Carpenter et al., 1995). Similarly, peer/adult group adolescent offenders were reported to have less psychosocial deficits than child group offenders (Hunter, Figueredo, Malamuth, & Becker, 2003), and to have higher degrees of narcissism and arrogance and to be more interpersonally exploitive than child group offenders (Carpenter et al.). In regard to gender attitudes, Epps, Haworth, and Swaffer (1993) found that adolescent sexual offenders targeting adults do not differ significantly from delinquent adolescents convicted of nonsexual violent crimes in terms of attitudes toward women or rape myth endorsement.

While studies have suggested that peer/adult group adolescent offenders have a decreased rate of childhood sexual victimization as compared to child group adolescent offenders (Awad & Saunders, 1991; Nisbet et al., 2004; O'Brien, 1991), Worling (1995) found no significant between-group differences in this regard. Interestingly, however, Knight and Prentky (1993) found that, among adult males convicted of rape, those who had histories of peer/adult-directed sexual offenses as adolescents were more likely to have experienced childhood neglect than those who did not have juvenile histories of sexual offending.

Delinquency and peer/adult-directed sexual coercion

It has been proposed that there is a significant association between nonsexual delinquent behaviors and juvenile sexually coercive behaviors toward peers and/or adults. Richardson et al. (1997) found that peer/adult group adolescent offenders had higher levels of antisocial behavior and delinquency and associated with peer groups with higher delinquency levels as compared to both child group adolescent offenders and a mixed group who offended across categories. Similarly, Hunter et al. (2000) reported that peer/adult group adolescent offenders were more likely to commit sexual offenses along with other criminal activities (e.g., burglary), act in a group with other offenders, and have higher levels of aggression and violence than child group adolescent offenders or adult sexual offenders. Peer/adult group adolescent offenders, in contrast to child group offenders, have also been found to be significantly more likely to be convicted for nonsexual crimes as adults (Nisbet et al., 2004). Such studies concerning delinquent behaviors in adolescent sexual offenders targeting peers and adults corroborate longitudinal findings of Thornberry, Huizinga, and Loeber (2004) regarding delinquent youth, which indicate that many delinquent youths engage in multiple forms of delinquency. As suggested by Thornberry et al., general delinquency may be one pathway (i.e., "Overt Pathway"; Thornberry et al., p. 5) through which youths develop sexually coercive behaviors.

The Relational-Cultural Model and Sexually Coercive Behavior in Adolescent Males

Overview of the relational-cultural model

The relational-cultural model (see Jordan, Kaplan, Miller, Stiver, & Surrey, 1991; Miller, 1976; Miller & Stiver, 1997) is proposed as a relevant framework from which to understand sociocultural influences on gender role development and the development of sexually coercive behavior toward peers and adults. The foundation of the model is the idea that meaningful, shared connection with others leads to the development of healthy self-identity. Psychological health and maturity is conceptualized as evolving through increasing relational complexity and mutuality, and through reciprocal and authentic exploration of conflict in relationships (Jordan et al., 1991). This premise is in contrast to traditional models, which emphasize the importance of the separation-individuation process in developing self-identity (Miller & Stiver, 1997).

Underlying constructs of the relational-cultural model include four characteristics that represent core aspects of connected, growth-enhancing relationships: (a) mutual engagement, defined as mutual involvement, commitment, and sensitivity to the relationship; (b) authenticity, defined as the freedom to be genuine in the relationship; (c) empowerment, defined as the capacity for action and sense of personal strength that emerges from the relationship; and (d) the ability to deal with conflict, defined as the ability to express, receive, and process diversity in the relationship (Liang, Tracy, Taylor, Williams, Jordan, & Miller, 2002). It is theorized that relationships encompassing these four constructs support and inform the evolution of a healthy self-identity. An absence of these qualities in relationships results in a lack of interpersonal connection and a sense of isolation leading to distress (Jordan & Dooley, 2001).

A key tenet of the relational-cultural model is the "central relational paradox" (Miller & Stiver, 1997, p. 81). Because some individuals encounter chronic and serious disconnections in relationships, they learn to hold important aspects of self out of relationships in order to remain safe. For example, an individual with a history of childhood abandonment might withhold feelings in significant adult relationships to avoid possible rejection. Miller and Stiver label such survival mechanisms "strategies of disconnection" (p. 106). Walker (2004) describes these strategies as retaining "an appearance of connection while lacking its substance" (p. 9). Caught in this struggle, the individual simultaneously yearns for and is terrified by genuine connection, resulting in the relational paradox (Miller & Stiver; Walker).

The influence of Western sociocultural norms on gender role development is integrated throughout the model. Specific to the development of males, for example, is the view that men's identity and self-esteem are socioculturally shaped through a process of fostering competition or comparison with others at the expense of relational development (Bergman, 1991). In response to the sociocultural expectation that men will be autonomous, independent, and unique, men sacrifice relational skill development (Bergman). This pattern is in contrast to women, who have often been taught to carry primary relational responsibility and, as a result, may sacrifice authenticity in order to maintain relationships (Brown & Gilligan, 1992; Miller, 1976).

The Relational-Cultural Model and Sexually Coercive Behavior Toward Peers and Adults

Dooley and Fedele (2004) discuss the sociocultural pressure on young males to follow gender role norms, including pressures regarding separation, autonomy, and the primacy of meeting their own needs at all costs. Compliance with this shaping process is necessary for young males to achieve and maintain acceptance within "boy culture" (Dooley & Fedele, p. 222). This pressure is particularly detrimental when young males are not provided opportunities for authentic connection within significant relationships: "…if deprived of sufficient opportunities to learn how to make real connections, (boys) try to meet these needs in superficial and manipulative ways" (Dooley & Fedele, p. 222). Miller (1976) described the consequence of this individual shaping process as reinforcing the broader "power-over culture" (Miller & Stiver, 1997, p. 59), a culture in which those with power work to maintain their power through maintenance of the status quo and of dominant-subordinate relationships, thus perpetuating an existing system of privilege. Miller and Stiver underscore the cyclical nature of these patterns, stating "All forms of oppression are also relational oppression" (p. 49).

Of course, relationships with parents can be of primary importance to young men in limiting the damaging impact of a power-over culture. Unfortunately, though, fathers may be ill-equipped to foster youths' relational development because they were also the recipients of the same sociocultural messages experienced by their sons (Bergman, 1991). Mothers experience a similar pressure in that they are pushed to disengage emotionally from sons in response to the sociocultural message emphasizing male separation from mothers in order to avoid being labeled as a "girl", "wimp", or "mama's boy" (Dooley & Fedele, 2004).

The consequence of boys growing up within this power-over culture is that, by adolescence, "social, physical, and sexual dominance replaces authentic interactions" (Dooley & Fedele, 2004, p. 242). Specifically, Dooley and Fedele propose that this dynamic can result in behaviors including aggressive physical behavior, dealing with interpersonal anxiety through the use of drugs and alcohol, and sexually dominating behaviors such as date rape.

An essential aspect of this model as it informs our understanding of peer/adult-directed sexually coercive behavior in male adolescents is that it goes beyond the theory of abuse of societal power (Lee et al., 1996; Tangri, Burt, & Johnson, 1982) as an etiological factor in the development of sexually coercive behavior. (See Lee et al. & Tangri et al. for comprehensive reviews of theoretical formulations regarding sexually coercive behavior.) Rather, experiences of authentic connection and relational growth are conceptualized as critical components in achieving individual psychological health and, more broadly, a culture emphasizing shared power vs. power-over behaviors (Miller, 1976; Miller & Stiver, 1997). Accordingly, the therapeutic relationship itself is an essential tool for change in working with male adolescents who engage in peer/adult-directed sexually coercive behavior.

Treatment Implications

Ryan and Lane (1997) discuss the impact of abusive relational experiences and relational disconnections on youth who engage in sexually abusive behavior, pointing to the value of the therapeutic relationship in providing youth with a reparative experience. There are many difficulties in achieving this goal, however. For example, the probability of involuntary referral, the power imbalance inherent in the therapeutic relationship, and limitations on confidentiality present particular challenges (Ryan & Lane). Furthermore, the emphasis on cognitive and behavioral interventions in the literature may result, often unintentionally, in minimization of the need to develop genuine, mutual connections with youth. Unfortunately, the combination of these factors may result in the neglect of the relationship in our work with these youths (R. E. Longo, personal communication, October 7, 2004).

The relational-cultural model provides a working framework from which to understand and develop effective interventions in working with male adolescents engaging in peer/adult-directed sexually coercive behavior. Approaching our work with these youths from the theoretical orientation of this model does not imply that strategies grounded in other orientations (e.g., restructuring cognitive distortions, relapse prevention strategies) cannot be utilized (although it should be noted that there is an absence of outcome literature regarding effective treatment approaches in working with this population). Instead, the model offers an overarching philosophy or orientation through which relational development can be understood and fostered. The following are offered as possible applications of the relational-cultural model to treatment with male adolescents who are sexually coercive toward peers and adults.

Reframing of accountability and responsibility

Promoting accountability and responsibility for sexually coercive behavior is a core tenet of the philosophy of most treatment programs and providers working with youth who have engaged in sexually coercive behavior. Often accountability is pursued via confrontive or even punitive and shaming interventions. From the perspective of the relational-cultural model, accountability and responsibility are reframed as essential to relational respect. The underlying message to be communicated is, "In our relationship, I have respect for you and your ability to accept responsibility for your behavior. If I didn't hold you responsible, that would be like saying you are not capable of responsibility. I expect you to have the same respect for me—let me know if you think I am not taking responsibility. Accepting responsibility is part of being strong and powerful."

Dealing with cultural marginalization

Many youths engaging in sexually coercive behavior are marginalized by our culture as a result of their behavior and labeling as juvenile delinquents or sexual offenders. Furthermore, some may be marginalized due to their race or socioeconomic status. The concept of a power-over culture provides language to help youths understand their experience of marginalization and the personal impact of their multiple and intersecting self-identities (e.g., gender, race, sexual identity). Dooley and Fedele (2004) describe the importance of helping youth develop "psychological mindedness" (p. 245), which allows them to understand the influence of sociocultural patterns on individual roles and how to deal with that influence. The insights that emerge from such discussion can then be applied to their own sexually coercive behavior. That is, saying "You've talked about how you think you've been treated and how that makes you feel. What about the person you hurt—are there any ways she/he might feel a similar way?" can foster an increased understanding of how and why they marginalize others, including those they sexually victimized.

Gendered relationships among professionals

The relational-cultural model underscores the importance of the images youth form of gendered relationships. These youth are keen observers of adult male-female interactions and relationships they are exposed to in residential treatment centers, group homes, and community treatment settings. Thus, attention of professionals to the gendered aspects of their work relationships is critical. For example, male staff interrupting or interfering in interactions occurring between youth and female staff, "rescuing" behavior on the part of male toward female staff, and female staff capitulating to or being dependent on male staff in dealing with difficult behaviors in youth are not uncommon behaviors in group treatment settings. If we expect youth to examine and change their power-over behaviors and the ways those behaviors inform their gendered self-identity, we have a responsibility to do the same work. This can be accomplished in a variety of ways, including staff meetings in which discussion of gender role norms and their impact on staff behaviors are discussed, as well as through valuing and encouraging the discussion of conflicts between staff rather than supporting disconnection from conflicts.

Connection through conflict

In a discussion of mother-son relationships, Dooley and Fedele (2004) point out, "Even if interactions seem to be conflicts and disagreements, the dialogue itself moves the relationship out of silence and distance into connection" (p. 244). This is also a different way to think about conflict in working with adolescents who engage in sexually coercive behaviors. Conflicts regarding rules, boundaries, and minimizing behaviors, as well as the myriad of other invitations to conflict that invariably occur in work with these youth, are often regarded as resistances that must be dealt with through "laying down the rules." However, the real relational opportunity in dealing with conflict may be the continuing dialogue of disagreement rather than silencing through rule-setting. This is not meant to imply that setting boundaries is unnecessary or that engaging in continual arguing with youth regarding compliance with boundaries is helpful. Rather, it suggests that professionals reframe their thinking about conflict as a disconnecting experience to conflict as a step toward reconnection (Miller & Stiver, 1997) and a way to support growth rather than enforce authority (Walker, 2004).

Some, perhaps many, of the youth we work with who have engaged in sexually coercive behavior have had family experiences of conflict that reinforced power-over relationships, led to the withdrawal of nurturing, or signified the end of a relationship. Reframing dialogue regarding conflict as a connecting or growth-enhancing relational opportunity can be an enormous paradigm shift for such youth. Here the underlying message is, "I understand that you don't agree with or want to follow this rule. It's still the rule. Nevertheless, let's keep communicating about what you think and feel about the rule because I value each of us hearing the other's viewpoint, even if we don't agree."

Relational courage

The reframing of strength and courage as involving emotional sharing, honesty in relationship, and the provision of psychological support to family and friends is an important application of the relational-cultural model (Dooley & Fedele, 2004). When working with youth who engage in sexually coercive behavior, however, this must be balanced with an awareness of the environmental context of their lives. For some of these youths, presenting a tough, aggressive façade is a survival mechanism. This does not imply that we cannot reframe strength in relational terms, but that we must acknowledge the realities of their lives and talk with youth about specific ways relational strength can be safely implemented in their daily lives. For example, one activity might involve youths identifying the components of "boy culture" (Dooley & Fedele, p. 222; perhaps more acceptably labeled as "man culture" in this setting) as it applies to their school, neighborhood, and family. Discussion can then ensue regarding specific strategies that demonstrate relational courage and strength but also incorporate an awareness of valid safety and survival issues.

The mother-son relationship

The relational-cultural model clearly has many implications applying to family interactions and professionals' counseling interventions with families (see, for example, Walker & Rosen, 2004, for various clinical applications of the model). Only one of these issues, the development of the mother-son relationship, will be briefly discussed here.

The model suggests the existence of sociocultural messages that encourage mothers to relationally move away from rather than toward sons when boys are quite young (Dooley & Fedele, 2004). Bergman (1991) proposes that the consequence of this early emotional disconnection for boys and men is isolation and dread regarding emotional intimacy and connection (see Bergman for a detailed discussion of the concept of "relational dread" in men's relationships). Dooley and Fedele conceptualize the mother-son relationship as an important arena for teaching boys relational skills, partially because women have been shaped to be the caretakers of relationships in many Western societies. Of course, interventions in this area must also honor differing cultural worldviews regarding the mother-son role, which places responsibility on the professional to be knowledgeable about and competent in multicultural counseling (e.g., Sodowsky, Kuo-Jackson, Richardson, & Corey, 1998).

Sociocultural messages often present a paradox to mothers, particularly those who are carrying the primary responsibility for parenting due to either physical or psychological absence of a partner. They may be disparaged as being failures as mothers and labeled as "emotionally detached" or "overly involved". As professionals, we frequently undervalue the fact that the mother may be the one parent who is present. The implication is not that mothers should be over idealized. Rather, frank discussion of cultural messages about mothering and genuine acknowledgement of mothers' willingness to maintain some level of connection with their sons (particularly in the physical or psychological absence of the father) promotes discourse that does not pathologize and alienate mothers. This level of communication can open the way to frank and honest discussion of the mothers' own relational disconnections and the impact of their personal relational experiences on the mother-son relationship.

Summary

This chapter explored three bodies of literature related to male adolescent sexually coercive behavior targeting peers and adults: the literature relating to sexual harassment, date and acquaintance sexual violence, and identified juvenile sexual offender populations. It was suggested that the lack of integration across these bodies of literature limits our understanding of peer and adult-directed sexually coercive behavior in adolescents. The broad review of the literature regarding the sexually coercive and exploitive behavior evidenced by these youths informed further examination of the relational impact of such behavior. The relational-cultural model (e.g., Jordan et al., 1991; Miller & Stiver, 1997) was presented as a framework from which to conceptualize such behavior. Treatment implications emerging from the philosophical orientation of this model were discussed.

References

Alexander, M. A. (1999). Sexual offender treatment efficacy revisited. *Sexual Abuse: A Journal of Research and Treatment*, 11, 101-116.

American Association of University Women Educational Foundation (AAUW). (1993). *Hostile hallways: The AAUW survey on sexual harassment in America's schools* (Research Report No. 923012). Washington, DC: Harris/Scholastic Research.

American Association of University Women Educational Foundation (AAUW). (2001). Hostile hallways: *Bullying, teasing, and sexual harassment in school*. Retrieved May 20, 2004, from http://aauw.org

Arriaga, X. B., & Foshee, V. A. (2004). Adolescent dating violence: Do adolescents follow in their friends', or their parents', footsteps? *Journal of Interpersonal Violence, 19,* 162-184.

Association for the Treatment of Sexual Abusers. (2000). *The effective legal management of juvenile sexual offenders.* Retrieved July 7, 2004, from http://www.atsa.com/ppjuvenile.html

Awad, G. A., & Saunders, E. B. (1991). Male adolescent sexual assaulters: Clinical observations. *Journal of Interpersonal Violence, 6,* 446-460.

Becker, J. V. (1990). Treating adolescent sexual offenders. *Professional Psychology: Research and Practice, 21,* 362-365.

Bergman, S. J. (1991). *Men's psychological development: A relational perspective* (Work in Progress No. 48). Wellesley, MA: Wellesley College, Stone Center.

Boyd, N. J., Hagan, M., & Cho, M. E. (2000). Characteristics of adolescent sex offenders: A review of the research. *Aggression and Violent Behavior, 5,* 137-146.

Brown, L. M., & Gilligan, C. (1992). *Meeting at the crossroads.* New York: Ballantine.

Carpenter, D. R., Peed, S. F., & Eastman, B. (1995). Personality characteristics of adolescent sexual offenders: A pilot study. *Sexual Abuse: A Journal of Research and Treatment, 7,* 195-203.

Chaffin, M. & Bonner, B. (1998). "Don't shoot, we're your children": Have we gone too far in our response to adolescent sexual abusers and children with sexual behavior problems? *Child Maltreatment, 3,* 314-316.

Davis, T. C., Peck, G. Q., & Storment, J. M. (1993). Acquaintance rape and the high school student. *Journal of Adolescent Health, 14,*220-224.

Dooley, C., & Fedele, N. M. (2004). Mothers and sons: Raising relational boys. In J. V. Jordan, M. Walker, & L. M. Hartling (Eds.), *The complexity of connection: Writings from the Stone Center's Jean Baker Miller Training Institute* (pp. 220-249). New York: Guilford.

Epps, K. J., Haworth, R., & Swaffer, T. (1993). Attitudes toward women and rape among male adolescents convicted of sexual versus nonsexual crimes. *The Journal of Psychology, 127,* 501-506.

Feiring, C., Deblinger, E., Hoch-Espada, A., & Haworth, T. (2002). Romantic relationship aggression and attitudes in high school students: The role of gender, grade, and attachment and emotional styles. *Journal of Youth and Adolescence, 31,* 373-385.

Feltey, K. M., Ainslie, J. J., & Geib, A. (1991). Sexual coercion attitudes among high school students: The influence of gender and rape education. *Youth & Society, 23,* 229-250.

Fineran, S., & Bennett, L. (1998). Teenage peer sexual harassment: Implications for social work practice in education. *Social Work*, 43, 55-64.

Fineran, S., & Bennett, L. (1999). Gender and power issues of peer sexual harassment among teenagers. *Journal of Interpersonal Violence*, 14, 626-641.

Fitzgerald, L. F., & Hesson-McInnis, M. (1989). The dimensions of sexual harassment: A structural analysis. *Journal of Vocational Behavior*, 35, 309-326.

Foshee, V. A. (1996). Gender differences in adolescent dating abuse prevalence, types and injuries. *Health Education Research: Theory & Practice*, 11, 275-286.

Foshee, V. A., Linder, F., MacDougall, J. E., & Bangdiwala, S. (2001). Gender differences in the longitudinal predictors of adolescent dating violence. *Preventive Medicine*, 32,128-141.

Frey, L. L. (2005). Girls don't do that, do they? Adolescent females who sexually offend. In R. Longo & D. Prescott (Eds.), *Current perspectives: Working with aggressive youth and youth with sexual behavior problems.* Holyoke, MA: NEARI Press.

Hand, J. Z., & Sanchez, L. (2000). Badgering or bantering? Gender differences in experience of, and reactions to, sexual harassment among U. S. high school students. *Gender & Society*, 14, 718-746.

Herman, J. L. (1990). Sex offenders: A feminist perspective. In W. L. Marshall, D. R. Laws, & H. E. Barbaree (Eds.), *Handbook of sexual assault: Issues, theories and treatment of the offender*. London: Plenum.

Hilton, N. Z., Harris, G. T., & Rice, M. E. (2003). Adolescents' perceptions of the seriousness of sexual aggression: Influence of gender, traditional attitudes, and self-reported experiences. Sexual Abuse: *A Journal of Research and Treatment*, 15, 201-214.

Hird, M. J. (2000). An empirical study of adolescent dating aggression in the U. K. *Journal of Adolescence*, 23, 69-78.

Hird, M. J., & Jackson, S. (2001). Where 'angels' and 'wusses' fear to tread: Sexual coercion in adolescent dating relationships. *Journal of Sociology*, 37, 27-43.

Hsu, L. K. G., & Starzynski, J. (1990). Adolescent rapists and adolescent child assaulters. *International Journal of Offender Therapy and Comparative Criminology*, 34, 23-31.

Hunter, J. A., Figueredo, A. J., Malamuth, N. M., & Becker, J. V. (2003). Juvenile sex offenders: Toward the development of a typology. Sexual Abuse: *A Journal of Research and Treatment*, 15, 27-48.

Hunter, J. A., Figueredo, A. J., Malamuth, N. M., & Becker, J. V. (2004). Developmental pathways in youth sexual aggression and delinquency: Risk factors and mediators. *Journal of Family Violence*, 19, 233-242.

Hunter, J. A., Hazelwood, R. R., & Slesinger, D. (2000). Juvenile-perpetrated sex crimes: Patterns of offending and predictors of violence. *Journal of Family Violence,* 15, 81-93.

Jackson, S. M., Cram, F., & Seymour, F. W. (2000). Violence and sexual coercion in high school students' dating relationships. *Journal of Family Violence,* 15, 23-36.

Jordan, J. V., & Dooley, C. (2001). *Relational practice in action: A group manual.* Wellesley, MA: Stone Center Publications.

Jordan, J. V., Kaplan, A., Miller, J. B., Stiver, I. P., & Surrey, J. L. (1991). *Women's growth in connection: Writings from the Stone Center.* New York: Guilford.

Knight, R. A., & Prentky, R. A. (1993). Exploring characteristics for classifying juvenile sex offenders. In H. E. Barbaree, W. L. Marshall, & S. M. Hudson (Eds.), *The juvenile sex offender* (pp. 45-83). New York: Guilford.

Lee, V. E., Croninger, R. G., Linn, E., & Chen, X. (1996). The culture of sexual harassment in secondary schools. *American Educational Research Journal,* 33, 383-417.

Liang, B., Tracy, A., Taylor, C. A., Williams, L. M., Jordan, J. V., & Miller, J. B. (2002). The Relational Health Indices: A study of women's relationships. *Psychology of Women Quarterly,* 26, 25-35.

Lodico, M. A., Gruber, E., & DiClemente, R. J. (1996). Childhood sexual abuse and coercive sex among school-based adolescents in a Midwestern state. *Journal of Adolescent Health,* 18, 211-218.

Marciniak, L. M. (1998). Adolescent attitudes toward victim precipitation of rape. *Violence and Victims,* 13, 287-300.

Maxwell, C. D., Robinson, A. L., & Post, L. A. (2003). The nature and predictors of sexual victimization and offending among adolescents. *Journal of Youth and Adolescence,* 32, 465-477.

Miller, J. B. (1976). *Toward a new psychology of women* (2nd ed.). Boston: Beacon.

Miller, J. B. (1991). The development of women's sense of self. In J. V. Jordan, A. G. Kaplan, J. B. Miller, I. P. Stiver, & J. L. Surrey (Eds.), *Women's growth in connection: Writings from the Stone Center* (pp. 11-26). New York: Guilford.

Miller, J. B., & Stiver, I. P. (1997). The healing connection: *How women form relationships in therapy and in life.* Boston: Beacon.

Murphy, W. D., & Page, I. J. (2000). Relapse prevention with adolescent sex offenders. In D. R. Laws, S. M. Hudson, & T. Ward (Eds.), *Remaking relapse prevention with sex offenders: A sourcebook* (pp. 353-368). Thousand Oaks, CA: Sage.

Nisbet, I. A., Wilson, P. H., & Smallbone, S. W. (2004). A prospective longitudinal study of sexual recidivism among adolescent sex offenders. *Sexual Abuse: A Journal of Research and Treatment*, 16, 223-234.

O'Brien, M. J. (1991). Taking sibling incest seriously. In M. Q. Patton (Ed.), *Family sexual abuse: Frontline research and evaluation* (pp. 75-92). Thousand Oaks, CA: Sage.

O'Keefe, M. (1997). Predictors of dating violence among high school students. *Journal of Interpersonal Violence*, 12, 546-568.

O'Keefe, M., & Treister, L. (1998). Victims of dating violence among high school students. *Violence Against Women*, 4, 195-223.

Poitras, M. & Lavoie, F. (1995). A study of the prevalence of sexual coercion in adolescent heterosexual dating relationships in a Quebec sample. *Violence and Victims*, 10, 299-313.

Richardson, G., Kelly, T. P., Bhate, S. R., & Graham, F. (1997). Group differences in abuser and abuse characteristics in a British sample of sexually abusive adolescents. Sexual Abuse: *A Journal of Research and Treatment*, 9, 239-255.

Rosenthal, D. A. (1997). Understanding sexual coercion among young adolescents: Communicative clarity, pressure, and acceptance. *Archives of Sexual Behavior*, 26, 481-492.

Ryan, G., & Lane, S. (1997). Integrating theory and method. In G. Ryan & S. Lane (Eds.), *Juvenile sexual offending: Causes, consequences, and correction* (pp. 267-321). San Francisco: Jossey-Bass.

Schwartz, M., O'Leary, S. G., & Kendziora, K. T. (1997). Dating aggression among high school students. *Violence and Victims*, 12, 295-305.

Smith, W. R., & Monastersky, C. (1986). Assessing juvenile sex offenders' risk for reoffending. *Criminal Justice and Behavior*, 13, 115-140.

Sodowsky, G. R., Kuo-Jackson, P., Richardson, L. F., & Corey, A. T. (1998). Correlates of self-reported multicultural competencies: Counselor multicultural social desirability, race, social inadequacy, locus of control racial ideology, and multicultural training. *Journal of Counseling Psychology*, 45, 256-264.

Tangri, S. S., Burt, M. R., & Johnson, L. B. (1982). Sexual harassment at work: Three explanatory models. *Journal of Social Issues*, 38, 33-54.

Thornberry, T. P., Huizinga, D., & Loeber, R. (2004). The causes and correlates studies: Findings and policy implications. *Juvenile Justice*, IX, 3-19.

Timmerman, G. (2003). Sexual harassment of adolescents perpetrated by teachers and by peers: An exploration of the dynamics of power, culture, and gender in secondary schools. *Sex Roles*, 48, 231-244.

United States Department of Justice. (1997). *Sex offenses and offenders: An analysis of data on rape and sexual assault* (No. NCJ-163392). Retrieved October 17, 2004, from http://www.ojp.usdoj.gov/bjs/pub/pdf/soo.pdf

United States Equal Employment Opportunity Commission (EEOC). (1990). *Policy guidance on current issues of sexual harassment* (No. N-915-050). Retrieved 10/14/04 from http://www.eeoc.gov/policy/docs/currentissues.html

Walker, M. (2004). How relationships heal. In M. Walker & W. B. Rosen (Eds.), *How connections heal: Stories from relational-cultural therapy* (pp. 3-21). New York: Guilford.

Walker, M., & Rosen, W. B. (Eds.). (2004). *How connections heal: Stories from relational-cultural therapy.* New York: Guilford.

Worling, J. R. (1995). Sexual abuse histories of adolescent male sex offenders: Differences on the basis of the age and gender of their victims. *Journal of Abnormal Psychology,* 104, 610- 613.

CHAPTER TEN

GIRLS DON'T DO THAT, DO THEY?
ADOLESCENT FEMALES WHO SEXUALLY ABUSE

LISA L. FREY

Introduction

This chapter presents a critical review of the literature on adolescent females who sexually abuse. The chapter highlights the invisibility of this problem in adolescent females and explores the possible influences of gender socialization and gender role stereotypes. Etiological theories and clinical presentation are reviewed. The research comparing female adolescents who sexually abuse to other groups of adolescent offenders and nonoffenders is critically analyzed and suggestions are made for future research and theory development. The role of feminist psychology in increasing our understanding of adolescent females who sexually abuse is emphasized. Three topics of interest to feminist psychology, gender identity development, gender role stereotypes and attitudes, and gender-responsive treatment, are discussed in terms of their applicability to this population.

For those practitioners and researchers working with female adolescents who sexually abuse, it is not unusual to encounter colleagues who insist that this population does not exist, at least not in their geographical area. While the intent of this response may be facetious, its frequency suggests otherwise. Chesney-Lind and Okamoto (2001) point out, "girls' capacity for aggression and violence has historically been ignored, trivialized or denied" (p. 3). Nowhere is this attitude more obvious than when considering the issue of females and sexually abusive behavior.

Interestingly, at a time when feminist psychologists are being challenged to acknowledge the role of women's aggression in intimate relationships, the issue of adolescent females and sexually abusive behavior remains largely ignored in the general psychological literature. The dilemma in exploring this issue is that researchers and theorists are urged to accept the existence of female sexually abusive behavior but are expected to do so within a sociocultural context in which women and girls' capacity for violence is simultaneously minimized (Schwartz & Cellini, 1995) and demonized (McDonald & Chesney-Lind, 2001). The field of feminist psychology, which has had a long-standing commitment to confronting the sociocultural and sociopolitical influences on identity and behavior, has much to offer in the effort to better understand sexually abusive behavior in adolescent females. Increased attention to this issue in the literature would contribute to a better understanding of the role feminist psychology can play in the assessment and treatment of these young women. This chapter is offered to further this effort.

Defining the Population

This review will concentrate on adolescent females aged 13-18 years old who have engaged in sexually abusive behavior, defined as "any sexual behavior which occurs 1) without consent; 2) without equality; or 3) as a result of coercion" (National Task Force on Juvenile Sexual Offending, 1993, p. 11). Included in this definition is a range of sexual behaviors, including sexual aggression (i.e., sexually abusive behavior that involves intimidation, threats of harm, or the use of force; National Task Force on Juvenile Offending, p. 11). The target of the sexually abusive behavior may be unable to give legal consent, such as in the case of children, or may not give voluntary consent due to coercive factors such as threat, physical force, verbal persuasion, verbal argument, or manipulation on the part of the abuser, as is evidenced in peer or dating abuse (Shaw, 1999). The terminology "offense" or "offender," referring to behavior that is criminal or illegal (National Task Force on Juvenile Sexual Offending), overlaps with the construct of sexually abusive behavior in much of the literature related to adolescent sexually abusive behavior. Specifically, the literature's use of this terminology does not necessarily imply that the behavior has been labeled as an offense by the legal system. Within the limits imposed by the reviewed literature, however, care has been taken to be as consistent as possible in the language used in the review.

Subsequent to the parameters outlined above, the literature focused on adult women, including college women, was determined to be beyond the scope of this review. The rationale underlying this decision was two-fold. First, minor adolescents and adult women, including college students who often are living independently, demonstrate significant developmental differences related to sexual behavior and identity. Second, the body of literature pertaining to adult and adolescent males who engage in sexually abusive behavior has established that important differences exist between the two populations and that adult findings cannot necessarily be generalized to adolescents (e.g., Association for the Treatment of Sexual Abusers, 2000; Becker, Hunter, Stein, & Kaplan, 1989; Center for Sex Offender Management, 1999; Chaffin & Bonner, 1998; Hunter, Goodwin, & Becker, 1994). Therefore, empirical studies that did not differentiate adolescents from adults in the results (e.g., Miccio-Fonseca, 2000; Spitzberg, 1999) were not included. Likewise, literature regarding female children was excluded unless the mean age of the sample group fell within the adolescent age range noted previously.

A final definitional issue is related to the differentiation between adolescent females who abuse children and those who abuse peers or older individuals. Coercion and consent are key constructs to consider in this regard (refer to following section for further discussion of this issue). The review will focus on those who abuse children or younger, more vulnerable individuals. This is not intended to minimize the problem of adolescent females who abuse peers. Rather, it is a function of the lack of research beyond prevalence data that specifically explores this population. For example, O'Keefe (1997) reported 3% of the 14-20 year old females (n = 554) in her study stated they had forced sexual activities on a partner. However, in subsequent analyses

O'Keefe collapsed this behavior and other types of physical aggression into one variable. Results of other studies were limited by: (a) not separating sexually abusive behavior from other types of physically aggressive behavior in reports of dating violence perpetrated by females (Foshee, Linder, MacDougall, & Bangdiwala, 2001); (b) indicating that male adolescent participants reported sexually abusive behavior in dating relationships but without providing specific prevalence data (Hird, 2000), (c) restricting sexual behavior in the general category of physically aggressive behavior to "kissing against will" (Feiring, Deblinger, Hoch-Espada, & Haworth, 2002); or (d) reporting the incidence of forced sexual experiences in female and male adolescents without differentiating between involvement as a victim or a perpetrator (Davis, Peck, & Storment, 1993). Poitras and Lavoie's (1995) study investigating sexual coercion in heterosexual dating relationships among 15-19 year olds (female n = 336, male n = 308) in Quebec provided some detail regarding the use of force by this population, finding that the female adolescents who inflicted an unwanted sexual experience most frequently used verbal coercion to do so. With this exception, however, the studies in this area have emphasized the existence of female adolescent sexually abusive behavior targeting peers, but not investigated the characteristics of the females engaging in this behavior.

The purpose of this chapter is three-fold. First, the invisibility of the problem of sexually abusive behavior in adolescent females will be discussed. This will include overviews of prevalence and gender role stereotypes that impact responses to these adolescents. Second, the recent literature relevant to the etiology and clinical presentation of adolescent females who sexually abuse children will be reviewed and critically analyzed. A focus will be on comparing the characteristics of female adolescents who sexually abuse to other groups of adolescent offenders and nonoffenders. The third purpose is to offer suggestions for future research and theory development, including a discussion of the role of feminist psychology in this endeavor.

Do Adolescent Females Who Sexually Abuse Really Exist?

Delineating the problem

Kasl (1990) discussed the definitional problems associated with delineating sexually abusive behavior in females. When the abuser is a female it may be the victim who is forced to perform penetration, as in the case of a male victim who is engaged in intercourse by a female adolescent abuser. Therefore, the power differential in the relationship becomes an even more salient issue. Kasl recommended that definitions of female sexual abusing need to consider the power differential, motivational issues, and an identification of whose needs were met. This is particularly true when the commonly cited research standard of a 3 to 5 year age difference between abuser and victim is applied to adolescents. In adolescents, developmental differences may be more salient than age. Consider, for example, the significant developmental differences between a 13-year-old female and a 10-year-old child who is engaged by the female in sexual activity. The confusion is compounded by the omission of operational definitions of sexually abusive behaviors in many of the studies focused on female adolescents who sexually abuse children. These definitional problems make it difficult to ascertain the prevalence and characteristics of sexually abusive behavior in this population.

What we know about prevalence

The Federal Bureau of Investigation (FBI) Uniform Crime Report (2002) indicates that 1385 females under the age of 18 were arrested for forcible rape or other sexual offenses (excluding prostitution) in 2002. Additionally, 1998-2002 arrest trends indicate increases of 74% in forcible rape and 12% in other sexual offenses (excluding prostitution) committed by females under 18 years old, as compared to a decrease of 15% and an increase of 9%, respectively, committed by males under 18 years old. According to the Office of Juvenile Justice and Delinquency Prevention (OJJDP; 1999), in 1997 females accounted for 2% of 5,500 total arrests of juveniles under 18 years old for forcible rape and 9% of 18,500 total arrests for other sexual offenses (excluding prostitution). It is important to note that these statistics underrepresent the extent of this problem for several reasons. First, they tell us little about the actual numbers of individuals who have been victimized by these young women. A low percentage of female adolescents who commit a sexual offense still results in large absolute numbers of individual victims. For example, according to the OJJDP statistics, females accounted for 1775 arrests (or, arguably, a minimum of the same number of victims) for rape or other sexual offenses. When one considers that each female adolescent who sexually abuses may have more than one victim (refer to Table 2), the number of victims increases even further. In addition, it is believed that the statistics are deflated by the perception that sexual offending is a "male problem," resulting in underreporting by victims and decreased responsiveness to allegations of abuse perpetrated by females (Allen, 1991; Bumby & Bumby, in press; Elliott, 1993; Schwartz & Cellini, 1995). Last, because these statistics are based on arrest trends that are influenced by sociocultural factors (see next section), they underestimate the number of young women under the age of 18 who have histories of sexually abusive behavior.

The Influence of Gender Socialization and Gender Role Stereotypes

Influences on juvenile court processes

The theoretical and empirical literature on delinquency suggests gender disparities in the way adolescent females and males are processed in the juvenile justice system, a system that has been described as gendered and paternalistic (Kempf-Leonard & Sample, 2000). In an empirical study examining over 85,000 family court cases in Hawaii, MacDonald and Chesney-Lind (2001) found that charge seriousness impacted female and male adolescents equally during early decision-making in the court process but, once a female reached disposition, she was "likely to be more harshly sanctioned than her male counterparts" (p. 189). It has also been hypothesized that, because female adolescents are viewed as less dangerous than males (Bumby & Bumby, in press), juvenile justice resources are directed toward dealing with male adolescents, frequently through community-based programs, while female adolescents with conduct problems are placed in psychiatric facilities (Chesney-Lind, 1995). While at first glance this may suggest that female adolescent sexual abusers actually receive preferential treatment, in truth placement in general psychiatric facilities often adds to the invisibility of their sexually abusive behavior by denying access to targeted services. There often are not many alternatives, however. Certainly, placing an adolescent female who sexually abuses in a program for adolescent males is not a good choice for many reasons, as will be discussed further in this review.

These problems are all too familiar to clinicians working with these adolescents. For instance, consider the case of L., a female adolescent who was placed in a private psychiatric program after sexually abusing two young family members. Although L.'s boyfriend was also involved in the abuse, L. disclosed she instigated the incidents. Despite this disclosure, the boyfriend was charged with sexual assault and sent to a community-based program for juvenile sexual offenders. L. was not charged and was placed in a psychiatric facility, where she received no treatment targeting her sexual behavior problems. In contrast was another adolescent female, P., who was referred for a psychosexual assessment prior to disposition on a founded charge of sexual abuse of an elementary-aged boy. Risk indicators suggested that P. would be appropriate for community-based outpatient treatment, which was available and recommended. However, she was sent to a training school because, according to the rationale provided by a juvenile court official, a female should know better than to sexually abuse a minor. As these case examples illustrate, female adolescents who sexually abuse may be in a double bind. On one hand, their behavior may be minimized and, as a result, their access to targeted intervention services limited. Yet once their behavior rises to the level of more active juvenile court intervention, the consequences may be harsher than for adolescent males.

It is a valid point that the increased numbers of male versus female adolescents who sexually abuse suggest it is reasonable to direct the majority of juvenile justice resources to programs targeting male adolescents. However, this reasoning also overlooks some important factors. First, both 5-year and 10-year arrest trends indicate a significant increase in sexual offenses committed by female adolescents, with increases exceeding those of males (FBI, 2002; see previous section). Second, it assumes that the resources that are directed toward female adolescents are gender-responsive rather than models developed for males and applied to females. Chamberlain (2003) pointed out that the basis of most theories of criminality is rooted in the characteristics and sociocultural experiences of males. Thus, the salient issue is not simply resource allocation but attention to gender disparities and the lack of gender-responsive services at many levels of system intervention. That is, it is an issue of quality not just quantity.[1]

Influences of culturally shaped gender roles

It would be a disservice to hold the juvenile justice system alone responsible for such gender disparities. After all, such systems are a microcosm of the overall societal structure. In the field of psychology, feminist scholars have long challenged the gender bias inherent in developing counseling theories and treatment models based on primarily male populations, and then applying them to females without consideration of gender-based differences (e.g., Gilligan, 1982, 1993; Gilligan, Rogers, & Tolman, 1991; Miller & Stiver, 1997; Mirkin, 1994). In this case, doing so simply helps perpetuate gender role stereotypes regarding female sexuality.

Several gender role stereotypes contributing to extreme responses to sexually abusive behavior in females have been mentioned in the theoretical literature. For example, societal ambivalence regarding females as sexual beings (Bumby & Bumby, in press; Schwartz & Cellini, 1995) and the belief that men are in control of sex while women are sexually passive and receptive (Schwartz & Cellini) may result in either a failure to intervene in female adolescents' sexually abusive behavior (Bumby & Bumby) or a tendency to demonize such violent behavior (MacDonald & Chesney-Lind, 2001). These stereotypes regarding female sexuality also make it difficult for victims to disclose abuse perpetrated by a female (e.g., Blues, Moffat, & Telford, 1999; Bumby & Bumby), preclude clinicians asking questions of female adolescent clients regarding sexually abusive behavior (Blues et al.), and make it difficult for young women to overcome their own internalized gender role stereotypes in order to seek help for sexually abusive thoughts or behaviors (Blues et al.). In addition, reinforcement of the care-taking role of females (e.g., babysitting) and a resultant acceptance of a wide range of legitimate intimate contact between females and children (e.g., Allen, 1991; Bumby & Bumby; Schwartz & Cellini) have been pointed to as factors that may obscure the boundaries between inappropriate and appropriate contact.

What We Know (Or Think We Know) About Female Adolescents With Sexual Behavior Problems

Etiological theories

Although several studies have offered typologies and etiological theories regarding females who sexually abuse, the majority have focused on girls under the age of 12 (Johnson, 1989), adult females (McCarty, 1986), or samples collapsing adult, child, and/or adolescent females into one group (Faller, 1995; Matthews, 1987). An exception is a study by Matthews, Hunter, and Vuz (1997), who proposed three preliminary subtypes of adolescent females who sexually abuse based on a descriptive comparison of juvenile female and male sexual abusers. The first identified subgroup involved a small number of young women who engaged a nonrelated child in a single or a few sexually abusive incidents, generally involving fondling and oral sex. The behavior occurred primarily within the context of babysitting and was related to sexual curiosity rather than individual psychopathology or past maltreatment. The second group was described as engaging in more extensive sexually abusive behavior, often preceded by personal experiences of victimization and motivated by mild to moderate individual psychopathology and family dysfunction. This group of adolescents, who constituted about a third of the sample, tended to replicate their own victimization experiences in their victimizing behavior and reported few sexual experiences with peers. Last, approximately half of the female adolescents were described as experiencing moderate to severe levels of individual psychopathology and family dysfunction, and were victims of extensive, repetitive sexual victimization. These adolescents demonstrated significant levels of conduct disordered behavior, deviant sexual arousal, and impairment in attachment. This typology, while useful in providing some structure to the preliminary study of adolescent female sexually abusive behavior, has not been subjected to empirical analysis and is therefore limited in its applicability.

Theorists (e.g., Goodwin & Divasto, 1979; James & Nasjleti, 1983) have also discussed the need for emotional connection and nurturance as a dynamic in the sexually abusive behavior of females. For instance, M. Turner and T. Turner (1994) theorized that some females sexually abuse because, as a consequence of their own victimization, they developed a distorted perception of abuse as a way to establish relational connection and get intimacy needs met. The impact of this dynamic on adolescent females has not been theoretically or empirically explored, however.

Table 1: Summary of Studies with a Primary Focus on Adolescent Females Who Sexually Abused Children

	N of Offender Sample	Sample	Comparison Group	Data Analysis
Kubik, Hecker, & Righthand (2002)				
Study I	11	Department of Corrections cases; placement not specified	Adolescent females with non-sexual offenses ($n = 11$)	Descriptive; Chi-squares; t-tests
Study II	11[a]	Department of Corrections cases; placement not specified	Adolescent male sexual offenders ($n = 11$)	Descriptive
Bumby & Bumby (1997)				
Study I	12	General psychiatric in-patient	None reported	Descriptive
Study II	18	General psychiatric in-patient	Adolescent female nonoffenders ($n = 36$); adolescent male sexual offenders ($n = 18$); adolescent male nonoffenders ($n = 24$)	Unknown; test statistics not reported
Matthews, Hunter, & Vuz (1997)	67	Targeted residential treatment (24%); targeted community-based (76%)	Adolescent male sexual offender ($n = 70$)	Descriptive
Fromuth & Conn (1997)	22	College students[b]	Female students who did not self-report history of sexual offending ($n = 524$)	Descriptive; Chi-squares
Hunter, Lexier, Goodwin, Browne, & Dennis (1993)	10	Residential treatment (targeted 80%; general 20%)	None reported	Descriptive
Fehrenbach & Monastersky (1988)	28	Targeted out-patient evaluation & treatment program	None reported	Descriptive

Note. Targeted treatment=treatment focused on sexually abusive behavior. General treatment=general psychiatric or psychological treatment. [a]Same female participants as used in Study I. [b]Survey asked college students to self-report their behavior as adolescents.

Characteristics of Female Adolescents Who Sexually Abuse Children

Table 1 provides a summary of research studies focusing on adolescent females who have sexually abused children. To be included, the study had to provide, at a minimum, summary descriptive data, identify children as the primary victims of the sexually abusive behavior, and focus on reports of abusive behavior perpetrated in adolescence. As can be seen in Table 2, which presents select descriptive data from these studies, some studies provided limited descriptive details (Bumby & Bumby, 1997; Kubik, Hecker & Righthand, 2002) or included a few adolescent or adult victims as targets of the sexually abusive behavior (Fehrenbach & Monastersky, 1988; Matthews et al., 1997; refer to Table 2 for age ranges of victims). The number of studies is limited, and most are descriptive in nature and characterized by small sample sizes. It is also difficult to compare differences in characteristics across the studies due to variability in sampling and lack of clarity in operational definitions. For example, the age range for adolescence differs, with some authors including 10 or 11 years olds in the sexual abuser sample group (Fehrenbach & Monastersky; Mathews et al.).[2] Over half of the studies provided inadequate or no detail regarding participant ethnicity. This is a significant omission in view of recent studies suggesting disparities between adolescent females of color and white adolescent females in terms of juvenile justice system treatment (e.g., MacDonald & Chesney-Lind, 2001).

Although such factors limit the generalizability of the studies, they do provide some guidance regarding preliminary hypotheses. One notable finding is that the victims of female adolescents tend to be known to the young women, often siblings or other family members (Bumby & Bumby, 1997; Fehrenbach & Monastersky, 1988; Fromuth & Conn, 1997; Hunter, Lexier, Goodwin, Browne, & Dennis, 1993; Matthews et al., 1997). Also, studies comparing adolescent females who sexually abuse to other groups of adolescents suggest an increased rate of childhood maltreatment in the female sexual abuser group (see later discussion of this finding). Thus, though flawed, the studies are useful in that they bring attention to a population that has been neglected in the literature and provide preliminary information suggesting directions for more rigorous future research.

Adolescent female sexual abusers, adolescent female nonsexual offenders, and adolescent female nonoffenders

Kubik et al. (2002) compared adolescent female sexual abusers to adolescent female nonsexual offenders who had charges ranging from theft and criminal mischief to assault, endangering the welfare of a child, and conspiracy to terrorize. They found that the nonsexual offender group had significantly more problems with alcohol and drug abuse, school problems, and fighting. In addition, the female sexual abuser group was significantly more likely to resist intervention aimed at their problems and engaged in their first incident of sexually abusive behavior at a younger age than the age at which the nonsexual offenders committed their first offense. Relatively higher percentages of the sexual abuser group as compared to the nonsexual offender group reported a history of physical abuse (n = 7/11 and 4/11, respectively) and sexual abuse (n = 7/11 and 6/11, respectively). It should be noted that, although there is a greater difference between the two groups in rates of physical as compared to sexual abuse, this did not represent a statistically significant difference (Kubik et al.). In addition, a difference has not been reported in other studies comparing rates of physical and sexual abuse in groups of adolescent females.

Bumby and Bumby (1997) compared adolescent female sexual abusers with adolescent female nonoffenders. Significantly higher levels of anxiety, depressive symptoms, and suicidal thoughts and behaviors, and significantly lower overall self-concept, were found in the abuser group.

In a unique approach to studying adolescent female sexually abusive behavior, Fromuth and Conn (1997) asked female college students to self-report incidents of sexually abusive behavior perpetrated as adolescents, and then compared this group to students who did not report this behavior. No significant differences between the two groups were found on instruments measuring family relationships, psychological adjustment, attitudes toward interpersonal violence, or sexual beliefs. Differences were found in two areas, however. First, the sexually abusive group reported a significantly increased sexual interest in children. Second, this group reported a significantly higher incidence of childhood sexual victimization. Of course, the validity of this study is limited by the self-report and retrospective nature of the data.

Table 2: Characteristics of Adolescent Females Who Sexually Abused Children: Select Descriptive Data

	Kubik et al. (2002)		Bumby & Bumby (1997)		Matthews et al. (1997)	Fromuth & Conn (1997)	Hunter et al. (1993)	Fehrenbach & Monastersky (1988)
	Study 1	Study 2	Study 1	Study 2				
N	11	11	12	18	67	22	10	28
Race (%)								
Caucasian	100	a			86.6	80	80	
African American					8.9		20	
Asian					3			
Hispanic					1.5			
Unspecified						20		
Mean Age of Adolescent	16.24[b]	a		14.9	14.3		15	13.6
Age range	13-18	a			11-18	17-21[c]	13-17	10-18
Mean Age at 1st Offense	11.18	a				12	9.5 (*Mdn*)	
Mean # of Victims			2		2.3	1.09	2.5 (*Mdn*)	
Mean Age of Victims						6	5.5 (*Mdn*)	5.2
Age range					0-11=87%; 12-17=11%; Adult=1%	1-9	1-13	<12 with exception of 1 adult
Sex of Victim (%)								
Female		27.3	42		23.9	30	39.4	57.1
Male		36.4	25		44.8	70	60.6	35.7
Both		36.4	33		31.3			7.1
Victims Relation to Adolescent (%)[d]								
Stranger		9.1	0		8.6		39.4	0
Acquaintance		72.7			15.2		12.1	57.1
Relative		27.3			21.2		18.2	14.3
Sibling/half-sibling		27.3			35.1		30.3	10.7
Step/foster-sibling		9.1						17.9
Family			83			69		
Nonfamily			25					
Abuser was babysitter					19.9			
Type of Sexual Behavior (%)								
Vaginal intercourse		27.3					70	
Anal intercourse		18.2					10	
Oral sex							70	
Fondling		90.9				46	100	46.4
Rape: specific behavior not noted								53.6
Level of Coercion (%)[d]								
Verbal threat		27.3						
Physical threat/restraint		18.2						
Instrumental aggression[e]		18.2						
Physical aggression		54.5						
Weapon use		9.1						
Co-offender present		18.2						
Force: specific type not noted					19.4	8	40	
Maltreatment History (as victim; %)								
Physical abuse	63.6	a	75		60		80	21.4
Sexual abuse	63.6	a	100	100	77.6	77	100	50
Exposure to family violence		62.5						
Neglect	63.6	a	42					
Nonsexual Behavior Problems (%)								
Alcohol abuse	10	a	75					
Drug abuse	10	a	58					
Alcohol/drug abuse[d]					25.4		50	
Running away	45.5	a	58		33.3		60	
Truancy			58					
Stealing			33					
Self-mutilation	36.4	a						
Suicide ideation or attempt	45.5	a			43.9		60	
Homicidal ideation							60	
Vandalism	30	a						
Fighting	30	a						
Fire-setting		9.1						

Note: [a] Female participants the same in both studies. Study II contained additional detail regarding characteristics. [b]Mean and range is for entire sample, including female sexual abusers and female nonsexual offenders. [c]Survey asked college students to self-report their behavior as adolescents. [d]Categories overlap due to differences in category definition in the studies. [e]No specific definition of instrumental aggression provided.

Adolescent female sexual abusers, adolescent male sexual abusers, and adolescent male nonoffenders

Three research studies were found comparing adolescent female sexual abusers with groups of adolescent males. Matthews et al. (1997) compared adolescent female and male sexual abusers and reported similarities in perpetration characteristics between the two groups, including similarities in victim selection characteristics and the magnitude and frequency of abusive behaviors. The principal difference observed between the two groups was the increased incidence of experiences of severe sexual and physical victimization in the female abuser group. Distinguishing characteristics of the sexual victimization history included a younger age at the time of first victimization, more frequent reports of multiple perpetrators, and an increased rate of force being used during the experiences. Other studies comparing adolescent female and male sexual abusers have found similar maltreatment characteristics (Bumby & Bumby, 1997; Kubik et al., 2002). Interestingly, Matthews et al. also reported over three times as many females as males reported being sexually abused by a female perpetrator. Similarly, Hunter et al. (1993) indicated 60% (n = 6) of the female adolescent abusers in their descriptive study reported a female victimizer, although provided no comparison group. The authors theorized that prior sexual victimization by a female may be an etiological factor in the development of sexually abusive behavior in female adolescents due to female modeling of aggression and eroticization of victimization experiences involving a female perpetrator. The degree to which this result is significant rather than an artifact of the specific sample groups remains to be seen.

Bumby and Bumby (1997) compared adolescent female sexual abusers with two groups of adolescent males, a sexual abuser group and a nonoffender group. With the exception of incidence of sexual victimization, as noted previously, few significant differences were found among these groups. The female group was found to have increased rates of drug abuse and "sexual promiscuity" (which was not defined) as compared to the male sexual abuser group. However, no notable differences were reported among the groups in terms of school history, delinquent behaviors, or self-destructive behaviors. Similarly, Kubik et al. (2002) compared adolescent female and male sexual abusers and found no notable differences between the groups in terms of psychosocial and criminal histories or characteristics of their sexually abusive behavior. Unique to this study, treatment factors (e.g., lack of remorse, use of denial, distorted thoughts about sexually abusive behavior) were also examined, with no outstanding differences reported between the groups. The single difference that did emerge in the study was, again, the increased incidence of childhood maltreatment in the female as compared to the male group. In particular, the females were more likely to be abused by multiple perpetrators and by someone they knew, as well as more likely to have been penetrated during sexual abuse experiences.

Adolescent female sexual abusers and childhood maltreatment

A consistent finding in the five research studies comparing females who have sexually abused with various control groups is the increased rate of childhood maltreatment noted in the female sexual abuser group. This result must be viewed with some caution because, as noted previously, the available studies are significantly limited in number and sample size, and statistical analyses supporting significant differences are lacking. However, some support for the validity of this finding in adolescent female sexual abusers is provided by studies documenting the increased frequency of maltreatment in adolescent female nonsexual offenders as compared to adolescent male nonsexual offenders (e.g., Artz, 1998; McCormack, Janus, & Burgess, 1986).

Adolescent female sexual abusers and physical aggression

Kubik et al. (2002) pointed to the use of physical aggression as a coercive factor in sexually abusive behavior, reporting that their male and female adolescent sample groups were similar in this regard (n = 5/11 and 6/11, respectively). Further questions regarding the overlap between sexually abusive and physically aggressive behavior arise when examining studies reporting rates of nonsexual physically aggressive behaviors among adolescent females who sexually abuse. Two studies reported these adolescents engaged in behaviors including assault and fighting (Kubik et al.), and "physical aggression" (Hunter et al., 1993, p. 324). It is difficult to come to any conclusions regarding the interaction between physical aggression and sexually abusive behavior in intimate relationships among adolescent females, however, until researchers examine this issue in more detail.

While overall these studies suggest that there are similarities between adolescent males and females who sexually abuse in terms of their abusive patterns, their adjustment, and in relation to treatment factors, this does not suggest that our existing treatment models for adolescent male sexual abusers can simply be applied to females. Indeed, Kasl (1990) warns against viewing sexual abuse perpetrated by females as the mirror image of that perpetrated by males because of gender differences in power dynamics and socialization. Similarities in characteristics do not imply that the etiological dynamics underlying behavioral or psychological responses are identical. For example, the concept of identification with the aggressor (i.e., an unconscious identification with and internalization of the aggressor as powerful), long believed to be a dynamic in the victim to victimizer cycle, is hypothesized to operate differently in some females as compared to males (Mayer, 1992). For some females who sexually abuse, the dynamic underlying identification with the aggressor may be the unconscious belief that molesting someone will be evidence of their own "badness," a personal defect that caused their victimization in the first place. Mayer provided an example of such an unconscious self-message: "I did it. It's my fault I got molested. Therefore, I'm bad and I'll do it again to prove I'm bad. I'll molest someone" (p. 73).

What More Do We Need to Know?

As had been previously noted, conceptual and methodological problems exist in the limited empirical literature relating to the topic of adolescent females who sexually abuse. In addition, the few theoretical models that have been offered, although based on clinical experience and records, have not been subject to statistical analysis. These problems limit the applicability and generalizability of both the theory and research. One of the real challenges in developing rigorous empirical studies with this population, however, is obtaining an adequate sample size. At this point in time, adolescent females who sexually abuse are simply not well identified. The use of research methods such as serial measures, replication studies with homogeneous and heterogeneous sample groups, and matching of abuser and nonabuser participants on key demographic variables may be helpful in overcoming some of the limitations imposed by small sample sizes. In addition, it is important for researchers to operationally define key constructs (e.g., sexual abuse, sexual offense) and clearly identify study parameters. For example, studies that combine female adolescents who abuse adults and those that abuse children limit the interpretation of results and, consequently, important research questions remain unanswered. These questions involve issues such as the frequency with which adolescent females demonstrate victim age preference (i.e., target both child and peer or adult victims) and the characteristics that differentiate among those who demonstrate age preference and those who don't.

A related generalizability problem is that those adolescent females who are identified as sexually abusive (and, thus, subject to recruitment as research participants) may represent a subset of the most serious abusers. In other words, if it is true that one consequence of gender role stereotyping is denial or minimization of sexually abusive behavior in adolescent females, those who are actually identified as sexual abusers by authorities and/or professionals may not be representative of adolescent female sexual abusers in general.

An important research need is related to the empirical investigation of the roles gender disparity and stereotyping may play in juvenile justice responses to sexually abusive behavior in adolescent females. MacDonald and Chesney-Lind's (2001) study is an example of a research design examining gender differences at multiple levels of juvenile justice intervention, including petition, adjudication, and disposition, that takes into account the multiplicity of factors (e.g., ethnicity, age, socioeconomic factors, crime seriousness) that impact juvenile court processing. One option might be to extend such studies through collateral examinations of juvenile justice personnel involved at all stages of court processing. Valuable insights might be gained, for example, through a research study examining juvenile justice officials' ranking of critical factors related to adjudication and disposition decisions in specific cases. Another study might involve the collection of data from juvenile justice officials regarding key variables theoretically related to gender disparities in decision-making (e.g., acceptance of gender stereotypes, patriarchal attitudes toward females), followed by analysis of the predictive relationships between these variables and juvenile court outcomes.

On a broader scale, efforts must be made to increase professional and public awareness regarding this unique population of adolescent females. Interestingly, OJJDP recently announced the organization of a group of researchers and practitioners focused on the overall problem of female delinquents (U.S. Department of Justice, 2003). Attention to the problem of female adolescent sexual abusers will hopefully be included in this project. On a more personal level, professionals offering to speak at conferences regarding this topic, advocating in pertinent conferences and meetings for the identification and gender-responsive treatment of adolescent females, acknowledging that some of the female adolescent clients we work with have engaged in sexually abusive behavior and not hesitating to assess for this, asking both female and male clients about personal experiences of abuse perpetrated by females—all of these actions can have an impact.

Concluding Remarks: The Role of Feminist Psychology

A central debate in the current literature on adult female aggression concerns gender-neutral versus gender-difference approaches to investigating issues such as sexual aggression (e.g., Hare-Mustin & Maracek, 1990; Muehlenhard, 1998; White & Kowalski, 1994). For example, White and Kowalski advocate for a single feminist theory of aggression that acknowledges variations in sociocultural influences on females and males. Muehlenhard points out that there are positive and negative consequences, whether explanations of female sexual aggression emphasize gender similarities or differences. She suggests the importance of taking into account the multiplicity of experiences and identities that interact with gender and influence sexual aggression. This debate is also pertinent to adolescent females who sexually abuse and informs the following discussion of three topics of interest to feminist psychology.

First, gender identity development in adolescents is a topic that is particularly salient to feminist psychology and adolescents who sexually abuse. In regard to female adolescents, many theorists (e.g., Archer, 1985; Gilligan, et al., 1991) have pointed to adolescence as a critical time in gender identity development. Gilligan (1982, 1993) suggests, for instance, that during adolescence females experience a "relational impasse" (p. xx) related to contradictions between socioculturally influenced gender expectations and their inner experience of the world. Resistance, defined by Abrams (2003) as the "conscious and unconscious rejections of social and cultural mandates concerning gender, race, class, and other axes of social difference" (p. 65), has been pointed to as playing a key role for adolescent females in maintaining authentic connection to self and others and in opposing cultural norms (Gilligan et al.; Miller & Stiver, 1997). Discussion of the multiple contexts of young women's lives is further enriching our understanding of gender identity development and the forms that resistance can take in young women, in particular pointing out that gender interacts with numerous contextual factors (e.g., race, ethnicity, class, geographic region) to result in many possible patterns of resistance in young women (Abrams). Specific to sexual aggression, Muehlenhard (1998) emphasizes the importance of examining the interaction between gender and other identities in striving to better understand sexually aggressive behavior in females. These issues suggest a number of questions related to female adolescents who sexually abuse. How is the sexually abusive behavior of these young women incorporated into their gender identity development? Is it possible that the desire to maintain some type of relational connection is an etiological factor in young women who experience alienation (e.g., due to family dysfunction, identifying as lesbian or bisexual, etc.) from their family, social group, and the larger societal context? If it is true that a large number of young women who sexually victimize have also been victimized, what role does resistance play in their sexually abusive behavior? For example, Abrams described a group of female adolescents whose resistance to suburban white community norms took the form of a "masculine stance" (p. 72) of aggression and externalizing behavior.

A related topic is that of gender role stereotypes and attitudes, which have been discussed previously in some detail. Muehlenhard (1998) cautions that theories of sexual aggression must move beyond a narrow focus on gender roles and socialization. Thus, it is essential to locate such examinations within a multidimensional model of sexual aggression. For instance, it would be helpful to develop a better understanding of how gender role stereotypes interact with other variables related to sexually abusive behavior in influencing the developmental trajectory of abusive behavior in adolescent females. On a systemic level, examining the impact of such stereotypes on patterns of community responsivity and the availability of targeted services for young women who sexually abuse would be very useful.

Last, feminist psychology can take a leadership role in advocating for treatment that addresses the special needs of adolescent females who sexually abuse. As discussed previously, although the increased prevalence of male versus female adolescents who sexually abuse supports the need to allocate more resources to males, it makes sense to also direct some resources toward the development of quality gender-responsive intervention models for female adolescents. This is particularly vital when one considers the arrest trends discussed previously. The National Institute of Corrections (NIC; 2003) report regarding adult female offenders includes many recommendations that are applicable to adolescent females. The NIC calls for the development of comprehensive assessment and treatment services that are gender-responsive and take into account individual factors and the social issues of poverty, abuse, and race and gender inequalities. Specific recommended approaches, such as the availability of female role models and mentors who are sexually, racially, and ethnically diverse and the implementation of gender-specific primary treatment groups (NIC), are strategies that are compatible with the principles and goals of feminist psychology.

Feminists have struggled with acknowledging the issue of sexually abusive behavior in females for many reasons, including concerns that male abusive behavior will be minimized, females who are already marginalized based on gender will be further marginalized, and patriarchal models of problem analysis and treatment will be imposed on female abusers (Kasl, 1990; Muehlenhard, 1998). However, these are the very reasons that feminist psychology must actively confront this problem. If we do not, the danger is that others who may be far less knowledgeable about and committed to women's well being will take the lead. As Babcock, Miller, and Siard (2003) pointed out in discussing adult females who engaged in physical violence, "A feminist perspective should be wholistic, examining both the positive and negative sides of women's behavior. Bringing attention to some women being in the role of perpetrators...involves viewing women as they are, not as we would wish them to be" (p. 160).

End Notes

[1]A comprehensive discussion of this complex issue is beyond the scope of this chapter. For a more complete discussion see, for example, Chamberlain (2003), Chesney-Lind and Pasko (2004), Horowitz and Pettieger (1991), and MacDonald and Chesney-Lind (2001).

[2]Note, however, that the mean age of each sample group is within study parameters previously described.

References

Abrams, L. S. (2003). Contextual variations in young women's gender identity negotiations. *Psychology of Women Quarterly*, 27, 64-74.

Allen, C. (1991). *Women and men who sexually abuse children*. Orwell, VT: Safer Society Press.

Archer, S. L. (1985). Identity and the choice of social roles. *New Directions for Child Development*, 30, 79-99.

Artz, S. (1998). *Sex, power, and the violent school girl*. Toronto: Trifolium Books.

Association for the Treatment of Sexual Abusers. (2000). *The effective legal management of juvenile sexual offenders*. Retrieved July 7, 2004, from http://www.atsa.com/ppjuvenile.html

Babcock, J. C., Miller, S. A., & Siard, C. (2003). Toward a typology of abusive women: Differences between partner-only and generally violent women in the use of violence. *Psychology of Women Quarterly*, 27, 153-161.

Becker, J. V., Hunter, J. A., Stein, R. M., & Kaplan, M. S. (1989). Factors associated with erection in adolescent sexual offenders. *Journal of Psychopathology and Behavioral Assessment*, 11, 353-363.

Blues, A., Moffat, C., & Telford, P. (1999). Work with adolescent females who sexually abuse: Similarities and differences. In M. Erooga & Masson, H., *Children and young people who sexually abuse others: Challenges and responses* (pp. 168-182). New York: Routledge.

Bumby, N. H., & Bumby, K. M. (1997). Adolescent female sexual offenders. In B. K. Schwartz & H. R. Cellini (Eds.), *The sex offender: Corrections, treatment, and legal practice* (pp. 10.1–10.16). Kingston, NJ: Civic Research Institute, Inc.

Bumby, N. H., & Bumby, K. M. (in press). Bridging the gender gap: Addressing juvenile females who commit sexual offenses. In G. O. O'Reilly, W. L. Marshall, R. Beckett, & A. Carp (Eds.), *Handbook of clinical intervention with juvenile sexual offenders*. London: Routledge.

Center for Sex Offender Management. (1999). *Understanding juvenile sexual offending behavior: Emerging research treatment approaches and management practices*. Retrieved July 7, 2004, from http://www.csom.org

Chaffin, M., & Bonner, B. (1998). "Don't shoot, we're your children": Have we gone too far in our response to adolescent sexual abusers and children with sexual behavior problems? *Child Maltreatment*, 3, 314-316.

Chamberlain, P. (2003). Antisocial behavior and delinquency in girls. In P. Chamberlain, *Treating chronic juvenile offenders: Advances made through the Oregon multidimensional treatment foster care model* (pp. 109-127). Washington D.C.: American Psychological Association.

Chesney-Lind, M. (1995). Girls, delinquency, and juvenile justice: Toward a feminist theory of young women's crime. In B. R. Price & N. Sokoloff (Eds.), *The criminal justice system and women* (pp. 71-88). New York: McGraw-Hill.

Chesney-Lind, M., & Okamoto, S. K. (2001). Gender matters: Patterns in girls' delinquency and gender responsive programming. *Journal of Forensic Psychology Practice*, 1(3), 1-28.

Davis, T. C., Peck, G. Q., & Storment, J. M. (1993). Acquaintance rape and the high school student. *Journal of Adolescent Health*, 14, 220-224.

Elliott, M. (1993). *Female sexual abuse of children*. New York: Guilford.

Faller, K. C. (1995). A clinical sample of women who have sexually abused children. *Journal of Child Sexual Abuse*, 4(3), 13-30.

Federal Bureau of Investigation. (2002). *Crime in the United States*. Retrieved October 31, 2003, from ttp://www.fbi.gov/ucr/02cius.htm

Fehrenbach, P. A., & Monastersky, C. (1988). Characteristics of female adolescent sexual offenders. *American Journal of Orthopsychiatry*, 58(1), 148-151.

Feiring, C., Deblinger, E., Hoch-Espada, A., & Haworth, T. (2002). Romantic relationship aggression and attitudes in high school students: The role of gender, grade, and attachment and emotional styles. *Journal of Youth and Adolescence*, 31, 373-385.

Foshee, V. A., Linder, F., MacDougall, J. E., & Bangdiwala, S. (2001). Gender differences in the longitudinal predictors of adolescent dating violence. *Preventive Medicine*, 32, 128-141.

Fromuth, M. E., & Conn, V. E. (1997). Hidden perpetrators: Sexual molestation in a nonclinical sample of college women. *Journal of Interpersonal Violence*, 12, 456-465.

Gilligan, C. (1982, 1993). *In a different voice: Psychological theory and women's development*. Cambridge, MS: Harvard University Press.

Gilligan, C., Rogers, A. G., & Tolman, D. L. (1991). *Women, girls, & psychotherapy: Reframing resistance*. New York: Harrington Park Press.

Goodwin, J., & Divasto, P. (1979). Mother-daughter incest. *Child Abuse and Neglect*, 3, 953-957.

Hare-Mustin, R. T., & Maracek, J. (Eds.). (1990). *Making a difference: Psychology and the construction of gender*. New Haven, CT: Yale University Press.

Hird, M. J. (2000). An empirical study of adolescent dating aggression in the U.K. *Journal of Adolescence*, 23, 69-78.

Hunter, J. A., Goodwin, D. W., & Becker, J. A. (1994). The relationship between phallometrically measured deviant sexual arousal and clinical characteristics in juvenile sexual offenders. *Behavior Research and Therapy*, 32, 533-538.

Hunter, J. A., Lexier, L. J., Goodwin, D. W., Browne, P. A., & Dennis, C. (1993). Psychosexual, attitudinal, and developmental characteristics of juvenile female sexual perpetrators in a residential treatment setting. *Journal of Child and Family Studies*, 2, 317-326.

James, B., & Nasjleti, M. (1983). *Treating sexually abused children and their families*. San Francisco: Consulting Psychologists Press.

Johnson, T. C. (1989). Female child perpetrators: Children who molest other children. *Child Abuse & Neglect*, 13, 571-585.

Kasl, C. D. (1990). Female perpetrators of sexual abuse: A feminist view. In M. Hunter (Ed.), *The sexually abused male: Prevalence, impact, and treatment* (Vol. 1; pp. 259-274). New York: Lexington Books.

Kempf-Leonard, K., & Sample, L. L. (2000). Disparity based on sex: Is gender specific treatment warranted? *Justice Quarterly*, 17, 89-128.

Kubik, E. K., Hecker, J. E., & Righthand, S. (2002). Adolescent females who have sexually offended: Comparisons with delinquent adolescent female offenders and adolescent males who sexually offend. *Journal of Child Sexual Abuse*, 11(3), 63-83.

MacDonald, J. M., & Chesney-Lind, M. (2001). Gender bias and juvenile justice revisited: A multiyear analysis. *Crime & Delinquency*, 47, 173-195.

Matthews, R. (May, 1987). *Female Sexual Offenders*. Address presented at Third National Adolescent Perpetrator Network Conference, Keystone, CO.

Matthews, R., Hunter, J. A., & Vuz, J. (1997). Juvenile female sexual offenders: Clinical characteristics and treatment issues. *Sexual Abuse: A Journal of Research and Treatment*, 9(3), 187-199.

Mayer, A. (1992). *Women sex offenders: Treatment and dynamics*. Holmes Beach, FL: Learning Publications.

McCarty, L. M. (1986). Mother-child incest: Characteristics of the offender. *Child Welfare*, LXV(5), 447-458.

McCormack, A., Janus, M. D., & Burgess, A. W. (1986). Runaway youths and sexual victimization: Gender differences in an adolescent runaway population. *Child Abuse and Neglect*, 10, 387-395.

Miccio-Fonseca, L. C. (2000). Adult and adolescent female sex offenders: Experiences compared to other female and male sex offenders. *Journal of Psychology and Human Sexuality*, 11(3), 75-88.

Miller, J. B., & Stiver, I. P. (1997). *The healing connection: How women form relationships in therapy and in life*. Boston: Beacon Press.

Mirkin, M. P. (1994). Female adolescence revisited: Understanding girls in their sociocultural contexts. In M. P. Mirkin (Ed.), *Women in context: Toward a feminist reconstruction of psychotherapy* (pp. 77-95). New York: Guilford.

Muehlenhard, C. L. (1998). The importance and danger of studying sexually aggressive women. In P. B. Anderson & C. Struckman-Johnson, *Sexually aggressive women: Current perspectives and controversies* (pp. 19-48). New York: Guilford.

National Institute of Corrections. (2003). *Gender-responsive strategies: Research, practice, and guiding principles for women offenders* (NIC Accession No. 018017).

National Task Force on Juvenile Sexual Offending. (1993). Revised report from the National Task Force on Juvenile Sexual Offending. *Juvenile and Family Court Journal*, 44(4), 3-108.

Office of Juvenile Justice and Delinquency Prevention. (1999). *Juvenile offenders and victims:1999 national report*. Retrieved October 31, 2003, from http://ojjdp.ncjrs.org

O'Keefe, M. (1997). Predictors of dating violence among high school students. *Journal of Interpersonal Violence*, 12, 546-568.

Poitras, M., & Lavoie, F. (1995). A study of the prevalence of sexual coercion in adolescent heterosexual dating relationships in a Quebec sample. *Violence and Victims*, 10, 299-313.

Schwartz, B. K., & Cellini, H. R. (1995). Female sex offenders. In B. K. Schwartz & H. R. Cellini (Eds.), *The sex offender: Corrections, treatment, and legal practice* (pp. 5.1 – 5.22). Kingston, NJ: Civic Research Institute, Inc.

Shaw, J. A. (1999). Sexually aggressive behavior. In J. A. Shaw (Ed.), *Sexual aggression* (pp. 3-40. Washington, DC: American Psychiatric Press.

Spitzberg, B. H. (1999). An analysis of empirical estimates of sexual aggression victimization and perpetration. *Violence and Victims*, 14(3), 241-260.

Turner, M. T., & Turner, T. N. (1994). *Female adolescent sexual abusers: An exploratory study of mother-daughter dynamics with implications for treatment*. Brandon, VT: Safer Society Press.

U.S. Department of Justice. (2003). Funding update. *OJJDP news at a glance*, II(6).

White, J. W., & Kowalski, R. M. (1994). Deconstructing the myth of the nonaggressive woman: A feminist analysis. *Psychology of Women Quarterly*, 18, 487-508.

CHAPTER ELEVEN

ADOLESCENT FEMALES WITH SEXUAL BEHAVIOR PROBLEMS

WHAT CONSTITUTES BEST PRACTICE[1]

SUSAN ROBINSON

Introduction

Learning that the treatment of female sexually abusive youth differs from the treatment provided to sexually abusive male youth, was a difficult lesson that came with a price in my clinical practice. The price: I lost the girl's trust. The therapeutic relationship was irreparably damaged and my error was confronting her too strongly. I confronted this particular girl to take responsibility for sexually abusing two young children before she was ready or willing. Because I, in effect, destroyed our relationship, my future efforts to work with her proved fairly futile. I learned that with girls, the therapeutic alliance is often fragile and due to a female adolescent developmental trait - all or nothing thinking - either there is a relationship or none at all; without one, no meaningful work will be done.

This is not to imply that the therapeutic relationship is not important for boys - clearly it is. However, a therapist working with girls appears to travail on a more precarious course; one which can easily be lost if close attention is not given to the relationship. The reason for this difference appears to be based on female relational development (Gilligan, 1982; Gilligan, Lyons, & Hammer, 1990; Jordan, Kaplan, Miller, Stiver, & Surrey, 1991). As Piper (1994) writes, "With girls this age, relationships are everything. No work can be done in the absence of mutual affection and regard. The first step… is helping the girl develop trust" (p. 254). It was this experience, in addition to many other ones with girls demonstrating a dissimilarity in treatment needs from boys, which led me to focus more on girls and develop treatment based on their behavior and development.

The need for feminine epistemology

Thus far, offense-specific treatment has been predominantly developed from clinical experience working with males and research conducted on male populations. These male treatment models were initially derived from working with incarcerated adult male sex offenders; they were then adapted to adolescent male sexually abusive youth. Because there were few female juveniles entering the system for sexually abusive behaviors, treatment was not conceptualized from a female standpoint. Rather, clinicians were left (myself included) applying the standard male treatment models, based on a masculine epistemology defined as "systems of knowledge that take the masculine perspective as if it were truly universal and objective" (Kaschak, 1992, p. 11), to females. The problem with this perspective is that it subsumes females: If the assumption exists that the dynamics of female sexual abuse and the treatment of sexually abusive female youth are the same as for males, ineluctably important distinctions and perspectives will be missed. In masculine epistemology, the female voice is silent, yet I believe that best practice means keenly listening for girls' perspectives in their own right, rather than viewing girls as the Other (defined as not male or differing from males) (de Beauvoir, 1949). It means learning from their narratives and developing treatment based on what they have to say, rather than molding male treatment models to them. Through the use of feminine epistemology, the uniqueness of female sexually abusive behavior is learned and acknowledged.

This chapter explores the idea of best practice for sexually abusive girls. (Although I refer to sexually abusive girls throughout this chapter for consistency purposes, much of the chapter is applicable to girls with general sexual behavior problems, i.e., promiscuity or repeated unsafe sex.) The chapter begins with an overview of female adolescent development and sexuality, and then explores the pathways to female delinquency, protective factors, and female sexually abusive behavior. Best practice for sexually abusive girls is informed by an understanding of these areas since the needs and issues germane to this population guide the assessment and treatment process. Subsequently, issues of, and suggestions for, the assessment and treatment of female sexually abusive youth are discussed in order to inform our practice towards a more female-specific foundation, one that resides in feminine epistemology.

An overview of female adolescent development and its accompanying vulnerabilities

The purpose of providing an overview on female adolescent development lies in its importance in grounding and guiding our practice with girls; understanding the needs and issues impacting adolescent girls allows us to be perspicacious in our work with girls and help them feel better understood. Perhaps the most important starting point is appreciating that female development is relational; that is, it is through relationships and meaningful connections that girls derive their identities (Brown & Gilligan, 1992; Gilligan, 1982; Gilligan et al., 1990; Gilligan, Rogers, & Tolman, 1991; Jordan, et al., 1991; Miller & Stiver, 1997). Likewise, female moral development is often based on the ethics of care and relational bonds (Gilligan, 1982). Conversely, male development is geared more towards separation and independence (Erickson, 1950, 1968; Kohlberg, 1981; Levinson, 1978). In addition to differing socialization processes, biological differences further explain the tendency for females to follow a relational course. On average, males have twenty times more testosterone than females. Higher levels of testosterone are associated with more aggression, greater self-assertion, greater self-reliance and independence, and more libido (Gurian, 2001, 2002). On the other hand, estrogen (far more dominant in females) is associated with lower levels of aggression, competition, self-assertion, and self-reliance (Gurian, 2001). Gurian (2002) refers to the female drive towards intimacy as the "intimacy imperative" (p. 53) dictated, in part, by female hormones that work together in such a way for females to be more naturally inclined towards "connectivity, empathy, and conciliation" (p. 90). Baron-Cohen (2003) also describes the differences between the female and male brain in that females are predisposed towards empathy, a distinct attribute of their relational development.

Moreover, research indicates that during female adolescence, girls lose their pre-adolescent authentic self and develop a false presentation (Brown & Gilligan, 1992; Gilligan, 1982; Hancock, 1989; Pipher, 1994; Shandler, 1999, Stern, 1991). In donning masks and acting untrue to themselves, girls become adept at being chameleons - changing and behaving in certain ways according to their environment and the people they are with. This process makes it difficult for girls to know who they are underneath their external presentation (Haag, 1999). When girls are inundated with depictions of how they are supposed to behave and look, it becomes more difficult to rely on internal resources to maintain an accurate view of themselves. As one girl described: "...Being yourself, in actuality it's fairly difficult. Media messages tell us to be a certain shape and size, our friends and peers want us to like certain things, our parents wish we'd act a specific way. With all the different messages from all different angles, it is sometimes hard for a girl just to find the person she really is" (quoted in Haag, 1999, p. 12). Many girls, however, are successful at resisting such scripts and developing their identities without succumbing to cultural pressures or losing their voice (Brown, 1998; Leadbeater & Way, 1996).

Self-confidence declines during female adolescence, yet as boys continue in adolescence, their self-esteem increases (American Association of University Women [AAUW], 1995; Orenstein, 1994; Commonwealth Fund, 1997). In the *Commonwealth Fund Survey* (1997), only 39% of high school girls appeared highly confident. This self-confidence drop is predominant among Caucasian, Hispanic, and Asian-American girls. African-American females are better able to sustain their confidence as they enter adolescence (Sadker & Sadker, 1994; Commonwealth Fund). One of the sources of decreased self-confidence is body dissatisfaction and distress. In the *Commonwealth Survey*, 53% of high school girls reported not being at the "right weight"; one-third believed they were overweight and this finding was twice the rate than for boys. Over half of high school girls dieted. Unrealistic standards of thinness and idealized media depictions foster unhealthy comparisons: Girls compare themselves with supermodels and in their failure to measure up, depression, decreased self-esteem, and body dysphoria set in. This body dissatisfaction results in "disordered eating" patterns (Hales, 1999) and eating disorders. The use of laxatives, diet pills, and compulsive exercise are other means that girls attempt to solve the problem of not being thin enough. Abused girls are also more vulnerable to eating disorders: In the *Commonwealth Survey*, they were three times more likely to binge and purge than non-abused girls.

Because girls are more likely to internalize their feelings than boys, different behavioral problems result. Harris, Blum, and Resnick (1991) describe girls engaging in behaviors of "quiet disturbance" (p. 119), for example, eating disorders, substance abuse, and suicide attempts. They are more likely than boys to attempt suicide (National Center on Addiction and Substance Abuse [NCASA], 2003; Peterson, Zhang, Lucia, King, & Lewis, 1996; Rosenthal, 1981; Simons & Murphy, 1985;

Wunderlich, Bronisch, Wittchen, & Carter, 2001) - about three times as likely (Canetto & Lester, 1995) - and girls who abuse substances are even more at risk for suicide (NCASA, 2003). Delicate self-cutting also predominates among female adolescents (Kaplan, 1991) and is often used to mitigate emotional pain. Conversely, boys tend to externalize their feelings and the mental health diagnoses more common among boys reflect this externalization process, e.g., conduct disorder, oppositional defiant disorder, and attention deficit and hyperactivity disorder (Harris et al., 1991; Leschied, Cummings, Van Brunschot, Cunningham, & Saunders, 2000; Loeber & Stouthamer-Loeber, 1998; Perry, 1997; Perry, Pollard, Blakley, Baker, & Vigilante, 1995).

One manifestation of girls' internalization response is depression. Many girls struggle with depression during their adolescence and at a greater rate than their peer aged males (Allgood-Merten, Lewinsohn, & Hops, 1990; Commonwealth Fund, 1997; NCASA, 2003; Nolen-Hoeksema, 1990; Rutter, 1986). Caucasian, Hispanic, and Asian American girls are the hardest hit by depression; African-American girls are far less likely to have depression (Commonwealth Fund, 1997). Approximately 25% of teenage girls exhibit depressive symptoms, compared to 16% of boys (Commonwealth Fund). Allgood-Merten et al. (1990) found that girls reported greater self-consciousness, negative body image, and poor self-esteem than boys, and these factors correlated to depression. Solomon (2001) notes that twice as many women have depression - a gender difference that unfolds at puberty. The gender difference appears to be a result of hormonal and social differences. In the female brain, sadness encompasses an area eight times larger than in the male brain (discussed in Hales, 1999). Higher levels of testosterone are associated with less depression (Gurian, 2002). Understandably, abused girls are more vulnerable to depression: The *Commonwealth Fund Survey* found that 46% of abused girls manifested depressive symptoms, almost twice the rate of non-abused girls.

Adolescent girls are also at risk for anxiety disturbances, especially those girls who have been traumatized (Perry et al., 1995; Wunderlich et al., 2001). Interestingly, according to the National Comorbidity Survey (cited in Hales, 1999) research shows that women are three to four times more likely to develop phobias; two to three times more likely to develop a panic disorder; and are at twice the risk for developing generalized anxiety disorder or posttraumatic stress disorder. Davis and Breslau (1998) have found that females are far more vulnerable to developing posttraumatic stress disorder: When faced with assaultive violence, females experience a larger number of PTSD symptoms than males; the lifetime prevalence of PTSD is approximately twice as high for females than for males; and the duration of symptoms for females is longer (four times longer than in males). In one study Davis and Breslau describe, following exposure to assaultive violence, females were at a greater risk of PTSD (36%), compared to males (6.2%).

Substance abuse is another behavior impacting adolescent girls. The extensive study, *The Formative Years: Pathways to Substance Abuse Among Girls and Young Women Ages 8-22* (NCASA, 2003), found that 45% of high school girls drink alcohol, 26.4% binge drink, 27.7% smoke cigarettes, 20% use marijuana, 3.7% use cocaine, and 4.2% use inhalants. Girls are more likely than boys to abuse prescription painkillers, stimulants, and tranquilizers. The reasons for substance use, the risk factors, and the subsequent medical problems for girls are different than those for boys. General risk factors associated with girls - depression, suicidal ideation, physical and sexual abuse, early puberty, dieting and eating disorders - increase substance abuse risk. Frequent moving and times of transition (i.e., from middle school to high school) also raise substance abuse risk for girls. Many girls use substances to reduce stress, mitigate depression, improve mood, lose weight, increase confidence, or enhance sex; conversely, boys typically use drugs for heightened social status and sensation seeking. Substance use can become more rapidly substance abuse for girls, and girls who abuse substances are at greater physiological risk than boys: Liver disease, lung damage, alcohol-induced brain damage, and cardiac problems develop quicker in females. Unprotected sex, unwanted pregnancies, sexually transmitted diseases, and sexual assault are also consequences of female substance abuse. Further, substance-abusing girls are at risk for reproductive and gynecological problems, i.e., infertility, vaginal infections (Nelson-Zlupko, Kauffman, & Dorr, 1995).

Finally, anger tends to be managed and expressed differently in males and females due to socialization processes that teach girls to deny and hide their anger. Girls learn to be "submissive peacekeepers" (Borysenko, 1996, p. 70). Boys are provided far more latitude in their expression of anger; physical fights, for example, are viewed more as a normal and necessary part of male development. Simmons (2002) maintains it is because our culture does not allow the overt expression of female conflict, that females resort to alternative means to display their anger; body language and relationships become tools for aggression rather than fists, guns, or knives. It is because of this that adolescent females are more likely to resort to indirect aggression than physical aggression when compared to boys (Bjorkqvist, Lagerspetz, & Kaukiainen, 1992; Bjorkqvist, Osterman, & Kaukiainen, 1992; Owens & MacMullin, 1995). Similarly, girls are more likely to engage in relational aggression than boys (Crick & Grotpeter, 1995; Simmons). Although these terms are often used interchangeably, indirect aggression is covert behavior that does not involve direct confrontation of a victim, e.g., spreading a rumor about someone or gossiping. Relational aggression refers to the dynamic of harming someone by damaging or threatening to damage the relationship: Social exclusion, negative body language, the silent treatment, avoidance, shunning, and threatening to end a relationship unless the aggressor gets what she desires, are all forms of relational aggression. Relational aggression is often indirect, but indirect aggression is not necessarily relational.

Social constructions of adolescent female sexuality

One of the areas of greatest gender divergence is sexuality. Kaschak (1992) notes, "[Girls'] sexuality is based on appearance and performance, on desirability rather than desire, on restraint rather than exploration. Sexuality is perhaps the most obviously gendered realm of functioning in this society" (p. 56). This perspective has been mirrored by many (Debold, 1991; Debold, Tolman, & Brown, 1996; Fine, 1988; Phillips, 2000; Thompson, 1990, 1995; Tolman, 1991, 1994, 1999, 2002; Wolf, 1997; Young-Eisendrath, 1999). The realm of female adolescent sexuality is complex and mired with contradictions. On the one hand, one cultural script teaches girls to use and flaunt their sexuality to attain power and manipulate males. Two popular female singers, Brittany Spears and Cristina Aguilera, are shining examples of females who use their sexuality to sell themselves and wield a considerable amount of power; many girls view them as their female role models. On the other hand, girls' psyches are flooded by a different cultural sexual script that teaches them to be sexually passive and inexperienced. If they take responsibility for their sexuality and demonstrate initiative, if they have had multiple sexual partners, or if they are not naïve enough, they are at risk for developing negative reputations and being labeled a "slut" or a "whore." There are no equivalent labels for male adolescents; not as pejorative, boys with such initiative are referred to as "players" and "studs." Additionally, male adolescents learn sexual entitlement and the sexual bravado many of them acquire is indicative of this. The dichotomies inherent in female adolescent sexuality are obvious: virgin/slut, Madonna/whore, good girl/bad girl, sexy/ugly are a few. Being unprepared for sex is one way girls demonstrate they are "nice" girls; girls who use birth control and are thus, prepared to have sex, are often viewed as "bad" since they are not conforming to the cultural script that teaches them to be sexually inexperienced or passive. Additionally, Phillips (as cited in Haag, 1999) describes how many girls feel pressured to say no in order to maintain a "good" girl image, when they really want to say yes.

A developmental dilemma for girls is the dilemma of desire: A girl is supposed to be desirable, but not desiring (Tolman, 2002). Sexually desiring girls are left feeling deviant (Lamb, 2001). In their need to become desiring, girls become objects of desire, which leaves them disconnected from their bodies through a process of self-objectification: They view their bodies through the eyes of others and define their sexuality through their desirability. Debold et al. (1996) refer to this process as "subjectivity-as-object" (p. 109). They also note, "In [a] socially condoned construction of sexuality, agency is all male and female sexuality seems limited to looking good" (p. 109). Girls internalize the importance of this male desire and believe that their success is equivalent to the attention they receive from males (Artz, 1997). Through observing eyes, female bodies are idealized, but simultaneously devalued, objectified, and violated.

Although they want to be wanted, girls also want to be assured of safety, yet their sexuality is an unsafe haven. Girls' desire to be attractive is used against them and seen as proof that they "wanted it" or "asked for it" (sexual harassment or assault). As a result, many girls also view themselves as responsible for what happens to them sexually. They blame themselves for being raped - for not resisting enough or dressing too provocatively - and consider themselves gatekeepers of male sexuality (Tolman, 2002). Because male adolescents are seen as being overwhelmed by their sexual impulses, girls are "supposed" to keep male sexual advances at bay; by regulating their own and boys' sexual impulses, they remain "good" girls.

The result of the social constructions pertaining to female adolescence is that females are left insecure about, and unaware of, their sexuality. Although masturbation is viewed as a norm of male adolescence and commonly joked about, girls do not as readily, or as easily, discuss or explore their own bodies. In one study, for example, results indicated that women masturbate far less than men; twice as many men than women ever masturbated and males that did, masturbated three times more frequently during their early adolescence and young adulthood than females masturbating during the same age periods (Leitenberg, Detzer, & Srebnik, 1993). They concluded that masturbation is not as reinforcing for females as it is for males, and the gender difference may be due to the fact that females are more socialized to link sex with romance, relationships, and emotional intimacy, in addition to biological factors which may have some bearing. I have heard girls speak of their genitalia with far more embarrassment and abashment than boys with whom I have worked. When speaking of masturbation, I often hear a chorus of girls saying "grooooooss" with red faces. Although many girls do masturbate, their shame, in addition to the notion that it is gross for girls to masturbate, prevents them from positively acknowledging it. Not surprisingly, many girls learn about their own bodies through their relationships with boys; a boy may find a girl's clitoris before she does (Farber, 2002). Furthermore, since cultural scripts teach girls to be passive and many girls are unsure of their sexuality, girls tend to place their partner's sexual needs before their own. They become masterful accommodators to more typically, male partners. Essentially, sex becomes a "performance for the benefit of boys" (Wolf, 1997, p. 70).

Sexual subjectivity is an adolescent developmental task, one that many girls fail to meet (Tolman, 2002). It is girls' lack of confidence and unawareness about their sexuality that often leads them to precarious and accommodating situations, demonstrating this lack of sexual agency and subjectivity. In a 1996 survey of 720 teenage girls, most girls stated that girls have sex because if they do not, they believe they will lose their boyfriends; girls also have sex because of the sexual pressure they receive from boys (discussed in Hales, 1999). Further, Thompson (1990, 1995) found from interviewing 400 teenage girls, that most girls are un-knowing when it comes to their sexuality. This amnesia is a result of developmental and social conditions that constrain girls' sexuality. Only one quarter of her sample consisted of girls who felt positive about their sexuality ("pleasure narrators") and demonstrated healthy sexuality. Other girls found themselves having unprotected sex or complying with boyfriends to have sex before they felt ready.

Finally, girls are left developing their sexuality in a culture replete with "male sexual imagination" (Young-Eisendrath, p. 82); the pornography industry is evidence of this. The result of the confluence of all these sexual scripts and behaviors is a lack of discourse of female sexual desire and the likelihood that female sexuality will continue to be denied and silenced unless sexual education encompasses healthy choices for female sexual expression and decision making. The question then becomes: Is there a relationship between these gendered expectations and sexual social scripts, and female adolescent sexual aggression? What does female adolescent sexuality tell us about female adolescent sexual offending? This relationship will be described in a subsequent section.

Understanding female pathways to delinquent behavior

Cavanagh (2002) writes: "[A]ggressiveness is gendered and ...attention must be devoted to the particularities of male and female violence" (p. i). Given this, attention should also be paid to the particular pathways to delinquent behavior for girls. Victimization appears to be a key pathway to girls' criminal behavior (Acoca, 1999; Leschied et al. 2000; Watts & Ellis, 1993). Acoca & Dedel (1998) maintain, "Victimization is the critical dynamic underlying girls' involvement in crime and other problem behaviors" (p. 116). Posttraumatic stress disorder leads to high distress levels and low self-restraint, which in turn, increase the risk of behavioral problems and offending behaviors (Cauffman, Feldman, Waterman & Steiner, 1998). And, PTSD is more common among delinquent female juveniles than males: Cauffman et al.,

(1998) found that incarcerated juvenile females were 50% more likely than incarcerated juvenile males to exhibit current PTSD symptomatology.

The role of internalized disturbances appears to play a distinct role in the development of female juvenile aggression. Leschied et al. (2000) and Leschied, Cummings, Zerwer, and Saunders (2002) conclude that unlike male aggression, the development of female aggression is accompanied by depression, suicidal ideation, and generalized anxiety disorders. Young, depressed girls are nearly four times more likely to act aggressively than boys (Leschied et al., 2000). Other studies have also identified a strong connection between female depression and aggressive behaviors (Obeidallah & Earls, 1999; Paikoff, Brooks-Gunn, & Warren, 1991; Zoccolillo & Rogers, 1991). Additionally, Zoccolillo and Rogers found the majority of conduct-disordered girls in their sample had anxiety disorders. They concluded that specific to females, depression and anxiety disorders often coincide with conduct disorder and antisocial personalities. Overall, females involved in the juvenile justice system have higher rates of mental health problems than males equally involved (Cauffman et al., 1998); this is not surprising given the role these problems appear to play in the development of female delinquency. Timmons-Mitchell et al. (as cited in Prescott, 1997) found that 84% of committed girls in their sample evidenced a need for mental health assistance; conversely, 27% of the boys needed such services. Girls' need for services increased over time.

Further, Chesney-Lind (as cited in Funk, 1999) has suggested that the origins of female delinquency reside in family problems. In Day, Franklin, and Marshall's (1998) study, a history of family violence was correlated to girls' aggression; they concluded that psychosocial variables may be more closely linked to aggression in females than males (male aggression was associated with a diagnosis of conduct disorder). Saner & Ellickson (1996) found a stronger correlation between low parental support and violence among girls than boys. Liu & Kaplan (1999) found that unconventional (criminal) values and peer influence on criminal behavior are less important for girls; rather, criminal behaviors among family members and extended family members carry a greater influence in the development of antisocial values in females than males (Cloninger, Christiansen, Reich & Gottesman, 1978). Further, Osborne and Fincham, and Paskaslahti et al. (as cited in Levene, Augimeri, Pepler, Walsh, Webster, & Koegl, 2001) note that a girl's problematic relationship with her mother can play an important role in the development of delinquent behavior.

Other pathways to female delinquency are noted in the literature. For example, some studies describe a relationship between early maturation and delinquency (Caspi, Lynam, Moffit, & Silva, 1993; Stattin & Magnusson, 1990). Obviously physical development is not always synchronized with emotional and mental development. Some girls experiencing early maturation have problems with body image. Other girls find that because of their early maturation, they do not easily fit in with their peers and experience peer ostracism, thus setting the stage for them to find relationships outside of a conventional peer group. At times these affiliations are with older males or delinquent peer aged males - some of whom take advantage of these girls and expose them to sexual intimacy (prior to being developmentally ready) and criminal behaviors. Caspi et al. (1993) offer other explanations for the association of early maturation and delinquency: Delinquency is "an effective means of knifing off childhood apron strings… [It is] an adaptive effort to secure adult privileges" (p. 28). Delinquent behaviors also result from a combination of stress affiliated with early maturation and preexisting behavior problems. They found that girls who experience early maturation and are also in mixed-school settings are at the greatest risk for delinquency: "[A]t least two factors are necessary for the initiation and maintenance of female delinquency: puberty and boys" (p. 26).

Additionally, according to Juon and Ensminger (1997), there appears to be an association for girls linking self-harm, i.e., suicide attempts, to physical harm towards others, however, it is not yet clear if suicidal behaviors can be viewed as a distinct pathway to delinquent behavior. Although given the preponderance of suicidality among delinquent girls (see Prescott, 1997), it is reasonable to speculate that girls who lack care about themselves, also do not necessarily care about harming others or at least, engaging in delinquent behaviors that cause further harm to themselves. Of note, a few studies on incarcerated adult females have found a correlation between self-injury and recidivism (see Blanchette & Motiuk, 1997; Bonta, Pang, & Wallace-Capretta, 1995), but a similar link has not yet been identified among female delinquents.

Another pathway to delinquency involves multiple risk factors. Cloninger et al. (1978) found that for females to engage in aggression or criminal behavior, a higher number of risk factors will be present than among their male counterparts. Mathews, Hunter, & Vuz (1997), in their study on female sexually abusive adolescents, summarized this idea by stating "biological and socialization factors create a higher threshold for the externalization of experienced developmental trauma in females than males" (p. 194). Finally, a pathway similar to boys is academic failure, which is considered to be the most significant risk factor relating to early onset delinquency (Office of Juvenile Justice and Delinquency Prevention [OJJDP], 1998). According to Ellickson et al., and Serbin et al. (as cited in Leschied et al., 2002), girls with lower academic achievement or who have dropped out of high school are at risk for engaging in violent or norm-violating behavior.

Protective factors

Despite the risks and vulnerabilities of adolescent females, there are protective factors that help girls navigate their way through adolescence and prevent the development of unhealthy and delinquent behaviors. These factors are important to consider when assessing and treating sexually abusive girls since treatment may involve nurturing these factors in order to build barriers to future inappropriate behavior. First, indicative of girls' relational development, their psychological strength is correlated to their strong connections to others. These connections can be extrafamilial with caring adults such as teachers (Hughes, Cavewill, & Jackson, 1999), or intrafamilial (Miller & Stiver, 1997; NCASA, 2003; Roberts, 1999). Jordan (2004) discusses the notion of "relational resilience," which is highly applicable to the discussion of protective factors. Relational resilience is a path built on "empathic mutuality" and healthy connections to others (p. 28). A strong relationship between a girl and her mother is especially protective (Harris et al., 1991; Levene et al., 2001; OJJDP, 1998). As Hales (1999) writes, "What matters most to a teenage girl, troubled or not, is her mother" (p. 148); girls with strong, supportive mothers are less likely to experience symptoms of depression and are more likely to feel positive about themselves.

Emotional expressiveness is an important protective factor and given that girls are socialized to identify and express their feelings more so than boys, girls have the advantage with this protective factor (J. Gilgun, personal communication, June 15, 2003). For girls, normative beliefs about aggression are protective, i.e., aggression is not considered acceptable female social behavior (Huesmann, Guerra, Zelli, & Miller, 1992). A religious or spiritual connection has also been identified as a protective factor for girls (Flansburg, 1991; NCASA, 2003; Pipher, 1994). Furthermore, more so with girls, moderating factors to aggression include cognitions about the consequences for the victim and the self (Perry, Perry, & Rasmussen, 1986). Similarly, Chase et al. (as cited in Leschied et al., 2002) found that empathy and the ability to engage in perspective taking are related to the suppression of aggression. Involvement in extracurricular activities, e.g., athletics (NCASA, 2003; Roberts, 1999), academic success or a positive orientation to school (Jessor, Van Den Boss, Vanderryn, Costa, & Turbin, 1995; OJJDP, 1998), and problem-solving abilities (Keltikangas-Jaervinen & Pakaslahti, 1999), decrease the potential of engaging in aggression and delinquent behaviors. Jessor et al. (1995) describe other protective factors including: an attitudinal intolerance for deviance, a positive orientation towards one's health, perceived regulatory controls in the social environment, and friends as models for conventional behavior. Further, resilience, the ability to self-regulate and self-soothe, a positive sense of self, and a hope for one's future serve as protective factors (Gilgun, 2001). Avenues for resisting the negative messages that permeate our culture and negatively impact adolescent girls can also be protective. These avenues include: "a strong ethnic identity…learning positive messages about oneself, trusting oneself as a source of knowledge, speaking one's mind… non-traditional sex typing, feminist ideas, and assertive role models" (Roberts, p. 409).

What We Do Know (And Don't Know) About Female Adolescent Sexually Abusive Behavior

What is known about female adolescent sex offending is exiguous due to the lack of research conducted on this population. For the most part, the studies that have been conducted consist of small sample sizes. The samples from which the data are drawn are often unrepresentative and are limited due to the lack of generalizability and an inability to meet strict scientific standards. Yet by examining the studies, consistent themes can be gleaned that subsequently inform the assessment and treatment of sexually abusive girls.

Sexual abuse histories

The most consistent theme is that many, if not most, sexually abusive girls have themselves been sexual abused (Bumby & Bumby, 1997; Fehrenbach & Monastersky, 1988; Howley, 2001; Hunter, Lexier, Goodwin, Browne, & Dennis, 1993; Johnson, 1989; Kubik, Hecker, Righthand, 2002; Mathews et al., 1997; Miccio-Fonseca, 2000; Ray & English, 1995; Turner & Turner, 1994). This is perhaps the greatest gender difference in the literature on sexually abusive youth. For example, Mathews et al. found that 77.6% of sexually abusive girls reported sexual abuse histories, whereas 44.3% of boys reported such a history. In Ray and English's sample, 93.5% of the girls versus 84.9% of the boys had sexual abuse histories. In Bumby and Bumby's study comparing 18 juvenile sex offending females to 18 juvenile sex offending males, all of the girls had been sexually abused versus 63% of the boys. Miccio-Fonseca found that 72% of sexually abusive females (adolescent and adult combined, n=18) had sexual abuse histories, compared to 50% of the sexually abusive males (n=332). In Kubik et al.'s (2002) study comparing 11 female sexually abusive adolescents to 11 male sexually abusive adolescents, 63.6% of the girls had histories of sexual abuse versus 50% of the boys. In Fehrenbach and Monastersky's study, 46.4% of their sample of 28 female adolescents had sexual abuse histories, compared to 18% of boys (from their 1986 study). 97% of girls in Howley's sample of 66 sexually abusive girls had been victims of child sexual abuse. Another significant finding is that sexually abusive girls tend to be sexually victimized at young ages (Hunter, 1993; Howley, 2001) and at younger ages when compared to boys (Mathews et al., 1997; Miccio-Fonseca, 2000). Hunter et al. found that the median age that the sexually victimized girls were abused was 4.5 years; Howley found it was 3.8 years. Girls in the Mathews et al. study were more likely to have been sexually victimized at the age of 5 years old or younger (64%), compared to 25.8% for boys.

Studies also indicate that many sexually abusive girls have been sexually victimized by more than one perpetrator (Bumby & Bumby, 1997; Howley, 2001; Hunter et al., 1993; Kubik et al., 2002; Mathews et al., 1997). In Howley's sample, 74% of the girls with sexual abuse histories had been abused by two or more perpetrators. Mathews et al. found that the mean number of perpetrators for the girls in their sample was 4.5; the mean for boys was 1.4. All the girls in Hunter et al.'s study had been sexually abused by more than one perpetrator (ranging from 2-7). Additionally, many sexually abusive girls have been sexually victimized by female perpetrators. A female perpetrator abused 32% of the sexually abused girls in Howley's study. In Hunter et al., a female perpetrator was present in 60% of the cases of the sexually abused girls. Mathews et al. found that over three times as many girls than boys reported having been abused by a female perpetrator. Further, those girls who have been sexually victimized are likely to have been abused repeatedly and severely. Kubik et al. found that 75% of the girls with sexual abuse histories had been victimized three or more times; the percentage for boys was 20%. 71.4% of the girls endured anal or vaginal penetration, compared to 22.2% of the boys. Yet this latter finding is not consistent with Mathews et al. who found that the sexually abusive boys who had sexual victimization experiences were more likely than their female counterparts to have experienced vaginal or anal intercourse (66.7% versus 58%, respectively). However, they also concluded that the sexually victimized girls were more often victims of offender aggression: 72.5% of the girls reported their sexual victimization experiences included force or aggression, compared to 45.2% of the boys.

Other maltreatment

Sexually abusive girls also tend to have experienced other forms of maltreatment, and studies suggest that these girls generally have more extensive abuse histories when compared to boys (Kubik et al., 2002; Mathews et al., 1997; Ray & English, 1995). Mathews et al. found that 60% of their sample of sexually abusive girls had physical abuse histories, compared to 44.9% of the boys. In Ray and English's study, 90% of the girls versus 80.2% of the boys had physical abuse histories. Moreover, 68% of the girls had been emotionally abused, compared to 48.4% of boys; 86.2% of girls versus 68.9% of boys had been neglected. Howley (2001) found that 82% of the girls in her study had physical abuse histories; 71% experienced general neglect. In Bumby and Bumby's (1997) sample, 75% of the girls had physical abuse histories; 42% had experienced emotional and physical neglect.

Mental health problems

Frequent among sexually abusive girls are mental health disturbances. In Hunter et al. (1993), 80% of the girls had received prior mental health services; 60% of the girls had histories of suicidal ideation and attempts. In Bumby and Bumby's sample (1997), 83% of the girls had received prior mental health treatment and 83% had histories of depression. Moreover, 58% of the girls had histories of suicide attempts. Miccio-Fonseca (2000) found that 44% of the sexually abusive females had attempted suicide, compared to 15% of males. Compellingly, 50% of the sexually abusive females came from families where someone had attempted suicide, compared to only 8% of the males. Mathews et al. (1997) found that over half their sample of 67 girls had a mood disturbance (i.e. depression or anxiety) and almost half met the diagnostic criteria for posttraumatic stress disorder. Kubik et al. found that 50% of their sample of sexually abusive girls had a diagnosis of PTSD, compared to only 9.1% of the sexually abusive boys. Interestingly, 45.5% of the boys had conduct disorder versus 9.1% of the girls.

Substance abuse

Another theme in the literature is substance abuse. In Hunter et al. (1993), 50% of the girls had histories of substance abuse. In Bumby and Bumby's (1997) study, 58% of the sexually abusive girls had histories of drug use and 75% had abused alcohol. Results of their comparison study showed that females abused drugs at a higher rate than males. Mathews et al. (1997) found that 25.4% of adolescent girls, compared to 14.3% of boys, had substance abuse histories. Over 1/3 (36%) of girls in Howley's (2001) sample had substance abuse problems. Yet Kubik et al. (2002) found that when compared to non-sexual offending girls, sexually abusive girls were less likely to have substance abuse problems. In their sample, only 10% of the sexually abusive females had a history of drug or alcohol abuse; conversely, 63.6% of the non-sex offending delinquent females had such a history. The lower levels of drug and alcohol abuse among sexually abusive girls in their study are unique when compared to the aforementioned studies and suggest the need for further research. In my clinical experience, the sexually abusive girls who receive residential treatment or are committed are far more likely to have substance abuse histories than those I see on an outpatient basis.

Other delinquent behaviors

Studies suggest that histories of stealing, truancy, and running away are not uncommon among sexually abusive girls (Bumby & Bumby, 1997; Hunter et al., 1993; Ray & English, 1995). Bumby and Bumby found in their original sample of 12 girls, that 33% of them had been arrested for stealing; a history of running away was evident in 58% of the cases. In Hunter et al., 60% of the girls had previously run away, whereas

Howley (2001) found that 49% had. Ray & English found higher rates of stealing and truancy among girls than boys in their study. 58% of the girls in Bumby and Bumby's study had histories of truancy and in their latter comparison study, the girls had higher truancy rates than the boys. Howley also found that 39% of girls in her sample engaged in truancy. In Kubik et al. (2002), only 9.1% of girls, versus 60% of sexually abusive boys, had previously been suspended from school: This finding is not surprising given that boys tend to engage in more overt behavioral displays resulting in suspension, e.g., fighting.

It is unclear to what extent sexually abusive girls resort to other aggressive means, i.e., physical. Among Bumby and Bumby's (1997) original sample, 67% of them had a history of aggressive behaviors with peers (although it did not describe the type of aggression). Similarly, Howley (2001) found that 76% of her sample had aggressive peer relationships. Yet Ray and English (1995) found that girls were less likely to engage in physically aggressive behaviors than stealing, truancy, or temper tantrums. Similarly, Kubik et al. found that when compared to non-sexual offending, delinquent adolescent girls, sexually abusive girls engaged in significantly less antisocial behaviors such as fighting (90.9% versus 30%), and displayed less serious anger problems (72.7% versus 27.3%). They concluded that sexually abusive girls do not appear to be as criminal or antisocial as non-sexual offending, delinquent girls. Compared to sexually abusive adolescent males, their female counterparts also engaged in less fighting and had less problems with peers. Mathews et al. (1997) described a subgroup of girls in their sample, approximately half of the girls, who were more conduct disordered and had engaged in delinquent behaviors, but there was no mention of physical aggression. In Fehrenbach and Monastersky's study, none of the girls had engaged in other bodily offenses such as assault. Relational and indirect aggression have not yet been examined in the histories of sexually abusive girls.

Dependency

It has been my experience that sexually abusive girls tend to be more dependent in their relationships, and are more often physically and/or emotionally abused in their intimate peer relationships than boys who abuse. Many girls stay in unhealthy relationships because from their perspective, it is better than being alone. They sacrifice their emotional well being for unhealthy and abusive relationships to mollify their internal states of emptiness and loneliness. Given that many sexually abusive girls have histories of abuse and poor boundaries, it is not surprising that they find themselves in re-victimizing relationships.

Academic problems

Learning problems are also noted in a few studies on sexually abusive girls. In one study, 83% of the girls experienced academic difficulties, yet only one had been classified as learning disabled (Bumby & Bumby, 1997). In their latter comparison study, Bumby and Bumby found that females were retained at least one grade in school at a significantly higher rate than males. Hunter et al. (1993) found that 40% of the girls had histories of learning disabilities. Moreover, Howley found that 60% of her sample of sexually abusive girls had below average IQs, and 50% of the girls received special education services (although this could have been for behavioral reasons).

Perpetrating age

Girls tend to sexually offend at young ages (Howley, 2001; Johnson, 1989; Ray & English, 1995). 50% of the girls in Ray & English's sample were 12 years old or younger when they offended, whereas 30% of the boys were. Fehrenbach and Monastersky (1988) also found that sexually abusive girls were younger (13.6 years) than sexually abusive males (14.8 years). Howley found that the average age of a girl's first offense was 10.65; 30% of the girls offended before the age of 10. Johnson's study consisted of pre-adolescent girls between the ages of 4-12. Finally, Kubik et al. (2002) found that sexually abusive girls offended at a significantly younger age (M = 11.18) when compared to non-sex offending delinquent adolescent females; for the delinquent females, the average age of their first non-sex victim offense was 14.45.

Victim selection

Also noted in the literature is the notion that girls tend to abuse family members (Johnson, 1989) or a child for whom they are in a caretaking position (Bumby & Bumby, 1997; Fehrenbach & Monastersky, 1988; Margolin, 1991; Mathews et al., 1997), therefore, they appear less likely than boys to abuse strangers. In Bumby and Bumby's study, 11 out of 12 of the sexually abusive girls offended while they were babysitting; none of the victims were strangers. The fact that females are more likely to offend on family members or children in their care is consistent with the literature on adult sex offending females (Faller, 1995; Mathews, Matthews, & Speltz, 1989; Saradjian, 1996; Syed & Williams, 1996). However, Hunter et al. (1993) found that 39.4% of the girls' victims were strangers (although 48.5% perpetrated against family members). A possible explanation for this finding is that these 10 girls in residential treatment comprise an unrepresentative sample and their behaviors are more severe than the average. Girls' cases are less likely than boys to result in residential treatment (Poe-Yamagata & Butts, 1996); when they do, the girls are generally more disturbed and their behaviors more severe than what is typically seen. Regarding gender selection, Kubik et al. (2002) and Mathews et al. (1997) found no differences among male and female sex offending adolescents: Like boys, girls are more likely to offend on the opposite sex.

Girls are more likely than boys to abuse children (Fehrenbach & Monastersky, 1988). This is consistent with my experience; boys are far more likely to engage in, and be adjudicated for, peer related offenses. There appears to be a double standard in this regard: In school settings, grabbing buttocks or other genital areas of the opposite sex is not so uncommon, yet boys are far more likely to be punished and held accountable for this. Although girls may engage in this behavior less often than boys, girls that do sexually touch or grab boys without consent should be held to the same level of accountability. I have only worked with one girl who was placed on probation for sexually touching a peer's genital area (over clothes) at school and the victim was a female. Yet I have worked with numerous male adolescents charged with a sexual offense for grabbing the buttocks or breasts of their female peers.

Use of force or violence

It is unclear to what extent girls use force or violence in their sexual offending behavior. Ray and English (1995) found that girls were less coercive and sophisticated in their sexual offending behavior than boys. In my experience, violent behavior is less common among sexually abusive girls than it is for sexually abusive boys. However, in Johnson's (1989) study, all of the girls used force or coercion to gain compliance of their victims: 23% of the girls used excessive physical coercion and other physical coercion was present in 15% of the cases (both forms of physical coercion involved restraining the victim). Furthermore, Hunter et al. (1993) found that 40% of the sexually abusive girls used force during at least one of their sex offenses. Finally, Kubik et al. (2002) found no differences between male and female sexually abusive adolescents in regards to their level of coercion.

Additionally, girls do not force others to sexually abuse with them as often as males, and it is rare for them to offend in concert with others. In the literature on adult sex offending, females coercing others to sexually abuse with them is the least common form of sexual abuse perpetrated by women (Saradjian, 1996), yet it is not uncommon to see males coercing their female partners to sexually offend. I have not yet worked on a case whereby a girl coerced another to offend with her. However, I have worked with boys that sexually offended females when part of a group: Group rape of a female is a behavior that primarily involves male instigation and participation. Although female gang members have been known to initiate and participate in a rape of another female gang member, this behavior is fairly rare (National Public Radio, 2003).

Offending behaviors

Male and female adolescents engage in similar offending behaviors. Kubik et al. (2002) found no differences among specific offense behaviors. Similarly, Mathews et al. (1997) found that sex offending female adolescents "engaged in offending behaviors comparable in frequency and magnitude to their male counterparts" (p. 192).

Cognitive distortions

Girls appear more likely to resort to caretaking and altruistic justifications for their offending behavior. This is understandable given the messages girls acquire in terms of needing to be caretakers, and the fact that many girls abuse while in caretaking positions. For example, one of my clients sexually abused her sister to "prepare" her for being sexually abused by their stepfather. My client had already been severely sexually abused by her stepfather and she believed he would soon begin offending on her sister. Although there were other reasons that contributed to my client's decision to sexually abuse her sister, this was her initial explanation. Another client explained her behavior by maintaining she was trying to "help" her sister overcome inappropriate masturbation. Her means of helping her sister was to have her sister lie on top of her and masturbate; this way, my client contended, she could explore with her sister why she was masturbating and "help the situation." Another girl recently asserted she touched her nephew's genitals and had him touch hers to clearly demarcate: "These are my private parts and those are your private parts and you don't let anyone touch them."

Perceptions of sexually abusive girls

Sexually abusive girls are viewed differently than their male counterparts in our society. On the one hand, they may be more harshly punished than boys since their behavior defies how girls are taught to behave; on the other hand, the criminal justice system treats them paternalistically, viewing them as victims needing protection or as girls who are mentally ill. Possibly as a result of the latter, girls are less likely than boys to enter the criminal justice system for sexual offending behavior. Howley (2001) found that only 21% of sexually abusive girls had been adjudicated in her sample. Ray & English (1995) found that only 2 girls (out of 34) compared to 93 boys (out of 237) were charged with sexual offending behavior. Ray & English concluded that when compared to boys, sexually abusive girls are more likely to be treated as victims: The girls in their sample were far more likely to have entered the Human Services system as possible or actual victims of child abuse and neglect, whereas the boys were significantly more likely to become involved with the system because of a concern for the safety of others. This apparent paternalistic response by the criminal justice system fails to hold girls accountable for sex offending behavior; it is a sexist response that helps no one, especially not the girls whose offending behavior is left unaddressed. I was recently informed about a case in which the judge ordered a girl, who was adjudicated for a sex offense, to attend therapy to address her victimization in lieu of offense-specific therapy. Although she was on probation for a sex offense, only her victimization history mattered. What message does this send to victims - their victimization does not matter?

Motivations

The motivations underlying juvenile female sex offending also appear, at times, to differ from their male counterparts. Noted in the literature on adult and adolescent sexually abusive females, females are more likely to offend for other reasons than sexual arousal and stimulation (Davin, 1999; Dunbar, 1999; Finkelhor & Russell, 1984; Howley, 2001; Johnson, 1989; Mathews et al., 1990; O'Connor, 1987; Saradjian, 1996; Turner & Turner, 1994; Wolfe, 1985). Johnson found that few, if any, of the preadolescent girls in her study were seeking sexual satisfaction, orgasm, or sexual pleasure. Howley also found that sex-offending behavior was far more about anger than sexual curiosity or stimulation.

Subsequently, girls' offending behavior often reflects relational aggression (Lamb, 2001; Leschied et al., 2000; Loeber & Stouthamer-Loeber, 1998; Simmons, 2002). Although relational aggression is not generally defined as physically or sexually abusive, my contention is that sexual abuse is a form of aggression that also is, by definition, relational; relational aggression better encompasses the motivation which often underlies sexual abuse. Salzman (1990) argues that when the attachment system is compromised in girls, their sexual system becomes a substitute venue to form attachments. This appears to play a distinct role in girls' sexual offending behavior, especially given the relational development of girls: sexual abuse becomes a means to reestablish a connection with someone or paradoxically, a means to disconnect from a relationship (Robinson, 2002). (A side note: I also believe much of male offending lies in relational dynamics and much of the treatment community has done a disservice to males by simply viewing their offending behavior in narrowly defined terms of deviant arousal, power, anger, and control. It may be that given their socialization, males are less inclined to describe their offending behavior in relational terms; conversely, since females are more relationally oriented, their language in describing their offending is more likely to denote relational motivations.)

Many girls I have worked with have described sex offending, in part, because they desperately wanted their mother's attention: Their mothers were frequently spending more time with their younger siblings and my clients were jealous of the attention their siblings received. Some girls were also angered by the attention their mothers' boyfriends received. Although they were also acting out of anger, there is a consistent theme of disconnected relationships with their mothers and a yearning to recover what was lost. For example, one client said "I wasn't getting enough attention…If I get these kids alone and I do something bad with them, then maybe my mom will pay more attention to me instead of her boyfriend." Other examples from clients depicting sexual abuse as a means of establishing a relationship include: "I felt lonely and angry…If I did this then I would be closer to them and less lonely," "I wanted a boyfriend but did not have one. I wanted somebody to talk to…I had no relationship," "I abused him so that I could feel that someone cared and loved me." Turner and Turner (1994) also described identification with the aggressor as having a distinct relational component: "It is from the relationship aspect of victimization that a female may commit abuse. That is, identifying with one's aggressor, taking on his or her characteristics, is a way of staying in the relationship" (1994, p. 16). Turner and Turner concluded that all the girls in their study were attempting to establish relationships: Perpetrating is "often motivated by the desire to establish or maintain an emotional relationship"(p. 41).

Conversely, some clients have described wanting to hurt their mothers for failing to protect them from sexual abuse. Abusing a younger sister, for example, becomes an effective vehicle to "get back" at a mother who did not protect her own daughter from being sexually abused by her sex-offending partner. Additionally, Turner and Turner (1994) found that "female offenders may have perpetrated in order to differentiate themselves from enmeshed, victim-identified mothers, and/or to act out rage at their mothers, who failed to protect them from other offenders" (p. 17). Howley (2001) found that girls predominantly offended due to anger, most often towards their main caretakers (approximately 60%). Johnson (1989) also bridged a girls' offending behavior to maternal-daughter relational dynamics. She describes that the mothers of the sexually abusive girls tended to be extremely dependent personalities; many of the mothers had been physically or sexually abused as children or adults, and adopted a victim stance in relating to the world. Role reversals were evident in the mother-daughter relationships whereby the mothers heavily depended on their daughters. Johnson hypothesized that the girls may have sexually abused due to a "reaction formation not only stemming from their own victimization but against the almost complete dependency and victim status which their mothers modeled for them" (p. 582).

Motivations for juvenile female sexual abuse are multifaceted. For those with severe abuse histories, sexual re-enactment can become rather compulsive in nature. Arousal to their sexual abuse victimization can serve as an impetus to sexually offend, and promote justifications for offending by believing their victims will enjoy the sexual contact. Furthermore, I believe that for some sexually abusive girls, there is a strong correlation between their sex-offending behavior and their female sexual development (just as male sexual aggression can stem from male sexual development and the messages they learn about their sexuality, i.e., entitlement, power, and initiative). When working with girls, viewing their behavior through the lens of female adolescent sexuality is imperative since it is the foundation of their sexual development and can be informative in helping us understand their sexual choices, including the decision to sexually abuse.

From this perspective, sexual offending for girls can be a resistance to a cultural script that teaches girls to be passive, inexperienced, naïve, and accommodating to boys. Likewise, it can be a rejection of cultural norms that teach girls to be silent and unaware of their own sexuality. Rather than being objects for the pleasure of males, they navigate their own avenues to learn about sex. One of my clients said her sexual offense was motivated by her desire to "learn more about sex in my own terms." Another client described her sex offending as a means to determine her sexual orientation; she thought she may be bisexual but did not want to experiment with female peers for fear of other peers finding out (which she believed would result in verbal jabs and ridicule). She was trying to protect herself from being labeled a lesbian. Girls who sexually offend do not have to worry about pleasing or accommodating their partner because they take from a victim instead. They do not have to worry about meeting their needs secondarily because their needs become primary. They do not have to worry about being labeled a "slut" or "whore" by their peers since they are not engaging in sexual behavior with peers. Finally, they do not have to worry about being victimized since they are the victimizers.

This victimizer dynamic is especially true for girls with significant abuse histories. Another one of my clients stated her reason to offend was to protect herself from sexual vulnerability. She said, "I will not be a victim or place myself in a position to be victimized." Her sexual aggression was a way of ensuring she would never again be abused by adopting a position of power.

Girls with other non-victim sexual behavior problems, e.g., promiscuity, may be motivated by power as well. Many girls learn to use their sexuality as a means to get what they want out of males, materially or in terms of attention. The danger in this is that subsequently many of them start defining themselves by their sexuality and external self, and consequently lose sight of their internal self. They can become masterful manipulators and learn to rely on others rather than their own internal resources. Promiscuity and unsafe sex also can be indicative of a significantly poor self-concept. The motivations underlying both can correspond to a lack of self-regard; such behavior further compromises one's self-worth and perpetuates a vicious cycle. Finally, as with sex-offending girls, girls with other sexual behavior problems may be acting out as a means to form attachments. Essentially, they are looking for love in the wrong places and relying on others to fill their feelings of inadequacy and/or loneliness. Some girls will specifically not use birth control in hopes they will become pregnant; they believe having a child will give them the unconditional love they believe they lack in their life and help them feel better about themselves. As long as female adolescent sexuality carries shame, harsh double standards, amnesic knowledge, and diminished agency (instead of healthy ownership and subjectivity), many girls will continue to find themselves in compromising situations involving poor sexual decision making. Sexual abuse and other sexual behavior problems can naturally evolve out of this dilemma because "[s]exual shame drives girls to do such things in closets and behind closed doors" (Lamb, 2001, p. 58).

In summary, there is still much we do not know in regards to juvenile female sexually abusive youth. The relationship between female juvenile sexual aggression and the use of violence and coercion remains unclear. Additionally, although some studies indicate that many sexually abusive girls have substance abuse histories, other studies find a lesser significance. It is also unclear to what extent the use of drugs or alcohol actually plays a role in girls' sex offending behavior. Whether sexually abusive girls tend to be more physically aggressive (in addition to sexually aggressive), or more generally passive, is an area requiring further examination. In my experience, only a small subgroup of the girls I have worked with have histories of acting physically aggressive towards others; rather, most of the girls are internalizers who have been passive and unable to set limits with others - this inability has resulted in repeat victimization experiences. This finding most likely reflects the outpatient population of girls with whom I work. Additionally, it remains unclear to what extent the desire for sexual arousal and stimulation motivates girls to sexually abuse. Although girls are viewed as less likely to offend for these reasons, how do we know this for sure? It may be that girls are less likely to disclose sexual arousal than boys due to a lack of awareness of their sexuality and arousal response, in addition to scripts that teach them to deny their sexuality. Clinician bias may also have a bearing on research results that view sexually abusive girls as less sexually driven than boys. The lack of physiological instruments to assess sexual deviancy in females makes the relationship between sexual abuse and deviant sexual arousal difficult to determine. What is needed are more studies that are consistent with the variables being examined (i.e., history of abuse, school functioning, family relationships, mental health problems), in addition to larger sample sizes. In the meantime, best practice involves being cognizant of the research to date, understanding its limitations, and listening with keen ears to the stories girls share.

Assessment issues and needs

The assessment process for a sexually abusive girl is guided by a thorough understanding of female development and the research conducted thus far on sexually abusive girls. (For a more extensive discussion of, and recommendations for, the assessment of sexually abusive girls, see Robinson, 2005). However, because of the lack of tools specific to this population, the assessment of juvenile sexually abusive youth has relied, and continues to rely, more on self-report (Hunter & Mathews, 1997). Overall, the assessment of girls involves paying close attention to their more subtle and covert behaviors, and internalization responses (i.e., self-mutilation, suicidal ideation, depression, eating disorders, hypercriticism, compulsive exercise), in addition to their more overt behavioral problems. First, because of the likelihood of prior victimization with these girls, assessing the type, extent, and severity of prior maltreatment, as well as the girls' relationships to their perpetrators, is essential. Second, a history of trauma lends itself to the development of mental health disturbances. Yet even those sexually abusive girls without abuse histories, will most likely evidence a mental health problem. As described earlier, delinquent girls often have comorbid diagnoses such as depression, PTSD, or anxiety disorders. Leschied et al. (2002) conclude, "More than for boys, when girls demonstrate violence, it appears important to assess for the presence of a possible underlying mental health disorder that may be coinciding with the higher violence potential" (p. 25). Tools that may be helpful in assessing mental health problems as well as responses to trauma include the Massachusetts Youth Screening Instrument (MAYSI-2; Grisso & Barnum, 2003), Trauma Symptom Checklist for Children (TSCC; Briere, 1996); and Reynolds Adolescent Depression Scale (RADS-2; Reynolds, 2002). Psychiatric consultation and medication management may also be important aspects of treatment for those girls faced with mental health disturbances.

A side note: it is important to be aware of the gender paradox that exists with certain mental health disturbances; that is, although boys are more often diagnosed with attention deficit and conduct disorder, girls with these diagnoses are considered to have more psychiatric disturbances than boys (Loeber & Keenen, 1994). Loeber & Keenen concluded that girls diagnosed with conduct disorder are at a higher risk for comorbid disorders including hyperactivity, anxiety, suicidality, and substance abuse. Further, Szatmari, Boyle, and Offord (1989) found that girls with attention deficit disorder were more likely than boys to develop conduct disorder: ADHD girls were 40 times more likely to develop conduct disorder than girls without ADHD; comparatively, ADHD boys were only 14.7 times more likely to develop conduct disorder than boys without ADHD. They concluded that the nature of ADHD in girls appears to be more indicative of a disruptive disorder, whereas in boys, it is more likely a part of a developmental disorder that may also correspond to a maturational delay. Moreover, Cohen (as cited in Loeber & Stouthamer-Loeber, 1998) found that conduct-disordered girls were more likely than boys to develop personality disorders. Another concern regarding conduct-disordered girls is their long-term prognosis. Zoccolillo and Rogers (1991), for example, found considerably poor outcomes among their sample of 55 adolescent girls with conduct disorder: some died violent deaths, the majority dropped out of school, many were pregnant before they reached their 17th birthday, many were rearrested, and several others sustained traumatic injuries.

Understanding this gender paradox, possible comorbid conditions, and long term outcomes related to girls are important given the possible implications for treatment. A treatment provider who is working with a girl with ADHD can hopefully provide therapy that will help interfere with the full development of conduct disorder by enhancing her protective factors, i.e., healthy support systems, pro-social activities, empathy, problem solving skills. Similarly, the treatment of conduct disorder would also encompass the additional focus on factors that protect against a personality disorder such as borderline personality disorder. Teaching the client self-soothing strategies, affect regulation, and cognitive techniques to counter all-or-nothing thinking would be appropriate (Linehan, 1993).

Clinicians also need to be cognizant of the gender differences in the presentation of attention deficit/hyperactivity disorder and conduct disorder. Females tend to demonstrate more inattention as opposed to the more overt behavioral problems manifested in boys (Biederman, Faraone, Mick, Williamson, Wilens, Spencer, Weber, Jetton, Kraus, Pert, & Zallen, 1999; Gaub & Carlson, 1997); consequently, an ADHD diagnosis is often overlooked in girls. Similarly, since girls with conduct disorder display less confrontational behaviors than their male counterparts (American Psychiatric Association, 2000), this disorder can also be easily overlooked. Zoccolillo

(1993) and Zoccolillo and Rogers (1991) also argue that the criteria for conduct disorder is not appropriate for girls and that sex-specific criteria should be developed. Lying, prostitution or promiscuous behavior, school problems, substance abuse, running away, truancy, and relational and indirect aggression are behaviors more prevalent among girls that support this diagnosis. Therefore, treatment providers need to ask about and pay closer attention to the types of symptoms and behaviors that indicate these disorders in girls, therefore, these diagnoses will less likely be overlooked and more likely appropriately addressed throughout the course of treatment.

Third, relational aggression is often neglected because of its subtle and covert nature; however, it requires attention because of the high presence among girls, the psychological damage inflicted on its victims, in addition to the fact it counters healthy relational development, a treatment goal for every sexual abusive girl. Henington, Hughes, Cavell, and Thompson (1998) found that relational aggression contributed to the prediction of overt aggression in girls (a small but statistically significant finding). Further, Leschied et al. (2000) conclude that assessing "aggression exclusive of this gender variant [relational aggression] is to overlook an important contribution in understanding how girls express aggression" (p. 57). The Relational and Direct Aggression Scale (RDAS; Cummings, Leschied, & Heilbron, 2002) is a tool to assist in this area.

Fourth, girls' relational development, in conjunction with their evolving identities and attachment styles, also require careful assessment since treatment involves helping each girl attain a normal adolescent track of female development. Many sexually abusive girls have injured attachments and have lacked healthy female role models to develop healthy identities. Relational instability, inchoate and disorganized identities, a loss of agency, a loss of voice, chameleon and disingenuous presentations, repeat victimizations, and low self-esteem are prevalent displays among these youth. Questions must be asked to determine the functioning of a girl's current peer and intimate relationships, the presence of healthy and supportive relationships and role models, the degree of dependency or tolerance of abuse, her view of herself, her ability to trust others, and the kind of boundaries she has (non-existent, walled, or healthy). The Relationship Questionnaire (Bartholomew & Horowitz, 1991) can be used to assess a girl's attachment style and the Piers-Harris Children's Self-Concept Scale (PHCSCS-2; Piers & Herzberg, 2002) can help understand a girl's attitudes about her behavior and attributes. Furthermore, due to the problematic dynamics often present between sexually abusive girls and their mothers, the role that these relational disturbances may play in a girl's sex offending behavior, and the importance this relationship holds in the healing process of a girl in treatment, the mother-daughter relationship (or caregiver-daughter relationship) warrants thorough assessment.

Fifth, requiring careful assessment is the overall sexual functioning of sexually abusive girls. Areas to focus on include a girl's degree of sexual desire, sexual experience (promiscuity or inexperience), trauma bond pairing sexual victimization and arousal, sexual ownership versus sexual passivity, placement in unsafe sexual situations and sexual re-victimization, an identity defined by sexuality and desirability, sexual shame and inadequacy, sexual knowledge, reproductive health, and healthy body image. The PHASE Sexual Attitudes Questionnaire (O'Brien, 1994), Multiphasic Sex Inventory II JF (MSI II JF; Nichols & Molinder, 1995), and Personal Sentence

Completion Inventory (Miccio-Fonseca, 1997), are tools available that assess sexual knowledge, development, beliefs, and a girl's sexual characteristics.

Finally, a girl's sex offending behavior warrants careful assessment but because of limitations noted in the assessment tools described below, there is more of a reliance on police reports and self-report. Because girls often offend against children to whom they are in a caretaking position, by paying attention to their victim selection and the relationship they have with the victim, important clues can be gleaned to determine their motivations to offend (i.e., jealousy of siblings, seeking a mother's attention, blocked opportunities for sexual exploration, anger, revenge). Further, sex offending should be viewed from multiple perspectives pertinent to girls to better understand each girl's underlying motivations; these perspectives involve examining cultural scripts, dependency issues, offending behavior as a form of relational aggression, sex as a means of attachment (sex = love), and trauma re-enactment. Cognitive distortions are less about a victim "asking for it" (as is commonly heard among boys) and are more likely to reflect caregiving justifications; the types of distortions a girl engages in provide information about needed treatment focus. Additionally, determining a girl's pathway to offending behavior (e.g., depression, victimization, early maturation) and her level of empathy lead to specific treatment needs. Finally, determining a girl's typology carries treatment implications. Although the development of female adolescent typologies is still in its infancy, there are a few categories appearing to have merit (see Mathews et al., 1997; Mathews, Matthews, & Speltz, 1990). For example, if she appears predisposed to offending because of a high level of psychopathology and significant trauma history, treatment will most likely be longer and require more focus on victimization issues than for a girl who sexually abused a young child on one occasion due to a desire to experiment sexually. These latter girls tend to be naïve but exhibit personality strengths and overall, have low levels of psychopathology. A minority of girls may fit into a peer-influenced category (Robinson, 2005); those that do may require more treatment focus on asserting themselves and self-efficacy.

The Use of Other Offense-Specific Assessment Tools and Their Applicability to Female Juveniles

Abel Screen

As of this writing, there is no information on the reliability or validity of the AASI with female adolescents (D. Jones, personal communication, November 3, 2003). Therefore, its use with female adolescents appears questionable. Furthermore, the validity of the instrument is even more in question with its use on girls when considering that the AASI is based on visual reaction time. Females are not as sexually responsive to visual stimuli as males: For males, sexual arousal is intricately connected with a visual response and this visual inclination may be related to testosterone levels (Blum, 1997). Due to biological and socialization factors, female sexual response is based less to a sexual act itself and more to the context and quality of a relationship, or the imagination of a sexual relationship (Hales, 1999; Ellis & Symons, 1990). These gender differences explain the proliferation of pornography, which largely lies in the domain of males, as opposed to romance novels being primarily the domain of females.

Photoplethysomography

Many sexually abusive male adolescents, primarily older ones, undergo a plethys-mograph to determine if they have any deviant sexual arousal needing to be addressed in treatment. The female equivalent to this is photoplethysomography; this physiological instrument measures genital blood flow in females. Given this tool is rarely utilized, it is considered experimental; consequently, this instrument should not be conducted on female adolescents (National Task Force on Juvenile Sexual Offending, 1993). Also worthy of consideration is the fact there is research suggesting genital arousal in females is not congruent with subjective sexual excitement (Laan, Everaerd, van Bellen, & Hanewald, 1994), therefore, measuring genital arousal in females may not be a valid measure of their sexual desires and interests. Hales (1999) hypothesizes that vaginal lubrication and blood flow increase as a result of either neg-ative or positive stimuli, and this may be an evolutionary biological reaction to pro-tect women during coerced or rough sex. More research is needed on female sexual response to support the use of photoplethysmography with sexually abusive female adolescents. Of course genital arousal does not necessarily equate to sexual interests for males either: Males can also experience sexual arousal to negative stimuli, e.g., when being sexually assaulted, simply because their bodies respond to the stimula-tion, not because of deviant sexual interests or arousal (Sarrel & Masters, 1982).

Polygraph

Polygraphs are often used for assessment and monitoring purposes in offense-specif-ic treatment (Colorado Sex Offender Management Board, 2002; Cross & Saxe, 2001). In my experience, the polygraph is a helpful tool, yet there are a few caveats in its use with girls. Most importantly, with some girls with extensive sexual abuse histories, the polygraph can generate a significant trauma response because of dynamics dur-ing the polygraph examination that may mirror prior abusive experiences. For exam-ple, the polygraph devices are physically constrictive; those being examined are not supposed to move because it interferes with the measured responses; there is a clear power differential between the examiner and the examinee; and, the examiners are often male and can be intimidating and act with authority, just as a girl's perpetrator may have been with her. All these things can produce a trauma response, especially one that is freezing. Therefore, the emotional cost of conducting a polygraph with some girls with trauma histories can outweigh the potential benefits and probably should not be recommended.

Furthermore, I have had some experiences where girls had actual emotional melt-downs in my office because they did poorly on a polygraph (i.e., a maintenance) but insisted they were honest. Their emotional hypersensitivity and significant personal-ization (two characteristics of adolescent female development), often from polygra-phers' confrontation and remarks, left them feeling traumatized by their polygraph experience and they demonstrated considerable fears about taking another one, almost phobic. Although their meltdown could be a form of manipulation, it is also true that for those girls who are being genuine, the emotional harm of redoing a poly-graph may surpass any benefits and therefore, be contraindicated. Because of their heightened anxiety and trauma reactions, their negative expectations about doing poorly may become a self-fulfilling prophecy. When these concerns are not present (or they are but due to a girl's risky behaviors the polygraph is still warranted), the polygraph should be used. Like boys, girls often do not easily disclose the extent of their offending behavior and the polygraph is one tool that aids the disclosure and accountability process for adolescents. My argument regarding the polygraph is not to excuse girls from the standards applied to boys; rather, it is to be sensitive to the possible problems associated with polygraph use and to assess its use on a case-by-case basis (as should be done for boys).

Risk assessments

To date, there are no risk assessments specific to sexually abusive juvenile females. The current risk assessments, the ERASOR (Worling & Curwen, 2001) and the J-SOAP-II (Prentky & Righthand, 2003) were derived from studies consisting of all males (Hagan & Cho, 1996; Sipe, Jensen, & Everett, 1998) or only relatively few females (Kahn & Chambers, 1991; Lab, Shields, & Schondel, 1993; Rasmussen, 1999; Worling & Curwen, 2000). As a result, the application of these risk assessments to the juvenile female population can be problematic. The highly utilized J-SOAP-II, for example, is a tool only designed for sexually abusive boys from age 12 to 18. We should not assume that males and females have the same risk factors, nor should we presume that these risk factors equally apply to both sexes: Female risk factors should not be subsumed under those identified for males for these reasons. Although Simourd and Andrews (as cited in Leschied et al., 2000) concluded that risk factors associated with male delinquency are also important for female delinquency, Funk (1999) found that female risk factors differ from those of males, and that a risk assessment specific to females predicts female recidivism more than twice as well as one designed for both sexes. Similarly, Bonta, Pang, & Wallace-Capretta (1995), in examining the applicability of a risk assessment designed for adult males to adult females, found that it had poor generalizability and there were distinct differences in risk factors. Although Funk's study did not focus specifically on a risk assessment for sexually abusive girls (it was for female delinquency in general), her argument that "the current state of risk assessment research treats the female group unfairly by failing to identify their specific risks for reoffending" (p. 62), is apropos to the field of sexual abuse. The different pathways to delinquency in males and females, and the differences in socialization and gender role expectations, suggest that risk factors will be different (Cunningham, 2002; Funk; Pate, n.d.).

Funk (1999) found that juvenile females, more than their male counterparts, "had family-related problems, including a poor relationship with parents, running away from home, victimization by child abuse or neglect, and parents who were involved in crime" (p. 56-57). Having a person-related offense (rather than total prior offenses) and a history of running away increased the likelihood of reoffending in girls, but not so with male juveniles. Additionally, an abuse history had a much stronger correlation to reoffending for girls than boys (r = 0.41 compared to .03).

Furthermore, in one study examining female recidivism among an incarcerated adult female sample, a history of self-injury, e.g., suicide attempts, was the strongest predictor of violent recidivism (referred to in Cunningham, 2002, and Blanchette & Motiuk, 1997). Bonta, Pang, & Wallace-Capretta (1995) also found a correlation between a history of self-injury and adult female recidivism. Furthermore, as described earlier, there appears to be a link between girls' self-harm and harm to others (Juon & Ensminger, 1997); research is necessary to determine whether or not a history of self-harm may apply to female juvenile recidivism as well.

Risk factors from the sex offending literature that do not appear as applicable to female sexually abusive youth include: a history of conduct disorder, juvenile antisocial behavior, evidence of sexual preoccupation or hypersexuality, a history of school behavior problems, multiple types of offenses, and pervasive anger. These risk factors do not have as much applicability since girls are less likely than boys to engage in overt behavioral displays, and girls are less likely to have paraphilias or use pornography (the latter are indicative of sexual drive and preoccupation in boys). As described earlier, female sex offending appears to be less about deviant sexual interests, arousal, or preoccupation (Davin, 1999; Dunbar, 1999; Finkelhor & Russell, 1984; Howley, 2001; Johnson, 1989; Mathews et al., 1990; O'Connor, 1987; Saradijian, 1996; Turner & Turner, 1994; Wolfe, 1985). Of course, if these factors are present in girls, they most certainly could contribute to increasing their sex offending risk, however, the point is, these risk factors do not capture girls' behavioral patterns or predispositions as much as boys, therefore, many girls not exhibiting these factors may be at a high risk to reoffend due to other factors not yet identified. Additionally, another risk factor for sexual recidivism is having a same sex victim, yet there is no evidence that a girl who chooses a female victim would be at an increased risk to reoffend.

General risk factors from the literature on female delinquency and the development of antisocial behavior in young girls include: a history of physical and/or sexual abuse (Acoca & Dedel, 1998; Funk, 1999); the use of relational aggression (Cummings, Leschied, & Heilbron, 2002; Henington et al., 1998); early maturation (Caspi et al., 1993; Stattin & Magnussin, 1990); depression (Leschied et al., 2000; Obeidallah & Earls, 1999); posttraumatic stress disorder (Cauffman et al., 1998); hyperactivity/impulsivity/attention deficits (see Levene et al., 2001); a lack of stable and supportive female role models (Mathews et al., 1997); caretaker-daughter relational disturbances (see Levene et al., 2001); and self-harm (see Blanchette & Motiuk, 1997; Bonta, Pang, & Wallace-Capretta, 1995; Juon & Ensminger, 1997). Naturally, these risk factors do not necessarily correspond to sex offending risk, however, they provide a starting point for the consideration of risk factors needing to be explored in sexually abusive girls - ones that may eventually be found to correlate to sexual recidivism.

Risk factors for boys that appear to correspond to females include caregiver inconsistency (a factor noted on the J-SOAP-II) and high-stress family environment (a factor on the ERASOR). These are applicable given the high levels of family dysfunction and poor environmental supports present in the lives of sexually abusive girls (Bumby & Bumby, 1997; Mathews, Hunter, & Vuz, 1997). Further, a risk factor noted on the ERASOR includes a lack of intimate peer relationships/social isolation. The importance of relational development to girls suggests that compromised functioning in this area would raise a girl's risk to engage in disturbing behavior. Because the risk factors of sexually abusive girls need to be further investigated, when determining risk specific to this population, it is best practice to consider the literature pertaining to adolescent sex offending risk (keeping in mind the gender limitations), as well as risk factors corresponding to general female delinquency. (See the appendix for a proposed risk assessment specific for sexually abusive girls.)

Concluding, assessment remains a difficult terrain with sexually abusive girls because of the reliance on self-report, the overall limitations with the tools available to determine a girl's sexual interest or arousal, the lack of gender-specific risk assessments, and the limited number of other assessment instruments designed for girls. These issues necessitate the development of specific measures for sexually abusive girls.

A Few Treatment Issues and Needs

On treatment approaches

The treatment of sexually abusive girls needs to be based on a model promoting healthy female identity formation, relational development, sexual efficacy, and for those with abuse histories, healing reparation. Previously I proposed an offense-relational model which encompasses multiple facets of a girl's life to improve her overall functioning and is based on female development and the issues relevant to girls (Robinson, 1999; 2002). This integrated approach is one way to conceptualize treatment to effectuate change. The model includes connections to the following domains: self, relational, social, sexual, healing, academic, and spiritual. All the above domains are addressed throughout treatment depending on the individual needs of each girl. Female juvenile sexual offending behavior is then examined and discussed in the context of all of the aforementioned areas.

Second, in addition to a gender-specific model based on the needs and issues of girls, also worthy of consideration are the learning styles of girls. Gurian (2001) wrote an entire book on the different learning styles of boys and girls, and asserts that these differences are based on chemical, hormonal, and structural differences of the brain. Of course there are many exceptions to these differences, however, it is important to be aware of these tendencies so therapists can provide treatment that is responsive to these dissimilarities. As he discusses, the frontal lobe and Broca's area are more active in females than in males, leading to better verbal communication. Likewise, the cerebellum has stronger connecting pathways in females leading to better language and intuition skills. Oxytocin, a hormone more present in females, is a bonding hormone that contributes to quick empathic responses. Both Gurian and Baron-Cohen (2003) discuss the predisposition of girls to be better able to emotionally process information and empathize than boys. Further, Belenky, Clinchy, Goldberger, and Tarule (1986) and Goldberger, Tarule, Clinchy, and Belenky (1996) have identified styles of female knowing; one of those styles, "connected knowing," an epistemological orientation towards relationship, utilizes empathy as a means of learning. Aligned with a verbal-empathic style of learning, is the process orientation so notorious among girls, as opposed to the task orientation often seen among males. Girls' process-orientation is not only an avenue from which they learn, but also decreases stress. Encouraging emotional expressivity is essential given that this is a protective factor; by helping girls learn to be emotionally expressive, the emotional constraint and inhibition seen in many of them can be reduced. Additionally, girls learn well through collaboration and cooperation. They tend to be more egalitarian, and less hierarchical and competitive in their learning than boys (Gurian, 2001); therefore, they are often receptive to exercises that involve working together to learn an aspect of treatment, e.g., the impact of abuse. The manner in which girls learn, then, is often in listening and responding to others share their feelings and thoughts, in addition to their own verbal expression. Girls learn and respond well to "tending and befriending" and by honoring their styles of learning, girls can build their empathy and in time, relational resilience (Jordan, 2004).

Third, treatment is relational; that is, the healing of a client most often comes from the relationship she has with her therapist. It is within the context of the relationship that emotional reparations are often made. The significance of the therapy relationship, especially for girls with abuse histories, should not be underestimated. Gil (1996) summarizes this well by stating: "The presence of a significant other who provides consistency of empathic care and continuity of attention is one of the most important variables in mitigating the negative effects of childhood abuse" (p. 19). At times, my role is to respond as a mother, other times a sister, or a caring and responsive friend. The girls project these roles on to the therapist due to their relational orientation and the dynamics associated with transference. However, this does not suggest, in any way, that the boundaries of the therapeutic relationship should be blurred or compromised. The therapeutic relationship with girls can be a double-edged sword: on the one hand, there is danger in bending the boundaries too much - that can lead to over dependency on, and manipulation of, the therapist - on the other hand, it is true that girls frequently want information about their therapists' lives because it is through this sharing that relationships are built. If the therapist is too secretive, the girl may not be willing to share. As one client once said to me, "You expect me to share everything in my life with you. Why would I do that when you don't tell me anything?" If there is no mutuality in the relationship, then there is not much of a relationship to provide a foundation that would incline a girl to want to share. A balancing act occurs here as well, whereby the therapist discloses enough to build a relationship, but withholds enough to keep the confines of the therapeutic relationship intact. Simply put, most of the time, girls demand that their therapists have a relationship with them: They will work no other way.

Fourth, just as many girls fare better in a same sex school environment (see Phillips, 1998), it is best practice to provide same sex offense-specific groups. Girls need a girls' group environment for multiple reasons. First and foremost is safety. Girls need opportunities to talk and process their feelings and experiences (OJJDP, 1998). However, the therapy environment must be safe in order for them to do so and it is incumbent upon the therapist to ensure such a group environment exists. Because many sexually abusive girls have been victimized themselves, and often by males, placing adolescent males - also in treatment for sexual offending issues and not yet healed themselves - in a group setting with females, may serve as an unwelcome triggering mechanism for re-experiencing trauma. This would be especially true for those girls who have not yet focused on their victimization issues and may have a diagnosis of PTSD. Some girls may endorse silence because of a perceived lack of safety, which will impede therapy. They may not feel safe enough to allow themselves to be vulnerable in sharing their intimate feelings and thoughts; therefore, they may not reveal their authentic self. Further, problematic dynamics could easily develop whereby some of the girls compete with one another in effort to acquire male attention by attempting to impress them or act seductively. Teenage male presence can become a significant impetus for distraction and invitation for drama. Many female clients are dramatic enough given some borderline and histrionic traits. It is simply too easy for girls to get off task and become disingenuous when males are present. Girls are already buffeted by a myriad of social, cultural, and hormonal forces during their adolescent development, why further complicate this by throwing adolescent males into the therapy pot, especially on such a sensitive issue as sex offending?

With this said, it may seem like a contradiction to then assert that best group practice would include a male-female co-facilitating team. The difference from having teenage males present is simple: A healthy male adult can serve as a base for a girl to work through her anger, rage, and mistrust towards males (if such feelings exist). A male co-facilitator can also serve as a base to help a previously abused girl recognize seductive or sexualized styles of relating to men, and with gentle confrontation, help her change this sexualized response. The transference issues are appropriately worked through to help the girl achieve resolution of prior traumas. Moreover, having an adult male in a position of trust who can be a role model, will help counter a script often adopted by abused girls and women - that all men are abusers. It helps the girls know that healthy men exist and they can find them for future relationships, rather than resorting to the unhealthy abusive relationships that many of them witnessed from their mothers.

An all girl offense-specific group is also a better conduit to address female-specific issues (e.g., female sexuality and arousal, teenage pregnancy, relational development, female pathways to abusive behavior, relational aggression, body image). Given the male/female differences in sociocultural processes, learning styles, issues, and pathways, it seems misguided to blend males and females into one group and not sufficiently justified. Without the stimulus of having male group members, it is more likely that girls will get to the heart of the matter, and discuss the issues that matter most to them. Case in point: recently one of the girls in my group discussed her poor body image (namely feeling fat), and how she fears it will curtail any male attraction towards her. She also discussed how her body image related to her offending: Since she thought no male peer would ever be interested in her due to her weight, she decided to experiment sexually with children she was babysitting. Knowing this client, I am confident she would not have been honest about her issues of weight with male peers present. A caveat in group work with girls: even without the presence of boys, girls can use their process-orientation to avoid, divert, and distract from their offense-specific issues. A balance must be struck between affording them opportunities to bond and share, as well as ensuring they are staying on task and addressing their offending behavior and the underlying issues requiring attention. Yet in sum, the benefits of group therapy for girls far outweigh any negatives. Because many sexually abusive girls have empathy and relational deficits, it is through their shared expressions, emotional resonance, and intimate interactions in a safe group environment that the trust and empathy, which were once impaired, start rebuilding. Additionally, being in a group with other girls who have sexually abused, helps them overcome their feelings of shame and isolation, which often stem from their all-or-nothing thinking that they are the only female on the planet that sexually abused. Group therapy then, becomes an emotionally reparative experience.

Finally, as illustrated at the beginning of this chapter, confrontational approaches have less merit when working with girls. This has been found in the area of female substance abuse (NCASA, 2003; Nelson-Zlupko, Kauffman, & Dore, 1995) and is true for sexual abuse. Strong confrontation can feel victimizing to those girls with abuse histories. It can also irretrievably damage the therapist/client relationship due to characteristics of adolescent female development. Although the use of strong confrontation has been consistently used in sex offender treatment, it appears boys are better able to tolerate and respond to it (however, harsh confrontation, which can easily become overly punitive and abusive, should not be used for either sex). Confrontation is important - it is how therapists help their clients work through their denial and cognitive distortions, and increase accountability - but it must always be done with respect and sensitivity, and stem from a strong relationship with the client. It needs to be compassionately responsive, instead of punitively alienating.

On focal points of treatment

One of the primary needs for sexually abusive girls is the concomitant need to address their victimization and perpetration issues. Generally in the sexual abuse field, there has been a tendency to subscribe to the belief that perpetrating behavior has to be addressed prior to any focus on a client's victimization issues. This attitude still prevails today, yet this separation between victimization and perpetration treatment is unfortunate, especially given the strong relationship between victimization and perpetration for many clients. In her work with adult sex-offending females, Saradjian (1996) found that it is by focusing on the victimization issues of a perpetrator that an empathy-bridge is built: "The most effective therapy has been done walking the tightrope of the victim/perpetrator divide" (p. 221). In other words, if a girl who has been abused can allow herself to experience the feelings she had as a result of being abused, and connect her abuse with behavioral choices she has made, she will be better able to identify and empathize with the emotional and behavioral affects that her sexual offense had on her victim(s). The importance of addressing underlying victimization issues cannot be underestimated. In my experience, it is imperative and if left unaddressed, will heighten a girl's risk to reoffend. In this regard, processing and reframing emotional and cognitive aspects of "malignant memories" (Schwartz & Perry, 1994) can become a large focal point of treatment.

Other areas requiring extensive focus for sexually abusive girls include loss and female role modeling. Many of these girls have experienced multiple losses, often with primary caregivers who were unable to provide continuity of stability, support, and healthy role modeling. Prescott (1998) describes the multiple losses that many girls involved with the criminal justice system have endured: loss of self-esteem, loss of a childhood, loss of control over their bodies, loss of consistent and stable caretakers, loss of trust. Operating from a relational stance means that treatment considers the relational injuries (jealousy, betrayal, abandonment, rejection) that may have contributed to a girl's motivations to sexually offend: Often involving loss, these injuries are then grieved to aid in a girl's healing process; additionally, the grieving process can help them emotionally relinquish an unhealthy former self and envision the development of a healthier future self. Some mothers of these girls, for example, have lost their parental rights, and their daughters need to begin relying on others to provide a constructive template for their female development. Girls require female role models to assist in the substitution for these losses. (Of course they can also benefit from male role models, but same sex role modeling provides more assistance to their female development.) Additionally, female role models can serve to counter the negative depictions of females, e.g., as sex objects, prevalent in the general media.

Treatment is obviously dictated by the findings from the assessment process. Yet some treatment goals appear to be consistent threads in the lives of sexually abusive girls. Many of these girls need to develop their identity formation and improve their self-esteem. They need to develop healthy relational patterns, boundaries, social skills, and support systems. The disengagement from others that often results from trauma and its aftermath lack of trust, needs to be altered so risks are taken to enter healthy relationships and relational resilience is developed. Many of them need to develop self-care strategies which include taking care of their hygiene, developing self-soothing strategies, setting limits with others, and balancing their individual needs with the needs of their relationships. Most of them require information regarding female sexuality and the female body to develop a healthy sexual self and positive body image. Further, girls should examine and challenge the sociocultural context that can adversely affect them by perpetuating unrealistic standards of beauty, dictating how females "should" be, devaluing females, and sexualizing adolescent girls. Self-destructive behaviors, such as self-mutilation, substance abuse, and unsafe sex, should be decreased as much as possible, if not eliminated, and comorbid diagnoses have to be addressed. Ultimately, the goal of therapy is to prevent future victims by improving the overall functioning of each girl in therapy. In so doing, we help them become healthy and whole human beings, and teach them the skills necessary that will make their journey through life a bit easier. Working with girls is exhausting yet at the same time illuminating and energizing: It is often filled with drama and passion; trauma and pain; joyfulness and growth. It is multifaceted and challenging, and the work of therapy includes accompanying them, by being fully present in every moment that is shared with them, through their healing process.

Conclusion

My hope in writing this chapter has been to provide a basis of information that can assist treatment providers in fine-tuning their work with sexually abusive girls, as well as further an understanding that girls require treatment that revolves around their specific developmental paths and issues. In the area of substance abuse, and after considerable research, female pathways, risk factors, reasons for, and affects of substance abuse have found to be distinctly different when compared to boys (NCASA, 2003). It stands to reason, then, that in time we will also be clearer about the unique pathways, risk factors, motivations behind, and manifestations of juvenile female sexual abuse. One way this will be done is through an open-mindedness and willingness to bear witness to the stories these girls share. Best practice involves incorporating into clinical practice a thorough understanding of girls: their development, their strengths and vulnerabilities, the impact trauma has had on their lives, the sociocultural scripts that overtly and subtly influence them, and their behavioral patterns. Of course there are significant variabilities within all these areas, but there are tendencies and predispositions just the same. Juvenile female sex offending behavior needs to be viewed through a lens of being female, rather than viewing it from an androcentric position as simply differing from males. Such a male-based approach can dismiss and/or overlook particular aspects of female sex offending behavior and fail to integrate these distinctions into practice.

Appendix

Juvenile Female Risk Assessment for Sexual Abuse

This risk assessment is not empirically validated. It is based on clinical experience and the literature on female delinquency and sexual abuse. It is offered as a starting point in the development of a gender-specific risk assessment for girls by describing factors worthy of further examination.

Historical/Static Variables

1) Sexual trauma history
None	0
Single or few instances with 1 perpetrator	1
Multiple perpetrators and/or chronic abuse by one perpetrator	2

Rationale: Based on studies conducted thus far, sexual trauma is prominent among sexually abusive girls (Bumby & Bumby, 1997; Fehrenbach & Monastersky; Howley, 2001; Hunter et al., 1993; Johnson, 1989; Kubik et al., 2002; Mathews et al., 1997; Miccio-Fonseca, 2000; Ray & English, 1995; Turner & Turner). For many girls, the association between their victimization histories and sexual perpetration is significant and it can be argued that the more role modeling that has been provided in this regard, the more likely a girl's risk could be raised for further reenactment. Two studies, one by Sepsi and another by Shields (cited in Bonta, Pang, & Wallace-Capretta, 1995), found an association between sexual abuse and recidivism among female juvenile offenders. Therefore, a history of sexual abuse may serve a criminogenic need for females that also corresponds to recidivism.

2) Physical trauma and/or history of other maltreatment (neglect, emotional abuse)
None	0
Some evidence	1
Chronic and/or severe	2

Rationale: Studies on sexually abusive girls have found high levels of physical abuse, emotional abuse, and neglect in their histories (Bumby & Bumby, 1997; Howley, 2001; Mathews et al., 1997; Ray & English, 1995). Like sexual abuse, other forms of maltreatment appear to play a distinct role in the development of delinquent behaviors for girls, as is noted in the literature on female delinquency (Acoca & Dedel, 1998; Leschied et al., 2000). Funk (1999) found that an abuse history had a much stronger correlation to reoffending for girls than boys (although she did not specify the type of abuse). Just as the negative sequelae to trauma influence the development of a negative trajectory and abusive behavior, it can also play a role in future delinquent behaviors.

3) History of witnessed family violence or criminal behavior among family members
None	0
Some evidence	1
High evidence	2

Rationale: Some studies have found that delinquent girls have more disturbed home environments than boys (Wattenberg & Saunders and Cowie, Cowie, & Slater, as cited in Cloninger et al., 1978). Day, Franklin, & Marshall (1998) found a history of family violence was correlated to girls' aggressive behavior. Further, Cloninger et al. (1978) concluded that criminal behavior among family members and extended family members carries a greater influence in the development of antisocial values in females than males. Funk (1999) found higher levels of family problems among female delinquents than male (males had more delinquent peer associations). The result of negative family role modeling on a girl's development may influence antisocial attitudes that perpetuate further delinquent behaviors, including sexual.

4) Early maturation

Not applicable	0
Somewhat early	1
Very early	2

Rationale: Studies indicate that there is a relationship between early maturation and female delinquency (Caspi et al., 1993; Stattin & Magnusson, 1990). The EARL-21G (Levene et al., 2001) notes sexual development as a risk factor for future antisocial behavior for young girls, and this factor may be applicable to adolescent females as well. Levene et al. describe sexual development as one of two "key variables that appear to contribute to the antisocial trajectory of young girls" (p.xiii). Not surprisingly, many sexually abusive girls have histories of early maturation. Although the role early maturation may play in recidivism is not yet determined, it appears to be an area worthy of examination.

5) History of person-related offenses

One offense	0
A few offenses	1
Offenses on multiple victims	2

Rationale: Funk (1999) found that a history of person-related offenses increased the risk of reoffending for female delinquents, whereas the total number of prior offenses was determined to be a risk factor for boys. Since sexual abuse is a person-related offense, this history may increase a girl's risk of reoffending. Given that girls are socialized towards non-aggressive behaviors, girls that engage in assaultive behavior towards others may be more predisposed than males (Cloninger, 1978; Mathews et al., 1997); this predisposition could correspond with increased risk.

6) History of running away

No history	0
One or two instances	1
Several instances	2

Rationale: Funk (1999) found that a history of running away was associated with recidivism for female delinquent youths, but not so for male delinquents. Further, a history of running away is a common thread among female delinquents (Acoca & Dedel, 1998) and is associated with the development of delinquent behaviors.

7) History of self-harm, e.g., suicide attempts
    No history   0
    One or two instances   1
    Several instances   2

Rationale: Juon and Ensminger (1997) found an association between high assault behavior in adolescence and reported suicide attempts among females (there was no such association found for males). Further, for females there appears to be a link between self-harm and recidivism: Two studies on incarcerated adult females (Bonta, Pang, & Wallace-Capretta, 1995; Blanchette & Motiuk, as cited in Blanchette & Motiuk, 1997) found an association between a history of self-injury and recidivism. Although the results on incarcerated adult females cannot be generalized to female adolescence, given the high amount of suicidal ideation and attempts in the histories of sexually abusive girls (Bumby & Bumby, 1997; Hunter et al., 1993; Miccio-Fonseca, 2000), this is an area that may also apply to female adolescent recidivism.

8) History of inconsistent caregivers
    No history   0
    One or two instances before age 10   1
    Significant inconsistency/numerous foster care   2
    placements/or loss of parental rights

Rationale: Rutter & Wolkind (as cited in Cloninger et al., 1978) found that early removal from the family and residential care was pathogenic for girls (large sibling size and a lack of contact with a father were viewed as causal factors to antisocial behavior in boys). The involvement of multiple caregivers, and the losses associated with changing caregivers, can interfere with a child's attachment process and reduce their willingness to trust others. Caregiver consistency is a factor noted on the J-SOAP-II (Prentky & Righthand, 2003) and given the importance of female relational development and the negative sequelae associated with a compromised relational development, a history of inconsistent caregiving is particularly relevant to an assessment for girls.

Stable and Dynamic Factors

Sexual factors:

9) Evidence of sexual preoccupation
    No evidence   0
    Some evidence   1
    Significant evidence   2

Rationale: For males, sexual preoccupation is a noted risk factor for recidivism and is often associated with pornography use and the development of sexual paraphilias (Prentky & Righthand, 2003; Worling & Curwen, 2001). Yet paraphilias are less common among females (American Psychiatric Association, 2000), as is the use of pornography (Marshall & Eclles, 1993) and masturbation to deviant sexual fantasy (Saradjian, 1996). Deviant sexual interests, arousal, and preoccupation appear to be less associated with female sex offending (Davin, 1999; Dunbar, 1999; Finkelhor &

Russell, 1984; Howley, 2001; Johnson, 1989; Mathews et al., 1990; O'Connor, 1987; Saradjian, 1996; Turner & Turner, 1994; Wolfe, 1985). In fact, Saradjian found that many sexual offending adult females actually had low sexual drives further suggesting that for many females, their motivation to offend is not sexual gratification. Although sexual preoccupation can be a risk factor for sexually abusive girls, the elements associated with sexual preoccupation may differ from those of boys. For example, instead of an evidence of pornography, evidence of masturbation to victimization experiences may correlate more to female sexual recidivism. Trauma reenactment is pronounced among sexually abusive girls; many girls masturbate to their own victimization experiences which can fuel a desire to sexually offend. Additionally, girls who do describe having a high sexual drive, or those that use sex as a primary coping strategy, may also be at an increased risk for recidivism.

10) Evidence of sexual subjectivity

Evidence of healthy sexual agency	0
Some evidence of compromised sexual agency	1
Significant evidence of poor sexual agency	2

Rationale: The development of sexual subjectivity is an adolescent developmental task (Tolman, 2002), yet for many girls this is compromised due to unhealthy cultural sexual scripts that teach girls to be sexually inexperienced (Thompson, 1990, 1995; Tolman, 1999, 2002), sexual objects (Debold, Toman, & Brown, 1996; Young-Eisendrath, 1999), and sexually accommodating to male partners (Wolf, 1997). If a sexually abusive girl lacks healthy sexual agency - that is, if she lacks appropriate sexual knowledge and continues to demonstrate poor sexual decision making - the more likely she will resort to unhealthy sexual avenues, which could include reoffending. (Examples of deficient sexual agency include indiscriminate or precocious sexual involvements, and sexual intercourse without birth control or protection from sexually transmitted diseases.)

Factors of relational functioning:

11) Social isolation, rejection, and/or lack of social skills

Not applicable	0
Some	1
High	2

Rationale: Girls that lack peer relationships, experience peer ostracism and rejection, and are socially isolated, also lack opportunities to engage in peer sexual exploration. This blockage (Finkelhor, 1984) can lead to developing sexual relationships with non-peers and can be a factor associated with recidivism.

12) Use of relational aggression

No evidence	0
Some evidence	1
High levels	2

Rationale: Since female development is relational, when girls are on a healthy developmental course, they are less inclined to engage in behaviors that would negatively impact their relationships (Miller & Stiver, 1997). Relational aggression refers to the dynamic of harming someone by damaging or threatening to damage the relationship: Social exclusion, negative body language, the silent treatment, shunning, or threatening to end a relationship unless the aggressor gets what she desires, are all forms of relational aggression (Crick & Grotpeter, 1995; Simmons, 2002). Cummings, Leschied, and Heilbron (2002) found a correlation between relational aggression and direct aggression in girls. Henington et al. (1998) also found that the use of relational aggression was predictive of overt aggression in girls. Therefore, there may be a connection between the continued use of relational aggression, and further overt aggression (including sexual abuse) in girls.

13) Relationship to female caregiver

Healthy and strong/supportive	0
Some difficulties	1
High discord, absent, or unhealthy role modeling	2

Rationale: A strong, healthy relationship between a girl and her mother can be an important protective factor from the development of inappropriate behaviors (Harris et al., 1991; Levene et al., 2001; OJJDP, 1998). Conversely, Mathews et al. (1997) noted disturbed mother-daughter relationships and poor female role modeling in the lives of sexually abusive girls. On the EARL-21G, Levene et al. (2001) specified caregiver-daughter interaction as a primary variable contributing to antisocial disturbances in girls. The importance of same sex role modeling dictates that disturbances in a mother-daughter relationship and unhealthy role modeling by a mother, may compromise a girl's overall functioning and predispose her to inappropriate behaviors and the continuation of problematic behaviors. Problematic parent-offender relationships/parental rejection is a factor listed on the ERASOR (Worling & Curwen, 2001), furthering the importance of this variable. Although fathers are extremely important influences and if major disturbances with this relationship are present, these could increase a girls risk as well, the female caregiver is noted due to the significance of the same sex influence and the fact many sexually abusive girls have had absent fathers. Additionally, sexually abusive girls often describe their relationships with their mothers as having far greater influence on them.

14) Attachment style

Primarily secure	0
Some attachment deficits (i.e., avoidant/preoccupied)	1
Significant attachment disturbances (i.e., dismissive)	2

Rationale: Bartholomew (1990) developed a four-category model of attachment based on one's view of self and others. Ward, Hudson, Marshall, and Siegert (1995) applied Bartholomew's model to adult male sex offending behavior, however, this model is also relevant and can be applied to female sex offending (adult and juvenile). The relationship questionnaire (Bartholomew & Horowitz, 1991) is a tool to determine one's attachment style. Hypothetically, girls evidencing a secure attachment style would be less likely to engage in sexually abusive behavior; their secure attachments make them less vulnerable to a need/desire to harm others. Girls with a negative view of self and positive view of others (preoccupied attachment style) may have dependency issues which can relate to sex offending behavior (peer influenced category), and girls with a negative view of self and others (avoidant attachment style) may be predisposed to offend, most likely due to trauma backgrounds. Girls who have a positive view of themselves and negative view of others (dismissive attachment style) may be the most dangerous, and most likely to recidivate, because they lack a desire for close relationships and are emotionally cold and detached. Girls fitting into this category can also be predisposed to offend due to severe trauma histories; their severe attachment disturbances make it unlikely they will have empathy for potential victims or care enough to refrain from further sexually abusive behavior. Girls with compromised attachment systems often use sex as a substitute avenue for attachment (Salzman, 1990), therefore, girls with insecure attachment styles will be more likely to engage in inappropriate sexual behaviors.

Factors related to personal functioning:

15) Attitudes reflecting non-normative beliefs

No evidence	0
Some evidence	1
Entrenched attitudes	2

Rationale: For girls, normative beliefs about aggression, e.g., that aggression is not considered acceptable female social behavior, are protective against the development of aggressive behaviors (Huesmann et al., 1992). Therefore, a girl that continues to engage in non-normative or aggressive attitudes may be more inclined to engage in further aggressive behavior.

16) Emotional expressivity

High	0
Average	1
Low	2

Rationale: Emotional expressivity is a protective factor from developing aggressive/delinquent behaviors (Gilgun, 2001). The inclination of girls to "tend and befriend" is a hallmark of being female and has been seen as an advantage that females have when compared with males. Emotional expressivity is a component of this female tendency that when lacking can reduce a girl's status and result in peer rejection and negative labeling (Gurian, 2002). Because girls are socially and biologically oriented to this trait, a deficit in this area can be devastating: Girls with poor emotional expressivity tend to internalize their feelings which can lead to angry displays; additionally, the peer ostracism that some girls face can fuel their anger and frustration - this can also result in aggressive behaviors and recidivism.

17) Posttraumatic Stress Disorder

No symptoms	0
Some symptoms and/or mild disorder	1
Chronic and severe	2

Rationale: Many sexually abusive girls meet the diagnosis of PTSD. Kubik et al. (2002) found that 50% of their female sample had a diagnosis of PTSD. Similarly, Mathews et al. (1997) found that nearly 50% of the girls in their sample had PTSD. PTSD leads to high distress levels and low self-restraint, and increases the risk of behavioral problems and offending behaviors (Cauffman et al., 1998). Because of the close association between PTSD and female offending, a current diagnosis of PTSD (or a constellation of symptoms) could increase a girl's risk to reoffend.

18) Depressive Disorder
    No symptoms   0
    Some symptoms and/or mild disorde   1
    Chronic and severe   2

Rationale: Several studies have shown a link between female depression and aggressive behavior (Obeidallah & Earls, 1999; Paikoff, Brooks-Gunn, & Warren, 1991; Zoccolillo & Rogers, 1991). Not surprisingly, depression is present among many sexually abusive girls (Bumby & Bumby, 1997; Mathews et al., 1997). Therefore, if a girl presents with this diagnosis, she may be more vulnerable to further delinquent and/or sexually abusive behaviors.

19) Conduct Disorder
    No symptoms   0
    Some symptoms and/or mild disorder   1
    Chronic and severe   2

Rationale: Although girls are less likely to be diagnosed with conduct disorder, girls with conduct disorder are viewed as having high levels of psychiatric comorbidity (Loeber & Keenan, 1994), which can lead to poor self-regulation and increased behavioral disturbances. Conduct disordered girls are also viewed as having poor outcomes (Zoccolillo & Rogers, 1991). In Zoccolillo and Rogers, many of the girls were rearrested supporting the notion of recidivism among these girls.

20) Anxiety Disorder
    No symptoms   0
    Some symptoms and/or mild disorder   1
    Chronic and severe   2

Rationale: Mathews et al. (1997) found that over half the girls in their sample had a mood disturbance (depression or anxiety). Leschied et al. (2000, 2002) also concluded that female aggression is often accompanied by depressed, suicidal ideation, and generalized anxiety disorders. Zoccolillo and Rogers (1991) found that the majority of conduct-disordered girls in their sample had anxiety disorders: They concluded that specific to girls, depression and anxiety disorders often coincide with conduct disorder.

21) Hyperactivity/impulsivity/inattention
    No symptoms   0
    Some symptoms and/or mild disorder   1
    Chronic and severe   2

Rationale: The purpose of listing HIA, rather than ADHD, is because the manifestation of ADHD in females often differs from the more overt, hyperactive displays characteristic of males; girls exhibit more inattention than boys - although as Loeber and

Keenan (1994) state, it has not yet been determined to what extent inattention is related to conduct disordered behavior. Levene et al. (2001) incorporated HIA into their risk assessment for young girls and it appears pertinent to adolescent females as well. Girls with ADHD are far more likely than boys to have conduct disorder (Loeber & Keenan, 1994; Szatmari, Boyle, & Offord, 1989). Further, girls with high levels of impulsivity, as with boys, will be less likely to think or consider the possible consequences before they act out; this factor, therefore, could raise their risk level.

22) Other diagnosis of concern: _____

No symptoms	0
Some symptoms and/or mild disorder	1
Chronic and severe	2

Rationale: Numerous studies have shown that girls involved with the criminal justice system have significant mental health concerns (Cauffman et al., 1998; Leschied et al., 200; Prescott, 1997). For sexually abusive girls, this also holds true (Bumby & Bumby, 1997; Hunter et al., 1993; Mathews et al., 1997; Kubik et al., 2002). It is hypothesized that the more mentally unstable a girl is, the less likely she will be able to cope and modulate her affect effectively; as a result, her risk to engage in inappropriate behaviors would be increased.

23) Investment in school

High or risk factor not applicable	0
Average	1
Low and/or dropped out	2

Rationale: Academic failure is considered to be the most significant risk relating to delinquency (OJJDP, 1998). Ellickson et al., and Serbin et al. (as cited in Leschied et al., 2002) found that girls with lower academic achievement or who dropped out of school were at risk for norm-violating or aggressive behaviors. A continued lack of school investment may indicate a lack of future orientation, low self-efficacy, and an increased likelihood to engage in delinquent behaviors, which could include sexual.

Factors related to treatment responsivity:

24) Empathy/ability to engage in perspective taking

Strong ability	0
Some deficits apparent	1
Significant deficits	2

Rationale: A person's ability to engage in empathic recognition and response is known to be a powerful mitigating force for the development of abusive behaviors (Ryan, 1998, 2003). Empathy (or specifically the lack thereof) is a risk factor on the J-SOAP-II (Prentky & Righthand, 2003) and is also pertinent to a risk assessment for girls. The more a girl can empathize, the less likely she will engage in the kind of behavior that harms others or her relationships (Miller & Stiver, 1997).

25) Internal motivation to change
      High internal motivation to change   0
      Some internal motivation to change   1
      Significantly lacks internal motivation   2

Rationale: The more a girl is internally driven to refrain from abusive behavior, the more likely she will take the necessary steps to prevent it from occurring. Internal motivation is a factor listed on the J-SOAP-II (Prentky & Righthand, 2003) and seems equally applicable to sexually abusive female juveniles.

Environmental factors:

26) Stress within the family environment
      No or low stres   0
      Moderate amounts of stress   1
      High levels of stress   2

Rationale: Given the relational orientation of girls, and the fact several studies have found that delinquent girls have more disturbed home environments than delinquent boys (see Cloninger et al., 1978), high stress family environments have a significantly negative impact on girls and their overall functioning. Such environments may be correlated to further delinquent behaviors.

27) Involvement in extracurricular activities
      At least one involvement in a positive activity,
          e.g., athletics, music   0
      No extracurricular activities   1
      No extracurricular activities and no desire to
      pursue any   2

Rationale: Involvement in extracurricular activities serves as a protective factor for the development of delinquent behaviors (NCASA, 2003; Roberts, 1999). Therefore, a lack of activities could promote apathy, low self-efficacy, boredom, a lack of focus, and a negative trajectory leading to inappropriate behavior, all of which could also correspond to reoffending.

End Notes

[1]Portions of this chapter are based on similar sections previously written for a chapter on assessment: Robinson, S. (2005). Considerations for the assessment of female sexually abusive youth. In M. Calder (Ed.) *Children and young people who sexually abuse: New theory, research, and practice developments.* Dorset, UK: Russell House Publishing.

References

Acoca, L. (1999, October). Investing in Girls: A 21st Century Strategy. *Juvenile Justice,* 6(1), 3-13. Retrieved November 16, 2002, from http://www.ncjrs.org/html/ojjdp/jjournal1099/invest2.html

Acoca, L., & Dedel, K. (1998). *No place to hide: Understanding and meeting the needs of girls in the California juvenile justice system.* Oakland, CA: The National Council on Crime and Delinquency.

Allgood-Merten, B., Lewinsohn, P. M., & Hops, H. (1990). Sex differences and adolescent depression. *Journal of Abnormal Psychology,* 99(1), 55-63.

American Association of University Women (AAUW). (1995). *How schools short-change girls – The AAUW report: A study of major findings on girls and education.* New York: Marlowe & Company.

American Psychiatric Association. (2000). *Diagnostic and statistical manual of mental disorders* (4th ed.). Washington, DC: Author.

Artz, S. (1997). On becoming an object. *Journal of Child and Youth Care,* 11(2), 17-37.

Baron-Cohen, S. (2003). *The essential difference: The truth about the male & female brain.* New York: Basic Books.

Bartholomew, K. (1990). Avoidance of intimacy: An attachment perspective. *Journal of Social and Personal Relationships,* 7, 147-178.

Bartholomew, K., & Horowitz, L. M. (1991). Attachment styles among young adults: A test of a four-category model. *Journal of Personality and Social Psychology,* 61(2), 226-244.

Belenky, M. F., Clinchy, B. M., Goldberger, N. R., & Tarule, J. M. (1986). *Women's ways of knowing: The development of self, voice, and mind.* BasicBooks.

Biederman, J., Faraone, S. V., Mick, E., Williamson, S., Wilens, T. E., Spencer, T. J., Weber, W., Jetton, J., Kraus, I., Pert, J., & Zallen, B. (1999). Clinical correlates of ADHD in females: Findings from a large group of girls ascertained from pediatric and psychiatric referral sources. *Journal of the American Academy of Child & Adolescent Psychiatry,* 38, 966-975.

Bjoerkqvist, K., Lagerspetz, K. M., & Kaukiainen, A. (1992). Do girls manipulate and boys fight? Developmental trends in regard to direct and indirect aggression. *Aggressive Behavior,* 18, 117-127.

Bjorkqvist, K., Osterman, K., & Kaukiainen, A. (1992). The development of direct and indirect aggressive strategies in males and females. In K. Bjorkqvist & P. Niemela (Eds.), *Of mice and women: Aspects of female aggression* (pp. 51-64). New York: Academic Press, Inc.

Blanchette, K., & Motiuk, L. L. (1997). *Maximum-security female and male federal offenders: A comparison.* Retrieved February 2, 2004, from http://www.csc-scc.gc.ca/text/rsrch/reports/r53/r53e_e.shtml

Blum, D. (1997). *Sex on the brain: The biological differences between men + women.* New York: Penguin Books.

Bonta, J., Pang, B., & Wallace-Capretta, S. (1995). Predictors of recidivism among incarcerated female offenders. *The Prison Journal,* 75(3), 227-293.

Borysenko, J. (1996). *A woman's book of life: The biology, psychology, and spirituality of the feminine life cycle.* New York: Riverhead Books.

Briere, J. (1996). *Trauma symptom checklist for children (TSCC): Professional manual.* Lutz, FL: Psychological Assessment Resources, Inc.

Brown, L. M. (1998). *Raising their voices: The politics of girls' anger.* Cambridge, MA: Harvard University Press.

Brown, L. M., & Gilligan, C. (1992). *Meeting at the crossroads: Women's psychology and girls' development.* New York: Ballantine Books.

Bumby, K. M., & Bumby, N. H. (1997). Adolescent female sexual offenders. In B. K. Schwartz & H. R. Cellini (Eds.), *The sex offender: Vol.2. New insights, treatment innovations and legal developments* (pp. 10.1-10.16). Kingston, NJ: Civic Research Institute.

Canetto, S. S., & Lester, D. (1995). Gender and the primary prevention of suicide mortality. *Suicide and Life-Threatening Behavior,* 25(1), 58-69.

Caspi, A., Lynam, D., Moffitt, T. E., & Silva, P. A. (1993). Unraveling girls' delinquency: Biological, dispositional, and contextual contributions to adolescent misbehavior. *Developmental Psychology,* 29(1), 19-30.

Cauffman, E., Feldman, F., Waterman, J., & Steiner, H. (1998). Posttraumatic stress disorder among female juvenile offenders. *Journal of the American Academy of Child and Adolescent Psychiatry,* 37(11), 1209-1217.

Cavanagh, S. (2002). Preface. In A. L. Cummings & A. W. Leschied (Eds.), *Research and treatment for aggression with adolescent girls* (pp. i-iii). Queenston, ON: The Edwin Mellen Press.

Cloninger, C. R., Christiansen, K. O., Reich, T., & Gottesman, I. (1978). Implications of sex differences in the prevalence of antisocial personality, alcoholism, and criminality for familial transmission. *Archives of General Psychiatry,* 35, 941-951.

Colorado Sex Offender Management Board (2002, July). *Standards and guidelines for the evaluation, assessment, treatment and supervision of juveniles who have committed sexual offenses.* Denver, CO: Colorado Department of Public Safety.

Commonwealth Fund (1997, September). *The Commonwealth Fund survey of the health of adolescent girls.* Retrieved July 19, 2000, from http://www.cmwf.org/programs/women/factshet.asp

Crick, N. R., & Grotpeter, J. K. (1995). Relational aggression, gender, and social-psychological adjustment. *Child Development, 66,* 710-722.

Cross, T. P., & Saxe, L. (2001). Polygraph testing and sexual abuse: The lure of the magic lasso. *Child Maltreatment, 6*(3), 195-206.

Cummings, A. L., Leschied, A. W., & Heilbron, N. (2002). Assessing relational and direct aggression in adolescent girls. In A. L. Cummings & A. W. Leschied (Eds.), *Research and treatment for aggression with adolescent girls* (pp. 103-130). Queenston, ON: The Edwin Mellen Press.

Cunningham, A. (2002). Adolescent female aggression: A proposal for a research agenda. In A. L. Cummings & A. W. Leschied (Eds.), *Research and treatment for aggression with adolescent girls* (pp. 187-207). Queenston, ON: The Edwin Mellen Press.

Davin, P. A. (1999). Secrets revealed: A study of female sex offenders. In P. A. Davin, J. C. Hislop, & T. Dunbar, *The female sexual abuser: Three views* (pp. 9-134). Brandon, VT: Safer Society Press.

Davis, G. C., & Breslau, N. (1998, July). Are women at greater risk for PTSD than men? *Psychiatric Times, 15*(7). Retrieved January 30, 2004, from http://www.psychiatrictimes.com/p980765.html

Day, H., D., Franklin, J. M., & Marshall, D. D. (1998). Predictors of aggression in hospitalized adolescents. *Journal of Psychology, 132*(4), 427-434.

de Beauvoir, S. (1949). *The second sex.* Middlesex, U.K.: Penguin.

Debold, E. (1991). The body at play. In C. Gilligan, A. G. Rogers, & D. L. Tolman (Eds.), *Women, girls & psychotherapy: Reframing resistance* (pp. 169-183). Binghamton, NY: Harrington Park Press.

Debold, E., Tolman, D., Brown, L. M. (1996). Embodying knowledge, knowing desire: Authority and split subjectivities in girls' epistemological development. In N. Goldberger, J. Tarule, B. Clinchy, & M. Belenky (Eds.), *Knowledge, difference, and power: Essays inspired by women's ways of Knowing* (pp. 85-125). New York: Basic Books.

Dunbar, T. (1999). Women who sexually molest female children. In P. A. Davin, J. C. Hislop, & T. Dunbar, *The female sexual abuser: Three views* (pp. 311-393). Brandon, VT: Safer Society Press.

Ellis, B. J., & Symons, D. (1990). Sex differences in sexual fantasy: An evolutionary psychological approach. *Journal of Sex Research,* 27(4), 527-556.

Erickson, E. H. (1950). *Childhood and society.* New York: W. W. Norton.

Erickson, E. H. (1968). *Identity: Youth and crisis.* New York: W. W. Norton.

Faller, K. C. (1995). A clinical sample of women who have sexually abused. *Journal of Child Sexual Abuse,* 4(3), 13-31.

Farber, S. K. (2002). *When the body is a target: Self-harm, pain, and traumatic attachments.* Northvale, NJ: Jason Aronson, Inc.

Fehrenbach, P., & Monastersky, C. (1988). Charcteristics of female adolescent sexual offenders. *American Journal of Orthopsychiatry,* 58(1), 29-52.

Fine, M. (1988). Sexuality, schooling, and adolescent females: The missing discourse of desire. *Harvard Education Review,* 58(1), 29-52.

Finkelhor, D. (1984). *Child sexual abuse: New theory & research.* New York: The Free Press.

Finkelhor, D., & Russell, D. (1984). Women as perpetrators: Review of the evidence. In D. Finkelhor, *Child sexual abuse: New theory and research* (pp. 171-187). New York: The Free Press.

Flansburg, S. (1991). *Building a self: Teenaged girls and issues of self-esteem.* Washington, DC: Women's Educational Equity Act Publishing Center.

Funk, S. (1999). Risk assessment for juveniles on probation: A focus on gender. *Criminal Justice and Behavior,* 26(1), 44-68.

Gaub, M., & Carlson, C. L. (1997). Gender differences in ADHD: A meta-analysis and critical review. *Journal of the American Academy of Child and Adolescent Psychiatry,* 36(8), 1036-1046.

Gilgun, J. F. (2001, May). Protective factors, resilience and child abuse and neglect [Electronic version]. *Healthy Generations,* 2(1). 4-5.

Gil, E. (1996). *Treating abused adolescents.* New York: The Guilford Press.

Gilligan, C. (1982). *In a different voice: Psychological theory and women's development.* Cambridge, MA: Harvard University Press.

Gilligan, C., Lyons, N. P., & Hammer, T. J. (Eds.). (1990). *Making connections: The relational worlds of adolescent girls at Emma Willard school.* Cambridge, MA: Harvard University Press.

Gilligan, C., Rogers, A. G., & Tolman, D. L. (Eds.). (1991). *Women, girls & psychotherapy: Reframing resistance*. Binghamton, NY: Harrington Park Press.

Goldberger, N., Tarule, J., Clinchy, B., Belenky, M. (Eds.). (1996). *Knowledge, difference, and power: Essays inspired by women's ways of knowing*. New York: Basic Books.

Grisso, T., & Barnum, R. (2003). *Massachusetts youth screening instrument – Version 2 (MAYSI-2): User's manual and technical report*. Sarasota, FL: Professional Resource Press.

Gurian, M. (2001). *Boys and girls learn differently! A guide for teachers and parents*. San Francisco: Jossey-Bass.

Gurian, M. (2002). *The wonder of girls: Understanding the hidden nature of our daughters*. New York: Atria Books.

Haag, P. (1999). *Voices of a generation: Teenage girls on sex, school, and stuff*. Washington, DC: AAUW Educational Foundation.

Hagan, M. P., & Cho, M. E. (1996). A comparison of treatment outcomes between adolescent rapists and child sexual offenders. *International Journal of Offender Therapy and Comparative Criminology*, 40, 113-122.

Hales, D. (1999). *Just like a woman: How gender science is redefining what makes us female*. New York: Bantam Books.

Hancock, E. (1989). The girl within. New York: Fawcett Columbine.

Harris, L., Blum, R. W., & Resnick, M. (1991). Teen females in Minnesota: A portrait of quiet disturbance. In C. Gilligan, A. G. Rogers, & D. L. Tolman (Eds.), *Women, girls & psychotherapy: Reframing resistance* (pp. 119-135). Binghamton, NY: Harrington Park Press.

Henington, C., Hughes, J. N., Cavell, T. A., Thompson, B. (1998). The role of relational aggression in identifying aggressive boys and girls. *Journal of School Psychology*, 36(4), 457-477.

Howley, D. (2001, May). *A descriptive study of sexually abusive female juveniles in residential treatment*. Workshop presented at the annual conference of the National Adolescent Perpetration Network, Kansas City, MO.

Huesmann, L. R., Guerra, N. G., Zelli, A., & Miller, L. (1992). Differing normative beliefs about aggression for boys and girls. In K. Bjorkqvist & P. Niemela (Eds.), *Of mice and women: Aspects of female aggression* (pp.77-87). New York: Academic Press, Inc.

Hughes, J., Cavewill, T., & Jackson, T. (1999). Influence of the teacher-student relationship on childhood conduct problems: A prospective study. *Journal of Clinical Child Psychology*, 28(2), 173-184.

Hunter, J. A., Lexier, L. J., Goodwin, D. W., Browne, P. A., & Dennis, C. (1993). Psychosexual, attitudinal, and developmental characteristics of juvenile female sexual perpetrators in a residential treatment setting. *Journal of Child and Family Studies, 2*, 317-326.

Hunter, J. A. & Mathews, R. (1997). Sexual deviance in females. In R. D. Laws & W. O'Donohue (Eds.), *Sexual deviance: Theory, assessment and treatment* (pp. 465-480). New York: The Guilford Press.

Jessor, R., Van Den Bos, J., Vanderryn, J., Costa, F. M., & Turbin, M. S. (1995). Protective factors in adolescent problem behavior: Moderator effects and developmental change. *Developmental Psychology*, 31, 923-933.

Johnson, T. C. (1989). Female child perpetrators: Children who molest other children. *Child Abuse & Neglect*, 13, 571-589.

Jordan, J. V. (2004). Relational resilience. In J. V. Jordan, M. Walker, & L. M. Hartling (Eds.), *The complexity of connection: Writings from the Stone Center's Jean Baker Miller Training Institute* (pp. 28-46). New York: The Guilford Press.

Jordan, J. V., Kaplan, A. G., Miller, J. B., Stiver, I. P., & Surrey, J. L. (1991). *Women's growth in connection: Writings from the Stone Center.* New York: The Guilford Press.

Juon, H., & Ensminger, M. E. (1997). Childhood, adolescent, and young adult predictors of suicidal behaviors: A prospective study of African Americans. *Journal of Child Psychology and Psychiatry*, 38(5), 553-563.

Kahn, T. J., & Chambers, H. J. (1991). Assessing reoffense risk with juvenile sexual offenders. *Child Welfare*, 70, 333-345.

Kaplan, L. J. (1991). *Female perversions: The temptations of Emma Bovary.* New York: Doubleday.

Kaschak, E. (1992). *Engendered lives: A new psychology of women's experience.* New York: Basic Books.

Keltikangas-Jaervinen, L., & Pakaslahti, L. (1999). Development of social problem-solving strategies and changes in aggressive behavior: A 7-year follow-up from childhood to late adolescence. *Aggressive Behavior*, 25(4), 269-279.

Kohlberg, L. (1981). *The philosophy of moral development.* San Francisco: Harper & Row.

Kubik, E. K., Hecker, J. E., & Righthand, S. (2002). Adolescent females who have sexually offended: Comparison with delinquent adolescent female offenders and adolescent males who sexually offend. *Journal of Child Sexual Abuse*, 11(3), 63-85.

Laan, E., Everaerd, W., van Bellen, G., Hanewald, G. (1994). Women's sexual and emotional responses to male- and female-produced erotica. *Archives of Sexual Behavior*, 23(2), 153-170.

Lab, S. P., Shields, G., & Schondel, C. (1993). Research note: An evaluation of juvenile sexual offender treatment. *Crime & Delinquency, 39*, 543-553.

Lamb, S. (2001). *The secret lives of girls: What good girls really do – sex play, aggression, and their guilt.* New York: The Free Press.

Leadbeater, B. J. R., and Way, N. (Eds.). (1996). *Urban girls: Resisting stereotypes, creating identities.* New York: New York University Press.

Leitenberg, H., Detzer, M. J., & Srebnik, D. (1993). Gender differences in masturbation and the relation of masturbation experience in preadolescence and/or early adolescence to sexual behavior and sexual adjustment in young adulthood. *Achives of Sexual Behavior, 22*(2), 87-99.

Leschied, A., Cummings, A., Van Brunschot, M., Cunningham, A., & Saunders, A. (2000). *Female adolescent aggression: A review of the literature and the correlates of aggression* (User Report No. 2000-04). Ottawa: Solicitor General Canada.

Leschied, A. W., Cummings, A. L., Zerwer, M., & Saunders, A. (2002). Correlates of aggression with adolescent girls. In A. L. Cummings & A. W. Leschied (Eds.), *Research and treatment for aggression with adolescent girls* (pp. 3-39). Queenston, ON: The Edwin Mellen Press.

Levene, K. S., Augimeri, L. K., Pepler, D. J., Walsh, M. M., Webster, C. D., & Koegl, C. J. (2001). *Early assessment risk list for girls, Earl-21G (Version 1 – consultation edition).* Toronto, ON: Earlscourt Child and Family Centre.

Levinson, D. (1978). *The seasons of a man's life.* New York: Alfred A. Knopf.

Linehan, M. (1993). *Cognitive-behavioral treatment of borderline personality disorder.* New York: Guilford Press.

Liu, X., & Kaplan, H. B. (1999). Explaining the gender difference in adolescent delinquent behavior: A longitudinal test of mediating mechanisms. *Criminology, 37*, 195.

Loeber, R., & Keenan, K. (1994). The interaction between conduct disorder and its comorbid conditions: Effects of age and gender. *Clinical Psychology Review, 14*, 497-523.

Loeber, R., & Stouthamer-Loeber, M. (1998). Development of juvenile aggression and violence: Some common misconceptions and controversies. *American Psychologist, 53*(2), 242-259.

Margolin, L. (1991). Child sexual abuse by nonrelated caregivers. *Child Abuse & Neglect, 15*, 213-221.

Marshall, W. L., & Eccles, A. (1993). Pavolovian conditioning processes in adolescent sex offenders. In H. E. Barbaree, W. L. Marshall, & S. M. Hudson (Eds.), *Juvenile sex offending* (pp. 118-142). New York: The Guilford Press.

Mathews, R., Hunter, J. A., & Vuz, J. (1997). Juvenile female sexual offenders: Clinical characteristics and treatment issues. *Sexual Abuse: A Journal of Research and Treatment*, 9(3), 187-200.

Mathews, R., Matthews, J., & Speltz, K. (1990). Female sexual offenders. In M. Hunter (Ed.), *The sexually abused male: Vol.1. Prevalence, impact, and treatment* (pp. 275-293). New York: Lexington Books.

Miccio-Fonseca, L. C. (2000). Adult and adolescent female sex offenders: Experiences compared to other female and male sex offenders. *Journal of Psychology and Human Sexuality*, 11(3), 75-88.

Miccio-Fonseca, L. C. (1997). *Personal sentence completion inventory: User's guide.* Brandon, VT: Safer Society Press.

Miller, J. B., & Stiver, I. P. (1997). T*he healing connection: How women form relationships in therapy and in life*. Boston: Beacon Press.

National Center on Addiction and Substance Abuse at Columbia University (NCASA). (2003). *The formative years: Pathways to substance abuse among girls and young women, ages 8-22*. New York: Author.

National Public Radio (2003). *From rubies to blossoms: A portrait of American girlhood* (part one). Retrieved February 27, 2003, from http://www.npr.org/programs/atc/features/feb/girl_gangs/index.html

National Task Force on Juvenile Sexual Offending (1993). The revised report from the National Task Force on Juvenile Sexual Offending [Special issue]. *Juvenile & Family Court Journal*, 44(4).

Nelson-Zlupko, L., Kauffman, E., & Dore, M. M. (1995). Gender differences in drug addiction and treatment: Implications for social work intervention with substance-abusing women. *Social Work*, 40(1), 45-54.

Nichols, H. R., & Molinder, I. (1995). *Mutiphasic sex inventory II: Adolescent female form*. Tacoma, WA: Authors.

Nolen-Hoeksema, S. (1990). *Sex differences in depression*. Standford, CA: Stanford University Press.

Obeidallah, D. A., & Earls, F. J. (1999, July). Adolescent girls: The role of depression in the development of delinquency. *National Institute of Justice Research Preview*. Washington DC: U. S. Department of Justice.

O'Brien, M. (1994). *PHASE treatment manual*. St. Paul, MN: PHASE Program.

O'Connor, A. (1987). Females sex offenders. *British Journal of Psychiatry*, 150, 615-620.

Office of Juvenile Justice and Delinquency Prevention (1998, October). *Guiding principles from promising female programming: An inventory of best practices.* Washington, DC: Author.

Orenstein, P. (1994). *Schoolgirls: Young women, self-esteem, and the confidence gap.* New York: HarperPerennial.

Owens, L. D., & MacMullin, C. E. (1995). Gender differences in aggression in children and adolescents in South Australian schools. *International Journal of Adolescence & Youth*, 6, 21-35.

Paikoff, R. L., Brooks-Gunn, J., & Warren, M. P. (1991). Effects of girls' hormonal status on depressive and aggressive symptoms over the course of one year. *Journal of Youth and Adolescence*, 20, 191-215.

Pate, K. (n.d.). *The risky business of risk assessment.* Retrieved October 25, 2003, from http://www.elizabethfry.ca/risky/1.htm

Perry, B. D. (1997). Incubated in terror: Neurodevelopmental factors in the "cycle of violence." In J. D. Osofsky (Ed.), *Children in a violent society.* New York: The Guilford Press.

Perry, B. D., Pollard, R. A., Blakley, T. L., Baker, W. L., & Vigilante, D. (1995). Childhood trauma, the neurobiology of adaptation, and "use-dependent" development of the brain: How "states" become "traits." *Infant Mental Health Journal*, 16(4), 271-291.

Perry, D. G., Perry, L. C., & Rasmussen, P. (1986). Cognitive social learning mediators of aggression. *Child Development*, 57(3), 700-711.

Peterson, B. S., Zhang, H., Lucia, R. S., King, R. A., & Lewis, M. (1996). Risk factors for presenting problems in child psychiatric emergencies. *Journal of the American Academy of Child and Adolescent Psychiatry*, 35(9), 1162-1173.

Piers, E. V., & Herzberg, D.S. (2002). *Piers-Harris 2: Piers-Harris children's self-concept scale manual* (2nd ed.). Los Angeles: Western Psychological Services.

Phillips, L. (1998). *The girls report: What we know and need to know about growing up female.* New York: The National Council for Research on Women.

Phillips, L. M. (2000). *Flirting with danger: Young women's reflections on sexuality and domination.* New York: New York University Press.

Pipher, M. (1994). *Reviving Ophelia: Saving the selves of adolescent girls.* New York: Ballantine Books.

Poe-Yamagata, E. & Butts, J. A. (1996, September). *Female offenders in the juvenile justice systems: Statistics summary* (NCJ Report No. 160941). Washington, DC: U. S. Department of Justice.

Prentky, R., & Righthand, S. (2003). *The juvenile sex offender assessment protocol-II (J-SOAP-II) manual* (Publication No. NCJ 202316). Retrieved January 16, 2004, from http://www.ncjrs.org/pdffiles1/ojjdp/202316.pdf

Prescott, L. (1997, December). *Adolescent girls with co-occurring disorders in the juvenile justice system.* Delmar, NY: The GAINS Center.

Prescott, L. (1998, June). *Improving policy and practice for adolescent girls with co-occurring disorders in the juvenile justice system.* Delmar, NY: The GAINS Center.

Rasmussen, L. A. (1999). Factors related to recidivism among juvenile sexual offenders. *Sexual Abuse: A Journal of Research and Treatment*, 11, 69-85.

Ray, J. A., and English, D. J. (1995). Comparison of female and male children with sexual behavior problems. *Journal of Youth and Adolescence*, 24(4), 439-451.

Reynolds, W. M. (2002). *RADS-2: Professional manual.* Lutz, FL: Psychological Assessment Resources, Inc.

Roberts, M. C. (Ed.). (1999). A new look at adolescent girls: Strengths and stresses. In N. G. Johnson, M. C. Roberts, & J. Worell (Eds.), *Beyond appearance: A new look at adolescent girls* (pp. 405-432). Washington, DC: American Psychological Association.

Robinson, S. (2005). Considerations for the assessment of female sexually abusive youth. In M. C. Calder (Ed.), Children and young people who sexually abuse: *New theory, research and practice developments* (pp.171-195). Dorset, UK: Russell House Publishing.

Robinson, S. (2002). *Growing beyond: A workbook for sexually abusive teenage girls (treatment manual).* Holyoke, MA: NEARI Press.

Robinson, S. (1999). An offense-relational model for female adolescent sex offending. *Newsletter of the National Organization of Forensic Social Work*, 3(7), 1-5.

Rosenthal, M. J. (1981). Sexual differences in suicidal behavior of young people. *Adolescent Psychiatry*, 9, 422-442.

Rutter, M. (1986). The developmental psychopathology of depression: Issues and perspectives. In M. Rutter, C. Issard, & P. Reads (Eds.), *Depression in young people: Developmental and clinical perspectives* (pp. 3-30). New York: Guilford Press.

Ryan, G. (2003). Hindsight: Cause for change or respite from fear? *Journal of Sexual Aggression*, 9(2), 125-133.

Ryan, G. (1998). The relevance of early life experience to the behaviour of sexually abusive youth. *The Irish Journal of Psychology*, 19(1), 32-48.

Sadker, M., & Sadker, D. (1994). *Failing at fairness: How our schools cheat girls.* New York: A Touchstone Book.

Salzman, J. P. (1990). Save the world, save myself: Responses to problematic attachment. In C. Gilligan, N. P. Lyons, & T. J. Hammer (Eds.), *Making connections: The relational worlds of adolescent girls at Emma Willard School* (pp. 110-146). Cambridge, MA: Harvard University Press.

Saner, H., & Ellickson, P. (1996). Concurrent risk factors for adolescent violence. *Journal of Adolescent Health*, 19, 94-103.

Saradjian, J. (1996). *Women who sexually abuse children: From research to clinical practice*. New York: John Wiley & Sons.

Sarrel, P. M., & Masters, W. H. (1992). Sexual molestation of men by women. *Archives of Sexual Behavior*, 11(2), 117-131.

Schwartz, E., & Perry, B. D. (1994). The post-traumatic response in children and adolescents. *Psychiatric Clinics of North America*, 17(2), 311-326.

Shandler, S. (1999). *Ophelia speaks: Adolescent girls write about their search for self*. New York: HarperPerennial.

Simmons, R. (2002). *Odd girl out: The hidden culture of aggression in girls*. New York: Harcourt, Inc.

Simons, R., & Murphy, P. I. (1985). Sex differences in the causes of adolescent suicide ideation. *Journal of Youth and Adolescence*, 14(5), 423-434.

Sipe, R., Jensen, E. L., & Everett, R. S. (1998). Adolescent sexual offenders grown up: Recidivism in young adulthood. *Criminal Justice and Behavior*, 25, 109-124.

Solomon, A. (2001). *The noonday demon: An atlas of depression*. New York: A Touchstone Book.

Stattin, H., & Magnusson, D. (1990). *Pubertal maturation in female development*. Hillsdale, NJ: Erlbaum.

Stern, L. (1991). Disavowing the self in female adolescence. In C. Gilligan, A. G. Rogers, & D. L. Tolman (Eds.), *Women, girls & psychotherapy: Reframing resistance* (pp. 105-118). Binghamton: New York: Harrington Park Press.

Syed, F., & Williams, S. (1996, December). *Case studies of female sex offenders in the correctional service of Canada*. Retrieved January 16, 2004, from http://www.csc-scc.gc.ca/text/pblct/sexoffender/female/female-01_e.shtml

Szatmari, P., Boyle, M. H., & Offord, D. R. (1989). ADDH and conduct disorder: Degree of diagnostic overlap and differences among correlates. *Journal of the American Academy of Child & Adolescent Psychiatry*, 28(6), 865-872.

Thompson, S. (1990). Putting a big thing into a little hole: Teenage girls' accounts of sexual initiation. *Journal of Sex Research*, 27, 341-361.

Thompson, S. (1995). *Going all the way: Teenage girls' tales of sex, romance and pregnancy*. New York: Farrar, Straus & Giroux.

Tolman, D. L. (1991). Adolescent girls, women and sexuality: Discerning dilemmas of desire. In C. Gilligan, A. G. Rogers, & D. L. Tolman (Eds.), *Women, girls & psychotherapy: Reframing resistance* (pp. 55-69). Binghamton, NY: Harrington Park Press.

Tolman, D. L. (1994). Daring to desire: Culture and the bodies of adolescent girls. In J. M. Irvine (Ed.), *Sexual cultures and the construction of adolescent identities* (pp. 250-284). Philadelphia, PA: Temple University Press.

Tolman, D. L. (1999). Female adolescent sexuality in relational context: Beyond sexual decision making. In N. G. Johnson, M. C. Roberts, & J. Worell (Ed.), *Beyond appearance: A new look at adolescent girls* (pp. 227-246). Washington, DC: American Psychological Association.

Tolman, D. L. (2002). *Dilemmas of desire: Teenage girls talk about sexuality*. Cambridge, MA: Harvard University Press.

Turner, M. T., & Turner, T. N. (1994). *Female adolescent sexual abusers: An exploratory study of mother-daughter dynamics with implications for treatment*. Brandon, VT: Safer Society Press.

Ward, T., Hudson, S. M., Marshall, W. L., & Siegert, R. (1995). Attachment style and intimacy deficits in sexual offenders: A theoretical framework. *Sexual Abuse: A Journal of Research and Treatment, 7*(4), 317-335.

Watts, D. W., & Ellis, A. M. (1993). Sexual abuse and drinking and drug use: Implications for prevention. *Journal of Drug Education, 23*, 183-200.

Wolf, N. (1997). *Promiscuities: The secret struggle for womanhood*. New York: Random House.

Wolfe, F. (1985, March). *Twelve female sexual offenders*. Paper presented at the Next Steps in Research on the Assessment and Treatment of Sexually Aggressive Persons, St. Louis, MO.

Worling, J. R., & Curwen, T. (2000). Adolescent sexual offender recidivism: Success of specialized treatment and implications for risk prediction. *Child Abuse & Neglect, 24*, 965-982.

Worling, J. R., & Curwen, T. (2001). *The "ERASOR" (Estimate of Risk of Adolescent Sexual Offense Recidivism – Version 2.0)*. Thistletown Regional Centre: SAFE-T Program.

Wunderlich, U., Bronisch, T., Wittchen, H. U., Carter, R. (2001). Gender differences in adolescents and young adults with suicidal behavior. *Acta Psychiatrica Scandinavica, 104*(5), 332-339.

Young-Eisendrath, P. (1999). *Women and desire: Beyond wanting to be wanted*. New York: Harmony Books.

Zoccolillo, M. (1993). Toward a developmental perspective on conduct disorder [Special issue]. *Development & Psychopathology, 5*(1-2), 65-78.

Zoccolillo, M., & Rogers, K. (1991). Characteristics and outcome of hospitalized adolescent girls with conduct disorder. *Journal of the American Academy of Child and Adolescent Psychiatry, 30,* 973-981.

CHAPTER TWELVE

GROUP TREATMENT OF YOUNG PEOPLE WITH INTELLECTUAL IMPAIRMENT WHO SEXUALLY HARM

DAVE O'CALLAGHAN

Introduction

This chapter presents a rationale, framework and core elements of a group treatment programme for young people with intellectual impairment or developmental disability who sexually harm others. The material is based on the work of the Challenge Group at the G-MAP (Greater Manchester Adolescent Programme) Service in Manchester, UK and offers a practical description of the principal challenges and strategies involved in the delivery of an effective group treatment service. G-MAP is a specialist service for young people who sexually harm, offering both residential and community-based programmes. It promotes a holistic approach throughout its programmes with a strong emphasis on tailoring the intervention response to the particular needs of the young person, and their parents/carers.

The chapter opens with a brief review of the significance and impact of intellectual impairment and developmental disability amongst young people who sexually harm, before going on to highlight key challenges in the assessment and treatment of this population. The main body of this chapter, however, describes the use of group work to address six core therapeutic goals:

- Abuse specific
- Social Functioning
- Sexuality
- Family
- Influences on Participation
- Non-sexual Behavioural Problems

Intellectual disability and young people who sexually harm

To date the specific needs of young people with intellectual disabilities have received limited attention in the literature devoted to adolescents who sexually harm. Research data from forensic and treatment services in the UK working with youth who sexually offend demonstrate an apparent over representation of adolescents with developmental disabilities, with numbers ranging between a third up to fifty percent of samples surveyed (Edwards et al 2003; Vizard et al, in press; Dolan et al 1996). The variability in definitional criteria in many studies where scholastic or behavioural problems are combined with young people with pervasive developmental disabilities may confuse the picture. Nevertheless, there is clear evidence to suggest that a significant sub-section of young people who sexually harm do present with assessed intellectual impairments and that there is a particular gap in services for these young people.

In the UK context the definition of developmental impairment (the commonly used term being *learning disability*) is defined as:

> *A significantly reduced ability to understand new or complex information, to learn new skills and impaired intelligence (an IQ measurement of 70 or below), plus*

> *Reduced ability to cope independently (impaired social functioning) which started before adulthood and has a lasting effect on development (Department of Health 2001).*

This definition reflects a wide range of ability, stretching from individuals who can live independently with low levels of support to those with profound and possibility multiple impairments requiring high levels of care. This chapter considers work with adolescents and young adults who have a mild to moderate level of developmental disability and have some literacy, communication and retention skills. The terms that will be used throughout are that of developmental disability or intellectual impairment.

Available evidence suggests that the developmental adversities associated with the onset of problematic sexual behaviours in youth generally (such as trauma, disruption of attachment bonds, and family dysfunction) are also features of the life histories of intellectually disabled sexual offenders (Day, 1993; Lindsay, 2001; Thompson & Brown, 1998). However, particular issues that may adversely affect the development of positive sexual identities for intellectually disabled youth include a limited opportunity for social development, social isolation, limited sexual education, a lack of privacy, a lack of opportunity to experience normative and appropriate sexual interactions, specific difficulties in communication, and the impact of specific genetic and medical factors (Thompson & Brown 1998; Herzog & Money 1993). Media images do not generally provide positive representations of disability and young people with intellectual impairments may be more vulnerable to misconceptions and forming literal interpretations of the images of sexuality presented in film, TV and music videos.

Families and carers may feel uncertain about preparing young people for peer relationships and sexual activity, anxious about the potential for exploitation or inaccurately viewing the adolescent as too childlike to develop into a sexual person. Youth with developmental impairments are more likely to have their lives monitored by adults and have less privacy within which to engage in exploratory sexual behaviours with peers, and their capacity to form appropriate relationships may be inhibited by social functioning and communication deficits. We are increasingly aware of the heightened risk children and adults with all forms of disability have to sexual victimisation (Cooke & Sinason 1998) and this does appear to be a significant factor in the histories of those intellectually impaired individuals who sexually offend (Lindsay 2001). Lastly children with disabilities are at an increased risk of experiencing separation due to respite or full-time substitute care and those with developmental disabilities who sexually offend frequently appear to present with a history of disrupted attachments (Thompson & Brown 1998; Corbett 1996).

Assessment

Clinical assessment of offenders with intellectual disabilities must take account of the following four factors (Claire, 1994; Gudjonsson, 1993):

1) General literacy difficulties and problems in the comprehension of complex language;
2) specific deficits in speech and communication, such as limited vocabulary, or need to use signs or symbols to facilitate communication;
3) level of conceptual understanding; presence of memory deficits; and
4) level of suggestibility.

The majority of assessment frameworks developed for young people who sexually abuse do not specifically address the needs of developmentally disabled youth. The framework most widely employed within the UK is the model developed for the AIM project (Assessment, Intervention and Moving on), in Greater Manchester (Print et al 2001). The AIM model utilises two continuums; the first considers factors viewed as indicative of concern or risk and the second evaluates strengths present in the young person, their family or environment/support structure. An important aspect of the AIM assessment framework is that it combines an 'offence' specific focus with a wider assessment of the developmental, family and social context and needs of the young person.

O'Callaghan (2002a) has produced an assessment model specifically for intellectually impaired adolescents based upon a detailed developmental and behavioural review which covers each of the nine areas outlined below:

1) *Family of Origin Factors.* Including parent's level of intellectual functioning; development and functioning of siblings; family attitudes towards sexuality (particularly in respect of the child with a learning disability); and current family relationships and level of contact.
2) *Personal Health History.* Including specific known genetic conditions such as fragile X, Downs Syndrome, autistic spectrum disorders; other medical factors impacting on development, such as brain trauma; use of medication; and impact of other physical conditions if present.
3) *Developmental History.* Including point at which developmental delay was identified; and other behavioural problems that have been following a developmental trajectory.
4) *Care History.* Including bonding and attachment experiences; issues related to loss or separation, such as being subject to respite, substitute or hospital care; care concerns such as neglect, lack of stimulation, abuse, trauma, lack of supervision, and response of parents to their child being identified as having a learning disability.

5) *Educational History.* Including attendance at mainstream or special schooling; point at which Statement of Special Educational Needs was drafted; academic and social experience of schooling to date; and behaviour within the school setting.

6) *Assessment of General Cognitive Functioning.* Including memory and retention of information skills; attention and concentration skills; problem solving abilities; language, communication, and literacy skills; capacity for conceptual thinking; and ability to transfer and generalise solutions.

7) *Social Functioning.* Including access to social networks; activities and opportunities; relationships with peers; independence skills (such as mobility within the community, and use of public transport); level of supervision in the community; and assertiveness skills.

8) *Psycho-Sexual History.* Including known information on sexual maturity, for example when did the young person experience the onset of puberty, physical development, erectile response, use of masturbation; information known on the young person's past sexual experiences, and known experiences of sexual victimisation.

9) *History and Meaning of Problematic Sexual Behaviour.* This includes the range of behaviours demonstrated (exposure or contact offences). Key questions involve: at whom has the behaviour been targeted to date (children or adults, was the direction of the behaviour gender specific or not); relationship to those victimised (was the person a family member, fellow student, fellow service user, neighbour, or stranger); how has the young person gained access or made contact with those victimised; what were the settings and circumstances of the behaviour, and was there evidence of planning or targeting specific and more vulnerable people such as less able peers or certain care staff.

An important issue is consideration of whether the reported behaviour is genuinely sexually motivated. With this group of adolescents there appears an increased likelihood both of interpreting normative sexual behaviours as unacceptable, or of under-responding to offensive or abusive sexual conduct. Apparent sexual behaviours may in fact reflect a number of non-sexual needs or responses such as; attention seeking; evidence of distress; avoidance of undesired demands; controlling behaviours; and under-stimulation. Interpretation may be particularly difficult in more significantly disabled individuals with communication impairments. Evaluation of personal and sexual relationships involving intellectually impaired individuals can be complex and interactions may be located across a continuum from mutual and consenting through insensitive; exploitative to abusive. Key areas to consider are:

- The extent of the young person's appreciation of the general rules and conventions concerning sexual and interpersonal behaviour
- The young person's ability to distinguish between acceptable and unacceptable sexual behaviour
- Sexual experiences and influences, including sexual abuse
- An evaluation of sexual interests
- The opportunities the young person has to express their sexuality in a non-problematic manner
- The understanding the young person has of the potential consequences for sexually abusive/offensive behaviours

- How meaningful are future potential consequences
- Any specific skill deficits or knowledge deficits which may impact upon the young person's ability to express their sexuality in a healthy and non-problematic manner
- The support available from the young person's family or carers to the concept of them developing a healthy sexual identity
- What responses have adults and involved agencies made to problematic sexual behaviours to date (have they been ignored, attempts made to distract the young person from the behaviour, has the young person been subjected to sanction, restriction, or removal, have the police been involved, and is the young person subject to legal sanction?); have there been any previous attempt at therapeutic intervention.

Using the AIM framework (O'Callaghan 2002b) the information gained from the assessment can then be analysed in terms of the degrees of strengths and concerns. Young people with high concerns and low strengths present a much bigger management challenge than those with high concerns but where there are also high strengths. The value of this holistic assessment framework is that it not only provides pointers as to management decisions such as placement, or prosecution but also provides the basis for future service and therapeutic planning.

Challenges in Treatment Delivery

Practitioners need to develop intervention with reference to the specific needs of this group such as limited literacy skills; difficulties in the comprehension of complex language and concepts; possible speech and communications problems; memory deficits; and a potential for suggestibility. Commonly developmentally disabled individuals experience poor self-esteem and will find gaining and generalising new skills a particular challenge. Adaptive skills are likely to be dominated by strategies for coping in situations of demand, uncertainty or stress. It may be that resistance to or poor engagement in treatment may reflect an anxiety with attempts to move individuals on from established coping strategies. Addressing anxiety and creating a climate of comfort and safety is the foundation for work with intellectually impaired clients.

Treatment approaches

Treatment methodologies need to be participative, active and make use of multi-sensory techniques to maximise interest/engagement and to link emotion to learning. Drama, games and entertaining or novel approaches will increase the likelihood of retention. Practitioners need to ensure that treatment messages are explicit and regularly reinforced and that they check on retention throughout the programme. Examples employed should be concrete and relevant and identifiable in young people's everyday lives. The programme should clearly label desired vs. negative behaviours and aim to promote a model of healthy sexual expression rather than exclusively focus on the elimination/suppression of problematic sexual behaviours. The culture of programmes should value participation and mark and celebrate small gains in all areas of functioning and behaviour, not just those related to sexual misconduct. The development of ritual, iconography and familiar routines within the treatment context adds to a sense of predictability and security and will assist in fostering openness and provide an environment in which individuals are more likely to attempt new activities. It is important to design practical tools and resources that allow participants to continue learning and rehearsal outside of the treatment setting. Carers and other significant members of the young person's network need to be briefed on how to use these resources and understand the key messages that the treatment work is seeking to deliver.

Treatment methodologies

As yet there is a lack of controlled treatment evaluation studies relating to the developmentally disabled who sexually abuse, either adult or adolescent. The limited but evolving literature base (for a review see O'Callaghan 2004 in press) suggests that intervention is most effectively delivered within an ecological framework in which a variety of treatment components (individual, group, family/carer work) are delivered in concert. These should include educative, cognitive and skill development components, as well as work with parents/carers to support them and to identify how they can reinforce the treatment work. The emphasis on lifestyle and skills based approaches underscore the potential value of group work intervention with a strongly educative and competency development approach.

Programmes developed within the Applied Behavioural Analysis (ABA) tradition have been widely used within the field of intellectual disability to modify a range of challenging behaviours and also to promote skills development (Emerson, 2001). The ABA model assumes that all behaviour, including challenging behaviour, has a function, which can be assessed through an analysis of the setting events and background factors that precede the behaviour and the consequences that follow from it. In the case of challenging behaviour, once its function is understood, the individual can be taught new behaviours that achieve the same purpose. Descriptions of cognitive behavioural group-work programmes (Rose et al 2002; Lindsey et al 1998; Allam et al 1997) suggest these can be a potentially useful treatment component, though there is need to adapt delivery to the specific learning needs of the group. However, certain programme elements commonly included in a sexual offender treatment group curriculum, for example victim empathy, appear of limited relevance when working with individuals with intellectual disabilities.

Individual and family work

Although this chapter focuses primarily on group work there is always a need to undertake individual and family/carer work with young people alongside group work. The importance of the role and influence of parents/carers cannot be emphasised too strongly. Even where the young person is living away from home, parents continue to exercise significant influence particularly in their attitude to, and support for, the young person's involvement in therapeutic work. The nature of the parents/carers role will vary but it is essential at a minimum that the young person is supported and encouraged during the therapeutic work by at least one carer. In other cases where the young person is living at home or likely to return home, there will be a need for a more intensive involvement of parents/carers in family work alongside the group work.

Note: Readers who are interested in gaining a more detailed understanding of individual work may wish to see O'Callaghan (In press) AIM Guide to Intervention Work with Young People with Learning Disabilities who Sexually Harm. In relation to family work readers are referred to Duane, Y; Morrison, T (2004) Families of Young People Who Sexually Abuse: Characteristics Context and Considerations in W. Marshall, R. Beckett, A. Carr, and G. O'Reilly (Eds), Handbook of Clinical Intervention with Juvenile Sexual Abusers, Brunner Routledge. or Morrison, T; Wilkinson, L (in press) Family Assessment and Intervention Guide to be published by AIM (aimproject@msn.com).

The G-MAP Challenge Programme

In designing the G-MAP group programme for young men with intellectual disabilities and problematic sexual behaviour, known as the Challenge Group, we developed a modular structure with the following eleven programme blocks:

- Beginning the group
- Sexual development
- What is sexual abuse
- Four steps to abusive behaviour
- Old life/new life
- The consequences of sexual abuse
- Communication
- Relationships with others
- Staying safe/staying in control
- Being assertive/coping with anger

Making choices

The core messages of the group concern, are taking responsibility for sexual behaviour problems, being honest and being respectful of others. Concurrent individual work is a requirement of the group programme and is provided by members of the G-MAP clinical team. Throughout each topic block the link with individual therapy is focused around three questions. These are: (a) how does this help me understand my sexual behaviour problem?; (b) how can I get better at some things or learn more about them?; and (c) how will these help me better manage my sexual behaviour problem? The ethos of the group is supportive rather than confrontational and group members are encouraged to bring current issues for consideration and advice.

In the Challenge Group activities are dynamic and interactive with use of expressive mediums such as role-play, video, sculpting, games, drawing and collage. Group leaders join in many of the activities, particularly fun games aimed solely at warm-up and tension release. For any given programme module group leaders frequently provide the initial role-plays. Group members then vote on what they have seen in the role-plays (for example they may be asked to judge whether the behaviours that were role played were OK, not OK, or if they fall into a "not sure" category). Although activities that involve physical movement are encouraged for their benefit in promoting client participation (for example 'voting' is by running to labelled corners of the room), they do not involve touch between group members. Where text is used there is an emphasis on clear and simple language (such as; "what helps" or "what does not help" in managing anger).

Example of an ice-breaker exercise: The Bus Stop Game

This can be used in a variety of ways to cover a multitude of topics. The game consists of all the young people queuing at a bus stop to get on the bus. When the bus stops the driver (one of the group facilitators) asks the young person to state their name and answer a question relevant to the topic that is the focus of the particular block of work e.g., 'something that I have done this week which has been fair to others. Once on the bus, the young person is encouraged to take a seat and put on a seat belt (in order to emphasise keeping themselves safe). They are then asked to follow the verbal instructions for the journey given by the driver, which are given on an individual basis until all of the young people and the group facilitators are sat on the bus. The aim of this is to alleviate the stress of starting group or engaging in a new block of work. The questions asked as they get on the bus can be varied to reflect the topics under discussion. Thus during the Relationships Block (see below) the driver might ask the young person to say one important thing to remember about meeting people such as 'be polite' or 'keep personal space'. During the work concerned with staying safe (see below), the bus driver might ask each member to identify one way in which they have kept themselves or others safe during the past week.

Group members have portfolios with sections for each of the programme blocks. They save their work in this along with summaries of the key points from sessions. These are then reviewed and elaborated within individual sessions and made accessible to carers. At the outset of a topic block each participant commits to a relevant behavioural goal (for example, to improve their relationship with a particular individual). At the outset of each session group members provide feedback on how they have progressed with their goal. Each topic block lasts for six weeks, and the concluding session is attended by the young person's carer. Group members take a lead in presenting what the group has learned from the topic block and group members' individual therapists participate in this group process. These group review sessions are followed up in subsequent individual group members are helped to consider specific issues, such as what the young person has gained from the block and targets for the next block.

Topic blocks are designed as self-standing modules. New group members can enter at the outset of a programme block and progress through all modules from this point. The group is seen as only one intervention component that is part of a broader intervention plan. It may be used during the early stages of individual therapeutic intervention to enhance early messages or after a considerable amount of individual therapy when a young person is functioning at a level where they can gain most from the group. There is very limited focus within the group on the details of each group members own offences, although all group members provide summaries of their offending behaviour.

In the following sections the key aspects of group work undertaken during each of the 11 programme blocks will be highlighted:

1. Beginning the group

Careful pre-group selection and preparation of group members are essential. At the start of the group itself, group rules are very important and provide boundaries that ensure participants feel safe and encourage participation. In the Challenge Group the following rules are applied.

No name-calling.
> Don't be rude to each other.
> Let people finish what they are saying.
> We all listen to each other.

No swearing.
No bullying.
> Say what you want to say.
> Try your best.
> Say if you find it difficult.
> Group members should not talk about each other outside
>   of group.
> Try to be honest.

2. Sexual development: Establishing a baseline for sexual knowledge

A precursor to beginning detailed work on issues of sexual behaviour is to establish with the group an agreed and understood language concerning sexuality and the human body. Basic topics include terminology for male and female parts of the body; clarity as to acceptable language and agreement that certain terms are offensive and inappropriate; clarity - exploring a variety of sexual behaviour and addressing orientation and the basic facts of changes through puberty. It is important to begin discussion of these topics from a positive perspective emphasizing the normality and acceptability of sexual expression, excepting where it is illegal and harms others. Young people may have confusion around issues such as masturbation or the acceptability of homosexual orientation and these sessions are an opportunity to provide clear messages around these areas. Distinguishing between public and private behaviours and environments is additionally important. Many developmentally impaired adolescents experience high levels of adult supervision across all aspects of their lives and may have contravened acceptable standards by presenting non-problematic behaviours (for example masturbation) in public settings.

Sexual health is another important component of this block and will need to be tailored to the developmental level of the individuals in group. Emphasis will generally need to be upon clear, simple messages and practical education such as the demonstration of how to use a condom. A core message for young people during this block is that confusion and uncertainty are normal but that the therapeutic environment is a safe setting in which to explore these muddles and gain helpful information. Emphasis is placed on the importance of taking responsibility for one's own health and that of other peoples. Lastly, the block will begin to identify that thoughts and feelings are a central part of sexual behaviour.

3. What is sexual abuse?

For adolescents within the mild to borderline category of intellectual disability most can be assisted to employ the concepts of fair, unfair and abusive in labelling sexual behaviours and interactions. For more significantly impaired individuals a distinction between YES and NO as to sexual behaviour may be more applicable. For example on the YES list are criteria such as:

Over 16
Consent [say yes – want to]
Boyfriend/girlfriend
Husband/wife
Happy
Private place

On the NO list:

Under 16
Family members
Strangers
Carers/staff
Not asked
Don't understand
They say no
Sad
Upset
Scared
Angry

The general message is that abuse occurs when the other person: is forced, not asked; is too young or unable to understand. For developmentally disabled adolescents it may be particularly difficult to apply these criteria to other, more intellectually impaired peers who appear to be passive or accepting of sexual interactions. Teaching by role-play, narrative accounts or storyboarding can promote a better understanding and improved skills in establishing that the other individual is offering clearly informed consent. Emotional labelling is an important aspect of this block, in that abusive or unfair sexual interactions are characterised by emotions of fear, confusion and anxiety, whilst genuine consensual interactions have a more positive emotional quality. Carers and supporters can be identified as important sources of clarification to help young people check out whether to proceed with certain interactions or behaviours. Work completed in this block will also assist adolescents to identify what was abusive and unacceptable in their own behaviour.

4. The four steps of abusive behaviour
Work in this area is effectively a precursor to relapse management components using Finklehor's (1984) concept of four preconditions to abusive sexual behaviour that include: motivation to abuse; overcoming internal inhibitors; overcoming external inhibitors, overcoming the victim's resistance. This model is adapted and employed as an aid to individuals to offer an external description of thoughts, feelings and behaviours that precede sexually abusive behaviours. The Challenge Group has constructed four substantial wooden blocks of increasing size and employ the following terminology to represent the four steps (preconditions) to abuse:

Wanting to
Thinking about it
Getting the chance
Doing it

Figure 1: The 4 Step model adapted from Finkelhor's Four Preconditions to Sexual Abuse

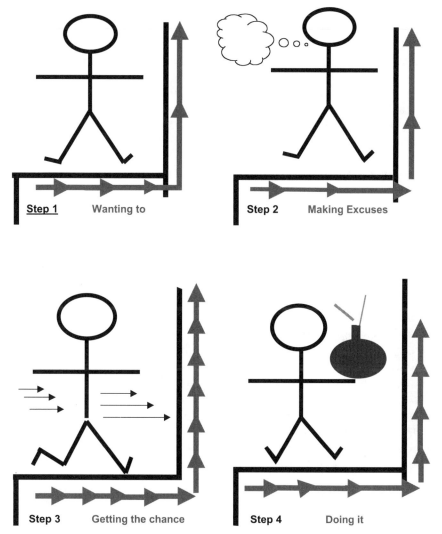

Step 1   Wanting to

Step 2   Making Excuses

Step 3   Getting the chance

Step 4   Doing it

Each group member is given a situation, such as observing a child whilst out on an activity. He is then asked whether this situation would move him on to step 1 (wanting to) and if the answer is affirmative the young person steps on to the first block and provides a description of the physical sensations associated with wanting to. These are likely to include experiencing an erection, heart beating faster, feeling butterflies in the stomach, hands getting sweaty, face getting red. The young person is then asked whether in that situation he would move up to the next step which is 'thinking about it', i.e., thinking about sexual contact with the child. Once again if the young person agrees to such thoughts he climbs on to the next step and provides an account of what he might think. Commonly this would include thoughts such as 'is the child alone? I could go over to them. Perhaps I could touch them.' The young person moves up to the next step and describes actions they may take to give them an opportunity to gain proximity to the child or to make some kind of contact with the child. They are now in a situation where they have a chance to abuse.

The young person is then asked at this point whether he would be likely to continue on to step 4 and act on the urges and thoughts if there was no care/supervisor present to prevent that. In most cases the young person agrees this would happen. The young person does not physically go up on to step 4 and the external restraint is represented by the group leader putting his/her arm across in front of the last step and encouraging the group to identify the negative consequences of taking the last step.

By repeated use in group sessions and the observation of other group members undertaking the exercise, the 4 Steps becomes a familiar method by which the young person can describe thoughts and sensations associated with the progression towards sexual offending. This can then be built upon by considering what external features are observable by carers/supporters as an indication that the young person is experiencing risky thoughts and feelings. Openness and honesty is the primary goal here.

The safety and familiarity of the process frequently allows young people to identify situations and feelings as being risky that they have previously been resistant to discuss. At this point the group leaders are likely to emphasise labelling of the problem and supporting and praising honesty and openness, rather than attempting to explore any self-management strategies. At this stage the focus is on external management as being the main component to prevent the young person from offending.

5. Old Life - New Life: The roadway to new life

The organising concept for the development of positive personal goals in the group is that of New Life/Old Life (see Figure 2 below). This visual framework provides a central concept of the Challenge Programme aims and is consistent with the growing recognition in the field of sex offender treatment that treatment goals must grow out of an individuals goals and aspirations (e.g. Ward & Stewart, 2003; Longo, 2001). Haaven and colleagues (Haaven 1990) developed the concept of old me, new me in their work with developmentally disabled adult sex offenders. This terminology has latterly been adopted within the sex offence treatment programme run in British prisons for sexual offenders with a mild learning disability (Hill and Hordell 1999).

In adapting this concept for use with intellectually disabled adolescents our intention was to use it in a dynamic manner that facilitated the following:
  • Recognition that change is an on-going process that allows incidents of Old Life behaviours not to lead to a sense of hopelessness but provide an opportunity for participants to reaffirm their positive goals and learn how to cope with the occurrence of negative and risky behaviours
  • Through use of a New Life rather than a New Me concept, acknowledgement that others, such as family-members and carers, have a significant role to play in shaping the quality of a young person's life and will need to contribute to the change process
  • Provision of a method for clearly labelling negative Old Life and positive

New Life behaviours
- Monitoring of progress by young people in the programme
- Exploration of ideas and behaviours that young people struggle to label as reflecting either Old or New Life.

The Old Life - New Life concept thus incorporates three elements: 1) the individual's own goals; 2) the potential contribution of others; and 3) behavioural signposts marking either progression towards those goals or behaviour that was regressive.

Figure 2: Old Life – New Life diagram

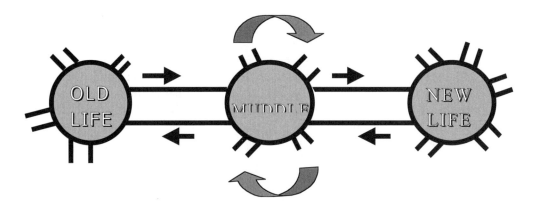

In the Challenge group the roadway is laid out on roles of paper with sufficient space for group members to place their own posters around it, depicting both Old Life experiences and New Life hopes. Posters, collages, drawings, photographic and video resources are all employed to assist in the articulation of Old Life experiences and New Life hopes. Simple drawings can often have a vivid emotional resonance, for example, one young man drew an image of the belt his stepfather used to hit him with. Another drew himself as a stick figure at the window of a burning house, recalling an incident where his mentally ill mother had locked him in his bedroom and set fire to the house. New Life hopes are often striking for bare simplicity and modesty, with young people drawing pictures of themselves being able to go to the shops on their own, go swimming, ride a bike or have a girlfriend. A similar exercise with more able adolescents would generally produce images of fast cars and dreams of success or fortune through sport or music.

The terminology of Old Life and New Life allows exploration of change, not just at the level of the individual but of family members, carers and other supporters who can assist the young person towards their New Life goals. Sadly in some cases the changes that young people may identify as New Life hopes from family members are unlikely to occur due to families' inability or unwillingness to change. Never the less such aspirations are important to acknowledge and the young person helped to understand how they can manage if others do not engage in desired change.

As can be seen from Figure 2 the centre of the New Life roadway is bisected by 'muddle roundabout' which provides a forum for considering those confused thoughts, feelings and behaviours that young people struggle to label as positive or regressive. This may relate for example to uncertainties about sexual responses to carers, family members, peers or ambivalent feelings about adults who have sexually victimized them or confusion around specific boundaries and acceptability of certain behaviours. On either lane of the New Life roadway colour coded road signs can be placed so that, for example, green road signs (go) can denote progression towards New Life goals and red road signs (stop) indicate Old Life behaviours.

These may be generalised within a group work context and then further specifically customised in individual work sessions. Examples can include red signs denoting behaviour such as collecting pictures of children, not being honest with staff; or walking away from staff. Positive indicators denoted by green road signs might include 'talking before I blow up', 'being honest about risky feelings', 'asking for help when I need it'. The roadway can subsequently be used for individuals to track their own progress in employing the green sign behaviours and avoiding the red sign behaviours. Although most young people are likely to begin with an over-optimistic evaluation of their ability to achieve such goals, over the course of the programme they generally become much more realistic, often spending much of the period of work focusing on the 'muddle' roundabout frequently indicating uncertainty or ambivalence about the potential for change.

6. Consequences of sexually harmful behaviour

The current consensus of clinical practice would suggest that the traditional sex offender treatment programme concept of victim empathy has limited utility with individuals who have developmental impairment. Emphasis is generally on ensuring consequences for the individual are vivid, meaningful and resonant. Within the Challenge Programme young people explore the negative impact on their life thus far of sexual offending; how it has affected those close to them such as family and what would be the consequences envisioned for further offending. Posters and artwork can be valuable activities but experience suggests the most resonant and memorable approach is the use of role play, which can be video taped for subsequent review.

The familiarity of the 4 Steps model established earlier in the programme is used to consider what would happen to the individual if he did reach the fourth step. We return to the concept of placing the individual in a risky situation and having him describe the pattern of thoughts and feelings as he proceeds towards acting out sexually. However on this occasion the young person is permitted to reach the fourth step. As he physically walks up each step the previous step is removed, until the individual is left standing alone on step 4 (the tallest of all four blocks). This is to symbolize that the young person cannot go back down the four steps once they have acted out sexually.

A new direction is now laid out as the young person walks along the 'consequences path' where we role play the arrest by police, being taken to the police station, interviewed and then a significant person (parent/carer) coming to the police station and asking the young person what has happened. This focus on immediate consequences generally has the most impact as young people are more able to imagine what would happen at the point in which they are detected in the commission of a crime. They imagine the anger of people in the immediate environment and the distress of a parent or carer having to come to the police station.

The idea of police involvement may be a new concept for many young people who have not experienced any legal sanctions resulting from their offensive behaviour to date. Often the only consequences imagined by young people may be that of being told off, kept in or having to see a Head Teacher at their school. During this block we also provide clear messages about the harm caused to the victim of sexual abuse, which may be further illustrated by reference to young people's own experiences of victimisation. The young people's ability to form such a connection or to experience an emotionally empathic reaction is, however, generally limited by the individual's intellectual impairment and thus the more effective focus, in terms of consequences, is generally egocentric in the terms of consequences for the individual himself.

7. Communication
Clearly many adolescents with developmental disabilities will have some degree of impaired communication skills resulting from difficulties with complex language and concepts. This is frequently exacerbated by levels of anxiety, poor self esteem or compromised further by additional speech or hearing impediments or a tendency to communicate in stereotypical ritualised forms common to many individuals on the autistic disorder spectrum. This is therefore an important element of the programme given that the development of relapse management skills involves working cooperatively and communicating honestly and openly with carers and supporters.

Group work environments allow for the extensive rehearsal of varying scenarios looking at helpful (New Life), unhelpful (Old Life), and confusing (muddled) forms of communication. The feedback to the young person's external network is essential in order to assist the individual to practice specific skills and to identify to carers and supporters particular communication methods established with the young person, especially around difficult issues such as negative or risky feelings. Three key messages for young people are that: 1) communication involves both expressing one's thoughts, wishes and feelings and listening to others; 2) feelings such as anger or arousal can prevent effective listening; and 3) improved communication can be helpful, particularly in risky situations.

8. Relationships with others
Many young people with developmental disabilities have a limited understanding of the varying degrees of intimacy and boundaries that can exist within relationships. In seeking friendships, they may be prone to inappropriate disclosure and to assume that all friendly individuals are instantly their friends. This may be discomfiting for others or indeed lead the young person into situations of vulnerability. For example, one young man was contacted by an adult male after he had taken part in a disabled sports activity. The young man believed that he had gained a 'best friend' but the adult male then abused the young man and engaged him in abusing an even less able peer. Group exercises can be utilised that identify what are appropriate and inappropriate approaches to establishing friendships and regulating boundaries. For instance members can be asked to identify the different types of relationships they have with different people, e.g., parents, teachers, friends, or the person who owns the video shop. They can then evaluate what is or is not appropriate in these different settings.

In running groups for developmentally disabled youth it is notable that the group itself becomes a key social contact for the young people involved who may otherwise lead very isolated lives. The young people can develop friendships with other group members and the group allows for the rehearsal of relationship skills. Additionally group members can be helped to recognise how relationships with supporters can be essential in helping the young person work towards New Life Goals.

9. Staying safe staying in control

A primary goal of therapy is the reduction of problematic sexual behaviours through the development of self-management or relapse prevention (RP) skills. Risk of continuing sexual aggression may be conceptualised in three domains:

- Predisposing Risks: Such as traumatic sexualisation; attachment/intimacy/ empathy problems; and general difficulties with social functioning.
- Precipitating Risks: Such as arousal; impulsivity; and opportunity.
- Perpetuating Risks: Such as lack of support or supervision; the absence of a model of healthy sexuality; and poor social and self-regulatory skills.

Overall progress may result from positive gains in all three domains but self-management strategies are best if they focus on precipitating factors (for example, developing specific responses to high risk situations that are the immediate precursors to offending). Individuals with intellectual disabilities can develop self-management skills but require a framework that recognises and adapts to particular difficulties.

Effective risk management requires four key skills: firstly the ability to identify risky situations, thoughts and feelings; secondly the motivation to avoid acting on the drive to offend, thirdly a preparedness to be open and honest about risky thoughts and feelings, and fourthly the retention and employment of specific skills and strategies in managing and minimising risk. This section of the group work programme focuses upon three areas:

1) clear labelling of risky thoughts and behaviours
2) identification of possible alternatives
3) developing confidence with specific risk management skills.

The first phase reinforces the work undertaken by young people in the 4 Steps section and considers the type of feelings that might be generated by specific situations. Experience suggests that it is usually not productive to spend time with the group in attempting to analyse why a young person may be in a particular situation, or focusing on the strength of risky responses for example, whether they include arousal. It is more effective for the young person to identify his feelings in the particular situation and then to focus on his choices in terms of thinking (e.g., between new life and old life thoughts?), and doing.

Figure 3 below is a diagrammatic representation of the connections between situations, feelings, thoughts and behaviours. Figures 4 and 5 are examples of the model's use in group.

Figure 3: Model of connections between situation, feelings, thoughts and behaviours

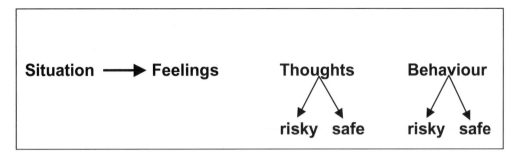

Figure 4: Example one of the use of the model

Figure 5: Example two of the use of the model

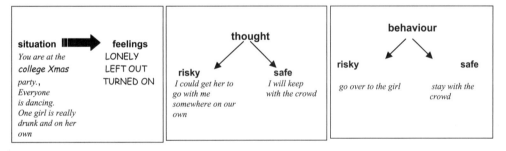

The Challenge Toolkit

Once young people have developed a consistent ability to identify and label risky thinking and behaviours and produce safe and appropriate alternatives, it is possible to move on to the Challenge Toolkit. This contains the principle skill set involved in developing risk management competencies. The toolkit comprises a series of six icons which the young men have available within their own portfolios and on wallet cards as well as posters and worksheets. Each icon represents one of the following

1. Danger   (identifying dangerous situations or thoughts).

2. Stop   (any activity that is increasing risk or is wrong)

3. Escape   (get out of risky situations).

4. Talk   (go to someone and discuss your risky behaviour).

5. Listen   (to what they say or to your own safe thoughts).

6. Think   (about what is said).

Rehearsing the Toolkit: 'Risky and Safe Islands'

Rehearsal of the Toolkit skills is primarily through the exercise of 'risky islands'. In this a group member stands upon a tilting circular board, which for many young people with impaired gross motor skills can feel somewhat unsafe. The young person is presented with a 'risky island' situation. This might be visiting home when a neighbour calls in with a young child, during which the young person realises that as his mother and neighbour are busy talking that he could touch the young child without being observed. The young person has to cross the room from the 'risky' to a 'safe' island (a stable flat board) by use of the Toolkit as steppingstones. Each group member is holding up an element of the Toolkit and the young person has to choose which items to use to cross to 'safe-island'. Through frequent rehearsal group members develop a highly critical mindset and will only provide a particular element of the Toolkit as a steppingstone if the young person can convince them he is using it appropriately and honestly.

One powerful aspect of the repetition is the ability of young people to develop a quick response to a risky situation and identify initial steps that will hold or minimise the risk while they think their way through the situation more comprehensively. Young people who make less progress often display an uncertainty about the initial steps, which appears to reflect ambivalence, about the desire to leave 'risky island.'

During the rehearsals elements of the Toolkit can be used in any order and as many times as the young person can identify a valid method of employment. Emphasis is placed on the individual describing exactly how he would employ that tool. For example if a young person is asking to talk to someone about a risky feeling, he would be asked by other group members to identify who he wishes to talk to, exactly what he would say and how honest he is prepared to be. Beginning with hypothetical examples young people can progress to describe and debrief recent or previous real 'risky island' incidents. They can also use worksheets to plan how to stay safe and in control in new or forthcoming situations. Clearly the familiarity of carers and supporters with this framework and the individual risk management strategies of the young person are essential if the young person is to generalise these skills into an external environment.

10. Assertiveness and anger management

Young people with developmental disabilities are prone both to being generally under-assertive and over-compliant, and to display aggression and poor self-regulation in situations of stress or frustration. As part of addressing this issue, it is important to teach young people how to recognise different feelings states accurately. One simple method is to pin up labels of different feelings and have the group facilitators act these out. The task for the members is to identify which behaviour is linked to which feeling. As well as recognising others' feelings they must also learn to recognise their own. This can be done by asking group members to develop coloured posters depicting what makes them 'happy/sad/frustrated' etc., using the format of 'I get frustrated when…'.

Key messages for young people are that feelings of anger, sadness or frustration are part of everyday life but individuals have choices as to how to act when upset and angry. The development of assertion skills in the group is designed to provide young people with clear messages as to their rights to express their views and communicate their wishes.

11. Making Choices

Dependent on the degree of their impairment many young people may have limited abilities to make choices in their lives. This concluding block of the programme aims to identify the significance of different choices and highlight ones in which young people may need to gain advice, information or support particularly around issues of safety and risk.

One exercise is called 'My desert island choices'. This involves providing each member with a large sheet of paper with an outline of a desert island that they are asked to fill in with details of their imaginary island (rivers, fish, animals etc.) They are then given six tokens representing money, which can be spent at an imaginary shop that sells provisions that may both be useful or useless on the island. Thus the shop sells tent/food/matches/fresh water but also cars and computers, each of which is represented by a pre-cut picture from a magazine. The group members are then asked to spend their items using their tokens one at a time, and placing the picture of the purchased item on their island. This gets the group to think about safe and appropriate choices in a dynamic and visual fashion which can then be the subject of discussion.

Working in Conjunction with Families, Carers, and Supporters

If treatment messages and skills initiated in therapeutic settings are to have value and the potential to be transferred and generalised by the young persons to the 'real world' then the role of carers and allied supporters is critical. As a foundation it is important for treatment providers to meet with carers and spend time addressing their concerns and questions. This is particularly important when young people are living with parents who may have adopted a policy of containment to address inappropriate sexual behaviours and require support to considerer the potential of the young person to develop an appropriate and healthy sexual identity. We find it is usually important to provide some separate time for parents/carers to offer them support and gain understanding of the particular stresses and difficulties they experience. Parents/carers need to gain a familiarity with the philosophy and key messages of the programme and then have direct opportunity to experience the strategies taught in therapy. In particular we have found that it is particularly important that parents/carers understand and share in the philosophy of positive reinforcement for all examples of progress and New Life behaviours.

The most productive approach is to directly involve carers in all or a proportion of the sessions undertaken. Young people can demonstrate skills learnt and opportunities for rehearsal can be planned and debriefed. Levels of supervision are frequently the most anxiety provoking issue for carers who will often need clear guidance and feedback of how to make decisions on what level of restriction, management and supervision is appropriate for a young person and how these may be gradually reduced as the young person makes progress. A typical programme for increasing autonomy is outlined below:

- Predisposing Stage 1 - Young Person goes into local shop with carer observing from the outside
- Predisposing Stage 2 - Young Person goes into local shop with carer observing from across the road
- Predisposing Stage 3 - Young Person walks to shops with carer following from a distance
- Predisposing Stage 4 - Young Person walks to local shops with carer monitoring half way
- Predisposing Stage 5 - Young Person walks to local shops and returns unaccompanied with agreed time limits

This general approach can be transferred to a range of activities. It is important that each phase is a fairly discrete task that can be implemented, monitored and evaluated over a relatively short timescale. Clinicians should meet with carers and the young person to debrief on the individual stages and look for indicators that the young person has applied self-management strategies.

Honesty and the ability of the young person to communicate about risk is a key variable. Carers will report that although they have identified external cues, for example the young person staring at children, they have attempted to raise this directly but faced denial. Often young people will subsequently confirm the impressions of their carers to therapists' but state that they found raising the issue directly or accepting the challenge by the carer at the time too difficult. One approach we have found useful is the use of the 'Four Step' cards. These are a series of four cards, which use visual icons to mirror the Four Steps towards abusive behaviour that young people will have rehearsed in the programme i.e. Wanting To; Thinking About It; Getting The Chance; and Doing It. Carers will hold the cards and the young person is given the responsibility to ask for the relevant card should he begin to experience sexual feelings and thoughts. When in possession of the card the young person is given an opportunity to devise a simple exit or coping strategy and if able to do so then returns the card to the carer. The skill and commitment of carers in providing a range of opportunities, encouraging the young person to employ strategies, and praising examples of efforts towards progress is an essential factor.

The goal for the young person is to identify risk at the earliest stage and ask the carer for the appropriate card. The young person then identifies a strategy to escape or manage the risk e.g. by looking away from children on a bus; leaving a shop in which children are present; moving to a different part of the park. He then returns the card to the carer to note he has successfully dealt with the situation. If the young person is only able to communicate the risk but not provide an escape strategy carers can offer one. Situations can be rehearsed in sessions, problems debriefed, and successes celebrated.

Conclusion

This chapter has sought to provide a practical description of a group treatment programme designed to meet the needs of young people with intellectual impairment who sexually harm others. Given the lack of services in general for these young people and practice descriptions in particular, it is hoped that this chapter will encourage more practitioners to develop more services. Our experience suggests that not only is it possible to do so, but that it is of significant benefit in assisting these young people with a range of both sexual and non sexual problems, and developing strategies that will enable them to establish safe and healthy lifestyles. The cornerstone of such group work is a detailed and holistic assessment at the outset, a customised programme utilising expressive and dynamic media, attention to repetition and reinforcement, and close liaison with, and support of, parent and carers.

References

Allam, J., Middleton, D. and Browne, K. (1997) Different clients, different needs?: practice issues in community based treatment for sex offenders. *Criminal Behaviour and Mental Health*, Vol 7 69--84.

Clare, I. (1993) "Issues in the assessment and treatment of the male sex offender with mild learning disabilities". *Journal of Sexual and Marital Therapy* 8 (2) 167-180.

Cooke, L.B. and Sinason, V. (1998) Abuse of people with learning disabilities and other vulnerable adults. *Advances in Psychiatric Treatment* 4, 119-125.

Corbett, A. (1996) The role of attachment in working with people with learning disabilities who commit sexual offences. *NAPSAC Bulletin* March, 14-17.

Demetral, G.D. (1994) Diagrammatic assessment of ecological integration of sex offenders with mental retardation in community residential facilitates. *Mental Retardation* 32, 141-5.

Department of Health (2001) *Valuing People: A New Strategy for Learning Disability for the 21st Century*. Department of Health Publications, London

Dolan, M., Holloway, J., Bailey, S., and Kroll, L. (1996) The psychosocial characteristics of juvenile sexual offenders. *Medicine, Science and the Law*. 36 (4) 342-352.

Duane, Y.; Morrison, T. (in press 2004) Families of Young People Who Sexually Abuse: Characteristics Context and Considerations. In G. O'Reilly, W. Marshall, A. Carr, & R. Beckett (Eds), *Handbook of clinical intervention with juvenile sexual abusers*. Hover and New York: Brunner-Routledge.

Edwards, R. (2003). *Predicting Dropout from a Residential Programme for Adolescent Sexual Abusers using Pre-Treatment Variables and Implications forRecidivism: Towards the development of a scale*. Presentation of the paper Predicting Dropout from a Residential Program for Adolescent Sexual Abusers using Pre-Treatment Variables and Implications for Recidivism (Edwards, R., Beech, A., Bishopp, D., Erikson, M., Friendship, C. & Charlesworth L. at the Home Office and DOH Conference on Young People who Sexually Abuse – 17/10/03

Emerson, E (2001) *Challenging Behaviour: Analysis and Intervention in People with Severe Learning Disabilities*. UK: Cambridge Press.

Finkelhor, D. (Ed.) (1984) *Child Sexual Abuse: New Theory and Research.* New York: Free Press.

G-MAP (2001) *A Modular Groupwork Manual for Intellectually Disabled Youth who Sexually Harm.* G-MAP, Manchester, England (Unpublished).

Gudjonsson, G., Clare, I., Rutter, S., et al (1993) *Persons at Risk During Interviews in Police Custody: The Identification of Vulnerabilities.* London: Royal Commission on Criminal Justice, HMSO.

Haaven, J., Little, R. and Petre-Miller, D. (1990) *Treating Learning Disabled Sex Offenders*: A Model Residential Programme. Orwell, VT: The Safer Society Press.

Haaven, J., and Coleman, E. (2000). Treatment of the Developmentally Disabled Sex Offender. In D. R. Laws: S. M. Hudson & T. Ward (Eds) *Remaking Relapse Prevention with Sex Offenders: A Sourcebook.* Thousand Oaks, CA: Sage.

Herzog, D and Money, J (1993) Sexology and social work in the case of Klinefelters (47 XXY) syndrome. *Mental Retardation* 3 (3) 161–2.

Hill, J., and Hordell, A. (1999) The Brooklands sex offender treatment programme. Learning Disability Practice, 1 (4) 16-23.

Lindsay, W.R., Neilson, C.Q., Morrison, F., and Smith, A.H (2001) A comparison of physical and sexual abuse histories of sexual and non-sexual offenders with intellectual disability. *Child Abuse and Neglect* 25(7) July: 989-995.

Longo, R. (2001) *Paths to Wellness: A holistic approach and guide for Personal recovery.* Holyoke, MA: NEARI Press

Morrison, T; Wilkinson, L (in press 2004) Family Assessment and Intervention Guide to be published by AIM aimproject@msn.com)

O'Callaghan, D. (1999) Young abusers with learning disabilities: towards better understanding and positive intervention. In M. Calder (ed) *Working with Young People who Sexually Abuse: New Pieces of the Jigsaw.* Brighton, UK: Russell House Publishing.

O'Callaghan, D (2002a). Providing a research informed service for young people who sexually harm others. In . M. Calder (Ed) *Young People who Sexually Abuse: Building an Evidence Base for Your Practice*, Brighton, UK: Russell House Publishing.

O'Callaghan, D. (2002b) A framework for undertaking assessment of young people with intellectual disabilities who present problematic/harmful sexual behaviours. In *The AIM Project: Working with Children and Young People who Display Sexually Harmful Behaviour - Assessment Manual.* The AIM Project, Manchester.

O'Callaghan, D (2004) Adolescents with Intellectual Disabilities who Sexually Harm: Intervention Design and Implementation. In G. O'Reilly, W. Marshall, A. Carr, & R. Beckett (Eds), *Handbook of clinical intervention with juvenile sexual abusers.* Hover and New York: Brunner-Routledge.

O'Callaghan, D (in press) A Guide to Intervention and Treatment Work with young people with intellectual disabilities who present problematic/harmful sexual behaviours. to be published by AIM aimproject@msn.com)

Print, B., Morrison, T., Henniker, J. (2001) An Inter-agency Assessment Framework for Young People who sexually abuse: Principles, Processes and Practicalities in Calder, M. (ed) (2001) Juveniles and Children who Sexually Abuse: Frameworks for Assessment Second Edition. RHP

Rose, J., Jenkins, R., O'Connor, C., Jones, C., Felce, D.,(2002) A group treatment for men with Intellectual Disabilities who Sexually Offend or Abuse. *Journal of Applied Research in Intellectual Disabilities* 15, 138 – 150

Thompson, D. and Brown, H. (1998) *Response-ability: Working with men with learning disabilities who have difficult or abusive sexual behaviours.* Brighton, England. Pavilion.

Vizard, E., French, L., Hickey, N., and Bladon, E. In press. Severe personality emerging in childhood: a proposal for a new developmental disorder. Criminal Behaviour and Mental Health.

Ward, T. & Stewart, C. A. (2003)   *Good lives and the rehabilitation of sex offenders.* In Ward, T., Laws, D. R., & Hudson, S. H.   (Eds.)Sexual deviance: Issues and controversies (pp21-44).   Thousand Oaks, CA: Sage.

CHAPTER THIRTEEN

BUILDING A HOLISTIC APPROACH IN THE TREATMENT OF YOUNG PEOPLE WHO SEXUALLY ABUSE

TONY MORRISON

Introduction

This chapter describes the context, drivers, challenges, and building blocks involved in the development of a holistic approach to the assessment, management and treatment of young people who sexually abuse others. It draws on both clinical work at the GMAP programme and wide experience of project and policy consultation work both in the United Kingdom (UK), and in other jurisdictions. GMAP (Greater Manchester Adolescent Programme) is a specialist treatment facility for young people with sexually harmful behaviour problems, offering both community and residential provision with a strong emphasis on holistic and systemic approaches. Although the chapter is located in the context of the UK child welfare and youth justice systems, it is hoped that the material will be generalisable to readers working in other jurisdictions. For whilst important contextual variables exist, experience suggests we face shared challenges and recognise very similar problems. Moreover given the relative youth of this field and the paucity of literature and research about what works, it is essential that we share our different approaches in order to widen the pool of knowledge and practice wisdom in a field that can attract such powerful public opprobrium and professional anxiety.

What follows therefore, is a discussion of work in progress rather than a prescription for holistic methodology. Indeed the very nature of holistic practice cautions against claims of finality or certainty whilst holding firmly to developmental and ecological principles and processes. Nevertheless the chapter offers a practical and not just theoretical discussion of holistic approaches, which will resonate with many of the other contributions in this book.

The chapter opens with a discussion of some important legal and organisational features of the UK and an overview of the current state of the art with regard to the UK service context before addressing a number of questions. These include:

- What are the drivers and barriers to a holistic approach in this field?
- Why is a holistic approach important and how does it differ to the way in which this field has developed in the UK?

- What are the macro, mezzo and micro level constituents of a holistic approach?
- What might it look like on the ground based on the work of the AIM and GMAP programmes in Greater Manchester?

Features of the UK Context

Readers of this book are likely to be drawn from a variety of contexts and jurisdictions, as far apart as the USA, Canada, New Zealand, Australia, UK, and Ireland as well as other European countries. This will have considerable implications for how the material will need to be translated into the reader's own context.

For instance, criminal justice systems in much of Europe and New Zealand follow a restorative justice approach in contrast to North America and Australia who follow an adversarial system. In the UK, also an adversarial system, there is increasing attention being paid to restorative justice approaches. Within the different criminal justice systems there are wide variations in the powers and disposals available to the courts; for instance, how far parents may be compelled to engage with services. This reflects wider cultural differences about how the problem of young people who sexually abuse is seen at a political and societal level which is in turn further influenced by public attitudes towards youth crime more generally.

Higher degrees of societal anxiety about youth crime are likely to be reflected in more punitive and less child-centred responses. For instance, Chaffin and Bonner's editorial (1998) in a special edition of *Child Maltreatment* on juvenile sexual offenders was entitled: "Don't shoot, We're Your Children: Have we gone too far in our response to adolescent sexual abusers and children with sexual behaviour problems?" The editorial went on to warn: "We should be on our guard against the potentially punitive aversive and absolutist tone inherent in some of our treatment beliefs. Punitive approaches must be considered within the context of a current political climate that exaggerates our fear of juvenile crime, and energises corresponding movements to punish children and youth as we would do hardened adults" (p.3-4). Programmes, especially those seeking more holistic approaches must be acutely aware of the wider socio-political context in which they work and how these impact on professional's responses.

There are also major differences in the degree to which services are provided, mainly in public and voluntary (not for profit) sectors in contrast to private providers financed either by insurance or personal fee systems, and the degree to which central, rather than local, government prescribes systems, services and standards.

In the United States the private provider sector accounts for well over half of all services. In contrast, in the UK this sector accounts for a much smaller proportion of services. The UK also has a much stronger tradition than most other countries of centrally prescribed guidance on inter-agency collaboration identified in documents such as *Working Together to Safeguard Children* (Department of Health, 1999) and the UK's national *Framework for the Assessment of Children in Need and their Families* (Department of Health, 2000). At the local authority level the UK has a well established system of Children's Service Planning processes and Local Childrens' Safeguarding Boards.

The latter are responsible for the coordination at a strategic level of inter-agency policies, services, training, and auditing in relation to child protection issues, and who
have been a key forum through which services for young abusers have been coordinated. Taken together, the public sector base to service delivery and the strong
emphasis on inter-agency collaboration across child welfare and youth justice fields,
offers in theory at least, a firm foundation for holistic work.

This is potentially further enhanced by current policy proposal entitled Every Child
Matters (DOH 2003) from the English and Welsh governments which emphasises the
importance of early support to vulnerable children and families, delivered through
integrated services. The policy envisions social services, education and parts of the
health system merging as organisations called Childrens' Trusts to deliver services to
vulnerable and at risk children. Having provided an overview of the policy context in
which UK services operate we turn now to look more specifically at the state of service development for young people who sexually abuse.

Services for Young People Who Sexually Abuse: A UK Overview

In the UK the National Children's Home Report (NCH Report, 1992) provided the
first comprehensive picture of how young abusers were being managed in the UK. It
painted a gloomy picture highlighting: conflicts concerning the definition of juvenile
sexual abuse; the absence of a coordinated management structure which resulted in
individual agencies intervening without reference to others, decisions being made
without the involvement of professionals with expertise in sexual abuse issues;
absence of policy; uncertainty about the legitimacy of the work; clashes of philosophy
especially between juvenile justice and child protection approaches; inadequate data
about the nature, scope and effects of the problem; an absence of internal and inter-
agency policy and practice guidance; lack of clarity about assessment and intervention models; absence of services for young abusers; placement problems and risks
arising from victims and abusers being placed in the same accommodation; inadequate supervision and training; and isolation for front line workers trying to tackle
the problem. It recommended the need for a comprehensive national strategy.

Over a decade later, there is still no national strategy. Nevertheless there have been
significant improvements. A large scale research exercise to map professional
approaches attitudes and services has been conducted (Hackett, Mason, and Phillips,
2002), replicating in part the taskforce on juvenile sex offenders coordinated by Ryan
in the US several years earlier. This has demonstrated significant changes in attitude
from a decade ago when young people with sexual behaviour problems were treated
as if they were simply 'mini' adult sex offenders in the waiting. In contrast in this survey there were high measures of inter-professional consensus that, whilst focus on the
protection of other children, is the over-arching goal:

- A developmental approach rather than using adult models is required
  (98%)
- Children/young people are not mini adult sex offenders (97%)
- Young people need emotional competence and skills (93%)
- Promoting the well being of these young people is a key goal (90%)

- Equipping parents to offer supervision and emotional care is very important (90%)
- Vast majority will not become adult sex offenders (90%)
- A focus on living environment is as important as individual treatment (85%)
- Signs that old orthodoxies are no longer holding such a dominant sway e.g., young people are always responsible for their behaviour (69%)
- Need to focus in detail on sexually abusive behaviour (50%)

Despite the promising ground that both these research findings suggest, and the broader UK child welfare policy context, there remain many challenges and frustrations in the pursuit of a holistic approach. Policy and attitude do not necessarily translate into action. Lovell (2002:41) presents a salutary conclusion as to the current state of play with regards to services to these young people: "Ten years on from the Committee of Enquiry Report (NCH 1992), many of the policy calls of the Committee have still not been acted upon, and others lack funding and monitoring. Recent legislation and guidance are not adequate and in some cases are contradictory. They do not provide a coherent strategy. The result is an ad hoc system in which there is a lack of consistent response to these young people; agencies do not work together; and children and young people frequently do not receive appropriate treatment and support."

The inquiry into the case of DM (Bridge Child Care 2001), who was convicted of the sexual assault and murder of a ten year old boy only six months after completing a three year residential treatment programme arising from convictions for sexual offences when DM was younger, provided a sharp reminder of continuing gaps. These were particularly around the lack of a holistic assessment framework incorporating needs, especially health and education, as well as risks, and including attention to issues of loss, trauma and attachment disruption. There were also familiar failings, around information exchange between agencies, and inadequate case planning and review requirements. The road to holistic services is clearly a long and only partially built route, full of promise but with many pitfalls and potholes to navigate.

Barriers to Holistic Services

1) *Impact of anxiety*: Given the prime facie appeal of a holistic approach across the whole spectrum of social and health care problems, explanations as to why it is such an elusive ambition to achieve are complex. In the field of risk, whether from dangerous diseases, or dangerous people, much of the explanation lies with the impact of anxiety and the increasing expectations on government, especially after the events of 09/11/01 to manage and eliminate risk.

In England the death of Victorie Climbie and the subsequent public inquiry (Lord Laming 2002) was only the latest in a long line of headline grabbing child protection disaster stories. It is the anxiety-driven political reaction to such public exposures of failing systems that have shaped legislative and professional responses to child protection practice over the past thirty years, and which by extension permeate the field of young people who abuse as well. Similarly public and media concern about youth crime has pressurised politicians to come up with a ready quick fix.

Anxiety runs like a vein throughout the child protection process. It is present in the anxious or unrewarding attachment that forms the family context in which abusive attitudes and behaviour take root. It is present in the highly charged atmosphere of the parents' first encounter with professionals concerned about the abusive behaviour of their child. It is present too within the professional system, as sexual abuse represents a crisis not only for the family, but also for the professional and inter-agency network. Banks (2002) in his study of specialist workers noted how their anxiety to ensure that young people took 'responsibility' was reflected in the ways in which workers dominated sessions, talking ten times as much as the young person.

However anxiety exists not just at the level of the individual, but also as an organisational phenomenon (Menzies, 1970). In other words, anxiety is reflected in the institutional and judicial responses to young people who abuse. Finally, in the current climate of radical public sector reform and change, anxiety about managing risk is compounded in many organisations by the struggle for their own survival.

The institutional consequences are defensiveness, high levels of gate-keeping, rationalisation of role and resource, over-reliance on procedures and rules, inward focus, and responses that may either minimise and ignore or catastrophise the concern, the latter leading to highly inconsistent responses to these young people.

Alongside these underlying anxieties, additional factors in this field include:

- Lack of organisational and multi-agency ownership
- Funding uncertainties
- Inadequate services
- Lack of experienced supervisors
- Lack of policy and practice frameworks
- Mystification arising from inadequate training, supervision and the role of 'experts'
- Personal impact arising from the nature of the sexual behaviour

2) *Complexity and challenges of changing practice:* A second but related issue is the sheer complexity and difficulty of engineering large scale changes in professional behaviour towards a more holistic approach. We can see this by looking at the experience of implementing the Children Act 1989 in the UK. This act was a comprehensive and radical piece of child welfare legislation designed to change the whole approach to statutory child welfare practice to a more preventative, inclusive and needs-led approach. Its underpinning ethos was the requirement to work in partnership with families, by focusing more on needs than risks, involving families in decision making processes, and seeking to reduce the levels of judicial intervention through more preventative strategies.

By 1995 a highly influential report called Messages From Research on the outcomes of twenty research studies commissioned to evaluate the implementation of the Children Act concluded that whilst existing processes were generally effective in protecting children, there remained a need for a better relationship between family support approaches to children and safeguarding approaches (DOH 1995). In other words six years after the Children Act, the forensic and investigative nature of the child protection system was largely unchanged with still too little support offered to families with children in need.

In a study undertaken to explore why practitioners, who intellectually endorsed the move to a more needs-led and partnership-based approach, in practice found themselves operating more conservatively, Spratt (2001) identified a number of barriers to making the shift:

- A gap between intellectual/professional beliefs and anxiety-driven behavioural responses in the reality of the workplace.
- Recategorising criteria for child protection referrals so as to 'reduce' the high profile of child protection in the agency's caseload whilst failing to provide family support services for cases who no longer met the child protection criteria. Thus a superficial shift was achieved through a technical rather than practice change.
- The anxiety of referring agencies who continued to categorise all referrals as child protection believing that only by doing so could they access social services' attention and resources.
- The low levels of multi-disciplinary collaboration for cases not reaching the child protection caseload. Thus practitioners seeking to manage a case outside the child protection system using a family support approach found themselves bereft of the high levels of inter-disciplinary assessment planning and monitoring which underpin the child protection system. The consequence was that worried professionals dealing with complex needs were more isolated and anxious than if they had used the child protection system.
- The lack of a robust needs-led inter-agency assessment framework.
- The continued reliance on a risk dominated assessment framework in the UK until 2000 reinforced professionals' "investigative" mind sets. Spratt (2001) noted that social workers in their contact with other agencies continued to focus on risk, rarely asking other professionals such as schools and health visitors what needs the child might have.

Finally, to complicate matters more, a number of high profile child abuse inquiries into the deaths of children during the late 1990s revealed concerns as to whether in the shift towards 'family support' child protection issues had been marginalised. An analysis of children under two years old who had suffered serious injuries with discrepant injuries by Dale et al. (2002) concluded that "Some parents were more skilled than the professionals in negotiating the partnership in a way which compromised child protection decisions. This cohort of families are different to the assumption in Messages from Research (DOH 1995) that abusing parents are helpless, poor and doing the best they can."

3) *Competing and conflicting priorities:* The third set of barriers to holistic practice concerns conflicting and competing priorities set by government departments for individual agencies. The link between meeting government targets, publication of league table results about the performance of individual agencies, and funding levels has been a driving force behind agency behaviour. The very public consequences of a failure to meet such expectations has resulted in chief officers' being pre-occupied by the achievement of individual targets to the detriment of achieving those outcomes which depend on collaboration with other agencies, such as services for children in need.

An example of this has been the government's targets for health service providers to cut waiting list times whilst there is still not a single health performance indicator relating to children's health or safety. Similarly the focus on examination pass rates has dominated the agenda of head teachers at the cost of considering the needs of children who are at risk of exclusion due to emotional and behavioural problems. Until these conflictual and separate targets are reconciled with more holistic and needs led approaches, holistic approaches will be driven not by organisational or political imperatives, but by the goodwill and personal commitment of individuals.

4) *Stable responsive workforce:* Perhaps the biggest single problem facing the public sector is the recruitment and retention of competent and motivated staff. In a recent survey of 151 child welfare staff in Kentucky, Anderson (2000: 844) found that 62% scored in the high range for both emotional exhaustion and depersonalisation 'indicating a strong trend towards burnout' and *appreciably higher* than a comparison group surveyed in 1986.

Shapiro et al. (1999) found that job satisfaction to be "lower in professionals whose own personal or sexual issues intrude into their work with clients or who were preoccupied with their jobs and their performance to the exclusion of non-work involvements." The nature of the workers' coping strategies and beliefs about their work had a considerable effect on job satisfaction. This is particularly relevant when dealing with young people who commit sexual offences. Naive optimism, escape/avoidance, confrontative coping and accepting too much responsibility were all associated with higher rates of stress. As Anderson points out, the greater the threat, the less likely that problem-focused coping will occur (Anderson, 2000: 841). Unless we can recruit, retain, and develop a responsive and committed workforce, the capacity to move from risk-dominated to needs-led approaches will be seriously compromised.

In making a shift towards a more holistic approach to young people where the management of their sexually risky behaviours is a key issue, the parallel experience of implementing the UK Children Act 1989 is very instructive. What we may take from that major change experience are the following lessons:

- The need to address professional and agency anxieties both about the clinical issues and the change process itself.
- A recognition of how hard change is. Hamblin et al. (2001:17) estimate that about 80% of organisational culture change programmes fail!
- The need for robust inter-agency strategic, and operational collaboration to ensure that the commitment of the different services upon which a holistic service depends is delivered.
- The shift required is not from a risk-only to a needs-only approach, but is about paying equal attention to needs, strengths, and risks. A holistic approach must include a robust approach to the management of risk.
- There is a need to re-configure performance targets in collaborative and holistic terms.
- Making the change to a more holistic service depends on the ability of agencies to recruit and retain stable, motivated and responsive practitioners.

Rationale and drivers for holistic approaches

One of the principle drivers for a holistic approach has been the emerging under-standing about the difference between adult and juvenile sex offenders. This, com-bined with research about the multiple needs of young people who sexually abuse, makes a powerful case for a holistic and ecological approach. We may summarise this research as follows.

Differences between adult and adolescent sex offenders

- The recidivism rate for young people who sexually offend is significantly lower than that of adult sex offenders. (Alexander, 1999; Hagan et al., 1994; Kahn & Chambers, 1991; Quinsey et al., 1995). Alexander (1999), for example, analysed the data of over 1000 young people who had sexually offended in a 3-5 year follow up study and found an overall recidivist rate of 7.1% as com-pared to an adult overall rate of 13%. Indeed the non-sexual non violent recidivism rate for adolescent sex offenders is higher than their sexual recidi-vism (Chaffin 2003).

- Adolescent experimentation in a range of antisocial (sexual and non-sexual) behaviours is not uncommon. Research (Blumstein et al., 1988) indicates that most do not continue such behaviours into adulthood.

- Young people are unlikely to have established a fixed pattern of sexual thoughts and behaviours. Their sexual preferences, fantasies and behaviours are often in a state of flux and, as yet, research has not been able to determine whether inappropriate sexual thoughts are significantly linked to the risks of re-offending against adults, peers or children (Prentky, 2000).

- Given the nature of adolescence, actuarial risk models which have been used extensively in the management of adult sex offenders, are far less effective with young people. As Bailey (2002) states, "Adolescence is characterised by profound and pervasive changes where contextual, dynamic and proximal risk factors are equally if not more predictive future violence than static or historical factors." Amongst these factors the role of family is of special importance.

- Young people are subject to greater influence, and management by others than adults. Most young people have parents/carers, teachers, peer groups and other adults who can exert influence and set boundaries. This signifi-cantly assists the implementation of risk management plans and strategies.

Developmental History and Pathways forYoung People Who Sexually Abuse

Most young people who sexually abuse others have been subject to some form of trauma or abuse themselves. (Kobayashi et al., 1995; Spaccarelli et al., 1997; Skuse et al., 1998). Van Ness (1984) found that 41% had been physically abused or neglected, as compared with 15% in a group of non-sexual delinquents. Smith, Monastersky, and Deisher (1987) found that 36% had a history of sexual or physical abuse, and 30% had a sexual offender living within their extended family. Griffin (2003) reported that a third of young people have witnessed domestic violence. Studies of incarcerated male adolescent sexual abusers (Lewis et al., 1981) report even higher rates of histories of physical abuse (75%) and having witnessed family violence (79%).

A history of loss, attachment disruption, and discontinuity of care has been reported in the lives of many of these young people (Skuse et al., 1998). This is in line with research on the experience of non-sexual adolescent offenders. In a study of 1000 young offenders, 92% had suffered one significant loss or rejection, 46% had experienced two episodes, and 11% had suffered four or more episodes of loss or rejection (Youth Justice Trust, 2003).

Many reports have noted a range of social and psychological problems in adolescent sexual abusers, including poor school attainment (Gomes-Schwartz, 1984), low self esteem, social isolation, loneliness, fear of intimacy and poor social skills (Prentky and Knight 1993, and Fehrenbach et al., 1986). A significant proportion (30%) of young sex offenders, have learning disabilities (Griffin and Beech, 2004). In a survey of 1000 young offenders (all types) 82% were identified as requiring medium to high maintenance whilst at school compared to 9% of the general school population (Youth Justice Trust, 2003). Other research has pointed to the incidence of conduct disorder and a history of interpersonal aggression amongst these young people (Spacarelli et al., 1997, Becker Kaplan et al., 1986). Katz (1990) in a matched study of adolescent sex offenders, non-sexual offenders and normals concluded that adolescent sex offenders were more socially incompetent, had more problems with loneliness, social anxiety, assertiveness, negative self evaluation, self consciousness, depression and low self esteem. They perceived social situations as threatening, and doubted their ability to perform well in them, and were more easily threatened by heterosexual relationships.

High rates of family instability, disorganisation and violence are also reported (Awad & Saunders, 1989; see Duane and Morrison (2004) for a review of the literature on family factors). This is in line with other research on the role of family factors in adolescent delinquency, which have come to a consistent set of conclusions summarised by Haapasalo and Pokela (1999: 111), "From the finding of the longitudinal studies poor child rearing practices especially corporal punishment, authoritarian and power assertive parental discipline, rejection, abuse and neglect have come up repeatedly as factors related to aggression, criminal and anti-social behaviour. Additional important factors are poor supervision, lack of interaction between parents and child, parental conflicts and disagreement on child rearing methods, separations, socio-economic difficulties, and parental criminality, alcoholism and mental health problems."

Social Ecological Approaches: Risk and Resilience

The multiple needs of these young people, and the influence of developmental and contextual factors points strongly to an approach which locates individual behaviour within a social and ecological context of family, school, culture and community. This is supported by one of the only controlled research studies into treatment effectiveness with young people who sexually abuse, which found that multi-systemic approaches (MST) were more effective than individual counselling (Borduin et al., 1990). MST has been shown to be an effective intervention with general delinquency and is based on the idea that family in particular are key change agents. This is supported by Bailey (2002) and Chaffin (2003) who identify that many of the key protective and malleable factors lie not within the individual, but in his family or care context. These include: positive attachments; consistent parental guidance and supervision; parental modelling of positive problem solving; development of emotional expressiveness; parental support for the young person's learning and education; positive engagement in the intervention work with the young person; and assisting the young person's engagement in the community.

Of particular importance in assessment and treatment work is the identification not only of needs and risks, but of the resilience factors or assets that are available in a young person, his family and his environment. Supporting and developing the strengths of a young person and his family are likely to prove significant in reducing risk. Interventions that focus solely on offence-related behaviours do not fully address the development of the range of skills and abilities that are generally required to lead an abuse-free lifestyle. Holistic interventions need to promote competence, coping skills, positive life goals and to enhance protective factors.

In short, the message is that many models developed for work with adult sex offenders are unlikely to be suitable for work with adolescents or younger children. New, developmentally appropriate models that are holistic in approach are required. As Ryan (1999:427) has indicated, in contrast to work with adult offenders where the task can be seen as lifetime management of the propensity to relapse, with adolescent offenders, the focus is more on enabling a return to a more normative developmental pathway. We need an approach which combines offence-specific work on fantasy, planning, selection, grooming, distortions with holistic interventions that focus on defusing affective triggers, increasing developmental competence and self efficacy, countering hopelessness, and increasing psychological safety in relationships, (Ryan 1999: 427).

Towards a Holistic Approach: Definition and Three Levels of Intervention

Having discussed some of the main challenges and drivers we turn now to consider what the principle elements of a holistic approach might be. Three levels of context will be considered: societal (macro); inter-agency (mezzo); and practice delivery (micro). But first a tentative definition of holistic work is offered:

> *A holistic approach seeks to understand and address the YP/child's sexually problematic behaviour within the totality of his/her context and needs, by working in partnership with the young person/child and his/her significant others including family, school, and social support network to promote the healthy and sustained development of the young person/child.*

It is an approach in which risk is understood in relation to unmet need, and in which strengths and protective factors are given equal attention alongside risks. The shift is summarised in this table which characterises the differences between risk dominated and holistic approaches, both at the level of language and focus of action.

Table 1

Risk Dominated Approaches	Holistic Approaches
Search for certainty	Acceptance of uncertainty
Reach for experts	Share the risk between agencies
Focus on diagnosis & categorisation	Understanding problem in family, social, cultural context
Assessment: 'problem risk deficit'	Holistic assessment: concerns, needs, strengths, protective factors
Family as source of information	Family as partners
Focus on the individual	Focus on individual in context
Control and management	Containment and boundaries
Method & programme	Process and care plan
Goal: Risk reduction	Competence, esteem & self control
Focus on offence specific areas & avoidance of abusive behaviour	Focus on competence, esteem, self management, attachments, trauma
Impact on workers: increase mystique, 'specialness' of the work	Identify commonalities to other work with troubled/troubling youth

1) *Societal (macro) level:* At this level the focus is on the role of government in addressing factors to do with societal attitudes to, and understanding of, sexual health in particular and more broadly the environment in which children grow up. It concerns the detoxification of a socially toxic environment in which:

- One in three children live in poverty
- One in four children live in poor housing
- Three out of five children in every classroom have witnessed domestic violence
- More than one in three 12-15yr olds are assaulted each year
- 12% of 11-15yr olds have used drugs in the previous year
- One in ten children have mental health problems
- Mortality is twice as high for unskilled workers as for professional families
- African Caribbean children are five times more likely to be excluded but no more likely to be truant (Local Government Association, 2002).

Space permits only a brief discussion of this major issue but the foundation lies in the commitment of government to the principles and practices of the UN Convention on the Rights of the Child (UN 1989), and the establishment of government structures (Hodgkin and Newall, 1996) that place the needs of children at the heart of public policy. In England the recent appointment of a Minister for Children and Families is a small step in the right direction but there is a long way to go. It is also about the degree to which government supports families in bringing up their children, in particular the availability of child care services and family support services for parents who are isolated and struggling. In a recent survey of family support services in England and Wales (National Family and Parenting Institute 2001) one of the largest gaps was for the parents of adolescents.

The same survey also identified a lack of support services for parents at the point of transition into school. Given the crucial role of education in supporting the development of children from vulnerable or at risk populations, and the often poor education experiences of those parents, helping parents to develop positive relationships with schools is an important goal. Policies and interventions to support at risk students and to minimise exclusions from school are also crucial as it is known that low achievement in school is a major predictor of youth crime (Youth Justice Board 2001). For young people who sexually abuse others, school exclusion makes the supervision and structuring of their time a major problem which in combination with boredom increases the likelihood of becoming sexually pre-occupied.

Education also has a vital role to play in the social, moral, personal and sexual development of children in terms of relationship skills, gender roles, sexual information and the capacity to problem solve. There is a growing awareness of the role of emotional and not just cognitive intelligence as a key predictor of life chances. Goleman (1997) defines emotional intelligence as "sensing what others are feeling, and handling relationships effectively" and is comprised of five main domains:

1) Self awareness – knowing what one feels
2) Self management – regulating one's emotions
3) Motivation – the capacity for goal directed behaviour
4) Awareness of others – both in terms of empathic ability and awareness of one's obligations to others
5) Inter-personal skills – the capacity to manage relationships well.

Research on young sex offenders has identified both poor social skills and isolation (Prentky and Knight, 1993), and emotional dysregulation as major factors in the pathways to sexual offending (Gilgun, 2003). Hence focusing on the development of emotional intelligence throughout the education process is a powerful tool not only in the longer term prevention of abusive behaviours and relationships, but also in helping vulnerable and at risk children to engage with school. This wider focus on emotional health would thus locate sexual education within a broader programme of relationship development which includes a focus on the prevention of abusive (sexual and other types) practices through protective behaviours and anti-bullying programmes.

Finally, there is a need to improve sexual health services. A recent survey of services reported in the Guardian newspaper (Bosely, 2003) in England revealed a chaotic and under-funded service. Adolescents reported that they felt they had nowhere to go for advice on sexual matters, especially if they wished to discuss matters to do with sexual orientation. A number of young people with sexual behaviour problems have very confused sexual identity and feel they cannot talk to their parents or care-givers.

2) Inter-agency (mezzo) level: Whereas societal (macro) level intervention seeks to create the conditions for the healthy development of children, mezzo level intervention focuses on strategic, rather than clinical, responses to children and young people who display sexually abusive behaviour problems. It also involves responses and services to victims of sexual abuse. The multiple needs of these young people requires strategic level collaboration between agencies such as social services (both government and non government), police, education, health and youth offending services at both national and local levels. It is not sufficient for committed individuals from different agencies to work together (multi-disciplinary work), if when those individuals leave, they are replaced by practitioners who do not bring the same commitment to collaboration. In other words, multi-disciplinary work is a necessary but not sufficient condition for collaboration which requires committed agencies (inter-agency) to work together. Practitioners need clear mandates, frameworks and structures to work effectively and purposefully across agency boundaries.

How this occurs will vary across jurisdictions dependent on government structures and legislation. In the UK, there is a strong role for government that has played a key role in creating national inter-agency guidance in the child protection and youth justice fields. The UK Children Act (1999) mandates agencies to map the needs of, and provide services for, 'children in need' defined as children whose health and development will be avoidably impaired if services are not provided. This population of young people clearly fits these criteria. Given that the majority of young people who commit sexual offences are not prosecuted, it is essential that strategic responses do not rely solely upon youth justice and criminal justice agencies. Regardless of context, therefore, there are a number of areas which require inter-agency clarity and commitment. These include:

- Arrangements for the joint management of cases based on clarity as to the roles of social services, police, youth justice and other agencies with these young people.
- Thresholds for referral of cases to police and/or social services.
- A holistic multi-disciplinary assessment framework.
- Judicial processes that provide for differential responses based on a multi-disciplinary assessment of the young person.
- Multi-disciplinary case assessment, planning, monitoring, and review protocols.
- Provision and funding of community based treatment resources. Holistic practice by definition is embedded in family/carer and social networks. Too often resources are directed to a small number of expensive specialist placements for high risk cases, usually many miles away from family and social networks.
- Provision of training and supervision for practitioners.

Note: For a fuller account of service development issues and strategies see Morrison, T. (2004) Preparing Services and Staff to work with Young People who Sexually Abuse: Context; Mandate; Pitfalls and Frameworks.

An example of Holistic Inter-agency Strategic Intervention

One of the largest examples in the UK of a strategic inter-agency intervention approach based on holistic principles is the AIM project in Greater Manchester. This project, in operation since 1999, covers a conurbation (city) of four million people across ten social services departments, ten youth offending services, a single police force, local health and education authorities and a large non government child protection agency. The project's mission is to establish an effective inter-agency, investigation, assessment and treatment response to children and young people displaying sexually harmful behaviour. Through the creation of a development officer, an inter-agency trustee board and commissioning of the GMAP service for young abusers, and a project consultant (myself), the project has thus far established the following elements:

1) Four initial AIM assessment tools based on a strengths and concerns model. The assessment process yields a two by two matrix combining strengths and concerns:

- High concern – low strength (high risk)
- High concern – high strength (high risk, but with strengths, and potentially more manageable in the community)
- Low concern – high strengths (emerging sexual problem)
- Low concern – low strengths (low sexual risk but more general concerns about unmet needs and impaired development)

Each of the AIM assessment tools considers four domains: the young person's abusive behaviour, developmental needs, parents/carers' capacities and social and environmental factors. The four initial assessment tools cover:

- Young people (Print, Morrison and Henniker 2001);
- Children under 10 displaying sexually problematic behaviour (Carson and Wilkinson, 2001);
- Young people with learning difficulties (O'Callaghan, 2001);
- Parents/carers of young people (Morrison and Wilkinson, 2001). A key emphasis in this model is on immediate engagement of parents/carers and their involvement in treatment work.

2) An inter-agency set of procedures for assessments, initial decision-making and placement based on all cases, regardless of whether they enter the criminal justice process, being subject to an AIM assessment. The police will thus request an AIM assessment prior to a decision as to whether to charge, or follow an alternative disposition. All AIM assessments are co-worked by social workers and youth justice or health professionals and result in a multi-agency planning meeting which involves the family.

3) Guidance for schools about the recognition, referral and management of pupils displaying sexually harmful behaviour.

4) Comprehensive training for practitioners and managers from social services, youth justice, police and other agencies.

5) A protocol for the adaptation of family group conferences in adolescent sex offender cases for both convicted and non-convicted young people.

6) An evaluation of the needs of black and Asian young people with sexual behaviour problems (Mir & Okotie, 2002). Another important facet of a holistic programme is attention to the needs of different groups. An evaluation of the needs of young females who sexually offend is currently underway in addition to the above work in advanced stages for three other services.

7) Three treatment guides covering work with young people, children under 10 years old, and parents.

8) The establishment of four community based group programmes based around clusters of neighbouring local authority departments and the development of a specialist group for young people with learning disabilities.

9) A research programme has also been established, using both local and external researchers to identify practitioners and service users' experience of the project as well as to evaluate the assessment tools. Initial research based

on a sample of 75 cases has revealed a high level of endorsement and compliance by practitioners with the tools (75% of cases showed all 10 steps of the AIM protocol were followed). Evaluation of the assessment procedure revealed that it correctly identified the four young people who have re-offended (one for sex offences and three for other offences) as being in the high concern/low strength category (Griffin and Beech 2004).

10) Finally, the next stage in this project is to map and address the needs of victims.

Note: For readers interested in a fuller account of the AIM Project see Morrison and Henniker (In Press).

3) *Practice Delivery (micro) level: Characteristics of Holistic Services.*
In many ways this is the simplest to describe, but crucially depends on the degree to which the macro and mezzo elements described above are in place. The less that these higher level factors are addressed the harder it is for individual services, let alone practitioners to operate in an holistic manner. Nevertheless the movement towards holistic practice cannot wait for the rest of the system to be aligned and we can certainly begin to identify important features of holistic practice. They might offer a basic checklist for a service.

a) Services seek to remove barriers to services in terms of accessibility, availability beyond office hours, and willingness to work in local communities and not just from an office base.

b) The proactive engagement of family or carers as partners and change agents, not just as sources of information.

c) An equal focus on risks, needs, strengths and protective factors from the outset in the assessment process.

d) A focus on the *whole* of a young person's experience and identity, not just their sexual behaviour problem.

e) Responsive and customised services in which choice of method is secondary to a full engagement and assessment of the young person and their family/carers; and attention to the needs of different groups such as young people with disabilities, or from different cultural or religious backgrounds.

f) A choice of methods: individual, family and group and an avoidance of a "one size fits all" approach. This may mean that family work becomes as significant as the traditional emphasis on group work.

g) Close attention to collaborative process, engagement and relationships, in particular seeking to ensure continuity of service and workers and seeking regular feedback from service users.

h) A focus on developing social and emotional competence as much as on the traditional offence specific areas of sexual fantasy and distorted thinking.

i) Ensuring that victims as well as abusers receive services.

j) Multi-disciplinary delivery based on an appreciation that these young people are not just the responsibility of one agency.

So what does it take to create the environment in which practitioners feel supported and equipped to work in these ways?

a) Strong supportive leadership who are willing to engage other agencies as partners.

b) Positive organisational cultures in which staff feel connected to the agency, clear about roles and responsibilities and involved in service planning.

c) Properly trained staff and well supervised staff.

d) Emotionally competent and reflective practitioners who are aware of what they bring to this work, have come to terms with the work and have good self care strategies.

e) Evidence-based, rather than anxiety driven practice.

f) Healthy and 'well teams' who can innovate and model what they practice.

Conclusion

This chapter has approached the development of holistic services from an ecological perspective. It has argued that the development of holistic practices cannot be separated from legislative, policy and cultural contexts. Each jurisdiction's understanding of, and movement towards holistic practices will be its own. What is presented here is an account of the context, drivers and barriers to holistic practice using the UK and more precisely England as one example. It is hoped that readers from different contexts can relate their own experiences to this account. We have made progress and have developed at least mezzo level models that suggest some optimism for the future. Nevertheless one remains mindful that in the current climate one case that goes wrong, attracting media criticism, could throw the pendulum back to conservative and punitive practices. It thus behoves all those advancing the cause of holistic practice to remain grounded in research based practice and committed to the evaluation of what works.

References

Alexander, M.A. (1999). Sexual offender treatment efficacy revisited. *Sexual Abuse: A Journal of Research and Treatment*, (11) 2.

Anderson, D. (2000). Coping strategies and burnout amongst veteran child protection workers. *Child Abuse and Neglect* 24(6) 839-848.

Awad, G. & Saunders, E.B. (1989). Male adolescent sexual assaulters, *Journal of Interpersonal Violence* 6: 446-60.

Bailey, S. (2002). Is it possible to assess risks – Practical approaches. NOTA *Conference Lancaster*. UK.

Banks, N; (2002). Unconscious processes in practitioners who work therapeutically with children and young people who sexually abuse. *Unpublished doctoral thesis: University of Sussex*.

Becker, J.V., Kaplan, M.S., Cunningham-Rathner, J., & Kavoussi, R. (1986). Characteristics of adolescent incest sexual perpetrators: Preliminary findings. *Journal of Family Violence* 1 (1): 85-87.

Blumstein, A., Cohen, J., and Farrington, D.P. (1988). Criminal career research: its value for criminology, *Criminology* 26, 1-35.

Borduin, C. M., Henggeler, S.W., Blaske, D.M. & Stein. R.J. (1990). Multisystemic treatment of adolescent sexual offenders. International *Journal of Offender Therapy & Comparative Criminology*. 34(2) 105-113.

Bosely, S. (2003). The crisis in our sexual health services. Guardian 19 June.

Bridge Child Care Development Service (2001). Childhood Lost: Part 8 Case Review Overview Report DM. *Bridge Publishing Haye on Wye.*

Carson, C. and Wilkinson, L. (2001). *Initial assessment of children under 10 years with sexually problematic behaviour*. AIM Project Manchester.

Chaffin, M. & Bonner, B. (1998). 'Don't shoot – We're your children' *Child Maltreatment* 2(3) 314-316.

Chaffin, M. (2003). *Working with young people who have sexual behaviour problems: Lessons from risk and resilience.* Paper presented at GMAP Conference: Working Holistically with Young People who Sexually harm. Bolton UK 26 June 2003.

Dale, P., Green, R., and Fellows, R. (2002). Serious and fatal injuries to infants with discrepant explanations: Some assessment and case management issues. *Child Abuse Review* 11 296-312 .

DOH (1995). *Child protection: Messages from research.* London: HMSO.

DOH (1999). *Working together to safeguard children: A guide to inter-agency arrangements to safeguard and promote the welfare of children.* London: The Stationary Office

DOH (2000). *Framework for the assessment of children in need and their families,* London: TSO

Treasury (2003). *Every child matters.* Cm 5860. TSO

Duane, Y. & Morrison, T. (2004). Families of young people who sexually abuse: Characteristics, context, and considerations. In G. O'Reilly, W. Marshall, A. Carr, & R. Beckett (Eds), *Handbook of clinical intervention with juvenile sexual abusers.* Hover and New York: Brunner-Routledge.

Fehrenbach, P., Smith , W., Monastersky, C., & Deisher, R. (1986). Adolescent sex offenders: Offenders and offence characteristics. *American Journal of Orthopsychiatry*, 56:225-233

Gomes-Schwartz, B. (1984). Juvenile sex offenders. In *Sexually exploited children: Service and research project.* Washington DC: US Dept. of Justice.

Gilgun, J. (1999). CASPARS: Clinical assessment instruments that measure strengths and risks in children and families. In M. Calder (Ed) *Working with young people who sexually abuse: New pieces of the jigsaw.* Dorset, England: Russell House.

Griffin, H Beech, A. (2004). *Evaluation of the AIM Framework for the assessment of adolescents who display sexually harmful behaviour.* Youth Justice Board and Youth Justice Trust.

Haapasalo, J., Pokela, E., (1999). Child rearing and child abuse antecedents of criminality. *Aggression and Violent Behaviour* 4(1) 107-127.

Hackett, S., Mason, H. & Phillips, S. (2002). *Mapping and exploring services for children and young people who have sexually abused: Final report.* University of Durham and University of Huddersfield.

Hagen, M., King, R., & Patros, R. (1994). Recidivism among adolescent perpetrators of sexual assault against children. *Young Victims, Young Offenders.* 127 - 137. I

Hamblin, Keep, and Ask (2001). *Organisational change and development.* Financial Times Prentice Hall

Hodgkin, R. and Newall, P. (1996). *Effective government structures for children.* London: Calouste Gulbenkian Foundation.

Kahn, T.J. & Chambers, H.J. (1991). Assessing reoffense risk with juvenile sexual offenders. *Child Welfare* LXX (3): 333-345.

Katz, R., (1990). Psycho-social adjustment in adolescent child molesters. *Child Abuse and Neglect* 14 (4): 567-575.

Kobayashi, J., Sales, B.D., Becker, J.V., Figueredo, A.J. and Kaplan, M.S. (1995). Perceived parental deviance, parent child-bonding, child abuse, and child sexual aggression. *Sexual Abuse: A Journal of Research and Treatment* 7(1): 25-43.

Local Government Association (2002). *Serving Children Well – A New Vision for Childrens Services.* LGA.

Lord Laming, H. (2003). *The Victoria Climbie Inquiry: Report of an Inquiry* Cmd 5730. TSO.
Lewis, D., Shanok, S., Pincus, J. (1981). Juvenile male assaulters, In D. Lewis (ed) *Vulnerabilities to delinquency* pp 89-105, Jamaica, N.Y: Spectrum Pubs.

Lovell, E. (2002). *I think I might need some more help with this problem: Responding to children and young people who display sexually harmful behaviour.* London: NSPCC.

Menzies, I., (1970). *The Functioning of social systems as a defence against anxiety,* London: Tavistock Institute of Human Relations.

Mir, B. Okotie, E. (2002). T*he Study of the Experiences of Black and Asian People who Behaviour is Sexually Harmful to Others.* NSPCC.

Morrison, T. & Henniker, J. (In Press). Building a comprehensive inter-agency assessment and interventional system for young people who sexually abuse: The AIM project. In Erooga, M. & Masson, H. (Eds.), *Children and young people who sexually abuse others. 2nd Edition.* Routledge.

Morrison, T. (2004). Preparing services and staff to work with young people who sexually abuse: Context; Mandate; Pitfalls and Frameworks. In G. O'Reilly, W. Marshall, A. Carr, & R. Beckett (Eds), *Handbook of clinical intervention with juvenile sexual abusers.* Hover and New York: Brunner-Routledge.

Morrison, T; and Wilkinson, L. (2001). *Initial assessment of families of young people who sexual abuse.* Manchester, England: AIM.

NCH (1992). *Children and young people who sexually abuse other children and young people.* London: NCH

National Family and Parenting Institute (2001). *National Mapping of Family Services in England and Wales: A Consultation Document.* London: NFPI.

O'Callaghan, D. (2001). *Initial assessment of young people with learning difficulties who sexually abuse others.* Manchester, England: AIM Project.

Prentky, R.A. & Knight, R.A. (1993). Age of onset of sexual assault: criminal and life history correlates. In G.C. Hall, R. Hirschman, J.R. Graham, & M.S. Zaragoza (Eds), *Sexual aggression: Issues in etiology, assessment and treatment.* Washington, DC: Taylor & Francis.

Prentky, R., Harris, B., Frizzell, K., & Righthand, S. (2000). An actuarial procedure for assessing risk with juvenile sex offenders. *Sexual Abuse: A Journal of Research and Treatment,* 8, 279-289.

Print, B., Morrison, T. & Henniker, J. (2001). An inter-agency assessment framework for young people who sexually abuse: Principles, processes and practicalities. In M. Calder (Ed). *Juveniles and children who sexually abuse: Frameworks for assessmen. Second Edition.* Lyme Regis, England: Russell House Publishing.

Quinsey, V., Lalumiere, M., Rice, M., & Harris, G. (1995). In J. Campbell (Ed) *Assessing Dangerousness.* Beverley Hills. CA. Sage.

Ryan, G. (1999). Treatment of abusive youth: The evolving consensus, *Journal of Interpersonal Violence* 14(4) 422-436.

Skuse, D., Bentovim, A., Hodges, J., Stevenson, J., Andreou, C., Lanyado, M., New, M., Williams, B., & McMillan, D. (1998). Risk factors for the development of sexually abusive behaviour in sexually victimised adolescent boys: cross sectional study, *British Medical Journal,* 317, 175-189.

Shapiro, J., Dorman, R., Burkey , W. & Welker, C. (1999). Predictors of job satisfaction and burn out in child abuse professionals: coping, cognition and victimization history. *Journal of Child sexual Abuse* 7(4) 23-42.

Smith, W.R., Monastersky, C., & Deisher, R. M. (1987). MMPI-based personality types among juvenile sex offenders. *Journal of Clinical Psychology*, 43, 422-430.

Spaccarelli, S., Bowden, B., Coatsworth, J.D., & Kim, S. (1997). Psychosocial correlates of male sexual aggression in a chronic delinquent sample. *Criminal Justice and Behavior*, 24, 71-95.

Spratt, T (2001). The Influence of Child Protection Orientation on Child Welfare Practice. *British Journal of Social Work*, 31: 933-954.

United Nations (1989). The Convention on the Rights of the Child Geneva: *Defence for Children International/UNICEF Geneva.*

Van Ness, S.R. (1984). Rape as instrumental violence: A study of youth offenders. *Journal of Offender Counselling Services and Rehabilitation*, 9, 161-170.

Youth Justice Board. Risk and Protective Factors associated with Youth Crime: Communities that Care (2001). *Youth Justice Board.*

Youth Justice Trust (2003). On the case: Survey of over 1000 children and young people under supervision by youth offending teams in Greater Manchester and W. Yorkshire. *Youth Justice Trust. Manchester.*

CHAPTER FOURTEEN

ATTACHMENT STYLES AND SEXUAL ABUSE

WILLIAM FRIEDRICH
AND
LESLIE SIM

Introduction

Research has firmly established the vital role that attachment plays in the adaptive functioning of the child. In particular, a secure attachment is central to the development of a positive and accurate view of oneself, empathic and sensitive interactions with others, as well as adaptive and flexible emotion regulation skills (Cassidy & Shaver, 1999). Unfortunately, children who have been sexually abused are at a unique risk for problems in their attachment relationships (Cicchetti & Toth, 1995). In fact, the sexual abuse of a child is often associated with a parent who has been sexually abused, a sexualized home environment or one in which sexuality is avoided, and/or the experience of other forms of abuse (Friedrich & Sim, 2003). In addition, maternal sexual abuse tends to be associated with psychopathology, limited self-knowledge, and unresolved feelings of anger and sexuality (Dozier, Stovall, & Albus, 1999). Of special concern, is the disorganized and faulty parenting that occurs when a parent has a history of unresolved abuse, in which they are frightened by or frightening to their child.

Clearly, these problems place a child at risk for insecure and disorganized attachment relationships and corresponding behavior problems. These problems in functioning can include subsequent victimization, sexual behavior problems, and even sexually intrusive behavior, particularly when predisposing factors such as cumulative adversity, modeling of coercion, and proneness to acting out are present (Friedrich, Davies, Feher, & Wright, 2003). As such, sexual abuse is typically one of several factors in the lives of victimized children that place them at risk for problems in later life.

In this chapter, we attempt to use an attachment perspective to explain how children who have been sexually abused are at special risk to experience subsequent problems, particularly in regards to child sexual behavior. We first provide a brief overview of attachment theory and then review a model of attachment that explains how cognition and affect become integrated. Next, we describe the research on attachment and sexual abuse, as well as the research on attachment and child outcome. Finally, we present a case study to illustrate the dynamic relationship between maternal sexual abuse and child sexual behavior.

Attachment

Attachment is a central component of research in the field of developmental psychopathology. One reason for its primacy is that maladaptive functioning is best studied in the context of development and relationships. Attachment is an instinctual process that guarantees most children a felt security and sets the stage for emotional regulation. Attachment security is enhanced when parents are committed to their child, act in a sensitive and attuned manner, and make efforts to repair ruptures in felt security. Over time, the attachment dynamics are internalized and aid the child in behaving in a more automatic and efficient manner. This process results in an internal working model, in which both the cognitive and affective components of attachment relationships are encoded (Crittenden, 1995).

The attachment relationship primarily reflects the affective qualities of the parent-child relationship in the first months of the infant's life. However, the infant is also beginning to appreciate the sequences of behavior and developing a rudimentary, cognitive understanding of the nature of relationships. In most situations, negative affect does not become too overwhelming to the child because of efforts by the parent to modulate the intensity of the affect. Positive affect is maximized, but it too is modulated.

The development of attachment constitutes an increasingly sophisticated integration of cognition with affect (Crittenden, 1995). The infant begins to recognize a relationship between maternal behavior and the child's feelings. The child also starts to appreciate the communicative/predictive effect of their affective signals on maternal behavior. As the child matures, they are more capable of integrating these affective signals. Interaction with attachment figures influence infants to preferentially attribute meaning to some types of information as opposed to others.

Although the majority of children in non-clinical settings have secure attachments to their caregivers, nearly one-third have insecure attachment styles (Ainsworth, Blehar, Waters, & Wall, 1978). There are three common forms of failure in the parent-child relationship that leads to an insecure attachment (Fonagy et al., 1995). First, the parent may not recognize negative affective signals (failure of attunement). Secondly, they may locate the source of the distress but fail to attend to the quality of the distressing affect, and then fail to reflect a combination of congruent affect and mastery in response to the infant/child. Thirdly, the parent may fail to respond empathically to early manifestations of individuation and intentionality on the part of the infant.

Based on this faulty care giving, attachment styles take several forms including avoidant, resistant, and a more recent designation, disorganized attachment (Ainsworth, et al., 1978; Lyons-Ruth & Jacobvitz, 1999). Typically, the avoidantly-attached child has had a primary caregiver that was routinely frustrating to the child. Infants who become avoidant by one year of age typically experience maternal rejection when they display affective signals indicative of a desire for closeness to their mothers. In the Strange Situation assessment paradigm (Ainsworth et al., 1978), the avoidant child keeps her distance from the parent since she has learned that interaction with the parent is frustrating and the parent is not necessarily a consistent answer to her distress. This results in the inhibition of affect and teaches infants that the expression of affect is counterproductive. Since the mothers of avoidant infants use affective signals in confusing ways, this is further reason why affect is discounted. The avoidant child is less likely to display distress and consequently her affect is often thought to be false, although her cognitions generally are accurate.

The resistant child has typically had an inconsistently reinforcing caregiver, sometimes quite capable and other times frustrating. The mother's affective signals may be clearer than the mother of the avoidantly-attached child, but she is inconsistently responsive to her infant's signals. In the Strange Situation paradigm, the child responds with frustration upon the caregiver's return, alternately seeking and rejecting the parent's offers of support (Ainsworth et al., 1978). When infants cannot predict their parental response, they become anxious and angry, which has been aptly described as ambivalently attached. As the infant becomes a toddler, ambivalent infants have been reinforced for affective behavior but have not learned a cognitive organization that reduces the inconsistency of maternal behavior. As such, they tend to display very genuine affect when distressed, but differ from the avoidantly-attached child in that their cognition is less accurate.

For this chapter, the disorganized child seems to have the most relevance. A relatively recent discovery, this type of insecure attachment is associated with parents who have a history of unresolved trauma/maltreatment, prolonged absences from this child, substance abuse, and/or major psychiatric problems (Lyons-Ruth & Jacobvitz, 1999). Caregivers with this type of history will be frightening to the child, and the intimacy of the parent-child relationship may also frighten the parent. The infant's need for security will result in an insoluble dilemma in which the parent is not the child's solution to safety and he or she is often frightening. This contradiction between desire and actuality is too much for the child to integrate into a coherent working model at this early stage of their life. Consequently, their behavior in infancy and toddlerhood often is paradoxical and Strange Situation behavior may contain some elements suggestive of secure attachment but other behaviors that are confusing, such as wandering aimlessly at reunion (Main & Solomon, 1990). By school age, the child with disorganized attachment more consistently falls into one of two categories, controlling-punitive and controlling-caregiving (Lyons-Ruth & Jacobvitz, 1999). Both of these types are at high risk for externalizing behavior problems. Moreover, these insecurely attached, disorganized children are considerably less likely than securely attached children to have accurate and positive views of themselves, interact with others empathically and sensitively, as well as regulate their emotions and describe their feelings accurately. This is concerning given that these qualities are notably absent among individuals who sexually offend (Marshall, 1993).

Affect, cognition, and psychopathology

According to Crittenden (1995), there is more variability in attachment styles based on the integration of affect and cognition. In contrast to Ainsworth's categorical description, Crittenden has designed a dimensional model, which illustrates the nuances in the relationship between parental behavior and child outcomes (See Figure 1). At the top of the figure, one can see that the secure (B) children have accurate or true affect and cognition and these components are integrated. There is some variability in the secure children, with the reserved infants B1-2 possibly reflecting some combination of temperament and also maternal affective behavior that requires a small amount of self-modulation. Moving down the left side are examples of defended or avoidantly (A) attached children. The inhibited group A1-2 is more likely to have parents who are intrusive and the child has learned to be close but not intimate with them. However, the caregiving and compliant groups have parents who need to be actively solicited into the parenting process because they are often withdrawn and truly unavailable (e.g. neglectful). The child has to work hard to elicit maternal caregiving and so may become a caregiver themselves or even hypercompliant, jumping to the smallest cue from the parent. This comes at the cost of false affect but yet more accurate cognitions about what is likely to occur in interpersonal relationships. Avoidant children deny and push away the anger and sad feelings that are a natural outcome of ineffective and isolating parenting.

Figure 1: Crittenden's (1995) Dimensional Model of Attachment based on the Integration of Affect and Cognition

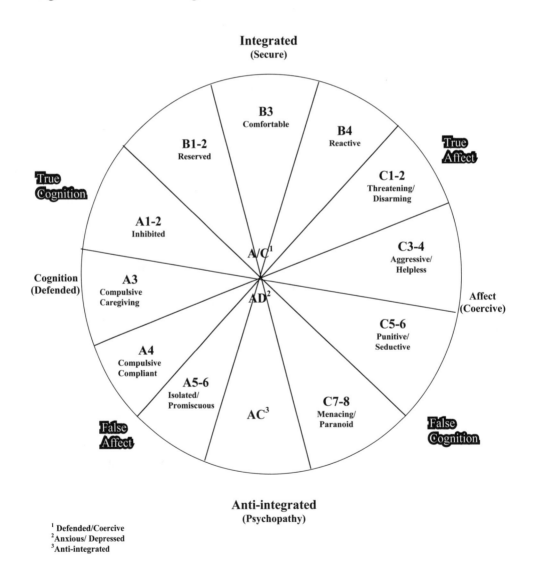

[1] Defended/Coercive
[2] Anxious/ Depressed
[3] Anti-integrated

The right side of Crittenden's model illustrates what occurs when the parent's unpredictability makes cognition suspect but affective responses are more predictable and understandable. The coercive child (C) is also likely to include coy and manipulative features in their behavior. Their angry outbursts, designed to elicit parental response, may be modulated by a quick smile once that parent has responded. In fact, coercive children experience anger concurrently with fear and a desire for comfort. However, the punitive child C5-6 is much more likely to use anger without modulation, and runs the risk of angry parental retaliation that only further solidifies their angry behavior. Both punitive and coercive children engage in much less integration and reorganization in response to new information. Because so much information is regarded as unreliable, these children often fail to recognize discrepancies, and thus fail to integrate this new information into a reorganized attachment strategy. Crittenden (1995) adds seductive as a modifier of punitive since children in this group are even more likely to be good at tricking and even seducing parents and others into behaving in a certain manner. The seductive strategy, as well as the isolated/promiscuous subtype in the avoidant group has the most relevance to our discussion of sexually intrusive children, given the ease with which these categories translate into sexual behavior.

Attachment and sexual abuse

The sexual abuse of a child reflects a disturbed pattern of relating on the part of the perpetrator. In fact, it has been reported that at least 95% of maltreated children have insecure attachment with the maltreating parent (Cicchetti & Toth). Moreover, research on the attachment security of perpetrators suggests that child molesters were more likely to have preoccupied or fearful styles of attachment whereas rapists were more often dismissing-avoidant (Ward, Hudson, & Marshall, 1996).

One hopes that a child's attachment quality with the non-offending parent is more often secure than insecure. However, there is little systematic research using appropriate assessment techniques (e.g. Strange Situation) on the attachment quality of children with a sexual abuse history with the nonoffending parent. Nevertheless, there is ample evidence to suggest the non-offending parent is likely to have their own psychiatric difficulties and abuse history, factors that may seriously interfere with the quality of attachment with their child. To our knowledge there are relatively few studies that formally assessed the relationship between the attachment quality of children with their nonoffending parent and subsequent child outcomes, and that include sexually abused children. Two studies come from longitudinal research at the Institute of Child Development, University of Minnesota. The first study examined those children in this high-risk sample who were maltreated (Erickson & Egeland, 1987). In particular, this study found that sexually abused children invariably were victims of other abuses in their home environment, including neglect, as well as emotional and physical abuse. Presumably, the mother inflicted some of the other abuses, but equally important is the suggestion that sexual abuse is rarely the only adversity in the child's life.

A second set of studies from this project found a subset of mothers who exhibited seductive behavior with their child during a play observation (Sroufe & Ward, 1980). Interestingly, these mothers typically reported a history of sexual maltreatment that had never been treated. Followed over time, children with seductive mothers were rated as the most disturbed subset of children in the sample, with some of the mothers admitting to the sexual abuse of this child (Sroufe, Jacobvitz, Mangelsdorf, DeAngelo, & Ward, 1985). Clearly, the presence of a sexual abuse history in the mother suggests unresolved victimization and disorganized attachment which has implications for this mothers' relationship with her own children.

In an observational study of children and their mothers with a sexual abuse history, Burkett (1991) found that these mothers tended to be self-focused rather than child-focused, and they appeared to use their children as a source of emotional support. Interestingly, this role reversal, a dynamic that is often described in incestuous families, appears to be present even when the abuse occurred in the previous generation.

Research of mothers' responses to the Adult Attachment Interview (AAI), a widely accepted strategy to assess attachment status, found that those with unresolved trauma, including sexual abuse, provided narratives to the AAI that violated numerous rules of discourse (Hesse, 1999). In particular, this research found that these were mothers of disorganized infants and children who failed to see their child accurately, and did not provide the type of interaction that allows the child to think accurately about itself or be aware of the motivations for their behavior.

Another study using the AAI examined the attachment security of foster and adoptive mothers of 4-6 year old maltreated children (Steele, Hodges, Kaniuk, Hillman, & Henderson, 2003). After 3 months of placement, maltreated children were influenced by their adoptive mother's security of attachment. In particular, children of securely attached adoptive mothers were significantly less likely to have attachment stories with themes of aggressivity and catastrophe than children with insecurely attached adoptive mothers. Clearly, these results suggest that the internal working model of young children's relationships can be positively influenced by a securely attached caregiver.

Parent sexual abuse history and child outcomes

There are many more studies that have examined the victimization history and psychopathology in parents of children who have sexually abused and those with sexual behavior problems. These studies are relevant since psychopathology interferes with normal parenting (Rutter & Quinton, 1984). Parents can influence their child's functioning along several pathways: 1) dyadic interaction between parent and child, 2) coaching and teaching about relationships, and 3) providing an environment which nurtures social activities (Dodge, 1990). Dyadic interaction in parents who are depressed or who have other psychopathology may be frustrating. They may offer the child few models of how to solve conflict, share with others, and be empathic. Clearly, parental psychopathology interferes with the quality of teaching and coaching a parent can do, or even the child's willingness to share failures and then together learn from experience. Finally, parents might expose their child to positive peer influences and structure their child's schedule to accommodate social and academic concerns, but these tasks can be formidable for a single, overwhelmed parent.

A study of the MMPI profiles of three groups of mothers found that mothers of sexually abused children were more likely than mothers who were receiving outpatient mental health services or mothers with no psychiatric history to have 4-3 and spike-4 profiles (Friedrich, 1991). This was particularly true for mothers of sexually abused children who had a history of sexual abuse. The MMPI code-types of these parents have implications for attachment. In particular, the elevation on Scale 4 is often related to issues with sexuality, as well as expression of anger. The addition of Scale 3 can be seen to reflect problems with the understanding of the self, particularly with regard to the understanding of one's sexual and angry feelings (Friedrich, 2002). Clearly, these unresolved sexual issues and angry feelings may translate into coercive parent-child behavior. In particular, a child's normal sexual behavior may be quite provocative to a parent with these unresolved feelings. As a result, the parent may over-respond or become quite punitive to a child's normal sexual behavior, thus setting the stage for a negative series of interactions. Moreover, these parents may also have partners who sexualize relationships, thus modeling overt sexuality in the home. Since they have problems with understanding themselves and others, this parent is also likely to have problems understanding the world from their child's point of view. Consequently, they do not contribute to a frame of mind that is essential for secure attachment (Fonagy et al., 1995).

In addition, parents with a sexual abuse history may take one of two routes to their own sexuality, hypersexual or inhibited (Merrill, Guimond, Thomsen, & Milner, 2003). Each path may have unique effects on child outcome. For example, the hypersexual parent may contribute to a sexualized home environment. In particular, they may misinterpret normative sexual behaviors exhibited by their child, or their relationship with their child may become sexualized. In addition, a hypersexual parent is likely to have abuse that is unresolved, which may affect their relationship and behavior toward their child. A recent study compared juvenile sex offenders to youth with conduct disorders (Tabacoff, Baker, Eisenstadt, & Tornusciolo, under review.). Sex offenders were more likely than conduct disordered youth to have mothers with a history of sexual abuse and reside in a sexualized home environment, including exposure to pornography, sexual activity among adults, and sexualized behavior toward the child, and having been sexually abused.

In contrast to the hypersexual parent, parents who respond to sexual abuse through inhibited sexuality (Merrill, Guimond, Thomsen, & Milner, 2003) are at risk for rejecting their child because the parenting relationship is so intimate that it is dysregulating to the parent.   They may also reject their child further because of normative sexual behaviors, and this can contribute to the creation of a coercive interaction between the parent and the child.

To illustrate, New, Stevenson, and Skuse (1999) studied the mothers of boys, ages 11-15, who had victimized other children or who had a sexual abuse history. Mothers of perpetrators reported higher rates of sexual victimization in their own childhood (55%) than mothers of victims (30%). Moreover, both mothers of perpetrators (72%) and mothers of victims (50%) reported high rates of domestic violence.   The authors also found a surprisingly high frequency of what they called "repressive coping style" in these mothers which they believed was related to the psychological absence of these parent figures.

Research has examined the relationship between child sexual abuse and sexual behavior problems (Hall & Mathews, 1996). An examination of the top twenty-five risk factors finds that twelve are suggestive of impaired attachment. These include a history of physical and emotional abuse of the child in question, role reversal with parent, PTSD in the mother, maternal competition with child, maternal boundary problems with the child, history of physical neglect in the mother, and history of domestic violence in paternal childhood.

A variety of other studies have also examined attachment-related variables in the parents of sexually abused children. For example, compared to mothers with sexual abuse whose child had not been sexually abused and mothers without a sexual abuse history whose child was sexually abused, mothers with a sexual abuse history whose child was also sexually abused had more disturbed relationships with their victimized children and a more negative rearing history (Leifer, Kilbane, & Grossman, 2001; Leifer, Kilbane, & Kalick, 2004; Paredes, Leifer, & Kilbane, 2001). In addition, parental support consistently has been found to be associated with the sexually abused child's adjustment (for a review see Elliott & Carnes, 2001). Clearly, a parent's history of sexual abuse, attachment problems, and/or current psychopathology may significantly interfere with the level of support they can offer to their sexually abused child.

Current research

Using a consecutive sample of 391 children admitted to a psychiatric unit, our research has examined the relationship between maternal victimization history and child outcome (Friedrich & Sim, 2003). In particular, we have used a standard set of measures to assess critical aspects of the parent child relationship including child internalizing and externalizing behavior, child sexual behaviors, maternal victimization history, maternal depression, and maternal social support, as well as discipline tactics used by the mother, and maternal negative attributions towards the child. Overall, we found that mothers with a sexual abuse history, compared to those without an abuse history, perceived themselves as having lower levels of social support and higher levels of depression. They also reported having more negative feelings toward their children, and used more coercive discipline techniques (Table 1). In addition, the children of mothers with a sexual abuse history, were more likely to have been sexually abused (35%) than those whose mother did not have a sexual abuse history (17.8%) (chi2=13.58, p < .001). These children also had experienced more negative life events and exhibited more symptoms of PTSD, as well as increased externalizing and internalizing behaviors than children whose mother was not abused (Table 1). There were no differences between the groups on child sexual behaviors, which may have been due to some victimized mothers being avoidant of sexuality and less likely to report these behaviors in their children.

Table 1: Means and Standard Deviations of Maternal Characteristics for Mothers with a History of Abuse and those without a History of Sexual Abuse

	Group		t-value	df
	No Maternal History of Sexual Abuse (N = 222)	Maternal History of Sexual Abuse (N = 132)		
Coercive Discipline Tactics (CTS)	.99 (.74)	1.21 (.82)	-2.58**	348
Maternal Negative Attributions (PCFS)	3.31 (.74)	3.15 (.66)	-2.12*	350
Maternal Social Support (Satisfaction item)	2.38 (.79)	1.92 (.97)	4.81***	237
Depression (Brief BDI)	.28 (.37)	.52 (.44)	-5.37***	234
Child Life Events (LEC)	.14 (.14)	.22 (.14)	-4.88***	352
Child Sexual Behavior (CSBI)	.21 (.31)	.29 (.38)	-1.25	112
Child Intrusive Sexual Behavior (CSBI-Intrusive Behavior Items)	.00 (.23)	.18 (.37)	-1.53	112
Child Externalizing Behavior (CBCL-Externalizing Subscale)	60.6 (12.92)	64.3 (12.27)	2.37*	287
Child Internalizing Behavior (CBCL-Internalizing Subcale)	64.1 (11.92)	67.80 (10.45)	-2.67**	287
Child PTSD symptoms (CBCL-PTSD Scale)	.58 (.43)	.70 (.43)	-2.34*	294

Note. Means are presented followed by standard deviations in parentheses. CTS = Conflict Tactics Scale (Straus, et al, 1998); PCS = Parentification of Children Scale (Friedrich & Reams, 1987); Brief BDI = 13 Items from Beck Depression Inventory (Beck et al., 1996); LEC = Life Events Checklist (Coddington, 1972); CSBI = Child Sexual Behavior Inventory (Friedrich, 1997); CSBI Intrusive = Intrusive Items from the Child Sexual Behavior Inventory (Friedrich, 1997); CBCL = Child Behavior Checklist Parent Report (Achenbach, 1991).
***$p < .001$, **$p < .01$, *$p < .05$

Case study

> *Aaron was a 5-year old boy living with his unmarried biological parents and his paternal uncle. His pediatrician referred him because of his sexual behavior, which his mother described as "The Whizzie Dance." During the first interview, Aaron's mother described the "game" as an activity in which Aaron would drop his pants, expose himself to whoever was in the room, and then dance and jump around telling people to look at his "whizzie." He did this several times per day on average.*

*He would often run outside into the back yard when chased by his mother and con-
tinue the "dance" there. This behavior typically occurred only at home but Aaron
had done this in other settings on a less frequent basis. His father's usual response
was to ignore it or tell him to stop, and his mother's response was usually to cover
her eyes, scream and react in a relatively histrionic manner. Both parents were victims of sexual abuse as children, neither had received therapy for this, and his
father, who was more than 20 years older than the mother, was also a Vietnam veteran who because of his experiences in the war had one time received a diagnosis of
PTSD.*

*Aaron's mother reported that they had tried a number of strategies, and that "none
of them worked." These included time out, spanking, ignoring, and promise of
rewards. She did report that if his father yelled and threatened, Aaron would usually stop for the rest of the day but that he preferred not to yell at his son. Since
Aaron was due to start kindergarten, the parents were increasingly motivated to
eliminate the problem and had purchased a motorized tricycle which they promised
him if he could stop the "dance" for one week. Aaron was discovered riding it the
day after it was brought home. Although the parents hid the tricycle and its battery
separately, he would search for both until he found them and then would ride it, an
almost daily occurrence. His mother stated she felt helpless at stopping him from
either riding the tricycle or stopping his "dance." She also described getting little to
no support from his father, who worked long hours. She also reported that she was
probably starting to yell more and react more strongly to Aaron since she was
increasingly worried about getting his behavior under control by the start of school.*

*Both parents were quite protective of Aaron because of their history. Consequently,
he had never attended daycare and his only baby-sitter was his uncle, his father's
oldest brother who was on medical disability. She was convinced Aaron had not
been sexually abused and she reported that Aaron exhibited no other worrisome sexual behaviors or problems with toileting or sleeping. In fact, he was generally well
behaved other than for his "dance" and the resistant behavior surrounding it. To
her credit, his mother reported that she and Aaron spent regular time together playing games, working on activities, learning numbers and letters, and conflict rarely
emerged at these times.*

*An older brother and his friend perpetrated the sexual abuse of Aaron's mother and
this initially involved the two of them exposing themselves to her. This eventually
led to their fondling her and her having to either masturbate them or perform oral
sex. The source of her over-reactivity seemed quite clear to the interviewer. Aaron's
mother was already partially aware that her sexual abuse was connected to her
over-reaction to Aaron, but felt helpless at changing her response. She reported that
she was avoidant of sexuality, and she and Aaron's father were rarely intimate. His
lack of interest was a relief to her although she reported some embarrassment at
reporting this fact.*

*The interviewer explained to the mother that people were avoidant of reminders of
previous traumas and so her wish not to be reminded of her abuse by the "dance"
was completely understandable. As a mother, she was entitled to have a different
response than the one she had as a child. She agreed with this and following some*

*in-session coaching, she demonstrated that she could turn her head away in a neu-
tral fashion and state, matter of factly, "I was hoping to play with you but now
we'll have to wait," and walked into another room. These directions were typed out
and she was sent home to practice.*

*She brought Aaron in the following week and was eager to report that she had fol-
lowed directions and had noticed that the overall frequency had decreased and each
episode was now shorter. Aaron played appropriately with the interviewer and no
emotional themes were evident. In the final portion of the session, his mother and I
demonstrated to him, using small dolls as props, how she was learning to teach him
that he was getting too old for the "dance."*

*Two weeks later, his mother reported an almost total drop-off in the "dance." She
was praised for that progress and encouraged to seek out a support group for
women with her history. Telephone follow-up at six weeks confirmed that the
"dance" had extinguished, no other behavior problems had emerged, and all family
members felt Aaron was ready for kindergarten. While the improvement demonstrated by this family was relatively rapid, the case study illustrates the relationship
of victimization history to child behavior. With guidance and support, parental
responses related to the victimization history thought to reinforce the child's behavior can be modified.*

Conclusion

The sexual abuse of a child is often predated by a greater than normal likelihood of
the child having one or more parents with a history of sexual abuse, living in a home
environment in which sexuality is either overly present or avoided, and growing up
with other types of abuse. All of these variables contribute to insecure attachment
and disrupted parent-child relationships. Of particular concern is the parenting that
occurs when a parent has a history of unresolved abuse, wherein they are frightened
or frightening to their child. This contributes to disorganized attachment, and is characterized in adult life by the over expression of severe Axis II disorders, substance
abuse, unemployment, criminal involvement, and abusive parenting (Lyons-Ruth &
Jacobvitz, 1999). While insecure attachment is not directly related to subsequent victimization or perpetration, the addition of distorted sexuality into the equation certainly can tilt the pathology in that direction, especially when predisposing factors,
e.g. cumulative adversity, modeling of coercion, and proneness to acting out are present (Friedrich et al., 2003).

Clinicians are best served when they conceptualize attachment as a multigenerational
process and maintain a three-generational perspective in their diagnostic interviews
and therapy (Friedrich, 2002). Attachment-related questions that we recommend
include the following: (1) Does the child's primary caregiver have a history of sexual abuse or other victimization?; (2) If so, has the parent ever received treatment?; and
(3) Does the parent have accurate and generally positive attributions about this child
and the child's sexual behavior? Clinicians should also pay close attention to how the
parent describes their relationship with the child's grandparents. Since attachment is
a secure-base phenomenon and secure attachment emerges with caregivers that provide safety, it is also important to assess for the safety and security of the child's home.
The Safety Checklist (Friedrich, 2002) is one measure that assesses the safety and secu-

rity of the child's home environment.

The behavior of the child or adolescent can also provide clues to the nature of their attachment. Controlling behavior by the child toward caregivers, the presence of severe externalizing disorders, self-injurious behavior, dissociation, and confusing and contradictory behavior towards and/or descriptions of their parents are all suggestive of disturbed attachment (Friedrich, 2002). Children who are cruel to others have a failure in empathy and are particularly likely to have disturbed attachment relationships and consequently, are at risk for future sexual offending. In fact, one of the reasons why the relationship between prior sexual abuse and subsequent sexual offending is so variable is that research has probably focused on too narrow a variable, i.e. prior history of sexual abuse and neglected the assessment of internal working models through which sexual abuse is processed. Sexual offending is a classic model of disturbed relating in a manner similar to disturbed attachment, especially disorganized attachment.

References

Ainsworth, M.D.S., Blehar, M.C., Waters, E., & Wall, S. (1978). *Patterns of attachment: A psychological study of the Strange Situation.* Hillsdale, NJ: Lawrence Erlbaum.

Burkett, L.P. (1991). Parenting behaviors of woman who were sexually abused as children in their family of origin. *Family Process*, 30, 421-434.

Cicchetti, D. & Toth, S.L. (1995). A developmental psychopathology perspective on child abuse and neglect. *Journal of the American Academy of Child and Adolescent Psychiatry*, 34, 541-565.

Crittenden, P.M. (1995). Attachment and psychopathology. In S. Goldberg, R. Muir, & J. Kerr (Eds.), *Attachment theory: Social, developmental, & clinical perspectives* (pp. 367-406). Hillsdale, NJ: Analytic Press.

Dodge, K. (1990). Developmental psychopathology in children of depressed mothers. *Developmental Psychology*, 26, 3-6.

Dozier, M., Stovall, K.C., & Albus, K.E. (1999). In J. Cassidy & P.R. Shaver (Eds.) *Handbook of attachment* (pp. 497-519). New York: Guilford.

Elliott, A.N. & Carnes, CN (2001). Reactions of nonoffending parents to the sexual abuse of their child: A review of the literature. *Child Maltreatment*, 6, 314-331.

Erickson, M.F. & Egeland, B. (1987). A developmental view of the psychological consequences of child maltreatment. *School Psychology Review*, 16, 156-168.

Fonagy, P., Steele, M., Steele, H., Leigh, T., Kennedy, R., Mattoon, G., & Target, M. (1995). Attachment, the reflective self, and borderline states: The predictive specificity of the Adult Attachment Interview and pathological emotional development. In S. Goldberg, R. Muir, & J. Kerr (Eds.), *Attachment theory: Social, developmental, & clinical perspectives* (pp. 233-278). Hillsdale, NJ: Analytic Press.

Friedrich, W.N. (1991). Mother's of sexually abused children: An MMPI study. *Journal of Clinical Psychology*, 47, 778-783.

Friedrich, W.N., Sim, L. (2003). Sexual abuse victims as mothers: relationship to coping resources, perceptions of the child, discipline practices, and behavior problems. *Paper presented at the 8th International Family Violence Research Conference,* Portsmouth, NH, July 14, 2003.

Friedrich, W.N., Davies, W.H., & Feher, E. & Wright, J. (2003). Sexual behavior problems in preteen children. *Annals of the New York Academy of Science*, 989, 95-104.

Hesse, E. (1999). The Adult Attachment Interview. In J. Cassidy & P.R. Shaver (Eds.) *Handbook of attachment* (pp. 395-433). New York: Guilford.

Leifer, M., Kilbane, T., & Grossman, G. (2001). A three-generational study comparing the families of supportive and unsupportive mothers of sexually abused children. *Child Maltreatment*, 6, 353-364.

Leifer, M., Kilbane, T., & Kalick, S. (2004). Vulnerability or resilience to intergenerational sexual abuse: the role of maternal factors. *Child Maltreatment*, 9, 78-91.

Lyons-Ruth, K. & Jacobvitz, D. (1999). Attachment disorganization. In J. Cassidy & P.R. Shaver (Eds.) *Handbook of attachment* (pp. 520-554). New York: Guilford.

Main, M. & Solomon, J. (1990). Procedures for identifying infants as disorganized/disoriented during the Ainsworth Strange Situation. In M.T. Greenberg, D. Cicchetti, & E.M. Cummings, (Eds), *Attachment in the preschool years* (pp. 121-160). Chicago: University of Chicago Press.

Marsa, F., O'Reilly, G., Carr, A., Murphy, P., O'Sullivan, M., Cotter, A., & Hevey, D. (2004). Attachment styles and psychological profiles of child sex offenders in Ireland. *Journal of Interpersonal Violence*, 19, 228-251.

Marshall, W. (1993). The role of attachment, intimacy, and loneliness in the aetiology and maintenance of sexual offending. *Sexual and Marital Therapy*, 8, 109-121.

Merrill, L.E., Guimond, J.M., Thomsen, C.J., & Milner, J.S. (2003). Child sexual abuse and number of sexual partners in young women: The role of abuse severity , coping style, and sexual functioning. *Journal of Consulting and Clinical Psychology*, 71, 987-996.

New, M.J.C., & Stevenson, J., & Skuse, D. (1999). Characteristics of mothers of boys who sexually abuse. *Child Maltreatment*, 4, 21-31.

Paredes, M., Leifer, M., & Kilbane, T. (2001). Maternal variables related to sexually abused children's functioning. *Child Abuse and Neglect*, 25, 1159-1176.

Rutter, M. & Quinton, D. (1984). Parental psychiatric disorder: Effects on children. *Psychological Medicine*, 14, 853-880.

Sroufe, L.A. & Ward, M.J. (1980). Seductive behavior of mothers of toddlers: Occurrence, correlates, and family origins. *Child Development*, 51, 1222-1229.

Sroufe, L.A., Jacobvitz, D., Mangelsdorf, S., DeAngelo, E., & Ward, M.J. (1985). Generational boundary dissolution between mothers and their preschool children: A relationship systems approach. *Child Development*, 56, 317-325.

Steele, M., Hodges, J., Kaniuk, J., Hillman, S., & Henderson, K. (2003). Attachment representations and adoption: associations between maternal states of mind and emotion narratives in previously maltreated children. *Journal of Child Psychotherapy*, 29, 187-205.

Straus, M. A., Hamby, S. L., Finkelhor, D., Moore, D. W., & Runyan, D. (1998). Identification of child maltreatment with the Parent-Child Conflict Tactics Scales: Development and psychometric data for a national sample of American parents. *Child Abuse & Neglect*, 22, 249-270.

Tabacoff, R., Baker, A.L., Eisenstadt, M., & Tornusciolo, G. Violent and sexualized family environments: A comparative study of juvenile sex offenders and youth with conduct disorders. (under editorial review).

Ward, T., Hudson, S., & Marshall, W. (1996). Attachment styles in sex offenders: A preliminary study. *Journal of Sex Research*, 33, 17-26.

CHAPTER FIFTEEN

CHILDREN AND ADOLESCENTS WITH PROBLEMATIC SEXUAL BEHAVIORS: LESSONS FROM RESEARCH ON RESILIENCE

JANE GILGUN

Introduction

Children and adolescents with problematic sexual behaviors typically have experienced adversities, but this by itself does not account for their inappropriate behaviors. If there were a direct route between adversities and outcomes, then all persons with risks for sexual behavior problems would have them. This is not the case. Such a simple observation leads to a search for factors that moderate the effects of adversities on behaviors. Developmental psychopathology provides many important ideas about outcomes, risks, vulnerability, and protective factors that moderate the effects of risks.

This subfield of developmental psychology studies high-risk groups, usually longitudinally, for the purpose of identifying factors that lead to good and poor outcomes under adverse conditions (Luthar, 2003). Individuals who don't have the negative outcomes associated with risks they have experienced are termed *resilient*. Thus, children and adolescents who are at risk for developing sexually inappropriate behavior patterns do not do so because they have resources to help them to cope with, adapt to, and overcome these risks.

The purpose of this chapter is to show how research and theory on resilience contribute to assessment and treatment planning for children and adolescents with sexual behavior problems. This body of knowledge has a great deal to offer practitioners who are looking for good ideas to use in therapy and psychoeducation programs. An increasing number of programs are incorporating these ideas to the advantage of clients.

Young people have ideas about their own resilience. The task of practitioners is to find the "hidden" resilience in behaviors that are harmful and sometimes illegal (Gilgun & Abrams, in press; Ungar, 2004). The overview of youth perspectives later in this chapter demonstrates that effective interventions start where clients are; that is, treatment providers should seek to connect with clients' points of view and build assessments and treatment plans from there.

Research on resilience

Research on resilience has much to offer treatment professionals. Foremost is an optimistic message that persons can recover from adversities, a view that is backed by substantial research evidence (Curtis & Cicchetti, 2003; Egeland, Carlons, & Sroufe, 1993; Gilgun, 1996; 1999c; Gilgun, Klein, & Pranis, 2000; Masten & Wright, 1998; Richters & Martinez, 1993; Rutter, 2000; Shields & Cicchetti, 1998; Werner & Smith, 1992; Widom, 1991). The effects of adversities, such as childhood abuse and neglect, parental abandonment and death, and forced migration can be life-long and have serious effects on quality of life. Studies have shown, however, that most individuals manage to cope with adversities and carry on with their lives in productive, pro-social, and law-abiding ways. This research has documented the existence of protective processes, which by definition, are factors that moderate the effects of adversities and are associated with capacities for personal well-being and competence.

Adaptation, vulnerability, and dysregulation

When individuals experience adversities, they generally adapt. These adaptations fit the types of adversities they experience. For example, being on the alert for the sound of footsteps and the angry utterances of a drunk parent with abusive tendencies will lead children to hide or escape the family home until the drunk person passes out or leaves. Such situations can result in hypervigilance, which can be protective when it leads individuals to avoid future frightening and dangerous situations. Children who behave this way are displaying adaptive behaviors whose purpose is to ensure their well-being and even survival. They are coping with and adapting to noxious events. Such children are vulnerable to anxiety in situations that are safe but trigger expectations that a drunk, violent parent is about to arrive.

Vulnerabilities represent residual emotional and psychological hurt. These hurts can be thought of as psychic wounds that may require life long effort to manage. These wounds are like "hot buttons" that environmental cues may touch, activating the reliving of past trauma and other troubling responses. Many individuals have resources such as supportive families and a history of secure attachments, which result in capacities for coping with this hurt. Despite the availability of resources, persons with psychic wounds are vulnerable to dysregulation when they are in situations that evoke earlier adversities.

When dysregulated, children experience a sense of unmanageability of their thoughts, emotions, and behaviors (Shields & Cicchetti, 1998). Their autonomous nervous systems, too, may be dysregulated. They are likely to display such emotional states as anxiety, depression, withdrawal, lethargy, hyperactivity, bouts of crying, bed wetting, sleep disturbances, and oppositional behaviors.

When dysregulated, individuals seek to re-regulate. They seek to regain self-efficacy, control, and mastery over themselves and their various environments (Gilgun, in press). Re-regulation can occur in three general ways: pro-social, anti-social, and self-injurious.

- **Pro-social efforts** to re-regulate include seeking comfort and affirmation from attachment figures, talking to someone about the hurt and confusion, channeling the negative affect into positive behaviors such as physical exercise and artistic expression. They may also seek ways to redirect implications of the hurt away from the self as worthless and helpless toward a sense of self as good and competent.

- **Anti-social** efforts to re-regulate include effacement and destruction of property, teasing and taunting others, bullying, physically aggressive, acting in sexually inappropriate ways, stealing and other oppositional behaviors. These may provide temporary relief from the subjective distress of dysregulation. School shootings are extreme examples of young people using anti-social methods of re-regulation. From the individuals' perspective, anti-social acts are typically attempts to restore a sense of honor or self-respect, and are a form of impression management. They may be strongly motivated to show others that they are not wimps and sissies but strong, forceful, and worthy of respect or even awe.

- **Self-injurious** efforts at re-regulation include cutting or other self injury, anorexia, bulimia, use of drugs or alcohol, suicide attempts, recklessness, and playing with guns or other weapons. These behaviors also provide a sense of relief and restore the sense of self. The consequences of these behaviors show another aspect of the human dilemma wherein solutions can become part of the problem. The relief is temporary and may lead to further dysregulation and a cycle of self-destructive behaviors.

Efforts at coping take place over time and often contain a mixture of these general classes of behaviors. For example, the immediate response to a noxious event, such as an incident of being sexually abused, might be intrapsychic numbing, followed by self-destructive negative thoughts, overeating, aggression toward others, or seeking comfort from an attachment figure. Individuals may cope successfully with some adversities, but find their capacities to be overwhelmed by others. Positive coping and resilience are not all-or-nothing processes. They are situational and dependent upon the meanings the noxious events have to individuals affected, the other risks that are activated, and the availability of supportive resources.

Protective processes

Research has shown that children and adolescents who experience adversities tend to manage well in a variety of situations if they have engaged in protective processes (Curtis & Cicchetti, 2003; Gilgun, 1996; 1999; Gilgun, Klein, & Pranis, 2000; Masten & Wright, 1998; Rutter, 2000; Shields & Cicchetti, 1998; Werner & Smith, 1992). These can include a long-term caring relationship with at least one other person with whom they share personal and painful experiences. These friends or confidants also model pro-social behaviors that they encourage and reward in younger partners, who, in turn want to emulate these positive persons. The younger partners thus internalize favorable working models of themselves, others, and how the world works. These working models are likely to guide them toward pro-social ways of dealing with other stressors and adversities, or minimally, serve to counteract inner working models that channel thoughts, emotions, and behaviors toward destructive actions.

Emotional expressiveness is the single most important protective factor that differentiates persons with problematic sexual behaviors from persons who do not have these behaviors (Gilgun, 1990, 1991, 1992, 1996a, 1996b, 1999; 2000). Other protective processes associated with good outcomes under adverse conditions include:

- **A confidant(e)** who may be a peer or an adult, either inside or outside of the family with whom the at-risk person reciprocates a sense of closeness, seeks for support and counsel during times of stress or fear, and freely shares painful personal issues. Typically individuals who show resilience have relationships of more than two years with both peers and adults, who may be parents, siblings, peers, coaches, teachers, or parents of friends. Supplemental confidants may be journals, diaries, or other verbal expres sion such as writing poetry or stories. Nonverbal avenues of emotional expression include playing musical instruments, drawing, sculpture, etc. Some young people have no one to confide in for many years, but they know that they are stressed and hurting. They also do not hurt other peo ple, and they seek situations where they feel safe, such as libraries or the corner pool hall. When they finally find someone whom they think is safe, they do confide sensitive personal information.
- **A strong desire to be pro-social,** which is characteristic of individuals who consciously and actively seek to do no harm to others. Thoughts of hurting others may evoke their own psychological pain, and they do not want to inflict this pain on others. Theories of human agency recognize that indi viduals have choices, but these choices are limited by personal experience occurring at particular times, places, and settings. These choices are further influenced by gender, social class, age, income, and a range of other status variables.
- **A favorable sense of self** that challenges inner representations of the self as bad and powerless. These positive inner working models develop from secure attachments, long term caring relationships, confidant relationships, and a personal sense of competence in such areas as emotion regulation and forming relationships.
- **Doing something positive really well** such as reading, athletics, drawing, riding a bike, etc. and getting positive attention for these accomplishments helps individuals to cope with adversity. Research on self-efficacy and com petence have emphasized how important this quality is for surviving adversities and developing resilience (Masten & Coatsworth, 1998).
- **The ability to engage in self-soothing behaviors**, such as listening to music, engaging in affirming self-talk, physical activity, and imagining a fulfilling future is another proactive process that offers good outcomes.
- **Affirming gender, ethnic or cultural identity** shape who we are. In cul tures that convey an "us and them" mentality, children and adolescents who are typed as "other", are at risk for adverse outcomes. They may inter nalize negative stereotypes and for a variety of reasons act out these inner representations of self, others, and how the world works.
- **Hope** for a positive future, capacities to imagine a positive future, and seek ing and using resources that build that positive future may arise as a pro tective process. Some young people who have experienced multiple adver sities develop unrealistic expectations about what they can achieve. Examples might include wanting to be a movie star or a multi-millionaire athlete. Hope, resources to achieve dreams, and efforts that engage these resources are significant components of this protective factor.

Key elements of protective processes include whether young people want to behave in pro-social ways and whether they engage with the personal, familial, and social resources that are available to them (Gilgun, in press).

Researchers and practitioners have observed these protective processes in natural environments, where young people have developed them in response to the resources available to them. Practitioners can seek to foster these processes in treatment and psychoeducation programs. Typically, a combination of factors lead to pro-social outcomes, but it is unlikely that pro-sociality comes about without capacities for emotional intelligence (Goleman, 1995), both in terms of knowing and expressing one's own emotions in appropriates ways, as well as connecting to and having empathy for the emotions and situations of others.

Most children and adolescents with sexual behavior issues have experienced substantial adversities, and these must be identified and dealt with if treatment is to be effective. The younger the person when their problematic sexual behaviors first appear, the more likely they have experienced adversities, such as being victims of child sexual abuse, that adults leave unattended or mismanage. Immediate, constructive responses to children who have been sexually abused greatly reduce the risk of long-term harm and of the child perpetrating child sexual abuse themselves.

Treatment professionals must develop strategies to deal with the messages that young people receive from within their cultures about appropriate behaviors, life goals, and how to achieve them. For children and adolescents with sexual issues, these culture-based messages are usually gendered in that certain behaviors are encouraged in females and others in males, with both rewards and sanctions meted out according to how well individuals live up to these gendered, culture-based expectations (Brody, 1999).

Children and adolescents recognize expectations for themselves as females and males, and they understand that non-conformity may subject them to ridicule and social isolation. They learn how to behave as gendered persons not only from how other people treat them and how their behaviors influence the responses of others, but also from observations of the gendered behaviors of others, including representations in mass media. They notice and internalize which behaviors are valued and which are not. Gender is a core identity and frequently operates outside of awareness.

Unfortunately, gender stereotypes about males discourage expression of emotions such as fear, hurt, compassion, and shame. Admitting weaknesses, backing down from a fight, and crying invite ridicule and social isolation. Emotional expressiveness, therefore, is difficult for many boys and young men to attain because of social pressures. As a result, they may distance themselves from resources that might help them to cope with, adapt to, and overcome adversities and other factors that put them at risk for problematic outcomes. They may see the acting out of gender stereotypes as a more acceptable way of restoring a sense of personal power and integration when they are dysregulated, than expressions of distress and vulnerability. They may come to rely on physical and even sexual aggression to restore an integrated sense of self and self respect, however temporary these outcomes may be.

Girls receive a more positive reception of their expressions of hurt and powerlessness, and therefore are at lower risk to resort to aggressive sexual behaviors to deal with the effects of the adversities they experience. Female stereotypes encourage help-seeking behaviors and direct efforts to relieve their psychological pain as compared to male stereotypes. As a result, girls appear to be less likely to develop sexually inappropriate behaviors that harm others, first because they are positioned to deal directly with hurt and vulnerability, and second because gender stereotypes discourage sexual and physical aggression. How individuals absorb these stereotype varies a great deal. For this reason, each young person in treatment must be carefully and individually assessed to see if and how gender stereotypes play a role in problematic sexual behaviors.

There are major variations in the risks and resources that male children and adolescents bring with them as they enter treatment. They are also likely to be faced with learning how to cope more effectively with adversities, and re-learning what it means to be male in this culture. By engaging in treatment, male children and adolescents confront the difficult task of changing deep-seated ideas that go to the core of their identities as males and as worthy human beings.

Girls, on the other hand, are less likely to be referred to treatment for sexual acting out. If and when they are, they often have several mental health diagnoses and may be far more disordered and confused than most boys who are in treatment for inappropriate sexual behavior. Girls' mental health issues may be more prominent in treatment than how they internalize and act out gender stereotypes.

In treatment, practitioners could develop protocols to guide the identification of environmental cues that activate stereotyped, gender-based styles of coping. Once children, adolescents, and people with whom they frequently interact identify indicators that result in harmful actions, children and adolescents may be closer to managing their sexuality in appropriate ways.

Identifying these "hot buttons", however, is only part of the processes that young people have to undergo. They have to reexamine and re-interpret the adversities they have experienced, which can be a long-term and painful process. They may have to develop new ideas about what it means to be male and female. Family members and other people with whom they interact are essential to the profound changes that treatment requires. Sadly, many children and young people in treatment for sexually inappropriate behaviors do not have families who will engage in treatment and processes of change.

Seeing resilience in inappropriate sexual behaviors

Another challenge for treatment professionals is to see resilience—or positive qualities—in inappropriate sexual behaviors. In order to build on client strengths, practitioners have to identify and engage these strengths. If strengths are embedded in behaviors that are destructive, then we need strategies for extricating them and putting them to more positive uses. For example, a great deal of thought and planning often goes into acting out sexually. Though the outcomes for others and the self are harmful, thought and planning are positive capacities. When children and young people trick and manipulate others, this shows creativity, ingenuity, and common sense.

Although it does not excuse the harm, it does require some talent. Most individuals want to have a sense of personal power and control, which often is part of the motivation for sexually acting out.

How can treatment professionals channel these capacities away from destructive behaviors to constructive behaviors? Pleasure-seeking and/or self-soothing often motivate sexually inappropriate behaviors. On the other hand, how can clients achieve this while enhancing the well-being of others and of the self? There is nothing unacceptable about any of these goals, but using and abusing others sexually to attain them is harmful. Perpetrators of these acts are subject to strong legal and social sanctions, and victims experience harm.

Research on resilience guides practitioners to do even-handed assessments that lead to the identification of strengths and risks that sometimes are intertwined. Practitioners would do well to show clients where their strengths are, even if clients use their strengths to meet particular goals that are harmful. Their deeper motivations could be the same goals that most, if not all people have—personal power and control, a sense of self-efficacy, pleasure, and well-being. So, if harmful sexual behaviors have three dimensions; 1) motivations that most people have, 2) strengths, and 3) outcomes that are harmful, then two of three of these elements are positive qualities that practitioners can build on, at the same time as starting where clients are.

Resilience from the Point of View of Young People

Research on resilience can direct attention to the positive elements of typical attitudes that young people bring with them into treatment. The following examples of young people's attitudes should generated further thinking along these lines.

Don't treat me like a dummy

Young clients want recognition for their capacities. When they think others consider them stupid or inadequate, they are likely to respond with hostility and withdrawal—hardly a basis for collaborative working relationships. Research on resilience provides many ideas for identifying and engaging clients' talents and attributes while not minimizing the negative effects of some of their behaviors. For example, taking responsibility for one's own behavior is a major strength that practitioners can encourage in young clients if they behave toward clients in ways that affirm their capacities for doing so.

I'm protecting myself when I don't tell you everything

Treatment professionals know all too well that many young clients withhold a great deal of information not only about their sexual behaviors but also about other parts of their lives that might be relevant to effective treatment. Their motivations may be self-protection and a desire to maintain some control. They do not want to feel the shame they believe is associated with their behaviors, and they want to feel as if they have control over something. Connecting with young people may require that practitioners recognize these motivations and devise strategies that support youngsters in managing shame and maintaining control. This is not a simple matter, but such an approach is a logical application of research on resilience that guides practitioners to see the strengths in client resistance to treatment.

I am more than my inappropriate sexual behaviors

Many youngsters may fear that their inappropriate sexual behaviors define them in the eyes of others, and they may define themselves as hopeless deviants and social outcasts. Although reactions of others certainly reinforce these self-appraisals, another dimension to consider is young people's tendency toward all-or-nothing thinking that sets them up for these self-appraisals. They may also contend, in hostile or passive-aggressive ways, that they are more than their inappropriate behaviors. As another logical application of research on resilience, practitioners have the challenge of figuring out how to let young people know that they do have positive attributes, that their sexual behaviors do not define them, and that they can use their positive attributes to manage their sexuality and cope with the shame and sense of being deviant.

I want what everyone else wants

Earlier in this chapter it was argued that the deep motivations driving inappropriate sexual behaviors are no different from motivations that drive any number of other behaviors. Young people get in trouble when the means they use to attain these ends are harmful. Thus, application of resilience research suggests that practitioners might consider these motivations as assets, at the same time the strategies of inappropriate sexual behaviors are unacceptable because of the consequences.

You're not helping me if you don't know your own blind spots

Young people are quick to spot deficits in others, and they may be most adept when they appraise those who have authority and power over them. We can dismiss these negative appraisals as additional forms of resistance and desire for control, or we can look at ourselves from their perspectives, acknowledge our blind spots, and then address them. We can admit our own mistakes to young people and call upon our own resources to deal with them. By such role modeling, young persons learn to admit and deal with their own deficits. Such self-disclosures require clinical skill and must arise naturally in treatment.

The sexually unhealthy cultures that we tolerate as adults are chief among our blind spots. Young people who grow up in sexually healthy families and communities have one less risk for inappropriate sexual behaviors to face. Young people with sexual issues have absorbed conflicting and harmful messages about sexuality that they internalize and act out. As a result, treatment programs have a responsibility to provide young people not only with information about sexual physiology but also with the meanings of desire, how love and sexuality are connected, and how we can use our sexuality to enhance our well-being and the well-being of others. We have a long way to go in figuring out how to promote the sexual well-being of young people, including those who are in treatment for sexually inappropriate behaviors.

We have many other blind spots, such as our tolerance of the gender stereotypes that undermine boys' capacities for emotional expressiveness and, instead, foster the channeling of hurt, stress, and trauma into gendered, stereotypical behaviors that are harmful. Research on resilience leads to the principle that adults are positioned to model appropriate behaviors, including how to deal with our own blind spots and take responsibility for their consequences. Furthermore, we as adults have the responsibility to offer children and adolescents sexuality education that promotes their well-being and the well-being of others.

It's not fair

Adolescents and often younger children have a keen awareness of injustices in their personal lives and in society as a whole. Though they may use the phrase, "It's not fair", as a way of deflecting their responsibility for their own behaviors, they have a point about fairness. Research on resilience can be applied to suggest that we agree with young people when they think the adversities they have experienced are unfair. They have experienced injustices. They have no responsibility for the abuse and neglect perpetrated on them. Nor is it fair when they blame themselves for parental abandonments, deaths, and other adversities they may have experienced.

Treatment has to go beyond fostering an understanding of the injustices children and adolescents personally experience. Once they have some understanding that life has not been fair to them, it is up to them to make choices that will not perpetrate injustices on others. They might be able to recognize that their perpetrating behaviors put them at risk for additional negative consequences. Understanding the many dimensions of unfairness that they have experienced and perpetuated, then, is an important dimension of treatment and draws upon positive capacities for grappling with painful life events and willingness to emulate the pro-social behaviors that are in their various environments but that they have not emulated when their behaviors are harmful to others.

There are many other ideas and attitudes that children and adolescents bring with them to treatment. Research on resilience directs clinical attention to elements we can use to engage youth in developing their capacity to manage their behaviors and transform their lives – no small task. We are better positioned to be helpful when we start where clients are. These attitudes often go to the core beliefs that young people have. Finally, we will be effective with young people if we uphold in our own lives the principles that we want them to emulate in their own.

Discussion

Research on resilience has a great deal to offer treatment programs for children and adolescents with problematic sexual behaviors. Typically, these young people have experienced adversities that contribute to their problematic behaviors. However, simply having been subjected to adversities does not entirely account for problematic behaviors. If this were so, all people at risk for inappropriate sexual behaviors would have them, and this is not the case. When outcomes are pro-social, we can assume the presence of factors that moderated the effects of adversities. Research on resilience uses the terms *protective factors* or *protective processes*, and has identified many of them.

When outcomes are harmful to self and others, we can assume that protective processes were insufficient to the risks, were unavailable, or individuals chose not to activate them.

Unfortunately for males, gender-based stereotypes often work against the qualities research has identified as associated with resilience -- namely finding comfort and affirmation by confiding in others, emotional expressiveness that includes awareness and empathy for one's own and others' emotions, and the rejection of gendered stereotypes that give permission for physical and sexual aggression.

It is possible that some problematic sexual behaviors are unconnected to adversities that persons have experienced, and may instead be primarily the outcome of socialization. Thus, some aspects of research on resilience may not apply to treatment of youth with sexual behavior problems.

When we examine "hidden" resilience in behaviors and attitudes of young people, we can apply the idea that being even-handed means to identify both positives and negatives wherever possible, even in behaviors that are illegal and harmful. Children and adolescents can show considerable skill and intelligence in problematic behaviors. Taking this idea a step further, we can also take a good look at our own deficits and manage them as well as we can. In doing so, we provide young people with models of conduct that might help them manage their sexuality in ways that promote their well being and the well being of others.

The applications of research on resilience to treatment programs for children and adolescents with sexually inappropriate behaviors are vast. This chapter suggests some of these applications. I hope that other professionals discover many others.

References

Berk, Laura E. (2003). *Child development* (6th ed.). Boston: Allyn & Bacon.

Brody, Leslie R (1999). *Gender, emotion, and the family.* Cambridge, MA: Harvard University Press.

Cicchetti, Dante & Norman Garmezy (1993). Editorial: Prospects and promises in the study of resilience. *Development and Psychopathology, 5,* 497-502.

Cicchetti, Dante, Fred A. Rogosch, Michael Lynch, & Kathleeen D. Holt (1993). Resilience in maltreated children: Processes leading to adaptive outcomes. *Development and Psychopathology, 5,* 629-647.

Egeland, Byron, E. Carlson, Elizabeth, & L. Alan Sroufe (1993). Resilience as process. *Development and Psychopathology, 5,* 517-528.

Gilgun, Jane F. (in press). Evidence-based practice, descriptive research, and the resilience-schema-gender-brain (RSGB) assessment. *British Journal of Social Work.*

Gilgun, Jane F. (2000, June). *A Comprehensive Theory of Interpersonal Violence,* paper presented at the conference on the Victimization of Children and Youth: An International Research Conference, Durham, NH, June 25-28.

Gilgun, Jane F. Christian Klein, & Kay Pranis. (2000). The significance of resources in models of risk, *Journal of Interpersonal Violence,* 14, 627-646.

Gilgun, Jane F. (1999). Mapping resilience as process among adults maltreated in childhood. In Hamilton I. McCubbin, Elizabeth A. Thompson, Anne I. Thompson, & Jo A. Futrell (Eds.), *The dynamics of resilient families.* (pp. 41-70). Thousand Oaks, CA: Sage.

Gilgun, Jane F. (1996a). Human development and adversity in ecological perspective: Part 1: A conceptual framework. *Families in Society,* 77, 395-402.

Gilgun, Jane F. (1996b). Human development and adversity in ecological perspective, Part 2: Three patterns. *Families in Society,* 77, 459-576.

Gilgun, Jane F. (1992). Hypothesis generation in social work research. *Journal of Social Service Research,* 15, 113-135.

Gilgun, Jane F. (1991). Resilience and the intergenerational transmission of child sexual abuse. In Michael Q. Patton (Ed.), *Family sexual abuse: Frontline research and evaluation* (pp. 93-105). Newbury Park, CA: Sage.

Gilgun, Jane F. (1990). Factors mediating the effects of childhood maltreatment. In Mic Hunter (Ed.), *The sexually abused male: Prevalence, impact, and treatment* (pp. 177-190). Lexington, MA: Lexington Books.

Gilgun, Jane F. & Laura S. Abrams (in press). Gendered adaptations, resilience, and the perpetration of violence. In Michael Ungar (Ed.), *Youth resilience around the world. Toronto:* University of Toronto Press.

Goleman, Daniel (1995). *Emotional intelligence: Why it can matter more than IQ.* New York: Bantam.

Kaufman, Joan & Edward Zigler (1987). Do abused children become abusive parents? *American Journal of Orthopsychiatry,* 57, 186-192.

Luthar, Sunyia (2003). Resilience and vulnerability: *Adaptation in the context of childhood adversities.* New York: Cambridge University Press.

Masten, Ann S. (1994). Resilience in individual development: Successful adaptation despite risk and adversity. In M. C. Wang & E. W. Gordon (Eds.), *Educational resilience in inner-city America: Challenges and prospects* (pp. 3-23). Hillsdale, NJ: Erlbaum.

Masten, Ann. S. & J. Douglas Coatsworth (1998). The development of competence in favorable and unfavorable environments: Lessons from research on successful children. *American Psychologist,* 53, 205-220.

Masten, Ann S. Karin M. Best & Norman Garmezy (1991). Resilience and development: Contributions from the study of children who overcome adversity. *Development and Psychopathology*, 2, 425-444.

Resnick, Michael. D., L. J. Harris, & Robert W. Blum (1993). The impact of caring and connectedness on adolescent health and well-being. *Journal of Pediatrics and Child Health*, 29, suppl.1, 53-59.

Richters, John E. & Pedro E. Martinez (1993). Violent communities, family choices, and children's chances: An algorithm for improving the odds. *Development and Psychopathology*, 5, 609-627.

Rutter, Michael (1990). Commentary: Some focus and process considerations regarding effects of parental depression on children. *Developmental Psychology*, 26, 60-67.

Shields, Ann & Dante Cicchetti (1998). Reactive aggression among maltreated children: The contributions of attention and emotion dysregulation. *Journal of Clinical Child Psychology*, 27, 381-395.

Ungar, Michael (2004). *Nurturing hidden resilience in troubled youth.* Toronto: University of Toronto Press.

Werner, Emme E. & Ruth S. Smith (1992). *Overcoming the odds: High risk children from birth to adulthood.* Ithaca, N.Y.: Cornell University Press.

Widom, Cathy Spatz (1991). Avoidance of criminality in abused and neglected children. *Psychiatry*, 54, 162-174.

CHAPTER SIXTEEN

TRAUMA AND NEUROBIOLOGY: CONSIDERATIONS FOR THE TREATMENT OF SEXUAL BEHAVIOR PROBLEMS IN CHILDREN AND ADOLESCENTS

KEVIN J. CREEDEN

Introduction

Over the past 10 years, there have been significant advances in research which have focused on the development and function of the human brain. Aspects of this research that examine the neuro-developmental process through childhood and adolescence have garnered widespread scientific and public interest, offering new perspectives on education and parenting and new insights into what influences the decision making, emotional fluctuations, and behaviors of children. Greater understanding of the neuro-developmental process has dovetailed with progress in understanding the connection between exposure to trauma and the emotional, behavioral, and cognitive difficulties exhibited by some children (Perry, 1995; Streeck-Fischer and van der Kolk, 2000; DeBellis, 2001; Bremner, 2002).

Given that a large number of the children and adolescents who are referred to treatment for sexual behavior problems present with significant histories of abuse, neglect, and other traumatic experiences (McMakin, et al., 2002), the neurobiology of trauma and its connection to subsequent psychopathology in children would appear to be of direct importance to researchers and clinicians in our field. However, to date, very little of this research has been incorporated into either the assessment or treatment protocols utilized in clinical practice (Ryan, 1999; Fago, 2003).

This chapter first identifies some of the research related to the neuro-developmental impact of trauma which appears particularly relevant to our work with children and adolescents exhibiting sexual behavior problems. Then it will consider ways in which assessment and treatment protocols might be changed in order to incorporate some of these findings into how we understand and help these children.

Brain organization and development

Before we examine the neuro-developmental research it is useful to outline a basic framework for understanding brain organization and maturation. Looking at the brain vertically, it can be described as being divided into 3 major regions: the brain stem, the limbic system, and the cortex. This perspective on brain development is referred to as the triune brain (MacLean, 1990). These regions mature in a hierarchical manner that mirrors their evolutionary development. Therefore the brain stem matures first and is the oldest while the cortex matures last and is, from an evolutionary standpoint, the newest region.

The brain stem is responsible for regulating basic cardiovascular functions, level of arousal, and some reflexes. Included in this region is the *cerebellum* which helps coordinate movement and in turn a variety of social, emotional and cognitive functions. The limbic system is frequently referred to as the "emotional brain" as it functions as the center for processing urges, appetites, and emotions. The limbic system contains a variety of structures important for understanding the individual's response to stress and trauma. The *amygdala* monitors incoming stimuli for possible threats and stores information regarding threatening stimuli. The amygdala also serves to activate the threat response when danger is detected. The *hippocampus* serves as a hub for memory and learning and appears to be involved in the processing of all conscious memory. The *thalamus* is a structure at the center of the brain just above the brain stem. It acts as the relay station for incoming stimuli and allows for the senses to be used in combination. The *hypothalamus* lies just below the thalamus, working to maintain homeostasis and functioning as the main center for information exchange between the brain and the body (Stien and Kendall, 2004, p.27). When Perry (2002) discusses brain organization he refers to the thalamus and hypothalamus as constituting the mid-brain.

The third region of the brain is the cortex or the "thinking brain". This is where thinking, reasoning, and cognition take place. More recently in evolutionary terms, the frontal lobes expanded to give us the *neocortex*. This created the capacity for symbolic language, conscious awareness, and metacognition, the capacity to think about our thoughts. (Stien and Kendall, 2004). Typically, as humans develop, the cortex exerts control in regulating limbic and brain stem responses. It serves to develop or "fine tune" more specific, creative, and adaptive problem solving approaches through the analysis of novel stimuli in the environment and by learning from the outcomes of previous experiences. Many of the difficulties we see in our clients might be understood as stemming from problems of the cortex effectively or adaptively processing and regulating limbic responses.

The other organizational feature of the brain that becomes important in understanding the impact of trauma, is that the brain is divided into two hemispheres, a right and a left. These hemispheres are connected at the cortical level by a large tract of neural fibers called the *corpus callosum* and at the subcortical level by the *anterior commissure*. Schiffer (1998) and Ratey (2001) discuss a variety of research studies indicating that the two hemispheres are associated with different functions and characteristics. The left hemisphere is typically the dominant hemisphere for most humans by the time they reach their late adolescence or early adulthood. The left hemisphere specializes in analytical and sequential thinking and it also tends to be the dominant hemisphere for language. The left hemisphere tends to provide a detailed perspective whereas the right hemisphere provides a more global perspective. The right hemisphere tends to be involved in processing non-verbal communication, imagery, and visual-spatial information while the left hemisphere largely processes words, verbal communication, and numbers. In terms of emotional information, the right hemisphere has been shown to be more involved in negative or pessimistic emotions (e.g. fear, despair) while the left hemisphere mediates the more positive emotions (e.g. happiness, joy). Not surprisingly, the left hemisphere seems more involved in the motivation to approach and explore while the right hemisphere is more inclined to withdraw and avoid. For our further discussion it is important to note that the right hemisphere also appears to be more involved in the experience and recall of trauma (Schiffer, Teicher, and Papanicolaou, 1995; Rauch, et al., 1996; Schore, 2002).

While the two hemispheres normally work in concert through an exchange and integration of information, different or dominant styles of information processing will clearly have an impact on personality style, emotional expression, preferred problem solving approaches, skills, interests, and a host of other individual strengths and differences.

The neurobiology of trauma

Studies of posttraumatic stress disorder have demonstrated that the age at which a child is first traumatized, the frequency of traumatic exposure, and the availability (or lack thereof) of caretakers as supportive resources all have a significant impact on the extent of the psychological consequences experienced by the child. These consequences are frequently expressed through problems with self-regulation, aggression against self and others, problems with attention and dissociation, physical problems, difficulties in self-concept, and the capacity to negotiate satisfactory interpersonal relationships (van der Kolk, 2003, p. 293). These studies suggest that the neurobiological impact of trauma will not express itself through a fixed set of cognitive, emotional, or behavioral difficulties/deficits, but rather along a continuum of structural or functional neurological responses influenced by the developmental stage at which the child experiences trauma and the availability of supportive resources provided by primary caretakers to the child.

Bremner (2002) argues that the physiological responses to stress result in common changes in neurological function that underlie the symptoms frequently seen in the aftermath of trauma. Bruce Perry and his colleagues (Perry, Pollard, Blakely, Baker, Vigilante, 1995; Perry, 2001) suggest that adaptive physiological responses to traumatic experiences become a central feature of how brain structure and function are organized when individuals endure repeated trauma and trauma cues in childhood. They highlight this fact by noting changes in baseline heart-rates for individuals with significant trauma experiences.

Research into the neurological consequences of repeated exposure to traumatizing experiences has shown both structural and functional neurological differences between traumatized and non-traumatized individuals. Martin Teicher and his colleagues (2002) through their own work and a review of other studies examining the neurodevelopmental impact of trauma have identified five major areas where these differences are most pronounced.

Limbic irritability

As noted earlier, the limbic system is the area of the brain that serves to process and regulate sensory information from the brain stem and the mid-brain. It filters or prioritizes information with regard to urges, appetites, and emotions that determine what sensory input requires further mental processing (van der Kolk, 2003). In particular, the limbic system will prioritize information relevant to preservation and procreation (Le Doux, 1995; Gallistel, et al., 1991). The amygdala, in particular, appraises sensory input relevant to threat, giving an emotional valence to the incoming stimuli that organizes the nature and intensity of the self-protective behaviors deemed necessary. The amygdala initiates autonomic responses such as increased heart rate and blood pressure and activates primary defensive responses such as freeze, fight, and flight. This level of defensive responsiveness bypasses the cortex allowing for immediate responses to strong threat cues (Le Doux, 1994, van der Kolk, 2003).

Teicher, et al., (2002) identified increased levels of activation in the amygdala of those individuals with trauma histories when compared to those who had not been traumatized. These persistent levels of amygdala activation generate a kindling effect where the individual can become hypervigilant in scanning for threat cues and over-interprets or misinterprets mildly difficult or even innocuous cues as being significantly threatening. This pattern of amygdala response has a variety of consequences such as general difficulties in affect regulation; problems in effectively learning from highly charged emotional situations, and applying that learning to new or novel stimulus; decreased activation of the speech center of the brain, contributing to difficulties in expressive/receptive language difficulties and auditory processing; social and relational problems generated by inaccurately reading social cues; attentional problems generated by a focus on scanning the environment for threat while simultaneously dismissing information as unimportant when it is not viewed as being threat (or safety) related.

Hippocampus

A part of the limbic system, the hippocampus plays a significant role in verbal and context related memory. Persistent activation of the amygdala appears to have an inverse effect on the hippocampus, especially the left hippocampus (Teicher et al., 2002). In a variety of clients with PTSD, hippocampal volume was smaller compared to control samples (Bremner, Randall, et al., 1997). This atrophy in the hippocampus due to persistent stress is believed to be associated with problems in short term memory, verbal memory, dissociative disorders, and context dependent memory (Bremner, 2002; Fanselow, 2000; DeBellis, et al., 1999, Stein, et al., 1997). Teicher and his colleagues (2002) also suggest that the lack of development in the left hippocampus may contribute to the increased language difficulties and lower verbal memory scores seen when samples of abused clients are compared with non-abused controls.

Deficient left hemisphere development

Teicher et al., (2002) found that not only was there underdevelopment in the left hippocampus of abused clients but a general lack of development and differentiation throughout the left hemisphere. In non-abused controls, Teicher found that the left cortex was more developed (greater volume, more neuronal growth) than the right whereas in his sample of clients who had experienced early trauma, the hemispheric asymmetry was generally found to be greater on the right. As noted earlier, the right hemisphere processes more non-verbal emotional communication and imagery; processes more negative emotions; has limited capacity to think analytically; and is more motivationally engaged in withdrawal and avoidance. Evidence that trauma-tized clients may be right hemisphere dominant, combined with indications of less right/left hemispheric integration in the sample of abused clients, suggests greater difficulties in analyzing and understanding both their own and other's behavior; decreased verbal skills; greater risk for pathological responses involving anger, fear, avoidance, withdrawal, and depression; and a decrease in available coping responses.

Lack of hemispheric integration

Teicher found that during memory recall there were marked shifts in hemispheric activity. He notes that when adults with an abuse history were asked to recall neutral memories, their left hemispheres seemed to be activated but when they were asked to recall unpleasant or traumatic memories, their right hemispheres were predominant. This was compared to Teicher's control (non-abused) sample that appeared to have a predominantly bi-lateral response (Teicher, et al., 2002). Further examination found that the corpus callosum was significantly smaller in the client sample that had expe-rienced early childhood abuse.

Both the underdevelopment of the left hemisphere and the lack of integration between the right and left hemisphere suggests the possibility that experience (and memory) for traumatized individuals may be more compartmentalized, less available for analysis and change (especially through language), and therefore less available for broader learning when those experiences are perceived as more emotionally charged or threatening. This might lead to more rigid and perseverative coping responses that remain despite negative outcomes. It might also lead to that experience by both clini-cians and other social supports that the traumatized individual "just doesn't get it" despite a large number of treatment interventions and negative consequences to par-ticular behaviors.

Abnormal activity in the cerebellar vermis

Teicher, et al., (2002) noted that not only does the cerebellum play an important role in motor functions such as posture, balance, and rhythmic movement but that the cerebellar vermis also serves in regulating emotional instability by controlling activa-tion and irritability in the limbic system. Everyday evidence for this is available in the soothing side-to-side rocking of an infant by their parent; in the head to toe rocking afforded by a rocking chair or swing; or in the activation of rocking movements when many clients are overwhelmed by the immediate experience or triggering of trauma.

Teicher notes that a variety of studies have demonstrated that the cerebellum plays a critical role in attention, language, cognition, and affect (Riva and Giorgi, 2000; Allen, et al., 1997; Schmahmann, 1991). In their own studies Teicher, et al., (2002) found that in the individuals with an abuse history there were indications of functional impair-ment in the activity of the cerebellar vermis.

Attachment and neurobiology

In his early formulation of attachment theory, Bowlby (1969) described an evolved behavioral process by which the attached person sought out a potentially protective attachment figure during periods of danger or threat. Attachment theory holds that the primary function of attachment relationships is to provide safety and security to the infant. In infancy, the ability to engage a nurturing, available caretaker is the fundamental coping response to stress. Through the process of infant-caregiver attunement, the caregiver highlights and stimulates positive states of excitement, joy, and pleasure and minimizes states of stress and anxiety. The caretaker serves as the infant's affect regulator and in turn this allows the infant to develop the neurological connections that will eventually allow the child to regulate their own affective states (Siegel, 1999). Persistent experiences of threat or stress in the absence of regulation and nurturance from the caregiver results in abnormal secretions of cortisol and can have an adverse influence on brain development (DeBellis, 1999; Hart, Gunnar, and Cicchetti, 1995). Schore (2002) has particularly focused attention on the right orbitofrontal cortex. He notes research by McEwen (2000) suggesting that chronic levels of stress contribute to fewer neural connections between the prefrontal cortex and the amygdala. Without regulation from the prefrontal cortex, sub-cortical processing of fear, especially through the amygdala, proceeds without conscious, inhibitory control.

We would therefore concur with van der Kolk (2003) when he writes, "it is virtually impossible to discuss trauma in children without addressing the quality of the parental attachment bond... The security of attachment bonds seems to be the most important mitigating factor against trauma-induced disorganization" (p. 294).

Attachment styles

Bowlby (1980) expanded and refined attachment theory to include developmental processes that culminate in adaptive or maladaptive functioning. Bowlby believes that the child's experience of early caretaking relationships results in the individual developing an "internal working model" or a framework for experiencing oneself in relation to others and that this "working model" is largely sustained throughout the individual's life.

Observing toddlers and their mothers in a laboratory experience described as "the strange situation", Ainsworth and her colleagues (1978) began to identify distinct attachment patterns, generally defined as secure, avoidant, ambivalent, and disorganized. *Secure* behavior was associated with a history of responsive and nurturing caretaking by the parent. The child experiences their parent as consistently and predictably available to meet both physical and emotional needs. Behaviorally, these children are emotionally and cognitively engaged, using their parent as a secure base from which to explore their environment. *Avoidant* behavior was associated with a history of rejection, neglect, or emotional distance by the caretaker. The child experiences the parent as emotionally unavailable or rigid. Behaviorally, these children frequently present with a blunted or flattened affect or are rigidly responsive to the specific expectations and demands of the environment. *Ambivalent* behavior was associated with a history of inconsistency by the parent. Behaviorally, these children frequently present as clingy, tense, and angry and with greater difficulties around impulse control. Main and Solomon (1990) later described the fourth category of attachment as disorganized. *Disorganized* behavior was associated with a parent's history of loss or severe trauma and has been found to predominate in children with a history of abuse, neglect, and family chaos. Behaviorally, these children present with contradictory approach/avoidance behavior associated with frightening or frightened behavior by the parent (Alexander and Anderson, 1997).

Attachment styles and neurological function

Patricia Crittenden writes that the infant attachment patterns identified by Ainsworth and her colleagues are reflected in identifiable patterns of mental processing (Crittenden, 1997; Ainsworth, et al., 1978). Crittenden proposes a model for understanding attachment that incorporates neuro-processing with observations of affect and behavior.

Crittenden would define *secure* attachment as the ability to effectively integrate the sub-cortical (limbic and lower brain) emotional responses to environmental stimuli with accurate cognitive transformation and discrimination of those emotions regarding their meaning. *Secure* attachment styles of processing information are likely to yield greater specificity in terms of responses to complex situations as well as greater flexibility in the individual's capacity to adapt behavioral responses to changing environmental cues. *Avoidant* attachment styles are likely to have developed cortical pathways that may "over-modulate" limbic and lower brain input, creating a limited and often rigid cognitive transformation of emotional stimuli. Cognitive representations of emotions are less specific, less flexible, and less responsive to context. *Ambivalent* attachment styles correspond to the development of cortical pathways which "under-modulate" affect related behavior. These pathways may respond more quickly and with greater intensity to a broad range of fear eliciting stimuli. These responses bypass the cortex, leading to less discriminatory inhibition of behavioral responses and as with the avoidant style, less specificity and flexibility in response to context. Crittenden writes of *disorganized* attachment (occurring when caregivers are frightened and/or frightening), as placing the child in the untenable situation of gravitating to the source of their threat as a way of coping with their traumatic experiences. Other researchers have suggested that these circumstances may lead to the development of dissociative responses in the child.

Initially for the child, these processing and behavioral patterns may have led to the development of successful strategies for effectively identifying and avoiding/decreasing/resolving dangerous conditions. However, cognitive attributions which may have been accurate and responses which may have been protective in the context in which they were first learned, may prove to be erroneous, maladaptive, and even dangerous when applied in a different context. Attachment patterns which can not effectively integrate affective responses from the limbic system and lower brain with appropriate levels of modulation and adaptation from the cortex, create obstacles for individuals in recognizing and/or adapting to those changes in context.

Crittenden's model of attachment is useful in that it reflects the neurobiological difficulties of cortical regulation and integration highlighted by Schore, Teicher and others. It views attachment not only as a coping response or a relational process but as a brain based process that has a profound impact on future neurological development. One of the ramifications of trauma may be the development of neurological obstacles to establishing secure attachment relationships.

Trauma, attachment and sexual behavior problems

There have been a variety of factors suggested as being contributory or causal in explaining the origins of sexually abusive behavior (Daversa, 2004; Schwartz, 1995; Finkelhor, 1984). While studies continue to examine the importance and influence of a number of developmental experiences and psychological dynamics, certain variables appear to persist as being essential to our understanding of the etiology of sexual behavior problems. I contend that these persistent variables are:

> 1) The presence, in childhood, of some type of trauma. This is especially true if we define trauma to include not only incidents of physical and sexual abuse, but also neglect, abandonment, witnessing domestic violence, and other experiences that the child may view as overwhelming or life threatening (Daversa, 2004; Friedrich, et al., 2003; McMackin, Leisen, Cusack, LaFratta, and Litwin, 2002; Prentky, Knight, Sims-Knight, 1989).
>
> 2) The deficits abusers appear to experience in intimacy, social competency, and empathy which, from our perspective, are best understood as problems offenders experience in their attachment relationships (Hudson and Ward, 2000; Marshall and Marshall, 2000; Burk and Burkhart, 2003).

A number of studies have examined the causal connection between a child's history of being sexually abused and later sexually abusive behavior. Much of this research on the trauma histories of offenders appears to be either explicitly or implicitly driven by a social-learning theory of sexual offending (Ryan, 1989; Garland and Dougher, 1990; Burton, Miller, and Shill, 2002). While this research provides evidence for a correlation between histories of sexual victimization and later sexual offending behaviors, these studies do not account for the majority of sexual abuse victims who do not go on to sexually offend. Neither does it account for those offenders who experience trauma other than sexual abuse but go on to be sexually abusive.

Hall, Mathews, and Pearce (1998) established a variety of risk factors associated with the emergence of sexually abusive behaviors. Some of these were clearly related to the child being eroticized or sexualized by older children or adults in their environment. However, most were factors associated with a broader range of traumatic experience (physical abuse), higher degrees of family stress (frequent moves, financial difficulties), or obstacles to developing secure attachment relationships (PTSD and attachment problems in mothers). In examining the research, Friedrich, et al., (2003), have written that sexual abuse appears to be a frequent but not essential contributor to sexual behavior problems in both teens and adults. Even when sexual abuse is present, it remains unclear what aspects of the abuse (i.e. trauma, sexualized behavior, violence, etc.) contribute to the eventual emergence of later sexually abusive behavior. Again, this will likely vary depending on the nature of the abuse, the developmental age at victimization, available adult supports, and the presence or absence of other environmental stressors.

Marshall and Marshall (2000) suggest that the origins of sexual offending behavior are found in the poor attachment relationships that offenders experience with their parents. They postulate that these poor relationships increased the risk of the offenders being sexually abused and led to offenders being more sexually preoccupied, less self-confident in relationships, and more likely to use sexualized behaviors as a preferred coping mechanism to manage stress in their lives. Marshall and Marshall highlight the importance of attachment in their model, with disrupted attachment providing the framework for the social learning process which ensues after victimization. While providing safety to the child is a fundamental function of early attachment relationships, the impact of poor attachment as described by Marshall and Marshall appears to identify only one of the pathways to sexual offending behavior in which disrupted or insecure attachment may play a part.

Along with maintaining proximity to a secure and trusted figure during periods of perceived danger and stress, developing and sustaining secure attachment relationships has been noted as increasing feelings of security, mastery, self-esteem, and social competence. By contrast, the loss, inconsistency, or unavailability of secure attachment can lead to sorrow, anxiety, anger, and confusion (Bowlby, 1969; Bowlby, 1980). Without specifically defining it as *attachment*, Baumeister and Leary (1995) write that the need for intimacy and connection is as fundamental a human need as food and sex. One could argue that the need to develop attachment relationships is a biological imperative for humans, since the failure of a human infant to engage a caretaker, on at least a minimal level, would threaten the infant's existence. It is important to note that experiences that are perceived as a threat to one's life or sense of personal integrity are the very definition of trauma. This leads to our belief that sexually abusive behavior arises in large part from a fundamental need for attachment (safety, attunement, nurturance, acceptance, care) and that it is the process that some individuals follow to meet this need that can become distorted and abusive. To understand abusive behavior we need to view it in the context of attachment and relationship and to appreciate the anxiety that is elicited when attachment is lacking or lost. To understand how the process becomes distorted, we need to at least begin with an understanding of the neurological impact of trauma and disrupted attachment.

Ward and Hudson (2000) contend that the difficulties offenders experience in intimacy, empathy, social skills, and cognitive distortions can be understood as the consequences of their poor attachment relationships. This view is consistent with research by Webster and Beech (2000) and Fernandez and Marshall (2003). These authors have suggested that, what was previously defined as a lack of empathy in offenders, might more accurately be viewed as a lack of integration between affective and cognitive responses in the offender (cognitive distortions) rather than a broader inability to be emotionally responsive to others. This lack of integration is consistent with what Crittenden (1997) describes in her discussion of neuro-processing patterns associated with insecure attachment styles.

Marsa, et al., (2004) found that 93% of the sexual offenders in their study evidenced an insecure attachment style and that secure attachment was less common in the sex offender group than in any of the other three groups studied (violent, non-sex offenders; non-violent, non-sex offenders; and community controls). Wahlberg, Kennedy, and Simpson (2003) in studying adolescent sexual offenders suggested that impairment in sensory-emotional integration contributed to a greater likelihood of violent behavior in their sample.

Galski, et al., (1990) linked both violent and non-violent manifestations of disordered sexuality to a wide range of deficits in brain functioning. When comparing the quantitative EEG's (QEEG) of non-sex offending and sex offending subjects, Corely, et al., (1994) specifically identified EEG abnormalities in the left hemisphere of the sex offender sample. These findings are consistent with the Teicher, et al., (2002) findings of a lack of differentiation and development in the left hemisphere of his trauma victims.

Raine and Buchsbaum (1996) reviewed 14 brain imaging studies indicating that frontal to temporal lobe dysfunction appears to be related to violence and sexual offending behavior, with frontal lobe dysfunction more closely related to violence while temporal lobe dysfunction was more aligned with sexual offending behavior. Gillespie and McKenzie (2000) found evidence suggesting left fronto-temporal dysfunction in their mentally disordered sex offender sample when compared to a mentally disordered, non-sex offender sample. These studies might be viewed as highlighting the difficulties in prefrontal cortex development and function identified by Schore (2002).

Impaired hemispheric integration and diminished prefrontal cortex regulation as a consequence of trauma and/or attachment difficulties may also have a direct connection with difficulties and distortions in how individuals process sexual information and stimuli. The brain does not treat all information equally. Rather, there are *hard wired* preferences for the rapid processing of information that is relevant to danger and reproduction (Le Doux, 1995; Gallistel, et al., 1991). Human brains also transform certain privileged information into affect largely through processes centered in the limbic system (and the sensory cortices). This affective learning indicates context *where* there are greater than usual probabilities for experiencing danger and anxiety or for generating safety and experiencing comfort (Le Doux, 1995; MacLean, 1990). Anxiety producing cues have been shown to consist of stimuli such as; darkness, sudden loud noises, being alone, being entrapped. These anxiety producing cues are not necessarily associated with a specific threat, but experienced as *free floating* or unfocused anxiety that nonetheless encourages the individual to either flee or prepare to defend themselves. Comforting stimuli include close bodily contact, stroking, and rocking motions, behaviors frequently associated with early infant/caretaker attachment. These behaviors promote a sense of safety and tend to encourage exploratory behavior (Lang, 1995; Le Doux, 1994; Bowlby, 1973; Seligman, 1971).

This affective or contextual learning also occurs with cues that elicit sexual arousal, which signals opportunities for reproduction. As with cues that elicit protective behaviors, the stimulus that gets associated with sexual arousal can prove either predictive or erroneous. We see this frequently in particular fetish types of behavior. Crittenden writes that "there is also a considerable overlap in the experiential features of anxiety and sexual arousal and of comfort and sexual satisfaction; these can lead to an overlap of the sexual and attachment behavioral systems" (Crittenden, 1997, p.40). Environmental stimuli associated with threat and/or sexuality may be processed by the cortex in an over-modulated or under-modulated manner creating either distorted and rigid cognitive representations or more impulsive, sub-cortical responses with little (if any) cortical control. Crittenden would suggest that this over-modulated and under-modulated neuro-processing respectively parallels avoidant and ambivalent attachment styles. If the experiential features of the stimuli associated with threat and sexuality have considerable overlap, it would appear to create even greater possibilities for misrepresentation, distortion, and faulty learning in individuals whose neurological functioning creates obstacles for contextual learning, affect regulation, and greater degrees of integration.

Aggressive, violent, and anti-social behavior

Many of the clients we treat present with problems of aggression and violence in conjunction with, or in addition to, identified problems with sexually inappropriate behavior. Numerous studies have identified neurological problems that appear to contribute to the expression of aggressive and violent behavior which mirrors the neurological consequences of trauma and insecure attachment. In addition, different types of aggressive behavior (instrumental/proactive; emotional/reactive) appear to be different types of neuro-processing styles that are consistent with Crittenden's (1997) model of rigid, over-modulation of sub-cortical responses and impulsive, under-modulation of sub-cortical responses.

Emotional/reactive aggression in children appears to be particularly associated with a history of abuse when compared to both other clinically referred children and a non-clinical sample. In addition, the abused sample also evidences significantly more problems in information processing, especially verbal processing (Connor, et al., 2003). Blair and James (2001) indicated that reactive aggression appeared to develop more from difficulties in the orbito-frontal cortex's capacity to regulate emotions in a socially adaptive manner, while proactive aggression appeared to result from difficulties in contextual learning that could allow for accurate interpretation and integration of responses to threat/distress cues. Frontal lobe dysfunction or differences have also been associated with broader anti-social and criminal behavior. However, there appear to be differences in the type of anti-social behaviors depending on whether sub-cortical responses are over-modulated or under-modulated (Dolan, et al., 2002; Brower and Price, 2001; Bigler, 2001; Kiehl, et al., 2001).

Neuropsychological deficits have also been identified in a number of studies involving delinquent youth (Morgan and Lilienfield, 2000; Teichner and Golden, 2000; Aguilar, Sroufe, Egeland, and Carlson, 2000; Moffitt, 1997; Moffitt, 1993). Particularly, verbal abilities appear to be affected in adolescents identified as anti-social or delinquent, with delinquent youth frequently showing significantly lower Verbal IQ's than Performance IQ's on standardized tests of cognitive abilities (Hirischi and Hindelang, 1977; Bleker, 1983; Grace and Sweeney, 1986; Lyman, et al., 1993; Teichner and Golden, 2000; Teichner, et al., 2000). In addition to verbal deficits, delinquent youth are frequently identified as having difficulties in "executive" functioning. Executive functioning relates to a variety of brain functions that support effective learning and problem solving. These functions include: attention, concentration, anticipation, planning, abstract reasoning and concept formation, cognitive flexibility, and the ability to control impulsive, unsuccessful, and inappropriate behavior. A recent review of the literature by Morgan and Lilienfield (2000) indicates that anti-social groups performed significantly lower than comparison groups on tests of executive functioning.

Perhaps the neurological issue which has received the most attention from researchers in this area has been examining the correlation of attention-deficit hyperactivity disorder (ADHD) with adolescent and adult anti-social behavior (Biederman, Newcorn, and Sprich, 1991; Klein and Manuzza, 1991; Lynam, 1996; Kafka and Prentky, 1998; Fago, 2003). In discussing the impact of trauma on children, Perry (1997) and Pynoos (1990) have argued that the symptoms in these individuals frequently identified as indicative of ADHD are instead attentional problems generated by the trauma victims' hypervigilant scanning of the environment for threat cues. They can also ignore other stimuli as "unimportant" when it is not associated with threat. These children may have their attention problems precipitated or compounded by difficulties with auditory and visual spatial processing. In particular environments, most notably school settings, where the demands for processing language and visual input are especially high, individuals who process language slowly or inaccurately, and individuals who have difficulties with visual-spatial organization may find themselves quickly overwhelmed and/or frustrated by these demands. For many of these individuals, the manifestations of ADHD symptoms (e.g. inattentive, disorganized, can't finish tasks, loses things, fidgety) are likely to appear. Along with the obvious problems these neurological difficulties create in academic and job performance, the additional consequences with regard to self-esteem, social acceptance, and impulsive behaviors generate a significant number of risk factors for engaging in delinquent or anti-social behavior. In addition to distinguishing between delinquent and non-delinquent groups, Vermeiren, et al., (2002) have presented data to suggest that comparing overall IQ, verbal abilities, and executive functioning skills may also help distinguish different levels of recidivism risk among delinquent populations.

Implications for assessment and treatment

Much of the research identifying the impact that trauma may have on neurodevelopment and on the function of specific areas of the brain is relatively new. However, there has been considerable writing and research on language deficits, executive functioning problems, attachment difficulties, and trauma focused treatment, in relation to children with abuse histories and behavioral difficulties. Much has been available for a number of years (Foa, 1997; Perry, 1997; Crittenden, 1997; Schore, 1994; Lyons-Ruth, et al., 1993; Lyman, et al., 1993; Sroufe, 1988; Green, Voeller, Gaines, 1981). To a large degree, the more current research has supported and elaborated on the neurological underpinnings of processing or behavioral difficulties identified in earlier writings. While this research is clearly pertinent to treating children and adolescents exhibiting sexual behavior problems, it has not been generally integrated into assessment or treatment protocols (Creeden, in press; Fago, 2003). Recently, there has been discussion of broadening our treatment perspective or developing more "holistic" approaches to treatment (Ryan, 1999; Longo, 2002), but there is little evidence that these discussions have resulted in widespread changes to how we conceptualize or treat sexual behavior problems in adolescents (Burton et al., 2000). To a large degree, cognitive behavioral models, including the Relapse Prevention Model (Pithers, 1990), continue to dominate both the structure and the specific interventions of treatment programs for adolescent and adult abusers. This remains true despite concerns that these models have some serious limitations (Ward and Hudson, 1996; Chaffin and Friedrich, 2000; Laws, Hudson, Ward, 2000). I believe that a working understanding of the research on the neurological impact of trauma, coupled with a theoretical approach garnered from both the trauma and attachment fields, supplies a framework for assessment and treatment with our population that is both developmental and holistic. I have previously described one possible treatment model that attempts to integrate both the trauma and attachment research into a program for treating sexual behavior problems in children and adolescents (Creeden, 2004; Creeden, in press). This treatment model uses as its framework a phase-oriented trauma treatment approach and attempts to integrate interventions from biofeedback, EMDR, drama therapy, DBT, occupational therapy, and cognitive-behavioral treatment among others. It is also a treatment model that is still evolving. In our work at Whitney Academy, we have seen promising results and significant shifts in behavior that have occurred as we've adapted our treatment from a more straightforward relapse prevention approach but, despite our belief that we are on the "right track", our treatment approach is still a work in progress. Therefore, rather than offering a specific treatment program, I hope to identify treatment considerations which take into account the neurological impact of early trauma and attachment issues.

Arousal control/regulation

One of the primary considerations in the work with sexual abusers has been in identifying, diminishing, or eliminating "deviant" arousal patterns. Primarily, this work has looked at sexual arousal to a variety of stimuli (e.g. young children, violence, etc.) that was identified at placing the individual at risk for further engaging in abusive behaviors. Masturbatory satiation, aversion therapies, cognitive-behavioral approaches (e.g. Stop and Switch stories, tapes) have all attempted to identify the sexual stimulus or trigger and then make that stimulus less appealing or reinforcing.

What the neurological research appears to suggest and our own experience more frequently bears out, is that the children and adolescents we treat have problems with arousal control in general as opposed to sexual arousal difficulties in particular. Often, we witness sexually inappropriate behavior stemming from generalized anxiety or arousal states which can become sexualized as one of a variety of options for discharging or addressing the arousal (physical and verbal aggression, self-injury, eating, and dissociation are among other options). The triggers or precipitants for these anxiety or arousal states are not necessarily or even predominantly sexual. Since the range of stimuli that might trigger anxiety/arousal can be quite broad, a focus on broad-based arousal control and regulation would appear to be an important element of treatment.

In this regard we have found that our clients have difficulty accurately identifying when their arousal states are high. We have begun the use of biofeedback approaches both to help clients recognize increased arousal and also as a tool which will allow them to monitor success and progress in using particular arousal control interventions (e.g. yoga, breathing, movement, weighted vests, and visualization).

I also feel that the neurological research which identifies higher levels of amygdala activity with consequent higher levels of autonomic arousal states (Teicher, et al., 2003; Perry, et al., 2001), raises questions about the conclusions we draw from the physiological measures currently utilized in assessment and treatment. As the field continues to incorporate polygraphs, viewing time, and phallometry into its assessment and treatment protocols, I believe we need to fully understand the neurological response to trauma and trauma cues and incorporate that understanding into interpreting the result of these assessments.

Language deficits

It is understood that past research shows evidence of significant Verbal and Performance IQ differences in delinquent populations, and that language difficulties stem from the lack of left hemisphere development and differentiation in those who experience early and persistent trauma. Therefore, consideration should be given to how receptive/expressive language disorders and auditory processing disorders impact our clients' ability to effectively utilize treatment. Since most treatment approaches with adolescents and adults tend to be strongly loaded with the need to process language, we may be using a modality for therapy that is least accessible to our clients. In addition, since many of the children and adolescents with whom we work come from families with histories of trauma and abuse, we are likely to be treating or giving information to parents who might also have serious obstacles in effectively processing verbal information.

Consideration should be given to making all aspects of the treatment process multi-modal (verbal, visual, movement, kinesthetic, music). This should not only facilitate greater degrees of integrating the treatment experience/information but it also serves to help clients feel more competent, motivated, involved, and understood throughout the treatment process.

Language problems not only have an impact on academic performance and treatment involvement but also impact work performance, organization, attention, the capacity to respond to compliance commands (behavior) and almost every other facet of social interaction. Because language problems can create a wide range of obstacles to daily living and treatment success, consideration should be given to including a screening for auditory processing difficulties and other language based problems as a standard part of assessment protocols.

Executive functioning skills

Impulsivity, disorganization, rigidity in problem solving approaches, misreading social cues and poor attention and concentration are frequently seen as problems to be addressed in our treatment population. Many of the children and adolescents whom we treat present with a diagnosis of Attention Deficit Disorder. Quite often, we rely on pharmacological interventions to address these issues or develop behavior management interventions to address the problems resulting from these difficulties. The underlying assumption of many of these behavior management programs is that the disruptive behavior stems from a lack of motivation on the part of the child and therefore the right combination of consequences and reinforcers will induce the child to engage in better behavior.

The neurological research would suggest that a child's trauma and attachment history may have a significant impact on the development, integration, and functioning of the pre-frontal cortex, an area of the brain that is highly involved in these executive functioning skills.

These executive function difficulties, along with the behavioral problems they may generate, might best be viewed as obstacles that the child must manage and/or overcome rather than viewed as bad choices that the child must learn to change. In this light, some assessment of executive functioning skills might be considered as a regular part of the evaluation process and interventions to help the child/adolescent increase their capacity for concentration, organization, flexible problem solving, etc. can also be developed to meet the needs of the individual client. Some of these capacities will improve by helping the child decrease their overall level of anxiety and arousal. Other areas (e.g. organizational skills) will help the child/adolescent feel less overwhelmed and confused and generally more competent and in control. The difference, I believe, is understanding that these children may have real deficits in these areas and therefore need specific interventions to improve these skills if they are to make better behavioral choices in the future.

Trauma

Historically, our field has sought to separate the trauma experiences of our clients from the abuse they have inflicted on others. Many treatment approaches continue to demand that a client address their abusing/offending behavior before they can talk about their own victimization histories. I suggest that our clients' trauma experiences are strongly intertwined with their abusive behavior and not just, or even primarily, from a social-learning perspective. Consideration might be given to the notion that our clients' abusive behavior is linked to their own trauma histories through anxiety, fear, abandonment, anger, shame, and other frequently overwhelming affective states. The experience of these overwhelming emotional states might also be the source of some of the cognitive distortions, incomplete memory or detail in offense reporting, lack of emotional integration or response, and many of the other presentations we identify in our clients as being avoidant behaviors.

As opposed to thinking that addressing a client's trauma history will inhibit or delay their ability to take responsibility for their own abusive behavior, I have come to believe that not addressing the impact of the client's own trauma will simply impede the learning and effective use of skills we are teaching them to control/change their inappropriate and abusive behavior (Creeden, 2004). Examining how a phase-oriented trauma treatment model might be adapted to address sexual behavior problems is a worthwhile endeavor for the offender treatment field in general to consider. I believe adopting a trauma-focused approach will be especially productive for treating children and adolescents with sexual behavior problems.

Conclusion

There are profound advances occurring in our ability to examine and understand the neuro-developmental process and specific neurological functions. Our understanding of this research literature offers possibilities for changing the way we understand sexually abusive and inappropriate behavior, as well as informing changes in both our assessment protocols and treatment interventions. Perhaps more importantly, this research can lead us to viewing our clients' trauma histories and attachment relationships as essential elements in treating abusive behavior and developing pro-active, preventive interventions that focus on addressing trauma experiences and attachment disruptions in young children.

References

Aguilar, B.; Sroufe, L.A.; Egeland. B. and Carlson, E. (2000). Distinguishing the early onset/persistent and adolescence-onset antisocial behavior types: From birth to 16 years. *Development and Psychopathology*, 12, 109-132.

Allen, J.G. (2001). *Traumatic Relationships and Serious Mental Disorders*. New York: Wiley and Sons.

Allen, G., Buxton, R., Wong, E., et al. (1997). Attentional activation of the cerebellum independent of motor movement. *Science*, (275), 1940-1943.

Alexander, P.C. and Anderson, C.L. (1997). Incest, Attachment, and Developmental Psychopathology. In Cicchetti, D. and Toth, S. (Eds.). *Rochester Symposium on Developmental Psychopathology*. 8, 343-377. Rochester, NY: University of Rochester Press.

Ainsworth, M.D.S., Blehar, M.C., Waters, E., and Wall, S. (1978). *Patterns of attachment: A psychological study of the strange situation*. Hillsdale, NJ: Erlbaum.

Baumeister, R.F. and Leary, M.R. (1995). The need to belong: Desire for interpersonal attachments as a fundamental human motivation. *Psychological Bulletin*. 117, 497-529.

Biederman, J., Newcorn, J., Sprich, S. (1991). Comorbidity of attention deficit hyperactivity with conduct, depressive, anxiety, and other disorders. *American Journal of Psychiatry*, 148, 564-577.

Bigler, E. (2001). Frontal lobe pathology and antisocial personality disorder. *Archives of General Psychiatry*, 58(6), 609-611.

Blair, R. and James, R. (2001). Neurocognitive models of aggression, the antisocial personality disorders, and psychopathy. *Journal of Neurology, Neurosurgery, and Psychiatry*, 71(6), 727-731.

Bleker, E.G. (1983). Cognitive defense style and WISC-R P>V sign in juvenile recidivists. *Journal of clinical Psychology*, 39, 1030-1032.

Bowlby, J. (1980). *Attachment and Loss. Volume III*. New York: Basic Books

Bowlby, J. (1973). *Attachment and Loss. Volume II: Separation: Anxiety and Anger.* New York: Basic Books.

Bowlby, J. (1969). *Attachment and Loss. Volume I: Attachment*. New York: Basic Books.

Bremner, J.D. (2002). *Does Stress Damage The Brain?* New York: Norton

Bremner, J.D. and Narayan, M. (1998). The effects of stress on memory and the hippocampus throughout the life cycle: Implication for childhood development and aging, *Development and Psychopathology*, 10, 871-888.

Bremner, J.D., Randall, P., Vermetten, E., Staib, L., Bronen, R., Capelli, S., Mazure, C., McCarthy, G., Innis, R. and Charney, D. (1997). MRI based measurement of hippocampal volume in posttraumatic stress disorder related to childhood physical and sexual abuse: A preliminary report. *Biological Psychiatry*, 41, 23-32.

Brower, M. and Price, B. (2001). Neuropsychiatry and frontal lobe dysfunction in violent and criminal behavior: A critical review. *Journal of Neurology, Neurosurgery, and Psychiatry*, 71(6), 720-726.

Burk, L. and Burkhart, B. (2003). Disorganized attachment as a diathesis for sexual deviance: Developmental experience and the motivation for sexual offending. *Aggression and Violent Behavior*, 8 (5), 487-511.

Burton, D., Miller, D., and Shill, C. (2002). A social learning theory comparison of the sexual victimization of adolescent sexual offenders and nonsexual offending male delinquents. *Child Abuse and Neglect*, 26, 893-907.

Burton, D., Smith-Darden, J., Levins, J., Fiske, J., Longo, R. (2000). *The 1996 nationwide survey of treatment programs and models: Serving abuse reactive children and adolescent and adult offenders*. Brandon, VT: Safer Society Press.

Chaffin, M. and Friedrich, W. (2000). Developmental-systemic perspectives on children with sexual behavior problems. Keynote speech presented at the annual meeting of ATSA, November, San Diego, CA.

Chu, J.A. (1992). The therapeutic roller coaster: Dilemmas in the treatment of childhood abuse survivors. *Journal of Psychotherapy: Practice and Research*. 1, 351-370.

Connor, D., Doerfler, L., Volungis, A., Steingard, R., and Melloni, R. (2003). Aggressive Behavior in Abused Children. *Annals of the New York Academy of Sciences*, 1008, 79-90.

Corley, A., Corley, M.D., Walker, J., Walker, S. (1994). The possibility of organic left posterior hemisphere dysfunction as a contributing factor in sex offending behavior. *Sexual addiction and Compulsivity*, 1, 337-346.

Creeden, K. (in press). Trauma, Attachment and Neurodevelopment: Implications for Treating Sexual Behavior Problems. In B. Schwartz (Ed.), *The Sexual Offender, Volume V*. Kingston, NJ: Civic Research Institute.

Creeden, K. (2004). Integrating Trauma and Attachment Research into the Treatment of Sexually Abusive Youth. In M.C. Calder (Ed.), *Children and young people who sexually abuse: New theory, research, and practice developments*. Lyme Regis, Dorset: Russell House Publishing.

Crittenden, P.M. (1997). Toward an Integrative Theory of Trauma: A Dynamic-Maturation Approach. In Cicchetti, D. and Toth, S. (Eds.). *Rochester Symposium on Developmental Psychopathology*. 8, 33-84. Rochester, NY: University of Rochester Press.

Daversa, M. (2004). Assessing Developmental Antecedents Using the MIDSA. Seminar presented at the annual meeting of ATSA, October, Albuqurque, NM.

DeBellis, M.D. (2001). Developmental traumatology: the psychobiological development of maltreated children and its implications for research, treatment, and policy. *Development and Psychopathology.* 13, 539-564.

DeBellis, M.D., Keshavan, M., Clark, D., Casey, B., Giedd, J., Boring, A., Frustaci, K., and Ryan, N. (1999). Developmental traumatology. Part II: Brain development. *Biological Psychiatry,* 45, 1271-1284.

Deckel, W., Hesselbrock, V., Bauer, L. (1996). Antisocial personality disorder, childhood delinquency, and frontal brain functioning: EEG and neuropsychological findings. *Journal of Clinical Psychology,* 52 (6), 639-650.

Dolan, M., Deakin, W., Roberts, N. and Anderson, I. (2002). Serotonergic and cognitive impairments in impulsive aggressive personality disordered offenders: Are there implications for treatment? *Psychological Medicine,* 32(1), 105-117.

Fago, D.P. (2003). Evaluation and Treatment of Neurodevelopmental Deficits in Sexually Aggressive Children and Adolescents. *Professional Psychology: Research and Practice.* 34(3), 248-257.

Fanselow, M. (2000). Contextual fear, gestalt memories, and the hippocampus. *Behavioral Brain Research,* 110(1-2), 73-81.

Fernandez, Y.M. and Marshall, W.L. (2003). Victim Empathy, Self-Esteem, and Psychopathy in Rapists. *Sexual Abuse: A Journal of Research and Treatment.* 15(1), 11-26.

Finkelhor, D. (1984). *Child Sexual Abuse.* New York: Free Press.

Foa, E.B. (1997). Psychological processes related to recovery from trauma and effective treatment of PTSD. In Yehuda, R. and McFarlane, A.C. (Eds.), *Psychobiology of posttraumatic stress disorder.* Vol. 823, 410-424. New York: New York Academy of Sciences.

Friedrich, W., Hobart Davies, W., Feher, E. and Wright, J. (2003). Sexual Behavior Problems in Preteen Children, *Annals of the New York Academy of Sciences,* 989, 95-104.

Galderisi, S. and Mucci, A. (2000). Emotions, Brain Development, and Psychopathology Vulnerability, *CNS Spectrums,* 5(8), 44-48.

Gallistel, C., Brown, A., Carey, S., Gelman, R., and Keil, F. (1991). Lessons from animal learning for the study of cognitive development. In S. Carey and R. Gelman (Eds.), *The epigenesis of mind: Essays on biology and cognition* (pp. 3-36). Hillsdale, NJ: Erlbaum.

Galski, T., Thornton, K., Shumsky, D. (1990). Brain dysfunction in sex offenders. *Journal of Offender Rehabilitation*, 16, 65-80.

Garland, R. and Dougher, M. (1990). The abused/abuser hypothesis of child sexual abuse: A critical review of theory and research, In J. Fierman (Ed.), *Pedophilia: Biosocial Dimensions* (pp.488-509). New York: Springer-Verlag.

Gillespie, N. and McKenzie, K. (2000). An examination of the role of neuropsychological deficits in mentally disordered sex offenders. *Journal of Sexual Aggression*, 5, 21-29.

Grace, W.C. and Sweeney, M.E. (1986). Comparisons of P>V sign on the WISC-R and WAIS-R in delinquent males. *Journal of Clinical Psychology*, 42, 173-176.

Green, A., Voeller, K., and Gaines, R. (1981). Neurological impairment in maltreated children. *Child Abuse and Neglect*, 5, 129-134.

Hall, D., Mathews, F. and Pearce, J. (1998). Factors associated with sexual behavior problems in young sexually abused children. *Child Abuse and Neglect*, 22, 289-312.

Hart, J., Gunnar, M., and Cicchetti, D. (1996). Altered neuroendocrine activity in maltreated children related to symptoms of depression. *Development and Psychopathology*. 8, 201-214.

Herman, J. (1992). *Trauma and Recovery*. New York, Basic Books.

Hoffman-Plotkin, D. and Twentyman, C. (1984). A multimodal assessment of behavioral and cognitive deficits in abused and neglected pre-schoolers. *Child Development*, 55, 794.

Hirichi, T. and Hindelang, M. (1977). Intelligence and delinquency: A revisionist review. *American Sociological Review*, 42, 571-587.

Hudson, S.M. and Ward, T. (2000). Interpersonal competency in sex offenders. *Behavior Modification*, 24(4), 494-527.

Kafka, M.P. and Prentky, R.A. (1998). Attention deficit/hyperactivity disorder in males with paraphilias and paraphilia-related disorders: A comorbidity study. *Journal of Clinical Psychiatry*, 59, 388-396.

Kiehl, K., Smith, A., Hare, R., Mendrek, A., Forster, B., Brink, J., Liddle, P. (2001). Limbic abnormalities in affective processing by criminal psychopaths as revealed by functional magnetic resonance imaging. *Biological Psychiatry*, 50(9), 677-684.

Klein, S. and Manuzza, S. (1991). Long term outcome of hyperactive children: A review. *Journal of the American Academy of Child and Adolescent Psychiatry*, 30, 1120-1134.

Lang, P. (1995). The emotion probe: Studies in motivation and attention. *American Psychologist*, 50, 372-385.

Laws, R., Hudson, S., and Ward, T. (2000). *Remaking relapse prevention with sex offenders: A sourcebook.* Thousand Oaks, CA: Sage.

Le Doux, J.E. (1994). Emotion, memory, and the brain : Neural routes underlying the formation of memories about primitive emotional experiences, such as fear, have been traced. *Scientific American*, June, 50-57.

Le Doux, J.E. (1995). In search of an emotional system in the brain: Leaping from fear to emotion and consciousness. In M. Gazzaniga (Ed.) *The Cognitive neurosciences*, p. 1049-1061. Boston: MIT Press.

Leguizamo, A. (2002). The Object Relations and Victimization Histories of Juvenile Sex Offenders. In Schwartz, B. (Ed.), *The Sex Offender, Volume IV.* Kingston, NJ: Civic Research Institute.

Lisak, D. and Ivan, C. (1995). Deficits in intimacy and empathy in sexually aggressive men. *Journal of Interpersonal Violence*. 10(3), 296-308.

Longo, R. (2002). A Holistic/Integrated Approach to Treating Sex Offenders. In B. Schwartz (Ed.), *The Sex Offender, Volume IV*. Kingston, NJ: Civic Research Institute.

Lott, D. (2003). Brain development, attachment and impact on psychic vulnerability. *Psychiatric Times*, 15(5), 1-5.

Lynam, D. (1996). Early identification of chronic offenders: Who is the fledgling psychopath? *Psychological Bulletin*, 120, 209-234.

Lynam, D., Moffitt, T. and Stouthamer-Loeber, M. (1993). Explaining the relation between IQ and delinquency: Class, race, test motivation, school failure or self-control? *Journal of Abnormal Psychology*, 102, 187-196.

Lyons-Ruth, K., Alpern, L., and Repacholi, B. (1993). Disorganized infant attachment classification and maternal psycho-social problems as predictors of hostile aggressive behaviorin the pre-school classroom. *Child Development*, 64, 572-585.

MacEwen, K. (1994). Refining the intergenerational transmission hypothesis. *Journal of Interpersonal Violence*, 9 (3), 350-365.

MacLean, P.D. (1990). The triune brain in evolution: *Role in paleocerebral functions.* New York: Plenum Press.

Main, M. and Soloman, J. (1990). Procedures for identifying infants as disorganized/disoriented during the Ainsworth strange situation. In M. Greenberg, D. Cicchetti, and M. Cummings (Eds.), *Attachment in the Preschool Years: Theory, Research, and Intervention.* Chicago: University of Chicago Press.

Marsa, F., O'Reilly, G., Carr, A., Murphy, P., O'Sullivan, M., Cotter, A., Hevey, D. (2004). Attachment styles and psychological profiles of child sex offenders in Ireland. *Journal of Interpersonal Violence*, 19, 228-251.

Marshall, W.L., Hudson, S.L., Jones, R. and Fernandez, Y.M. (1995). Empathy in sex offenders. *Clinical Psychology Review*. 15(2), 99-113.

Marshall, L.E. and Marshall, W.L. (2002). The role of attachment in sexual offending: an examination of pre-occupied attachment style offending behavior. In Schwartz, B. (Ed.), *The Sex Offender, Volume IV*. Kingston, NJ: Civic Research Institute.

Marshall, W.L. and Marshall, L.E. (2000). The origins of sexual offending. *Trauma, Violence, and Abuse: A Review Journal*, 1, 250-263.

McEwen, B.S. (2000). The neurobiology of stress: from serendipity to clinical relevance. *Brain Research*. 886, 172-179.

McMackin, R.A., Leisen, M., Cusack, J.F., LaFratta, J. and Litwin, P. (2002). The relationship of trauma exposure to sex offending behavior among male juvenile offenders. *Journal of Child Sexual Abuse*, 11(2), 25-40.

Meichenbaum, D. (1994). *A clinical handbook/practical therapist manual for assessing and treating adults with posttraumatic stress disorder*. Waterloo, Ontario: Institute Press.

Moffitt, T.E. (1997). Neuropsychology, antisocial behavior, and neighborhood context. In J. McCord (Ed.), *Violence and childhood in the inner city* (pp. 116-170). Cambridge, England: Cambridge Criminology Series.

Moffitt, T.E. (1993). The neuropsychology of conduct disorder. *Development and Psychopathology*, 5(1-2), 135-151.

Morgan, A. and Lilienfield, S. (2000). A meta-analytic review of the relation between anti-social behavior and neuropsychological measures of executive function. *Clinical Psychology Review*, 20, 113-136.

Murray, G., McKenzie, K., Quigley, A., Matheson, E., Michie, A, Lindsay, W. (2001). A comparison of the neuropsychological profiles of adult male sex offenders and non-offenders with a learning disability. *Journal of Sexual Aggression*, 7, 57-64.

Ogden, P. and Minton, K. (2000). Sensorimotor psychotherapy: one method for processing traumatic memory. *Traumatology*, 6 (3).

Ornstein, R. and Thompson, R.E. (1984). *The amazing brain*. New York: Houghton-Mifflin.

Perry, B., Pollard, R., Blakely, T., Baker, W., Vigilante, D. (1995). Childhood trauma, the neurobiology of adaptation, and "use dependent" development of the brain: How states become traits. *Infant Mental Health Journal*. 16, 271-291.

Perry, B. (2001). The neurodevelopmental impact of violence in childhood. In Schetky, D. and Benedek, E. (Eds.) *Textbook of Child and Adolescent Forensic Psychiatry.* Washington, D.C.: American Psychiatric Press.

Perry, B. and Pate, J.E. (1994). Neurodevelopment and the psychobiological roots of post-traumatic stress disorders. In L. Kozoil and C. Stout (Eds.) *The Neuropsychology of Mental Illness: A Practical Guide*

Pithers, W.D. (1990). Relapse prevention with sexual aggressors. In Marshall, W.L., Laws, D.R., and Barbaree, H.E. (Eds.), *Handbook of Sexual Assault.* 343-361. New York: Plenum Press.

Prentky, R.A., Knight, R.A., Sims-Knight, J.E., Straus, H., Rokous, F. and Cerce, D. (1989). Developmental antecedents of sexual aggression. *Development and Psychopathology.* 1, 153-169.

Pynoos, R. (1990). Post-traumatic stress disorder in children and adolescents. In B. Garfinkel, G. Carlson, and E. Weller (Eds.) *Psychiatric Disorders in Children and Adolescents* (pp. 48-63). Philadelphia: W.B. Saunders.

Raine, A. and Buchsbaum, M.S. (1996). Violence, brain imaging, and neuropsychology. In D. Stoff and R. Cairns (Eds.) *Aggression and violence: Genetic, neurobiological, and biosocial perspectives* (pp. 195-217). Mahwah, NJ: Erlbaum.

Ratey, J. (2001). *A user's guide to the brain.* New York: Pantheon Books.

Rauch, S., van der Kolk, B., Fisler, R., Alpert, N., Orr, S., Savage, C., Fischman, A., Jenike, M. and Pitman, M. (1996). A symptom provocation study of posttraumatic stress disorder using positron emission tomography and script driven imagery. *Archives of General Psychiatry,* 53, 380-387.

Resick, P.A. and Schnicke, M.K. (1992). Cognitive processing therapy for sexual assault victims. *Journal of Consulting and Clinical Psychology,* 60, 748-756.

Riva, D. and Giorgi, C. (2000). The cerebellum contributes to higher functioning during development: Evidence from a series of children surgically treated for posterior fossa tumors. *Brain,* 123, 1051-1061.

Rubin, K.H. and Rose-Krasnor, L. (1986). Social-cognitive and social behavioral perspectives on problem solving. In M. Perlmutter (Ed.) *Cognitive Perspectives on Children's Social and Behavioral Development.* Minnesota Symposium on Child Psychology, v. 18. Hillsdale, NJ: Erlbaum.

Ryan, G. (1989). Victim to victimizer: Rethinking victim treatment. *Journal of Interpersonal Violence,* 4, 325-341.

Ryan, G. (1999). Treatment of sexually abusive youth: The evolving consensus. *Journal of Interpersonal Violence,* 14, 422-436.

Schiffer, F. (1998). *Of two minds: The revolutionary science of dual-brain psychology.* New York: Free Press.

Schiffer, F., Teicher, M., and Papanicolaou, A. (1995). Evoked potential evidence for right brain activity during the recall of traumatic memories. *The Journal of Neuropsychiatry and Clinical Neurosciences, 7,* 169-175.

Schmahmann, J. (1991). *The cerebellum and cognition.* New York: Academic Press. Schore, A.N. (1997). Early organization of the nonlinear right brain and development of a predisposition to psychiatric disorders. *Development and Psychopathology. 9,* 595-631.

Schore, A.N. (2002). Dysregulation of the right brain: a fundamental mechanism of traumatic attachment and the psychopathogenesis of posttraumatic stress disorder. *Australian and New Zealand Journal of Psychiatry, 36,* 9-30.

Schwartz, B.K. (1995). Theories of sex offenses. In B.K. Schwartz and H.R. Cellini (Eds.) *The Sex Offender: Corrections, Treatment, and Legal Practice.* Kingston, NJ: Civic Research Institute.

Shapiro, F. (1995). *Eye Movement Desensitization and Reprocessing: Basic principals, protocols, and procedures.* New York: Guilford.

Siegel, D. (1999). *The developing mind: toward a neurobiology of interpersonal experience.* New York: Guilford Press.

Smallbone, S. and Dadds, M.R. (2000). Attachment and coercive sexual behavior. *Sexual Abuse,* 12(1), 3-15.

Sroufe, L.A. (1988). The role of infant-caregiver attachment in development. In J. Belsky and T. Nezworski (Eds.), *Clinical Implications of Attachment.* Hillsdale, NJ: Lawrence Erlbaum.

Stien, P. and Kendall, J. (2004). *Psychological Trauma and the Developing Brain.* New York: Haworth Press.

Stone, M. and Thompson, E. (2001). Executive function impairment in sexual offenders. *Journal of Individual Psychology, 57,* 51-59.

Streeck-Fischer, A. and van der Kolk, B. (2000). Down will come baby cradle and all: Diagnostic and therapeutic implications of chronic trauma on child development. *Australian and New Zealand Journal of Psychiatry, 34,* 903-918.

Teicher, M., Andersen, S., Polcari, A., Andersen, C., Navalta, C. (2002). Developmental neurobiology of childhood stress and trauma. *Psychiatric Clinics of North America, 25,* 397-426.

Teichner, G. and Golden, C. (2000). The relationship of neuropsychological impairment to conduct disorder in adolescence: A conceptual review. *Aggression and Violent Behavior, 5,* 509-528.

Teichner, G., Golden, C., Crum, T., Azrin, N., Donohue, B., Van Hasselt, V. (2000). Identification of neurological subtypes in a sample of delinquent adolescents. *Journal of Psychiatric Research*, 34, 129-132.

Uvnas-Moberg, K. (1998). Oxytocin may mediate the benefits of positive social inter-action and emotions. *Psychoneuroendocrinology*, 23, 819-835.

van der Kolk, B. (2003). The neurobiology of childhood trauma and abuse. *Child and Adolescent Psychiatric Clinics of North America*, 12, 293-317.

van der Kolk, B., Mc Farlane, A., and Weisaeth, L. (1996). *Traumatic Stress. The effects of overwhelming experience on mind, body, and society.* New York: Guilford Press.

van der Kolk, B. A., McFarlane, A.C., and van der Hart, O. (1996). A general approach to the treatment of posttraumatic stress disorder. In van der Kolk, B., Mac Farlane, A.C. and Weisaeth, L. (Eds.), *Traumatic Stress: The effects of overwhelming experience on mind, body, and society.* 417-440. New York: Guilford Press.

van der Kolk, B.A. and Ducey, C.P. (1989). The psychological processing of traumatic stress. Rorschach patterns in PTSD. *Journal of Traumatic Stress*, 2, 259-265.

van der Hart, O., van der Kolk, B.A., and Boon, S. (1998). Treatment of dissociative disorders. In Bremmer, J.D. and Marmar, C.R. (Eds.). *Trauma, memory, and dissocia-tion.* 253-283. Washington, D.C.: American Psychiatric Press.

Vermeiren, R., De Clippele, A., Schwab-Stone, M. , Ruchkin, V. , Deboutte, D. (2002). Neuropsychological characteristics of three subgroups of Flemish delinquent adoles-cents, *Neuropsychology*, 16 (1), 49-55.

Wahlberg, L., Kennedy, J., and Simpson, J. (2003). Impaired sensory-emotional inte-gration in a violent adolescent sex offender. *Journal of Child Sexual Abuse*, 12(1), 1-15.

Ward, T., Hudson, S. and McCormack, J. (1997). Attachment style, intimacy defcits, and sexual offending. In Schwartz, B. and Cellini, H. (Eds). *The Sex Offender*, Vol. II. Kingston, NJ: Civic Research Institute.

Ward, T. and Hudson, S. (1996). Relapse prevention: A critical analysis. *Sexual Abuse: A Journal of Research and Treatment*, 8(3), 177-200.

Webster, S.D. and Beech, A.R. (2000). The nature of offenders' affective empathy: a grounded theory analysis. *Sexual Abuse: A Journal of Research and Treatment.* 12(4), 249-262.

CHAPTER SEVENTEEN

DISCOVERING INTEGRITY: WORKING WITH SHAME WITHOUT SHAMING YOUNG PEOPLE WHO HAVE ABUSED

ALAN JENKINS

Introduction

The experience of shame is a primary influence in the lives of young people who have abused. The sense of disgrace that accompanies shame may feel toxic to the point of annihilation, with an enormous amount of time and energy spent in desperate strategies to avoid the experience of shame. These can range from practices which produce emotional detachment, including a wide range of sexualised preoccupations and fantasies, to anti-social activities that include excessive drug and alcohol use.

Increasingly driven and desperate practices to avoid the experience of shame result in cycles of despair and paralysis, which foster a sense of identity as "loser" that is characterised by feelings of worthlessness, insufficiency, and self-deprecation. Such self-paralysing practices invite shaming judgements and interactions by family members, members of the community, and representatives of the justice system. Young people inevitably become increasingly trapped in vicious cycles of despair and passivity.

We cannot avoid working with the experience of shame. Intervention requires ethical practices that allow for shame (and shame-related practices) to be re-positioned from restraining and disabling concepts and experiences to ones that might be enabling and facilitate reclaiming a respectful sense of self. Facing shame can be experienced as disabling or enabling. However, it is an inevitable and vital component of the young person's ethical journey and we are obliged to help provide safe passage. In an enabling context, facing shame is often the catalyst for reclamation and restoration with the young person and his community.

What is shame?

Shame can be defined as the experience associated with the realisation that one has acted in a way that is dishonourable. This experience generally involves a pervasive judgement of oneself as dishonourable, unworthy, or lacking in integrity. Thus the experience of shame generally promotes a challenge to personal integrity. The experience of shame can be distinguished from the act of shaming. Shaming (to shame) is the attempt to disgrace or make ashamed; to influence, force, or compel through the use or attribution of shame. One is a subjective experience, the other a political act of power. They are, of course, strongly interconnected and inter dependent in ways which are often hidden or invisible to the individuals concerned. There is a political paradox in the dilemma posed by the idea of making one's own realisation (attributing shame to the self) which requires a social context in which the behaviour is regarded as shameful. However, the distinctions between shame and shaming can be enlightening and are, in fact, vital to considerations of ethical practice for young people and workers alike.

The problem with shame

Most young people have the capacity to face shame and make their own judgements of personal dishonour or disgrace, but are restrained by pervasive practices designed to avoid the experience of shame. Shame poses a frightening challenge to the young person's sense of worth and integrity. Without supporting and enabling structures, he will most likely act to protect himself through practices of avoidance.

Attempts to avoid shame attribution and a sense of worthlessness and personal dishonour can involve:

- Complete or partial denial of the dishonourable action
- Attempts to minimise, justify or excuse the dishonourable action, including attempts to blame other people or circumstances beyond his sphere of influence
- Strategies to prevent or distract thinking about the dishonourable action. These can include alternative preoccupations which retreat into a fantasy world of self-aggrandisement and impersonal and objectifying sexualised ideas and activities
- Withdrawal from family and community life and activities
- Excessive drug and alcohol use

And in the extreme:

- Aggression and violence towards others, particularly those regarded as having attributed dishonour or disrespect
- Self-harm

Such avoidance practices inevitably lead to increasingly paralysing cycles of detachment, desperation, and futility. They become increasingly desperate, ineffective and self-destructive and always serve to hint at or point towards judgements of a sense of identity of "loser".

These avoidance strategies are generally interpreted by others as indications that the young person is shameless or lacking in responsibility, empathy, or compassion. Such attributions frequently lead to attempts by family, community, and statutory systems to confront or correct the young person with shaming interactions and discourses. A vicious cycle of desperation, avoidance, and disability becomes more deeply entrenched.

Shame avoidance practices are a reflection of a more widespread community or social concern. Intervention workers with young people often pay little attention to the experience of shame, and may themselves avoid the issue leaving it entirely off the agenda.

Like any set of experiences and practices which relate to power, shame has both repressive and creative aspects. However, dominant ideas in popular culture and modern psychotherapy; ideas which are generally informed by dominant ideologies concerning enlightenment through individual growth, self-expression, and self-actualisation, have emphasised the repressive at the expense of the creative potential of shame (Schneider, 1992). Shame has tended to be regarded as repressive and restrictive; something to be overcome or overthrown along with all oppressive structures, or an obstacle to enlightenment and liberation of the self.

Schneider invites us to challenge this conservative view by situating self-development in a context of community and highlighting that "shame is not a disease... it is a mark of our humanity." Shame can be valued as "a pointer of value awareness" whose "very occurrence arises from the fact that we are valuing animals." Shame is vital in social relations because it is "aroused by phenomena that would violate the organism and its integrity." "To extirpate shame is to cripple our humanity." Shame offers us a means of warning regarding potential violation and can enable the protection of privacy. " To avoid the witness of shame" is regarded as akin to removing the brakes on a motor vehicle because they slow it down (Schneider, 1992).

It can be helpful to distinguish between *"discretion shame"*, which can enable the anticipation and prevention of a potential shameful act, and *"disgrace shame"*, which may follow its enactment. Both forms have an adaptive and creative potential in the maintenance of respectful relationships (Schneider, 1992). Effective intervention allows for a young person to appreciate and develop a sense of discretion shame in future relationships, through facing disgrace shame regarding his past abusive acts. Most forms of inquiry in intervention discussed in this chapter invite the young person to address disgrace shame.

Shame can only be adaptive in this way when certain actions are regarded as shameful within a culture and when there are effective and accessible means for evaluating its discretion and disgrace aspects. Here lies the paradox of shame. Despite some ambivalence, sexual assault of children is generally regarded as a shameful conduct in most cultures. However, culturally sanctioned shaming practices particularly when they are excluding or marginalizing of the young person, frequently result in patterns of avoidance of shame.

Mistaken shame

Disadvantaged young people who have been subjected to injustice and oppression face an additional challenge, which can result in extreme confusion through their ongoing and pervasive subjection to shaming discourses. It is one thing to experience shame as the result of realisations about one's own dishonourable actions. In this context, shame might be regarded as appropriately attributed. However, the politics of disadvantage allows for shame to be attributed to disadvantaged young people, when the dishonourable acts have been perpetrated by those with greater privilege in a context of fixed and imbalanced power relations, not by the young person himself.

Disadvantaged young people can, for example, experience a sense of failure in relation to not achieving certain culturally sanctioned life goals despite unequal access to resources. A sense of shame may be mistakenly attributed with these experiences of disadvantage or failure. Such attributions can be the result of cultural expectations and ideologies (eg. "not being man enough") or specific attributions of culpability and worthlessness (as often experienced by those who have been abused by a significant other). This might be referred to as *"mistaken shame"*, in that there is no discernible, dishonourable act which has been carried out by the young person in this context.

Mistaken shame is perhaps similar to Nietzsche's concept of "false shame" which is "a product of fear and embarrassment, not love and respect," resulting from "having mistaken oneself…having underestimated oneself…a lack of reverence for oneself," often as a result of "wrongful humiliation" (Nietzsche, 1967; Schneider, 1992).

Finding safe passage

Widespread practices of avoidance and confusion, in relation to the issue of shame, can make it difficult for young people, caregivers, and workers to find constructive and enabling pathways in their journeys towards respect. It can be extremely difficult to establish an enabling context, which allows for shame to be understood and addressed in ways that might promote a sense of agency and might foster realisation, restoration, reclamation, and redemption. There appear to be few safe places and few opportunities available, in which a young person can face appropriately attributed shame in ways that might foster a respectful sense of identity.

A safe environment is required to assist the young person to draw several distinctions so that shame can be repositioned or re-contextualised from a restraining experience to an enabling experience:

- This environment should promote the capacity to identify and name dis honourable acts and the power relations which determine them, in order to responsibility and shame accordingly. This can enable the young person to address the question, "Whose shame is it?"; to face shame associated with dishonourable acts he has carried out and define and reattribute the shame he may have mistakenly carried on behalf of others or in the service of unhelpful cultural and gendered expectations.
- The young person should be helped to recognize the distinctions between the dishonourable *act* and the *person* who has carried out the act. The young person can be assisted to discover new possibilities in means of evaluating himself as a person, through his realisations and the positions he takes in relation to the abusive act. This generally involves a gradual transition from an initial state of dishonour and disgrace in judgements of self towards judgements of his actions as dishonourable and disgraceful.
- The person-act distinction can enable new understandings about the nature and process of facing appropriately attributed shame. If facing and

accepting responsibility for dishonourable actions can be regarded as honourable or virtuous (in accordance with the young person's stated ethics), then the painful processes involved in facing shame might be regarded as significant and worthwhile contributions towards developing a sense of honour, integrity, and inner strength. Facing shame might be regarded as an honourable process concerned with restitution and restoration in relation to a dishonourable action. This can clear the way for potential, alternative judgements of self as honourable in the light of personal assessment and critique of the significance of courageous steps, taken willingly, to face disgrace-shame which inevitably accompanies responsible acknowledgement and realisation. What becomes possible is the recognition that, "I *committed a terrible act*", together with the understanding, earned through processes of reclamation, that "*I am not a terrible person.*"

- The vital distinction, concerning the initiative or motivation of the young person, in the context of external political expectations for him to address his abusive behaviour. The young person may be invited to face responsibility for his abusive actions and thereby invited to face shame. He may decline or accept such invitations. There is a significant difference in enabling possibilities, when a young person chooses to face shame, as opposed to accommodating to experiences of coercion or shaming by others.

An adaptive sense of shame requires cultural attributions of shame towards the perpetration of abusive acts. However, shaming justice or therapeutic interventions may serve only to further confuse the distinctions between person and the act and foster accommodation or avoidance strategies. The choice to face shame with appropriate supports can enable respectful action, which is likely to be owned by the young person and incorporated into a respectful sense of identity.

The processes involved in addressing and taking responsibility for abusive behaviour require a journey, which entails facing shame. It is not possible to understand the political nature of abuse, to develop empathy and compassion for others, or to engage in any meaningful form of restoration or reclamation of self, without facing shame.

Attempts to bypass the issue of shame serve only to promote avoidance or a sense of accommodation or "going through the motions" of restorative action. The young person's sense of identity remains based on avoidance strategies and on the edge of "loser" or self-contempt ideology. It is in this context that popular formulations which attempt to draw distinctions between "shame" and "guilt", have been rejected as being unhelpful for an invitational model. These conceptualisations tend to regard "guilt" as a developmentally "mature" feeling of regret which focuses upon the abusive action. The action is judged to be bad or wrong. Thus "guilt" is privileged and regarded as a more desirable focus than "shame," which involves a judgement of the identity of the person who has carried out the action. The person is judged to be bad or wrong. The possibilities of restoration and growth are therefore regarded as greater, in the supposedly more self-enhancing context of "guilt" (Fossum & Mason, 1986).

One can appreciate the spirit of such formulations in attempting to draw the person-act distinction. However, they can serve to privilege "guilt" and promote bypassing or attempting to rush the significant developmental journey of transition from a shameful judgement of self to a shameful judgement of the act, and the social role that this gradual transition can serve for all concerned. It might be regarded as "mature" for a person who has abused to experience shameful judgements of himself - indications that he perhaps is experiencing some understanding of the seriousness and gravity of the act of abuse - along with the potential impact upon the abused person. This level of judgement may be helpful in the context of the principle of accountability and restitution to the abused person who could feel somewhat affronted by the abuser too readily embracing "guilt" and bypassing "shame". "Guilt" is a concept which has meaning in a legal context, but little relevance as a reference point in therapeutic intervention, where it can obscure the importance of facing shame in the journey.

If the young person decides to face and address abusive behaviour and make significant efforts towards atonement, restitution and restoration, he cannot do this without facing shame. Addressing abuse requires embarking on a journey in which the young person is assisted to position himself in relation to shame, so that he can "look shame squarely in the eye". This is an inevitable and necessary part of this journey. The therapist's role is to remain highly attuned to windows of opportunity, throughout intervention in which the young person can be assisted to consider enabling means to address shame and decline means which are likely to be disabling to self and others.

How does shame show its face? – The initial contact

Evidence of shame is usually apparent right from the initial contact with the young person, but generally in the form of avoidance behaviours. The young person may not have the understanding or language to name and address the experience of shame and is desperately preoccupied with attempts to avoid its potentially disabling consequences. The therapist, however, is in a position to interpret and respond to indicators or signs of shame.

> On introduction to the therapist, Jake (aged 15) roles his eyes upwards and defiantly exclaims, "Whatever."

> Peter (aged 14) averts his eyes downwards and asserts, "It didn't hurt her."

> Kevin (aged 14) picks up a pen and begins to tap the arm of the chair loudly and rhythmically.

> Keith (aged 15) glances frequently out of the window and then towards his watch and demands, "When's this going to be finished?"

> Mike (aged 14) responds to all inquiries by looking downwards and responding, "I dunno."

A disabling interpretation might underestimate the young person's capacity to experience shame and suggest that this initial behaviour is an indication of "conduct disorder" or deficits in empathy and compassion. Such an interpretation might then inform confronting responses and a desire to challenge and correct the young person's minimizations and irresponsible attitudes.

inform confronting responses and a desire to challenge and correct the young person's minimizations and irresponsible attitudes.

Interpretations and responses which are enabling will perhaps be based on recognition that the young person's avoidance responses and reactions may, in fact, be informed by an underlying sense of shame and anticipation that intervention will most likely be a shaming process.

The young person is not likely to be in any position to be able to address abusive behaviour and face shame, given the politics of intervention, unless we first establish a context for fairness (Chapter Five "The Politics of Intervention"). Any expectation that the young person will show remorse, at this point, will only serve to create a more shaming context, which in turn leads to avoidance, further minimizations, justifications, denial, and even the possibility of aggressive behaviour in the interview.

> *Jake knows he has forced his little step-sister to submit to practices which have hurt her. He knows his abuse of one of her friends during a sleep over is an undisclosed secret. He knows that he has recently beaten up his mother. He will be desperate to avoid intense shame associated with these actions. On top of this, he carries unimaginable, mistaken shame - in relation to a sense of culpability associated with letting his family down - in the context of his step-father's abuse and through feelings of failure and worthlessness regarding his own life goals.*

If we inadvertently shame a young man like Jake by attempting to coerce him to demonstrate remorse and then label his resistance to our efforts as pathological or deviant, we are perpetrating abuse in the service of therapeutic intervention. Shame should be rightfully attributed to ourselves.

When we focus on fairness and decline invitations to shame the young person, we pay respect to shame. We allow space for avoidance strategies and try to see them for what they are. Such declinations implicitly serve to recognise that the young person's shame may be real and intense and are evidence of, or a pointer to, honour and integrity of the young person despite his dishonourable actions. In this way we begin to respect rather than demonise shame.

Interventions which are based on confrontation and correction tend to intensify shaming discourses. This leads to shame becoming increasingly inaccessible to the young person and avoidance strategies becoming more and more entrenched. The only safe option for a young person, in this context, is to accommodate or "go through the motions" of submission to the demands of the therapeutic program, by learning the language and behaving in ways that mimic political correctness, in order to ensure survival. This is not an unfamiliar process for young disadvantaged people who have learnt to submit and accommodate in order to survive a wide range of oppressive circumstances.

However, intervention processes which ignore or attempt to bypass or "protect" the young person from shame, also serve to distance him from his own sense of shame, whilst simultaneously intensifying shame.

In the service of respectful and accountable intervention, we can only attempt to establish enabling conditions under which shame can be safely and courageously faced. In such a journey, the young person must experience judgements of self, including the initial judgement of dishonour and unworthiness, before moving towards a judgement of the dishonourable action and the recognition of his own capacity to act in honourable ways. It is through facing the painful aspects of shame, learning to draw the distinctions between self and action, and recognising honour and integrity in facing abuse that the young person is able to reclaim himself and further a sense of identity based on respect and integrity.

Young people who engage in patterns of avoidance behaviour are generally used to being cajoled and shamed and they will anticipate this kind of interaction in an intervention program. Many of these young people have been shamed by "experts" in the past and they will be wary and ready to defend themselves with us. If we can recognise the indications of shame, allow space for avoidance, decline invitations to confront or correct, and focus on establishing a context for fairness, then we may be able to help to open up an enabling way to face shame.

Naming abuse and naming shame

If we maintain patience and persevere with genuine efforts to promote a context of fairness, a range of windows of opportunity will open for assisting the young person to face shame. As injustices and abuses experienced by the young person are recognised, ethics are named, and responsibility overloads are addressed, then opportunities will become increasingly frequent. The young person has less need to employ such confrontational methods of avoidance. However, he will continue to be watchful, wary and distrustful of the therapist's motives, perhaps wondering, *"What are they setting me up for?* This underscores the importance of inviting and legitimising protest in the context of intervention (see Chapter Five "The Politics of Intervention").

In a fair and ethical context, indications of shame will often be evident, when reference is made to the abuse perpetrated by the young person. These indications are usually non-verbal, e.g. eyes averted downwards, head down, wetness in the eyes, faltering in speech. They afford opportunities to begin to name and make meaning of the experience of "shame."

> *Tim (aged 14) had greatly minimised his abuse of his five-year-old half sister in interviews with the police and statutory authorities. Despite initial defiance, Tim was eventually able talk about his experience of watching his step-father tyrannise and abuse his family, particularly his mother. He had attempted at times to stand by and protect his mother when she was being abused. This conversation led to acknowledgement of injustice, hurt, and betrayal to which Tim and his family had been subjected, along with consideration of ethics of concern and care and a desire to stick up for someone being abused by a bigger person.*

A responsibility overload was highlighted:

> *"People expect you to face up to what you did to your sister and understand how this affected her, but has anyone stopped and thought about what it was like for you when your dad was running amok in your family?"*

"How fair is this?"

Tim was invited to consider his ethics:

> *"Who understands how worried you were about your Mum and how much you tried to stick up for her?"*

> *"Why was it so important for you to try to stand up for your Mum?"*

> *"What is it that is important to you that you had to stand up for?"*

The naming of overloads and the clarification of ethics promote intense dilemmas for young people like Tim. The dissonance between ethics and abusive actions is felt, as shame comes closer to the surface of awareness.

At this point, it may be appropriate to make direct enquiries about the young person's abusive behaviour. These enquiries are informed by a vigilant appreciation of any evidence of respectful and honourable actions in the face of adversity. Thus a focus on integrity is maintained.

> *"Tim, can I ask you something about what you did to your sister?"*

> *"How did you manage to find what it takes to start to face up to what you did to Peta?" (Tim had previously acknowledged to police that he had touched Peta but denied numerous allegations of penetration and other abusive acts.)*

> *"What stopped you from running away from it and calling her a total liar?"*

A focus on evidence of acknowledgement, rather than denial, can be maintained throughout the process of inquiry.

These initial inquiries may also focus upon the young person's intent:

> *"Tim, did you want to hurt Peta and make her feel bad, or did you not realise that what you were doing would hurt her when you first started?"*

> *"If what you did has hurt Peta, would that worry you?"*

Through these inquiries about intent, the young person is given the opportunity to position himself in relation to his intent regarding his abusive actions. The distinctions between "cruel intent" and "self-centred lack of consideration" for the younger child, are important in the clarification of ethics and in addressing and challenging disabling attributions by others.

As such inquiries promote increasing dissonance between stated ethics and abusive actions, non-verbal indications of shame are likely to be evident. These signs afford opportunities for naming and making meaning of shame through processes called "talking about talking about it".

> *Tim declared that he had not intended nor wanted to hurt his sister.*
> *When asked, " If Peta was hurt by what you did, would it worry you?", Tim's eyes*
> *had began to water and he averted them downwards.*
> *I responded, "Tim, you look like you don't feel proud about what you did?"*
>
> *Tim gave a very brief nod and kept his head down.*
>
> *I enquired, "What are you realising Tim?"*
>
> *Tim tearfully responded, "She was my sister."*

Even within the restraining context of a young person's limitations of vocabulary and verbal expression and familiar patterns of avoidance, he can begin to identify and name shame in relation to his abusive actions. These become named as actions he "doesn't feel proud of" or "feels bad about," because "she is my sister." In this way, he can further situate his abusive actions in a context of violation of personal and family ethics, concerning loyalty, and standing by those in vulnerable circumstances.

In our impatience to address abuse, we can easily overlook or underestimate the enormous significance of initial acknowledgements and realisations. They may be inadequate as they stand, however, they are substantial beginnings and should be open to recognition, further inquiry and honouring.

It can be tempting to immediately pursue lines of inquiry about what it is that Tim feels bad about in order to deepen his experience and move him further along the path of facing his abusive actions. However, we run the risk of overwhelming him with attempts to coerce movement at our pace in accordance with our sense of readiness. If we can assist him instead to develop his own framework and rationale for interpreting these initial steps, he may develop a sense of readiness which enables him to take further steps towards achieving his own goals because he feels safe enough and is convinced that this is the right direction for him to take.

The process of inquiry called "talking about talking about it" invites the young man to reflect upon and attribute meaning to the step he has just taken in order to critique this step and determine whether it is a step he would want to own because it fits with his own ethics. The therapist might pursue lines of inquiry like the following:

> *"Tim, would anyone else know how bad you feel about what you did?"*
>
> *"Have you ever told anyone before?"*
>
> *"Would anyone be surprised to learn about how bad you really feel?"*
>
> *"Would anyone realise how hard it is to face up to what you are starting to realise?"*
>
> *"What does it take to begin to speak out about the truth?"*

"How are you able to begin to think about what you did to Peta when you've been through such hard times yourself?"

An opportunity may now exist for young men like Tim to begin to make new meanings out of facing shame:

"What does it say about you that you are not only beginning to realise that you hurt your sister, but that you are also beginning to speak out about it?"

Tim responded, *"I don't know. I guess I'm stupid."*

Like most young people, Tim does not yet have an enabling framework for making sense of shame. However, his response does give an indication of the meaning he attributes to shame - one which challenges his entire worth and integrity as a person - "I'm stupid." This response is typical for young people when they initially try to make sense of the experience of shame. The therapist might further enquire:

"Would a stupid person begin to stop and think about what he put the little guy through, or would he just be thinking about himself?"

"What would it say about you, if you didn't feel bad about what you did to Peta?"

In this way, the young person is invited to consider the meaning of experiencing shame in relation to his ethics and in the context of what might fit with honour and integrity.

After some consideration, Tim decided that it would be "pretty callous" not to feel "bad".

The therapist might further enquire:

"Does it fit with the kind of person you are, that you do feel bad when you have let a little person in your family down?"

"What qualities about yourself does it fit with - things that you really believe in?"

"How does it fit with caring? Would a caring person feel bad?"

The young person can be invited to speculate about other people's views regarding his feelings of remorse and shame:

"What would other people in your family think, if they knew you feel bad?"

We can invite the young person to choose names for the ethics he is experiencing:

"Anyone can hurt another person or let them down, but maybe it takes real guts to face up to it. Is "guts" the right word or is it something else that it takes?"

Tim responded, *"It's because I love her."*

It is vital that we do not colonise a young person's experience by attempting to define and name it for him. It is important that we help to create opportunities for the young person to name the experience and their ethics. In this case, Tim declared that "love" was the ethic informing his facing up. This shocked some members of Tim's family, who had not imagined that he might experience feelings of love, let alone declare them. However, other family members felt relief that Tim was reclaiming values in himself that were important for the family.

Patterns of avoidance that accompany the experience of shame can remain paralysing for some young people, even when significant efforts have been made to establish a context of fairness through highlighting ethics and responsibility overloads.

> *Mike (aged 14) has been able to speak openly and frankly about having witnessed abuses by his father and his uncles and about the ethics implicit in the protective stance he took in standing up for his younger siblings. However, attempts to invite Mike to address his abusive behaviour towards two younger cousins have resulted in distracted behaviour and attempts to change the subject which progress towards a paralysed silence with his body increasingly slumped, occasionally punctuated with "I don't know" responses. This pattern of behaviour is familiar to members of Mike's family who generally react with corrective responses whilst labelling him as uncooperative and uncaring, in the face of his abusive behaviour.*

Attempts to *externalise* avoidance behaviour or shame itself may be helpful in this context. Externalisation processes can assist the young person to separate himself from the avoidance behaviour, to enable him to examine the behaviour, and, to take a position in relation to his ethics. This position might involve challenging or standing apart from avoidance practices (White, 1995).

> *"Mike, something happens when we start to talk about what you did to Emma and Jeff. You seem to phase out and then you stop talking. Something happens and you slump over and can only say, 'I don't know.' Have you noticed?"*

The conversation is kept at a level which is light and non-blaming. Sometimes humour may disrupt avoidance patterns and prevent bogging down in the familiar paralysis.

> *"It's kind of like something comes in and shuts you down or spaces you out - like a big hand coming down and switching a computer into sleep mode. What do you reckon it's like?"*

> *"Does it try to get you in other places or at other times?"*

The processes of externalisation can lead to conversations about restraining events in which the young person can participate without a sense of being judged. He can be invited to name the restraining experience. A generic name such as "the thing" or "it" is often chosen. Ways in which "the thing" operates can be noticed and examined. Others reactions to "the thing" might also be explored.

> *Mike established that others in his family regard the presence of "the thing" as an indication that he doesn't care about his abusive actions.*

Processes of externalisation allow "the thing" to be examined and understood. An invitation may be offered to watch out for any signs that might indicate that "the thing" is coming. Signals may be agreed upon to announce "the thing's" presence. Agreements can be made to take a break or check out just what "the thing" is about, when it shows its face.

These inquiries may lead to speculation about "the thing's" purpose or meaning. This involves inquiry about intent.

After some reiteration of Mike's stated ethics about caring and concern for the people he has hurt and his desire to make restitution, I made some inquiries about "the thing":

> *"Mike, is it a mean, 'I don't give a stuff, kind of thing', or is it more like an "I care but it's too hard to think about it kind of thing?"*

> *"Does 'the thing' care about what happened or not give a stuff about what happened?"*

> *"Is 'the thing' worried about the abuse or not worried about the abuse?"*

> *"Does 'the thing' worry about you or does it not give a damn about you?"*

Such conversation can assist Mike to separate an ethical sense of self from the influence of "the thing," whilst paying respect to a possible need for avoidance strategies and the potentially intense impact of shame. It was established that "the thing" was in fact protective of Mike and concerned about "not wanting to bring me down."

Further enquiry established that 'the thing' was concerned that Mike might be 'brought down,' if he faced his abusive actions because people would think, "I'm stupid."

This inquiry led to jointly agreed upon strategies to "slow down" when "the thing" tries to take over. The thing needed to be reassured, "I did a stupid thing but I'm not a stupid person." "I have done a bad thing, but I'm not a bad person."

Of course, these assertions require an accompanying question, "What is the proof of this?" Mike needed to constantly reassure "the thing" that the evidence for his integrity lay in the efforts he was making to face and stop abuse and to make restitution to those he had victimized.

Empathy and compassion are not qualities that are either present or deficient as personality traits in young people. They are context-dependent and require a patient, step by step process to be uncovered, noticed, expressed, and valued. When the young person is gradually assisted to find enabling ways to face his abuse and face shame, he can understand the nature of abuse and its impact upon others, and engage in meaningful acts of restitution and restoration. The intervention process must establish a context for facing shame, largely through "talking about talking about it" in relation to ethics. This process establishes meaning and rationale for the whole concept of addressing abusive behaviour. Each step the young person takes must have meaning in relation to his own ethics, if this step is to be owned and incorporated into a respectful sense of identity. Facing shame enables the discovery and strengthening of ethical values and qualities, which in turn enables further steps to be taken in acknowledging and understanding abusive behaviour and its effects upon others. The young person is continually invited to understand and appreciate the steps he is taking in a context of demonstrating to himself and others his ethics and integrity as a person.

Facing shame – seeing abuse like it really is

The invitational language used by the therapist follows a progression which is attuned to the young person's readiness to name his actions appropriately and face the accompanying shame. If we attempt to encourage the young person to name abusive behaviour accurately and without minimisation prematurely, we only invite protest and denial because the young person does not yet have an enabling context or means for facing shame.

Initial invitations tend to be vague and non-specific, e.g. "Can I ask you about what happened with Emma?" As the young person engages in therapeutic intervention, these inquiries may progress to: "People may expect you to face what you did to Emma." Later still, the abuse may be referred to in terms of, acts which may have hurt Emma. These acts will eventually be named as abuse or molestation, when the young person is ready to embrace these labels, understand their significance, and face the accompanying shame. The use of such a progression in naming practice is enabling in itself and prevents the young person from initially "painting himself into a corner" of denial and minimisation from which he will experience humiliation and a loss of face when feeling compelled to depart.

As the young person is open to or accepting of a new label which is more accurate and direct, he is invited to speculate about the meaning of taking on this new terminology. This is referred to as "seeing it like it really is"; a move towards facing shame and acting with integrity.

> *"What difference does it make, when you start to see it like it really is, rather than pretend that it wasn't so bad?"*

> *"What does it take to start to see it like it really is and tell it like it really is?"*

> *"Is this the right way for you to go or would it be better for you to pretend?"*

> *"Will this make you stronger or weaker as a person?" "How will it?"*

> *"Does this fit with who you are and the direction that you want to take?"*

> *"What do you respect more?"*

Particular sets of terminology and their meanings can be explored:

> *"Can you handle calling what you did to Amy by it's proper name, sexual abuse?"*

> *"What makes it sexual abuse?"*

> *"How hard is it to use the name sexual abuse?"*

> *"What difference does it make when you call it sexual abuse?"*

The young person is invited to examine the differences in power and vulnerability, between the person he has abused and himself, and to make meaning of what he is doing in the contexts of shame and personal integrity:

> *"How old are you? How old is Amy?"*

> *"How much were you trusted with Amy?"*

> *"How much did Amy trust you/look up to you?"*

> *"Who's idea was it in the first place?"*

> *"What did you say to Amy?"*

> *"Was that fair, or was it a trick or a lie?"*

> *"What makes it a trick or a lie?"*

> *"What difference does it make when you call it a trick?"*

These inquiries will of course be accompanied by the "seeing it like it really is" style of inquiry.

We seldom confront the young person with evidence of minimisation or denial and invite the inevitable protest. The young person is encouraged to refrain from making acknowledgment of or naming abuse until he has an adequate sense that doing so would not only fit with his own sense of ethics, but will have benefit to himself and others.

> *"If there is more truth to come out (and there usually is), you'd be nuts to face it unless you knew for sure that it would,*
> > * *help the kid you did it to*
> > * *and help you.*
> *unless you knew for sure that,*
> > * *it wouldn't be used against you*
> > * *it wouldn't be used to put you down or make you feel small.*
> > *How would you know if it was safe to speak out?"*

433

Facing shame - naming the impact of abuse

As the young person is beginning "to see the abuse like it really is," name tricks and lies, and recognise exploitation in the context of differences in power and vulnerability between the person he abused and himself, evidence of shame will become increasingly apparent.

Inquiries such as, *"What are you realising?"* might lead to responses like, *"She was only a little kid"*; *"He looked up to me, like a father."* Such realisations invoke deep shame and require careful attention to enable their meanings and significance to be safely explored. For example, if ethics relating to "courage" have been previously named, realisations may be examined in this context:

> *"How much courage is it taking to see it like it really is? Like you are starting to do now?"*

> *"What are you up against?"*

The young person may be invited to choose a feeling label (from a list provided) which he thinks best describes the "bad" feeling that he is experiencing:

> *"How big (out of ten) is the ashamed feeling that goes with seeing it like it really is?"*

> *"So how big (out of ten) is the courage you need to face it?"*

> *"Did you know that you had that much courage?"*

> *"Does anyone else know that you have that much courage?"*

Inquiries that relate to intent and the person-act distinction may be conducted:

> *"If you could talk about it and not feel that much shame, what sort of person would you be?"*

> *"What does it say about you that you do feel this much shame?"*

> *"Are you feeling more like you are a terrible person or more like you did a terrible thing?"*

> *"Would a terrible person stop and face up to it, like you are doing?"*

> *"What are you proving, about the kind of guy you really are?"*

The *"connections through difference"* style of inquiry, can be helpful with young people who have witnessed or been subjected to past abuses:

> *"Do you think that your step-father ever took the time or trouble to stop and think and feel about what he did to you and your family; like you are starting to do now for your sister?"*

"Do you realise that you are doing something that maybe he never had the guts to do?"

"What does this say about you and the direction you are taking?"

Similarly, inquiry may be conducted in the spirit of honour in the face of adversity:

"Do you think that you are taking the tough path or the easy path?"

"How are you managing to do this when you have been through so many hard times yourself?"

"How are you managing to think about other people's hurt feelings when you have been hurt so much yourself?"

"How is this changing you? What are you learning about yourself?"

"How does it fit with the kind of guy you really are?"

"Can you feel the strength and courage, along-side the shame?"

"Can you feel strength and courage growing or shrinking, as you face up?"

"Is facing up making you stronger or weaker?"

"Is carrying shame on your shoulders making them stronger or weaker?"

"Does facing up or running away fit best with showing your true colours?"

The young person can be invited to situate facing shame in the context of a healing journey or journey of reclamation of self:

"Facing up always hurts."

"How can you make sure you turn shame into strength and not weakness?"

"How can you put shame on your side?"

"What things will you need to remind yourself about to do this?"

In this context a range of affirmative concepts concerning shame, which relate to ethics and integrity, can be documented and referred to when facing up is particularly challenging and painful. Facing shame and feeling the pain:

- proves I care
- gives me training in mental toughness
- means I'm facing up and not running away
- means I'm not leaving it for my little sister to worry about
- means I'm not trying to hide behind the little guy
- means I'm being a big brother

- means I'm being true to myself
- means I'm earning the trust and respect of others

In a respectful, step by step, invitational context where shame can be safely faced as integrity and honour are affirmed, the young person may eventually be able to consider the enormous significance and potential impact of his abusive actions. He may become ready to face inquiries which expose the terrible effects of sexual exploitation:

Jeff had begun to describe how his little brother, Mick, had never had a father who was there for him and how Mick looked up to him "as a father." In response to inquiries about how he introduced sexual abuse to Mick, Jeff described ways in which he pretended to be interested in playing with Mick or pretended to be helping to bathe Mick in order to subtly introduce sexual touching. When Mick felt uncomfortable and asked, "What are you doing?" Jeff would reassure his brother and tell him it was a game and great fun.

As Jeff described this pattern of deception and exploitation, he was asked:

> *"What would it be like to look up to your big brother, to see him like the father you never had, to trust that he would look out for you, and then find he set you up and just used you like you were a magazine to get off on?"*

> *"What would it do to you?"*

> *"What would it be like to discover that he had tricked you - that he was only pretending to care for you, when what he really wanted was to use you?"*

> *"How would this make you think and feel about yourself?"*

Young men like Jeff may be invited to imagine themselves "in the younger child's shoes" and be interviewed, as though they were the little child, responding as they imagine the little child might respond to inquiry about the development of a pattern of abuse and the nature and effects of deception, betrayal, and exploitation.

Each bold step taken by the young person to "look shame squarely in the eye," must be critiqued in an ethical context of meaning, in terms of the young person's sense of honour and integrity.

Facing shame – restitution and restoration

Shame is of vital importance in family and community settings where mutual obligations between the young person and others are required in order to allow for both personal and community restoration following abuse.

Sexual abuse must be regarded as shameful in the family and community, if shame is to fulfil its adaptive function in the maintenance of respectful relationships. However, caregivers and community members must avoid shaming practices, especially those which reject, exclude, or isolate the young person from the community.

The participation of caregivers and community members in intervention practices is vital in a young person's journey towards respect. Caregivers are invited to address disabling attributions and shaming interaction, in order to assist the young person to reclaim and restore a sense of honour and integrity by choosing to face his abusive actions and his sense of shame in accordance with his own ethics.

Parents and family members are frequently restrained by their own avoidance practices which are associated with a sense of shame, regarding unsatisfactory parenting or mistakenly-attributed shame, which is linked to a sense of culpability for the young person's abuse and judgements of personal or family dishonour and disgrace. Patterns of denial, blame, and disengagement are common, especially when parents have felt shamed in previous encounters with authorities. The young person may then be left unsupported to face his abusive actions, or family members may collude in denial of the abuse or of the need to address it.

Caregivers are invited to attribute meaning to significant steps taken by the young person, which require facing shame in a context which is honouring:

> *"What do you think it is taking for Peter to face up to (specific step)?"*

> *"What do you think he is up against?"*

> *"How do you think he is managing to do it, in the face of (specific challenges or adversities)?"*

> *"What do you think this says about Peter?"*

> *"Did you know that Peter feels ashamed about (specific realisation)?"*

> *"Is this the first time he has let you know?"*

> *"What do you think it is taking for him to let you know?"*

> *"What does it say about him that he does feel ashamed?"*

> *"What would it say about him if he didn't feel ashamed?"*

> *"What difference does it make to know that he feels ashamed?"*

> *"Does it fit with a pathway that you can respect?"*

The young person is invited to document his realisations about the nature and potential impact of his abusive actions upon others, and to consider his ethical stance in relation to providing restitution to those he has hurt. In relation to specific realisations, the young person may be asked:

> *"Have you let anyone in your family know what you realise you put your sister through?"*

"What would it tell them about you?"

"Who would respect it if you did?"
"What would it prove to you about yourself?"

"What would you respect most in yourself, speaking out or keeping quiet?"

Acts of restitution are much more than apologies. They require deep levels of realisation about the exploitative nature of abusive actions and the effects these actions have upon all family and community members.

"What would it mean if you left it for your sister/your family to sort out on their own? How fair would this be?"

"How much do you owe it to them to think deeply about what you have put them through?"

"What would saying sorry mean if you hadn't thought much about what you put them through?"

Restitution can involve sharing realisations or simply respecting other's privacy and staying away from them. Restitution requires consideration of other's feelings and of the destructive effects of abuse upon one's community. In the absence of significant steps of restitution, it is difficult to imagine any meaningful form of personal restoration (reclaiming of one's own integrity and honour) or meaningful contribution to assisting in the healing of hurts suffered. Acts of restitution help to restore a balance or harmony that has been damaged by abuse within communities. Close scrutiny and study of the nature and effects of abuse, along with meaningful restitution practices, enables the development of a sense of discretion-shame and its protective function to be realised in individuals and in their communities.

A more detailed description of theory and practice concerning restitution and restoration in the context of child sexual abuse, has been previously documented (Jenkins et al., 2002).

Facing shame – mistaken shame

A substantial focus in therapeutic intervention concerns the distinctions between disgrace shame and mistaken shame. These are inevitably confused in the experience of young people and members of their families and communities. The goals are simple; disgrace shame must be faced, and mistaken shame must be reattributed. However, the processes can be complex and challenging.

Young men are steeped in traditions of shaming as a means of differentiating power relations and determining relative positions in social hierarchies. The art of put down, sarcasm and practices of humiliation in social relations have generally been practised and honed over years. They are often taken for granted as appropriate and familiar strategies for connection. Every male is faced with the challenge posed by the ubiquity of these dominant shaming traditions, if he is genuinely interested in developing an ethic of care and concern for others which privileges their feelings and needs. Therapeutic intervention processes which are highly confronting can inadvertently reproduce and support such shaming practices. For example, group processes which encourage young men to develop "bullshit detectors" in order to challenge minimisations and justifications in other's descriptions of their abuses can undermine an ethic or care and concern for others and promote hegemonic patterns of relating in the guise of caring.

The effects of past shaming practices require careful attention in intervention practice. In our enthusiasm to further their journeys towards respect, we can easily overwhelm young people and underestimate the effects of shaming.

> *John (aged 15) described a pattern of shaming by his father throughout his early childhood. His father would try to encourage him to engage in rituals of humiliation towards his mother: "Tell your mother she's stupid." "Doesn't she cook shit?" etc. John would never participate. He would burst into tears and run away to try to hide from his father, whereupon his father would ridicule him, calling him a "wimp" and "pathetic".*

> *In my enthusiasm to highlight ethics, I exclaimed, "You were really brave!" John looked at me bewildered and annoyed. He regarded himself as "weak" and this experience proved it. I was attempting to colonise his ethics, to impose my interpretations upon him, just as his father had done to him.*

I needed to enquire:

> *"Why didn't you say those things to your mum?"*

> *"Why didn't you go along with your dad?"*

> *"Wouldn't it have been easier to do what he said than have him put you down?"*

> *"Was it better to cop to it yourself, than see your mum suffer?"*

> *"What stopped you from causing hurt to your mum?"*

> *"What is it about you?"*

> *"Do you think your dad ever thought this way?"*

I needed to refrain from underestimating John's capacity to discover and name his ethical stance and establish conditions where he might determine and name this stance and its significance for himself.

Young people who have been subjected to sexual abuse themselves can be invited to separate and examine disgrace shame and mistaken shame in ways which mutually promote responsibility for abuse perpetrated and ameliorate the effects of abuse suffered.

Corey (aged 14 years) disclosed that his uncle had sexually abused him between the ages of nine and eleven, when he was meant to be providing child care for Corey's parents. Corey had begun to examine the political context of this abuse. Conversation with Corey included inquiries like the following:

"Whose idea was it?"

"How old were you; how old was he?"

"What was his job? What was your job?"

"What did he do to get your trust?"

"How did he set up opportunities?"

"How did he try to convince you that it was OK?"

"How did he try to trick you into thinking that it was a game/friendship?"

"How did he try to get you to keep it secret?"

"How did he try to set you up to feel responsible/like it was your fault?"

"Whose shame is it?"

"How did he try to trick you into carrying his shame?"

These inquiries may assist the young person to examine his experience from a perspective of power relations and relative responsibilities in order to locate ownership of shame appropriately with the person who perpetrated the abuse. Such inquiries also run parallel with a similar set concerning the abuse perpetrated by the young person. It can be enlightening for the young person to be invited to switch focus from one to the other, especially in the spirit of "connections through difference" style inquiries. In this way, a deeper sense of empathy and compassion regarding the abused person is reached through reference to the young person's own experience of exploitation, betrayal, and hurt feelings.

"Did your uncle ever stop and think about your feelings, like you are now doing for your little sister?"

"Did he ever try to do anything about the hurt he was causing you?"

"What does this say about the path you are taking?"

Similarly, the young person is invited to name factors that make it hard for him to speak out about the abuse done to him. For example:

He said he would go to gaol, if I told.

I thought that no-one would believe me.

People would think I'm gay.

I should have stopped it earlier.

I brought shame on my family.

He is invited to attribute responsibility and shame in accordance with a developing political understanding of abuse. He may become more able to understand some of the dilemmas faced by the child that he abused. Disgrace shame may be addressed and faced and mistaken shame can be appropriately attributed.

Facing shame – The statutory context

A fair statutory justice process will be informed by the concept that sexual abuse is a shameful act. However, it will not rely on shaming as a means of deterrence or promoting respectful behaviour. The young person will be afforded opportunities to:

- choose respectful directions which are accountable to those he has hurt;
- participate in supportive community networks and intervention programs which do not serve to marginalise, exclude, or isolate him; and
- establish his ethics and make respectful realisations in his own time frame, but in a statutory context which expects that abusive behaviour will be addressed and which monitors and documents responsible goal attainment, thus holding the young person accountable for his actions.

Braithwaite (2000), has proposed theory and reviewed research which supports the use of statutory justice processes, which communicate shamefulness of specific behaviours in a respectful manner, as opposed to shaming processes which are degrading, humiliating, and rejecting.

The collaborative youth conferencing and remand processes previously discussed, can greatly assist fair, respectful, and accountable intervention.

References

Braithwaite, J. (2000). Shame and criminal justice. *Canadian Journal of Criminology,* July: 281-298.

Fossum, M.A. & Mason, M.J. (1986). *Facing shame: Families in recovery*. NY: Norton

Jenkins, A., Hall, R., & Joy, M. (2002). Forgiveness in child sexual abuse: A matrix of meanings. In The Question of Forgiveness. *International Journal of Narrative Therapy and Community Work*. Issue 1.

Nietzsche, F. (1967). *The will to power*. NY: Random House.

Schneider, C.D. (1992). *Shame, exposure and privacy.* NY: Norton.

White, M. (1995). *Re-authoring lives.* Adelaide, Australia: Dulwich Centre Publications.

CHAPTER EIGHTEEN

FAMILY VIOLENCE AND SEVERE MALTREATMENT IN SEXUALLY REACTIVE CHILDREN & ADOLESCENTS

BARBARA SCHWARTZ
DEBORAH CAVANAUGH
ROBERT PRENTKY
AND
ANN PIMENTAL

Do you hear the children weeping
Oh my brothers
The Cry of the Children
Elizabeth Barrett Browning

Introduction

The world today is a manifestly violent place. Intra-state wars have left hundreds of thousands dead, and inter-state violence in the form of terrorism takes countless lives and leaves a blanket of fear over our everyday life. Street and gang violence have become a way of life in many places in the world. The United States has, until quite recently, been relatively immune from orchestrated acts of terrorism, and the last domestic war with horrific casualties was the Civil War, almost 150 years ago. The United States has not been as fortunate, however, with respect to family violence. Indeed, the level and magnitude of family violence in the United States, as well as the increasingly instrumental use of violence as a strategy for resolving foreign conflicts, is so high that "representatives from Christian faith communities around the globe launched a year-long effort to confront and overcome violence in the United States" (World Council of Churches, 2004). Communities of faith from around the world pledged to pray specifically that the citizens and the government of the United States will abandon their addiction to violence.

We are focally concerned in this chapter with violence expressed within the family and with the child victims of that violence. Clearly, the victimization of children is not new. As De Mause (1974) observed, "The history of childhood is a nightmare from which we have only recently begun to awaken. The further back in history one goes, the lower the level of child care, and the more likely children are to be killed, abandoned, beaten, terrorized, and sexually abused" (p.6). More recently, Hartman (1990) commented that, "The plight of millions of children in this country is so desperate and overwhelming that the American public may be using psychic numbing to protect itself from the pain and terror, in the same way that we have defended against knowing and believing in the possibility of a nuclear holocaust" (p. 14).

It is thus of no surprise that the home is the most violent place in America (Straus, 1974). The rates of violence and trauma in the United States are alarmingly high (Chu, 1998, 2001). In 1995, the FBI reported that 27% of all violent crime involved family member on family member violence, 48% involved family acquaintances with the violence most often occurring in the home (National Incident Based Reporting System, Uniform Crime Reporting Program, 1999). According to Perry, (2001a) less than 5% of all domestic violence results in a criminal report, leaving these figures grossly underestimated. Additionally researchers have estimated that each year at least 3.3 million children in the U.S. are exposed to domestic violence between adult intimate partners (Rosado, 1999). There is a significant link between witnessing domestic violence and being a victim of abuse (Fantuzzo & Mohr, 1999). Domestic and intra-familial abuse accounts for the majority of physical and emotional violence experienced by children in this country (Horowitz, Weine, and Jekel, 1995; Koop and Lundberg, 1992).

There are more than three million allegations of childhood abuse and neglect each year (Teicher, 2000, 2002). Three children die each day in the United States as a result of abuse or neglect at the hands of his or her caretaker (Fromm, 2001) compared to one child per day as reported by Karr-Morse in 1996, including the two thousand children who are murdered by their parents each year (Garbarino, 1999). Serious chronic trauma including neglect, physical, sexual, and emotional abuse has profound immediate and long-term effects upon a child's development, including attachment difficulties, low self-esteem, academic problems, poor peer relationships, anger, developmental delays, and increased dependency (American Academy of Pediatrics, 2002; Child Trend and Center for Child Health Research, 2004a, 2004b; Damon & Eisenberg, 1998; DeBellis, 1999; Egeland & Farber, 1984; Garbarino, 1999; Perry, 2001a, Perry, 2002b, 2002; Teicher, 2000; 2002; van der Kolk, 1997).

Relation Between Family Violence and Delinquent Behavior

It is certainly no surprise that violent children often come from violent families (Widom & Weeks, 1998). Other research has demonstrated that an abused child is four to seven times more likely to commit a violent act than a non-abused child. Further, physical abuse during the first five years of life increases the likelihood of later developing clinically significant conduct problems by about four-fold (Dodge, Pettit & Bates, 1997). Similarly, according to van der Kolk (1997), "Boys who witness violence by their fathers have a 1,000 percent greater likelihood of growing up to abuse their partners than men who were not exposed to marital violence when they were young" (p. 83). As may be noted in the data presented in this chapter, of the 720 abuse reactive children studied, an overwhelming number of them were neglected, psychologically, physically and/or sexually abused by their primary caretakers.

Witnessing domestic violence

Although direct abuse of a child within the family system can have devastating consequences, so too witnessing domestic violence can produce significant pathology as well. Edelson (1999) identified 31 studies, which met rigorous methodological criteria, and found that children who were exposed to domestic violence, even when they themselves were not the intended victims, consistently exhibited behavioral and emotional problems including depression, anger, impaired self-esteem as well as deficient social skills. Indeed violence begets violence as Singer and associates (1998) found in their study of over 2,000 children exposed to violence in their homes. Not surprisingly, the children who were both abused and who witnessed abuse fared the worst, demonstrating a variety of significant emotional problems (Hughes, Parkinson & Vargo, 1989; Singer, Miller, Guo, Slovak, & Fuerson, 1998). The US Department of Justice (1998) reported that a little more than half of all women who were victims of intimate violence lived in households with children under the age of twelve, and Carlson (1984) reported that between three and ten million children in the United States witness some form of domestic violence per year. In our sample 84% of the girls and 74% of the boys had witnessed domestic violence in the home.

Neglect

High levels of abuse and neglect are common among juveniles with sexually offending behaviors (Awad, Saunders & Levene, 1984; Borduin, Henggeler, Blaske, & Stein, 1990; Center for Sex Offender Management, [CSOM], 1999; Ford & Linney, 1995; Hirschberg & Riskin, 1994; Knight & Prentky, 1993; Kobayashi, Sales, Becker & Hunter, 1997). These rates range from 25% in a study conducted with boys (Becker & Hunter, 1997), to 100% in a study conducted with girls (Hirschberg & Riskin, 1994).

Most studies do not differentiate neglect from abuse and lump them all together into the general category of child maltreatment or abuse. However, neglected children do show some significant differences from their directly abused peers. According to Howes-Plotkin and Twentyman (1984) neglected children tend to be more passive and isolated from their peers whereas physically or sexually abused children are more actively aggressive. The neglected children appear to be modeling their behavior after their passive and ineffective parental role models. Another early study revealed significant developmental delays in neglected preschoolers who exhibited deficient coping skills, higher levels of frustration, anger and non-compliance than their non-neglected peers (Egeland & Farber, 1984). These children were less likely to engage in problem solving activities, more likely to be portrayed by their pre-school teachers as lacking in "persistence, initiative, and confidence to work on their own. They were more dependent upon the teacher, somewhat helpless, passive, withdrawn, and at times angry" (Egeland, 1999, p. D14-D15).

Psychological abuse

It is a challenge to separate the effects of psychological abuse from that of other types of abuse, as some degree of psychological abuse is inherent in all types of maltreatment. However, children can be subjected exclusively to emotional abuse in apparently "normal" families. According to the International Conference on Psychological Abuse of Children and Youth (Garbarino, Guttman, & Seely, 1986), psychological abuse includes the following:

- Rejecting
- Degrading/devaluing

- Terrorizing
- Isolating
- Corrupting
- Exploiting
- Denying essential stimulation, emotional responsiveness, or availability
- Unreliable and inconsistent parenting

Garbarino (1999) in his book, *Lost Boys: Why Our Sons Turn Violent and How We Can Save Them* stated that, "Psychological maltreatment, particularly rejection, is a primary cause of the developmental problems that result in violent acts on the part of the children and youth" (p. 186).

In 1974 Byron Egeland became involved in the *Minnesota Studies: Parenting Styles and Personality Development*. Until that time Sroufe and associates were examining only middle-class families. Sroufe was interested in the correlates of secure and insecure attachment styles, and Egeland was interested in risk factors associated with child abuse. Egeland introduced a new population, and recruited lower income families to participate in their longitudinal study (Egeland & Farber, 1984; Egeland, Sroufe & Erickson, 1983; Karen, 1998). This research indicated that children raised by unloving, unresponsive and otherwise emotionally neglectful caretakers are at risk for serious disruption of their capacities to relate to others. Damon and Eisenberg (1998) described children reared with a lack of parental warmth and affection as more likely to suffer behavioral problems in later life. The American Academy of Pediatrics (2002) reported that affectionless parenting could cause children to develop low self-esteem, academic deficits, antisocial behaviors and impaired physical health.

Physical abuse

Physically abused children are much more likely to behave in a violent manner than their non-abused peers (Alessandri, 1991; Cicchetti, Lynch, Shank & Manly, 1992; Crittenden, Claussen & Sugarman, 1994; Haskett & Kishner, 1991; Kaufman & Cicchetti, 1989; Williamson, Borduin & Howe, 1991). In a recent meta-analysis of sexually reactive children, Burton and Schatz (2003) found that 38% of 7,261 youth (from 30 studies) had been physically abused, 44% of 522 youth (from 4 studies) had been emotionally abused, and 32% of 2,879 youth (from 10 studies) had been neglected. In our sample of 720 abuse reactive children and adolescents, 82% of the boys and 85% of the girls had been physically abused. 47% of the boys and 54% of the girls had been subjected specifically to psychological abuse, over and above the psychological abuse inherent in any type of abuse or maltreatment. In our study, psychological abuse indicated an event where the child was put in danger, or feared for their lives, were humiliated, degraded, or specifically made to feel worthless and/or undeserving of the love and care every child is entitled to. 91% of the boys and 95% of the girls had been neglected.

Sexual abuse

According to many studies, juveniles with sexually offending behaviors have higher than normal rates of sexual abuse victimization (Cooper, Murphy & Haynes, 1996; Groth 1977; Hunter & Figueredo, 2000; Ryan, 1989). While findings indicate that not all of the juveniles who have sexually offended have been sexually abused with one study reporting a rate as low as 19% (Fehrenbach, Smith, Monastersky, & Deisher, 1986), most studies have in fact found quite high rates of sexual abuse (Center for Social Work Research, 1997; Friedrich, Beilke & Urguiza, 1987; Gale, Thompson, Moran & Stack, 1988; Goldston, Turnquist & Knutson, 1989; Kolko, Maser & Weldy, 1988; Milloy, 1994), ranging from 39% to 81% (Friedrich & Luecke, 1988). In the meta-analysis previously mentioned, Burton and Schatz (2003) reported that 43% of 9,597 youths from 49 different studies had been sexually victimized. When sexually reactive children under the age of 12 were examined, the rates of sexual victimization were even higher, ranging from 65% to 100% (Burton, Nesmith & Badten, 1997; Friedrich & Luecke, 1988; Gil & Johnson, 1994). When young sexually reactive females have been examined, the rate was as high as 100% (Hirschberg & Riskin, 1994). The high rate of discrepancy can be partially explained by the different methodologies utilized in these studies. Burton & Schatz (2003), in trying to account for these differences, conducted a study combining data from over 50 studies with a combined sample of 8,135 adolescents with sexually offending behaviors and found an overall sexual victimization rate of 40.28%. This rate is almost three times the rate found among adolescents without sexual offending behaviors reporting a rate of 14.8% in a sample of 5,811 subjects during the same analysis. In community samples of non-abusive, non-delinquent youth, a rate of 10%-15% for sexual abuse victimization was reported (Crouch, Hanson, Saunders, Kilpatrick, & Resnick, 2000; Finkelhor, Hotaling, Lewis, & Smith, 1990). In our sample 65% of the boys and 83% of the girls had been sexually abused.

In addition to these high rates of sexual abuse, most of these children have had more than one individual perpetrate against them. In a study by Mathews and associates (1989) 80% of the boys and 75% of the girls were assaulted by more than one individual. However, the girls had a higher average number of offenders (4.1 for the females compared with 1.4 for the males) and were subjected to more severe abuse categorized by greater use of force and earlier onset (Mathews, Mathews, & Speltz, 1989). Other studies have confirmed this higher rate of abuse against girls (Bumby & Bumby, 1997; Hunter, Lexier, Goodwin, Browne, & Dennis, 1993; Kubik, Hecker, & Righthand, 2002; Mathews, Matthews, & Speltz, 1989; Ray & English, 1995). 58% of the females and 80% of the males were molested by male perpetrators only, while 4% of the females and 13% of the males were molested by only female perpetrators. 38% of the females and 7% of the males were molested by perpetrators of both genders (Mathews, Hunter & Vuz, 1997). In our sample, significantly more girls, 69%, versus 44% of the boys had been sexually molested by more than one perpetrator. The girls also were significantly more likely to be penetrated during the abuse, 67% versus 51% of the boys. To highlight the severity of these percentages, Fergusson, Horwood, & Lynskey (1996) reported sexual abuse rates of 10-25% for females and 2-10% for males, and when penetration was involved, the percentages declined to 5.6% for females and 1.4% for males. Fergusson's study was based on self-report data of 18-year-old adolescents from New Zealand, generally considered to be the most reliable method of gathering sexual abuse statistics. However, for our subjects to have been coded for sexual abuse, clear documentation of the abuse was necessary, such as a supported investigation by the Department of Social Services, trauma evaluations or self-report along with supporting evidence the abuse occurred.

Youthful perpetrators have typically been exposed to pornography at an early age. Only 11% of Becker and Stein's (1994) sample of boys reported they did not use pornography, while 42% of Ford and Linney's (1995) sample and 76% of Wieckowski, Hartsoe, Mayer & Shortz' (1998) sample had been exposed to pornography by age seven. A high rate of pornography exposure was also observed among sexually inappropriate juvenile females (Mathews, Hunter & Vuz, 1997). Case records of our sample indicated that 19% of the boys and 16% of the girls had been exposed to pornography during their sexual abuse, although 42% of the boys and 12% of the girls indicated an interest in viewing porn. It is possible that these low figures were more an artifact of the reporting system rather than a complete account of the abuse.

The psychological consequences of child sexual abuse have been documented by a number of studies. An increase in psychiatric symptoms and substance abuse have been documented by Fergusson, Horwood & Lynsky (1996), Molnar, Berkman & Buka (2001), Mullen, Martin, Anderson, Romans, & Herbison (1993), and Stein, Golding, Siegel, Burnam & Sorenson (1988), to name a few. Briere and Elliott (2003) found such consequences even when other family conditions were controlled for. According to the literature, this population showed an increase in mood disorders (Brown, Cohen, Johnson & Smailes, 1999; Molnar et al., 2001), suicidal ideation (Brown et al., 1999; Fergusson et al, 1996; Molnar, Berkman, & Buka, 2001; Mullen et al., 1993) and diagnoses of PTSD (Boney-McCoy & Finkelhor, 1995, 1996). Three studies were able to locate twin cohorts of whom only one was sexually abused. Results indicated the twin who was molested displayed more psychopathology including suicidal ideation in the males (Dinwiddie et al., 2000), were more likely to develop mental health problems and substance abuse disorders (Kendler, Bulik, Silberg, Hettema, Myers & Prescott, 2000; Nelson et al., 2002). Smallbone & McCabe (2003) cite insecure attachment, early onset of masturbation and sexual offending as being correlated with childhood sexual abuse.

Despite these high rates of sexual abuse found in sexually inappropriate children, these figures may still be underestimated due to under-reporting for several reasons. According to the literature, older adolescent males do not report being victims of sexual abuse at the same rate as younger males (Campis, Hebden-Curtis, & Demaso, 1993). Males also may not disclose due to a fear of being labeled "gay" (Mathews, 1996), and may feel incompetent for not being able to protect themselves (Pelsuo & Putnam, 1996). However, Worling (1995) reported increased rates of disclosure of sexual abuse with adolescent males once they have been in treatment for a while and start to develop a trusting relationship with their therapist. In Worling's (1995) study, using pre-treatment and post-treatment data the percentage of males disclosing sexual abuse rose from 22 to 52 percent.

Disturbance in Attachment: An Outcome of Maltreatment

Obviously child maltreatment disrupts the relationship with the abusive caretaker, leading to a variety of difficulties. John Bowlby was one of the first to suggest the importance of the early relationships on the social and emotional development of children (Bowlby, 1940, 1944). His theory conceptualized attachment as biologically and evolutionarily based. During evolution, in order to insure the survival of the species, infants are born with the capability of exhibiting certain cues during the first years of life that encourage the proximity of the caregiver. In other words, our brains are designed to promote relationships. Certain parts of the brain respond to emotional cues, such as facial expression, touch, and scent, which allow us to receive pleasure from positive human interactions (Perry, 2001). Bowlby suggested these behaviors were biologically based and referred to them as "signaling behaviors." These signaling behaviors are critical in inducing individuals to approach, and thus increase proximity and physical contact with their caretakers (Wilson, 2001). Infant signaling behaviors include crying, smiling, babbling, sucking, and following, with crying being the dominant behavior during the first phase of attachment (Crain, 2000, Wilson, 2001). When the caregiver is appropriately available and responsive, this system promotes a balance between maintaining proximity to a caregiver and enhancing the child's confidence in exploring their environment. Bowlby identified an attachment cycle, which occurs in four phases during the first few years of life (Bowlby, 1969). An important concept in Bowlby's theory is the "internal working model" described as a cognitive representation of attachment relationships. These relationships are internalized in infancy and early childhood and serve as a lens or filter through which all future relationships are interpreted (Bowlby, 1973).

When attachment develops normally, the child receives pleasure from interacting with other people. Bowlby classified this group as having a "secure" attachment style. Those who have negative experiences such as not having their needs met in a consistent and timely manner are classified as demonstrating an "insecure" attachment style (Bowlby, 1969, 1973, 1980). During infancy, this interaction is focused on the primary caregiver, and as the child matures, branches out to include other people, usually to individuals within the family. The degree of pleasure received during this interaction is related to the degree of attachment that has developed. It is the parent's/caregiver's job to teach the child emotional, social, and cognitive tasks which promote responsibility, empathy, and other prosocial behaviors. The strongest rewards for a child are the attention, approval, praise, and recognition of the parent. In contrast, if a child feels he/she has not pleased the parent on a consistent basis this can have devastating consequences (Patterson & Moran, 1988; Perry, 2001).

With consistent, sensitive, and nurturing care, an infant will most likely form a secure attachment to their primary caregiver, most commonly the mother. This early connection is crucial to the development of a foundation for later relationships and appears to predict the quality of these later interpersonal relationships. A positive attachment with a caregiver is thought to influence the construction of mental states, which raises the expectations of the reliability of others and enhances a sense of self-worth. These are critical aspects of personality development (Smallbone & Dadds, 2000). Consistent alleviation of an infant's needs by the caregiver is crucial in order to foster a sense of trust and security, which is imperative for attachment to occur (Lieberman & Zeanah, 1995).

Ainsworth and colleagues (1978) elaborated on Bowlby's theory and went on to develop the most widely used research method for assessing the quality of a baby's attachment. She and her colleagues were among the first to empirically test Bowlby's theory. The method she developed is referred to as the "Strange Situation" a classification system that involves a twenty-minute laboratory procedure based on the infant's reactions to separation and reunion with the caregiver. This research lead to the development of three distinct patterns of attachment (A) *Insecure/Avoidant*, (B) *Secure*, (C) *Insecure/Resistant* (Ainsworth, Blehar, Waters & Wall, 1978). Main and Solomon (1986) later developed a fourth group, (D) *Disorganized/Disoriented* that describes those infants who displayed no coherent pattern in their coping strategies during the strange situation.

Attachment disorder results when there is an interruption in the bonding between parent (caregiver) and child, most often due to abandonment, neglect, abuse, or early trauma. It involves a disturbance of social interaction due to the neglect of the child's basic physical and emotional needs. Getting one's needs met provides the foundation for the capacity to regulate one's internal biological systems. This includes learning how to soothe oneself during times of stress (van der Kolk, 1994). Attachment is related to teaching children how to regulate those systems. In attachment disorders, the child has not learned how to regulate their emotions.

Another risk factor for attachment disorders results from the child having multiple caregivers, which prevents the child from forming consistent bonds. This creates serious emotional and behavioral conditions that have the potential to manifest themselves in anti-social behaviors, or could turn inward to destructive acts against the self, such as suicide, suicidal gestures, and other self-injurious behaviors. According to Prentky, Knight, Sims-Knight, Straus, Rokous, & Cerce (1989), caregiver instability has important implications for attachment styles in adult sex offenders and was found to be highly predictive of the severity of future sexual aggression. Prentky et al. (1989) also found that a history of sexual victimization, and deviation in the home is highly predictive of sexual aggression. A consistent theme among the caregivers in the Prentky et al. (1989) study was drug abuse and involvement in the criminal justice system, which would be consistent with an inability to provide consistent caregiving or parenting.

Other consequences of an attachment disorder may include violence to self or others, fire-setting, sexual deviation, and cruelty to animals. The child lacks the ability to trust others or to form reciprocal loving relationships. If left untreated, most likely, the child will have little impulse control and may not develop a conscience. Their anti-social behavior will only escalate, resulting in violence, or total isolation from society (Lieberman & Zeanah, 1995; Teicher, 2000, 2002).

The risk of neglect to infant/child increases with isolation from society and the lack of any type of support to the parent, either from family, friends, or the community. Lack of parenting skills, having teenage parents, or having a caregiver who suffers from some form of cognitive or emotional disability are all risk factors for disrupted attachment. Other documented risk factors include:

- Insufficient pre-natal care
- Poor nutrition
- Mother's age (less than 19 and over 35)
- Mother's reproductive history
- Mother's drinking and smoking habits
- Adverse pre-natal environment
- Parental depression or stress
- Drug exposure

All these factors have a cumulative affect on the child and can be quite damaging to the child's development (Child Trends, 2004; Greenough, Gunnar, Emde, Massinga, & Shonkoff 2001; Herschkowitz, Kagan, & Ziles 1999; Shore, 1997; Szilagyi, 1998).

Reactive attachment disorders and sexually abusive behavior

The main component of Reactive Attachment Disorder (RAD) is developmentally inappropriate social relatedness in most contexts and is associated with severe and chronic childhood abuse and neglect (American Psychiatric Association [APA], 2000). There are two sub-types of RAD: (1) *Inhibited Type*, involves a persistent failure to respond to most social interactions, especially during times of stress, and (2) *Disinhibited Type*, involves the lack of selectivity in the choice of caregivers or attachment figures, especially during times of stress. These two subtypes are opposites. The child with an *Inhibited* type RAD will avoid all contact with individuals, even when the individual is trying to soothe or comfort the child. Conversely, the *Disinhibited* RAD type child will actively seek out any individual, regardless of familiarity, in order to receive comfort or attention (Haugaard & Hazan, 2004). Children diagnosed with RAD are often misdiagnosed with behavioral disorders such as ADHD, Conduct Disorder, Oppositional Defiant Disorder, or Anxiety Disorder due to the aggressive behaviors and frequent temper tantrums commonly seen in children diagnosed with RAD (Alston, 2000; Hauggaard, & Hazan, 2004; Wilson, 2001). Due to the association between attachment disorders and antisocial behaviors, scientists have conducted research to determine a possible correlation between sexual offending behaviors and attachment styles. Marshall (1989, 1993; Marshall & Marshall, 2000) observed that a large number of sexual offenders were found to have insecure adult attachment bonds. He proposed that insecure attachment may result in deficits in interpersonal relationship skills, self-confidence, and empathy, which could all interfere with courtship behaviors (Marshall, 1989). This observation has led to more research in the area of attachment theory and sexual offending (Smallbone & Dadds, 1998; Ward, Hudson, Marshall, & Siegert, 1995).

Marshall, Serran, & Cortoni (2000) found sex offenders to suffer deficits in intimacy, report high levels of loneliness, and exhibit poor adult attachment styles. They also exhibited insecure attachments to their parents and used inadequate coping strategies to deal with their problems. This theory suggests that poor parent/child relationships produce various dysfunctional adult interpersonal styles that lead to sexual offending behaviors (Marshall, Serran, & Cortoni, 2000). Marshall and Marshall (2000) go so far as to propose the "origins of sexual offending lie in the offender's experience of poor quality childhood relationships with their parents. This is said to increase their risk of being sexually abused, which in turn, feeds into the sexual fantasies they entertain, particularly during adolescence" (p. 250).

Smallbone and Dadds (2000) examined the relationship between childhood attachment styles and coercive sexual behaviors. Subjects consisted of 162 male undergraduates who completed self-report measures of childhood maternal attachment, childhood paternal attachment, adult attachment, antisociality, aggression, and coercive sexual behaviors. As predicted, an insecure childhood attachment, especially paternal, was associated with antisociality, aggression, and coercive sexual behaviors. Insecure childhood attachment independently predicted coercive sexual behavior after controlling for antisociality and aggression. These results are consistent with research linking adverse family experiences with offending behaviors and lends support to an attachment-theoretical framework for understanding offending behavior in general, and sexual offending behavior in particular (Marshall, 1989, 1993; Marshall & Marshall, 2000; Marshall, Serran, & Cortoni, 2000; Prentky, et al., 1989; Smallbone & Dadds, 2000).

Developmental Traumatology

Given the relationship between the various types of familial abuse, disruption of the bonding experience and subsequent behavioral disorders, it becomes advisable to try to identify specific processes, which may help explain this linkage. As Shield and Cicchetti (1998) have stated, "By studying processes leading to maladaptation among at-risk individuals, researchers stand to gain a more comprehensive understanding of the pathways to developmental competence and psychopathology." (p. 381). In an attempt to do this, the field of Developmental Traumatology has emerged, which according to DeBellis (1999), is defined as "the systematic investigation of the psychiatric and psychological impact of overwhelming and chronic interpersonal violence on the developing child" (p. 1). This relatively new area of study synthesizes knowledge from an array of scientific fields including developmental psychopathology, developmental neuroscience, and stress and trauma research (DeBellis, 1999; DeBellis, Baum, & Birmaher, 1999; DeBellis, Keshavan, Clark, Casey, Giedd, Boring, Frustaci, & Ryan, 1999).

Teicher (2000, 2002) has reported on a series of studies conducted at McLean Hospital on the effects of childhood abuse and the developing brain. He argues that "childhood maltreatment exerts enduring negative effects on the developing brain, fundamentally altering one's mental capacity and personality and while it may be possible to compensate for these abnormalities – to succeed in spite of them – but it is doubtful they can actually be reversed in adulthood" (pg. 64). Teicher describes how childhood abuse can cause a collection of permanent brain abnormalities in which there are four major components including: (1) limbic irritability, (2) deficient development and differentiation of the left hemisphere, (3) deficient left/right hemisphere integration, and the (4) abnormal functioning of the cerebellar vermis (Teicher, 2000, 2002). Although a thorough discussion of neurobiological consequences of abuse on the developing brain is not possible here, some of the consequences are outlined below.

Being unable to modulate emotional responses including anger and depression, having difficulty interpreting social situations, and having difficulty with consequential thinking might contribute to impulsivity, antisocial behavior and sexual misconduct.

Table 1: The Neurobiology of Child Abuse.

Brain Structure	Purpose	Impairment
Left Hemisphere	Regulation and oversight of logical responses to a situation; control and mediation of emotional responses generated by the right hemisphere.	Diminished control of emotional responses resulting in poor or inappropriate reactions to emotional responses; angry outbursts, self-destructive or suicidal impulses; paranoia, psychosis and a tendency to pursue intense, ultimately unstable, relationships.
Prefrontal Cortex	Internal editor of emotional states, consequential thinking, moral reasoning. and reactions to emotional crises.	Increased potential for depression, delinquency and criminal behavior.
Corpus Collosum	Communication between the brain s two hemispheres.	Significantly smaller in neglected and abused children causing non--integrated, inappropriate responses to everyday situations.
Temporal Lobe	Regulation of emotion and verbal memory.	Poor modulation of emotions, increased chance for temporal lobe epilepsy.
Amygdala	Creates emotional content of memories; mediating depression, hostility/ aggression; and governs reactions and responses to fear.	Significantly smaller for neglected and abused children raising the risk for depression, irritability, and hostility/ aggression. Incorrect emotional memories , absence of fear conditioning and increased chance of psychopathic tendencies.
Hippocampus	Formation and retrieval of verbal and emotional memories.	Lower performance on verbal memory tests, mental problems during adult years.
Cerebellar Vermis	Modulates the production and release of neurotransmitters; has a significant number of receptor sites for stress-related hormones.	Increased potential for risk for psychiatric symptoms such as depression, psychosis, hyperactivity, ADHD and in rare cases, psychosis.

Training and Research Institute, Albuquerque, New Meixco, 2004.

The Relationship Between Abuse, Attachment, Developmental Traumatology and Outcome

Abuse of children sets into motion an interaction that may well have tragic outcomes. Physical, psychological and sexual abuse within the family, as well as the witnessing thereof, not only provides negative learning experiences but also disrupts the very dynamics that allow individuals to connect with others (Perry, 2001a, 2001b). Children diagnosed with PTSD due to chronic abuse during early childhood suffer alterations of biological stress systems. Increased levels of stress hormones, such as catecholaminergic neurotransmitters and steroid hormones, adversely affect brain development. In a study conducted by DeBellis and associates (1999) subjects who had been diagnosed with PTSD were subjected to MRI brain scans and these scans revealed smaller intracranial and cerebral volumes than their matched controls. Disruption of this bonding experience actually produces neurological changes in the developing brain, which manifest themselves as psychiatric symptoms, antisocial behavior, including sexually inappropriate conduct (DeBellis, 1999; Marshall & Marshall, 2000). This highly complex interaction may produce a variety of outcomes dependent upon the age the abuse occurs and protective factors in the environment as well as resilient personality factors, which the child may be fortunate enough to be born with, or otherwise develop (DeBellis, 1999, Perry, 2002). A greatly simplified illustration of this interaction is presented below.

MODEL

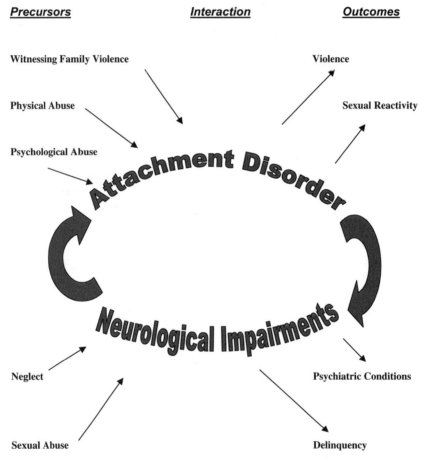

Maltreatment of a young child may interfere with his/her ability to attach to the caregiver, which then manifests itself in a variety of behaviors such as emotional instability, impulsivity, aggression, lack of empathy and affective remoteness which further contributes to the failure of the bonding experience. This then results in dysfunctional behaviors including, but not limited to, a variety of sexually inappropriate behaviors (DeBellis, 1999; DeBellis et al., 2001; Perry 2001a, 2001b, 2002).

Applying Theory to Reality

The principles of *developmental traumatology* are being applied in an ongoing investigation of a large sample of severely abused, abuse-reactive children in the custody of the Massachusetts Department of Social Services (DSS). The preliminary findings reported in this chapter are based on the analyses of 720 of those children. The Commonwealth of Massachusetts and the National Institute of Justice funded this research project, initiated in February 2001.1 The vast majority of these children have been abused in a variety of ways in addition to being subjected to disruptions in their caregiving and living situations. Recent findings in developmental neuroscience and their implications for future behavior can enlighten our understanding of the subsequent sexually inappropriate behavior of these children and can inform both therapeutic and public policy approaches to this severely abused population.

In 1998, a state budget appropriation in Massachusetts established a program with the principle mandate of examining children and adolescents involved with the Department of Social Services (DSS), who have been flagged for either firesetting or sexually inappropriate behaviors. The program, Assessment for Safe and Appropriate Placement (ASAP), was designed to improve the management and care of these children who because of their behaviors are now at risk to physically endanger or to sexually victimize other children in either their own homes, foster homes, or group/residential settings. The current research project deals only with those who have exhibited sexually inappropriate behaviors.

In studying the effects of family violence upon sexual misconduct in children, this group represented the ideal research sample. 83% of these children had been physically abused with 56% having been kicked, punched, or beaten with objects and 8% having been burned, strangled, rendered unconscious or sustaining broken bones. The remainder had either no physical injuries or sustained cuts, bruises, or abrasions. 49% had been psychologically abused, over and above the psychological abuse inherent in neglect, physical or sexual abuse, or being exposed to domestic violence. 51% of these children were exposed to threats with the intention of scaring or frightening them, and/or being forced to endure humiliation and degradation from their primary caretaker. 69% were sexually abused with 64% of these children being assaulted by family members and 55% endured penetration during the abuse. 91% had been neglected with 40% being severely and chronically denied basic needs. 76% were exposed to domestic violence with 29% witnessing extreme and chronic violence in the home.

Although comparisons could not be drawn between the children who had experienced the many aspects of family violence, basically because they all had been exposed to this in one form or another, differences did emerge between children with regard to extreme forms of different types of abuse. It should be noted that these categories are not mutually exclusive.

Witnessed domestic violence

The majority of the parents of children who were exposed to domestic violence were never married, 52%, and 44% are currently divorced or separated, 7% are separated due to the death of one spouse, another 4% are institutionalized, either in prison or psychiatrically hospitalized. Only 4% of the parents are currently still married. Due to the level of violence in these homes, the Department of Social Service (DSS) placed significantly more of these children in foster homes.

According to the American Psychiatric Association (2000), by definition a diagnosis of PTSD is associated directly with having been exposed to a traumatic event in which both of the following are present:

> 1) The individual experienced, witnessed, or was confronted with an event or events that involved actual or threatened death or serious injury, or a threat to the physical integrity of self or others; and
> 2) The individual's response involved intense fear, helplessness or horror.

The abuse is a description of the everyday lives of these children who have witnessed every manner of violence between the adults in their lives including sexual abuse and even murder of one parent by another. It is no wonder that they show significantly more expressed anger as defined as (a) verbal aggression and/or angry outbursts, (b) threatening and/or intimidating behavior, (c) non-sexual assaults and/or fighting involving peers, caretakers, teachers or other "authority figures," (d) destruction of property, (e) suspensions or expulsions from school due to anger, and (g) cruelty to animals.

Table 2: Impact of Witnessing Domestic Violence

	Did <u>Not</u> Witness Family Violence	Witnessed Family Violence	Witnessed <u>Severe</u> Family Violence	2
Foster care [a]	6%	63%	25%	12.09**
PTSD diagnosis [b]	10%	58%	23%	26.19***
Observed sexual deviance [a]	20%	27%	13%	26.80***
Psychological abuse [a]	16%	41%	17%	23.46***
Physical abuse [a]	8%	66%	27%	37.10***
Sexual abuse [a]	10%	55%	22%	10.92**
Neglect [a]	4%	72%	28%	27.95***
Caretaker Instability [b]	1%	75%	29%	15.36**

Note. [a] df = 2, [b] df = 4. *p<.05; **p<.01; ***p<.001.

Children who witnessed domestic violence began to act out sexually at a younger age, approximately a year younger than those children who had not witnessed domestic violence. As such these behaviors were identified earlier as revealed by the significantly earlier age at time of ASAP referral. These ages followed an assumed pattern, where the domestic violence was more extreme and chronic, the younger the age of sexually acting-out. Other significant findings in regard to witnessing domestic violence were a younger age at first residential placement, and having more caretakers being involved in the lives of these children. To qualify as a "caretaker" the child must have lived in the home with the same caretaker for at least six months. As shown in Table 2, the children who witnessed domestic violence were significantly more likely to be subjected to neglect, psychological, physical and sexual abuse, and to have witnessed sexual deviance in the home. Along with those findings, these children were also subjected to more severe psychological abuse and neglect, and for the abuse to have occurred at a significantly younger age (physical, sexual, neglect, and psychological).

Table 3: Witnessed Domestic Violence and Age of Inappropriate Sexual Behavior, Onset of Abuse, Placements, and Severity of Abuse

	No Exposure to Family Violence	Exposed to Moderate Family Violence	Exposed to Severe Family Violence	F	df
Age of 1st sexually inappropriate behavior [a]	M = 10.4	M = 9.6	M = 9.2	6.13**	2, 587
Age of 1st hands-on sexualized behavior, including a victim [b]	M = 10.8	M = 9.10	M = 9.6	5.24**	2, 538
Age at time of ASAP referral [c]	M = 13.0	M = 12.3	M = 11.5	10.31***	2, 696
Age at first residential placement	M = 12.3	M = 11.6	M = 11.2	4.74**	2, 569
Total number of different caretakers	M = 4.1	M = 4.4	M = 4.8	3.83*	2, 696
Age at onset of physical abuse	M = 6.0	M = 5.2	M = 4.4	5.99**	2, 455
Age at onset of psychological abuse	M = 6.9	M = 5.4	M = 5.0	3.89*	2, 269
Age at onset of sexual abuse	M = 6.3	M = 5.2	M = 5.2	4.29*	2, 364
Age at onset of neglect	M = 4.3	M= 3.5	M = 2.6	6.85***	2, 580
Severe psychological abuse	M = 1.5	M = 1.2	M = 1.6	3.40*	2, 301
Severe neglect	M = 1.1	M = 1.2	M = 1.5	11.79***	2, 630
Having victims of both genders					

Note. [a] $df = 2, 587$; [b] $df = 2, 538$, [c] $df = 2, 696$ $*p<.05; **p<.01; ***p<.001$.

Physical abuse and delinquent behaviors

Not surprisingly, children who had been physically abused displayed behaviors characterized by antisocial or delinquent behaviors. They were significantly more likely to exhibit behaviors consistent with conduct disorder prior to age 10, verbal bullying of peers, truancy, and being arrested prior to age 16.

Table 4: Physical Abuse and Delinquent Behaviors

	No Physical Abuse	Yes Physically Abused	χ^2
Conduct disorder prior to age 10 [b]	12%	68%	9.64**
Verbal bullying [b]	12%	66%	5.81*
Arrest prior to age 16 [b]	9%	27%	10.11**
Truancy [a]	8%	28%	5.56*

Note. [a] df = 1, [b] df = 2.   *p<.05; **p<.01; ***p<.001.

Psychological abuse

Significantly more psychologically abused children had been diagnosed with PTSD. These children were also of a significantly younger age when first seen for outpatient mental health treatment, and were of a younger age at first foster home placement. They also had significantly more caretakers. Psychologically abused children also had significantly more changes in living situations, more victims, and more separate incidents of sexually inappropriate behaviors.

Table 5: Psychological Abuse

	No Psych Abuse	Yes Psych Abuse	*F*	*df*
Diagnosed with PTSD	M = .41	M = .92	8.81***	1, 684
Age 1st sought mental health treatment	M = 7.7	M = 6.9	8.55**	1, 660
Age 1st foster home placement	M = 8.1	M = 6.9	8.46**	1, 545
Total number different caretakers	M = 4.2	M = 4.7	9.57**	1, 685
Total changes in living situations	M = 9.6	M = 10.7	6.65**	1, 676
Number of sexual abuse victims	M = 2.9	M = 3.4	4.12*	1, 674
Total number of separate Incidents of sexually inappropriate behavior	M = 8.7	M = 10.7	4.20*	1, 642

*p<.05; **p<.01; ***p<.001.

Severe neglect

Consistent with the literature on severely neglected children and the impact on the developing brain, these children were significantly more likely to be diagnosed with PTSD and learning disorders and also had significantly lower IQ scores, indicative of developmental delays. They also were seen for mental health treatment at a younger age. Due to the disregard for the welfare of the child, both before and after birth, significantly more of the mothers of the severely neglected children had abused drugs and alcohol during their pregnancies. They were also significantly more likely to be exposed to domestic violence and sexual deviance in the home and to be victims of psychological abuse. Due to the severity of neglect, they were significantly more likely to be placed in a foster home and at an earlier age. Due to the number of placements, they also spent less time with their biological mothers, had significantly more foster home placements, and as a result were subjected to more changes in living situations.

Table 6: Severe Neglect

	No	**Yes**	2
PTSD diagnosis [b]	10%	65%	9.43**
Learning disorder [b]	5%	44%	5.84*
Alcohol abuse during pregnancy [a]	1%	16%	4.51*
Drug abuse during pregnancy [a]	1%	20&	11.36***
Foster care [a]	9%	75%	14.12***
Exposed to family violence [b]	9%	70%	12.38**
Exposed to sexual deviance [a]	2%	32%	19.50***
Psychological abuse [a]	5%	47%	6.00*

Note. [a] $df = 1$, [b] $df = 2$, $*p<.05$; $**p<.01$; $***p<.001$.

Table 7: Analysis of Variance (ANOVA) Severe Neglect and Development Factors

	No	**Yes**	**F**	**df**
IQ scores	M = 93.9	M = 89.9	3.80*	1, 507
Time spent w/ bio mother (months)	M = 117	M = 92	17.73***	1, 633
Age first sought mental health treatment	M = 8.2	M = 7.1	6.61**	1, 626
Age at first foster home placement	M = 9.3	M = 7.1	14.12***	1, 536
Total number of foster homes	M = 3.5	M = 4.9	6.97**	1, 534
Total changes in living situations	M = 8.9	M = 10.5	4.93*	1, 640

$*p<.05$; $**p<.01$; $***p<.001$.

According to the literature, most children who are severely neglected tend to be more passive and withdrawn in comparison with more actively abused children. The severely neglected children in this sample did display some significant antisocial behaviors; however, of the children who were severely neglected, 47% had also been psychologically abused, 75% physically abused, and 63% subjected to sexual abuse. This could explain the high rates of antisocial behaviors identified in this group of children. They were significantly more likely to have problems in grammar school, be involved in non-prescription drug abuse, and have a Child In Need of Services, (CHINS) filed against them. In the Commonwealth of Massachusetts, a CHINS is filed with the juvenile court by a parent, legal guardian, or teacher when a child is displaying chronic behavioral problems such as truancy, running away, or non-compliance with rules at home or at school. These behaviors are considered "status offenses", not criminal offenses, and unlike a delinquency, do not appear on a juvenile's criminal record. However, research has demonstrated a strong correlation between CHINS status offenses and subsequent delinquency (Wen, 2004). The severely neglected children were also significantly more likely to be arrested prior to age 16, be involved in firesetting behaviors, and to carry or own a weapon.

Table 8: Severe Neglect and Antisocial Behaviors

	No	Yes	2
Problems in grammar school [c]	10%	74%	7.95*
Non-prescription drug abuse [a]	5%	21%	4.26*
CHINS [A]	7%	29%	12.51***
Arrested prior to age 16 [b]	6%	28%	6.35*
Firesetting behaviors [d]	7%	41%	14.07*
Carries a weapon [b]	4%	16%	8.63*

Note. [a] $df = 1$, [b] $df = 2$, [c] $df = 3$, [d] $df = 5$. *$p<.05$; **$p<.01$; ***$p<.001$.

[A] CHINS, Child In Need of Services, a document filed in Massachusetts for delinquent behaviors.

Sexual abuse

Sexually abused children who acted out in a sexually inappropriate manner were significantly different from children who were not sexually abused but also engaged in sexually inappropriate behavior in a variety of ways. They had a more extensive history of physical and emotional problems than their non-abused peers. Significantly more of these children were classified as physically disabled, suffered from enuresis, and to have participated in special education classes. They were more likely to have a history of psychiatric hospital admissions and at a significantly younger age, 9.4 years, versus 10.8 years. The reasons reported for the psychiatric admissions were 31% for suicidal or other self-injurious behaviors, 22% for extreme management problems, 33% for multiple reasons, and 8% for sexually inappropriate behaviors. The remaining 6% were coded as "other" for psychiatric admission reason. This group was also significantly more likely to have been prescribed psychotropic medications. The average age of their first mental health contact was almost two years younger than the non-sexually abused sample, having had their first mental health contact at 6.9 years. The mean time spent in residential placement for children who were sexually abused was 27.5 months versus a mean of 17.7 months for the non-sexually abused group. The sexually abused group was also significantly more likely to have been exposed to domestic violence, and sexual deviance in the home, and their mothers were more likely to have abused alcohol during their pregnancy. They were much more likely to be diagnosed with PTSD and Anxiety Disorders.

More sexually abused children engaged in both consenting and non-consenting sexual activity. For example, they were more likely to have participated in consenting foreplay with age mates. However, they were also more likely to have exposed themselves to age mates, engage in frottage and simulating intercourse, kissing genitals, touching genitals, physically forced their victims to submit to being masturbated, forcing the victim to masturbate the subject, performing oral sex on their victims, and forced anal penetration. The sexually abused children displayed a significantly higher degree of sexual aggression, had significantly more victims, had more male child victims, defined as at least four years younger than the subject, and to have been involved in more separate incidents of sexualized behaviors than those children who engaged in sexually inappropriate conduct but had not been abused themselves. Consistent with the literature, the sexually abused group began their sexually inappropriate behavior and their first hands-on sexualized behavior an average of two years earlier than the non-sexually abused group.

Table 9: Sexual Abuse: Maltreatment, Sexualized Behaviors, and Development Factors

Maltreatment:	No	Yes	^{2}
Exposed to family violence [b]	21%	55%	10.92**
Observed sexual deviance [a]	5%	26%	34.02***
Alcohol abuse during pregnancy [a]	3%	12%	4.55*
Sexualized Behaviors:			
Consensual foreplay with agemates [a]	8%	26%	7.47**
Exposing self to agemates [a]	12%	34%	9.67**
Frottage [c]	8%	25%	9.85*
Kissing genitals [b]	3%	16%	13.93***
Genital touching without permission [a]	20%	56%	20.41***
Subject masturbated victim [b]	3%	13%	7.84*
Victim masturbated subject [b]	2%	11%	9.68**
Subject performed oral sex on victim [b]	3%	19%	24.27***
Forced anal penetration [b]	3%	14%	9.97**
Developmental Factors:			
Special classes [a]	21%	53%	5.31*
Physical disabilities [a]	< 1%	5%	8.05**
Psychiatric hospital admissions [a]	18%	47%	6.21*
Psychotropic medications [a]	24%	60%	8.00**
Anxiety disorder [b]	8%	23%	7.69*
PTSD [b]	17%	55%	64.21***
Enuresis [b]			

Note. [a] $df = 1$, [b] $df = 2$, [c] $df = 3$. *$p<.05$; **$p<.01$; ***$p<.001$.

Unique Patterns of Behavior in Maltreated Children

Child maltreatment of all types leads to a variety of negative consequences for the victim. When a parent or caregiver perpetrates the abuse, one of the most significant results is the disruption of the child's attachment to the caretaker. Thus begins a vicious cycle, beginning with the disruption of the emotional bond, which can then produce not just psychological consequences but can actually alter the neurological development of the child. This can then produce deficits, which may then alienate the caretaker even more, and thus results in further abuse. The child may manifest symptoms of ADHD including hyperactivity, impulsivity, and poor judgment. Disruption of the function of the left hemisphere has been associated with difficulty in controlling emotions, angry outbursts, and difficulty reacting appropriately to minor stressors. Disruption of the attachment bond impairs the ability to interact with others, and because this relationship does not provide reinforcement, the child ceases to conform their behavior to the expectations of others, thus making it more difficult to facilitate positive interpersonal experiences. Adult sex offenders have been found to have symptoms associated with insecure attachment patterns, predisposing these individuals to inappropriate sexual behavior (Marshall, 1989, 1993; Marshall & Marshall, 2000).

Table 10: Analysis of Variance (ANOVA) Sexual Abuse: Psychiatric Factors, Placement Factors, and Sexualized Behaviors

Psychiatric Factors:	No	Yes	F	df
Age of first psychiatric admission	M = 10.8	M = 9.4	18.35***	1, 417
Number of psychiatric admissions	M = 2.4	M = 3.7	13.80***	1, 367
Age of first mental health treatment	M = 8.4	M = 6.9	25.90***	1, 619
Placement Factors:				
Time spent with bio mother (months)	M = 112.8	M = 95.5	14.46***	1, 629
Time spent with bio father (months)	M = 82.7	M = 59.6	9.86**	1, 454
Age first foster home placement	M = 8.4	M = 7.1	10.95***	1, 512
Total number different caretakers	M = 4.1	M = 4.6	7.82**	1, 645
Total number different living situations	M = 9.1	M = 10.5	8.07**	1, 637
Number residential placements	M = 1.7	M = 2.2	12.98***	1, 645
Time in residential placements (months)	M = 17.7	M = 27.5	16.82***	1, 491
Age first residential placement	M = 12.4	M = 11.4	14.06***	1, 523
Sexualized Behaviors:				
Number of sexual abuse victims	M = 2.5	M = 3.5	13.25***	1, 635
Number of male child victims †	M = 1.3	M = 1.4	5.69*	1, 278
Sexualized aggression	M = .62	M = .81	9.55**	1, 632
Age first inappropriate behavior	M = 11.0	M = 9.2	40.35***	1, 550
Age first hands-on inappropriate behavior	M = 11.1	M = 9.6	25.77***	1, 509
Total separate incidents	M = 6.8	M = 11.6	18.55***	1, 605

Note. [a] df = 1, [b] df = 2, [c] df = 3. *p<.05; **p<.01; ***p<.001.

†Male child must be at least 4 years younger than subject.

Following the model that we have discussed in this chapter, children who are subjected to abuse and neglect have a high likelihood of developing an attachment disorder associated with behavioral problems which may be learned or may be the outcome of biologically-based impairments. The pattern of these behavioral disorders may then be different, based upon the different types of abuse or neglect or a combination thereof. To assess this theory the patterns of physically, sexually, severely psychologically abused, and severely neglected children as well as children who had witnessed domestic violence, all of whom had engaged in sexually inappropriate behavior, were studied.

This study does suffer from some methodological limitations. The subjects were children whose custody had been assumed by the Department of Social Services, either before or as a consequence of sexually inappropriate behavior, and had been subjected to multiple types of abuse. This chapter simply compares children who experienced the most severe forms of each type of abuse but there was much overlap in the sample. The interaction of abuse variables and protective variables will help us to understand the variety of outcomes.

Conclusion

This chapter has explored the effects of different types of familial abuse on a group of children with sexualized behaviors, who are under the custody or care of the Massachusetts Department of Social Services. All of these children had engaged in some type of sexually inappropriate behavior. Additionally, the vast majority of these children had been born into highly dysfunctional families. This chapter has explored the theoretical relationship between the maltreatment these children received in these families and their subsequent patterns of behavior.

We have discussed a model that starts with specific types of abuse, which may lead to disruption of the attachment bond, resulting in maladaptive behavior, which further aggravates the already disturbed relationship to the caretaker. At some point the relationship may become so dysfunctional that the child is removed from the home and placed in an alternative living situation. Whether as a result of the child's negative behavior or the vagaries of the child welfare system, the child may be subjected to multiple placements, which further impedes the likelihood that the child will be able to form a stable emotional bond to others. Depending upon the nature of the child's abusive background, a variety of problematic behaviors emerge. Eventually an adult may be produced who is neither able to relate to or care about others or desires to conform his behavior so as to gain the approval and affection of his fellow human beings. Furthermore, his ability to tolerate stress, engage in problem solving behaviors, modulate his emotions, or follow the dictates of society may have been severely compromised.

The authors have received a federal grant that will allow further exploration on how many of these youngsters have gone on to commit crimes as adults and perhaps to identify relevant risk factors that predict future dysfunctional behavior. In the meantime, this study provides a glimpse at the incredible expenditure in terms of resources and human suffering that child abuse may produce.

References

Ainsworth, M. D. S., Blehar, M. C., Waters, E., & Wall, S. (1978). *Patterns of attachment: A psychological study of the strange situation.* Hillsdale, NJ: Erlbaum.

Alessandi, S. M. (1991). Play and social behavior in maltreated preschoolers. *Development and Psychopathology, 3,* 191-205.

Alston, J. (2000). Correlation between childhood bipolar I disorder and reactive attachment disorder, disinhibited type. In T. Levy (Ed.), *Handbook of attachment interventions* (pp. 193-242). San Diego, CA: Academic Press.

American Academy of Pediatrics (2002). *Failure to make children feel valued and loved causes lasting damage.* Retrieved January 8, 2004 online at: www.childtrends.org

American Psychiatric Association (2000). *Diagnostic and statistical manual of mental disorders,* 4th Edition, Revised. Washington, DC: American Psychiatric Association.

Awad, G. A., Saunders, E. & Levene, J. (1984) A clinical study of male adolescent sex offenders. *International Journal of Offender Therapy and Comparative Criminology,* 20, 105-116.

Becker, J. V. & Hunter, J. A. (1997). Understanding and treating child and adolescent sexual offenders. *Advances in Clinical Child Psychology,* 19, 177-197.

Becker, J. V., & Stein, R. M. (1994). Is sexual erotica associated with sexual deviance in adolescent males? *International Journal of Law and Psychiatry,* 14, 85-95.

Boney-McCoy, S., & Finkelhor, D. (1995). Psychosocial sequelae of violent victimization in a national youth sample. *Journal of Consulting and Clinical Psychology,* 63, 726-736.

Boney-McCoy, S., & Finkelhor, D. (1996). Is youth victimization related to trauma symptoms and depression after controlling for prior symptoms and family relationships? A longitudinal, prospective study. *Journal of Consulting and Clinical Psychology,* 64, 1406-1416.

Borduin, C. M., Henggeler, S. W., Blaske, D. M. & Stein, R. J. (1990). Multisystemic treatment of adolescent sexual offenders. *International Journal of Offender Therapy and Comparative Criminology,* 34(2), 105-113.

Bowlby, J. (1940). The influence of early environment in the development of neurosis and neurotic character. *International Journal of Psycho-Analysis,* 1, 154-178.

Bowlby, J. (1944). Forty-four juvenile thieves: Their characters and home-life. *International Journal of Psycho-Analysis,* 25, 19-52.

Bowlby, J. (1969). Attachment and loss: Vol. 1: *Attachment.* NY: Basic Books.

Bowlby, J. (1973). Attachment and loss. Vol. 2: *Separation.* NY: Basic Books.

Bowlby, J. (1980). Attachment and loss. Vol. 3: *Loss, sadness and depression.* NY: Basic Books.

Briere, J., & Elliott, D. M. (2003). Prevalence and psychological sequelae of self-reported childhood physical and sexual abuse in a general population sample of men and women. *Child Abuse & Neglect,* 27, 1205-22.

Brown, J., Cohen, P., Johnson, J. G., & Smailes, E. M. (1999). Childhood abuse and neglect: Specificity of effects on adolescent and young adult depression and suicidality. *Journal of the American Academy of Child and Adolescent Psychiatry,* 38(12), 1490-6.

Bumby, K. M., & Bumby, N. H. (1997). Adolescent female sexual offenders. In B. K. Schwartz & H. K. Cellini (Eds.). *The sex offender: Volume II: New insights, treatment innovations, and legal developments,* (pp. 10.1-10.16). NJ: Civic Research Institute.

Burton, D. L., Nesmith, A. A., & Badten, L. (1997). Clinical views on sexually aggressive children and their families: A theoretical exploration. *Child Abuse and Neglect,* 21, 157-710.

Burton, D. L., & Schatz, R. (2003). *Meta-analysis of the abuse rates of adolescent sexual abusers.* Paper presented at the 8th International Family Violence Conference. Portsmouth, NH.

Campis, L.B., Hebden-Curtis, J. & Demaso, D.R. (1993) Developmental differences in detection and disclosure of sexual abuse. *Journal of the American Academy of Child and Adolescent Psychiatry,* 32,920-924.

Carlson, B. E. (1984). *Children's observations of interpersonal violence: A risk factor for lifelong problems among a nationally representative sample of American men and women.* Report of the Twenty-Third Ross Roundtable. Columbus, OH: Ross Laboratories.

Center for Sex Offender Management. (1999). U*nderstanding juvenile sexual offending behavior.* Silver Springs, MD: Author.

Center for Social Work Research. (1997). Retrieved online 11/25/03 at: http://www.utexas.edu/research/cswr/projects/pj0027.html

Child Trends and Center Research (2004a). *Child abuse and neglect: Media handbook.* Washington, DC: Child Trends.

Child Trends and Center Research (2004b). *Early child development in social context: A chart book.* New York: The Commonwealth Fund.

Chu, J. A. (2001). A decline in the abuse of children? *Journal of Trauma and Dissociation,* 2 (2), 1-4.

Chu, J. A. (1998). *Rebuilding shattered lives.* NY: Wiley & Sons.

Cicchetti, D., Lynch, M., Shank, S. & Manly, J. (1992). An organizational perspective on peer relations in maltreated children. In R. D. Parke & G. W. Ladd (Eds.). *Family-peer relationships: Modes of linkage.* (pp. 345-383). Hillsdale, NJ: Lawrence Erlbaum Associates, Inc.

Cooper, C.L., Murphy, W.D. & Haynes, M.R. (1996). Characteristics of abused and non-abused adolescent sexual offenders. *Sexual Abuse: A Journal of Research and Treatment,* 8, 105-119.

Crain, W. (2000). *Theories of development: Concepts and applications.* (4th Ed.). NJ: Pearson Education.

Crittenden, P.M., Claussen, A.H. & Sugarman, D.B. (1994). Physical and psychological maltreatment in middle childhood and adolescence. *Development and Psychopathology*, 6, 145-164.

Crouch, J. L., Hanson, R. F., Saunders, B. E., Kilpatrick, D. G., & Resnick, H. S. (2000). Income, race/ethnicity, and exposure to violence in youth. Results from the National Survey of Adolescents. *Journal of Community Psychology*, 28, 625-641.

Damon, W., & Eisenberg, N., (Eds.), (1998). *Social, emotional and personality development: Handbook of child psychology* (p. 817). New York: Wiley and Sons.

DeBellis, M. D. (1999). Developmental traumatology: Neurobiological development in maltreated children with PTSD. *Psychiatric Times*, 16 (9), 1-5.

DeBellis, M. D., Baum, A.S., & Birmaher, B (1999). A.E. Bennett Research Award. Developmental traumatology. Part 1: Biological stress systems. *Biological Psychiatry* 45(10), 1259-1270.

DeBellis, M. D., Keshavan, M. S., Clark, D. B., Casey, B. J., Giedd, J. N., Boring, A. M., Frustaci, K. and Ryan, N. D. (1999). Developmental traumatology: Brain development, Part 1. *Biological Psychiatry*, 45, 1259-1270.

DeMause, L. (1974). The evolution of childhood. In L. DeMause (Ed.) *The history of childhood*. New York: Souvenir Publishing.

Dinwiddie, S., Heath, A. C., Dunne, M. P., Bucholz, K. K., Madden, P. A.,Slutske, W. S., Bierut, L. J., Statham, D. B., & Martin, N. G. (2000). Early sexual abuse and lifetime psychopathology: A co-twin-control study. *Psychological Medicine*, 30, 41-52.

Dodge, K.A., Pettit, G.S. & Bates, J. E. (1997). How the experience of early physical abuse leads children to become aggressive. In D. T. Cicchetti (Ed.), *Rochester Symposium on Developmental Psychology*, 263 Rochester: Rochester University Press. (p. 277).

Edelson, J.L. (1999). Problems associated with Children's witnessing domestic violence. Retrieved online on 1/23/2004 from: http://www.vaw.umn.edu/documents/vawnet/witness/witness.html

Egeland,B. & Farber, E.A. (1984). Infant-mother attachment: Factors related to its development and changes over time. *Child Development*, 55, 753-771.

Egeland, B., Sroufe, L. A. & Erickson, M. (1983). The developmental consequences of different patterns of maltreatment. *Child Abuse & Neglect*, 7, 459-469.

Fantuzzo, J. W. & Mohr, W. K. (1999). Prevalence and effects of child exposure to domestic violence, in R. E. Behrman (Ed.). *The future of children: Domestic violence and children*. Los Altos, CA: The David and Lucile Packard Foundation (Winter, 1999), 21-32.

Fergusson, D. M., Horwood, L. J., & Lynskey, M. T. (1996). Childhood sexual abuse and psychiatric disorder in young adulthood: II. Psychiatric outcomes of childhood sexual abuse. *Journal of the American Academy of Child an Adolescent Psychiatry*, 34, 1365-1374.

Fehrenbach, P. A., Smith, W. Monastersky, C. & Deisher, R. W. (1986). Adolescent sex offenders: Offender and offense characteristics. *American Journal of Orthopsychiatry*, 56(2), 225-233.

Finkelhor, D., Hotaling, G., Lewis, J. A. & Smith, C. (1990). Sexual abuse in a national survey of adult men and women: Prevalence, characteristics, and risk factors. *Child Abuse and Neglect*, 14, 19-28.

Ford, M. E. & Linney, J.A. (1995). Comparative analysis of adolescent sexual offenders, violent non-sexual offenders, and status offenders. *Journal of Interpersonal Violence*, 10, 56-70.

Friedrich, W. N., Beilke, R. L., & Urquiza, A. J. (1987). Children from sexually abusive families: A behavioral comparison. *Journal of Interpersonal Violence*, 2, 391-402.

Friedrich, W. N., & Luecke, W. J. (1988). Young school-age sexually aggressive children. *Professional Psychology: Research and Practice*, 19(2), 155-164.

Fromm, S. (2001). *Total estimated cost of child abuse and neglect in the United States: Statistical evidence.* Retrieved online January 2, 2005 at www.preventchildabuse.org.

Gale, J., Thompson, R. J., Moran, T., & Sack, W. H. (1988). Sexual abuse in young children: Its clinical presentation and characteristic patterns. *Child Abuse and Neglect*, 12, 163-171.

Garbarino, J. (1999). *Lost boys: Why our sons turn violent and how we can save them.* New York: The Free Press.

Garbarino, J. Guttman, E. & Seely, J. (1986). *The psychologically battered child: Strategies for identification, assessment and intervention.* San Francisco, CA: Jossey-Bass.

Gil, E. & Johnson, T. C. (1993). *Sexualized children: Assessment and treatment of sexualized children and children who molest.* Rockville, MD: Launch Press.

Goldston, D. B., Turnquist, D. C. & Knutson, J. F. (1989). Presenting symptoms of sexually abused girls receiving psychiatric services. *Journal of Abnormal Psychology*, 98, 314-317.

Greenough, W., Gunnar, M., Emde, N., Massinga, R., Shonkoff, J. P. (2002). The impact of the caregiving environment on young children's development: Different ways of knowing. *Zero to Three*, 21, 16-23.

Groth, A. N. (1977). The adolescent sexual offender and his prey. *International Journal of Offender Therapy and Comparative Criminology*, 21, 249-254.

Hartman, R.L. (1990). Children in a careless society. *Social Work*, 35, 482-487.

Haskett, M.E. & Kishner, J.A.(1991). Social interactions and peer perceptions of young physically abused children. *Child Development*, 62,979-990.

Haugaard, J. J., & Hazan, C. (2004). Recognizing and treating uncommon behavioral and emotional disorders in children and adolescents who have been severely maltreated: Reactive Attachment Disorder. *Child Maltreatment*, 9(2), 154-160.

Herschkowitz, N., Kagan, J., & Zilles, K. (1999). Neurobiological bases of behavioral development in the second year. *Neuropediatrics*, 30, 221-230.

Hirschberg, D. & Riskin, K. (1994). *Female adolescent sexual offenders in residential treatment: Characteristics and treatment implications.* Retrieved online 11/25/03 from www.germainelawrence.org/web/fasot.html

Horowitz, K., Weine, S., & Jekel, J. (1995). PTSD symptoms in urban adolescent girls: Compounded community trauma. *Journal of the American Academy of Child and Adolescent Psychiatry* 34, 1353-1361.

Howes-Plotkin, D., & Twentyman, C. (1984). A multimodel assessment of behavioral and cognitive deficits in abused and neglected preschoolers. *Child Development*, 55, 794-802.

Hughes, H. M., Parkinson, D., & Vargo, M. (1989). Witnessing spouse abuse and experiencing physical abuse: "A double whammy?" *Journal of FamilyViolence*, 4, 197-209.

Hunter, J.A. & Figueredo, A. J. (2000). The influence of personality and history of sexual victimization in the prediction of juvenile perpetrated child molestation. *Behavior Modification*, 24, 241-263.

Karen, R. (1998). *Becoming attached: First relationship and how they shape our capacity to love.* New York: Oxford University Press.

Karr-Morse, K. (1996). *The state of America's children.* Washington, DC: Children's Defense Fund.

Kaufman, J. & Cicchetti, D. (1989). Effects of maltreatment on school-age children's socio-emotional development: Assessment in a day-care setting. *Developmental Psychology*, 25, 516-524.

Kendler, K. S., Bulik, C. M., Silberg, J., Hettema, J. M., Myers, J., & Prescott, C. A. (2000). Childhood sexual abuse and adult psychiatric and substance use disorders in women: An epidemiological and co-twin control analysis. *Archives of GeneralPsychiatry*, 57, 953-959.

Knight, R. A. & Prentky, R. A. (1993). Exploring characteristics for classifying juvenile sex offenders. In H. E. Barbaree, W. L. Marshall, & S. M. Hudson (Eds.), *The juvenile sex offender* (pp. 45-79). New York: The Guilford Press.

Kobayashi, J., Sales, B. D., Becker, J. V., Figueredo, A. J. & Kaplan, M. S. (1995). Perceived parental deviance, parent-child bonding, and child sexual aggression. *Sexual Abuse: A Journal of Research and Treatment, 7,* 25-44.

Kolko, D. J., Maser, J. T. & Weldy, S. R. (1988). Behavioral/emotional indicators of sexual abuse in psychiatric inpatients: A controlled comparison with physical abuse. *Child Abuse and Neglect,* 12, 529-541.

Koop, C. E., & Lundberg, G. (1992). Violence in America: A public health emergency. *Journal of the American Medical Association,* 22, 3075-3076.

Kubik, E. K., Hecker, J. E. & Righthand, S. (2002). Adolescent females who have sexually offended: Comparisons with delinquent adolescent female offenders and adolescent males who have sexually offended. *Journal of Child Sexual Abuse,* 11 (3), 63-83.

Lieberman, A. F., & Zeanah, C. H. (1995). Disorders of attachment in infancy. *Child and Adolescent Psychiatric Clinic of North America,* 4(3), 571-587.

Main, M., & Solomon, J. (1986). Discovery of an insecure-disorganized/disoriented attachment pattern. In T. B. Brazelton & M. Yogman (Eds.), *Affective development in infancy* (pp.95-124). Norwood, NJ: Ablex.

Marshall, W. L. (1989). Intimacy, loneliness and sexual offenders. *Behavioral Research and Therapy,* 27, 491-503.

Marshall, W. L. (1993). The role of attachment, intimacy, and loneliness in the etiology and maintenance of sexual offending. *Sexual and Marital Therapy,* 8, 109-121.

Marshall, W. L. & Marshall, L. E. (2000). The origins of sexual offending. *Trauma Violence and Abuse,* 1,(3), 250-263.

Marshall, W. L., Serran, G. A., & Cortoni, F. A. (2000). Childhood attachments, sexual abuse, and their relationships to adult coping in child molesters. *Sexual Abuse: A Journal of Research and Treatment,* 12, 17-26.

Mathews, F. (1996). T*he invisible boy: Revisioning the victimization of male children and teens.* Toronto: Health Canada.

Mathews, R., Matthews, J.K. & Speltz, K. (1989). *Female sexual offenders: An exploratory study.* Orwell, VT: The Safer Society Press.

Mathews, R., Hunter, J. A. & Vuz, J. (1997). Adolescent female sexual offenders: Clinical characteristics and treatment issues. *Sexual Abuse: A Journal of Research and Treatment,* 9, 187-199.

Milloy, C. D. (1994). A comparative study of adolescent sex offenders and non-sex offenders. *Washington State Institute for Public Policy.*

Molnar, B. E., Berkman, L. F., & Buka, S. L. (2001). Psychopathology, childhood sexual abuse and other childhood adversities: relative links to subsequent suicidal behaviour in the US. *Psychological Medicine*, 31, 965-77.

Molnar, B. E., Buka, S. L., & Kessler, R. C. (2001). Child sexual abuse and subsequent psychopathology: results from the National Comorbidity Survey. *American Journal of Public Health*, 91, 753-60.

Mullen, P. E., Martin, J. L., Anderson, J. C., Romans, S. E., & Herbison, G. P. (1993). Childhood sexual abuse and mental health in adult life. *British Journal of Psychiatry*, 163, 721-732.

National Incident Based Reporting System, Uniform Crime Reporting Program, (1999). Washington, DC: Bureau of Justice Statistics, Office of Justice Programs, United States Department of Justice.

Nelson, E. C., Heath, A. C., Madden, P. A., Cooper, M. L., Dinwiddie, S. H., Bucholz, K. K., Glowinski, A., McLaughlin, T., Dunne, M. P., Statham, D. J., & Martin, N. G. (2002). Association between self-reported childhood sexual abuse and adverse psychosocial outcomes: Results from a twin study. *Archives of General Psychiatry*, 59 (2), 139-45.

Patterson, R. J., & Moran, G. (1988). Attachment theory, personality development, and psychotherapy. *Clinical Psychology Review*, 8, 611-636.

Peluso, E. & Putnam, N. (1996). Case study: Sexual abuse of boys by females. *Journal of the American Academy of Child and Adolescent Psychiatry*, 35, 51-54.

Perry, B. D. (2001). *Violence and childhood: How persisting fear can alter the developing child's brain.* Retrieved 1/24/04 online at: http://www.childhoodtrauma.org/CTAMATERIALS/Vio_child.asp

Prentky, R. A., Knight, R. A., Sims-Knight, J. E., Straus, H., Rokous, F., & Cerce, D. (1989). Developmental antecedents of sexual aggression. *Development and Psychopathology*, 1, 153-169.

Ray, J. A., & English, D. L. (1995). Comparison of female and male children with sexual behavior problems. *Journal of Youth and Adolescents*, 24, 439-451.

Rosado, L. M. (1999). *The pathways to youth violence: How child maltreatment and other risk factors lead children to chronically aggressive behavior.* Philadelphia: American Bar Association Juvenile Justice Center.

Ryan, G. (1989). Victim to victimizer: Rethinking victim treatment. *Journal of Interpersonal Violence*, 4, 325-341.

Shield, A. & Cicchetti, D. (1998) Reactive aggression among maltreated children: The contributions of attention and emotional dysregulation. *Journal of Clinical Child Psychology*, 27(4), 381-395.

Shore, R. (1997). *Rethinking the brain: New insights into early development.* New York, NY: Families and Work Institute.

Singer, M.I., Miller, D.B., Guo, S., Slovak, K. & Fuerson, T (1998). T*he mental health consequences of children's exposure to violence.* Cleveland, OH: Cayahoga County Community Mental Health Research Institution, Mandel School of Applied Social Sciences. Case Western Reserve University.

Smallbone, S.W. & Dadds, M. R. (2000). Child attachment & coercive sexual behaviors. *Sexual Abuse: A Journal of Research and Treatment,* 12(1), 3-15.

Smallbone, S. W. & McCabe, B. A. (2003). Childhood attachment, childhood sexual abuse and onset of masturbation among adult sexual offenders. *Journal of Research and Treatment,* 15, 1-10.

Stein, J. A., Golding, J. N., Siegel, J. M., Burnam, M. A., & Sorenson, S .B. (1988). Long-term psychological sequelae of child sexual abuse. In G. E. Wyatt & G. J. Powell (Eds.), *Lasting effects of child sexual abuse* (pp. 135-154). Newbury Park, CA: Sage Publications.

Straus, M. (1974). Cultural and organizational influences on violence between family members. In R. Prince & D. Barried (Eds.), *Configurations: Biological and cultural factors in sexuality and family life.* Washington, D.C. Health.

Szilagyi, M. (1998). The pediatrician and the child in foster care. *Pediatric Review,* 19, 39-50.

Teicher, M.H. (2000). Wounds that time won't heal: The neurobiology of child abuse. *Cerebrum: The Dana Forum on Brain Science,* 50-67.

Teicher, M. H. (March, 2002). Scars that won't heal: The neurobiology of child abuse. *Scientific American,* 68-75.

U.S. Department of Justice (March, 1998). *Violence by intimates: Analysis of data on crimes by current or former spouses, boyfriends, and girlfriends.* Bureau of Justice Statistics. Washington DC: Author.

van der Kolk, B.A. (1994). The body keeps the score: Memory and the evolving psychobiology of posttraumatic stress. *Harvard Review of Psychiatry,* 1, 253-265.

van der Kolk, B.A. (1997). The psychobiology of posttraumatic stress disorder. *Journal of Clinical Psychiatry,* 58, 16-24.

Ward, S.M., Hudson, S.M., & Marshall, W.L. (1996). Attachment style in sex offenders: A preliminary study. *The Journal of Sex Research,* 33, (1), 17-26.

Wen, P. (2004). Cruel bargain: Parents lose custody to aid teens. *The Boston Globe.* Boston, MA. December 19, 2004.

Widom, C. S. & Weeks, R. (1998). *Early childhood victimization among incarcerated male felons.* Washington, DC: US Department of Justice, National Institute of Justice.

Wieckowski, E., Hartsoe, P., Mayer, A., & Shortz, J. (1998). Deviant sexual behavior in children and young adolescents: Frequency and patterns. *Sexual Abuse: A Journal of Research and Treatment,* 10, (4), 293-304.

Williamson, J.M., Borduin, C.M. & Howe, B.A. (1991). The ecology of adolescent maltreatment: A multilevel examination of adolescent physical abuse, sexual abuse and neglect. *Journal of Consulting and Clinical Psychology,* 59,449-457.

Wilson, S. L. (2001). Attachment disorders: Review and current status. *Journal of Psychology,* 135, 37-52.

World Council of Churches Press Update, (2004). "WCC launches year to focus on overcoming violence in the US during service honoring Dr. Martin Luther King, Jr." January 13, 2004.

Worling, J. R. (1995). Sexual abuse histories of adolescent male sex offenders: Differences on the basis of the age and gender of their victims. *Journal of Abnormal Psychology,* 104, 610-613.

CHAPTER NINETEEN

DOMESTIC VIOLENCE, CHILDHOOD PHYSICAL ABUSE, AND JUVENILE SEX OFFENSE

MELISSA M. SISCO
JUDITH V. BECKER
MATTHEW SANDERS
AND
DAVID HARVEY

Introduction

Youth in our society are subjected to various forms of victimization. Finkelhor, Ormrod, Turner, and Hamby (2005), conducted a comprehensive national survey of children between the ages of 2 and 17 living in the United States to estimate a one year incidence of childhood victimization across gender, race, and developmental stage. Information was obtained through telephonic interview with children and parents. Results indicated that of every 1,000 children, 530 had experienced a physical assault in the study year, 82 had experienced sexual victimization, and 357 had witnessed violence or experienced some form of indirect victimization during the study year. Of those physically abused, in 83% of the cases, the perpetrator had been a family member. In respect to lifetime abuse and exposure to domestic violence, one in eight children had been the victims of maltreatment during the study year (Finkelhor & Ormrod, 2001). Child physical abuse makes up about 22% of all maltreatment situations reported to police (Perry, Mann, Palker-Corell, Ludy-Dobson, Schick, 2002) and 19% of all violent crimes committed against juveniles (Finkelhor & Ormrod, 2001). Approximately 5 to 15% of males and 20 to 25% of women experience childhood sexual abuse (Berliner & Elliot, 2002), while approximately 25% of U.S. children witness domestic violence during childhood (Osofsky, 2003).

The prevalence of abuse and domestic violence exposure among juvenile sex offenders is substantially higher. In an assessment of 256 juvenile sex offenders, ranging in age from 13 to 18, from court affiliated treatment programs across five states, 66.4% of these youth reported being physically abused by a father or step-father, 70% reported childhood sexual abuse, approximately 75% had been exposed to some form of sexual or physical violence toward females, and 53% had witnessed a male relative physically assault a female (Hunter, Figueredo, Malamuth, Becker, & Mack, 2003). These significantly higher rates of victimization and exposure to violence among juvenile sex offenders raise the following questions: a) Is there a relationship between domestic violence, childhood victimization, and youthful sexual offending? b) If so, what is the nature of these associations? and c) What are the implications of these findings for assessment and intervention in a clinical setting? This chapter will review literature delineating factors that place youth at risk of sexually offending with a specific focus on domestic violence and childhood physical abuse.

To explore the possible relationship between domestic violence, childhood physical abuse, and juvenile sexual crimes, this chapter will discuss: 1) definitions, theories, and consequences of domestic violence; 2) definitions, theories, and co-occurrence of childhood physical abuse; and 3) definitions, theories, and factors associated with juvenile sexual offenses.

Domestic violence defined

Definitions of domestic violence differ within various theoretical frameworks. Feminist ideologies emphasize the central nature of the victimized woman by using terms such as "battered women's syndrome", a controversial term that is not always legally permissible in court. Among systems driven theories, domestic violence is termed "familial violence" or "partner abuse", indicating the important systemic context that shapes the act. The clinical classification system uses the term "domestic violence", which is defined as the presence of one *severe* act or two moderate acts of physical aggression occurring within one year that lead one's partner to be fearful or to sustain injury to an extent that requires medical attention (American Psychiatric Association, 2002). Though straight forward, this definition is limited in that it only focuses on the marital or intimate partner relationship and it also seems to miss the most damaging facets of domestic violence, psychological and sexual aggression.

Women are typically the focus of domestic violence theories since women are victimized eight times more frequently than men in this manner (Greenfield, Rand, Craven, Flaus, Perkins, Ringel, Warchol, Maston, & Fox, 1998) and typically in an array of modalities. In a recent meta-analysis, Tjaden & Thoennes (2000) found that, while 7.7% of women reported being victimized solely through spousal sexual abuse and 22.1% reported solely physical assault, the majority (24.8%) had experienced both spousal sexual and physical assault by intimate partners during the lifetime. Psychological abuse accompanied physical abuse in the majority of cases. Simply put, half of U.S. women have experienced domestic violence in which sexual violence and psychological manipulation occurred more often than not (Marshall & Holtzworth-Munroe, 2000; Tjaden & Thoennes, 2000).

Theories of Domestic Violence

General aggression model

The general aggression model posits that all forms of inter-relational aggression stem from an overall predisposition towards aggression. This aggressive nature may stem from personality flaws, biological predisposition, or mental illness. In support of this theory, people who are physically and sexually aggressive towards a romantic partner also tend to be outwardly violent towards others and psychopathic (Kropp & Hart, 2000; Holtzworth-Munroe & Stuart, 1994; Marshall & Holtzworth-Munroe, 2000).

Status inconsistency theory

The family unit is a cohesive group of individuals each asserting a degree of control through decision making, purchasing of tangible goods, or associating with others contingent on the resources that each party provides (Kurz, 1989). Family members who feel insecure about their degree of resource contribution in comparison to social norms may enforce control over other members through more overt force if the subtler forms of control are perceived to be unavailable or ineffective. Violence against a domestic partner is thought to be one form of forceful family interaction that the perpetrator uses to counteract feelings of lack of control (Kurz, 1989). Researchers who endorse this model typically use the language of "family violence" to emphasize the central role of the family in creating situations of domestic violence (Yick, 2001).

Feminist power theory

Inequality between the sexes is at the base of all violence against women including physical, sexual, and emotional abuse in this model (Dobash & Dobash, 1979). The basic concept is that domestic violence is rooted in power and domination over women. For this reason, most researchers that subscribe to the feminist theory will use descriptive terms that emphasize the victimization of women (e.g., "wife beating") while avoiding terms that neutralize the gender message associated with violence (Yick, 2001). In feminist theory, the only way of eliminating violence against women is ensuring equality of the sexes.

Intergenerational transmission of violence

The notion of intergenerational violence describes why each one of the above theories would create aggression prone individuals, specifically offending youth from domestically violent homes. In this model, an abusive behavioral pattern is learned through exposure to domestic violence or personal victimization during childhood. This theory suggests that since identification with the aggressor circumvents feeling victimized, children from abusive homes may opt to model abusive behaviors. Bevan and Higgins (2002) recently found that the level of childhood abuse, neglect, and exposure to parental domestic violence each directly increased the frequency of domestically violent behaviors in current relationships.

Child Physical Abuse Defined

The Third National Incidence Study of Child Abuse and Neglect defined physical abuse as present when a person under the age of 18 was injured or was at great risk of being injured as a result of having been hit with the hand or other object, kicked, shaken, thrown, burned, stabbed, or choked by a parent or surrogate-parent (Sedlak & Broadhurst, 1996).

There is a high probability that domestic abusers will also abuse their children. In fact, 30 to 59% of abusers target both spouses and children (Carlson, 1984; Wright, Wright, & Isaac, 1997). In addition to the risks associated with marital conflict (Shipman, Rossman & West, 1999), the probability of child abuse is increased by parental histories of childhood victimization (Clarke, Stein, Sobota, Marisi, & Hanna 1999), caregiver depression or distress (Hazen, Connelly, Kelleger, Landsverk, & Barth, 2004; Shipman et al., 1999) and parental illegal behaviors (Child Welfare League of America, 2001). The family structure also seems to impact the risk of child abuse; when the biological father is absent, children are twice as likely to be mal-treated (Mash & Wolf, 1991; Radhakrishna, Bou-Saada, & Hunter, 2001).

Certain characteristics further increase the risk that a child will be targeted for mal-treatment; younger children are more prone to neglect while increasing age brings greater risk for sexual assault, as does being female. Children with disabilities or dif-ficult temperaments are more prone to all types of abuse (e.g., Blackson, Tarter, & Mezzich, 1993; Schilling & Schinke, 1984).

Though there are many factors that seem to increase the co-occurrence of domestic violence and child abuse, it is unclear why some domestic violence perpetrators sole-ly target the spouse while others also target their children and how to predict this col-lateral type of victimization (Shipman et al., 1999).

Theories of Child Physical Abuse

Overall, physical abuse is theorized as an exaggeratedly aggressive parental reaction to stress in conjunction with a distorted perception of insult or threat (Kolko, 2002). The following three theories discuss some of the mechanisms that may explain these phenomena:

The stress and coping model

Hillson and Kupier (1994) noted that child physical abuse hinges on the multi-level interactions of the individual, family, and social-system. Specifically, this model hypothesizes that the psychological state of the individual, familial hostility, mal-adaptive styles of communication, limited availability of social support resources, and situational stress culminate to create a circumstance conducive to child physical abuse. Domestic violence would heighten the risk of child abuse according to this model since family hostility would be high and family interactions would be charac-terized by ineffective communication tactics and social isolation.

Social information-processing model

Milner (2000) posits that abuse takes place in a series of three stages. The first stage involves the parent observing the behavior of the child, the second involves the par-ent interpreting that behavior in the given social context, and finally, the parent reacts to the conception formed in these first two stages. If the first two stages result in feel-ings of distress or threat, the parent may react in an explosive fashion regardless of the validity of the initial interpretation. Due to the generally reactive nature of domes-tic violence perpetrators or possibly the hypervigilance incurred on ongoing victims of domestic violence, childhood gestures may be more likely to be perceived as insulting and punished more severely by both parents in domestically violent families.

Discipline mediation model

Greenwald, Bank, Reid and Knutson (1997) hypothesized that childhood physical abuse stems from inadequate parental development of child management and discipline skills. In support of this hypothesis, Greenwald and colleagues (1997) found that disciplinary strategy mediated the relationship between stress and physically punitive tactics. The chaotic boundaries associated with domestic violence may account for inconsistent discipline and thus sporadic severely punitive repercussions in this model.

The Consequences of Domestic Violence and Physical Abuse

Exposure to violence has major ramifications on the physical and psychological development of children. The negative effects of child abuse have proven to be amplified by exposure to additional trauma such as domestic violence (Edleson, 1999). Impacts of child physical abuse and domestic violence exposure include the following:

Developmental delay. Childhood abuse and exposure to domestic violence have been found to impede language development (McLaren & Brown, 1989), social competence (Katz, 1992), emotional expression and development, and psychosocial growth (Hunter, Figueredo, Malamuth, & Becker, 2003). These delays may, in turn, decrease a child's resources for relieving frustration and receiving social support, thus, decreasing a child's ability to cope with a toxic home environment.

Poor academic progress. Children who have witnessed domestic violence or experienced abuse are at increased risk of academic failure, truancy, and poor educational communication skills (Berliner & Elliot, 1996; Shipman et al., 1999). These children may be limited to lowered socioeconomic status as adults due to a lack of academic requisites necessary to secure higher paying employment.

Teenage parenthood. Herrenkohl, Herrenkohl, Egolf, and Russo (1998) found that early parenthood was directly related to childhood abuse and neglect. Since dropping out of school so commonly follows teenage pregnancies, abused children are at an even higher risk for unsuccessful education, poor employment outcomes, and reduced resource availability.

Depression and anxiety. Childhood victimization leads to an increased risk of low self-esteem, depression and anxiety disorders (Herrenkohl et al., 1998; Mancini, Van Ameringen, & MacMillan, 1995). Interestingly, this increased risk of depression is compounded when a person self-identifies his/her childhood experiences as abusive (Carlin, Kemper, Ward, & Sowell, 1994).

Suicidality. Children who witness or are subjected to physical violence exhibit more feelings of hopelessness, worthlessness, and insufficient attachment than non-exposed children (Fantuzzo, 1990). In turn, abused children are more likely to endorse suicidal ideation and thoughts of self-harm (Baldry, & Winkel, 2003). For instance, sexually abused girls are 2 to 4 times more likely to attempt suicide in adulthood while sexually abused boys are 4 to 11 times more likely (Molnar, Berkman, & Buka, 2001).

Aggression and externalizing behaviors. Children who have been exposed to domestic violence commonly misinterpret non-threatening situations as dangerous and, as a result, respond in a chronically aggressive fashion (Dodge, Pettit & Bates, 1997; Kolko, 2002; Shipman et al., 1999). This phenomenon is particularly evident in resistance to interactions with adults. Failure to properly connect with authority figures in combination with this propensity to respond aggressively may predispose a child to fail in structured settings, thus heightening risks of antisocial peer groups, behavioral and emotional problems, conduct disorder, and delinquency (Rogers & Miglani, 2001).

Perpetration of future partner violence. A 20-year follow-up study found that witnessing domestic violence during childhood was the strongest predictor of perpetrating domestic violence in adulthood (Ehrensaft, Cohen, Brown, Smailes, Chen, & Johnson, 2003). Experiencing sexual or physical violence in childhood or witnessing a parent experience either abuse doubled the likelihood of becoming a domestic violence perpetrator, for men, and a victim, for women, in adulthood. Experiencing all four conditions increased this risk four fold. (Whitfield, Anda, Dube, & Felitti, 2003).

Antisocial symptoms, personality disorder, and subsequent youthful offending. Luntz and Widom (1994) found that childhood victimization was a strong predictor of lifetime antisocial behavior and diagnosis of antisocial personality disorder. The more violence a child experienced, the more likely the child was to participate in increasing amounts of antisocial behaviors, regardless of socioeconomic status, race, gender, or age. Specifically, childhood neglect was the strongest predictor of adult arrest (Grogan-Kaylor & Otis, 2003). In addition, exposure to physical violence predicted drug abuse (McClellan, Farabee, & Crouch, 1997). Famularo, Kinscherff, Fenton, and Bolduc (1990) found that 52% of non-criminal troubled youth and 42% of criminal delinquents had substantiated histories of abuse. Exposure to domestic violence has shown to directly predict more frequent offenses, subsequently increasing the likelihood of youthful sexually coercive behaviors (Hunter, Figueredo, Malamuth, & Becker, 2003).

Antagonistic hypermasculinity. Experiencing physical abuse is indirectly predictive of belief in negative gender stereotypes that embody subjugation of women and value aggressive masculine tactics (Hunter et al., 2003). These beliefs are highly correlated with the perpetration of sexual crimes (Burt, 1980).

Youthful sexually coercive behaviors. Kobayashi, Sales, Becker, Figueredo, and Kaplan (1995) found that physical abuse perpetrated by the father against a male child increased the risk of youthful perpetration of sexually coercive behaviors. In addition, Kobayashi and colleagues (1995) noted several factors that may mediate the role from physical abuse and exposure to domestic violence to the perpetration of sexual violence in youth such as 1) extent of attachment to the family, 2) gender of the primary abuser, and 3) bonding with parents.

The body of literature reviewed above indicates that youth who are exposed to domestic violence and/or physical abuse are at increased risk for experiencing mental health problems and engaging in norm violating behaviors. The exact mechanisms through which this occurs remain in need of future study.

Juvenile Sex Offenses Defined

In general, a sexually motivated behavior may be defined as criminally offensive if the age, familial relation, consent status, or types of contact between the parties are not in line with societal norms and legislation. Sexual crimes vary in degree ranging from hands on crimes like rape to non-contact crimes like indecent sexual exposure. For the purposes of this chapter, sexual offenses are defined as sexually motivated behaviors towards another individual who is unable or unwilling to consent to such acts.

In 2002, 2.3 million children under the age of 18 were arrested in the U.S.; 24,120 of these arrests were for sexual crimes (Snyder, 2004) and approximately 3 out of 4 juvenile rape convictions resulted in a sentence of incarceration (Rainville & Smith, 2003). Juveniles were responsible for 12% of all rapes committed in the U.S. during 2002 (Rainville & Smith, 2003). Research has been ongoing in an attempt to delineate the etiologies of juvenile sexual offending behavior and to determine what factors place youth at greater risk of re-offending (Hunter, Figueredo, Malamuth, & Becker, 2004). Though not all juveniles will pursue ongoing criminal habits, many will revisit the mental health and/or correctional systems. In one study, youthful sexual offenders were significantly more likely to commit sexual offenses in early adulthood than their delinquent counterparts, 10% and 3% respectively (Sipe, Jensen, & Everett, 1998).

Theories of Juvenile Sexual Violence

"There are as many definitions of the term 'sex offender' as there are individuals doing the defining" (Schwartz, 1997). As pointed out by Chaffin, Letourneau, and Silovsky (2002), many juvenile sexual offenders share little more in common than a prosecution for a sexual offense. Though clinical samples of juvenile sexual offenders have been generally characterized by poor social skills, nonsexual delinquency, learning disabilities, depression, and impulse dysregulation, Hunter, Figueredo, Malamuth, and Becker (2003) found evidence to support dimensional etiological differences among juvenile sexual offenders. The primary dimension splits the types of offenders who target prepubescent children, from those who target individuals who have reached or exceeded puberty. In addition, juvenile sex offenders were divided according to whether the aggressive act was committed "reactively" in response to misinterpreted cues or "proactively" without provocation. Finally, the level of aggression utilized during the offense is a vital categorical descriptor of the offender.

These conceptualizations form the basic classification system used to determine the treatment and legal punishment that will be established for youthful offenders. Another consideration that plays a prominent role in the legal system is motivation (i.e., causation). Causation of sexual violence can be thought of along several paradigms; biological predisposition, ego imbalance, evolutionary adaptation, neurosis, learned behavior, diathesis stress induced, or a combination of the above. In addition to these considerations, it is currently unclear whether there are differences between the causes of youthful and adult sexual violence. Some of the theories of juvenile sexual crimes are as follows:

Conditioned response

Theoretically, repetitive behaviors in childhood shape the development of the hypothalamus and endocrine systems which indirectly regulate sexual behaviors (Allen, 1940). In childhood, the family provides the framework for which behaviors are appropriate to be repeated and which are not. Through adolescence and early adulthood, children begin to experiment with different sexual strategies repeating only those that produced rewarding responses. Thus, sexual acts may become part of one's sexual repertoire through experimentation, fantasy, forced repetition, or by modeling if the act was followed by a pleasurable physiological or emotional response. If a child consistently receives sexual gratification in response to a specific behavior, he/she may begin to opt for that specific behavior (Schwartz, 1997).

Learning theory

Children learn a system of interpreting the world through aligning with familial/cultural beliefs, media norms, and peer interactions. As a whole, U.S. families are commonly plagued with unspoken expectations about how boys should act; strong, sexually focused, and emotionally inexpressive. The media seems to bolster displays of these characteristics. For example, a recent study found that exposure to popular violent music increased overt displays of aggression in teens (Miller, 1991) and heightened hostility in college students (Anderson, Carnagey & Eubanks, 2003).

Many programs treating individuals who have committed sexual offenses involve a behavioral plan for reducing the recurrence of inappropriate sexual behaviors. It has been hypothesized that these behaviors are maladaptive coping strategies in response to the traumas of familial abuse (Schwartz, 1997). In support of this hypothesis, adverse family environments have been found to correlate with increasing frequencies of juvenile offending (Ge, Donnellan, & Wenk, 2001). This being the case, and especially considering that domestic violence is most typically perpetrated against women and is rarely an isolated event, youth who are exposed to domestic violence against women may be at risk for modeling that behavior.

Theory of cognitive distortions

The cognitive distortion model hypothesizes that sexual offense patterns predominantly result from the ability to ignore the negative consequences of sexual coercion through excusing or rationalizing one's inappropriate behaviors. A study by Lonsway and Fitzgerald (1995) found that believing that women are innately incapable or wicked and that they must be guided by a man's "instructive" aggression predicted almost 40% of the variation in acceptance of rape. It might be hypothesized that if children endorse these beliefs that they are exposed to in the family of origin, they may be at risk to commit sexual offenses. The general idea coincides with differential association theories of delinquency in which deviant patterns of thoughts and behavior are thought to be the byproducts of successfully socializing in a criminally deviant surrounding (Miner & Crimmins, 1997). Cognitive distortions are commonly targeted in relapse prevention since they seem to maintain criminal patterns.

Social control theory

This theory hinges on the concept that humans are born essentially self-serving and hedonistic. It is only the value that one learns to place on the community and the needs of others that control this drive towards hedonistic activities. In this model, juveniles that sexually offend may not have sufficient enough ties to the community, family, or societal system to overpower the drive for self fulfillment (Miner & Crimmins, 1997).

Developmental model

Malamuth, Sockloskie, Koss, and Tanaka (1991) hypothesized that the true root of youthful sexually coercive behaviors can often begin in home experiences of physical and sexual abuse. In addition to this primary cause, Malamuth and colleagues (1991) hypothesized two pathways that may increase the likelihood of adolescent perpetrations of sexual coercion. Males who endorse a strong machismo characteristic known as hypermasculinity and express social dominance through sexuality are at increased risk of perpetrating sexually coercive acts.

Diathesis stress model

Attitudes and behavioral patterns are clearly learned to a large extent, yet the shared genetic quality between the perpetrator of domestic violence and his aggressive child raises the concept of biological determinism. In such cases, hormonal, chromosomal, or neurological dysfunction may be transmitted from parent to child genetically. These physiological risk factors may create a lowered ability to deal effectively with certain types of situations. However, not all children who inherit the physiological predisposition would necessarily become aggressive since only persons who inherit the risk factors and are exposed to particular types of stress would commit acts of sexual aggression. In support of this theory, situational stresses from personal frustration, poverty, isolation, lack of familial support, or relationship discord have been found to increase the likelihood of interpersonal violence including coercive sexuality (Bishop & Leadbeater, 1999; Demaris, Benson, Fox, Hill, & Van Wyk, 2003; Masser & Abrams, 1999; Sedlak & Broadhurst, 1996).

Though the majority of findings indicate some relation between physical abuse and exposure to domestic violence and later expressions of aggression, most of these endeavors employed relatively small samples. The following section evaluates the impact of family violence on sex offending behavior.

The Relationship of Domestic Violence, Physical Abuse, and Sex Offenses

To explore the effects of childhood victimization and court interactions, English and Widom (2003) cataloged all child dependency petitions that were filed in an Urban Midwest county between 1980 and 1984. Although 2,262 petitions had been filed, 187 cases were excluded because further transcripts were not available and 1,198 cases were excluded because the children were not made dependants of the county. This left 877 children, ranging in age from 1 to 11 years of age, who were referred to the court due to neglect, physical abuse, emotional abuse, sexual abuse, or abandonment. A control group was matched to the dependency group based on gender, ethnicity, and approximate socioeconomic status (n=877). All children were reevaluated in 1998.

As indicated by the original findings of English and Widom (2004), childhood physical abuse was associated with a greater number of arrests in childhood and a greater number of arrests for violent crimes throughout the time span in all except Native American children.

Given the paucity of research on domestic violence and sex offending among youth, the data set was accessed through the University of Michigan's NACJD archival library and reanalyzed. We executed a multiple regression to explore the impact of the presence of domestic violence, as indicated in the original court dependency petition, on the presence of childhood physical abuse, the number of juvenile arrests, and arrests through the follow-up period for violent crimes and/or sexual crimes. There were a total of 1,754 cases available in the original data set (English & Widom, 2004) of which 1,357 were excluded due to missing data. Subsequently, 397 children, 237 boys and 133 girls, were included in this analysis. Exposure to domestic violence was hypothesized to be associated with greater numbers of juvenile arrests, arrests for violence, and sexual crimes during the follow-up. In addition, children who were exposed to domestic violence were hypothesized to be more likely to experiences personal physical victimization. The results indicated that experiences of childhood physical abuse (b=0.031, p=0.07) and arrests for sexual crimes through young adulthood (b=0.013, p=0.052) were associated with exposure to domestic violence, but not at a statistical significant level. The other variables appeared unrelated.

Pearson's correlation matrixes were produced separately for girls and boys to examine response to domestic violence and physical abuse. From the Pearson correlation matrix of the boys (see table 1), juvenile violence was positively correlated to the number of juvenile offenses. All other correlations were not significant. From the Pearson correlation matrix for girls (see table 2), exposure to domestic violence was related to increasing amounts of juvenile arrests, the presence of violence in the juvenile arrest record, and sexual arrests during young adulthood. Girls who had been exposed to domestic violence were slightly more likely to have also experienced physical abuse than their non-exposed counterparts. For girls, physical abuse was positively related to juvenile violence and sexual offenses. In addition, girls who committed more crimes were more likely to commit juvenile violence and were more likely to commit sexual crimes during early adulthood. Juvenile violence was positively correlated to sex crimes.

Table 1: Pearson's Correlation Matrix for boys (n=237). A re-analysis of a dataset accessed through the University of Michigan's NACJD Archival library (English & Widom, 2003). The top row indicates the correlation and the second row in each cell represents the significance level.

	DV	Physical Abuse	Juvenile Arrests	Juvenile Violence	Sexual Arrests
DV	1.00000				
Physical Abuse	0.0116 0.8504	1.00000			
Juvenile Arrests	0.0225 0.7154	0.0280 0.6493	1.00000		
Juvenile Violence	0.0622 0.3113	0.0622 0.3113	**0.5508** **<0.0001**	1.00000	
Sexual Arrests	-0.0556 0.3658	-0.1139 0.0631	0.0155 0.8013	0.0631 0.3042	1.00000

Table 2: Pearson's Correlation Matrix for girls (n=130). A re-analysis of a dataset accessed through the University of Michigan's NACJD Archival library (English & Widom, 2003). The top row indicates the correlation and the second row in each cell represents the significance level.

	DV	Physical Abuse	Juvenile Arrests	Juvenile Violence	Sexual Arrests
DV	1.00000				
Physical Abuse	**0.3083** **0.0004**	1.00000			
Juvenile Arrests	**0.3006** **0.0005**	0.1230 0.1634	1.00000		
Juvenile Violence	**0.2850** **0.0010**	**0.4114** **<0.0001**	**0.4050** **<0.0001**	1.00000	
Sexual Arrests	**0.3075** **0.0004**	**0.1776** **0.0433**	**0.55806** **<0.0001**	**0.2307** **0.0083**	1.00000

Several limitations of the re-analysis must be noted. First, a large portion of the sample was not included in the current data due to missing information. Only 84 cases reported acts of domestic violence, so the sample size was relatively small. This sample may have failed to detect a large degree of criminality due to lack of the follow-up sample size and selection bias of those who remained in contact. Second, the original data set combined arrests for prostitution with indecent exposure. Approximately half of the people who had been arrested for sex offenses fell into this category. The way the data set was collected made it unclear how many of these arrests were due to prostitution. Third, the multiple regression used only examines direct relationships. The small associations may imply either that other key variables were excluded from the current analysis or that an unexplored indirect relationship among current variables exists. Finally, all variables are defined by a stipulated portion of court records. This limited view of criminality results in a greatly conservative estimate of the abusive events that initially placed the child in contact with the court system as well as the ongoing criminal behaviors that the individual may have engaged in without being detected by law enforcement.

Discussion

Experiencing physical abuse as a youth and witnessing domestic violence have major mental health implications for children including depression, anxiety, poor social skills, learning problems, and juvenile delinquency. The secondary data analysis presented did not support a strong direct relationship for boys between perpetration of sexual offenses in young adulthood and exposure to domestic violence and/or physical abuse. There were, however, several factors that may have made these findings an artifact of the procedure and thus the current findings may not be truly representative. Interestingly, the finding that exposure to domestic violence does not directly predict the prevalence of sexual offenses mirrors a study of recidivism among convicted juvenile sex offenders conducted by Hunter, Figueredo, Malamuth, and Becker (2003) that implied an indirect impact. Domestic violence may have an indirect effect on juvenile sex offending through the creation of psychosocial deficits which mediate the influence of domestic violence exposure on both sexual and nonsexual juvenile offenses (Hunter et al., 2004). Johnson and Knight (2000) found that sexual abuse, physical abuse, juvenile delinquency, and alcohol abuse, preceded aggressive acts and hostile masculinity all indirectly predicted acts of sexual coercion. Specifically, physical abuse indirectly increased the risk of coercive sexual behaviors through increasing juvenile delinquency, alcohol abuse, peer aggression, misogynistic fantasy, and hypermasculinity.

For girls, domestic violence was related positively to an increased likelihood of general arrests, juvenile violence, and sexual crimes during the follow-up period. Physical abuse was positively related to increased risks of juvenile violence and sex crimes during young adulthood.

Little is known of the specific risk factors that increase the likelihood of youthful sexual violence though several factors may decrease these risks (see chapter 13). More research is needed to determine the impact that domestic violence may have on youthful sexual offending.

Clinical implications

The importance of improving domestic violence and abuse screening techniques is imperative with consideration of detrimental effects of domestic violence and physical abuse. Implementation of standard abuse screening in a pediatric setting has increased recognition of possible cases of abuse 1,500% (Sisk, 2002). When abuse is detected, victims may be unwilling to verify such acts in order to protect the offender-family union or in fear of further retaliation. The victim may also be unable to recognize the acts as abusive (Mihalic, & Elliott, 1997). Treatment providers must be educated in an effort to minimize the offender's influence over the family's ability to *safely* disclose incidents of violence. Screening in environments where the offender is not likely to be present, like a medical office or school, may be the only means of effectively assessing the true home environment (AAPCCAN, 1998). Efforts must be made to correct the practical issues such as lack of time, knowledge, or office protocol that make effective screening uncommon (Erickson, Hill, & Siegel, 2001; Lapidus, Beaulieu, Cooke, Gelven, Sherman, Duncan, & Banco, 2002; Wright et al., 1997). In addition, parents should be surveyed for concerns about any of their children's current conduct including sexual behaviors. Adolescents should be asked if they have had any thoughts or have engaged in any sexual behaviors that they are concerned about. Providers treating juveniles who have committed sexual offenses need to do in-depth assessments as to whether these youth have witnessed domestic violence or experienced physical abuse. As part of a comprehensive treatment program, any personal victimization or exposures to violence need to be addressed in treatment.

In cases where sexual offenders have experienced abuse or domestic violence, treatment providers have long debated the viability of including victimization in the therapeutic focus arguing that victim posturing will dilute responsibility. Conversely, McMackin, Leisen, and Cusack (2002) found that 95% of juvenile males currently in a sex offense treatment program had been exposed to a trauma which was perceived to "trigger" their current sexual offense in 85% of the cases. In 62.5% of the cases, the trauma involved domestic violence. Normally, defenses exist to protect us from intense emotional pain, but they can run awry if excessively relied upon (Vaillant, 1998). Without intervention, many of these dysfunctional defenses remain intact throughout the lifetime. For many offenders, early exposure to violence manifests as immature and sometimes explosive responses to interpersonal conflict. In short, violence experienced in childhood often predisposes young men to resolve conflicts with aggression. However controversial, origins of powerlessness must be addressed in order to prevent perpetration of future sexual violence.

In conclusion, domestic violence was found to be highly correlated to the frequency of childhood crimes, the presence of juvenile violence, and the occurrence of sexual crimes during young adulthood for girls. In addition, physical abuse was correlated to the presence of juvenile violence and sexual crimes in early adulthood for girls. Boys did not exhibit a direct effect from domestic violence or physical abuse in relation to juvenile criminality, juvenile violence, or sexual crimes in young adulthood. Girls who committed more crimes and/or crimes of violence were more likely to commit sexual crimes in young adulthood. More research is needed to understand the difference between the impact of domestic violence and physical abuse on girls versus boys. The lack of direct relation from domestic violence to juvenile patterns of sexual criminality may indicate the need to explore mediating and moderating factors that would change the way boys were impacted by domestic violence. Both abuse and exposure to domestic violence have been found to be extremely detrimental on the development of healthy social skills and personal boundaries and may indirectly encourage youthful sexual crimes. More research is needed to determine the exact impact of domestic violence on youthful sexual behaviors.

References

Allen, C. (1940). *The sexual perversions and abnormalities: A study of the psychology of paraphilias.* London: Oxford University Press.

American Academy of Pediatrics Committee on Child Abuse and Neglect (AAPC-CAN) (1998). The role of the pediatrician in recognizing and intervening on behalf of abused women. *Pediatrics,* 101, 1091-1092.

American Psychiatric Association (2002). *Diagnostic and statistical manual of mental disorders- Text revision* (4th ed.). Washington, DC: Author.

Anderson, C.A., Carnagey, N.L., & Eubanks, J. (2003). Exposure to violent media: The effects of songs with violent lyrics on aggressive thoughts and feelings. *Journal of Personality & Social Psychology,* 84 (5), 960-971.

Baldry, A.C., & Winkel, F.W. (2003) Direct and vicarious victimization at school and at home as risk factors for suicidal cognition among Italian adolescents. *Journal of Adolescence,* 26 (6), 703-716.

Berliner, L., & Elliott, D. (1996). Sexual abuse of children. In J. Briere, L. Berliner, J. Bulkley, C. Jenny, & T. Reid (Eds.), *The APSAC handbook on child maltreatment* (pp. 55-78). London: Sage Ltd.

Bevan, E., & Higgins, D.J. (2002). Is domestic violence learned? The contribution of five forms of child maltreatment to men's violence and adjustment. *Journal of Family Violence,* 17 (3), 223-245.

Bishop, S., & Leadbeater, B. (1999). Maternal social support patterns and child maltreatment: Comparison of maltreating and nonmaltreating mothers. *American Journal of Orthopsychiatry,* 69, 172-181.

Blackson, T.C., Tarter, R.E., & Mezzich, A.C. (1993). Interaction between childhood temperament and parental discipline practices on behavioral adjustment in preadolescent sons of substance abuse and normal fathers. *American Journal of Drug & Alcohol Abuse,* 22(3), 335-348.

Burt, M.R. (1980). Cultural myths and support for rape. *Journal of Personality and Social Psychology,* 38, 217-230.

Carlin, A.S., Kemper, K.J., Ward, N.G., & Sowell, H. (1994). The effect of differences in objective and subjective definitions of childhood physical abuse on the estimates of its incidence and relationship to psychopathology. *Child Abuse & Neglect,* 18 (5), 393-399.

Carlson, B. (1984). Children's observations of interparental violence. In A. R. Roberts (Ed.), *Battered women and their families* (pp. 147- 167). New York: Springer Press.

Chaffin, M., Letourneau, E., Silovsky, J.F. (2002). Adults, adolescents, and children who sexually abuse children: A developmental perspective. In J. Briere, L. Berliner, J. Bulkley, C. Jenny, & T. Reid (Eds.), *The APSAC handbook on child maltreatment* (pp.205-232). London: Sage Ltd.

Child Welfare League of America (2001). *Alcohol, other drugs, & child welfare.* (2001/0-87868-839-0/#8390). Washington, DC: Author.

Clarke, J., Stein, M., Sobota, M., Marisi, M., & Hanna, L. (1999). Victims as victimizers: Physical aggression by persons with a history of childhood abuse. *Archives of Internal Medicine,* 159, 1920-1924.

DeMaris, A., Benson, M.L., Fox, G.L., Hill, T., & Van Wyk, J. (2003). Distal and proximal factors in domestic violence: A test of an integrated model. *Journal of Marriage and Family,* 65 (3), 652-667.

Dobash, R.E., & Dobash, R.P. (1979).*Violence against wives: A case against the patriarchy.* New York: Free Press.

Dodge, K.A., Pettit, G.S., & Bates, J.E. (1997) How the experience of early physical abuse leads children to become chronically aggressive. In D. Cicchetti, & S.L. Toth (Eds.), *Developmental perspectives on trauma: Theory, research, and intervention* (pp.263-288). Rochester: University of Rochester Press.

Edleson, J.L. (1999). Children's witnessing of adult domestic violence. *Journal of Interpersonal Violence,* 14 (8), 839-870.

Ehrensaft, M.K., Cohen, P., Brown, J., Smailes, E., Chen, H., & Johnson, J.G. (2003). Intergenerational transmission of partner violence: A 20-year prospective study. *Journal of Consulting and Clinical Psychology,* 71 (4), 741-753.

English, D.J., & Widom, C.S. (2003). Childhood victimization and delinquency, adult criminality, and violent criminal behavior in a large urban county in the northwest united states, 1980-1997 [Computer file]. ICPSR version. Seattle, WA: State of Washington Department of Social and Health Services, Office of Children's Administration Research [producer]. Ann Arbor, MI: Inter-university Consortium for Political and Social Research [distributor].

Erickson, M.J., Hill, T.D., & Siegel, R.M. (2001). Barriers to domestic violence screening in the pediatric setting. *Pediatrics,* 108, 98-102.

Famularo, R., Kinscherff, R., Fenton, T., & Bolduc, S.M. (1990). Childhood matreatment histories among runaway and delinquent children. *Clinical Pediatrics,* 29 (2), 713-718.

Fantuzzo, J.W. (1990). Behavioral treatment of the victims of child abuse and neglect. *Behavior Modification,* 14 (3), 316-339.

Finkelhor, D., & Ormrod, R. (2001). Child abuse reported to police. *Juvenile Justice Bulletin*. Washington, DC: Office of Juvenile Justice and Delinquency Prevention.

Finkelhor, D., Ormrod, R., Turner, H., & Hamby, S.L. (2005). The victimization of children and youth: A comprehensive, national survey. *Childhood Maltreatment*, 10 (1), 5-25.

Ge, X., Donnellan, M.B., & Wenk, E. (2001). The development of persistent criminal offending in males. *Criminal justice and behavior*, 28 (6), 731-755.

Greenfield, L.A., Rand, M.R., Craven, D., Flaus, P.A., Perkins, C.A., Ringel, C., Warchol, C., Maston, C., & Fox, J.A. (1998). *Violence by intimates: Analysis of data on crimes by current or former spouses, boyfriends, and girlfriends.* (NCJ-167237). Washington, DC: U.S. Department of Justice.

Greenwald, R.L., Bank, L., Reid, J.B., & Knutson, J.F. (1997). A discipline-mediated model of excessively punitive parenting. *Aggressive Behavior*, 23, 259-280.

Grogan-Kaylor, A., & Otis, M.D. (2003). The effect of childhood maltreatment on adult criminality: A tobit regression analysis. *Child Maltreatment: Journal of the American Professional Society on the Abuse of Children*, 8 (2), 129-137.

Hazen, A.L., Connelly, C.D., Kelleger, K., Landsverk, J., & Barth, R. (2004). Intimate partner violence among female caregivers of children reported for maltreatment. *Child Abuse & Neglect*, 28 (3), 301-319.

Herrenkohl, E.C., Herrenkohl, R.C., Egolf, B.P., & Russo, M.J. (1998). The relationship between early maltreatment and teenage parenthood. *Journal of Adolescence*, 21 (3), 291-303.

Hillson, J.M.C., & Kupier, N.A. (1994). A stress and coping model of child maltreatment. *Clinical Psychology Review*, 14 (4), 261-285.

Holtzworth-Munroe, A., & Stuart, G.L. (1994). Typology of male batterers: Three subtypes and the differences among subtypes. *Psychological Bulletin*, 116, 476-497.

Hunter, J.A., Figueredo, A.J., Malamuth, N.M., Becker, J.V., & Mack, J. (2003). *Juvenile sex offender typology.* Washington, DC: OJJDP.

Hunter, J.A., Figueredo, A.J., Malamuth, N.M., & Becker, J.V. (2003). Juvenile sex offenders: Toward the development of a typology. *Sexual Abuse: A Journal of Research and Treatment*, 15 (1), 27-47.

Hunter, J.A., Figueredo, A.J., Malamuth, N.M., & Becker, J.V. (2003). Juvenile sex offenders: Toward the development of a typology. *Sexual Abuse: A Journal of Research and Treatment*, 15(1), 27-48.

Hunter, J.A., Figueredo, A.J., Malamuth, N.M., & Becker, J.V. (2004). Developmental pathways in youth sexual aggression and delinquency: Risk factors and mediators. *Journal of Family Violence*, 19 (4), 233-242.

Johnson, G.M., & Knight, R.A. (2000) Developmental antecedents of sexual coercion in juvenile sexual offenders. *Sexual Abuse: A Journal of Research and Treatment* 12(3), 165-178.

Katz, K.B. (1992). Communication problems in maltreated children: A tutorial. *Journal of Childhood Communication Disorders*, 14 (2), 147-163.

Kobayashi, J., Sales, B.D., Becker, J.V., Figueredo, A.J., & Kaplan, M.S. (1995). Perceived parental deviance, parent-chlid bonding, child abuse, and child sexual aggression. *Sexual Abuse: A Journal of Research and Treatment*, 7(1), 25-44.

Kolko, D. (2002). Child physical abuse. In J. Briere, L. Berliner, J. Bulkley, C. Jenny, & T. Reid (Eds.), *The APSAC handbook on child maltreatment* (pp.21-50). London: Sage.

Kropp, P.R., & Hart, S.D. (2000). The Spousal Assault Risk Assessment (SARA) guide: Reliability and validity in adult male offenders. *Law and Human Behavior*, 24 (1), 101-118.

Kurz, D. (1989). Social science perspective in wife abuse: Current debates and future directions. *Gender & Society*, 3, 489-505.

Lapidus, G., Beaulieu, E., Cooke, M., Gelven, E., Sherman, K., Duncan, M., & Banco, L. (2002). A statewide survey of domestic violence screening behaviors among pediatricians and family physicians. *Archive of Pediatry & Adolescent Medicine*, 156, 332-336.

Lonsway, K.A., & Fitzgerald, L.F. (1995). Attitudinal antecedents of rape myth acceptance: A theoretical and empirical reexamination. *Journal of Personality and Social Psychology*, 68 (4), 704-711.

Luntz, B.K., & Widom, C.S. (1994). Antisocial personality disorder in abused and neglected children grown up. *American Journal of Psychiatry*, 151 (5), 670-694.

Malamuth, N.M., Sockloskie, R. J., Koss, M.P., & Tanaka, J.S. (1991). Characteristics of aggressors against women: Testing a model using a national sample of college students. *Journal of Consulting and Clinical Psychology*, 59, 670-681.

Mancini, C., Van Amerigen, M., & MacMillan, H. (1995). Relationship of childhood sexual and physical abuse to anxiety disorders. *Journal of Nervous & Mental Disease*, 183 (5), 309-314.

Marshall, A.D., & Holtzworth-Munroe, A. (2000). Varying forms of husband sexual aggression: Predictors and subgroup differences. *Journal of Family Psychology*, 16 (3), 286-296.

Mash, E.J., & Wolfe, D.A. (1991). Methodological issues in research on physical child abuse. *Criminal Justice & Behavior*, 18 (1), 8-29.

Masser, B., & Abrams, D. (1999). Contemporary sexism: The relationship among hostility, benevolence, and neosexism. *Psychology of Women Quarterly, 23*, 503-517.

McClellan, D.S., Farabee, D., & Crouch, B.M. (1997). Early victimization, drug use, and criminality: A comparison of male and female prisoners. *Criminal Justice & Behavior, 24* (4), 455-476.

McLaren, J., & Brown, R.E. (1989). Childhood problems associated with abuse and neglect. *Canada's Mental Health, 37* (3), 1-6.

McMackin, R.A., Leisen, M.B., Cusack, J.F., & Litwin, P. (2002). The relationship of traumatic exposure to sex offending behavior among male juvenile offenders. *Journal of Child Sexual Abuse, 11* (2), 25-58.

Mihalic, S.W., & Elliott, D. (1997). If violence is domestic, does it really count? *Journal of Family Violence, 12* (3), 293-311.

Miller, M.A. (1991). *The Effects of music videos on adolescent meaning construction and attitudes toward physical violence as a method of conflict resolution.* Casper, WY: Counseling and Student Services.

Milner, J.S. (2000). Social information processing and child physical abuse: Theory and research. In D.J. Hansen (Ed.), *Nebraska symposium on motivation 46, 1998: Motivation and child maltreatment* (pp.39-84). Lincoln: University of Nebraska.

Miner, M.H., & Crimmins, C.L.S. (1997). Adolescent sexual offenders: Issues of etiology and risk factors. In B. K. Schwartz & H.R. Cellini (Eds.), *The sex offender: New insights, treatment innovations and legal developments* (pp. 9-1-9-15). Kingston, NJ: Civil Research Institute.

Molnar, B.E., Berkman, L.F., & Buka, S.L. (2001). Psychopathology, childhood sexual abuse and other childhood adversities: Relative links to subsequent suicidal behaviour in the US. *Psychological Medicine, 31* (6), 965-977.

Osofsky, J.D. (2003). Prevalence of children's exposure to domestic violence and child maltreatment: Implications for prevention and intervention. *Clinical Child & Family Psychology Review, 6* (3), 161-170.

Perry, B.D., Mann, D., Palker-Corell, A., Ludy-Dobson, C., & Schick, S. (2002). Child physical abuse. In D. Levinson (Ed.), *Encyclopedia of Crime and Punishment* (pp.197-202). Thousand Oaks: Sage publications.

Radhakrishna, A., Bou-Saada, I.E., & Hunter, W.M. (2001). Are father surrogates a risk factor for child maltreatment? *Child Maltreatment: Journal of the American Professional Society on the Abuse of Children, 6* (4), 281-289.

Rainville, G.A., & Smith, S.K. (2003). Juvenile felony defendants in criminal courts. *Bureau of Justice Statistics Special Report.* Washington, DC: Office of Justice Programs.

Rogers, K.M. & Miglani, J.K. (2001). Socially and emotionally maltreated youth. In H.B. Vance, & A. Pumariega (Eds.), *Clinical assessment of child and adolescent behavior* (pp.450-472). New York: John Wiley & Sons.

Schilling, R.F., & Schinke, S.P. (1984). Personal coping and social support for parents of handicapped children. *Children & Youth Services Review*, 6 (3), 195-206.

Schwartz, B.K. (1997) Theories of sex offenders. In B.K. Schwartz & H.R. Cellini (Eds.), *The sex offender: New insights, treatment innovations and legal developments* (pp. 2-1-2-32). Kingston, NJ: Civil Research Institute.

Sedlak, A., & Broadhurst, D. (1996). *Third national incidence study of child abuse and neglect: Final report.* Washington, DC: U.S. Government Printing Office.

Shipman, K.L., Rossman, B.B.R., & West, J.C. (1999). Co-occurrence of spousal violence and child abuse: Conceptual implications. *Childhood Maltreatment: Journal of the American Professional Society on the Abuse of Children*, 4 (2), 93-102.

Sipe, R., Jensen, W.L., & Everett, R.S. (1998). Adolescent sexual offenders grown up: Recidivism in young adulthood. *Criminal Justice and Behavior*, 25 (1), 109-124.

Sisk, D. (2002, June 4). *Domestic violence screening in a pediatric clinic.* Arizona's Child Abuse Infocenter. Retrieved April 4, 2004 from http://www.ahsc.arizona.edu/acainfo/index2.htm

Snyder, H. (2004). Juvenile arrests 2002. *Juvenile Justice Bulletin.* Washington, DC: OJJDP.

Tjaden, P., & Thoennes, N. (2000). *Full report of the prevalence, incidence, and consequences of violence against women* (Rep. No. NCJ 183781). Rockville, MD: Office of Justice Programs, National Institute of Justice.

Vaillant, G.E. (1998). Adaptation to life (pp.383-386). London: Harvard University Press.

Whitfield, C.L., Anda, R.F., Dube, S.R., & Felitti, V.J. (2003). Violent childhood experiences and the risk of intimate partner violence in adults. *Journal of Interpersonal Violence*, 18 (2), 166-185.

Wright, R.J., Wright, R.O., & Isaac, N.E. (1997) Response to battered mothers in the pediatric emergency department; a call for an interdisciplinary approach to family violence. *Pediatrics*, 99, 186-192.

Yick, A.G. (2001). Feminist theory and status inconsistency theory. Violence Against Women, 7 (5), 545-559.

CHAPTER TWENTY

FAMILY MATTERS: THE IMPORTANCE OF ENGAGING FAMILIES IN TREATMENT WITH YOUTH WHO HAVE CAUSED SEXUAL HARM

JOANN SCHLADALE

Introduction

The purpose of this chapter is to address the importance of engaging family members, as an integral part of social support and healing, into treatment with youth who have caused sexual harm. It begins with research findings about family life experiences that place youth at risk for sexual harm and is followed by descriptions of numerous barriers to adequate family assessment and involvement. Solutions for overcoming such challenges are then illustrated in a collaborative approach for both residential and community-based settings. Descriptions of specific ideas such as educational material, family genograms, the trauma outcome process, narratives and therapeutic fun are examples of ways to enhance successful treatment outcomes.

This model invites youth and their family members to explore strengths and resources for healing the pain of sexual abuse. It provides practical information for integrating best practices even when resources and advanced training are limited. Ideas are predicated on research indicating that paraprofessional staff can greatly influence successful treatment outcomes (Miller, Hubble and Duncan, 1995). This approach honors the efforts of so many hard working staff who maintain a commitment to respectfully include parents, siblings, extended family, and significant others from a youth's school, church and community in the healing process.

This chapter introduces a framework embracing leading edge research in family therapy that can inform interventions with youth who have been sexually aggressive and their families. Each topic is broken down into sections with guidelines for staff from all departments. While there is significant overlap in service provision, youth care workers facilitate a broad range of interaction among children and their family members while licensed mental health clinicians facilitate intimate healing processes through structured therapy sessions. Administration and education also play critical roles in establishing a comprehensive ecological approach to stop youthful sexual harm. Each section distinguishes challenges associated with family involvement and identifies tasks necessary for successful treatment outcomes.

Family Issues Relating to Youthful Sexual Aggression

Treatment with sexually aggressive youth and their families remains an under-investigated topic in the field of mental health (Chaffin & Bonner, 1998). Interventions have often been based upon research with incarcerated adult sexual offenders that do not take into account the developmental and life cycle differences of adolescents and children. During the last fifteen years clinicians and researchers have been working diligently to make sense of complex dynamics involved in the development of sexually abusive behavior (Hermann, 1992; Ryan & Lane, 1997), ways to prevent recidivism (Knight and Prentky, 1993; Prentky, Harris, Frizzell & Righthand 2000; Minor & Crimins, 1995) and curb the tide of sexual abuse.

Literature now includes comprehensive, multidisciplinary models addressing the full continuum of care (Bengis, 1986; Henggeler, Schoenwald, Broduin, Rowland & Cunningham, 1998; Trepper & Barrett, 1989). In 1988, and 1993, the National Task Force on Juvenile Sexual Offending published reports outlining guidelines for treatment with these youth. Those documents have served as standards for agencies interested in responding to the need for treatment with this population but do not provide empirically based data for application. Efforts to piece together the therapeutic puzzle required to respond effectively to the needs of these children and families remains a significant challenge.

Research indicates that multisystemic family therapy (MST) is an empirically tested approach that influences successful treatment outcomes with delinquent youth and is cost effective. A study using MST with sexually aggressive youth shows promise with this population (Borduin, Henggeler, Blaske & Stein, 1990). Concepts derived from family systems theory, which provide the foundation for multisystemic treatment, can be integrated into all service provision. Family focused interventions need not be limited to the intensive home-based approach created by Henggeler and his colleagues. Programs do not have to struggle with an either/or dilemma of providing MST, or limiting interventions to traditional responses based primarily on outdated conventional wisdom.

Agencies intent on providing a therapeutic response to youthful sexual harm based upon best practice strategies can integrate core effective components into a broad range of settings. The potential for more cost effective, successful treatment outcomes can easily be integrated into the fabric of all service provision.

Family life experiences

Several studies of juvenile sexual offending have identified distinguishing factors prevalent in families of youth in treatment (Bagley & Shewchuk-Dann, 1991; Miner, Siekert and Ackland, 1997; Morenz & Becker, 1995). They have been described as dysfunctional (Araji, 1997), pathological (Bagley & Shewchuk-Dann, 1991), chaotic (Minor, Siekert, & Ackland, 1997) and unavailable (Smith & Isreal, 1987). Sexually aggressive children are growing up in families characterized by poor communication (Morenz & Becker, 1995; Stith & Bischof, 1996), instability, disengagement and poor attachment (Weinrott, 1996; Minor & Crimmins, 1995), high levels of parent-child conflict and marital stress (Bagley & Shewchuk-Dann, 1991; Kimball & Guarino-Ghezzi,

1996), substance abuse and mental health problems (Minor, Siekert, & Ackland, 1997). These families also have high incidences of family members who are both perpetrators and victims of sexual abuse (Pithers, Gray, Busconi & Houchens, 1998a). Pithers' study also revealed high levels of poverty in the youth's families of origin. After identifying a litany of problematic characteristics that describe families with sexually aggressive children, Araji has identified the family as the "primary source of the problem"(1997, p.87). Families of these children are often described in negative and demeaning ways.

Family centered intervention can provide the primary focus for harm reduction. All service providers can develop skills for assessing strengths and observing compassionate action that honors a family's ability to support their child and stop sexual harm.

Histories of childhood abuse, most often experienced within the family context, and witnessing family violence, are correlated with juvenile sexual aggression (Kobayashie, Sales, Becker, Figueredo & Kaplan, 1995; Ryan, Miyoshi, Metzner, Krugman & Fryer, 1996). Furthermore, Ryan and colleagues (1996) identify anger, boredom and family problems as "triggers" identified by youth who committed sexual offenses. All three factors are common elements of family experience. One study found that sexually aggressive youth who were victims of child abuse perceived a lack of family support after disclosing their victimization (Hunter & Figueredo, 1999). Factors such as age of onset of victimization, type of abuse and severity have been identified as etiological factors relating to decisions to commit sexual crimes (Prentky et al., 2000). The fact that child abuse occurs primarily within the context of family relationships that may involve intimate partner violence, parent-child harm and neglect, indicates the importance of addressing such salient factors within treatment venues that are family centered. It is only through family involvement that parents can learn and practice conflict management, boundary identification and benevolent parenting in order to reduce risk factors for sexual offending, and enhance protective factors that may deter further aggression.

Deficits in social interaction, peer relationships and isolation have been identified as significant risk factors for juvenile sexual offending (Becker, 1990; Knight & Prentky, 1993; Fehrenback, Smith, Monastersky & Deisher, 1986; Katz, 1990; Minor and Crimmins, 1995). Interpersonal skills are initiated and developed in family constellations. Additionally, antisocial behaviors and an unstable home life are predictors of recidivism (Prentky, et al., 2000; Minor, Siekert & Ackland, 1997). Issues such as these punctuate the need to intervene with the family where life skills can be enhanced and practiced. Wise staff model pro-social and benevolent behavior for parents in order to create a foundation for maintaining therapeutic change long after treatment has ended. It is imperative that interventions focus on ways to reduce antisocial behavior and counter negative influences that support such dangerous conduct. Promoting social competency across all facets of a child's ecological context can be a keystone of treatment.

Literature addressing youthful sexual aggression has consistently illustrated the importance of involving families in the therapeutic process (Bonner, Marx, Thompson & Michaelson, 1998; Gray & Pithers, 1993; Stevenson, & Wimberley, 1990; Ryan &

Lane, 1997). Recommendations are made for involving parents or guardians in the assessment and treatment process (Araji, 1997; Morenz & Becker, 1995; Becker & Hunter, 1997) and eliciting their cooperation (Gray and Pithers, 1993). Rasmussen (1999) maintains that family involvement is a critical component of effective programming and prevention of reoffenses.

We can no longer afford to pretend that utilizing group therapy as the primary treatment modality for these children is the recommended intervention of choice (Dishion, McCord & Poulin, 1999). While group and individual therapy continue to comprise the bulk of interventions with sexually aggressive youth, opportunities to impact ecological change remain woefully underutilized. By focusing on the context in which children live, and the primary relationships in their lives, we can provide much greater service to victims, the youth we serve, their families and communities (Thornton, Craft, Dahlberg, Lynch & Baer, 2002). Individual therapy still provides an avenue for confronting private struggles with honor, for considering and planning new initiatives, and for building partnership based upon support and assistance. Group therapy remains a forum for learning healthy responses to difficult interpersonal situations, processing new knowledge and receiving public support for successful initiatives. Group processes can enhance mindfulness by eliciting peer support for motivation to change.

Restraints to involving families

For the purposes of this chapter, restraints are defined as anything that gets in the way of implementing best practices for intervention. Jenkins describes restraints as "traditions, habits, and beliefs" (p.32, 1990) that prevent people from taking responsibility for their own actions. In this context restraints represent traditions, habits and beliefs that inhibit family involvement in reducing youthful sexual harm.

Systems of care

It is hard to change established patterns of care. While many professionals are committed to the idea of engaging families in treatment with sexually aggressive youth, traditional systems of care have not been conducive to family involvement. Many children are placed in residential treatment facilities significant distances from their homes, sometimes in out of state locations very far away. Financial limitations impose transportation barriers and time constraints to meaningful participation in the treatment process. Tightly packed therapeutic schedules also limit both visitation and time for family meetings.

Treatment settings for youth who have caused sexual harm can be scary places for families. Professional jargon that requires a glossary of terms to understand can be intimidating and disrespectful. Subtle elements of disregard and disdain may distinguish staff attitudes towards parents. Settings in which space limitations threaten confidentiality can restrict development of the safety and trust necessary to build therapeutic relationships.

A historical emphasis on residential care has only recently begun to give way to community-based programs. Even community-based programs focus predominantly on individual and group processes with inadequate family involvement. Logistical concerns about getting family members to attend sessions abound. Services predominately maintain a traditional focus of scheduled office visits for 'talk" therapy.

Considering home-based interventions as a primary modality for treatment flies in the face of conventional wisdom (Chaffin & Bonner, 1998). Mythology that programs should either provide MST, or maintain traditional treatment services, creates a false dichotomy and limits potential for enhancing successful treatment outcomes and exploring more cost effective interventions. When multisystemic therapy is not an option, families can still play an integral role in contributing to successful treatment outcomes regardless of where a child is receiving services.

A program's inability to provide basic introductory information and expectations for family involvement can further hinder already hesitant parents from initiating and maintaining contact. Lack of defined treatment goals for family involvement can cause confusion among all parties and result in confounding parents and creating feelings of demoralization and estrangement. Such barriers are unnecessary in service provision.

Staff

While many agency staff members provide tremendous support, care, and concern for these youth and their families, some have difficulties that can stem from transference, counter transference and experiences of parallel processes with the clients they serve (Goocher, 1994; Etgar, 1996). It is not unusual to hear well-meaning service providers refer to families in derogatory terms; engage in parent blaming; and make excuses for not involving parents in the treatment process. Behind closed doors, in clinical supervision, some staff share fears about families, and a sense of being overwhelmed by perceptions of abusive power attributed to parents and extended family members.

Professional and childcare staff seldom receive adequate specialized training for providing a therapeutic response with families of youth who have committed sexual offenses. A lack of family involvement may be characterized as "sabotage" by clients and parents, when agencies have made little effort to engage family members in warm, empathic, non-judgmental ways.

Families

Many family members have significant restraints to participation in treatment. As previously mentioned, geography can wreak havoc on involvement. Even when families have time and financial recourses, distance can be a great barrier to intimate involvement in the therapeutic process. Parental feelings of shame and guilt, and perceptions of blame, often inhibit a family's willingness to consider involvement in their child's treatment. Family secrets that may include current experiences of abuse can prevent family involvement.

Engagement

The primary treatment goal for eliminating sexually harmful behavior is to support these youth in assuming responsibility for their behavior in order to prevent future abuse. The first priority is to engage all participants in such a way that they are motivated to integrate positive change into their lives. This task involves everyone in service delivery. Clinicians, youth care workers, administrators and support staff are challenged to provide a congruent approach to all children and family members in order to provide a comprehensive therapeutic message that reflects a research based philosophy of care.

Webster's New World Dictionary defines the word "engage" as "committed to, or actively supporting a cause" (Guralnik, 1986 cite). Therapeutic engagement refers to a shared commitment between agency personnel and family members to actively support a child's effort to stop harmful sexual behavior. The rationale for such collaboration is to affirm a clear message that loving and caring adults can work together in the youth's best interest. Providing a range of services for families, and maintaining genuine commitment to engaging parents in the therapeutic process, can occur in a variety of creative and cost-effective ways.

The process of engagement is the most important step to insure successful treatment outcomes (Jenkins, 1990; Miller, Hubble & Duncan, 1995). Key elements include warmth, empathy, genuiness, and a nonjudgmental attitude (Miller et al., 1995). Therapeutic engagement involves introducing and modeling interaction based upon respect, care and concern for other human beings. This issue is well documented in family therapy literature (Durrant, 1993; Freidrich, 1990; Haley, 1976; Minuchin, 1981) and can be modeled by all staff in a treatment setting.

Engaging families in treatment is not simply providing a social stage in which introductions and superficial conversation introduce a therapeutic process (Haley, 1976). Nor is it a marketing ploy, or cheerleading effort, to convince wary family members that their child's treatment program has all the answers to their family's problems. Therapeutic engagement is not compliance. Engagement occurs when participants embark on a reciprocal therapeutic process that guides a collaborative effort at harm reduction. It is challenging, rewarding, and can make work much more fun while influencing successful treatment outcomes.

Successful therapeutic engagement embraces distrust and resistance that is normative in the early stages of treatment with youth who have caused sexual harm and their families. Open recognition of restraints to addressing the pain of sexual abuse creates a context of respect, care and concern for the development of trust in therapeutic relationships.

Family members can be prepared for a range of positive and negative affect that revelations of sexual abuse can bring about. Providing a therapeutic environment that invites participants to attend to their pain in an emotionally and physically safe manner may prevent it from being acted out in harmful ways. Program personnel and families have the ability to collaborate in the best interest of all children, family cohesion, and community safety. Courage and honesty are elicited as a means to address and heal the pain of sexual abuse in the family.

A collaborative approach

A collaborative approach is founded on the premise that youth often face the task of harm reduction in the very environment that influenced their initial decisions to commit acts of sexual harm. Historically, youth who return to their home communities after residential treatment have been alone in their efforts to maintain therapeutic change. Involving family members as a guiding principle of treatment, rather than an adjunct component, can influence an ecological effort to stop sexual abuse. Ecology is simply the relationship between a person and the various elements of their environment. In this case, a youth's ecology is made up of his or her family, neighbors, school, church, and community.

This approach has evolved, in part, from exploration of common factors that influence successful treatment outcomes in psychotherapy (Hubble, Duncan & Miller, 1999; Miller et al., 1995). Recent analyses of outcome studies indicate four primary factors that influence successful change in psychotherapy (Hubble et al., 1999). The central indicator (40%) for success is the client, in this case, the youth and family we serve. A child and his or her family member's strengths, resources, social support, living environment and serendipitous experiences are all critical contributions to change. Each client's perception of the therapeutic relationship contributes 30% towards effective results. This perception is defined by a participant's ideas of warmth, trustworthiness, affirmation, encouragement of therapeutic risk taking, respect and empathy. Identifying positive expectations of the therapeutic process and instilling a sense of hope for the future account for 15% of therapeutic impact. Finally, therapeutic techniques also influence 15% of successful outcomes. Preparing and supporting youth and family members to learn to take good care of themselves by risking exploration into new understanding; embracing difficult emotions and vulnerability; and taming violent and sexually aggressive behavior are critical elements of psychotherapy. A collaborative approach, congruent with the four factors, attempts to engage youth and families through a respectful and courteous process of introducing clearly defined program information and structure, such as program descriptions, handbooks, policies and procedures. Utilizing the factor of hope and expectancy can influence service providers to share stories of successful treatment experiences with other families involved in the process. Staff can model open, direct communication and desired behavior for the youth and family members.

One critical element of a collaborative approach involves identifying and assessing potential social support network members who will help a youth throughout the treatment process. One young man told staff that he wanted his imprisoned father to be an active part of his treatment and social support network. Upon investigation, corrections personnel revealed that the youth's father was incarcerated for sexually abusing his daughter, the client's sister. Of equal concern was information in the court reports indicating that the youth may have been involved in the molestation. The young man expressed a high level of anger when the treatment team would not support his father's involvement with the youth until the father was actively taking responsibility for his own criminal behavior and participating in the sexual offender treatment program in the prison. Staff worked diligently with the youth to identify, and involve other family members who could act as role models and mentors to provide clear messages opposing sexual aggression.

Collaboration with this youth and family involved assessing dangerousness; acknowledging intergenerational dynamics of abuse; addressing anger brought about by destructive family ties and loyalty; supporting the youth's ambivalence about criminal behavior; and helping him to explore other avenues for support and encouragement. Collaboration can require restrictions on family involvement that threatens successful outcomes.

A competency-based foundation (Berg, 1994; Durrant, 1993; Waters & Lawrence, 1993) reinforces strengths that each youth and his or her family members reveal in an effort to stop sexual abuse. This approach assumes a continuous process of assessment based upon all available resources (Bonner et al., 1998; Ryan & Lane, 1997; Prescott, in press). All staff can maintain vigilance for indications of competence and skills that clients reveal in day-to-day interactions.

Integrating underlying assumptions of systems theory (Hoffman, 1981) is central to a collaborative approach. Maintaining a belief that the sum is greater than the whole of its parts, illustrates the importance of engaging an entire family in a commitment to stop sexual abuse. This philosophy embraces an assumption that many people working together have a greater opportunity for success than a few working in isolation. It also illuminates the phenomenon that parents actively influence similar emotional states in children (Stein & Kendall, 2004). While negative parent-child experiences hinder development and brain functioning, positive therapeutic interactions can facilitate restorative processes that promote stress reduction, memory retention, maturation, well-being and healing. Such interaction has a ripple effect in which all family members can embrace and support a commitment for holistic harm reduction within the entire family system. This assumption has potential to influence intergenerational healing from an array of painful experiences that may enhance long-term successful treatment outcomes.

This model embraces a paradox that by slowing down we get there faster. Problems with understaffing and overloaded therapeutic schedules place extreme limitations on time spent in meaningful dialogue with parents and caregivers. Most families have weathered a judicial experience or social service process that has brought shame to their family. By taking time to elicit parental concerns and listen to fears, worries and restraints, staff can maximize core effective factors relating to clients and the therapeutic relationship. While time is a premium in all programs, thoughtful management of time with clients and their families can actually streamline improvement. Immediately clarifying expectations about clearly addressing all elements of sexual harm allows youth and family members to get directly to the point and remain focused throughout the course of treatment. While everyone slows down to grapple with delicate issues, maintaining focus on clearly defined elimination of harm prevents unnecessary deviation that can impede progress.

Learning to ask family members about their experiences and perceptions, rather than attempting to tell them what they should be doing, can enhance a sense of feeling valued as an important contributor to the healing process. Well meaning staff can confuse responsibility to support families with a myth that they are supposed to "fix" each youth and his or her family. It is important to remember that education does not equal therapeutic change. Telling people what is in their best interest does not guarantee that they will heed such advice. As a reminder to practice this change, one treatment team created a sign for the staff lounge that simply said "Ask. Don't tell."

While offense specific treatment challenges each youth to stop harmful behavior, families receive support to make sense of painful experiences that have impacted their lives in negative ways. These youth and their families learn to destroy powerful secrets of sexual abuse that may have influenced their lives for generations. Treatment addresses struggles with power, control, connection and secrecy that have often dominated the lives of these youth and their families.

Collaborating with family members in the creation of treatment goals, and monitoring progress towards those goals, solidifies a working relationship based upon constructive interdependence. Such an approach can reduce restraints to engagement and create a context for therapeutic reciprocity and mutual affirmation. As youth progress through treatment, families are encouraged to focus on reconciliation through atonement and forgiveness. When staff from every department work together to provide such collaboration, everyone benefits. Children and families get treatment needs met and staff experience the satisfaction of a job well done.

Therapeutic Tools

Educational material

Programs providing services for youth who have caused sexual harm and their families should have a comprehensive array of information and educational material that illustrates best practice research in a user friendly manner for everyone involved. Unfortunately, some programs offer a hodge-podge of paperwork that may be poorly written, difficult to comprehend, and meaningless for over stressed family members. A haphazard approach not only confuses children and families, but also staff, referral sources and accrediting bodies who have to struggle to make sense of an array of seemingly unrelated yet necessary information.

A variety of documents can provide important information that enhances successful treatment outcomes. General information, such as program descriptions, client handbooks, and phases of treatment, can provide important introductory material with clear expectations that enhance meaning, compliance and participation. Every document should clearly illustrate an agency's philosophy and mission while meeting licensing, accreditation and liability requirements. All legal documents, such as personal rights, confidentiality and consent forms should be easy to read and understand.

Resources that can ease stress for a family should be provided as soon as a youth is referred for treatment. A variety of introductory material geared towards reducing barriers to participation can be mailed or provided during the referral process. Parent and child handbooks that provide a program description and philosophy of care can help families learn about the agency's treatment approach and understand what to expect. These materials should be written in language that does not reflect clinical jargon, or multisyllabic words that have little meaning for families experiencing the complex stressors related to youthful sexual aggression.

Integrating the factor of hope and expectancy into all educational material throughout the full continuum of care is essential. Answers to frequently asked questions help normalize the challenge of being involved in the treatment process. Brief staff biographies (including photos) describing how each person will be helpful, can enhance the introductory experience through understanding and the creation of positive anticipation for successful treatment outcomes. An organizational chart can illustrate players on the treatment team, help families visualize the interrelated nature of the program, and grasp how they can all work together to support harm reduction and healing.

Workbooks relating to the tasks of therapy can be provided and facilitated with children through a collaborative effort among adult family members and treatment team staff. These may include topics such as anger management, social skills development, understanding the dynamics of abuse, and human sexual development. Programs can create a reference library in order for parents to access resources in the most cost effective way. Copies of each workbook should be available so that parents have an opportunity to understand the rationale for each, what material is being presented, the developmentally appropriate nature of the content, and how all of the educational resources illustrate research contributing to successful treatment outcomes.

Educational materials represent a significant financial investment that should involve cost benefit analysis. Therapeutic workbooks should be evaluated for age appropriate comprehension and values congruent with the agency mission and philosophy. Each workbook is a personal account of a child's healing experience and a confidential part of the treatment process. Unfortunately some agencies violate copyright laws by illegally copying material in an effort to save money. Not only is such practice illegal, it sets dangerous precedent for modeling illegal practice with children who are in treatment as a result of potentially illegal sexual behavior. Most importantly, these children and their families often receive inadequate materials illustrating the implicit message that they deserve nothing better. To provide them with inferior educational and material resources confirms a lack of regard and concern. Offering developmentally appropriate, research-based, optimistic resources conveys a commitment to respectful representation of factors that influence successful treatment outcomes.

All agency departments can work together to create and maintain excellence in material resources. Administration can budget adequate funding for both the creation and purchase of leading edge material to help children and families prepare for and heal throughout the treatment experience. Visionary managers can facilitate steering committees for the creation and maintenance of program documents, workbook evaluation, purchasing decisions and quality assessment. These steering committees should be comprised of staff representing all departments and include the issue of time management for staff to meet with children and families when they receive materials and are digesting all of the information.

Clinical, education and direct care staff can collaborate on the presentation of materials. Direct care staff may serve as the primary welcoming committee and focus on introducing program documents. Throughout treatment they can support children's workbook activities during designated times. Teachers or medical staff may provide the bulk of sexuality education and help children to receive school credit for any life skills material that pertains to educational requirements. Clinical personnel help children and families heal the intimate pain of sexual abuse through facilitation of confidential information that may be contained in any of the material resources. Children and family members should be able to communicate with any personnel about all agency documents and everyone can work together to enhance understanding and therapeutic change.

Family systems and ecological assessment

Community safety, victim justice and sensitivity are the primary concern of any treatment model. This principle guides all intervention. It is important to note that tools for facilitating assessment require specialized clinical training. Evaluating dangerousness involves thoughtful consideration of family dynamics that can impact outcomes. Problems inherent in misusing therapeutic tools involve the possibility of making matters worse in vulnerable family systems by inadvertently reopening deep wounds among family members. Moving too fast, or making therapeutic errors in the application of these tools can potentially cause further problems for these youth and their families. Ethical guidelines are provided by all licensed mental health professions and professional bodies such as the Association for the Treatment of Sexual Abusers (ATSA), *"First do no harm."*

An effective family systems assessment provides an understanding of how a youth came to cause sexual harm; family strengths and vulnerabilities that can influence outcomes; static and dynamic risk factors for recidivism; and protective factors that mitigate risk. It involves collection of any information pertinent to a child's treatment experience and is analogous to piecing together parts of a puzzle. Because family assessments are conducted for a variety of reasons in a range of settings, the following issues are taken into consideration. If a youth is being adjudicated a pre-sentence assessment can enhance disposition by providing information pertinent for location of services. Family support influences recommendations for service provision in a youth's home, community, residential, or secure facility. Family dynamics inform decisions about treatment modality (individual, group, family therapies). Family assessments are used through formal or informal process as meaningful working documents throughout the full continuum of care.

Facilitating a family systems assessment can be conducted while introducing a youth and family to the program. A child's primary clinician with the aid of a case manager usually collects this information and maintains vigilance in identifying strengths and resources that will influence harm reduction. The process begins immediately upon referral and continues throughout the entire process of treatment, including aftercare. Engaging parents, siblings and significant people in a child's life, while collecting salient information, serves to streamline orientation into the therapeutic experience. Collaboration may result in obtaining information that would not have been forthcoming through a less hospitable process. During an initial family meeting, a client's nine-year-old brother, who had not been identified as having sexual behavior problems, revealed participation in acts of bestiality. This information enabled the treatment team to address the problem as part of a holistic process for harm reduction and healing. That opportunity illustrated the importance of engaging the entire family in a commitment to stop sexual abuse.

A family systems assessment explores all facets of family life in an ecological context. Ecology is the relationship between a person and his or her environment. A child's ecology includes biological and extended family, relevant neighbors, church, school and community members. It takes into consideration issues of gender, race, socioeconomic status, religion and culture. This approach stresses comprehensive evaluation of a youth's ecological foundation and integrates findings with individualized assessment methods such as the J-SOAP-II, Protective Factors Scale and ERASOR for harm reductions (Prescott, In Press). Ecological assessment is woven into the ongoing fabric of services and guides continuous treatment planning and progress.

There is a disproportionate representation of sexually aggressive youth in the juvenile justice system that live in a social context of poverty and racism (Becker and Kaplan, 1993). Knowledge of the unique cultural experiences of each family, which takes into consideration race, socioeconomic status, gender and ethnicity, is explored in an effort to support the understanding of coping strategies and the development of sexually aggressive behavior. Social, cultural and family beliefs about the use of violence in relationships can contribute to the creation of a high risk setting in which sexual abuse occurs. Understanding such influences can decrease the likelihood of reoffending (Trepper & Barrett, 1989).

Exploring tenets of social learning theory (Bandura, 1973) enable youth to make sense of influences in their environment that impacted decisions to sexually offend. All of the messages that children receive about values, beliefs, growing up and how to behave are social learning. Knowing how and what youth learn about sexuality and sexual harm influences treatment planning.

Creating a family genogram (McGoldrick & Gerson, 1985; Hardy, 1995) and timelines of salient family events reveal histories of family life experience that can lead to greater understanding of stressors and issues of pride and shame. These therapeutic tools can help identify strengths, resources, vulnerabilities and resiliency throughout the family system. A genogram is simply a family map that illustrates a minimum of three generations and punctuates family relationships and information about health and well being.

A timeline traces the chronological order of significant family events that can illustrate connections and developments in the evolving family history. Timelines should focus equally on positive and negative events in order to obtain a comprehensive balance of information. Positive experiences can provide helpful memories and illuminate important resources to counter bad things that happened.

These techniques are used to assist families in understanding the impact that sexual abuse has had on their lives. They reveal a vast array of information that can help participants distill patterns of strength and vulnerability, harm and good. Factors that influence resiliency, such as supportive relationships, can be explored through the genogram and used as a foundation for engendering strength to continue in the therapeutic process.

Most importantly, they provide opportunity to evaluate family events and legacies that reveal intergenerational patterns. It is reasonable to expect disclosures through the genogram and timeline of traumatic experiences that may include significant family disruption, poverty, violence, substance abuse, racism, physical and mental illness. Genograms and time lines poignantly illustrate family history and provide a springboard for considering therapeutic change.

Once the initial assessment is completed, designated members of a treatment team meet with the child and family to share observations, reflections and begin the process of creating an individualized treatment, or service plan. This information, combined with a youth's individual assessment, is the foundation for clinical work. As treatment progresses and therapeutic change occurs, ongoing assessment influences changes in service planning.

Trauma outcome process

As mentioned in the introduction, these families have experienced disproportionate amounts of trauma. Such vulnerabilities often create restraints to participation in treatment. All family members are faced with the task of discerning the complex dynamics of sexual abuse with regard to the impact of perpetration and victimization. Understanding the effects that sexual abuse has on victims, family members, the youth being served, social services agencies, the criminal justice system and the community at large, broadens the foundation for harm reduction. Conversely, understanding the context in which sexual abuse occurs can help service providers influence therapeutic change within the intimate family circle that may prevent recidivism.

A therapeutic tool that can help children and families make sense of pain in their lives, and the impact it has on behavior, is the trauma outcome process (Burton, Rasmussen, & Christopherson, 1998; Schladale, 2002). The trauma outcome process is a conceptual framework for mapping the influence of previous trauma on the lives of children and their family members. It provides a framework for tracking sequential patterns of behavior and exploring strategies for developing new patterns that no longer involve harm to self or others.

Eliminating patterns of destructive behavior is the foundation for intervention and can easily be broadened to include any destructive behavioral patterns across the breadth of the family system. Family members are encouraged to explore how bad things that happen in life can have grave consequences for very long periods of time in a family's history. Participants are challenged to explore how individual coping strategies affect the lives of all family members. They are supported in their efforts to embark on a journey towards self-care that focuses on honor, integrity, empathy and compassion.

All staff can influence how each youth's trauma outcome process can shift from getting into trouble to exploring solutions for staying out of trouble. Administration can provide a commitment for supporting staff to help families address and heal from trauma that influenced their child's need for services. This can be done by providing training and allocating time necessary to help children and their families explore the trauma outcome process. Training for all staff on research-based responses to problematic behavior can enhance safe therapeutic communities, reduce physical management and liability, streamline progress and increase satisfaction and well-being among staff and clients. Standardizing an approach for responding to harmful behavior across all areas of a youth's life, increases cohesiveness that helps children know what to expect and how to predict the behavior of helping adults.

Narratives

A narrative is simply a story, or account of something. In this context narrative is used to facilitate understanding of the story, or account of a child's life experiences. Exploring and making sense of how life experiences influence harmful behavior, provides a foundation for helping children to learn how to change their life stories in order to stop causing harm. van der Kolk (2004) refers to a similar approach as "trauma scripting" in order to reframe and reduce emotional intensity related to traumatic experience. The purpose of using narratives is to help youth and families create a "new" story, based upon honor and integrity, in order to eliminate the "old" harmful story.

Narrative techniques (White and Epston, 1990) provide a way of talking about experiences related to destructive behavior in order to explore exceptions to sexually aggressive behavior. When a young boy's father was arrested and incarcerated, the young boy was told that he was now the king of the house. Several years later while receiving treatment for sexually aggressive behavior, he was able to explore for the first time, the impact of such a message. The young man identified how such a belief contributed to a sense of destructive entitlement that influenced his decisions to commit sexual crimes. Through examination of abusive power, control, connection and secrecy, the young man was able to consider the need to give up such destructive power and control. He decided to abdicate the *throne* in his desire to establish his rightful place in the family, that of first born son, not king of the house. The narrative journey led him to a place of congruent hierarchy (Minuchen and Fishman, 1981) in which he was able to make sense of how the inappropriate position of king had caused confusion and misunderstanding about his position in the family.

Another young man, whose father was incarcerated out of state, and could not be contacted in any other way, was encouraged to write him. His father responded promptly and they began correspondence that influenced the young man's participation in treatment. His father consistently encouraged his son to embark on a different journey that focused on abiding by the law and learning to manage his anger in ways that no longer caused harm.

Children can be encouraged to communicate with family members even when they are far away and have had little contact in the past. Once a treatment team has established that contact will do no harm, encouraging meaningful dialogue can support healing. These clinical experiences provide an opportunity to create a new story based upon courage, honor, and a willingness to reject the young person's sexually abusive lifestyle.

Story telling is a very important and compelling part of life. Childcare staff, educators, clinicians, parents and volunteers can powerfully influence therapeutic changes through the use of narratives and story telling (Spees, 2002). Restorative family processes can also be enhanced through creation of story time (Spees, 2002). Family members are encouraged to tell stories, or read aloud and discuss the meaning of famous children's books such as, *The Velveteen Rabbit,* and *The Little Engine that Could.* Metaphors and therapeutic themes evolve from such practice and support youth as they grapple with the challenges of taming harmful behavior. Narratives also introduce elements of playfulness and fun to the serious consideration of problems. Both children and adults benefit from the rich expression of personal narrative. Biographies can also provide poignant opportunities to learn how others overcome obstacles in order to pursue dreams and become the people that they really want to be.

Media support

Media support represents creative ways that programs can utilize technology to enhance successful treatment outcomes. Children today are often more media savvy than adults and live in a media saturated world that greatly influences their reality. Using the media to meet children where they are, can influence relationship building and the exploration of client characteristics that will ultimately determine treatment outcome.

A variety of options remain for families who are unable, or seemingly unwilling, to participate directly in the treatment process. Several years ago, the Commonwealth of Kentucky initiated an innovative approach for involving families whose children received services far away from home. Designated community-based staff received specialized training and were provided with a camcorder and VCR/monitor that fit in the trunk of a car. Residential staff joined in partnership with children in facilities and created videotapes of the program that served as an orientation for parents. Parents received the videos, created a corresponding tape with the community worker, and sent it to the child. This process serves to maintain connection with a youth's family of origin; put faces to names for staff and family members; keep everyone abreast of changes in all of the family members' lives; help families to feel valued by treatment teams; maintain open avenues for communication; and assist with family reunification.

Children and families can be assigned to watch designated commercial movies and television episodes and discuss how they are related to therapeutic issues in treatment. Depending upon the age of children, motion pictures such as *Ground Hog Day*, can illustrate a vast array of therapeutic topics relating to patterns of destructive behavior and healing relationships. The classic Abbott and Costello comedy skit, *"Who's On First"*, is a wonderful illustration of communication problems. Treatment teams can use it to enhance the orientation process for clients through discussion of challenges that they may face throughout the therapeutic process. Younger children are able to explore the metaphors used in a host of animated movies such as *Shrek* and *The Lion King*, in an effort to create a parallel process to their own experiences.

Television episodes can provide comic illustration of serious concerns. The Simpson's episode entitled *"Homerphobia"* is used to address sexual identity development. An episode of *Dinosaurs* entitled, *"The Quest For Male Supremacy"*, provides a humorous opportunity for addressing gender roles, sexism and destructive entitlement.

Music is also a media resource with evocative healing power. Informal music appreciation that takes into consideration everyone's interests, can help youth to identify meaningful lyrics and explore the influence that music can have on the development of healthy lifetime coping strategies. Music enhances integration of brain functions that promote self-soothing and support affect regulation (van der Kolk, 2004; Stien & Kendall, 2004).

Childcare staff, educators and clinicians can work collaboratively to utilize media resources throughout the fabric of treatment. Children and families receive important therapeutic messages in a nonthreatening manner since media sources are often an entertainment outlet of choice. It is important to have content reviewed and approved for age appropriate viewing. Adherence to rating systems can ensure protection from harmful material.

Therapeutic Fun

"Play is children's work."
~ Uri Bronfenbrenner

Many young people who are in treatment for sexual behavior problems have suffered from way too little playtime in their lives, and are sometimes punished for having fun in treatment. Service providers can suffer from a heavy burden of responsibility for preventing further victimization by the children they serve. They can also suffer from a myth that all intervention must demonstrate a serious attitude with no room for nonsense.

Play is considered a critical element of child development that influences social participation and problem solving (Rubin, Coplan, Nelson & Lagace-Sequin, 1999). Children learn through play and figure out lessons through metaphor and experiential activity (Freeman et al., 1997; Gil, 1994; Schaefer & Carey, 1994). An important tool for everyone involved is therapeutic fun. Treatment programs that employ expressive therapists, recreation specialists, and staff trained in experiential and wilderness therapies do well to integrate such activities into family activities and therapy.

Therapeutic fun provides a playful approach for addressing serious issues. Examples include introduction to therapy through the creation of a personal shield to use as a metaphor that normalizes the basic human need for self-protection throughout the treatment process. Masks are often used to illustrate a variety of therapeutic issues such as different parts of the self that reflect internal and external focus, victim and perpetrator, vulnerability and aggression. Art activities that reveal struggles with power and control through the use of mixed media such as clay, various types of paint, building materials and natural elements, can loosen restraints to emotional expression.

Creating meaningful rituals and celebrations to punctuate treatment progress embraces all elements of the four factors that influence successful treatment outcomes. Such techniques can instill a sense of hope while engaging a client and family in collaborative relationship. Ritual can punctuate a myriad of emotions that are often elicited in the process.

Families are invited to create their own healing rituals and rituals of transition throughout their time in therapy, in order to punctuate unique family characteristics, strengths and resources that will aid their ongoing healing process. Poignant experiences often occur when youth successfully complete treatment and say good-bye to valued service providers. Families are invited to work with the child to create celebrations reflecting their experience of the therapeutic process. These activities provide an opportunity for everyone to share genuine feelings and reminisce about personal growth, successful initiatives, and future challenges.

The use of ritual can also help when children and families are struggling in therapy. One family used a baseball metaphor about a team player being in a "slump" when their son was "striking out" in treatment. They worked with the treatment team to create extra practice and more focused coaching to keep the youth in the game and find the courage to continue getting up to bat. Teachers joined in the process as the youth was having trouble in school and everyone worked together to help the boy get some hits that led to becoming a more active player in the game.

Conclusion

While there remains a great need for more research in this field of treatment, there is enough available to identify and integrate common threads for successful therapeutic outcomes with youth who have caused sexual harm and their families (Henggeler et al., 1998; Rasmussen, 1999; Weinrott, 1996). When professionals allow research from all mental health disciplines to inform interventions, potential for influencing successful outcomes, facilitated in the most cost efficient ways, is greatly enhanced. Service providers will do well to explore strengths and resources that everyone in a youth's social support network can bring to the effort of reducing sexual harm. Utilizing a systemic approach that takes into consideration the need for all family members to heal from the pain of sexual abuse increases opportunity to stop intergenerational patterns of sexual harm.

References

Araji, S. (1997). *Sexually aggressive children: coming to understand them.* Thousand Oaks, California: Sage Publications.

Bagley, C. & Shewchuk-Dann, D. (1991). Characteristics of 60 children and adolescents who have a history of sexual assault against others: Evidence from a controlled study. *Journal of child and youth care* (Fall Special Issues): 43-52.

Bandura, A. (1973). *Aggression: A social learning analysis.* Englewood Cliffs, New Jersey: Prentice Hall.

Becker, J. (1990). Treating adolescent sexual offenders. *Professional psychology: Research and practice,* 21(5): 362-365.

Becker, J. & Hunter, J. (1997). Understanding and treating child and adolescent sexual offenders. In T. Ollendick & R. Prinz (Eds.), *Advances in clinical child psychology,* 19 (pp.177-197). New York: Plenum Press.

Becker, J. & Kaplan, M. (1993). Cognitive behavioral treatment of the juvenile sexual offender. In H. Barbaree, W. Marshall, & S. Husdon (Eds), *The juvenile sexual offender.* New York: Guilford Press.

Bengis, S. (1986). *A comprehensive service delivery system and continuum of care.* Brandon, Vermont: Safer Society Press.

Berg, I. (1994). *Family based services: A solution-focused approach.* New York: W.W. Norton.

Bonner, B., Marx, B., Thompson, J. & Michaelson, P. (1998). Assessment of adolescent sexual offenders. *Child Maltreatment,* 3 (4), 374-383.

Borduin, C., Henggeler, S., Blaske, D. & Stein, R. (1990). Multisystemic treatment of adolescent sexual offenders. *International Journal of Offender Therapy and Comparative Criminology,* 34, 105-113.

Burton, J., Rasmussen, L., & Christopherson (1998). *Treating children with sexual behavior problems.* Haworth Press.

Chaffin, M. & Bonner, B. (1998). Don't shoot, we're your children: Have we gone too far in our response to adolescent sexual abusers and children with sexual behavior problems. *Child Maltreatment,* November, 314-316.

Dishion, T., McCord, J. & Poulin, F. (1999). When interventions harm: Peer groups and problem behavior. *American Psychologist,* 54 (9), 755-764.

Durrant, M. (1993). *Residential treatment.* New York: W.W. Norton.

Etgar, T. (1996). Parallel processes in a training and supervision group for counselors working with adolescent sex offenders. *Social work with groups,* 19 (93/4), 57-69.

Fehrenback, P., Smith, W., Monastersky, C., & Deisher, R. (1986). Adolescent sexual offenders: Offender and offense characteristics. *American Journal of Orthopsychiatry,* 56 (2), 225-233.

Freeman, J., Epston, D., & Lobovits, D. (1997). *Playful approaches to serious problems.* New York: W.W.Norton.

Freidrich, W. (1990). *Psychotherapy of sexually abused children and their families.* New York: W.W. Norton.

Gil, E. (1994). *Play in family therapy.* New York: Guilford Press.

Goocher, B. (1994). Some comments on the residential treatment of juvenile sex offenders. *Child & Youth Care Forum,* 23 (4), 243-250.

Gray, A., Busconi, A., Houchens, P. & Pithers, W. (1997). Children with sexual behavior problems and their caregivers: Demographics, functioning, and clinical patterns. *Sexual Abuse: A Journal of Research and Treatment, 9* (4), 267-290.

Gray, A. & Pithers, W. (1993). Relapse prevention with sexually aggressive adolescents and children: Expanding treatment and supervision. In H. Barbaree, W. Marshall, & S. Hudson (Eds.), *The juvenile sex offender* (pp. 289-319). New York: Guilford Press.

Guralnik, D. (Ed.)(1986). *Webster's New World Dictionary.* New York: Prentice Hall.

Haley, J. (1976). *Problem solving therapy.* San Francisco: Jossey-Bass.

Hardy, K. & Laszloffy, T. (1995). The cultural genogram: key to training culturally competent family therapists. *Journal of Marital and Family Therapy,* 21(3), 227-237.

Hoffman, L. (1981). *Foundations of family therapy.* New York: Basic Books.

Henderson, J., English, D., & MacKenzie, W. (1989). Family centered casework practice with sexually aggressive children. *Treatment of sex offenders in social work and mental health settings.* New York: Haworth Press, Inc.

Henggeler, S. (1998, April/May). Family-based services and juvenile justice: An effective family-based alternative to incarceration proves its worth. *Family Therapy News,* 9.

Henggeler, S., Schoenwald, S., Broduin, C., Rowland, M., & Cunningham, P. (1998). *Multisystemic treatment of antisocial behavior in children and adolescents.* New York: The Guilford Press.

Hermann, J. (1992). *Trauma and recovery.* New York: Basic Books.

Hubble, M., Duncan, B., & Miller, S. (1999). T*he heart and soul of change.* Washington, D.C.: American Psychological Association.

Hunter, J., & Figueredo, A. (1999). Factors associated with treatment compliance in a population of juvenile sexual offenders. *Sexual Abuse: A Journal of Research and Treatment, 11* (1), 49-67.

Jenkins, A. (1990). *Invitations to responsibility: The therapeutic engagement of men who are violent and abusive.* Adelaide, South Australia: Dulwich Centre Publications.

Kimball, L. & Guarino-Ghezzi, S. (1996). *Sex offender treatment: An assessment of sex offender treatment within the Massachusetts Department of Youth Services* (Juvenile Justice Series Report No. 10). Boston, Massachusetts: Northeastern University, Privatized Research Management Initiative.

Katz, R. (1990). Psychosocial adjustment in adolescent child molesters. *Child Abuse and Neglect,* 14 (4), 567-575.

Knight, R., & Prentky, R. (1993). Exploring characteristics for classifying juvenile sex offenders. In H. Barbaree, W. Marshall, & S. Hudson (Eds.), *The juvenile sex offender* (pp. 45-83). New York: Guilford Press.

Kobayashi, J., Sales, B., Becker, J. Figueredo, A., & Kaplan, M. (1995). Perceived parental deviance, parent-child bonding, child abuse, and child sexual aggression. *Sexual Abuse: A Journal of Research and Treatment, 7* (1), 25-43.

Lord, A., & Barnes, C. (1996). Family liaison work with adolescents in a sex offender treatment programme. *The Journal of Sexual Aggression* 2 (2), 112-121.

McGoldrick, M., & Gerson, R. (1985). *Genograms in family assessment.* New York: W.W.Norton.

Miller, S., Hubble, M., & Duncan, B. (1995). No more bells and whistles. *Family Therapy Networker* 19 (2), 52-58.

Miner, M., Siekert, G., & Ackland, M. (1997). *Evaluation: Juvenile sex offender treatment program, Minnesota Correctional Facility-Sauk Centre* (Final Report-Biennium 1995-1997). Minneapolis, Minnesota: University of Minnesota, Department of Family Practice and Community Health, Program in Human Sexuality.

Minor, M. & Crimmins, C. (1995). Adolescent sex offenders: Issues of etiology and risk factors. In B. Schwartz & H. Cellini (Eds.), *The sex offender: Vol. 1. Corrections, treatment and legal practice* (pp. 9.1-9.15). Kingston, New Jersey: Civic Research Institute.

Minuchen, S., & Fishman, H. (1981). *Family therapy techniques.* Cambridge, Massachusetts: Harvard University Press.

Morenz, B. & Becker, J. (1995). The treatment of youthful sexual offenders. *Applied and Preventive Psychology* 4 (4), 247-256.

National Adolescent Perpetrator Network. (1988). Preliminary report from the National Task Force on Juvenile Sexual Offending. *Juvenile and Family Court Journal,* 38 (2), 1-67.

National Adolescent Perpetrator Network. (1993). The revised report from the National Task Force on Juvenile Sexual Offending. *Juvenile and Family Court Journal,* 44 (4), 1-120.

Pithers, W., Gray, A., Busconi, A., & Houchens, P. (1998). Caregivers of children with sexual behavior problems: Psychological and familial functioning. *Child Abuse and Neglect,* 22 (2), 129-141.

Prentky, R., Knight, R., Sims-Knight, J., Straus, F., Rokous, F., & Cerce, D. (1989). Developmental antecedents of sexual aggression. *Development and Psychopathology,* 1,153-169.

Prentky, R., Harris, B., Frizzell, K., & Righthand, S. (2000). An actuarial procedure for assessing risk with juvenile sex offender. *Sexual Abuse: A Journal of Research and Treatment*, 12, 71-94.

Prescott, D. (in press). *Emerging strategies for risk assessment of sexually abusive youth: Theory, controversy, and practice.*

Rasmussen, L. (1999). Factors related to recidivism among juvenile sexual offenders. *Sexual Abuse: A Journal of Research and Treatment*, 11, (1), 69-85.

Rubin, K., Coplan, R., Nelson, L., & Lagace-Seguin, D. (1999). *Peer relationships in childhood.* Developmental psychology an advanced textbook. Mahwah, New Jersey: Lawrence Erlbaum Associates, Publishers.

Ryan, G. & Lane, S. (Eds.). (1997). *Juvenile sexual offending.* San Francisco: Jossey-Bass Publishers.

Ryan, G., Miyoshi, T., Metzner, J., Krugman, R., & Fryer, G. (1996). Trends in a national sample of sexually abusive youths. *Journal of the American Academy of Child and Adolescent Psychiatry*, 31 (1), 17-25.

Schaefer, C., & Carey, L. (1994). *Family play therapy.* Northvale, New Jersey: Jason Aronson Inc.

Schladale, J. (2002). *The T.O.P.* workbook for taming violence and sexual aggression.* Freeport, Maine: Resources for Resolving Violence.

Sefarbi, R. (1990). Admitters and deniers among adolescent sex offenders and their families: A preliminary study. *American Journal of Orthopsychiatry*, 60 (3), 460-465.

Smith, H., & Isreal, E. (1987). Sibling incest: A study of dynamics of 25 cases. *Child Abuse and Neglect*, 11 (1), 101-108.

Spees, E. (2002). Word movies: Strategy and resources for therapeutic storytelling with children and adolescents. *Annals of the American Psychotherapy Association*, January/February 2002, 14-21.

Stien, P. & Kendall, J. (2004). *Psychological trauma and the developing brain.* New York: The Haworth Press.

Stith, S. & Bischof, G. (1996). Communication patterns in families of adolescent sex offenders. In D. Cahn & S. Lloyd (Eds.), *Family violence from a communications perspective.* Thousand Oaks, California: Sage.

Thornton, T., Craft, C., Dahlberg, L., Lynch, B., & Baer, K. (2002). *Best practices of youth violence prevention: a sourcebook for community action* (rev.). Atlanta: Centers for Disease Control and Prevention, National Center for Injury Prevention and Control.

Trepper, T., & Barrett, M.J. (1989). *Systemic treatment of incest.* New York: Brunner Mazel.

Waters, D., & Lawrence, E. (1993). *Competence courage and change: An approach to family therapy.* New York: W.W. Norton.

Weinrott, M. (1996). *Juvenile sexual aggression: A critical review.* Boulder, Colorado: University of Colorado, Institute for Behavioral Sciences, Center for the Study and Prevention of Violence.

White, M., & Epston, D. (1990). *Narrative means to therapeutic ends.* New York: Brunner Mazel.

CHAPTER TWENTY-ONE

FROM FAMILY RESEARCH TO PRACTICE

JERRY THOMAS
AND
WILSON VIAR, III

Introduction

Although the socialization of children developed from the interaction over time of countless influences, personal characteristics, situational factors, and the sometimes inexplicable vagaries of life, it is generally accepted that the family and family environment are primary factors in that process. These are not the only factors, of course. There are countless other factors (sometimes multidimensional) that take place in every individual's life. However, the family and its environment represent a child's primary developmental influence and provide the context of time and space in which the other factors occur.

Sexuality is inherent. Sexual attitudes and behaviors are not. Attitudes and behaviors about sex – just like other attitudes and behaviors - develop in a particular context of circumstances, experiences, and parental models that begin in the early home environment. It bears repeating that while the family/family environment is influential in that development, this does not mean it is directly causal. In general, the family and the family environment simply encourage, allow, support, and/or fail to provide the inhibitors needed to preclude development of sexually abusive behavior. The families of sexually abusive youth are not more unhealthy or pathological than the families of other populations of youth.

In actuality, family systems range on a continuum of types and categories from basically healthy to seriously disturbed. There are parents who would if they could (but don't know how to) intervene when they observe sexual behavior. When you don't know how to differentiate normal age appropriate sexual behavior from problematic sexual behavior it is easier to take the line of least resistance and just ignore all sexual behavior. There are families incapable of taking the steps to correct problematic sexual behaviors. There are also families that provide a fertile ground for the development and maintenance of that behavior. Parental influences range from active to passive, from deliberate to unwitting. Even otherwise good intentions are sometimes guided by poor, erroneous, or misleading information and result in harm, however unintended. There are basically healthy families who live in a time and place where outside variables are the most dominating influence. There are even cases in which a child's characteristics and experiences are pivotal in their development, thus producing otherwise unexpected results. In most cases, however, families appear to be doing the best that they can considering their present circumstances, degree of knowledge/skills and access to professional help.

As early as 1984, Troupe and Ruther reminded us that, "Many behaviors should be understood not as distortions derived from abnormal processes but instead as normal processes that were distorted by atypical circumstances or experiences." This concept helps us in understanding the families for whom we provide services - sexually abusive behavior can develop in any family, even our own. This recognition should be humbling to all professionals, particularly those of us who are parents. It is one of the realizations that may serve to eliminate some of the barriers between "us" and "them".

This chapter discusses the need to base our treatment in the reality of our clients. It also provides a theoretical background and review of the existing literature as a context for that treatment. Throughout this discussion we provide examples from our practice. We discuss ideas for exploiting our field's expanding knowledge base, and thoughts for putting it into practice. We then discuss some ideas for structuring a family assessment and treatment plan in order to operationalize our knowledge base.

Making treatment reality based

Keeping treatment as reality based as possible is one of the primary reasons for involving the family or the family situation in treatment programs for sexually abusive youth. When the treatment focus is on the context in which children live and on their primary relationships, we base our treatment on their reality base. Why would anyone attempt to treat a young person in a bubble when this isn't the context of his life?

If we do not involve parents, parental figures, and/or entire families in the treatment process, who will provide the support needed by a child – or adult for that matter – in what is a painful and difficult process? Who will help families to understand what has happened or teach them how to regain control of their lives? How will the family heal from the tremendous impact of personal and familial victimization? And where will they find the information needed to develop an environment that both provides barriers to sexually abusive behavior and supports non-offending, non-abusive behavior?

Reality is composed of numerous small realities and is much more than the single reality of sexual abuse. The problem of sexual abuse does not define youth, their families, or even the professionals who work with them. In order for us to provide reality-based treatment, we must keep this belief at the forefront lest we become consumed by what is really only one finite part of a family and of ourselves as professionals. It is an easy trap for all of us to fall into and leaves all of us without much hope for a full life. We must confess that at times we have let this work define us. When one family anguished that their lives were consumed by child sexual abuse and the sexually abusive behavior of one family member – we think - so is ours. If we are to be grounded in health rather than illness, we need to see the families that we work with as much more than that one reality. To remain reality based, to see the whole picture rather than just part of it, our obligation to them and ourselves is to rid ourselves of tunnel vision and provide all of us with the hope that is necessary before life can be full and healthy.

Looking back, I can identify several times and ways in which I, as a very young mother, may have placed my own children in risky situations – not through neglect, but as the result of a lack of information. Just as most families, I was doing the best that I could with what I knew at the time. It was only years later that I began to wonder about the babysitter who my boys said forced them to take baths. Probably this was only because most little boys love to get dirty and hate to take baths, but if I had known then what I know now I would have asked different questions instead of simply telling the children that they had to mind the babysitter.

Ironically, I can also remember several times and ways in which I as a parent very likely over-reacted, a behavior not uncommon among sexual abuse professionals. At one time I believed, and publicly stated in front of my son and colleague, that the only two people in the world that I was sure weren't sexually abusive were my mother and I. It didn't occur to me that I had also just made the shocking observation that my colleague and son were questionable. At the time, my intentions were to underscore how unreliable the clichés about child-sexual abusers are and to emphasize that they can't be identified by their overall social performance or "likeability". Since there are no studies on the subject, one has to wonder how these attitudes affect the children of child sexual abuse professionals.

Learning in context: communication variables

> *"There are three kinds of men, the ones that learn by reading, the ones who have to be taught, the few that learn by observation, and the rest of them have to pee on the electric fence themselves." ~ Will Rogers*

What, where, and when we learn is sometimes an unexpected gift. I have learned important lessons gained valuable information from clients and their families. Professional colleagues have graced me with their wisdom in many ways – advising, producing research, writing important clinical literature, and most importantly by being good role models. I have learned by success and by failure, as ironically, the tragedies teach the most important lessons. I first learned and continue to learn from my family, my biological family, the family I birthed, and the one I have chosen as mine. Relationship is the basis of all of these different ways to learn... even if the relationship is between you and the electric fence. It is my mother who can testify that I have spent more time than necessary setting off the electric fence.

Clients have often told me that relationships are more important to them than cognitive behavioral therapy, relapse prevention planning, family therapy, or individual counseling. Even when asked on discharge surveys, what part of the treatment program was most influential in helping you to change, the answer given most often was simply the name of a particular person. This person was sometimes the primary therapist, sometimes a family member, not always someone I would have expected. One young man named a professional gardener who supervised the work program at the residential treatment center saying, "He believed I was worthwhile, he gave me hope." This may be the kind of communication that has been rare in that child's life.

We generally agree that good communication is one of the attributes of any positive interpersonal relationship. Inadequate or faulty communication is often cited in both research and the professional literature as a common deficit in the families of sexually abusive youth. This is all true but it is not always this simple. There are times, however, that the results of poor communication are not negative and that excellent and timely communication does not result in a positive outcome.

Three examples

As a child, the absence of any discussion about sex or sexuality in my family, particularly my mother's inability of to even mention the existence of such things, proved to be a positive when taken in context. In another person's life the same flaws in communication might have produced entirely different results. I grew up in the 1950s in a small southern town where the general belief among my peers was that sex was something mysterious that not only must, but *could* happen, only after marriage. There were no televisions or movies with graphic messages about sex or constant portrayals of sex. There were no magazines or books available to me that depicted anything sexual. The few vaguely sexual things my mother did talk about – such as the kind of women who pierced their ears – made such an impression that they left me with a life long inability to pierce my own.

For the most part, however, sex was simply not discussed in my home. Yet this didn't occur in a sexually repressive context. There was no stigmatization of sex; it was simply not polite or appropriate to discuss such things with or in front of children. There was also no avoidance of touch in my home, hugs, both comforting and affectionate, came regularly. Another mitigating factor was that, while I was a town rather than country girl, it was a small town with no great distance in space or lifestyle from the farms that surrounded it. We had chickens, dogs, and horses ourselves, and though the particulars of sex may not have been discussed, we were probably more aware of the basics of procreation than most urban children today.

As a result of these and many other contextual factors, while I grew up without much positive information about sex and sexuality, I also had even less in the way of negative information. What I did learn was that sex was normal, sex was good, and sex was a part of married life. I learned this much from church school – strange as that may seem. So one must consider that my beliefs about sex and sexuality are the culmination of where I come from, the family I was born into, and the time and place in which I lived. They involve the culture that surrounded me, the adult and peer group that I associated with, and my own unique experiences in life.

In fact, I grew up without any strong preconceived notions about sex, positive or negative, unless you count pierced ears. Considering how often a deficit in the ability to communicate about sex and sexuality is identified as a contributing problem in the families of sexually abusive youth, this is particularly interesting.

The second example comes from my professional life, which is full of instances of parents' inability to communicate openly and honestly about sex. In some cases communication about sex was developmentally inappropriate, and in others, all communication was sexualized. Generally this had very negative consequences. Early in my career, I worked with a family that for all intents and purposes was healthy and functional. This family consisted of parents in their early thirties and three children aged thirteen, seven and five. The couple had no major marital problems. Family members were active in the community, their church, and the children's school. The thirteen year old was especially active in scouts, an activity enthusiastically supported by his father who himself was a former Eagle Scout as well as a personal friend of the scoutmaster. Relatively conservative and religious, sex wasn't discussed in the home, and overt sexuality - particularly homosexuality - was stigmatized as an ill of society at large.

When the scoutmaster began sexually abusing Scott, he didn't know what to do, who to tell or where to turn. Although there was an absence of any communication about sex, his father often had professed a great deal of respect for the scoutmaster, and Scott was actively encouraged to spend time with him. Scott's attempt to make sense of this vacillated from believing that his father knew and approved of the sexual abuse to his belief that if his father and mother found out they would be disgusted and rejecting as well as blaming and disowning.

As Scott grew older, however, the scoutmaster's attention turned to younger boys and Scott's own abuse stopped. Although very ashamed of the sexual abuse and unable to talk about it to anyone, Scott had become unhealthily sexualized as a result. He found himself missing the closeness and arousal associated with the abuse. He began to fantasize about doing the same things to his younger brother and sister. He actively fantasized for over six months before he finally acted on those fantasies. When Scott's abuse of his younger siblings was accidentally discovered, a report was made, and he was adjudicated. The only treatment available in a three-state area was residential, and so Scott was placed in a residential, treatment facility for adolescents who had been sexually abusive.

Learning to communicate openly and honestly about sex and sexuality was one of the foci of family treatment. Eventually, Scott and his parents were able to talk quite openly – the kind of communication that might have either prevented the abuse or stopped it soon after it began. Ironically, Scott's father disclosed for the first time (in family treatment) that a baseball coach had sexually abused him as a young boy. This disclosure freed Scott from fear of his father's rejection and his father from many years of secrecy. As a consequence of this disclosure both Scott and his father, as well as the entire family, not only benefited, but it was a pivotal point in the change process for everyone.

The third example comes from the lives of professional colleagues and personal friends. All four of the parents involved worked in the child sexual abuse field in some capacity. One of the mothers developed sexual abuse prevention programs. The two sets of parents had prided themselves on developing open and direct lines of communication with all of their children. One day the daughters of the two couples, ages twelve and thirteen, were walking down the street not very far from their homes.

A man stopped his car, opened the car door and exposed himself to them. They remembered one of the lessons of the prevention talk – yell and get away. They did so immediately. However, they didn't tell their parents, later saying they were too embarrassed and ashamed.

The good news is that they did eventually tell one of the girls' older sisters. Imagine the feelings of those four parents – giving their children the most up to date prevention information, concentrating on developing open communication patterns with them, and still the girls didn't go to them when this event occurred. What a lesson for all of us. Good prevention programs and open honest communication are sometimes not enough. With all the prevention programs in the world and all the communication in the world it cannot be left up to children alone to protect them. This underscores not only why prevention efforts must be comprehensive but also what motivates us in this work.

I give these three examples for this reason: to point out the importance of the many variables involved in all situations. It is not the absence of communication or the presence of communication, but the interaction of the many individual variables that determines the outcome. Understanding this perhaps we can stop looking at parents as either to blame or blameless. We can then focus our energies on supporting them through this awful experience, identify the family system issues which may have laid some of the groundwork for the offending behavior, and help them to build family dynamics that will support non-offending behavior and provide the barriers to offending behavior.

Examining the pathways to offending

There are practical reasons to examine the pathways to offending. For example: 1) this knowledge guides the development of assessment protocols, treatment plans, treatment interventions, and discharge criteria not only for the family but for the youth; 2) this knowledge supplies the information needed to develop early intervention programs, child care and child placement decision making, and to structure prevention programs; and 3) this knowledge has serious implications for the development of residential treatment centers, group and foster home environments, and juvenile justice environments. Understanding the factors that help grow or support abusive behavior means that we can help avoid replicating an environment in out-of-home treatment settings or placements where the dynamics support, encourage, or help maintain sexually abusive behavior. If familial environment is crucial, then so are the familial environments provided in out-of-home treatment settings.

1) Theoretical concepts
Some of the attempts to identify and understand the development of sexually abusive or deviant behavior are theoretical. In *Juvenile Sexual Offending, Causes and Consequences* (Ryan & Lane, 1997), Ryan identified a number of those concepts, and seven of them are either closely or directly connected to the family of origin or whatever served as that family constellation. None, however, suggest that the family lives in a vacuum. Let's look at a number of them:

- *The family systems model* – The focus is on the assumption that the health of one component of a social system will effect and/or arise from other processes or components of that social system. Prevention, treatment, and the maintenance of health of juveniles consequently will require an appreciation and attention to their family system as a whole.

- *The learning theory model* - effectively defined by the following statement: "The ways in which people manifest their sexuality are learned."
- *The developmental theory model* – based on the belief that "learning depends on what has gone before."
- *The cognitive theory model* - focuses upon the cognitive distortions that support sexually offending behavior and promotes cognitive behavior techniques can prove important to efforts to extinguish and replace dysfunctional sexual learning in both abusive youth and their families.
- *The addictive theory model* – depends upon the concepts of reward and learning, cognitive distortion, and compulsivity and upon physiological factors. In this perspective sexual behaviors become unmanageable or out of control in a man ner generally similar to traditional substance addictions.
- *The trauma model* – developed as a result of the basic belief that the failure to master a childhood trauma can create a need to repeat or reenact that trauma through life stages, and the trauma then becomes reinforced.
- *The sexual abuse cycle* – built on the concept that antecedent thoughts, feelings, and behaviors culminate in sexually abusive acts, and this becomes a cycle of abusive behavior.
- *The integrative model* – exactly what the name implies. Instead of a single source for the development of sexually abusive behavior, this model integrates several theories together into a comprehensive model.

In addition to these and other theoretical concepts, we also have a growing body of information from research, literature, and clinical experience that is informative. Although at times the results of clinical studies may appear to be widely divergent, this is almost invariably an artifact of the specific populations that were the subjects of those studies. In a population that is extremely heterogeneous and that is treated in a continuum of settings, from the least restrictive to the most restrictive, this is to be expected and taken into consideration.

2) Concepts from research and clinical studies:
   A) Information about environment and functioning:

- In sibling incest families, parents are often physically and emotionally inaccessible, parental control lax, and the climate secretive and sexually stimulating (Smith & Israel, 1987).
- Results of study showed that 25.5% of families had a "lack of sexual boundaries", and 33.3% of the families kept sexually explicit materials (Manocha & Mezey, 1998).
- Families often function at extremes - either disengaged or enmeshed (Serfabi, 1990; Graves et al., 1996).
- Family environments are "chaotic" (Miner, Siekert, & Ackland, 1997).
- Family instability, disorganization, and violence are noted to be prevalent (Bagley & Shewchuk-Dann, 1991; Miner, Siekert, & Ackland, 1997; Morenz & Becker, 1995).

- Various studies suggest that many juvenile sex offenders have experienced physical and/or emotional separations from one or both of their parents (e.g., Kahn & Chambers, 1991; Fehrenbach et al., 1986; Smith & Israel, 1987).

B) Child maltreatment histories:

- The quality of care in families is often poor, and relationships often disrupted (Ward et al., 1995).
- This Ward et al. study described 29.4% of the parents as "uncaring" Manocha & Mezey (1998).
- Relationships with parents are often disrupted, leading to the formation of inadequate attachments (Ward et al., 1995).
- Instability, disengagement, and poor attachment shows up frequently (Minor & Crimmins, 1995).
- Poor social judgment and social anxiety are characteristic which point to the importance of interventions that maximize the ability to build interpersonal attachments, as these reduce the propensity to engage in sexually abusive and aggressive behaviors (Miner & Crimmins, 1995).
- A lower level of perceived family support is one predictor of the development of sexual offending behavior (Smith & Monastersky, 1986).

And to sum it up Araji (1997) comments, "The evidence... points to family interactions as a primary source of the problem."

C) Information about communication styles:

- Families have patterns of negative communication, aggressive statements and interruptions, as well as a lack of supportive communication and dialogue (Blaske, Borduin, Henggeler, & Mann, 1989).
- Communication between parents and children of sexually abusive youth are lower compared to normative samples (Stith & Bischof, 1996; Morenz & Becker, 1995).
- The age of onset, number of incidents of abuse, period of time elapsing between the abuse and its first report, and perceptions of familial responses are all relevant in understanding why some sexually abused youth go on to commit sexual assaults while others do not (Hunter & Figueredo, 1999).

D) Childhood histories of abuse:

- Physical abuse, neglect, and witnessing family violence have been independently associated with sexual violence in juvenile offenders (Kobayashi et al., 1995; Ryan et al., 1996).
- Experiences of sexual abuse range from 40% to 80% depending on the study and the population studied (Hunter & Becker, 1998; Kahn & Chambers, 1991).
- A retrospective case review of 100 young people who had been sexually abusive determined that 47% had either experienced or witnessed family violence of some kind (Richardson et al., 1997).
- Histories of developmental trauma resulting from rejection and/or abuse are shown as direct contributors to the development of sexually aggressive

behavior (Marshall, 1989; Bentovin, 1998).
- The age of onset of victimization, the type of abuse and the severity of the abuse are identified as etiological factors (Prentky et al., 2000).
- Exposure to family violence is linked to the likelihood of sexually offending as an adolescent, as well as the severity of psychosexual disturbance (Fagan & Wexler, 1988; Smith, 1986).

E) Parental histories:

- High levels of personal victimization. (Kaplan et al, 1988).
- High levels of childhood sexual victimization among the mothers in their samples (25.5% and 55% respectively; Manocha & Mezey, 1998).
- Criminality, mental health problems, economic disadvantage, substance and alcohol abuse, and medical problems prevalent in families (Hsu & Starzynski, 1990; Graves et al., 1996; Browne & Falshaw, 1998; Bagley, 1992; Dolan et al., 1996; Manocha & Mezey, 1998; Pithers et al., 1998; Gray et al., 1999).

F) Family make up:
The makeup of families can range from single unwed parents to married biological parents. Studies done on diverse populations show:

- Approximately 70% of juvenile sex offenders lived in two-parent homes at the time their abusive behavior was discovered (Cellini, 1995).
- One third of juvenile sex offenders in a sample resided with both birth parents (Kahn & Chambers, 1991; Fehrenbach et al., 1986).
- 16% of a study of incarcerated sexually abusive juveniles came from intact families (Miner, Siekert, & Ackland 1997).
- Reported parental separation was in 41% of a sample studied by Sheridan and McGrath (1999).
- There were findings of high rates of parental separation, single parent homes, and in particular, absent father homes (Kaplan et al., 1990; Graves et al., 1996; O'Reilly et al., 1998; Hsu & Starzynski, 1990; Browne & Falshaw, 1998; Manocha & Mezey, 1998; Gray et al., 1999).
- Juveniles who committed sexual assaults against victims who were their peers or older were more likely to come from single-parent homes (78%) than those who committed "pedophilic" offenses (44%) or mixed offenses (37%). 53% of those who committed pedophilic offenses, however, lived with foster or blended families (Graves et al., 1996).
- Physical and/or emotional separations from one or both of the parents was experienced by many juveniles (Kahn & Chambers, 1991; Fehrenbach et al., 1986; Smith & Israel, 1987).

G) Social competence:

- Significant deficits in social competence was found in sexually abusive youth (Becker, 1990; Knight & Prentky, 1993; Ryan et al., 1996).

- Inadequate social skills, poor peer relationships, and social isolation are some of the difficulties identified by Fehrenbach et al. (1986), Katz (1990), Miner & Crimmins (1995), and Miner, Siekert, & Ackland (1997).
- Antisocial behaviors and an unstable home life are predictors of recidivism (Prentky et al., 1993).

H) Influence of kind of maltreatment:
The kind and the degrees of sexually offending behavior are correlated with the type of offending as shown in the following studies:

- Rapists and child molesters who began offending as juveniles had higher rates of emotional neglect and sexual victimization as children than those who began in adulthood. Their sexually abusive experiences also generally began at younger ages and were more severe (Knight & Prentky, 1993).
- Levels of sexual aggression appear to be inversely related to the degree of positiveness of the relationships between the juveniles and their mothers (Kobayashi et al., 1995).
- Family instability and problems in parent-child attachment are associated with more intrusive forms of juvenile sex offending (Weinrott, 1996).

I) Comparing the families of juvenile sexual offenders with the families of delinquents and other youth populations

In contrast to delinquent youth, sexually abusive juveniles:

- Were exposed to pornographic material at younger ages on the average, and to "harder core" pornography, than either status offenders or violent non-sex offending youths (Ford & Linney, 1995).
- Typically come from intact, "hothouse" families who evidenced severe pathology, including child maltreatment; have experienced less family instability (as defined by multiple male adult caregivers and/or desertions by their father figure); come from families with higher levels of marital stress; are more likely to have parents with mental health problems that require intervention; have fathers who evidence slightly greater rates of alcohol abuse; and are more likely to have parents who are overly ambitious for their children and excessively critical of poor grades (Bagley & Shewchuk-Dann, 1991).
- Are more likely to be disengaged from their families than other juveniles and, consequently, may have been cut off from possible sources of emotional support as well as less able to form positive attachments (Miner & Crimmins, 1995).
- Have a higher incidence of exposure to family violence and more frequent occurrence of physical and sexual abuse (Van Ness, 1984; Davis & Leitenberg, 1987; Lewis et al., 1979, 1981; Rubenstein et al., 1993; Ford & Linney, 1995).
- Observed intra-familial violence (79%) compared with 20% of their non-violent delinquent comparison group (Lewis et al., 1979).
  Had twice the number of victims (if sexually or physically abused) than the non-abused group, began their sex offending 1.6 years earlier, were more likely to have both female and male victims, and were less likely to limit their offending to family members (Cooper, Murphy, & Haynes, 1996).

- Were more socially maladjusted and evidenced more social anxiety and fear of heterosexual interactions than the two comparison groups - juvenile delinquents who had not committed sex offenses and a random group recruited from a local high school (Katz, 1990).
- Have fathers who were more rejecting and twice as lax with parental control as fathers of non-sexual offending adolescents. (Awad, Saunders, & Levene, 1984).
- Had mothers who were significantly more likely than mothers of non-incest perpetrators to report a personal history of early sexual victimization, a later sexual dysfunction, and to have received psychotherapy (Kaplan et al., 1990).
- Had mothers (36%) and fathers (10%) who were sexually victimized themselves, compared to only 9% of the mothers and 5.5% of the fathers of non-incest perpetrators (O'Brien, 1991).

3) Integration of concepts into models:
As the research and professional literature has become more substantial, theoretical models that integrate information from a broad variety of sources and professional fields have developed. Because these models take advantage of a richer, more complex information base, they are better able to account for and cope with the tremendous variety of youth and family systems.

They provide useful guides as well as organizational tools. These are the tools that help professionals to gather, process, and interpret the great and varied amount of information that is generated by a family assessment. Considering the number of interacting psychological, social, and physiological factors involved, the individual responsivity and pre-existing behavior patterns of any given youth and their families, as well as the immediate individual responses of a host of others they interact with, such tools and guides are a critical asset.

The following are some examples of integrated models – each developed by different and respected researchers and clinicians:

A) The Becker and Kaplan Model (1993) is based on the belief that: "Sexual behavior results from a combination of individual, family and social environmental variables". According to this hypothesis, those who develop a pattern of abusive behavior do so because they found the experience pleasurable, experienced no or minimal consequences, and experienced reinforcement through masturbatory activity coupled with fantasies.

B) The Barbaree et al. Model (1998) is based on the following: Development of sexually abusive behavior is considered the product of a number of causal factors including, disruption or inadequate attachment, childhood abuse, dysfunctional family patterns, and various temperamental factors. Here the focus is on unhealthy family systems, childhood trauma, and individual characteristics that provide vulnerability to the interruption of the normal developmental process. The theory is that the family is important both as an active source of negative influences and as a passive environment that provides the impetus to the development of sexual offending.

C) The Prentky and Knight Model (1989) states that: "There are four common deficits in the lives of sexually abusive youth: caretaker inconsistency;

institutionalization; family instability; and physical/sexual abuse. All four of these types of developmental deficits have a significant impact on a child's ability to form healthy and stable attachments."

There are models that focus on the identification of protective factors rather than on the identification of risk. One of these is the following:

4) Protective factors model (Bremer, 1998)
In 2001, Janis Bremer developed a Protective Factors Model that was initially designed as a scale which could be used to evaluate the adequacy of initial youth placement along the continuum of care. This is a ten-factor measure that looks at personal, social, sexual, and environmental assets in a given youth's life. Dr. Bremer was influenced by the work of Michael Rutter (1983) on delinquency, and the efficacy of a protective factors perspective in reducing the risk of delinquency. Rutter suggests that protective factors research will prove important both in identifying factors that support positive development individually and in interaction, mitigating the impact of adverse life experiences.

Protective factors are also useful in identifying the factors that are important to the provision of a non-offending non-abusive environment. Three of the protective factors directly address the family and the others involve the general living situation. These are:

A) Caregiver stability

Rutter (1972) found that caregiver stability was a central factor in the development of healthy social orientation and the ability to conceive of another in an empathic, humanized fashion. The literature to date continues to reinforce this finding, as well as the finding that the presence of multiple childhood caregivers is a strong predictor of delinquent behavior in adolescence. Hawkins et al. (1998) found that disrupted parent-child relationships were linked to subsequent violent behavior. Harris et al. (1993), in a study of violent adult recidivists, concluded that parent-child separation prior to age sixteen was a predictor of later violence. Farrington (1991) concluded the same about separation prior to age ten.

B) Family style

The ability of juveniles and young adults to behave in a healthy, safe and productive fashion in the community at large has been conclusively and repeatedly linked to whatever constituted/ constitutes family in their lives. The availability of structure and support are particularly crucial (Bremer, 2001), as are family support, communication, and parental involvement in children's lives (Benson et al., 1998).

C) Variables

Combining aspects of both Bremer's Family Style and Caregiver Stability categories, a wide range and number of studies show consistently that primary caregiver substance abuse, mental problems, and criminal behavior are linked to poor social, psychological, and behavioral development. Primary caregivers with these characteristics are generally not providers of stable care. The things they are often most inconsistent in providing are structure, support, communication, and reliable involvement in their dependent children's lives. An Al-Anon cliché often cited is this, "No matter what she did when she was drunk, I swear Mom was wonderful when she was straight. It was like she was two different people." Essentially, what this cliché indicates is that some children regularly suffer the deficits of serial multiple caregivers and the instability that involves without ever physically changing parents.

Exploiting our growing knowledge base

Even with all of the information available to us, we still cannot point to just one answer for our question. Where and why did this kind of behavior originate? None of the different theories, research, or clinical knowledge are really predictive devices. They are very useful organizational tools. These tools empower treatment providers not by making the job easy, but by making it easier to do the job well.

As Becker and Kaplan (1993) point out, "there are many different and diverse paths which both singly and in combination effect the development of sexually aggressive behavior. In fact, there may be as many developmental paths as there are sexually abusive youth."

The pathways to offending are not and probably never will be simple and straightforward. We do not know what variables need to be present, in what combinations, in what relationship to each other, at what critical points of development, with what intensities, and in what context in order for sexual abuse to occur and be maintained. In fact, it is probably unrealistic to speak of anything but risk factors and the broadest generalizations when considering the etiology of sexually abusive juveniles (Becker & Kaplan, 1993).

Given the great heterogeneity of the youth and of their families as well as the fact that individuals react differently to highly similar objective circumstances, it would be illogical for treatment providers to think that there are any pegs that will fit predefined holes, no matter how many "unique" holes one may allow for. The goal is not to find the best hole to peg these youth and their families but to find the particular path to health that their particular path to illness requires.

Our growing knowledge base about the individuality of the population enhances our ability to perform the tasks of assessing, evaluating, and treating youth and their families. A broad range of possibilities and solutions make treatment planning more individual and focused.

A case that demonstrates the essential individuality of every youth's developmental history involves fraternal twins admitted to different program tracks housed in the same residential facility. One twin was admitted as the result of several attempted suicides. The other had sexually abused an infant, the abuse characterized by a great deal of anger and aggression. He subsequently described fantasies, before and after the abuse, of bashing the child's head against the wall.

These twins came from a relatively stable and healthy family environment, and no significant differences in the ways they were parented were ever found. Both boys had been sexually abused at six by the same babysitter in the same way, twice a week for six months. The adolescent male sitter abused the twins one at a time, putting each into a separate room to do so. The child not being abused could hear the screams of the child being abused, was helpless to do anything about it, and knew that his turn was coming next. Both youths described feelings of anger against their parents for not protecting them and feeling helpless to protect either themselves or their sibling.

This outwardly identical experience appeared to be central to both twins' problems, but one boy had turned his anger on himself and his brother had turned his anger on others. Same babysitter, same family, same peers, identical genetic makeup – what was different?

After conducting copious clinical interviews with parents, siblings, grandparents, and schoolteachers, and gathering all the information apparently available, we could find no evidence of parental abuse, separation, or family system dysfunction. The boys went to the same school, had the same friends, and were thought by everyone to have much the same personality characteristics. Obviously there was some distinguishing variable that had had a significant impact on how the twins acted out their anger and feelings of helplessness. We simply couldn't find it. It may, in practical terms, never have been discoverable.

The intensive assessment process, however, had provided ample information about the boys, their family, and their social environments to intelligently plan their individual and family treatment. One great advantage in both of the boys' treatment was the fact that their family was fairly healthy, supportive, and readily engaged in treatment. The protective lapses that had led to the twins' victimization revolved in part around the parents' lack of accurate information about sexual abusers - information that was not generally available at the time. It may have been that even if they had talked with the boys about self-protection and self-disclosure it would not have been effective. Second, the parents were slightly repressive about sex. Though the lack of sex education and discouragement of discussing sexual matters had helped maintain the abusive relationship, their sexual attitudes were well within cultural norms.

The treatment plans for the twins were quite different and quite involved. The treatment plan for the family, however, was fairly simple and included the following: 1) basic information about child sexual abuse and its consequences as well as parental interventions; 2) education about depression and suicidal ideation, including parental interventions; 3) education about sexually abusive behavior, the development of family support systems, building relapse prevention plans and providing a non-offending family environment; 4) the development of family communication skills, particularly about sex and sexuality; 5) family therapy focus on the twins' feelings of being unprotected by their parents, and not being able to trust them to protect; 6) inclusion of the siblings of the twins, who feared that their parents couldn't protect them, didn't care about their problems, their fears about the twins' behaviors, and the community response to their siblings behaviors; 7) addressing and resolving the parents' feelings of helplessness, self-blame, and guilt about employing the babysitter; and 8) addressing and resolving the parents' feelings about the twins' behaviors and the humiliation the parents felt within their neighborhood, church and community because they felt like and believed they were perceived as bad parents.

This was not a high-risk family system. Without conducting a thorough assessment, and utilizing what we know about the families of sexually abusive youth (including the risk factors involved), we could not have intelligently planned treatment. We could not have identified either the underlying reason why an abusive babysitter was able to gain access, or that the abuse continued for some time without being discovered.

The family dynamic that supported the abuse was the parents' inability to talk to the twins about sexual issues, the common belief that every nice, hardworking teen would be a safe babysitter, the common parental practice of saying "do everything the babysitter tells you to do", and the absence of good prevention information and personal empowerment. These parents were doing the best that they could with the skills and information that they had, and so describing them as causal, much less blameworthy would be inaccurate. Yet it would also be inaccurate to say that the parents and family system did not play a role, however innocent, in the development and maintenance of the problem behaviors.

In turn, it would have been a serious mistake if we had not worked to engage the family as part of treatment, which would have left the family not only inadequately equipped to support the twins, but in many ways less functionally healthy than they were before the disclosure. As a consequence of the family involvement, the effectiveness of the twins' treatment and post-treatment prospects were greatly improved. The parents' feelings of helplessness were reduced as they learned and applied new skills. As an additional bonus, parents and siblings learned how to get their needs met and deal with their own need for healing.

The complexity and uniqueness of each specific youth's history simply underscores the importance of conducting a thorough and individualized assessment and evaluation of their family. Without client-specific, open-ended, and multi-modal assessment, treatment planning becomes a ship without a rudder.

Operationalizing research

Historically, our response to the problem of sexually abusive behavior in children and youth has been to base all assessment protocols, treatment philosophies, modalities and interventions on adult models. Professionals with a child welfare and/or child development background and familiar with the research on childhood development, childhood learning disabilities, family systems, delinquency, etc., protested this direction but were decidedly in the minority. Eventually, however, we began to pay serious attention to research and clinical experience in fields that complimented our own, and even to conduct our own studies based on the same subjects. As a result our direction began to slowly change. However, our acknowledgment that children and adolescents were not small adults, that children were not small adolescents, and that neither was defined by their sexual behavior took some time. When that finally happened – not one but two distinct fields had emerged – one dedicated to children and one dedicated to adolescents.

Although tunnel vision has been characteristic of our field for years, there have always been treatment programs and professionals who understood the clients and their problems from a holistic and child oriented point of view. In the early eighties it was noticeable that treatment programs for youth developed in agencies whose background was child welfare oriented, were more effective than the programs developed in agencies whose background was grounded in adult sexual aggression. It seemed to be easier for child welfare professionals to incorporate knowledge about sexually abusive behavior into their treatment models than for professionals with a background in adult sexual aggression to incorporate knowledge and expertise about child development into theirs. What was only an observation years ago now makes perfect sense.

One very significant example of the changes in treatment direction is the inclusion of families in treatment as well as the operational response to the research in many areas that is child centered. Of particular interest is our current knowledge about attachment and attachment disorders. The awareness that large numbers of youth in the mental health, juvenile justice, and child welfare populations presented with a history of physical, emotional and sexual trauma, or witnessing of domestic violence encouraged researchers to look at the possible connection between early childhood abuse and later behavior. Simultaneously, our growing understanding of the effects of early trauma, particularly structural and functional changes in the brain, gave us access to new ways of understanding and addressing the problems that resulted from early childhood abuse.

Three programs: operationalizing attachment theory

A child learns interactional skills and intimacy behavior that enables him to satisfy their social and intimacy needs in a way that is mutually satisfying and respectful of the needs of others. If a child learns to see intimidation, violence, and other abuses of power as normal and effective within the family, then the child will, in turn try to form relationships with others outside the family based on these strategies. An abusive environment that also facilitates the disruption of attachment with primary caregivers has a ripple effect, resulting in the child learning a maladaptive, coercive, aggressive and manipulative strategy for interpersonal interactions. The effect increasingly pervades more and more of the child's perceptions and behaviors, coloring their social and psychological development, self confidence, self esteem, and his ability to form extrafamilial attachments (Barbaree et al., 1998).

Several respected treatment professionals were asked to discuss how their understanding of attachment theory had shaped the programs at their different treatment programs.

1) The following is from a personal conversation with Dr. Phil Rich, the clinical director of the Stetson School in Barre, Massachusetts. The Stetson School is a 111 bed, long-term residential treatment center for sexually reactive children and juvenile sexual offenders, ranging from age nine to twenty-one, serving cognitively impaired students, as well as those with average and higher cognitive functioning.

"It has long been clear to me that relationships transform people from unsocialized

beings with little sense of either self or others into social, interactive individuals capable of rational and intentional behavior, and it is through relationships that we find, not just others, but our own self. In normal child development we see this process unfold, of symbiosis and individuation, separation and attachment, differentiation and bonding. It is through developmental pathology that we see the results of a failure to form meaning-ful relationships early in life, and resulting weaknesses in the capacity to understand, or even recognize, the minds of others and limited capacity for a sense of self agency or self efficacy. Driven nevertheless to get needs met, we develop behaviors that are, almost by necessity, asocial, and not infrequently antisocial and socially deviant. Failing to recog-nize the humanity of others, we are thus able to commit crimes against them, but we can only fail to recognize their humanity when we are unable to feel the connection and essential satisfaction normally derived through relationships.

Treatment programs, then, that consider social attachment and affiliation to be central to treatment will not simply pursue relationships through cognitive-behavioral exercises, psycho educational material, completion of workbooks, and individual and group thera-py that discuss relationships. These programs will build treatment environments that foster relationships, between treatment staff and clients, between clients and other clients, and between clients and their families. The seeking of attached relationships is a goal in these programs, in which staff absorbs difficult client behavior, provide client support, reflect back to clients their self worth, and help build social relationships in which clients start seeing themselves as capable and stop seeing others as objects. Clients thus build the skills of distress tolerance and self-regulation, learn to become attuned and empathic to others, and experience themselves as capable of setting and accomplishing goals (efficacy and agency). They come to recognize they are connected to others, and in so doing that others are connected to them."

2) Kevin Creeden, Director of Assessment and Research at the Whitney Academy in East Freetown, Massachusetts has long been a vocal proponent of the utility of attach-ment theory in the treatment of sexually abusive youth. He and his colleagues have integrated their understanding of the attachment research into a comprehensive treat-ment model at Whitney Academy, a residential treatment program for males ten to twenty-two. He says the following:

"Understanding the brain's response to both trauma and disorganized attachment expe-riences also directs us to interventions that are developmental, holistic, humanistic, and strength-based on both an individual and systemic level. It proposes that children are remarkably resilient; that regular engagement in caring, consistent relationships can alter attachment styles; and that thoughtful, persistent stimulation of neural pathways can change brain function and possibly brain structure.

The model reflects a belief that all types of abusive behavior (sexual, physical, and emo-tional) are essentially reflective of a striving to meet basic relational needs. Our treat-ment approach assumes that sexually abusive behavior arises in large part (but not sole-ly) from a fundamental, even universal, need that individuals have for safety, attention, acceptance, nurturance, and care from other human beings. Sexually abusive behavior is only the process that some individuals follow to meet these needs that can become dis-torted, abusive, or even deviant. Therefore what in the end makes abusive behavior abu-sive is not that the needs being met are different or perverse but that the process for meeting those needs lacks the attunement, trust, and mutuality that eventually distinguishes positive from negative human relationships.

We also believe that the fundamental goal in treating abusive behavior should not be defined merely as the absence of abuse in relationships, but as the increased capacity to engage and maintain stable, mutual, and intimate relationships with others. Attachment difficulties are not only seen as a treatment issue; they are a treatment obstacle in that they interfere with the development of the trust, safety, openness, and attunement, which we feel are essential for learning, integration, and change to occur. Likewise, we believe that our student's trauma experiences are inextricably intertwined with their attachment difficulties, learning problems, general behavior problems, and more specifically their sexually abusive behavior. As opposed to thinking that addressing the student's trauma history will inhibit or delay their ability to address their own sexually abusive behavior, we have come to believe that not addressing the impact of the student's own trauma will simply impede the learning and (more importantly) the effective use of skills we are teaching them to control/change their inappropriate and abusive behavior."

(The previous excerpt is part of a chapter giving a comprehensive overview of attachment theory and its utilization at Whitney Academy. The chapter entitled "Integrating Trauma and Attachment Theory into the Treatment of Children who sexually Abuse" is found in *Children and Young People Who Sexually Abuse: New Theory, Research and Practice Developments* edited by Martin C. Calder and published by Russell House Publishing, Lyme Regis, Dorset.)

3) The third program that shared information, New Hope Treatment Centers in Charleston, South Carolina, has also made significant changes in programming based on their understanding of the impact of developmental/attachment issues on sexually abusive youth. Their 52-bed program for sexually aggressive males, The Waypoint Program, is located in Summerville, South Carolina. Jim Grady, MCJ, the Executive Director of New Hope Charleston, and Sherri Reynolds, LPC, the Director of Clinical Services, had this to say about their program:

"The Waypoint Program, in their treatment of sexual aggression, emphasizes developmental and relational processes. Focus on areas such as attachment, trauma, family systems, individuation, and biological conditions are vital. The primary clinical focus of the program is understanding the individual needs of the patient and developing specific, effective interventions promoting self-regulation, healthy coping strategies, and overall wellness.

The primary importance of therapeutic relationships forms the philosophical base for the New Hope program. Several years ago, we made programmatic changes in response to our understanding of the attachment research and also as the result of our observation that a significant number of the clients admitted to New Hope suffered from a disruption of fundamental attachment relationships.

We believe that by identifying the need for support, building trust, and establishing relationships we are providing not only a safe entry into treatment but a primary treatment intervention as well. The relationship includes the therapist/ staff as role model of expected treatment outcomes – for example all of the healthy interpersonal processes including communication skills, conflict resolution, and boundary negotiation, etc., to name a few.

In residential treatment, it is always a primary responsibility of staff to provide a safe environment and to provide safety in relationships. It is the caregiver's task to integrate nurturing, stimulation, and limit-setting into those relationships. This means, among other things that counter transference/ transference issues between direct care staff and residents have to be constantly identified and directly addressed. Since many clients have delayed processing abilities, their ability to appraise relationships is limited, and thus there is a need for additional and constant guidance and help."

The following are some of the programmatic changes:

1) *Environment* – More child friendly, developmentally appropriate, less "sterilization" and "control" over ambiguous areas like touch, music, pictures; amount of structure is determined by the individual ability to self regulate.
2) *Relationships* – Continuous encouragement of healthy relationships; training on such relationship areas as boundaries and boundary negotiation, healthy touch, transference/counter transference, and values clarification. Humor is used in daily functioning. Activities are integrated with both staff and resident participation.
3) *Types of Interventions* – Emphasis on verbal process when residents exhibit problematic behavior; continuous training as to attachment styles, traumatic attachment, relational dynamics, and trauma reenactment in relational style.
4) *Assessments/Diagnostics* – Psychosocial assessment: on admission, an assessment protocol called an Interactive Timeline establishes a collaborative therapeutic relationship between staff and client. The client is "in control" of his own timeline and controls the information he gives to the program instead of the program using archival information, thus building trust and rapport right from the beginning.
5) *Process of Performance Improvement* – Resident Satisfaction Surveys: changes are made based on client feedback furthering the building of trust and client ownership of the program. Current examples include resident task teams on the food menu and aesthetics.
6) *Therapeutic Community Process* – Therapeutic community is built and maintained by residents who have a vocal role in all decision-making.
7) *Training and Small Group Supervision* – Process oriented in delivery.

There are many other programs and issues that could be examined. These three programs, however, represent excellent examples of how research and clinical knowledge can and should be operationalized.

Family assessment and evaluation

Prior to putting any of our newly acquired knowledge to use we have to know exactly what that particular knowledge has to do with the individual youth and families we serve, and how that knowledge can help in the development of useful treatment interventions.

All knowledge-based treatment programs begin with the assessment, evaluation and treatment planning of the clients involved. Although this is a very basic task in any family program, many professionals find it a difficult one, and some even skip it altogether. The following material on assessment, evaluation, and treatment planning below is a compilation of the information published in other professional literature, as well as the addition of new materials. I continue to repeat this information because many treatment professionals find the assessment and evaluation steps complicated and confusing, and some will even ignore them completely. Without accomplishing these steps, however, there is really nothing to serve as a basis for treatment. For this reason, I continue to try to simplify and clarify them as much as possible. In order to serve a useful purpose they must be both practical and functional.

These are the previous publications that have covered material on assessment and treatment planning with families: 1) "Essentials of a Good Treatment Programme for Sexually Abusive Juveniles. Part Four. A Programme for Working with the Parents of Sexually Abusive Juveniles," in Gary O'Reilly et al. [Eds.] *Handbook of Clinical Intervention with Juvenile Abusers*, Wiley Publishing, London, England, 2004; 2) "Family Reunification in Sibling Incest", Calder, M.C. (Ed.) (2004), *Children and young people who sexually abuse: new theory, research and practice developments*. Dorset: Russell House Publishing. (In publication); and 3) "The Adolescent Sex Offender's Family in Treatment," In G. Ryan & S. Lane [Eds.] (1997), *Juvenile Sexual Offending: Causes, Consequences and Correction*, Lexington, MA: Lexington Books.

To begin at the beginning: just who is family and what is assessment

The major goal of assessment is to develop the fullest possible understanding of family circumstances and problems so that the treatment provider can plan the interventions that will be helpful in solving those problems. Although there are formal instruments that assess family dynamics, in general the family itself is the most important and richest source of information. This is only logical, given the highly individualized nature of the families of this population. An extensive clinical interview by a competent family therapist as well as the gathering of all pertinent collateral information available should provide the data necessary for the treatment plan. If other assessments are needed, these will be identified during the course of the clinical interviews.

Clinical interviews serve many uses other than data collection. For example, they serve as an entry into treatment and as a treatment intervention. They provide excellent opportunities for forming relationships, establishing mutual trust, observing family dynamics, checking out collateral information, and establishing professional competency. Since one of the goals in family treatment is to join in a collaborative effort with all parties involved, the relationships formed are as important as the information received. In fact without such a relationship and the engagement of the family it produces, treatment cannot even begin. A critical mistake in family therapy is to begin treatment before a relationship is established.

The idea of family must be viewed in a larger and inclusive rather than exclusive context. The traditional definition of family isn't always realistic in the 21st century. Parents and/or family may be blood kin, but sometimes are simply our primary support system. They can be the people that we live, work, and/or play with, that we can count on, that are there when we are happy and support us when we are suffering and that sometimes serve as parental or familial surrogates. Working with this inclusive definition of family can extend even further what is meant by extended family. This is not uncommon in the southern United States where aunts and uncles are often just close family friends or someone who fulfills the function of an aunt or uncle. One of my colleagues was once characterized as my play brother thus defining our relationship in a way that fit the dynamics rather than the bloodlines. Another colleague, who has no children of her own, is an "aunt" to her best friend's son.

Family also includes absent family members or systems, or simply the lingering impact of family dynamics. An absent family or family member can be present in ways that are very real, and helpful or damaging.

All of us have unique family circumstances and this includes sexually abusive youth. By this I mean the people who are considered members of the family group, current living situations, socio-economic status, ethnic, cultural and regional attributes, family support or non support, to name only a few examples. Some families will readily cooperate in treatment; others will need to be actively encouraged; and still others will either provide no support or will actively sabotage. Not all family assessments will be clear and straightforward and many will require not only complex data collection but informed interview techniques as well.

Structuring assessment and evaluation

Prior to discussing the structuring of assessments and evaluations, it is important to clarify the meaning of those terms – both in definition and in operation. It is not unusual to find these terms used interchangeably although their meaning is actually quite different. The clearest and most comprehensive definition of assessment and evaluation was made by Maddock and Larson (1995): "Assessment is the process of gathering information and applying expert knowledge in order to judge the status of a client's problem and to understand the context within which the problem is occurring. Evaluation is the application of some criteria and forming of judgments. Data gathering is the obtaining of information about the client. Observation is looking at patterns of language, non-verbal behavior and behavior as a whole. A pattern is a process of behavior that is observed over a period of time."

A second misconception is that assessment and evaluation are time limited. In actuality assessment is not a procedure at all but a process, which takes place in a series of stages and interviews and will continue throughout treatment. New data emerges over time, the accuracy and reliability of information changes as the family's trust in the treatment provider grows.

Third, an assessment is much more than a collection of facts. For example: 1) The subjective perceptions of family members, both collectively and individually, are as important to the family system as any objective facts. 2) The observation of behavior is just as important a source of information as any verbalizations. 3) Awareness of the professional self is important because the same data can be interpreted in different ways; their interpretation affected by the professional and personal perceptions, preconceptions, and beliefs of the assessor.

For all of the above reasons, the best working policy for therapists is to operate from a blank slate, giving youth and families the benefit of the doubt until the test of time and really truly objective evidence indicates otherwise. For example when young children appear out of control this does not always mean the children are spoiled or the parents are poor disciplinarians, but it could mean that the children are frightened, feeling helpless, have a stomach ache, or a host of other explanations.

Finally, understanding any particular family means that it is just as necessary if not more to know the family's strengths, assets, and resources just as well as their problems. Parents with a strong marital relationship will provide each other support and comfort during this painful experience, and good individual and couple stress management skills will sustain them. Parents who have good verbal communication skills will be able to manage the myriad of systems involved with more ease. Their strengths will determine outcome.

No information is static – not from our clients or from our professional resources. Information and beliefs change as we grow in knowledge and understanding. In this chapter's discussion of assessment and evaluation we encourage the family therapist to make active use of the current information about families and children from theory, research, clinical experience, and professional literature, whether it is from the child development field or the field of youthful sexual aggression.

The following is a review of some of the information that will be important to capture during family assessments. The course of treatment and the outcome will be effected in significant ways by their presence, absence, or degree. Any assessment protocol should look for these dynamics. These include but are not limited to:

- physically and/or emotionally inaccessible parents
- physical and emotional neglect
- physical, mental, and/or sexual abuse
- family or domestic violence
- numerous living situations
- lax parental control, family disorganization, inadequate quality of care
- a culture of secrecy
- a sexualized environment, lack of sexual boundaries, presence of sexually explicit materials
- "uncaring" parents
- family boundaries that are either disengaged or enmeshed
- environments characterized by chaos
- relationships with parents disrupted, leading to the formation of inadequate attachments
- familial anxiety and poor social judgment
- negative communication patterns, aggressive statements and interruptions, the lack of supportive communication
- lower levels of perceived family support
- parents with high levels of victimization, domestic violence, mental health problems, criminal behaviors, substance and alcohol abuse, economic disadvantage, and medical problems

After capturing the information in the assessment necessary, a formal evaluation of that information is generally produced in written form. Then one takes that evaluation in order to develop an individualized family treatment plan. Although family treatment actually begins with the first contact made between the persons involved – clients and professionals – it is the family treatment plan that will establish the individual family goals of treatment and the objectives necessary to reach those goals.

Creating a family treatment plan

A treatment plan is a road map. This road map identifies the following for the family and the treatment provider: 1) your destination; 2) the roads to take to get to your destination; 3) the benchmarks along that road; and 4) indicates how much further it is to journey's end. This map serves to focus the treatment provider, the youth, the family, and other interested parties on the tasks necessary to be accomplished in order to reach the goals for family health. It serves as a guide but in actuality is also an accountability measure for the youth, his/her family, and for the treatment provider.

Keep in mind that a treatment plan is a living breathing entity that will very likely change in the course of treatment, that everyone's goals may not always coincide, and that all people reach goals at different times and in different ways.

Treatment planning has been made simple and practical in a book entitled, *Child and Adolescent Psychotherapy Treatment Planner* (Jongsma, Peterson, & McInnis, 1996). The authors recommend that the process of developing treatment plans take place in a logical series of steps, effectively taking away the mystery behind all treatment planning.

Since family systems fall on a continuum that runs from healthy to pathological and from supportive to hostile, the amount and intensity of the work needed varies greatly. The composition of any given family can range from a traditional nuclear unit, to single parent, to parents of the same sex, to community groups as parents, to foster care, and so on. They could be comprised primarily of organizations and professionals who fill the roles and provide the services traditionally provided by a family unit. The behavior disclosed can be the result of one event or the result of intergenerational events. These and other variables will determine the length and complexity of plans.

One thing is constant: the primary goal of all family treatment plans is to provide the family with the skills and the experiences necessary to interrupt family dynamics that may support or encourage offending behavior and replace them with patterns and environments that support a non-offending lifestyle. This would include the self-management skills to live that non-offending lifestyle. Short of this goal there are other acceptable goals for the family, but these are rarely identified at the outset of planning and many times only become clear as treatment progresses. These goals are called family resolution or the reconciling of family issues, but are no less important than the primary goal, which may not always be the most beneficial goal.

Family treatment planning: the ten steps

Step One: Treatment plan development. Developing the plan involves the family therapist, and/or the treatment team, the youth, and the youth's family in a collaborative effort. In some cases there may be other members, such as the victim's therapist, foster parents, group home parents, foster services case manager, probation or parole, etc. As each situation is different so the players will be different. A collaborative effort not only gives more input, more information, and more cooperation but also gives everyone involved a motivation to problem solve and to be invested in the outcome. This is a particularly important issue with families who may be feeling helpless and out of control of their own lives and of their families. It is only reasonable that everyone involved in living the plan needs to be involved in making the plan.

Families can be completely overwhelmed – sometimes just with day to day survival. Something that the therapist may see as a small change may be a huge accomplishment for the family involved. Or what to the therapist might seem an impossible achievement may be just another obstacle to overcome – one of many, to some families.

Several years ago I worked with a family that was facing overwhelming problems. The mother worked full time at a minimum wage job and was the family's sole support. The father was in a wheelchair, a disabled Vietnam veteran. The victimized sibling was in St. Jude Hospital dying of cancer. Their four-year-old had just been diagnosed with juvenile diabetes, and their son – my client, was in a secure residential treatment program for sexually abusing his dying sister. Simply on the basis of the above circumstances I would not have asked or expected very much of this family, but by collaborating with them in the treatment planning process I learned of their incredible strength and spirit. This family taught me that it can be a mistake not only to overestimate the capabilities of any individual family, but to underestimate those capabilities as well. This family was one of those teaching families – not only for the treatment provider but also for the other families in their multi family group.

Step Two: Select the problem. Keep foremost in mind the findings of research and clinical studies identifying high-risk factors in the family systems of sexually abusive youth. As you gather data during the family assessment phase these are the factors most important to identify and target for change. Although it is tempting to over generalize these characteristics in treatment planning the first rule of thumb is to simplify and then simplify some more. For example, a dysfunctional family system covers many different levels and degrees of problems. Changing a dysfunctional family system appears both an impossible and overwhelming task to the family as well as the family therapist, but changing the different characteristics that make up a dysfunctional family system appears doable. For example, identify the meaning of dysfunction in each particular family by breaking this down into the problems that make up that dysfunction. State problems in terms that are realistic and establish goals that are achievable.

Step Three: Define the problem. This simply means that you define how this problem is evidenced in the family. Family dysfunction is not a single discrete phenomenon and all of the factors that make up family dysfunction may not appear in every family. It is important to break this term down into the various dynamics that are characteristic of a particular dysfunctional family system. Descriptors should be in clear and behavioral terms avoiding such terminology as poor, inadequate, or inappropriate as these terms are not descriptive at all. In the Smith family, dysfunction is displayed in the following ways: A pattern of acting out feelings of anger and frustration, an inability to share feelings on a verbal level, family members being emotionally detached from each other and displaying limited nurturing behaviors. Problem-solving is approached by the use of physically abusive behaviors, and the parental figures are unable to set limits and follow through on consequences. In the Jones family, dysfunction is displayed by the social isolation of the family from the community and the social isolation of family members from each other. It is displayed in the parentification of the children, the sexualized modes of compensation used by mother and father, and in the absence of any parental supervision or guidance. By avoiding global terminology and stating family dysfunctions in simple behavioral terms, interventions can be developed that are focused and individualized.

Step Four: Indicate strengths. No family is without some strengths, it is only that some have more than others. It is the task of the treatment provider to identify and utilize those strengths or to facilitate their development. Individual or collective strengths will provide the tools necessary to endure, accept, and/or overcome the problems facing families of sexually abusive youth. For example, a strong community support system is of immense help to families in times of trouble. If this is already available, then it is a given strength and can be utilized to further treatment success. If it is not available, then it should be targeted as an area to be developed, as it is one of the characteristics of a functional family.

Step Five: Develop the goals. Goals are global, stated in measurable and behavioral terms and intended for the resolution or the desired outcome of the problem dynamics that you have targeted in the treatment plan. Goals must also be achievable given the family's strengths and liabilities, and the length of treatment time available to accomplish those goals. Objectives are the small steps that need to be taken in order to reach the indicated goals. If it is less confusing you can speak of objectives as the small goals that must be accomplished before you can reach the final goal. For example, open and honest communication may be an ultimate goal. The objectives to reach that goal can include learning to express opinions in a direct, non-aggressive manner, learning to manage and express anger in a way that is healthy and non-abusive, and learning how not to personalize disagreements. In a real sense these are also goals but in the language of treatment planning they are called objectives.

Step Six: Construct the objectives. Objectives are steps that are stated in terms of measurable behaviors that are both manageable and achievable. Treatment in and of itself is not an objective unless the client has refused to participate in treatment. For example, attendance at multi-family group is not an objective unless the family's participation has been indicated as a critical to the treatment plan and they have refused to attend. In this instance, gaining their trust and preparing them for attending the group would an objective.

Treatment planning can be very difficult if you don't break the problem down and keep breaking it down into understandable and clear constructs. For example, sex offending may be what brings a youth and their family into treatment, but to simply label that as a problem area is too broad. This behavior includes many and numerous problem areas such as familial denial, minimization and projection of blame, cognitive distortions, etc. Each problem must be addressed and completed and others added in order to reach the ultimate goal.

Each goal and associated objectives are developed as a step toward attaining the over-all treatment aims. Objectives are prioritized in the manner that will be realistic in facilitating the family's growth without creating blocks to working other problem areas. Plans that are difficult to understand often indicate that the problems and objectives have not been broken down enough to be manageable.

Step Seven: Create the interventions. The interventions identified to reach the objectives are the actions of those involved in creating the treatment plan. They are designed to help the family complete the objectives. They are described in observable, measurable terms to enable the staff to implement the intervention in a consistent fashion and to be accountable for their work. Interventions should be selected on the basis of the family's needs as well as the treatment provider's therapeutic skills and can come from a wide variety of approaches; cognitive, developmental, dynamic, behavioral, etc.

Step Eight: Modalities. Modalities are simply the components in which the interventions will be provided, and can range from a group teaching modality to the every-day living environment. The modalities utilized are those that will fit the individual needs of the clients. For example, some families who are socially isolated will benefit from multifamily therapy group, and families who have a background of mixed criminal and mental health issues might not.

Step Nine: Person responsible for the intervention. This simply identifies the person responsible for delivering the intervention.

Step Ten: State the proposed target date. Each objective should have a target date for it to be achieved. If after review on this target date the objective hasn't been reached the target date would be extended.

Outcome: a living, breathing treatment plan

These ten steps are not finite. Since issues can change during treatment, the plan should be seen as a dynamic document, which can and must be updated regularly to reflect any major change of problem, goal, objective, or intervention. Regular reviews also help families to see in concrete terms what has been accomplished, what work is still in progress or ongoing, and what objectives remain unaddressed.

As a treatment plan is an action plan, reviews and updates, which are periodic evaluations of whether or not the treatment plan is working, are a necessary part of the plan's success. During an update the plan is reviewed and documented as accomplished, extended, or changed to another plan. This documentation states the date of the review of the treatment plan, by whom it was reviewed, and with whom the information was shared.

Because plans are meant to be used by the youth and the youth's family as well as professional staff, they are not really useful if they are based on professional terminology. Some therapists write the treatment plan with the family present and ask to use their terminology. This can be done quite easily if one is proficient with a computer. This involvement of the family in planning shows your respect for their opinions, gives them ownership in the plan, and is empowering to family members at a point in the process when they feel most helpless and out of control.

A treatment plan is not difficult to understand – it is just an outline of goals, the objectives necessary to meet those goals, the interventions that will be utilized to meet those objectives, the modalities, staff members, and time frame for completion of those interventions.

Conclusion

This chapter has tried to give you the information that you need as a base for the establishment of a family treatment program. My mother used to say, "Old age is not for sissies". Neither is the work of a family therapist. It will be helpful, however, to start with as much knowledge as possible about the families of sexually abusive youth in general, and then gather as much knowledge as possible about the particular family for whom you are providing services. Then take that knowledge and map out your plan of action.

References

Araji, S. (1997). *Sexually aggressive children: coming to understand them.* Thousand Oaks, CA: Sage Publications.

Awad, G.A., Saunders, E. & Levene, J. (1984). A clinical study of male adolescent sexual offenders. *International Journal of Offender Therapy and Comparative Criminology.* 28(1), 105-115.

Bagley, C. (1992). Characteristics of 60 children and adolescents with a history of sexual assault against others: evidence from a comparative study. *Journal of Forensic Psychiatry.* 3, (2).

Bagley, C. & Shewchuk-Dann, D. (1991). Characteristics of 60 children and adolescents who have a history of sexual assault against others: Evidence from a controlled study. *Journal of Child and Youth Care.* Fall, 43-52.

Barbaree, H., Marshall, W., & McCormack (1998). The development of sexually deviant behaviour among adolescents and its' implications for prevention and treatment. *The Irish Journal of Psychology.* 19, 1, 1-31.

Becker, J. (1990). Treating adolescent sexual offenders. *Professional Psychology Research and Practice.* 21, 362-365.

Becker, J.V. & Hunter, J.A. (1997). Understanding and treating child and adolescent sexual offenders. In T.H. Ollendick and R.J. Prinz (Eds.) *Advances in Clinical Child Psychology* 19. NY: Plenum Press.

Becker, J. & Kaplan, M. (1993). Cognitive Behavioral Treatment of the Juvenile Sex Offender. in H. Barbaree, W. Marshall and S. Hudson (Eds.). *The Juvenile Sex Offender.* NY: Guilford Press.

Benson, Peter, Galbraith, J. and Espeland, P. (1998). *What kids need to succeed: proven practical ways to raise good kids*. Minneapolis, MN: Free Spirit Publishing.

Benson, P.L. (1993). *The troubled journey: a profile of American youth*. Minneapolis, MN: Search Institute.

Bentovim, A. (1998). Cleveland 10 years on: a mental health perspective. *Family Law*. April, pp. 202-207.

Bischof, G., Stith, S., & Wilson, S. (1992). A comparison of the family systems of adolescent sex offenders and non-sexual offending delinquents. *Family Relations*. 41, 318-323.

Bischof, G.P., Stith, S.M., & Whitney, M.L. (1995). Family environments of adolescent sex offenders and other juvenile delinquents. *Adolescence*, 30, 117, 157-170.

Blaske, D. M., Borduin, C. M., Henggeler, S. W., & Mann, B. J. (1989). Individual, family, and peer characteristics of adolescent sex offenders and assaultive offenders. *Developmental Psychology*. 25, 846-855.

Blaske, D.M., Borduin, C.M., & Henggeler, S.W. (1989). Individual, family and peer characteristics of adolescent sex offenders and assaultive offenders. *Developmental Psychology*, 25, 5, 846-855.

Browne, K. & Falshaw, L. (1998). Treatment work with young people in secure care. *The Irish Journal of Psychology*. 19, 1, 208-225.

Bremer, J.F. (1998). Challenges in the assessment and treatment of sexually abusive adolescents. *The Irish Journal of Psychology*, 19, 1, 82-92.

Cellini, H.R. 1995. Assessment and treatment of the adolescent sexual offender. In B.K. Schwartz and H.R. Cellini (Eds.). *The Sex Offender: Vol. 1. Corrections, Treatment and Legal Practice*. Kingston, NJ: Civic Research Institute, pp. 6.1-6.12.

Cooper, C., Murphy W.D., & Haynes, M.R. (1996). Characteristics of abused and non-abused adolescent sexual offenders. *Sexual Abuse: A Journal of Research and Treatment*. 8, 2, 105-119.

Davis, G.E., & Leitenberg, H. (1987). Adolescent sex offenders. *Psychological Bulletin*.101, 3, 417-427.

Dolan, M., Holloway, J., Bailey, S. & Kroll, L. (1996). The psychosocial characteristics of juvenile sexual offenders. *Medicine, Science and the Law*. 36, 4, 343-352.

Farrington, D.P. (1991). Childhood aggression and adult violence: Early predictors and later-life outcomes. In D.J. Pepler & K.H. Rubin (Eds.). *The development and treatment of childhood aggression* (pp. 5-29). New Jersey: Lawrence Erlbaum Associates.

Farrington, D.P., Loeber, R., Elliot, D., Hawkins, J.D., Kandel, D.B., Klein, M.W., McCord, J., Rowe, D.C., & Trembley, R.E. (1990). Advancing knowledge about the onset of delinquency and crime. In B.B. Lahey & A.E. Kazdin (eds.). *Advances in Clinical Child Psychology* (pp. 283-342). New York: Plenum.

Fehrenbach, P.A., Smith, W., Monastersky, C., & Deisher, R.W. (1986). Adolescent sexual offenders: Offender and offense characteristics. *American Journal of Orthopsychiatry* 56(2): 225-233

Ford, M.A. & Linney, J.A. (1995). Comparative analysis of juvenile sexual offenders, violent non-sexual offenders and status offenders. *Journal of Interpersonal Violence.* 10, 56-70.

Graves, R., Openshaw, D., Ascione, F., & Erickson, S. (1996). Demographic & parental characteristics of youthful sex offenders. *Individual Journal of Offender Therapy and Comparative Criminonology.* 40(4), 300-317.

Gray, A., Pithers, W.D., Busconi, A., & Houchens, P. (1999). Developmental and etiological characteristics of children with sexual behaviour problems: treatment implications. *Child Abuse & Neglect.* 23, 6, 601-621.

Harris, G.T., Rice, M.E., & Quinsey, V.L. (1993). Violent recidivism of mentally disordered offenders: the development of a statistical prediction instrument. *Criminal Justice and Behavior.* 20, 315-335.

Hawkins, J.D., Herrenkohl, T., Farrington, D.P., Brewer, D., Catalano, R.F., & Harachi, T.W. (1998). A review of predictors of youth violence. In R. Loeber & D.P. Farrington (Eds.), *Serious and violent juvenile offenders: Risk factors and successful interventions* (pp. 106-146). Thousand Oaks, CA: Sage.

Hsu, L.K.G. & Starzynski, J. (1990). Adolescent rapists and adolescent child sexual assaulters. *International Journal of Offender Therapy and Comparative Criminology.* 34, 23-31.

Jongsma, A. Peterson, M. & McInnis, W. (1996). *Child and adolescent psychotherapy treatment planner.* NY: Wiley & Sons.

Kahn, T.J., & Chambers, H.J. (1991). Assessing reoffense risk with juvenile sexual offenders. *Child Welfare* LXX (3): 333-345.

Kaplan, M.S., Becker, J.V. & Cunningham-Rathner, J. (1988). Characteristics of parents of adolescent incest perpetrators: Preliminary findings. *Journal of Family Violence.* 3, 183-191.

Kaplan, M., Becker, J. & Martinez, D. (1990). A comparison of mothers of adolescent incest vs. non-incest perpetrators. *Journal of family Violence.* 5, 3, 209-214.

Katz, R.C. (1990). Psychosocial adjustment in adolescent child molesters. *Child Abuse and Neglect.* 14 (4) 567-575.

Knight, R.A. & Prentky, R.A. (1993). Exploring characteristics for classifying juvenile sex offenders. In Barbaree, Marshall & Hudson (Eds.), *The Juvenile Sex Offender* (pp.45-83). NY: Guildford Press.

Kobayashi, J. Sales, B.D., Becker, J.V, Figueredo, A.J. & Kaplan, M.S. (1995). Perceived Parental Deviance, Parent-Child Bonding, Child Abuse and Child Sexual Aggression. *Sexual Abuse: A Journal of Research and Treatment.* v7 n1 p25-44.

Lewis, D.O., Shankok, S.S. & Pincus, J.H. (1979). Juvenile sexual assaulters. *American Journal of Psychiatry.* 136, 1194 -1196.

Manocha, K.F. & Mezey, G. (1998). British adolescents who sexually abuse: A descriptive study. *The Journal of Forensic Psychiatry.* 9, 3, 588-608.

Marshall, W.L. (1989). Invited essay: Intimacy, loneliness and sexual offenders. *Behaviour Research and Therapy.* 27, 491-503.

Miner, M.H. & Crimmins, C.L.S. (1995). Adolescent sex offenders: Issues of etiology and risk factors. In B.K. Schwartz and H.R. Cellini [Eds.] *The Sex Offender: Vol. 1. Corrections, Treatment and Legal Practice,* Kingston. NJ: Civic Research Institute, pp. 9.1-9.15.

Miner, M.H., Siekert, G.P., & Ackland, M.A. (1997). Evaluation: *Juvenile Sex Offender Treatment Program, Minnesota Correctional Facility—Sauk Centre.* Final report—Biennium 1995-1997. Minneapolis, MN: University of Minnesota, Department of Family Practice and Community Health, Program in Human Sexuality.

Morenz, B., & Becker, J.V. (1995). The treatment of youthful sexual offenders. *Applied and Preventive Psychology.* 4, (4), 247-256.

New, M.J., Stevenson, J. & Skuse, D. (1999). Characteristics of mothers of boys who sexually abuse. *Child Maltreatment.* 4, 1, 21-31.
O'Brien, M. (1991). Taking sibling incest seriously. in Quinn-Patton, M. (ed.) *Family Sexual Abuse: Frontline Research and Evaluation.* Beverly Hills, CA: Sage.

O'Reilly, G., Sheridan, A., Carr, A., Cherry, J., Donohoe, E., McGrath, K. Phelan, S., Tallon, M. & O'Reilly, K. (1998). A descriptive study of adolescent sexual offenders in an Irish community-based treatment programme. *The Irish Journal of Psychology.* 19, 1, 152-167.

Pithers, W.D., Gray, A., Busconi, A. & Houchens, P. (1998). Caregivers of children with sexual behavior problems: Psychological and familial functioning. *Child Abuse & Neglect.* 22, 43-55.

Prentky, R., Harris, B., Frizzell, K., & Righthand, S. (2000). An Actuarial Procedure for Assessing Risk with Juvenile Sex Offenders. *Sexual Abuse: A Journal of Research and Treatment.* 12, 2, 71-93.

Richardson, G., Kelly, T.P., Bhate, R. & Graham, F. (1997). Group differences in abuser and abuse characteristics in a British sample of sexually abusive adolescents. *Sexual Abuse: A Journal of Research and Treatment.* 9, 3, 239-257.

Rubenstein, M., Yeager, C.A., Goodstein, B.A. & Lewis, D.O. (1993). Sexually assaultive male juveniles: a follow-up. *American Journal of Psychiatry.* 150, 262-265.

Rutter, M. (1972). *Maternal Deprivation Reassessed.* Middlesex, England: Penguin Books, Ltd.

Rutter, M. & Giller, H. (1984). *Juvenile Delinquency: Trends and Perspectives.* NY: The Guilford Press

Ryan, G. & Lane, S. (1997). *Juvenile sexual offending: causes, consequences and correction.* Lexington, MA, Lexington Books.

Ryan G., Miyoshi, T. Metzer, J., Krugman, R. & Fryer, G. (1996). Trends in a national sample of sexually abusive youths. *Journal of the American Academy of Child and Adolescent Psychiatry.* 35 (1).

Serfabi R. (1990). Admitters and deniers among adolescent sex offenders and their families: a preliminary study. American Journal of *Orthopsychiatry.* 60, 460-465.

Smith, H. & Israel, E. (1987). Sibling incest: a study of the dynamics of 25 cases. *Child Abuse & Neglect.* 11, pp. 101-108.

Smith, W.R., and Monastersky, C. 1986. Assessing juvenile sexual offenders' risk for reoffending. *Criminal Justice and Behavior.* 13(2), 115-140.

Stith, S. & Bischof, G. (1996). Communication patterns in families of adolescent sex offenders. In Cahn, D. & Lloyd, S. (Ed.s) *Family Violence from a communication Perspective.* Chap. 6, pp. 108-126. Sage Publications.

Thomas, J & Viar, W., (2004). Essentials of a good treatment programme for sexually abusive juveniles. Part four. A programme for working with the parents of sexually abusive juveniles. In Gary O'Reilly, et al., (Eds.) *Handbook of Clinical Intervention with Juvenile Abusers.* Wiley Publishing, London, England, 2004;

Thomas, J. & Viar, W. (2003). Family reunification in sibling incest. In M.C. Calder (Ed.). *Children and young people who sexually abuse: new theory, research and practice developm1yents.* Dorset: Russell House Publishing

Thomas, J. (1993). The adolescent sex offender's family in treatment. In G. Ryan & S. Lane (Eds). *Juvenile Sexual Offending: Causes, Consequences and Correction.* Lexington, MA: Lexington Books.

Van Ness, S. (1984). Rape as instrumental violence: A study of youth offenders. *Journal of Offender Counseling Services and Rehabilitation.* 9, 161-170.

Watson, J (2000) personal communication.

Ward, T., Hudson, S. Marshall, W., & Siegert, R. (1995). Attachment Style and Intimacy Deficits in Sexual Offenders. Sexual Abuse: *A Journal of Research and Treatment.* v7 n4.

Weinrott, M. (1996). *Juvenile sexual aggression: a critical review.* Boulder, CO: University of Colorado, Institute for Behavioral Sciences, Center for the Study and Prevention of Violence.

CHAPTER TWENTY-TWO

INNOVATIVE USES OF PSYCHODRAMA WITH SEXUALLY ABUSIVE ADOLESCENTS: EXPANDING THE HOLISTIC APPROACH

MARLYN ROBSON
AND
IAN LAMBIE

Introduction

SAFE Network began specifically as a specialist community based agency to provide treatment, support, and education for adults and adolescent sexual offenders. They come from across the social, ethnic and cultural spectrum of Auckland. It specializes in assisting offenders to choose an abuse free lifestyle. The thinking about the development of sexually abusive behaviour recognizes that it happens for many different reasons. Therefore the treatment process has to be broad based and holistic (Ryan and Lane, 1991). They reported that since initially there were no scientifically based theories or models for adolescent sexual offender programs they were mostly designed around trial and error. They incorporated some features from adult programs, and some from juvenile delinquent programs. The SAFE treatment program's initial format was a 10 day wilderness program, which incorporated hiking in the wilds, challenging outdoor activities and group therapy in outdoor settings. Over time, staff traveled to conferences, visited other programs overseas, and constantly reviewed the latest research. Today the current program is based, as are most of overseas programs, on cognitive behavioural principles, but as it has since its inception, our program also incorporates family therapy and the theory and practice of psychodrama. (Lambie, Robson, and Simmonds 1997; Robson and Lambie 1995; Robson 1998).

At SAFE Network, the treatment program tries to make it safe for offenders to re-experience their feelings of being both a victim and perpetrator. This includes an active attempt to address the shame, to enhance responsibility, restructure distorted cognitions, develop empathy, control deviant fantasy and to develop relapse prevention strategies for themselves. In this work at SAFE, we have also incorporated the psychodramatic techniques of role playing, concretisation, mirroring, doubling, modeling and role reversal. The results validate that of van der Kolk and McFarlane (1996) who suggested that, used in a safe and mindful way, techniques like psychodrama can internalize past traumatic experiences by taming the associated terrors and desomatising the memories. Elliott, Greenberg and Lietaer (2001) believe the important characteristic of experiential therapies is they promote in-therapy "experience" of emotions, rather than just talking about them; that people are wiser than their intellect alone.

Psychodramatic practice central to the development of self in adolescents

There are several important psychodramatic concepts developed by Jacob Moreno that are incorporated into the treatment program for adolescent sexual offenders at SAFE. These seem to encourage the development of embryonic roles which can be underdeveloped in the adolescent. Roles are relational and situational and have a thinking, feeling and action component and by definition, a psychodramatic role is the functioning form an individual takes (Moreno, cited in Fox, 1961). Roles need to be encouraged or created in order to allow emotional and cognitive processing of trauma to happen and growth in these roles to occur. This helps in the development of a clearer sense of self, and therefore the ability to make better choices. The concepts used are warm up, doubling, mirroring, modeling, role reversal, and spontaneity.

Adolescents who have suffered trauma have little concept or sense of self (of who they are). There also appears to be significant gender difference in group work. Girls can usually access and name feelings reasonably easily and only need to move physically to dissipate strong feelings. Close observation shows that with boys, concretisation, physical movement, and games are needed for them to warm up more to themselves and thus facilitate access to their feelings. Once aware of their feelings they too can learn to name them, tie them to experiences, perhaps make more sense of them and discover something about themselves.

There is often a fear among professionals untrained in experiential therapies that clients will get too warmed up or re-traumatised. Unfortunately "talk" therapy is often not enough to stir the old right brain memory. The principles of trauma therapy are that the client should be able to look through the window of the memory and move back (Briere, 1996). Put simply, the amygdala is triggered without the hypocampus being overwhelmed, so that cortical processing can happen. Rothschild describes helping clients learn to put on the brakes (2003). However, experience is needed to warm up enough and not too much. In our experience, a great deal of doubling and mirroring are needed to build up enough ego strength or sense of self, before small role reversals or vignettes can be handled. The aim is to bring everyone back to present space and time before group ends, having processed the experiences that have happened. We also involve parents and caregivers so that they can be sensitive and supportive if clients are excited at the end of group, provide containment and boundaries, and contact the individual therapist if necessary.

The process of warm-up

The concept of "warm-up" is important with these adolescent boys because they do not want to be in group facing the shame and consequences of their actions. As athletes warm up before a race to achieve their full potential, so group members have to warm up to being in group (Williams, 1989). Also, if there are attachment deficits, being in a group can create overwhelming abandonment feelings of no one caring enough. It feels as if there is not enough "mummy and daddy" (i.e., the facilitators) to go around. It may be possible to warm up these types of boys to feeling cared about. However, if not, then more role development may be needed in individual therapy before they can handle being in a group.

The boys need to warm up to being in group, to warm up to the idea of change, to warm up to us and to each other. Usually therapy groups are just talking, however with these adolescents, as action methods help them warm up to themselves, their bodies remember what their minds have forgotten. The adolescents whether staunch, terminally "cool", or just plain stubborn are actively encouraged by various activities to use their bodies and by doing so, their emotions are also stimulated, bringing about a balance of action and feeling in their warming-up process. Boys generally have difficulty connecting to their feelings and action encourages this.

Warming up attends to the development of appropriate thoughts, feelings and actions. Tavron (1998) notes that inadequate warm-up leads to an inadequate drama, and though at this stage we are using the psychodramatic concept of action to warm up the self rather than for actual dramas, an inadequate warm up will lead to a less than adequate development of different roles that have fully present thinking, feeling and action components. Warm up assists a great deal in lowering anxiety and facilitating an environment where trust can be reborn. With adequate warm up, spontaneity will increase and the level of increased spontaneity will determine how they will react to new situations. Bergman and Hewish (2003) discuss an excellent selection of purposeful effective experiential exercises that will encourage the increase of warm up and emotion.

Van der Kolk (1996) suggests that after trauma, individuals respond to high levels of emotional arousal with an inability to properly evaluate and categorise the experience, or to make sense of it and that this can create a fragmented warm up. The boys may have difficulty taking in and processing information or with learning from experience. He states that their altered psychobiology may cause them to react with aggression or withdrawal. Therefore, this warm-up process needs to be carefully monitored by noticing voice levels, interruptions, body movements and general anxiety levels, as too much can result in fragmentation of the individual or group through the emotional dysregulation.

As the boys in the group warm up more to who they are and their relationships with each other, there is more chance that spontaneity will be present enough for them to have a new insight, a new learning, a new experience, or act in a new way. A new role emerges or an embryonic one develops. They may, as Moreno (1934) said, have a new response to an old situation or an adequate response to a new situation and new roles may emerge or develop more strongly.

Sometimes warm-up can occur around external events. For example, after the bombing of the Twin Towers in New York on September 11, 2001, we facilitated a sociodrama on this issue and all the group participated amazingly well. This was not "talking about themselves." It was about others and they warmed up fully to all the issues involved; the horror, the terror, the loss, the grief and the powerlessness of it all. Active "games" and sociodramas all help to increase warm up and thus their ability to step into other's shoes is enhanced. This expands in turn their experience, their thoughts, ideas and feelings. Possibly because of this, there will be some development of empathy, which may in turn help them make different choices. Warm up may lead to increased spontaneity and the development of new social attunement, empathy and new roles.

Doubling, mirroring, and modelling

To assist a client's self discovery, the SAFE program uses Moreno's (1972) developmental stages of doubling, mirroring, and modelling. It is catching the tiny moments, doubling in a stuck pause, mirroring the glimpse of an emerging role, and practicing modeling a new behaviour that helps the self develop.

The double is speaking and acting as if one were the other person, the way the mother names the baby's experience before the baby can speak. It is the basis of empathic attunement and in this way one can speak the unspoken. This concept of the double is very helpful in this work, and many of our boys may have missed out on this developmental stage in their life. The ideas developed by Hudgins (1998) of the containing double are of special value. These ideas have been a central part of her therapeutic spiral work with trauma survivors. About 30-40% of SAFE boys are sexual abuse survivors but all are survivors of other traumas such as physical abuse, emotional abuse, and severe attachment deficits.

There are three strands in developing the containing double. The first is learning to reflect on the process or on what is happening in any given moment. This ability to observe is frequently absent in our boys. A common phrase is "it just happened", so becoming aware is very important.

The second strand of development is learning what is involved in being able to express the containing statement e.g., "I'm okay; I can handle this; I do have some skills; I can do it; or I think I can even begin to look at what happens when."

The third strand to the development of the containing double is the anchor in the here and now (i.e., awareness of changes in the body and awareness of the possibility of change). The boys become sexually aroused almost without awareness, and certainly without the skills to de-arouse themselves. It is incredibly empowering for them to become aware that they don't necessarily have to act on their arousal, and that they can learn other ways of behaving. The awareness might be of the incredible loss or sadness that is always present in their lives. The containing double is a bit like having a strong accepting loving mother beside you who notices what is happening and totally believes in you. The containing double is a very helpful role relationship for the adolescents to develop so that they can be safe in facing their own trauma, and safe in facing their own aggressive impulses towards others.

Mirroring is the name of the process given to reflecting the role of another so they can experience themselves as seen by others. In psychodrama, to help a protagonist check out their reality, the protagonist will be asked to stand at a distance from the action while an auxiliary is asked to act out exactly the same movements, expressions, words and sounds. It is as if the protagonist is looking in a mirror and can see and experience himself as others do. The observation of oneself being portrayed at a distance can give one a different experience or a new clarity of understanding, an "Ah-ha" moment, which then has the possibility of being integrated into new behaviour, (i.e., a new adequacy of being). It helps develop a new relationship with the self that is experiential rather than cognitive. For example, a boy in the group was acting aggressively but refused to accept this view of himself. The behaviour was re-enacted using two other boys from the group. One being aggressive and displaying the behaviour as they'd observed it; the other responding, to demonstrate the effect on them of the aggressive behaviour. Seeing himself mirrored as being angry and aggressive, and also how the other boy responded by being frightened, closed off or scared, allowed the aggressive boy to feel and accept his anger and understand how others were affected by him at these times. Mirroring is something that mothers often do when they interact with their children, smiling back at them and naming the feeling, or frowning and saying, "You do look angry". This way children learn that their feelings are seen, understood and that someone cares enough to notice. It is an important learning for the boys in our groups.

Tavron (1998) states that in Morenian theory, unity and integration come first before there is differentiation; then comes the important discovery of the child of a sense of self, and only then can one place oneself in another's shoes. The mirror is the stage at which information from the outside contributes to the formation of self. The mirror supplies information from the outside that is not necessarily congruent with the inner voice. It can help us to see this disparity between how we know ourselves and how others see us. Early traumatisation leads to little or no capacity for self perception (Friedrich, 1995). There is little or no development of the observing ego. Doubling, mirroring and empathy in therapy, increases the skill of self perception and the development of the observing ego role. It also helps to decrease the self criticism and shame that bind adolescent sexual offenders into repeating damaging behaviors.

Spontaneity

Spontaneity is the catalyst for creative activity. Moreno had a profound belief in the infinite spontaneity and creativity of human beings (1972). Without it, it is impossible to develop new roles and continue the development of a self that can make good choices.

At the moment of birth, as the infant moves from the safety of the uterus and being nurtured by the placenta, down the birth canal to a world where all is different, strange and possibly dangerous, a new response is required immediately. Adjustment to this totally different environment, "this response of an individual to a new situation and the new response to an old situation" is called by Moreno spontaneity, (1972, p.50).

The response of the baby to the new situation must be at least adequate for survival. This is the first big test of spontaneity. From this moment onward in life there are critical moments of testing, moment to moment, day to day, year to year. New roles develop. Dependent upon the child's experience in relation initially to a primary caregiver and gradually to a wider world, there will be defences built up against responding with adequate spontaneity. Some boys have experienced abandonment, neglect and violence as children. They have built huge defences against the new or different situations which might hurt them again.

"Spontaneity is the ability of a subject to meet each new situation with adequacy" (Moreno, 1972, p. 81). Often the boys have no experience or confidence of ever doing the right thing at the right time. Moreno talked of spontaneity as being a kind of energy but that we have no reservoir and cannot store it, it is either present in the moment or it is not. It can enable new acts, choices and decisions, which lead to inventiveness and creativity. The presence of spontaneity is vital for the development of new or embryonic roles in the personality and helps us integrate the various dimensions of life in our ongoing journey. When anxiety or resistance is high, as it often is in the therapy groups for reasons that have already been described, then spontaneity is low and the chance of new role development is low. At these moments it is important work to increase the warm up of spontaneity present in ways described in the warm up section, (refer to page 3) which then allows adequate creative responses to emerge from the boys.

Often, when discussing the actual moment of offending, shame is high, spontaneity is low and boys have difficulty talking about what they did to their victims. Here is a moment to break off from the task, do something active to increase their warm up to themselves, then when returning to sit and talk in group, it is easier, their spontaneity has increased, and a different role has emerged that allows for more responsibility taking.

Experience showed that for therapy to be successful with this population, the process of self-discovery needs to include a catharsis of integration that touches upon the emotional, cognitive and behavioural levels of a person at one and the same time. Psychodrama offers a powerful opportunity to change old self defeating patterns through the creation of new learning experiences.

The use of group work and issues for consideration

A new group begins, and the usual issues of "Who's here?", "How can I trust anyone?" and "Is it safe be here?" arise. Groups at SAFE try to have male and female co-facilitators, and it is often an unspoken but powerful fact that it is hard to share "mummy and daddy" with other group members. However, the self has to develop in a social context, and group experience mimics their experience of society. There will be acting out and also healing moments as new roles develop in this context. Adolescent boys need to move. Sitting still and talking in group for two hours is unnatural, which is why so many games and physical warm ups are used. The games also allow for gradual introductions without words. Boys who sexually abuse, are often disconnected from their environment and insensitive to others' reality. The idea of action methods is that they are experiential rather than instructional. Little children get to know each other and learn through play, and the same happens in the groups as the boys push and pull and compete and laugh. Through this, gradually new roles seem to emerge. They get to know each other better as their sociometric relationships develop. As social isolates they learn the social roles of interaction. It is vital to see as large a range of roles as possible developing including all the hidden ones, so that all can be worked with. Everyone has experienced failure in their lives, so fear of further failure is very present in any group. However, learning in groups helps because there is modeling from others. If one person gets stuck on an issue, others in the group can offer other roles, other experiences, ideas, and this group centered approach lowers anxiety, "I don't have to do this all on my own." The staff look for memories and experiences of competence to build on, the embryonic progressive roles, and encourage the boys to realize that it is a life long process to learn to live safely.

To work therapeutically with traumatized children, clinicians need to provide consistency, containment, have boundaries, be hypervigilant to what is going on, and titrate their therapeutic interventions with skill and thoughtfulness related to developmental needs.

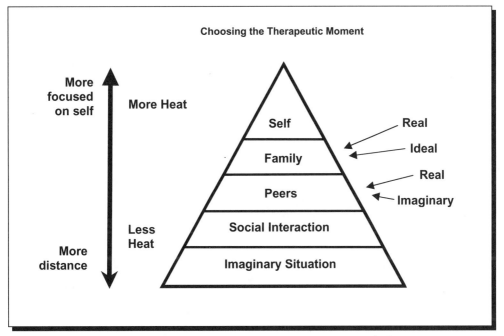

Diagram courtesy John Bergman

Too much experiencing too soon can re-traumatise the adolescent. It is important to inspire in clients a sense of connection, compassion, coherence, creativity and community; to help self knowing, to somehow make sense, and to create a new narrative that helps to connect past, present and future. The aim of therapy is to provide a new experience from which new roles can emerge, always remembering that clients with attachment trauma can experience a fundamental difficulty in being able to use the helping relationship.

There are special problems when working with adolescents who sexually abuse. For example, according to the focal conflict theory of Whittaker and Lieberman (1964), there is a disturbing motive to encourage change and an equally reactive fear of change. An enabling solution needs to be found for change of behaviour to occur. Adolescent sexual offender groups tend to be stuck in a position of conflicting tensions. While they may wish for change (because they are in trouble with the police, they have been removed from home, they have been expelled from school, etc.), however there is also a reactive fear of change because that would involve adopting new behaviour that is unusual and strange to them. Much motivational work needs to happen in group to enable them to feel less fearful of the new.

Application of the offending cycle

Concurrently we introduce the basic content of the program which consists of understanding what we call the offending cycle, looking at why and how sexual offending happened, and encouraging the development of new roles so the adolescents can think, feel and act in different ways and hopefully choose to remove themselves from the cycle.

Case Study: Mark's Story

Let me introduce you to Mark, who's story depicts the offending cycle, the various interventions that were made, and the overall impact on his behaviour and the development of his sense of self.

Mark's History

When we first met him he was a big angry looking 15 year old boy. How could we begin to form a relationship with this boy who clearly by his behaviour and attitude disliked and distrusted adults? How could we warm him up to us, himself and the possibility of life being different? From his case notes and reports I knew the bare bones of his history, which on the cycle are 'Lifestyle Problems.' His mother was in a violently abusive relationship with his alcoholic father and eventually left when Mark was three years old. She then remarried another physically abusive man who constantly beat and humiliated Mark. Child, Youth, and Family Services stepped in for care and protection and Mark was then placed with successive family members from whom he either ran away or behaved in such a way that he was removed because the adults couldn't cope. At eight years old an older girl cousin introduced him to sexual play, playing with his penis and encouraging him to put his penis into her vagina, and he became sexualized earlier than is developmentally normal. He subsequently sexually abused eight younger cousins over the next 6 years in six different placements.

Analysis of Mark

From his history and the original meeting I suspected that his attachment style was Insecure Avoidant because he seemed to have turned off his need for connectedness, was detached and tense. "Who needs you? I can manage on my own," were the attitudes he emanated. Mark's mother had failed in her role of nurturer and protector, failed to protect him from the constant abuse from his father and step-father, and he had been sexually abused by another female. His mistrust of women was inevitably going to be present in our relationship. So, where and how to begin with treatment?

Mark's treatment program: a sequential description of what was actually done with Mark

To help to develop a therapeutic relationship that was non threatening yet had containment and boundaries, we spent many weeks drawing his life on a huge piece of paper, almost as long as the room. We sat on the floor together as he drew and wrote the important events in his life. This was a form of concretization, a symbolisation, a way of making clear and external what was inside him. It was also this consistent relationship with the therapist who was attuned to his emotions and needs, that encouraged the possibility of new behaviour. He could not and would not just talk about his life but as we co-created this pictorial representation of his life, he gradually warmed up more to himself and all he knew and felt about it. Bringing forward and exposing his intrapsychic drama was the first healing step as he experienced feelings, ideas, flashbacks and shared them with me on the paper. His story of betrayal, guilt, shame, fear, confusion and anger touched us both as we shared it together. He had a distorted cognitive idea of himself as helpless and bad, he experienced persistent flashbacks of trauma, he felt fearful and hopeless about his future, the angry way he expressed his feelings usually resulted in criticism, rejection and isolation, and this led to huge difficulties in interpersonal relationships, where he always expected to be abandoned. However, during this process of concretizing his life story on paper, in a slow gentle contained way, where he was not shamed or abandoned by me for admitting his behaviour, and where his feelings were acknowledged and held without criticism, some trust began to develop. At this stage he displayed much dry humour to deflect us away from touchy places. When the going became too tough, when we were too near to painful material, Mark would take care of himself by making jokes and deflect us away from his excruciating pain with acid humour. He seemed like a hedgehog, tough, spikey and dangerous on the outside with a soft vulnerable underbelly.

Concurrently with individual work, Mark was in group, where he consistently disrupted the process and had an ongoing battle with the male co-facilitator whom he experienced as a powerful authority figure and at some level reminded him of the trauma experienced at the hands of his father and stepfather. Throughout his life Mark had difficulty making meaningful relationships with his peers. It was the same here, where he either ignored some boys, or joked inappropriately with smart remarks, irritating others. His sociometry with the others in the group was generally negative, however, at moments he could become the star, by sharing incredibly insightfully and encouraging others to do so too. The others noticed him profoundly in these moments and drew closer to him. If praised for this leadership he became disruptive again, sharing that if people expect too much of him he will always let them down. Mark's spontaneity for new behaviour was low.

In a vignette, or small enactment, Mark was encouraged to show exactly what had happened in a fight with another inmate at his house. The other boy in the enactment held up a cushion for Mark to punch. He then came out of the action and watched as another group member re-enacted the fight. "I'm not that violent" he said immediately. He was encouraged to return to the action and do it again. As he warmed up to himself with action and dialogue he replayed the fight almost identically. Outside the drama and seeing himself mirrored again, he ruefully admitted that perhaps he was violent. With mirroring he not only had the chance to see himself as others do, but also had an opportunity to make an assessment about his behaviour. A new role may emerge, and he may perhaps have a choice to behave differently in the future. The development of new roles enhances the development of a sense of self since the self emerges from roles (Moreno, 1972).

In spite of his resistance to being in group there were times when Mark could be reluctantly encouraged to participate. One day the group had been drawing life stories and sharing them, warming up to themselves. Mark was being hypervigilant and unceasingly fidgety, scanning the room and looking as if he wished to escape. It is his turn to share. His anxiety hits high, his body, arms and legs, move endlessly, he tells his horrendous story of endless traumatic experiences at a hundred miles an hour in one minute flat. I move beside him and say to him:

> Marlyn: "Its time to show us a moment of your life, are you willing?

> Mark nods.

> Marlyn: (placing a hand on his shoulder and pointing to the rest of the room,) "I will be here with you and we will create the moment out there", pointing to the rest of the room. "You will see it again but not be in it. There will be a distance between us and the action. It will be like watching a video, and you can press the stop button if you wish."

> Mark: "OK."

This helped to create safety, containment, some boundaries, and some possibilities. He agreed.

> Marlyn: "What moment are you remembering?"

> Mark: "I was 5 years old and mum was trying to escape with me in the car and my stepfather was attacking us in the car with a chainsaw." He looks around the group, and laughs nervously.

> Group Member: "It's the Chainsaw Massacre" (—some tension is released and more importantly he has checked out he is connected to the group—he is not doing this on his own.)

> Marlyn: "Create the car, choose people to be you and your mother in the car and your stepfather."

(As he sets the scene, he clearly warms up more, his colour changes, he is concentrating and is very careful and exact about where everyone goes.)

> Marlyn: "Role reverse with your stepfather and warm up the auxilliary to be that role fully."

> Mark does this and comes out to his observer role with me once more. He stares but says nothing.

Marlyn: (as the double) "It's terrifying, we're going to be hurt, killed, we can't escape, I can do nothing."

Mark: "Yes", (quiet tears pouring down his cheeks.)

Marlyn: "You were very little then, totally powerless, and very afraid, you have more skills now and you have survived."

Mark: "Yes, and I don't want to be a man like my stepfather."

I ask for the scene to be cleared and as we sit in the group and all share our experiences of the moment. Mark is more settled in his body, his arms and legs still and he listens intently to what the others share with him as they all reconnect as a group. By observing an incident from his life, getting mirroring from others, experiencing the emotional content and making some sense of it in his head, Mark had some healing of the trauma and gained some insight into who he is. This helped him develop his sense of self.

Two years into the program Mark had become more relaxed and less hypervigilant for danger, particularly in group where he was friendly and polite, participated well, and could manage to interact appropriately with the facilitators. He had completed a further education computer course and was living on his own, cooking, cleaning and budgeting for himself. He was beginning to be able to see a future for himself with work and a car. He had had an inappropriate relationship with a slightly older woman but this had been helpful in shifting his sexual fantasies from his child victims to more age appropriate girls. He still became smart mouthed and distracting if challenged by the male facilitator but was more aware of why and was working on making better choices. He had a dread of freedom and having to interact with his peers in his home area because he believed that he would be led in drugs and drinking to excess like his father and stepfather. His confidence around making good choices in this area was low. All is not healed in two years.

At his "moving on" ceremony a few months later, he spoke clearly and with confidence, in front of twenty family, friends, and SAFE staff, about all he had learnt, and his safety plans for the future. But he was most eloquent about how he himself had changed, how he believed in himself now, and that he felt he was a worthwhile person who could make good choices in his future even though the choices might be hard. He is still an adolescent, his roles are still developing, but there was a clear sense that he had a good feel for the person or "self" that he is as he walks toward his future.

The voyage of discovery of who I am?

The development of the self, acquiring self perception, and the discovery of the "I", are parts of an important life journey. As new roles emerge and develop the understanding of "Who am I?" changes and grows. Boys enter the SAFE program believing they are one sort of person ? bad ? and as they journey through, staff observe their perception of themselves change. They discover that it is possible to be different. As they develop new roles their self expands and they have more choices about good or bad behaviour.

"Who am I?" is an important question on every adolescents journey. The therapist has to consider whether the sense of self the adolescent has developed so far is useful. It is often emotional, based on perception of someone else's judgment of them. A way of concretizing these aspects of self, bringing the internalized feelings and beliefs out into the open where they can be seen and acknowledged, is by creating masks. The mask they show to the world and the mask of that which is hidden. This is a good example of differentiating between the social roles which are known to most, and the psychodramatic roles which are in their inner private worlds. Initially as they start painting the blank white masks there is frivolity and much hilarity, however as they gradually warm up to the task and themselves the concentration becomes intense and the group quiet. In the sharing, each boy is intensely warmed up to himself and who he is, what he shows to the world and what he hides. In Mark, anger and aggression were painted on the outside mask to hide the deep sadness and despair. In another, anger is hidden by a cheeky clown; yet another has a totally blank outside mask hiding black badness inside.

The act of painting warms them up enough to themselves so that the hidden, shameful beliefs that they hold about themselves can be brought out into the open, the emotions experienced, and some cognitive processing allows possible integration of new beliefs. Psychodramatic methods can enable these boys who have experienced trauma in their lives, to come to terms with their experiences, develop a new story that makes more sense, and develop a clearer sense of themselves as new roles emerge. If this self is more congruent and integrated, then it should be possible to make more sensible choices about all of their behaviour, including their sexual behaviour. This is a very useful development to occur in any adolescent.

The sense of self is reliant on autobiographical or explicit memory which doesn't begin to form until around three to four years of age. In people who have experienced trauma in childhood earlier than this, there may be explicit memory, implicit memory, or experiential memory. Anxious or frightening feelings can come for no apparent reason. These memories may be fractured, open to doubt about their reality, or come and go with barely any perceived stimuli. Siegel (1999) talks of memory forming "the foundation for both implicit reality (behavioural responses, emotional reactions, perceptual categorization, schemata of the self and others in the world, and possibly body memories) and explicit recollections of facts and of the self across time. In this way we must understand the many layers of memory in order to comprehend other persons' present and past life experiences, and the ways they anticipate and plan for the future" (p. 60). Disruptive and damaging interpersonal relationships produce incoherent functioning of the individual mind. Just being in group, or a quasi family situation, can trigger implicit memories of early childhood rejections, fears, and hurts. In other words, there are no actual memories of particular incidents but the person can be awash with the swirling feelings of abandonment or terror. The feelings of babies and toddlers are of being in a situation that is overwhelmingly life threatening. When this is triggered in a boy in group he will either close down or act out, usually without understanding why. Moreno (1934) has taught us that roles are learnt in relationship to other people. This connection between interpersonal and individual process is an important aspect of memory and what we remember and tell about our life stories, and how we make sense of it and the sense of our self.

A boy in group had developed a survival mechanism of closing off and hiding from tall men with dark beards because they reminded him of the perpetrator of his victimisation. When a tall, dark bearded colleague from overseas visited our group, this boy had no idea why he experienced such terror and discomfort. He doubted his sense of reality. This visitor seemed friendly and kind. Why is he so terrified? Perhaps he really is mad, bad, and wrong, as everyone is always telling him. Not only does he doubt himself, he critisises himself and feels shame. The truth came later when talking to his mother.

Childhood trauma has a profound impact because uncontrollable and frightening experiences may have their strongest effect when the central nervous system and cognitive functioning are not yet fully developed (Cicchetti & Toth, 1998). People who were traumatized as children have shown a tendency to react rather than reflect, and abused children have a marked impairment in their capacity to describe affect states in words. Since a sense of "self" is derived from the interactions between the child and his caregivers and is founded on the important relationships of early childhood, trauma during this period interferes with the development of ego identity and with the capacity to develop trusting and collaborative relationships (Cole and Putnam, 1991; Herman, 1992). This parallels Moreno's (1961) notion of social and cultural atom, and role and personality development.

Conclusion

This chapter has shown that the use of psychodramatic methods and an understanding of psychodramatic theory is an important part of our treatment program at SAFE to help change sexual offending behaviour. As adolescents learn to develop a relationship with the therapists, both in individual and group work, there is enough trust built up to allow them to explore and develop new roles so that their personality or self expands, and therefore they have more possibility to make better behavioural choices in the future. As part of the program, boys in group are continually encouraged to enact respectful behaviour, both in group and in everyday life. Sexual offending was very disrespectful of their victim, so one of the measures of change is noticing change in present day life. However, it often feels as if they are asking, "How can I make good choices about my behaviour when I don't know who I am?" The boys in our program feel they lack choice. There is only one predictable way of behaving, "this is how I've always been." Spontaneity is encouraged in the ways previously described, to try to expand their role structures which will expand their choice about who they are and how they behave. At SAFE the work is to make their roles more congruent and therefore more effective. For example, a role that allows someone to hurt someone else may have a very distorted but small cognitive component, (consequences may not be considered), a large action component, and very little feeling component. In group work, with doubling and mirroring to challenge their actions, feelings and beliefs, their roles will become more congruent, they develop a clearer sense of who they are, which will allow more sensible and clearly thought out choices. So much of the group work is around, "If I learn to know who I am, accept and like who I am in other words develop a sense of self, then I may have some choice about what I do."

The SAFE program provides many examples of adolescents who have experienced trauma in their lives. Yet with psychodramatic interventions it allows them to develop a clearer sense of self and from there, develop the ability to make better choices about their behavior and live more respectful and positive lives.

References

Bergman, J and Hewish, S.(2003). *Challenging Experiences, An Experiential Approach to the treatment of Serious Offenders.* Oklahoma City, OK; Wood N' Barnes.

Briere, J.(1996). *Therapy for adults molested as children.* Springer Publishing Company.

Cicchetti, D., and Toth, S.(Eds.). (1995). Risk, trauma, and memory (special issue).*Development and Psychopathology,* 10(4).

Clayton,M.(1994). Role theory and its application in clinical practice. In Holmes, P., Karp, M., and Watson, M. (Eds). *Psychodrama Since Moreno: Innovations in Theory and Practice.*

Cole, P.M., and Putnam, F. W. (1991). Effect of incest on self and social functioning: A developmental psychopathology perspective. *Journal of Consulting and Clinical Psychology,* 60, 174-184.

Daniels, M. and Thornton, D. (1998) Using role play to develop victim empathy: Experience from a large scale trial. *Presentation at A.T.S.A. 17th Annual Research & Treatment Conference,* 1998.

Elliot, R., Greenberg, L.S., and Lietaer, G. (2001). Research on Experiential Psychotherapies. *In Handbook of psychotherapy and behaviour change,* Lambert, M., Bergin, A., & Garfield, S. (Eds). New York: Wiley.

Fox, J. (1987). *The Essential Moreno.* New York: Springer Publishing Company.

Friedrich, W.N. (1995). *Psychotherapy with Sexually Abused Boys.* London: Sage.

Herman, J.L. (1992). *Trauma and recovery.* London, Pandora.

Hudgins, M.K., & Drucker, K.(1998). The Containing Double as part of the Therapeutic Spiral model for treating trauma survivors. *The International Journal of Action Methods,* 51 (2), 63-74.

Hudgins, M.K. (1998). Experiential psychodrama with sexual Trauma. In L.S. Greenberg, J.C. Watson & G. Lietaer, (Eds.). *Handbook of Experiential Psychotherapy,* (pp.328-348). New York: Guildford Press.

Lambie, I., Robson, M. & Simmonds, L. (1997). Embedding psychodrama in a wilderness group program for adolescent sex offenders. *Journal of Offender Rehabilitation,,* 26, 89-107.

Moreno, J.L. (1914). Einladung zu einer Bebgnung. Vienna: Anzengruber Verlag. Translated by J.L.Moreno.

Moreno, J.L. (1934). *Who Shall Survive?* Foundations of Sociometry, Group psychotherapy and Sociodrama. Washington D.C. Nervous and Mental Diseases Publishing Co.

Moreno, J.L. (1961). The Role Concept, a Bridge between Psychiatry and Sociology. From *American Journal of Psychiatry* 118(1961), 518-523.

Moreno, J.L. (1972) *Psychodrama, Volume 1*. New York: Beacon House. (Original work published 1946).

Robson, M. & Lambie, I. (1995) Using psychodrama to facilitate victim empathy in adolescent sexual offenders. *Journal of the Australian and New Zealand psychodrama association*, 4, 13-19.

Robson, M. (1998). Action Insight: The treatment of adolescent sexual offenders. *Journal of the Australian and New Zealand psychodrama association*, 7, 41-57.

Rothschild, B.(2003).*The Body Remembers Casebook: Unifying Methods and Models in the Treatment of Trauma and PTSD*. New York, Norton .

Ryan, G. & Lane, S. (1991). *Juvenile Sexual Offending*. Massachusetts, Lexington Press.

Siegel, D. (1999) *The Developing Mind*. New York: Guildford Press.

Tavron, K.B. (1998).The Principles of Psychodrama, in Karp, M., Holmes, P., & Tavron, K.B..(Eds.) *The Handbook of Psychodrama*, p.30. Routledge.

Williams, A. (1989). *The Passionate Technique*. Tavistock/Routledge, London and New York.

Whitaker, D.S., & Lieberman, M.A. (1964). *Psychotherapy through the group process*. New York: Atherton Press.

van der Kolk, B. & McFarlane, A. C. (1986).The black hole of trauma. In B. A. van der Kolk, A. C. McFarlane, & L. Weisaeth (Eds).*Traumatic Stress: the effect of overwhelming experience on mind, body, and society*. (1,3-23) New York: Guildford Press.

van der Kolk, B.A. (1986). The complexity of adaptation to trauma. In B.A. Van der Kolk, A.C. McFarlane, & L. Weisaeth (Eds) *Traumatic Stress: The effects of overwhelming experience on mind, body, and society*. (9,182-213) New York: Guildford Press.

CHAPTER TWENTY-THREE

MULTISYSTEMIC THERAPY WITH JUVENILES WHO SEXUALLY ABUSE

LISA SALDANA
CYNTHIA CUPIT SWENSON
AND
ELIZABETH LETOURNEAU

Introduction

Multisystemic therapy (MST) is a family and community-based approach to treating youth who have serious clinical problems and their families. Specifically, MST was designed to intervene with youth engaging in antisocial activities. More recently, however, MST has been identified as a potentially effective means of treating juvenile sexual offending behaviors (Borduin, Henggeler, Blaske, & Stein, 1990; Borduin & Schaeffer, 2002). A thorough description of the MST model and techniques is found in a treatment manual (Henggeler, Schoenwald, Borduin, Rowland, & Cunningham, 1998) and is based on nine treatment Principles (Table 1). A supplement is being developed to describe the adaptations made when working with youth who have sexually abused others. The present chapter: (a) describes the theoretical underpinnings of MST; (b) summarizes the empirical support for MST; (c) explains the rationale for applying MST to juvenile sexual offending behavior; (d) presents outcomes of randomized controlled trials applying MST to youth who have sexually abused others; (e) summarizes the clinical aspects of MST; and, (f) illustrates via a case example, the use of MST with juveniles who exhibit sexual offending behavior.

Theoretical Basis for Multisystemic Therapy

Theory of social ecology

Theoretically, MST is based on Bronfenbrenner's (1979) social ecological theory of human development. The social-ecological philosophy assumes that an individual is imbedded within a greater context and set of nested systems. At its most basic foundation, therefore, the MST perspective views an individual youth not in isolation, but rather as the core of imbedded systems that include family, peers, school, neighborhood, and community (see Figure 1). The relationship between the child and each system are such that the closer in proximity that a system is to the child, the greater influence that system has on the child. Using this theory, the caregivers and family have the greatest influence over a child whereas treatment providers, who are in the community, have the least amount of influence on the child. Given this underlying foundation for the MST model, assessment and interventions logically target the reciprocal relationship between the child and family, followed by the child and peers, child and school, child and community. Furthermore, the influence of the relationship between each of these systems with one another, as it relates to the target youth, is assessed and involved in intervention (e.g., between family and school, the social support network of the caregivers who might provide parenting suggestions). It is essential that in this process, assessment and intervention not target each of these systems individually, but rather also evaluate the bi-directional relationship between each of them (Henggeler & Borduin, 1990).

Pragmatic family therapies

In practice, the MST model draws upon strategic (Haley, 1976) and structural (Minuchin, 1974) family therapies. From within these models, behavior problems are viewed as developing out of normal life stressors or crises that were not handled well by family members. Problematic behaviors: a) are related to patterns of family interaction; b) occur as a result of difficulty in the management of developmental transitions and life stressors; and, c) have a functional component that is somehow reinforced. Both strategic and structural family therapies are compatible with the MST model in: a) their use of problem-focused and change-oriented interventions; b) the recognition that there are multiple paths to achieve a desired outcome; c) the ownership of the focused, action-oriented direction of treatment being the responsibility of the therapist; d) the development of interventions that conceptualize the problem in the context of the current environment; and, e) the view of long-term behavior change being dependent on changing interactions between individuals across multiple systems.

Empirical support for MST

MST has been identified by several federal entities (National Institute on Drug Abuse, 1999; President's New Freedom Commission on Mental Health, 2003; USDHHS, 1999) as a treatment model that demonstrates effectiveness for treating youth antisocial behavior and substance abuse. The Surgeon General (USPHS, 2001) reported MST to be one of only three empirically supported treatments for serious juvenile offenders. In comparison with control conditions, MST has consistently achieved significant reductions in rates of rearrest (Borduin, Henggeler, Blaske, & Stein, 1990; Borduin et al., 1995; Henggeler et al., 1986; Henggeler et al., 1991; Henggeler, Melton, & Smith, 1992; Henggeler, Melton, Brondino, Scherer, & Hanley, 1997; Henggeler, Pickrel, & Brondino, 1999) with follow-ups ranging from 1.7 to 13.7 years (Henggeler et al., 1997; Schaeffer & Borduin, 2004). MST has also been successful at reducing rates of out-of-home placement and related costs, with the Washington State Institute on Public Policy concluding that this treatment approach produced more than $130,000 per youth in savings in placement, criminal justice and crime victim costs (Aos, Phipps, Barnoski, & Lieb, 2001).

In addition to showing effectiveness in the treatment of antisocial behavior, outcomes from MST randomized controlled trials have demonstrated promising results in the treatment of adolescent alcohol and marijuana abuse (McBride, VanderWaal, Terry, &

VanBuren, 1999; Stanton & Shadish, 1997), an important component to the treatment of conduct disorders as one of the strongest correlates of juvenile offending is substance abuse (Howell, 2003). Indeed the National Institute on Drug Abuse (1999) and the Center for Substance Abuse Prevention (2001) have declared MST as one of the few empirically supported treatments for adolescent substance abuse.

MST With Juveniles Who Sexually Abuse

Ecological perspective

Consistent with findings in the general delinquency literature (Loeber & Farrington, 1998), the correlates of juvenile sexual offending behavior not only consist of individual characteristics of youth, but also include characteristics of the social contexts in which they are embedded (i.e., family, peer, school). An ecological approach to treatment, such as MST, that provides clinical interventions for problems occurring within and between all systems, therefore, might be particularly effective with this population. As will be described, family, peer, and school systems, in addition to individual characteristics, appear to be facets of the sexually abusive youth's environment that should be targeted for assessment and intervention.

Family relations

Juveniles who sexually abuse others often have tenuous family relations. Ageton (1983) found that juveniles who sexually abuse others reported more family disruptions (e.g., divorce) than youth who did not report a history of abusive behaviors. Moreover, controlled studies (i.e., studies with control or comparison groups) have reported that families of adolescents who committed sexual offenses have less positive communication and warmth (Bischof, Stith, & Whitney, 1995; Blaske, Borduin, Henggeler, & Mann, 1989) and more parental violence (Ford & Linney, 1995) than do families of other juvenile offenders. Given these findings, there is reasonable support for the hypothesis that family factors might be involved in sexual delinquency.

Peer relations

In the life of the adolescent, peer relationships are of particular importance. The peer relations of youth involved in sexually abusive behaviors show important differences from those of other juvenile offenders and nondelinquents. In general, juveniles who have committed sexual offenses tend to have peer deficits that are more characteristic of youths with internalizing problems and high levels of peer rejection including social isolation, low bonding with peers, low popularity, and low association with deviant peers (Blaske et al., 1989; Ford & Linney, 1995; Milloy, 1994). Furthermore, adolescents who offend against young children tend to be immature relative to same-age peers (Graves, Openshaw, Ascione, & Ericksen, 1996). Consistent with this perspective, juveniles who victimized a peer, versus those who molested a younger child have been shown to be more likely to associate with deviant peers (Ageton, 1983). Unlike other delinquents, therefore, interventions regarding peer relationships for youth who sexually abuse others are less likely to target changing deviant peer groups and more likely to focus on social skills training and developmentally appropriate relationships.

School functioning

Although poor school functioning is a risk factor for delinquency in general, such problems do not seem to be related to sexual offending in particular. Despite several uncontrolled studies indicating that juveniles who sexually offend have academic deficits (Awad & Saunders, 1989; Fehrenbach, Smith, Monastersky, & Deisher, 1986), controlled studies have found no evidence for intellectual or achievement differences between these youth and other juvenile offenders (Ford & Linney, 1995; Jacobs, Kennedy, & Meyer, 1997). Youth who sexually abuse others, therefore, show similar school difficulties as other delinquents including behavioral and learning problems (Jacobs et al., 1997; Righthand & Welch, 2001).

Individual characteristics

Juveniles who commit sexual offenses have long been assumed to have deviant sexual arousal patterns and cognitive distortions regarding their crimes. Research over the last decade, however, has shown that these youth demonstrate variable patterns of sexual arousal (Hunter, Goodwin, & Becker, 1994) that neither consistently differentiate them from other delinquents (Smith & Fischer, 1999) nor correlate with other important clinical characteristics (Becker, 1998). Moreover, there is no empirical evidence supporting the notion that juveniles who sexually abuse others endorse more deviant sexual fantasies than delinquent and non-delinquent control groups (Daleiden, Kaufman, Hilliker, & O'Neil, 1998). Similarly, research does not support the view that youth who commit sexual offenses have more cognitive distortions regarding their crimes than do other delinquents (Ageton, 1983; Hastings, Anderson, & Hemphill, 1997).

On the other hand, several individual differences have been observed between youth who have sexually abused others and other delinquents. Although sexually abusive youth are more likely to have experienced sexual victimization than non delinquents (Davis & Leitenberg, 1987), there is mixed evidence in the literature regarding juveniles who commit sexual offenses and other delinquents' experiences with sexual victimization. At present, some studies report equal rates of victimization between sexually offending youth and other delinquents while other studies indicate greater rates of sexual victimization for sexually offending youth (Awad & Saunders, 1989; Milloy, 1994). Juveniles who sexually abuse others also have been found to have higher rates of internalizing problems (e.g., anxiety, depression) than both delinquents and non-offending controls (Blaske et al., 1989; Kempton & Forehand, 1992). Lastly, sexually offending youth report similar or lower rates of alcohol and illicit substance use as compared with other delinquents (Ageton, 1983; Milloy, 1994).

MST with Sexually Abusive Youth: Empirical Evidence

Although at present MST has been validated only for use with delinquency populations, there is promising evidence for use of this treatment with juveniles who sexually abuse others. Two randomized controlled trials (RCTs) conducted to examine the efficacy of MST versus "usual services" (usually court-ordered treatment services) when working with juvenile delinquents, have included subsamples of youth who had committed sexual offenses whose data were analyzed separately from the main

study analyses (Borduin et al., 1990; Borduin & Schaeffer, 2002). Both trials were conducted as part of the Columbia, Missouri MST program (PI: Borduin), and have limitations preventing the generalization of results. Namely, both trials were "efficacy"
as opposed to "effectiveness" studies. Efficacy studies offer a preliminary examination of whether a treatment works under ideal conditions, and such studies generally precede "effectiveness" trials, where the treatment is employed in real world settings. Thus, the initial randomized trials were conducted with doctoral graduate students as the MST therapists who were supervised by one of the developers of MST. In
addition, the sample sizes were small and assessments were limited to pre-treatment
and post-treatment, preventing analyses of mid-treatment effects. Nonetheless, outcomes from these projects suggest favorable results and are the basis of a currently ongoing larger RCT specifically examining effectiveness of MST with youth who sexually offend (PI: Henggeler).

Outcomes with sexually abusive adolescents

In the first of two randomized clinical trials comparing MST with usual services provided to sexually abusive adolescents (Borduin et al., 1990), 16 adolescents and their
families were randomly assigned to home-based MST services ($n = 8$) or to outpatient
individual therapy in the local community ($n = 8$). Three-year recidivism data were
collected from juvenile court, adult court, and state police records. None of the adolescents had moved out of the area at follow-up. Recidivism for sexual offenses was
12.5% for adolescents who received MST ($n = 1$; mean = 0.12 sexual arrests per adolescent) and 75% for adolescents who received individual therapy ($n = 6$; mean = 1.62
sexual arrests per adolescent). Recidivism for nonsexual offenses was 25% for MST
adolescents ($n = 2$; mean = 0.62 arrests per adolescent) and 50% for adolescents in the
individual therapy condition ($n = 4$; mean = 2.25 arrests).

More recently, Borduin and his colleagues completed a larger study with a longer follow-up (Borduin & Schaeffer, 2002). Adolescents who had raped peers or adults ($n =
24$) or molested younger children ($n = 24$) were randomly assigned to MST or usual
services. Adolescents in the usual services condition received mandated court referrals including one or more stipulations (e.g., individual or group therapy at local
agencies, alternative schooling, curfew), and adherence to these stipulations was
monitored weekly by deputy juvenile officers. At posttreatment, adolescents in the
MST condition had fewer behavior problems, less self-reported criminal offending,
more positive family relations, improved peer relations, and better grades in school
than did adolescents in the usual services condition. Caregivers in the MST condition
reported decreased symptomatology relative to those in the usual services condition.
In addition, adolescents in the MST condition spent an average of 75 fewer days in
out-of-home placements during the first year following referral to treatment than did
adolescents in the usual services condition.

For both offender types (peer/adult rapists and child molesters) in the second study
(Borduin & Schaeffer, 2002), recidivism was about 3 times greater for youth in the control group than in the MST condition. Importantly, offender type did not moderate
MST treatment effectiveness, with youth in both typologies evidencing significant
treatment gains. Eight years following referral, adolescents in the MST condition were
less likely than their usual services counterparts to have been arrested for sexual

(12.5% vs. 41.7%) or nonsexual (29.2% vs. 62.5%) crimes and spent one third as many days in adult incarceration facilities. These recent findings replicated and extended those of Borduin et al. (1990) and provide support for the efficacy of MST with adolescents who sexually abuse others.

Clinical Aspects of MST

The MST structure

Given MST's empirical basis, there is considerable effort made to ensure that implementation of the model is sound. Currently, approved MST programs operate in 34 states across the United States and seven countries around the world, comprising 300 teams. Maintenance of an MST operating license is based, partially, on quality assurance and adherence to the model. To help guide adherence, nine MST principles have been developed (Table 1) to guide therapists', supervisors', and consultants' behavior. Adherence ratings are gathered monthly (by an independent data collection agency) regarding family perceptions of therapist behaviors and therapist perceptions of supervisor behaviors. Standardized measures are utilized to monitor the therapeutic teams' consistency with the nine principles and to provide feedback to help increase adherence with the goal of achieving better outcomes. Each component of the quality assurance process is supported by a manualized protocol developed for clinicians (Henggeler et al., 1998), supervisors (Henggeler & Schoenwald, 1998), consultants (Schoenwald, 1998), and organizations (Strother, Swenson, & Schoenwald, 1998). Research on treatment fidelity suggests that the quality assurance procedures imbedded within MST are effective at preventing therapist "drift" from the MST model. For example, caregiver reports of therapist treatment adherence (using a well-validated adherence measure) cluster in the "high" range of the measure, indicating good adherence over the course of treatment (e.g., see Schoenwald, Sheidow, & Letourneau, 2004; Schoenwald, Sheidow, Letourneau, & Liao, 2003). Indeed, adhering to the MST model is a significant predictor of positive behavior change in families (Huey, Henggeler, Brondino, & Pickrel, 2000; Schoenwald et al., 2004; Schoenwald et al., 2003).

MST team

The MST therapist works as a member of a therapeutic team. Each team typically is comprised of three to four therapists, a supervisor, and a consultant. Therapists and supervisors are typically Masters level social workers or clinical counselors. The supervisor provides weekly supervision to the entire team and is also available on-call 24 hours a day to provide additional supervision when needed. In addition, the supervisor is available to attend sessions with the therapist to help assess barriers to change when progress is limited, or during particularly challenging or potentially dangerous situations. The consultant is a doctoral level MST expert who provides consultation on active cases at least once a week, generally by telephone. In addition, the consultant provides quarterly on-site booster training for the team on topics that are posing particular challenges with the population being served.

Session arrangement

Given the ecological approach to intervention suggested by the MST model, one of the key elements of implementation is full use of the ecology in assessment and treatment sessions. Conducting sessions within a typical office setting provides barriers to including all family members (including extended members if deemed necessary), peers, teachers, and other individuals who are important within the multiple systems of the child. Furthermore, the typical outpatient session limits the therapist's ability to assess the child's environment, witness the maladaptive interactions as they occur in their natural context, and coach the involved members toward more adaptive functioning. MST assessments and interventions, therefore, occur in the natural setting of the participants. Most often sessions are in the family home; however, they also may occur with teachers at the school or any other place that will provide the most direct route to client information and change.

In addition to being flexible with session location, it is necessary for the MST therapist to be flexible with other aspects of the therapeutic time. Sessions occur during times that are convenient for families, including weekends, mornings, and late in the evening. The MST therapist is not bound by the typical 50 minute session, but rather must be willing to meet with families for as little or as long of time as is necessary to complete the goals of the session, and for as many or few times during the week as is needed. In addition, a member of the MST team is available on-call 24 hours a day, 7 days a week. In the event that a family experiences a crisis or challenging situation with the youth, the on-call therapist is available to coach the family on the phone, or if necessary, to meet them at their home. This "in vivo" strategy allows for interventions to occur "in the moment" and when they are most salient to participants.

Therapeutic interventions

Although the MST therapist must be flexible and strength focused, interventions target well defined irresponsible behavior and utilize empirically validated strategies for creating behavior change (e.g., contingency management, solution focused problem-solving). Furthermore, as an ecological model, MST interventions encompass a broadrange of treatments for various problems experienced by the youth and members of the ecology. More specifically, the MST therapist does not broker services with other agencies, but rather, utilizes empirically supported techniques for addressing problems as part of service delivery (e.g., a caregiver who is using substances will receive substance abuse treatment from the MST therapist).

As noted within the nine MST principles, one of the key elements of the MST model is the conceptualization of the "fit" assessment. Drawing from information gathered across each of the ecological systems of the identified youth, the MST therapist develops a list of strengths and needs for each of the systems. Given that the family has the greatest influence over the youth, the caregiver and family system is emphasized in the strengths and needs assessment. The assessment information is then utilized to develop a "fit circle" or a structured method of conceptualizing the factors that are maintaining problem behavior. Figure 2 provides an example of a fit assessment for a sexually offending youth and will be described further in the case example provided.

Case Example

The following example is based on a conglomeration of cases seen during the course of one of the clinical trials evaluating MST with sexually abusive youth. Identifying information has been altered to protect the confidentiality of the youths and families involved.

Referral behaviors. Doug P., a 15-year-old, White (non-Hispanic) male, was referred by the local juvenile office following his discharge from the Juvenile Justice Center. Doug had been arrested for exposing himself and masturbating in front of female peers on the school bus (the index offense). During his psychological evaluation at the juvenile center, Doug acknowledged that he had engaged in sexually aggressive behaviors prior to the current referral incident. Upon follow-up with Doug's parents, the assessor learned that Doug had been sexually aggressive toward his 7-year-old sister, April (i.e., had coerced her to orally stimulate him). Prior to the index offense, Doug already was being followed by the juvenile office for a shoplifting incident that occurred six months previously.

Conceptualization. Following the MST principles, the initial goal of the MST therapist was to assess the strengths and needs of each of the youth's ecological systems in order to derive a "fit" assessment (Principle 1; see Figure 2). In doing so, the therapist learned that Doug had been sexually inappropriate with April on multiple occasions, with her report of several incidents of fondling. Doug's step-father and mother, Mr. and Mrs. W., acknowledged being aware of some, but not all, of the incidents of inappropriate behavior. April denied feeling fearful of her brother, instead reporting that she was embarrassed about the behavior and knew it was "bad." Doug reported knowing the sexual acting out was inappropriate, but simultaneously reported he did "not know" why he engaged in the behaviors. He appeared ashamed of himself and reported feeling worried about returning to school where his peer relationships were already limited.

Given the new allegations of sexual acting out toward his sister, a mandated report to Child Protective Services (CPS) was necessary. The MST therapist worked with Mr. and Mrs. W. to help them make the hotline report together. The report was taken, but CPS chose not to prosecute due to Doug's involvement in active treatment for his sexual behavior problems.

In addition, during the course of discussion about sexually inappropriate behavior, it was disclosed that Doug and his cousins had been sexually abused by his biological paternal uncle when he was eight years old. In the year following Doug's parents' separation, he had visited his father, who was living with Doug's uncle. Doug recalled having been molested during three of those visits by his uncle. He had disclosed his abuse to his mother upon returning from one of the visits and visitation was ceased. The incident was reported to the authorities and the reason for lack of follow-through was not clear to Mrs. W. Doug had not seen his father since the allegation and his father had not attempted to contact him. In addition, his father had never attempted to contact April, with whom Mrs. W. was pregnant at the time of separation. Mrs. W. reported leaving the relationship due to domestic violence, with the last incident occurring after she had revealed her pregnancy. The step-father, Mr. W., became involved with the family two years later. He clearly stated that he considered the children to be his "own" despite their non-biological relationship.

Given the MST approach to rely heavily on family involvement (Principles 3 & 7), family members and the therapist worked together to develop overarching goals for treatment. The primary goal, as endorsed by all systems, was to reduce the risk for future sexual offenses across environments. Overarching goals including (1) increasing parental monitoring (Mr. and Mrs. W.: "We want to keep track of things better and keep him from messing with his sister."); (2) increasing parent-child positive affect (Doug: "I want to spend more time with my [step-] dad and learn about man stuff."); (3) increasing positive peer relationships; (4) increasing school social and academic performance; and (5) decreasing Doug's symptoms of depression (Mrs. W.: "I would like for him to stop being so mopey."). Examining Figure 2, it is apparent that by addressing the well-defined contributors to each of the overarching needs (i.e., the drivers sustaining the problems), multiple goals can be addressed simultaneously (Principles 1, 4, & 5).

Interventions.   Over the course of five months, the therapist worked closely with Doug and his family to address each of the identified overarching goals. Interventions capitalized on individual and systemic strengths (e.g., Mr. and Mrs. W.'s expressed concern for Doug and strong desire for him to succeed, Doug's artistic strengths, Mr. W.'s strong work ethic, Mrs. W.'s creativity) to help promote change within and across systems (Principle 2). Throughout the process, the fit assessment (Figure 2) was referred to and revised as necessary when new information was learned (Principle 8). For example, it was learned that Mrs. W. had an untreated sexual abuse history that provided a barrier to her ability to (a) communicate openly with Doug about his sexual acting out, (b) be involved in protecting April's physical safety, and (c) overcome her depression. Once this driver was identified, the therapist adjusted the fit assessment, and targeted "treatment of mother's sexual abuse history" as one of the intermediary goals necessary to obtain other overarching goals.

Interventions targeted by the therapist included all family members, as well as other key individuals in Doug's ecology (Principles 5 & 9). Parenting sessions were conducted to help Mr. and Mrs. W. learn the skills necessary to promote parenting behavior changes such as 1) increase their parental monitoring (e.g., developing a well defined plan to eliminate times that Doug and April were left alone together, even if the parents were in the next room), 2) increase their understanding of Doug's victimization as well as his offending behavior (e.g., he was traumatized and developed fears as a result of his own abuse, while he also cannot be allowed to re-enact his negative experience against others), and 3) increase their realistic developmental expectations (e.g., April cannot take on the adult role of supervision or preventing Doug's sexual acting out and Doug cannot be expected to engage in abstract thinking). Family sessions were conducted to help increase communication skills (e.g., solution focused problem solving), to facilitate family activities (e.g., homework assignments prescribing "family night"), and to increase all family members' emotional and physical safety (e.g., development of a safety plan). Individual time was spent with each of the family members to help coach them regarding their broader interactions and to establish the foundation for greater interventions (e.g., helping Mr. W. discuss appropriate sexual behavior with Doug; addressing Mrs. W.'s trauma symptoms and depression resulting from her own sexual abuse and domestic violence; helping Doug learn how to assert himself appropriately with his peers). Because Doug's index offense occurred during school hours and was directed toward his classmates, school sessions were conducted with school faculty to help educate the teachers and school officials about Doug's role as both victim and offender and to help address their concerns regarding the safety of having Doug interact with peers. School meetings between school faculty and Doug's parents were conducted to establish a monitoring plan to reduce the likelihood of Doug being in high risk situations (e.g., initially being driven to school by a parent instead of riding the bus and being monitored when changing classes and during free periods), to help Mr. and Mrs. W. advocate for Doug to be allowed to participate in prosocial extracurricular activities (e.g., art club), to establish a behavioral plan promoting more responsible academic behavior (e.g., turning in homework), and to help increase the level of positive communication between the school and caregivers (e.g., having scheduled meetings to discuss Doug's progress).

Given the treatment team's availability 24 hours a day, Doug and his family were able to receive services whenever they were most needed. In addition to keeping regularly scheduled appointment times, the therapist was available by phone (or if necessary in person) to help monitor family adherence to behavioral plans, to provide support to family members during challenging times, and help problem solve when interventions were not successful (Principle 8). For example, in the second month of treatment the therapist received a call from Mrs. W. who was highly distressed after she walked in on Doug who had April on his lap as he read her a story. The therapist went to the home and helped the family understand where their safety plan had unraveled (Mr. W. was working late and Mrs. W. lost track of time while on the phone and left the children unattended; Doug had not followed the rule of staying out of April's room). The therapist also helped Mrs. W., in the moment, deliver the predetermined immediate consequence to Doug for his rule violation (i.e., Doug had to remain in the same room as one of his parents for 24 hours, which included sleeping on the floor of their room. Doug also lost his video games for two weeks and earned them back one at a time as days passed where he avoided unmonitored contact with April). On the other hand, by being available during this time, the therapist was able to identify strengths in the interaction (e.g., Doug had not acted out sexually, although his behaviors bordered on grooming and were inappropriate; Mrs. W. had identified the situation as inappropriate and asked for assistance) and provide support to all family members.

As treatment progressed, the therapist systematically transferred the responsibility of monitoring strengths and needs over to Mr. and Mrs. W. The caregivers were encouraged to develop interventions on their own, with the therapist serving only as a guide and to provide feedback and indirect monitoring (Principle 9). Mr. and Mrs. W. were charged with the task of conducting school meetings without the facilitation of the therapist. They were encouraged to identify consistent strengths in their children and to deliver positive consequences in addition to negative sanctions. Termination was sought when each of the overarching goals were addressed successfully and the family demonstrated the skills necessary to sustain progress.

Treatment outcomes. At the time of termination, the MST therapist reviewed treatment gains with the key participants and encouraged them to accept responsibility for the positive changes. At this time it was noted that there were no new reports of inappropriate sexual behavior at school, home, or the neighborhood, since the time that Doug was found with April on his lap. Mr. and Mrs. W. had successfully developed and maintained a reliable plan for monitoring April's safety, and there were no obvious trauma related symptoms endorsed by April. The positive relationship between all family members was stronger, in particular between Doug and his parents. Both Doug and Mrs. W. self-reported a decrease in symptoms of depression, and were observed by the therapist to be happier. Although Doug still was not excelling academically, he had shown improvement in turning in homework assignments and seeking additional assistance after school. Doug also was successful in developing a positive relationship with two boys in his art club, and was asked to participate in a local art competition. Both his and his parents' relationship with school officials was more positive and Doug had not experienced any school infractions in over three months. In addition, Doug had not experienced any further non-sexual violations (e.g., shoplifting).

Conclusion

Multisystemic therapy is an ecologically-focused family and community based treatment, with services delivered in the home. Although MST only has been empirically validated for the treatment of serious juvenile nonsexually offending delinquents, preliminary outcomes are promising for the effectiveness of MST with juveniles who have sexually abused others. Two small randomized controlled trials have demonstrated that sexually abusive youth who receive MST have lower recidivism rates for both sexual and criminal offenses than offenders who receive usual services. These findings have been established up to eight years post-referral.

One of the key factors to successful treatment within the MST framework is adherence to the model. As a result, a strict adherence protocol has been established for treatment providers to ensure that all members of the therapeutic team faithfully abide by the nine principles of MST. As illustrated through the case example provided, the MST therapist is flexible both with time and structure of sessions, while maintaining the use of empirically supported treatment strategies that are individualized to meet the needs of families. The MST protocol may be particularly effective in working with juveniles who have committed sexual offenses and their families, as these systems require vigilant monitoring and structured intervention strategies. The effectiveness of MST over usual services with sexually abusive youth is the topic of an on-going large scale randomized controlled trial, the results of which will aid in the decision regarding dissemination of the model for use with this special population of youth.

References

Ageton, S. S. (1983). *Sexual assault among adolescents.* Lexington, MA: Lexington Books.

Aos, S., Phipps, P., Barnoski, R., & Lieb, R. (2001). *The comparative costs and benefits of programs to reduce crime* (Document 01-05-1201). Olympia, WA: Washington State Institute for Public Policy.

Awad, G. A., & Saunders, E. B. (1989). Adolescent child molesters: Clinical observations. *Child Psychiatry & Human Development, 19*, 195-206.

Becker, J.V. (1998). What we know about the characteristics and treatment of adolescents who have committed sexual offenses. *Child Maltreatment: Journal of the American Professional Society on the Abuse of Children, 3*, 317-329.

Bischof, G. P., Stith, S. M., & Whitney, M. L. (1995). Family environments of adolescent sex offenders and other juvenile delinquents. *Adolescence, 30, 157-170.*

Blaske, D. M., Borduin, C. M., Henggeler, S. W., & Mann, B. J. (1989). Individual, family, and peer characteristics of adolescent sex offenders and assaultive offenders. *Developmental Psychology*, 25, 846-855.

Borduin, C. M., Henggeler, S. W., Blaske, D. M., & Stein, R. J. (1990). Multisystemic treatment of adolescent sexual offenders. *International Journal of Offender Therapy and Comparative Criminology, 34*, 105-113.

Borduin, C. M., Mann, B. J., Cone, L. T., Henggeler, S. W., Fucci, B. R., Blaske, D. M., et al., (1995). Multisystemic treatment of serious juvenile offenders: Long-term prevention of criminality and violence. *Journal of Consulting and Clinical Psychology*, 63, 569-578.

Borduin, C. M., & Schaeffer, C. M. (2002). Multisystemic treatment of juvenile sexual offenders: A progress report. *Journal of Psychology and Human Sexuality*, 13, 25-42.

Bronfenbrenner, U. (1979). *The ecology of human development: Experiments by design and nature.* Cambridge, MA: Harvard University Press.

Center for Substance Abuse Prevention (CSAP) (2001). *Exemplary substance abuse prevention programs award ceremony.* Washington, DC: CSAP, Substance Abuse and Mental Health Services Administration.

Daleiden, E. L., Kaufman, K. L., Hilliker, D. R., & O'Neil, J. N. (1998). The sexual histories and fantasies of youthful males: A comparison of sexual offending, nonsexual offending, and nonoffending group. *Sexual Abuse: A Journal of Research and Treatment, 10*, 195-209.

Davis, G. E., & Leitenberg, H. (1987). Adolescent sex offenders. *Psychological Bulletin, 101*, 417-427.

Fehrenbach, P. A., Smith, W., Monastersky, C., & Deisher, R. W. (1986). Adolescent sexual offenders: Offender and offense characteristics. *American Journal of Orthopsychiatry*, 56, 225-233.

Ford, M. E., & Linney, J. A. (1995). Comparative analysis of juvenile sexual offenders, violent nonsexual offenders, and status offenders. *Journal of Interpersonal Violence, 10*, 56-70.

Graves, R. B., Openshaw, D. K., Ascione, F. R., & Ericksen, S. L. (1996). Demographic and parental characteristics of youthful sexual offenders. *International Journal of Offender Therapy & Comparative Criminology, 40*, 300-317.

Haley, J. (1976). *Problem solving therapy.* San Francisco: Jossey-Bass.

Hastings, T., Anderson, S. J., & Hemphill, P. (1997). Comparisons of daily stress, coping, problem behavior, and cognitive distortions in adolescent sexual offenders and conduct-disordered youth. *Sexual Abuse: Journal of Research & Treatment, 9*, 29-42.

Henggeler, S. W., & Borduin, C. M. (1990). *Family therapy and beyond.* Pacific Grove, CA: Brooks/Cole Publishing Co.

Henggeler, S. W. & Borduin, C. M., Melton, G. B., Mann, B. J., Smith, L. Hall, J. A., et al. (1991). Effects of Multisystemic Therapy on drug use and abuse in serious juvenile offenders: A progress report from two outcome studies. *Family Dynamics of Addiction Quarterly, 1*, 40-51.

Henggeler, S. W., Melton, G. B., Brondino, M. J., Scherer, D. G., & Hanley, J. H. (1997). Multisystemic Therapy with violent and chronic juvenile offenders and their families: The role of treatment fidelity in successful dissemination. *Journal of Consulting and Clinical Psychology, 65*, 821-833.

Henggeler, S. W., Melton, G. B., & Smith, L. A. (1992). Family preservation using Multisystemic Therapy: An effective alternative to incarcerating serious juvenile offenders. *Journal of Consulting and Clinical Psychology, 60*, 953-961.

Henggeler, S. W., Pickrel, S. G., & Brondino, M. J. (1999). Multisystemic treatment of substance abusing and dependent delinquents: Outcomes, treatment fidelity, and transportability. *Mental Health Services Research, 1*, 171-184.

Henggeler, S. W., Rodick, J. D., Borduin, C. M., Hanson, C. L., Watson, S. M., & Urey, J. R. (1986). Multisystemic treatment of juvenile offenders: Effects on adolescent behavior and family interactions. *Developmental Psychology, 22*, 132-141.

Henggeler, S. W., & Schoenwald, S. K. (1998). *The MST supervisor manual: Promoting quality assurance at the clinical level.* Charleston, SC: MST Services.

Henggeler, S. W., Schoenwald, S. K., Borduin, C. M., Rowland, M. D., & Cunningham, P. B. (1998). *Multisystemic treatment of antisocial behavior in children and adolescents.* New York: Guilford Press.

Howell, J. C. (2003). *Preventing and reducing juvenile delinquency: A comprehensive framework.* Thousand Oaks, CA: Sage Publications.

Huey, S. J., Henggeler, S. W., Brodino, M. J., & Pickrel, S. G. (2000). Mechanisms of change in Multisystemic Therapy: Reducing delinquent behavior through therapist adherence and improved family and peer functioning. *Journal of Consulting and Clinical Psychology, 68*, 451-467.

Hunter, J. A., Goodwin, D. W., & Becker, J. V. (1994). The relationship between phal-lometrically measured deviant sexual arousal and clinical characteristics in juvenile sexual offenders. *Behavioral Research and Therapy, 32,* 533-538.

Jacobs, W. L., Kennedy, W. A., & Meyer, J. B. (1997). Juvenile delinquents: A between-group comparison study of sexual and nonsexual offenders. *Sexual Abuse: Journal of Research & Treatment, 9,* 201-217.

Kempton, T., & Forehand, R. L. (1992). Suicide attempts among juvenile delinquents: The contribution of mental health factors. *Behaviour Research & Therapy.* 30, 537-541.

Loeber, R., & Farrington, D. P. (Eds.). (1998). *Serious and violent juvenile offenders: Risk factors and successful interventions.* Thousand Oaks, CA: Sage Publications.

McBride, D. C., VanderWaal, C. J., Terry, Y. M., & VanBuren, H. (1999). *Breaking the cycle of drug use among juvenile offenders.* Washington, DC: National Institute of Justice, NCJ 179273.

Milloy, C. D. (1994). *A comparative study of juvenile sex offenders and non-sex offenders.* Olympia, WA: Washington State Institute for Public Policy.

Minuchin, S. (1974). *Families & family therapy.* Cambridge, MA: Harvard University Press.

National Institute on Drug Abuse. (1999). *Principles of drug addiction treatment: A research-based guide.* NIH Publication No. 99-4180.

President's New Freedom Commission on Mental Health (2003). *Achieving the prom-ise: Transforming mental health care in America.* Rockville, Maryland.

Righthand, S., & Welch, C. (2001). *Juveniles who have sexually offended: A review of the professional literature.* Washington, DC: Office of Juvenile Justice and Delinquency Prevention.

Schaeffer, C. M., & Borduin, C. M. (in press). Long-term follow up to a randomized clinical trial of Multisystemic Therapy with life course persistent offenders. *Journal of Consulting & Clinical Psychology.*

Schoenwald, S. K. (1998). *Multisystemic therapy consultation guidelines.* Charleston, SC: MST Institute.

Schoenwald, S. K., Sheidow, A. J., & Letourneau, E. J. (2004). Toward effective quali-ty assurance in evidence-based practice: Links between expert consultation, thera-pist fidelity and child outcomes. *Journal of Clinical Child and Adolescent Psychology, 33,* 94-104.

Schoenwald, S. K., Sheidow, A. J., & Letourneau, E. J., & Liao, J. G. (2003). Transportability of multisystemic therapy: Evidence for multi-level influences. *Mental Health Service Research, 5,* 223-239.

Smith, G., & Fischer, L. (1999). Assessment of juvenile sexual offenders: Reliability and validity of the Abel Assessment for Interest in Paraphilias. *Sexual Abuse: A Journal of Research and Treatment, 11,* 207 – 216.

Stanton, M. D., & Shadish, W. R. (1997). Outcome, attrition, & family-couples treatment for drug abuse: A meta-analysis and review of the controlled comparative studies. *Psychological Bulletin, 122,* 177-191.

Strother, K. B., Swenson, M. E., & Schoenwald, S. K. (1998). *Multisystemic Therapy organizational manual.* Charleston, SC: MST Institute.

U.S. Department of Health and Human Services (1999). *Mental health: A report of the Surgeon General.* Rockville, MD: U.S. Department of Health and Human Services, National Institutes of Health, National Institute of Mental Health.

U.S. Public Health Service (2001). *Youth violence: A report of the Surgeon General.* Washington, DC: Author.

Table 1: Nine MST Principles

1) The primary purpose of assessment is to understand the fit between the identified problems and their broader systemic context.

2) Therapeutic contacts emphasize the positive and use systemic strengths as levers for change.

3) Interventions are designed to promote responsible behavior and decrease irresponsible behavior among family members.

4) Interventions are present focused and action oriented, targeting specific and well-defined problems.

5) Interventions target sequences of behavior within and between multiple systems that maintain the identified problems.

6) Interventions are developmentally appropriate and fit the developmental needs of the youth.

7) Interventions are designed to require daily or weekly effort by family members.

8) Intervention effectiveness is evaluated continuously from multiple perspectives with providers assuming accountability for overcoming barriers to successful outcomes.

9) Interventions are designed to promote treatment generalization and long-term maintenance of therapeutic change by empowering caregivers to address family members' needs across multiple systemic contexts.

Figure 1: Social-ecological model of the child environment.

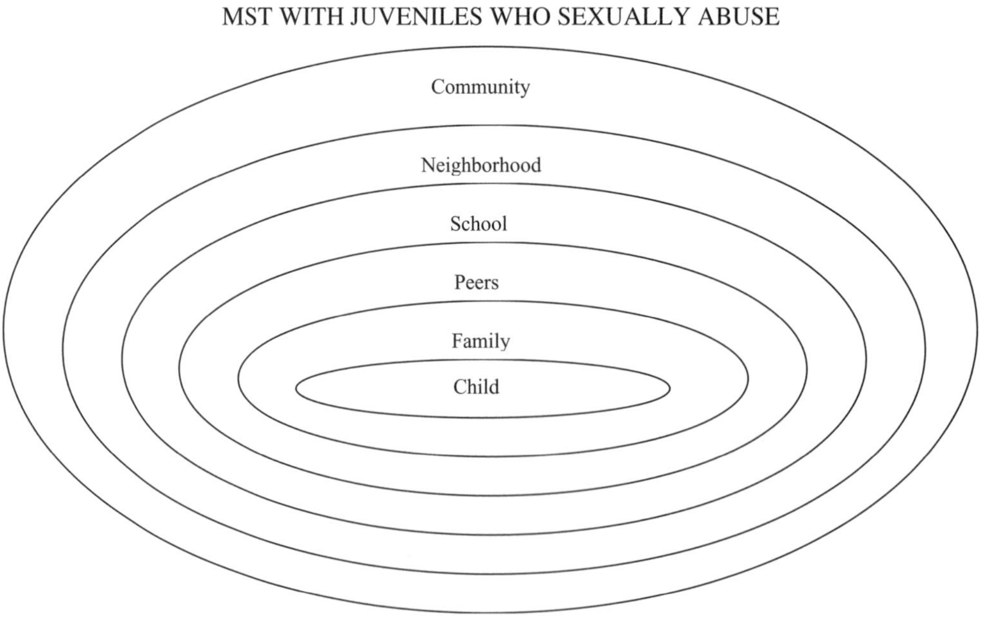

MST WITH JUVENILES WHO SEXUALLY ABUSE

Bronfenbrenner, U. (1979). The ecology of human development. Cambridge, MA: Harvard University Press.

Figure 2: Fit circle used for conceptualization of youth's sexual offending behaviors.

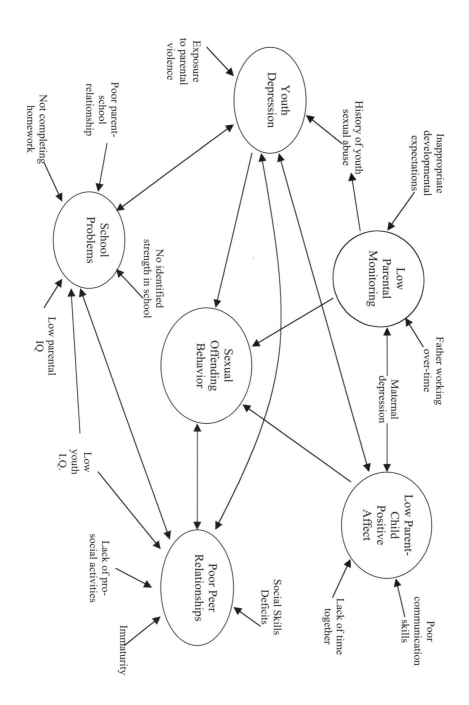

Overarching goals target well-defined problem behaviors (depicted in circles) that are maintained by reinforcers from the youth's ecology (depicted as "drivers" or arrows).

CHAPTER TWENTY-FOUR

BEYOND PSYCHOLOGY: BRAIN-BASED APPROACHES THAT IMPACT BEHAVIOR, LEARNING AND TREATMENT

STEVEN M. BENGIS
AND
PENNY CUNINGGIM

Introduction

Since its inception in the mid 1980's, the child/adolescent sex abuse-specific field has been gradually evolving away from the "one size fits all" cognitive-behavioral-relapse prevention model (CBRP) towards a more individualized, holistic or eclectic approach. This latter approach more accurately incorporates both the developmental realities of children and youth and the complexity of the diagnostic profiles of those who engage in abusive/offending behaviors. Certain central tenets of this specialized field have remained consistent (i.e., protecting future victims, ensuring safety and appropriate levels of containment within which to conduct treatment, developing continuum of care services, and providing specialized assessments conducted by qualified practitioners). However, finding the most effective treatment interventions remains a fluid and ever-expanding realm within which practitioner creativity and research-based outcomes continue to co-exist in creative/destructive tension. Practitioners who understand that sex abusing is a behavior, not a diagnosis, continue to seek the most effective treatment approaches for a wide spectrum of children/youth engaging in similar behaviors, i.e., those with mood and personality disorders, PDD/aspergers/autisim, learning disabilities, ADHD and other neurological disorders. Common themes amongst many of these varied treatment approaches are: maximizing the likelihood that inappropriate behaviors can be stopped; enhancing the likelihood that various concepts/information can be learned; and, healing the impact of life experiences that contribute to sexually abusive behaviors. Given this change we would suggest that to accomplish these goals, we must incorporate brain-based principles into our conceptualization, assessment and intervention approaches.

In parallel with the development of the abuse-specific field, brain-based knowledge has also been expanding rapidly over the past twenty-plus years. As Eric Jensen (1998), one of the leaders in the "brain-compatible movement" put forth, "With the arrival of MRI, NMRI, PET Scans, CAT Scans, EEG, X-Rays and other 'brain mapping' techniques, fields like genetics, physics, and pharmacology were seamlessly woven into scientific journal articles on the brain." He continues by saying; "drawing from a body of technical knowledge about the brain, a whole new way of thinking about the organ developed. While we don't yet have an inclusive, coherent model of how the brain works, we do know enough to make significant changes in how we teach."[1]

This new knowledge has applicability beyond the common understanding of the word "teach" (although most professionals are engaged in one way or another in trying to convey a body of information/knowledge to their clients/students and, therefore, are "teachers"). It also includes the ways we assess, intervene, and conduct therapy/counseling. In this chapter, we hope to encourage this expansion. Our goals are to: 1) introduce our colleagues in the sex abuse-specific field to some alternative brain-based constructs and intervention techniques; 2) raise questions about the ways in which we have both interpreted a number of behaviors and chosen to intervene with the behaviors we have observed; and, 3) encourage the field to join with us and others in an open and critical exploration of this rich and rapidly growing area of brain-based assessment and treatment/intervention. Personally, we feel we have entered a whole new realm of conceptualization and implementation. It is a realm that is somewhat daunting, vast and rapidly expanding. Jeri Janowky, a top learning and memory neuroscientist at Oregon Health Sciences University in Portland, says, "Anything you learned two years ago is already old information… neuroscience is exploding." (Jensen, 1998). In our view, it is essential to cross-fertilize our own abuse-specific work with that of this "exploding" brain-based field. This cross-fertilization can only increase the effectiveness of our assessment and intervention approaches. This will contribute to enhancing both the safety and protection of victims and the management and healing of those who abuse.

Some Examples of Alternative Brain-Based Constructs and Intervention Techniques

For purposes of this discussion, we would like to share some examples of brain-based approaches to treatment intervention. For us, the working definition of "brain-based" is:

> *"…acknowledging and embracing the brain's rules for meaningful learning, and organizing teaching [and counseling] with those rules in mind."*[3]

There is an array of technological and teaching/counseling approaches that synchronize with this definition. For this chapter, our own explorations have focused on a small, but fairly representative sample of these approaches. Specifically, we will talk about vestibular stimulation, vision work, auditory stimulation, and dominance-based learning styles. What follows are brief descriptions of each of these areas and the types of interventions that may be used to remediate/resolve any identified deficits:

Vestibular stimulation

Definition: The vestibular system is a sensory-motor system that connects the semicircular canals of the inner ear, brain stem, eyes and core muscles. It regulates our equilibrium, our sense of space, our movement, and even our eye-hand coordination. It helps our brain remain alert. It is involved in waking or stimulating the brain and preparing the brain to receive new information.

Vestibular dysfunction: Some signs that one's vestibular system is not working optimally include: poor posture, clumsiness, fidgety movements, poor handwriting, poor listening ability, auditory discrimination and processing problems, delayed speech and reading skills, inattention, hyperactivity, and poor sensory integration.

Diagnostic techniques: Sample kinds of assessments one would use include: observation and interviews regarding childhood neuro-developmental delays and blocks; reflexes; balance, coordination, and whole-body, gross motor movement weaknesses.

Remediation techniques: Interventions to address vestibular problems include the use of specially developed exercises involving movements of the head, as well as balancing, spinning, rolling, and crawling that can activate and "grow" the vestibular system. An example of vestibular development that lead to enhanced reading scores is as follows: Although a student may have excellent athletic skills in basketball and gymnastics he may be unable to crawl bi-laterally, i.e., when asked to crawl with his left leg and right arm forward, he can only use a leg and arm on the same side of his body. Such an inability often is an indication of an underdeveloped vestibular and an inability to move across the midline, an imaginary line going from the middle of the skull down to the floor through the center of the body. With such a disability, the eyes often are unable to smoothly track across the midline of a page of print, making reading difficult, i.e., the eyes stop in the center of the page and then must start again from the middle to the end. By involving a youngster in repeated exercises that increase his ability to use opposite extremities when crawling, he builds brain connections between the right and left sides of the brain. Research has shown that such exercises translate into enhanced ability to cross midline while reading with a concomitant increase in reading readiness skills as evidenced on standardized reading tests. These increases occur in the absence of any additional reading instruction.

Application/impact: All learning depends in part on the maturity of the vestibular system. From infancy, the brain's vestibular system is developing through rocking, crawling, walking, touching and other kinds of basic motor stimulation. When these opportunities are limited either by too much sitting time (in front of a TV, in a car seat or walker), or by other kinds of problems, e.g., trauma, injury, poor nutrition, etc., the brain is less ready for learning. Sensory motor skill development impacts on our ability to read, write, attend, remember, move our bodies, as well as our motivation and ability to become and remain alert.[4] Last, certain kinds of planned exercises can produce chemical and neurological changes in our brain that increase brain functioning and health.

Vision

Definition: Vision involves both one's ability to see (20/20 vision), and one's ability to give meaning to visual information. We take in more information visually than through any other sense. "The eyes contain nearly 70% of our body's receptors and send millions of signals every second along the optic nerves to the visual processing centers of the brain."[5] The visual cortex or occipital lobes take in information from our eyes and processes that data in many ways. Then we process this data in a variety of brain areas that relate to our scanning, stereo-vision, distance, depth and visual perceptive abilities[6]. Visual information aids us in remembering, analyzing, and expressing our thoughts. Its proper processing and expression are crucial to success in life.

Vision dysfunctions: Problems with vision can manifest as learning difficulties in the areas of reading, writing, and math; problems with relating to others, following instructions, inattention; coordination, spatial relationships, and poor self image and lack of confidence. Clinical issues have also been treated successfully with vision aids for clients with developmental delays, learning disabilities, depression, insomnia, chronic fatigue syndrome and hyperactivity.

Diagnostic techniques: Some useful tools include vision screens, light/sound machines for determining the nature of over/under-stimulation; the Telebinocular vision screen (eye teaming, fusion, convergence, etc.), vision examination by a developmental or behavioral optometrist; light sensitivity and color preference overlays, and symptom checklists.

Remediation techniques: Natural light profoundly impacts our health. In the past century we have begun to see a vast increase in the uses of light to enhance learning, social interactions, our mental health and general well being. Some of the techniques now available include: special eye glasses (for 20/20 sight or to correct vision problems, i.e. lens with prisms); full spectrum light panels and tubes for home, school and office; therapies that combine motion, light and sound; educational software and clinical optometry light therapy equipment and related treatment modalities, eye movement exercises, computer software that trains visual tracking, scanning, and visual discrimination skills, etc., audio-visual entrainment, and use of visual exercises and aids in class like scanning and fusion exercises, colored overlays, colored paper, and a host of other vision related aids, like special printed word, visual maps, film, drawings, pictures, organizational webs, collages, computers, diagrams, charts and other graphic representations, etc. An example of using vision work is a youngster with 20/20 vision, as measured on standardized vision tests, and who is unable to read, and frequently rubs his eyes, becomes agitated when pushed to read for any length of time, and also squints. By using a Telebinocular assessment tool, vision problems with fusion and accommodation, among others, are identified, i.e., the student's eyes do not work together and his eyes cannot focus and refocus quickly. By sending the student to a developmental optometrist who provides him with vision therapy exercises, his eyes begin to strengthen and function appropriately. Together with Irlen color screens that help with light sensitivity, i.e., a youngster whose normal experience of the printed word includes swirling, jumping and moving letters, the student's reading ability begins to advance. For the first time in his life, reading becomes the same task that it is for other students rather than a complex task of catching moving letters, not seeing whole words, etc. The changes can be dramatic and the resulting increase in learning ability enhances not only academic achievement but also self-image and self-esteem.

Application/impact: Without the ability to make accurate and understandable mental pictures of data and concepts, clients and students often are unable to achieve in math, reading, and other academic areas. All these areas require one's ability to encode and decode what is read, solve problems, manipulate symbols and concepts. In study and counseling groups students are expected to be able to express their concerns and talk about concepts, alternative choices and behaviors, when sometimes these students do not have mental tools in their heads to analyze and compare, or form cues to anchor their words. When using visual aids they often are able to organize and articulate their ideas more clearly in a variety of media.

Listening

Definition: Listening is not the same as hearing. Hearing is a passive process whereby we detect the sounds in the environment around us. On the other hand, listening is an active process. It involves the meaning sounds give us. One can have perfect hearing but still be a poor listener. Good listeners hear both the sounds and their nuanced meanings clearly. Good listeners can push extraneous or irrelevant noises out of the way and focus on the sounds that are important to the task they are currently completing.[7]

Dysfunction: Poor listeners cannot tune out irrelevant sounds. Problems with our listening function result in many varying kinds of learning problems. Some include stuttering, hesitant speech, poor word recall, difficulty with mood swings and focus; and with a range of affective problems, including hypersensitivity, low motivation, and inability to interact effectively with others. Sounds that enter the inner ear affect the vestibular, so problems related to vestibular dysfunction mentioned above (coordination, whole body movement) can come from a problem in listening. Careful use of sound can address symptoms related to autism, PDD, ADD, ADHD, dyslexia, and central auditory processing disorders. Also, as with vision problems, listening interventions have helped students without such pervasive labels but nevertheless with problems with coordination and balance, focus and attention, and reading and writing as well. In order to read, we need to be able to listen to the sound vibrations in the inner ear. These sounds are what we "hear" as language right before we speak. Poor listeners also have the inability to tune out sounds in the environment. This results in poor attention, distractibility, and feelings of being overwhelmed. Last, the more desirable, high frequency sounds increase our physical energy, whereas, low frequency sounds drain our physical energy away.

Diagnostic techniques: Some assessments include hearing tests, listening screens, language and speech assessments, and auditory processing and discrimination tests.

Remediation techniques: A sample of techniques include specially designed hardware, sound making devices, music and sound tapes to stimulate and enhance hearing and listening capacity (increase ability to hear high frequency sound), and to reprogram the way we speak and listen for meaning; use of rhythm, rhyme and tone in popular song and classical music to learn new information, enhance memory, increase joy and relax the brain and body. Paper and pencil work, auditory tapes and computer software to train auditory processing. Reading books and instructions aloud as view text and using books on tape for silent reading time. Joshua Leeds describes many of these methods in, *The Power of Sound*.[8] An example of a listening remediation is as follows: a young seventeen year-old woman frequently misunderstands instructions and has developed elaborate defenses against being held responsible for not paying attention. She cannot follow what happens in class and cannot understand any interactive social conversation without interrupting. She is anxious and talks loudly and is underperforming in school in all major subjects. These auditory deficits exist in spite of normal hearing because they are based in brain-processing inabilities rather than basic "hearing" capacity. She is provided with a sophisticated computer-based program that enhances auditory discrimination through the use of interesting and engaging software games. As her auditory discrimination skills develop, her response time to auditory stimuli has increased. She is now able to recognize a wider variety of consonant sounds than she could identify prior to the training. Her ability to engage in conversations has increased along with enhanced academic achievement. Her motivation to remain in school has increased where she had considered dropping out prior to the auditory training.

Application/impact: Sound and music are the elixirs of life. They put us in touch with the living world around us. Based on extensive research and for clients/students who are stressed, resist instruction and have trouble staying focused, music provides an important source of remedies. For students with autistic symptoms, learning disabilities, and problems with coordination and muscle-use, sound therapies provide a range of solutions. They provide memory cues and promote relaxed attention for patterns that enhance reasoning capacity. Music can be used to both stimulate and, alternatively, calm the brain as well as affect. It can enliven our curiosity and motivation or it can relax our bodies, minds and spirits.

Dominance

Definition: Dominance is a learning styles tool based on the work of Paul Dennison[9] that takes an individual's specific lateral dominances (and taken together, pattern) of brain, ear, eye, hand and foot preference and uses them to suggest more effective ways for that individual to learn difficult material, interact, and respond to stress. Carla Hannaford, who studied with Paul Dennison, describes 32 dominance profiles in her book *The Dominance Factor.*[10] She tells us the senses provide the raw information that the brain uses to learn about and respond to the world. Each person's sensory dominance profile tells him/her the preferred way he/she receives, processes, assimilates and expresses information. One's profile also aids in understanding why one behaves as one does, responds to new situations and information in certain ways, and reacts to highly stressful events with particular patterned actions. This dominant profile is innate. By becoming conscious of our own unique dominance profiles we can improve our learning and relationship capacities.

Dominance problems: Problems with dominance begin when we do not have a natural learning or dominance profile that fits how we must function. This functioning might be related to our home culture to ensure parental approval, how we are taught in school, or how we are asked to relate in groups. For instance, most schools value left brain thinking: analytical, organized, sequential learners who have good reading, language and articulation skills. But much research tells us that in many schools at least half the learners can be right brain, global, non-sequential processors, who need to move around, flourish when provided visual input, require lessons that are immediately and clearly relevant to their lives, and who tend to approach problems non-conventionally.

Besides these differences in general brain functioning, in certain cases, one's responses to the world are not optimal because the dominant brain (whether right or left) does not work smoothly with the dominant eye, ear, hand or foot. For example, for easiest functioning, it is best to have a cross-over pattern, whereby the dominant eye, hand, foot and ear each communicate with the opposite (and dominant) brain hemisphere. When this does not occur, one is operating in what is known as a unilateral or weaker state, which makes learning and coping harder under certain circumstances. During stress only the dominant eye, ear, hand and foot opposite the dominant brain side will be good at processing what is happening to us. As a result, knowing such weaknesses, as well as the ways in which our dominances serve us best, is important. When learners have unilateral functioning instead of integrated brain and body dominance (everything works together with appropriate cross-overs), they could have much frustration with, as well as significant deficiencies in, reading, writing, speaking, relating, processing information, and responding appropriately to stressful events. Yet, such problems go unseen and unresolved because learners' behaviors are seen as attitudinal or the result of their limited I.Q., that is, their "low innate intelligence."

As so many theorists have pointed out in the past half-century, there is no such thing as immutable intelligence. There are no best learning styles either. Each is just different, but if educational and social institutions prefer certain styles over others, and disregard learners whose dominance patterns result in weaker functioning under certain conditions, then we find ourselves not only trying to adapt, but trying to become something we are not. In doing so, we create other problems for ourselves, both in school and in other settings.

Assessment tools: Good tools include: paper and pencil assessments, dominance exercises, observation, muscle testing for dominance, and laterality assessments found as part of the work of Hannaford, Dennison, Vitale, Buzan, etc. In addition there are a number of learning styles questionnaires not based on the Dennison dominance paradigm, but on other research regarding one's biological, sociological, environmental and psychological preferences. One example is the work of Rita and Kenneth Dunn, who have compiled extensive research studies and written numerous books on their approach to learning style strengths.[11]

Remediation techniques: To support a preferred style of learning, one can provide environmental and instructional/counseling aids that match the learner's specific strengths. For example, right brain students who respond to the larger picture, or the global view, often like whole-body or hands on activities, and need purpose and meaning when learning and interacting. For these students it makes sense to share the larger purposes and goals of a lesson or activity, make sure the lesson provides relevant examples, and emphasize tactile and whole-body learning options as part of the lesson. In addition, research tells us there are many other aids for enhancing right brain learners' performance that include: an informal, not formal, environment; opportunities to eat and drink as part of learning; access to music and visuals while learning; opportunity to do more than one task at a time (right-brainers enjoy juggling and tend to get bored quickly); and the "space" to talk to themselves as they study.

For left brain, more analytic students and clients, when beginning new tasks, it makes sense to explain what will occur in an orderly sequenced manner and provide clear steps towards completion. Such students often enjoy debate and often like lectures and textbook assignments. They like to study in bright light and often do not need food or drink in order to concentrate.

For either group of students, incorporating learning methods that support their specific styles can give them a motivational boost to try difficult tasks. It also can give them the sense that their (different) ways of working, relating and living are not aberrations, but genuine preferences or strengths that others hold as well. Not only are they not alone, but they have the potential to learn as much and as well as their successful, "studious", "smarter" peers.

Application and impact: Knowing our preferred learning style enables us to better prepare for situations we know will tax our brain wiring. It suggests ways to increase our chances of success in classroom or job. It provides instructors and parents with valuable information about the young people in their care. With this knowledge they can both choose teaching methods, and provide guidance, that enhances learning and motivation for difficult tasks they will inevitably encounter.

All these areas of brain-based research and their related methods overlap. Which lens one works through, which set of treatment tools one tries is based both on the assessment of primary versus secondary problems and on what tools clients respond to most positively. Because you do not know where the dysfunction originates, nor what tools will be most useful, it is important to keep learning about new brain-based methods, while refining the use of tools currently part of one's treatment or teaching approach.

Of course, a basic part of this work is to understand how a wide variety of problematic behaviors might be viewed through this brain-based lens in the first place. The next section shares some thoughts on this topic.

For those of us working with sexually abusive children/youth, the above information may be intriguing, but how relevant is it to our need to assess and treat those who abuse? After twenty-plus years of work, we have gained sophisticated diagnostic and treatment skills. We are managing behaviors with psychopharmacology and a combination of behavior management techniques. We differentiate amongst those children/youth with long-term sexual behavior problems and those with problematic but less entrenched patterns. We have integrated elements of CBRP techniques for those youth who need them, integrated many of the newest trauma reduction interventions, and fundamentally learned to mix and match our approaches to meet the needs of our clients. So, what do brain-based perspective and related strategies bring us that twenty years of clinical and research work doesn't already produce?

First, we owe it to all our clients to accurately diagnose the behaviors that we are observing. We think that too often the most commonly observed acting-out behaviors (i.e., impulsivity, oppositionality, resistance, inattention, distractibility, irritability, hyperactivity) that may be important contributing factors to a child/adolescent's sexual acting-out, are misunderstood, misdiagnosed and mistreated. Second, too many of these behaviors are being attributed to ADD/ADHD/bi-polar conditions and being treated with medicine. Medicine may well be a component of a holistic intervention approach, but too often, of late, it has become the "sine qua non" of symptom removal. The art of careful and systematic diagnosis is being lost to the "quick fix", "take care of the symptoms" approach to treatment. Yet, the same symptomatology that results in a DSM diagnosis may well be attributed to a brain-based condition. If a psychiatric problem, appropriate psychopharmacological intervention is central to an overall treatment plan. However, in other circumstances, the failure to understand the learning disability, neurological or other brain-based condition that may be underlying acting-out behaviors may:

- limit the effectiveness of certain treatment approaches.
- contribute to the misattribution of attitudinal problems where none exits (and such misattribution often results in negative consequences to these children/youth).
- may result in treatment failures, over lengthy treatment in costly residential services, or even further sexual acting-out.

What follows are some commonly observed behaviors and the possible brain-based problems that may be contributing to/causing them. As you read through this behavioral list, think about the clients whom you have assessed or treated and the diagnosis that you were inclined to make based on these behavioral realities. In many cases, as with our own experience, these behaviors may have far different causes than those that we had previously considered. Such a realization is sobering.

Irritability/resistance: These behaviors are often seen as indicative of an attitude problem, oppositionality, and conduct disorder. But they may be a function of: a lack of resonance between brain dominance and task; failure to adapt learning mode to learning style; a vision problem; an auditory processing problem; ADHD; a sensory-motor integration problem; or allergies. For example, a seventeen-year old ADHD student refuses to engage in language arts classes, walks out, is often confronted and occasionally restrained. She is constantly irritable and resistant to classroom participation, although she is very intelligent. Assessments identified that she was right-brain and left-ear dominant. As such, her preferred perceptual mode was auditory. To increase her motivation and attention to reading, she was allowed to use ear phones and music as well as to sit comfortably in a beanbag chair during silent reading time. Almost immediately, her interest in/willingness to read books increased significantly. She remained on task throughout a class and the need to intervene with her was sharply reduced.

Impulsivity/hyperactivity: These are seen mostly as frontal lobe ADHD or a component of bi-polarity. They may be a sign of a(n): auditory processing problem; vision processing problem; or vestibular development problem. For example, a thirteen year-old female student talks incessantly, has symptoms of ADHD and interjects herself into the business of other students frequently. Through the use of the AVE machine (audio-visual entrainment) this young woman began to demonstrate reduced talking, less intrusive behaviors with others, greater calm and an increase in overall happiness.

Resistance/oppositionality/disruptive behaviors: These are seen as an attitude problem, or an indication of ODD or CD. They may be a function of: a visual processing problem; auditory processing problem; sensory/motor integration problem; vestibular development problem; learning styles or brain dominance problem. For example, a young person who is extremely irritable and acts out in manner that appears to be based on an attitude problem, (i.e., they are choosing to misbehave, don't care, could stop if they chose), actually is warding off anxiety and panic that comes from an inability to process the sensory information that is coming through their senses, (i.e., through eyes, ears, touch, etc.). By providing the youngster with a "sensory ball", rocking chair or pressure blanket or vest, anxiety is reduced and the youngster stops being resistant and oppositional.

Anxiety/depression: Often seen as evidence of either external, psychological stress or biochemical imbalance. They may be a sign of an auditory or visual processing problem; sensory-motor integration problem; or vestibular or neuro-developmental problem. For example, a youngster who appears clinically depressed may be struggling with massive input overload and disorganization. By increasing the level of brain alertness by taking short breaks, moving around, listening to activating music and singing, or increasing water or protein intake, the brain is stimulated and concentration and performance increases. As the amount of stimuli the youngster can handle increases, the overload and concomitant depression decreases.

Inability to read: This is often seen as an indication of dyslexia. This may be result of a(n): visual processing problem; auditory processing problem; vestibular brain development problem; or a pattern of unilateral rather than cross-dominance, (i.e., being left-eyed and left brained or having dominant right ear, eye, hand, and foot, but right-brained). An example as previously discussed is a youngster who labors with serious light sensitivity who, in spite of the use of several reading programs, continues to be a non-reader. However, with the introduction of Irlen color overlays and developmental optometric exercises begin to increase vision efficiency and enhance reading ability.

Many of the behaviors/problems with which we deal each day have these multiple etiological possibilities. We all tend to understand what we observe through the lens of the discipline/knowledge base in which we have been trained. Psychologists/therapists tend to use clinical/DSM categorizations, while many educators use the lens of traditionally understood learning disabilities. These remain important and at times the most accurate lenses, since there are youth whose behaviors/problems are generated by ADHD, bi-polarity, and/or cognitive disorders. But as our knowledge of even a limited range of brain-based etiological conditions deepens, these more generally understood traditional views appear significantly over-diagnosed and their brain-based counterparts seriously overlooked. It is also very difficult to consider alternatives when the diagnostic tools that we have been trained to use do not assess a large variety of brain-based problems.

However, with a limited amount of additional training and without the need for additional advanced degrees, practitioners can learn to use:

- a telebinocular machine to diagnose vision-processing problems.
- observational and motor tests to establish brain dominance and sensory motor integration problems.
- simple auditory diagnostic tools to identify potential auditory processing problems.
- observation and question and answer tests to establish learning style pref erences.

Once identified, these problems can be remediated either through referral to a specialist (e.g., a developmental optometrist in the case of vision processing problems) and/or through the use of techniques that clinicians/educators/others can learn in specialized training workshops (e.g., use of special musical tones, audio tapes, dietary changes, use of light and sound devices and use of computer-based brain development software).

Mostly, we all need to begin to question the certainty with which we are diagnosing and classifying the behaviors/problems that we encounter in our work on a daily basis. With a sex abuse-specific population, this diagnosis becomes even more imperative. Maximizing the possibility for successful treatment outcomes is a victim protection necessity. Failure to understand any component of an individual's capacity to apprehend the knowledge/skills he/she will need to prevent relapse, increases re-offense risk. It is equally harmful to fail to understand the role of vision/hearing to an individual's behavioral profile as it is to miss the etiological role of trauma. These are "misses" that we can ill afford to be making.

Outcomes

It is too early for us to proffer research-based results of our ongoing efforts to incorporate brain-based principles into our sex abuse assessment and intervention approaches. But, in each of the brain-based areas identified above, i.e., vision, hearing, vestibular, and dominance, the founders and their colleagues in these fields have put forth extensive objective research demonstrating the efficacy of their approaches. As a simple introduction to a new field, we have chosen not to put forth a formal literature review. For those interested in the objective research, we encourage you to read the primary texts identified in the footnotes to this chapter. Those sources will lead you to hundreds of other research studies available in the world of brain-based learning.

We would, however, like to offer some of our own anecdotal evidence for consideration. After several years of learning style and other brain-based modifications, we have some remarkable success stories in our work with severely emotionally disturbed and behaviorally disordered children and adolescents.

1) A first in a twenty-year history, seventy-five percent drop in the number of restraints over a six-month period for youth in our Juniors Program (ages 8-13).[12]

2) A significant increase in reading scores ranging from six month to 2.5 year jumps within a ten-month time period.[13] (Generally, our students make no or minute progress in one year's period of time.)

3) The remediation of a significant sleep disorder after six sessions of light-sound therapy (audio visual entrainment) in a youth for whom sleep had been a major problem for years and for whom a variety of medications over several years of time had proven ineffective in addressing this condition.

4) A dramatic reduction in oppositionality and acting-out in a bright yet highly impulsive student after her learning style was diagnosed and modifications made in seating, auditory input, and lighting.

5) A dramatic change in behaviors (i.e., a marked reduction in hyperactivity and distractibility; significant reduction in chronic "baiting" of other youth; significant increase in eye contact; and a dramatic increase in reading scores) in a student who spent three months, three times a week engaged in individual vestibular stimulation exercises.

6) Students choosing to spin (a daily vestibular exercise in which students engage at our school) when under stress and informing parents that it helped them relax.

7) Improved vision and a jump in reading performance for two youth who had never worn glasses but were diagnosed with vision eye teaming problems on the telebinocular machine. With the addition of glasses, different seating arrangements, and individualized eye/hand exercises, these youth are performing much more successfully in their academics.

These are very preliminary observations, but they parallel what the research predicts. These observed impacts provide us with encouragement to continue our brain-based work. Within the next few years, we would hope to have more quantitative and qualitative results to share with our colleagues.

Conclusion

Personally, we are in the infancy of our understanding of the impact of brain-based approaches to our work with sexually abusive and other children/youth. As our knowledge and "aha" experiences increase, we are convinced that brain-based research and intervention is the cutting-edge of work with complex, severely disturbed acting-out children/youth. We believe the failure to use these approaches to diagnose and treat such clients will be viewed similarly to our failure to identify and treat sexual abuse twenty-years ago. We can well remember the sophisticated psychodynamic formulations we constructed for some of our deeply disturbed youth that never even mentioned sexual abuse. Yet, in retrospect, such abuse was the core of the treatment issue for these kids, and we missed it entirely.

But we can only know what we know at the time that we are asked to make the best judgments of which we are capable. The last twenty years of brain-based research in combination with the work of practitioners in the brain-based field, has convinced us that we are now obligated to study this literature, learn the appropriate intervention techniques, and integrate them into the important "traditional" psychological/behavioral/special education approaches that have guided our work to date. We anticipate that just as sex abuse-specific work for children/youth has moved from the fringes of the field to become accepted mainstream practice, so too will brain-based work. In our view, such mainstream acceptance holds enormous promise for our clients as well as for victim prevention. We look forward to the coming journey and hope as many of you as possible will join us in the search for ever more effective treatment of these children/youth.

End Notes

[1]Jensen, Eric (1998). *Teaching with the brain in mind*. Alexandria, Virginia: Association for Supervision and Curriculum Development.

[2]Ibid, Jensen, p.2

[3]Caine, Renate Nummela and Caine, Geoffrey (1994). *Making connections*, Menlo Park, California: Innovative Learning Publications; Alternative Publishing Group of Addison-Wesley Publishing Company.

[4]Ayres, Jean (1999). *Sensory integration and learning disorders*. Los Angeles: Western Psychological Services, 1999.

[5]Wolfe, Patricia (2001). *Brain matters: Translating research into classroom practice*. Alexandria, VA: ASCD, p. 152.

[6]Carter, R. (1998). *Mapping the mind*. Los Angeles: University of California Press.

[7]Tomatis, Alfred A. (1991). *The conscious ear*. Barrytown, NY: Station Hill Press.

[8]Leeds, Joshua (2001). *The power of sound*. Rochester, VT: Healing Arts Press.

[9]Dennison, Paul(1985). *Brain learning for the whole person*. Ventura, California: Edu-Kinesthetics, Inc.

[10]Hannaford, Carla (1997). *The dominance factor*. Arlington, Virginia: Great Ocean Publishers.

[11]See The Dunn and Dunn website for extensive information on their work: learningstyles.net.

[12]Unpublished daily restraint data collection at the New England Adolescent Research Institute (NEARI) in Holyoke, MA. Available upon request.

[13]Unpublished reading score data collected at NEARI. Available upon request.

John Bergman with Saul Hewish, Marlyn Robson and Patrick Tidmarsh

---

CHAPTER TWENTY-FIVE

EXPERIENTIAL TREATMENT RESISTANCE IN THE USE OF DRAMA THERAPY WITH ADOLESCENTS WHO SEXUALLY OFFEND

JOHN BERGMAN
WITH
SAUL HEWISH
MARLYN ROBSON
AND
PATRICK TIDMARSH

Introduction: A Primer on Experiential Therapies in Treating Adolescent Offenders ~ John Bergman

The Western psychological arts are young compared to the non-Western traditions of the therapist/healer, the curandero or the shaman. But experiential therapies in Western cultures, especially drama as therapy, have been a potent part of the history of treatment and have historical roots at least as far back in Europe as the eighteenth century. Patients in Ticehurst Asylum in England were encouraged to do theatre "to restore health to diseased minds."

Progress in the use of drama therapy came rapidly during the late nineteenth century. In 1891 Dr. Janet used drama in re-enactments to work with trauma, and in 1908 Moreno began his creative drama work with children in Vienna. By the 1920's his practical investigations had become the body of work now known as psychodrama.

Meanwhile in the United Kingdom, Brian Slade, an early drama therapy practitioner, focused on using drama with children. He recalled that he first began to think of drama as "therapy" about 1926. He began serious experiments in 1931, developing his drama techniques with medical advice from 1938 to 1941. During the 1950's he advanced the notion that drama therapy could be used for working with delinquency and "maladjustment". Simultaneously there were already articles such as, "The Use of Drama in Psychology", written by a medical doctor, William Kraemer in 1949 (Slade, 1958), that enthusiastically endorsed the notion that "there is hardly any psychotherapist or educational psychologist who is not aware of the great value of the several arts to the practice of modern psychology."

Drama therapy is, to use the National Association of Drama Therapist's more classical definition, "the systematic and intentional use of drama processes and products to achieve the therapeutic goal of symptom relief. It is an active, experiential approach."

Experiential techniques include such disciplines as gestalt, psychodrama, body-centred psychotherapy, and emotion focused therapy amongst a significantly growing body of work.

Despite the not inconsiderable resistance to the use of experiential therapies from more cognitive based treatment providers, Elliott and Greenberg (2001) have done a massive study of the experiential field that conclusively proves the effectiveness of a variety of experiential approaches. At the very least, experiential therapies are, for many types of clients, equally if not more effective than standard cognitive-behavioural therapies.

As detailed by Eliot and Greenberg in 2001, "A significant centre of controversy involves assumptions shared by many academic or cognitive-behavioural oriented psychologists that experiential therapies are inferior to cognitive-behavioural treatments... analyses indicated that, for the sub-sample of 28 studies analysed here, experiential therapies showed larger pre-post effects than cognitive-behavioural (CB) therapies. On the other hand, the 46 studies comparing experiential to CB therapies revealed a mean difference of -.11, which was clinically equivalent (i.e., statistically significantly less than the ±.4 minimum difference but not significantly different from zero). Thus, these data support the claim that experiential therapies in general are equivalent to CB therapies in effectiveness" (Elliot, Greenberg, 2001).

The two authors go further and state that "the existing research is now more than sufficient to warrant a positive valuation of experiential therapy conclusion in four important areas: depression, anxiety disorders, trauma, and marital problems even using the strict version of effectiveness put forward by Chambless and Hollon's (1998) additions to the APA Division 12 Criteria."

Experiential techniques emphasize active experiencing, emotional experiencing and "commitment to a phenomenological approach that flows directly from this central interest in experiencing" (Elliott, R., Greenberg L., & Lietaer, G., 2001). This has particular relevance in that some experiential treatment of sexually abusing adolescents takes its theoretical underpinning from the fields of attachment, neurobiology of the brain, and trauma based treatment. In these fields, especially in neurobiology, it is a sine qua non that experience and experiencing mediate meaning, and therefore change. Siegel explains that:

> *"Integrative interpersonal interactions may produce linkages among neural networks that reinforce their very nature. It is in this way that interpersonal communication may facilitate a direct effect on the organization of the complexity of neural structure"* (Siegel, 1999).

The drama therapist's action/experiencing tools are functional elements of process that work with many types of clients including adolescent sexual abusers. These experiential/drama therapy tools are supportive and support many types of theory-based process treatment. Some of drama therapy's most basic units of interpersonal/experiencing are well used, well researched, and even ubiquitous in treatment literature. Role-play, for example, a common drama therapy technique, has been used in a variety of therapeutic strategies including anger management with police (Novaco, 1977; Sarason, Johnson, Berberich, & Siegel, 1979), stress inoculation for adolescents (Feindler & Fremouw, 1983), in the treatment of borderline personality disorder (Linehan 1993), in skills training for problem behaviours with adolescents (Goldstein, A.P., Glick, B., Reiner, S.C., Zimmerman, D. & Coultry, T.M., 1987) and with problem drinkers (McCrady, Dean, & Dubreuil 1985). Most recently role-plays were used in the treatment of conduct disordered adolescents in an affect regulation and attachment intervention for incarcerated adolescents and their parents (Keiley, 2002).

Role-play exists within a precise continuum in drama therapy of a variety of tools for creating experiencing. These range from the carefully inducted role-play, as used in trauma work, to finely sculpted reframes of earlier narrative based experiences, to group or community based simulations. There are even some historically "notorious" examples of simulations including Zimbardo's Stanford prison study (Haney 1973), and Professor Stanley Milgram's (Milgram, 1983) experiment on "conformity and obedience."

Role-play is, in fact, a calculated tool that generates, as Moreno (1972) suggests, experiencing in the here and now. Role-play generates new experience in the "now". Yardley-Matwiejczuk K. (1997), in her careful examination of the function of role-play, clearly defines its functioning as "generative action, spontaneous and experienced action as produced by purposive human beings, rather than behaviour that is the result of following a script or responding without volition to a stimulus." In other words, Yardley-Matwiejczuk approximates Siegel's concept of the importance of "integrative, interpersonal interaction."

Experience and experiencing mediate meaning and therefore mediate change. Experiential therapies use techniques that emphasize experiencing and emotional experiencing. We believe that drama therapy is the pragmatic use of tools such as role-play, sculpts, and structured improvisations, that create interpersonal "experiencing" which when amplified by affect leads to direct neurological learning and possible changes of behaviour.

Drama therapy is potent because it creates intentional interpersonal action, loaded with titrated emotion, which codes powerfully in the brain. Trauma, similarly, is strongly preceded by intense interpersonal experiencing and stressful emotions. Siegel implies that interpersonally experienced emotion helps sculpt meaning and growth in the brain. Therefore, at its best, the potent, affectively controlled role-play may well force new axonic connections, leading to new meaning and a possible change, for example, in old self-abusive narratives.

Resistance and adolescent sexual abusers

However, as with many treatment tools, it is our experience that experiential processes, such as drama therapy, can be strongly resisted. These resistances are often presented by adolescents who have been sexually abusive and are in group for treatment. They are also often significantly different to the resistance shown by antisocial violent offenders. Why? What might this signify about these processes, and how do drama therapists understand this, and thus reduce the resistance?

The intrinsic reason for resistance is simple. Adolescents who sexually offend are much more likely to have experienced abusive early experiences which generally lead to more resistant behaviours. Sexually abusing children report experiences of being hurt at very high rates. These experiences include neglect, physical abuse, and emotional abuse such as being present during repeated acts of violence in the family setting. In addition, sexually abusive adolescents may also show signs of early inadequate attention to their physical health, malnourishment, and the constant impact of pornography.

Becker and Hunter (1997), cite high percentages of sexually abusing adolescents who have been sexually abused (25-50%) or physically abused (40-80%). Athens speaks very persuasively of the impact of violence, humiliation, and unjustified beatings on young children. Hunter and Figueredo (1999) also speak of the impact of violence committed on children and how this affects the development of sexually abusive adolescents. The trauma may also be intensified by the lack of confidantes for children experiencing abuse, the duration and intensity of sexually assaultive experiences, and the young age of many of the children at the time of these assaults on them. Neglect is as dangerous in its impact as any of the more obviously assaultive experiences, especially since it interrupts the attachment drive of the child and fails to sequentially stimulate the child's emotional experiencing and understanding, or map of human relationships.

The evidence supports the notion that there is damage from assaults and neglect on at least two fronts – neurobiological and attachment, leading to attachment disorders and trauma formation. Attachment theory is based on an assumption that "humans innately strive for connection with others" (Diamond & Stern, 2003). Attachment is learned in infancy through experiential interaction with parents or caregivers. It includes mirroring, turn-taking, attunement, and holding, generally between mother and child. The mirroring "completes emotional exchanges" between parent and child. These interactions increase in significance in the second six months of a child's life when there is a notable increase in activity in the limbic centres, and a huge increase in dendritic activity. Children at this age begin to experience connections to their emotions as well as experiencing increased social interactivity. "Attachment is the primary source of a child's security, self-esteem, self-control, and social skills" (Hughes, 1997).

If successful, the attachment experiences with the parent/caregiver supply the child with a permanent strategy to manage stress, and a model of the world and itself in that world (Kieley, 2003).

Yet there is clear evidence that many of the adolescents who sexually abuse have experienced very unstable or even violent family relationships (Miner, Siekert & Akland 1997; Bagley, Shewchuk-Dann, 1991). Miner et al., (1997) noted in a study of these children's families that the parents themselves and siblings had a range of serious behaviours, criminal histories, substance abuse behaviours, and psychiatric problems. This degree of violence and dysfunction, paired with the high rates of abuse reported by children, can be theorised to impair whatever secure attachment experiences the adolescents had. Family violence impairs children and may leave them vulnerable to sexually abusive behaviour. Smallbone and Dadds (2000), state that paternal avoidant attachment, for example, correlates strongly to coercive sexual behaviour.

Creeden and Howland (1998), have made a strong theoretical connection between attachment disorders and trauma as it relates to sexually abusing adolescents. They suggest that "attachment difficulties may represent some of the most profound consequences of experiencing early childhood trauma." Siegel (1999), in discussing children who have experienced abuse of all types, noted high incidences of disorganized attachment and a "likelihood of having clinical difficulties in the future, including affect regulation problems, social difficulties, attentional problems, and dissociative symptomatology."

Trauma has profound effects on the physiological system. Since parental mediation helps "ease the powerful physiological/emotional states of distress to which a child is so vulnerable" (Knopp, F. & Benson, 1996), young children with limited defences to intense emotional and physiological arousal experience significant physiological damage. Beatings and severe emotional humiliations, if there are no caring, holding, hugging parents to reduce the stress, are recorded throughout the physiological system. In studies of the impact of trauma on the brain, the amygdala, the whole limbic system, and the hippocampus at the minimum are implicated. In van der Kolk's work looking at PET scans of patients with PTSD listening to their own trauma stories, he noted that the brain's emotion-processing areas were powerfully affected (Rauch, van der Kolk, et al., 1996). Over-arousal may reduce the hippocampus' processing of traumatic arousal/emotional information. Significantly for the experiential/drama therapist, the speech centre, Broca's area, remains shut down when clients try to remember traumatic events. Trauma "stays stuck in the brain's nether regions – the nonverbal, nonconscious regions… where they are not accessible to…the understanding, thinking, and reasoning parts of the brain" (van der Kolk, 1996).

Abuse experiences are not easy to quantify, but there is consensus of agreement that many sexually abusing adolescents come from abusive family experiences. Perry (1995), refers to "persisting flight or fight states", created in aggression-filled family environments. He notes the intense impact that trauma has on the amygdala, and that the amygdala must be healthy in order to generate "emotional information that is important in the regulation of anxiety." Constant states of fear force the traumatized child to focus continuously on non-verbal cues to allay the perceived danger. Attachment is easily disrupted by any violence which interrupts the attaching process, since there are very "narrow windows, critical periods, during which specific sensory experience is required for optimal organization and development of any brain area" (Singer, 1995; Thoenen, 1995). Absent such experience and development, dysfunction is inevitable.

Controlled and purposeful experiencing is therefore critical to generating new meaning with new affectively supportive antecedents. The drama therapist tries to sort out the information, in part provided by resistance, in part through the client's self-report, in part through his responses to action based experiential work, and in part through the evidence of social history records. The information shapes the nature of the tools used, whether to treat simple skills (role-play for addictions for example), or to create interpersonal experiencing between client and client, or client and therapist in a more affectively intense mode (gestalt, controlled experiential trauma work with sculpting or masks for example).

Resistance is clearly a reactivity bred sometimes from violence, or from the body's attempt to cope with significant disruption, or from a fragmented attempt to make a new map of meaning of human relationships that is fearful, avoidant and suspicious.

Creeden and Howland (2001), note, "intense emotions are experienced without being named, and are encoded in a fragmented, sensorial way."

What the Experiential Therapists Understand by Resistance

Drama therapists and experiential therapists who use strategies such as psychodrama, drama therapy, and somatosensory therapy, must understand, cope with, and reduce resistance. Experienced drama therapists have a working knowledge of possible resistance antecedents that they gauge into experiential work. I have known Patrick Tidmarsh, Saul Hewish, and Dr. Marlyn Robson for many years. They are all experiential therapists of long standing. In this chapter, they explain how they respond to resistance demonstrated by sexually abusing adolescents, during the use of drama therapy and psychodrama. These therapists now react instinctively to maintain the child's experiencing while focusing intently on individual and group safety. Many of their experiences are classic, and the resistances very simple to classify.

Dr. Marlyn Robson is a psycho-dramatist with many years of experience in treatment of adolescent sexual abusers. Dr. Robson sees the issues of resistance in the context of group work, and meaning-making in creating trauma-sensitive and attachment-sensitive work. The experiential therapist understands "the group" as a living force in which the multiple meanings of resistance are played out. Dr. Robson outlines the major elements of resistance in the context of its impact on the concept of group.

Resistance and the Meaning of Group ~ Marlyn Robson

Adolescents who have been sexual abusers do not choose to be in group therapy. They are sent to treatment by the statutory bodies of a society that disapproves of their behaviour. They are often resistant to participation or change because their abusive sexual behaviour meets some of their needs. It is the job of the facilitators to motivate these boys to choose to change.

They may wish to change because of outside influences (removal from home, being in trouble with the police, or possible legal charges), but they will also have defences against change. They will have to give up behaviours that meet certain needs and there will be grief about that loss, (Whitaker and Lieberman's Focal Conflict theory, 1964).

Some adolescents have resistance to participating in group because, depending on the construct, they may have limited self capacities, inadequate ego strengths, inadequate personality development, or trauma memories. The experience of being with unknown and potentially dangerous other people in a group is too scary for them to concentrate on the tasks required. These boys may need one to one attention first to build up the capacity to be able to handle the demands of social interaction in group. When you are used to using your eyes and ears to watch out for danger then it is hard to concentrate on learning new behaviours. Van der Kolk (1996), suggests that after trauma, individuals may have altered psychobiology causing them to react with aggression or withdrawal.

They may be responding to the high levels of emotional arousal of being in a group. They may be called "resistant to treatment" by staff, but actually have an inability to properly evaluate and categorise the experience, and have difficulty taking in and processing information or learning from the experience because of their hypervigilance.

Resistance may be the adolescents' cognitive distortions about their sexually abusive behaviour. Adolescents have needs for intimacy and sex, particularly sex, (especially given the normal surge of testosterone in adolescence). However, if they are social isolates that have difficulty forming peer relationships and exploring intimacy and sex with same-age friends, they may have previously met these needs with younger children. There will be resistance to relinquishing these relationships and re-experiencing the consequent loneliness. Learning new ways and new skills of connection will be taxing and frightening. There is always the possibility of failure. Depressed children feel this more intensely, though it may only be based on the meaning given by their brain chemistry.

One of the main tasks of being in group in attachment terms is to elicit and explore the working models of oneself and significant others. Each of the attachment strategies implies resistance to others. The insecure resistant or ambivalently attached boy will present as needy, manipulative or "attention-seeking", and quite untrusting of the adult facilitators. He will resist. Adults may not understand the resistance, feel irritated or exhausted by this behaviour, and want to push the boy away or shut him up.

The boy assessed as insecure avoidant will present as cut off from others, day dreaming or apparently compliant, but really untrusting of the facilitators and resistant to any new experiences. Children who have had to use their eyes and ears to watch out for danger in their lives will not concentrate on new learning until they can feel safe. For all of these clients we must encourage the climate of safety and lower resistance. And safety will also mean there will have to be boundaries and consistency in group before their hypervigilance for danger reduces. It is always a question of connection, interpersonal connectivity and affectively driven meaning.

The biggest resistance of all may well be the oldest we know – the normal adolescent rebellion against adult authority. It is a cruel developmental task to discover one's own identity different from the adults around one. The group is both home and enemy, an entity to rebel against and a home base to find meaning.

The adolescent is resistant, the group is resistant, and the adolescent is resistant to the group. When a group is functioning well it is working towards what Whitaker and

Lieberman (1964) have called an "enabling solution" to its focal problem. This is in contrast to a "restrictive solution" where a group is dealing with fear and may appear resistant to change. Motivation and exploration of these fears are an important part of group work. But resistance or apparent compliance may subvert the real behaviour change needed – changing sexually abusive behaviour. Behaviours that are entrenched and are notoriously difficult to change – just like eating and smoking.

Foulkes (1964) talks about how we are not individuals in isolation but beings who are firstly in a primary family unit, which is enlarged by extended family first, and then ancillary relationships are added throughout life. Marrone (1998) says that one of the main tasks of being in a group is to explore how we function developmentally in a social context. Damaged children in a group that has a purpose, will experience forces which will cause it to move towards and away from fulfilling its purpose (Bion, 1961). The group is a living entity that the experiential therapists must watch and adjust as one would adjust a family learning to make intensive connections. It must pass through resistance. The essence of mankind is social. We are group and tribal animals.

Patrick Tidmarsh has worked for ten years with sexually abusing adolescents at the Male Adolescent Program for Positive Sexuality (based in Melbourne, Australia and serving only adolescent boys), and is the recent and long term director of the program. He is a working therapist, who has used drama and drama therapy for many years. He was a founding member of Geese Theatre Company, U.K. He knows well the practical resistances of the clients. Here Patrick notes the "classic" types of resistance and how to respond "in situ" to the adolescent sexual abuser's reactivity.

The Classic Resistances - What a Drama Therapist Can Typically Encounter ~ Patrick Tidmarsh

The experience of drama therapy can sometimes lead people to the distressing axis of truth and change. Few people wish to be there – at least not for long. The truth is that at some point, a client won't like the intensity of change and he may resist. That is where the real work often starts.

There are some classic resistances to drama therapy, as there are to any experiential work:

The standard resistance is based on Fearfulness

Most clients are afraid of us (therapists), especially those young people with early childhood trauma. Drama therapy makes visible moments of early truth, and therefore is terrifying. For groups where fragility is an issue, we teach the young people how to say "No". Once they know how to do that, and they experience that this is safe, then their own safety net can broaden. Early experiential processes have to make the group emotionally secure. You can't rush this process. Otherwise, feelings of fear will be so dominant that other emotions will be inaccessible. They cannot connect to us, even marginally, without the feeling state of safeness.

One of the other most common resistances comes from Anxiety

Anxiety occurs during much of the uncovering process. Anxiety blocks the clients from experiencing their discoveries fully. Experiencing is the heart of drama therapy work. Anxiety leads to a reduced spontaneity and therefore limited interpersonal learning. We use non-verbal work, and simple metaphor creation that helps the client maintain some sense of affective distancing.

One of the very strong and complex resistances is Inertia

All adolescent groups in treatment can "bring" inertia. Some clients will attempt to alter the energy of the group to a state of listless apathy and defeat. Trauma and insecure attachment can create defences that include distractibility, dissociation, rigidity and vagueness.

The session runs on group energy. It is essential for experiential therapies. Adolescents in group may take some shifting if there is a strong push towards fearful preoccupation internally. In these groups, especially in the early stages, the young will sit down and/or resist at any opportunity. If you pause for breath in the middle of a warm-up, you might find that you have to start all over again.

Our experiential treatment answer is to increase the levels of constant motion with mild competition and laughing. In other words, focused work and safe connection in the form of interpersonal experiencing.

One of the classic resistances is Denial

All groups have issue specific denial. One only has to think of eating disorder groups, or domestic abuse groups. Shameful feelings about behaviour can act in a powerful way on the client to keep silent and therefore keep the therapist, victims, families, or even self, from rejecting the client. Experiencing new feelings of meaning is the most effective way to deal with this. We use a basic role reversal strategy to teach/show the young client the essence of how he injured another person. It is a "here and now" experience that powerfully undermines the intellectualising of denial. Unlike defiance, denial needs only the persistent creation of calculated experiencing.

Noting that the persistent resistance can simply be an Unmet Need

When other obvious resistant factors are not present, but a participant insists on holding up the process, it's really worth pausing to listen. On occasion it is simply an unmet need. In one session, a participant role-playing the partner of another participant kept looking to the facilitator to stop the scene. She was related to the participant and was worried about hurting her friend's feelings. Reassured by the other participant and the group facilitator of her role in the process, she continued. The obvious is easily forgotten in our rush to analyse or dismiss.

The most dangerous resistance - when it's really "No!"

For the drama therapist, as for the verbal therapist, these moments are moments of acute danger. When no is delivered with either wild-eyed terror or determined calmness, the experiential therapist must take strong action. The safest action is the following: stop, and lower the emotional intensity of the experience (my partner checks the rest of the group, and I remain comfortably in place to help the young man grapple with finding a calming self-statement). *No* is a major indicator of real connection issues. We use this information to understand his map of meaning. Resistance is a road sign.

When the resistance is the time waster or diversion known as Words

Theatre is a "doing" process. Words are often used to inhibit, stall or obscure the processing. In experiential exercises, most warm-ups and trust exercises focus first on the kinetic, then visual, then verbal. Non-verbal role-play and other techniques are an essential precursor to any "feeling" based process and give clients confidence that they can describe what they feel in a new way.

Drama Therapy Needs Basic Environmental Support to Cope with the Intense Meanings of Resistance

There are practical steps to working with resistance: using the process of the group; making a place and process of safety; working gradually with increasing levels of client anxiety; and finally, dispelling unmet needs. But the art is to know when, in drama therapy, to stay put.

Saul Hewish, has worked for nearly twenty years in the field of adolescent and adult sexual offending. His work is strongly influenced by his long term work with many types of children at risk. He is a renowned forensic drama specialist who relies strongly on experiential and drama therapeutic experiences to help adolescents resolve their issues. Here, Saul examines in more depth, the practical issues of drama therapy work with resistant clients.

The Drama Therapist Deals with Resistance ~ Saul Hewish

Resistance from adolescent sex offenders to taking part in experiential exercises should be considered a "normal" response to the challenge of something new and unknown, in the same way that during the early stages of treatment, it might be "normal" for these young people to minimise and deny the extent of the harm they have caused.

In a recent study of children and young people accused of sexually abusing a child in one English city, Taylor (2003) observed that 44% had been referred to a professional for an emotional or behavioural problem, and 70% had a least one problem at school. The most common problems at their schools were undisciplined behaviour, underachievement, aggression and bullying, and isolating. Taylor cites other studies showing similar results.

Since many adolescent sex offenders have shown some degree of emotional and behavioural difficulty in school or at home, it is not strange that such difficulties occur within the context of a group dealing with sexual offending. But whilst these behaviours might be considered to signify resistance to treatment, they may also be symptoms of pre-existing conditions (i.e., ADHD, Asperger's Syndrome, attachment disorders, PTSD). There are many strategies for dealing with such behaviours (Munden & Arcelus, 1999; Attwood, 1998). In drama therapy, there is also a gradually growing, but smaller body of literature focusing on issues which are specific to the treatment of these problems (i.e., trauma) and the problems of resistance, action, and meaning that we encounter (Kellermann & Hudgins, 1988). Resistance is the epicentre of the task of change with adolescents.

The experiential drama therapist works on using strong felt senses (Gendlin, 1978) of the connectivity and affect of the group. A good drama therapist takes the "emotional temperature" of a group all the time. Adolescence is a time when the approval of one's peers is much more significant than the approval of adults. If an activity is believed by the participant to be "childish" or too individually exposing, then he will resist. Such resistance can be heard in statements such as, "I'll just watch" or "No one said I was going to have to do this", or even somatic aches and pains to prevent participation. (It is important to check with the client to see that he has no real physical infirmities.)

These early interactions are crucial for establishing the experiential rapport supporting a healthy sense of participation in the activity in the group. But, active or realized resistance to experiential work forms part of the transferential and counter transferential matrix for supporting the affective connecting that allows new meanings for the client and new meaning for the group. Resistance is to be worked with, not beaten. In role-play training there is a simple mantra for trainees – "at all times say yes to what you are given by the other role-player!"

When the drama therapist accepts that there will be varying degrees of reluctance from all group members it is then easier to create a "public" sense that there will be participation without the need for negative authority. This means that if a member of the group wishes to sit out an exercise I can make a fast verbal contract with him that he will take part in the next exercise. His reluctance/fear/freezing is acknowledged without punishment, isolation or rejection. The contract I make with the client is done in front of the group. We do not foster secrecy. The client is drawn in usually as he gains confidence that the work is within his competencies, or that the group reward is higher than his anxious resistance. If the most powerful peer for the day, or hour, invests in the work, then it is easier for the young person to overcome his anxiety.

Young people, especially defiant young people, see adults as hopelessly invested in being proved right. In addition, we carry the stain of "oldness". It is a mark against us. Antisocial adolescents who sexually offend will use the smallest perceived insult to add their beliefs to a vast stockpile of beliefs about our lack of efficacy due to age, or our sense of being right when they are perceived to be wrong. Is there a grain of truth in what some of these clients say? Allowing a young person to sit out until he is comfortable is considered, by some therapists, a failure! In drama therapy we learn to change the channel, move from drama, to art, to words until we find a channel of connection. We do not cede, we try to find the right learning style for the fear or misperception that we sense the client has.

All my groups tend to begin with participants seated in a circle of chairs. Initially the group does not know what is going to happen. Clients regularly tell us that it is easier to sit and talk, if rather frantically, and nod in passive agreement rather than engage both physically and mentally with an active exercise.

It is therefore important at the outset to acknowledge the clients' feelings and even emphasize that some of the exercises they will be asked to do may evoke "strange" or unusual feelings. However, it is crucial that they try and stay open to the exercises. It is the experience, and in the reflection on the experience, that the learning takes place. We choose exercises very carefully to give clients' specific experiences that induce affective and cognitive reframing through experiencing. Talking just will not do.

During warm-up and low-intensity group-based exercises, you may experience many types of resistance. This is a brief, but well known list of classic resistances.

Deliberate sabotage of an exercise. This might be done in order to take the pressure off other members of the group, or alternatively, for the client to avoid having to do that particular exercise himself because of the self-exposure he may fear.

Passive participation. The client does everything that is asked of him in an exercise but does so without making any real emotional engagement. When asked to talk about the experience during the processing stage he responds with "Just like he said", or something similarly disparaging. Attachment disordered children and highly traumatized children are deliberately "vague" about their feelings, or slightly dissociate when there may be subtle cues to the past.

Making jokes at inappropriate times and/or breaking the "momen"' of an exercise. This may be a reaction to either a sense of the client's own possible fear of failure, or a need for a different type of connection because of the dangerousness of the experience.

Engaging in an activity that is "off-task". When asked to prepare a piece of work for the rest of the group to view, the client spends much of the time talking about issues which are unrelated to the work. Loss of control is key for some young people despite the inappropriateness of the surrounding. It is, interestingly, typical of reactive attachment disorder.

Dismissive statements about the quality of any of the following:

> The exercises – "This is kid's shit", "This is boring";
> Other group members – "They're all muppets";
> The group staff – "You're mad", "You live on another planet";
> The victim – "She/he asked for it"; and
> The system – "I've been stitched up" "They just want to make an example of me."

The dismissive attachment style of these children is all too easily apparent. The work needs clarity and the maintaining of connection with the young person. Here it may be necessary to work in pairs.

Rogers (2000) gives a number of strategies for dealing with these types of behaviours in a school setting, many of which are immediately applicable in an experiential group work setting. Key to these is remaining focused on the primary behaviour and not getting drawn into discussions and arguments concerning secondary behaviour, no matter what your treatment goals for the child really are. If you ask someone to focus on the presentation of a scene to the rest of the group, choose to ignore getting drawn into defensive arguments from the group about such things as whose fault it is that the group is not ready. Equally, try not to react to sulky behaviours when you ask the group to stop talking and pay attention to what others are doing. From the adolescent's perspective, engaging in secondary behaviour and dialogue about such behaviour is a powerful and well used strategy to keep group staff away from real issues that carry connection at the heart of them.

Drama therapists use a variety of strategies to overcome resistance. Obviously we recognise that resistance is the crucial reactivity that the therapists must acknowledge as part of the client's repertoire of responses to stress. Resistance is a type of isolating, perhaps sometimes family derived. Hence, we use intensive experiential strategies to keep the client connected with us in the heart of their experiencing.

Staff who use experiential approaches on a regular basis, regularly discuss the very intense resistance at the heart of the adolescent's sexual offending. This shows clearest in their avoidance and deflection of attempts to take part in empathy-based exercises. There is a variety of common resistant behaviours ranging from a perceived difficulty in staying "in-role", through to flat refusal to take part in the exercise at all.

Sometimes this resistance may be because the exercise has been introduced too early or because of the fear and shame in the young person of where the exercise might go and what might be discovered in doing so. Many adolescent sex offenders have a vested interest in maintaining the secret of their behaviour, since if it is exposed then they might have to accept a degree of culpability and responsibility for it. They may feel embarrassed, guilty and/or ashamed of what they have done, and may be complying with treatment only because of external sanctions rather than a strong motivation to address and change behaviour (Graham, Richardson, & Bhate, 1997).

I commonly use role reversal in this work. In victim empathy work, "slipping out of role" occurs when the participant suddenly switches from talking as the victim (or other members of a family, for instance) and instead, begins talking as himself. It is common for him then to slide straight back to the present and to try to control the "here and now" by changing it all to "then and there".

We gently reassure the client that it is alright, that he won't get hurt, and that there is so much more to do. We are really saying that we will not reject him. But, implacably, we refocus the young man back into the victim that they are trying to understand, asking him simple questions about who he is supposed to be playing and getting him used to first person statements. By beginning with simply asking questions that are affect neutral: Where are you? Where is the tree? Where is the door? What time is it? Where are you sitting?; and constantly using the victim's name, the client calms and focuses. So one can begin to eliminate the resentment, rage to control and profound sense of being controlled that makes the work so intense for these young men.

In groups where resistance to this type of work is high, staff may find it useful to begin by modelling the exercise(s) themselves using a fictional character. For example, in disclosure work a member of staff can play someone who is being questioned by other members of the group. Ask the group to take on the role of the therapist and get them to ask questions that they think should be asked. As soon as they think the character of the abuser is not being completely honest then they should say so. That group member is then asked to explain why they thought the offender was not telling the truth. At some point the clients themselves are asked to do the same exercise but directly from their own perspective or based on their own experiences.

Whilst this resistance is especially prevalent when doing the more intensive work, it can also occur in other areas as well. It is quite common for individuals to work on a group scene and then talk, in the third person, about the scene they are going to do. They tell you the scene rather than actually playing the scene and engaging with the emotions which might occur in it. In these situations you need to instruct them to not tell you anything about the scene – but rather, you want to the scene to "tell" its own story.

We are always amazed at the number of therapists who pay little attention to the environment that they are working in. Space, light, colour, interest, energy are all part of the supporting ingredients of this work. Few architects and correctional systems really understand the dynamics of active experiential group work. Group rooms are merely seen as just one more box.

Any drama therapist will tell you that the nature of the space can create resistance. If possible, work in places which have good outside light and have chairs which are easy to move around but are not too comfortable. There must be sufficient space for the clients to do active experiential game work and to do quiet intimate private experiences.

Dealing with resistance in experiential work means creating a safe place where participants know that they can take risks and not be exposed or ridiculed for doing so. It also means being confident in the setting of exercises. One must be clear about the rules of a game, or the requirements of a role-play. Staff should introduce exercises without too much preamble. If you want the group standing, then just ask them to push all the chairs to the side so you can begin. You do not need to explain at this stage why.

If the group has members whose concentration span is limited then make sure you vary the type of exercises. A mixture of group and individual focus exercises during a session will help maintain interest and reduce the resistance caused by trauma based cognitive confusion. Sometimes we remind ourselves to why we are doing an exercise and what we want the clients to learn from the experience. If you don't know, the client will sense your confusion and it will frighten him into frozen resistance. And most important for all of us: check your own resistance levels beforehand.

John Bergman has worked for twenty four years in correctional settings using drama as a therapeutic tool. He is a drama therapist. Here he discusses the issues surrounding drama therapy and attachment and trauma problems in sexually offending adolescents.

When the Drama Therapist Must Deal with Trauma-Based or Attachment-Based Resistance ~ John Bergman

Children who commit sexual offences, even criminally sophisticated children, are fragile. Many have learnt how to survive within a narrow range of life experiences. If their lives have been dangerous, then their life experiences often reflect a sophisticated but distorted knowledge of interpersonal dangerousness. Dangerous, alienating experiences retard complex affective interactions and interpersonal learning skills. Resistance is one of many signs.

Children in trouble with the law, or coping with danger, may not show us the mistaken or tragic ways that they try to understand the world. They may not show us their sadness, their crying, their wails of incomprehension. They may have put these away, suppressed them, or tried to forget them. Young adolescents who have been emotionally or sexually violated, may still have to survive with dignity amongst their own friends, or with apparent fierceness if they are in an institution. But the bottom line is likely to be that they survive in secret. If we probe in these areas we may get, unsurprisingly, a very powerful resistance.

Various traumas can, for some children, ease the process of forgetting. Attachment traumas become glossed over by traumas from other violent experiences. Violent beatings, continual humiliation, and murderous events, change the focus of the child's brain chemistry from develop to protect. These children's minds can either crumple with shame when reminded of the past, or just as speedily protect themselves with vagueness. And despite their internal screaming, all that we might see is the vague distancing that hints at the chaos of the chemically and fear-induced limbic system's defences. These reactions can be triggered by an apparently simple therapy question, and can turn a ubiquitous session into a child's experience of a dangerous invasion of guarded territory. Our very words in therapy may also be the enemy. "Words can't integrate the disorganized sensations and action patterns that form the core imprint of trauma" (van der Kolk, 2003).

Resistance is a litmus paper that the experientialist and drama therapist must read when treating the adolescent offender. It may be the only sign that dangerous territory has been breached. It is not always easy to recognise the "why" of it.

Drama therapy, like all "now-centred" work, is a calculated action to engender interpersonal experiencing. For many children who sexually offend and who have attachment and trauma issues, drama therapy quickly highlights deficits in interpersonal experiential strengths, creating sometimes fear or even the imprints of old memories. This may be the traumatised mind responding very quickly to stimulus. Resistance therefore can be very fast, acute, and vital.

There are many other situations where reading the resistance is complex. For instance, where a culture has a negative interpretation about the expression of affect, it may well be that affective expressivity in daily life is powerfully suppressed, which may in turn intensify the clients' sensations of feeling "strange" during drama therapy work.

Sometimes it is easier to gauge resistance from a cognitive perspective, though being accurate is also problematic. Resistance might be indicative of core beliefs being challenged, or that a schema is being breached, or that the client's victim stance is being weakened and the client needs validation to continue (Leahy, 2001).

Sometimes the resistance is best read from analysing the information from the viewpoint of group dynamics. The client may be part of the peer storming process, or the group process has perhaps become too rigid and the client is merely expressing his/her/the group's distrust or discomfort. It may even be that the adolescent is looking for safety from the group's censure.

Or perhaps the resistance is just a portrait of the client's map of meaning derived from the earliest experiencing of his parent or family dynamics. In that case it may be a picture of trauma.

Resistance as evidence of trauma

So many adolescents who we work with in the justice systems around the world are strongly reactive to affect, or have intense affective responses without any seeming abilities to self-regulate. Sexually abusive children find many emotions excessively uncomfortable or paralysing. Apparently, fearing loss of control because of the intensity or confusion of the interpersonal stimulus, fearing crying and without the "skills" to talk about what may be encoded physically rather than verbally (van der Kolk (1996), some children will very obviously "shut down", "freeze", "smile inanely", "grimace" or mimic the facial leads of the adult working with them. Many of these responses are absolutely typical of trauma responses.

The list of "signs" of trauma is lengthy: frozen movement when affective experiencing is intense; the inability to break eye contact, physiological anxiousness; hyperarousal, physical rigidity, constant scanning, minimal eye contact accompanied by poor concentration; and of course dysregulated affect. These reactivities form a core set of objectives for much of the drama therapists' work with adolescents who sexually offend, especially where there is strong supporting evidence of the client's traumatisation. The resistance must be read rather than subsumed as in standard cognitive work on behaviour change.

Experiential therapists, trained in the physiological processing of clients' affective experiencing, often use the "bottom-up" analogy of Damasio (2000) to understand the processing of experiencing used by the client. Drama therapists understand that traumatized children's body/mind processing may be interrupted on its journey to the frontal cortex. "...the sensorimotor reactions of arousal and defensive responses... leave traumatized persons at the mercy of their bodies" (Ogden & Minton, 2000).

The experiential therapist or drama therapist has one basic task; to reduce the level of arousal of trauma-based reactions so that the client can engage without fear with the therapist (or other clients) and experience successful interpersonal experiencing with controlled affective reaction. This means, in practice, knowing the child's history, engaging with the client in a verbal contract before any trauma work begins, creating a basic safe place or safe memory similar to Hudgins' sense of the containing double, putting the client in charge of the pace of intensive work, and covering small segments of experience and meaning first. Acute trauma responses prior to any treatment may mean that the client must do private sessions with a therapist before translating some of the affective gains into the peer successes that group can generate.

The drama therapist, in practice might use any of the following action-based responses to trauma resistances:

A) Asking a client to role-play alternative behaviours, but with a focus on reducing his physiological stress sensations. The client might be taught a stress reduction strategy, or a simple bio-feedback strategy first, and then begin an exercise such as standing on a chair pointing at someone. He is asked to maintain his sense of calm. He reports during this about what he is physically experiencing. Any reduction in his sense of well-being means stopping the exercise. If he remains comfortable, he will slowly assume the position of the one who he pointed at. He comes down slowly from the chair, and moves gradually to the reverse role position. He comments on his sensations. Again, any significant change, or even appearance of physiological symptoms of distress and the exercise must be slowed or stopped. He then processes his new sensations as he experiences being pointed at. He may use his bio-feedback skills during this. Finally he discusses what well-being and distress feel, where and how it can be contained.

B) Most drama therapists will fluctuate from therapist to therapist-in-role to promote trust. They will often model more affectively intense exercises. The explanation of the exercise may sometimes be repeated with varying degrees of approach to the clients – that is closer or farther away in the space, or with more or less eye contact. The drama therapist working with traumatised clients must model not just safeness but their own genuineness. He must also find ways to help bypass or calm the traumatising brain.

C) Drama therapists often use a set of secondary objects such as masks or toys to work with the client to co-create or strengthen new defences. We begin from a neutral exercise such as slow motion walking, or making controlled faces, (make a huge face, make a very small face, make a bored face). We then ask the client to choose an object, toy, doll, or mask that can represent his old self, or his old fear, and then something to represent his new stronger self. We then work with him and the group to create a wall, or a barrier between the old and the new. It may be that the clients in the group are then used to create the battle between the old and the new, with the script being supplied by the client. We continually focus him on being in touch with his physiological responses. The drama is enacted while the client attempts to maintain his physiological comfort. Over time the barrier is gradually reduced between the old and new, until he can feel calmer and be involved directly in his own drama.

D) Drama therapists use multiple creative strategies to help clients learn to cope. For instance we might create minimal stress conditions during a simulation, i.e., you are cooking a fast meal when the toaster breaks down. Convert this stress to laughter. These simulations are gradually repeated with a focus on eliciting more intensive consequences (the house is burning) while working with the client to maintain his felt sense of self-control.

E) We often begin our session with giving clients increased physiological skills, such as slow motion walking, while maintaining a rolled tongue, or a clenched jaw; then doing this again but without the clenched jaw. We try to get the client to focus his consciousness on specific experiences and to be able to change these and through the group experience praise for doing this.

Many of these exercises are designed to re-focus the traumatic resistance into a managed marker for self-referral about physiological change. They are slow steps towards making self, and the early work before managing more intense trauma memories.

Resistance as evidence of attachment or as a result of attachment disorders

The essence of much experiential and drama therapy work is the creation of active interconnection and new safe affectively controlled pathways for clients. But this terrorizes some children. The attachment disordered child fears connection. He/she fears not just the potential of connection, but of being enveloped again in the dangerousness of a connection that may lead to being abandoned. Resistance is always more likely with such adolescents.

Therefore many "resistances" are potential clues to the maps of relationship meaning that attachment disordered children have created. Sarcasm, controlling shrugs, dismissive responses, seductive behaviours, passive scowls, accusatory outbursts or vague smiling and dissociative-appearing behaviours occurring in any interaction can be easy markers for disturbed attachment maps.

In the warm up phase of a drama therapy session it is painfully easy to stimulate these types of attachment map resistances. Why? Delaney (1988) notes, "The maltreated child views himself as worthless, unsafe and impotent… he views caretakers as unreliable, unresponsive and dangerous". All strangers and their actions are a threat. All strangers are to be resisted. Many attachment disordered children believe that the stranger will try to get close enough to cause hurt.

The resistance we experience in our work is sometimes the reaction to our blundering around in the complex maps of meaning of relationship of these frightened and angry children. It is simply, what some adolescent sexual offenders do when humans get too close.

Finding a "correct" stance is difficult. It is our experience that the open ended, flex-responses of some therapists, practicing a watered down version of "therapeutic alliance" is, in the end, just as dangerous to these types of children. Equally, pretending to the child that he/she can "attach" to the therapist is a cruel hoax. In fact, without a strong sense of boundary of yes and no, the sexually offending adolescent has no sense that the therapist will "stay" in place. He/she perceives such therapists as people who cannot be trusted and may not really deal with his/her specialness. Some therapists seem determined to undermine their own voice of authority, of knowing, of setting the limit. The anxious adolescent responds aggressively to the therapist's own avoidance. The vague intimation of affective connection, the lack of clarity of the therapist's tone enrages and frightens the insecurely attached client. Treatment of sexual offenders takes engagement, connection, and direct and spontaneous dialogue.

Secure connections, rather than ill-defined attachment, define the ground in a collaborative effort, which is also sensitive to authority and its boundaries. It is compassion tempered with the sense of the client's need to move on, to connect with others and therefore to be accepted and to understand his self.

The beginning of a drama therapy session with attachment disordered adolescents must be quite slow and simple, focussed on simply warming up the clients to the idea of a work session. The drama therapist reframes his exercises so that the level of interpersonal experiencing while possibly reduced in directness is still adequate for new meaning. Exercises will have to be made simpler, giving the child less reason for the distrust that hides attachment terror. A cooler, less connecting version of an experiential exercise may ratchet the degree of affective connection up or down and therefore be more "safe".

The drama therapist accomplishes this task through the use of a drama therapy devise called aesthetic distance. Aesthetic distance is really a measure of how certain theme material, certain contexts, certain simulated relationships, or certain drama therapy strategies create more or less affective arousal in the client. Non-competitive games, for instance, create limited interpersonal arousal, and mostly safe physiological sensations. A simulation or role-play occurring on the moon is rarely emotionally dangerous, nor considered by clients to be interpersonally threatening. But a role conflict between a client and a remembered violent grandfather is clearly very potentially intensive, threatening the client's control of his _____ to the group for example. Anger, shame, and rejection are likely affective reactions. Many therapists working with these children use controlled distancing devices in intense work. Hughes (1997) notes that in dealing with anger, for instance, he helps children name the emotions, name what they are thinking, and thereby reduce the resistance as he sees it coming on.

As mentioned previously, we always begin our sessions for these adolescents with games, without winners, to try to activate safe physiological arousal. Every experiential action is a test of our "safeness". Drama therapy exercises must take into account contradictory responses – I want to do that/I don't want to do that. Some of these adolescents who sexually offend "lack any coherent, organized strategy for stress or separation"(Lyons-Ruth & Jacobovitz, 1999). We are directive and supportive, trying to prove over and over that we will stay very clearly in one "place of connection". This premise is tested by the clients time and again. Each time we raise the intensity of a sculpt, or a simulation, we have to re-attach with the clients from that safe connection space. This may take one staff member never leaving their chair, or having a doll or toy that is always associated with laughter. This is hard to do with teenage clients.

But the clients are also calmed by the rules of drama therapy ? it is only a group room, you don't have to act, and there is no grading of your "performance". We make it clear that the staff will maintain their correct place in the adolescents' lives while the clients are there. We work on self-mapping, experiencing and adding to the meaning of safe interpersonal experiencing. We use drawing exercises of self in relation to others, drawings of getting across a "difficult place" for example, or exploring a new place or relationship as the basis for graduated improvised experiences. We process using other drama therapy experiences. We check in constantly in the here and now with the clients. Drama therapy exercises are not holy events. This therapy is extremely malleable.

Gradually the attachment disordered adolescent must feel safer to do more intense experiential connecting. Keiley (2002) states, "...new emotional experiences and interactions with others are necessary for change to occur in internal working models and hence in relations with significant others." The work of the experiential therapist is to create for the clients real-time situations in the group room that can support the client in his search for affective control and increased meaning. Such experiences have included a role-play of coping with a mother blaming the client for the family's distress, confronting the client's severe sense of stuckness, and separating himself from sensation of deadness which led ultimately to a confrontation with his long departed father played by one of the therapists.

Drama therapy processes assist the therapist in a minute-to-minute titrating of the level of experiential intensity and safety for the client. It uses, for example, non verbal processes to reduce or intensify interpersonal connectivity – or more obvious techniques such as adjusting the proximity between himself, the therapist, and the client in the group room, lowering his voice to the edge of hearing and so on. Any improvised role-play can easily be switched from the intensity of dealing with family distress to a scene of coping with one's football team losing in the face of the opposition's barracking. But, each scene needs the child to make connection.

The drama therapist must be alert on many fronts simultaneously. Reactive attachment disordered children can become violent, even fight physically to maintain control. They may be more than just sullen, and may act with a vengeful sarcastic superiority challenging the therapist for control of the group. Control, for attachment disordered clients, is critical to ensuring that there is no simulation of the earliest experience of abandonment. The therapist must make it clear that he/she is the therapist in the group, that there are rules but that he is *STILL* affectively connected to the adolescent. Humane, normal rules of behaviour and the rules of the drama therapy work make the session safer for these children. But these children are often canny and distrustful. If the therapist is too obvious about the objectives of his/her work that day, if he cannot make the client feel at ease, if he spooks the group, or uses words that are outside the comfortable knowledge of the client, then the client may fearfully race ahead of the therapist's questions, guessing/sensing the answer. If the predicted answer is a perceived attack on his sense of core control then the child will resist.

We have spoken predominantly of reactive attachment, but insecurely attached children also choose many avenues of resistance to the experiential therapist – ducking a question or action, refusing but without much apparent affect, or ignoring the presented drama experience entirely. Their signals are hard to read. Lyons-Ruth & Jacobvitz (1999) explain that in their early childhood insecurely attached children, "experience inherently contradictory tendencies to both flee and approach the caregiver, resulting in an experience of fright without solution."

Insecure attachment covers a multitude of attachment pathways from ambivalent and avoidant to resistant and disoriented. Insecure children can resist with a range of responses including the situationally foolish, adopting the peer group's "dumb" play of defiance, all the way to staring into space with an aggressive passivity. These adolescents are extremely fragile. They must learn the message of safety over and over. Much of the early drama therapy work is on expanding the range of responses that they could cognitively and affectively give to a role-play situation.

Typically we might begin by posing a role-play where one person is seated, frozen, on a chair in a very "dramatic" pose – slumped over for instance, or with his fists out. Then we ask the group to arrange themselves one by one in relation to the posed actor in a staged photograph. As soon as the adolescents have solved this problem, we create another. The work is done very swiftly with great humour. For many of these clients, responding to a problem but not having to use words is a huge relief. We work with any freezing by simply including the freeze in the role-play. Gradually over time, the client will kinetically examine the feelings behind the freezing, and work on finding non-verbal alternatives.

Theoretically this is similar to the responsivity principle used in cognitive skill work. Clients have risks that are matched to needs. These needs are satisfied for the client by providing action strategies that match his/her learning style. Drama therapy uses art, action, and words to solve action based problems. Hence our early work is slow.

To win over these children's resistance takes continued patience, humour, and the ability to work closely with changes from the client that may make you angry. We must remember that our disappointment confirms their map, or "internal working model of attachment" (Bowlby, 1988).

Resistance seen through rage or in antisocial behaviour

Rage is a sweet dish for some sexually offending children, and comes in a variety of guises. *It is* resistance. It functions excellently to achieve the client's goals – power, safe space between the treatment experience and himself, safety, control, or even the excitement of creating fear.

Rage occurs both in those children who have experienced physical family violence and emotional family violence, as well as children who were brutalized, or confused by their own sexual abuse. Rage also has multiple attachment and developmental pathways including neglect (reactive attachment disorder) and caregiver terror (disoriented attachment).

Extreme statements of hatred are remarkable expressions. They seem to give some clients a temporary rest from hurt. But these violent responses are dangerous to the group, to the client and to the free world. Drama therapists must use a variety of techniques to derail the intensity of the interior monologues that fuel the client's rageful sensations.

Rage is a complex resistance that reduces the chance of a defended child being out of step with antisocial peers, or being vulnerable to peers and adults. The drama therapist must quickly reduce the anxiety in the group room, and find the reason for the outburst. Drama therapy has been seen to be effective in the reduction of anger in clients even when used for only five days, and despite re-testing three months later using the STAXI (Reiss et al., 1998).

A classic drama therapy response would, once the instant reaction to explosive reaction was over, be a gentle retracing of steps with the client, and a replay first in a cool way of the event and its alternatives, and then a deeper look at the "persona" of "ragefulness". Then we would start the job of defusing and understanding the role of rage in the client's connective experiencing. But we do not turn away from rageful responses. Resistance is the chance to see the problem!

Violent angry resistances can have many pathways. Children, who have been called stupid, or dumb, try to maintain total control of their intellectual safeness in every moment. Therapy and therapists are a challenge. Group work only intensifies the adolescent's unease, the need to be on guard and always correct. It is an obsession bordered by rage. The emotionally slandered child cannot afford to let any replication of the hurtful memories of being wrong and humiliated reoccur. The slander might only be a few years old in his/her history, or a birth slander as old as the child's parental birth rejection. The humiliated child never forgets. Experiential work in victim empathy shows us how intensely the memory of being scorned, or bullied or demeaned is encoded and how easily it is recalled.

The simplest question *from us* may be a trip wire for these slandered children. They must win, if need be, in defiance of the demands of the real situation. At the worst, the therapists must be taught a lesson by the client. The right answer, as opposed to their wrong answer is a challenge, perhaps even to the validity of the rejection of their former tormentor. Such children may play one-upmanship games, create an answer that is magically inappropriate (a poem for a role-play) or insist that they are right. The antisocial client will eventually make this his way to power and intimidation and control. Rage, scorn, and sudden threats coming with a staggering speed, are the humiliated adolescent's safest response to the perceived hell of humiliation and shaming. It is the only defence to being thought stupid. And we sometimes label it resistance because we have so few tools to gauge the real meaning.

Lonnie Athens (1997), in his work on the creation of violent men notes a very clear process of "family violentisation" in the early rearing of young dangerous people. The process as he outlines it includes "ridicule, torment, coercion, fear, and haranguing, incessant melodrama." It is an intensely fearful process of desensitisation, and terrorizing. The end result is simple. Rage and intimidation become the primary strategies to control fear, or fear of fear. Drama therapists trying to read this rage will look for such emotions as disgust, or phrases such as "anyone would do what I did" or "I only taught him a lesson." Disgust may be by far the more dangerous unspoken resistance signalling the possible fusion of frustration and anger.

Hanna (1999) discusses a simple strategy for angry resistant children, especially those who are also antisocial. Hanna focuses the child on his use of anger to control sensations of hurt and affective pain. By remaining fixed on asking the child why he "needs" anger, and by not flinching at his resentment and intimidation, the child is helped to reason his way into perceiving how he nurses his pain and simultaneously guards against reducing his anger.

Our version of this approach is found in our use of narrative therapy, a very common tool in drama therapists' work. Narrative therapy can separate the client from the problem, and reframe his self-narratives so that he can find new meanings, new outcomes (Morgan, 2000). The client is not the problem, the problem is the problem. Resistance may well come from the client identifying himself as the problem and creating a narrative that must use rage or violence for defence. By deconstructing the old narratives and constructing new ones, the client is sometimes relieved of these violent older self meanings. A client will create a drama for the group based on a classic violent situation that he experienced at home. He then watches the scene replayed by the group from different perspectives. Most typically we play the father as somewhat incompetent, unable to provide the safety that the child needed because he was incapacitated through chemical dependency. This work is very delicate and must be done slowly. The child must gradually reduce his need to defend himself and his discomfort through aggression.

Another common experiential technique is to ask the client to knock on the therapy door as if he was going to a social service agency for help. He waits for someone to come to the door. The therapist then appears and apologises, "for not having been there to protect him, for not having heard his cries, and for society's deafness" (Bergman, 2003). This action experiencing creates great internal movement. It is the apology the client has often waited for. It is the first sign that not everyone in society is bad and self-centred. It is a sign of honesty. This sometimes releases violent resistance from its central place in the client's survival pantheon.

Resistance learnt from criminal adults or because of class based narratives

Sometimes children imitate successful resistances that they learn from dysfunctional adults, parents, and relatives. The children can learn from these adults that there are complex and even criminal uses of the word respect. Especially in criminal households, respect is a word that often accompanies threats of violence. Sometimes respect is just code for trust, sometimes it conveys disgust and reinforces the need to maintain control. When an adolescent from a more antisocial background says, "I have no respect for you", he may mean that the therapist has broken a code of expected interaction, or is merely different, or has asked a question that disgusted or offended the client. The word is on a sliding scale of meaning to be invoked when the session is becoming too intense, or merely to keep the therapist at a distance. It may accord with the client's notion of his right to keep secrets, or his sense of power at being able to keep the therapist at bay so simply.

Some adolescents will very quickly resist drama therapy strategies claiming that they are "disrespectful". The words must be very carefully read.

Sometimes the use of the word respect as used in resistance to experiential work may be linked to family notions of what is right and proper behaviour in the world. Many of our clients are working class, and many of the therapists are middle class. A common belief in some working class households is that what happens in the house, stays in the house. Many middle class workers are often more elastic about family issues and may talk with little prompting about their intimate issues. Such talk would be considered, on the part of many of our clients, disrespectful, a little like sedition and certainly likely to get disapproval from the family. Adolescents may find themselves in a confused state of mind about drama therapy work that not only asks the client to discuss his family but even more, to enact part of the family experiences.

Drama therapists have a variety of antidotes to these problems. For instance we might use a very simple three-sided role-play in which we see two people together – A and B. A tells B a secret that concerns C and that may well cause harm to C. C is a friend of B. We then put B and C together and let the group coach B through the experience. It is a form of drama therapy called sociodrama and a very quick way for a group to have critical discussions that can challenge or contradict the family message of secrecy.

Resistance, what we feel and what we set up, a check-list

Resistance is just that. It arrests therapeutic flow and sometimes the therapist's imagination. Some resistances can be the very antithesis of what we feel that we can stand. They can linger in the mind and memory of the calmest therapist. Supervision is simply the safest way to process and understand the emotions that just will not go away. Much of this has been discussed in the literature on burn-out, but the impact of the resistances can help derail the next session and lay the groundwork for more resistances. The usual signs are:

- Dwelling on the event.
- Thoughts of getting back at the client.
- Seeing the event all in terms of what he/she did to you.
- Not wanting to focus or do work with the client in the session.
- Trying to influence other staff to see it your way.
- Not feeling at all comfortable with how you feel.
- Experiencing fear, or not being able to talk about the client without anxiety, or even tears.
- Not being able to create relevant dramas for the client.

We influence the process of resistance. We can even initiate the actions that generate the resistance. It sometimes seems to take so little. The following will tip the scales sometimes:

- Resisting their suggestions in an experiential session.
- Giving the experiential answer that you think is the best.
- Cutting into the clients simulation/role-play/sculpt without acknowledgement.
- Distrusting the client. Distrusting what they say occurred, for instance in a sexual assault.
- Fearing or not liking the client.
- Ignoring the signals of a client but doing it intentionally because it feels as if it would take up too much time. The client exhausts you.
- Ignoring the client because he/she has, in your eyes, been rude or not "obeyed" the rules.
- Sarcastic responses.

Some Conclusions

In their article on client resistance to group counselling, Carter, Mitchell, and Krautheim (2001), note that, "developmentally, adolescents are dealing with issues of competence and managing emotions and identity within their social contexts." The irony of the comments is that the authors are talking about students and not sexually offending adolescents. Yet adolescent sexual offenders must also cope with such issues. The issues of resistance in these children are complex and confused. In adolescent sexual offenders what part of resistance is just differentiation, peer connection and self definition? Which part of resistance is trauma, or attachment disorders, or just a reaction to therapist and environmental inconsistencies?

It is clear that when we talk of resistance it is still a Pandora's box of issues from a multitude of disciplines. Here are just a few more theories. Resistance may be due to interactional variables (Sottman & Leiblum, 1974), or the client's sense that we will continue to thwart his sexual needs. The client's "I don't care" resistance may even be because we sent a message that his resisting is too hard for us to understand. Critelli (2004) calls adolescent apathy the "defiant adolescent's central defence" and suggests that this resistance is an indicator of pain and how hard it is for the client to manage. Resistance, in other words, forms the heart of a huge literature of understanding how to work past these clients' issues.

Experiential therapies have proven effective in getting past adolescent resistances. Keiley (2002) works with incarcerated conduct disordered adolescents who have attachment disorder issues with their families. Resistant to the usual change strategies, she works with the families using live and pre-recorded role-plays to stimulate connection and change. Quantitative analysis shows marked improvement in these clients in a range of affective tests. Yet despite such successes, and the proven effectiveness of role-play, Hewish, Tidmarsh, and Robson have all spoken of the intense complexities of resistance both to group work and to the experiential work of change.

Experiential therapists, especially drama therapists, must pay great attention to a wide range of possible meanings of resistance. Resistance contributes to the very quality and meaning of the experiential activities. The drama therapist interprets the client's resistance in the moment and responds with drama therapy strategies to ease the client past his affective block. If the client is successful he can expand his repertoire of interpersonal coping and alter his map of relationship meaning.

Group work is always complex especially with sexually abused children who "tend to be less socially competent" (Briere, 1994). Many adolescent sexual offenders are in fact fragile, afraid, sometimes paralysed with shame, or on the road to sexualised revenge. The experiential therapist reviews not only the adolescent's fearful or rageful resistance, but his unspoken needs to generate new meanings, and new relationships through affective interpersonal experiencing. No matter what the resistance, the client's need for change is often acute. But the road to change is through coping with sometimes unspeakable experiences. Drama therapy is the positive practice, in a safe place of these new meanings.

At this point we want to strongly underline the issues of closure work. Though Hewish and Bergman have lectured extensively on correct closure procedure, it is my responsibility as the lead author to remind readers that this work needs to be done, as with all treatment, with due and appropriate care.

In my shared book with Hewish, Challenging Experience (2004) we devote a segment to closure. Appropriate care includes the following: not beginning any experiential exercise late in a session, nearly half the session's time for processing, pre-closure work with the rest of the group and closure exercises that both reduce the affective and cognitive intensity, and provide appropriate cognitive containers for further processing. Again, in our book we note what caliber of staff we consider are appropriate to do this work. It is based entirely on experience.

No treatment is neat and tidy, and having good relations with unit staff and doing processing work with such staff after group work is a normal part of the real work of doing any therapy, including experiential and drama therapy.

"They cry, feel anger, hope – these are not experienced as fictional. Real tears are wept. Real anger is vented – at the same time it is within a fictional construct"(Jones, 1996).

Once the resistance is surfaced and discovered in the drama therapy space, it can always be re-worn, re-adapted, re-worked and eventually resisted. The narrative is adaptable. The heart of drama therapy is the connecting and experience-making and meaning-making that may make resistance no longer necessary.

References

Athens, L. (1997). *Violent Criminal Acts and Actors Revisited.* Urbana: University of Illinois Press.

Attwood, T. (1998). *Asperger's Syndrome: A Guide for Parents and Professionals.* London: Jessica Kingsley Publishers.

Bagley, C., & Shewchuk-Dann, D. (1991). Characteristics of 60 children and adolescents who have a history of sexual assault against others: Evidence from a controlled study. *Journal of Child and Youth Care,* (Fall Special Issue), 43-52.

Becker, J. V., & Hunter, J. A. (1997). Understanding and treating child and adolescent sexual offenders. *Advances in Clinical Child Psychology,* 19, 177-197.

Bergman,.J. & Hewish, S. (2003). *Challenging Experience.* Oklahoma City: Wood 'N' Barnes.

Bion,W.R. (1961) *Experiences in group and other papers,* London: Tavistock.

Bowlby, J. (1988). *A secure base.* New York: Basic Books.

Bowlby, J. (1980) *Attachment and loss: Vol. 3. Loss, sadness and depression.* New York: Basic Books.

Briere, J. & Elliott, D.M. (1994). Immediate and long-term impacts of child sexual abuse. *The Future of Children,* 4, 54-69. [A publication of the Center for the Future of Children, the David and Lucile Packard Foundation].

Carter, E., Mitchell, S. & Krautheim, M. (2001). Understanding and addressing clients' resistance to group counseling. *The Journal for Specialists In Group Work.* Vol.26, No.1, March. Pp.66-80.

Casson, J. (1997). Drama therapy history in headlines: Who did what, when, where? *In Drama therapy* Vol. 19 No.2 Autumn.

Creeden, K . & Howland, J. (2001). Integrating Trauma and Attachment Research into the Treatment of Child and Adolescent Sexual Behaviour Problems. *Masoc/Matsa Annual conference.*

Critelli, J. (2004). *Sometimes A Sock In The Dryer Is Just A Sock.* MASOC/MATSA Conference, Marlboro, MA.

Damasio, A. (2000). *The Feeling Of What Happens.* London: Vintage.

Delaney, R., (1998). *Fostering Changes, Treating Attachment Disordered Foster Children.* Oklahoma City: Woods 'N' Barnes.

Elliott, R., Greenberg L., & Lietaer, G. (2001). Research on Experiential Psychotherapies. In M. Lambert, A. Bergin, & S. Garfield (Eds.) *Handbook of psychotherapy and behavior change* (5th ed.) New York:Wiley.

Feindler, E. & Fremouw, W. (1983). Stress inoculation training for adolescent anger problems. In D. Meichenbaum and M. Jaremko (eds), *Stress Reduction and Prevention.* New York: Plenum

Foulkes, S.H. (1964). *Therapeutic Group Analysis,* London: Allen & Unwin.

Gendlin, E.T., (1978). *Focusing.* Bantam Books.

Goldstein, A.P., Glick, B., Reiner, S.C., Zimmerman, D. & Coultry, T.M. (1987). *Aggression Replacement Training.* Champaign, IL: Research Press.

Graham, F., Richardson, G., & Bhate, S. (1997). Assessment. In Hoghugi, M.S., Bhate, *S.R., and Graham, F. (Eds.) Working with Sexually Abusive Adolescents* London: Sage.

Haney, C., Banks W.C., & Zimbardo, P.G., (1973). Interpersonal dynamics in a simulated prison. *International Journal of Criminology and Penology,* 1, 69-97.

Hanna, F., Hanna C., Keys, S., (1999). Fifty Strategies for counseling defiant, aggressive adolescents: reaching, accepting and relating. *Journal of Counseling and Development,* Fall vol.77 pp. 395-404.

Harvey, S. (1995). Sandra: the case of an adopted sexually abused child. In F .Levy, J. Fried, & F. Leventhal (Eds). *Dance and Other Expressive Therapies.* London: Routledge.

Hughes, D., (1997). *Facilitating Developmental Attachment.* New Jersey: Aronson.

Hunter, J.A., Jr., & Figueredo, A.J. (1999). Factors associated with treatment compliance in a population of juvenile sexual offenders. *Sexual Abuse: A Journal of Research and Treatment,* 11(1), 49-67.

Jones, P. (1996). *Drama As Therapy*: New York: Routledge.

Keiley, M. (2002). The development and implementation of an affect regulation and attachment intervention for incarcerated adolescents and their parents. T*he Family Journal and Counseling and Therapy for Couples and Families,* Vol. 10, No2, April 2002, pp.177-189, Sage.

Knopp, F. & Benson, A. (1996). *A primer on the complexities of traumatic memory of childhood sexual abuse.* Brandon, VT: Safer Society Press.

Kraemer, W. (1958). Untitled chapter.

Leahy, R. (2001). *Overcoming Resistance in Cognitive Therapy.* Guilford Press: New York.

Linehan, M.M. (1993). *Cognitive-Behavioral Treatment of Borderline Personality Disorder.* New York: The Guilford Press. pp. 334 – 336.

Lyons-Ruth, K. & Jacobovitz, D. (1999). Attachment disorganization: Unresolved loss, relational violence, and lapses in behavioural and attentional strategies. In J. Cassidy and P. Shaver (Eds.) *Handbook of Attachment: Theory, Research, and Clinical Implications* (pp.520-554). New York: Guilford.

Marrone, M. (1998). *Attachment and Interaction.* London: Jessica Kingsley.

McCrady, B.S., Dean, L., Dubreuil, E. & Swanson, S. (1985). The problem drinkers' project: A programmatic application of social-learning-based treatment. In G.A. Marlatt and J.R. Gordon (Eds.), *Relapse Prevention.* New York: The Guilford Press. pp. 448.

Milgram, S., (1983). *Obedience to Authority: An experimental view.* New York: Harper/Collins.

Miner, M.H., Siekert, G.P., & Ackland, M.A. (1997). Evaluation: Juvenile Sex Offender Treatment Program, Minnesota Correctional Facility —*Minneapolis, MN: University of Minnesota.*

Moreno, (1972). Psychodrama, Vol. 1, NY: Beacon House.

Morgan, A., (2000). *What is Narrative Therapy.* Adelaide: Dulwich Centre.

Munden, A. & Arcelus, J. (1999). *The ADHD Handbook: A Guide for Parents and Professionals.* London: Jessica Kingsley Publishers New York: Wiley.

Novaco, R. (1977). A stress inoculation approach to anger management in the training of law enforcement officers. *American Journal of Community Psychology,* 5 pp. 327 – 346

Ogden, P., & Minton, K. (2000). *Sensorimotor processing: the role of the body in trauma recovery.* Hakomi Somatics Institute.

Perry, B. (1995). *Maltreated Children: Experience, Brain Development and the Next Generation.* NY: W.W. Norton.

Rauch, S., van der Kolk, B.A., (1996). A symptom provocation study of post traumatic stress disorder using positron emission tomography and script driven imagery. *Archives of General Psychiatry,* 53, 380-387.

Reiss, D., Quayle, M., Brett, T. & Meux, C. (1998). Drama therapy for mentally disordered offenders: changes in levels of anger. *Criminal Behaviour and Mental Health* (8) 139-153.

Rogers, B. (2000). *Behaviour Management: A Whole School Approach* London: Paul Chapman Publishing Ltd.

Sarason, I., Johnson, J., Berberich, J., and Siegel, J. (1979). Helping police officers to cope with stress: A cognitive-behavioral approach. *American Journal of Community Psychology,* 7, pp. 593 – 603.

Siegel, D. (2001). Toward an interpersonal neurobiology of the developing mind: attachment relationships "mindsight" and neural integration. In *Infant Mental Health Journal,* Vol. 22 (1-2), 67-94. Michigan.

Siegel, D. (1999). *The Developing Mind.* New York: Guilford.

Singer, W. (1995). Development and plasticity of cortical processing architectures. *Science,* 270, 758-764.

Slade, P. (1958). *An Introduction to Child Drama London:* University of London Press.

Smallbone, S.W., & Dadds, M.R. (2000). Attachment and coercive sexual behaviour. *Sexual Abuse: A Journal of Research and Treatment.* 12 (1).

Sottman, J. & Leiblum, S. (1974). Resistance. Chap.7. *In: How to do Psychotherapy and how to evaluate it.* Holt, Rinehart and Winston.

Stock Whitaker, D. (1985/1989). *Using Groups to Help People.* London: Routledge.

Taylor, J.F. (2003). Children and young people accused of child sexual abuse: A study within a community. *Journal of Sexual Aggression,* 9(1), 57–70.

Thoenen, H. (1995). Neurotrophins and neuronal plasticity. *Science,* 270, 593-598.

van der Kolk, B.A. (1996). The body keeps the score: approaches to the psychobiology of posttraumatic stress disorder. In B.A. van der Kolk, A.C. McFarlane, and L. Weisaeth (Eds.). *Traumatic Stress: the effect of overwhelming experience on mind body and society.* (9). NY: Guildford Press.

van der Kolk, B. A. (1996). The complexity of adaption to trauma. In B.A. van der Kolk, A.C. McFarlane, and L. Weisaeth (Eds). *Traumatic Stress: the effect of overwhelming experience on mind body and society.* (9). NY: Guildford Press.

van der Kolk, B. & McFarlane, A.C. (1986). The black hole of trauma. In B.A. van der Kolk, A.C. McFarlane, and L. Weisaeth (Eds.). *Traumatic Stress: the effect of overwhelming experience on mind, body and society.* (1, 3-23).NY: Guildford Press.

Whitaker, D.S. & Lieberman, M.A.(1964). *Psychotherapy through the group process.* NY: Atherton Press.

Yardley-Matwiejczuk, K. (1997). *Role-play Theory and Practice.* London: Sage.

CHAPTER TWENTY-SIX

WORDS FROM THE HEART: THE PROCESS OF CHANGE WITH SEXUALLY ABUSIVE YOUTH

IAN LAMBIE
AND
MARLYN ROBSON

"There is always one moment in childhood when the door opens and lets the future in."
~ The Power and the Glory, Graham Greene

Introduction

It is not surprising that when faced with telling something they are ashamed and embarrassed about, that most kids would prefer not to talk about it. Let's face it, who would? Few of us can say that we didn't do things as a child that looking back we now regret. When faced with talking about it at the time, things such as shame and guilt came flooding into our consciousness, and we either lied about it or minimised what we had done. Distorting the truth is part of human nature, and in fact such behaviour is commonly modelled internationally across television screens by numerous people including politicians, leading celebrities, sports persons, etc.

So what would motivate someone to firstly, talk about something considered amongst the most taboo in society, and secondly, to talk about it at a level whereby they are able to get some help? In this chapter we will discuss key factors that we have found to be important in assisting our clients to talk about their problems – basically what we have found to work. Some of this may be common sense, but despite many years experience working with adolescents, sometimes we still forget what we often preach to others.

Like adults, adolescents who have been sexually abusive will often lie and minimise their offending in order to avoid detection or the consequences of what they have done. Yet, what lies behind such behaviour is often fear, shame, and embarrassment. Another reason they may not wish to talk about their offending is fear of the reaction of the victim's family. In cases of sibling incest this is further complicated by their anxiety and uncertainty as to whether they will be supported by their parents or ostracised by their family. Finally, there may be a real fear that they may go to prison or a residential centre and be removed from their family and friends.

A young person may ask questions such as: Will they take the law into their own hands and seek retribution? Will they talk about the offense in public? These issues are of real concern when they see media reporters and the public taking vigilante action to deal with sex offenders. This makes it even more important that the relationship practitioners develop with adolescents is one that does not shame them. Instead, it must support them in talking about their offending and dealing with the challenge of motivating them to change their behaviour. One of the key things that we aim for in therapy is for the person to talk about their offending and not to be "compliant." It is all too common to see young people who are well versed in what to say, and say what we want to hear, but in therapy their behaviour fails to correspond to what they say. Specifically, they may still be engaging in high risk and antisocial behaviour.

What makes a difference to the outcome of an interview?

A decade ago catch phrases like "breaking down denial" and "confronting denial" were not uncommon. Over a decade ago conference presenters would talk about breaking adolescents down, and that it was not until this was done that we could then really get to the bottom of what had happened. Thankfully, the field has progressed and clinicians now recognize the need to develop more sensitive, sophisticated, and ethical approaches to treatment, if they are going to effectively help clients change. One of the major concerns of using confrontative approaches is that clients are more likely to be "compliant" to therapists and that some of the client's cognitions contribute to their offending may actually go "underground" as the client places their energies in "defending themselves against the therapist."

What affects whether adolescents do or do not talk about their offending? Like any other psychotherapeutic relationship, it is influenced by the client factors (e.g., presenting problem, gender, age, culture, counter transference, etc.) and the therapist factors (e.g., experience, personal history, transference, etc.). It is very important that clinicians recognize the impact of these issues on a client's ability and receptiveness to therapy. Culturally in New Zealand, the way practitioners and psychologists who work with adolescents present themselves, may be very different from the way their counterparts present themselves in other countries. For example, we would never dress formally, such as wearing a suit and tie. In our country, clients are less likely to respect you if you are formally dressed as opposed to more casually dressed. The respect that our clients give us is vitally important as it forms a basis for how open they are with us and is also likely to have a positive influence on the outcome of therapy.

The Process of Change

What is apparent in working with any client group is the role of "psychotherapeutic factors" in assisting change within the client. A significant body of research indicates that the effectiveness of therapy may in fact have more to do with process issues (e.g., client-therapist relationship), as opposed to therapeutic "techniques" (Ackerman and Hilsenroth, 2003; Hubble, Duncan & Miller, 1999; Martin, Garske, & Davis, 2000; Orlinsky, Grawe, & Parks, 1994). The therapeutic relationship has been reported to impact positively on treatment outcome (Martin et al., 2000). Indeed many authors in the field refer to the work of Bordin (1979) when describing what the therapeutic alliance entails. Bordin described to it as being the agreement of therapeutic goals with a client, the assigning of therapeutic tasks to facilitate change, and finally, the development of a therapeutic relationship that facilitates change in the client. While recently sex offender treatment has started focusing on process variables (e.g., Marshall et al., 2003), comparatively little attention has been paid to process issues with children and adolescents who are sexually abusive. Indeed this is also true of the general psychotherapy field (Shirk & Karver, 2003), though the therapeutic process issues such as the relationship is considered critical in child therapy outcome research (Russell & Shirk, 1998).

We are talking about therapist personal attributes that impact on another person. In their review of therapist characteristics and techniques that impact positively on the therapeutic relationship throughout therapy, Ackerman and Hilsenroth (2003, p. 28) found specific attributes on therapies (see Table 1) that have a positive impact on the development and maintenance of a strong relationship. Interestingly, Ackerman and Hilsenroth found little difference between different therapists in the impact on the therapeutic relationship regardless of what therapeutic model was used. They suggested this was because the therapeutic relationship was the "pan-theoretical construct impacting psychotherapy process on multiple levels".

Table 1: Summary of therapist's attributes and techniques found to contribute positively to the therapeutic alliance

PERSONAL ATTRIBUTES	TECHNIQUE
Flexible	Exploration
Experienced	Depth
Honest	Reflection
Respectful	Supportive
Trustworthy	Notes past therapy successes
Confident	Accurate interpretation
Interested	Facilitates expression of affect
Alert	Active
Friendly	Affirming
Warm	Understanding
Open	Attends to client's experience

Lambert (1992) proposed that therapy comprised of four therapeutic factors. He called these: (a) extra-therapeutic factors: (b) therapeutic techniques; (c) relationship factors; and (d) expectancy or placebo factors.

Extra-Therapeutic Factors: Lambert (1992) argued that extra-therapeutic factors, or client factors, are the most important of the factors that exist amongst psychotherapies. Extra-therapeutic factors are the ones clients bring with them to therapy, along with environmental influences. These may include the client's strengths, social supports, the sense of personal responsibility, the severity and type of problem, the motivation to change, the strength of social supports, and the presence or absence of co-morbidity. Commonly, adolescent offenders present with co-morbid disorders and mental health problems that typically include; conduct disorder, attention-deficit hyperactivity disorder, substance abuse, and post-traumatic stress disorder (Bourke & Donohue, 1996; Lightfoot & Barbaree, 1993; Morenz & Becker, 1995; Ryan, Miyoshi, Metzner, Krugman, & Fryer, 1996). The presence of these disorders and the afore-mentioned factors can affect whether there is a positive or negative outcome in psychotherapy. Co-morbid disorders left untreated can lead to significant impairment and distress that likely impact negatively on treatment. High levels of trauma reported by these adolescents are also likely to impact negatively on the outcome of treatment, possibly through subsequent dysregulation of emotional states and a resulting hyper-arousal to stimulus in their environment (Friedrich, 1995).

Research suggests that client factors change at varying rates and may account for as much as 40% of the outcome in psychotherapy (Bergin & Garfield, 1994). For example, motivation may vary quite rapidly as opposed to personality variables that may remain relatively stable over time. What is evident is that clients who show the most improvement believe the results of their gains are primarily due to themselves as opposed to therapist or other external factors. Factors include:

Therapeutic Relationship: A significant factor that contributes to the process of change in clients is the relationship between therapist and client. These include a positive regard towards the client, genuineness, and congruence with the client. Other factors, such as being able to express empathy and affirmation towards the client when appropriate, also impact on treatment outcome. Relationship factors are thought to account for up to 30% of the treatment outcome in counselling. Some of these factors include warmth, caring, empathy, acceptance, mutual affirmation, and encouragement. Lambert and Bergin (1994) proposed that these probably account for the most gain in psychotherapy.

Bordin (1976), suggested that there are three important components of the therapeutic alliance that impact the outcome goals, tasks, and bonds. The goals of therapy are the objectives that both the client and therapist agree on, while the tasks are the nuts and bolts of a therapy session that include both behaviors and processes. For a strong therapeutic alliance to happen, it is important that both therapist and client view these as important. Finally, therapeutic bonds are the positive relationship between a client and therapist that includes trust, confidence, and acceptance.

For adolescent offenders, the therapeutic relationship may be even more important than for adult therapy, as they seldom want to talk about their offending, are often coerced into coming to therapy, and fail to acknowledge they have a problem. Hence, developing a therapeutic relationship with adolescents can often be an overwhelming challenge (Shirk & Russell, 1998). Alongside this aspect is the need to respect and value the adolescent's developmental need for increasing autonomy from adults which can also serve as another challenge in developing a close therapeutic relationship (DiGiuseppe, Linscott & Jilton, 1996).

In their review of psychotherapy outcome, Shirk and Karver (2003) found the same relationship between therapeutic relationship and treatment outcome in child and adolescent therapy as in adult therapy. "Taken together, results suggest that the therapeutic relationship was modestly associated with outcome, not only across divergent types of treatment but also across levels of development as well". (p. 461).

Therapeutic Technique: This describes factors that are specific to the therapy the client is undergoing. It includes the therapy model (e.g., in adolescent sexual offender treatment the predominant models are cognitive behavioural and family systems model). Despite many studies that compare one model with another, surprisingly little evidence has been found for one model being superior over another (Lambert, 1992). In the field of adolescent sex offender treatment, the research is still in its infancy, and comparative studies of one therapeutic model over another still need to be undertaken. Lambert (1992) suggested that the therapeutic technique may account for approximately 15% of the outcome in psychotherapy.

Expectancy/Placebo Factors: The final set of factors is placebo, hope, and expectancy. This involves clients gaining improvement based on the knowledge that they are being treated and their assessment that the therapist is credible. One common factor that influences all medicine and psychotherapeutic outcomes is that treatment in itself offers people hope that change can take place. Lambert (1992) argued that hope and expectancy of change may be as important in producing change as technique. It is thought to account for up to 15% of the variance in client change. Lambert, Weber, and Sykes (1993) reviewed studies looking at the effect sizes of psychotherapy, placebo, and no-treatment controls. They found that the average client placed in placebo treatment has a 66% greater improvement compared with no-treatment controls, while an average client undergoing psychotherapy is better off than 79% of clients who do not receive any treatment.

Motivational Interviewing Strategies with Adolescents

An important early development in understanding process issues when interviewing offenders has been the use of motivational interviewing (Garland & Dougher, 1991; Miller & Rollnick, 2002; Prochaska & DiClemente, 1984). Motivational interviewing is a model of assisting clients who may be experiencing resistance to change through a variety of techniques. Through these the clinician can increase the internal motivation of clients towards change, and assist clients to sustain new behaviours and avoid relapse.

Two key assumptions of motivational interviewing are that a client's "resistance" typically stems from their environment, and that motivation to change behaviour (or to overcome their resistance) is elicited from within the client rather than being imposed externally. While these issues may arise for adolescents, there are also maturational processes that may be unique to this client population, such as anti-authoritarian issues. In addition, engagement in therapy is often dependent upon the client being mandated to attend treatment, and over time their motivation often increases.

The role of the clinician is not to persuade or convince the client to change or resolve a client's ambivalence. Rather, the clinician's task is to quietly direct the client towards examining that ambivalence and to develop discrepancy and dissonance in the client about his situation. Arguments with clients are to be avoided; resistance is not to be directly confronted. Instead the clinician is encouraged to argue indirectly, to "roll with" the client's resistance in much the same way as a martial arts fighter might roll with their opponent's momentum and use it to make their opponent's position less secure. At the same time, clinicians must operate from a position of empathy with their clients. They must create for the client a sense that change is both desirable and achievable, and that efforts towards change will be based on a collaborative effort between them rather than be imposed and directed by the clinician. There are six stages of motivational interviewing that have been identified with adolescents and are often referred to as the "wheel of change" (Miller & Rollnick, 1991). When working with adolescents we don't stick rigidly to these, but at times use them as a guide. It can be useful to reflect on and take to supervision. The stages are:

Pre-contemplation: The person has not yet realised the need for change, though someone else may be aware that he has a problem. Often what people at this stage require is information and feedback in order to raise their level of awareness.

Contemplation: Clients may be weighing the pros and cons of the status quo as compared to making the required changes.

Preparation: Clients may begin to experiment with change, or make plans to change; they may even make some initial changes. At some point during this stage, they have made a decision to change.

Action: Clients are making changes and trying out new ways of behaving.

Maintenance: Clients are attempting to sustain the changes and beginning to implement strategies that will prevent their relapsing into old behaviours.

Relapse: A relapse is usually accompanied by a return to earlier change stages such as pre-contemplation during which the client questions his motivation and rationale for change. Following a relapse, the client will need to revisit all the stages of the wheel of change rather than simply begin again at the action stage.

"It's more about process of me and them as opposed to doing something fancy"

In adolescent development they are making dramatic changes to be different from the adults in their lives. What often complicates therapy with adolescents is the "normal" rebellious nature that adolescents have as they make the transition from dependence to independence. In the process of assessment and therapy, creative ways need to be employed that not only engage the adolescent but also to allow for the important issues in sex offender treatment to be addressed.

Tips to STOP you Tripping

There are a number of issues that therapists need to be cognisant of when working with adolescents. These tips are important to remember as they form the basis for much of our work with young people. They require some level of self-awareness, and a degree of opening up themselves.

1) Just because you were young once, it does not mean that you can understand children. Remember that time moves on and they are not like us. They think and act very

differently from us. It is important not to overly identify with their issues and make our history theirs! We believe a healthy awareness of transference and counter-transference issues that may arise in the course of therapy is important.

2) Humour is a must in therapy with young people. Let's face it, they don't want to be there. Talking with adolescents and using humour can be a critical tool in the engagement process. Make the adolescent feel as comfortable as possible through verbal and non-verbal communication. Despite it being a really difficult thing to talk about, laughter is a wonderful tool.

3) Make it easier for yourself by finding something you like about the adolescent, what interests you have in common, and in what ways your own personal life may be similar to theirs. Start off talking about what they are good at, interested in, find amusing, or did over the weekend. If all this fails, then talk about the most exciting and fastest film playing at the movies. This is the great thing about working with young people. It gives you a real excuse to go out and go to the movies - a movie that you might otherwise might not have chosen to see!

4) Enter the client's model of the world. This idea was coined by J. Hayley in his book on strategic family therapy called *Uncommon Therapy* (Hayley, 1973). This means meet the client at their level.

5) Step into their shoes. Ask yourself, "How would I feel if I was an adolescent, being interviewed at this moment?" "What would help me to talk more? What would help me to talk less?"

6) Remember to ask yourself: "In what ways is my client similar to me?" and "How might this assist and/or hinder my work with them?"

7) If you were in the adolescent's shoes, what would warm you up to talking about your offending? What would shut you down and not make you want to talk about your offending?

8) Treat them how you would like to be treated.

9) Be aware of how your behaviour may impact negatively on your clients.

10) Remember the key issues from motivational interviewing that are useful with adolescents. Roll with resistance. Avoid arguing for change.

11) Get regular supervision. Consider videotaping sessions in order to improve your interview skills.

12) It's not about interrogation – clinicians who are starting out often emphasise that the goal of an interview is to get a full disclosure. Personally, our goal when we interview an adolescent is to develop enough rapport to get them to come back a second time and at some stage to get them to talk honestly to you about their offending.

Everyday Interviewing Strategies

Filling the void

Use your interpersonal skills that you learnt before the age of fifteen to help the young person talk about what's going on for them. This may be using music, talking about the latest sporting results, super cars, or video games. We use whatever works and only have in our minds that it needs to be sensitive and matched to our client's needs.

Look before you leap

Prior to the interview, read all documentation (cumulative summaries) available on the adolescent, their family, the victim's disclosure, etc. You may also want to discuss the referral with your colleagues and/or supervisor as required.

It's all about relationships

Putting the client at ease will increase the likelihood of honesty in counselling. This is the crucial stage of any interview and it is often necessary to talk about everything else except the reason they are there. Remember the aim is not compliance but honesty. The clinician should state from the beginning of the interview that they have experience with other adolescents who have sexually abused and will not be shocked by what they might be told. This assists in establishing credibility and control of the interview. Statements such as: "It's tough being here having to talk to grown-ups about what you've done"; "Lots of boys like you feel so much shame and embarrassment that it's hard to talk honestly"; "Sometimes it's easier to get it off your chest all at once"; "It will get easier to talk more about your offending the more you get to know me and the more times you come"; "Many of the other guys that I talk to describe how pleased they are when they have talked about it all. Its like they've taken a huge load off their shoulders." The clinician can seem especially credible if they can predict what the adolescent might be thinking and the extent of their behaviour.

Treat others the way you would like to be treated

The principal that we try to adhere to is to treat the adolescent as we would want a family member of ours to be treated. This means both verbal and non-verbal behaviour in the interviews. The clinician should create a context for respectful behaviour in the interview and model this for the adolescent. For example, only respectful sexually explicit language should be allowed (no sexually aggressive terms for body parts, etc.). Don't talk down to them. If challenging the adolescent's cognitive distortions, the clinician could say: "I respect you and believe you deserve a better life than that of continuing your sexually abusive behaviour, so I want to be really honest with you about your offending." By doing this, the clinician models both respect and honesty. While we acknowledge the very sensitive nature of sexual offending, the clinician should take care not to distance the adolescent by showing strong emotional reaction to their disclosures and take any issues that need to be processed to supervision.

The interview should be prefaced by the clinician talking about the difficulty and importance of honesty, along with the consequences for them should they choose not to be honest. Clinicians should be aware of the importance of not only under disclosing but also of over disclosing their offending, as the young person may want to "please the professionals" and tell them what they "think" the clinician wants to hear. This is particularly true of younger children and clients who are intellectually disabled.

Remember, more does not necessary equal a more honest disclosure, nor a better one! The clinician should support and praise disclosures made by the young person for being honest as this increases the likelihood that they will be more honest in the future.

Don't speak in tongues – talk to me in language that I can understand

While this may seem obvious, it's important to use open-ended questions and non-jargon, down to earth language. This is especially important in allowing adolescents to talk about their offending in as much detail as possible and to allow them sufficient time to do this. And remember, while we may understand what we are saying, the young person may have no idea. Our goal is to use language that is even more straightforward than the young person may need to help them understand. Be aware also that adolescents have little respect for people who patronise them and who use long words that go right over their heads.

Embarrassment and shame is part of the game

Most of us have done something that we are ashamed and embarrassed about something illegal such as stealing from shops, taking money from our parents, driving over sports fields in our parents' cars, or whatever. Looking back on these experiences we are likely to think that it's lucky we did not get caught and to feel some shame about what we did. Such feelings are normal. An important distinction here is to support the young person to like them, but not condone their abusive behaviour. Talking about it is hard but it's also the start of dealing with the shame. That is one of the reasons why it's so important to talk about the offending as fully and as early in the assessment/therapy process as possible. Giving the young person more room to move later in therapy by acknowledging that there is likely to be more they can talk about is a strategy we often use. In real terms this means that it is perfectly understandable if they change their disclosure of what happened later to a more honest one and that this would not be surprising. It is also common for adolescents to remember more details of their offending the more they talk about it. The more they are able to do this, the more we are able to help them and make sure they do not end up reoffending. It can be useful to be prepared for cognitive distortions that the adolescent may make and to remember the motivational interviewing slogan of "rolling with resistance", which is useful when faced with clear denial and minimisation of offending.

Finally, knowing that adolescents who have sexually offended do not have three heads and are human beings, can assist in dispelling the myths that they are freaks, totally weird, and the only individual who has done this behaviour.

Offering hope of a good future and that things can change through therapy

Therapy may provide adolescents who have been sexually abusive with the first real opportunity to change. Because of this, it's important to provide hope as to their ability to be different, as well as the positive things about changing. Stating the positive aspects that you notice about their personality is important as it strengthens their motivation and provides a platform from which they are able to be different. Remember, it is really difficult, if not impossible for someone to change who does not receive the motivation and support required.

Working with cognitive distortions

Working through cognitive distortions is essential in ensuring that offenders change their behaviour. As we have seen in the earlier section on motivational interviewing, to effect change, the challenging should not be forceful or hostile, but respectful. Creating dissonance by repetition, reframing, rephrasing, interrupting, and information-giving are all useful ways in which to challenge the young person's thoughts and offending behaviour. Ways of enabling the challenging to occur while maintaining rapport include: acting more warmly at the time; using plenty of humour; making joining comments; using simple, non-jargon language; and reinforcement when appropriate. Remember, if an adolescent goes "underground" in his story, it can increase the difficulty of successfully completing treatment.

A clearer picture can always comes from the horse's mouth – using reframing and the seeding of ideas

It is always useful to hear the adolescent's account of his offending, regardless of what you already know about the offence. This is useful in that it often marks the first step in the young person taking responsibility for his offending. It also allows you to develop an understanding of the level of honesty they have and the degree to which they may minimise their offending. Throughout this stage of interviewing we find it useful to employ strategies such as reframing and seeding ideas. The notion of reframing comes from the work of Watzlawick, Weakland, & Fisch (1974), and it refers to redefining the meanings or beliefs associated with a particular behaviour. In work with adolescents it can be reframing "being caught" as an opportunity to change and be different. Being honest and fronting up to what they have done does not indicate failure, but success on which the adolescent is to be congratulated for being brave enough to talk about their offending and to be different. Reframing can also include ways of working with cognitive distortions. Adolescents who may deny planning their offending (e.g., the adolescent says, "it just happened"), might be challenged by the clinician suggesting that, if they have no control over their sexual behaviour, "then why didn't you offend on a busy street?", or it indicates a high level of risk and you may require residential care.

On the other hand, seeding ideas (Haley, 1973) was a technique first used by Milton Erickson who during hypnotic inductions would mention an idea and later develop it. When working with adolescents you may seed ideas by asking questions such as, "How did you trick the victim?" or "How did you pull the wool over her eyes?" We also take the opportunity to seed ideas about the importance of being honest, the effects of sexual abuse, etc. We may also wish to seed ideas about how they made the victim feel guilty and not talk about it. This assists in their clearly recognizing that they are responsible for the abuse and the negative impact of offending on the victim.

How big is the iceberg?

The adolescent may have a history of sexual offending over and above those that you know about. It is important that the belief is not put on the adolescent of "the more disclosures you say, the better it is." What is important is that they tell the truth, at the same time realising it is not unlikely for them to have offended previously. The use of open ended questions here is particularly important. These may include questions such as: "When did you first offend? How many months or years have you been offending for? How many other children have you sexually abused? What other sexually inappropriate behaviour have you engaged in?"

Always check for potential suicidal ideation and depression

While the clinician should request a mental health assessment if there are genuine concerns for the offender's mental health, it is always useful to at least assess for depression and suicidality. This would include current and past mood level and mental state, detailing any current suicide plans or past attempts, whether there is positive family history, and whether they have known someone who has committed suicide. Using validated risk assessment measures to accompany clinical interviews can be really useful. Suicidal ideation and/or intent should not be downplayed or ignored, and clinicians should always seek further specialist assessment.

There is a need to be aware that on very rare occasions an adolescent may use the threat of suicide in an attempt to manipulate the clinician's sympathies in this situation, and as a way of taking the pressure off them or averting the attention away from their offending. An important part of any risk assessment for depression and suicide is case consultation and supervision, which should be routinely undertaken.

Interviewing an Adolescent's Family

An adolescent's family or caregivers can be powerful forces to support them in talking honestly about their abusive behaviour. As a consequence, it is essential that the family, extended family, and/or caregivers are involved in all stages of counselling the adolescent.

As a rule, it is advisable to meet briefly first with the adolescent and their family together, then have a period alone with the adolescent, and finally, bring them all back together. Frequently, the family will be having great difficulty in accepting the reality of the adolescent's behaviour. If the family and adolescent both strongly deny the offending, despite conclusive evidence to the contrary, it is useful to interview them separately early in the interview process. Throughout the interview with the family there are a number of strategies that can help prepare the adolescent to disclose offending.

Prepare the family for the shock of disclosure and create a context for honesty

It is essential that the family be prepared in the event that an adolescent is likely to disclose their offending. This can be facilitated by joining with the family in the first instance and then acknowledging the anger, disbelief, shame, and embarrassment of learning that their child has sexually offended. Offer hope, dispel myths, give information, be educational, and particularly, be supportive and show compassion. The clinician should be trying constantly to encourage the family to make supportive comments about the adolescent being honest. The type of questions you might ask include: "Would you rather your son was honest or dishonest about his behaviour? Would you respect your son if he was more honest?" Explain that their reaction will greatly affect the adolescent's ability to be honest. Support the family with respect to their being able to tell the adolescent that they will be able to handle the disclosure. Present to the family the consequences of not getting the necessary help. The clinician might say, "Would you want your son to have a future where he grows up to be an adult sex offender and ends up in jail?" In some situations, the use of some form of leverage may be needed to convince the family to appreciate the seriousness of the issue.

Prepare the family for talking explicitly about sex

For many adolescents who sexually offend, their families may be ambivalent about discussing sexuality. By preparing the family for detailed discussion on sexual matters, the clinician is also giving permission for the adolescent to speak explicitly and potentially break the family norms.

Be sensitive to the possibility of other victims within the family

Often other victims of abuse within the family will be present and, understandably, may find these sessions extremely difficult. Sometimes their experiences can be helpful in confronting the offender. Their personal stories can begin to create a climate for further honest disclosures from the adolescent. Respect for the feelings of victims must be shown at all times. It would be inappropriate to have both the offender's siblings and victims of abuse at a family interview. It is important that the family is also offered support. This enables them to continue to see treatment as valuable, to motivate the adolescent towards change, and to more effectively monitor the adolescent's behaviour in the family.

Inform the family of potential relapse

Always discuss with the family the risk of the adolescent re-offending. If the victim is within the same household, discuss the need for the adolescent to spend some time outside the home. This is especially relevant in the initial stages of counselling and if younger children are living at home. The family must have safety rules in place around the adolescent and these rules need to be discussed with the clinician. It is also important that the family is informed that keeping safe is the offender's rather than the family's responsibility and that their role is to support him in carrying this out. Statutory child welfare agencies must be involved to ensure that the safety measures are followed.

Provide information and support

It is really useful to provide information on what help is available to the adolescent and his family. Even if they are all still denying any abusive behaviour at the end of their first interview, the clinician should take the opportunity to educate both the adolescent and their family or caregivers about the effects of sexually abusive behaviour on both victims and perpetrators, and also about their need for therapy. Alongside this is the potential for negative effects if they do not receive treatment.

Conclusion

In an age where communication is being carried out with the ever increasing speed of internet access, let us not forget the most important thing in human nature: being in relationship with each other. As researchers strive with an ever increasing drive towards evidence-based practice, let us not forget that communication and relationships are important fundamentals to change.

This chapter provides a summary of process issues and effective and practical techniques that we have found useful in our clinical work with adolescents. While interviewing adolescents requires one to be on one's feet and often "two steps ahead", the joy when compared to adult offenders is that their cognitive distortions are significantly less, and they are often more responsive to counselling. We believe the development and maintenance of the therapeutic relationship with the adolescent and the involvement of their family are the keys to ensuring the success of therapy for adolescents who have been sexually abusive.

References

Anderson, E.M., & Lambert, M.J. (1995). Short-term dynamically oriented psychotherapy: A review and meta-analysis. *Clinical Psychology Review*, 9, 503-514.

Bergin, Allen E. (Ed); Garfield, Sol Louis (Ed). *Handbook of psychotherapy and behavior change* (4th ed.). [Edited Book] (1994). Washington: American Psychological Association.

Bordin, E.S. (1976). The generalizability of the psychoanalytic concept of the working alliance. *Psychotherapy: Theory, Research and Practice*, 16, 252-260.

Bourke, M.L., & Donohue, B. (1996). Assessment and treatment of juvenile sex offenders: An empirical review. *Journal of Child Sexual Abuse*, 5, 47-70.

Burke, B., Arkowitz, H., & Dunn, C. (2002). The efficacy of motivational interviewing. In W.R. Miller & S. Rollnick (eds.), *Motivational interviewing: Preparing people to change addictive behavior* (2nd ed., pp. 217-250). New York: Guilford Press.

Garland, R.J., & Dougher, M.J. (1991). Motivational interviewing in the treatment of sex offenders. In W.R. Miller, & S. Rollnick, *Motivational interviewing: Preparing people to change addictive behavior* (pp. 303-313). New York: Guilford Press.

Haley, J. (1973). *Uncommon Therapy*. New York: W.W. Norton & Co.

Hubble, M.A., Duncan, B.L., & Miller, S.D. (1999). Introduction. In M.A. Hubble, B.L. Duncan, & S.D. Miller (Eds.), *The heart and soul of change: What works in therapy* (pp. 1-32). Washington: American Psychological Association.

Lambert, M.J. (1992). Implications of outcome research for psychotherapy integration. In J.C. Norcross & M.R. Goldstein (Eds.), *Handbook of psychotherapy integration* (pp. 94-129). New York: Basic Books.

Lambert, M.J., & Bergin, A.E. (1994). The effectiveness of psychotherapy. In A.E. Bergin & S.L. Garfield (Eds.), *Handbook of psychotherapy and behavior change* (4th ed., pp. 143-189). New York: Wiley.

Lambert, M.J., Weber, F.D., & Sykes, J.D. (1993, April). *Psychotherapy versus placebo.* Poster presented at the annual meetings of the Western Psychological Association, Phoenix, AZ.

Lightfoot, L.O., & Barbaree, H.E. (1993). The relationship between substance use and abuse and sexual offending in adolescents. In H.E. Barbaree, W.L. Marshall & S.M. Hudson (Eds.), *The Juvenile Sex Offender* (pp 203-224). New York: Guilford.

Miller, W.R., & Rollnick, S. (1991). *Motivational interviewing: Preparing people to change addictive behavior.* New York: Guilford Press.

Miller, W.R., & Rollnick, S. (2002). *Motivational interviewing: Preparing people to change addictive behavior* (2nd ed.). New York: Guilford Press.

Morenz, B., & Becker, J. (1995). The treatment of youthful sexual offenders. *Applied and Preventive Psychology, 4,* 247-256.

Luborsky, L., Singer, B., Luborsky, L. (1975). Comparative studies in psychotherapy. *Archives of General Psychiatry, 32,* 995-1008.

Prochaska, J.O., & DiClemente, C.C. (1984). *The transtheoretical approach: Crossing the traditional boundaries of therapy.* Malabar, FL: Krieger.

Ryan, G., Miyoshi, T.J., Metzner, J.L., Krugman, R.D., & Fryer, G.E. (1996). Trends in a national sample of sexually abusive youths. *Journal of the American Academy of Child and Adolescent Psychiatry, 35*(1), 17-25.

Watzlawick, P., Weakland, J., & Fisch, R. (1974). *Change: Principles of Problem Formation and Problem Resolution.* W.W. Norton & Co., New York.

CHAPTER TWENTY-SEVEN

TELLING STORIES:
IMPROVING YOUTHS' ABILITY TO ACCESS TREATMENT[1]

DAVID S. PRESCOTT

Introduction

This chapter demonstrates how the timeless and universal phenomenon of story-telling can engage youth in treatment. In individual interactions and group therapy situations, the right story can focus young people on "what's real" rather than what others are doing, and get stalled groups moving again. Methods, stories, and strategies for managing distractions are presented, along with fundamental values to guide practitioners. While not a specific model requiring strict adherence to be most effective (e.g., *Dialectal Behavior Therapy*, Linehan, 1993), some elements of storytelling may be particularly powerful with people who remain ambivalent about their own treatment.

The Author's Story

I began working with sexually abusive youth in the mid-1980s. Without any specific interest in the field, I entered simply because I liked the people who interviewed me for the position. As a protective services caseworker overseeing many youth who had sexually abused, I had the opportunity to tour and work with many programs treating this population.

The treatment that I saw at that time was often very confrontive. Many therapists seemed to have a particular license to be harsh in the pursuit of disclosure, and disclosure often seemed to be the only appropriate starting point for treatment. Many clinicians shied away because the treatment seemed to focus only on the behavior. Beliefs such as "sexual abuse is about power and control" seemed to apply to all of our clients. Revelations that many adult offenders reported an adolescent onset to their offending (e.g., Abel, Becker, Cunningham-Rathner, Mittelman, Murphy, & Rouleau, 1987) led many to the mistaken belief that the kids we worked with were likely on a pathway to adult havoc and mayhem. This retrospective bias belied what was not yet known: that successful youthful sexual abusers often have quite low rates of detected re-offense (Worling & Curwen, 2000; Alexander, 1999).

Throughout these first years, I wondered what was missing from the clinical picture. What I saw did not seem to steer young people towards success, but only to avoid failure. A strong emphasis was placed on continually holding young people accountable at a time in their life when they rarely understood what accountability was.

I eventually took a position at a residential treatment center where a premium was placed on collaboration with the youth served (Prescott, 2001). However, a fundamental problem remained. Even though it is possible to reduce coercion (Jenkins, 1990), embrace resistance (Miller & Rollnick, 2002), and situate relapse prevention into a context of developing good lives (Ward & Stewart, 2002), kids are kids and can have difficulty settling in to a group situation. Further, they often have comorbid Axis I conditions (e.g., Attention Deficit Hyperactivity Disorder, Post Traumatic Stress Disorder) that make participating in group treatment particularly difficult. While I am a great believer in adapting treatment strategies to the needs of youth, there are times when adults are obliged to help kids access the treatment that is available to them.

Further, in the earliest days in the field, there existed for many an attitude that group therapy is an opportunity for change, and that if the student were disruptive or disrespectful of the group, they would simply be asked to leave. This certainly makes sense at face value. Sexual aggression is grounds for serious concern and intervention, and those who actively undermine the treatment available to them should not be allowed to undo the hard work of others. However, two points are worth considering.

First, not every act of defiance or disruption signals an overarching resistance to change. For many youth, these actions belie difficulty in trusting adults and/or the treatment we espouse, even after long periods of time. For many, it is as though they are inviting the leader to remove them from group in order to confirm their world view of adults as hostile and rejecting (Mann & Beech, 2002). Ward and Stewart (2002), point out that by entering treatment, an individual is essentially asking how they might become a different person. Given that virtually all adolescents are in the throes of coming to terms with who they are, it is therefore hardly surprising that they should express ambivalence about the treatment process, even after the establishment of a therapeutic rapport (Blanchard, 1995).

Second, research suggests that failure to complete treatment not only signals a higher level of risk, but can also elevate risk independently of other variables (Hanson & Bussiere, 1998; Hunter, 1999). For this reason alone, I believe that treatment providers assume a responsibility to do what they can to keep youth in treatment once they have started, and to view their work not so much as "an opportunity to change" that is either taken or not, but as a process of inviting and shepherding youth through a treatment sequence.

Putting this perspective into practice, however, is often not nearly as easy as it seems. Young people can be defiant for any number of reasons and can act out anxiety and anger despite our best efforts. Often, creating connections with young people requires having any number of skills and techniques at the ready in order to quickly meet challenges with poise, grace, patience, and a humanitarian stance. Questions I've found helpful include:

- How can I go beyond and stay beyond mere lip service to the importance of therapeutic engagement?
- How can I eliminate all forms of coercion in engaging youth in treatment?
- What do I bring to those moments when growth is really happening?
- What skills can I take with me into any situation that will re-orient youth toward their own treatment, strengthen the therapeutic relationship, and promote the sense of a healthy future?

To this end, I've found that simply being an adult with many stories to tell can be extraordinarily helpful, for reasons outlined below.

Clearly, there are many ways to incorporate stories into treatment. Many clinicians have found that published works make for good discussion. However, for purposes of this chapter I will discuss only those uses of memorized stories that can contribute to moving an individual or group through a difficult point in treatment.

The Problems

Many of us have experienced the difficult or seemingly impossible group. There are the kids who just don't want to attend or who want to bring their schoolbooks, friends, families, lawyers, etc. Young people, and the adults who treat them, are subject to distractibility, and there are always concerns around exposing youth to each other's distorted thinking and procriminal attitudes.

More intractable, however, can be those who genuinely don't see how abuse-specific treatment applies to them. Youth sometimes enter group inviting facilitators to throw them back out. Others might enter a group situation needing to dominate, withdraw, or posture themselves as unwilling or unable to attend. Others simply appear to attend more to distractions than to the material.

If these problems were as simple as outright disobedience, it might be practical to simply set limits. However, it is easy to forget that virtually all young people are anxious about sex and sexuality. It is also easy to forget that it can be quite natural for them to joke around and engage in horseplay at the start of any new situation. For these reasons, many clinicians struggle with where to draw the line in moving a group forward.

A potential pitfall to telling stories is our own belief that young people, particularly adolescents, will not respond to the art of storytelling. Nothing could be further from the truth. One has only to look at the enormous appeal of soap operas and outer space movies to find examples of stories that can become interesting quickly.

Why Tell Stories?

Telling stories can introduce kindness, soothing, and even a hypnotic effect to a group process that is easily marked by its proximity to shameful past events, conflict with the legal system, and problems with adults in general. We are all familiar with the tradition of storytellers: Parents often enjoy reading to their children as much as the children enjoy listening. Prior to electronic entertainment, storytelling was both a method of education and recording history, and ranged as far and wide as *Aesop's Fables* and *The Icelandic Sagas*. It is said that in some rabbinical traditions, good questions would be answered with stories. The idea of the storyteller in modern times often brings up visions of grandparents speaking to children held in rapt attention. Other images might include actors using props and costumes that conjure up images from long ago and far away.

For purposes of group treatment of delinquent youth, telling stories can offer the following advantages:

Well-told stories have a universal appeal and are easy to listen to. They can be as calming or as entertaining as the teller wishes. Stories can tame groups of young people, as well as the abuse youth often invite us to experience in treatment.

Telling stories can set up an atmosphere of generosity and nurturing. This is especially true among youth who have often experienced little of this themselves.

Telling stories quickly focuses the attention of youth on the storyteller rather than on each other. Many group therapy leaders, educators, and residential line staff are familiar with the problem of distractions and disruptions that serve to get kids off task.

Telling stories establishes adults as adults and kids as kids. It borrows from the tradition of elders providing wisdom to children without using the often authoritarian stance of teachers or sex offender therapists. It can therefore quickly, and often dramatically, bridge the gap between "us and them."

Telling stories can covertly introduce and emphasize lesson material. It can draw young people into discussions without the direct instruction of adults (and therefore with less resistance).

A smooth storytelling voice can focus different kinds of participants simultaneously. It can bring disruptive and impulsive youth together at the same time as it gets the attention of those who come into a situation with a defensive strategy of acting bored or ignoring material.

Telling stories reduces anxiety around talking in group. Many young people feel that coming to group means having to talk about difficult topics. Most appear to appreciate the reprieve that a story brings. Once the story brings a level of unity to a group situation, it can be easier for them to participate.

Telling stories can make young people more ready to respond to other interventions. It can improve the match between youth and treatment strategies that contribute to reduced likelihood of future misconduct, such as cognitive-behavioral treatment and the development of relapse prevention and safety plans.

Telling stories can slow down the over-eager participant. Many clinicians have observed the phenomenon of the individual who wants to address every painful issue in their life in a short period of time, only to leave a session and decompensate in their living environment.

Telling stories can covertly move young people closer to the substantive issues in their life. For those youth who can spot a therapeutic process a mile away and swerve to avoid it, stories can be a powerful tool for engagement. Treatment curricula and manuals can only provide so much if their user is too guarded against change. It is this author's experience that stories can move kids closer to what's real rather than simply what the adult wants them to learn.

Telling stories is less threatening than other interventions. Many clinicians have taken interest in the emerging trend of experiential treatment with sexually abusive youth. However, many youth may find this kind of work threatening. Telling stories can serve to make youth ready to engage in other forms of constructive risk-taking and alternative means of education and treatment.

Telling stories provides little opportunity for detrimental effects. At a time when many have concerns around bringing "deviant" youth together (Dishion, McCord, & Poulin 1999; Jones, 2002), a well placed story may well counteract this effect by focusing youth on the story and its discussion rather than on other problematic elements.

Telling stories creates invitation. A well placed story can emphasize a "come as you are" stance rather than a "thou shalt not" stance (Laws, 2002).

Finally, for the therapist:

Telling stories can be a method for improving clinical skills that is not emotionally charged. Many of us know how draining working around sexual abuse can be. By collecting stories and practicing storytelling, clinicians can sharpen their skills even at times when they need a break from their work.

What it's not

In order for telling a story to work most effectively, I recommend the following guidelines:

Storytelling is not a role-play. It is well known that large numbers of sexually abusive youth have, themselves, been physically and sexually victimized. Many have experienced various kinds of neglect, and many have intense difficulty trusting adults. For this reason, I advise against turning a story into a role-play. Many of us have images of storytellers as being distinguished by their costumes, hats, properties, etc. For purposes of working with sexually abusive youth, I prefer to place storytelling in the context of who I am as an adult and a clinician. I believe that most of the young people I've worked with have had enough adults in their life that seemed to turn into somebody else or act differently that I do not need to be among that number. By being myself throughout the treatment sequence I can better transmit a sense of safety and predictability. For these reasons I advise that instead of setting one's self up to be a storyteller, it may be more effective to consider a set of stories to be an invisible toolbox brought to every situation.

Telling stories is not a coercive tactic. Rather, it is a powerful invitation to treatment that often takes considerable faith to initiate. Stories are often most useful at that moment when groups are about to become disruptive and disengaged. While many clinicians might quickly set limits or raise their voice, the most effective means of engaging youth can be through a story (a specific method for this situation is supplied below).

Telling stories is not "cool". Most providers seek to establish rapport with sexually abusive youth. Many newer providers feel a need to prove that they are somehow of the same generation or can speak the same language. While it is natural for people to establish common interests, the appearance of being cut from the same cloth as the youth can quickly become a restraint against subsequent treatment. As Ward and Stewart (2002) have observed, an implicit question participants ask in treatment is how to live their life differently. By ensuring that the adults in their life do not fall into the trap of being "cool", youth are ensured of one less restraint to their progress.

Storytelling is not a pulpit, and stories should not be cautionary tales. Although many adults have lessons they hope that young people will learn, stories might best be used as a soothing method for having youth explore their own evolving sense of values.

Storytelling is not manipulation. All adults engage in some form of manipulation, and treatment providers certainly pay attention to the most effective ways to move youth through treatment. However, it is vital that stories be used for others to access and not to corner a young person into participation. An example might be the temptation to tell a story based on the life of a group member as an effort to gain participation. It is the author's opinion that as telling stories can have such a powerful effect on youth, manipulation can easily replicate dynamics of secrecy or coercion.

Storytelling is not self-disclosure. While there is a time and place for self-disclosure, it is recommended that stories not be made up of personal material, even in third person (e.g., "I knew this guy who always drove too fast."). In this way, the focus can be on the story, and not our attempts to maintain personal boundaries.

Storytelling is not a rambling dissertation. Stories are best thought out in advance based on the treatment needs of youth. While we all improvise from time to time, carefully embedding a story with elements relevant to treatment ensures their impact.

Storytelling is not permission to get off topic. Storytelling should not replace the essential elements of treatment.

Storytelling is not the same as campfire ghost stories. In choosing a story, one should remember that their soothing element is essential for moving a group forward.

Telling a Story

As mentioned above, beginning a group can be quite a struggle. A terse statement of what the day's lesson plan and discussion will be often costs the participation of some members, while allowing a discussion to arise out of the initial greetings runs the risk of difficulty focusing. I typically use an exercise borrowed from the work of Schladale (2002), in which each member answers the question "how is your life better than the last time we were all together." At a time when I notice a point of agitation that could easily escalate into conflict or disruption, I turn to whom I believe is the most receptive member and say "You know, Jerry, I'd like to tell you a story about a young man who…"

This requires no small amount of faith on the part of the clinician. It is easy to revert to a position of authority and limit setting. However, I believe that there is a fundamental curiosity and desire on the part of others to become involved when something interesting is happening. One teacher in our program would move to the center of the classroom and begin sweeping the floor when his students became distracted. There is a classic episode of Abbot and Costello in which comedian Lou Costello has a problem with his neck so that he constantly appears to be looking up. While stopped in the street, numerous passersby stop to see what he was looking at. One conference presenter is able to re-focus her audience after a break by whispering "Hello… I simply can't raise my voice any more." When asked what she means, she explains that she has a problem with her throat and is physically incapable of shouting as a means of gaining attention. However, she is able to hold people's attention time and again.

I have found that by simply starting the story and having one youth become interested, the others become involved quickly. If a student asks what's going on, I will simply say, "I'm telling Jerry about a young man who…" The keys to making this strategy work are persistence and a deep sense of confidence in the universal appeal of stories. Genuine interest in telling the story and an overall spirit of inquiry are also vital to its success. An example of a story for the beginning of a group is as follows:

Theme of attachment and trust

"You know, Jerry, I'd like to tell you a story about a young man who lived in a small village by the side of a lake, way, way up North. It was so far up North that winter lasted for many months. Early one morning this young man wandered away from his home. He went exploring out across the ice-covered lake, deep into the woods on the other side. He brought some food with him, but not much…

He spent the night out in the deep woods. He knew he really shouldn't, but this was a time of great adventure. When he came back to the lake, the ice was much thinner. He started to go out across it, but he fell through, into the frigid water below. He struggled for some time, and managed to get back to the shore. He built a fire and ate the last of his food. He sat and he wondered for a long time. At one point, he thought he could hear his family calling for him in the distance. He knew he wasn't supposed to spend the night out in the deep woods, and now he couldn't get back. And most of all, he knew he would never go out onto the lake again.

The winter quickly turned into the spring, and the boy stayed on the other side of the lake. He learned about finding things to eat, and he kept warm and dry by a campfire. He knew he'd be in trouble if he ever returned, so he gradually learned to be happy with what he had. Some days he could hear sounds from the faraway village.

One day, some men came out in a boat. When they saw him by the campfire, they called his name and came after him. The young man ran into the woods and hid behind a huge pine tree. They found him, but he ran to hide behind some other trees farther back in the woods. When the men caught up with him, they told him they were there to bring him back across the lake.

The boy was terrified. He never wanted to go on the lake again. He was afraid of what would happen if he went to the village, and he was afraid of these big men. They grabbed him, carried him back to the boat, and told him it was going to be all right. But the more they talked, the more furiously he fought because he was afraid. He was afraid of the thing that he longed for the most. He was afraid to go back to the village…"

The group typically sits quietly at the end of this story for a few seconds. Depending on how the participants look one might wait for a response or ask a question about a seemingly irrelevant aspect of the story. For purposes of demonstration, let's imagine a moderately hostile response:

> Youth: *And your point is?*
>
> Adult: *My point is (turning to a student that is looking at me, but not Jerry or the youth who asked the question) … What do you think the grown-ups in that story should have done?*

This, again, keeps the focus off the participants and on the story. It also explores the notion of responsibility, as presumably the adults are in a position to be responsible. The rest of the following dialogue is summarized from past discussions, and edited for brevity:

> Jerry: *They should have told him it would be OK.*
>
> Adult: *But he was so afraid of the lake and the village. How could they make all of that OK for the kid?*
>
> Another student: *Well, they could have calmed him down instead of just grabbing him.*
>
> Adult: *Can you tell me how to do that?*
>
> Jerry: *Make him feel… welcome.*
>
> Adult (noticing that moderately hostile student is no longer fidgeting): *You guys have some good ideas. (Turning to moderately hostile student) Billy, what could the grown-ups do better?*
>
> Billy: *They could get that he's afraid.*

By this point, Billy has let us know what's really going on, just as the others have, in their own way, stated what they need. Although it may be presumptuous, it might benefit the group process if the facilitator understands that Jerry needs to feel welcomed, the second student (Tommy) needs to feel safe from intrusion, and Billy's scared. However, they are participating, and their contributions can be fed back to them using the same words later on. For the time being, seeing that the moderately hostile student, Billy, is more involved, the facilitator can now move the group closer to an affectively charged element.

Adult: Is there any part of that story that people can relate to?

Tommy: Yeah. It's hard to trust people. I've been stabbed in the back. I know how it is.

Jerry: I don't know… it's hard to communicate. They should have tried to communicate.

Adult: How is that story like being in this group?

Tommy: Like I said, how do you do it without getting shit from people?

Adult: Billy?

Billy: How do you know that you're really like other people or that they've got the same issues?

By this point the group is focused on the group. It is far from being the sum of its distractions and can be moved in whatever relevant direction is helpful. Although virtually every members' responses are worthy of a separate discussion, keeping the focus moving quickly from one member to another ensures that nobody is the subject of undue attention or scrutiny at a time when the group is still coming together. Later on in the discussion one could ask Jerry how he knows when he's really welcomed, how Tommy keeps himself together in a world that feels intrusive, and how Billy finds courage in the face of being afraid. Whatever the situation, in engaging a group, I typically try to continue the discussion a little further than is necessary with the belief that *the slower you go, the faster you get where you want to go.* One can then move into the next stage of a group by asking: What would it be like if we discussed some difficult things? Some things closer to home? Can you handle that?[2]

Ending the story

The ending of the story is, obviously, a critical juncture in the group process. As indicated in the above story, pausing for a period of time while reading the faces of group members can give the leader a chance to assess his or her next move, and to get a sense of the mood of the participants. As with starting a story, the timing is often more a matter of art than science. I advocate finishing with silence for at least several seconds, and encourage group leaders, if possible, to maintain an attitude of respect, wonder, and curiosity throughout this silence in order to guide the process quietly to its next level. Possible questions and avenues for further inquiry include:

How is everybody? This question can be helpful when the group's response is uncertain, allowing the leader to gain additional information and decide how best to proceed. It also expresses concern and compassion, particularly when asked from a standpoint of curiosity and wonder.

Does anybody have a response? Although this question might appear obvious, it is phrased quite openly. It doesn't limit responses in the way that "what do you think about this story?" would (i.e., negates feelings) or "what did you feel listening to that story?" (i.e., focuses only on feelings). Its open nature does not easily invite a derogatory response such as "It was boring."

Is there any part of that story that is like being in treatment? This is essentially an invitation for students to bring up concerns around what the treatment process means to them. It can also serve as an invitation to bring the discussion of the story closer to their own lives.

What should the adults have done? This question can yield useful information regarding the youths' experiences with adults and initiate discussions regarding values that the youth hold around their own impending adulthood.

Improvising

In some instances, other themes present themselves. Sometimes, the initial story does not successfully engage the group to its fullest potential, while a second story does. The successful group leader will want to have any number of stories "at the ready" for difficult situations. However, in the absence of pre-arranged stories, the following themes may be useful for improvising:

How people's attitudes shape their world. Adults know that our world view can shape our thoughts and behavior: "A long time ago there was a young man that grew up with a lot of people telling him he was no good. He wasn't much of a student and no one ever gave him a chance at sports. Somewhere along the line, though, he knew that the world could be a better place…"

Another possibility is to start a story that takes place on a river far, far away. All the fish in the river thought that it was the *only* place to live. The crocodiles thought that it was a good place to live, but they also liked the river's banks. The forest creatures thought that the river was a nice place to visit, but they wouldn't want to live there. They looked at the river as a nice place to catch fish! The birds thought the river was a nice place to catch the little rodents that thought the river was a nice place to live near, etc. The moral of the story is that everybody looked at the river differently. How is that like being in treatment? Like living in the city? The country? The world?

A theme that can be helpful is an example of putting hardships into a more positive light. A story about Thomas Edison can be useful:

Thomas Edison was the guy that invented the electric light bulb. We take it for granted today, but this has been one of the most significant contributions in world history. He built a huge factory, the size of three football fields, for inventing things. When he was in his 60s, it caught on fire, and burned to the ground. The story is told that instead of getting upset, he told his kids – "Kids, go get your mother, quickly. She'll never seen another fire like this one."

Individuals' relationships with the world. The combination of attitudes and world view of group members can often be made into stories when no others seem to fit the bill. For example: "There was once a young man who had nothing, and I mean nothing. He had no supports anywhere, and when he moved out on his own, he came to expect that no one would ever be kind to him, or be nice to him in any way. And because he expected the world to be a cold and hostile place, he never saw that things could be any different. Once in a while, a stranger might smile, or a co-worker would start up a conversation, but he wouldn't respond. In his world view they might just be trying to take advantage of him. All the others around him thought that he was being cold and detached, and they couldn't see that he was just trying to protect himself because he lived in a cold and dark universe. What he didn't know is that the more he thought he was right about the world, the less he was willing to consider that things could be different for him."

How others have taken good care of themselves. Improvised stories with Horatio Alger themes where diligence and hard work pay off risk appearing corny, but reflect many of the values underlying treatment: "You guys all know about Michael Jordan and all the other great basketball players that are around today. They seem to have all the talent in the world. A few years ago, there was a guy named Larry Bird. He was famous not so much for his natural talent, but for the fact that he practiced all the time. Sometimes he'd be practicing shots for hours, and I mean hours, before his teammates would show up. But most importantly, Bird knew when to stop and rest and relax..."

Becoming the person they want to be. Beyond simply praising kids for their accomplishments, their treatment sequence itself can be made into a story: "Hey Scooter, would it be OK if I told the Scooter X story? When Scooter was a younger guy and just getting started at building a successful life, he used to have a hard time making it to group. One day, Scooter had some hard conversations with the adults in his life, and began to make some tough decisions for himself. What he didn't know then is that a whole lot of becoming the people we want to be is about exactly that... tough decisions and hard conversations with the people we care about. As Scooter moved forward, his life got a bit easier, because the more you practice these things, the better you get..."

Simple cooperation. Sometimes, a short and seemingly bizarre story can diffuse a counter-therapeutic process. The following[3] includes a theme of cooperation despite all odds:

A porcupine was walking through the woods. Things were peaceful enough. The only animal a porcupine needs to be afraid of is the fisher. The fisher doesn't fish, but it does have a way of eating porcupines without getting hurt by their quills. A hunter came along and said: "Hey! You! Porcupine! Get up in that tree over there and I'll tell you why later on." The porcupine did as he was told. Along came a fisher, who said: "Hey! Porcupine! I'm coming up there to knock you down." The fisher climbed right up the tree and into the hunter's trap. The hunter said: "OK, Porcupine, that's it. Get down from up there. We have more fishers to catch in those trees over there. Come on, let's go..."

Managing interruptions

Even the best storytellers have to deal with disruption and defiance. The most destructive of these can be the student who says merely, "this is stupid." Many leaders will view this as a direct affront and power struggle. However, it may be more useful to consider this an invitation to get off track and an implicit statement that the youth is not ready to participate. In any event, an underlying value that the only mission of the group leader is to keep the treatment sequence moving, and allow disruption and defiance to be what they are, may be beneficial in looking beyond the momentary power struggles.

It may also be useful to look at interruptions and objections as little more than anxiety as well as a lack of readiness to engage in treatment. For this reason, it may be most beneficial to manage interruptions by talking for a long period of time. In doing so, the leader is preventing further objections that make the youth's position more intractable, and allowing the youth to remain silent until he is ready to participate more substantively. If youth are anxious about talking, it can be useful to ask them implicitly not to talk. Rather than become sidetracked by interruptions and objections, there are a number of techniques that may be useful:

"I'm glad you brought that up." Very often, if not all the time, objections to storytelling and treatment in general contain very prosocial elements. By starting a response with, "I'm glad you brought that up," the leader can focus on these acceptable elements and support the youth rather than engage in a struggle (i.e., "no it's NOT stupid!"). Examples of this include:

> Youth: *This is stupid.*

> Leader: *I'm glad you brought that up, because a lot of things, even a lot of people, look stupid until we really get to know them. On the other hand, lots of the things people do seem like a good idea at the time until later when they seem really stupid. Wait until you here what happens next!*

> Youth: *I thought we're supposed to talk about issues.*

> Leader: *I 'm glad you brought that up. Some of the issues are really complicated. They're really hard. Do you think you can handle that? Excellent... watch out, because they're coming right up.*

> Youth: *What does this have to do with my getting out of here?*

> Leader: *I'm glad you brought that up, because it shows how much you want to move forward with your life, and oh my, this story has everything to do with that. Just wait until you hear the end.*

> Youth: *My parents are going to be mad that we're wasting time like this.*

> Leader: *I'm glad you brought that up because it tells me how much you're connected to your family, and even when you're away from them you're looking out for their best wishes.*

"Yes, that's really important, because..." This is essentially a variation on the same theme, but emphasizes that even the least contribution to the process is valuable. In some cases, it may even be beneficial to ask whether you could share that objection with others because of all the prosocial elements it contains. In this way, the leader places a very strong emphasis on "what's right" with the youth. For example: "Yes, that's really important, because it shows how much you value your time and your family. Sometime, would it be OK if I shared how much you're concerned for their well being?"

"Excellent point, and that has a lot to do with the end of the story." This is best used with anxious youth who try to engage in discussion before they're actually ready. While this is a judgment call on the part of the leader, a student's willingness to interrupt a story should serve as a signal that separate motivations may be at work.

Use of hands to say "whoa." This simple gesture can keep a youth on track while conveying a calm and soothing attitude. It consists of holding both hands with the fingers pointing up and the palms facing the student, and moving the hands up and down in such a way as to get the clear message out: "Hold on because I'm going to respect your concerns and get you through this." Although this may seem simplistic, there is value in keeping your hands where youth can see them.

The *"this is stupid balloon."* In this situation, the leader comes prepared with a balloon, mumbles "Aha... I have just the thing...", inflates the balloon, and hands it to the student, saying: "This is your 'this is stupid' balloon. If you think this is stupid, it's between you and your balloon. I have a great story to tell. Please feel free to sit there with your balloon, or listen and have fun, or both. It's up to you." If a balloon is unavailable, or would be too distracting, a couch pillow (or any other object) can work. In some cases, young people have gone on to hug the couch pillow or use it as a kind of stress relief object by fidgeting with it.

It is critical that the leader be lighthearted and deferential, maintaining an attitude that he is giving back the defiance to the youth. Even a trace of anger or frustration can turn this into a manipulative ploy or aggravated struggle. It may be advisable to follow this up with a statement such as: "I mean no disrespect. I simply am too old to hold on to 'this is stupid'. My job is to keep kids safe, and that includes my group. If there is anything that even looks like abuse, I'm going to have to ask it to leave the room."

"I'm sorry, but the abuse has just entered the room." As in the previous example, this statement can separate the youth from his actions. While a statement such as "I will not tolerate your abuse" can appear more confrontational than necessary, this wording reinforces the notion that the only enemy is the abuse itself. A variation on the following may also be effective:

"I'm sorry, but I'm concerned that if we let the abuse enter the room we'll all be in for trouble. Here's what I mean... When I was a young clinician, I would try to do groups where kids would try to communicate with each other, try to disrupt each other, and try to get the group off track. I used to think some of it was to be expected. But the more time I've spent helping people resign from a lifestyle that permits abusiveness, the more I've come to value getting rid of anything that even looks like abuse. I would like to invite you all, and everyone in this program, to think along the same lines. In the meantime, a big part of my job is to keep all of you guys safe, and for that reason, I can't have anything that even looks like abuse enter this room. Sorry about that."

Finally, in some cases, interruptions can signal that the group is simply not ready to move on, and at these times, it can simply help to say, *"You know, that reminds me of another story, a different story about…"*

Courage and honor

I have found this story useful in drawing young people into discussions about treatment, growing up, and what masculinity means to them. It can be used to help initiate conversations on images of manhood that the media portrays:

Long, long ago, there was a young man who lived far to the North, where winter lasts much longer. Cold and hunger haunt those who are unprepared in this part of the world. One day, he left his home in search of food and adventure. Like many young men, he felt trapped inside himself, and wanted to go out and make his mark…

He left his warm home and set out into the open places where one cloud covers the whole sky, and it is hard to tell the direction. This is the land of the "snow snakes" – where the wind blows the snow into weird forms that can confuse the unwary and take away all sense of the four directions, leaving you shivering and totally lost.

The young man made his way and came upon some moose tracks. It was late in the winter, and the snow was crusty on top, but powdery underneath. It was tough going, even on snowshoes. But this was all right. He figured that if it was tough going for him, it was tough going for the moose, and he would catch up. He tracked, and he tracked, and he tracked. Finally, he came to the end of the tracks, and there was … a rabbit! The rabbit looked at him, shivered, and said … "This has been a very difficult winter."

After some time, the rabbit explained that in the frozen lands ahead was a place from which no man had ever returned. The young man decided that if he couldn't have any food he could at least have some adventure and make his mark. They went closer, and the sky grew darker. They arrived at a frozen swamp and stood silently.

All of a sudden, a huge ugly arm broke through the ice and started to grab at the young man and the rabbit. They backed up, but the horrible creature disappeared again under the ice. The young man said … "This must be the place!"

In one group, the discussion went as follows:

> *Leader: How is everyone.*
>
> *All: Silent (look mystified)*
>
> *Leader: What do you think about the monster?*

Young man #1: Umm... Maybe that was the person the young man had told on, coming back for revenge. (Note: this young man had been abused by an individual who was subsequently incarcerated. The diagnostic relevance of this statement is of obvious importance.)

Young man #2 (after a pause): I don't know... a talking rabbit is a pretty weird idea (everyone laughs).

Leader: What does that story have to do with being in group? (Group is silent. One member starts to smile. Leader redirects question to him.)

Young man #2: They both take a lot of strength and they're both a lot of hard work... courage AND bravery. (Others nod in agreement.)

Leader: One example of bravery is right here in this room (looks at young man #1)... being able to talk about really awful things. It takes strength to bring that up...

Faking it

The following story can be useful in helping those kids who want to appear as though they're doing well even though they aren't. It can be broken down into its two elements (hiding victimization and hiding abusive acts) or told as is:

A long, long time ago there was a young man who made it seem like he was doing well, but he really wasn't. When he was younger, a lot of bad things happened to him. He got hurt really badly by some people he cared about... people he was supposed to be able to trust. He didn't tell anybody because he didn't think it would make any sense. He was afraid he might get into trouble and he was afraid the people who mistreated him might get into trouble. He saw other families who seemed to have it all together and he felt different. People would tell him he was a good kid, but he couldn't accept it because in his mind he knew differently. People told him he could be whoever he wanted to be, but he knew differently. He would go to the dance and everything would seem so sweet and innocent, and that just made him feel even more different. He would go to games at school and see the other kids with their families and he felt even more different.

It got worse. Whenever he got good grades, he felt that the teachers had missed something, because he was different. Whenever he got bad grades he felt different, and wondered if the mean people in his life weren't right about him after all. He came to wonder if the whole universe wasn't simply a bunch of people faking it – that no one can really be happy. Or was it just him?

Whatever the case, he felt different from the top of his head to the bottom of his feet, and as his body and mind changed as he went through puberty, he felt even more different still, like he didn't know who he was, only that he was different and, most importantly, that he never deserved the nice things that people said about him.
Well, you know that all young people want to be loved, but he felt so different. Some days he was lonely, and some days he was angry. Other days he felt that there was

nothing in the world he was good at. It was like he was living on the edge of a knife... he couldn't stand it, but he was afraid of falling off. One day he got into serious trouble by hurting someone, and he wound up in a place kind of like this.

Sooner or later, he was able to talk to others about what he'd done but he was afraid to tell the whole story. He didn't want to get into deeper trouble or have others get into trouble. He did what people asked, and they told him he was doing a good job. But he couldn't accept their kind words, because he knew he still had some secrets he was keeping. They told him he was good in school, but he still felt different because he had some awful secrets. They told him he had lots of talents, but it didn't mean anything to him because he was holding on to all these secrets. Worst of all, they told him he was a good kid, but all he could think is "they're just not seeing the real me. They just don't know. If they did know, they wouldn't accept me..."

Some questions that might help move a dialogue after this most powerful story include:

- If he were sitting here, what advice would you give him?
- What should the adults have done?

The leader will need to be sensitive to the fact that bad things are done by people the kids love and admire. Youth will often say in this third-party situation that the protagonist should have talked to people, whereupon the leader can say:

- But what if these people were really special to him? What if he said, "You know, my Dad's really a good guy."

Obviously, this story can provoke the strong emotional responses that it was designed to do. The leader will need to be highly sensitive to issues around both victimization as well as aggression.

Empathy

Marshall (2002) has defined 4 elements of empathy:

1) Recognition of another's emotional state
2) Taking the perspective of the other person
3) Experiencing the same or similar emotion
4) Taking some action to ameliorate the other person's distress

Within this conceptualization, Fernandez, Marshall, Lightbody, and O'Sullivan (1999) have used brief vignettes in the construction of an empathy measure for child molesters. With some introductory questions, these modified vignettes can be of clear benefit in discussing matters related to empathy:

1) Introduction
Hey, I saw that game last night. What do you guys think when you win a game? How do you feel?

What do you think when you lose a game? How do you feel?

2) Crash victim
Speaking of this, I'd like to tell you about a person who was involved in a really nasty car accident. This person just woke up in the hospital one day and couldn't remember a thing that happened. The only thing he knew is that he'd gotten hurt. What do you suppose he were thinking? What kinds of emotions do you suppose he was feeling? I know a lot of us don't like to put words into others' mouths, but just for the sake of discussion, what do you think?

If the answer is "I don't know", a useful response can be "Well, if you did know, what do you suppose that person would be experiencing?" It is hard for this vignette not to engage young people, since at least one of them has known someone who has been in a traffic accident. Care should be taken to ensure that no one has lost a close relative or dear friend in an accident. In those cases, a different kind of accident can be chosen.

3) Victim of sexual abuse
Well, let me take this a step further. Can you handle that? Imagine that someone has been sexually abused. What do you think he'd be telling himself the next day? How about a year later? What kind of emotions might he have? What kind of fears?

4) Specific victim
Well, with your permission, I'd like to invite you to imagine the story of what the person you hurt was thinking, was feeling, was experiencing. What do you think they thought at the time, and what do you imagine they might think about it in a few years?

Obviously, a sizeable portion of this exercise involves discussion as well as actually telling a story, but it indicates one way that a story can be turned into a more interactive and substantive element of the group.

The big noise

The "big noise" story can build on the empathy vignettes above. Although other versions have been told elsewhere, we all have similar stories to tell:

There was once a two-year-old boy. He was just a little guy, and didn't know much about the world. His mom and dad loved him a lot. One day, they went to another state, and helped some family move into a new home. This home had belonged to someone who had installed a big security system.

It was a long day of moving things around, and the boy got very tired and fell asleep in his mother's arms. Just at the moment he started to dream, his older cousin upstairs found a button to push, and this set off the burglar alarm. The noise sounded like a hundred fire engines, all in the same room. It woke up the little boy, who had never heard anything like it. He was terrified. The grown-ups quickly turned off the alarm, but the boy didn't know how to understand it, because he was just a little guy.

His mom and dad calmed him down, but because he didn't really know much about talking yet, all he could say was "BIG noise... BIG NOISE!"

And when he woke up the next morning, again he said "BIG noise... BIG NOISE!" And his mom and dad held him and told him things would be all right. Then he saw his aunt and uncle, and he told them "BIG noise... BIG NOISE!" And they told him it was all over. The next day at day care, he told the grown-ups "BIG noise... BIG NOISE!" and they told him he was OK.

What would you have told him? If you were his mom or dad, what would you have done?

Is it possible that when bad things happen to all of us... that we have to tell our stories over and over again until we really understand them? Until we really understand ourselves?

Re-visioning values

The following[4] may be useful vignettes for exploring and discussing the values of individual group members:

The eels and the fishes. There once was a huge lake that no one had ever visited. It was a beautiful lake that held vast numbers of fishes and eels. One day, some fishermen came upon it and began to fish. The fish in the lake got excited and arrogant. They told the eels that they were the special ones because only they were selected to feed mankind. They said that they had a higher purpose than just swimming around in the lake. But the eels said that the fish were crazy... it was they who were the special ones because they didn't have to be the ones eaten by man. They had a special purpose, and it was to swim around in their lake and enjoy their life.

Questions: Which one was right? Which one had the higher value?

The brothers. Once upon a time there were two brothers. One of them was born with a condition that left him paralyzed in a wheelchair. He got used to this and went on to study computers and was quite good with them. The other brother joined the army and went away to war. He was proud to serve his country, and others in his town were proud of him. He died at the front lines in a battle.

Questions: Which of the brothers was more fortunate? Was one better than the other?

The sisters. There were once two sisters. One was very beautiful, and the other was not. They were both exceptional students who wanted to become very successful. The more beautiful sister was consistently harassed by the boys in their school and often felt misunderstood... like others couldn't see past her good looks. The other sister often felt as though she was completely unnoticed and that because she wasn't pretty, no one could see she was in fact very talented. As a result, she often felt very misunderstood.

Questions: Which of the girls was more fortunate? How come?

The brother and the sister. A brother and sister were each beaten terribly by their father. The younger brother was hurt, told his teacher, and had to be hospitalized for his wounds. Later, he was put in foster care. His sister never said a word, and stayed at home. Although she was afraid of her father, she was also afraid to tell.

Questions: Which one of them handled the situation better? Who was more fortunate?

Final Thoughts

It will be up to the reader to be either good at telling stories or to be boring. Due to the sensitive nature of the topic, it is suggested that group leaders may wish to refrain from over zealousness or role-playing, as this level of activity may actually create distance. At the same time, being a bit "corny" can help adults establish themselves as safe adults rather than as overly friendly or unnecessarily authoritative. A calm and soothing approach marked by a lighthearted curiosity and sense of wonder can embody as well as promote the spirit of inquiry that can lead to a more substantive treatment outcome. In any case, when dealing with disruptive youth, the story itself can function as an invisible group leader or supportive adult.

Ultimately, the goal of treating aggressive youth should be to assist victims, prevent future abuse, and develop the integrity that will allow therapeutic gains to persist across time. Given the severity of the problem, it is no surprise that treatment providers are frequently asked to help those who are inherently poor candidates for treatment. By looking past elements such as disruption, defiance, and denial, many seemingly impossible youth can be invited to participate in their own lives.

End Notes

[1] The author is indebted to the work of Joann Schladale, Alan Jenkins, Howard Norman, Everett Spees, and to Orville W. Prescott, who in 1965 edited *A Father Reads to his Children*, and to Peter S. Prescott, who in 1988 edited *The Norton Book of American Short Stories*. Many portions of the stories in this chapter are borrowed from other, often long-forgotten and sometimes third-party sources encountered over time. Credit is given where possible.

[2] For further discussion on this point, see Jenkins (1992).

[3] Based on a Swampy Cree story; Norman, (1982).

[4] Many of these stories have biblical origins, and many have been re-worked into vignettes by Spees (2002).

References

Abel, G.G., Becker, J.V., Cunningham-Rathner, J., Mittelman, M.S., Murphy, W.D., & Rouleau, J.L. (1987). Self-reported sex crimes of nonincarcerated paraphiliacs. *Journal of Interpersonal Violence*, 2, 3-25.

Alexander, M. (1999). Sexual Offender Treatment Efficacy Revisited. *Sexual Abuse: A Journal of Research and Treatment*, 11, 101-116.

Blanchard, G.T. (1995). The difficult connection: The therapeutic relationship in sex offender treatment. Brandon, VT: Safer Society.

Dishion, T.J., McCord, J., and Poulin, F. (1999). "When interventions harm: peer groups and problem behavior". *American Psychologist*, 54, (9), 755-764.

Fernandez, Y., Marshall, W.L., Lightbody, S., & O'Sullivan, C. (1999). The child molester empathy measure: description and examination of its reliability and validity. *Sexual Abuse: A Journal of Research and Treatment*, 11, (1), 17-32.

Hanson, R.K., & Bussiere, M.T. (1998). Predicting relapse: a meta-analysis of sexual offender recidivism studies, *Journal of Consulting and Clinical Psychology*, 66 (2), 348-362.

Hunter, J. (1999). Understanding Juvenile Sexual Offending Behavior: Emerging Research, Treatment Approaches, and Management Practices. Center for Sex Offender Management. available at www.csom.org

Jenkins, Alan (1990). *Invitations to Responsibility.* Adelaide, Australia: Dulwich Centre Publications.

Jones, R. (2002). Research and practice with adolescent sexual offenders: Dilemmas and directions. In Ward, T. Laws, R.D., & Hudson, S.M. (Ed.s) Sexual Deviance: Issues and Controversies. Thousand Oaks, CA: Sage.

Laws, D.R. (2002). Harm reduction and sexual offending: Is an intraparadigmatic shift possible? In Ward, T. Laws, R.D., & Hudson, S.M. (Ed.s) *Sexual Deviance: Issues and Controversies.* Thousand Oaks, CA: Sage.

Linehan, M. (1993). *Cognitive behavioral treatment of borderline personality disorder.* New York: Guilford Press.

Mann, R. E., & Beech, A.R. (2002). Cognitive distortions, schemas, and implicit theories. In Ward, T. Laws, R.D., & Hudson, S.M. (Ed.s) *Sexual Deviance: Issues and Controversies.* Thousand Oaks, CA: Sage.

Marshall, W. L. (2002). Historical foundations and current conceptualizations of empathy. In Fernandez, Y. (Ed.) *In their shoes: Examining the issue of empathy and its place in the treatment of offenders.* Oklahoma City: Wood'N'Barnes.

Miller, W.R. & Rollnick, S. (2002). Motivational interviewing: *Preparing people for change, 2nd edition.* New York: Guilford Press.

Norman, H. (1982). *Where the Chill Came From: Cree Windigo Tales and Journeys.* San Francisco: North Point Press.

Prescott, D.S. (2001). Collaborative treatment for sexual behavior problems in an adolescent residential treatment center, in Miner, M.H., & Coleman, E. (eds.) *Sex Offender Treatment: Accomplishments, Challenges, and Future Directions.* Binghamton, NY: Haworth Press.

Schladale, J. (2002). The T.O.P. (Trauma Outcome Process) *Workbook for Taming Violence and Sexual Aggression.* Freeport, ME: Self-published and available at www.resourcesforresolvingviolence.com

Spees, E. (2002). Word movies: Strategy and resources for therapeutic storytelling with children and adolescents. *Annals of the American Psycotherapy Association,* January/February 2002, 14-21.

Ward, T., Laws, D.R., & Hudson, S.M. (2002). *Sexual Deviance: Issues and Controversies.* Thousand Oaks, CA: Sage Publications.

Ward, T. & Stewart, C.A. (2002). Good lives and the rehabilitation of sexual offenders. In Ward, T. Laws, R.D., & Hudson, S.M. (Ed.s) *Sexual Deviance: Issues and Controversies.* Thousand Oaks, CA: Sage.

Worling, J.R. & Curwen, T., (2000). Adolescent sexual offender recidivism: success of specialized treatment and implications for risk prediction. *Child Abuse and Neglect,* 24, 965-982.

CHAPTER TWENTY-EIGHT

CAN WE DEVELOP EVIDENCE-BASED PRACTICE WITH ADOLESCENT SEX OFFENDERS?

MARK CHAFFIN[1]

Introduction

Evidence-based practice (EBP) is a relatively new but increasingly dominant perspective in behavioral and health care services. EBP was born out of the recognition that many treatment practices or services are based more on clinical lore or "clinical proof" than they are on scientific outcome research. We all are familiar with broadcast or magazine advertisements reporting that some product is "clinically proven" to accomplish some benefit. We would do well to understand what this term means, and the standard of evidence it describes. "Clinically proven" simply means that practitioners have observed that people receiving the intervention seem to get better. In other words, it is a correlational, not a causative, standard of evidence. This is probably the most common basis for clinical practice traditions, and adolescent sex offender treatment is no exception. EBP, on the other hand, refers to practices supported by more carefully controlled research evidence. EBP strives to bring services more into line with the best available controlled research and promote practices supported by causative rather than simply correlational evidence. This chapter will briefly review some of the basic tenets of EBP, the arguments of its proponents and critics, and describe the strengths and limitations of differing types of evidence for evaluating a given practice. Next, the chapter will examine the current state of adolescent sex offender (ASO) treatment outcome research and evidence, and the research from related populations. The chapter will conclude by examining some of the difficulties and possible solutions to developing an evidence-based approach to ASO treatment, including how we measure outcomes, how research is organized and finally reconsidering how we define our field and how we think about adolescent sex offenders.

Defining Evidence-Based Practice

EBP can be defined as *the competent and high-fidelity implementation of practices that have been demonstrated safe and effective, usually in randomized controlled trials (RCTs).* Much of the controversy surrounding EBP among practitioners involves the parameters of what is meant by "high-fidelity implementation." Fidelity to an intervention protocol raises questions of how strictly protocols or manuals must be followed and the extent to which practitioner creativity, idiosyncratic practice styles, and individualized treatment approaches can be retained in EBP.

The term "evidence-based" has grown tremendously in use over the last decade. For example, in the behavioral science literature, the term was used in approximately three publication titles or abstracts in 1994, but a decade later was being used in close to 600 annually, as shown in Figure 1.

Figure 1: Use of term "evidence-based" in behavioral science literature, 1994 -2003

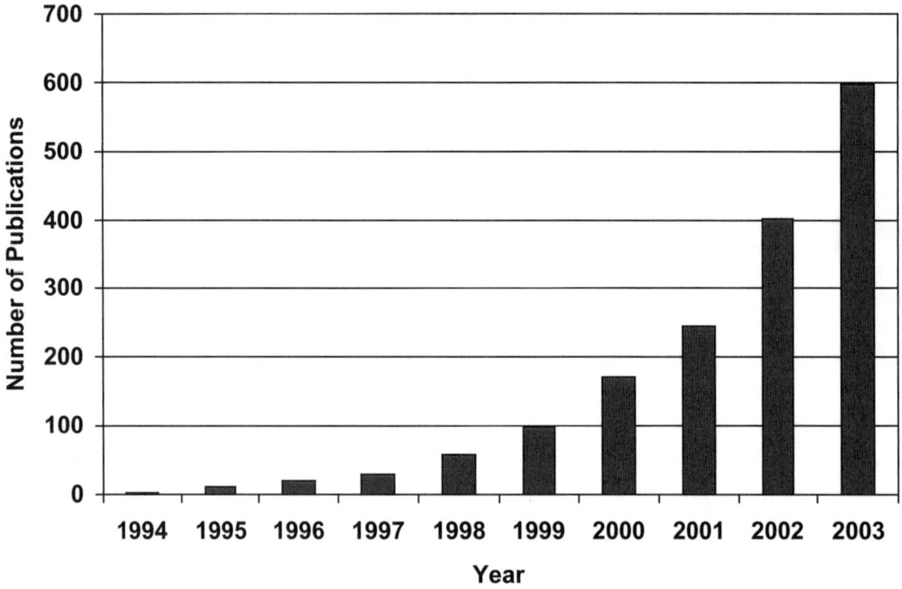

Funding sources and government agencies are increasingly emphasizing EBP, and promoting infrastructure for exporting EBP's from the laboratory to field settings (NIMH National Advisory Council, 2002). As the EBP movement spreads across behavioral health care and social services systems, there is the risk that it will become merely a gratuitous shibboleth or a slogan; ill defined, often invoked, applied to virtually everything, but rarely actually understood or practiced. Indeed, if one were to ask practitioners, "do you use practices based on scientific knowledge about what works", the large majority probably would respond with an enthusiastic, "yes". Yet, expert reviews of field services appear to have come exactly to the opposite conclusion (Saunders, Berliner & Hanson, 2004; Kauffman Best Practices Project, 2004; NIMH National Advisory Council, 2002), and suggest that most behavioral and mental health services provided in field settings are not based on any clear evidence that the service model actually works or is among the better supported available models. In fact, it is common in the youth violence field for models to be widely implemented despite fairly strong evidence that they do not work or are actually harmful (USD-HHS, 2001). Similarly, many field practitioners appear to have never heard of, let alone use, better supported intervention models.

As with any movement challenging established practice traditions, the move toward EBP has been met with some degree of reticence or resistance. A few clinical traditionalists appear averse to science in general and intervention outcome research in particular, arguing that practice is inherently subjective and too complex to be evaluated with the blunt instrument of clinical science (Clemens, 2002). For them, science is of almost no value when it comes to psychosocial interventions, a field they perceive as one of the humanities rather than one of the sciences. Other practitioners, perhaps the majority, take more of a middle ground and would consider themselves judicious consumers of science as well as practitioners of the art of therapy. For these practitioners, scholarly or scientific information is consumed, weighed, combined with clinical experience and used ideographically and creatively to articulate an *ad hoc*, case-by-case intervention plan. The resulting practice behaviors reflect both unique aspects of the case and the unique personal characteristics of the practitioner. In this approach, the practitioner is an expert whose own personality, own unique assessment of the individual case and own unique read of the scientific evidence, are what drives practice. This approach to using scientific information might be termed "evidence-informed practice" or "evidence-suggested practice"[2]. However, the evidence-informed or evidence-suggested approach is quite distinct from EBP as defined here. The evidence-informed or suggested process is far more subjective, far less structured and prescribed, and more driven by personal values, changing practice fashions, popular theories, charismatic opinion leaders, and political or social contexts.

One criticism of the evidence-suggested or evidence-informed perspective is that it is difficult to know what it *doesn't* describe, given that some sort of indirect evidence can be cited to support virtually any intervention imaginable. All behavioral or mental health interventions have proponents who are able to articulate a practice rationale or logic model, usually one that infers its conclusions from various bits and pieces of scientific evidence, however indirect. Treatment rationales based on indirect or inferential scientific evidence may obscure the fact that the intervention is based more on ideological, cultural or entrepreneurial agendas than on demonstrated efficacy. For example, in the 1980's, there was widespread public fear of juvenile delinquency. Advocates and politicians argued that the "soft" juvenile justice system was unable or unwilling to take control of young criminals. This gave rise to using boot camps or fear-based programs, such as "Scared Straight", which proliferated around the country, including programs and facilities run by for-profit corporations with a financial interest in portraying their programs as effective. These sorts of intervention models were able to articulate a coherent and plausible logic model. They were able to marshal indirect or inferential scientific evidence to support core propositions. They had anecdotal stories of success. The logic seemed intuitively correct to many front-line practitioners and policy makers eager to bring a "tougher" approach to delinquency. The approach had articulate expert proponents. The approach might easily have been described as evidence-informed or evidence-suggested. As it turned out in later controlled trial outcome research, boot camps did not produce better outcomes, and fear-based programs such as "Scared Straight" were shown to be deleterious and produced worse outcomes than doing nothing at all (Petrosino, Turpin-Petrosino & Finckenauer, 2000).

The central difficulty with evidence-informed practice is that the bar is set too low; so low in fact that inert or harmful practices can qualify, especially given reasonably articulate proponents and a rationale that resonates with current social values. This is not to suggest that no evidence-informed practices work. Some evidence-informed practices probably do work, while others do not. Unfortunately, there is no basis or process within the evidence-informed framework to confidently separate the two. A second overarching problem caused by the low bar of the evidence-informed approach is that it yokes intervention development and practice evolution to the vicissitudes of random fashion rather than to a program of clear, step-by-step cumulative progress towards the ultimate goal of improved outcomes. A generation ago, one of the fathers of empirical psychology, Paul Meehl (1978), noted, "it is simply a sad fact that in soft psychology, theories rise and decline, come and go, more as a function of baffled boredom than anything else, and the entire enterprise is characterized by a disturbing lack of cumulative character…". Thus, in the traditional evidence-informed practice culture, we can expect only that tomorrow's interventions will look different from today's. We cannot confidently expect that they will work any better.

From the EBP perspective, social consensus and changing values do have a place. However, their place lies more in setting ultimate goals for programs (e.g., reducing sexual re-offenses) rather than selecting the programmatic means to reach those goals (e.g., group therapy or learning "cycles"). Systematic science is required in order to define the methods that are effective at achieving whatever ultimate benefits that society and our clients hope to obtain. The promise of EBP is that it puts the selection of programmatic means on a road where cumulative progress can be made, and the reliable expectation that we will obtain better outcomes tomorrow than we obtain today. Indeed, cumulative progress has been the hallmark of the experimental scientific fields over the last century.

A summary emphasizing some contrasts between EBP and traditional clinical practice are shown in Table 1.

Having punctuated and emphasized some of the differences between EBP and traditional clinical practice, it also is important to note their commonalities. Both EBP and traditional practice are governed by common codes of good clinical practice and professional ethics. Both recognize the importance of core non-specific intervention practices, such as the importance of establishing a working client-practitioner relationship, having good interpersonal skills, and respect for client dignity. Both recognize that individual characteristics of the therapist or interventionist are important. Indeed, it is not protocols or models alone that yield efficacy. Some individual providers are more successful than others, and there is significant variation in client outcomes from one provider to the next, both within traditional models and EBP models (WSIPP, 2004). A significant amount of provider-to-provider variation in EBP results appears to be related to how faithfully the provider adheres to the specified EBP protocol (Schoenwald, Shiedow & Letourneau, 2004). Multiple service dimensions are probably important for achieving results: personal provider characteristics, non-specific provider skills, the quality of the model itself, and the fidelity and quality with which the model is implemented. Although outcomes may be multiply determined, and factors aside from the intervention model may contribute, this should not obscure the fact that model selection and model fidelity matter.

Table 1: Contrasting EBP and Traditional Approaches

	Traditional Clinical Practice	**Evidence-Based Practice**
Source of Knowledge	Accumulated subjective experience with individual cases. Opinion about practice outcomes emphasized. "In my experience…".	Well designed, randomized trials and other controlled clinical research. Facts about practice outcomes emphasized. "The data show that…".
Knowledge Location and Access	Hierarchical. Knowledge is possessed by opinion leaders and gurus. Charismatic expert driven.	Democratic. Knowledge is available to anyone willing to read the published scientific research or research reviews. Information technology driven.
Method of Achieving Progress	Haphazard, fortuitous, based on changing values, fads, fashions and leaders.	Systematic, predictable, based on incremental and cumulative programs of outcome research.
Practitioner Expertise	Quasi-mystical personal qualities and intuition.	Specific, teachable, learnable skills and behaviors.
View of Practice	Art. Creative artistic process with fluid boundaries.	Craftsmanship. Creativity within the boundaries of the supported models and protocols.
Research Practice Link	Indirect. Inferential.	Direct. Integral and fundamental to practice.
How is Research Summarized and Applied to Practice	Individual subjective practitioner synthesis of whatever literature is consumed.	Best practices workgroup or collaborative summary based on exhaustive reviews of the outcome research and meta-analysis.
Program Evaluation	Inputs (e.g., credentials of practitioners) and Process (e.g., treatment assignments completed or desired attitudes endorsed).	Outcomes (measurable "bottom-line" client benefits, such as improved school performance or reduced recidivism).
Location of Research	Mostly in laboratory settings and divorced from actual practice.	Field clients routinely enrolled in trials in order to test benefits and refine services.
Quality Control	Focuses on how well service rationales are conceptualized and the credentials of who provides them.	Focuses on how well services are behaviorally delivered *vis a vis* a prescriptive protocol.
Practice Visibility	Actual practice is seldom observed by anyone other than the practitioner and the client.	Direct peer or consultant observation of actual practice, and specific feedback is common.
Assumptions About Outcomes	Faith. Service programs in general are seen as good and are assumed to be beneficial.	Skepticism. Knowledge that interventions may be inert or even harmful. Benefit must be empirically demonstrated, not assumed.

Finally, it is important to note that EBP has been questioned on ethical grounds. Most criticism centers on two main points. The first is that EBP may be viewed as cookbook, lock-step and inflexible. This view sees EBP as requiring slavish adherence to manuals which ultimately results in poor services if client needs are not strictly in line with the manual. This criticism is based on the fact that EBP is an attempt to bring some of the consistency found in laboratory outcome trials into field practice. Some have suggested that failure of EBP to completely customize the intervention for the individual client is ethically questionable. Many of these critics advocate for more free-form services; basically a defense of what I have described as the evidence-informed position.

To a certain extent, this criticism presents an inaccurate caricature of EBP and of controlled trial research. Part of the difficulty may be that traditional practitioners and clinical scientists move in different worlds. Many traditionalists have limited direct experience with clinical trials. Practitioners who have delivered services within the confines of a controlled clinical trial would probably find these critiques rather amusing, and certainly would not consider themselves automatons slavishly bound to a manual, or required to sacrifice ethics and humanity in order to achieve lock-step model fidelity. The reality is that no manual or protocol runs nearly as smoothly or lock-step as it might appear on the surface or in a scientific article. At ground level, both EBP and clinical trials are very human activities, and few cases are without complications, surprises, or complexities. Considerable fluency with the intervention protocol, its underlying theory model, and good general clinical practices are necessary to execute EBP competently and adapt to case-by-case idiosyncrasies. This is true regardless of whether one is working in a research laboratory or in field practice.

Second, the argument that protocol-driven practice produces inferior results compared to highly customized, *ad hoc* and eclectic services runs counter to considerable research evidence. Some might argue that individualized case-by-case treatments have never been and cannot be empirically tested. I would argue that eclectic, *ad hoc* services are probably the single most tested service model in the entire outcome research literature. They are simply known under another name. They are called "standard community care." Anyone examining the outcome research literature will not come away optimistic about the effectiveness of standard community care (Weiss & Weisz, 1995; Weisz, Donenberg, Han & Weiss, 1995).

What kind of evidence counts?

When talking about EBP it is critical to understand what is meant by "evidence." Not all evidence is created equal, at least when it comes to determining intervention effectiveness. Certain types of evidence are inadequate for establishing effectiveness. For example, client testimonials or client satisfaction ratings may be poor indicators of effectiveness. Naturally, it is desirable for clients to feel satisfied with the services they receive. However, high client satisfaction can be obtained from inert or placebo treatments if they are delivered with confidence. Even demonstrable quackery or proven deleterious interventions can proffer many satisfied customers and testimonials describing miraculous cures. Client satisfaction actually tells us more about how friendly, pleasing or engaging the services are than about their efficacy. This is not unimportant—other things being equal, friendly, pleasing and engaging services are obviously better than rude, aversive or disengaged services. Services that fail to engage or that drive clients away may have little chance of success. However, simply because disengaged customers may benefit little does not imply that satisfied customers benefit more. High client satisfaction and testimonials provide little information for discriminating the truly effective from the ineffective.

EBP assigns little evidentiary value to clinical experience, such as the experience of seeing clients get better over the course of a certain type of intervention. Practitioners, of whom I am one, should not take this personally. It is more the nature of clinical data, rather than a matter of personal failure. If clinical data could be characterized in terms of its experimental design, it most closely approximates a simple one-group pre-post change paradigm. Both clinical experience and pre-post experiments suffer from a lack of equivalent comparisons. The limitations of pre-post change evidence have been well known for decades (Campbell & Stanley, 1966). Absent key comparison conditions, spontaneous improvement may be confused with intervention benefits, and prevented deterioration may be confused with intervention failure. In short, without comparisons, whether or not clients appear to get better during treatment is irrelevant to the question of treatment effectiveness. One cannot know how one's clients might have fared with an alternative, competing intervention or with no intervention at all, so causal effects cannot be determined. Finally, clinical experience and similar sorts of data are vulnerable to a variety of biases, including expectancy effects, demand effects or confirmatory bias. In other words, we may tend to see things selectively—to see what we wish to see, see what influential others want us to see, or see that which confirms what we already believe. These sorts of threats to validity are inherent to clinical experience. Again, this is not to suggest that practitioners are any more biased than other human beings, but only to suggest that we are human beings.

Comparisons are essential, but not all types of comparisons are equal. Evaluations that involve non-randomized comparisons also have potential comparison group problems. Although non-randomized comparisons using statistical adjustment procedures (e.g., covariance, case-mix adjustment, propensity analyses) may sometimes replicate the findings of true randomized trials, they often don't, and it can be difficult to know when non-randomized and statistically adjusted comparisons are equivalent in their findings to true randomized trials and when they are not (Glazerman, Levy & Myers, 2002; Ioannidis et al., 2001). Ultimately, obtaining confident evidence of intervention benefit involves well-designed and controlled true randomized trials. According the U.S. Office of Management and Budget's recommendations for program evaluation, "well-designed and implemented RCTs [randomized controlled trials] are considered the gold standard for evaluating an intervention's effectiveness across many diverse fields of human inquiry, such as medicine, welfare and employment, psychology, and education" (OMB, 2004, p. 4). Typically, early tests are conducted in controlled settings or under fairly ideal circumstances, sometimes but perhaps misleadingly called laboratory trials. These tests demonstrate efficacy, or the ability for the intervention to yield effects under ideal circumstances. Efficacy trials determine whether an intervention *can work*. A different type of trial is known as an effectiveness study. Effectiveness trials typically take place in actual field settings and under somewhat looser controls, and answer the question of whether the model *will work* when it is put to use in actual practice settings. Ideally, effectiveness trials follow efficacy trials as an intermediate step between initial efficacy testing and widespread dissemination. In practice, this important step is often skipped.

Acceptable evidence of benefit also depends on what outcomes are measured. Benefits should include tangible, bottom-line, functional outcomes that directly reflect ultimate program goals. For example, a treatment designed to help children with posttraumatic stress disorder should actively reduce traumatic stress symptoms. For ASO treatment programs, reduction in future sexual offenses is the obvious bottom-line outcome, although other bottom-line outcomes arguably are important too, including reduced levels of non-sexual delinquency and improved functioning. Outcome evidence based on soft outcomes, such as psychological tests tapping presumed mediators of ultimate benefits, is less persuasive. For example, a program designed to reduce future sexual offending against children might measure changes in the presumed mediating variable of social competence with peers. Although improving peer social competence is probably a good outcome that stands on its own merits, one should not infer that the program was effective in reducing sex offenses solely because it impacted the theoretically linked outcome of improving peer social competence. Understanding mediators of benefit, or the how and why of efficacy, is important. However, tests of why something works, or what mediates effects, should extend and follow bottom-line effectiveness tests, not substitute for them.

It is important to note that EBP does not necessarily mean that only practices meeting the highest possible criteria for scientific support should be used. Nor does it imply that a complete body of rigorous research must exist for all potential outcomes or with all potential population subgroups before EBP can be embraced. This is a particularly critical point for the ASO treatment field at our current stage of development. No ASO intervention models meet the generally accepted standards required to designate a model as "well supported"[3] or "empirically validated." If we concluded that only well-supported models should be employed with ASO's we would quickly find that none existed and would have to close virtually all current treatment programs. Fortunately, EBP doesn't imply this. EBP simply means favoring the *best supported available practices*. Where well-supported or empirically validated treatments are available, they may be synonymous with EBP. Where there are no fully supported interventions, one must pick from among competing models with varying levels of support.[4] For example, there might be one model tested in a single well-conducted randomized laboratory trial, along with a few quasi-experimental field studies or single-case multiple baseline studies, and with a robust clinical literature. This model would be clearly preferable to competing models having no randomized trials and only anecdotal or single-group outcome support. In this example, the first model might not meet full criteria as empirically validated, but compared to competing models, would clearly be the *best supported* and could be consistent with EBP, at least for the time being.

In circumstances where many of the available models have little or no controlled efficacy testing on which to base decisions, there can be no assurances that the EBP approach will necessarily result in selecting the most effective model. Untested models, once tested, ultimately may prove better than the currently best supported model. However, adopting the EBP framework does offer some protection against employing inert or downright harmful models. More importantly, adopting the EBP practice culture creates a demand that intervention models prove themselves empirically, not simply rhetorically, and creates a context for cumulative progress.

EBP and ASO Treatment Outcome Research

Overview

A major obstacle to applying EBP to ASO treatment programs is the fact that the field has produced very little controlled outcome research, despite over two decades of program proliferation, increased public awareness of the problem, and the success of specialized professional societies such as ATSA and NOTA in bringing practitioners and researchers into close affiliation. Somewhere in the neighborhood of five RCT's have been conducted in the entire modern sex offender treatment content area; two with children (Bonner, Walker & Berliner, 2000; Pithers, Gray, Busconi & Houchens, 1998) two with teenagers (Borduin, Henggeler, Blaske & Stein, 1990; Borduin & Schaeffer, 2001) and one with adults (Marques, et al., 2005).

Although only one ASO intervention model has been tested in an RCT, a wide variety of clinical treatment approaches for adolescent sex offenders have been described in the literature, including behavioral conditioning approaches (Kaplan, Morales & Becker, 1993; Weinrott, Riggan & Frothingham, 1997), pharmacological approaches (Bradford, 1993; Galli, Raute, McConville & McElroy, 1998), family systems approaches (Bentovim, 1998), Rational-emotive therapy (Whitford & Parr, 1995), music and art therapy (Gerber, 1994; Skaggs, 1997), "cycle" based approaches (Ryan, Lane, Davis & Issac, 1987), cognitive-behavioral or CBT approaches (Becker & Kaplan, 1993; Kahn, *1996*), relapse prevention CBT approaches (Steen, 1993, Gray & Pithers, 1993), holistic perspectives (Longo, 2001) and ecological multi-systemic approaches (Swenson et al., 1998). A number of programs have tracked their sexual and non-sexual recidivism outcomes. However, except for Multisystemic Therapy (MST), none have employed any controlled comparison conditions, thereby precluding judgments about program effectiveness. What is clear from this body of literature, however, is that officially detected sexual recidivism tends to be low, while non-sexual recidivism tends to be substantially higher. Figure 2 depicts a summary of multiple U.S.-based, single-group follow-up studies.[5] All of the studies followed at least 50 youth for at least one year (mean follow-up of five years), but employed a range of different intervention models. Although consistently low rates of sexual recidivism might convey optimism about treatment, the optimistic conclusion that treatment works is only one of several plausible interpretations. The findings could be explained by consistent effectiveness, consistent ineffectiveness, consistent iatrogenesis, a complex mixture of subgroup by treatment type interactions, or the possibility that treatment matters little beyond the impact of the usual juvenile justice system procedures.

Figure 2: Sexual and non-sexual recidivism in single-group U.S. follow-up studies of ASO's (average of 5-year follow-up).

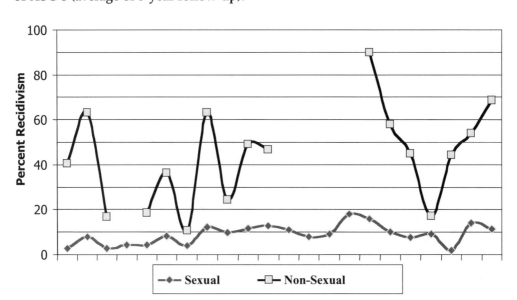

Multisystemic Therapy

The MST model is unique among ASO intervention approaches because it has been evaluated in two RCT's (Borduin, Henggeler, Blaske & Stein, 1990; Borduin & Schaeffer, 2001), the first a very small trial and the second a moderate-sized trial. MST is an intensive, low-caseload, short-term, home-based, ecologically oriented model. Briefly, the model focuses on factors known to be associated with general delinquency, such as low parental monitoring and delinquent peer affiliation. MST works with and through parents, parent surrogates or others in the youth's social ecology rather than focusing primarily on intra-individual factors. When implemented faithfully, MST appears to be effective in reducing delinquent and related behaviors among seriously delinquent youth (average effect size = .51; Curtis, Ronan & Borduin, 2004). It would appear that a substantial number of youth in the MST sex offender trials fit this description of seriously delinquent youth.

MST is the leading candidate model for any program wanting to adopt an EBP orientation to treating adolescent sex offenders. However, there are a number of challenges that might be involved in adopting MST and a few caveats. First, adopting MST involves a substantial financial investment in staff training and licensing. It also requires adopting prescribed quality control procedures designed to insure fidelity to the MST model. Adopting the model also may require changes in how a community handles adjudicated delinquent youth such as setting a priority on keeping youth in the community and engaging families rather than relying on residential placement. The treatment is expensive to deliver, although for serious or chronic delinquents, cost analysis suggests that these expenses are recaptured after a few years (Mihalic Irwin, Elliott, Fagan & Hansen, 2001). Also, it is important to note that standard MST inclusion criteria preclude using the standard MST model with certain types of adolescent sex offenders. For example, youth who are considered "primary" sex offenders, without substantial concomitant non-sexual delinquency, may not be considered candidates for standard MST. A sex-offender specific version of MST has been developed and is currently being tested in a randomized trial (Henggeler, 2004), but application of expanded inclusion criteria or use of the modified ASO protocol may need to await findings from this ongoing study. Similarly, because MST works largely with and through parents or parent surrogates, youth who are nearing adulthood or who do not have at least one committed adult in a long-term parenting and supervisory role may not be candidates for MST. However, for mid-adolescent youth who are generally delinquent in addition to their sexual offense, and for whom at least one committed long-term adult caretaker can be found, MST would appear to be well suited and probably the best supported available model. It remains less clear how well MST might work with youth whose problems are more paraphilic in nature rather than related to general delinquent proclivities, and it is not clear how cost-effective any intensive intervention like MST would be for low-risk youth whose sexual behavior is largely experimental and who are more socially immature than generally delinquent.

Aggregate residential placements

Growing evidence suggests that one traditional intervention model applied to adolescent sex offenders, residential care, may be among the least supported and most poorly suited models for delinquent youth or youth who are susceptible to delinquent influences. Although residential placement of delinquent youth offers the advantage of short-term community protection, the long-term effectiveness of residential placement has been questioned. The Surgeon General's Report on Youth Violence (USDHHS, 2001) concluded that although correctional and residential placements "appear to have positive effects on youth as long as they remain in the institutional setting, research demonstrates consistently that these effects diminish once young people leave" (p. 118). The NIMH National Advisory Workgroup reached similar conclusions (2001). Residential care, along with boot camps and shock programs, was categorized by both reports as among the proven ineffective approaches. Most of the studies supporting these conclusions have been with generally delinquent youth. This probably includes some youth who have committed sex offenses. However, studies of specialized ASO residential programs have not been conducted. Furthermore, because residential programs vary considerably in quality, findings may apply to some, but not all, programs.

Perhaps the most parsimonious mechanism for explaining the poor outcomes of residential placements is that aggregating delinquent youth together inadvertently promotes affiliation with delinquent peer groups within the facility, resulting in socialization into delinquent attitudes, beliefs and a delinquent peer culture. It is not simply a matter that any out-of-home placement produces poor results. For example, a randomized trial found that group home placement resulted in higher rates of future violent and delinquent behavior compared to a non-aggregate treatment foster care placement (Eddy, Whaley & Chamberlain, 2004). There is widespread evidence that peer groups have a major influence on adolescent behavior, and affiliation with delinquent peer groups plays an important role in the development of delinquency and violence (Elliott, Huizinga & Ageton, 1985; Thornberry, Krohn, Lizotte & Chard-

Wierschen, 1993). Studies have repeatedly found that affiliation with deviant peers is the most proximal influence on the onset and escalation of delinquent and violent behavior (Dishion, Andrews & Crosby, 1995; Hawkins, Catalano & Miller, 1992). Because aggregation of delinquents with other delinquents is an intrinsic feature of correctional centers, group homes and group therapy, countering this iatrogenic effect could prove impossible. Residential placements may be unavoidable for some youth. The community simply will not tolerate the behavior of some and there are a small number who are too psychiatrically ill or who simply pose too great a risk to remain in the community. However, there is currently no outcome research evidence demonstrating effectiveness of ASO residential treatment and a growing body of research suggesting the potential for harm. In short, residential placement can no longer be approached with a "better safe than sorry" justification.

Sex-offender specific cognitive-behavioral group therapy

For the past generation, the most commonly employed treatment model for all youth who have committed sexual offenses has been sex-offender specific cognitive-behavioral group therapy (SOS-CBT), often based on the relapse-prevention or "cycle" models. SOS-CBT can be applied in either community-based or residential settings. Although CBT approaches are generally short-term, the SOS-CBT model as it is currently applied is typically long-term, often one to two years or more, although there is little foundation for this length of treatment beyond clinical custom. SOS-CBT is rooted in intervention models originally developed for adult sex offenders, particularly adult child molesters whose behavior appears related to deviant sexual arousal and courtship interest patterns. Consequently, this approach may be known as the "deviancy model", although the extent of actual deviancy focus among SOS-CBT programs for adolescents may vary widely. Often, SOS-CBT focuses on detailed admission of offense behavior and deviant sexual interests, changing attitudes and beliefs about sexual behavior, increasing victim empathy, learning long-term self-monitoring strategies (e.g., relapse prevention) and enforcing long-term lifestyle modifications (e.g., avoiding contact with young children). Conditioning approaches for reducing specific deviant sexual interests may be used to varying extents. One central assumption of the SOS-CBT approach is that the problem is an internal or intra-individual one—for example, deviant interests, impaired empathy, cognitive distortions or compulsive cycles are all intra-individual problems. A second central assumption is that the problem is relatively fixed, specialized, and enduring. Consequently, the approach is similar to that for other presumably permanent diseases such as diabetes or alcoholism, and involves accepting one's diagnosis and implementing a lifetime program of vigilance and self-management. It is important to note that the core assumptions of SOS-CBT are distinct from the core assumptions embraced by most established evidence-based treatments for non-sexual delinquency. Most EBP models for general delinquency, such as MST, hold that social and ecological factors, not intra-individual psychopathology, are the proximal and most malleable leverage points for changing youth behavior.

At present, there is no controlled outcome evidence available to evaluate how well the SOS-CBT model works for ASO's, or more to the point, for particular ASO subgroups. Because the model is drawn from work with adult pedophiles and is focused in substantial part on more internal sexual problems, one might speculate that the SOS-CBT model's effectiveness would be concentrated in subgroups of ASO's who have, or who are rapidly developing, paraphilic disorders. However, it is not clear how many ASO's actually have deviant interests or incipient paraphilias. For that matter, it is not clear what range of sexual responses are normal for teenagers, or whether teenage sexual interest variations convey the same increased risk among adolescents that they do among adults. It appears that the percentage of ASO's with enduring sexual deviancy problems may be small (Hunter & Becker, 1994; Hunter, Figueredo, Malamuth & Becker, 2003; Hunter, Goodwin, et al., 1994). Moreover, it remains uncertain how well SOS-CBT works, even among the adult populations for whom it was originally developed. The sole RCT of the relapse prevention SOS-CBT model with adult populations has yielded discouraging results and the overall body of outcome evidence is equivocal (Berliner, 2002; Hanson, et al., 2002; Marques et al., 2005).

In short, although the SOS-CBT model or some of its variants ultimately may prove effective with ASO's or with particular ASO subgroups, this is far from established. In fact, the necessary research has yet to begin. This is not a reason for abandoning SOS-CBT. After all, it is not the case that the model has been tested and failed. But it is reason to modify our attitude toward it. In some states or communities, group-based SOS-CBT has been specifically prescribed by ASO treatment standards, along with prescriptions for specific treatment components, such as victim empathy training or learning one's cycle. Alternative approaches, especially those that are not "sex-offender specific" are discouraged or prohibited. Ironically, these sorts of standards would appear to preclude standard MST, which is the sole model with RCT evidence, because it contains no sex-offender specific components. From an EBP perspective, any specific treatment prescriptions are wildly premature at this point. There is simply not enough evidence to support them. Worse, they may inhibit development of ultimately more effective treatments, or deter beneficial innovation. Premature standards and widespread acceptance may reify untested assumptions and create a sense of false confidence that any treatment model so widely practiced and officially endorsed must be effective.

Obstacles to developing a body of ASO treatment outcome evidence

From the preceding review, it is probably evident that applying the EBP perspective to ASO treatment offers few prescriptive specifics at the present time because so little controlled outcome research has been conducted. Indeed, as EBP becomes the practice standard across fields, the ASO treatment field seems to find itself lagging behind. Paradoxically, the ASO field lacks neither scientific interest nor scientific talent. It is not the case that the field is averse to science or empiricism, at least within the major ASO treatment professional societies. In fact, it is anything but. So, is our research base really any less than that of similar fields and if so, why? First, let's consider the number of treatment outcome studies published in the twenty-year period between 1984 and 2003, comparing the number for sex offender and ASO treatment studies to those in our sibling areas of family violence, delinquency, alcoholism and addiction.[6] From Figure 3, it is clear that our knowledge base is considerably smaller than in these other fields. Similarly, let's compare the number of U.S. Public Health Service (NIH, CDC) funded research projects. These federally funded projects often are larger studies with the potential for major impact on practice. Figure 4 compares the number of federally funded projects for sex offender related topics with domestic violence topics, and suggests a substantial and growing discrepancy. The number of projects funded for delinquency, alcoholism and addiction are considerably higher still and dwarf those shown in Figure 4. All of these areas, other than sex-offender treatment, have seen increases in the numbers of funded projects over the past decade. In short, the knowledge discrepancy is large, and more disturbingly, growing.

Figure 3: Number of treatment outcome studies (controlled or uncontrolled) between 1984 and 2003 by topic area.

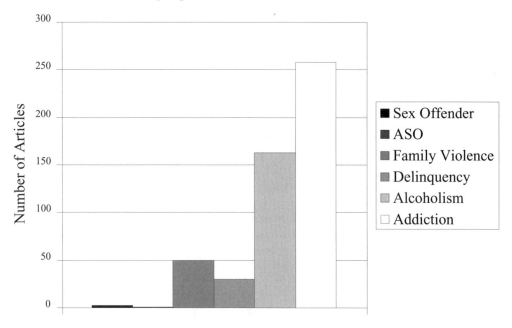

Figure 4: Number of U.S. PHS-funded research projects. Sex offender topics compared to domestic violence tpics.

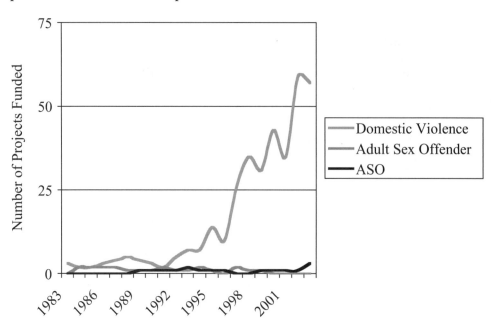

Although I cannot argue that adolescent sexual offending is as prevalent a problem as non-sexual delinquency, addiction or domestic violence, this disparity in the knowledge base does give some indication of how far behind our field is compared to other fields, and the comparative and growing disadvantage our field faces for adopting EBP.

There are obstacles to conducting quality ASO outcome research. First among these are the inter-related problems of small samples and low base rates for the ultimate (but not only) outcome of interest, i.e. subsequent sex offenses. Few individual treatment programs or researchers have access to sufficient numbers of youth to conduct even a simple two-arm RCT with adequate power to detect differences in a low base rate event. Moreover, official recidivism events require time to accrue, necessitating long-term follow-up. The most methodologically sophisticated study in the adult sex offender research literature, the Atascadero trial (Marques et al., 2005) took well over a decade to complete. The option of turning to "soft" or "proxy" outcomes might appear to offer a solution, but only at the price of circular reasoning and wasted effort. For example, we might easily compare intervention groups on their ability to apply relapse prevention concepts, or their self-reported attitudes and beliefs. But this begs the question of whether changes on these factors actually correspond to changes in future behavior. Proxy measures or measures of presumed mediators may only confirm *how* the intervention was designed to impact behavior (i.e., by changing attitudes or teaching relapse prevention), not *whether* the intervention impacted behavior.

Ultimately, we must grapple with the problem of how to measure not only the rare officially detected sexual re-offense but also the presumably less rare undetected sexual re-offense. Because most adolescent sex offending involves child sexual abuse, there is a delicate balance to be struck. Protecting research participant confidentiality and also respecting legal or ethical obligations toward child victims may require substantial thought. However, the only alternative to confronting this ethical and policy dilemma is to embrace a position of willful blindness. The traditional ethical position in research has often been "don't ask – don't tell." We don't ask, so we won't have to report; they don't tell, so they won't get in trouble. Progress is deferred and everyone, including victims, suffer. This solution, once examined, is hardly one with which we can remain ethically comfortable.

Additionally, the ASO treatment field, like many other fields treating relatively rare conditions, might organize its clinical research efforts. Few, if any, single sites have the patient population to generate substantial outcome research. This problem is exacerbated by the fact that ASO's are a heterogeneous population, comprised of at least three major population subtypes (Hunter, et al., 2003) and the optimal intervention for one subtype may be quite different from the optimal intervention for another. Other fields dealing with heterogeneous and relatively rare clinical conditions have encountered this same problem and have solved it by organizing into clinical research networks. For example, a generation ago, the small field of pediatric oncology organized into networks of centers, all of which implemented common clinical trial protocols. The result was remarkable progress in the treatment of childhood leukemia and other cancers. Affiliating into clinical research networks requires sacrifice. Local customs, entrepreneurial interests and individual practitioner preferences must be subordinated to the greater interests of protocol fidelity and experimental design in order to achieve progress. Given the largely entrepreneurial direction of ASO treatment, it is unclear whether these sacrifices would be feasible. For example, would a private-practice clinician or a corporation that depends on ASO treatment revenue be willing to implement a shorter and less expensive (i.e., less profitable) treatment trial protocol? Because few ASO programs are conducted in academic or clinical research settings, the sort of clinical research networks that have been so productive with some rare disorders in medicine might be especially difficult in our field.

Finally, we might advance our treatment evidence knowledge base by changing how we define ourselves as a field and how we define our clients. The field of ASO treatment exists as a demarcated specialty area because a generation ago we defined the ASO population as special and different. Certainly, we did not discover the problem of adolescent sexual offending. The population has long existed, in approximately the same proportions as today. It was simply never defined as special or different. Prior to defining these youth as special, they were simply known as "delinquents", and treated using the approaches of the larger delinquency field. The juvenile justice system and the delinquency treatment world have accepted the definition of these youth as different and special, and largely ceded them to the specialized field of adolescent sex offender treatment (Zimring, 2004). There is no controlled scientific evidence to suggest whether this has helped, hurt or made no difference. One thing, however, is certain. The general delinquency intervention field has moved rapidly forward in terms of EBP, and the specialized ASO treatment field has not. The general delinquency intervention field has generated a range of empirically well-supported, evidence-based practices (Mihalic, et al., 2001). In fact, identifying effective practices for delinquents is no longer the primary task. The primary task is to disseminate and implement known effective practices on a large-scale (Elliott & Mahalic, 2004; WSIPP, 2004). Perhaps we might ask what our field could gain from shifting back to viewing our ASO clients (or at least some of them) as generalists rather than a unique subpopulation with completely different and unique problems. Arguably, most ASO's have more in common with other delinquents or other behavior-problem youth than they do with pedophiles. Perhaps what we define as specialized sex offender treatment should be reserved for the small subpopulation of ASO's with demonstrable paraphilias. If the non-paraphilic majority of ASO's were given back to the general delinquency field, would they ultimately be better served? Would we better be able to develop effective evidence-based treatments if we focused on a single problem? Subspeciality practice areas, particularly those with a substantial entrepreneurial bent, naturally seek to expand their business, not narrow it. Nonetheless, downsizing in the interest of focusing on a core mission might allow us to do one thing well rather than many things poorly.

In summary, moving the ASO treatment field in the direction of EBP may require rethinking several aspects of business as usual. First, it should involve an honest appraisal of the level of evidence we have for the effectiveness of our established and routine clinical practices. It should involve coming to terms with the fact that, currently, the best supported practice model is radically different in its assumptions, theory and approach from our established and routine clinical practices. It should involve recognizing that many of our established and routine clinical practices are rooted in work with a problem (i.e., pedophilia) which it appears few ASO's, as we currently define them, actually have. It will involve replacing wishful thinking about sex offender treatment effectiveness with a hard look at the data. Rigorously testing SOS-CBT effectiveness should become our absolute top priority in the field, as well as that of our professional societies, and research funding agencies. The obstacles to generating randomized trial outcome evidence are considerable but not insurmountable. After all, the MST model, which is applied only with a small percentage of all ASO's has succeeded in organizing three RCT's. Finally, it may be time to think about which youth we seek to include under our domain, and which youth may best be served under other, more highly resourced domains. Twenty years ago, when many of us began specialized treatment programs for ASO's, very little was known about treatment effectiveness. Now, twenty years later, we still do not know much more (although we seem to believe we do). Twenty years from now, this will no longer be viable.

End Notes

[1]A portion of this manuscript, including Table 1,was drawn from a previously published article: Chaffin, M., & Friedrich, W. (2004). Evidence-based practice in child abuse and neglect. Children and Youth Services Review, 26, 1097-1113.
[2]These terms have various meanings. In other contexts, they may refer to practice based on lower-levels of evidence, such as quasi-experimental studies or case studies, rather than randomized trials.
[3]Designation as "well-supported" may require multiple randomized trials done by independent groups. For a discussion of the types and quantity of evidence required for various levels of empirical support, see Chambless and Ollendick, 2001.
[4]Conceivably, there could be a large number of well-supported and empirically validated models available, and the task of choosing would be much the same. However, this enviable circumstance is beyond the horizon at present.
[5]Some non-US studies have reported higher rates of sexual recidivism. However, it is not clear whether this reflects higher sensitivity in detecting offenses or differing population characteristics such as differing criteria for labeling a youth as a sex offender.
[6]Each of these areas is one in which criminal justice and behavioral health areas interface.

References

Becker, J.V. & Kaplan, M.S. (1993). Cognitive behavioral treatment of the juvenile sex offender. In H.E. Barbaree & W.L. Marshall (Eds.) *The juvenile sex offender.* New York: Guilford (pp. 264-277).

Becker, J.V. & Kaplan, M.S. (1988). The assessment of adolescent sexual offenders. *Advances in Behavioral Assessment of Children and Families,* 4, 97-118.

Bentovim, A. (1998). A family systemic approach to work with young sex offenders. *Irish Journal of Psychology,* 19, 119-135.

Berliner, L. (2002). Commentary, *Sexual Abuse: A Journal of Research and Treatment,* 14, 195-198.

Bonner, B., Walker, C. E. & Berliner, L. (2000). *Final report. Children with sexual behavior problems: Assessment and treatment.* Grant No. 90-CA-1469. National Clearinghouse on Child Abuse and Neglect: Washington, DC.

Borduin, C.M. & Schaeffer, C.M. (2001). Multisystemic treatment of juvenile sexual offenders: A progress report. *Journal of Psychology & Human Sexuality,* 13, 25-42.

Borduin, C.M., Henggeler, S.W., Blaske, D. M. & Stein, R. J. (1990). Multisystemic treatment of adolescent sexual offenders. *International Journal of Offender Therapy & Comparative Criminology,* 34, 105-113.

Bradford, J. (1993). The pharmacological treatment of the adolescent sex offender. In H.E. Barbaree (Ed.), *The juvenile sex offender* (pp.289-319). New York, NY: Guilford.

Campbell, D.T. & Stanley, J.T. (1966). *Experimental and Quasi-Experimental Designs for Research.* Chicago: Rand-McNally.

Chambless, D.L. & Ollendick, T.H. (2001). Empirically supported psychological interventions: Controversies and Practices. *Annual Review of Psychology,* 52, 685-716.

Clemens, N.A. (2002). [Review of the book Evidence in the Psychological Therapies: A Critical Guide for Practitioners] *Psychiatric Services,* 53, 221.

Curtis, N.M., Ronan, K. R. & Borduin, C. M. (2004). Multisystemic Treatment: A Meta-Analysis of Outcome Studies. *Journal of Family Psychology,* 18, 411-419.

Dishion, T.J., Andrews, D.W. & Crosby, L. (1995). Antisocial boys and their friends in early adolescence: Relationship characteristics, quality, and interactional process. *Child Development, 66 (1),* 139-151. Blackwell Publishing, United Kingdom.

Eddy, J.M., Whaley, R. & Chamberlain, P. (2004). The Prevention of Violent Behavior by Chronic and Serious Male Juvenile Offenders: A 2-Year Follow-up of a Randomized Clinical Trial. *Journal of Emotional & Behavioral Disorders,* 12, 2-8.

Elliot, D.S., Huizinga, D & Ageton, S. (1985) *Explaining Delinquency and Drug Use.* Beverly Hills, CA: Sage.

Elliot, D.S. & Mihalic, S. (2004). Issues in Disseminating and Replicating Effective Prevention Programs. *Prevention Science,* 5, 47-52.

Galli, V.B., Riggan, N., McConville, B.J. & McElroy, S.L. (1998). An adolescent male with multiple paraphilias successfully treated with fluoxetine. *Journal of Child and Adolescent Psychopharmacology,* 8, 195-197.

Gerber, J. (1994). The use of art therapy in juvenile sex offender specific treatment. *Arts in Psychotherapy,* 21, 367-374.

Glazerman, S., Levy, D.M. & Myers, D. (2002). *Nonexperimental replications of social experiments: A systematic review.* Washington, DC: Corporation for the Advancement of Policy Evaluation, Mathematica Policy Research, Inc.

Gray, A.S. & Pithers, W.D. (1993). Relapse prevention with sexually aggressive adolescents and children: Expanding treatment and supervision. In H.E. Barbaree (Ed.), *The juvenile sex offender* (pp.289-319). New York, NY: Guilford.

Hanson, R.K., Bloom, I. & Stephenson, M. (2004). Evaluating Community Sex Offender Treatment Programs: A 12-Year Follow-Up of 724 Offenders. *Canadian Journal of Behavioural Science*, 36, 87-96.

Hanson, R.K., Gordon, A., Harris, A.J.R., Marques, J.K., Murphy, W., Quinsey, V.L. & Seto, M.C. (2002). First report of the collaborative outcome data project on the effectiveness of psychological treatment for sex offenders. *Sexual Abuse: A Journal of Research and Treatment*, 14, 169-194.

Hawkins, J.D., Catalano, R.R., & Miller, J.Y. (1992). Risk and protective factors for alcohol and other drug problems in adolescence and early adulthood: Implications for substance abuse prevention. *Pscyhological Bulletin, 112 (1)*, 64-105.

Henggeler, S.W. (2004). *Effectiveness Trial: MST with Juvenile Offenders.* Abstract available for download from http://crisp.cit.nih.gov

Hunter, J.A., Figueredo, A.J., Malamuth, N.M. & Becker, J.V. (2003). Juvenile sex offenders: Toward the development of a typology. *Sexual Abuse: Journal of Research & Treatment*, 15, 27-48.

Hunter, J.A., Goodwin, D.W. & Becker, J.V. (1994). The relationship between phallometrically measured deviant sexual arousal and clinical characteristics in juvenile sexual offenders. *Behavior Research Therapy*, 32, 533-538.

Hunter, J.A. & Becker, J.V. (1994). The role of deviant sexual arousal in juvenile sexual offending. *Criminal Justice and Behavior*, 21, 132-149.

Ioannidis, J.P.A., Haidich, A., Papp, M., Pantazis, N., Kokori, S.I., Tektonidou, M.G., Contopoulos-Ioannidis, D.G. & Lau, J. (2001). Comparison of evidence of treatment effects in randomized and nonrandomized studies. *Journal of the American Medical Association*, 286, 821-830.

Kahn, T.J. & LaFond, M.A. (1988). Treatment of the adolescent sexual offender. *Child and Adolescent Social Work*, 5, 135-148.

Kaplan, M.S., Morales, M. & Becker, J.V. (1993). The impact of verbal satiation of adolescent sex offenders: A preliminary report. *Journal of Child Abuse*, 2, 81-88.

Kauffman Best Practices Project (2004, March). *Closing the quality chasm in child abuse treatment: Identifying and disseminating best practices: Findings of the Kauffman Best Practices Project to Help Children Heal from Child Abuse.* Charleston SC: National Crime Victims Research and Treatment Center.

Longo, R.E. (2001). *Paths to Wellness: A Holistic Approach and Guide for Personal Recovery.* Holyoke, MA: NEARI Press.

Marques, J. K., Wiederanders, M., Day, D.M., Nelson, C., & Van Ommeren, A. (2005). Effects of a relapse prevention program on sexual recidivism: Final results from California's sex offender treatment and evaluation project (SOTEP). *Sexual Abuse, 17,* 79-107.

Meehl, P. (1978). Theoretical risks and tabular asterisks: Sir Karl, Sir Ronald, and the slow progress of soft psychology. *Journal of Consulting and Clinical Psychology, 46,* 806-834.

Mihalic, S., Irwin, K., Elliott, D., Fagan, A. & Hansen, D. (2001). Blueprints for Violence Prevention. Juvenile Justice Bulletin, July, 2001. U.S. Department of Justice: Office of Juvenile Justice and Delinquency Prevention.

The National Advisory Mental Health Council Workgroup on Child and Adolescent Mental Health Intervention Development and Deployment (2002). *Blueprint for change: research on child and adolescent mental health.* Washington, D.C.: NIMH.

Petrosino, A., Turpin-Petrosino, C. & Finckenauer, J.O. (2000). Well-meaning programs can have harmful effects! Lessons from experiments of programs such as Scared Straight. *Crime & Delinquency, 46,* 354-379.

Pithers, W. D., Gray, A., Busconi, A. & Houchens, P. (1998). Children with sexual behavior problems: Identification of five distinct child types and related treatment considerations. *Child Maltreatment, 3,* 384-406.

Ryan, G., Lane, S., Davis, J. & Isaac, C. (1987). Juvenile sex offenders: Development and correction. *Child Abuse & Neglect, 11,* 385-395.

Saunders, B.E., Berliner, L. & Hanson, R.F. (Eds.). (2004). *Child physical and sexual abuse: guidelines for treatment* (Revised Report: April 26, 2004). Charleston, SC: National Crime Victims Research and Treatment Center.

Schoenwald, S.K., Shiedow, A.J. & Letourneau, E.J. (2004). Toward effective quality assurance in evidence-based practice: Links between expert consultation, therapist fidelity and child outcomes. *Journal of Clinical Child and Adolescent Psychology, 33,* 94-104.

Skaggs, R. (1997). Music-centered creative arts in a sex offender treatment program for male juveniles. *Music Therapy Perspectives, 15,* 73-78.

Steen, C. (1993). *The relapse prevention workbook for youth in treatment.* Brandon, VT: The Safer Society Press.

Swenson, C.C., Schoenwald, S.K., Randall, J., Henggeler, S.W. & Kaufman, K.L. (1998). Changing the social ecologies of adolescent sexual offenders: Implications of the success of multisystemic therapy in treating serious antisocial behavior in adolescents. *Child Maltreatment, 3,* 330-338.

Thornbery, T.P., Krohn, M., D., Lizotte, A.J., & Chard-Wierschem, D. (1993). The role of juvenile gangs in facilitating delinquent behavior. *Journal of Research in Crime & Delinquency, 30 (1),* 55-87.

U.S. Department of Health and Human Services. (2001). *Youth Violence: A Report of the Surgeon General.* Rockville, MD: National Center for Injury Prevention and Control; Substance Abuse and Mental Health Services Administration, Center for Mental Health Services; and National Institutes of Health, National Institute of Mental Health.

U.S. Department of Health and Human Services (1999). *Mental Health: A Report of the Surgeon General* (DHHS Publication No. USHHS/SAMHSA/CMHS/NIMH). Rockville, MD: U.S. Government Printing Office.

U.S. Office of Management and Budget (2004). *What constitutes strong evidence of program effectiveness.* Available from the U.S. OMB at http://www.whitehouse.gov/omb/part/2004_program_eval.pdf

Washington State Institute for Public Policy (2004). *Outcome evaluation of Washington state's research-based programs for juvenile offenders.* Olympia Washington: Washington State Institute for Public Policy.

Weinrott, M.R., Riggan, M. & Frothingham, S. (1997). Reducing deviant arousal in juvenile sex offenders using vicarious sensitization. *Journal of Interpersonal Violence,* 12, 704-728.

Weiss, B. & Weisz, J.R. (1995). Relative effectiveness of behavioral versus nonbehavioral child psychotherapy. *Journal of Consulting & Clinical Psychology.,* 63, 317-320.

Weisz, J.R., Donenberg, G.R., Han, S.W. & Weiss, B. Bridging the gap between laboratory and clinic in child and adolescent psychotherapy. *Journal of Consulting & Clinical Psychology,* 63, 688-701.

Whitford, R. & Parr, V. (1995). Uses of rational emotive behavior therapy with juvenile sex offenders. *Journal of Rational-Emotive & Cognitive Behavior Therapy,* 13, 273-282.

Zimring, F.E. (2004). *An American travesty: Legal responses to adolescent sex offending.* Chicago: University of Chicago Press.

CHAPTER TWENTY-NINE

YOUNG PEOPLE WHO SEXUALLY ABUSE: CELEBRATING PROGRESS AND LOOKING TOWARDS THE FUTURE

MARTIN C. CALDER

Introductory Comments

This chapter will review some of the progress that has been made in relation to children and young people who sexually abuse, as well as exploring areas where progress has been slow, concluding with some suggestions on what coordinated next steps are needed. Much of what is reported in the US literature fails to capture the work that has taken place in the UK, and this chapter attempts to redress this under the headings of context and operational issues.

Contextual Considerations

Governmental culpability

In the UK, the issue of young people who sexually abuse reached the professional and political agenda in the early 1990's when a landmark report (NCH, 1992) was published, coupled with a requirement in central government guidance (DOH, 1991) that Area Child Protection Committees (ACPC's) develop local procedures to govern the process of intervention.

The NCH Report highlighted that there was:

- No coordinated management structure.
- An absence of policy, practice or ethical guidance.
- An uncertainty regarding the legitimacy of the work.
- Clashes of philosophy relating to minimum intervention with this group.
- A lack of inter-agency coordination.
- An inadequate information base and a lack of evaluation.
- A paucity of training.
- Deficits in supervision.
- A shortage of consultation.

Working Together (DOH, 1991) clearly identified young people who sexually abuse as a child protection issue and stated that official responses and interventions should take place within child protection procedures. It recommended that ACPC's should coordinate the development of a strategic plan for dealing with this group, bring them into the child protection system, and devote a section of their annual report to outlining progress. These were welcomed as they provided a platform from which to build the UK response to address ongoing professional and societal resistance to recognizing that these were children in need. Unfortunately, the capacity to be creative allowed for multiple different systems to emerge and there remained a very powerful division of philosophy between the criminal justice and child protection camps (see figure 1 below).

Figure 1: Criminal justice and child protection: territorial disagreements (Calder, 2003).

Principles	Child Protection	Criminal Justice
	Interventionist approach. Grow into behaviour, which escalates over time. Legal mandate needed for the work to be completed.	Diversionary approach. Grow out of their behaviour. Innocent until proven guilty.
Supporting positions	Diversion is collusion, allowing the abuser and their family to minimise their behaviour. Diverted cases are more likely to re-offend.	Practice wisdom (e.g., most young people stop offending at 16-17 years of age). 80% cautioned do not re-offend. Those referred to court most likely to re-offend. Court confusion over change of approach.
Benefits	Broadens the focus of intervention away from only those convicted. Widens the available options. Reinforces this group as children "in need".	Allows a professional-young person partnership. Prevents stigma and labelling. Diversion avoids mixing delinquent youth together as a peer group.

There then followed a tremendous number of changes in the central government approach to youth crime and justice systems and views as to who should manage young people who sexually abuse. These did not resolve the original problems; they simply switched positions. Figure 2 highlights the key pieces of legislation and guidance that were issued by central government.

Figure 2: The current supra-structure: evidence of disjointed government and thinking (Calder, 2002).

Criminal Justice	Child protection
Sex Offenders Act (1997)	Working Together to Safeguard Children (DOH, 1998)
Crime and Disorder Act (1998)	
Home Office Guidance to Probation (Home Office, 2000)	Safeguarding Children (DOH, 1999)
Setting the boundaries (Home Office, 2000b)	Assessment Framework (DOH, 2000)
ASSET	

The detail of these is beyond the scope of this chapter (see Calder 2002 for a detailed discussion), although what has resulted has been the production of a supra-structure that has brought contradiction, confusion and consequences way beyond what could have been expected, as well as fuelling a general failure of agencies to work cooperatively and share responsibility. This has diverted attention from the frontline work at a time in which considerable interest in this topic was being shown.

There is also an issue of offering the community a false sense of security through the introduction of sex offender registration laws which are also counter-productive. Indeed, there are numerous problems associated with sex offender registration laws. The laws are not effective at preventing future sex crimes, leading to the public feeling a false sense of safety. The laws damage the lives of the young people who sexually abuse and their families, as well as others in a variety of ways. No law can ultimately stop behavior. Registration laws and public notification laws, especially as applied to young people, are not going to prevent sexually abusive and/or aggressive behavior from occurring. In fact, these laws may go on to not only damage these young lives, but also further delay their individual potential for healthy recovery (Longo and Calder, 2005). Clearly, if the registration system serves to increase the apprehension and resistance of parents to engage in treatment work, then the potential gains will have been more than outweighed by the alienation of the group most critical to the monitoring and management of juveniles and the parents.

Inter-agency practice

The work of Helen Masson (1995, 1998) in researching the experiences of practitioners involved with young people who sexually abuse identified a set of concerns relating to the systems, cooperation and communication that existed between agencies. Unless the local delivery was through a dedicated project then practitioners reported a relatively low degree of time allocated and a limited amount of clinical experience gained.

The need for a shared philosophy is essential to effective inter-agency practice. Sanders and Ladwa-Thomas (1997) surveyed staff in various agencies regarding perspectives on young people who sexually abuse. They identified a substantial agreement in relation to many of the perspectives across social work groups (child protection, child and family, youth justice and probation), although there was a strikingly different response from the police officers. A spread of opinion was found on a set of specified questions related to practice issues with this group and the greatest diversity related to:

- Whether young abusers should be seen as victims first and offenders second.
- Whether local authorities should have a register of children and young people who abuse others.
- To what extent children under the age of 10 understand their own sexuality.

Calder (1999) set out a conceptual model for standardizing the process of local resolution of processes and procedures in relation to this group (see figure 3) as well as advocating a consortium approach in which authorities as well as agencies at a regional level pooled resources to offer a service in this specialist area.

Figure 3: A framework for local responses (Calder, 1999; 2002).

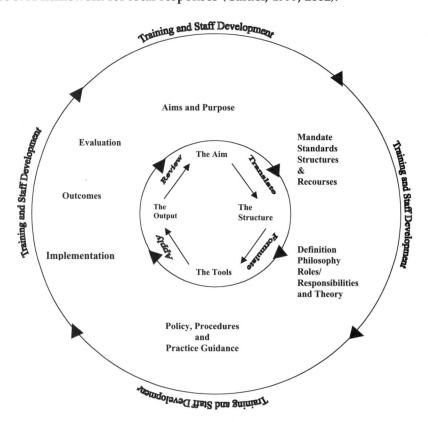

Organizational Considerations

Morrison (1995) has advocated a number of key building blocks for delivering a quality service to young people who sexually abuse divided into three tiers:

> 1) Strategic: at this level agencies must accept the validity of such provision, agree with inter-agency procedures and allocate adequate resources.
> 2) Managerial: staff concerned with this area of work require adequate training, supervision and consultation.
> 3) Practice: where work should be based on a written and accepted philosophy of intervention and reflect a holistic view of the young person and their developmental needs.

Morrison (1997) has also referred us to the concept of "emotional competence" to consider whether organizations provide practitioners with a safe structure to engage with the complex issues which arise in the sexual abuse field. Without this there is a danger that workers may drift into mirroring the distorted dynamics of young people and their families (Bankes, 2002).

Hackett (2002) has also written about the need for us to support workers in the personal context in order to equip them to deal with the costs of working with this group. Just as impact works on cognitive, affective and emotional levels, so our self-care responses need to be multi-levelled and multi-dimensional. Hackett's model promotes the following kind of questions (Hackett, 1999):

- In what way do my previous life and professional experiences influence my responses to young people and their families?
- How do my values, particularly in relation to sexuality and abuse, affect the way in which I conduct the work and make sense of my role in the task?
- What are my previous experiences of practice in this field? How do they influence my approaches and responses?
- What is happening in my external life/personal life currently?
- How does the environment I work in contribute to, or influence, the impact of my experience?
- What are the details of the interpersonal exchange I have with my clients?
- What are the particular themes and struggles associated with my direct contact with young people?
- What feelings are promoted in me? As a consequence of the work? About me, my work and my world view?
- What patterns and links can I trace in the web of feelings that emerge?
- What particular scripts and schemas are being projected upon me?
- In what ways are my thoughts, beliefs and attitudes being changed, eroded or strengthened through the experience of the work?
- What is different now about my behaviour than when I first engaged in this work?
- To what degree are my behaviours appropriate and effective ways of coping?
- To what extent are my behaviours, thoughts and feelings congruent to each other?

Figure 4 sets out examples of this.

Figure 4: Connecting impact on affective, cognitive and behavioural levels (Hackett, 2002). Reproduced with permission of the author.

Impact area	Dynamics	Affective domain	Cognitive domain	Behavioural domain
Sex and sexuality	• Worker is bombarded by sexual stimuli in the work place • Worker listens to accounts of abusive sexuality • Worker subject to sexually deviant fantasies • Young person's sexual behaviours force the worker to make an association between sex, children and abuse	• Repulsion by sexual issues • Worker feels victimised sexually • Worker feels like an abuser • Fear of being perceived an abuser • Own sexual development and experiences highlighted • Unresolved feelings about own victimisation experiences resurface • Feeling that all sex is dirty and sordid	• Re-evaluation of sexual values • Distorted views of sexual normality (abuse = the norm, or all sex = abuse) • Reading sex into everything • Over-salience of sex in cognitive schema • Sexual imagery intrudes into sexual experiences – affective flashbacks to the work/an account of abuse, especially during sex • Development of deviant fantasies	• Sexual abstinence • Questioning of sexual identity (positive and negative connotations) • Over-emphasis on sex • Sexual fixation and increased sexual drive • Arousal problems • Consensual sex becomes a behavioural fix- a way of cleansing self from influence of work • Relationship strain and break-up
Gender and personal identification	• Worker subject to overwhelming accounts of male sexual and non-sexual violence • Abuser attempts to recruit workers into exaggerated gender stereotypes; e.g., men into collusion to distortions about women, women into submissive roles, etc.	• Feelings of gender confusion • Feelings of loss; of innocence, of self, of elements of gender socialisation • Anger at abusers for damaging own gendered identity and gender assumptions • Fear of being associated as an abuser through commonality of gender or other personal aspect • Self guilt and gender shame (men) • Pride in new gender awareness • Personal isolation	• Distorted sense of responsibility for actions of all men • Distorted view of masculine and feminine roles • Review of self and own socialisation, leading to negative or positive new self-awareness • Male worker experiences a 'gender crisis' • Sense of distance from members of same gender (especially men)	• Career revision to cope with gender role strain • Exaggerated behavioural attempts to distance self from identification as abuser • Reluctance to engage in certain professional or personal life activities/ roles, e.g., bathing children • Review of external life activities, e.g., protection of own children
Power and powerlessness	• Abuser engages worker in power struggle • Worker is required to exercise an uncomfortable level of power and control over young person • Young person projects overwhelming level of need upon worker	• Worker feel overwhelmed by extent of young person's unmet need • Feelings of exaggerated power-euphoria • Feelings of exaggerated powerlessness- depression • Deep cynicism about society and the denial of sexual abuse issues • Desire for revenge – wish to right wrongs of victim	• Distorted sense of own power • Increased self confidence and increased level of self esteem • Non-abusive relationships given added value	• Punitive behaviours towards others • Increased respectful behaviours within own relationships • New-found assertiveness

Theoretical developments

At the time in the early 1990's when work with young people who sexually abuse started, there was a paucity of theory as well as practice wisdom in the UK. We were forced to import materials to help us work with the young people that were being referred for a service. This importation took several forms and included using the materials developed in North America and from the field of working with adult male sexual perpetrators. Practice could not wait for research answers or direction. Lessons were learned en route and sometimes in a hard way.

There has been a lot of criticism about adopting materials from both these sources. Steve Myers (1998) has argued that by importing the models and findings from the US, we have constructed a philosophical and practice base that reflects much of that particular construction of the young person who sexually abuses. For example, there was a use of the US model to support punitive and intensive responses to enforce compliance with intervention. Myers argued that experience does not support any greater compliance, contrition or acceptance of responsibility through legal intervention, and it can actually delay intervention. There is also evidence to neutralize the assertion that 50% of adult offenders begin their offending in adolescence. Apart from the problem with any assertion that young people have a fifty-fifty chance of growing into adult sexual offenders, we cannot necessarily transfer research findings from adults to young people. A more informative approach would be to longitudinally study a population of young people to determine their re-abusing behaviour. Where this has been done, the results have been somewhat different from the retrospective studies. Kahn and Chambers (1991) evaluated disparate types of intervention in young abusers' lives and found there was a re-offending rate of about 7%, which matched the other studies they had identified.

The assertion that young people who are left unchecked go on to increase their victims by 55 times is again a retrospective study of adults with juvenile offending histories and is made in such a manner as to suggest inevitability. Prentky and Knight (1993) found no correlation between the age at which people begin offending and the future frequency or seriousness of that offending, which immediately problematizes the above statement.

Lab et al., (1993) have been very critical of sex offender treatment programmes as they are arguably extending the net of social control over many youths who may not need help. Brannon and Troyer (1995) also found little or no difference in recidivism rates between those young people who had attended specialist cognitive-behavioural programmes and those who had been subject to more generalized therapeutic, welfare orientated approaches. This leads to their challenge on the need for specialized intervention programmes.

There has been some recognition that because of the developmental differences between young people and adults and because of the different pathways to their sexually abusive behaviour, the transplant of expertise between the two camps is not helpful. The following differences have been highlighted:

- Most juveniles have not yet developed a relatively fixed pattern of sexual arousal and interest which gives direction to consistent patterns of behaviour (Hunter and Becker, 1994).
- Juveniles have greater developmental fluidity, e.g., many more juveniles have victims of both genders and engage in multiple paraphilic behaviour (Calder, 1997).
- There appears to be considerable crossover between sexual abuse inside and outside the family in the juvenile population (Hunter and Becker, 1994, p. 536-7). For example, Becker et al., (1986) found that 41% of juveniles who abused within the family had also engaged in sexual offences outside the family, whilst Abel, Mittleman and Becker (1985) found that 50% of juveniles admitted to multiple sexual deviations. The most recent research from Monck and New (1996) has also highlighted the crossover across genders in the choice of victims. They found that whilst 83% of young people abused only one gender, some 17% abused both genders. These figures support a cautious approach to risk estimation. James and Neil (1996) found that whilst the majority of victims are female (83.3%), the more victims there are, the greater the probability that males will become the victims.

We also know that there are important differences between young people who sexually abuse and non-sexual offenders, and between child abusers and sexual assaulters. Barbaree et al., (1993) were astute enough to anticipate that the population of young people who sexually abuse may be every bit as heterogeneous as the population of adult sex offenders. O'Callaghan (2002) noted that we have seen a profound shift on focus and orientation concerning interventions with young people who sexually abuse. Perhaps the most significant thing has been the recognition that work with this group of young people has more similarities than differences with other young people who have significant emotional and behavioural disorders (Rich, 1998), with the advantage that we have drawn more heavily from their extensive literature base (e.g., Loeber and Farrington, 1998).

Despite these statements, the theory and practice of that time focused on the offence and the offending behaviour and the confrontational approaches so widely used with adults. It will come as no surprise that such an approach did not engage young people in the work. If there was a mandate, it usually succeeded in getting them to the sessions and contributed to parental cooperation being sustained, but did not facilitate their active involvement. Thus change was unlikely to follow. The key to engagement is the relationship between the worker and the young person and the environment of safety that is created (Calder, 2003b).

Kevin Epps (1999) has provided a very accessible summary of the theoretical terrain in this area (see figure 5). He identified the following influences from the adult field:

Figure 5: A theoretical overview (from Epps, 1999).

Single-factor models	Integrated models
Biological or medical models.	Four-factor model (Finkelhor, 1984).
Psychodynamic theories.	Offender cycle model (Wolf, 1984).
Behavioural theories.	Young Abusers Project Integrated
Social-cognitive theories.	Perspectives Model (Hawkes, 1999).
Social-emotional developmental	Developmental vulnerability models
theories.	(Becker and Kaplan, 1988).
Cognitive theories.	
Trauma theories.	
Family theories.	

Epps went on to name the essential requirements of a theory of young people who sexually abuse and included:

> • *Normal and abnormal development*: there has to be some guidance to help us differentiate between the "normal" and the "abusive" (see Calder, 1997). There are few characteristics of this group that distinguishes them from other young people.
> • *Characteristics of young people who sexually abuse*: there must be some way of explaining the association between the characteristics (such as psychosocial problems, e.g., low self-esteem, poor social skills, peer relationship difficulties, social isolation and loneliness, educational and academic problems, gender-identity confusion, family problems, substance abuse, etc.) found in young people who sexually abuse and their offending. At present, it remains unclear.
> • *Types of offence:* any adequate theory must account for the wide variety of sexually abusive behaviours. A range of offence-related variables could be used to place the abusers into subgroups:
> **Age of victim:** The range may be 2 years to 23 years.
> **Gender of victim:** Some choose boys or girls only, and some choose both. The vast majority of victims are female (69-84%), although as the age of the victim decreases, the victim is more likely to be male.
> **Relationship to victim:** Most of the victims are known to the abuser. However, the more sophisticated abusers may prefer victims who are less familiar, perhaps to avoid detection.
> **Use of force and violence:** Young men tend to use less coercion, force and violence than adult sex offenders. There is a gap in our knowledge about young people who commit serious sexual offences, such as torture and mutilation.

He concluded that there is no adequate theory of why young people sexually abuse. Why has this been so difficult? One answer might be that human behaviour is complex, influenced as it is by a wide range of factors ranging from the action of chemicals on the nervous system to the effect of information and ideas obtained through the media. These factors interact with one another to produce a complex myriad of variables, the effects of which are often difficult to identify and research in isolation. Complex human behaviours, such as sexual offending, are extremely difficult to explain and are seen to be the outcome of an interaction between individual and environmental factors. Trying to prove that one event (such as a particular thought) caused another (such as a particular behaviour) is difficult. Usually there are "hidden" variables that mediate between events. The situation becomes even more complex when events are separated by a long period of time.

Hudson and Ward (1997) and Ward and Hudson (1998) have recently offered a meta-theoretical framework for the construction and development of future theory in the sexual offending area. They pointed out that there has not been any integrated approach to theory building to date, resulting in an ad hoc proliferation of theories that often overlap as well as ignore each other's existence. Their framework takes into account a number of different theory construction principles and ideas. It differentiates between different levels of theory, and stresses the importance of distinguishing between distal and proximal causal factors. They begin to locate the existing theory within the framework and argue that an integrated approach using their framework will benefit workers and researchers significantly. This is needed if we are to neutralize the offenders power base and further invite them to accept responsibility for their behaviour.

Epps and Fisher (2004) have argued that we should now aim to group offenders according to offence and offender characteristics given the evidence that different clusters of physchosocial problems are associated with different types of sexual offending which, in turn, follow different developmental pathways. Identification of these pathways will have important implications for prevention, through early intervention and for treatment.

Typology is the study of a class or group that has common characteristics. Sex offender typologies can be helpful in distinguishing different groupings of offenders, recognising that there may be crossover between the different types of behaviour. Two problems with typologies is the tendency to fit a particular offender into a category that may not fit, or failure to acknowledge that an offender may exhibit behaviours from two or more categories (Cumming and Buell, 1997). Because of the heterogeneity of sexual offenders, typological frameworks have been attempted to construct homogeneous sub-groups and thus categorisations of sex offender. Tomison (1995) has argued that these typologies are crude and unreliable due to the extensive overlap of various behaviours by offenders. Epps (1996) also argued that they often involve an over-simplification of existing data, although they can be helpful to workers when having to choose between various forms of disposal and treatment options.

Terminology

Definitions are very important. If they are too narrow, they restrict our understanding, figures of incidence and prevalence as well as our intervention threshold. Conversely, if they are too broad, they are all embracing and often detract from focusing in on the highest risk cases. Sexual abuse is a cultural issue, a social issue, a political issue, an economic issue, a legal issue, a medical issue, a psychological issue, an educational issue, and a spiritual issue (Groth and Oliveri, 1989). Child sexual abuse is, therefore, a complex and multi-determined problem which can be viewed from a wide range of perspectives. This is reflected in the number and variance of definitions, most of which are rigorously defended by the originating discipline. Thus, whilst child sexual abuse falls within the remit of a wide variety of professional groups: social workers, teachers, health service workers, police and legal professionals – they rarely discuss the same phenomenon, tending to use criteria in line with the goals of their particular profession. There is often more consensus at the severe end of the continuum, whilst there are many differing and often divergent opinions when the consideration relates to non-penetrative acts. Child sexual abuse thus tends to be a blanket term for a multitude of vaguely defined acts (Haugaard and Reppucci, 1988, p. 17).

Another reason why we struggle to develop adequate theories is the lack of any consistent definition of the problem. Different terms have been used to describe the same behaviour, e.g., adolescent sex offenders, sexual aggressors, paedophiles, child molesters, etc.

Intervention (Print and Morrison, 2000)

Intervention can be considered at three different levels.

Primary intervention

Primary intervention involves societal based strategies aimed at changing familial and cultural understanding, attitudes and behaviours. We know that only a small percentage of cases come to the attention of professionals and thus dealing with these only would be dealing with the tip of the iceberg. In order to be effective, a comprehensive range of educative and information sharing strategies are required. For example, professionals and the public should have a much clearer understanding of: what is acceptable and developmentally "normal" sexual behaviour and what should be regarded as abusive; how individuals should respond if they have concerns; the professional services that are available and the resources they offer. There is a need for research to develop further insight into the role of pornography, patriarchy, and oppressive attitudes towards sexuality in promoting and maintaining sexually abusive behaviour. In addition, at an educative and awareness raising level, it is important for children and young people to be given the opportunity to explore issues of sexuality and sexually appropriate and inappropriate behaviour.

Secondary intervention

Secondary intervention involves specialized preventative intervention with groups of young people who are considered to be at increased risk of developing abusive behaviours. Whilst we are not able to predict accurately who will go on to sexually abuse, there is sufficient knowledge to direct preventative work towards some higher risk groups. For example, whilst the majority of victims of sexual abuse do not go on to sexually abuse others, it is known that a significant number of people who sexually abuse have been physically, sexually or emotionally abused and neglected themselves (see Way, 2002 for a detailed review). Until the professional system tackles this problem and provides specific prevention programmes as part of a therapeutic response to all children and young people who have been sexually abused, the scope for secondary intervention will remain limited.

Hackett (2002b) has articulated clearly how to work with the victim within the abuser in a way that acknowledges their own history but holds them accountable for their abusive behaviour. Hackett is supportive of the view that practitioners working primarily with abusive behaviours should build into their programmes opportunities to encourage the young person to explore the interconnections between the two elements of their experiences, their similarities and differences, and the young person's affective and behavioural responses to the totality of their abuse experiences. This element of work is therefore not meant as a stand-alone model of practice, nor should it be envisaged merely as a one-off session within the course of a "sex offence-specific" programme, but it is more a consistent theme or thread running throughout intervention designed to address a young person's abusive behaviour. Alan Jenkins' work on addressing the dual sexual abuse experience of young male abusers provides a helpful model for such an integrative approach (Jenkins, 1995). Adapting Jenkins' model slightly, we can conceive of a six-stage process in addressing victimisation experiences:

> 1) Acknowledge the significance of the young person's sexual abuse experience and the importance of its disclosure.
> 2) Help the young man reflect upon the impact of the abuse upon his development, attitudes, feelings and behaviours.
> 3) Encourage the young man to draw distinctions between his own abusive behaviour and his own abuse and abuser.
> 4) Acknowledge that facing abuse is a sign of maturity and respect (to self and others).
> 5) Help the young man to de-construct his experience of victimisation.
> 6) Help the young men to re-construct his experience of victimisation.

Table One demonstrates practitioner tasks within each of the stages, together with some suggested interventions.

Table One: Addressing Young Abusers' Sexual Victimisation Experiences (Jenkins, 1995, adapted by Hackett, 2002). Reproduced with permission of the author.

STAGE	THERAPIST'S TASKS	EXAMPLES OF INTERVENTION
1) Acknowledge the significance of the young person's sexual abuse experience and its disclosure.	Stress the young person's courage in being able to address both aspects of his abuse experience. Encourage the young person to own up to and quantify the pain, distress and unfairness of his abuse experience.	• *Is this the first time that you have talked about__?* • *What did it take for you to be able to speak out?* • *How has it been to keep your abuse inside?* • *How does it affect you to recall your abuse?* • *How much (out of ten) has the abuse hurt you?* • *What are you proving (to yourself and your abuser) by speaking out?* • *What difference will speaking out make to you/to your family/ to how others see you?*
2) Reflect the impact of the abuse upon the young man.	Reflect the impact of the abuse and mobilise it as a force for responsibility and behavioural change. Reflect the link between the abuse experience and the abusive behaviour.	• *Is it fair that you are expected to face up to your abuse, if no one has tried to understand what you have been through?* • *Who knows how hard it is for you to face up to what you have done to the victim?* • *How could coming to terms with your own abuse help you to face up to what you did to victim?* • *Who else is aware of how difficult it is to live with your offence when you know how it feels to be abused?*
3) Help the young man to draw distinctions between his own abusive behaviour and his own abuse and abuser.	Focus upon the abuser s lack of courage/ inability to stop. Highlight the difference between the young person facing the abuse and the abuser s denial.	• *Did your abuser ever face up to his abuse of you, like you are doing now about victim?* • *Do you think that your abuser has ever taken the time to think about you and what he did?* • *How do you feel about yourself now that you have had the courage to do something he has never done?* • *By starting to make changes and be committed to an abuse-free life, do you think that you are following his ways or are you breaking free from his influence?* • *What do you think your abuser would think to hear you breaking his secrets?* • *Will being honest about the things that have happened give him or you more power?*
4) Acknowledge that facing abuse is a sign of maturity and respect (self and others).	Acknowledge how the young person is showing self respect and respect to those he hurt. Stress the alternatives for dealing with the legacy of abuse other than to hurt others.	• *Do you know what I mean when I say that burying your hurt feelings usually ends up with you taking them out on someone else?* • *Have you ever faced your feelings of hurt and talked about them as maturely as you are doing today?* • *What ways are you learning not to take out hurt feelings on others?* • *What difference will this make?*
5) De-construct the young person s experience of victimisation.	Pick up on clues given by the young person. Help the young person split up the abuse experience into manageable bits. Avoid the young person being overwhelmed or flooded.	• *Whose idea was it?* • *How old were you when it started?* • *How old was your abuser?* • *How did your abuser trick you/set you up for the abuse?* • *How did he try to convince you it was OK?* • *How did he try to silence you?* • *How did he make you feel like you were responsible or to blame?* • *How did he make you carry his shame?*
6) Re-construct the young person s experience of victimisation.	Chart responses and build up a picture over time, e.g., timelines. Highlight the new meanings of the abuse.	• *What difference does it make to your memories and understandings?* • *What light does this shed on your choice to abuse victim?* • *How can we understand things differently now?* • *What does this free you up to achieve now?* • *Can you handle facing up to your abuse of the victim even though you still have painful memories of your own past?* • *What would it say about you if you could do this despite the pain your own abuse has caused?*

Tertiary intervention

Tertiary intervention is aimed at preventing continued offending by known abusers. This requires a coordinated central government response, a strategy for local interpretation, close inter-agency collaboration and an organizational environment in which agencies, managers and practitioners establish an infrastructure both within and between agencies.

Operational Considerations

Risk refinement and extension

The need to categorize risk is an essential part of the assessment process. Of concern therefore is the fact that workers have been forced to use for some considerable time invalidated instruments and toolkits in order to decide whether someone was high, medium or low risk in general rather than in specific terms. There was little hope of getting very many workers to make a low risk diagnosis. If they got it wrong and the young person reoffended, then there would be blame apportioned and further victims. High risk was the easy option: it covers backs and there are no professional consequences if you get it wrong. There are, however, immense consequences for the young person when they are labelled high risk in addition to their sexually abusive behaviour. They may then act to "the label" as they can see no way out. They have their denial entrenched and any potential for change is affected.

One of the proud achievements has been the progress made in relation to developing better frameworks for assessing risk with young people who sexually abuse and how this has now reached a level where it is informing developments needed in the adult sex offender field. As historically the case, the starting point was importing the developments from the adult sex offender field. These took the form of actuarial risk tools and the emergence of stable and dynamic risk factors so we did not concentrate exclusively on previous behaviour.

Static, stable and dynamic risk factors

We know that future behaviour can never be predicted with certainty. Nevertheless, a growing body of research indicates that well-informed practitioners can predict sexual recidivism with at least moderate accuracy. Hanson (1998; 1999) argued that risk assessments consider two distinct concepts: enduring propensities, or potentials to re-offend; and factors that indicate the onset of new offences. These offence triggers are not random, but can be expected to be organised into predictable patterns (offence cycles), some unique to the individual and some common to most sexual offenders.

Different evaluation questions require the consideration of different types of risk factors. *Static, historical variables* (e.g., prior offences, childhood maladjustment) can indicate deviant developmental trajectories and, as such, enduring propensities to sexually offend. Evaluating changes in risk levels (e.g., treatment outcome), however, requires the consideration of *dynamic, changeable risk factors* (e.g., cooperation with supervision, deviant sexual preferences). The relatively low recidivism rates of sexual offenders makes it difficult to detect dynamic risk factors. Over a 4-5 year period, approximately 10-15% of sexual offenders will be detected committing a new sexual offence (Hanson and Bussiere, 1998). Although age is sometimes considered a dynamic factor, the most important dynamic factors are those that respond to treatment. *Dynamic factors* can further be classified as *stable or acute*. *Stable factors* have the potential to change, but typically endure for months or years (e.g., personality disorder) and, as such, represent ongoing risk potential. In contrast, *acute factors* (e.g., negative mood) may be present for a short duration (minutes, days) and can signal the timing of offending. Most risk decisions require consideration of both static and dynamic risk factors. Calder (2000) has reviewed these concepts in detail as they relate to adult male sex offenders.

Prentky et al., (2000) and Ryan (2000) have started to consider the concept of dynamic and static risk factors with young people who sexually abuse (see figure 7 next page). Ryan has argued that the more research that becomes available with this group shows that they are not noticeably different from other groups of young offenders, such as those who self-harm or commit violent offences. She has provided us with a useful embryonic and at this stage hypothetical framework for considering factors relevant to abusive functioning. The usefulness of her framework is considerable as she has extended the concept of risk factors to include assets. This is an important extension of the concepts developed in the adult field and are consistent with the view that risk assessment is about balancing risks and assets, weighting them within the presenting situation and then coming to an informed conclusion. Jane Gilgun, in her work with children exhibiting sexual behaviour problems, developed a framework that also embraces assets alongside risks. She argued that it is important to have a framework that explores assets as well as risks (see figure 6 below). The ideal is that we protect children from risks. However, the power of risks can be moderated by creating an imbalance with greater assets. The child with high risks and high assets may be less dysfunctional than the child with few risks but few assets. The most dysfunctional outcome is likely to be the child with high risks and low assets.

Figure 6: Balancing risks and assets (Gilgun, 1999)

LOW ASSET LOW RISK	HIGH ASSET LOW RISK
LOW ASSET HIGH RISK	HIGH ASSET HIGH RISK

The material developed by Gail Ryan suggested the following (see figure 7) when assessing young people who sexually abuse.

Figure 7: Towards a framework for assessing risk in young people who sexually abuse (Ryan, 2000). Reproduced with permission of the author.

Static risk factors are historical and therefore unchangeable.

Static factors

RISKS	ASSETS
- Prenatal insults	- Prenatal care
- Premature/traumatic birth	- Normative birth
- Unempathic care	- Empathic care
- Caregiver loss/disruption	- Consistent caregiver(s)
- Trust failure	- Trustworthy relationship
- Disordered attachment	- Secure attachment
- Dysfunctional modelling	- Normal growth/development
- Witness domestic violence	- Functional modelling
- Abuse, neglect, failure to thrive, trauma	- Nurturance and protection

Stable risk factors are those that remain somewhat constant across the life-span. They are less changeable although they may be moderated.

Stable factors

RISKS	ASSETS
- Difficult temperament	- Easy/adaptive temperament
- Low functioning	- Average-high intelligence (IQ)
- Learning disability	- Positive internal working model
- Heritable psychiatric disorders	(self and others)
- Chronic PTSD reactivity	- Normative physical and neurological functioning

Dynamic risk factors are constantly changing, either purposefully or by chance. They are clearly changeable.

Dynamic risk factors

GLOBAL (foreseeable in life span)	CIRCUMSTANTIAL (specific/fluctuating daily)
- Constant/expected stressors	- Current/unexpected stressors (conflict or emotional trigger)
- Unresolved emotional issues	- Perceived threat vulnerability
- Unsafe environment/ persons	- Lowered self-esteem/efficacy
- Injury/illness	- Negative expectations
- Temporary disabilities	- Isolation/lack of support
- Lack of opportunity/support	- Mood dysregulation: anger, depression, anxiety
- Change/loss	- Projection/misattributions
- Sexual drive/arousal	- Limited options/skill deficits
- Abusive memories	- Abusive memory/fantasy
- Failed relationships	- Sexual arousal/thought
- Access to vulnerable persons	- Lowered inhibitions
	- Access to vulnerable persons

Ryan also sets out the following observable outcomes of evidence of change relevant to decreased risk:

- Consistently defines all abuse (self, others, property).
- Acknowledges risk (foresight and safety planning).
- Consistently recognizes/interrupts cycle (no later than the first thought of an abusive solution).
- Demonstrates new coping skills (when stressed).
- Demonstrates empathy (sees cues of others and responds).
- Accurate attributions of responsibility (takes responsibility for own behaviour and doesn't try to control the behaviour of others).
- Rejects abusive thoughts as dissonant (incongruent with self-image).

It is important that we simultaneously consider the outcomes related to increased health:

- Pro-social relationship skills (closeness, trust and trustworthiness).
- Positive self-image (able to be separate, independent and competent).
- Able to resolve conflicts and make decisions (assertive, tolerant, forgiving, cooperative, able to negotiate and compromise).
- Celebrates good and experiences pleasure (able to relax and play).
- Able to manage frustration and unfavourable events (anger management and self-protection).
- Works/struggles to achieve delayed gratification (persistent pursuit of goals, able to concentrate).
- Able to think and communicate effectively (rational cognitive processing, adequate verbal skills).
- Adaptive sense of purpose and future.

Actuarial risk tools

Actuarial methods utilise statistical techniques to generate risk predictors.

Since no single factor is sufficient to determine whether offenders will or will not re-offend, practitioners need to consider a range of relevant risk factors. There are three plausible methods by which risk factors can be combined into overall evaluations of risk:

> 1) Empirically guided clinical evaluations: which begins with the overall recidivism base rate, and then adjusts the risk level by considering factors that have been empirically associated with recidivism risk. The risk factors to be considered are explicit, but the method for weighting the importance of the risk factors is left to the judgement of the worker.
> 2) Pure actuarial predictions: in contrast, explicitly state not only the variables to be considered, but also the precise procedure through which ratings of these variables will be translated into a risk level. In the pure actuarial sense, risk levels are estimated through mechanical, arithmetic procedures requiring a minimum of judgement.

3) Clinically adjusted actuarial predictions: begins with a pure actuarial prediction, but then raises or lowers the risk level based on consideration of relevant factors that were not included in the actuarial method (see Quinsey et al., 1995). As research develops, actuarial methods can be expected to consistently outperform clinical predictions. With the current state of knowledge, however, both actuarial and guided clinical approaches can be expected to provide risk assessments with a moderate level of accuracy.

There are a number of strengths of adopting an actuarial approach to the work:

- They are consistent with the expectation of evidence-based social care interventions.
- They are useful in establishing those risk predictors which have a proven track record.
- They are useful in establishing the relevant base rates for clinical assessment.
- They are useful in increasing the accuracy of risk assessments.
- They increase the levels of consistency and reliability (adapted from Kemshall, 2001).

Equally there are a number of problems and potential pitfalls:

- Any tool has limitations if inappropriately used.
- Statistical fallacy is the problem when seeking to transfer the information about a population to an individual user under assessment.
- The use of meta-analyses (research based on the analysis of a large number of primary studies) to develop risk predictors can result in overly simple outcomes which fail to capture the complexity of the processes involved. We often require a human dimension to explain the behaviour.
- A further problem relates to the predictions of risk where there is a low incidence of risky behaviours in the population as a whole. This is especially true in the case of child sexual abuse (Kemshall, 2001).
- Collect accurate information in cases. In fact it may encourage a tick box approach.
- Cover all permutations of situations.
- Undertake compound predictions in complex situations. This arises from inevitable shortage of data and base rate problems (Hollows, 2003).
- Specific samples: either convicted or imprisoned people.
- Time of offending not addressed.
- Consequences not addressed (risk/dangerousness).
- Role of other behaviours ambiguous.
- Recidivism based on official report.
- Don't apply to women, young people or un-convicted men (Kennington, 2003).

Problems in the Application of Actuarial Frameworks to Young People Who Sexually Abuse

Print et al., (2001) have argued that these materials developed with adults cannot be easily transferred to young people. The reasons cited include the following:

- Research indicates that the recidivism rate for young people who sexually offend is significantly lower than that of adult sex offenders. Alexander (1999), for example, analysed the data of over 1000 young people who had sexually offended in a 3-5 year follow up study and found an overall recidivist rate of 7.1% as compared to an adult overall rate of 13%. This low rate of known re-offending makes actuarial risk protocols difficult to conduct. We cannot accurately predict future sexual offending behaviour of juveniles who participated in the non-violent sexual abuse of children.
- Young people are unlikely to have established a fixed pattern of sexual thoughts and behaviours. Their sexual preferences, fantasies and behaviours are often in a state of flux and, as yet, research has not been able to determine what inappropriate sexual thoughts are significantly linked to the risks of re-offending against adults, peers or children.
- Adolescent experimentation in a range of antisocial (sexual and non-sexual) behaviours is not uncommon. We know from research that most do not continue such behaviours into adulthood. It is important not only to identify the factors that increase the likelihood of persistent inappropriate behaviour but also those factors that inhibit such behaviour.
- Young people are subjected to greater influence and management of others than most adults. Most young people have parents/carers, teachers, peer groups and other adults who can exert influence in their day-to-day lives and thereby significantly impact on the implementation of risk management plans and strategies. Assessment and therapeutic interventions must therefore include attention to a young person's context and wider network.
- Most young people who sexually abuse others have been subject to some form of trauma or abuse themselves. For many this can mean that related short-term and longer-term effects of abuse may be present and require attention. Thus assessment and intervention must address a young person's physical and emotional health, educational and support needs.
- The system response to young people who sexually abuse is very different to adult sex offenders. The legal framework and the justice system are notably different for young people and in most cases multi-agency involvement is likely to be required, involving child care, youth justice, health, education and others.
- In short, these differences imply that many models developed for work with adult sex offenders are unlikely to be suitable for work with adolescents or younger children.

New, developmentally appropriate, models that are holistic in approach and that recognise this group of young people as "children in need" (DOH, 1999) are more likely to prove effective and useful in work with adolescents and younger children who sexually abuse.

The Development of a Clinically Adjusted Actuarial Risk Tool

Although research is in embryonic stages we are already identifying some primary signposts to factors associated with the persistence of reoffending. These include a general pattern of conduct disorder and other non-sexual offending, poor social functioning, discontinuity of care, trauma and neglect, high levels of family dysfunction, evidence of offence-planning or sexual pre-occupation and early drop out from treatment programmes (Bentovim, 2002; Rasmussen, 1999).

Despite such research developments in the field of young people who sexually abuse, research lags behind practice significantly. Specialist bodies such as G-MAP (Greater Manchester Adolescent Project based in Manchester, England) have analysed the cases that they have worked with over a decade and supplemented the deficit of research to produce a clinically adjusted actuarial risk tool (Print et al, 2001). This has now been extended to young people with a learning disability (O'Callaghan, 2001) and families (Morrison and Wilkinson, 2001). Similar developments have also emerged in Canada (Worling and Curwen, 2001) and in the US (Prentky et al., 2000).

The AIM (Assessment, Intervention and Moving On) model has utilised available research and literature to develop an initial assessment model that helps to provide a structured approach to the gathering and analysis of information about a young person, their problematic behaviour, their family and their environment. The model is intended as a framework that will assist practitioners in gathering and analysing relevant information in order to make initial recommendations about needs and risks.

This may include recommendations about placements, supervision requirements, case management, court disposal, plans for therapeutic work with individuals and families, and an initial prognosis for outcome. The model also usefully provides practitioners with a tool to assist them in articulating a structured basis for their opinions and thereby supporting the public exercising of professional judgement.

Figure 8: The four domains of AIM.

Offence Specific	**Developmental**
<ul><li>Nature of index sexual offence/abuse</li><li>Young person and family's attitude to victim</li><li>Amount and nature of offence planning</li><li>Use of threats, violence or aggression during commission of offence/abuse</li><li>Young person's offending and abusive behaviour history</li><li>Previous professional involvement with young person and family regarding offending/abusive behaviours</li><li>Motivation to engage with professionals</li></ul>	<ul><li>Resilience factors</li><li>Health issues</li><li>Experiences of physical/sexual/emotional abuse or neglect</li><li>Witnessed domestic violence</li><li>Quality of the young person's early life experiences</li><li>History of behaviour problems</li><li>Sexual development and interests</li></ul>
Family/Carers	**Environment**
<ul><li>Level of functioning</li><li>Attitudes and beliefs</li><li>Sexual boundaries</li><li>Parental competence</li></ul>	<ul><li>Young person's access to vulnerable others</li><li>Opportunity for further offending</li><li>Community attitudes to young person and family</li><li>Wider supervisory and support network</li></ul>

Once gathered the information can be used to identify which factors in the empirically/clinically based continuums are relevant to the young person, his abusive behaviour, his family and environment (see figure 9).

The concept of wellness and holistic treatment introduced by Longo (2002) is built upon a similar premise and the extension of relapse prevention to include a focus on strengths within a broader framework is refreshing and progressive.

Figure 9: Continuum of Indicators of Concerns (Print et al., 2001).

High Concerns A	Medium Concerns B	Medium Concerns C	Low Concerns D
1. * Young person has previous convictions for sexual offences or evidence of previous sexual offending	1. Young person has been suspected of previous sexual assaults	1. Young person has poor capacity for empathy	1. First known assault/one assault
2. * Formal diagnosis of conduct disorder or a history of interpersonal aggression	2. Early onset of severe behavioural problems	2. Young person denies responsibility for assault	2. Non-penetrative (including attempts) assault
3. * Very poor social skills / deficits in intimacy skills	3. Young person diagnosed with ADHD	3. Has difficulties in coping with negative feelings	3. No history of significant trauma or abuse
4. * Use of violence or threats of violence during assault	4. Cold callous attitude in commission of assault	4. Has poor sexual boundaries	4. Demonstrates remorse/empathy
5. * Self-reported sexual interest in children	5. Young person diagnosed with depression or other significant mental health problems	5. Parents express anger or no empathic concern towards victim	5. Assault appears to be experimental or peer influenced
6. * Young person blames victim	6. Young person has significant distorted thoughts about sexual behaviours	6. High level of parental / carer together with family denial	6. No significant history of non-sexual assaults
7. Persistently threatens to commit abusive acts	7. Obsessive/pre-occupation with sexual thoughts/ pornography	7. Social group is predominantly pro-criminal	7. Healthy peer relationships
8. Has persistent aggressive/sadistic sexual thoughts about others	8. Copes with negative emotions by use of sexual thoughts, behaviours or use of pornography/graffiti	8. Family members include Schedule 1 offences	8. No documented school problems
9. Has history of cruelty towards animals	9. Targets specific victims because of perceived vulnerability		9. No history of behavioural/ emotional problems
10. Little concern about being caught	10. * Pattern of discontinuity of care / poor attachments		
11. * High levels of trauma e.g., physical, emotional, sexual abuse, neglect or witnessing domestic violence	11. Unsupervised access to potential victims		
12. * High levels of family dysfunction / abusive or harsh child rearing regime	12. Young person regularly engaged in significant substance abuse		
13. * Evidence of detailed planning			
14. * Early drop out from treatment programme			

High Strengths

A

1. Young person has ability to reflect and understand consequences of offence behaviour
2. Young person is willing to engage in treatment to address abusive behaviour
3. Young person has positive plans / goals
4. Young person has positive talents and interests
5. Young person has good problem solving and negotiation skills
6. Young person has at least one emotional confidant
7. Young person has positive relationships with school or employers
8. Young person has experienced consistent positive care
9. Parents demonstrate good protective attitudes and behaviours
10. Family has clear, positive boundaries in place
11. Family demonstrates good communications
12. Family demonstrates ability to positively process emotional issues
13. Family is positive about receiving help
14. Young person lives in supportive environment
15. Network of support and supervision available to young person

Medium strengths

B

1. Young person has at least one parent/carer who supports and is able to supervise
2. Young person demonstrates remorse for offence (even if not accepting responsibility)
3. Parents/carers are healthy and there is no other family trauma or crisis
4. Parents demonstrate responsible attitudes and skills in family management
5. Parents/carers have no history of own abuse or abusive experiences are resolved
6. Family has positive social network
7. Community is neutral towards young person/family

Low Strengths (High Need)

C

1. Young person appears to not care what happens
2. Young person has poor communication skills
3. Young person has no support/is rejected by parents/carers
4. Young person has been excluded from school/unemployed
5. Isolated family
6. Absence of supportive/structured living environment
7. Parents/carers unable to supervise
8. Family is enmeshed in unhealthy social network
9. Family has high levels of stress
10. History of unresolved significant abuse in family
11. Family refuses to engage with professionals
12. Domestic violence in family
13. Community is hostile towards young person/family

Assessment Frameworks

Although not actuarially derived, Calder (1997; 2001) has formulated an evidence-based framework for conducting core assessments of young people who sexually abuse. The components of this framework are identified in figure 10 below:

Figure 10: A framework for core assessment (Calder, 2001)

Individual History
- Demographic data
- Educational-occupational history
- Peer relationships
- Interpersonal relationships/intimacy
- Attachment history
- Assertiveness
- Aggression
- Anger
- Self-esteem and self-concept
- Social competence
- Social skills and competence
- Health and medical history
- Non-sexual criminality
- Drug and alcohol abuse

Family composition and functioning
- Perceptions of family life
- Family problems, secrets, rules, boundaries and alliances
- Family interactions
- Support issues
- Coping strategies
- Marital relationship and violence
- History of child abuse/witnessing domestic violence

Sexual history, knowledge and attitudes
- Sex education and sexual knowledge
- Sexual experiences
- Masturbation history
- Sexual fantasies
- Cognitive distortions
- Sexual attitudes – to men, women and children
- Sexual beliefs
- Sexual values
- Sexual self-concept
- Attachment and intimacy
- Sexual interests and preferences
- Sexual arousal
- Sexual blocks and dysfunction
- Sexual orientation
- Effects of drugs, alcohol and pornography on sexual behaviour

The alleged abuse
- Aspects of preparation
- Election of victim(s)
- Level of consent and power relationships
- Creation of abusive situation(s)
- What they did to the victim
- What they required the victim to do
- The use of coercion
- Evidence of co-abusers

Denial and excuses
- What is the source of their denial?
- Is it a shifting denial?
- What are the consequences of addressing their abusive behaviour?
- Where are they on the denial continuum?

Victim empathy and awareness
- How aware are any young people of victim empathy?
- How might the young person's own experiences influence their thoughts and behaviour?
- Are we happy that re-abuse or victim retaliation is not a current issue for the young person?

Motivation to change
- Where are they on the motivation continuum?
- Do they know why it is important for them to change?
- Do they have the ability to change?
- Who do they want to support them in their efforts to change?

Feedback and report
- Should provide an appraisal of the information collected to inform treatment, disposal or mandate needed, risk management strategies needed, etc.

Clearly work is needed to ensure that such proposed frameworks are informed by the available research evidence, although the concerns about an exclusive focus on the "what works?" agenda does allow for such frameworks to retain a meaningful place in practice. However, the work of Worling (2002) has shown that such clinically derived models can indicate falsely assumed levels of risk. One frequently cited example is that of denial where workers have long noted its existence and believed that entrenched denial correlates with heightened risk, whereas recent research has found that denial and minimization have no relationship to sexual recidivism in relation to young people who sexually abuse (Worling, 2002) as well as adults (Hanson, 2003).

Culturally and Developmentally Sensitive Practice

Sexual aggression fundamentally reflects an abuse of inter-personal power. The wider societal context forms the background and often underpins the vulnerability of the group or individuals to exploitation or abuse. Young people who sexually abuse may at one and the same time be the most disadvantaged and powerless in society, whilst on an interpersonal level have exploited power over those weaker than themselves (O'Callaghan and Corran, 2004). Practitioners have frequently struggled to resolve these tensions, which may in part explain the paucity of provision or even discussion of services for young people who sexually abuse who have learning difficulties (O'Callaghan, 1999; 2004); those from ethnic minorities (save Abassi and Jamal, 2002; Lewis, 1999 and Mir and Okotie, forthcoming); or young females who sexually abuse (Blues et al., 1999; Robinson, 2005; Williams and Buehler, 2002). These areas are in need of significant development.

Hackett (1999) has argued that practitioners need to explore and critically appraise their own beliefs and attitudes in order to engage with young people who sexually abuse in ways that empower change.

Hackett (2000) developed a very useful framework for developing anti-oppressive practice in this field. He set out the following questions as an integral part of an anti-oppressive response for workers engaging in assessment and intervention:

- What have you done to critically examine your own values and perceptions regarding young people who sexually abuse, with specific regard to those from minority groups?
- How does your assessment make a distinction between the person's possible control of personal problems and external constraints beyond his/her control?
- Are you restricting your assessment because you think that there are no suitable resources for this particular person as a result of his/her difference or minority status?
- Is your assessment of the person's behaviour located within a clear child protection framework, where the needs of victims are the paramount concern?
- Is your assessment sensitive to the cultural implications, expectations and aspirations of the person without collusion on the basis of these cultural issues?
- Have you challenged and included critical assessment of racist and oppressive practice and procedures of other institutions and professionals involved?
- What steps have you taken to check whether your assessment is influenced by oppressive pathological or oppressive liberal approaches?

Figure 11 highlights some of these key steps within this multi-levelled approach for individuals wishing to developing anti-oppressive responses in sexual abuse work:

Figure 11: Preparing for anti-oppressive practice: a multi-leveled approach for the practitioner (Hackett, 2000). Reproduced with permission of the author.

LEVEL ONE: The Intra-personal (The Self)
- Personal acknowledgement of the existence of power imbalances within one's relationships with others.
- A readiness to focus on how one's own personal and professional power is used and experienced.
- Ownership of one's own personal power.
- An ability to maintain critical openness with respect to individual mothers and their families, etc.
- Recognition of others' difference and a willingness to validate and value this in contact with others.
- Scrutiny of personal values and behaviour, with specific regard to sex, sexuality, gender and race.

LEVEL TWO: The Organisational (Self-Organisation)
- An organisational framework which promotes partnership and values difference in all interactions with people who abuse and their families.
- Written aims and objectives to services for mothers, and an explicit philosophy agreed upon at organisational level to underpin practice.
- A clear and unambiguous policy on exchange of information and the limited nature of confidentiality
- An anti-oppressive statement, which has as its core prevention and protection of actual and potential victims, but which defines service users' rights.
- An agreed organisational risk management policy in respect of sexual abuse work.
- Power issues centre stage when planning services and when allocating resources within the organisation.

LEVEL THREE: The Interpersonal (Self-Other)
- An interpersonal approach which builds upon people's (and their family's) experiences to consolidate their strengths.
- A belief in the possibility of change and a desire to be a vehicle of change for the person who has abused.
- Practice which acknowledges and values the diversity of individual people's experiences of power, abuse and discrimination.
- A willingness to hear and embrace people's wider experiences, rather than a focus solely upon "the offence".
- Practice models which seek to understand the complex connections between people's experiences, context and abusive behaviour (Hackett, 2000).

Inclusion of Family

A major component of working with young people who sexually abuse is family work. While some clients may have families who are unwilling or unavailable to participate, whenever possible the family should be included in the treatment process and family treatment conducted routinely.

The reality in the UK is that family work is still largely under-recognized, under-funded, under-researched and unpublished. In other words, the point has not arrived where family work is accepted as a core part of any service to young people who commit sexual offences. Its status is that of an optional extra which depends on the commitment, orientation, and resources of individual practitioners. For those who are engaged in such work, it is largely a lone journey through uncharted waters, without compass, maps, or preparation, seeking by trial and error equally to avoid being sucked under by the sheer size and complexity of the task, or simply to lose direction and to run aground in the fog of organizational paralysis and inter-agency confusion (Duane and Morrison, 2004).

The consequences of not engaging families are considerable. Whilst for a small minority of these young people their futures may not lie at home, or they may not wish to return home, the majority will be un-convicted young people living at home, subject neither to family court proceedings (care or supervision orders) nor placed on child protection registers. In other words, their engagement and maintenance in any form of therapeutic work will hinge upon support and endorsement of such work from those who care for them. The longer the family is left without services and support the less likely it is that that they will engage when it is eventually offered. Even for those who are subject to court orders, at the psychological level the permission and support of parents remains far more significant in their engagement in therapeutic work than such external influences. The issue from the young persons' perspective is a simple one: will their parents be able to accept and love them if they reveal the true nature of their sexually abusive behaviour?

With regard specifically to the families of young people who have sexually abused, the research, although limited, provides some support for family environment as a discriminating variable. Family dysfunction, abuse and neglect may be predictive in the development of sexually offending behaviour (Vizard, Moncks & Mish, 1995). However, because of the wide variability in methodologies and samples, these studies are difficult to interpret. It is possible only to say that these factors may be linked to the development of sexually abusive behaviour in some young people.

Chaffin (1998) noted that, on the basis of clinical impressions of those working within the adult sex offender population, there are many assumptions accepted as conventional wisdom within the area of young people who sexually abuse. Included amongst these is the idea that all parents and families of young people who have sexually abused are generally dysfunctional and that personal victimization is usually present in the young person's history. However, the empirical support for these is limited. The research is in its infancy and while significant progress has been made, there is much ground yet to be covered. There are many gaps in the research and results need to be confirmed in well-designed larger controlled trials (Duane and Morrison, 2004).

Effectiveness of Intervention

An increasing consensus has been emerging that treatment intervention with young people who sexually abuse needs to be multi-systemic and located within the young person's developmental progress (Bourke and Donohue, 1996). This is in recognition that a "one size fits all" approach is not a useful one. To date however, the only randomised comparative study published in relation to young people who sexually abuse has been that evaluating the impact of multi-systemic therapy (MST) compared with a traditional counselling approach (Borduin et al., 1990).

MST is an ecologically focused treatment that addresses multiple determinants of behaviour. To improve community and family safety and to promote responsible behaviour in children and young people, effective treatments must be applied to the problems of young people who sexually abuse and child sexual behaviour problems. Prevailing treatments for young people who sexually abuse have limited empirical support. The lack of support does not necessarily equate to ineffectiveness; rather, additional research is sorely needed in this field (Letourneau, 2004).

Letourneau and Swenson (2004) have reviewed the literature around MST with both children and young people who sexually abuse and found considerable support as to its appeal as well as its apparent effectiveness. They argue that if we are to take seriously the problem of sexual abuse, we must take seriously the scientific evaluation of treatment. Preliminary evidence supports the efficacy of both MST and sex-offender specific (SOS) as used with young people who sexually abuse. Likewise, preliminary evidence supports the use of several treatment modalities with children, all of which have substantial caregiver components. We believe that any treatment that purports to address these problems, should at minimum, address factors across a youth's ecology rather than limiting the focus exclusively (or nearly so) on individual youth characteristics. Such a strategy seems insufficient in light of the multitude of factors associated with sexual offending and with sexual behaviour problems. However, only empirically rigorous research that compares well-defined treatments is capable of answering this question. Thus, additional randomised controlled trials should compare the prevailing treatments (e.g., SOS in the case of juvenile sexual offenders) with experimental treatments (e.g., MST) and should include long-term follow up on well-defined targeted behaviours.

Brown and Kolko (1998) in their critique of existing treatment studies noted that the treatment outcome literature is still developing; the relationship between risk assessment, treatment and recidivism warrants further investigation; and that we move toward the development of controlled clinical trials and bridging the gap between clinical trials and services on a systematic basis.

Evaluation of Services

Unfortunately there is a paucity of research reports on treatment outcome and those that exist were not controlled (Becker et al., 1988).

Monck and New (1996) in their survey of treatment services for sexually abused and sexually abusing young people found that services failed to build in systems that would facilitate an evaluation of their effectiveness. In particular, poor assessment and problem formation and poor record keeping hindered a consideration of the specific needs of the young person as judged on intake. Services generally failed to provide a description of the treatment provided and evaluation of the young person's functioning at the conclusion of the key points of their involvement with the service. Monck and New argued that clarity of assessment and integrated evaluation processes are essential, both to effective decision-making concerning an individual young person and to programme evaluation/development. Allam and Browne (1998) suggested that whilst "in-house" evaluation systems are of some value, professional understanding of the effectiveness of various interventions with specific sub-groups will only be achieved through large-scale independent research.

Taking Stock

As more research is emerging both here in the US about this group, several conclusions can be reached:

- The research is clearly demonstrating that a principal pathway to sexually abusive behaviour is family experience and perceptions of it. Attachment problems, rejection, witnessing domestic violence, multiple care moves, are all key examples. The problems of dysfunctional attachment are multiple and might include intimacy and relationship problems, communication difficulties etc. This suggests that there are some common linkages between the histories of adult sexual offenders and young people who sexually abuse and we may be able to learn some lessons across the two domains. The principal advantage to this is the reassurance to the worker that skills are transferable. We have to remain alert to the fact that there are critical differences, e.g., a lower level of recidivism with young people and developmental differences.
- The young person should be seen holistically. It is unhelpful to single out and target their sexually abusive behaviour in isolation from other key developmental areas, such as life experiences and communication and relationships skills, etc. Such an approach will only lead to partial assessments and will potentially alienate the young person. It is their behaviour and not their identity that needs to be addressed and labelled.
- Young people who sexually abuse are not fundamentally different from other young people who exhibit a wide range of problems, such as self-harm and violence. This should be good news, as we do not need to worry about searching out a unique and tailored service for this group. We can employ a holistic assessment of their needs and then address them all in order to make an impact. If we target their sexual abuse behaviours at the exclusion of all else then we will be unlikely to repair any damaged self from their own past and thus have not effected change that is likely to be sustained. However, we do need to have people who are specially trained and comfortable addressing the sexual and abusive aspects very directly as well.
- We should try and move away from categorizing someone as generally being high, medium, or low risk, as this is principally labelling for the purposes of worker self-protection rather than being a valuable aid to worker intervention. If we label someone high-risk then we are covered if they re-offend. If we label them low-risk and they re-offend then the workers may be held responsible for this. It is more helpful to try and identify broad risk bands which split this down into a context. For example, offence characteristics, their history/background, behavioural features, and attitudes, thoughts and fantasies. The focus should then be one of risk management.
- The development of more sophisticated risk tools should allow us to more effectively screen in and out cases according to the anticipated risk coupled with the potential for change. Decisions then have to be reached as to whether

to target the high risk group where the outcomes may be average or poor or target the middle group where the risk might not be so acute but where the projected outcomes are probably significantly better. That choice is probably being made for us by the public and the politicians who want certainty in controlling the young person exhibiting sexually abusive behaviour (Calder, 2000; 2003b).

Conclusions

Gerrilyn Smith (1996) set out the stages of our understanding to date:

Stage one - It doesn't happen. If it does it isn't harmful. It is either peer experimentation or exploration.

Stage two - Recognition that the problem exists, leading to a redefinition and the development of prognostic indicators.

Stage three - Providing guidelines, dealing with ambiguities, recognizing the simultaneous occupation of both the victim and victimizer roles, long-term consequences of criminalizing juveniles who sexually abuse.

Smith has argued that we have now moved into stage three with young people, where we can begin to address the real ambiguities of this area of work. If we added a fourth stage, this would be fundamentally reviewing whether we have over-identified the numbers being drawn into the system because of their sexual behaviours, particularly as an immediate access to precious resources. There is a considerable body of research demonstrating that the pathways to sexually abusive behaviour are multiple, and that many young people, like children, are responding to their family experiences, and we may need to reframe many cases as juveniles who are sexually reactive rather than abusive. This is not to minimize the seriousness of their behaviour, but it is about organizing young people along a continuum, reflecting the heterogeneity of the group.

Recommendations for the Future

Based upon the report of where we currently are across a wide range of areas within this relatively small and specialized field, the following recommendations are made for future developments:

> 1) We need to develop empirically-based risk assessment instruments for this group to allow us to more accurately identify those at risk for reoffending. These need to be developed using assets as well as strengths and which allow for the retention of professional judgment alongside actuarially-derived findings.
> 2) We need to systematically develop, implement and evaluate services rather than allowing services to develop on an ad hoc and unregulated basis.
> 3) There is a need to have a common definition of the problem adopted within practice and research and we unify future theoretical development within

an integrated ecological macro-framework.

4) There needs to be a coordinated review of guidance, legislation and responsibility from central government that assists frontline workers and their managers. Such a review should be informed by methodologically sound research findings.

5) There is a need for clarification of agency roles and responsibilities with this group and the use of the conceptual model for developing a local response (Calder, 1999) would assist in this as well as inviting regional collaboration to provide sufficient resources to this small, specialized group.

6) There is a need for organizational workers to have support with evidence-based materials to do the work and personal support to help them manage the potential impact personally of involvement in this field. There is also a need to explore a consortium approach to extend the resources available for service delivery. This should include provision of a "continuum of care" for young people who sexually abuse, ranging from community-based non-residential, to secure residential facilities.

7) There is a need for continued development of evidence-based interventions is essential and requires a partnership between researchers, theorists and frontline practitioners.

8) There is a need to require a better understanding of the sexual development of young people and the impact on them of sexism, pornography and patriarchal attitudes.

9) There is a need to raise public and professional awareness of the impact of sexual abuse by young people and improve public education on how parents might better protect their children. Parents should be provided with information regarding what behaviours should cause them concern and who they can approach for advice (see Hackett, 2001 for a superb text addressing this and other issues).

10) There needs to be more investment in prevention to reflect the fact that this is a public health issue and move towards secondary and primary intervention.

11) There is a need to refine our approaches toward engaging young people and their parents, since we know they are correlated with enhanced outcomes.

12) There is a need to provide specialized assessment, evaluation and treatment services for young people who sexually abuse that encourages early identification and appropriate assessment and intervention.

References

Abassi, K. & Jamal, S. (2002). South Asian adolescent sex offenders: effective assessment and intervention work. In Calder, M.C. (Ed.) *Young people who sexually abuse: building the evidence base for your practice.* Dorset: Russell House Publishing, 196-202.

Abel, G., Mittelman, M. & Becker, J. (1985). Sexual offenders: results of assessment and recommendations for treatment. In Ben-Aron, H., Hucker, S., and Webster, C. (Eds.) *Clinical Criminology,* Toronto, M&M Graphics, 191-205.

Alexander, M.A. (1999). Sexual Offender Treatment Efficacy Revisited. *Sexual Abuse: A Journal of Research and Treatment*, (11) 2.

Allam, J.A. & Browne, K.D. (1998). Evaluating community-based treatment programmes for men who sexually abuse children. *Child Abuse Review* 7: 13-29.

Barbaree, H.E., Hudson, S.M. & Seto, M.C. (1993). Sexual assault in society: the role of the juvenile offender. In Barbaree, H.E. et al., (Eds.), op cit, 1-24.

Barbaree, H.E., Marshall, W.E. & McCormick, J. (1998). The development of deviant sexual behaviour among adolescents and its implications for prevention and treatment. *The Irish Journal of Psychology* 19: 1-31.

Becker, J.V. & Kaplan, M.S. (1988). The assessment and treatment of adolescent sexual offenders. *Advances in Behavioural Assessmen of Children and Families* 4: 97 - 118.

Becker, J.V., Kaplan, M.S., Cunningham-Rathner, R.J. & Kavoussi, R. (1986). Characteristics of adolescent incest sexual perpetrators: preliminary findings. *Journal of Family Violence* 1 (1): 85 - 97.

Bentovim, A. (2002). Research on the development of sexually abusive behaviour in sexually abused males: the implications for clinical practice. In Calder, M.C. (Ed.) *Young people who sexually abuse: building the evidence base for your practice.* Dorset: Russell House Publishing, 345-354.

Blues, A., Moffat, C. & Telford, P. (1999). Work with adolescent females who sexually abuse: similarities and differences. In Masson, H. and Erooga, M. (Eds.) *Children and young people who sexually abuse others: challenges and responses.* London: Routledge, 168-182.

Borduin C, Hengeller S, Blaske, D. & Stein, R. (1990). Multisystemic treatment of adolescent sex offenders. *International Journal of Offender Therapy and Comparative Criminology* 34: 105-113.

Brannon, J. & Troyer, R. (1995). Adolescent sex offenders: investigating adult commitment rates four years later. *International Journal of Offender Therapy and Comparative Criminology* 39(4): 317-326.

Brown, E.J. & Kolko, D.J. (1998). Treatment efficacy and program evaluation with juvenile sexual abusers: a critique with directions for service delivery. *Child Maltreatment* 3(4): 362-373.

Calder, M.C. (1997). *Juveniles and children who sexually abuse: a guide to risk assessment.* Dorset: Russell House Publishing.

Calder, M.C. (1999). A conceptual framework for managing young people who sexually abuse: towards a consortium approach. In Calder, M.C. (Ed.) *Working with young people who sexually abuse: New pieces of the jigsaw puzzle.* Dorset: Russell House Publishing, 117-159.

Calder, M.C. (2000). *A complete guide to sexual abuse assessments*. Dorset: Russell House Publishing.

Calder, M.C. (2001). *Juveniles and children who sexually abuse: Frameworks for assessment (2nd edition)*. Dorset: Russell House Publishing.

Calder, M.C. (2002). Structural changes in the management of young people who sexually abuse in the UK. In Calder, M.C. (Ed.) *Young people who sexually abuse: Building the evidence base for your practice*. Dorset: Russell House Publishing, 265-308.

Calder, M.C. (2003) *From clarity comes chaos: the impact of government frameworks for young people who sexually abuse*. Keynote presentation to Durham ACPC conference, Durham, 13th June 2003.

Calder, M.C. (2003b). The Assessment Framework: A critique and reformulation. In Calder, M.C. and Hackett, S. (Eds.) *Assessment in childcare: Using and developing frameworks for practice*. Dorset: Russell House Publishing, 3-60.

Chaffin, M. & Bonner, B. (1998). "Don't shoot, we're your children": have we gone too far in our response to adolescent sexual abusers and children with sexual behaviour problems? *Child Maltreatment* 3(4): 314-316.

Cuming, G. & Buell, M. (1997). *Supervision of the sex offender*. Brandon VT: Safer Society Press.

DOH (1991). *Working Together under the Children Act 1989: A guide to arrangements for inter-agency co-operation for the protection of children from abuse*. London: HMSO.

DOH (1998). *Working Together to safeguard children: New government proposals for inter-agency co-operation*. London: HMSO.

DOH (1999). *Working Together to Safeguard Children: A guide to inter-agency working to safeguard and promote the welfare of children*. London: HMSO.

DOH (2000). *Framework for the assessment of children in need and their families*. London: The Stationary Office.

Duane, Y. & Morrison, T. (2004). Families of young people who sexually abuse: characteristics, context and considerations. In O'Reilly, G., Marshall, W.L., Carr, A., and Beckett, R.C. (Eds.) *The handbook of clinical intervention with young people who sexually abuse*. Chichester: John Wiley and Sons, 103-128.

Epps, K. & Fisher, D. (2004). A review of the research literature on young people who sexually abuse. In O'Reilly, G., Marshall, W.L., Carr, A. and Beckett, R.C. (Eds.) *The handbook of clinical intervention with young people who sexually abuse*. Chichester: John Wiley and Sons, 62-102.

Epps, K.J. (1999). Causal explanations: filling the theoretical reservoir. In Calder, M.C. (Ed.) *Working with young people who sexually abuse: New pieces of the jigsaw*. Dorset: Russell house Publishing, 7-26.

Epps, K.J. (1996). Sexually abusive behaviour in an adolescent boy with the 48, XXYY syndrome: a case study. *Criminal Behaviour and Mental Health* 6, 137-146.

Finkelhor, D. (1984). *Child Sexual Abuse: New Theory and Research.* NY: The Free Press.

Gilgun, J.F. (1999). CASPARS: Clinical assessment instruments that measure strengths and risks in children and families. In Calder, M.C. (Ed.) *Working with young people who sexually abuse: New pieces of the jigsaw.* Dorset: Russell house Publishing, 49-58.

Groth, A.N. & Oliveri, F.J. (1989). Understanding sexual abuse offence behaviour and differentiating among sexual abusers: basic conceptual issues. In Sgroi, S.M. (Ed.) *Vulnerable Populations (Volume 2).* Lexington: DC Health, 309-327.

Hackett, S. (1999). Empowered practice. In Erooga, M. and Masson, H. (Eds.) *Young people who sexually abuse others: Responses to an emerging problem.* London: Routledge, 225-243.

Hackett, S. (2000). Sexual aggression, diversity and the challenge of anti-oppressive practice. *The Journal of Sexual Aggression* 5(1): 4-20.

Hackett, S. (2001). *A guide for parents of children who have sexually abused.* Dorset: Russell House Publishing.

Hackett, S. (2002). Negotiating difficult terrain: The personal context to work with young people who sexually abuse others. In Calder, M.C. (Ed.) *Young people who sexually abuse: building the evidence base for your practice.* Dorset: Russell House Publishing, 73-83.

Hackett, S. (2002b). Abused and abusing: work with young people who have a dual sexual abuse experience. In Calder, M.C. (Ed.) *Young people who sexually abuse: building the evidence base for your practice.* Dorset: Russell House Publishing, 203-217.

Hanson, R.K. (1998). *Using research to improve sex offender risk assessment.* Keynote presentation to the NOTA National Conference, University of Glasgow, September 17th, 1998.

Hanson, R.K. (1999). Sex offender risk assessment. In Hollin, C.R. (Ed.) *Handbook of offender assessment and treatment.* Chichester: John Wiley and Sons Ltd.

Hanson, R.K. (2003). Empathy deficits of sexual offenders: a conceptual model. *Journal of Sexual Aggression* 9(1): 13-23.

Haugaard, J.J. & Reppuccind (1988). *The sexual abuse of children.* San Francisco, Ca: Jossey-Bass.

Hawkes, C. (1999). Linking thoughts to action. In H. Kemshall & J. Prichard (Eds.) *Good practice in working with violence.* London: Jessica Kingsley.

Hollows, A. (2003). *Beyond actuarial risk assessment: the continuing role of professional judgment.* Presentation to a one-day national conference 'Risk assessment: developing and enhancing evidence-based practice', TUC Congress Centre, London, 6th February 2003.

Home Office (2000). *Setting the boundaries: reforming the law on sex offenders.* London: Home Office.

Home Office/HM Inspector of Probation (1998). *Exercising constant vigilance: the role of the probation service in protecting the public from sex offenders.* London: Home.

Hudson, S.M. & Ward, T. (1997). Future Directions. In Laws, D.R. and O'Donohue, W. (eds) *Sexual Deviance: Theory, Assessment and Treatment.* NY: Guilford Press, 481-500.

Hunter, J.A. & Becker, J.V. (1994). The relationship between phallometrically measured deviant sexual arousal and clinical characteristics in juvenile sexual offenders. *Professional Psychology: Research and Therapy* 32: 533-538.

James, A.C. & Neil, P.C. (1996). Juvenile sexual offending: a one-year prevalence study within Oxfordshire. *Child Abuse and Neglect* 20(6): 477-485.

Jenkins, A. (1995). *Engaging adolescents who sexually abuse:* workshop notes. South Australia: NADA Consultants.

Kahn, T. & Chambers, H. (1991). Assessing re-offence risk with juvenile sexual offenders, *Child Welfare* LXX(3), 333-345.

Kemshall, H. (2001). Risk assessment and management of known sexual and violent offenders: *A review of current issues. Police Research Series Paper 140.* London: The Home Office.

Kennington, R. (2003). *Assessing men who sexually abuse.* Presentation to a one-day national conference 'Risk assessment: developing and enhancing evidence-based practice', TUC Congress Centre, London, 6th February 2003.

Lab, S., Shields, G. & Schondel, C. (1993). Research note: an evaluation of juvenile sexual offender treatment. *Crime and Delinquency* 39(4): 543-553.

Letourneau, E.J. & Swenson, C.C. (2004). Sexual Offending, Sexual Behavior Problems: Treatment with Multisystemic Therapy. In Calder, M.C. (ed.) *Children and young people who sexually abuse: new theory, research and practice developments.* Dorset: Russell House Publishing.

Letourneau, E.J. (2004). A comment on the first report: Letter to the editor. *Sexual Abuse: A Journal of Research and Treatment,* 16, 77-81.

Lewis, A.D. (1999). *Cultural diversity in sexual abuser treatment: issues and approaches.* Orwell, VT: Safer Society Press.

Loeber, R. & Farrington, D.P. (Eds.) (1998). *Serious and violent juvenile offenders: risk factors and successful interventions.* Thousand Oaks, Ca: Sage Publications.

Longo, R.E. (2002). A holistic approach to treating young people who sexually abuse. In Calder, M.C. (Ed.) *Young people who sexually abuse: building the evidence base for your practice.* Dorset: Russell House Publishing, 218-230.

Longo, R.E. & Calder, M.C. (2005). The use of sex offender registration with young people who sexually abuse. In Calder, M.C. (ed.) *Children and young people who sexually abuse: new theory, research and practice developments.* Dorset: Russell House Publishing.

Masson, H. (1995). Juvenile sexual abusers: A challenge to conventional wisdom about juvenile offending. *Youth and Policy 50,* Autumn 1995, 13-25.

Masson, H. (1997/8). Issues in relation to children and young people who sexually abuse other children: A survey of practitioners' views. *The Journal of Sexual Aggression* 3(2): 101-118.

Masson, H. (1998). Issues in relation to children and young people who sexually abuse other children: responses to an emerging problem. *The Journal of Sexual Aggression* 3(2): 101-118.

Mir, B. & Okotie, E. (forthcoming). A study of the experiences of Black and Asian youth whose sexual behaviour is abusive. In Calder, M.C. (Ed.) *Young people who sexually abuse: taking the field forward.* Dorset: Russell House Publishing.

Monck, E. & New, M. (1996).*Report of a study of sexually abused children and adolescents and young perpetrators of sexual abuse who were treated in voluntary agency community facilities.* London: HMSO.

Morrison, T. (1994). Context, constraints and considerations in practice. In Morrison, T., Erooga, M., and Beckett, R. (Eds.) *Sexual offending against children: Assessment and treatment of male abusers.* London: Routledge, 25-54.

Morrison, T. (1997). Emotionally competent child protection organisations: fallacy, fiction or necessity? In Bates, J., Pugh, R., and Thompson, N. (Eds.) *Protecting children: challenges and change.* London: Arena.

Morrison, T. & Wilkinson, L. (2001). The G-MAP *Family Service: A manual of assessment and intervention.* Manchester: G-MAP.

Myers, S. (1998). Young people who sexually abuse: is consensus possible or desirable? *Social Work in Europe* 5(1): 53-56.

National Children's Homes (1992). *Report of the committee of enquiry into children and young people who sexually abuse other children.* London: NCH.

O'Callaghan, D. (1998). Practice issues in working with young abusers who have learning disabilities. *Child Abuse Review.* 7: 435-448.

O'Callaghan, D. (1999). Young abusers with learning disabilities: towards better understanding and positive interventions. In Calder, M.C. (Ed.) *Working with young people who sexually abuse: New pieces of the jigsaw.* Dorset: Russell house Publishing, 225-249.

O'Callaghan, D. (2001). A framework for undertaking assessment of young people with intellectual disabilities who present problematic/harmful sexual behaviours. In: *Working with children and young people who display sexually harmful behaviour: assessment manual.* Manchester: AIM Project.

O'Callaghan, D. (2002). Providing a research informed service for young people who sexually abuse. In Calder, M.C. (Ed.) *Young people who sexually abuse: building the evidence base for your practice.* Dorset: Russell House Publishing, 5-25.

O'Callaghan, D. (2004). Adolescents with intellectual disabilities who sexually harm: intervention design and implementation. In O'Reilly, G., Marshall, W.L., Carr, A., & Beckett, R.C. (Eds.) *The handbook of clinical intervention with young people who sexually abuse.* Chichester: John Wiley and Sons, 345-368.

O'Callaghan, D. & Corran, M. (2004). The inter-agency management of children and young people who sexually abuse. In Bailey, S. & Dolan, M. (Eds.) *Handbook of adolescent psychiatry.* London: Blackwell Scientific Press.

Prentky, R. & Knight, R. (1993). Age of onset of sexual assault. In Nagayama-Hall, G., Hirschman, R., Graham, J., & Zaragoza, M. (Eds.) *Sexual aggression: issues in etiology, assessment and treatment.* Washington, DC: Taylor and Francis.

Prentky, R., Harris, A., Frizzell, B., & Righthand, S. (2000). An actuarial procedure for assessing risk with juvenile sex offenders. *Sexual Abuse: A journal of Research and Treatment* 12(2): 71-93.

Print, B. & Morrison, T. (2000).Treating adolescents who sexually abuse others. In Itzin, C. (Ed.) *Home truths about child sexual abuse: influencing policy and practice.* London: Routledge, 290-312.

Print, B., Morrison, T., & Henniker, J. (2001). An inter-agency framework for young people who sexually abuse: principles, processes and practicalities. In Calder, M.C. (Ed.) *Juveniles and children who sexually abuse: frameworks for assessment.* Dorset: Russell House Publishing (2nd edition), pp. 271-281.

Quinsey, V.L., Rice, M.E., & Harris, G.T. (1995). Actuarial prediction of sexual recidivism. *Journal of Interpersonal Violence* 10(1): 85-105.

Rasmussen, L.A. (1999). Factors related to recidivism among juvenile sexual offenders. *Sexual Abuse: A Journal of Research and Treatment* 11(1): 69-85.

Rich, S.A. (1998). A developmental approach to the treatment of adolescent sex offenders. *The Irish Journal of Psychology* 19: 101-118.
Robinson, S. (2005). Considerations for the assessment of female sexually abusive

Robinson, S. (2005). Considerations for the assessment of female sexually abusive youth. In Calder, M.C. (Ed.) *Children and young people who sexually abuse: new theory, research and practice developments*. Dorset: Russell House Publishing, pp. 175-199.

Ryan, G. (2000). *Early identification of factors which put children 'at risk' of becoming abusive and a continuum of intervention to improve outcomes*. Presentation to the positive outcomes conference, Manchester airport, 11-13th July, 2000.

Sanders, R.M. & Ladwa-Thomas, V. (1997). Inter-agency perspectives on child sexual abuse perpetrated by juveniles. *Child Maltreatment* 2(3): 264- 271.

Smith, G. (1996). *Brotherly love: Ambiguities of peer abuse*. Keynote presentation to the Barnardo's 'learning to change' conference, Liverpool Town Hall, 14 March 1996.

Vizard, E., Monck, E., & Misch, P. (1995). Child and adolescent sex abuse perpetrators: A review of the research literature. *Journal of Child Psychol. Psychiat.* 36(5): 731-756.

Ward, T. & Hudson, S.M. (1998). The construction and development of theory in the sexual offending area: A meta-theoretical framework. *Sexual Abuse: A Journal of Research and Treatment* 10(1): 47-63.

Way, I. (2002). Childhood maltreatment histories of male adolescents with sexual offending behaviours: a review of the literature. In Calder, M.C. (Ed.). *Young people who sexually abuse: building the evidence base for your practice*. Dorset: Russell House Publishing, 26-55.

Williams, D. & Buehler, M.P. (2002). A proposal for comprehensive community-based treatment of female juvenile sex offenders. In Calder, M.C. (Ed.). *Young people who sexually abuse: building the evidence base for your practice*. Dorset: Russell House Publishing, 251-264.

Wolf, S. (1984). *A multi-factor model of deviant sexuality*. Paper at 3rd International conference on victimology. Lisbon, Portugal, November, 1984.

Worling, J. (2002). Assessing risk of sexual assault recidivism with adolescent sexual offenders. In Calder, M.C. (Ed.) *Young people who sexually abuse: building the evidence base for your practice*. Dorset: Russell House Publishing, 365-375.